CHRYSLER

CARAVAN AND VOYAGER
1984-95 REPAIR MANUAL

CHILTON'S

Senior Vice President	Ronald A. Hoxter
Publisher & Editor-In-Chief	Kerry A. Freeman, S.A.E.
Executive Editors	Dean F. Morgantini, S.A.E., W. Calvin Settle, Jr., S.A.E.
Managing Editor	Nick D'Andrea
Senior Editors	Jacques Gordon, Michael L. Grady, Ben Greisler, S.A.E., Debra McCall, Kevin M. G. Maher, Richard J. Rivele, S.A.E., Richard T. Smith, Jim Taylor, Ron Webb
Project Managers	Martin J. Gunther, Will Kessler, A.S.E., Richard Schwartz
Production Manager	Andrea Steiger
Product Systems Manager	Robert Maxey
Director of Manufacturing	Mike D'Imperio
Editor	Martin J. Gunther

CHILTON BOOK COMPANY

ONE OF THE **DIVERSIFIED PUBLISHING COMPANIES,**
A PART OF **CAPITAL CITIES/ABC, INC.**

Manufactured in USA

Chilton Way, Radnor, PA 19089
ISBN 0-8019-8796-2
Library of Congress Catalog Card No. 96-84177
1234567890 5432109876

Contents

1 GENERAL INFORMATION AND MAINTENANCE

1-2 HOW TO USE THIS BOOK
1-3 TOOLS AND EQUIPMENT
1-6 SAFETY
1-8 FASTENERS
1-18 ROUTINE MAINTENANCE
1-52 FLUIDS AND LUBRICANTS
1-66 JUMP STARTING A DEAD BATTERY
1-67 JACKING
1-74 SPECIFICATIONS CHARTS

2 ENGINE PERFORMANCE AND TUNE-UP

2-2 TUNE-UP PROCEDURES
2-16 SPECIFICATIONS CHARTS
2-17 FIRING ORDERS
2-18 ELECTRONIC IGNITION
2-37 OPTICAL DISTRIBUTOR SYSTEM
2-38 DIRECT IGNITION SYSTEM (DIS)

3 ENGINE AND ENGINE OVERHAUL

3-2 BASIC ELECTRICAL THEORY
3-7 ENGINE ELECTRICAL
3-17 ENGINE MECHANICAL
3-20 SPECIFICATIONS CHARTS
3-107 EXHAUST SYSTEM

4 EMISSION CONTROLS

4-2 AIR POLLUTION
4-3 AUTOMOTIVE EMISSIONS
4-5 EMISSION CONTROLS
4-17 CHRYSLER SELF-DIAGNOSTIC SYSTEM
4-20 TROUBLE CODES
4-37 VACUUM DIAGRAMS

5 FUEL SYSTEM

5-2 BASIC DIAGNOSIS
5-2 CARBURETED FUEL SYSTEM
5-12 MULTI-POINT FUEL INJECTION
5-24 SINGLE POINT FUEL INJECTION
5-29 FUEL TANK
5-30 SPECIFICATIONS CHARTS

6 CHASSIS ELECTRICAL

6-2 UNDERSTANDING ELECTRICAL SYSTEMS
6-10 AIR BAGS
6-17 HEATING AND A/C
6-35 RADIO
6-37 WINDSHIELD WIPERS
6-41 INSTRUMENTS
6-53 LIGHTING
6-57 CIRCUIT PROTECTION
6-58 WIRING DIAGRAMS

Contents

7-2 MANUAL TRANSAXLE
7-49 CLUTCH
7-52 AUTO TRANSAXLE
7-58 POWER TRANSFER UNIT
7-59 REAR DRIVE LINE MODULE
7-66 SPECIFICATIONS CHARTS

DRIVE TRAIN **7**

8-2 FRONT SUSPENSION
8-2 WHEELS
8-16 SPECIFICATIONS CHARTS
8-17 REAR SUSPENSION
8-24 STEERING

SUSPENSION AND STEERING **8**

9-2 BRAKE SYSTEM
9-13 FRONT DISC BRAKES
9-24 REAR DRUM BRAKES
9-33 BENDIX SYSTEM 10 ABS
9-51 BENDIX SYSTEM 4 ABS
9-66 SPECIFICATIONS CHARTS

BRAKES **9**

10-2 EXTERIOR
10-13 INTERIOR

BODY AND TRIM **10**

10-31 GLOSSARY

GLOSSARY

10-35 MASTER INDEX

MASTER INDEX

SAFETY NOTICE

Proper service and repair procedures are vital to the safe, reliable operation of all motor vehicles, as well as the personal safety of those performing repairs. This manual outlines procedures for servicing and repairing vehicles using safe, effective methods. The procedures contain many NOTES, CAUTIONS and WARNINGS which should be followed along with standard procedures to eliminate the possibility of personal injury or improper service which could damage the vehicle or compromise its safety.

It is important to note that the repair procedures and techniques, tools and parts for servicing motor vehicles, as well as the skill and experience of the individual performing the work vary widely. It is not possible to anticipate all of the conceivable ways or conditions under which vehicles may be serviced, or to provide cautions as to all of the possible hazards that may result. Standard and accepted safety precautions and equipment should be used when handling toxic or flammable fluids, and safety goggles or other protection should be used during cutting, grinding, chiseling, prying, or any other process that can cause material removal or projectiles.

Some procedures require the use of tools specially designed for a specific purpose. Before substituting another tool or procedure, you must be completely satisfied that neither your personal safety, nor the performance of the vehicle will be endangered.

Although information in this manual is based on industry sources and is complete as possible at the time of publication, the possibility exists that some car manufacturers made later changes which could not be included here. While striving for total accuracy, Chilton Book Company cannot assume responsibility for any errors, changes or omissions that may occur in the compilation of this data.

PART NUMBERS

Part numbers listed in this reference are not recommendation by Chilton for any product by brand name. They are references that can be used with interchange manuals and aftermarket supplier catalogs to locate each brand supplier's discrete part number.

SPECIAL TOOLS

Special tools are recommended by the vehicle manufacturer to perform their specific job. Use has been kept to a minimum, but where absolutely necessary, they are referred to in the text by the part number of the tool manufacturer. These tools can be purchased, under the appropriate part number, from your local dealer or regional distributor, or an equivalent tool can be purchased locally from a tool supplier or parts outlet. Before substituting any tool for the one recommended, read the SAFETY NOTICE at the top of this page.

ACKNOWLEDGMENTS

The Chilton Book Company expresses appreciation to Chrysler Corporation for their generous assistance.

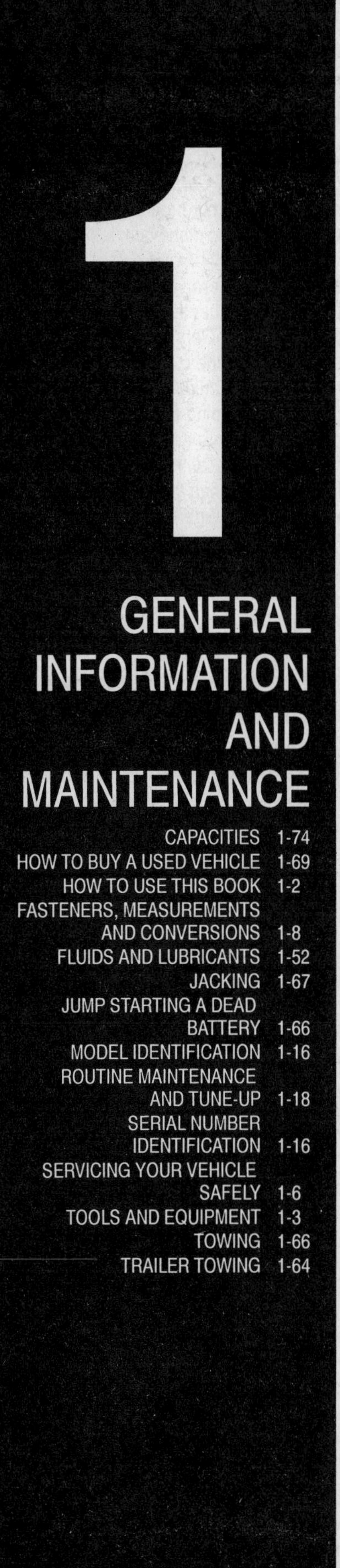

1 GENERAL INFORMATION AND MAINTENANCE

CAPACITIES 1-74
HOW TO BUY A USED VEHICLE 1-69
HOW TO USE THIS BOOK 1-2
FASTENERS, MEASUREMENTS AND CONVERSIONS 1-8
FLUIDS AND LUBRICANTS 1-52
JACKING 1-67
JUMP STARTING A DEAD BATTERY 1-66
MODEL IDENTIFICATION 1-16
ROUTINE MAINTENANCE AND TUNE-UP 1-18
SERIAL NUMBER IDENTIFICATION 1-16
SERVICING YOUR VEHICLE SAFELY 1-6
TOOLS AND EQUIPMENT 1-3
TOWING 1-66
TRAILER TOWING 1-64

FASTENERS, MEASUREMENTS AND CONVERSIONS
BOLTS, NUTS AND OTHER THREADED RETAINERS 1-8
STANDARD AND METRIC MEASUREMENTS 1-14
TORQUE 1-11
FLUIDS AND LUBRICANTS
BODY LUBRICATION 1-63
CHASSIS LUBRICATION 1-62
COOLING SYSTEM 1-58
DIFFERENTIAL 1-57
DRIVE LINE MODULE 1-58
ENGINE 1-52
FLUID DISPOSAL 1-52
FUEL RECOMMENDATIONS 1-52
MASTER CYLINDER 1-60
POWER STEERING PUMP 1-61
POWER TRANSFER UNIT (PTU) 1-57
REAR WHEEL BEARINGS 1-63
STEERING GEAR 1-62
TRANSAXLE 1-55
HOW TO BUY A USED VEHICLE
TIPS 1-69
HOW TO USE THIS BOOK
AVOIDING THE MOST COMMON MISTAKES 1-2
AVOIDING TROUBLE 1-2
MAINTENANCE OR REPAIR? 1-2
WHERE TO BEGIN 1-2
JACKING
JACKING PRECAUTIONS 1-69
JUMP STARTING A DEAD BATTERY
JUMP STARTING PRECAUTIONS 1-67
JUMP STARTING PROCEDURE 1-67
MODEL IDENTIFICATION 1-16
ROUTINE MAINTENANCE AND TUNE-UP
AIR CLEANER 1-18
AIR CONDITIONING 1-40
BATTERY 1-27
CRANKCASE VENT FILTER 1-26
CV-BOOTS 1-40
DRIVE BELTS 1-30
EVAPORATIVE CHARCOAL CANISTER 1-27
FUEL FILTER 1-20
FUEL SYSTEM PRESSURE 1-24
HOSES 1-38
PCV VALVE 1-25
TIRES AND WHEELS 1-47
WINDSHIELD WIPERS 1-43
SERIAL NUMBER IDENTIFICATION
ENGINE IDENTIFICATION NUMBER (EIN) 1-16
ENGINE SERIAL NUMBER 1-18
TRANSAXLE 1-18
VEHICLE IDENTIFICATION NUMBER (VIN) 1-16
SERVICING YOUR VEHICLE SAFELY
DO'S 1-8
DON'TS 1-8
SPECIFICATIONS CHARTS
AUTOMATIC TRANSMISSION APPLICATIONS 1-72
CAPACITIES 1-74
ENGINE APPLICATIONS 1-71
MANUAL TRANSMISSION APPLICATIONS 1-73
STANDARD (ENGLISH) TO METRIC CONVERSION CHARTS 1-76
STANDARD AND METRIC CONVERSION FACTORS 1-15
TORQUE SPECIFICATIONS 1-75
TOOLS AND EQUIPMENT
SPECIAL TOOLS 1-6
TOWING 1-66
TRAILER TOWING 1-64
COOLING 1-65
GENERAL RECOMMENDATIONS 1-64
HANDLING A TRAILER 1-65
HITCH (TONGUE) WEIGHT 1-64
TRAILER WEIGHT 1-64
WIRING 1-65

HOW TO USE THIS BOOK

Chilton's Total Car Care manual for the Chrysler Town & Country, Dodge Caravan and Plymouth Voyager is intended to help you learn more about the inner workings of your vehicle while saving you money on its upkeep and operation.

The beginning of the book will likely be referred to the most, since that is where you will find information for maintenance and tune-up. The other sections deal with the more complex systems of your vehicle. Operating systems from engine through brakes are covered to the extent that the average do-it-yourselfer becomes mechanically involved. This book will not explain such things as rebuilding a differential for the simple reason that the expertise required and the investment in special tools make this task uneconomical. It will, however, give you detailed instructions to help you change your own brake pads and shoes, replace spark plugs, and perform many more jobs that can save you money, give you personal satisfaction and help you avoid expensive problems.

A secondary purpose of this book is a reference for owners who want to understand their vehicle and/or their mechanics better. In this case, no tools at all are required.

Where to Begin

Before removing any bolts, read through the entire procedure. This will give you the overall view of what tools and supplies will be required. There is nothing more frustrating than having to walk to the bus stop on Monday morning because you were short one bolt on Sunday afternoon. So read ahead and plan ahead. Each operation should be approached logically and all procedures thoroughly understood before attempting any work.

All sections contain adjustments, maintenance, removal and installation procedures, and in some cases, repair or overhaul procedures. When repair is not considered practical, we tell you how to remove the part and then how to install the new or rebuilt replacement. In this way, you at least save the labor costs. Backyard repair of some components is just not practical.

Avoiding Trouble

Many procedures in this book require you to "label and disconnect . . . " a group of lines, hoses or wires. Don't be lulled into thinking you can remember where everything goes — you won't. If you hook up vacuum or fuel lines incorrectly, the vehicle will run poorly, if at all. If you hook up electrical wiring incorrectly, you may instantly learn a very expensive lesson.

You don't need to know the official or engineering name for each hose or line. A piece of masking tape on the hose and a piece on its fitting will allow you to assign your own label such as the letter A or a short name. As long as you remember your own code, the lines can be reconnected by matching similar letters or names. Do remember that tape will dissolve in gasoline or other fluids; if a component is to be washed or cleaned, use another method of identification. A permanent felt-tipped marker can be very handy for marking metal parts. Remove any tape or paper labels after assembly.

Maintenance or Repair?

It's necessary to mention the difference between maintenance and repair. Maintenance includes routine inspections, adjustments, and replacement of parts which show signs of normal wear. Maintenance compensates for wear or deterioration. Repair implies that something has broken or is not working. A need for repair is often caused by lack of maintenance. Example: draining and refilling the automatic transaxle fluid is maintenance recommended by the manufacturer at specific mileage intervals. Failure to do this can ruin the transmission/transaxle, requiring very expensive repairs. While no maintenance program can prevent items from breaking or wearing out, a general rule can be stated: MAINTENANCE IS CHEAPER THAN REPAIR.

Two basic mechanic's rules should be mentioned here. First, whenever the left side of the vehicle or engine is referred to, it is meant to specify the driver's side. Conversely, the right side of the vehicle means the passenger's side. Second, most screws and bolts are removed by turning counterclockwise, and tightened by turning clockwise.

Safety is always the most important rule. Constantly be aware of the dangers involved in working on an automobile and take the proper precautions. See the information in this section regarding SERVICING YOUR VEHICLE SAFELY and the SAFETY NOTICE on the acknowledgment page.

Avoiding the Most Common Mistakes

Pay attention to the instructions provided. There are 3 common mistakes in mechanical work:

1. Incorrect order of assembly, disassembly or adjustment. When taking something apart or putting it together, performing steps in the wrong order usually just costs you extra time; however, it CAN break something. Read the entire procedure before beginning disassembly. Perform everything in the order in which the instructions say you should, even if you can't immediately see a reason for it. When you're taking apart something that is very intricate, you might want to draw a picture of how it looks when assembled at one point in order to make sure you get everything back in its proper position. We will supply exploded views whenever possible. When making adjustments, perform them in the proper order; often, one adjustment affects another, and you cannot expect even satisfactory results unless each adjustment is made only when it cannot be changed by any other.

2. Overtightening (or undertightening). While it is more common for overtorquing to cause damage, undertightening may allow a fastener to vibrate loose causing serious damage. Especially when dealing with aluminum parts, pay attention to torque specifications and utilize a torque wrench in assembly. If a torque figure is not available, remember that if you are using the right tool to perform the job, you will probably not have to strain

yourself to get a fastener tight enough. The pitch of most threads is so slight that the tension you put on the wrench will be multiplied many times in actual force on what you are tightening. A good example of how critical torque is can be seen in the case of spark plug installation, especially where you are putting the plug into an aluminum cylinder head. Too little torque can fail to crush the gasket, causing leakage of combustion gases and consequent overheating of the plug and engine parts. Too much torque can damage the threads or distort the plug, changing the spark gap.

There are many commercial products available for ensuring that fasteners won't come loose, even if they are not torqued just right (a very common brand is Loctite®). If you're worried about getting something together tight enough to hold, but loose enough to avoid mechanical damage during assembly, one of these products might offer substantial insurance. Before choosing a threadlocking compound, read the label on the package and make sure the product is compatible with the materials, fluids, etc. involved.

3. Crossthreading. This occurs when a part such as a bolt is screwed into a nut or casting at the wrong angle and forced. Crossthreading is more likely to occur if access is difficult. It helps to clean and lubricate fasteners, then to start threading with the part to be installed positioned straight in. Then, start the bolt, spark plug, etc. with your fingers. If you encounter resistance, unscrew the part and start over again at a different angle until it can be inserted and turned several times without much effort. Keep in mind that many parts, especially spark plugs, have tapered threads, so that gentle turning will automatically bring the part you're threading to the proper angle, but only if you don't force it or resist a change in angle. Don't put a wrench on the part until it's been tightened a couple of turns by hand. If you suddenly encounter resistance, and the part has not seated fully, don't force it. Pull it back out to make sure it's clean and threading properly.

Always take your time and be patient; once you have some experience, working on your vehicle may well become an enjoyable hobby.

TOOLS AND EQUIPMENT

➧ See Figures 1, 2, 3, 4, 5, 6, 7, 8, 9, 10, 11, 12, 13 and 14

Naturally, without the proper tools and equipment it is impossible to properly service your vehicle. It would also be virtually impossible to catalog every tool that you would need to perform all of the operations in this book. Of course, It would be unwise for the amateur to rush out and buy an expensive set of tools on the theory that he/she may need one or more of them at some time.

The best approach is to proceed slowly, gathering a good quality set of those tools that are used most frequently. Don't be misled by the low cost of bargain tools. It is far better to spend a little more for better quality. Forged wrenches, 6 or 12-point sockets and fine tooth ratchets are by far preferable to their less expensive counterparts. As any good mechanic can tell you, there are few worse experiences than trying to work on a vehicle with bad tools. Your monetary savings will be far outweighed by frustration and mangled knuckles.

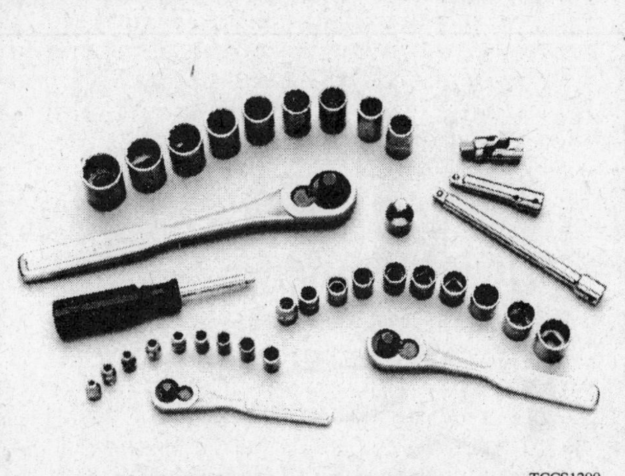

TCCS1200

Fig. 1 All but the most basic procedures will require an assortment of ratchets and sockets

Begin accumulating those tools that are used most frequently: those associated with routine maintenance and tune-up. In addition to the normal assortment of screwdrivers and pliers, you should have the following tools:

- Wrenches/sockets and combination open end/box end wrenches in sizes from $^1/_8$–$^3/_4$ in. or 3mm–19mm (depending on whether your vehicle uses standard or metric fasteners) and a $^{13}/_{16}$ in. or $^5/_8$ in. spark plug socket (depending on plug type).

➥ If possible, buy various length socket drive extensions. Universal-joint and wobble extensions can be extremely useful, but be careful when using them, as they can change the amount of torque applied to the socket.

- Jackstands for support.
- Oil filter wrench.
- Spout or funnel for pouring fluids.
- Grease gun for chassis lubrication (unless your vehicle is not equipped with any grease fittings — for details, please refer to information on Fluids and Lubricants found later in this section).
- Hydrometer for checking the battery (unless equipped with a sealed, maintenance-free battery).
- A container for draining oil and other fluids.
- Rags for wiping up the inevitable mess.

In addition to the above items there are several others that are not absolutely necessary, but handy to have around. These include Oil Dry® (or an equivalent oil absorbent gravel — such as cat litter) and the usual supply of lubricants, antifreeze and fluids, although these can be purchased as needed. This is a basic list for routine maintenance, but only your personal needs and desire can accurately determine your list of tools.

After performing a few projects on the vehicle, you'll be amazed at the other tools and non-tools on your workbench. Some useful household items are: a large turkey baster or siphon, empty coffee cans and ice trays (to store parts), ball of twine, electrical tape for wiring, small rolls of colored tape for tagging lines or hoses, markers and pens, a note pad, golf tees (for plugging vacuum lines), metal coat hangers or a roll of mechanics's wire (to hold things out of the way), dental pick or similar long, pointed probe, a strong magnet, and a small mirror (to see into recesses and under manifolds).

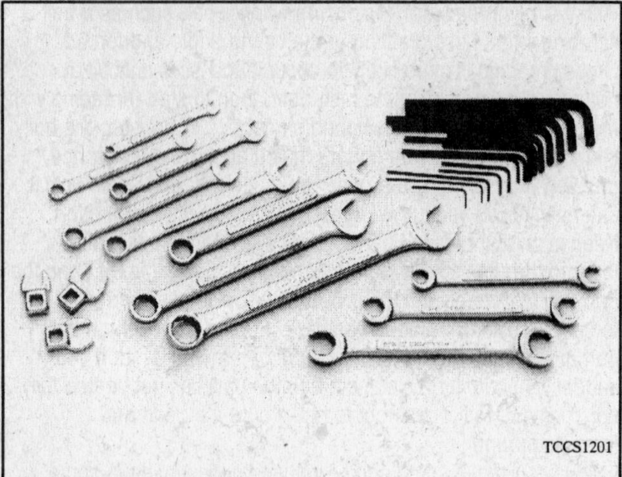

Fig. 2 In addition to ratchets, a good set of wrenches and hex keys will be necessary

Fig. 3 A hydraulic floor jack and a set of jackstands are essential for lifting and supporting the vehicle

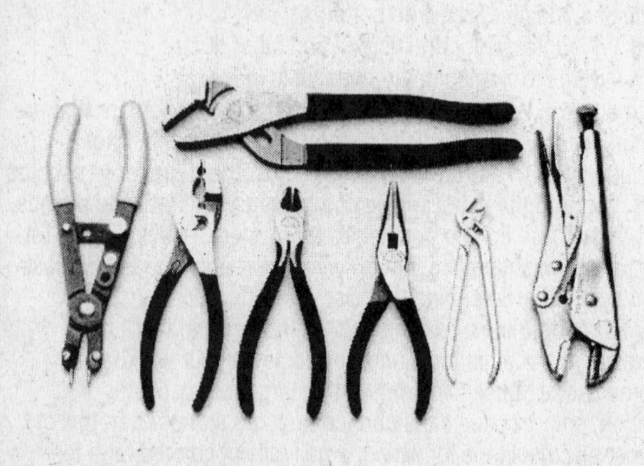

Fig. 4 An assortment of pliers, grippers and cutters will be handy, especially for old rusted parts and stripped bolt heads

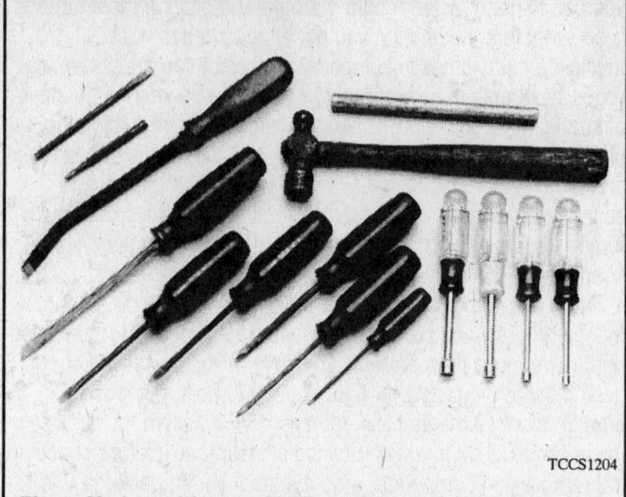

Fig. 5 Various drivers, chisels and prybars are great tools to have in your tool box

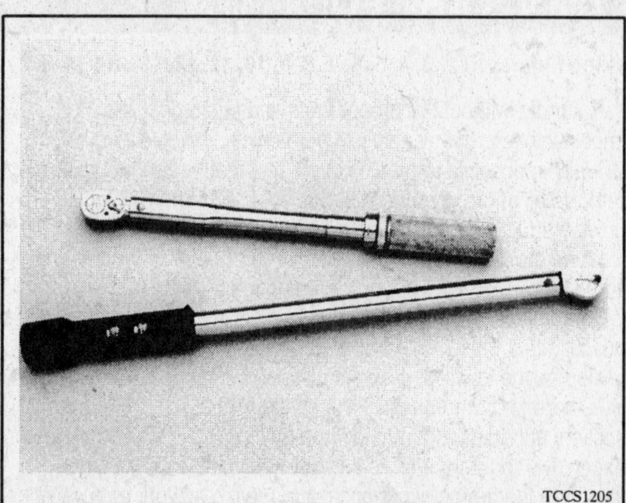

Fig. 6 Many repairs will require the use of a torque wrench to assure the components are properly fastened

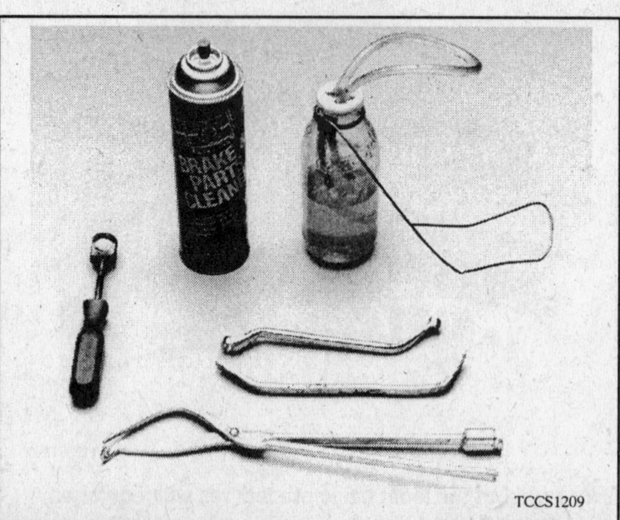

Fig. 7 Although not always necessary, using specialized brake tools will save time

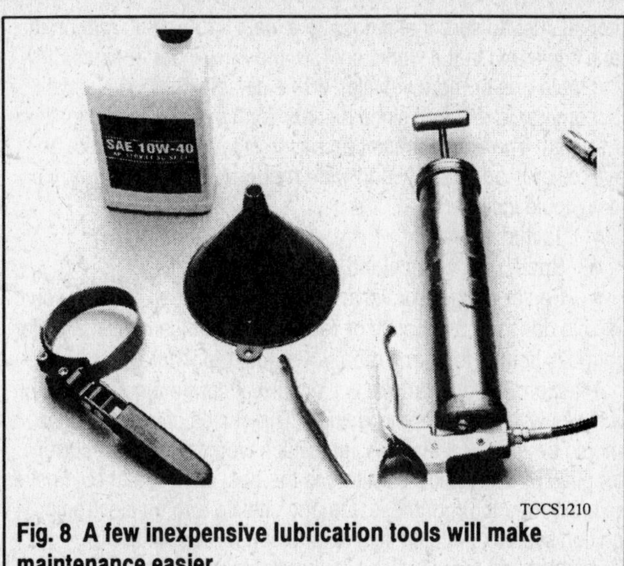

TCCS1210

Fig. 8 A few inexpensive lubrication tools will make maintenance easier

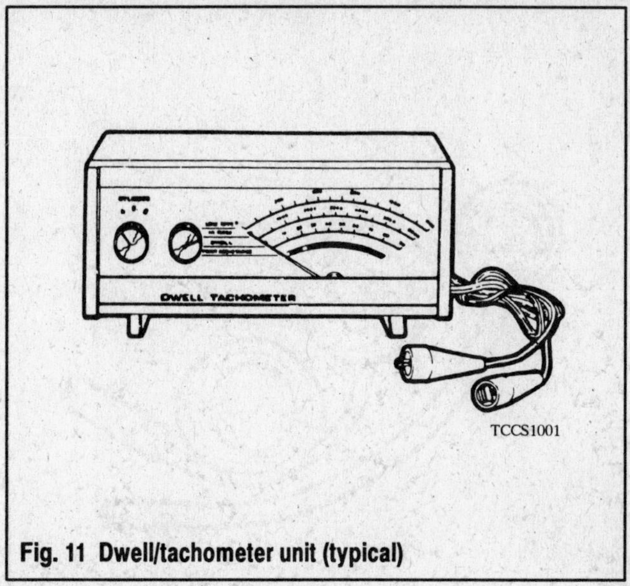

TCCS1001

Fig. 11 Dwell/tachometer unit (typical)

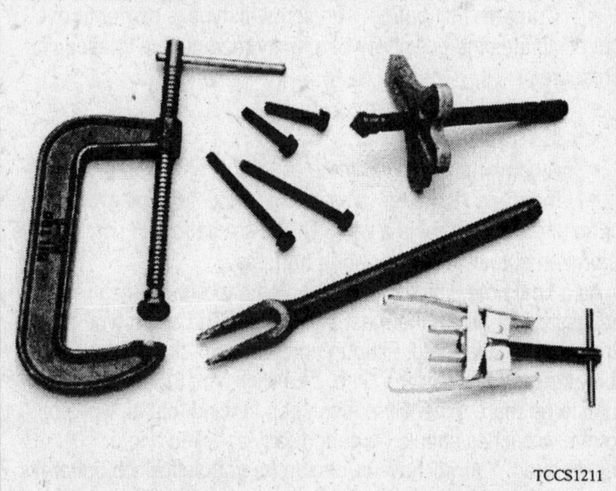

TCCS1211

Fig. 9 Various pullers, clamps and separator tools are needed for many larger, more complicated repairs

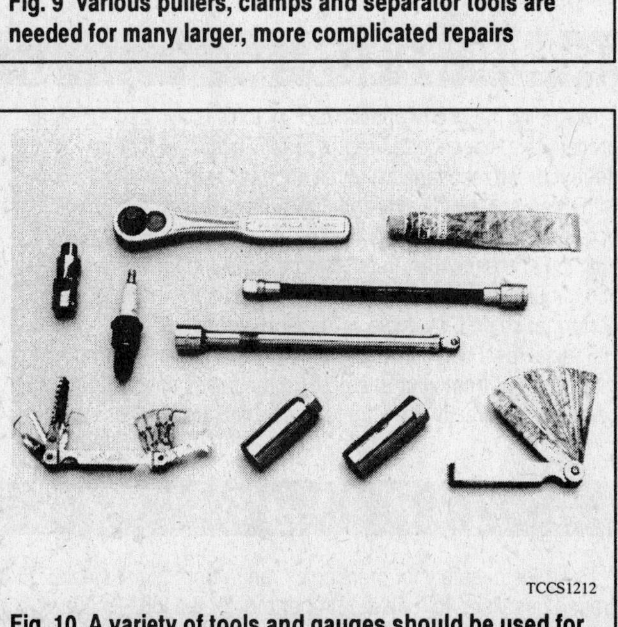

TCCS1212

Fig. 10 A variety of tools and gauges should be used for spark plug gapping and installation

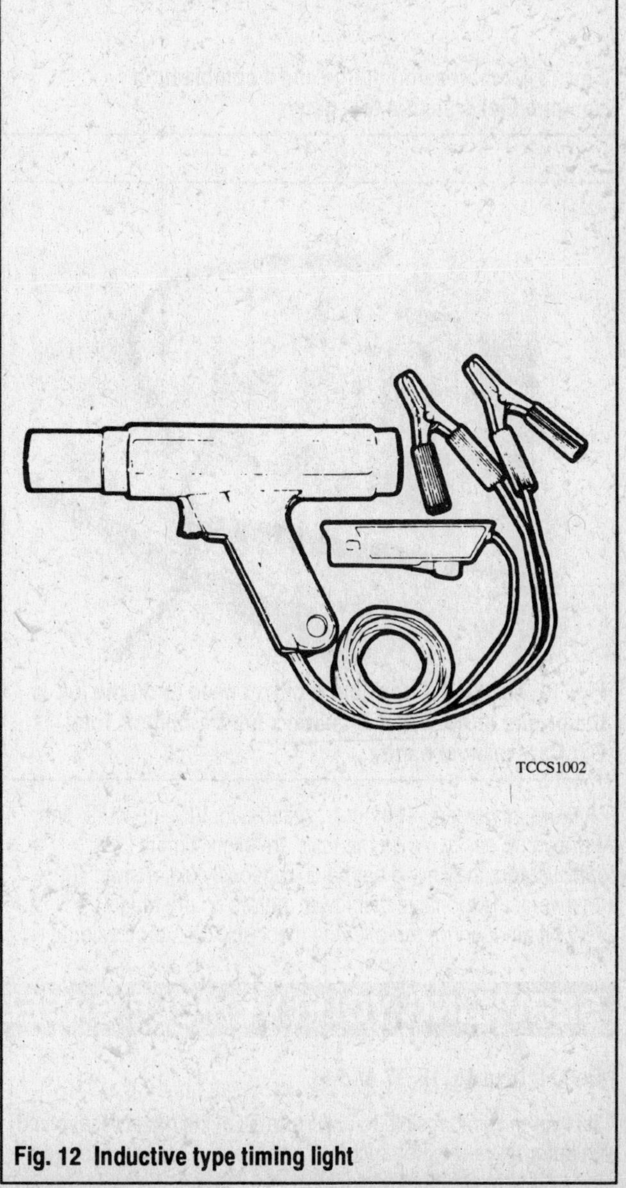

TCCS1002

Fig. 12 Inductive type timing light

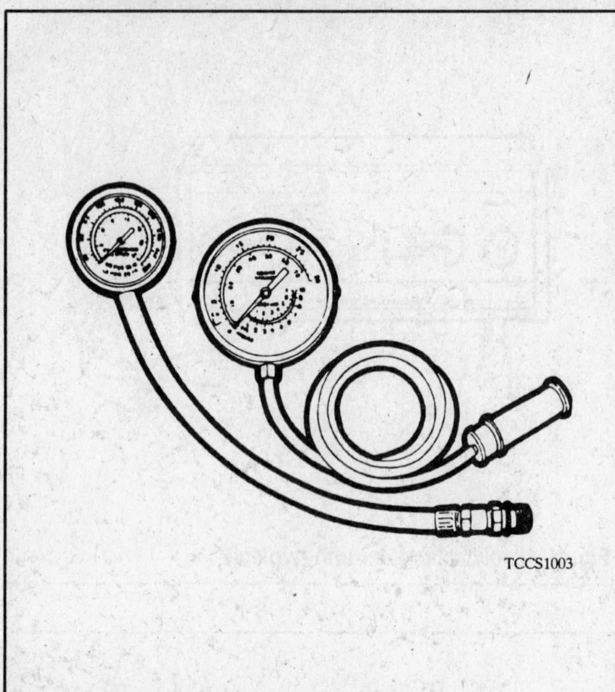

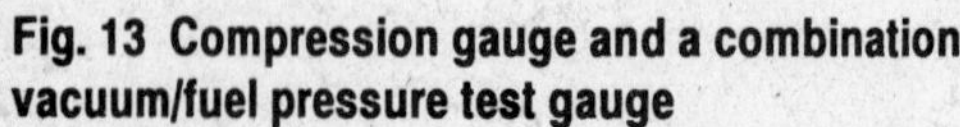
Fig. 13 Compression gauge and a combination vacuum/fuel pressure test gauge

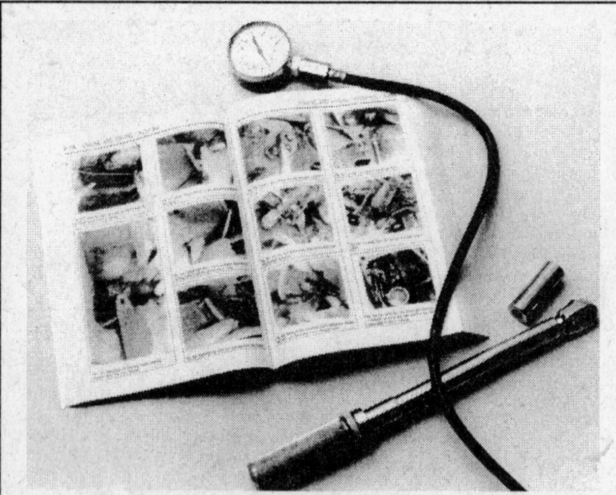

Fig. 14 The most important tool you need to do the job is the proper information, so always have a Chilton Total Car Care manual handy

A more advanced set of tools, suitable for tune-up work, can be drawn up easily. While the tools are slightly more sophisticated, they need not be outrageously expensive. There are several inexpensive tach/dwell meters on the market that are every bit as good for the average mechanic as a professional model. Just be sure that it goes to a least 1200–1500 rpm on the tach scale and that it works on 4, 6 and 8-cylinder engines. (If you have one or more vehicles with a diesel engine, a special tachometer is required since diesels don't use spark plug ignition systems). The key to these purchases is to make them with an eye towards adaptability and wide range. A basic list of tune-up tools could include:

- Tach/dwell meter.
- Spark plug wrench and gapping tool.
- Feeler gauges for valve or point adjustment. (Even if your vehicle does not use points or require valve adjustments, a feeler gauge is helpful for many repair/overhaul procedures).

A tachometer/dwell meter will ensure accurate tune-up work on vehicles without electronic ignition. The choice of a timing light should be made carefully. A light which works on the DC current supplied by the vehicle's battery is the best choice; it should have a xenon tube for brightness. On any vehicle with an electronic ignition system, a timing light with an inductive pickup that clamps around the No. 1 spark plug cable is preferred.

In addition to these basic tools, there are several other tools and gauges you may find useful. These include:

- Compression gauge. The screw-in type is slower to use, but eliminates the possibility of a faulty reading due to escaping pressure.
- Manifold vacuum gauge.
- 12V test light.
- A combination volt/ohmmeter
- Induction Ammeter. This is used for determining whether or not there is current in a wire. These are handy for use if a wire is broken somewhere in a wiring harness.

As a final note, you will probably find a torque wrench necessary for all but the most basic work. The beam type models are perfectly adequate, although the newer click types (break-away) are easier to use. The click type torque wrenches tend to be more expensive. Also keep in mind that all types of torque wrenches should be periodically checked and/or recalibrated. You will have to decide for yourself which better fits your purpose.

Special Tools

Normally, the use of special factory tools is avoided for repair procedures, since these are not readily available for the do-it-yourself mechanic. When it is possible to perform the job with more commonly available tools, it will be pointed out, but occasionally, a special tool was designed to perform a specific function and should be used. Before substituting another tool, you should be convinced that neither your safety nor the performance of the vehicle will be compromised.

Special tools can usually be purchased from an automotive parts store or from your dealer. In some cases special tools may be available directly from the tool manufacturer.

SERVICING YOUR VEHICLE SAFELY

➧ **See Figures 15, 16, 17 and 18**

It is virtually impossible to anticipate all of the hazards involved with automotive maintenance and service, but care and common sense will prevent most accidents.

The rules of safety for mechanics range from "don't smoke around gasoline," to "use the proper tool for the job." The trick to avoiding injuries is to develop safe work habits and to take every possible precaution.

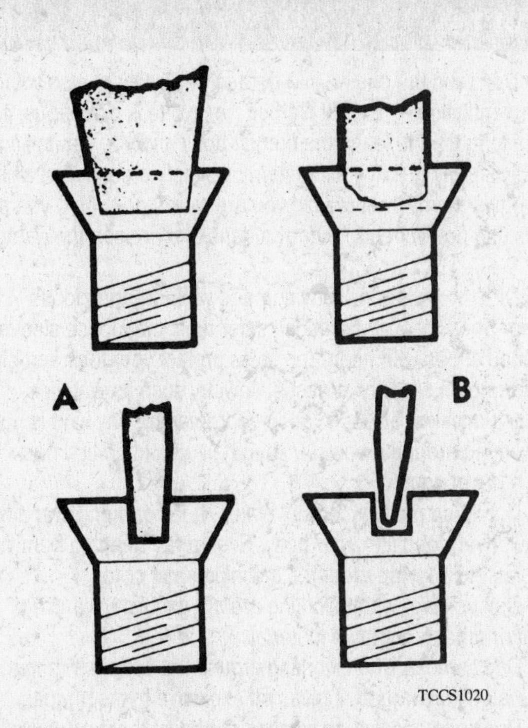

Fig. 15 Screwdrivers should be kept in good condition to prevent injury or damage which could result if the blade slips from the screw

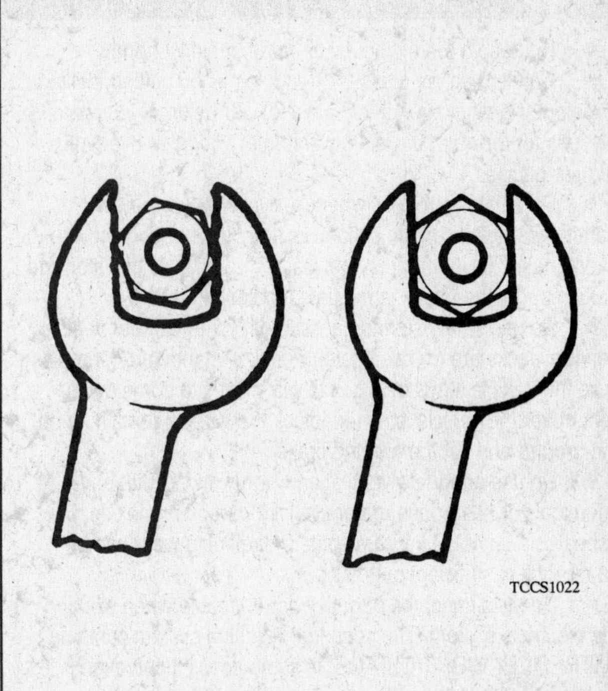

Fig. 17 Using the correct size wrench will help prevent the possibility of rounding-off a nut

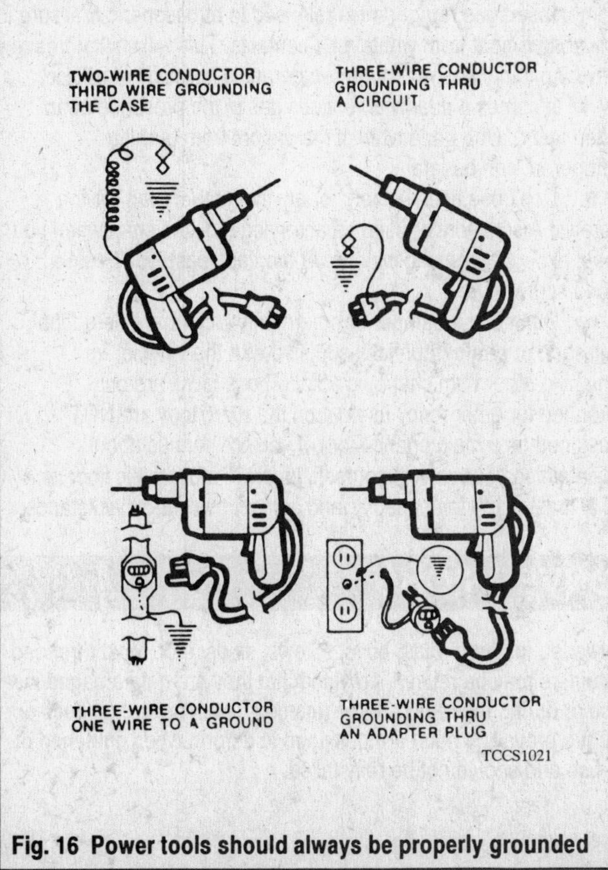

Fig. 16 Power tools should always be properly grounded

Fig. 18 NEVER work under a vehicle unless it is supported using safety stands (jackstands)

Do's

- Do keep a fire extinguisher and first aid kit handy.
- Do wear safety glasses or goggles when cutting, drilling, grinding or prying, even if you have 20-20 vision. If you wear glasses for the sake of vision, wear safety goggles over your regular glasses.
- Do shield your eyes whenever you work around the battery. Batteries contain sulfuric acid. In case of contact with the eyes or skin, flush the area with water or a mixture of water and baking soda, then seek immediate medical attention.
- Do use safety stands (jackstands) for any under vehicle service. Jacks are for raising vehicles; jackstands are for making sure the vehicle stays raised until you want it to come down. Whenever the vehicle is raised, block the wheels remaining on the ground and set the parking brake.
- Do use adequate ventilation when working with any chemicals or hazardous materials. Like carbon monoxide, the asbestos dust resulting from some brake lining wear can be hazardous in sufficient quantities.
- Do disconnect the negative battery cable when working on the electrical system. The secondary ignition system contains EXTREMELY HIGH VOLTAGE. In some cases it can even exceed 50,000 volts.
- Do follow manufacturer's directions whenever working with potentially hazardous materials. Most chemicals and fluids are poisonous if taken internally.
- Do properly maintain your tools. Loose hammerheads, mushroomed punches and chisels, frayed or poorly grounded electrical cords, excessively worn screwdrivers, spread wrenches (open end), cracked sockets, slipping ratchets, or faulty droplight sockets can cause accidents.
- Likewise, keep your tools clean; a greasy wrench can slip off a bolt head, ruining the bolt and often harming your knuckles in the process.
- Do use the proper size and type of tool for the job at hand. Do select a wrench or socket that fits the nut or bolt. The wrench or socket should sit straight, not cocked.
- Do, when possible, pull on a wrench handle rather than push on it, and adjust your stance to prevent a fall.
- Do be sure that adjustable wrenches are tightly closed on the nut or bolt and pulled so that the force is on the side of the fixed jaw.
- Do strike squarely with a hammer; avoid glancing blows.
- Do set the parking brake and block the drive wheels if the work requires a running engine.

Don'ts

- Don't run the engine in a garage or anywhere else without proper ventilation — EVER! Carbon monoxide is poisonous; it takes a long time to leave the human body and you can build up a deadly supply of it in your system by simply breathing in a little every day. You may not realize you are slowly poisoning yourself. Always use power vents, windows, fans and/or open the garage door.
- Don't work around moving parts while wearing loose clothing. Short sleeves are much safer than long, loose sleeves. Hard-toed shoes with neoprene soles protect your toes and give a better grip on slippery surfaces. Jewelry such as watches, fancy belt buckles, beads or body adornment of any kind is not safe working around a vehicle. Long hair should be tied back under a hat or cap.
- Don't use pockets for tool boxes. A fall or bump can drive a screwdriver deep into your body. Even a rag hanging from your back pocket can wrap around a spinning shaft or fan.
- Don't smoke when working around gasoline, cleaning solvent or other flammable material.
- Don't smoke when working around the battery. When the battery is being charged, it gives off explosive hydrogen gas.
- Don't use gasoline to wash your hands; there are excellent soaps available. Gasoline contains dangerous additives which can enter the body through a cut or through your pores. Gasoline also removes all the natural oils from the skin so that bone dry hands will suck up oil and grease.
- Don't service the air conditioning system unless you are equipped with the necessary tools and training. When liquid or compressed gas refrigerant is released to atmospheric pressure it will absorb heat from whatever it contacts. This will chill or freeze anything it touches. Although refrigerant is normally non-toxic, R-12 becomes a deadly poisonous gas in the presence of an open flame. One good whiff of the vapors from burning refrigerant can be fatal.
- Don't use screwdrivers for anything other than driving screws! A screwdriver used as an prying tool can snap when you least expect it, causing injuries. At the very least, you'll ruin a good screwdriver.
- Don't use a bumper or emergency jack (that little ratchet, scissors, or pantograph jack supplied with the vehicle) for anything other than changing a flat! These jacks are only intended for emergency use out on the road; they are NOT designed as a maintenance tool. If you are serious about maintaining your vehicle yourself, invest in a hydraulic floor jack of at least a 1½ ton capacity, and at least two sturdy jackstands.

FASTENERS, MEASUREMENTS AND CONVERSIONS

Bolts, Nuts and Other Threaded Retainers

See Figures 19, 20, 21 and 22

Although there are a great variety of fasteners found in the modern car or truck, the most commonly used retainer is the threaded fastener (nuts, bolts, screws, studs, etc). Most threaded retainers may be reused, provided that they are not damaged in use or during the repair. Some retainers (such as stretch bolts or torque prevailing nuts) are designed to deform when tightened or in use and should not be reinstalled.

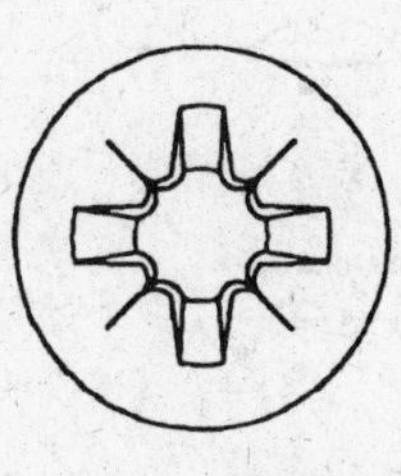

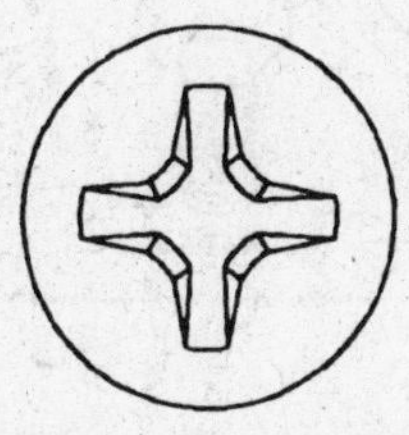

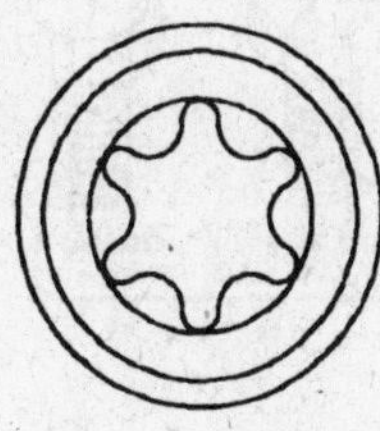

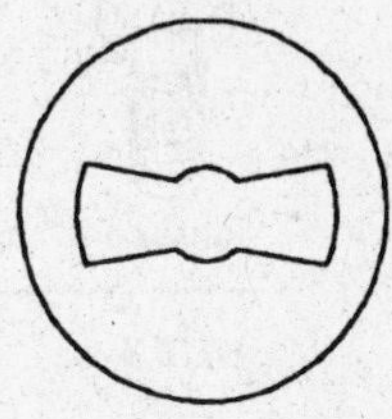

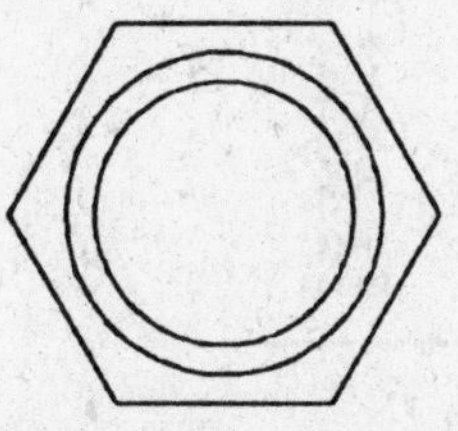
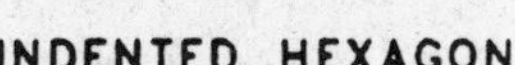

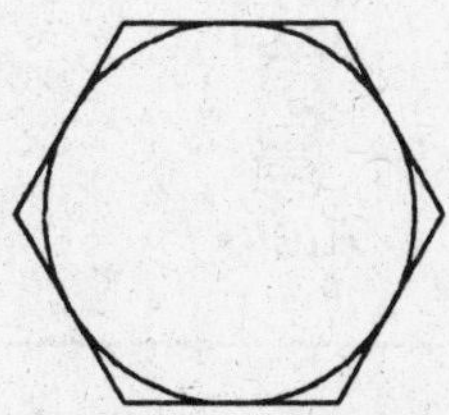

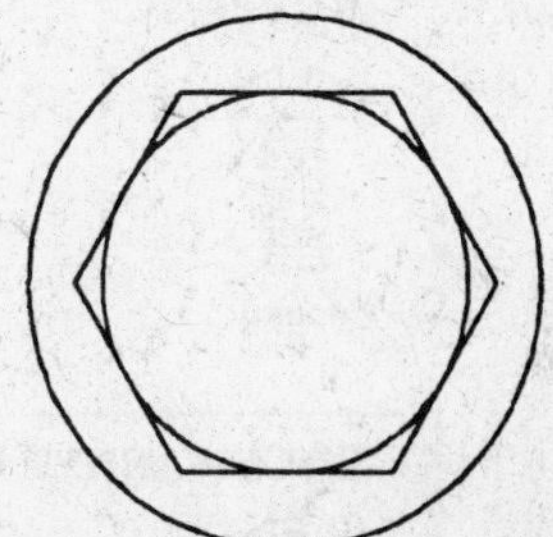

Fig. 19 Here are a few of the most common screw/bolt driver styles

Whenever possible, we will note any special retainers which should be replaced during a procedure. But you should always inspect the condition of a retainer when it is removed and replace any that show signs of damage. Check all threads for rust or corrosion which can increase the torque necessary to achieve the desired clamp load for which that fastener was originally selected. Additionally, be sure that the driver surface of the fastener has not been compromised by rounding or other damage. In some cases a driver surface may become only partially rounded, allowing the driver to catch in only one direction. In many of these occurrences, a fastener may be installed and tightened, but the driver would not be able to grip and loosen the fastener again. (This could lead to frustration down the line should that component ever need to be disassembled again).

If you must replace a fastener, whether due to design or damage, you must ALWAYS be sure to use the proper replacement. In all cases, a retainer of the same design, material and strength should be used. Markings on the heads of most bolts will help determine the proper strength of the fastener. The same material, thread and pitch must be selected to assure proper installation and safe operation of the vehicle afterwards.

Thread gauges are available to help measure a bolt or stud's thread. Most automotive and hardware stores keep gauges available to help you select the proper size. In a pinch, you can use another nut or bolt for a thread gauge. If the bolt you are replacing is not too badly damaged, you can select a match by finding another bolt which will thread in its place. If you find a nut which threads properly onto the damaged bolt, then use that nut to help select the replacement bolt. If however, the bolt you are replacing is so badly damaged (broken or drilled out) that its threads cannot be used as a gauge, you might start by looking for another bolt (from the same assembly or a similar location on your vehicle) which will thread into the damaged bolt's mounting. If so, the other bolt can be used to select a nut; the nut can then be used to select the replacement bolt.

In all cases, be absolutely sure you have selected the proper replacement. Don't be shy, you can always ask the store clerk for help.

**WARNING

Be aware that when you find a bolt with damaged threads, you may also find the nut or drilled hole it was threaded into has also been damaged. If this is the case, you may have to drill and tap the hole, replace the nut or otherwise repair the threads. NEVER try to force a replacement bolt to fit into the damaged threads.

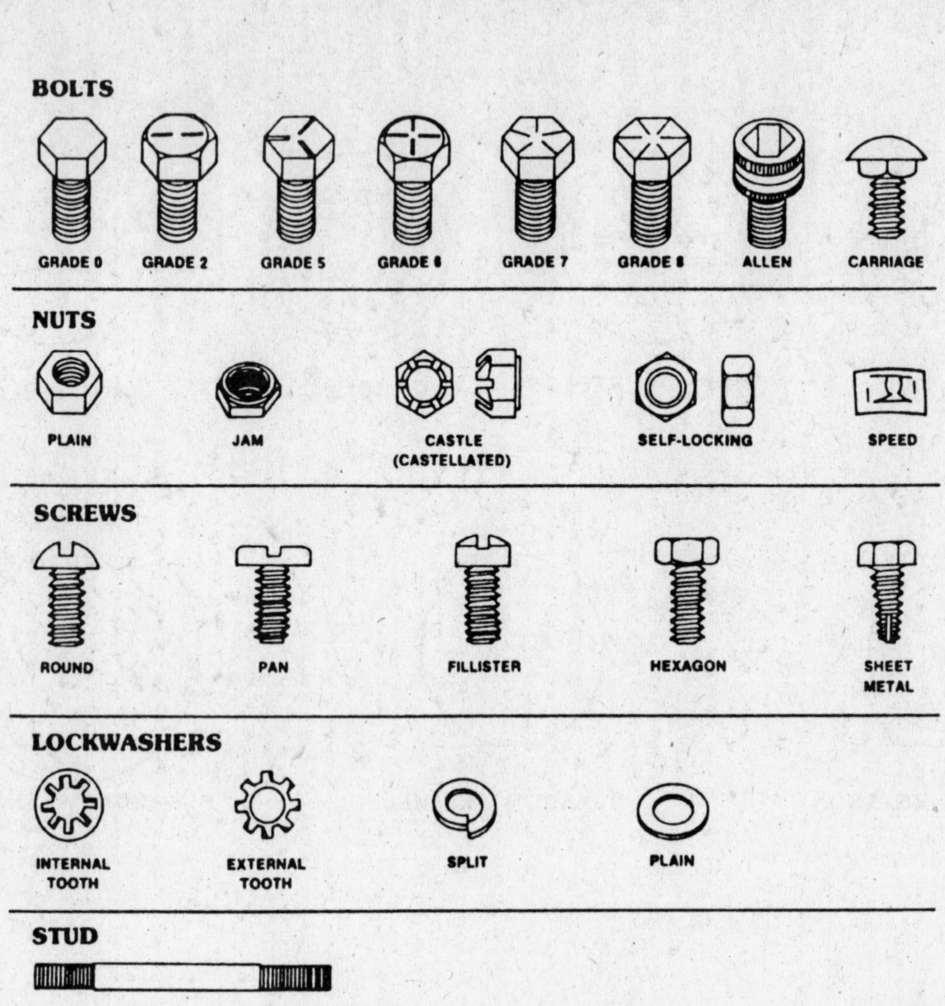

Fig. 20 There are many different types of threaded retainers found on vehicles

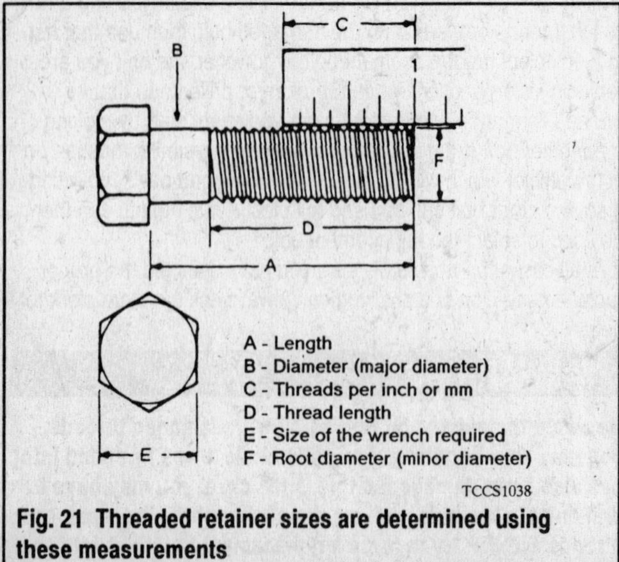

Fig. 21 Threaded retainer sizes are determined using these measurements

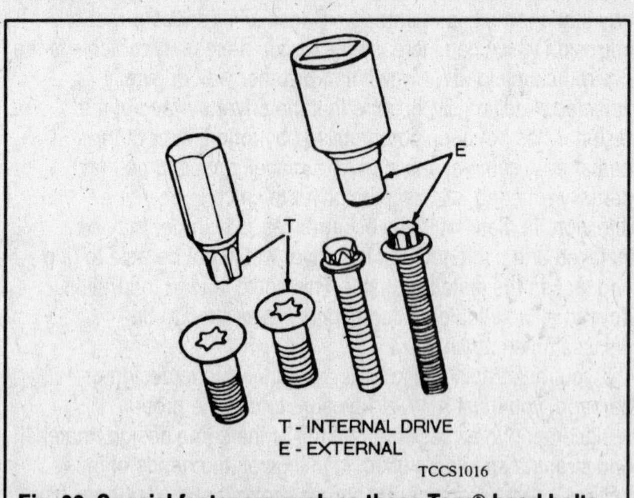

Fig. 22 Special fasteners such as these Torx® head bolts are used by manufacturers to discourage people from working on vehicles without the proper tools

Torque

Torque is defined as the measurement of resistance to turning or rotating. It tends to twist a body about an axis of rotation. A common example of this would be tightening a threaded retainer such as a nut, bolt or screw. Measuring torque is one of the most common ways to help assure that a threaded retainer has been properly fastened.

When tightening a threaded fastener, torque is applied in three distinct areas, the head, the bearing surface and the clamp load. About 50 percent of the measured torque is used in overcoming bearing friction. This is the friction between the bearing surface of the bolt head, screw head or nut face and the base material or washer (the surface on which the fastener is rotating). Approximately 40 percent of the applied torque is used in overcoming thread friction. This leaves only about 10 percent of the applied torque to develop a useful clamp load (the force which holds a joint together). This means that friction can account for as much as 90 percent of the applied torque on a fastener.

TORQUE WRENCHES

➧ See Figures 23 and 24

In most applications, a torque wrench can be used to assure proper installation of a fastener. Torque wrenches come in various designs and most automotive supply stores will carry a variety to suit your needs. A torque wrench should be used any time we supply a specific torque value for a fastener. A torque wrench can also be used if you are following the general guidelines in the accompanying charts. Keep in mind that because there is no worldwide standardization of fasteners, the charts are a general guideline and should be used with caution. Again, the general rule of""if you are using the right tool for the job, you should not have to strain to tighten a fastener" applies here.

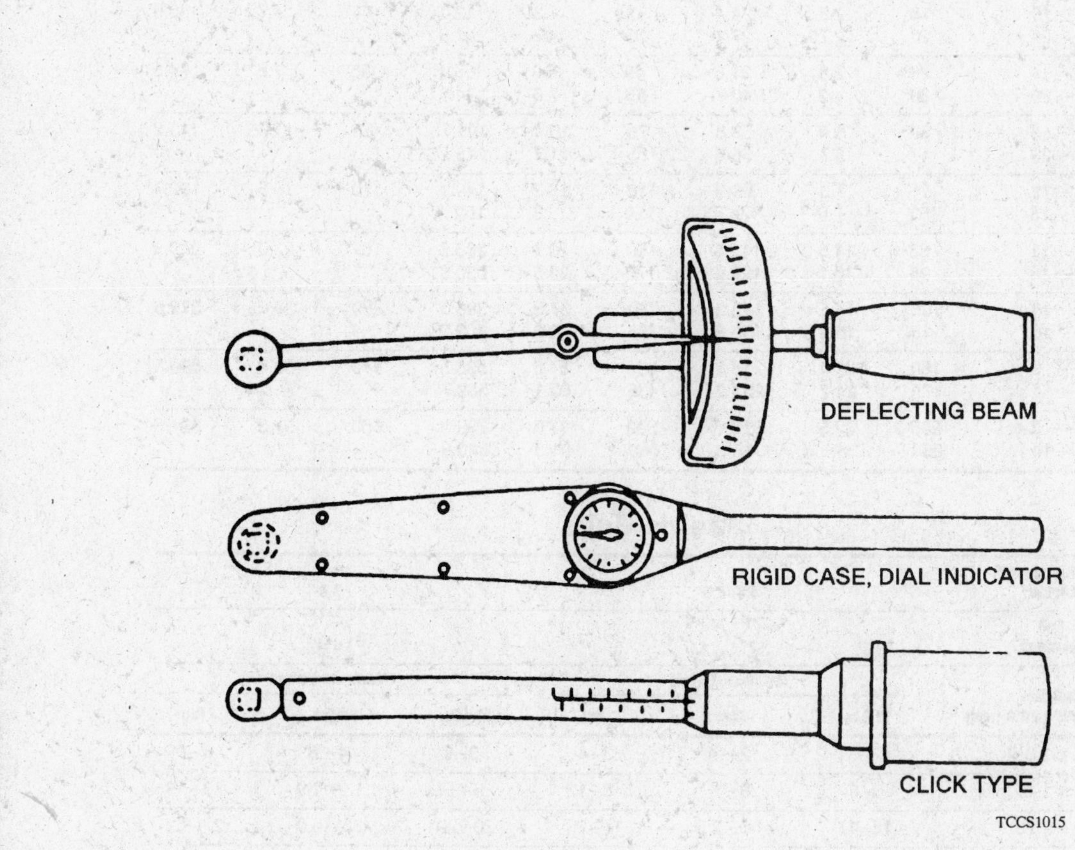

Fig. 23 Various styles of torque wrenches are usually available at your local automotive supply store

Standard Torque Specifications and Fastener Markings

In the absence of specific torques, the following chart can be used as a guide to the maximum safe torque of a particular size/grade of fastener.

- There is no torque difference for fine or coarse threads.
- Torque values are based on clean, dry threads. Reduce the value by 10% if threads are oiled prior to assembly.
- The torque required for aluminum components or fasteners is considerably less.

U.S. Bolts

SAE Grade Number	1 or 2			5			6 or 7		
Number of lines always 2 less than the grade number.									
	Maximum Torque			Maximum Torque			Maximum Torque		
Bolt Size (Inches)—(Thread)	Ft./Lbs.	Kgm	Nm	Ft./Lbs.	Kgm	Nm	Ft./Lbs.	Kgm	Nm
¼—20	5	0.7	6.8	8	1.1	10.8	10	1.4	13.5
—28	6	0.8	8.1	10	1.4	13.6			
5/16—18	11	1.5	14.9	17	2.3	23.0	19	2.6	25.8
—24	13	1.8	17.6	19	2.6	25.7			
⅜—16	18	2.5	24.4	31	4.3	42.0	34	4.7	46.0
—24	20	2.75	27.1	35	4.8	47.5			
7/16—14	28	3.8	37.0	49	6.8	66.4	55	7.6	74.5
—20	30	4.2	40.7	55	7.6	74.5			
½—13	39	5.4	52.8	75	10.4	101.7	85	11.75	115.2
—20	41	5.7	55.6	85	11.7	115.2			
9/16—12	51	7.0	69.2	110	15.2	149.1	120	16.6	162.7
—18	55	7.6	74.5	120	16.6	162.7			
⅝—11	83	11.5	112.5	150	20.7	203.3	167	23.0	226.5
—18	95	13.1	128.8	170	23.5	230.5			
¾—10	105	14.5	142.3	270	37.3	366.0	280	38.7	379.6
—16	115	15.9	155.9	295	40.8	400.0			
⅞— 9	160	22.1	216.9	395	54.6	535.5	440	60.9	596.5
—14	175	24.2	237.2	435	60.1	589.7			
1— 8	236	32.5	318.6	590	81.6	799.9	660	91.3	894.8
—14	250	34.6	338.9	660	91.3	849.8			

Metric Bolts

Relative Strength Marking	4.6, 4.8			8.8		
Bolt Markings						
	Maximum Torque			Maximum Torque		
Bolt Size Thread Size x Pitch (mm)	Ft./Lbs.	Kgm	Nm	Ft./Lbs.	Kgm	Nm
6 x 1.0	2-3	.2-.4	3-4	3-6	4-.8	5-8
8 x 1.25	6-8	.8-1	8-12	9-14	1.2-1.9	13-19
10 x 1.25	12-17	1.5-2.3	16-23	20-29	2.7-4.0	27-39
12 x 1.25	21-32	2.9-4.4	29-43	35-53	4.8-7.3	47-72
14 x 1.5	35-52	4.8-7.1	48-70	57-85	7.8-11.7	77-110
16 x 1.5	51-77	7.0-10.6	67-100	90-120	12.4-16.5	130-160
18 x 1.5	74-110	10.2-15.1	100-150	130-170	17.9-23.4	180-230
20 x 1.5	110-140	15.1-19.3	150-190	190-240	26.2-46.9	160-320
22 x 1.5	150-190	22.0-26.2	200-260	250-320	34.5-44.1	340-430
24 x 1.5	190-240	26.2-46.9	260-320	310-410	42.7-56.5	420-550

TCCS1098

Fig. 24 Standard and metric bolt torque specifications based on bolt strengths — WARNING: use only as a guide

Beam Type

➧ See Figure 25

The beam type torque wrench is one of the most popular types. It consists of a pointer attached to the head that runs the length of the flexible beam (shaft) to a scale located near the handle. As the wrench is pulled, the beam bends and the pointer indicates the torque using the scale.

Click (Breakaway) Type

➧ See Figure 26

Another popular design of torque wrench is the click type. To use the click type wrench you pre-adjust it to a torque setting. Once the torque is reached, the wrench has a reflex signalling feature that causes a momentary break-away of the torque wrench body, sending an impulse to the operator's hand.

Pivot Head Type

➧ See Figures 26 and 27

Some torque wrenches (usually of the click type) may be equipped with a pivot head which can allow it to be used in areas of limited access. BUT, it must be used properly. To hold a pivot head wrench, grasp the handle lightly, and as you pull on the handle, it should be floated on the pivot point. If the handle comes in contact with the yoke extension during the process of pulling, there is a very good chance the torque readings will be inaccurate because this could alter the wrench loading point. The design of the handle is usually such as to make it inconvenient to deliberately misuse the wrench.

➥ It should be mentioned that the use of any U-joint, wobble or extension will have an effect on the torque readings, no matter what type of wrench you are using. For the most accurate readings, install the socket directly on the wrench driver. If necessary, straight extensions (which hold a socket directly under the wrench driver) will have the least effect on the torque reading. Avoid any extension that alters the length of the wrench from the handle to the head/driving point (such as a crow's foot). U-joint or Wobble extensions can greatly affect the readings; avoid their use at all times.

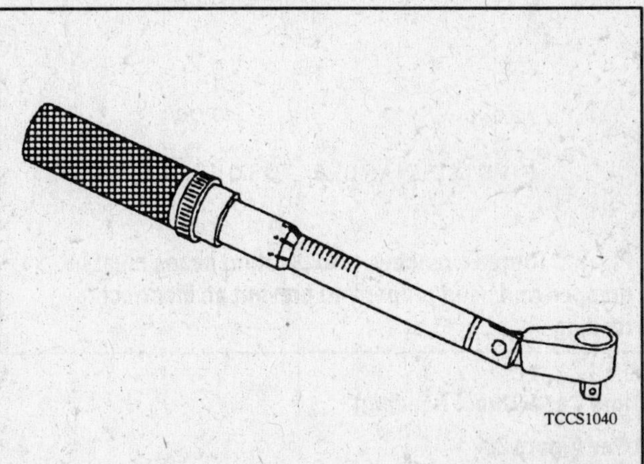

Fig. 26 A click type or break-away torque wrench — note this one has a pivoting head

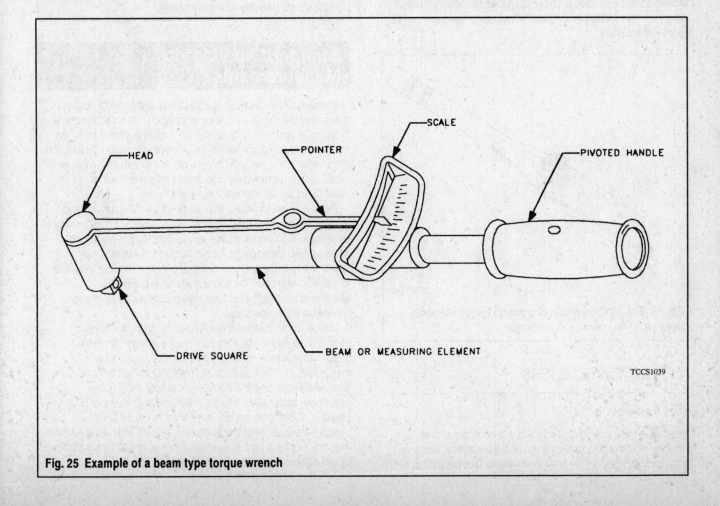

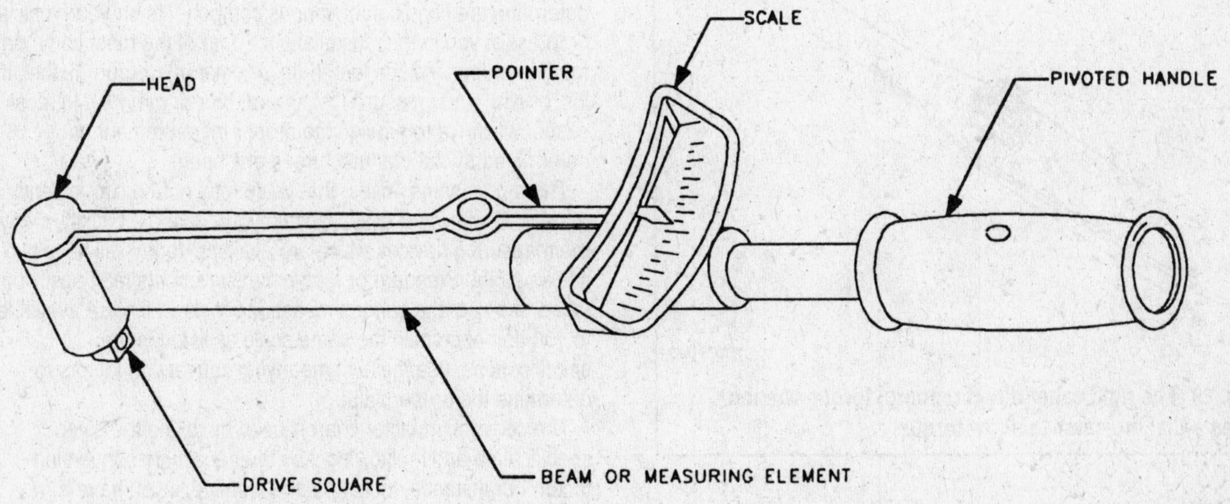

HEAD
POINTER
SCALE
PIVOTED HANDLE
DRIVE SQUARE
BEAM OR MEASURING ELEMENT
TCCS1039

Fig. 25 Example of a beam type torque wrench

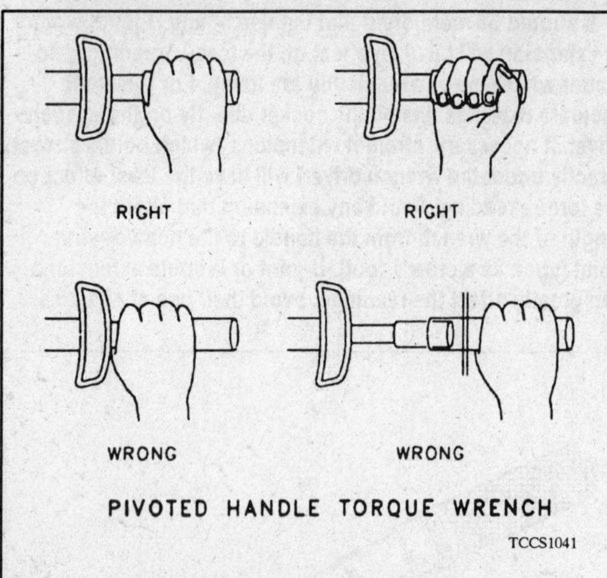

Fig. 27 Torque wrenches with pivoting heads must be grasped and used properly to prevent an incorrect reading

Rigid Case (Direct Reading)

➧ See Figure 28

A rigid case or direct reading torque wrench is equipped with a dial indicator to show torque values. One advantage of these wrenches is that they can be held at any position on the wrench without affecting accuracy. These wrenches are often preferred because they tend to be compact, easy to read and have a great degree of accuracy.

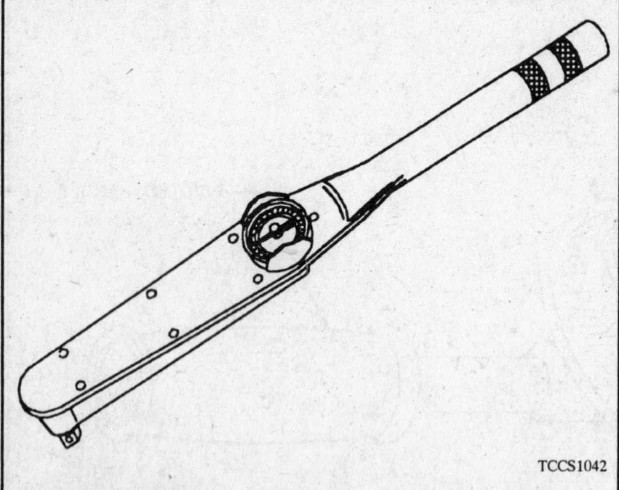

Fig. 28 The rigid case (direct reading) torque wrench uses a dial indicator to show torque

TORQUE ANGLE METERS

➧ See Figure 29

Because the frictional characteristics of each fastener or threaded hole will vary, clamp loads which are based strictly on torque will vary as well. In most applications, this variance is not significant enough to cause worry. But, in certain applications, a manufacturer's engineers may determine that more precise clamp loads are necessary (such is the case with many aluminum cylinder heads). In these cases, a torque angle method of installation would be specified. When installing fasteners which are torque angle tightened, a predetermined seating torque and standard torque wrench are usually used first to remove any compliance from the joint. The fastener is then tightened the specified additional portion of a turn measured in degrees. A torque angle gauge (mechanical protractor) is used for these applications.

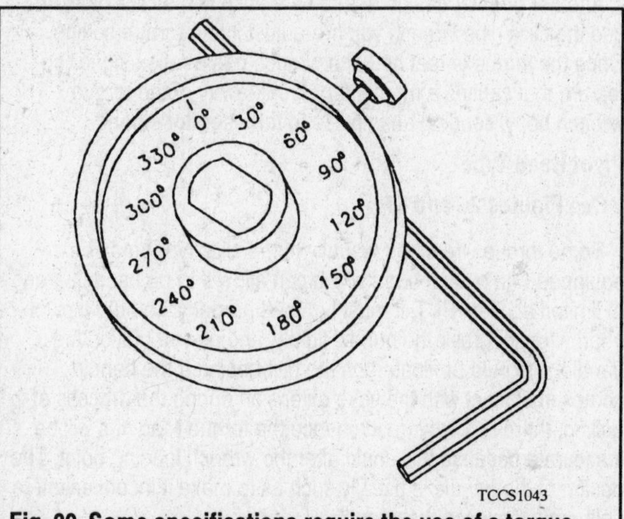

Fig. 29 Some specifications require the use of a torque angle meter (mechanical protractor)

Standard and Metric Measurements

Throughout this manual, specifications are given to help you determine the condition of various components on your vehicle, or to assist you in their installation. Some of the most common measurements include length (in. or cm/mm), torque (ft. lbs., inch lbs. or Nm) and pressure (psi, in. Hg, kPa or mm Hg). In most cases, we strive to provide the proper measurement as determined by the manufacturer's engineers.

Though, in some cases, that value may not be conveniently measured with what is available in your tool box. Luckily, many of the measuring devices which are available today will have two scales so the Standard or Metric measurements may easily be taken. If any of the various measuring tools which are available to you do not contain the same scale as listed in the specifications, use the accompanying conversion factors to determine the proper value.

The conversion factor chart is used by taking the given specification and multiplying it by the necessary conversion factor. For instance, looking at the first line, if you have a measurement in inches such as""free-play should be 2 in." but your ruler reads only in millimeters, multiply 2 in. by the conversion factor of 25.4 to get the metric equivalent of 50.8mm. Likewise, if the specification was given only in a Metric measurement, for example in Newton Meters (Nm), then look at the center column first. If the measurement is 100 Nm, multiply it by the conversion factor of 0.738 to get 73.8 ft. lbs.

CONVERSION FACTORS

LENGTH–DISTANCE

Inches (in.)	x 25.4	= Millimeters (mm)	x .0394	= Inches
Feet (ft.)	x .305	= Meters (m)	x 3.281	= Feet
Miles	x 1.609	= Kilometers (km)	x .0621	= Miles

VOLUME

Cubic Inches (in3)	x 16.387	= Cubic Centimeters	x .061	= in3
IMP Pints (IMP pt.)	x .568	= Liters (L)	x 1.76	= IMP pt.
IMP Quarts (IMP qt.)	x 1.137	= Liters (L)	x .88	= IMP qt.
IMP Gallons (IMP gal.)	x 4.546	= Liters (L)	x .22	= IMP gal.
IMP Quarts (IMP qt.)	x 1.201	= US Quarts (US qt.)	x .833	= IMP qt.
IMP Gallons (IMP gal.)	x 1.201	= US Gallons (US gal.)	x .833	= IMP gal.
Fl. Ounces	x 29.573	= Milliliters	x .034	= Ounces
US Pints (US pt.)	x .473	= Liters (L)	x 2.113	= Pints
US Quarts (US qt.)	x .946	= Liters (L)	x 1.057	= Quarts
US Gallons (US gal.)	x 3.785	= Liters (L)	x .264	= Gallons

MASS–WEIGHT

Ounces (oz.)	x 28.35	= Grams (g)	x .035	= Ounces
Pounds (lb.)	x .454	= Kilograms (kg)	x 2.205	= Pounds

PRESSURE

Pounds Per Sq. In. (psi)	x 6.895	= Kilopascals (kPa)	x .145	= psi
Inches of Mercury (Hg)	x .4912	= psi	x 2.036	= Hg
Inches of Mercury (Hg)	x 3.377	= Kilopascals (kPa)	x .2961	= Hg
Inches of Water (H_2O)	x .07355	= Inches of Mercury	x 13.783	= H_2O
Inches of Water (H_2O)	x .03613	= psi	x 27.684	= H_2O
Inches of Water (H_2O)	x .248	= Kilopascals (kPa)	x 4.026	= H_2O

TORQUE

Pounds–Force Inches (in–lb)	x .113	= Newton Meters (N·m)	x 8.85	= in–lb
Pounds–Force Feet (ft–lb)	x 1.356	= Newton Meters (N·m)	x .738	= ft–lb

VELOCITY

Miles Per Hour (MPH)	x 1.609	= Kilometers Per Hour (KPH)	x .621	= MPH

POWER

Horsepower (Hp)	x .745	= Kilowatts	x 1.34	= Horsepower

FUEL CONSUMPTION*

Miles Per Gallon IMP (MPG)	x .354	= Kilometers Per Liter (Km/L)
Kilometers Per Liter (Km/L)	x 2.352	= IMP MPG
Miles Per Gallon US (MPG)	x .425	= Kilometers Per Liter (Km/L)
Kilometers Per Liter (Km/L)	x 2.352	= US MPG

*It is common to covert from miles per gallon (mpg) to liters/100 kilometers (1/100 km), where mpg (IMP) x 1/100 km = 282 and mpg (US) x 1/100 km = 235.

TEMPERATURE

Degree Fahrenheit (°F)	= (°C x 1.8) + 32
Degree Celsius (°C)	= (°F – 32) x .56

TCCS1044

MODEL IDENTIFICATION

The Caravan and Voyager models covered in this manual have remained much the same since their introduction. There are a few variations on the basic model, these include the Mini Ram Van, the 1991 Chrysler Town & Country and the Plymouth Grand Voyager. All of these models are still based on the Caravan and Voyager, and are only different in trim configurations.

As of 1991, Chrysler began offering both anti-lock brakes and All Wheel Drive (AWD) as an option on the entire Caravan and Voyager line.

SERIAL NUMBER IDENTIFICATION

Vehicle Identification Number (VIN)

➧ See Figures 30 and 31

The vehicle identification number (VIN) consists of seventeen numbers and letters embossed on a plate, located on the upper left corner of the instrument panel, near the windshield.

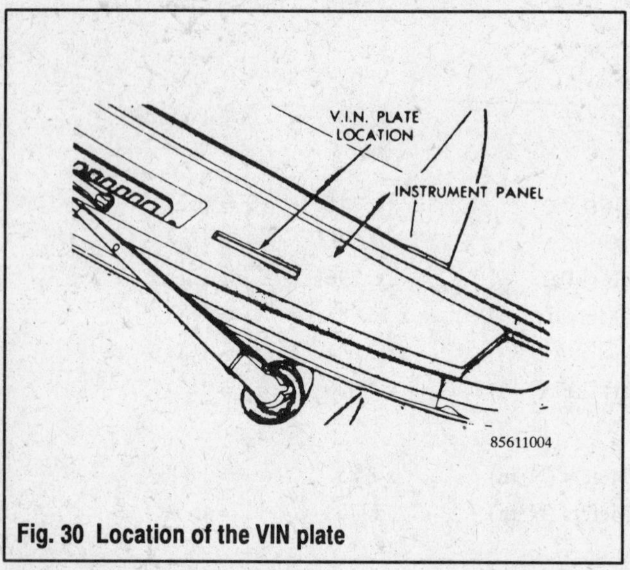

Fig. 30 Location of the VIN plate

Fig. 31 Example of a VIN plate

Engine Identification Number (EIN)

➧ See Figures 32, 33, 34, 35 and 36

All engine assemblies carry an engine identification number (EIN). On 2.2 liter and 2.5 liter engines, the EIN is located on the face of the engine block, directly under the cylinder head (left side of vehicle).

On 1984–90 2.6 liter, 3.0 liter and 3.3 liter engines, the EIN is located on the left side of the engine block between the core plug and the rear face of the block (radiator side of vehicle). On the 1991–95 3.0 liter, 3.3 liter and 3.8 liter engines, the engine serial number (E.I.N) is located on the rear face of the engine block, directly below the cylinder head.

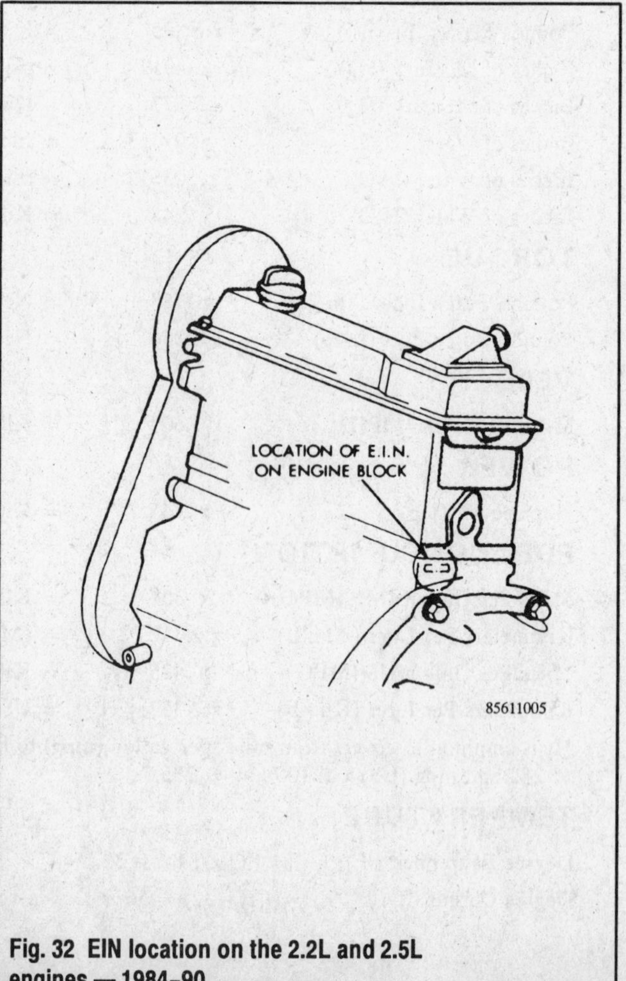

Fig. 32 EIN location on the 2.2L and 2.5L engines — 1984–90

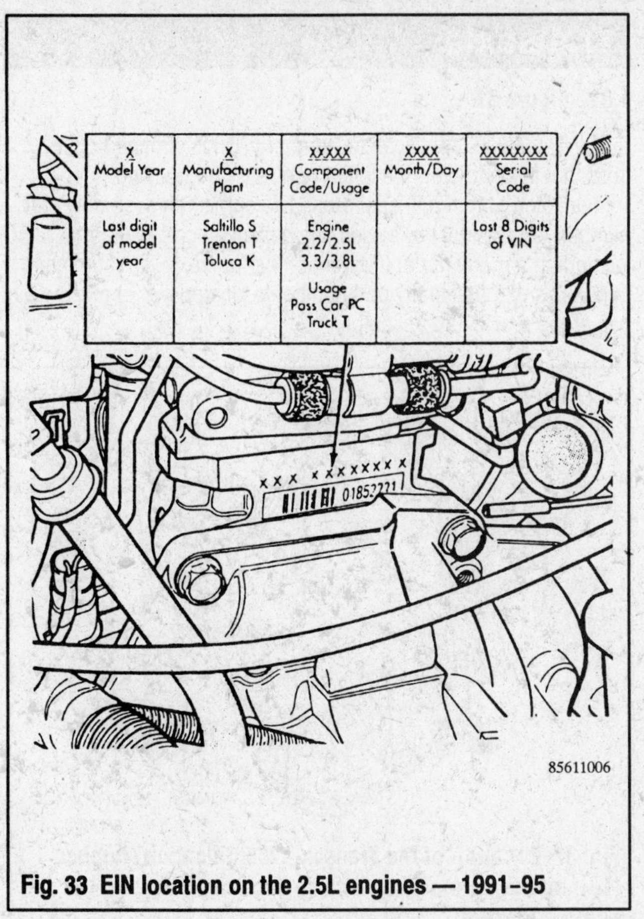

Fig. 33 EIN location on the 2.5L engines — 1991-95

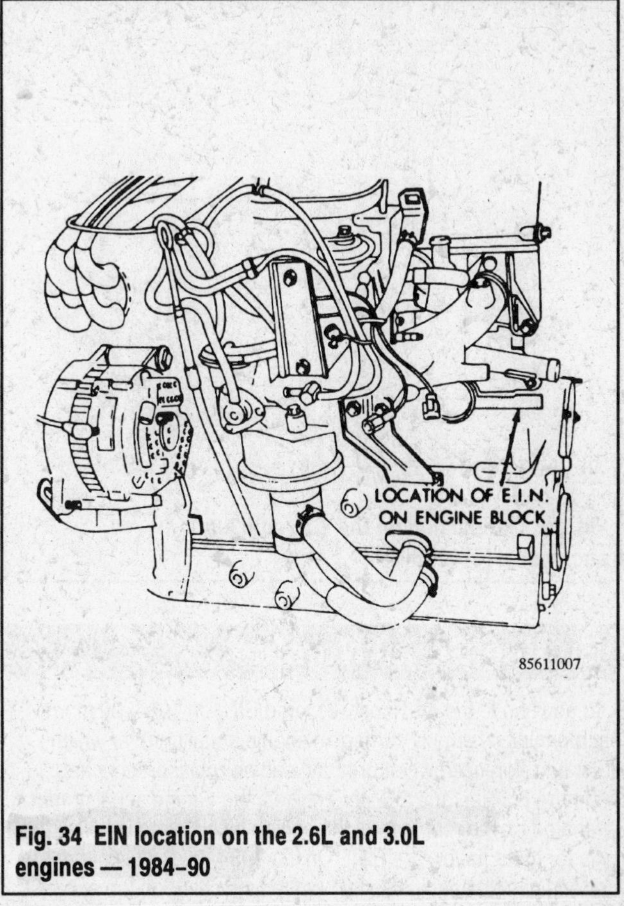

Fig. 34 EIN location on the 2.6L and 3.0L engines — 1984-90

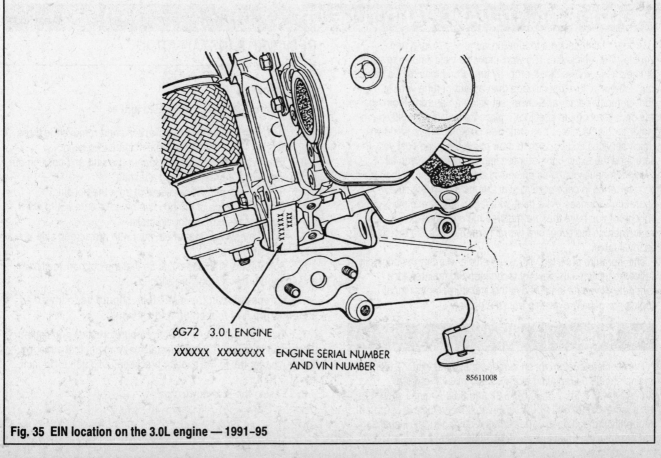

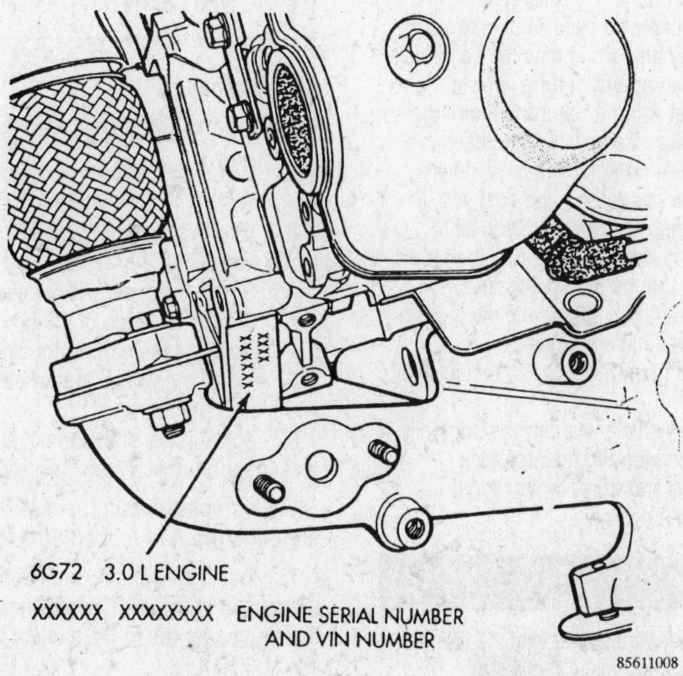

Fig. 35 EIN location on the 3.0L engine — 1991-95

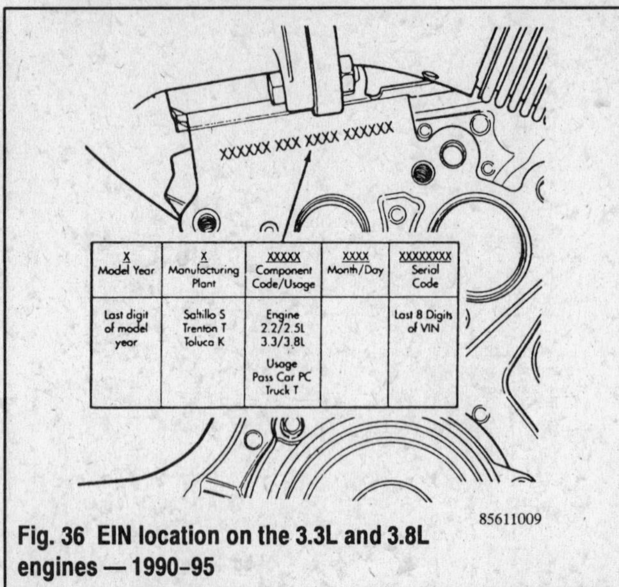

X Model Year	X Manufacturing Plant	XXXXX Component Code/Usage	XXXX Month/Day	XXXXXXXX Serial Code
Last digit of model year	Saltillo S Trenton T Toluca K	Engine 2.2/2.5L 3.3/3.8L Usage Pass Car PC Truck T		Last 8 Digits of VIN

Fig. 36 EIN location on the 3.3L and 3.8L engines — 1990–95

Engine Serial Number

In addition to the previously covered EIN, on 1984–90 models, each engine assembly carries an engine serial number which must be referenced when ordering engine replacement parts.

On the 2.2 liter, and 2.5 liter engines, the engine serial number is located on the rear face of the engine block, directly below the cylinder head (below the EIN). On the 1984–90 2.6 liter, and 3.0 liter engines, the engine serial number is located on the exhaust manifold stud (dash panel side of vehicle).

Transaxle

➧ **See Figure 37**

The Transaxle Identification Number (TIN) is stamped on a boss that is located on the left upper transaxle housing.

In addition to the TIN, each transaxle carries an assembly part number. On manual transaxles, the assembly part number is located on a metal tag at the front of the transaxle. On automatic transaxles, the assembly part number is located just above the oil pan at the rear of the assembly.

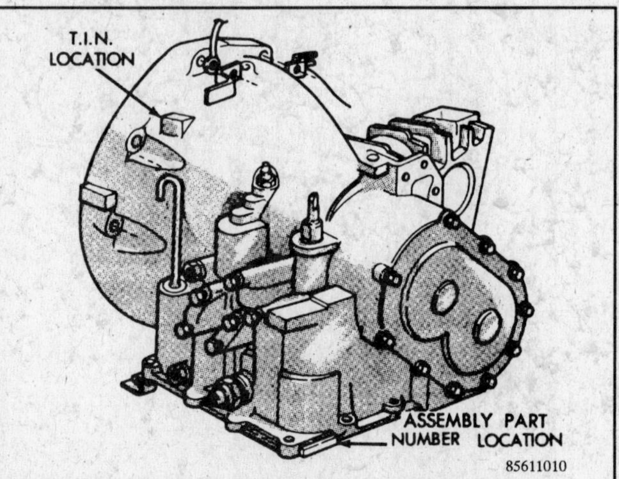

Fig. 37 Location of the Transaxle Identification Number (TIN) on the automatic transaxle and assembly part number location

ROUTINE MAINTENANCE AND TUNE-UP

Proper maintenance and tune-up is the key to long and trouble-free vehicle life. The work can also yield its own rewards. Studies have shown that a properly tuned and maintained vehicle can achieve better gas mileage than an out-of-tune vehicle. As a conscientious owner and driver, set aside a Saturday morning, say once a month, to check or replace items which could cause major problems later. Keep your own personal log to jot down which services you performed, how much the parts cost you, the date, and the exact odometer reading at the time. Keep all receipts for such items as engine oil and filters, so that they may be referred to in case of related problems or to determine operating expenses. As a do-it-yourselfer, these receipts are the only proof you have that the required maintenance was performed. In the event of a warranty problem, these receipts will be invaluable.

The literature provided with your vehicle when it was originally delivered includes the factory recommended maintenance schedule. If you no longer have this literature, replacement copies are usually available from the dealer.

Air Cleaner

The air cleaner element on vehicles equipped with 2.2 liter engine should be replaced every 52,000 miles. Vehicles equipped with 2.5L, 2.6L, 3.0L, 3.3L and 3.8L engines should be replaced every 30,000 miles. However, if the vehicle is operated frequently through dusty areas; it will require periodic inspection and/or replacement at least every 15,000 miles.

REMOVAL & INSTALLATION

2.2L Engines

➧ **See Figures 38, 39, 40, 41, 42, 43 and 44**

1. Unfasten the three hold-down clips and remove the three wing nuts that retain the top of the air cleaner housing.
2. Remove the top of the air cleaner housing and position out of the way with the breather hose attached.
3. Remove the air cleaner element from the housing.
4. Clean the inside of the housing but take care not to allow the dirt to enter the carburetor air intake.
5. Install a new air cleaner element with the screen side up into the plastic housing.
6. Position the steel top cover so that the hold-down clips and support bracket studs are aligned.

➥ **The procedures in the next steps should be followed as stated to prevent loosening and air leaks.**

7. Install the wing nuts on both carburetor studs and tighten them to 14 inch lbs. (1.6 Nm). Install the wing nut that attaches the air cleaner tab to the support bracket and tighten to 14 inch lbs. (1.6 Nm).
8. Fasten the hold-down clips.

85611011

Fig. 38 Before removing the air cleaner housing, disconnect the hoses from the housing retaining clips

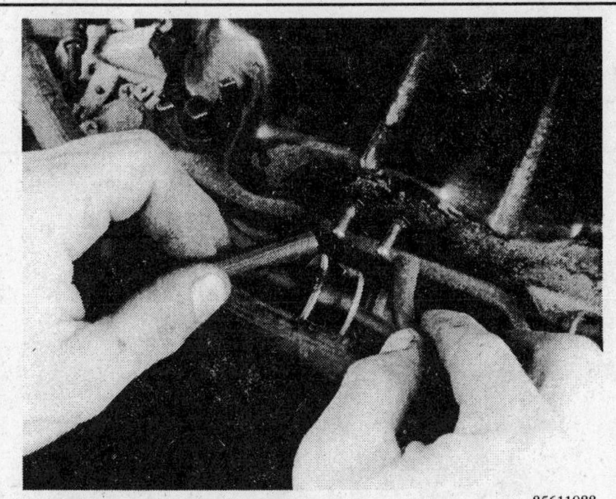
85611088

Fig. 39 Although not necessary, the hoses may be disengaged from the housing connectors

85611089

Fig. 40 Unsnap the spring clips from the air cleaner housing

85611090

Fig. 41 When removing the housing, remove this wingnut first. Install this wingnut last during installation

85611091

Fig. 42 During removal, loosen the two end wingnuts last. Install these nuts first during installation

85611092

Fig. 43 After unsnaping the clips and removing the nuts the air cleaner housing cover can be removed

Fig. 44 With the air cleaner housing cover removed the air filter element can easily be replaced

Except 2.2L Engines

See Figures 45, 46, 47, 48 and 49

1. Unfasten the hold-down clips that retain the air cleaner cover.
2. Remove the air cleaner housing cover with intake hose attached and position out of the way.
3. Remove the air cleaner element from the housing.
4. Clean the inside of the air cleaner housing.
5. Install a new cleaner element and position the cover on the air cleaner housing. Secure the hold-down clips.

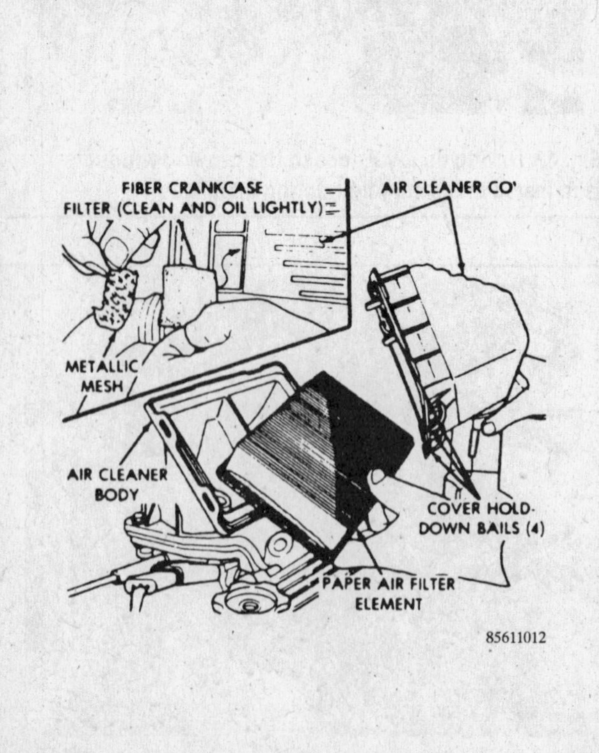

Fig. 45 Air cleaner assembly — 2.5L engines

Fig. 46 Air cleaner assembly — 2.6L engines

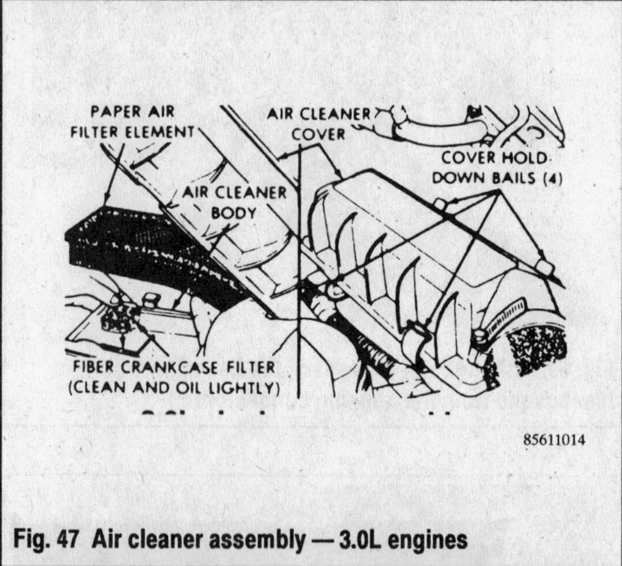

Fig. 47 Air cleaner assembly — 3.0L engines

Fuel Filter

**CAUTION

Don't smoke when working around gasoline, cleaning solvent or other flammable material. The hoses used on fuel injected vehicles are of a special construction due to the possibility contaminated fuel in the system. If it is necessary to replace these hoses, only hoses marked EFM/EFI may be used. The hose clamps used on fuel injected vehicles are of a special rolled edge construction to prevent the edge of the clamp from cutting into the hose, resulting in a high pressure fuel leak.

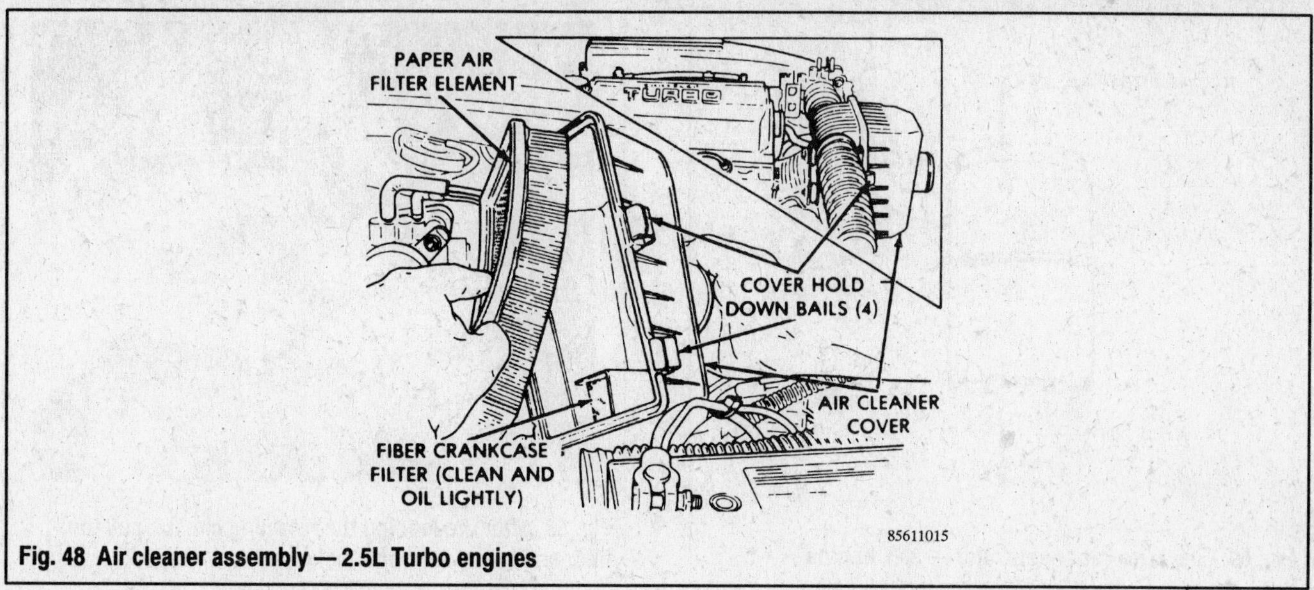

Fig. 48 Air cleaner assembly — 2.5L Turbo engines

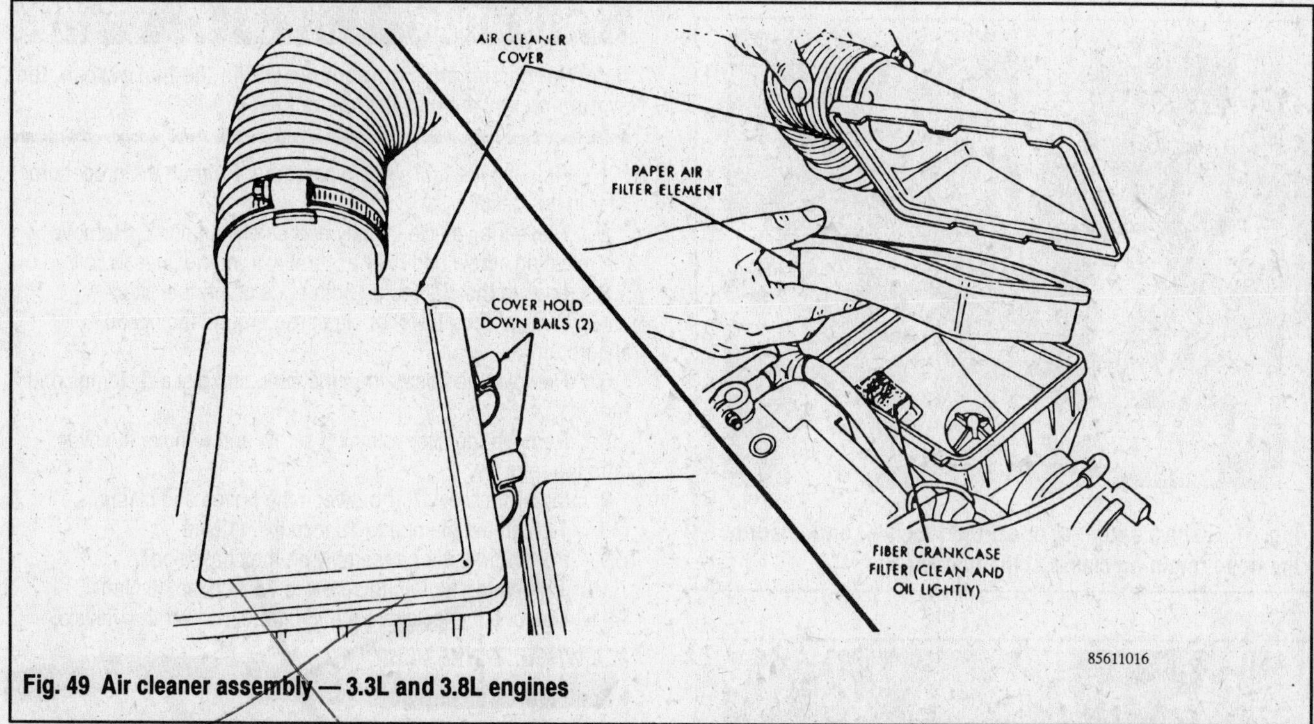

Fig. 49 Air cleaner assembly — 3.3L and 3.8L engines

The fuel system on all vehicles incorporate two fuel filters. One is part of the fuel gauge unit; located inside the fuel tank at the fuel suction tube. Routine servicing of this filter is not necessary. However, if limited vehicle speed or hard starting is exhibited, it should be inspected.

The second filter is located in the fuel line between the fuel pump and the carburetor or fuel injector rail. Replacement of this filter is recommended every 52,000 miles.

REMOVAL & INSTALLATION

2.2L and 2.6L Engines

➧ See Figures 50, 51, 52 and 53

1. Clean the area at the filter and clamps with a suitable solvent
2. Loosen the clamps on both ends of filter.
3. Wrap a shop towel or clean rag around the hoses to absorb fuel.
4. Remove the hoses from the filter, and discard the clamps and filter.
5. Install the new filter between the fuel lines and clamp.
6. Tighten the clamps to 10 inch lbs. (1 Nm)

2.5L, 3.0L and 3.3L Engines

EXCEPT ALL WHEEL DRIVE VEHICLES

➧ See Figure 54

The fuel filter on these vehicles is located along the chassis, mounted just ahead of the fuel tank. To remove the filter, the vehicle will have to be raised slightly.

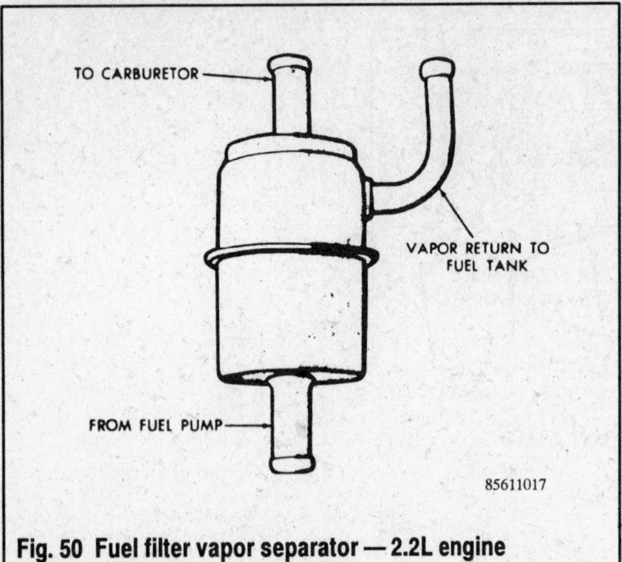

Fig. 50 Fuel filter vapor separator — 2.2L engine

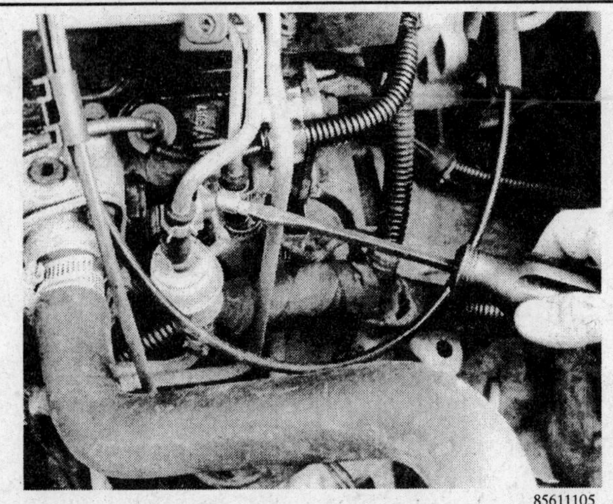

Fig. 51 Place a shop rag under the fuel filter and unscrew the hose retaining clamp at the fuel line

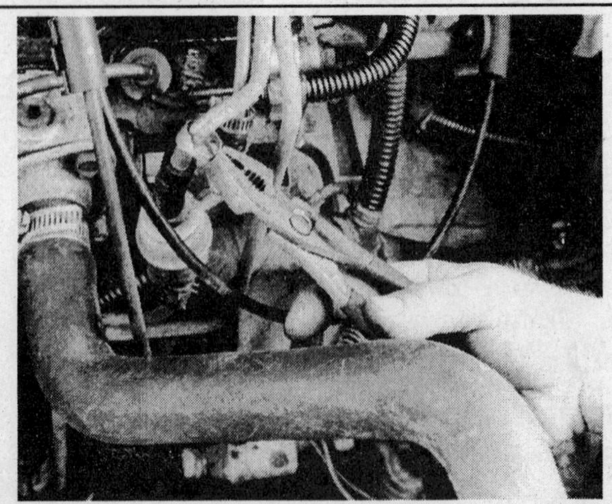

Fig. 52 Squeeze open the other hose retaining clamps with a suitable pair of pliers

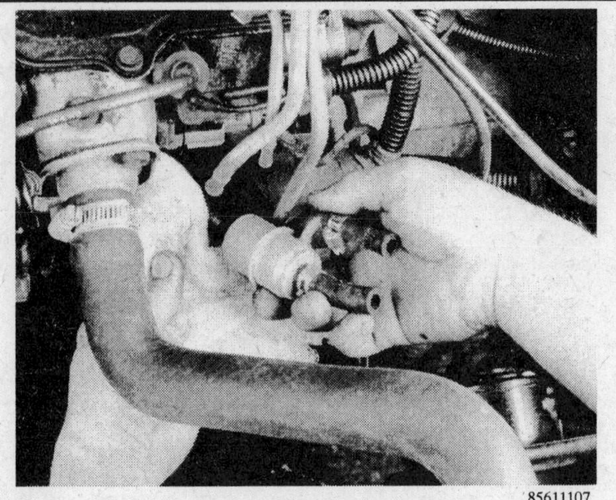

Fig. 53 After the loosing the retaining clamps pull the filter and hoses from the fuel pipes

****CAUTION**

Before servicing any components within the fuel system, the system pressure must first be released.

1. Release the fuel system pressure. Refer to the procedure later in this section.
2. Raise the vehicle slightly and safely support it. Remove the retaining screw and filter assembly from the chassis rail.
3. Loosen the clamps on both ends of the fuel filter.
4. Wrap a shop towel or clean rag around the hoses to absorb fuel
5. Remove the hoses from the filter, and discard clamps and filter.
6. Remove the filter retaining screw and remove the filter from the rail.
7. Install the new filter between the hoses and clamp.
8. Tighten the clamps to 10 inch lbs. (1 Nm).
9. Position the filter assembly on the chassis rail.
10. Tighten the mounting screw to 75 inch lbs. (8 Nm)
11. Remove the jackstands and carefully lower the vehicle.

ALL WHEEL DRIVE VEHICLES

See Figures 55 and 56

****CAUTION**

Before servicing any components within the fuel system, the system pressure must first be released.

1. Release the fuel system pressure. Refer to the procedure later in this section.
2. Raise the vehicle slightly and safely support it. Remove the retaining screw and filter assembly from the chassis rail.
3. Remove the converter support bracket.
4. Remove the exhaust pipe heat shield.
5. Loosen the clamps on both ends of the fuel filter.
6. Wrap a shop towel or clean rag around the hoses to absorb fuel

7. Remove the hoses from the filter, and discard clamps and filter.
8. Remove the filter retaining screw and remove the filter from the rail.
9. Install the new filter between the hoses and clamp.
10. Tighten the clamps to 10 inch lbs. (1 Nm).
11. Position the filter assembly on the chassis rail.
12. Tighten the mounting screw to 75 inch lbs. (8 Nm)
13. Install the exhaust pipe heat shield.
14. Install the converter support bracket.
15. Remove the jackstands and carefully lower the vehicle.

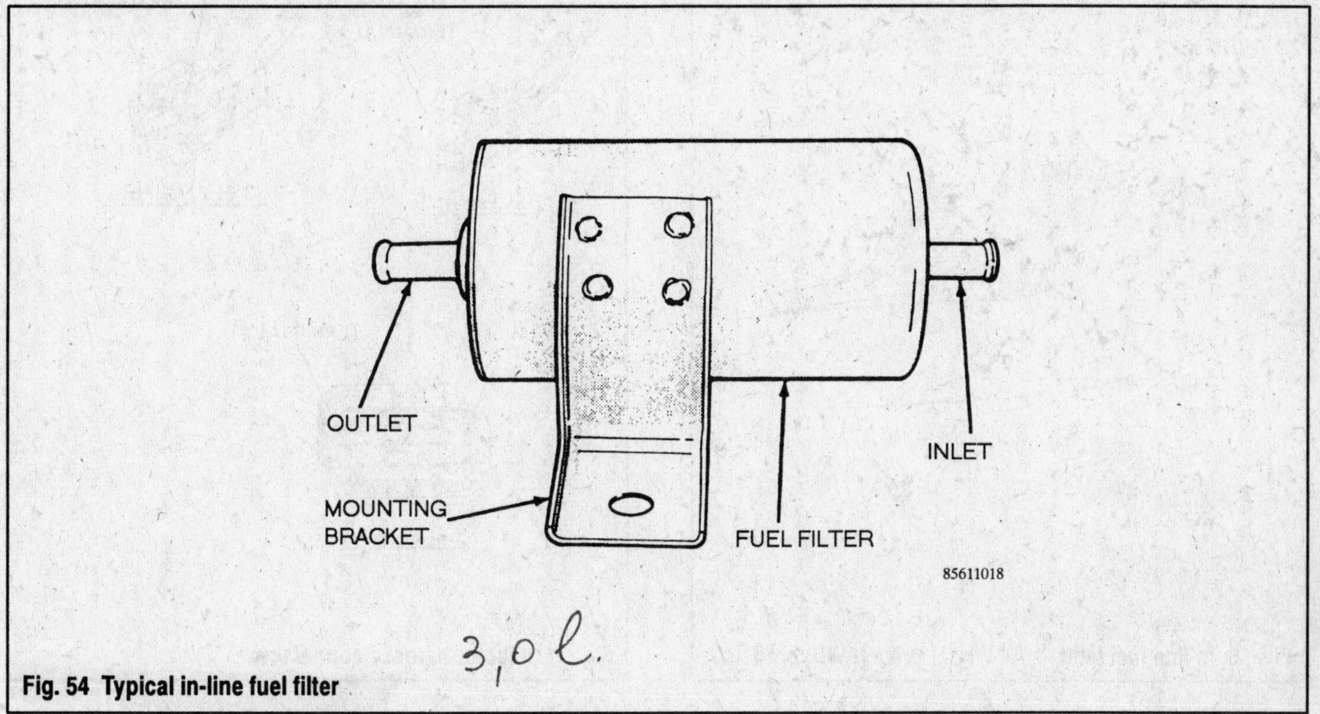

Fig. 54 Typical in-line fuel filter

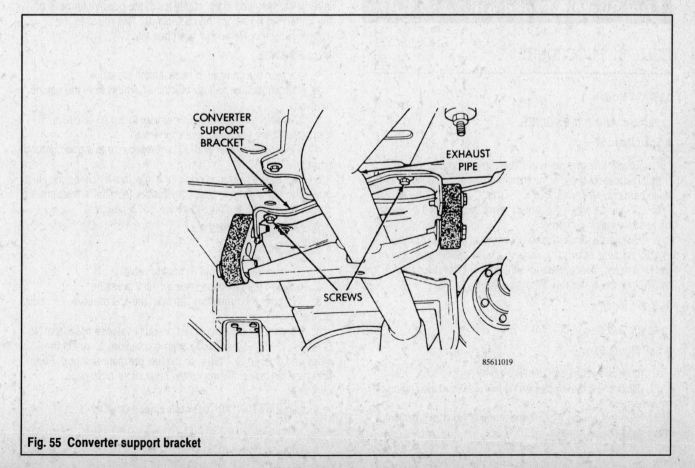

Fig. 55 Converter support bracket

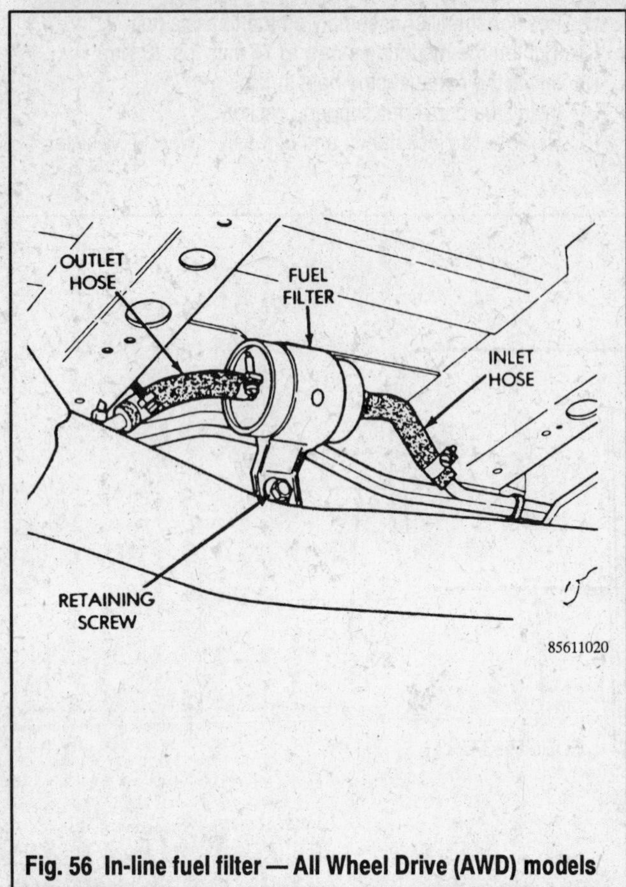

Fig. 56 In-line fuel filter — All Wheel Drive (AWD) models

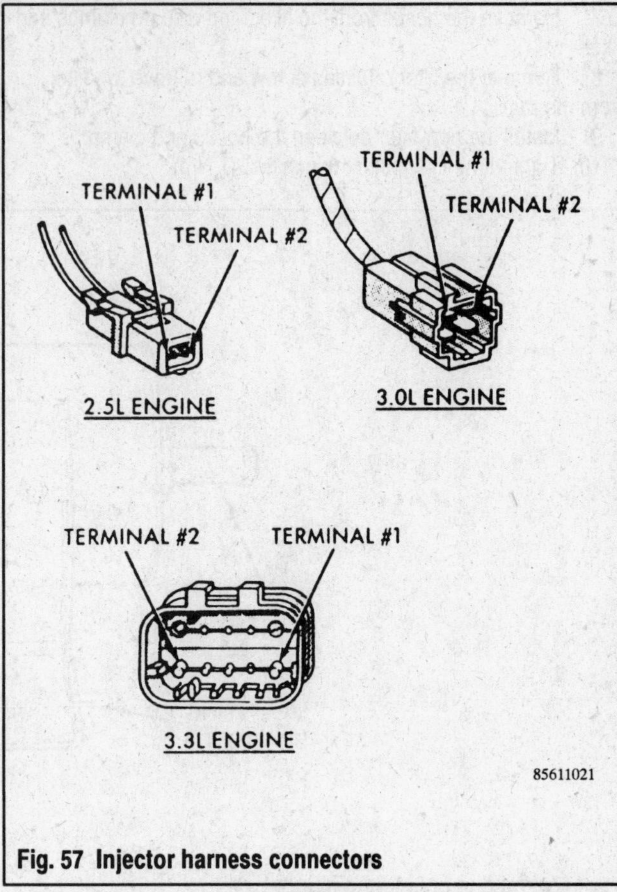

Fig. 57 Injector harness connectors

Fuel System Pressure

RELEASE PROCEDURE

1987-92 Models

2.5L, 3.0L AND 3.3L ENGINES

➧ See Figure 57

1. Loosen the gas cap to release tank pressure.
2. Disconnect the injector wiring harness from the engine or main harness.
3. Connect a jumper to ground terminal No. 1 of the injector harness to engine ground.
4. Connect a jumper to the positive terminal No. 2 of the injector harness and momentarily touch the positive terminal of the battery for no longer than 5 seconds. This releases the system pressure. Remove the jumper wires.

1993-95 Models

2.5L ENGINES

➧ See Figure 57

1. Loosen the gas cap to release tank pressure.
2. Disconnect the injector wiring harness from the engine or main harness.
3. Connect a jumper to ground terminal No. 1 of the injector harness to engine ground.
4. Connect a jumper to the positive terminal No. 2 of the injector harness and momentarily touch the positive terminal of the battery for no longer than 5 seconds. This releases the system pressure. Remove the jumper wires.

3.0L ENGINES

1. Loosen the gas cap to release tank pressure.
2. Disconnect the fuel rail electrical harness from the engine harness.
3. Connect one end of a jumper wire to the A142 circuit terminal of the fuel rail harness connector.
4. Connect the other end of the jumper wire to a good ground source.
5. Momentarily ground one of the injectors by connecting the other end of the jumper wire to an injector terminal in the harness connector. Repeat the procedure for 2 or 3 injectors.

3.3L AND 3.8L ENGINES

➧ See Figure 58

1. Disconnect the negative battery cable.
2. Loosen the gas cap to release tank pressure.
3. Remove the protective cap from the fuel pressure test port on the fuel rail.
4. Place the open end of fuel pressure release hose, tool No. C-4799-1, into an approved gasoline container. Connect the other end of hose C-4799-1 to the fuel pressure test port. Fuel pressure will bleed off through the hose into the gasoline container.

➔ Fuel gauge C-4799-A contains hose C-4799-1

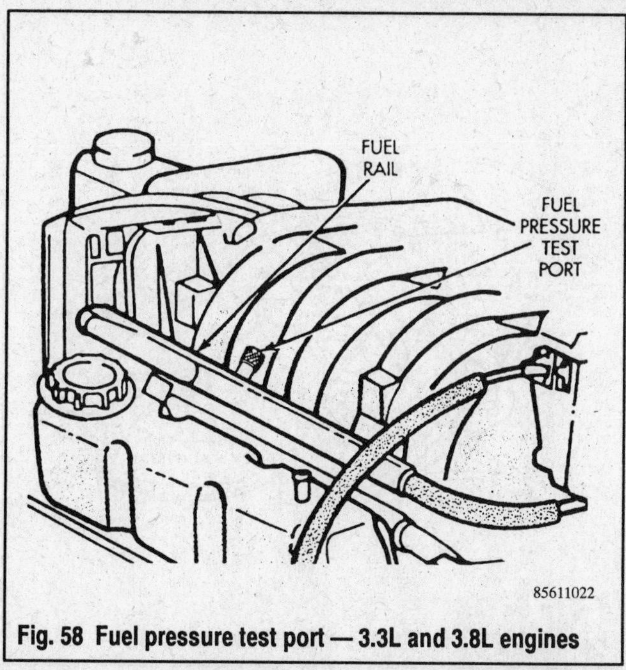

Fig. 58 Fuel pressure test port — 3.3L and 3.8L engines

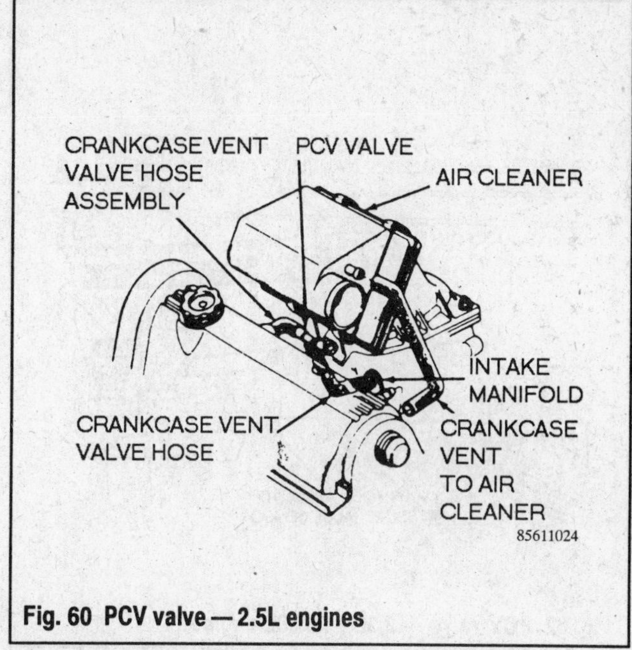

Fig. 60 PCV valve — 2.5L engines

PCV Valve

See Figures 59, 60, 61 and 62

OPERATION

Except 2.6L Engines

Crankcase vapors and piston blow-by are removed from the engine by intake manifold vacuum. The emissions are drawn through the PCV valve (usually located in the top of the engine valve cover) into the intake manifold where they become part of the air/fuel mixture. Crankcase vapors are then burned and pass through the exhaust system. When there are not enough vapors or blow-by pressure in the engine, air is drawn from the air cleaner. With this system no outside air enters the crankcase.

Fig. 59 Removing the PCV valve from the crankcase vent module

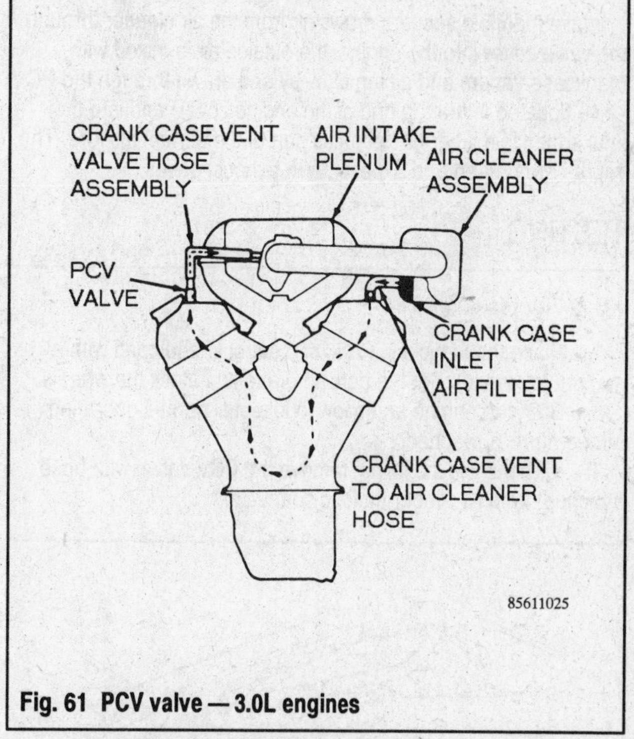

Fig. 61 PCV valve — 3.0L engines

The PCV valve is used to control the rate at which crankcase vapors are returned to the intake manifold. The action of the valve plunger is controlled by intake manifold vacuum and the spring. During deceleration and idle, when manifold vacuum is high, it overcomes the tension of the valve spring and the plunger bottoms in the manifold end of the valve housing. Because of the valve construction, it reduces, but does not stop, the passage of vapors to the intake manifold. When the engine is lightly accelerated or operated at constant speed, spring tension matches intake manifold vacuum pull and the plunger takes a mid-position in the valve body, allowing more vapors to flow into the manifold.

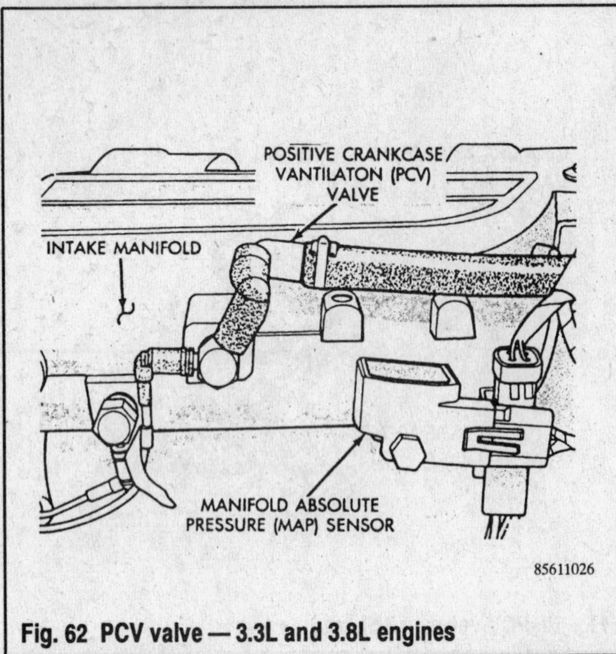

Fig. 62 PCV valve — 3.3L and 3.8L engines

2.6L Engines

Intake manifold vacuum draws air from the air cleaner through the valve cover into the engine, the outside air is mixed with crankcase vapors and piston blow-by and drawn through the PCV valve (located in the top end of the engine cover) and into the intake manifold where it becomes part of the air/fuel mixture. The vapors are burned and expelled with exhaust gases.

TESTING

➧ **See Figures 63 and 64**

1. Place the vehicle in Park, or Neutral (if equipped with a manual transaxle). Set the parking brake and block the wheels.
2. Start the engine and allow to idle until normal operating temperature is reached.
3. With the engine idling, remove the PCV valve, with hose attached, from its rubber molded connector.

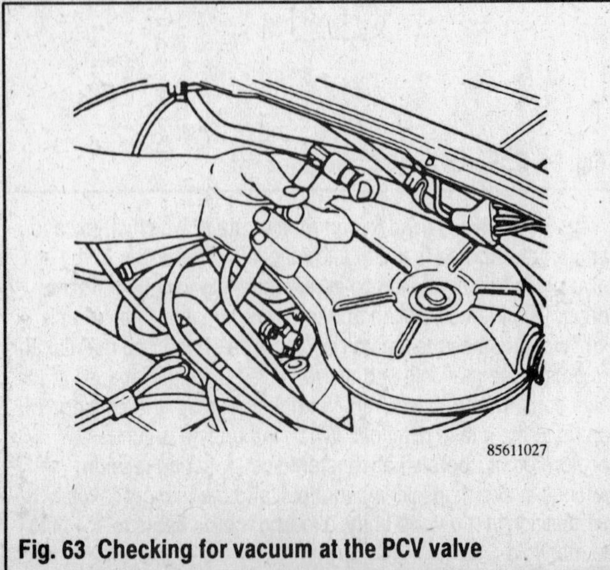

Fig. 63 Checking for vacuum at the PCV valve

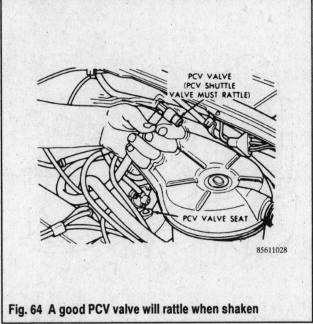

Fig. 64 A good PCV valve will rattle when shaken

4. When the PCV valve is free of its mounting, a hissing noise will be heard and a strong vacuum felt when a finger is placed over the valve inlet. When the engine is turned **OFF**, the valve should rattle when shaken. If the valve is not operating properly it must be replaced.

REMOVAL & INSTALLATION

1. With the engine **OFF**, clean PCV valve area with a suitable solvent.
2. Remove the PCV valve from the mounting grommet on the top cover (2.6L, 2.5L, 3.0L, 3.3L and 3.8L engines) or from the vent module (2.2L engines). Disconnect the hose from the valve.
3. Examine the vacuum hose and replace if the hose is cracked, broken or dried out. Always check the vent hose for clogging. If clogged, replace or clean as necessary.
4. Install a new PCV valve into the hose and install into mounting grommet.

Crankcase Vent Filter

All engines are equipped with a crankcase vent filter which is used to filter the outside air before it enters the PCV system. The filter is located in the air cleaner housing on 2.6L and 2.5L, or in the vent module on 2.2L engines. The filter is located inside the filter element box under the filter element on 3.0L engines and the filter element is located in the bottom of the filter element box on the 3.3L and the 3.8L engines. Replacement should be performed every 50,000–60,000 miles.

VENT FILTER SERVICE

1. On models equipped with the 2.2L engine, remove the PCV valve from the vent module and remove the vent module from the engine cover. Wash the module thoroughly in kerosene or safe solvent.
2. Lubricate or wet the filter with SAE 30 weight oil. Reinstall the module, PCV valve and hose.

3. On models equipped with the 2.5L or 2.6L engine, remove the vent filter from the air cleaner housing. Replace with a new element. Wet the new element slightly with SAE 30 weight oil before installation.

4. Models equipped with the 3.0L, 3.3L or 3.8L engine, remove the filter from the filter element box. Replace the filter.

Evaporative Charcoal Canister

All vehicles are equipped with a sealed, maintenance free charcoal canister, located in the wheel well area of the engine compartment. Fuel vapors, from the carburetor float chamber and from the gas tank, are temporarily held in the canister until they can be drawn into the intake manifold and burned in the engine.

SERVICING

Periodic inspection of the vent hoses is required. Replace any hoses that are cracked, torn or become hard. Use only fuel resistant hose if replacement becomes necessary.

Battery

GENERAL MAINTENANCE

All batteries, regardless of type, should be carefully secured by a battery hold-down device. If this is not done, the battery terminals or casing may crack from stress applied to the battery during vehicle operation. A battery which is not secured may allow acid to leak out, making it discharge faster; such leaking corrosive acid can also eat away components under the hood. A battery that is not sealed must be checked periodically for electrolyte level. You cannot add water to a sealed maintenance-free battery (though not all maintenance-free batteries are sealed), but a sealed battery must also be checked for proper electrolyte level as indicated by the color of the built-in hydrometer "eye."

Keep the top of the battery clean, as a film of dirt can completely discharge a battery that is not used for long periods. A solution of baking soda and water may be used for cleaning, but be careful to flush this off with clear water. DO NOT let any of the solution into the filler holes. Baking soda neutralizes battery acid and will de-activate a battery cell.

****CAUTION**

Always use caution when working on or near the battery. Never allow a tool to bridge the gap between the negative and positive battery terminals. Also, be careful not to allow a tool to provide a ground between the positive cable/terminal and any metal component on the vehicle. Either of these conditions will cause a short circuit leading to sparks and possible personal injury.

Batteries in vehicles which are not operated on a regular basis can fall victim to parasitic loads (small current drains which are constantly drawing current from the battery). Normal parasitic loads may drain a battery on a vehicle that is in storage and not used for 6–8 weeks. Vehicles that have additional accessories such as a cellular phone, an alarm system or other devices that increase parasitic load may discharge a battery sooner. If the vehicle is to be stored for 6–8 weeks in a secure area and the alarm system, if present, is not necessary, the negative battery cable should be disconnected at the onset of storage to protect the battery charge.

Remember that constantly discharging and recharging will shorten battery life. Take care not to allow a battery to be needlessly discharged.

BATTERY FLUID

➧ See Figures 65, 66 and 67

****CAUTION**

Battery electrolyte contains sulfuric acid. If you should splash any on your skin or in your eyes, flush the affected area with plenty of clear water. If it lands in your eyes, get medical help immediately.

The fluid (sulfuric acid solution) contained in the battery cells will tell you many things about the condition of the battery. Because the cell plates must be kept submerged below the fluid level in order to operate, maintaining the fluid level is extremely important. And, because the specific gravity of the acid is an indication of electrical charge, testing the fluid can be an aid in determining if the battery must be replaced. A battery in a vehicle with a properly operating charging system should require little maintenance, but careful, periodic inspection should reveal problems before they leave you stranded.

Fluid Level

Check the battery electrolyte level at least once a month, or more often in hot weather or during periods of extended vehicle operation. On non-sealed batteries, the level can be checked either through the case on translucent batteries or by removing the cell caps on opaque-cased types. The electrolyte level in each cell should be kept filled to the split ring inside each cell, or the line marked on the outside of the case.

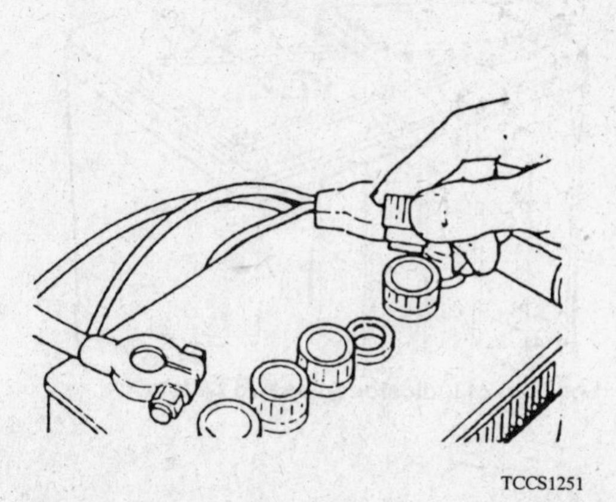

Fig. 65 On non-maintenance free batteries, the level can be checked through the case on translucent batteries; the cell caps must be removed on other models

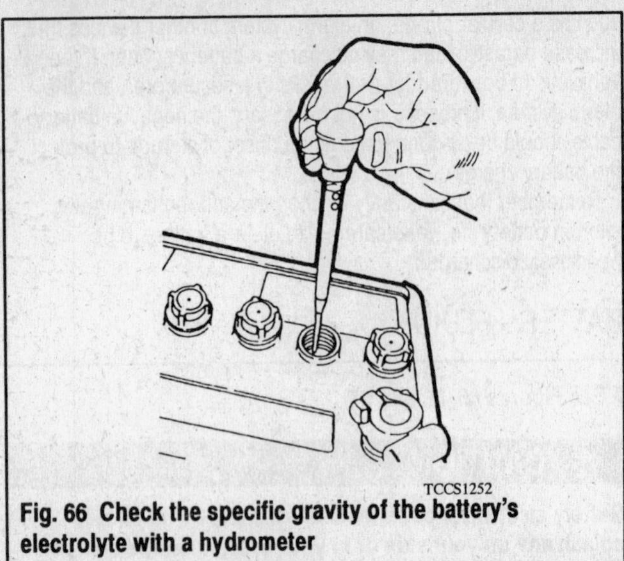

Fig. 66 Check the specific gravity of the battery's electrolyte with a hydrometer

If the level is low, add only distilled water through the opening until the level is correct. Each cell is separate from the others, so each must be checked and filled individually. Distilled water should be used, because the chemicals and minerals found in most drinking water are harmful to the battery and could significantly shorten its life.

If water is added in freezing weather, the vehicle should be driven several miles to allow the water to mix with the electrolyte. Otherwise, the battery could freeze.

Although some maintenance-free batteries have removable cell caps for access to the electrolyte, the electrolyte condition and level on all sealed maintenance-free batteries must be checked using the built-in hydrometer "eye." The exact type of eye varies between battery manufacturers, but most apply a sticker to the battery itself explaining the possible readings. When in doubt, refer to the battery manufacturer's instructions to interpret battery condition using the built-in hydrometer.

➔ Although the readings from built-in hydrometers found in sealed batteries may vary, a green eye usually indicates a properly charged battery with sufficient fluid level. A dark eye is normally an indicator of a battery with sufficient fluid, but one which may be low in charge. And a light or yellow eye is usually an indication that electrolyte supply has dropped below the necessary level for battery (and hydrometer) operation. In this last case, sealed batteries with an insufficient electrolyte level must usually be discarded.

Specific Gravity

As stated earlier, the specific gravity of a battery's electrolyte level can be used as an indication of battery charge. At least once a year, check the specific gravity of the battery. It should be between 1.20 and 1.26 on the gravity scale. Most auto supply stores carry a variety of inexpensive battery testing hydrometers. These can be used on any non-sealed battery to test the specific gravity in each cell.

The battery testing hydrometer has a squeeze bulb at one end and a nozzle at the other. Battery electrolyte is sucked into the hydrometer until the float is lifted from its seat. The specific gravity is then read by noting the position of the float. If gravity is low in one or more cells, the battery should be slowly charged and checked again to see if the gravity has come up. Generally, if after charging, the specific gravity between any two cells varies more than 50 points (0.50), the battery should be replaced as it can no longer produce sufficient voltage to guarantee proper operation.

On sealed batteries, the built-in hydrometer is the only way of checking specific gravity. Again, check with your battery's manufacturer for proper interpretation of its built-in hydrometer readings.

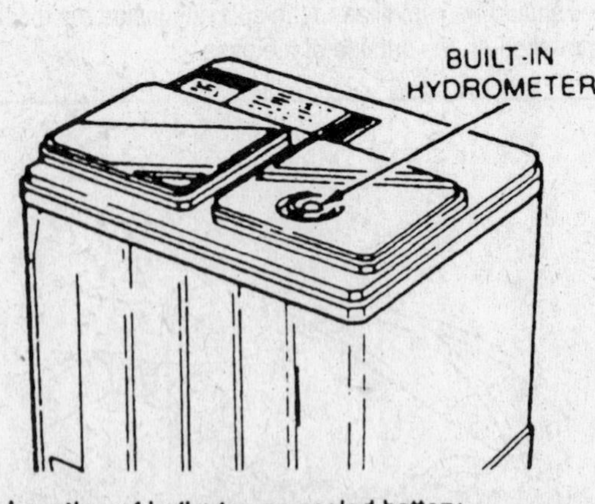

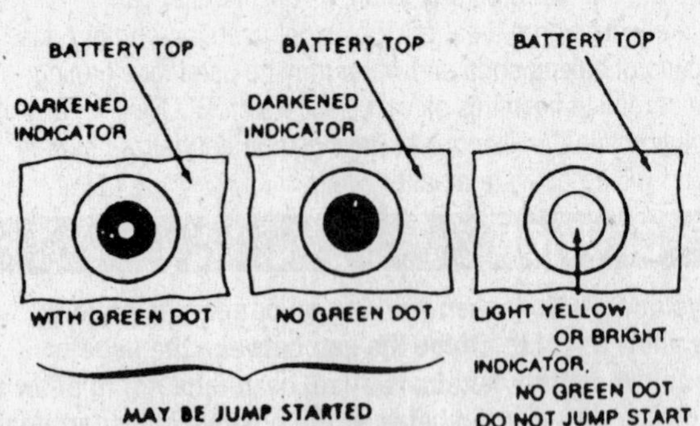

Fig. 67 A typical sealed (maintenance-free) battery with a built-in hydrometer — NOTE that the hydrometer eye may vary between battery manufacturers; always refer to the battery's label

CABLES

➧ **See Figures 68, 69, 70, 71, 72 and 73**

Once a year (or as necessary), the battery terminals and the cable clamps should be cleaned. Loosen the clamps and remove the cables, negative cable first. On batteries with posts on top, the use of a puller specially made for this purpose is recommended. These are inexpensive and available in most auto parts stores. Side terminal battery cables are secured with a small bolt.

Clean the cable clamps and the battery terminal with a wire brush, until all corrosion, grease, etc., is removed and the metal is shiny. It is especially important to clean the inside of the clamp (an old knife is useful here) thoroughly, since a small deposit of foreign material or oxidation there will prevent a sound electrical connection and inhibit either starting or charging. Special tools are available for cleaning these parts, one type for conventional top post batteries and another type for side terminal batteries.

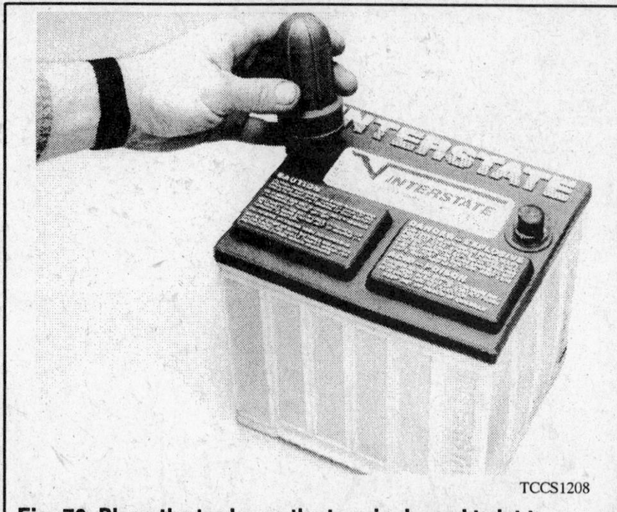

Fig. 70 Place the tool over the terminals and twist to clean the post

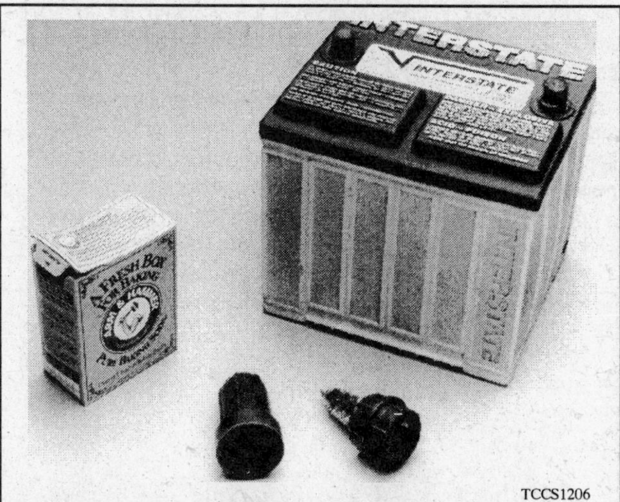

Fig. 68 Maintenance is performed with household items and with special tools like this post cleaner

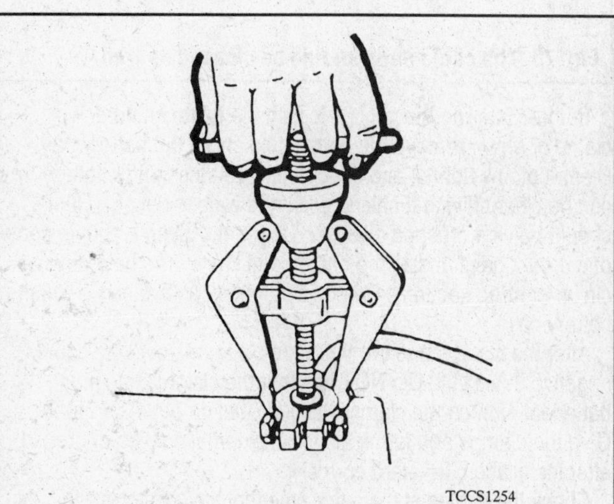

Fig. 71 A special tool is available to pull the clamp from the post

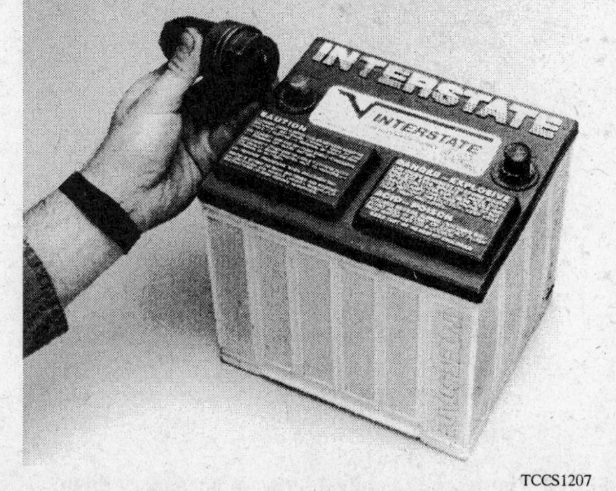

Fig. 69 The underside of this special battery tool has a wire brush to clean post terminals

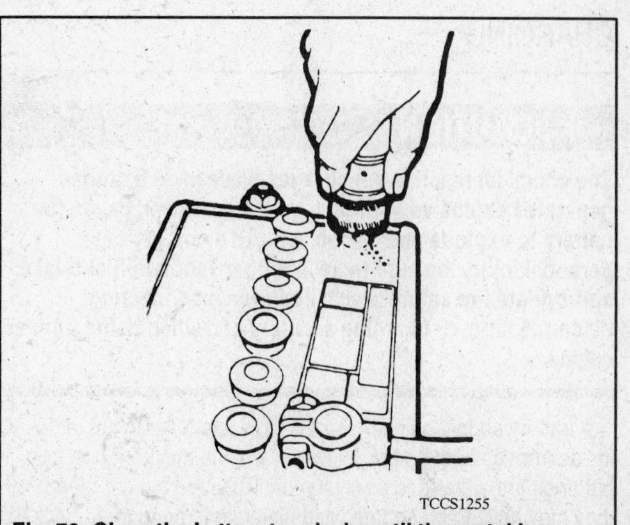

Fig. 72 Clean the battery terminals until the metal is shiny

Fig. 73 The cable ends should be cleaned as well

Before installing the cables, loosen the battery hold-down clamp or strap, remove the battery and check the battery tray. Clear it of any debris, and check it for soundness (the battery tray can be cleaned with a baking soda and water solution). Rust should be wire brushed away, and the metal given a couple coats of anti-rust paint. Install the battery and tighten the hold-down clamp or strap securely. Do not overtighten, as this can crack the battery case.

After the clamps and terminals are clean, reinstall the cables, negative cable last; DO NOT hammer the clamps onto post batteries. Tighten the clamps securely, but do not distort them. Give the clamps and terminals a thin external coating of grease after installation, to retard corrosion.

Check the cables at the same time that the terminals are cleaned. If the cable insulation is cracked or broken, or if the ends are frayed, the cable should be replaced with a new cable of the same length and gauge.

CHARGING

****CAUTION**

The chemical reaction which takes place in all batteries generates explosive hydrogen gas. A spark can cause the battery to explode and splash acid. To avoid serious personal injury, be sure there is proper ventilation and take appropriate fire safety precautions when connecting, disconnecting, or charging a battery and when using jumper cables.

A battery should be charged at a slow rate to keep the plates inside from getting too hot. However, if some maintenance-free batteries are allowed to discharge until they are almost “dead,” they may have to be charged at a high rate to bring them back to “life.” Always follow the charger manufacturer’s instructions on charging the battery.

REPLACEMENT

When it becomes necessary to replace the battery, select one with a rating equal to or greater than the battery originally installed. Deterioration and just plain aging of the battery cables, starter motor, and associated wires makes the battery’s job harder in successive years. The slow increase in electrical resistance over time makes it prudent to install a new battery with a greater capacity than the old.

Drive Belts

INSPECTION

See Figures 74, 75, 76, 77 and 78

Check the condition and tension of all drive belts every 12,000 miles, or at least once a year. Loose drive belts can lead to poor engine cooling and diminished alternator, power steering pump, air conditioning compressor, or emission air pump output. A belt that is too tight places a strain on the bearings in the driven component.

Replace any drive belt that is glazed, worn, cracked, or stretched to the point where correct adjustment tension is impossible. If two belts are used to drive a component, always replace both belts when replacement is necessary. After installing a new belt, run the engine for ten minutes, shut **OFF** the engine and recheck the belt tension. Readjust if necessary.

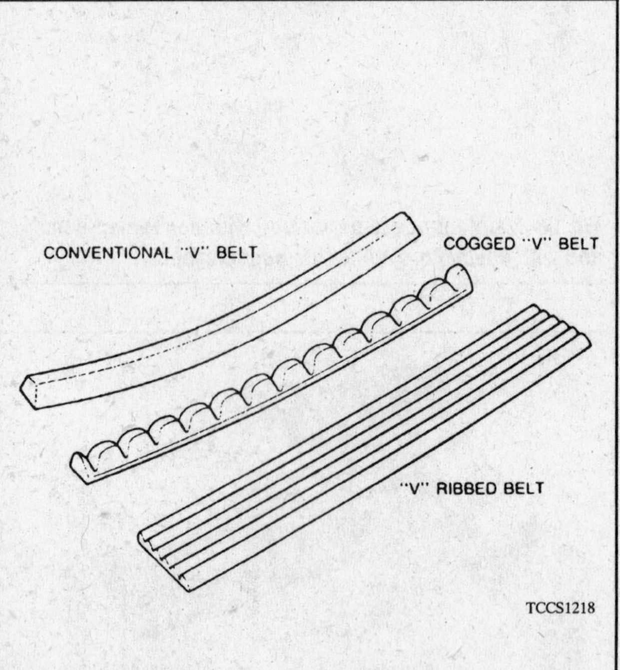

Fig. 74 There are typically 3 types of accessory drive belts found on vehicles today

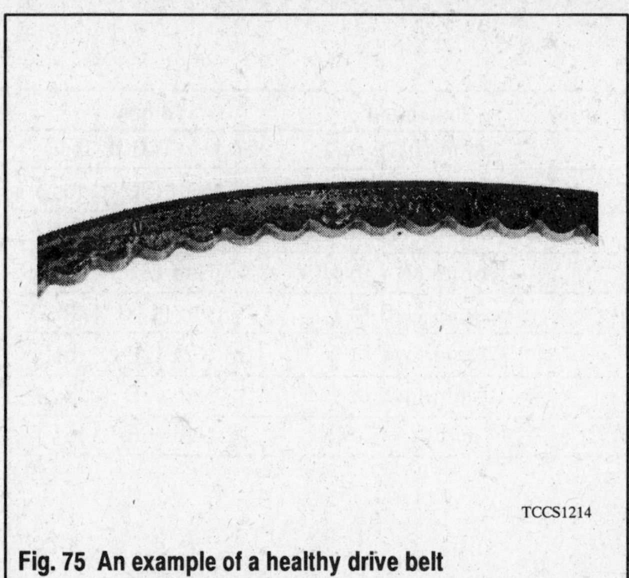
TCCS1214

Fig. 75 An example of a healthy drive belt

TCCS1215

Fig. 76 Deep cracks in this belt will cause flex, building up heat that will eventually lead to belt failure

TCCS1216

Fig. 77 The cover of this belt is worn, exposing the critical reinforcing cords to excessive wear

TCCS1217

Fig. 78 Installing too wide a belt can result in serious belt wear and/or breakage

ADJUSTMENT

➧ **See Figures 79, 80, 81, 82 and 83**

Two popular methods of checking drive belt adjustment are; the Belt Tension Gauge Method and the Belt Deflection Method. The former requires a special gauge and the latter requires a straight edge and scale or just a good eye for measurement. The deflection method will be used in the following belt replacement instructions. A rule of thumb for checking belt tension by the deflection method is to determine the midpoint between two pulleys of the drive belt and press down at that point with moderate thumb pressure. The belt should deflect to the measurement indicated in the following installation procedures. Adjustment is necessary if the belt is either too loose or too tight.

****WARNING**

A belt adjustment which is either too loose or too tight will eventually damage the accessory that belt is driving. A too loose adjustment allows free-play in the belt which could transfer a whipping motion or shock to the accessory drive pulley. Similarly, a belt which is too tight will preload the accessory bearings, leading to early failure.

Accessory Drive Belt		Gauge	Deflection	Torque
Air Conditioning Compressor	New	105 lb.	8mm (5/16 in.)	54 N·m (40 ft. lbs.)
	Used	80 lb.	9mm (7/16 in.)	41 N·m (30 ft. lbs.)
Air Pump	New	—	5mm (3/16 in.)	61 N·m (45 ft. lbs.)
	Used	—	6mm (1/4 in.)	47 N·m (35 ft. lbs.)
Alternator/Water Pump "V" Belt and Poly "V"	New	115 lb.	3mm (1/8 in.)	149 N·m (110 ft. lbs.)
	Used	80 lb.	6mm (1/4 in.)	108 N·m (80 ft. lbs.)
Power Steering Pump	New	105 lb.	6mm (1/4 in.)	102 N·m (75 ft. lbs.)
	Used	80 lb.	11mm (7/16 in.)	75 N·m (55 ft. lbs.)

85611043

Fig. 79 Engine belt tension chart — 2.2L engines

Accessory Drive Belt		Gauge	Deflection	Torque
Air Conditioning	New	105 lb.	8mm (5/16 in.)	54 N·m (40 ft. lbs.)
Compressor	Used	80 lb.	11mm (7/16 in.)	41 N·m (30 ft. lbs.)
Alternator/Water Pump	New	115 lb.	3mm (1/8 in.)	149 N·m (110 ft. lbs.)
Poly "V"	Used	80 lb.	6mm (1/4 in.)	108 N·m (80 ft. lbs.)
Power Steering Pump	New	105 lb.	6mm (1/4 in.)	102 N·m (75 ft. lbs.)
	Used	80 lb.	11mm (7/16 in.)	75 N·m (55 ft. lbs.)

85611044

Fig. 80 Engine belt tension chart — 1987-89 2.5L engines

Accessory Drive Belt		Gauge	Deflection	Torque
Power Steering Pump	New	95 lb.	6mm (¼ in.)	149 N·m (110 ft. lbs.)
	Used	80 lb	9mm (⅜ in.)	102 N·m (75 ft. lbs.)
Alternator	New	115 lb	4mm (3/16 in.)	—
	Used	80 lb.	6mm (¼ in.)	—
Alternator/Air Conditioning Compressor	New	115 lb.	6mm (¼ in.)	—
	Used	80 lb.	8mm (5/16 in.)	—
Water Pump	New	—	8mm (5/16 in.)	—
	Used	—	9mm (⅜ in.)	—

85611045

Fig. 81 Engine belt tension chart — 2.6L engines

BELT TENSION CHART

ACCESSORY DRIVE BELT		GAUGE	TORQUE
2.5L ENGINE			
AIR CONDITIONING COMPRESSOR	NEW	125 LB.	47 N•M (35 FT. LBS.)
	USED	80 LB.	27 N•M (20 FT. LBS.)
ALTERNATOR/WATER PUMP POLY "V"	NEW	130 LB.	
	USED	80 LB.	
POWER STEERING PUMP	NEW	105 LB.	58 N•M (43 FT. LBS.)
	USED	80 LB.	43 N•M (32 FT. LBS.)
3.0L ENGINE			
AIR CONDITIONING COMPRESSOR	NEW	125 LB.	
	USED	80 LB.	
ALTERNATOR/WATER PUMP/POWER STEERING PUMP	NEW USED	DYNAMIC TENSIONER	
3.3L ENGINE			
AIR CONDITIONING COMPRESSOR	NEW USED	DYNAMIC TENSIONER	
ALTERNATOR/WATER PUMP/POWER STEERING PUMP			

85611046

Fig. 82 Engine belt tension chart — 1990–93 models

BELT TENSION CHART

ACCESSORY DRIVE BELT		GAUGE	TORQUE
2.5L ENGINE			
AIR CONDITIONING COMPRESSOR	NEW	135 LB.	47 N·m (35 FT. LBS.)
	USED	80 LB.	27 N·m (20 FT. LBS.)
GENERATOR/WATER PUMP POLY "V"	NEW	135 LB.	
	USED	80 LB.	
POWER STEERING PUMP	NEW	105 LB.	58 N·m (43 FT. LBS.)
	USED	80 LB.	43 N·m (32 FT. LBS.)
3.0L ENGINE			
AIR CONDITIONING COMPRESSOR	NEW	125 LB.	
	USED	80 LB.	
GENERATOR/WATER PUMP/POWER STEERING PUMP	NEW USED	DYNAMIC TENSIONER	
3.3L AND 3.8L ENGINE			
AIR CONDITIONING COMPRESSOR	NEW USED	DYNAMIC TENSIONER	
GENERATOR/WATER PUMP/POWER STEERING PUMP			

85611047

Fig. 83 Engine belt tension chart — 1994–95 models

REMOVAL & INSTALLATION

➧ See Figure 84

➥ Raise the front of the vehicle, support on jackstands and remove the lower splash shield if access is hampered due to space limitations when changing drive belts.

2.2L Engines

A/C COMPRESSOR DRIVE BELT

➧ See Figures 85, 86 and 87

1. Loosen the idler pulley bracket pivot screw and the locking screw.
2. Remove the belt and install a replacement.

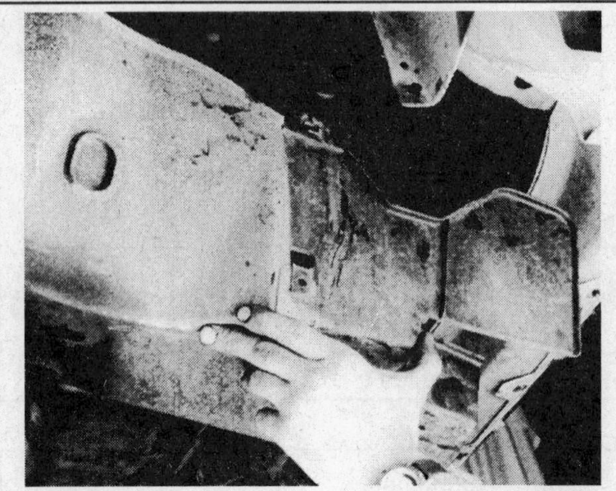

85611108

Fig. 84 Support the vehicle, then remove the lower right side splash shield for access to the drive belts

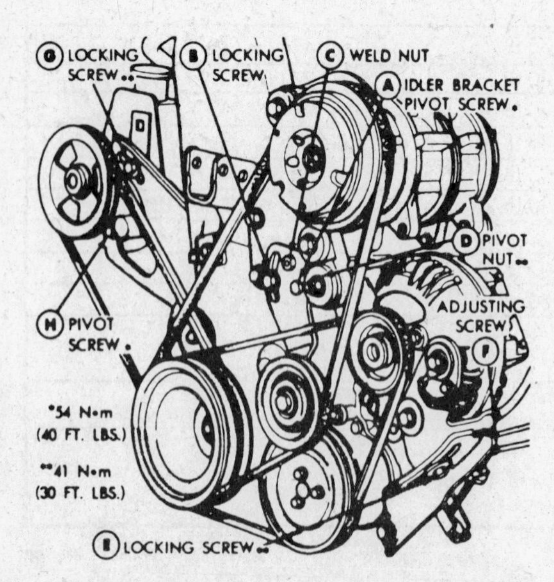

85611033

Fig. 85 A/C compressor drive belt adjusting points — 2.2L engines

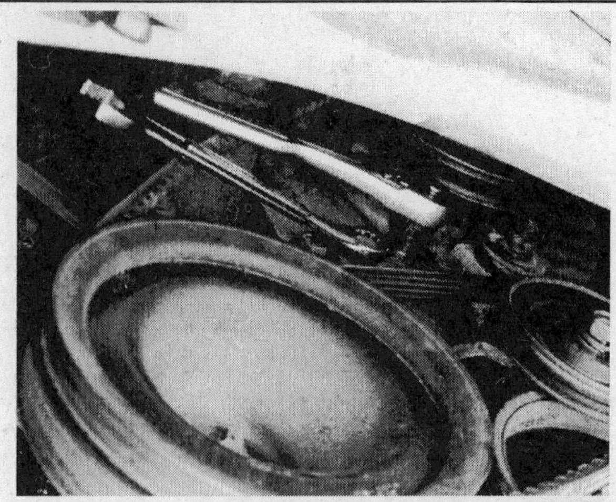

85611109

Fig. 86 Loosening the locking screws for A/C compressor drive belt removal

85611110

Fig. 87 Removing the A/C compressor drive belt from under the vehicle

3. Using a breaker bar and socket apply torque to the welded nut provided on the mounted bracket to obtain proper tension.
4. Tighten the locking screw first, followed by pivot screw. Tighten to 40 ft. lbs. (55 Nm).

ALTERNATOR DRIVE BELT (CHRYSLER TYPE)

➧ See Figures 88 and 89

If removal of the alternator belt is required, the A/C belt must first be removed.

1. Loosen the pivot nut, locking screw, and the adjusting screw.
2. Remove the belt and install a replacement.
3. Adjust to specification by tightening the adjusting screw.
4. Tighten the locking screw to 25 ft. lbs. (34 Nm).
5. Tighten the pivot nut to 30 ft. lbs. (41 Nm).

ALTERNATOR DRIVE BELT (BOSCH TYPE)

If removal of the alternator belt is required, the A/C belt must first be removed.

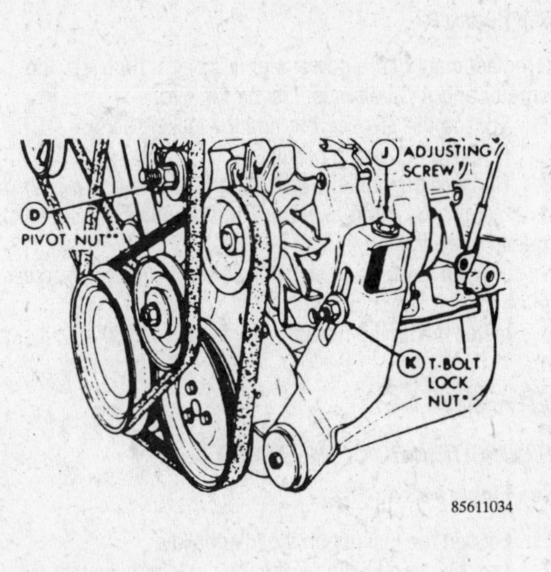

Fig. 88 Alternator belt adjustment — 2.2L engine

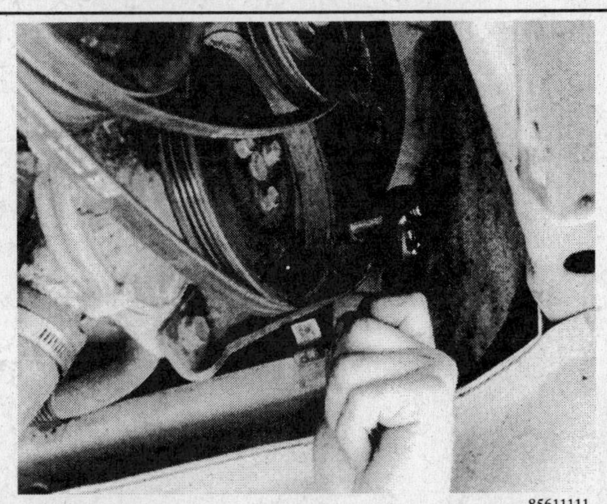

Fig. 89 Loosening the locking screw for alternator drive belt removal

1. Loosen the pivot nut, locking nut, and adjusting screw.
2. Remove the belt and install a replacement.
3. Adjust to specification by tightening the adjusting screw.
4. Tighten the locking nut to 25 ft. lbs. (34 Nm).
5. Tighten the pivot nut to 30 ft. lbs. (41 Nm).

POWER STEERING BELT

If removal of the power steering belt is required, the A/C and alternator belts must first be removed.

1. Loosen the locking screw, and pivot screw.
2. Remove the belt and install a replacement.
3. Install a 1/2 in. breaker bar into the pump bracket slot, apply pressure with the breaker bar and adjust the belt to specification.
4. Tighten the locking screw first, then the pivot screw. Tighten to 40 ft. lbs. (55 Nm).

AIR PUMP DRIVE BELT

See Figure 90

When servicing the air pump, use the square holes provided in the pulley to prevent camshaft rotation.

1. Remove the nuts and bolts retaining the drive pulley cover.
2. Remove the locking bolt and pivot bolt from the pump bracket, then remove the pump.
3. Remove the belt and install a replacement.
4. Position the pump, then install the locking bolt and pivot bolt finger-tight.
5. Install a 1/2 in. breaker bar into the bracket assembly (block the drive pulley to prevent camshaft rotation), and adjust the belt to specification.
6. Tighten locking bolt and pivot bolt to 25 ft. lbs. (35 Nm).

2.5L Engines

AIR CONDITIONING COMPRESSOR

See Figure 91

1. Loosen the idler bracket pivot screw and the locking screws to replace, or adjust belt.
2. Remove the belt and install a replacement.
3. Adjust the belt to specification by applying torque to weld nut on the idler bracket.
4. Tighten locking screw first, followed by the pivot screw. Tighten to 40 ft. lbs. (55 Nm).

ALTERNATOR BELT

See Figure 91

If replacement of the alternator belt is required, the A/C drive belt must first be removed.

1. Loosen the pivot nut, locking nut, and adjusting screw.
2. Remove the belt and install a replacement.
3. Adjust the belt to specification by tightening the adjusting screw.
4. Tighten the locking nut to 25 ft. lbs. (35 Nm).
5. Tighten the pivot nut to 30 ft. lbs. (40 Nm).

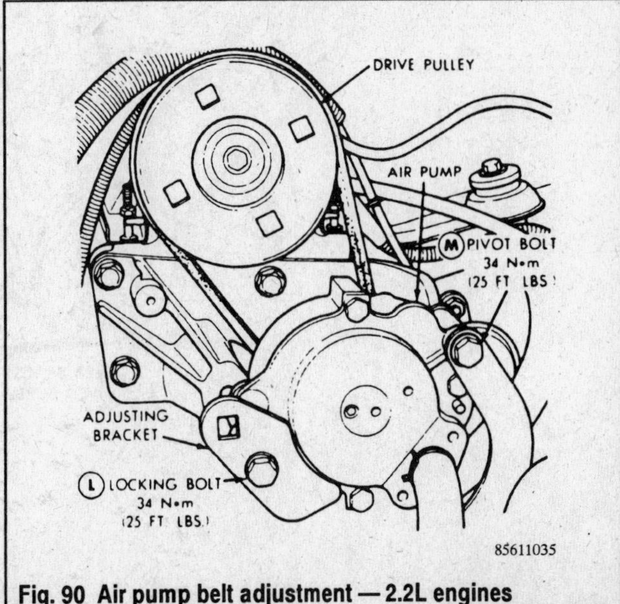

Fig. 90 Air pump belt adjustment — 2.2L engines

POWER STEERING PUMP

➧ See Figure 91

If replacement of the power steering belt is required, the A/C and alternator belts must first be remove.

1. Loosen the locking screw and pivot screw to replace, or adjust the belt.
2. Remove the belt and install a replacement.
3. Using a $^{1}/_{2}$ in. breaker bar positioned in adjusting bracket slot, adjust the belt to specification.
4. Tighten the locking screw followed by the pivot screw. Tighten to 40 ft. lbs. (55 Nm).

2.6L Engines

ALTERNATOR/AIR CONDITIONING COMPRESSOR BELT

➧ See Figure 92

1. Loosen the locking screw, jam nut, and pivot nut.
2. Loosen the adjusting screw.
3. Remove the belt and install a replacement.
4. Adjust the belt to specification by tightening the adjusting screw.
5. Tighten the locking screw followed by the pivot nut. Tighten to 16 ft. lbs. (22 Nm).
6. Tighten the jam nut to 21 ft. lbs. (28 Nm).

POWER STEERING PUMP BELT

➧ See Figure 92

If replacement of the power steering belt is required, the alternator and A/C belt must first be remove.

1. Loosen the pivot screw, and the locking screw.
2. Remove the timing pickup.
3. Remove the belt and install a replacement.
4. Install a $^{1}/_{2}$ in. breaker bar in the adjusting bracket slot, torque to specification.
5. Tighten the locking screw, followed by the pivot screw. Tighten to 40 ft. lbs. (55 Nm).
6. Install the timing pick-up, and tighten to 160 inch lbs. (18 Nm).

3.0L Engines

AIR CONDITIONING COMPRESSOR BELT

➧ See Figures 93 and 94

1. Loosen the locknut on the idler pulley.
2. Loosen the adjusting screw on the idler pulley.
3. Remove the belt and install a replacement.
4. Adjust to specification by tightening the adjusting screw.
5. Tighten the idler pulley locknut to 40 ft. lbs. (55 Nm).

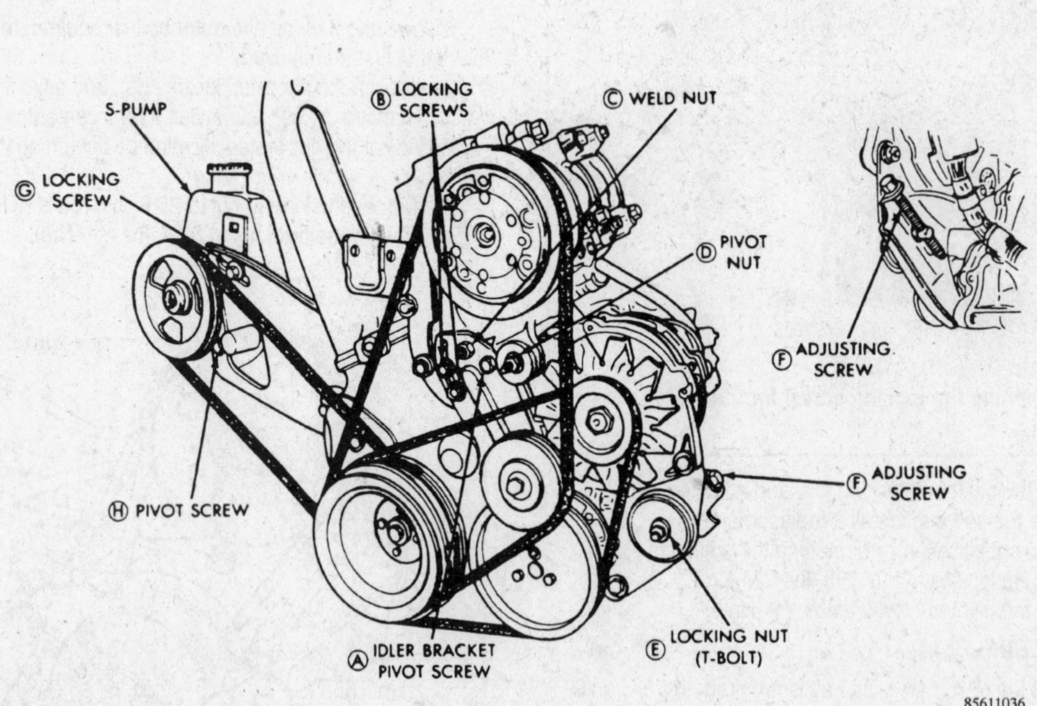

Fig. 91 Drive belt adjustment points — 2.5L engines

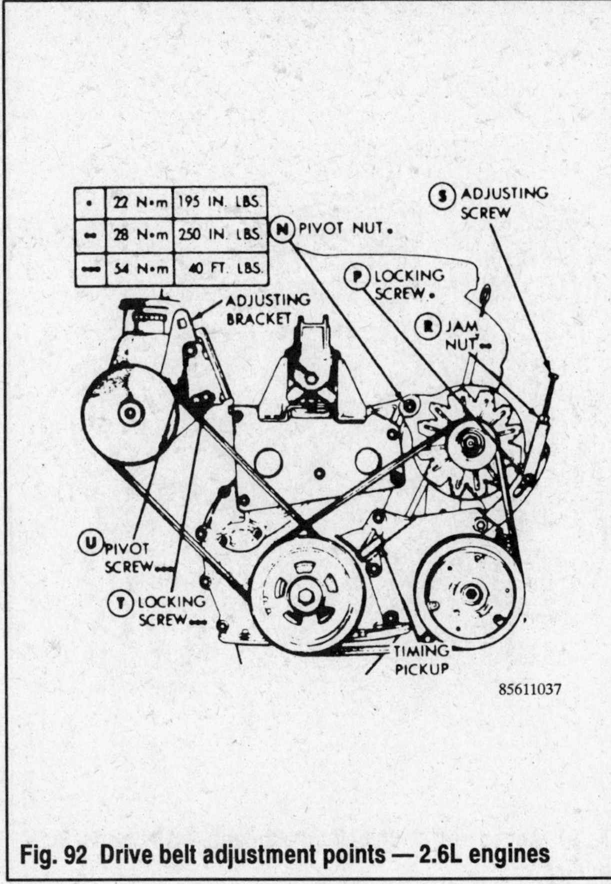

Fig. 92 Drive belt adjustment points — 2.6L engines

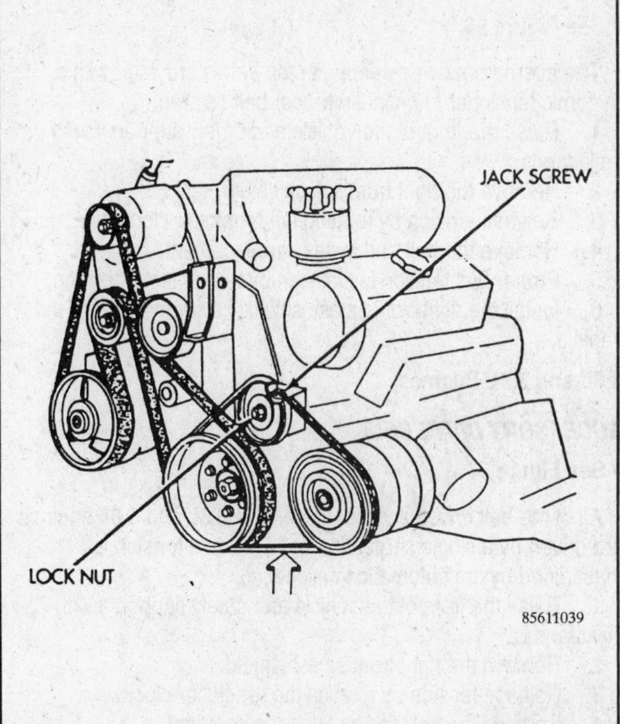

Fig. 94 Air conditioning compressor belt — 1991-95 3.0L engines

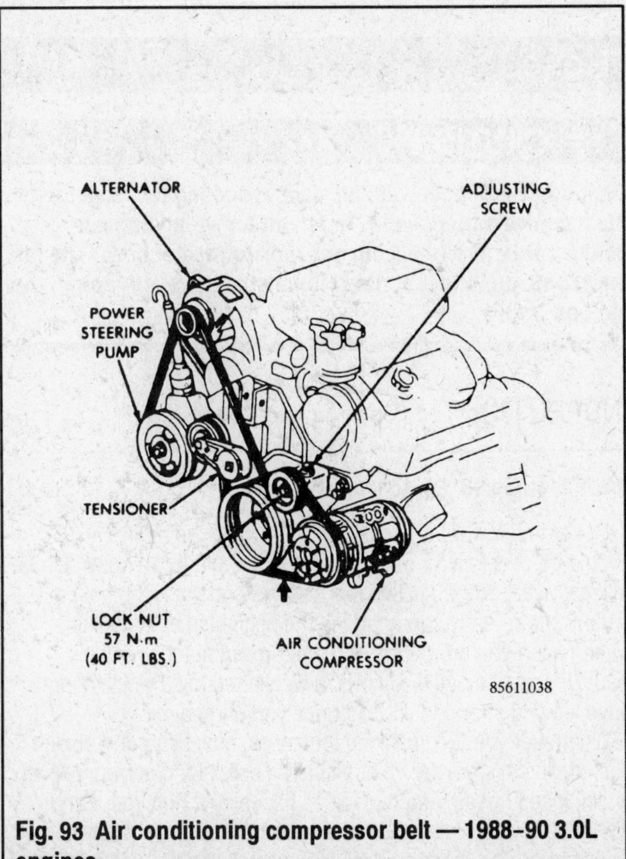

Fig. 93 Air conditioning compressor belt — 1988-90 3.0L engines

ALTERNATOR/POWER STEERING PUMP BELT — 1988-90 MODELS

➧ See Figure 95

If replacement of the alternator/power steering drive belt is required, the air conditioner drive belt must first be removed.

1. Install a $^1/_2$ in. breaker bar into the tensioner slot, and rotate counterclockwise to release belt tension.
2. Remove the belt and install a replacement.
3. Proper belt tension is maintain by the dynamic tensioner.

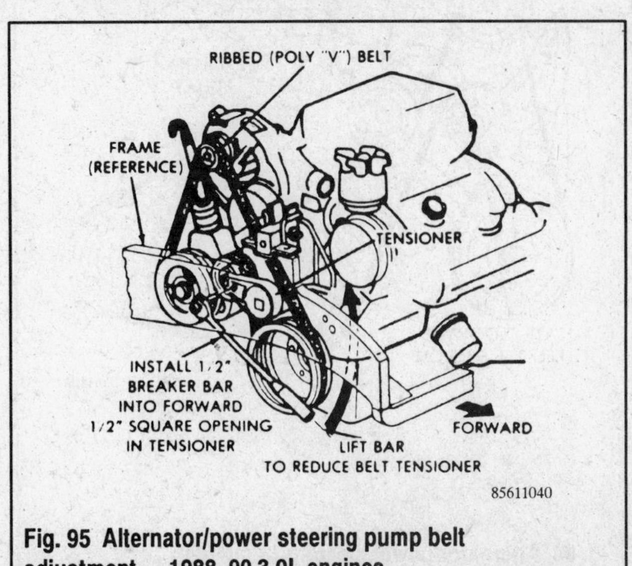

Fig. 95 Alternator/power steering pump belt adjustment — 1988-90 3.0L engines

ALTERNATOR/POWER STEERING PUMP BELT — 1991-95 MODELS

➧ See Figure 96

The alternator/power steering pump belt is provided with a dynamic tensioner to maintain proper belt tension.

1. Raise the front of the vehicle and safely support it with jackstands.
2. Remove the right front splash shield.
3. Release tension by rotating the tensioner clockwise.
4. Remove the belt and install a replacement.
5. Proper belt tension is maintain by the dynamic tension.
6. Install the right front splash shield. Lower the front of the vehicle.

3.3L and 3.8L Engines

ACCESSORY DRIVE BELT

➧ See Figure 97

All of the belt driven accessories on the 3.3L and 3.8L engines are driven by a single serpentine belt. The belt tension is maintained by am automatic tensioner.

1. Raise the front of the vehicle and safely support it with jackstands.
2. Remove the right front splash shield.
3. Release tension by rotating the tensioner clockwise.
4. Remove the belt and install a replacement.
5. Proper belt tension is maintain by the dynamic tension.
6. Install the right front splash shield. Lower the front of the vehicle.

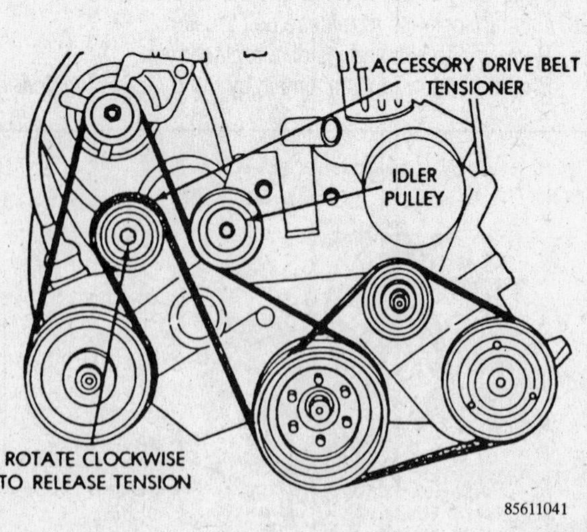

Fig. 96 Alternator/power steering pump belt adjustment — 1991-95 3.0L engines

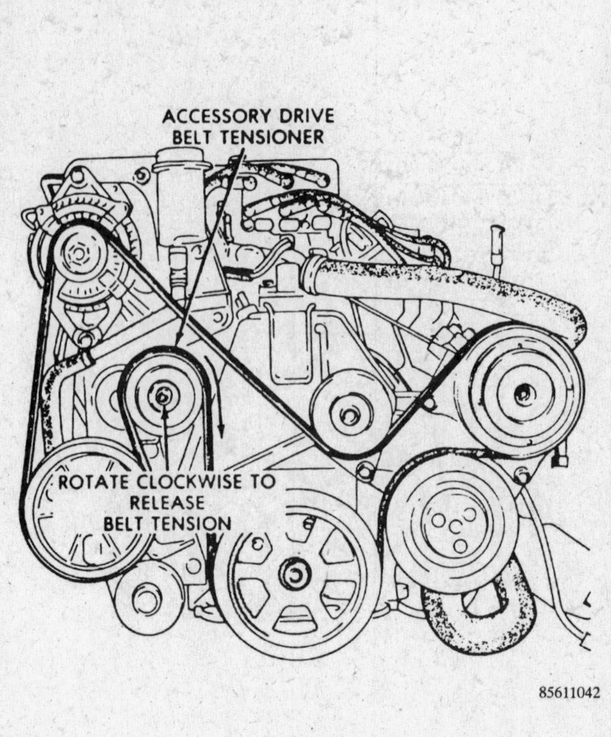

Fig. 97 Accessory drive belt adjustment — 3.3L and 3.8L engines

Hoses

✲✲CAUTION

On models equipped with an electric cooling fan, disengage the negative battery cable, or fan motor wiring harness connector before replacing any radiator/heater hose. The fan may come on, under certain circumstances, even though the ignition is OFF.

INSPECTION

➧ See Figures 98, 99, 100 and 101

Upper and lower radiator hoses along with the heater hoses should be checked for deterioration, leaks and loose hose clamps at least every 15,000 miles. It is also wise to check the hoses periodically in early spring and at the beginning of the fall or winter when you are performing other maintenance. A quick visual inspection could discover a weakened hose which might have left you stranded if it had remained unrepaired.

Whenever you are checking the hoses, make sure the engine and cooling system are cold. Visually inspect for cracking, rotting or collapsed hoses, and replace as necessary. Run your hand along the length of the hose. If a weak or swollen spot is noted when squeezing the hose wall, the hose should be replaced.

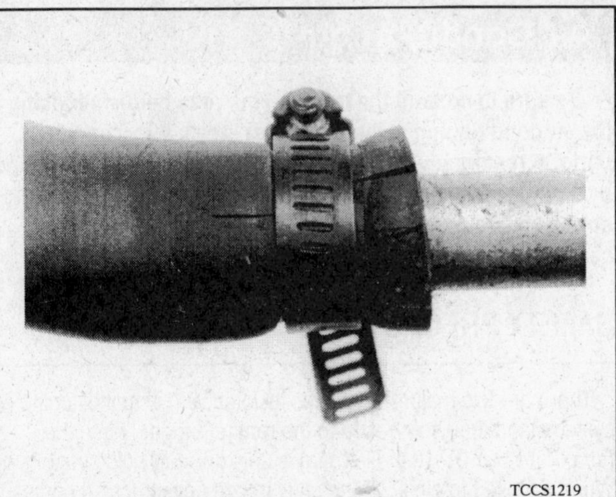
TCCS1219

Fig. 98 The cracks developing along this hose are a result of age-related hardening

TCCS1220

Fig. 99 A hose clamp that is too tight can cause older hoses to separate and tear on either side of the clamp

TCCS1221

Fig. 100 A soft spongy hose (identifiable by the swollen section) will eventually burst and should be replaced

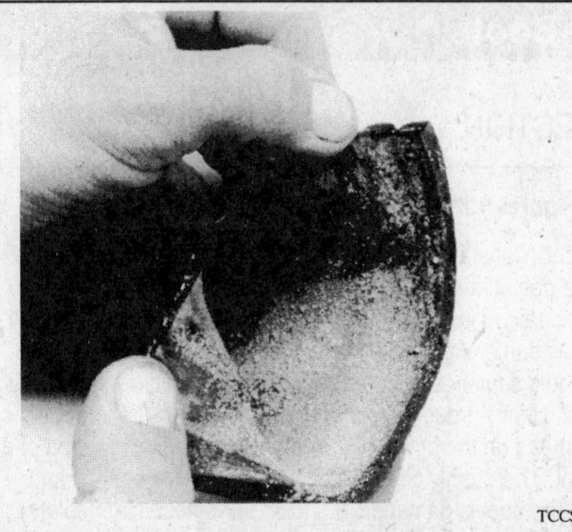
TCCS1222

Fig. 101 Hoses are likely to deteriorate from the inside if the cooling system is not periodically flushed

REMOVAL & INSTALLATION

Inspect the condition of the radiator and heater hoses periodically. Early spring and at the beginning of the fall or winter, when you are performing other maintenance, are good times. Make sure the engine and cooling system are cold. Visually inspect for cracking, rotting or collapsed hoses, replace as necessary. Run your hand along the length of the hose. If a weak or swollen spot is noted when squeezing the hose wall, replace the hose.

1. Drain the cooling system into a suitable container (if the coolant is to be reused).

****CAUTION**

When draining the coolant, keep in mind that cats and dogs are attracted by ethylene glycol antifreeze, and are quite likely to drink any that is left in an uncovered container or in puddles on the ground. This will prove fatal in sufficient quantity. Always drain the coolant into a sealable container. Coolant should be reused unless it is contaminated or several years old.

2. Loosen the hose clamps at each end of the hose that requires replacement.
3. Twist, pull and slide the hose off the radiator, water pump, thermostat or heater connection.
4. Clean the hose mounting connections. Position the hose clamps on the new hose.
5. Coat the connection surfaces with a water resistant sealer and slide the hose into position. Make sure the hose clamps are located beyond the raised bead of the connector (if equipped) and centered in the clamping area of the connection.
6. Tighten the clamps to 20–30 inch lbs. (2–3 Nm). Do not overtighten.
7. Fill the cooling system.
8. Start the engine and allow it to reach normal operating temperature. Check for leaks.

CV-Boots

INSPECTION

➧ **See Figures 102 and 103**

The CV (Constant Velocity) boots should be checked for damage each time the oil is changed and any other time the vehicle is raised for service. These boots keep water, grime, dirt and other damaging matter from entering the CV-joints. Any of these could cause early CV-joint failure which can be expensive to repair. Heavy grease thrown around the inside of the front wheel(s) and on the brake caliper/drum can be an indication of a torn boot. Thoroughly check the boots for missing clamps and tears. If the boot is damaged, it should be replaced immediately. Please refer to Section 7 for procedures.

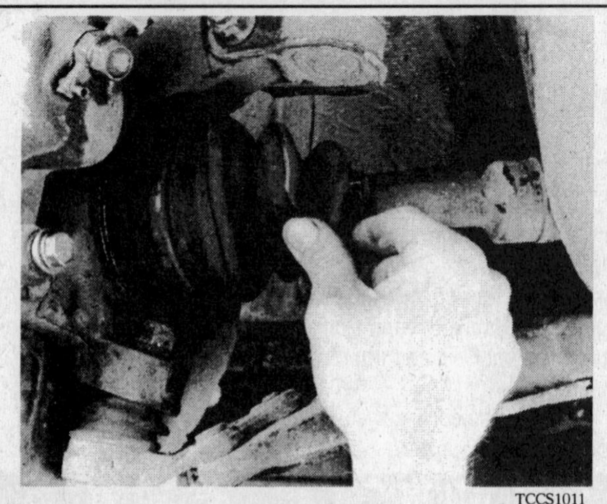
TCCS1011

Fig. 102 CV-Boots must be inspected periodically for damage

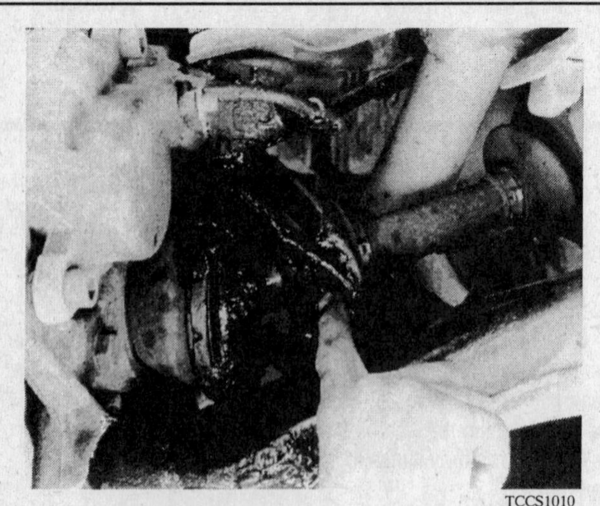
TCCS1010

Fig. 103 A torn boot should be replaced immediately

Air Conditioning

➔ **Be sure to consult the laws in your area before servicing the air conditioning system. In most areas, it is illegal to perform repairs involving refrigerant unless the work is done by a certified technician. Also, it is quite likely that you will not be able to purchase refrigerant without proof of certification.**

SAFETY PRECAUTIONS

There are two major hazards associated with air conditioning systems and they both relate to the refrigerant gas. First, the refrigerant gas (R-12 or R-134a) is an extremely cold substance. When exposed to air, it will instantly freeze any surface it comes in contact with, including your eyes. The other hazard relates to fire (if your vehicle is equipped with R-12. Although normally non-toxic, the R-12 gas becomes highly poisonous in the presence of an open flame. One good whiff of the vapor formed by burning R-12 can be fatal. Keep all forms of fire (including cigarettes) well clear of the air conditioning system.

Because of the inherent dangers involved with working on air conditioning systems, these safety precautions must be strictly followed.

- Avoid contact with a charged refrigeration system, even when working on another part of the air conditioning system or vehicle. If a heavy tool comes into contact with a section of tubing or a heat exchanger, it can easily cause the relatively soft material to rupture.
- When it is necessary to apply force to a fitting which contains refrigerant, as when checking that all system couplings are securely tightened, use a wrench on both parts of the fitting involved, if possible. This will avoid putting torque on refrigerant tubing. (It is also advisable to use tube or line wrenches when tightening these flare nut fittings.)

➔ **R-12 refrigerant is a chlorofluorocarbon which, when released into the atmosphere, can contribute to the depletion of the ozone layer in the upper atmosphere. Ozone filters out harmful radiation from the sun.**

- Do not attempt to discharge the system without the proper tools. Precise control is possible only when using the service gauges and a proper A/C refrigerant recovery station. Wear protective gloves when connecting or disconnecting service gauge hoses.
- Discharge the system only in a well ventilated area, as high concentrations of the gas which might accidentally escape can exclude oxygen and act as an anesthetic. When leak testing or soldering, this is particularly important, as toxic gas is formed when R-12 contacts any flame.
- Never start a system without first verifying that both service valves are properly installed, and that all fittings throughout the system are snugly connected.
- Avoid applying heat to any refrigerant line or storage vessel. Charging may be aided by using water heated to less than 125°F (50°C) to warm the refrigerant container. Never allow a refrigerant storage container to sit out in the sun, or near any other source of heat, such as a radiator or heater.

- Always wear goggles to protect your eyes when working on a system. If refrigerant contacts the eyes, it is advisable in all cases to consult a physician immediately.
- Frostbite from liquid refrigerant should be treated by first gradually warming the area with cool water, and then gently applying petroleum jelly. A physician should be consulted.
- Always keep refrigerant drum fittings capped when not in use. If the container is equipped with a safety cap to protect the valve, make sure the cap is in place when the can is not being used. Avoid sudden shock to the drum, which might occur from dropping it, or from banging a heavy tool against it. Never carry a drum in the passenger compartment of a vehicle.
- Always completely discharge the system into a suitable recovery unit before painting the vehicle (if the paint is to be baked on), or before welding anywhere near refrigerant lines.
- When servicing the system, minimize the time that any refrigerant line or fitting is open to the air in order to prevent moisture or dirt from entering the system. Contaminants such as moisture or dirt can damage internal system components. Always replace O-rings on lines or fittings which are disconnected. Prior to installation coat, but do not soak, replacement O-rings with suitable compressor oil.

GENERAL SERVICING PROCEDURES

➥ It is recommended, and possibly required by law, that a qualified technician perform the following services.

****WARNING**

Some of the vehicles covered by this manual may be equipped with R-134a refrigerant systems, rather than R-12. Be ABSOLUTELY SURE what type of system you are working on before attempting to add refrigerant. Use of the wrong refrigerant or oil will cause damage to the system.

The most important aspect of air conditioning service is the maintenance of a pure and adequate charge of refrigerant in the system. A refrigeration system cannot function properly if a significant percentage of the charge is lost. Leaks are common because the severe vibration encountered under hood in an automobile can easily cause a sufficient cracking or loosening of the air conditioning fittings; allowing, the extreme operating pressures of the system to force refrigerant out.

The problem can be understood by considering what happens to the system as it is operated with a continuous leak. Because the expansion valve regulates the flow of refrigerant to the evaporator, the level of refrigerant there is fairly constant. The receiver/drier stores any excess refrigerant, and so a loss will first appear there as a reduction in the level of liquid. As this level nears the bottom of the vessel, some refrigerant vapor bubbles will begin to appear in the stream of liquid supplied to the expansion valve. This vapor decreases the capacity of the expansion valve very little as the valve opens to compensate for its presence. As the quantity of liquid in the condenser decreases, the operating pressure will drop there and throughout the high side of the system. As the refrigerant continues to be expelled, the pressure available to force the liquid through the expansion valve will continue to decrease, and, eventually, the valve's orifice will prove to be too much of a restriction for adequate flow even with the needle fully withdrawn.

At this point, low side pressure will start to drop, and a severe reduction in cooling capacity, marked by freeze-up of the evaporator coil, will result. Eventually, the operating pressure of the evaporator will be lower than the pressure of the atmosphere surrounding it, and air will be drawn into the system wherever there are leaks in the low side.

Because all atmospheric air contains at least some moisture, water will enter the system mixing with the refrigerant and oil. Trace amounts of moisture will cause sludging of the oil, and corrosion of the system. Saturation and clogging of the filter/drier, and freezing of the expansion valve orifice will eventually result. As air fills the system to a greater and greater extent, it will interfere more and more with the normal flows of refrigerant and heat.

From this description, it should be obvious that much of the repairman's focus in on detecting leaks, repairing them, and then restoring the purity and quantity of the refrigerant charge. A list of general rules should be followed in addition to all safety precautions:

- Keep all tools as clean and dry as possible.
- Thoroughly purge the service gauges/hoses of air and moisture before connecting them to the system. Keep them capped when not in use.
- Thoroughly clean any refrigerant fitting before disconnecting it, in order to minimize the entrance of dirt into the system.
- Plan any operation that requires opening the system beforehand, in order to minimize the length of time it will be exposed to open air. Cap or seal the open ends to minimize the entrance of foreign material.
- When adding oil, pour it through an extremely clean and dry tube or funnel. Keep the oil capped whenever possible. Do not use oil that has not been kept tightly sealed.
- Purchase refrigerant intended for use only in automatic air conditioning systems.
- Completely evacuate any system that has been opened for service, or that has leaked sufficiently to draw in moisture and air. This requires evacuating air and moisture with a good vacuum pump for at least one hour. If a system has been open for a considerable length of time it may be advisable to evacuate the system for up to 12 hours (overnight).
- Use a wrench on both halves of a fitting that is to be disconnected, so as to avoid placing torque on any of the refrigerant lines.
- When overhauling a compressor, pour some of the oil into a clean glass and inspect it. If there is evidence of dirt, metal particles, or both, flush all refrigerant components with clean refrigerant before evacuating and recharging the system. In addition, if metal particles are present, the compressor should be replaced.
- Schrader valves may leak only when under full operating pressure. Therefore, if leakage is suspected but cannot be located, operate the system with a full charge of refrigerant and look for leaks from all Schrader valves. Replace any faulty valves.

Additional Preventive Maintenance

USING THE SYSTEM

The easiest and most important preventive maintenance for your A/C system is to be sure that it is used on a regular basis. Running the system for five minutes each month (no matter what the season) will help assure that the seals and all internal components remain lubricated.

ANTIFREEZE

See Figure 104

In order to prevent heater core freeze-up during A/C operation, it is necessary to maintain a proper antifreeze protection. Use a hand-held antifreeze tester (hydrometer) to periodically check the condition of the antifreeze in your engine's cooling system.

Antifreeze should not be used longer than the manufacturer specifies.

RADIATOR CAP

For efficient operation of an air conditioned vehicle's cooling system, the radiator cap should have a holding pressure which meets manufacturer's specifications. A cap which fails to hold these pressures should be replaced.

CONDENSER

Any obstruction of or damage to the condenser configuration will restrict the air flow which is essential to its efficient operation. It is therefore a good rule to keep this unit clean and in proper physical shape.

Bug screens which are mounted in front of the condenser (unless they are original equipment) are regarded as obstructions.

CONDENSATION DRAIN TUBE

This single molded drain tube expels the condensation, which accumulates on the bottom of the evaporator housing, into the engine compartment. If this tube is obstructed, the air conditioning performance can be restricted and condensation buildup can spill over onto the vehicle's floor.

TCCS1233

Fig. 104 An antifreeze tester can be use to determine the freezing and boiling level of the coolant in your vehicle

SYSTEM INSPECTION

R-12 refrigerant is a chlorofluorocarbon which, when released into the atmosphere, can contribute to the depletion of the ozone layer in the upper atmosphere. Ozone filters out harmful radiation from the sun.

The easiest and often most important check for the air conditioning system consists of a visual inspection of the system components. Visually inspect the air conditioning system for refrigerant leaks, damaged compressor clutch, compressor drive belt tension and condition, plugged evaporator drain tube, blocked condenser fins, disconnected or broken wires, blown fuses, corroded connections and poor insulation.

A refrigerant leak will usually appear as an oily residue at the leakage point in the system. The oily residue soon picks up dust or dirt particles from the surrounding air and appears greasy. Through time, this will build up and appear to be a heavy dirt impregnated grease. Most leaks are caused by damaged or missing O-ring seals at the component connections, damaged charging valve cores or missing service gauge port caps.

For a thorough visual and operational inspection, check the following:

1. Check the surface of the radiator and condenser for dirt, leaves or other material which might block air flow.
2. Check for kinks in hoses and lines. Check the system for leaks.
3. Make sure the drive belt is under the proper tension. When the air conditioning is operating, make sure the drive belt is free of noise or slippage.
4. Make sure the blower motor operates at all appropriate positions, then check for distribution of the air from all outlets with the blower on **HIGH**.

Keep in mind that under conditions of high humidity, air discharged from the A/C vents may not feel as cold as expected, even if the system is working properly. This is because the vaporized moisture in humid air retains heat more effectively than does dry air, making the humid air more difficult to cool.

5. Make sure the air passage selection lever is operating correctly. Start the engine and warm it to normal operating temperature, then make sure the hot/cold selection lever is operating correctly.

DISCHARGING, EVACUATING AND CHARGING

Discharging, evacuating and charging the air conditioning system must be performed by a properly trained and certified mechanic in a facility equipped with refrigerant recovery/recycling equipment that meets SAE standards for the type of system to be serviced.

If you don't have access to the necessary equipment, we recommend that you take your vehicle to a reputable service station to have the work done. If you still wish to perform repairs on the vehicle, have them discharge the system, then take your vehicle home and perform the necessary work. When you are finished, return the vehicle to the station for evacuation and charging. Just be sure to cap ALL A/C system fittings immediately after opening them and keep them protected until the system is recharged.

Windshield Wipers

ELEMENT (REFILL) CARE AND REPLACEMENT

➧ **See Figures 105, 106, 107, 108, 109, 110, 111, 112, 113, 114, 115 and 116**

For maximum effectiveness and longest element life, the windshield and wiper blades should be kept clean. Dirt, tree sap, road tar and so on will cause streaking, smearing and blade deterioration if left on the glass. It is advisable to wash the windshield carefully with a commercial glass cleaner at least once a month. Wipe off the rubber blades with the wet rag afterwards. Do not attempt to move wipers across the windshield by hand; damage to the motor and drive mechanism will result.

To inspect and/or replace the wiper blade elements, place the wiper switch in the **LOW** speed position and the ignition switch in the **ACC** position. When the wiper blades are approximately vertical on the windshield, turn the ignition switch to **OFF**.

Fig. 105 Bosch® wiper blade and fit kit

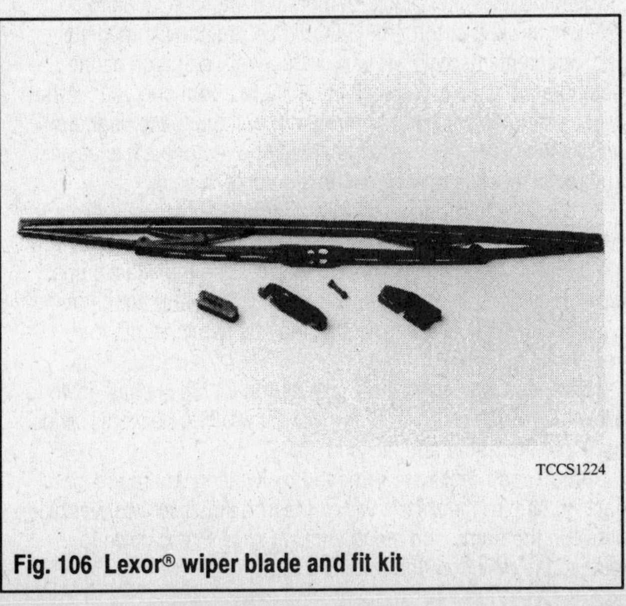

Fig. 106 Lexor® wiper blade and fit kit

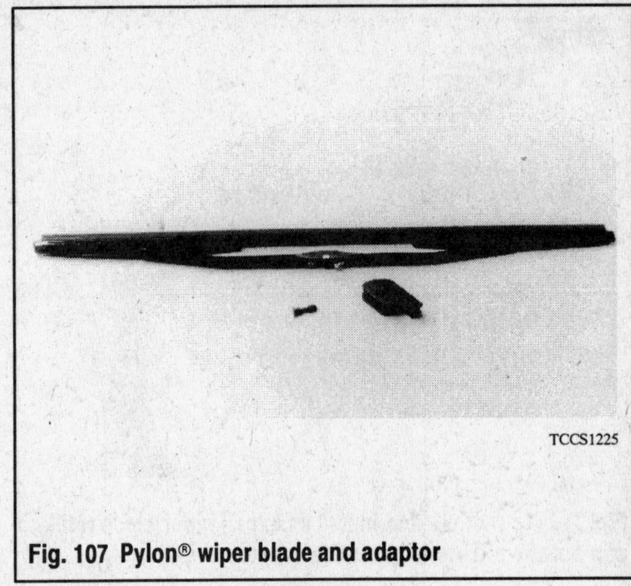

Fig. 107 Pylon® wiper blade and adaptor

Fig. 108 Trico® wiper blade and fit kit

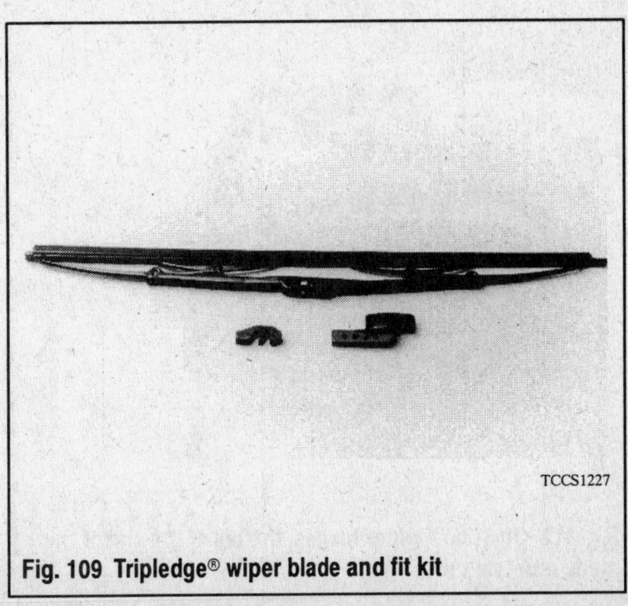

Fig. 109 Tripledge® wiper blade and fit kit

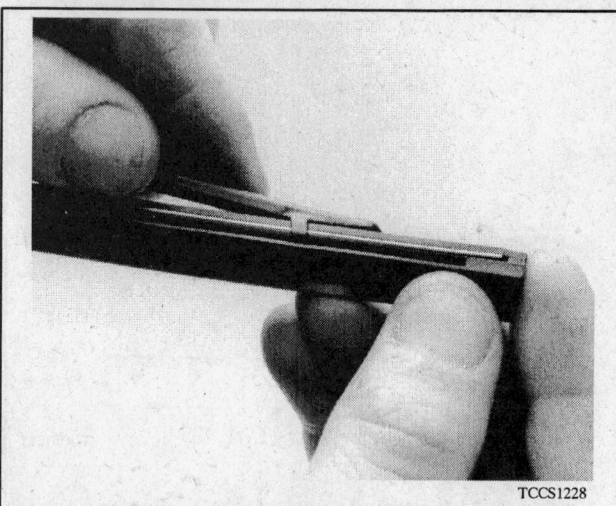

TCCS1228

Fig. 110 To remove and install a Lexor® wiper blade refill, slip out the old insert and slide in a new one

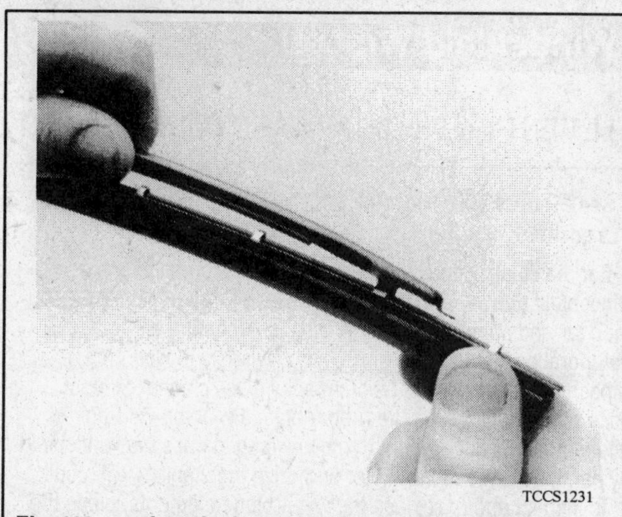

TCCS1231

Fig. 113 . . . then the insert can be removed. After installing the replacement insert, bend the tab back

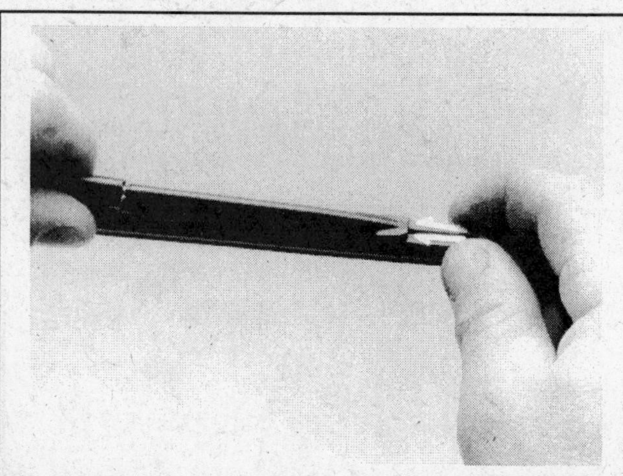

TCCS1229

Fig. 111 On Pylon® inserts, the end clip must be removed prior to the insert. Don't forget to install the clip after the new insert

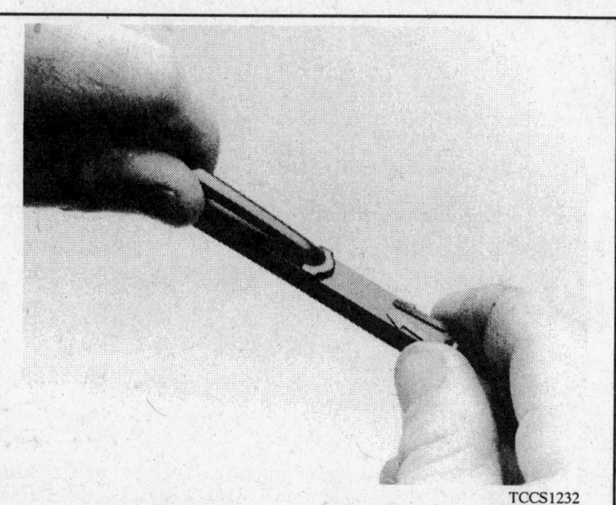

TCCS1232

Fig. 114 The Tripledge® wiper blade insert is removed and installed using a securing clip

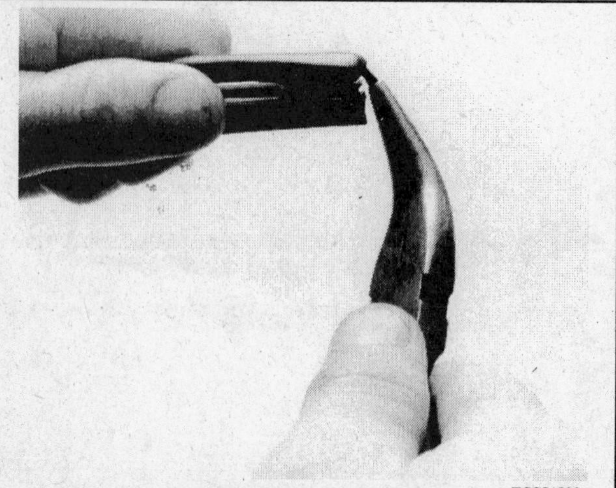

TCCS1230

Fig. 112 On Trico® wiper blades, the tab at the end of the blade must be turned up . . .

Examine the wiper blade elements. If they are found to be cracked, broken or torn, they should be replaced immediately. Replacement intervals will vary with usage, although ozone deterioration usually limits element life to about one year. If the wiper pattern is smeared or streaked, or if the blade chatters across the glass, the elements should be replaced. It is easiest and most sensible to replace the elements in pairs.

If your vehicle is equipped with aftermarket blades, there are several different types of refills and your vehicle might have any kind. Aftermarket blades and arms rarely use the exact same type blade or refill as the original equipment. Here are some typical aftermarket blades; not all may be available for your vehicle:

The Anco® type uses a release button that is pushed down to allow the refill to slide out of the yoke jaws. The new refill slides back into the frame and locks in place.

Some Trico® refills are removed by locating where the metal backing strip or the refill is wider. Insert a small screwdriver blade between the frame and metal backing strip. Press down to release the refill from the retaining tab.

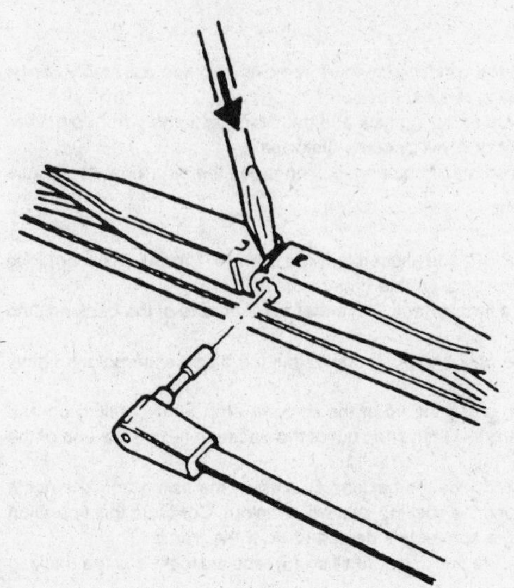

BLADE REPLACEMENT

1. CYCLE ARM AND BLADE ASSEMBLY TO UP POSITION-ON THE WINDSHIELD WHERE REMOVAL OF BLADE ASSEMBLY CAN BE PERFORMED WITHOUT DIFFICULTY. TURN IGNITION KEY OFF AT DESIRED POSITION.

2. TO REMOVE BLADE ASSEMBLY, INSERT SCREWDRIVER IN SLOT, PUSH DOWN ON SPRING LOCK AND PULL BLADE ASSEMBLY FROM PIN (VIEW A)

3. TO INSTALL, PUSH THE BLADE ASSEMBLY ON THE PIN SO THAT THE SPRING LOCK ENGAGES THE PIN (VIEW A). BE SURE THE BLADE ASSEMBLY IS SECURELY ATTACHED TO PIN

VIEW A

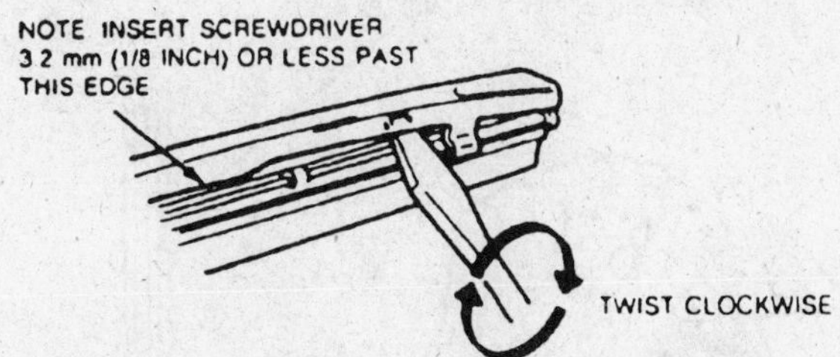

ELEMENT REPLACEMENT

1. INSERT SCREWDRIVER BETWEEN THE EDGE OF THE SUPER STRUCTURE AND THE BLADE BACKING DRIP (VIEW B) TWIST SCREWDRIVER SLOWLY UNTIL ELEMENT CLEARS ONE SIDE OF THE SUPER STRUCTURE CLAW

2. SLIDE THE ELEMENT INTO THE SUPER STRUCTURE CLAWS

VIEW B

4. INSERT ELEMENT INTO ONE SIDE OF THE END CLAWS (VIEW D) AND WITH A ROCKING MOTION PUSH ELEMENT UPWARD UNTIL IT SNAPS IN (VIEW E)

VIEW D

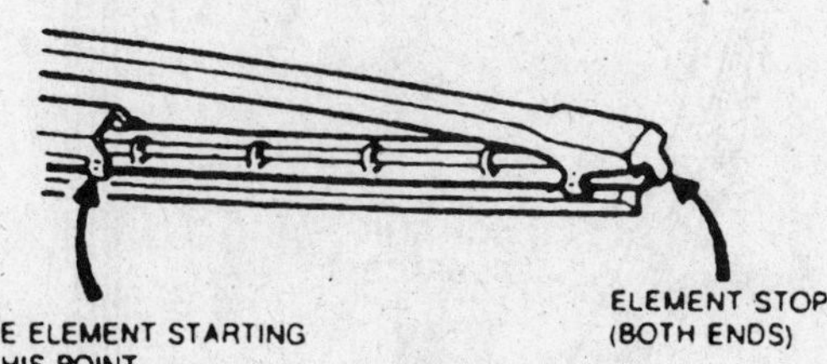

3. SLIDE THE ELEMENT INTO THE SUPER STRUCTURE CLAWS, STARTING WITH SECOND SET FROM EITHER END (VIEW C) AND CONTINUE TO SLIDE THE BLADE ELEMENT INTO ALL THE SUPER STRUCTURE CLAWS TO THE ELEMENT STOP (VIEW C)

VIEW C

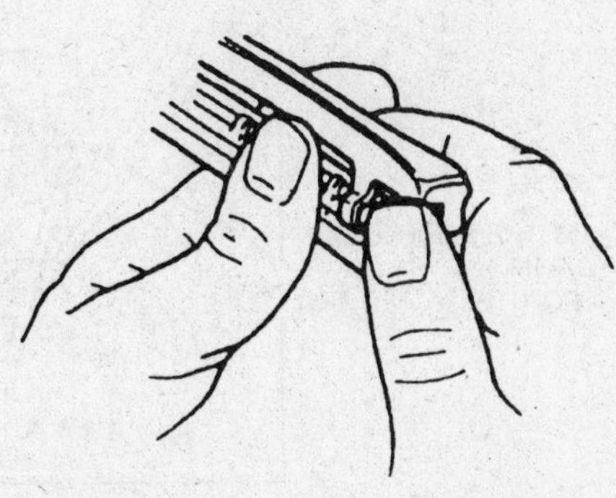

VIEW E

TCCS1236

Fig. 115 Trico® wiper blade insert (element) replacement

BLADE REPLACEMENT

1. Cycle arm and blade assembly to a position on the windshield where removal of blade assembly can be performed without difficulty. Turn ignition key off at desired position.
2. To remove blade assembly from wiper arm, pull up on spring lock and pull blade assembly from pin (View A). Be sure spring lock is not pulled excessively or it will become distorted.
3. To install, push the blade assembly onto the pin so that the spring lock engages the pin (View A). Be sure the blade assembly is securely attached to pin.

ELEMENT REPLACEMENT

1. In the plastic backing strip which is part of the rubber blade assembly, there is an 11.11mm (7/16 inch) long notch located approximately one inch from either end. Locate either notch.
2. Place the frame of the wiper blade assembly on a firm surface with either notched end of the backing strip visible.
3. Grasp the frame portion of the wiper blade assembly and push down until the blade assembly is tightly bowed.
4. With the blade assembly in the bowed position, grasp the tip of the backing strip firmly, pulling up and twisting C.C.W. at the same time. The backing strip will then snap out of the retaining tab on the end of the frame.
5. Lift the wiper blade assembly from the surface and slide the backing strip down the frame until the notch lines up with the next retaining tab, twist slightly, and the backing strip will snap out. Continue this operation with the remaining tabs until the blade element is completely detached from the frame.
6. To install blade element, reverse the above procedure, making sure all six (6) tabs are locked to the backing strip before installing blade to wiper arm.

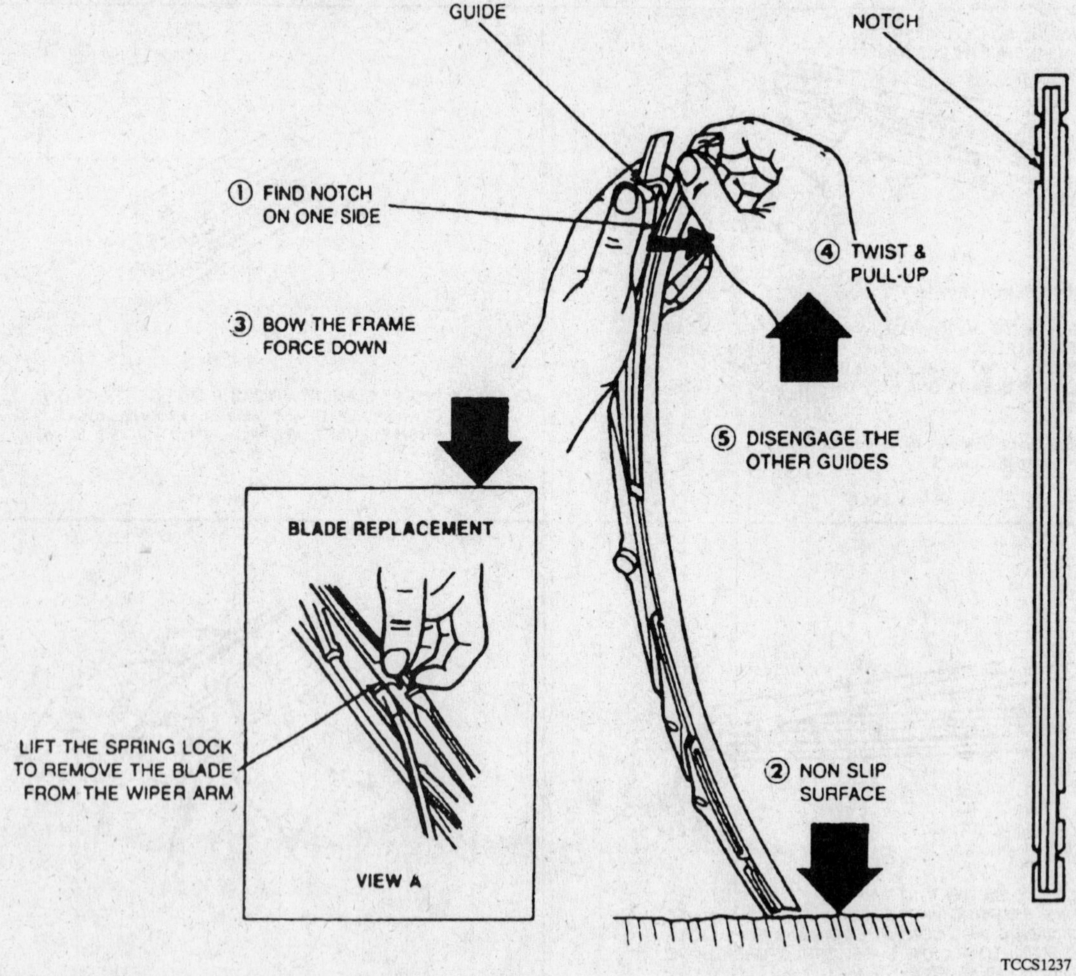

Fig. 116 Tridon® wiper blade insert (element) replacement

Other types of Trico® refills have two metal tabs which are unlocked by squeezing them together. The rubber filler can then be withdrawn from the frame jaws. A new refill is installed by inserting the refill into the front frame jaws and sliding it rearward to engage the remaining frame jaws. There are usually four jaws; be certain when installing that the refill is engaged in all of them. At the end of its travel, the tabs will lock into place on the front jaws of the wiper blade frame.

Another type of refill is made from polycarbonate. The refill has a simple locking device at one end which flexes downward out of the groove into which the jaws of the holder fit, allowing easy release. By sliding the new refill through all the jaws and pushing through the slight resistance when it reaches the end of its travel, the refill will lock into position.

To replace the Tridon® refill, it is necessary to remove the wiper blade. This refill has a plastic backing strip with a notch about 1 in. (25mm) from the end. Hold the blade (frame) on a hard surface so that the frame is tightly bowed. Grip the tip of the backing strip and pull up while twisting counterclockwise. The backing strip will snap out of the retaining tab. Do this for the remaining tabs until the refill is free of the blade. The length of these refills is molded into the end and they should be replaced with identical types.

Regardless of the type of refill used, be sure to follow the part manufacturer's instructions closely. Make sure that all of the frame jaws are engaged as the refill is pushed into place and locked. If the metal blade holder and frame are allowed to touch the glass during wiper operation, the glass will be scratched.

Tires and Wheels

TIRE INFLATION

See Figure 117

Check the air pressure in your vehicle's tires every few weeks. Make sure that the tires are cool. Air pressure increases with higher temperature, and will indicate false reading. A decal located on the glove box door or side door frame will tell you the proper tire pressure for the standard equipment tires.

Never exceed the maximum inflation pressure on the side of the tire. Also never mixed tires of different size or construction (Belted vs Bias-ply, or Radial vs Belted etc.).

It pays to buy a tire pressure gauge to keep in your vehicle, since those of service stations are often inaccurate or broken. While you are checking the tire pressure, take a look at the tread. The tread should be wearing evenly across the tire. Excessive wear in the center of the tread indicates over inflation. Excessive wear on the outer edges indicates under inflation. An irregular wear pattern is usually a sign of incorrect front wheel alignment or wheel balance.

A front end that is out of alignment will usually pull to one side when the steering wheel is released. Conditions which relate to front end alignment are associated by tire wear patterns. Tire treads being worn on one side more than the other, or wear on the tread edges may be noticeable. Front wheels which are incorrectly balance, is usually accompanied by high speed vibration.

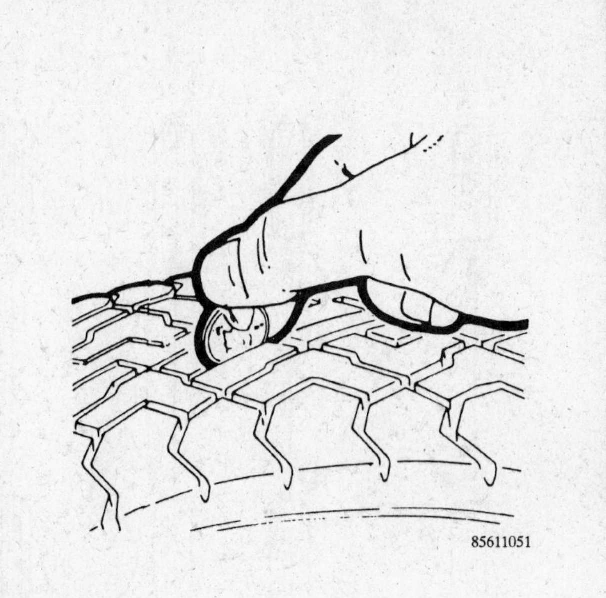

Fig. 117 Tread depth can be roughly checked with a Lincoln penny. If the top of Lincoln's head is visible, replace the tire

TIRE ROTATION

See Figure 118

Tires installed on the front or rear of any vehicle are subjected to different loads, breaking, or steering functions. Because of these conditions, tires develop uneven wear patterns. Rotating the tires every 6000 miles or so will result in increased thread life. Use the correct pattern for tire rotation. Refer to Tire Rotation Patterns chart.

Most automotive experts are in agreement that radial tires are better all around performers, giving prolonged wear and better handling. An added benefit which you should consider when purchasing tires is that radials have less rolling resistance and can give up to a 10% increase in fuel economy over a bias-ply tire.

It is recommended that you have the tires rotated and the balance checked every 6000 miles. There is no way to give a tire rotation diagram for every combination of tires and vehicles, but the accompanying diagrams are a general rule to follow. Some truck, foul-weather and high-performance tires have directional tread, indicated by arrows on the sidewalls; the arrow shows the direction of rotation. They will wear very rapidly if reversed.

Mark the wheel position or direction of rotation on direction tires before removing them.

If your van is equipped with tires having different load ratings on the front and the rear, the tires should not be rotated front to rear. Rotating these tires could affect tire life (the tires with the lower rating will wear faster, and could become overloaded), and upset the handling of the van.

When installing the wheels on the vehicle, tighten the lug nuts in a criss-cross pattern.

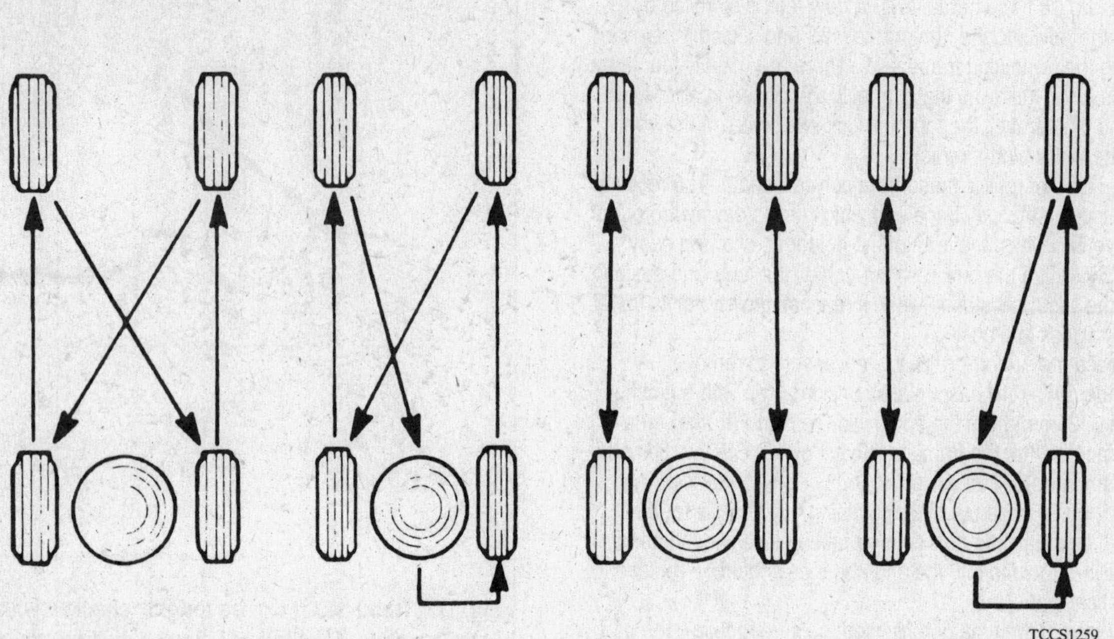

Fig. 118 Common tire rotation patterns for 4 and 5 wheel rotations

TIRE USAGE

The tires on your van were selected to provide the best all around performance for normal operation when inflated as specified. Oversize tires will not increase the maximum carrying capacity of the vehicle, although they will provide an extra margin of tread life. Be sure to check overall height before using larger size tires which may cause interference with suspension components or wheel wells. When replacing conventional tire sizes with other tire size designations, be sure to check the manufacturer's recommendations. Interchangeability is not always possible because of differences in load ratings, tire dimensions, wheel well clearances, and rim size. Also due to differences in handling characteristics, 70 Series and 60 Series tires should be used only in pairs on the same axle; radial tires should be used only in sets of four.

Many states have vehicle height restrictions; some states prohibit the lifting of vehicles beyond their design limits.

The wheels must be the correct width for the tire. Tire dealers have charts of tire and rim compatibility. A mismatch can cause sloppy handling and rapid tread wear. The old rule of thumb is that the tread width should match the rim width (inside bead to inside bead) within 1 in. (25mm). For radial tires, the rim width should be 80% or less of the tire (not tread) width.

The height (mounted diameter) of the new tires can greatly change speedometer accuracy, engine speed at a given road speed, fuel mileage, acceleration, and ground clearance. Tire manufacturers furnish full measurement specifications. Speedometer drive gears are available for correction.

Dimensions of tires marked the same size may vary significantly, even among tires from the same manufacturer.

The spare tire should be of the same size, construction and design as the tires on the vehicle. It's not a good idea to carry a spare of a different construction.

TIRE DESIGN

See Figure 119

For maximum satisfaction, tires should be used in sets of five. Mixing or different types (radial, bias-belted, fiberglass belted) should be avoided. Conventional bias tires are constructed so that the cords run bead-to-bead at an angle. Alternate plies run at an opposite angle. This type of construction gives rigidity to both tread and sidewall. Bias-belted tires are similar in construction to conventional bias ply tires. Belts run at an angle and also at a 90° angle to the bead, as in the radial tire. Tread life is improved considerably over the conventional bias tire. The radial tire differs in construction, but instead of the carcass plies running at an angle of 90° to each other, they run at an angle of 90° to the bead. This gives the tread a great deal of rigidity and the sidewall a great deal of flexibility and accounts for the characteristic bulge associated with radial tires.

When radial tires are used, tire sizes and wheel diameters should be selected to maintain ground clearance and tire load capacity equivalent to the minimum specified tire. Radial tires should always be used in sets of five, but in an emergency, radial tires can be used with caution on the rear axle only. If this is done, both tires on the rear should be of radial design.

****WARNING**

Radial tires should never be used on only the front axle!

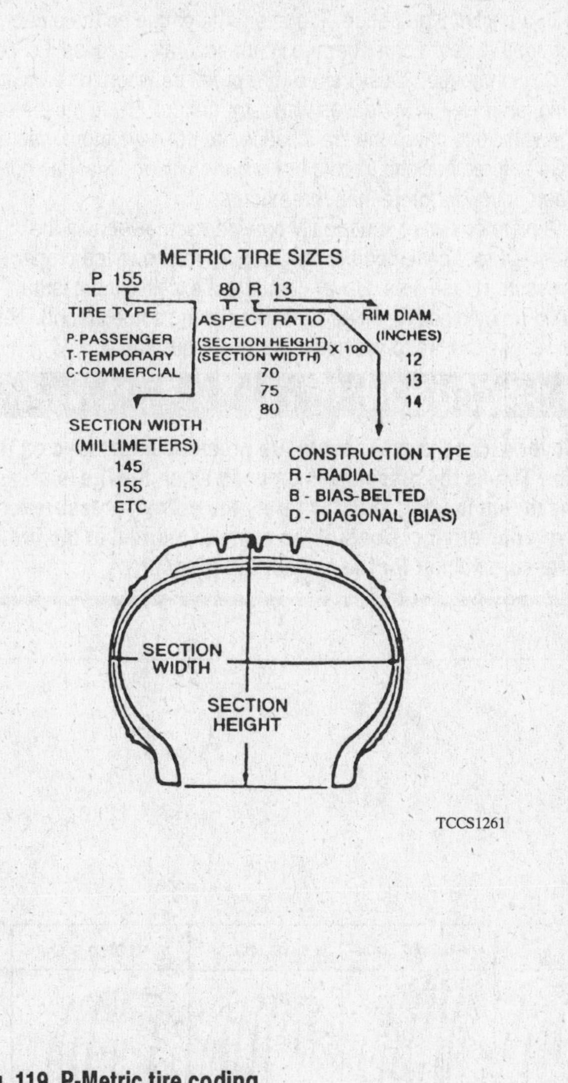

Fig. 119 P-Metric tire coding

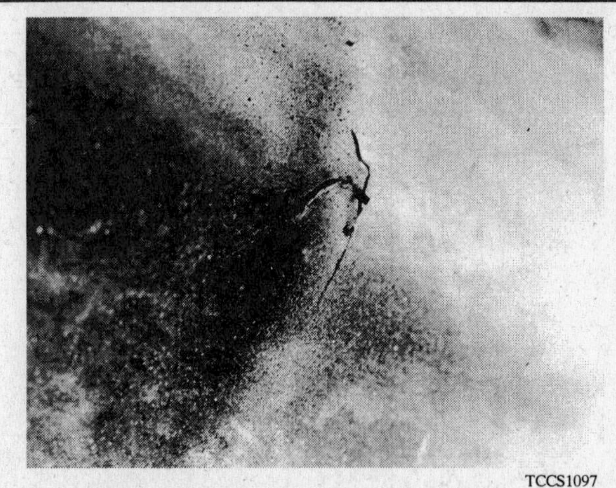

Fig. 120 Tires should be checked frequently for any sign of puncture or damage

Fig. 121 Tires with deep cuts, or cuts which show bulging should be replaced immediately

TIRE STORAGE

If they are mounted on wheels, store the tires at proper inflation pressure. All tires should be kept in a cool, dry place. If they are stored in the garage or basement, do not let them stand on a concrete floor; set them on strips of wood, a mat or a large stack of newspaper. Keeping them away from direct moisture is of paramount importance. Tires should not be stored upright, but in a flat position.

INSPECTION

➧ See Figures 120, 121, 122, 123, 124, 125, 126 and 127

The importance of proper tire inflation cannot be overemphasized. A tire employs air as part of its structure. It is designed around the supporting strength of the air at a specified pressure. For this reason, improper inflation drastically reduces the tires's ability to perform as intended. A tire will lose some air in day-to-day use; having to add a few pounds of air periodically is not necessarily a sign of a leaking tire.

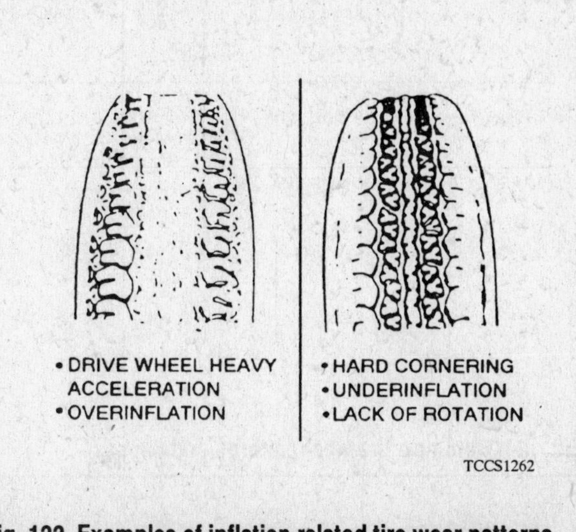

Fig. 122 Examples of inflation-related tire wear patterns

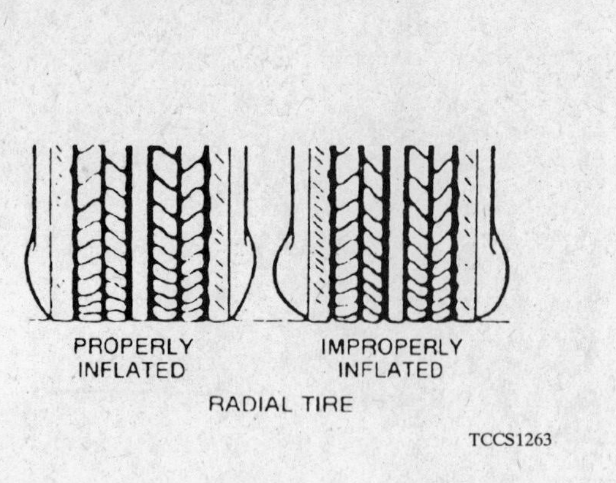

Fig. 123 Radial tires have a characteristic sidewall bulge; don't try to measure pressure by looking at the tire. Use a quality air pressure gauge

Two items should be a permanent fixture in every glove compartment: an accurate tire pressure gauge and a tread depth gauge. Check the tire pressure (including the spare) regularly with a pocket type gauge. Too often, the gauge on the end of the air hose at your corner garage is not accurate because it suffers too much abuse. Always check tire pressure when the tires are cold, as pressure increases with temperature. If you must move the vehicle to check the tire inflation, do not drive more than a mile before checking. A cold tire is generally one that has not been driven for more than three hours.

A plate or sticker is normally provided somewhere in the vehicle (door post, hood or tailgate) which shows the proper pressure for the tires. Never counteract excessive pressure build-up by bleeding off air pressure (letting some air out). This will cause the tire to run hotter and wear quicker.

****CAUTION**

Never exceed the maximum tire pressure embossed on the tire! This is the pressure to be used when the tire is at maximum loading, but it is rarely the correct pressure for everyday driving. Consult the owner's manual or the tire pressure sticker for the correct tire pressure.

CONDITION	RAPID WEAR AT SHOULDERS	RAPID WEAR AT CENTER	CRACKED TREADS	WEAR ON ONE SIDE	FEATHERED EDGE	BALD SPOTS	SCALLOPED WEAR
EFFECT	1. 2.						
CAUSE	UNDER-INFLATION OR LACK OF ROTATION	OVER-INFLATION OR LACK OF ROTATION	UNDER-INFLATION OR EXCESSIVE SPEED*	EXCESSIVE CAMBER	INCORRECT TOE	UNBALANCED WHEEL OR TIRE DEFECT*	LACK OF ROTATION OF TIRES OR WORN OR OUT-OF-ALIGNMENT SUSPENSION.
CORRECTION	ADJUST PRESSURE TO SPECIFICATIONS WHEN TIRES ARE COOL ROTATE TIRES			ADJUST CAMBER TO SPECIFICATIONS	ADJUST TOE-IN TO SPECIFICATIONS	DYNAMIC OR STATIC BALANCE WHEELS	ROTATE TIRES AND INSPECT SUSPENSION

*HAVE TIRE INSPECTED FOR FURTHER USE.

TCCS1267

Fig. 124 Common tire wear patterns and causes

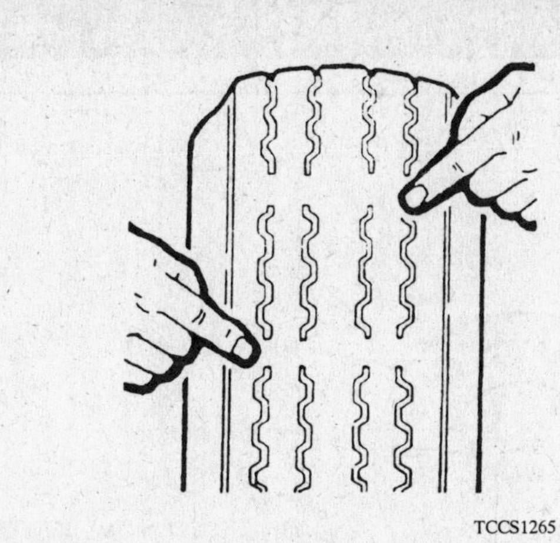

Fig. 125 Tread wear indicators will appear when the tire is worn

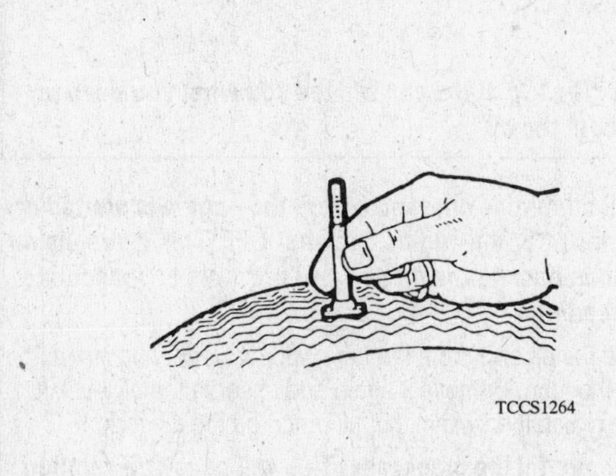

Fig. 126 Accurate tread depth indicators are inexpensive and handy

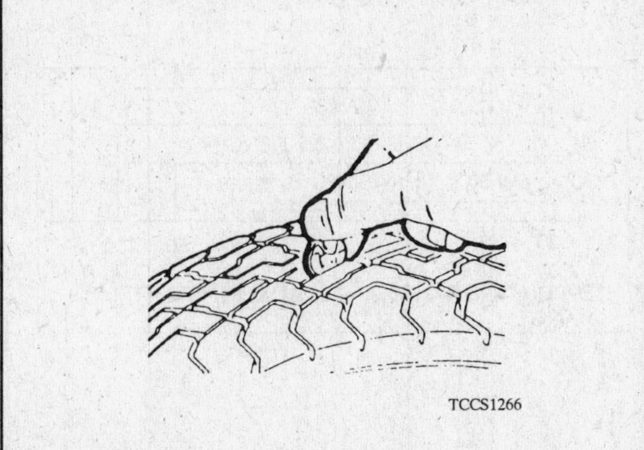

Fig. 127 A penny works well for a quick check of tread depth

Once you've maintained the correct tire pressures for several weeks, you'll be familiar with the vehicle's braking and handling personality. Slight adjustments in tire pressures can fine-tune these characteristics, but never change the cold pressure specification by more than 2 psi. A slightly softer tire pressure will give a softer ride but also yield lower fuel mileage. A slightly harder tire will give crisper dry road handling but can cause skidding on wet surfaces. Unless you're fully attuned to the vehicle, stick to the recommended inflation pressures.

All tires made since 1968 have built-in tread wear indicator bars that show up as $^1/_2$ in. (13mm) wide smooth bands across the tire when $^1/_{16}$ in. (1.5mm) of tread remains. The appearance of tread wear indicators means that the tires should be replaced. In fact, many states have laws prohibiting the use of tires with less than this amount of tread.

You can check your own tread depth with an inexpensive gauge or by using a Lincoln head penny. Slip the Lincoln penny (with Lincoln's head upside-down) into several tread grooves. If you can see the top of Lincoln's head in 2 adjacent grooves, the tire has less than $^1/_{16}$ in. (1.5mm) tread left and should be replaced. You can measure snow tires in the same manner by using the "tails" side of the Lincoln penny. If you can see the top of the Lincoln memorial, it's time to replace the snow tire(s).

CARE OF SPECIAL WHEELS

If you have invested money in magnesium, aluminum alloy or sport wheels, special precautions should be taken to make sure your investment is not wasted and that your special wheels look good for the life of the vehicle.

Special wheels are easily damaged and/or scratched. Occasionally check the rims for cracking, impact damage or air leaks. If any of these are found, replace the wheel. But in order to prevent this type of damage and the costly replacement of a special wheel, observe the following precautions:

- Use extra care not to damage the wheels during removal, installation, balancing, etc. After removal of the wheels from the vehicle, place them on a mat or other protective surface. If they are to be stored for any length of time, support them on strips of wood. Never store tires and wheels upright; the tread may develop flat spots.
- When driving, watch for hazards; it doesn't take much to crack a wheel.
- When washing, use a mild soap or non-abrasive dish detergent (keeping in mind that detergent tends to remove wax). Avoid cleansers with abrasives or the use of hard brushes. There are many cleaners and polishes for special wheels.
- If possible, remove the wheels during the winter. Salt and sand used for snow removal can severely damage the finish of a wheel.
- Make certain the recommended lug nut torque is never exceeded or the wheel may crack. Never use snow chains on special wheels; severe scratching will occur.

FLUIDS AND LUBRICANTS

Fluid Disposal

Used fluids, such as engine oil, antifreeze, transaxle oils and brake fluid are hazardous as waste material and must be disposed of properly.

Before draining any fluids, consult with your local municipal government. In may areas, waste oils are being accepted as part of the recycling program. A number of service stations, repair facilities and auto parts stores are accepting these waste fluids for recycling.

Be sure of the recycling center's policies before draining any fluids, as many will not accept different fluids that have been mixed together, such as oil and antifreeze.

Fuel Recommendations

Chrysler recommends that unleaded fuel only with a minimum octane rating of at least 87 be used in your vehicle. Since your vehicle is equipped with a catalytic converter, the use of unleaded gasoline is required in order to meet all emission regulations, and to prevent damage to the converter which would occur if leaded gas was to be used.

Fuels of the same octane rating have varying anti-knock qualities. Thus, if your engine knocks or pings, try switching brands of gasoline before trying a more expansive higher octane fuel.

Your engine's fuel requirements can change with time, due to carbon buildup which changes the compression ratio. If switching brands or grades of gas doesn't work, check the ignition timing. If it is necessary to retard timing from specifications, don't change it more than about 4°. Retarded timing will reduce power output and fuel mileage and increase engine temperature.

Engine

OIL RECOMMENDATIONS

See Figures 128 and 129

A high quality heavy-duty detergent oil having the proper viscosity for prevailing temperatures and a minimum SG/CC service rating should be used in your vehicle. A high quality SG/CC rated oil should be used for heavy duty service or turbocharged equipped engines. The SG/CC and SG/CD rated oil contain sufficient chemical additives to provide maximum engine protection.

Pick an oil with the viscosity that matches the anticipated temperature of the region your vehicle will be operated in before the next oil change. A chart is provided to help you with your selection. Choose the oil viscosity for the lowest expected temperature and you will be assured of easy cold weather starting and sufficient engine protection.

OIL LEVEL CHECK

See Figures 130, 131, 132, 133 and 134

The engine oil level is checked with the dipstick which is located on the radiator side of the engine.

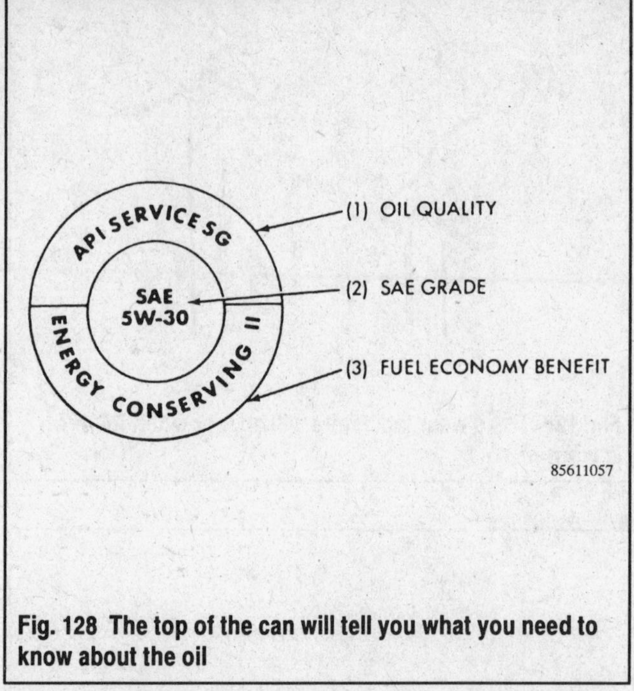

Fig. 128 The top of the can will tell you what you need to know about the oil

The oil should be checked before the engine is started or five minutes after the engine has shut OFF. This gives the oil time to drain back to the oil pan and prevents an inaccurate oil level reading.

Remove the dipstick from the tube, wipe it clean, and insert it back into the tube. Remove it again and observe the oil level. It should be maintained within the full range on the dipstick.

Do not overfill the crankcase. This will cause oil aeration and loss of oil pressure.

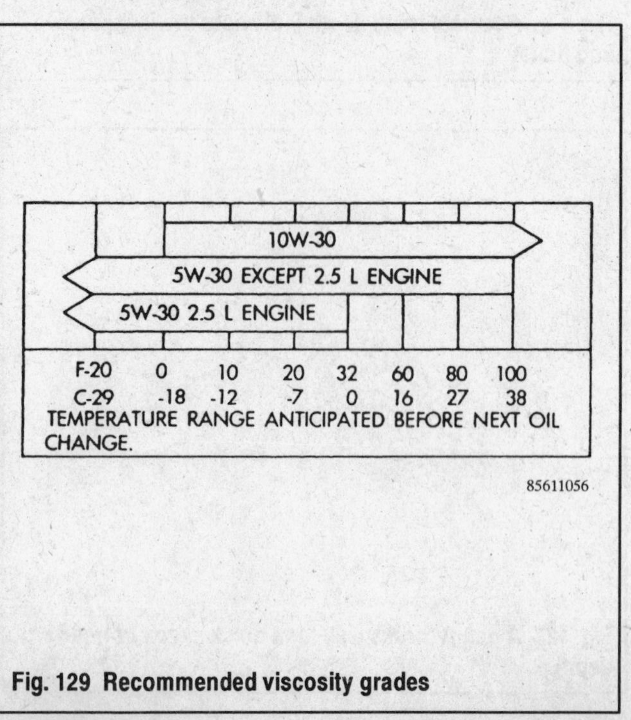

Fig. 129 Recommended viscosity grades

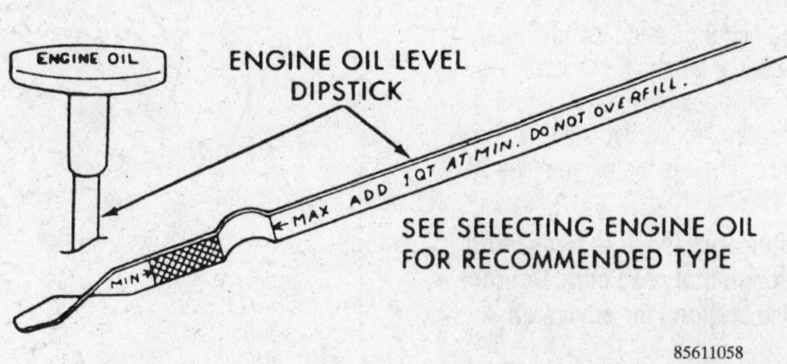

Fig. 130 Typical engine oil level indicator dipstick

Fig. 131 Removing the engine oil level dipstick from the tube

Fig. 133 Add oil through the fill cap in the valve cover. Always check the condition of the cap sealing gasket

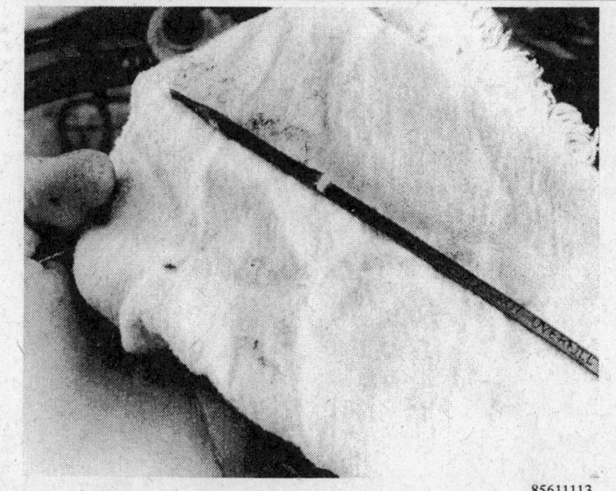

Fig. 132 Wipe the dipstick clean then insert it back into the tube

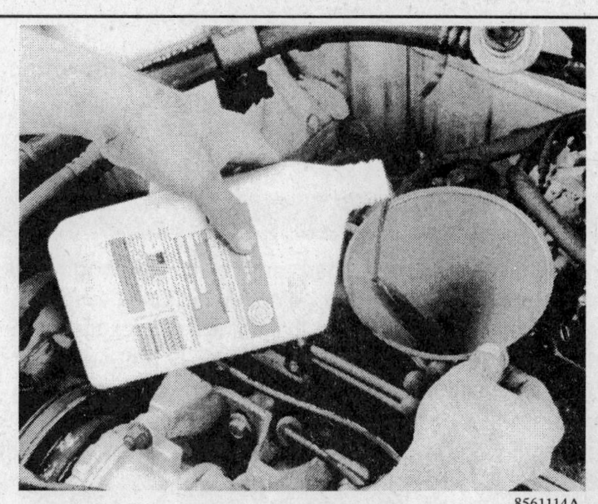

Fig. 134 For easier filling and to avoid spilling, use a funnel when adding engine oil

OIL AND FILTER CHANGE

See Figures 135, 136, 137 and 138

The recommended mileage figures for oil and filter changes are 7500 miles or 12 months whichever comes first, assuming normal driving conditions. If your vehicle is being used under dusty conditions, frequent trailer pulling, excessive idling, or stop and go driving, it is recommended to change the oil and filter at 3000 miles.

Improper disposing of all lubricants (engine, trans., and differential), can result in environmental problems. Contact your local dealerships or service stations for advice on proper disposal.

Always drain the oil after the engine has been running long enough to bring it to operating temperature. Hot oil will flow easier and more contaminants will be removed along with the oil than if it were drained cold.

Chrysler recommends changing both the oil and filter during the first oil change and the filter every other oil change thereafter. For the small price of an oil filter, it's cheap insurance to replace the filter at every oil change. One of the larger filter manufacturers points out in its advertisements that not changing the filter leaves as much as one quart of dirty oil in the engine. This claim is true and should be kept in mind when changing your oil.

1. Run the engine until it reaches normal operating temperature.
2. Raise the front of the vehicle and support on jackstands, remove the shield if it will cause interference.
3. Slide a drain pan of at least 6 quarts capacity under the oil pan.

CAUTION

The engine oil will be hot! Keep your arms, face and hands away from the oil as it drains out!

4. Loosen the drain plug. It is located in the lowest point of the oil pan. Turn the plug out by hand. By keeping an inward pressure on the plug as you unscrew it, oil won't escape past the threads and you can remove it without being burned by hot oil.
5. Allow the oil to drain completely and then install the drain plug. Don't over tighten the plug, it will result in stripped threads.
6. Using a strap wrench, remove the oil filter. Keep in mind that it's holding about one quart of dirty, hot oil.

CAUTION

The EPA warns that prolonged contact with used engine oil may cause a number of skin disorders, including cancer! You should make every effort to minimize your exposure to used engine oil. Protective gloves should be worn when changing the oil. Wash your hands and any other exposed skin areas as soon as possible after exposure to used engine oil. Soap and water, or waterless hand cleaner should be used.

7. Empty the old filter into the drain pan and dispose of the filter.

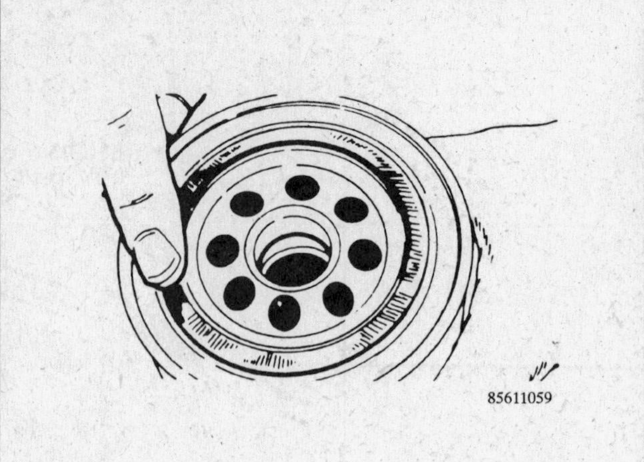

Fig. 135 Lubricate the gasket on a new filter with clean engine oil

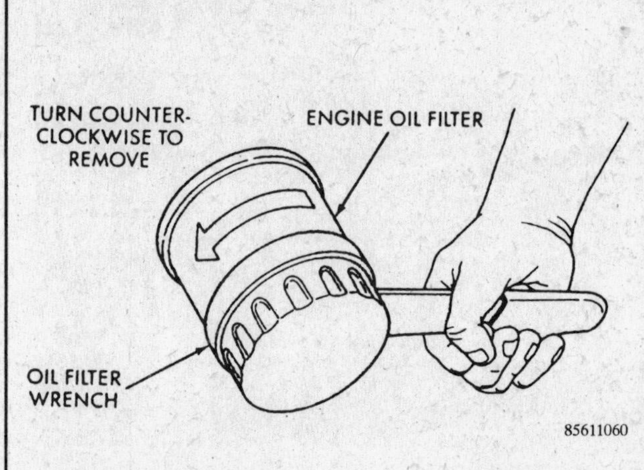

Fig. 136 The use of an oil filter wrench is strongly advised

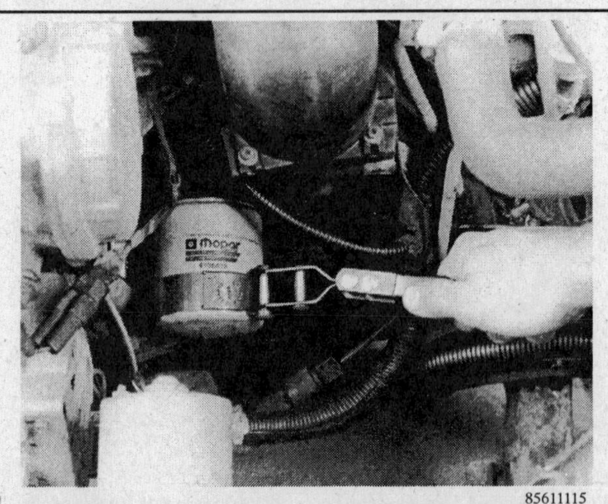

Fig. 137 The strap-type wrench works well, provided there is enough clearance

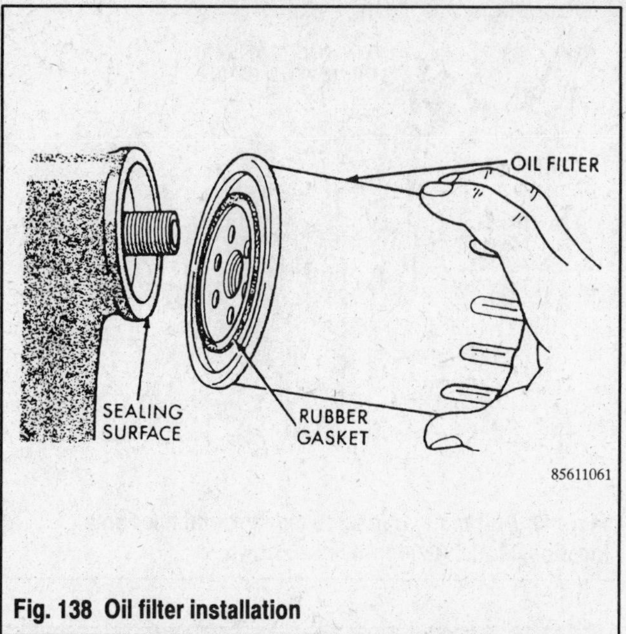

Fig. 138 Oil filter installation

8. Using a clean rag, wipe off the filter adapter on the engine block. Be sure that the rag doesn't leave any lint which could clog an oil passage.

9. Coat the rubber gasket on the filter with fresh oil. Spin it onto the engine by hand; when the gasket touches the adapter surface give it another $^1/_2$–$^3/_4$ turn. No more, or you'll squash the gasket and it may leak.

10. Remove the jackstands and carefully lower the vehicle.

11. Refill the engine with the correct amount of fresh oil. See the Capacities Chart in this section.

Refill the engine crankcase slowly, checking the level often. You can always add a little more oil, but removing some at this point would be a bother.

12. Run the engine at idle for approximately one minute. Shut the engine **OFF**. Wait a few minutes and recheck oil level. Add oil, as necessary to bring the level up to **Fill**.

****CAUTION**

You now have a few quarts of used engine oil. Please store this oil in a secure container, such as a 1 gallon windshield washer fluid bottle. Locate a service station, parts store, or garage which accepts used oil for recycling and dispose of it there.

Transaxle

FLUID RECOMMENDATION

The 1984–86 manual transaxles use Dexron®II type automatic transaxle fluid. The 1987–95 manual transaxles use SG or SG/CD SAE 5W-30 engine oil. All automatic transaxles use Dexron®II type automatic transaxle fluid. Under normal operating conditions, periodic fluid changes are not required. If the vehicle is operating under severe operating conditions change the fluid (M/T), or fluid and filter (A/T) every 15,000 miles.

FLUID LEVEL CHECK

Manual Transaxle

See Figures 139 and 140

1. The fluid level is checked by removing the fill plug on the end cover side of the transaxle.

2. The fluid level should be between the top of the fill hole and a point not more than $^1/_8$ in. (3mm) below the bottom of the fill hole.

3. Add fluid as necessary. Secure the fill plug.

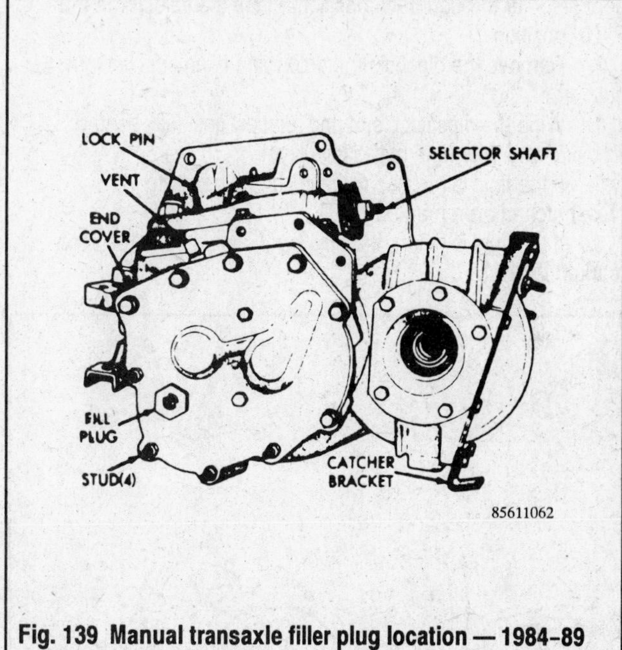

Fig. 139 Manual transaxle filler plug location — 1984–89

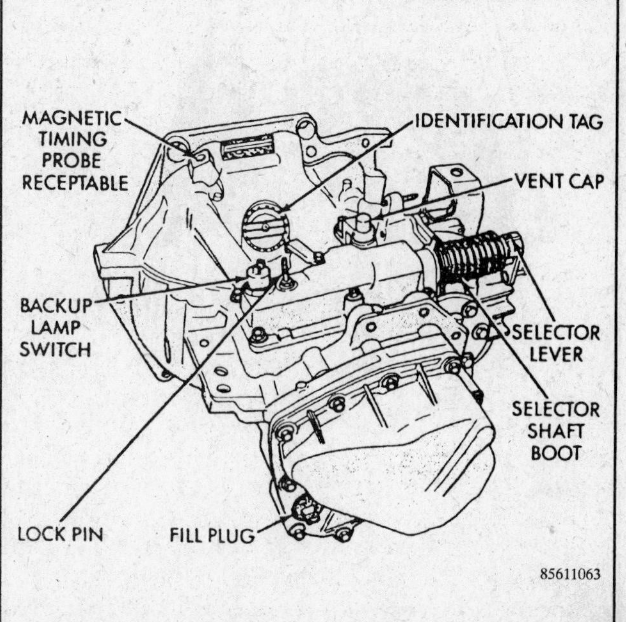

Fig. 140 Manual transaxle filler plug location — 1990–95

Automatic Transaxle

➧ See Figures 141, 142, 143, 144 and 145

➥ When checking the fluid level, the condition of the fluid should be observed. If severe darkening of the fluid and a strong odor are present, the fluid, filter and pan gasket (RTV sealant) should be changed and watched closely for the next few hundred miles. If the fresh fluid also turns color, the vehicle should be taken to a qualified service center.

1. Make sure the vehicle is on level ground. The engine should be at normal operating temperatures, if possible.
2. Apply the parking brake, start the engine and move the gear selector through each position. Place the selector in the PARK position.
3. Remove the dipstick and determine if the fluid is warm or hot.
4. Wipe the dipstick clean and reinsert until fully seated. Remove and take note of the fluid level.
5. If the fluid is hot, the reading should be in the crosshatched area marked **HOT**.
6. If the fluid is warm, the fluid level should be in the area marked **WARM**.

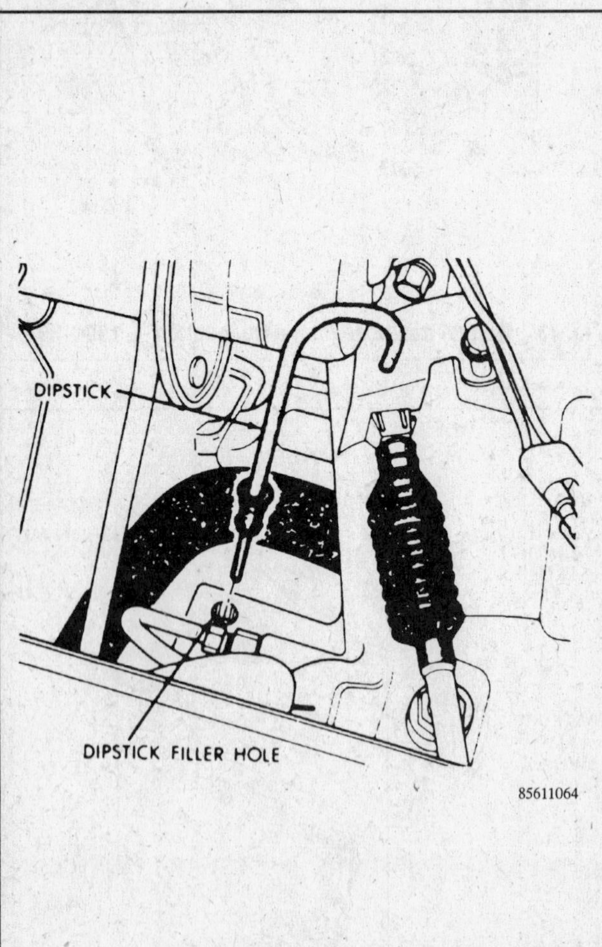

Fig. 141 Automatic transaxle dipstick and filler hole location, Model A413 transaxle shown

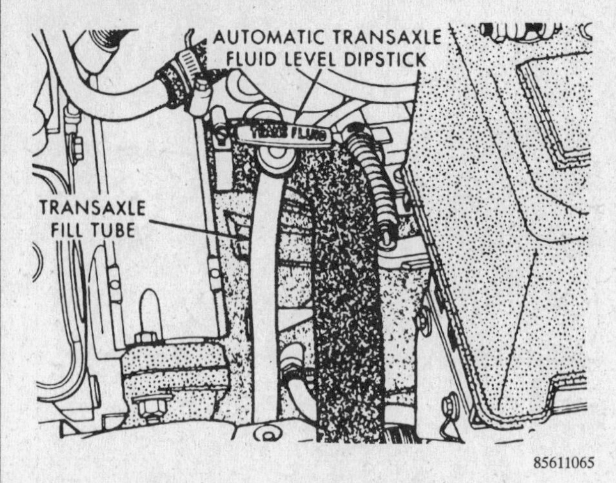

Fig. 142 Automatic transaxle dipstick and filler hole location, Model A604 transaxle shown

Fig. 143 Removing the automatic transaxle fluid level dipstick

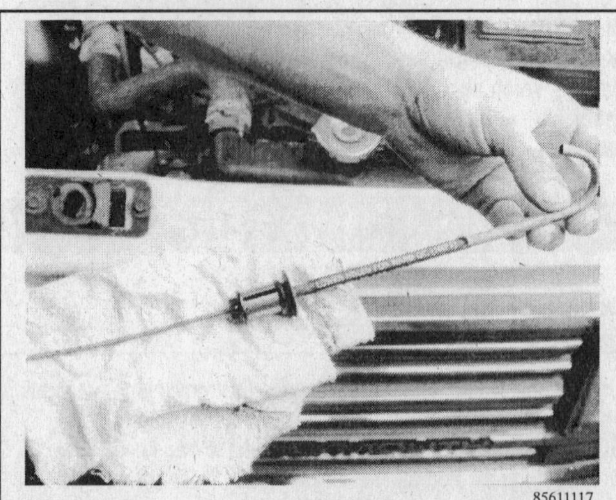

Fig. 144 Wipe the dipstick clean and reinsert it in the tube

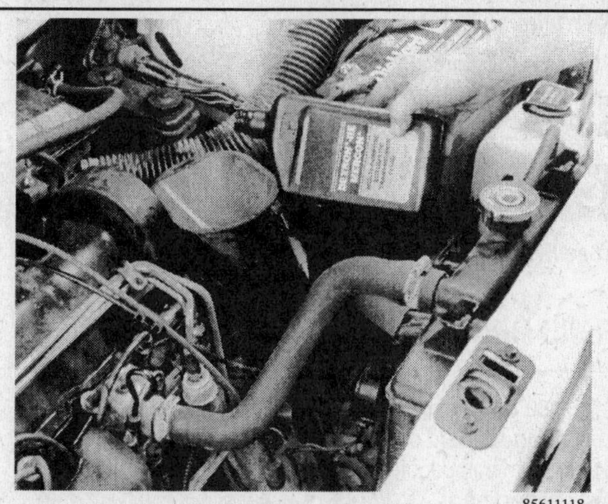

Fig. 145 Using a funnel with a long neck is necessary for adding fluid to the automatic transaxle

7. If the fluid level checks low, add enough fluid (Dexron II®) through the fill tube, to bring the level within the marks appropriate for average temperature of the fluid.

8. Insert the dipstick and recheck the level. Make sure the dipstick is fully seated to prevent dirt from entering. Do not overfill the transaxle.

DRAIN AND REFILL

Manual Transaxle

See Figure 146

1. Raise and support the front of the vehicle on jackstands.
2. Remove the undercarriage splash shield if it will interfere with fluid change.
3. Position a drain pan underneath the end of the transaxle and remove the differential end cover where the fill plug is located. Loosen the bolt slightly and pry the lower edge away so that the fluid will drain.
4. Remove the cover completely. Clean the gasket surfaces of the case and cover. Clean the magnet located on the cover.
5. Use an even 1/8 in. (3mm) bead of RTV sealant to form a gasket on the cover and reinstall on the transaxle case.
6. Refill the transaxle with the correct fluid. (Refer to Transaxle Fluid Recommendations earlier in this section.)

Automatic Transaxle

Filter replacement is recommended when the fluid is changed. Refer to Section 7 for required procedures.

Differential

The transaxle and differential share a common housing. Although manual transaxle fluid was covered earlier in this section, the fluid and filter changing procedure for the automatic transaxle and differential is covered in the Drive Train section.

Power Transfer Unit (PTU)

On models with All Wheel Drive (AWD), a power transfer unit is used that is connected to the transaxle. This unit is separate from the other drive train components.

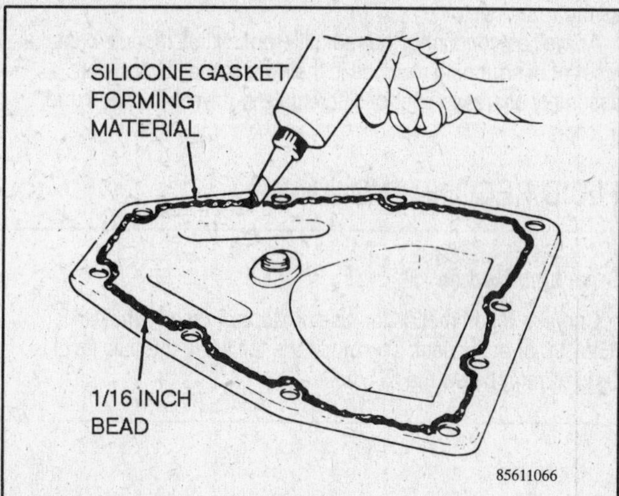

Fig. 146 Form a silicone gasket as shown for the manual transaxle cover

FLUID RECOMMENDATION

See Figure 147

Chrysler recommends the use of Mopar® Gear Lube, SAE 85W–90 or equivalent. The correct quantity of oil is 1.22 qts.

DRAIN AND REFILL

The PTU cannot be serviced. If fluid leakage is detected, the unit must be disassembled and the seals replaced.

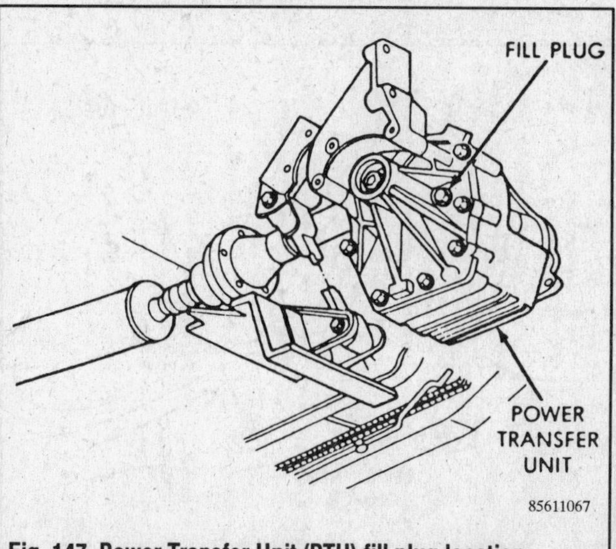

Fig. 147 Power Transfer Unit (PTU) fill plug location

Drive Line Module

➧ See Figures 148 and 149

On models with All Wheel Dive (AWD), the rear wheels are driven by shafts from the Drive Line Module. This module serves as the rear drive axle.

As well as containing the rear differential, this module contains a set of overrunning clutches in their own case. This clutch assembly serves to control differences in drive line speed and traction.

FLUID RECOMMENDATION

Drive Line Module

Chrysler recommends the use of Mopar® Gear Lube, SAE 85W-90 or equivalent. The module is full when the fluid level is $^1/_8$ in. (3mm) below the fill plug.

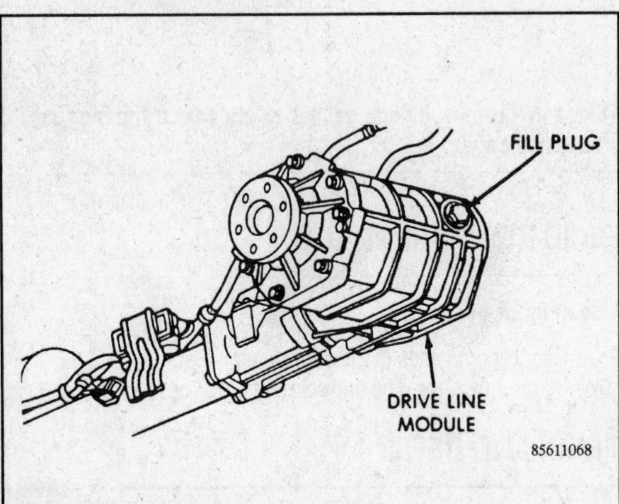

Fig. 148 Drive line module fill plug, All Wheel Drive equipped vehicles

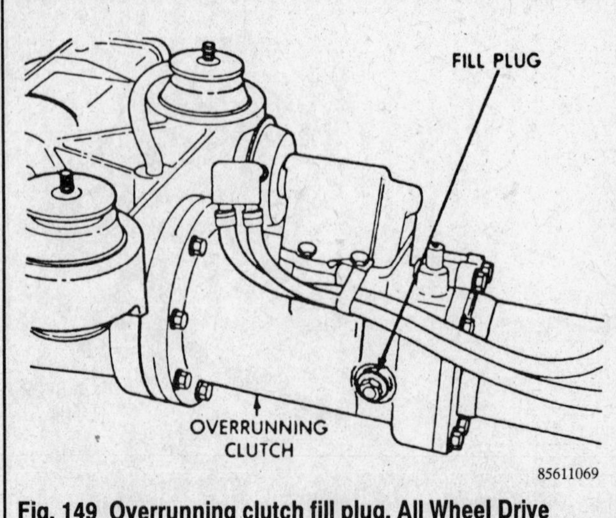

Fig. 149 Overrunning clutch fill plug, All Wheel Drive equipped vehicles

Overrunning Clutch

Chrysler recommends the use of Mopar® ATF type 7176 or equivalent. The oil level should be at the bottom of the oil fill opening.

Cooling System

➧ See Figures 150, 151, 152 and 153

FLUID RECOMMENDATION

A 50/50 mixture of water and ethylene glycol type antifreeze (containing Allguard or silicate type inhibitor) that is safe for use in aluminum components is recommended. The 50/50 mixture offers protection to -34°F (-37°C). If additional cold weather protection is necessary a concentration of 65% antifreeze may be used.

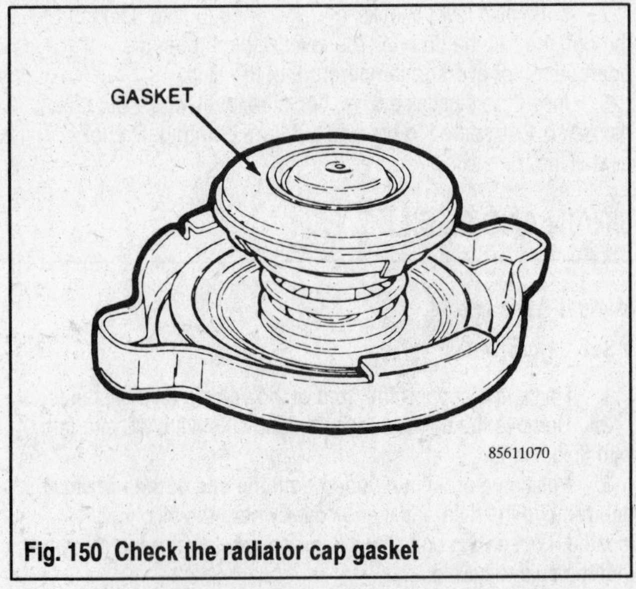

Fig. 150 Check the radiator cap gasket

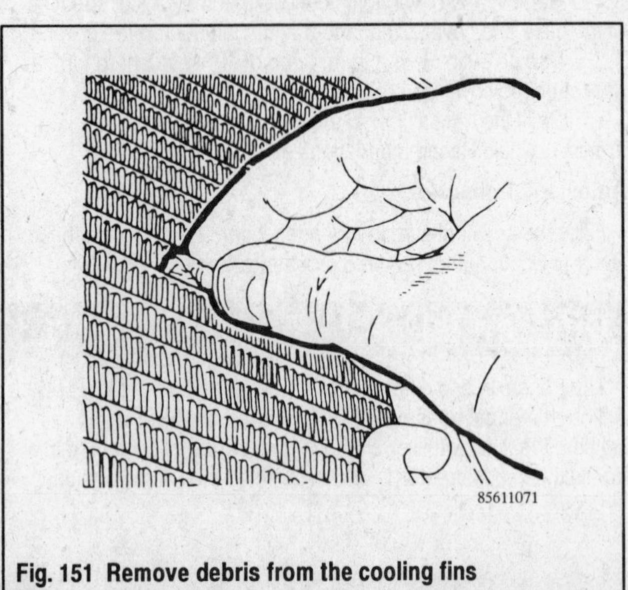

Fig. 151 Remove debris from the cooling fins

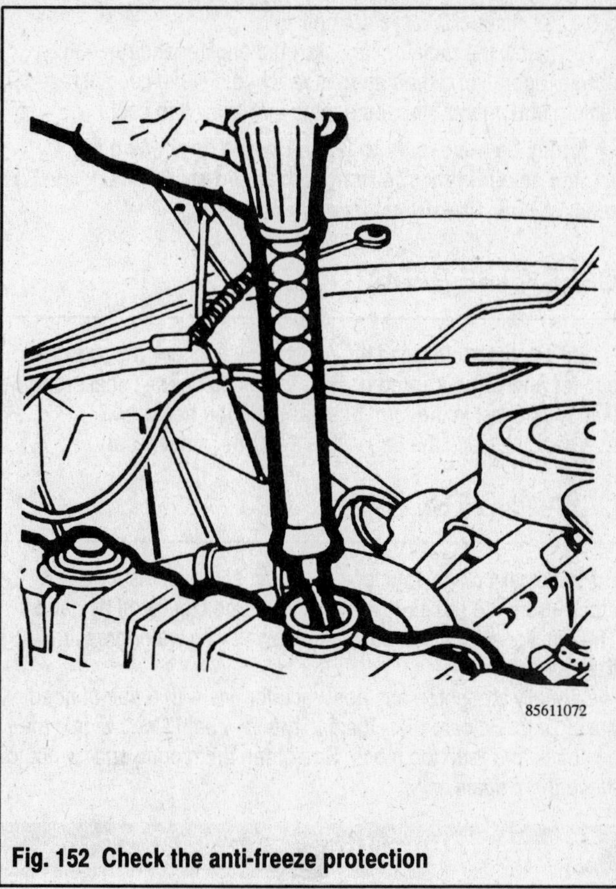
85611072

Fig. 152 Check the anti-freeze protection

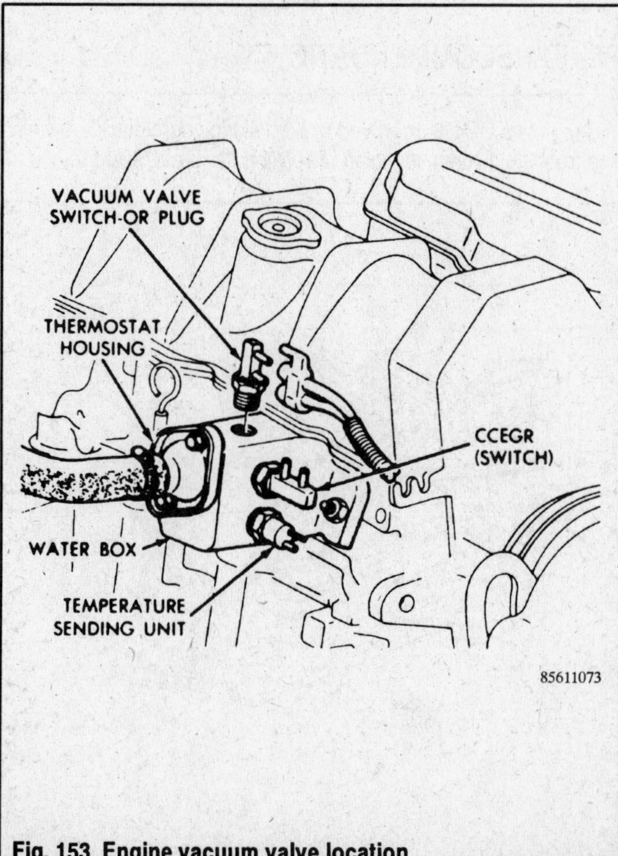

85611073

Fig. 153 Engine vacuum valve location

LEVEL CHECK

➧ **See Figure 154**

All vehicles are equipped with a transparent coolant reserve container. A minimum and maximum level mark are provided for a quick visual check of the coolant level.

1. Run the engine until normal operating temperature is reached.
2. Open the hood and observe the level of the coolant in the reserve.
3. Fluid level should be between the two lines. Add coolant, if necessary, through the fill cap of the reserve tank.

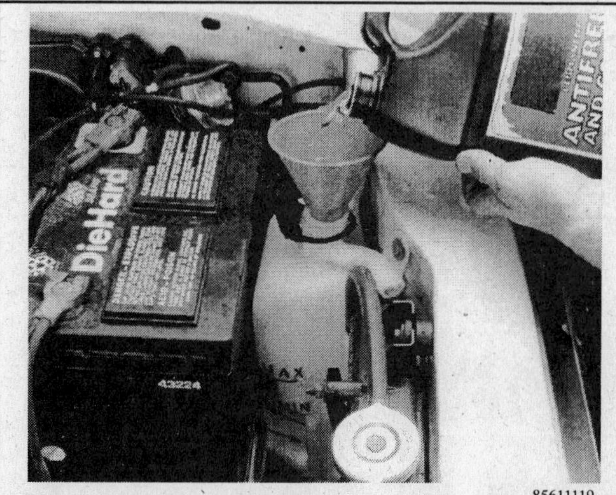
85611119

Fig. 154 Adding coolant through the fill cap of the reserve tank

DRAIN AND REFILL

➧ **See Figures 155 and 156**

✲✲CAUTION

When draining the coolant, keep in mind that cats and dogs are attracted by ethylene glycol antifreeze, and are quite likely to drink any that is left in an uncovered container or in puddles on the ground. This will prove fatal in sufficient quantity. Always drain the coolant into a sealable container. Coolant should be reused unless it is contaminated or several years old.

1. If the lower splash shield is in the way, remove it.
2. Place the heater control lever on the dash control to full on.
3. Place a drain pan under the radiator and open the drain cock. When the coolant reserve tank is drained completely, remove the radiator cap.

➥ The radiators used on some vehicles covered by this manual may not be equipped with a drain cock. If a quick inspection does not reveal one to you, loosen and disconnect the lower radiator hose from the radiator assembly in order to drain the cooling system.

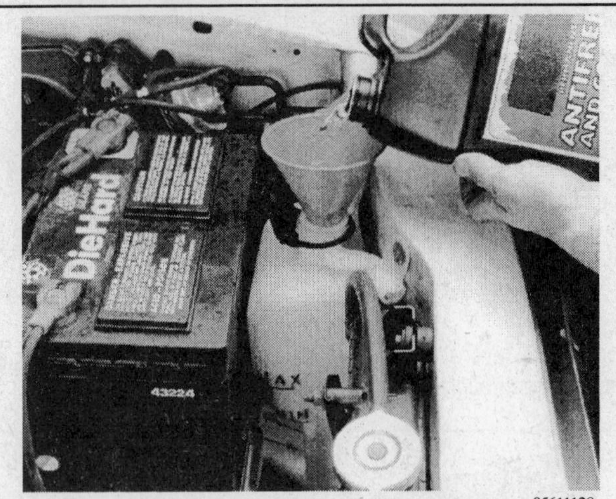

85611120

Fig. 155 Remove the radiator cap when the system is cool. Check the cap sealing gasket for deterioration

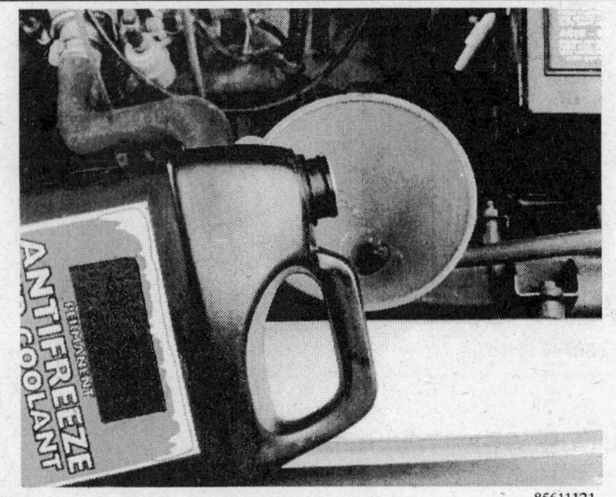

85611121

Fig. 156 Fill the system with a 50/50 mixture of ethylene glycol type antifreeze

4. If your vehicle is equipped with the 2.2L engine, removal of the vacuum valve (located above the thermostat housing), is necessary to provide air displacement. If your vehicle is equipped with the 2.5L engine, removal of the drain/fill plug (located above the thermostat housing), is necessary to provide air displacement.

➥ To remove the vacuum valve, disengage the hose connector plug, and carefully unscrew the valve using the proper size wrench.

5. After draining the system, refill with water and run the engine until normal operating temperature is reached. (See the following refill procedures). Drain the system again, repeat procedure until the drained water runs clear.
6. Close the radiator drain cock or connect the lower hose, as applicable.
7. Fill the system with a 50/50 mixture of ethylene glycol type antifreeze.
8. When the coolant reaches the hole in the water box at thermostat housing (2.2L and 2.5L engines), install the vacuum valve or drain/fill plug to 15 ft. lbs. (20 Nm).
9. Continue filling system until full.
10. Install the radiator cap, start the engine, and run until normal operating temperature is reached. Fill the coolant reserve tank to **Max** mark. Stop the engine and allow it to cool.

➥ It may be necessary to warm up and cool down the engine several times to remove trapped air. Recheck level in reserve tank, and adjust level if necessary.

CHECK THE RADIATOR CAP

While you are checking the coolant level, check the radiator cap for a worn or cracked gasket. If the cap doesn't seal properly, fluid will be lost in the form of steam and the engine will overheat. Replace the cap with a new one, if necessary.

CLEANING THE RADIATOR

Periodically clean any debris — leaves, paper, insects, etc. — from the radiator fins. Pick the large pieces off by hand. The smaller pieces can be washed away with water pressure from a hose.

Carefully straighten any bent radiator fins with a pair of needle nose pliers. Be careful — the fins are very soft! Don't wiggle the fins back and forth too much. Straighten them once and try not to move them again.

Master Cylinder

➧ See Figures 157 and 158

FLUID RECOMMENDATION

Use only a DOT 3 approved brake fluid in your vehicle. Always use fresh fluid when servicing or refilling the brake system.

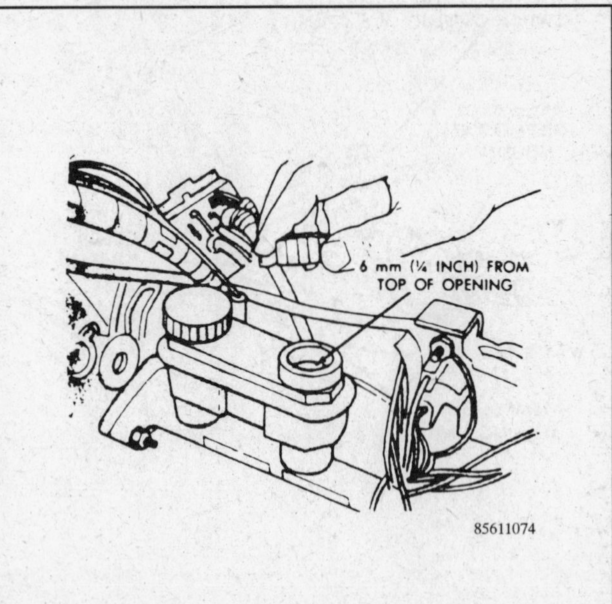

85611074

Fig. 157 Check the master cylinder fluid level

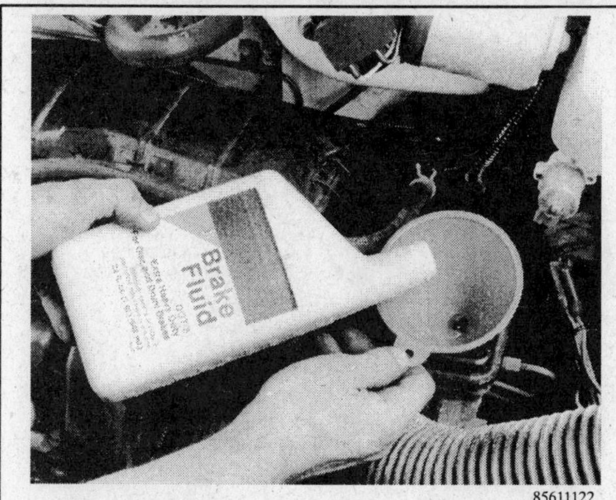

85611122

Fig. 158 Adding brake fluid to the reservoir. Use caution as brake fluid will remove paint from

LEVEL CHECK

The fluid level in both reservoirs of the master cylinder should be maintained at the bottom of the fill split rings visible after removing the covers. Add the necessary fluid to maintain a proper level. A drop in the fluid level should be expected as the brake pads and shoes wear. However, if an unusual amount of fluid is required, check for system leaks.

Power Steering Pump

See Figures 159, 160 and 161

FLUID RECOMMENDATIONS

Power steering fluid such as Mopar Power Steering Fluid (Part Number 4318055) or equivalent should be used. Only petroleum fluids formulated for minimum effect on the rubber hoses should be added. Do not use automatic transaxle fluid.

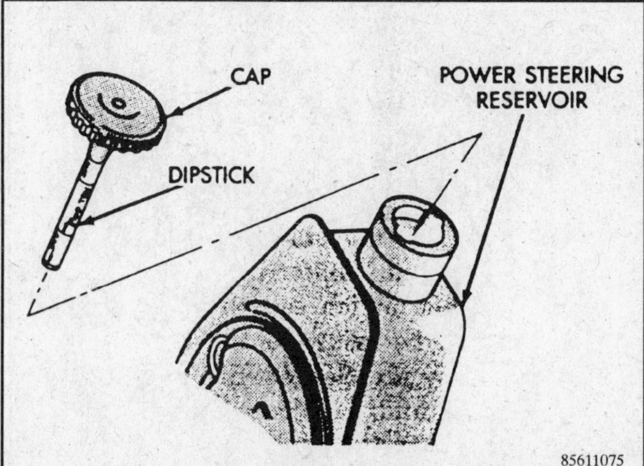

85611075

Fig. 159 Typical power steering reservoir dipstick — 2.2L, 2.5L, and 2.6L engines

CAUTION

Check the power steering fluid level with engine off, to avoid injury from moving parts.

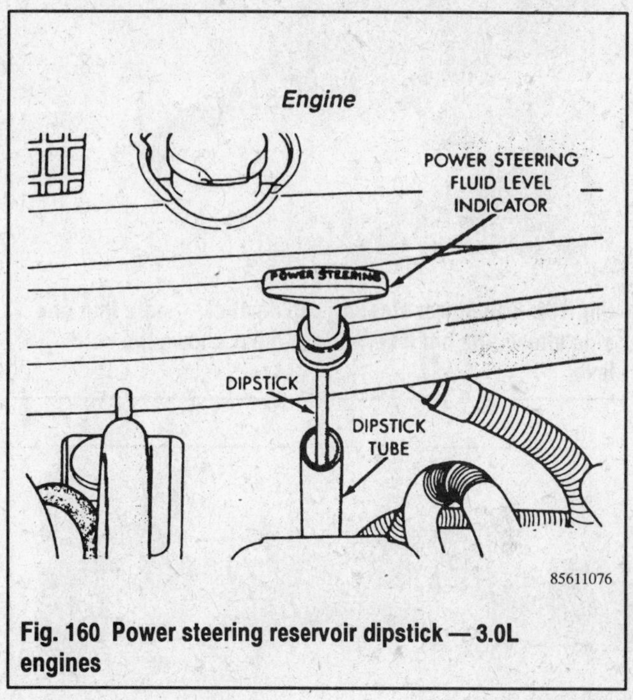

85611076

Fig. 160 Power steering reservoir dipstick — 3.0L engines

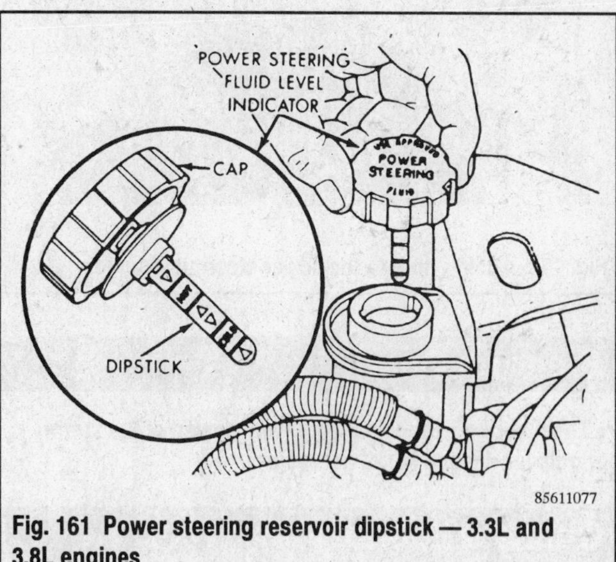

85611077

Fig. 161 Power steering reservoir dipstick — 3.3L and 3.8L engines

LEVEL CHECK

See Figures 162 and 163

1. Wipe off the power steering pump reservoir cap with a cloth before removal.
2. A dipstick is built into the cover. Remove the reservoir cover cap and wipe the dipstick with a cloth.
3. Reinstall the dipstick and check the level indicated.
4. Add fluid as necessary, but do not overfill.

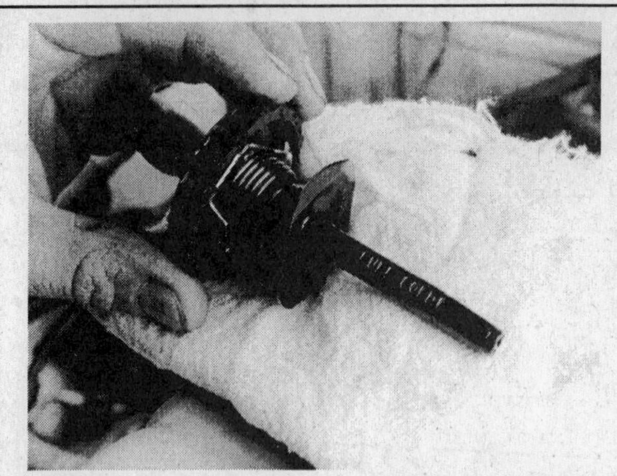

85611123

Fig. 162 The power steering cap dipstick — note that one side shows the hot level and the other shows the cold level

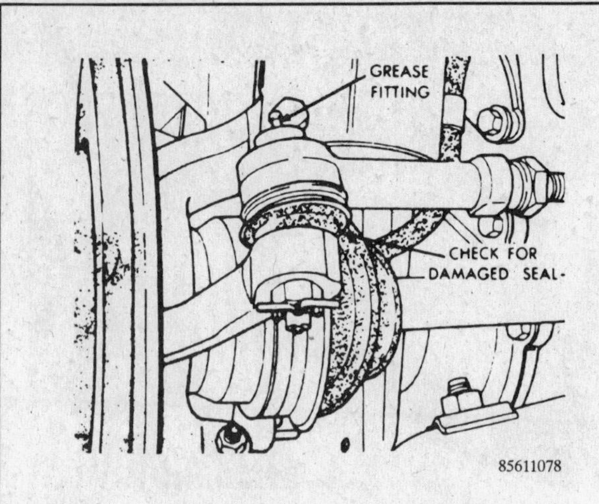

85611078

Fig. 164 Check the tie-rod end ball joint seals and lubricate at the grease fitting

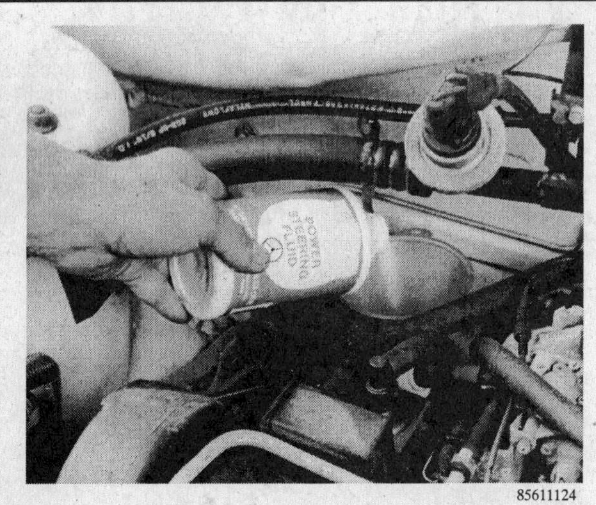

85611124

Fig. 163 Adding fluid to the power steering reservoir

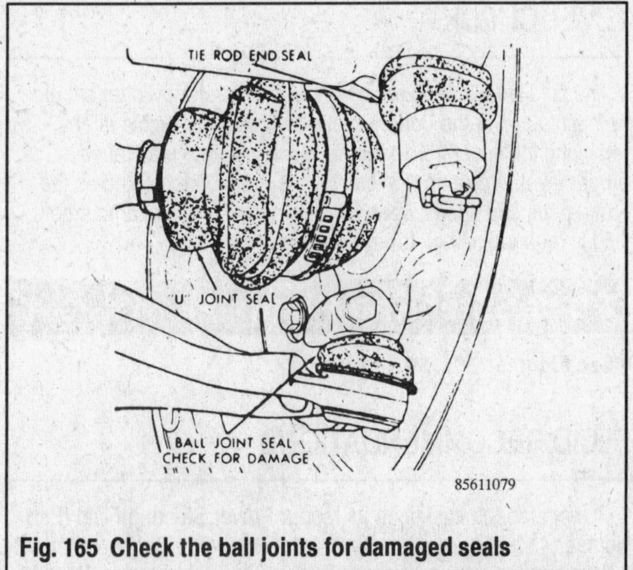

85611079

Fig. 165 Check the ball joints for damaged seals

Steering Gear

The steering gear is lubricated and sealed at the factory, periodic lubrication is not necessary.

Chassis Lubrication

See Figures 164, 165 and 166

All vehicles have two lower ball joints in the front suspension that are equipped with grease fittings as are the tie rod ends. Periodic lubrication (every 24,000 miles) using a hand grease gun and NLGI Grade 2, Multipurpose grease is required. Connect the grease gun to the fitting and pump until the boot seal on the tie rod ends or ball joints start to swell. Do not overfill until grease flows from under the boot edges.

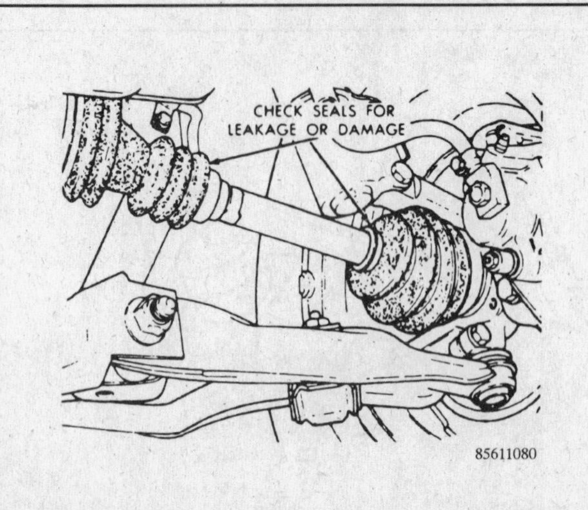

85611080

Fig. 166 Inspect CV-joint seals (boots) for cuts or damage

Body Lubrication

The following body parts and mechanisms should be lubricated periodically at all pivot and sliding points. Use the lubricant specified;

Engine Oil:

- Door Hinges at pin and pivot contact area.
- Hinges
- Liftgate Hinges
- Sliding Door at center hinge pivot.

White Spray Lube:

- Hood Hinge cam and slide
- Lock cylinders
- Parking Brake Mechanisms
- Window Regulator: remove trim panel
- Liftgate Latches
- Liftgate Prop Pivots
- Ash Tray Slide

Multi-purpose Lubricant (Water Resistant):

- Door Latch, Lock control Linkage and Remote Control Mechanism (trim panel must be removed)
- Latch Plate and Bolt

Multi-purpose Grease, NLGI Grade 2:

- Sliding Door: lower, center and upper tracks. Open position striker spring.
- Fuel Tank Door

Rear Wheel Bearings

The following procedure is intended for front wheel drive vehicles only. The front wheel bearings of all vehicles along with the rear wheel bearings on All Wheel Drive (AWD) vehicles are sealed units which do not require periodic removal, inspection and relubrication. For replacement procedures of all other wheel bearings, please refer to Section 8 of this manual.

The rear wheel bearings on all front wheel drive vehicles should be inspected and relubricated a minimum of every 22,000 miles (although it is probably a good idea to check them anytime the rear brake drum is removed). Vehicles used in any form of severe service should be checked and repacked more frequently, as-often-as every 9000 miles.

SERVICING

➧ See Figure 167

➥ Sodium-based grease is not compatible with lithium-based grease. Read the package labels and be careful not to mix the two types. If there is any doubt as to the type of grease used, completely clean the old grease from the bearing and hub before replacing.

Before handling the bearings, there are a few things that you should remember to do and not to do.

Remember to DO the following:

- Remove all outside dirt from the housing before exposing the bearing.
- Treat a used bearing as gently as you would a new one.
- Work with clean tools in clean surroundings.
- Use clean, dry canvas gloves, or at least clean, dry hands.

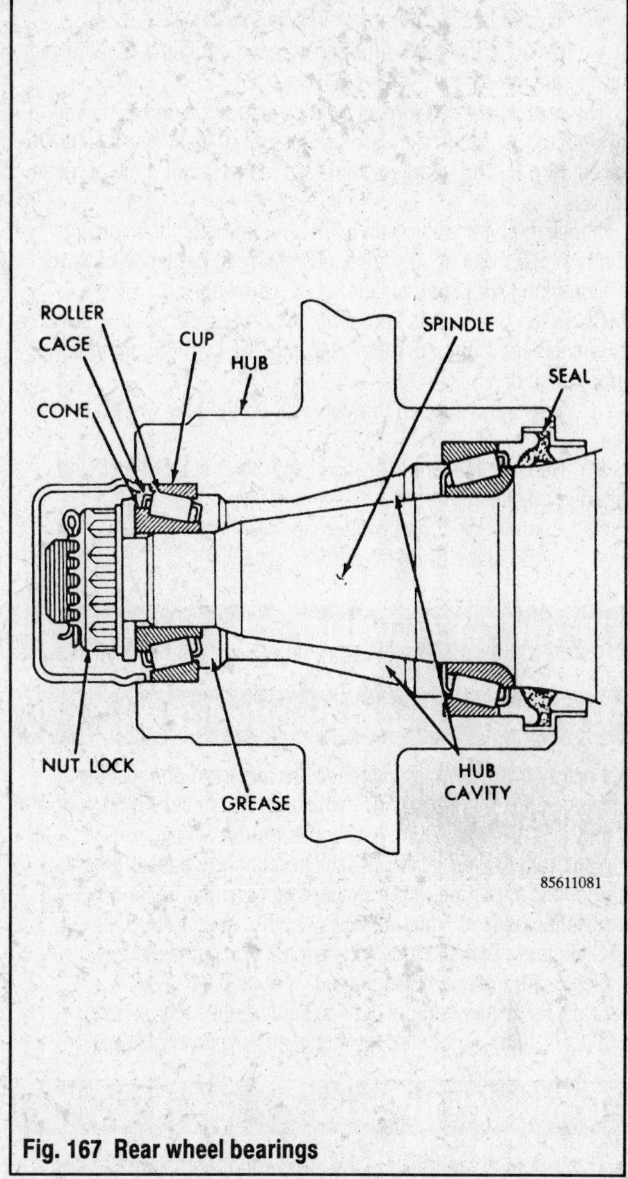

Fig. 167 Rear wheel bearings

- Clean solvents and flushing fluids are a must.
- Use clean paper when laying out the bearings to dry.
- Protect disassembled bearings from rust and dirt. Cover them up.
- Use clean rags to wipe bearings.
- Keep the bearings in oil-proof paper when they are to be stored or are not in use.
- Clean the inside of the housing before replacing the bearing.

Do NOT do the following:

- Don't work in dirty surroundings.
- Don't use dirty, chipped or damaged tools.
- Try not to work on wooden work benches or use wooden mallets.
- Don't handle bearings with dirty or moist hands.
- Do not use gasoline for cleaning; use a safe solvent.
- Do not spin-dry bearings with compressed air. They will be damaged.
- Do not spin dirty bearings.

- Avoid using cotton waste or dirty cloths to wipe bearings.
- Try not to scratch or nick bearing surfaces.
- Do not allow the bearing to come in contact with dirt or rust at any time.

The rear wheel bearings should be inspected and relubricated whenever the rear brakes are serviced or at least every 30,000 miles. Repack the bearings with high temperature multi-purpose grease.

Check the lubricant to see if it is contaminated. If it contains dirt or has a milky appearance indicating the presence of water, the bearings should be cleaned and repacked.

Clean the bearings in kerosene, mineral spirits or other suitable cleaning fluid. Do not dry them by spinning the bearings. Allow them to air dry.

1. Raise and support the vehicle with the rear wheels off the floor.
2. Remove the wheel grease cap, cotter pin, nut-lock and bearing adjusting nut.
3. Remove the thrust washer and bearing.
4. Remove the drum from the spindle.
5. Thoroughly clean the old lubricant from the bearings and hub cavity. Inspect the bearing rollers for pitting or other signs of wear. Light discoloration is normal.
6. Repack the bearings with high temperature multi-purpose EP grease and add a small amount of new grease to the hub cavity. Be sure to force the lubricant between all rollers in the bearing.
7. Install the drum on the spindle after coating the polished spindle surfaces with wheel bearing lubricant.
8. Install the outer bearing cone, thrust washer and adjusting nut.
9. Tighten the adjusting nut to 20–25 ft. lbs. (27–35 Nm) while rotating the wheel.
10. Back off the adjusting nut to completely release the preload from the bearing.
11. Tighten the adjusting nut finger-tight.
12. Position the nut-lock with one pair of slots in line with the cotter pin hole. Install the cotter pin.
13. Clean and install the grease cap and wheel.
14. Lower the vehicle.

TRAILER TOWING

General Recommendations

Factory trailer towing packages are available on most vans. However, if you are installing a trailer hitch and wiring on your van, there are a few thing that you ought to know.

Your vehicle was primarily designed to carry passengers and cargo. It is important to remember that towing a trailer will place additional loads on your vehicle's engine, drive train, steering, braking and other systems. However, if you decide to tow a trailer, using the proper equipment is a must.

Local laws may require specific equipment such as trailer brakes or fender mounted mirrors. Check your local laws.

Trailer Weight

The weight of the trailer is the most important factor. A good weight-to-horsepower ratio is about 35:1, 35 lbs. of Gross Combined Weight (GCW) for every horsepower your engine develops. Multiply the engine's rated horsepower by 35 and subtract the weight of the vehicle passengers and luggage. The number remaining is the approximate ideal maximum weight you should tow, although a numerically higher axle ratio can help compensate for heavier weight.

Hitch (Tongue) Weight

Calculate the hitch weight in order to select a proper hitch. The weight of the hitch is usually 9–11% of the trailer gross weight and should be measured with the trailer loaded. Hitches fall into various categories: those that mount on the frame and rear bumper, the bolt-on type, or the weld-on distribution type used for larger trailers. Axle mounted or clamp-on bumper hitches should never be used.

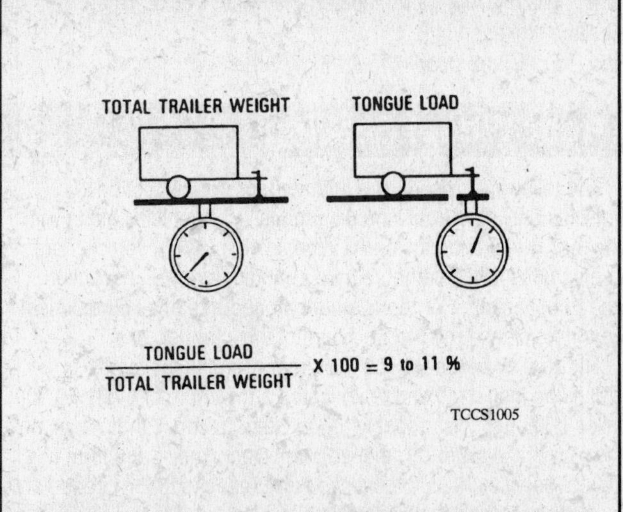

Fig. 168 Calculating proper tongue weight for your trailer

Check the gross weight rating of your trailer. Tongue weight is usually figured as 10% of gross trailer weight. Therefore, a trailer with a maximum gross weight of 2000 lbs. will have a maximum tongue weight of 200 lbs. Class I trailers fall into this category. Class II trailers are those with a gross weight rating of 2000–3000 lbs., while Class III trailers fall into the 3500–6000 lbs. category. Class IV trailers are those over 6000 lbs. and are for use with fifth wheel trucks, only.

When you've determined the hitch that you'll need, follow the manufacturer's installation instructions, exactly, especially when it comes to fastener torques. The hitch will subjected to a lot of stress and good hitches come with hardened bolts. Never substitute an inferior bolt for a hardened bolt.

Cooling

ENGINE

Overflow Tank

One of the most common, if not THE most common, problems associated with trailer towing is engine overheating. If you have a cooling system without an expansion tank, you'll definitely need to get an aftermarket expansion tank kit, preferably one with at least a 2 quart capacity. These kits are easily installed on the radiator's overflow hose, and come with a pressure cap designed for expansion tanks.

Flex Fan

Another helpful accessory for vehicles using a belt-driven radiator fan is a flex fan. These fans are large diameter units designed to provide more airflow at low speeds, by using fan blades that have deeply cupped surfaces. The blades then flex, or flatten out, at high speed, when less cooling air is needed. These fans are far lighter in weight than stock fans, requiring less horsepower to drive them. Also, they are far quieter than stock fans. If you do decide to replace your stock fan with a flex fan, note that if your vehicle has a fan clutch, a spacer will be needed between the flex fan and water pump hub.

Oil Cooler

Aftermarket engine oil coolers are helpful for prolonging engine oil life and reducing overall engine temperatures. Both of these factors increase engine life. While not absolutely necessary in towing Class I and some Class II trailers, they are recommended for heavier Class II and all Class III towing. Engine oil cooler systems usually consist of an adapter, screwed on in place of the oil filter, a remote filter mounting and a multi-tube, finned heat exchanger, which is mounted in front of the radiator or air conditioning condenser.

TRANSAXLE

An automatic transaxle is usually recommended for trailer towing. Modern automatics have proven reliable and, of course, easy to operate, in trailer towing. The increased load of a trailer, however, causes an increase in the temperature of the automatic transaxle fluid. Heat is the worst enemy of an automatic transaxle. As the temperature of the fluid increases, the life of the fluid decreases.

It is essential, therefore, that you install an automatic transaxle cooler. The cooler, which consists of a multi-tube, finned heat exchanger, is usually installed in front of the radiator or air conditioning compressor, and hooked in-line with the transaxle cooler tank inlet line. Follow the cooler manufacturer's installation instructions.

Select a cooler of at least adequate capacity, based upon the combined gross weights of the vehicle and trailer.

Cooler manufacturers recommend that you use an aftermarket cooler in addition to, and not instead of, the present cooling tank in your radiator. If you do want to use it in place of the radiator cooling tank, get a cooler at least two sizes larger than normally necessary.

➥ A transaxle cooler can, sometimes, cause slow or harsh shifting in the transaxle during cold weather, until the fluid has a chance to come up to normal operating temperature. Some coolers can be purchased with or retrofitted with a temperature bypass valve which will allow fluid flow through the cooler only when the fluid has reached above a certain operating temperature.

Handling A Trailer

Towing a trailer with ease and safety requires a certain amount of experience. It's a good idea to learn the feel of a trailer by practicing turning, stopping and backing in an open area such as an empty parking lot.

Wiring

Wiring the van for towing is fairly easy. There are a number of good wiring kits available and these should be used, rather than trying to design your own. All trailers will need brake lights and turn signals as well as tail lights and side marker lights. Most states require extra marker lights for overly wide trailers. Also, most states have recently required back-up lights for trailers, and most trailer manufacturers have been building trailers with back-up lights for several years.

Additionally, some Class I, most Class II and just about all Class III trailers will have electric brakes.

Add to this number an accessories wire, to operate trailer internal equipment or to charge the trailer's battery, and you can have as many as seven wires in the harness.

Determine the equipment on your trailer and buy the wiring kit necessary. The kit will contain all the wires needed, plus a plug adapter set which included the female plug, mounted on the bumper or hitch, and the male plug, wired into, or plugged into the trailer harness.

When installing the kit, follow the manufacturer's instructions. The color coding of the wires is standard throughout the industry.

One point to note, some domestic vehicles, and most imported vehicles, have separate turn signals. On most domestic vehicles, the brake lights and rear turn signals operate with the same bulb. For those vehicles with separate turn signals, you can purchase an isolation unit so that the brake lights won't blink whenever the turn signals are operated, or, you can go to your local electronics supply house and buy four diodes to wire in series with the brake and turn signal bulbs. Diodes will isolate the brake and turn signals. The choice is yours. The isolation units are simple and quick to install, but far more expensive than the diodes. The diodes, however, require more work to install properly, since they require the cutting of each bulb's wire and soldering in place of the diode.

One final point, the best kits are those with a spring loaded cover on the vehicle mounted socket. This cover prevents dirt and moisture from corroding the terminals. Never let the vehicle socket hang loosely. Always mount it securely to the bumper or hitch.

TOWING

The vehicle can be towed from either the front or rear. If the vehicle is towed from the front make sure the parking brake is completely released.

Manual transaxle vehicles may be towed on the drive wheels at speeds up to 30 mph (48 km/h), for a distance not to exceed 15 miles (24 km), provided the transaxle is in Neutral and the drive line has not been damaged. The steering wheel must be clamped in a straight ahead position.

****WARNING**

Do not use the steering column lock to secure front wheel position for towing.

Automatic transaxle vehicles may be towed on the drive wheels at speeds not to exceed 25 mph (40 km/h) for a period of 15 miles (24 km).

****WARNING**

If this requirement cannot be met the drive front wheels must be placed on a dolly. Also, if the transaxle is damaged, the vehicle should not be pulled on the drive wheels, use a dolly or flatbed.

JUMP STARTING A DEAD BATTERY

➧ See Figure 169

Whenever a vehicle is jump started, precautions must be followed in order to prevent the possibility of personal injury. Remember that batteries contain a small amount of explosive hydrogen gas which is a by-product of battery charging. Sparks should always be avoided when working around batteries, especially when attaching jumper cables. To minimize the possibility of accidental sparks, follow the procedure carefully.

****CAUTION**

NEVER hook the batteries up in a series circuit or the entire electrical system will go up in smoke, especially the starter!

Vehicles equipped with a diesel engine may utilize two 12 volt batteries. If so, the batteries are connected in a parallel circuit (positive terminal to positive terminal, negative terminal to negative terminal). Hooking the batteries up in parallel circuit increases battery cranking power without increasing total battery voltage output. Output remains at 12 volts. On the other hand, hooking two 12 volt batteries up in a series circuit (positive terminal to negative terminal, positive terminal to negative terminal) increases total battery output to 24 volts (12 volts plus 12 volts).

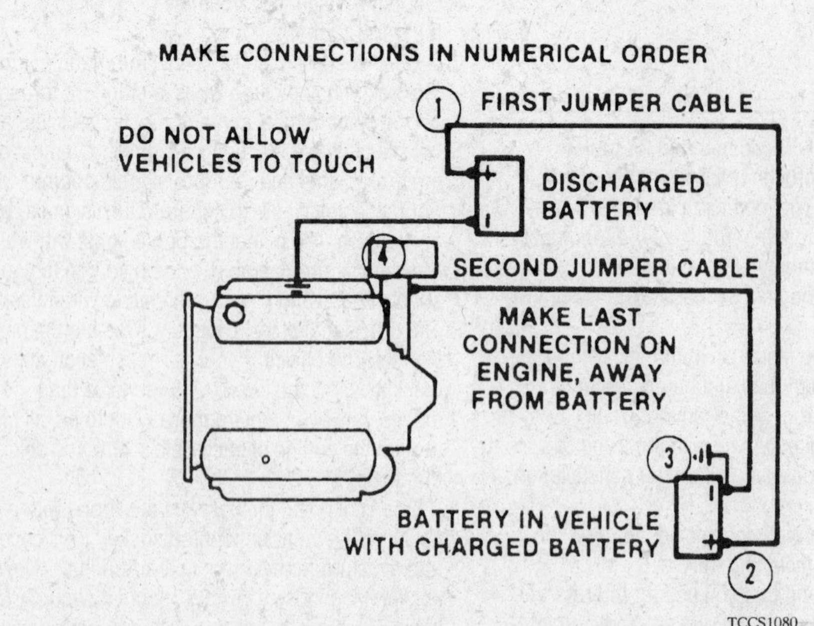

Fig. 169 Connect the jumper cables to the batteries and engine in the order shown

Jump Starting Precautions

- Be sure that both batteries are of the same voltage. Vehicles covered by this manual and most vehicles on the road today utilize a 12 volt charging system.
- Be sure that both batteries are of the same polarity (have the same terminal, in most cases NEGATIVE grounded).
- Be sure that the vehicles are not touching or a short could occur.
- On serviceable batteries, be sure the vent cap holes are not obstructed.
- Do not smoke or allow sparks anywhere near the batteries.
- In cold weather, make sure the battery electrolyte is not frozen. This can occur more readily in a battery that has been in a state of discharge.
- Do not allow electrolyte to contact your skin or clothing.

Jump Starting Procedure

1. Make sure that the voltages of the 2 batteries are the same. Most batteries and charging systems are of the 12 volt variety.
2. Pull the jumping vehicle (with the good battery) into a position so the jumper cables can reach the dead battery and that vehicle's engine. Make sure that the vehicles do NOT touch.
3. Place the transmissions/transaxles of both vehicles in **Neutral** (MT) or **P** (AT), as applicable, then firmly set their parking brakes.

➥ If necessary for safety reasons, the hazard lights on both vehicles may be operated throughout the entire procedure without significantly increasing the difficulty of jumping the dead battery.

4. Turn all lights and accessories OFF on both vehicles. Make sure the ignition switches on both vehicles are turned to the **OFF** position.
5. Cover the battery cell caps with a rag, but do not cover the terminals.
6. Make sure the terminals on both batteries are clean and free of corrosion or proper electrical connection will be impeded. If necessary, clean the battery terminals before proceeding.
7. Identify the positive (+) and negative (–) terminals on both batteries.
8. Connect the first jumper cable to the positive (+) terminal of the dead battery, then connect the other end of that cable to the positive (+) terminal of the booster (good) battery.
9. Connect one end of the other jumper cable to the negative (–) terminal on the booster battery and the final cable clamp to an engine bolt head, alternator bracket or other solid, metallic point on the engine with the dead battery. Try to pick a ground on the engine that is positioned away from the battery in order to minimize the possibility of the 2 clamps touching should one loosen during the procedure. DO NOT connect this clamp to the negative (–) terminal of the bad battery.

****CAUTION**

Be very careful to keep the jumper cables away from moving parts (cooling fan, belts, etc.) on both engines.

10. Check to make sure that the cables are routed away from any moving parts, then start the donor vehicle's engine. Run the engine at moderate speed for several minutes to allow the dead battery a chance to receive some initial charge.
11. With the donor vehicle's engine still running slightly above idle, try to start the vehicle with the dead battery. Crank the engine for no more than 10 seconds at a time and let the starter cool for at least 20 seconds between tries. If the vehicle does not start in 3 tries, it is likely that something else is also wrong or that the battery needs additional time to charge.
12. Once the vehicle is started, allow it to run at idle for a few seconds to make sure that it is operating properly.
13. Turn ON the headlights, heater blower and, if equipped, the rear defroster of both vehicles in order to reduce the severity of voltage spikes and subsequent risk of damage to the vehicles' electrical systems when the cables are disconnected. This step is especially important to any vehicle equipped with computer control modules.
14. Carefully disconnect the cables in the reverse order of connection. Start with the negative cable that is attached to the engine ground, then the negative cable on the donor battery. Disconnect the positive cable from the donor battery and finally, disconnect the positive cable from the formerly dead battery. Be careful when disconnecting the cables from the positive terminals not to allow the alligator clips to touch any metal on either vehicle or a short and sparks will occur.

JACKING

➧ See Figure 170

Your vehicle was supplied with a jack for emergency road repairs. This jack is fine for changing a flat tire or other short term procedures not requiring you to go beneath the vehicle. If it is used in an emergency situation, carefully follow the instructions provided either with the jack or in your owner's manual. Do not attempt to use the jack on any portions of the vehicle other than specified by the vehicle manufacturer.

The standard jack utilizes special receptacles or locator pins found along the body sills (just behind the front or in front of the rear wheels). They accept the scissors jack supplied with the vehicle, for emergency road service only. The jack supplied with the vehicle should never be used for any service operation other then tire changing. NEVER get under the vehicle while it is supported only by a jack.

****CAUTION**

Always block the wheels when changing tires. At the very least, block the wheel opposite the one being lifted.

The service operations in this book often require that one end or the other, or both, of the vehicle be raised and safely supported. The ideal method, of course, would be a hydraulic hoist. Since this is beyond both the resource and requirement of the do-it-yourselfer, a small hydraulic floor jack is recommended <#106>for most procedures which require access to the underbody of the vehicle. A floor jack can be used on various suspension and body-frame components (as detailed by the accompanying diagram).

Never place the jack under the radiator, engine or transmission components. Severe and expensive damage will result when the jack is raised. Additionally, never jack under the floorpan or bodywork; the metal will deform.

Whenever you plan to work under the vehicle, you must support it on jackstands or ramps. Never use cinder blocks or stacks of wood to support the vehicle, even if you're only going to be under it for a few minutes. Never crawl under the vehicle when it is supported only by the tire-changing jack or other floor jack.

➛ Always position a block of wood or small rubber pad on top of the jack or jackstand to protect the lifting point's finish when lifting or supporting the vehicle.

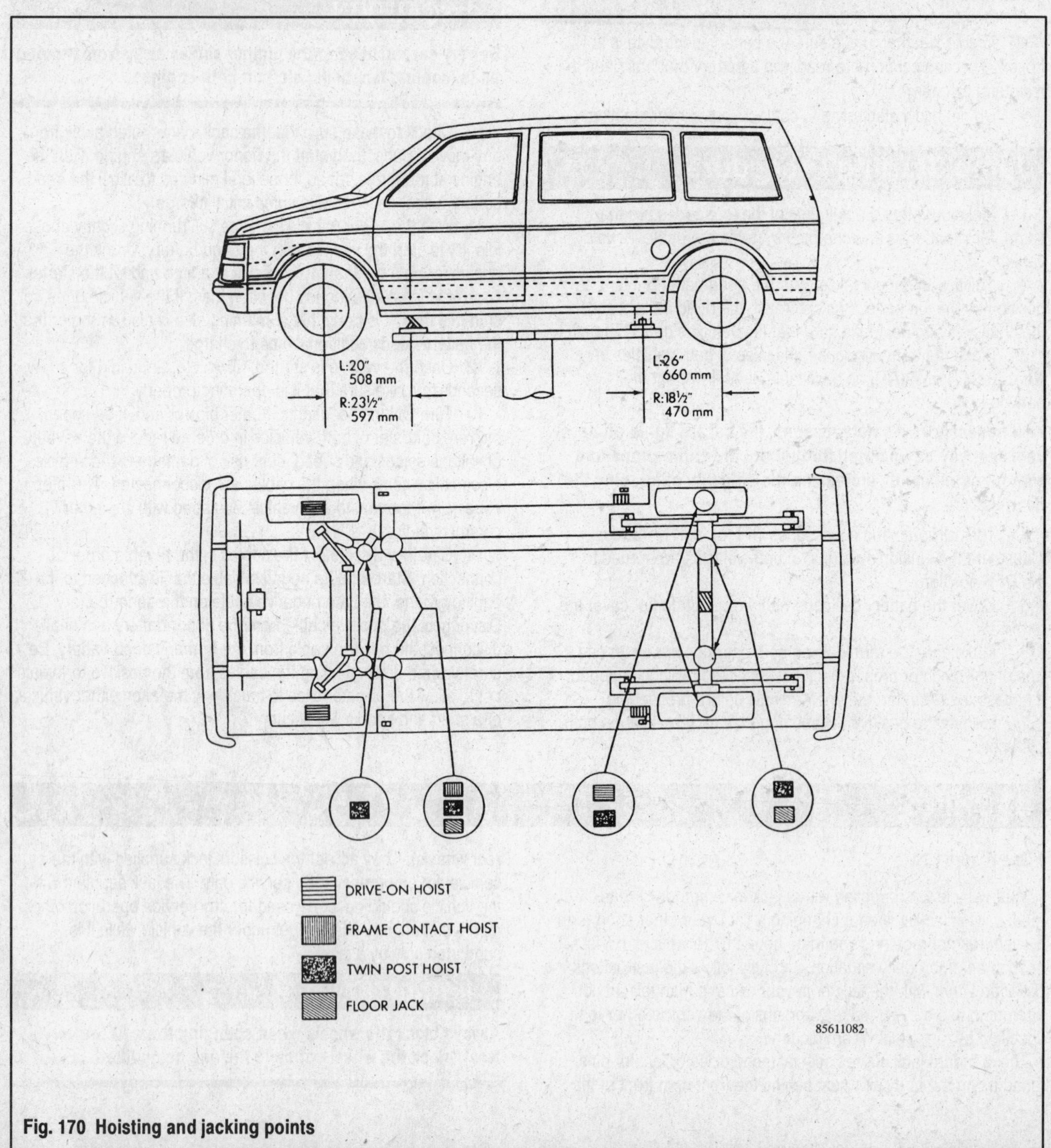

Fig. 170 Hoisting and jacking points

Small hydraulic, screw, or scissors jacks are satisfactory for raising the vehicle. Drive-on trestles or ramps are also a handy and safe way to both raise and support the vehicle. Be careful though, some ramps may be too steep to drive your vehicle onto without scraping the front bottom panels. Never support the vehicle on any suspension member (unless specifically instructed to do so by a repair manual) or by an underbody panel.

Jacking Precautions

The following safety points cannot be overemphasized:

- Always block the opposite wheel or wheels to keep the vehicle from rolling off the jack.
- When raising the front of the vehicle, firmly apply the parking brake.
- When the drive wheels are to remain on the ground, leave the vehicle in gear to help prevent it from rolling.
- Always use jackstands to support the vehicle when you are working underneath. Place the stands beneath the vehicle's jacking brackets. Before climbing underneath, rock the vehicle a bit to make sure it is firmly supported.

HOW TO BUY A USED VEHICLE

Many people believe that a two or three year old used car or truck is a better buy than a new vehicle. This may be true as most new vehicles suffer the heaviest depreciation in the first two years and, at three years old, a vehicle is usually not old enough to present a lot of costly repair problems. But keep in mind, when buying a non-warranted automobile, there are no guarantees. Whatever the age of the used vehicle you might want to purchase, this section and a little patience should increase your chances of selecting one that is safe and dependable.

Tips

1. First decide what model you want, and how much you want to spend.
2. Check the used car lots and your local newspaper ads. Privately owned vehicles are usually less expensive, however, you may not get a warranty that, in many cases, comes with a used vehicle purchased from a lot. Of course, some aftermarket warranties may not be worth the extra money, so this is a point you will have to debate and consider based on your priorities.
3. Never shop at night. The glare of the lights make it easy to miss faults on the body caused by accident or rust repair.
4. Try to get the name and phone number of the previous owner. Contact him/her and ask about the vehicle. If the owner of a lot refuses this information, look for a vehicle somewhere else.

A private seller can tell you about the vehicle and maintenance. But remember, there's no law requiring honesty from private citizens selling used vehicles. There is a law that forbids tampering with or turning back the odometer mileage. This includes both the private citizen and the lot owner. The law also requires that the seller or anyone transferring ownership of the vehicle must provide the buyer with a signed statement indicating the mileage on the odometer at the time of transfer.

5. You may wish to contact the National Highway Traffic Safety Administration (NHTSA) to find out if the vehicle has ever been included in a manufacturer's recall. Write down the year, model and serial number before you buy the vehicle, then contact NHTSA (there should be a 1-800 number that your phone company's information line can supply). If the vehicle was listed for a recall, make sure the needed repairs were made.
6. Refer to the Used Vehicle Checklist in this section and check all the items on the vehicle you are considering. Some items are more important than others. Only you know how much money you can afford for repairs, and depending on the price of the vehicle, may consider performing any needed work yourself. Beware, however, of trouble in areas that will affect operation, safety or emission. Problems in the Used Vehicle Checklist break down as follows:

- Numbers 1-8: Two or more problems in these areas indicate a lack of maintenance. You should beware.
- Numbers 9-13: Problems here tend to indicate a lack of proper care, however, these can usually be corrected with a tune-up or relatively simple parts replacement.
- Numbers 14-17: Problems in the engine or transmission/transaxle can be very expensive. Unless you are looking for a project, walk away from any vehicle with problems in 2 or more of these areas.

7. If you are satisfied with the apparent condition of the vehicle, take it to an independent diagnostic center or mechanic for a complete check. If you have a state inspection program, have it inspected immediately before purchase, or specify on the bill of sale that the sale is conditional on passing state inspection.
8. Road test the vehicle — refer to the Road Test Checklist in this section. If your original evaluation and the road test agree — the rest is up to you.

USED VEHICLE CHECKLIST

See Figure 171

The numbers on the illustrations refer to the numbers on this checklist.

1. Mileage: Average mileage is about 12,000-15,000 miles per year. More than average mileage may indicate hard usage or could indicate many highway miles (which could be less detrimental than half as many tough around town miles).
2. Paint: Check around the tail pipe, molding and windows for overspray indicating that the vehicle has been repainted.
3. Rust: Check fenders, doors, rocker panels, window moldings, wheelwells, floorboards, under floor mats, and in the trunk for signs of rust. Any rust at all will be a problem. There is no way to permanently stop the spread of rust, except to replace the part or panel.

If rust repair is suspected, try using a magnet to check for body filler. A magnet should stick to the sheet metal parts of the body, but will not adhere to areas with large amounts of filler.

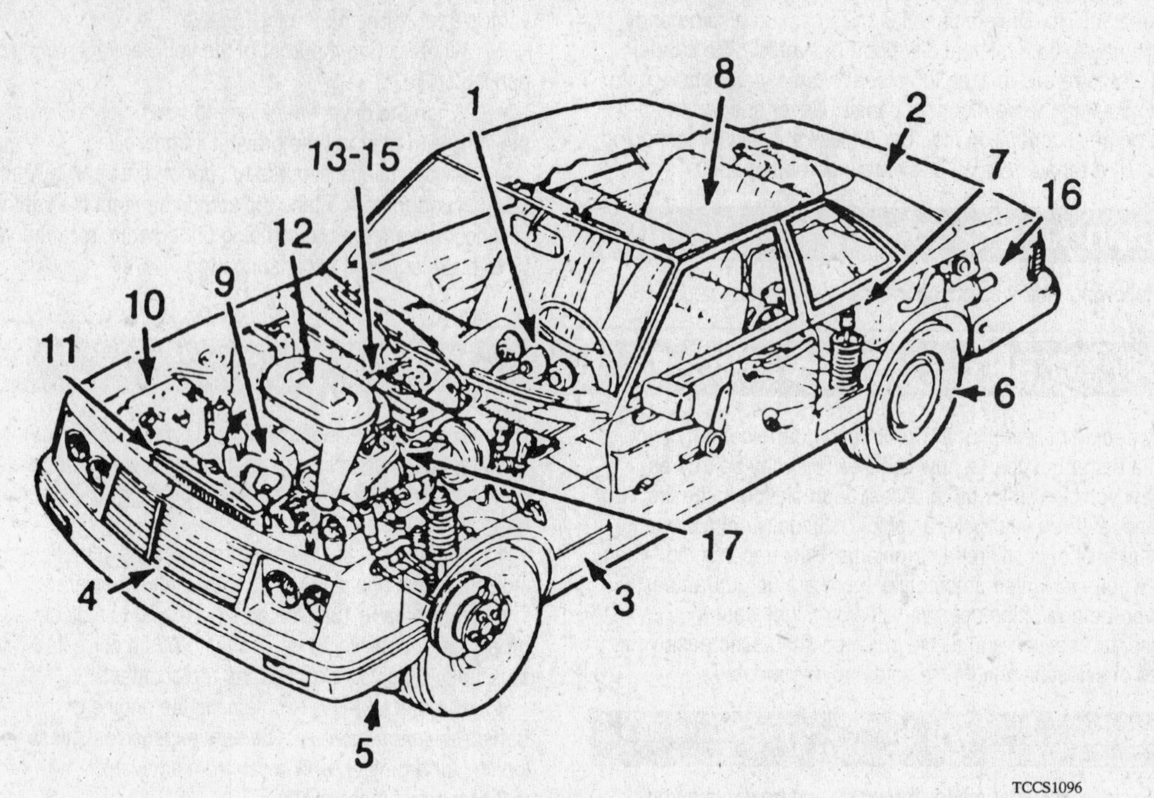

Fig. 171 Each of the numbered items should be checked when purchasing a used vehicle

4. Body appearance: Check the moldings, bumpers, grille, vinyl roof, glass, doors, trunk lid and body panels for general overall condition. Check for misalignment, loose hold-down clips, ripples, scratches in glass, welding in the trunk, severe misalignment of body panels or ripples, any of which may indicate crash work.

5. Leaks: Get down and look under the vehicle. There are no normal leaks, other than water from the air conditioner condenser.

6. Tires: Check the tire air pressure. One old trick is to pump the tire pressure up to make the vehicle roll easier. Check the tread wear, open the trunk and check the spare too. Uneven wear is a clue that the front end may need an alignment.

7. Shock absorbers: Check the shock absorbers by forcing downward sharply on each corner of the vehicle. Good shocks will not allow the vehicle to bounce more than once after you let go.

8. Interior: Check the entire interior. You're looking for an interior condition that agrees with the overall condition of the vehicle. Reasonable wear is expected, but be suspicious of new seat covers on sagging seats, new pedal pads, and worn armrests. These indicate an attempt to cover up hard use. Pull back the carpets and look for evidence of water leaks or flooding. Look for missing hardware, door handles, control knobs, etc. Check lights and signal operations. Make sure all accessories (air conditioner, heater, radio, etc.) work. Check windshield wiper operation.

9. Belts and Hoses: Open the hood, then check all belts and hoses for wear, cracks or weak spots.

10. Battery: Low electrolyte level, corroded terminals and/or cracked case indicate a lack of maintenance.

11. Radiator: Look for corrosion or rust in the coolant indicating a lack of maintenance.

12. Air filter: A severely dirty air filter would indicate a lack of maintenance.

13. Ignition wires: Check the ignition wires for cracks, burned spots, or wear. Worn wires will have to be replaced.

14. Oil level: If the oil level is low, chances are the engine uses oil or leaks. Beware of water in the oil (there is probably a cracked block or bad head gasket), excessively thick oil (which is often used to quiet a noisy engine), or thin, dirty oil with a distinct gasoline smell (this may indicate internal engine problems).

15. Automatic Transmission: Pull the transmission dipstick out when the engine is running. The level should read FULL, and the fluid should be clear or bright red. Dark brown or black fluid that has distinct burnt odor, indicates a transmission in need of repair or overhaul.

16. Exhaust: Check the color of the exhaust smoke. Blue smoke indicates, among other problems, worn rings. Black smoke can indicate burnt valves or carburetor problems. Check the exhaust system for leaks; it can be expensive to replace.

17. Spark Plugs: Remove one or all of the spark plugs (the most accessible will do, though all are preferable). An engine in good condition will show plugs with a light tan or gray deposit on the firing tip.

ROAD TEST CHECKLIST

1. Engine Performance: The vehicle should be peppy whether cold or warm, with adequate power and good pickup. It should respond smoothly through the gears.

2. Brakes: They should provide quick, firm stops with no noise, pulling or brake fade.

3. Steering: Sure control with no binding harshness, or looseness and no shimmy in the wheel should be expected. Noise or vibration from the steering wheel when turning the vehicle means trouble.

4. Clutch (Manual Transmission/Transaxle): Clutch action should give quick, smooth response with easy shifting. The clutch pedal should have free-play before it disengages the clutch. Start the engine, set the parking brake, put the transmission in first gear and slowly release the clutch pedal. The engine should begin to stall when the pedal is $\frac{1}{2}$–$\frac{3}{4}$ of the way up.

5. Automatic Transmission/Transaxle: The transmission should shift rapidly and smoothly, with no noise, hesitation, or slipping.

6. Differential: No noise or thumps should be present. Differentials have no normal leaks.

7. Driveshaft/Universal Joints: Vibration and noise could mean driveshaft problems. Clicking at low speed or coast conditions means worn U-joints.

8. Suspension: Try hitting bumps at different speeds. A vehicle that bounces excessively has weak shock absorbers or struts. Clunks mean worn bushings or ball joints.

9. Frame/Body: Wet the tires and drive in a straight line. Tracks should show two straight lines, not four. Four tire tracks indicate a frame/body bent by collision damage. If the tires can't be wet for this purpose, have a friend drive along behind you and see if the vehicle appears to be traveling in a straight line.

ENGINE APPLICATION CHART

Year	Engine Code	No. Cyl.	Actual Displacement Cu. In.	cc	Liters	Type	Fuel System	Built By
1984	C	4	135	2,212	2.2	OHC	2 bbl	Chrysler
	G	4	156	2,556	2.6	OHC	2 bbl	Mitsubishi
1985	C	4	135	2,212	2.2	OHC	2 bbl	Chrysler
	G	4	156	2,556	2.6	OHC	2 bbl	Mitsubishi
1986	C	4	135	2,212	2.2	OHC	2 bbl	Chrysler
	G	4	156	2,556	2.6	OHC	2 bbl	Mitsubishi
1987	C	4	135	2,212	2.2	OHC	2 bbl	Chrysler
	K	4	153	2,507	2.5	OHC	EFI	Chrysler
	G	4	156	2,556	2.6	OHC	2 bbl	Mitsubishi
	3	6	181	2,966	3.0	OHC	EFI	Mitsubishi
1988	K	4	153	2,507	2.5	OHC	EFI	Chrysler
	3	6	181	2,966	3.0	OHC	EFI	Mitsubishi
1989	K	4	153	2,507	2.5	OHC	EFI	Chrysler
	J	4	153	2,507	2.5	OHC	EFI ①	Chrysler
	3	6	181	2,966	3.0	OHC	EFI	Mitsubishi
1990	K	4	153	2,507	2.5	OHC	EFI	Chrysler
	J	4	153	2,507	2.5	OHC	EFI ①	Chrysler
	3	6	181	2,966	3.0	OHC	EFI	Mitsubishi
	R	6	201	3,294	3.3	OHV	EFI	Chrysler
1991	K	4	153	2,507	2.5	OHC	EFI	Chrysler
	3	6	181	2,966	3.0	OHC	EFI	Mitsubishi
	R	6	201	3,294	3.3	OHV	EFI	Chrysler
1992	K	4	153	2,507	2.5	OHC	EFI	Chrysler
	3	6	181	2,966	3.0	OHC	EFI	Mitsubishi
	R	6	201	3,294	3.3	OHV	EFI	Chrysler
1993	K	4	153	2,507	2.5	OHC	EFI	Chrysler
	3	6	181	2,966	3.0	OHC	EFI	Mitsubishi
	R	6	201	3,294	3.3	OHV	EFI	Chrysler
1994	K	4	153	2,507	2.5	OHC	EFI	Chrysler
	3	6	181	2,966	3.0	OHC	EFI	Mitsubishi
	R	6	201	3,294	3.3	OHV	EFI	Chrysler
	L	6	231	3,786	3.8	OHV	EFI	Chrysler
1995	K	4	153	2,507	2.5	OHC	EFI	Chrysler
	3	6	181	2,966	3.0	OHC	EFI	Mitsubishi
	R	6	201	3,294	3.3	OHV	EFI	Chrysler
	L	6	231	3,786	3.8	OHV	EFI	Chrysler

① Turbocharged Engine

85611C01

AUTOMATIC TRANSMISSION APPLICATION CHART

Year	Transmission	Models
1984	A-413 3 speed	Caravan, Voyager
	A-470 4 speed	Caravan, Voyager
1985	A-413 3 speed	Caravan, Voyager
	A-470 4 speed	Caravan, Voyager
1986	A-413 3 speed	Caravan, Voyager
	A-470 4 speed	Caravan, Voyager
1987	A-413 3 speed	Caravan, Voyager
	A-470 4 speed	Caravan, Voyager
1988	A-413 3 speed	Caravan, Voyager
	A-670 3 speed	Caravan, Voyager
1989	A-413 3 speed	Caravan, Voyager
	A-604 4 speed	Caravan, Voyager
	A-670 3 speed	Caravan, Voyager
1990	A-413 3 speed	Caravan, Voyager
	A-604 4 speed	Caravan, Voyager
	A-670 3 speed	Caravan, Voyager
1991	A-413 3 speed	Caravan, Voyager
	A-670 3 speed	Caravan, Voyager
	A-604 4 speed	Town & Country, Caravan, Voyager
1992	A-413 3 speed	Caravan, Voyager
	A-670 3 speed	Caravan, Voyager
	A-604 4 speed	Caravan, Voyager, Town & Country
1993	A-413 3 speed	Caravan, Voyager
	A-670 3 speed	Caravan, Voyager
	41TE 4 speed	Caravan, Voyager, Town & Country
1994	A-413 3 speed	Caravan, Voyager
	A-413 4 speed	Caravan, Voyager, Town & Country
1995	A-413 3 speed	Caravan, Voyager
	A-413 4 speed	Caravan, Voyager, Town & Country

85611C03

MANUAL TRANSMISSION APPLICATION CHART

Year	Transmission	Models
1984	A-460 4 speed	Caravan, Voyager
	A-465 4 speed	Caravan, Voyager
	A-525 5 speed	Caravan, Voyager
1985	A-460 4 speed	Caravan, Voyager
	A-465 4 speed	Caravan, Voyager
	A-525 5 speed	Caravan, Voyager
1986	A-460 4 speed	Caravan, Voyager
	A-525 5 speed	Caravan, Voyager
1987	A-460 4 speed	Caravan, Voyager
	A-520 5 speed	Caravan, Voyager
1988	A-520 5 speed	Caravan, Voyager
1989	A-520 5 speed	Caravan, Voyager
	A-555 5 speed	Caravan, Voyager
1990	A-523 5 speed	Caravan, Voyager
	A-568 5 speed	Caravan, Voyager
1991	NA	NA
1992	A-523 5 speed	Caravan, Voyager
1993	A-523 5 speed	Caravan, Voyager
1994	A-523 5 speed	Caravan, Voyager
1995	NA	NA

85611C02

CAPACITIES

Year	VIN	Engine No. Cyl. Liters	Crankcase Includes Filter (qts.)	Transmission (pts.) 4-sp	5-sp	Auto. ④	Power Transfer Unit (qts.) ⑧	Fuel Tank (gal.)	Cooling System (qts.) ③
1984	C	4-2.2L	4	4.8	—	①	—	15②	8.5
	G	4-2.6L	5	—	4.8	①	—	15②	9.5
1985	C	4-2.2L	4	4.8	—	①	—	15②	8.5
	G	4-2.6L	5	—	4.8	①	—	15②	9.5
1986	C	4-2.2L	4	4.8	—	①	—	15②	8.5
	G	4-2.6L	5	—	4.8	①	—	15②	9.5
1987	C	4-2.2L	4	4.8	—	①	—	15②	8.5
	K	4-2.5L	4	—	4.8	①	—	15②	8.5
	G	4-2.6L	5	—	4.8	①	—	15②	9.5
	3	6-3.0L	4	—	—	①	—	15②	10.5
1988	K	4-2.5L	4	—	5.0	①	—	15②	8.5
	3	6-3.0L	4	—	—	①	—	15②	10.5
1989	K	4-2.5L	4	—	5.0	①	—	15②	8.5
	J	4-2.5L	4	—	5.0	①	—	15②	8.5
	3	6-3.0L	4	—	—	①	—	15②	10.5
1990	K	4-2.5L	4	—	4.6	①	—	15②	8.5
	J	4-2.5L	4	—	4.6	①	—	15②	8.5
	3	6-3.0L	4	—	—	①	—	15②	10.5
	R	6-3.3L	4	—	—	①	—	15②	10.5
1991	K	4-2.5L	4.5	—	—	①	1.22	15②	8.5
	3	6-3.0L	4.5	—	—	①	1.22	15②	10.5
	R	6-3.3L	4.5	—	—	①	1.22	15②	10.5
1992	K	4-2.5L	4.5	—	4.8	⑤	1.22	⑥	9.5
	3	6-3.0L	4.5	—	4.8	⑤	1.22	⑥	10.0
	R	6-3.3L	4.5	—	—	⑤	1.22	⑥	10.0
1993	K	4-2.5L	4.5	—	4.8	⑤	1.22	⑥	9.5
	3	6-3.0L	4.5	—	4.8	⑤	1.22	⑥	10.0
	R	6-3.3L	4.5	—	—	⑤	1.22	⑥	10.0
1994	K	4-2.5L	4.5	—	4.6	⑤	1.22	⑥	9.5⑦
	3	6-3.0L	4.5	—	4.6	⑤	1.22	⑥	10.5⑦
	R	6-3.3L	4.5	—	—	⑤	1.22	⑥	10.5⑦
	L	6-3.8L	4.5	—	—	⑤	1.22	⑥	10.5⑦
1995	K	4-2.5L	4.5	—	4.6	⑤	1.22	⑥	9.5⑦
	3	6-3.0L	4.5	—	4.6	⑤	1.22	⑥	10.5⑦
	R	6-3.3L	4.5	—	—	⑤	1.22	⑥	10.5⑦
	L	6-3.8L	4.5	—	—	⑤	1.22	⑥	10.5⑦

① A413/A470 Transaxles (except Fleet): 17.8 pts.
A413/A470 Transaxles (Fleet): 18.4 pts.
A413/A460 Transaxles with Lockup Converter: 17.0 pts.
A604 Transaxles: 18.2 pts.

② Standard: 15 Gal.
Optional: 20 Gal.

③ Add 1 qt. when equipped with rear heater

④ Overhaul fill capacity with converter empty

⑤ Three speed except fleet: 17 pts.
Three speed fleet: 18.4 pts.
4 speed: 18.2 pts.

⑥ All wheel drive: 18 gal.
Front wheel drive: 20 gal.

⑦ Includes heater and coolant recovery bottle

⑧ All wheel drive vehicles

85611C04

TORQUE SPECIFICATIONS

Component	English	Metric
Air cleaner wing nut	14 inch lbs.	1.5 Nm
A/C Compressor		
Exc. 2.6L engine		
Locking and pivot screws	40 ft. lbs.	54 Nm
2.6L engine		
Locking screw and pivot nut	16 ft. lbs.	22 Nm
Jam nut	21 ft. lbs.	29 Nm
A/C Compressor idler pulley locknut		
3.0L engine	40 ft. lbs.	54 Nm
Air Pump locking and pivot bolts	25 ft. lbs.	34 Nm
Alternator		
Exc. 2.6L engine		
1984–89		
Locking screw	25 ft. lbs.	34 Nm
Pivot nut	30 ft. lbs.	41 Nm
1990–94 Locking & Pivot Nut	40 ft. lbs.	54 Nm
2.6L engine		
Locking screw and pivot nut	16 ft. lbs.	22 Nm
Jam nut	21 ft. lbs.	29 Nm
Carburetor stud nuts	14 inch lbs.	1.5 Nm
Cooling system hose clamps	20–30 inch lbs.	2–3 Nm
Cooling system vacuum valve or drain/fill plug	15 ft. lbs.	20 Nm
Fuel filter line clamps	10 inch lbs.	1 Nm
Fuel filter mounting screw	75 inch lbs.	8 Nm
Power Steering Pump locking and pivot screws	40 ft. lbs.	54 Nm
Wheel lug nuts	95 ft. lbs.	129 Nm

85611C05

ENGLISH TO METRIC CONVERSION: MASS (WEIGHT)

Current mass measurement is expressed in pounds and ounces (lbs. & ozs.). The metric unit of mass (or weight) is the kilogram (kg). Even although this table does not show conversion of masses (weights) larger than 15 lbs, it is easy to calculate larger units by following the data immediately below.

To convert ounces (oz.) to grams (g): multiply th number of ozs. by 28
To convert grams (g) to ounces (oz.): multiply the number of grams by .035

To convert pounds (lbs.) to kilograms (kg): multiply the number of lbs. by .45
To convert kilograms (kg) to pounds (lbs.): multiply the number of kilograms by 2.2

lbs	kg	lbs	kg	oz	kg	oz	kg
0.1	0.04	0.9	0.41	0.1	0.003	0.9	0.024
0.2	0.09	1	0.4	0.2	0.005	1	0.03
0.3	0.14	2	0.9	0.3	0.008	2	0.06
0.4	0.18	3	1.4	0.4	0.011	3	0.08
0.5	0.23	4	1.8	0.5	0.014	4	0.11
0.6	0.27	5	2.3	0.6	0.017	5	0.14
0.7	0.32	10	4.5	0.7	0.020	10	0.28
0.8	0.36	15	6.8	0.8	0.023	15	0.42

ENGLISH TO METRIC CONVERSION: TEMPERATURE

To convert Fahrenheit (°F) to Celsius (°C): take number of °F and subtract 32; multiply result by 5; divide result by 9

To convert Celsius (°C) to Fahrenheit (°F): take number of °C and multiply by 9; divide result by 5; add 32 to total

Fahrenheit (F)	Celsius (C)	Celsius (C)	Fahrenheit (F)	Fahrenheit (F)	Celsius (C)	Celsius (C)	Fahrenheit (F)	Fahrenheit (F)	Celsius (C)	Celsius (C)	Fahrenheit (F)
°F	°C	°C	°F	°F	°C	°C	°F	°F	°C	°C	°F
−40	−40	−38	−36.4	80	26.7	18	64.4	215	101.7	80	176
−35	−37.2	−36	−32.8	85	29.4	20	68	220	104.4	85	185
−30	−34.4	−34	−29.2	90	32.2	22	71.6	225	107.2	90	194
−25	−31.7	−32	−25.6	95	35.0	24	75.2	230	110.0	95	202
−20	−28.9	−30	−22	100	37.8	26	78.8	235	112.8	100	212
−15	−26.1	−28	−18.4	105	40.6	28	82.4	240	115.6	105	221
−10	−23.3	−26	−14.8	110	43.3	30	86	245	118.3	110	230
−5	−20.6	−24	−11.2	115	46.1	32	89.6	250	121.1	115	239
0	−17.8	−22	−7.6	120	48.9	34	93.2	255	123.9	120	248
1	−17.2	−20	−4	125	51.7	36	96.8	260	126.6	125	257
2	−16.7	−18	−0.4	130	54.4	38	100.4	265	129.4	130	266
3	−16.1	−16	3.2	135	57.2	40	104	270	132.2	135	275
4	−15.6	−14	6.8	140	60.0	42	107.6	275	135.0	140	284
5	−15.0	−12	10.4	145	62.8	44	112.2	280	137.8	145	293
10	−12.2	−10	14	150	65.6	46	114.8	285	140.6	150	302
15	−9.4	−8	17.6	155	68.3	48	118.4	290	143.3	155	311
20	−6.7	−6	21.2	160	71.1	50	122	295	146.1	160	320
25	−3.9	−4	24.8	165	73.9	52	125.6	300	148.9	165	329
30	−1.1	−2	28.4	170	76.7	54	129.2	305	151.7	170	338
35	1.7	0	32	175	79.4	56	132.8	310	154.4	175	347
40	4.4	2	35.6	180	82.2	58	136.4	315	157.2	180	356
45	7.2	4	39.2	185	85.0	60	140	320	160.0	185	365
50	10.0	6	42.8	190	87.8	62	143.6	325	162.8	190	374
55	12.8	8	46.4	195	90.6	64	147.2	330	165.6	195	383
60	15.6	10	50	200	93.3	66	150.8	335	168.3	200	392
65	18.3	12	53.6	205	96.1	68	154.4	340	171.1	205	401
70	21.1	14	57.2	210	98.9	70	158	345	173.9	210	410
75	23.9	16	60.8	212	100.0	75	167	350	176.7	215	414

TCCS1C01

ENGLISH TO METRIC CONVERSION: LENGTH

To convert inches (ins.) to millimeters (mm): multiply number of inches by 25.4

To convert millimeters (mm) to inches (ins.): multiply number of millimeters by .04

Inches	Decimals	Milli-meters	Inches to millimeters inches	mm	Inches	Decimals	Milli-meters	Inches to millimeters inches	mm
1/64	0.051625	0.3969	0.0001	0.00254	33/64	0.515625	13.0969	0.6	15.24
1/32	0.03125	0.7937	0.0002	0.00508	17/32	0.53125	13.4937	0.7	17.78
3/64	0.046875	1.1906	0.0003	0.00762	35/64	0.546875	13.8906	0.8	20.32
1/16	0.0625	1.5875	0.0004	0.01016	9/16	0.5625	14.2875	0.9	22.86
5/64	0.078125	1.9844	0.0005	0.01270	37/64	0.578125	14.6844	1	25.4
3/32	0.09375	2.3812	0.0006	0.01524	19/32	0.59375	15.0812	2	50.8
7/64	0.109375	2.7781	0.0007	0.01778	39/64	0.609375	15.4781	3	76.2
1/8	0.125	3.1750	0.0008	0.02032	5/8	0.625	15.8750	4	101.6
9/64	0.140625	3.5719	0.0009	0.02286	41/64	0.640625	16.2719	5	127.0
5/32	0.15625	3.9687	0.001	0.0254	21/32	0.65625	16.6687	6	152.4
11/64	0.171875	4.3656	0.002	0.0508	43/64	0.671875	17.0656	7	177.8
3/16	0.1875	4.7625	0.003	0.0762	11/16	0.6875	17.4625	8	203.2
13/64	0.203125	5.1594	0.004	0.1016	45/64	0.703125	17.8594	9	228.6
7/32	0.21875	5.5562	0.005	0.1270	23/32	0.71875	18.2562	10	254.0
15/64	0.234375	5.9531	0.006	0.1524	47/64	0.734375	18.6531	11	279.4
1/4	0.25	6.3500	0.007	0.1778	3/4	0.75	19.0500	12	304.8
17/64	0.265625	6.7469	0.008	0.2032	49/64	0.765625	19.4469	13	330.2
9/32	0.28125	7.1437	0.009	0.2286	25/32	0.78125	19.8437	14	355.6
19/64	0.296875	7.5406	0.01	0.254	51/64	0.796875	20.2406	15	381.0
5/16	0.3125	7.9375	0.02	0.508	13/16	0.8125	20.6375	16	406.4
21/64	0.328125	8.3344	0.03	0.762	53/64	0.828125	21.0344	17	431.8
11/32	0.34375	8.7312	0.04	1.016	27/32	0.84375	21.4312	18	457.2
23/64	0.359375	9.1281	0.05	1.270	55/64	0.859375	21.8281	19	482.6
3/8	0.375	9.5250	0.06	1.524	7/8	0.875	22.2250	20	508.0
25/64	0.390625	9.9219	0.07	1.778	57/64	0.890625	22.6219	21	533.4
13/32	0.40625	10.3187	0.08	2.032	29/32	0.90625	23.0187	22	558.8
27/64	0.421875	10.7156	0.09	2.286	59/64	0.921875	23.4156	23	584.2
7/16	0.4375	11.1125	0.1	2.54	15/16	0.9375	23.8125	24	609.6
29/64	0.453125	11.5094	0.2	5.08	61/64	0.953125	24.2094	25	635.0
15/32	0.46875	11.9062	0.3	7.62	31/32	0.96875	24.6062	26	660.4
31/64	0.484375	12.3031	0.4	10.16	63/64	0.984375	25.0031	27	690.6
1/2	0.5	12.7000	0.5	12.70					

ENGLISH TO METRIC CONVERSION: TORQUE

To convert foot-pounds (ft. lbs.) to Newton-meters: multiply the number of ft. lbs. by 1.3

To convert inch-pounds (in. lbs.) to Newton-meters: multiply the number of in. lbs. by .11

in lbs	N-m	in lbs	N-m	in lbs	N-m	in lbs	N-m	in lbs	N-m
0.1	0.01	1	0.11	10	1.13	19	2.15	28	3.16
0.2	0.02	2	0.23	11	1.24	20	2.26	29	3.28
0.3	0.03	3	0.34	12	1.36	21	2.37	30	3.39
0.4	0.04	4	0.45	13	1.47	22	2.49	31	3.50
0.5	0.06	5	0.56	14	1.58	23	2.60	32	3.62
0.6	0.07	6	0.68	15	1.70	24	2.71	33	3.73
0.7	0.08	7	0.78	16	1.81	25	2.82	34	3.84
0.8	0.09	8	0.90	17	1.92	26	2.94	35	3.95
0.9	0.10	9	1.02	18	2.03	27	3.05	36	4.07

TCCS1C02

ENGLISH TO METRIC CONVERSION: TORQUE

Torque is now expressed as either foot-pounds (ft./lbs.) or inch-pounds (in./lbs.). The metric measurement unit for torque is the Newton-meter (Nm). This unit—the Nm—will be used for all SI metric torque references, both the present ft./lbs. and in./lbs.

ft lbs	N-m	ft lbs	N-m	ft lbs	N-m	ft lbs	N-m
0.1	0.1	33	44.7	74	100.3	115	155.9
0.2	0.3	34	46.1	75	101.7	116	157.3
0.3	0.4	35	47.4	76	103.0	117	158.6
0.4	0.5	36	48.8	77	104.4	118	160.0
0.5	0.7	37	50.7	78	105.8	119	161.3
0.6	0.8	38	51.5	79	107.1	120	162.7
0.7	1.0	39	52.9	80	108.5	121	164.0
0.8	1.1	40	54.2	81	109.8	122	165.4
0.9	1.2	41	55.6	82	111.2	123	166.8
1	1.3	42	56.9	83	112.5	124	168.1
2	2.7	43	58.3	84	113.9	125	169.5
3	4.1	44	59.7	85	115.2	126	170.8
4	5.4	45	61.0	86	116.6	127	172.2
5	6.8	46	62.4	87	118.0	128	173.5
6	8.1	47	63.7	88	119.3	129	174.9
7	9.5	48	65.1	89	120.7	130	176.2
8	10.8	49	66.4	90	122.0	131	177.6
9	12.2	50	67.8	91	123.4	132	179.0
10	13.6	51	69.2	92	124.7	133	180.3
11	14.9	52	70.5	93	126.1	134	181.7
12	16.3	53	71.9	94	127.4	135	183.0
13	17.6	54	73.2	95	128.8	136	184.4
14	18.9	55	74.6	96	130.2	137	185.7
15	20.3	56	75.9	97	131.5	138	187.1
16	21.7	57	77.3	98	132.9	139	188.5
17	23.0	58	78.6	99	134.2	140	189.8
18	24.4	59	80.0	100	135.6	141	191.2
19	25.8	60	81.4	101	136.9	142	192.5
20	27.1	61	82.7	102	138.3	143	193.9
21	28.5	62	84.1	103	139.6	144	195.2
22	29.8	63	85.4	104	141.0	145	196.6
23	31.2	64	86.8	105	142.4	146	198.0
24	32.5	65	88.1	106	143.7	147	199.3
25	33.9	66	89.5	107	145.1	148	200.7
26	35.2	67	90.8	108	146.4	149	202.0
27	36.6	68	92.2	109	147.8	150	203.4
28	38.0	69	93.6	110	149.1	151	204.7
29	39.3	70	94.9	111	150.5	152	206.1
30	40.7	71	96.3	112	151.8	153	207.4
31	42.0	72	97.6	113	153.2	154	208.8
32	43.4	73	99.0	114	154.6	155	210.2

TCCS1C03

ENGLISH TO METRIC CONVERSION: FORCE

Force is presently measured in pounds (lbs.). This type of measurement is used to measure spring pressure, specifically how many pounds it takes to compress a spring. Our present force unit (the pound) will be replaced in SI metric measurements by the Newton (N). This term will eventually see use in specifications for electric motor brush spring pressures, valve spring pressures, etc.

To convert pounds (lbs.) to Newton (N): multiply the number of lbs. by 4.45

lbs	N	lbs	N	lbs	N	oz	N
0.01	0.04	21	93.4	59	262.4	1	0.3
0.02	0.09	22	97.9	60	266.9	2	0.6
0.03	0.13	23	102.3	61	271.3	3	0.8
0.04	0.18	24	106.8	62	275.8	4	1.1
0.05	0.22	25	111.2	63	280.2	5	1.4
0.06	0.27	26	115.6	64	284.6	6	1.7
0.07	0.31	27	120.1	65	289.1	7	2.0
0.08	0.36	28	124.6	66	293.6	8	2.2
0.09	0.40	29	129.0	67	298.0	9	2.5
0.1	0.4	30	133.4	68	302.5	10	2.8
0.2	0.9	31	137.9	69	306.9	11	3.1
0.3	1.3	32	142.3	70	311.4	12	3.3
0.4	1.8	33	146.8	71	315.8	13	3.6
0.5	2.2	34	151.2	72	320.3	14	3.9
0.6	2.7	35	155.7	73	324.7	15	4.2
0.7	3.1	36	160.1	74	329.2	16	4.4
0.8	3.6	37	164.6	75	333.6	17	4.7
0.9	4.0	38	169.0	76	338.1	18	5.0
1	4.4	39	173.5	77	342.5	19	5.3
2	8.9	40	177.9	78	347.0	20	5.6
3	13.4	41	182.4	79	351.4	21	5.8
4	17.8	42	186.8	80	355.9	22	6.1
5	22.2	43	191.3	81	360.3	23	6.4
6	26.7	44	195.7	82	364.8	24	6.7
7	31.1	45	200.2	83	369.2	25	7.0
8	35.6	46	204.6	84	373.6	26	7.2
9	40.0	47	209.1	85	378.1	27	7.5
10	44.5	48	213.5	86	382.6	28	7.8
11	48.9	49	218.0	87	387.0	29	8.1
12	53.4	50	224.4	88	391.4	30	8.3
13	57.8	51	226.9	89	395.9	31	8.6
14	62.3	52	231.3	90	400.3	32	8.9
15	66.7	53	235.8	91	404.8	33	9.2
16	71.2	54	240.2	92	409.2	34	9.4
17	75.6	55	244.6	93	413.7	35	9.7
18	80.1	56	249.1	94	418.1	36	10.0
19	84.5	57	253.6	95	422.6	37	10.3
20	89.0	58	258.0	96	427.0	38	10.6

TCCS1C04

ENGLISH TO METRIC CONVERSION: LIQUID CAPACITY

Liquid or fluid capacity is presently expressed as pints, quarts or gallons, or a combination of all of these. In the metric system the liter (l) will become the basic unit. Fractions of a liter would be expressed as deciliters, centiliters, or most frequently (and commonly) as milliliters.

To convert pints (pts.) to liters (l): multiply the number of pints by .47
To convert liters (l) to pints (pts.): multiply the number of liters by 2.1
To convert quarts (qts.) to liters (l): multiply the number of quarts by .95

To convert liters (l) to quarts (qts.): multiply the number of liters by 1.06
To convert gallons (gals.) to liters (l): multiply the number of gallons by 3.8
To convert liters (l) to gallons (gals.): multiply the number of liters by .26

gals	liters	qts	liters	pts	liters
0.1	0.38	0.1	0.10	0.1	0.05
0.2	0.76	0.2	0.19	0.2	0.10
0.3	1.1	0.3	0.28	0.3	0.14
0.4	1.5	0.4	0.38	0.4	0.19
0.5	1.9	0.5	0.47	0.5	0.24
0.6	2.3	0.6	0.57	0.6	0.28
0.7	2.6	0.7	0.66	0.7	0.33
0.8	3.0	0.8	0.76	0.8	0.38
0.9	3.4	0.9	0.85	0.9	0.43
1	3.8	1	1.0	1	0.5
2	7.6	2	1.9	2	1.0
3	11.4	3	2.8	3	1.4
4	15.1	4	3.8	4	1.9
5	18.9	5	4.7	5	2.4
6	22.7	6	5.7	6	2.8
7	26.5	7	6.6	7	3.3
8	30.3	8	7.6	8	3.8
9	34.1	9	8.5	9	4.3
10	37.8	10	9.5	10	4.7
11	41.6	11	10.4	11	5.2
12	45.4	12	11.4	12	5.7
13	49.2	13	12.3	13	6.2
14	53.0	14	13.2	14	6.6
15	56.8	15	14.2	15	7.1
16	60.6	16	15.1	16	7.6
17	64.3	17	16.1	17	8.0
18	68.1	18	17.0	18	8.5
19	71.9	19	18.0	19	9.0
20	75.7	20	18.9	20	9.5
21	79.5	21	19.9	21	9.9
22	83.2	22	20.8	22	10.4
23	87.0	23	21.8	23	10.9
24	90.8	24	22.7	24	11.4
25	94.6	25	23.6	25	11.8
26	98.4	26	24.6	26	12.3
27	102.2	27	25.5	27	12.8
28	106.0	28	26.5	28	13.2
29	110.0	29	27.4	29	13.7
30	113.5	30	28.4	30	14.2

TCCS1C05

ENGLISH TO METRIC CONVERSION: PRESSURE

The basic unit of pressure measurement used today is expressed as pounds per square inch (psi). The metric unit for psi will be the kilopascal (kPa). This will apply to either fluid pressure or air pressure, and will be frequently seen in tire pressure readings, oil pressure specifications, fuel pump pressure, etc.

To convert pounds per square inch (psi) to kilopascals (kPa): multiply the number of psi by 6.89

Psi	kPa	Psi	kPa	Psi	kPa	Psi	kPa
0.1	0.7	37	255.1	82	565.4	127	875.6
0.2	1.4	38	262.0	83	572.3	128	882.5
0.3	2.1	39	268.9	84	579.2	129	889.4
0.4	2.8	40	275.8	85	586.0	130	896.3
0.5	3.4	41	282.7	86	592.9	131	903.2
0.6	4.1	42	289.6	87	599.8	132	910.1
0.7	4.8	43	296.5	88	606.7	133	917.0
0.8	5.5	44	303.4	89	613.6	134	923.9
0.9	6.2	45	310.3	90	620.5	135	930.8
1	6.9	46	317.2	91	627.4	136	937.7
2	13.8	47	324.0	92	634.3	137	944.6
3	20.7	48	331.0	93	641.2	138	951.5
4	27.6	49	337.8	94	648.1	139	958.4
5	34.5	50	344.7	95	655.0	140	965.2
6	41.4	51	351.6	96	661.9	141	972.2
7	48.3	52	358.5	97	668.8	142	979.0
8	55.2	53	365.4	98	675.7	143	985.9
9	62.1	54	372.3	99	682.6	144	992.8
10	69.0	55	379.2	100	689.5	145	999.7
11	75.8	56	386.1	101	696.4	146	1006.6
12	82.7	57	393.0	102	703.3	147	1013.5
13	89.6	58	399.9	103	710.2	148	1020.4
14	96.5	59	406.8	104	717.0	149	1027.3
15	103.4	60	413.7	105	723.9	150	1034.2
16	110.3	61	420.6	106	730.8	151	1041.1
17	117.2	62	427.5	107	737.7	152	1048.0
18	124.1	63	434.4	108	744.6	153	1054.9
19	131.0	64	441.3	109	751.5	154	1061.8
20	137.9	65	448.2	110	758.4	155	1068.7
21	144.8	66	455.0	111	765.3	156	1075.6
22	151.7	67	461.9	112	772.2	157	1082.5
23	158.6	68	468.8	113	779.1	158	1089.4
24	165.5	69	475.7	114	786.0	159	1096.3
25	172.4	70	482.6	115	792.9	160	1103.2
26	179.3	71	489.5	116	799.8	161	1110.0
27	186.2	72	496.4	117	806.7	162	1116.9
28	193.0	73	503.3	118	813.6	163	1123.8
29	200.0	74	510.2	119	820.5	164	1130.7
30	206.8	75	517.1	120	827.4	165	1137.6
31	213.7	76	524.0	121	834.3	166	1144.5
32	220.6	77	530.9	122	841.2	167	1151.4
33	227.5	78	537.8	123	848.0	168	1158.3
34	234.4	79	544.7	124	854.9	169	1165.2
35	241.3	80	551.6	125	861.8	170	1172.1
36	248.2	81	558.5	126	868.7	171	1179.0

TCCS1C06

ENGLISH TO METRIC CONVERSION: PRESSURE

The basic unit of pressure measurement used today is expressed as pounds per square inch (psi). The metric unit for psi will be the kilopascal (kPa). This will apply to either fluid pressure or air pressure, and will be frequently seen in tire pressure readings, oil pressure specifications, fuel pump pressure, etc.

To convert pounds per square inch (psi) to kilopascals (kPa): multiply the number of psi by 6.89

Psi	kPa	Psi	kPa	Psi	kPa	Psi	kPa
172	1185.9	216	1489.3	260	1792.6	304	2096.0
173	1192.8	217	1496.2	261	1799.5	305	2102.9
174	1199.7	218	1503.1	262	1806.4	306	2109.8
175	1206.6	219	1510.0	263	1813.3	307	2116.7
176	1213.5	220	1516.8	264	1820.2	308	2123.6
177	1220.4	221	1523.7	265	1827.1	309	2130.5
178	1227.3	222	1530.6	266	1834.0	310	2137.4
179	1234.2	223	1537.5	267	1840.9	311	2144.3
180	1241.0	224	1544.4	268	1847.8	312	2151.2
181	1247.9	225	1551.3	269	1854.7	313	2158.1
182	1254.8	226	1558.2	270	1861.6	314	2164.9
183	1261.7	227	1565.1	271	1868.5	315	2171.8
184	1268.6	228	1572.0	272	1875.4	316	2178.7
185	1275.5	229	1578.9	273	1882.3	317	2185.6
186	1282.4	230	1585.8	274	1889.2	318	2192.5
187	1289.3	231	1592.7	275	1896.1	319	2199.4
188	1296.2	232	1599.6	276	1903.0	320	2206.3
189	1303.1	233	1606.5	277	1909.8	321	2213.2
190	1310.0	234	1613.4	278	1916.7	322	2220.1
191	1316.9	235	1620.3	279	1923.6	323	2227.0
192	1323.8	236	1627.2	280	1930.5	324	2233.9
193	1330.7	237	1634.1	281	1937.4	325	2240.8
194	1337.6	238	1641.0	282	1944.3	326	2247.7
195	1344.5	239	1647.8	283	1951.2	327	2254.6
196	1351.4	240	1654.7	284	1958.1	328	2261.5
197	1358.3	241	1661.6	285	1965.0	329	2268.4
198	1365.2	242	1668.5	286	1971.9	330	2275.3
199	1372.0	243	1675.4	287	1978.8	331	2282.2
200	1378.9	244	1682.3	288	1985.7	332	2289.1
201	1385.8	245	1689.2	289	1992.6	333	2295.9
202	1392.7	246	1696.1	290	1999.5	334	2302.8
203	1399.6	247	1703.0	291	2006.4	335	2309.7
204	1406.5	248	1709.9	292	2013.3	336	2316.6
205	1413.4	249	1716.8	293	2020.2	337	2323.5
206	1420.3	250	1723.7	294	2027.1	338	2330.4
207	1427.2	251	1730.6	295	2034.0	339	2337.3
208	1434.1	252	1737.5	296	2040.8	240	2344.2
209	1441.0	253	1744.4	297	2047.7	341	2351.1
210	1447.9	254	1751.3	298	2054.6	342	2358.0
211	1454.8	255	1758.2	299	2061.5	343	2364.9
212	1461.7	256	1765.1	300	2068.4	344	2371.8
213	1468.7	257	1772.0	301	2075.3	345	2378.7
214	1475.5	258	1778.8	302	2082.2	346	2385.6
215	1482.4	259	1785.7	303	2089.1	347	2392.5

TCCS1C07

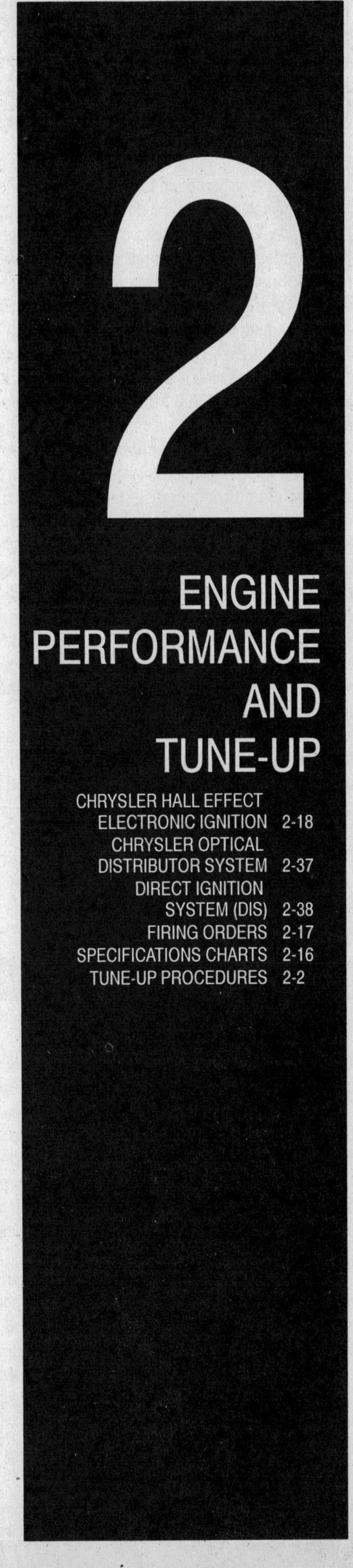

CHRYSLER HALL EFFECT ELECTRONIC IGNITION
- SINGLE MODULE ENGINE CONTROLLER (SMEC) AND SINGLE BOARD ENGINE CONTROLLER (SBEC) SYSTEMS 2-29
- SPARK CONTROL COMPUTER (SCC) SYSTEM 2-18
- SPARK CONTROL COMPUTER (SCC) SYSTEM — COMPONENT REPLACEMENT 2-24

CHRYSLER OPTICAL DISTRIBUTOR SYSTEM
- COMPONENT REPLACEMENT AND TESTING 2-37

DIRECT IGNITION SYSTEM (DIS)
- DIS SYSTEM COMPONENT REPLACEMENT 2-39
- DIS SYSTEM DIAGNOSIS AND TESTING 2-38
- GENERAL INFORMATION 2-38

FIRING ORDERS 2-17

SPECIFICATIONS CHARTS
- TUNE-UP SPECIFICATIONS 2-16

TUNE-UP PROCEDURES
- IDLE MIXTURE 2-14
- IDLE SPEED 2-11
- IGNITION TIMING 2-9
- SPARK PLUG WIRES 2-9
- SPARK PLUGS 2-2
- VALVE LASH 2-15

TUNE-UP PROCEDURES

Neither tune-up nor troubleshooting can be considered independently since each has a direct relationship with the other.

It is advisable to follow a definite and thorough tune-up procedure. Tune-up consists of three separate steps: Analysis, (the process of determining whether normal wear is responsible for performance loss, and whether parts require replacement or service); Parts Replacement or Service; and Adjustment, (where engine adjustments are performed).

The manufacturer's recommended interval for tune-ups on non-catalyst vehicles is 15,000 miles (24,000 km). Models with a converter, every 30,000 miles (48,000 km). Models equipped with a 2.6L engine require a valve lash adjustment every 15,000 miles (24,000 km). This interval should be shortened if the vehicle is subjected to severe operating conditions such as trailer pulling or stop and start driving, or if starting and running problems are noticed. It is assumed that the routine maintenance has been kept up, as this will have an effect on the result of the tune-up. All the applicable tune-up steps should be followed, as each adjustment complements the effects of the other. If the tune-up (emission control) sticker in the engine compartment disagrees with the information presented in the Tune-up Specifications chart in this section, the sticker figures must be followed. The sticker information reflects running changes made by the manufacturer during production.

Troubleshooting is a logical sequence of procedures designed to locate a particular cause of trouble. While the apparent cause of trouble, in many cases, is worn or damaged parts, performance problems are less obvious. The first job is to locate the problem and cause. Once the problem has been isolated, repairs, removal or adjustment procedures can be performed.

It is advisable to read the entire section before beginning a tune-up, although those who are more familiar with tune-up procedures may wish to go directly to the instructions.

Spark Plugs

➧ See Figure 1

A typical spark plug consists of a metal shell surrounding a ceramic insulator. A metal electrode extends downward through the center of the insulator and protrudes a small distance. Located at the end of the plug and attached to the side of the outer metal shell is the side electrode. The side electrode bends in at a 90° angle so that its tip is just past and parallel to the tip of the center electrode. The distance between these two electrodes (measured in thousandths of an inch or hundredths of a millimeter) is called the spark plug gap.

The spark plug does not produce a spark but instead provides a gap across which the current can arc. The coil produces anywhere from 20,000 to 50,000 volts (depending on the type and application) which travels through the wires to the spark plugs. The current passes along the center electrode and jumps the gap to the side electrode, and in doing so, ignites the air/fuel mixture in the combustion chamber.

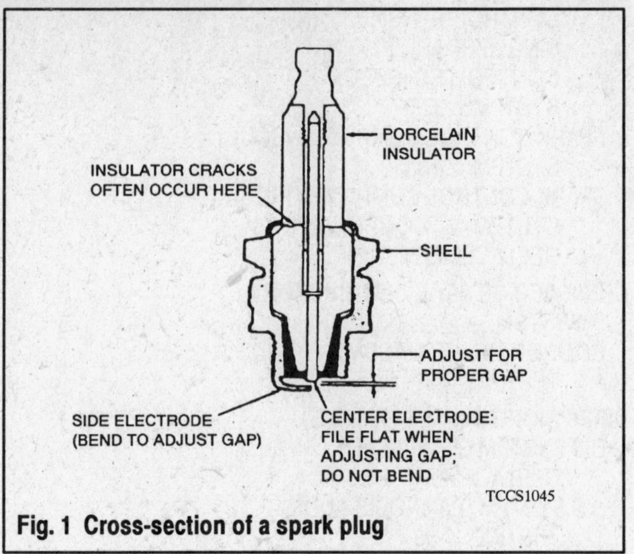

Fig. 1 Cross-section of a spark plug

SPARK PLUG HEAT RANGE

➧ See Figure 2

Spark plug heat range is the ability of the plug to dissipate heat. The longer the insulator (or the farther it extends into the engine), the hotter the plug will operate; the shorter the insulator (the closer the electrode is to the block's cooling passages) the cooler it will operate. A plug that absorbs little heat and remains too cool will quickly accumulate deposits of oil and carbon since it is not hot enough to burn them off. This leads to plug fouling and consequently to misfiring. A plug that absorbs too much heat will have no deposits but, due to the excessive heat, the electrodes will burn away quickly and might possibly lead to preignition or other ignition problems. Preignition takes place when plug tips get so hot that they glow sufficiently to ignite the air/fuel mixture before the actual spark occurs. This early ignition will usually cause a pinging during low speeds and heavy loads.

The general rule of thumb for choosing the correct heat range when picking a spark plug is: if most of your driving is long distance, high speed travel, use a colder plug; if most of your driving is stop and go, use a hotter plug. Original equipment plugs are generally a good compromise between the 2 styles and most people never have the need to change their plugs from the factory-recommended heat range.

REMOVAL & INSTALLATION

➧ See Figures 3, 4 and 5

➥ Remove the spark plugs and wires one at a time to avoid confusion and miswiring during installation.

1. Before removing the spark plugs, number the plug wires so that the correct wire goes on the plug when replaced. This can be done with pieces of adhesive tape.
2. Next, clean the area around the plugs by blowing with compressed air. You can also loosen the plugs a few turns and crank the engine to blow the dirt away.

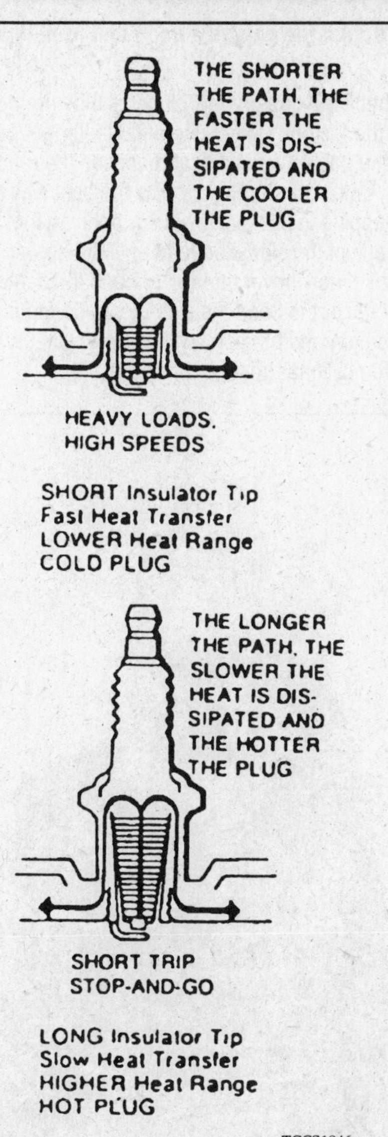

Fig. 2 Spark plug heat range

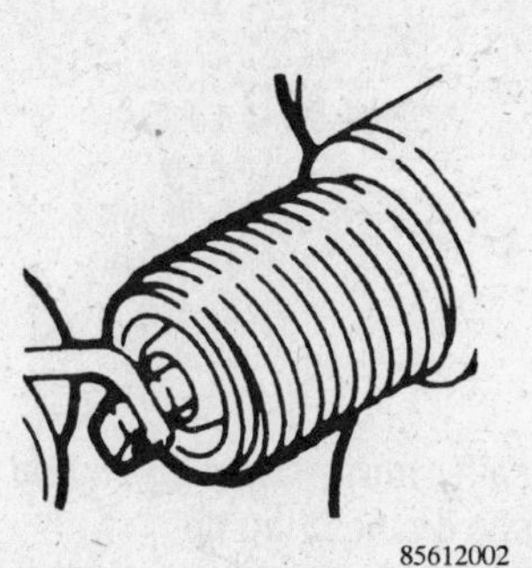

Fig. 3 Check the spark plug gap with a feeler gauge

Fig. 4 Disconnect the spark plug wire by pulling on the boot and not the wire

Fig. 5 Removing the spark plug using a rachet and extension

CAUTION

Wear safety glasses to avoid possible eye injury due to flying dust particles.

3. Disconnect the plugs wires by twisting and pulling on the rubber cap, not on the wire.
4. Remove each plug with a rubber insert spark plug socket. make sure that the socket is all the way down on the plug to prevent it from slipping and cracking the porcelain insulator.
5. After removing each plug, evaluate its condition. A spark plug's useful life is approximately 30,000 miles (48,000 Km). Thus, it would make sense to replace a plug if it has been in service that long.
6. If the plugs are to be reused, file the center and side electrodes flat with a fine, flat point file. Heavy or baked on deposits can be carefully scraped off with a small knife blade, or the scraper tool of a combination spark plug tool. However, it is suggested that plugs be test and cleaned on a service station sandblasting machine. Check the gap between the electrodes

with a round wire spark plug gapping gauge. Do not use a flat feeler gauge; it will give an inaccurate reading. If the gap is not as specified, use the bending tool on the spark plug gap gauge to bend the outside electrode. Be careful not to bend the electrode tool far or too often, because excessive bending may cause the electrode to break off and fall into the combustion chamber. This would require removing the cylinder head to reach the broken piece, and could also result in cylinder wall, piston ring, or valve damage.

7. Clean the threads of the old plugs with a wire brush. Lubricate the threads with a drop of oil.

8. Screw the plugs in finger tight, and then tighten them with the spark plug socket to 20 ft. lbs. (27 Nm). Be very careful not to over tighten them.

9. Reinstall the wires. If, by chance, you have forgotten to number the plug wires, refer to the Firing Order illustrations.

INSPECTION & GAPPING

See Figures 6, 7, 8, 9, 10, 11, 12, 13, 14, 15, 16 and 17

Check the plugs for deposits and wear. If they are not going to be replaced, clean the plugs thoroughly. Remember that any kind of deposit will decrease the efficiency of the plug. Plugs can be cleaned on a spark plug cleaning machine, which can sometimes be found in service stations, or you can do an acceptable job of cleaning with a stiff brush. If the plugs are cleaned, the electrodes must be filed flat. Use an ignition points file, not an emery board or the like, which will leave deposits. The electrodes must be filed perfectly flat with sharp edges; rounded edges reduce the spark plug voltage by as much as 50%.

Check spark plug gap before installation. The ground electrode (the L-shaped one connected to the body of the plug) must be parallel to the center electrode and the specified size wire gauge (please refer to the Tune-Up Specifications chart for details) must pass between the electrodes with a slight drag.

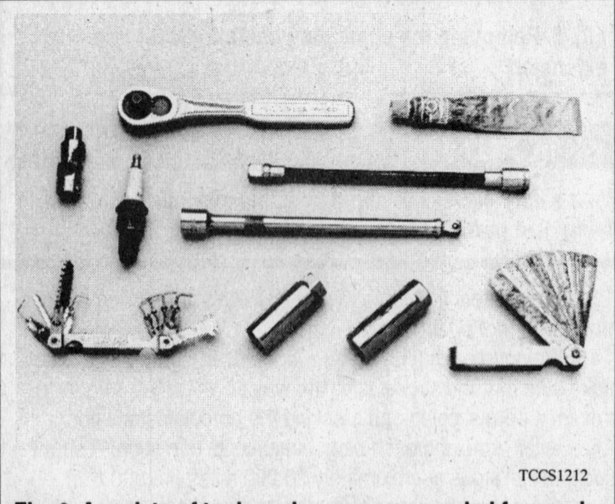

Fig. 6 A variety of tools and gauges are needed for spark plug service

NEVER adjust the gap on a used platinum type spark plug.

Always check the gap on new plugs as they are not always set correctly at the factory. Do not use a flat feeler gauge when measuring the gap on a used plug, because the reading may be inaccurate. A wire type gapping tool is the best way to check the gap. Wire gapping tools usually have a bending tool attached. Use that to adjust the side electrode until the proper distance is obtained. Absolutely never attempt to bend the center electrode. Also, be careful not to bend the side electrode too far or too often as it may weaken and break off within the engine, requiring removal of the cylinder head to retrieve it.

Fig. 7 A normally worn spark plug should have light tan or gray deposits on the firing tip

Tracking Arc
High voltage arcs between a fouling deposit on the insulator tip and spark plug shell. This ignites the fuel/air mixture at some point along the insulator tip, retarding the ignition timing which causes a power and fuel loss.

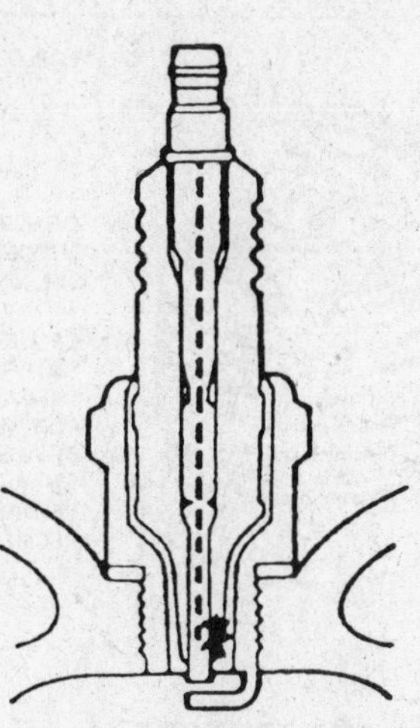

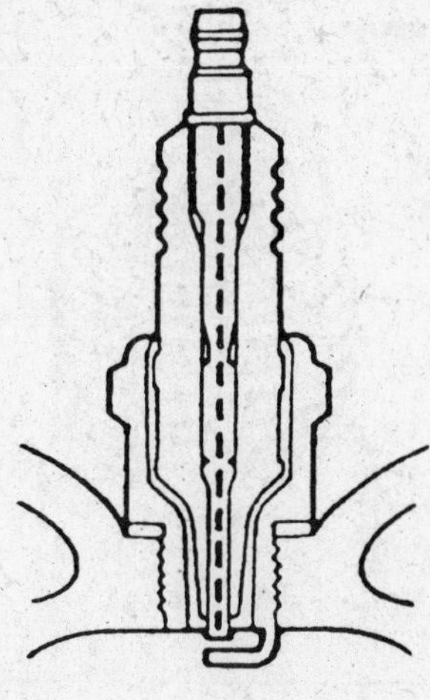

Wide Gap
Spark plug electrodes are worn so that the high voltage charge cannot arc across the electrodes. Improper gapping of electrodes on new or "cleaned" spark plugs could cause a similar condition. Fuel remains unburned and a power loss results.

Flashover
A damaged spark plug boot, along with dirt and moisture, could permit the high voltage charge to short over the insulator to the spark plug shell or the engine. A buttress insulator design helps prevent high voltage flashover.

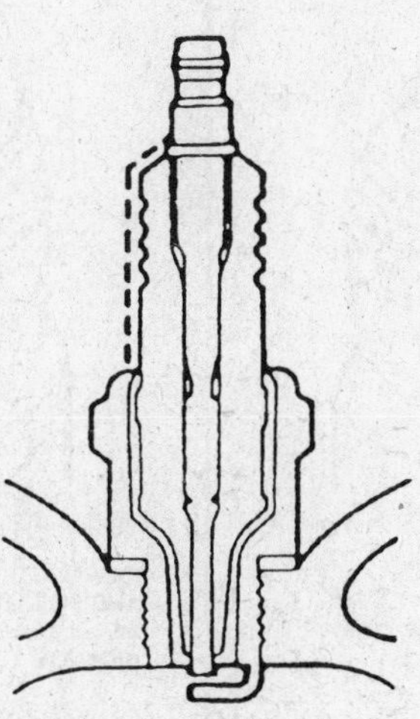

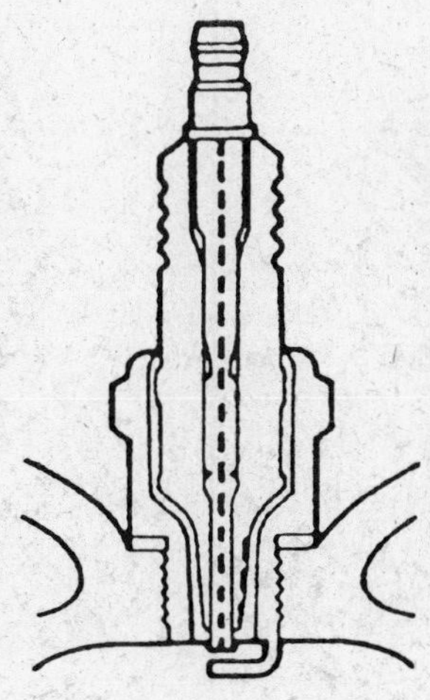

Fouled Spark Plug
Deposits that have formed on the insulator tip may become conductive and provide a "shunt" path to the shell. This prevents the high voltage from arcing between the electrodes. A power and fuel loss is the result.

Bridged Electrodes
Fouling deposits between the electrodes "ground out" the high voltage needed to fire the spark plug. The arc between the electrodes does not occur and the fuel air mixture is not ignited. This causes a power loss and exhausting of raw fuel.

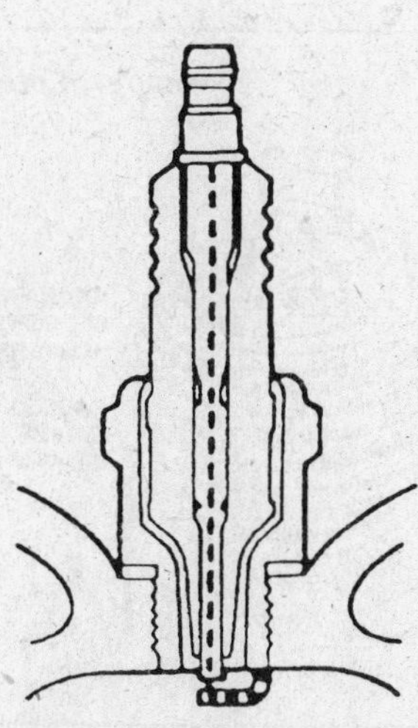

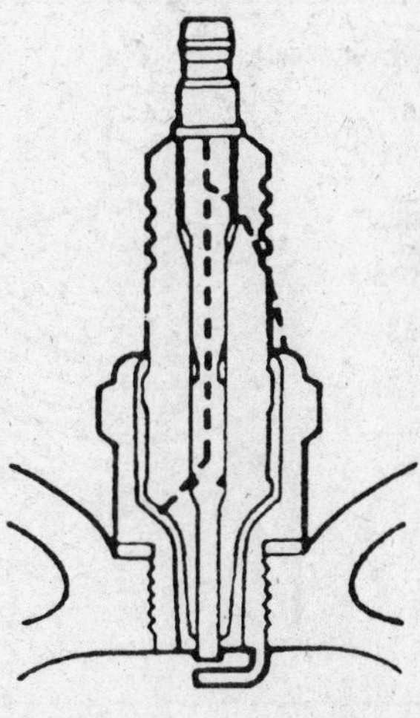

Cracked Insulator
A crack in the spark plug insulator could cause the high voltage charge to "ground out." Here, the spark does not jump the electrode gap and the fuel air mixture is not ignited. This causes a power loss and raw fuel is exhausted.

TCCS201A

Fig. 8 Used spark plugs which show damage may indicate engine problems

GAP BRIDGED

IDENTIFIED BY DEPOSIT BUILD-UP CLOSING GAP BETWEEN ELECTRODES.

CAUSED BY OIL OR CARBON FOULING. REPLACE PLUG, OR, IF DEPOSITS ARE NOT EXCESSIVE THE PLUG CAN BE CLEANED.

OIL FOULED

IDENTIFIED BY WET BLACK DEPOSITS ON THE INSULATOR SHELL BORE ELECTRODES.

CAUSED BY EXCESSIVE OIL ENTERING COMBUSTION CHAMBER THROUGH WORN RINGS AND PISTONS, EXCESSIVE CLEARANCE BETWEEN VALVE GUIDES AND STEMS, OR WORN OR LOOSE BEARINGS. CORRECT OIL PROBLEM. REPLACE THE PLUG.

CARBON FOULED

IDENTIFIED BY BLACK, DRY FLUFFY CARBON DEPOSITS ON INSULATOR TIPS, EXPOSED SHELL SURFACES AND ELECTRODES.

CAUSED BY TOO COLD A PLUG, WEAK IGNITION, DIRTY AIR CLEANER, DEFECTIVE FUEL PUMP, TOO RICH A FUEL MIXTURE, IMPROPERLY OPERATING HEAT RISER OR EXCESSIVE IDLING. CAN BE CLEANED.

NORMAL

IDENTIFIED BY LIGHT TAN OR GRAY DEPOSITS ON THE FIRING TIP.

PRE-IGNITION

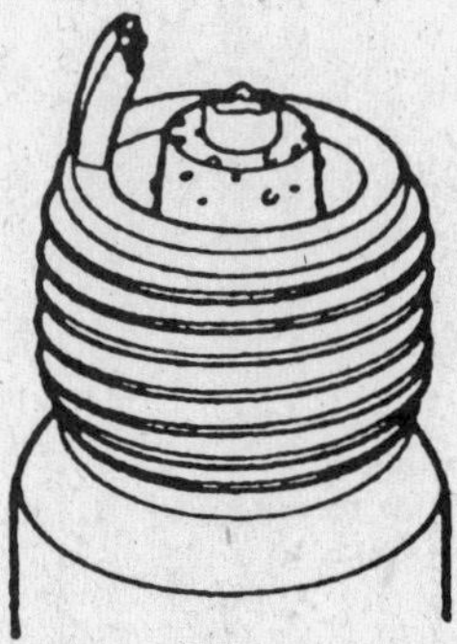

IDENTIFIED BY MELTED ELECTRODES AND POSSIBLY BLISTERED INSULATOR. METALIC DEPOSITS ON INSULATOR INDICATE ENGINE DAMAGE.

CAUSED BY WRONG TYPE OF FUEL, INCORRECT IGNITION TIMING OR ADVANCE, TOO HOT A PLUG, BURNT VALVES OR ENGINE OVERHEATING. REPLACE THE PLUG.

OVERHEATING

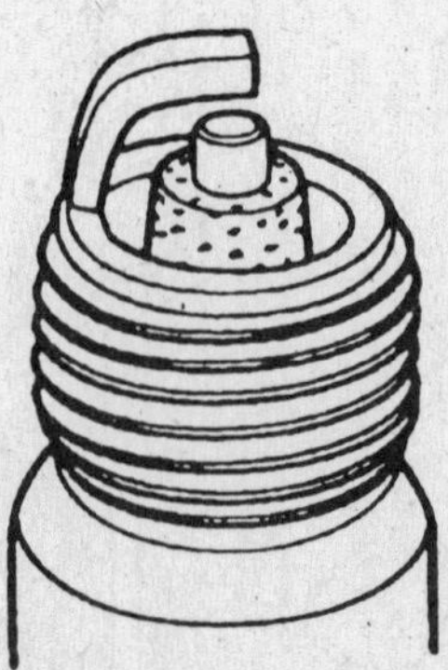

IDENTIFIED BY A WHITE OR LIGHT GRAY INSULATOR WITH SMALL BLACK OR GRAY BROWN SPOTS AND WITH BLUISH-BURNT APPEARANCE OF ELECTRODES.

CAUSED BY ENGINE OVER-HEATING, WRONG TYPE OF FUEL, LOOSE SPARK PLUGS, TOO HOT A PLUG, LOW FUEL PUMP PRESSURE OR INCORRECT IGNITION TIMING. REPLACE THE PLUG.

FUSED SPOT DEPOSIT

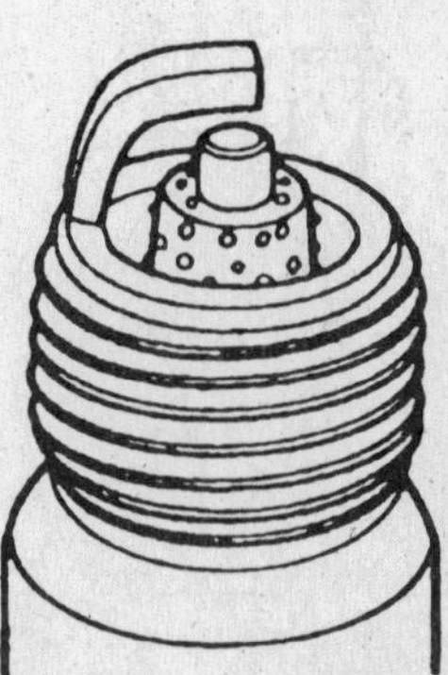

IDENTIFIED BY MELTED OR SPOTTY DEPOSITS RESEMBLING BUBBLES OR BLISTERS.

CAUSED BY SUDDEN ACCELERATION. CAN BE CLEANED IF NOT EXCESSIVE, OTHERWISE REPLACE PLUG.

TCCS2002

Fig. 9 Inspect the spark plug to determine engine running conditions

TCCS2136

Fig. 10 A carbon fouled plug, identified by soft, sooty, black deposits, may indicate an improperly tuned vehicle. Check the air cleaner, ignition components and engine control system

TCCS2137

Fig. 12 A physically damaged spark plug may be evidence of severe detonation in that cylinder. Watch that cylinder carefully between services, as a continued detonation will not only damage the plug, but could also damage the engine

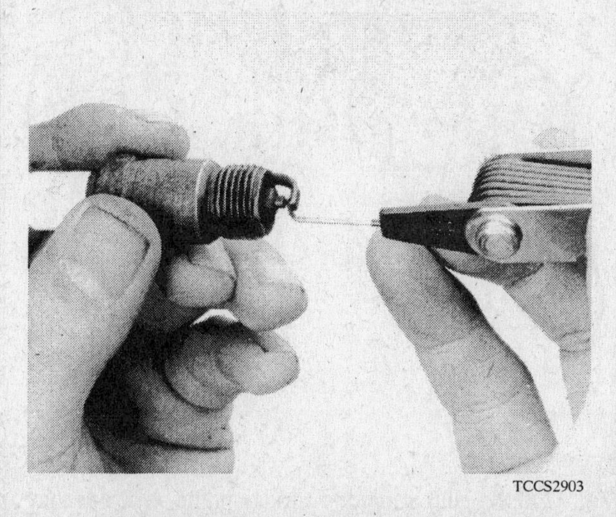

TCCS2903

Fig. 11 Checking the spark plug gap with a feeler gauge

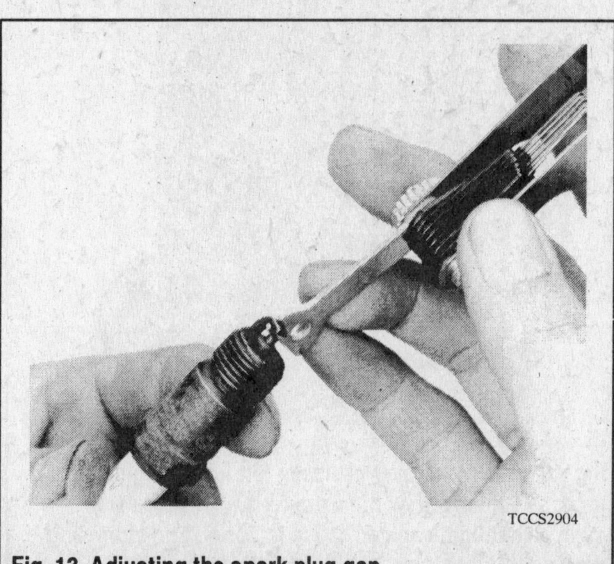

TCCS2904

Fig. 13 Adjusting the spark plug gap

Fig. 14 An oil fouled spark plug indicates an engine with worn piston rings and/or bad valve seals allowing excessive oil to enter the chamber

Fig. 16 A bridged or almost bridged spark plug, identified by a build-up between the electrodes caused by excessive carbon or oil build-up on the plug

Fig. 15 This spark plug has been left in the engine too long, as evidenced by the extreme gap — Plugs with such an extreme gap can cause misfiring and stumbling accompanied by a noticeable lack of power

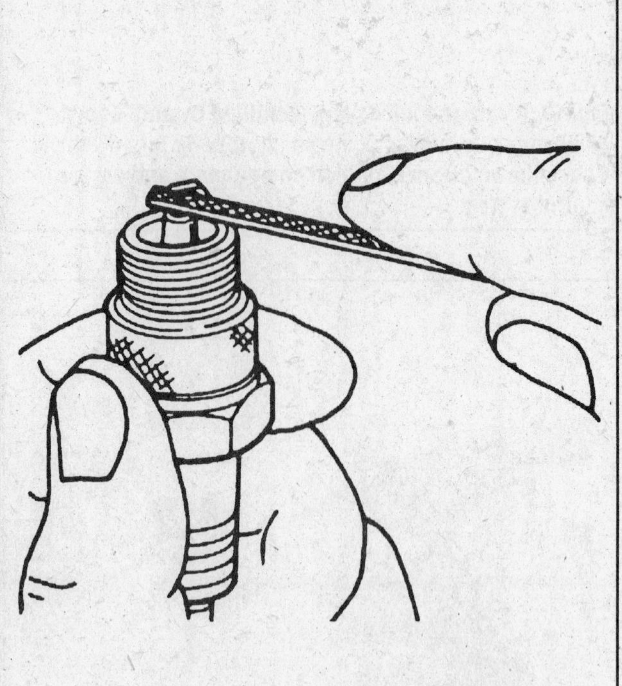

Fig. 17 If the plug is in good condition, the electrode may be filed flat and reused

Spark Plug Wires

See Figure 18

Check the spark plug wire connections at the coil, distributor cap towers, and at the spark plugs. Be sure they are fully seated, and the boot covers are not cracked or split. Clean the cables with a cloth and a non-flammable solvent. Check for brittle or cracked insulation, replace wires as necessary. If a wire is suspected of failure, test it with an ohmmeter.

Wire length can be used to determine appropriate resistance values:

- 0–15 in. — 3000–10,000Ω
- 15–25 in. — 4000–15,000Ω
- 25–35 in. — 6000–20,000Ω
- Wire over 35 in. — 6000–25,000Ω

Any wire with a resistance in excess of 30,000 ohms should be considered bad and replaced regardless of length.

1. Remove the plug wire from the spark plug. Twist the boot and pull. Never apply pressure to the wire itself.

The 3.3L and 3.8L engines are equipped with a distributorless electronic ignition system. The plug wires run directly from the coil pack to the spark plugs.

2. Remove the distributor cap from the distributor with all wires attached.

Do not pull plug wires from the distributor cap, they must first be released from inside of cap.

3. Connect an ohmmeter between the spark plug terminal, and the corresponding electrode inside the distributor cap. Resistance should be within limits of the resistance figures listed earlier. If resistance is not within specs, remove the wire from the distributor cap and retest. If still not within specs, replace the wire.
4. Install the new wire into the cap tower, then squeeze the wire nipple to release any trapped air between the cap tower and nipple.
5. Push firmly to properly seat wire electrode into the cap.
6. Install the plug end of the wire onto the plug until it snaps into place.

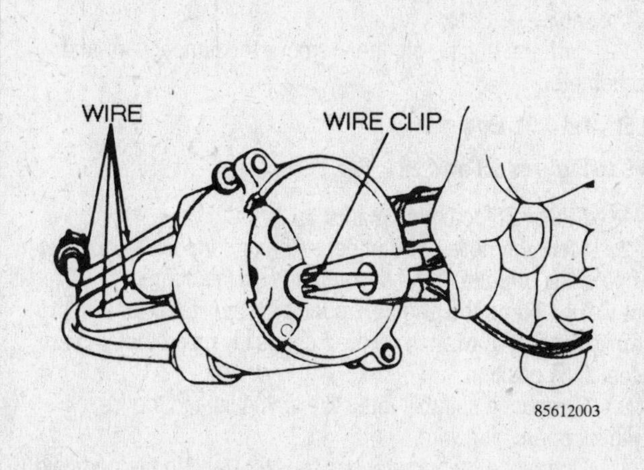

Fig. 18 Removing the plug wires from the distributor cap

WARNING

Do not allowed plug wires to contact exhaust manifold or any moving parts.

Ignition Timing

Basic timing should be checked at each tune-up in order to gain maximum engine performance. While timing is not likely to change very much with electronic ignition systems, it becomes a critical factor necessary to reduce engine emissions and improve driveability.

A stroboscopic (dynamic) timing light must be used, since static lights are too inaccurate for emission controlled engines.

Some timing light have other features built into them, such as dwell meters or tachometers. These are nice, in that they reduce the tangle of wires under the hood when you're working, but may duplicate the functions of tools your already have. One worthwhile feature, which is becoming more of a necessity with higher voltage ignition systems, is an inductive pickup. The inductive pickup clamps around the No. 1 spark plug wire, sensing the surges of high voltage electricity as they are sent to the plug. The advantage is that no mechanical connection is inserted between the wire and the plug, which eliminates false signals to the timing light. A timing light with an inductive pickup should be used on electronic ignition systems

ADJUSTMENT

CAUTION

Always apply parking brake and block wheels before performing any engine running tests.

2.2L and 2.6L Engines

See Figures 19, 20, 21 and 22

1. Clean off the timing marks.
2. Mark the pulley or damper notch and the timing scale with white chalk or paint. If the timing notch on the damper or pulley is not visible, bump the engine around with the starter or turn the crankshaft with a wrench on the front pulley bolt to get it to an accessible position.
3. Connect a suitable inductive timing light to number one cylinder plug wire.
4. Connect a tachometer unit with the positive lead to the negative terminal of the coil and the negative lead to a known good engine ground. Select the tachometer appropriate cylinder position.
5. Warm the engine to normal operating temperature. Open the throttle and release to make sure the idle speed screw is against its stop, and not on fast idle.
6. On vehicles equipped with a carburetor switch, connect a jumper wire between the carburetor switch and ground to obtain specified rpm. Disconnect and plug the vacuum hose at the Spark Control Computer (SCC). (Refer to the specifications decal under the hood for specific instructions).

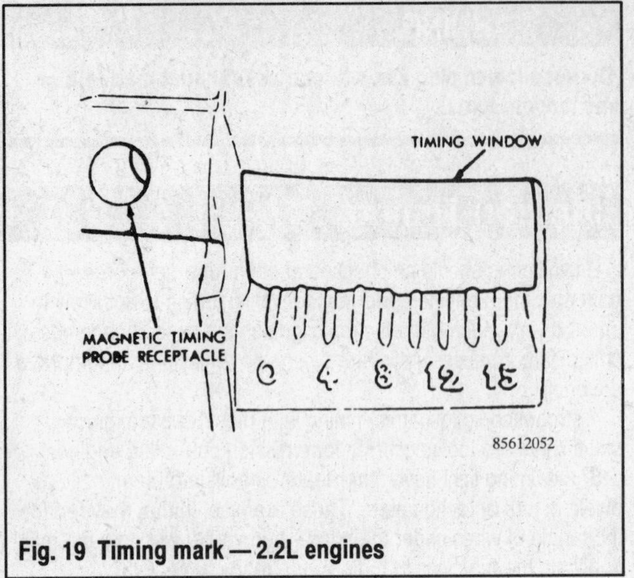

Fig. 19 Timing mark — 2.2L engines

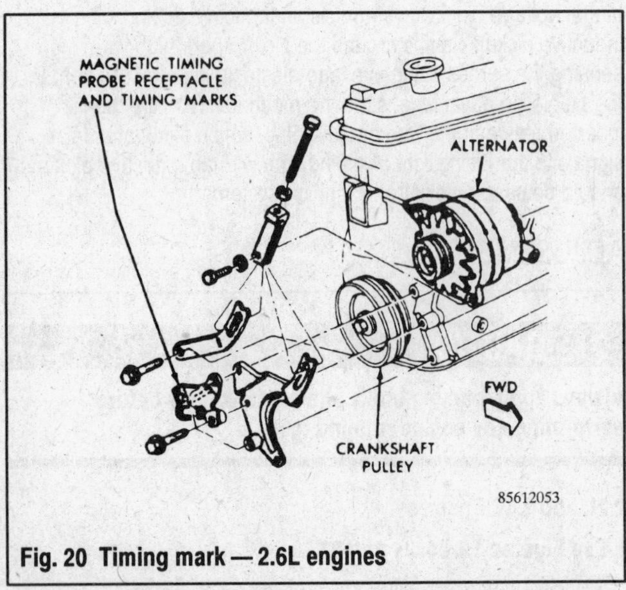

Fig. 20 Timing mark — 2.6L engines

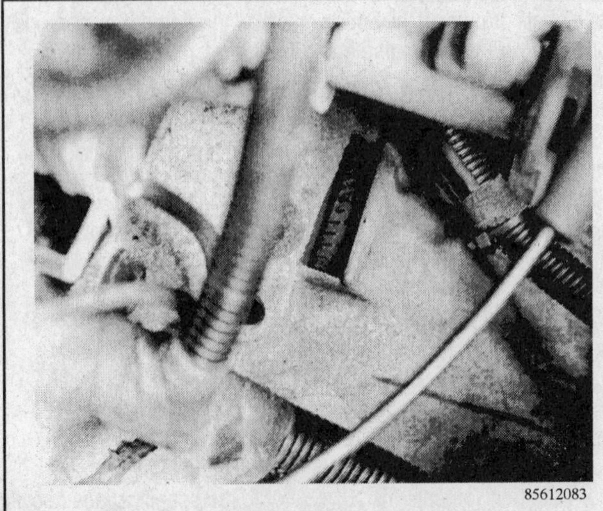

Fig. 21 Typical timing mark window

Fig. 22 Checking the timing with a timing light and adjusting by turning the distributor

7. Read the engine rpm on the tachometer's 1,000 rpm scale, and adjust the curb idle to the specification noted on the under hood label.

8. Aim the timing light toward the timing indicator, and read the degree marks. If the flash occurs when the timing mark is before the correct specification, timing is advanced. If the flash occurs when timing mark is after the correct specification, timing is retarded.

➜ Models equipped with the 2.2L engine have a notch on the torque converter or flywheel, with the numerical timing marks on the bell housing. Models equipped with the 2.6L engine have the timing marks on the front crankshaft pulley.

9. If adjustment is necessary, loosen the distributor hold-down screw. Turn the distributor slowly (while observing the timing marks with the timing light) until the timing mark is correctly aligned to the specified value. Once the timing is correct, tighten the hold-down screw. Recheck the timing and curb idle speed. If the curb idle speed has changed, readjust it to the specified value, then reset the ignition timing. Repeat the curb idle setting, and ignition timing until both are within specification.

10. Disconnect the timing light and install all vacuum hoses, if necessary.

11. Turn the engine off, then remove the jumper wire and tachometer.

2.5L and 3.0L Engines

➧ See Figures 23 and 24

1. Clean off the timing marks.
2. Mark the pulley or damper notch and the timing scale with white chalk or paint. If the timing notch on the damper or pulley is not visible, bump the engine around with the starter or turn the crankshaft with a wrench on the front pulley bolt to get it to an accessible position.
3. Connect a suitable inductive timing light to the No. 1 cylinder spark plug wire.
4. Connect a tachometer unit, positive lead to the negative terminal of the coil and the negative lead to a known good engine ground. Select the tachometer appropriate cylinder position.
5. Warm the engine to normal operating temperature.

6. With the engine at the normal operating temperature, disconnect the coolant temperature sensor. The radiator fan and instrument panel check engine lamp should come on. (See specifications decal under the hood for specific instructions).
7. Read the engine rpm on the tachometer's 1000 rpm scale. Adjust the curb idle to the specification noted on the underhood label.
8. Aim the timing light toward the timing indicator, and read the degree marks. If the flash occurs when the timing mark is before the specified value, timing is advanced. If the flash occurs when the timing mark is after the specification, timing is retarded.

Models equipped with the 2.5L engine have the timing marks visible through a window on the transaxle housing. Models equipped with the 3.0L engine have the timing marks on the front crankshaft pulley.

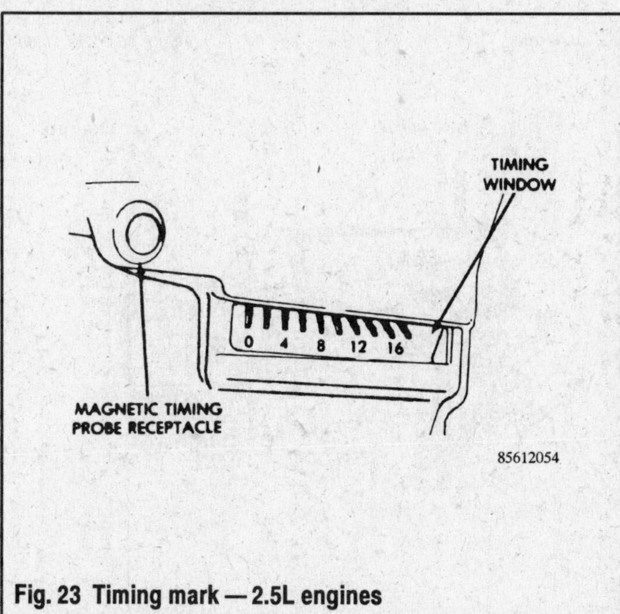

Fig. 23 Timing mark — 2.5L engines

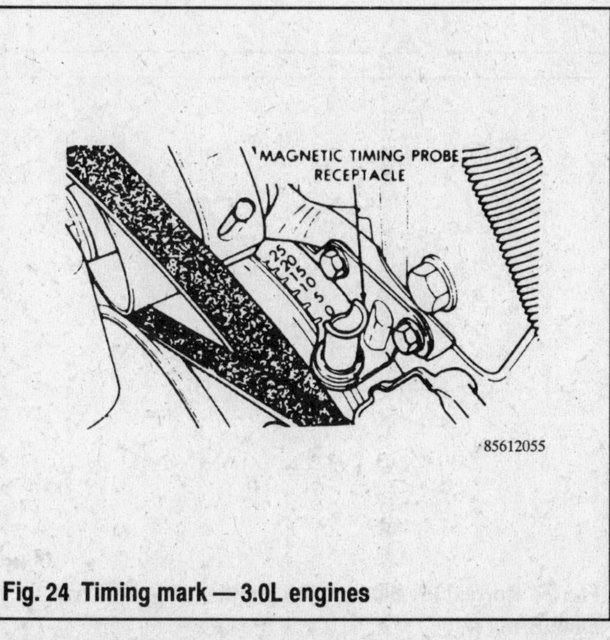

Fig. 24 Timing mark — 3.0L engines

9. If adjustment is necessary, loosen the distributor hold-down screw. Turn the distributor slowly to specified value, and tighten the hold-down screw. Recheck the ignition timing.
10. Turn the engine off. Remove the tachometer and timing light.
11. Connect the coolant temperature sensor.

Reconnecting the coolant temperature sensor will turn the check engine lamp off; however, a fault code will be stored in the SMEC. After 50 to 100 key on/off cycles the SMEC will cancel the fault code. The code can also be canceled by disconnecting the battery.

3.3L and 3.8L Engines

The 3.3L and 3.8L engine use an electronic distributorless ignition system. The ignition timing cannot be changed or set in any way.

Idle Speed

ADJUSTMENT

See Figures 25, 26, 27, 28, 29 and 30

****CAUTION**

Always apply the parking brake and block the wheels before performing idle adjustments, or any engine running tests.

Holley 5220/6520 Carburetors

2.2L ENGINES

1. Check and adjust the ignition timing.
2. Disconnect and plug the vacuum connector at the Coolant Vacuum Switch Cold Closed (CVSCC) located on the top of the thermostat housing.
3. Unplug the connector at the radiator fan and attach a jumper wire so that the cooling fan will run constantly. Remove the PCV valve from the engine and allow it to draw under hood air.
4. Connect a tachometer to the engine.
5. Ground the carburetor switch with a jumper wire.
6. On models equipped with a 6250 carburetor, unplug the oxygen system test connector on the left fender shield.
7. Start the engine and run until normal operating temperature is reached.
8. Turn the idle adjustment screw until required rpm is reached. (Refer to the Underhood Specification Label or Tune-Up Chart). Shut off the engine.
9. Reconnect the PCV valve, oxygen connector, vacuum connector (CVSCC) and remove the carburetor switch jumper. Remove the radiator fan jumper and reconnect the harness.

After Step 9 is completed, the idle speed might change. This is normal and the engine speed should not be readjusted.

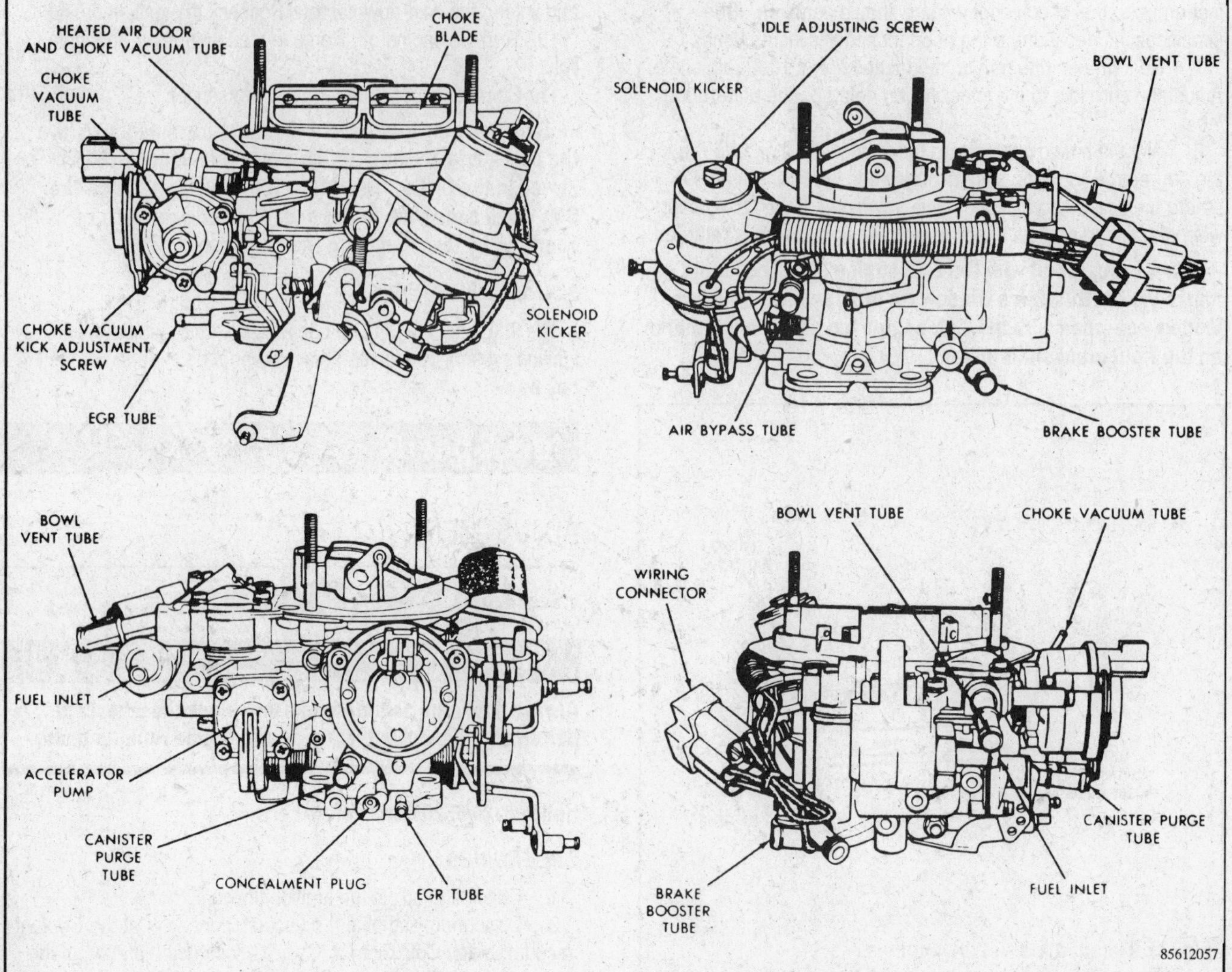

Fig. 25 Model 5220 carburetor

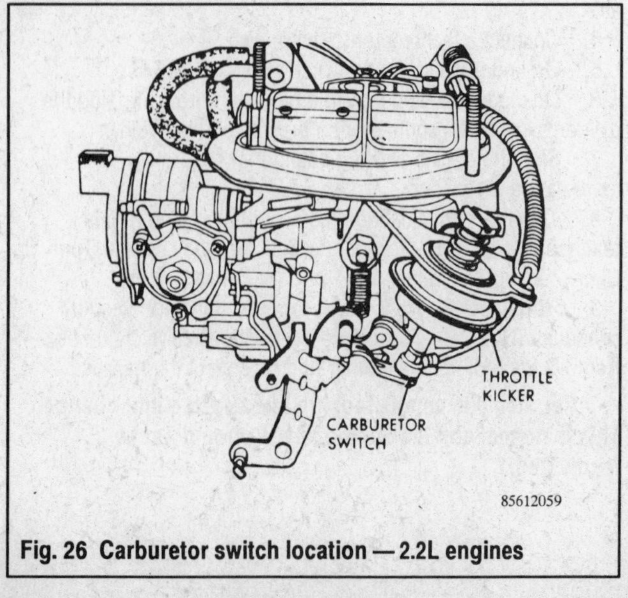

Fig. 26 Carburetor switch location — 2.2L engines

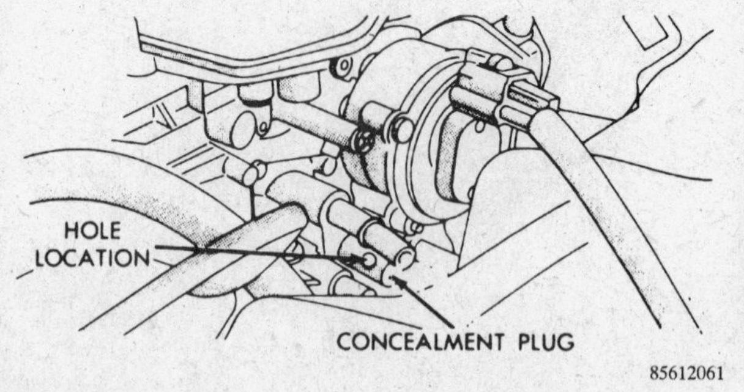

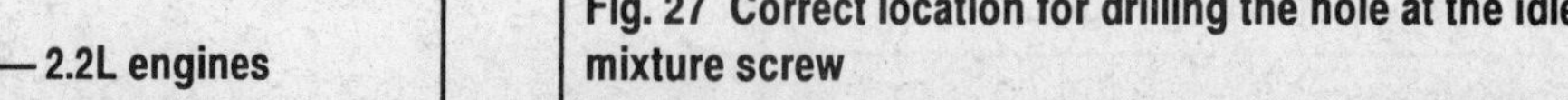

Fig. 27 Correct location for drilling the hole at the idle mixture screw

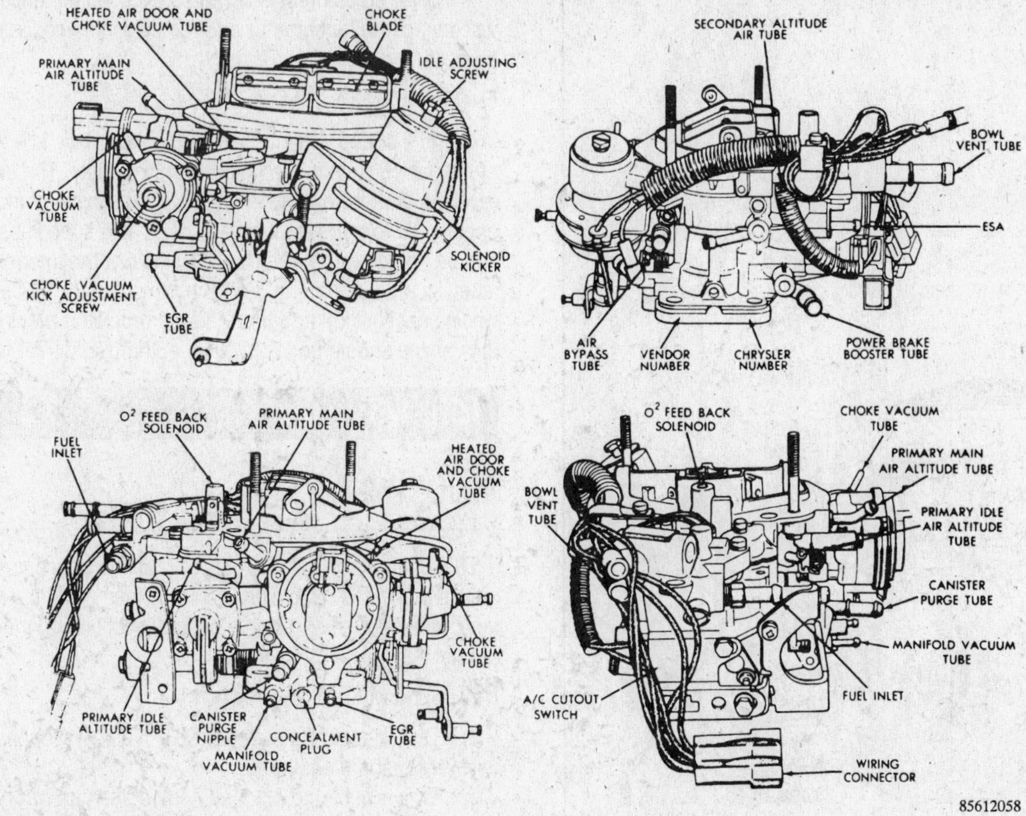

Fig. 28 Model 6520 carburetor

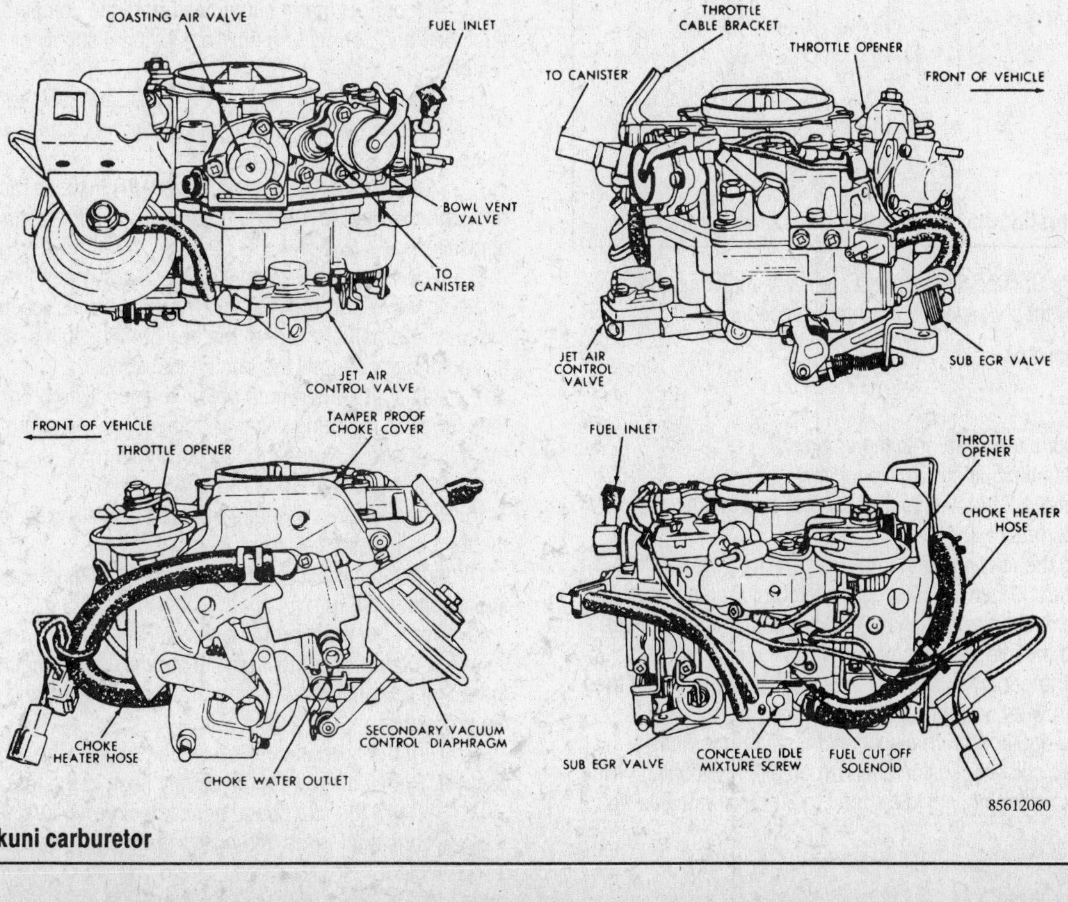

Fig. 29 Mikuni carburetor

Fig. 30 Adjusting the mixture using an Allen wrench

10. Refer to Section 5 for the fast idle, air conditioning idle speed check and choke kick adjustment procedures.

Mikuni Carburetor

2.6L ENGINES

1. Connect a tachometer to the engine.
2. Check and adjust the ignition timing.
3. Start and run the engine until normal operating temperature is reached.
4. Unplug the cooling fan harness connector.
5. Run at 2500 rpm for 10 seconds. Return the engine to idle.
6. Wait two minutes and check engine rpm indicated on the tachometer. If the idle speed is not within the specifications indicated on the underhood sticker or Tune-Up Chart, adjust the idle speed screw as necessary.
7. Models equipped with air condition, set temperature control lever to coldest position and turn on air conditioning. With the compressor running, set idle speed to 900 rpm with idle up screw.
8. After adjustment is complete, shut off the engine, disconnect the tachometer and reconnect the cooling fan harness.

Fuel Injected Engines

The idle speed is controlled by the Automatic Idle Speed (AIS) motor, which is controlled by the logic module. The logic module receives data from various sensors in the system and adjusts the engine idle to a predetermined speed. Idle speed specifications can be found on the Vehicle Emission Control Information (VECI) label, located in the engine compartment. If the idle speed is not within specification and there are no problems with the system, the vehicle should be taken to an authorized dealer for service.

Idle Mixture

ADJUSTMENT

The following procedure uses a propane enrichment method of adjusting the idle. Use extreme care when using the propane tank. Make sure that it is in a secure location and that the fittings are not leaking.

Holley and Mikuni Carburetors

1. Disconnect and plug the EGR hose. Disconnect the oxygen sensor, if equipped.
2. Disconnect and plug the hose at the canister.
3. Remove the PCV hose from the valve cover and allow it to draw under hood air.
4. Ground the carburetor switch with a jumper wire, if equipped.
5. Disconnect the vacuum hose from the computer, if equipped and connect an auxiliary vacuum supply of 16 in. Hg (54 kPa).
6. Remove the concealment plug. Disconnect the vacuum supply hose to the tee and install a propane supply hose in its place.
7. Make sure all accessories are **OFF**. Install a tachometer and start the engine. Allow the engine to run for 2 minutes to stabilize.
8. Open the main propane valve. Slowly open the propane metering valve until the maximum engine rpm is reached. When too much propane is added, the engine will begin to stumble; at this point back off until the engine stabilizes.
9. Adjust the idle rpm to obtain the specified propane rpm. Fine tune the metering valve to obtain the highest rpm again. If there has been a change to the maximum rpm, readjust the idle screw to the specified propane rpm.
10. Turn the main propane valve off and allow the engine to run for 1 minute to stabilize.
11. Adjust the mixture screw to obtain the smoothest idle at the specified idle rpm.
12. Open the main propane valve. Fine tune the metering valve to obtain the highest rpm. If the maximum engine speed is more that 25 rpm different than the specified propane rpm, repeat the procedure.
13. Turn the propane valves off and remove the propane canister. Reinstall the vacuum supply hose to the tee.
14. Perform the idle speed adjustment procedure.
15. Connect all wires and hoses that were previously disconnected.

Valve Lash

Valve lash adjustment determines how far the valves enter the cylinder, and how long they stay open and closed.

If the valve clearance is too large, part of the lift of the camshaft will be used in removing the excess clearance. Consequently, the valve will not be opening as far as it should. This condition has two effects: the valve train components will emit a tapping sound as they take up the excessive clearance and the engine will perform poorly because the valves does not open fully and allow the proper amount of gases to flow in and out of the engine.

If the valve clearance is too small, the intake valve and the exhaust valves will open too far and they will not fully seat on the cylinder head when they close. As a result, the valves will also become overheated and will warp, since they cannot transfer heat unless they are touching the valve seat in the cylinder head.

While all valve adjustments must be made as accurately as possible, it is better to have the valve adjustment slightly loose then slightly tight as a burned valve may result from overly tight adjustments.

ADJUSTMENT

Valve adjustment must be performed after any engine overhaul or when the valve train components emit a tapping sound requiring valve adjustment service.

****CAUTION**

Always apply the parking brake and block the wheels before performing any engine running tests.

2.2L, 2.5L, 3.0L, 3.3L and 3.8L Engines

The 2.2L, 2.5L, 3.0L, 3.3 and 3.8L engines use hydraulic lash adjusters. No periodic adjustment or checking is necessary.

2.6L Engines

WITH JET VALVES

See Figure 31

A jet valve is added on some models. The jet valve adjuster is located on the intake valve rocker arm and must be adjusted before the intake valve.

1. Start the engine and allow it to reach normal operating temperature.
2. Stop the engine and remove the air cleaner and its hoses. Remove any other cables, hoses, wires, etc., which are attached to the valve cover, remove the valve cover.
3. Disconnect the high tension coil-to-distributor wire at the distributor, and allow it to contact a known good engine ground.
4. Tighten the cylinder head bolts in the correct sequence and to the specified torque value. For more details, refer to Section 3.
5. Have a helper bump the ignition switch. Watch the rocker arms until piston No. 4 cylinder is at Top Dead Center (TDC) and adjust jet valves as follows:
   a. Back out the intake valve adjusting screw two or three turns.
   b. Loosen the locknut on the jet valve and back out the jet valve adjusting screw.
   c. Install a 0.005 in. (0.15mm) feeler gauge between the jet valve stem and the jet valve adjusting screw.
   d. Turn in the jet valve adjusting screw until it slightly makes contact with the jet valve stem. While holding the jet valve adjusting screw in place, tighten the jet valve locknut. Recheck the clearance.
6. Complete the adjustment by adjusting intake and exhaust valve clearance on the same cylinder as the jet valve you've finished. Refer to Valve Clearance Specification Chart.

WITHOUT JET VALVES

1. Start the engine and allow it to reach normal operating temperature.
2. Stop the engine and remove the air cleaner and its hoses. Remove any other cables, hoses, wires, etc., which are attached to the valve cover, remove the valve cover.
3. Disconnect the high tension coil-to-distributor wire at the distributor, and allow it to contact a known good engine ground.
4. Tighten the cylinder head bolts in the correct sequence and to the specified torque value. For more details, refer to Section 3.
5. Have a helper bump the ignition switch. Watch the rocker arms until the piston is at Top Dead Center (TDC) of the compression stroke (both valves closed).
6. Loosen the valve adjuster locknut. Back out the valve adjusting screw and install a feeler gauge between the adjusting screw and valve stem.
7. Turn in the valve adjusting screw until it slightly touches the feeler gauge. While holding the adjusting screw in place, tighten the adjusting screw locknut. Refer to the Valve Clearance Specification Chart.
8. Perform Steps 5–7 on the remaining three cylinders.

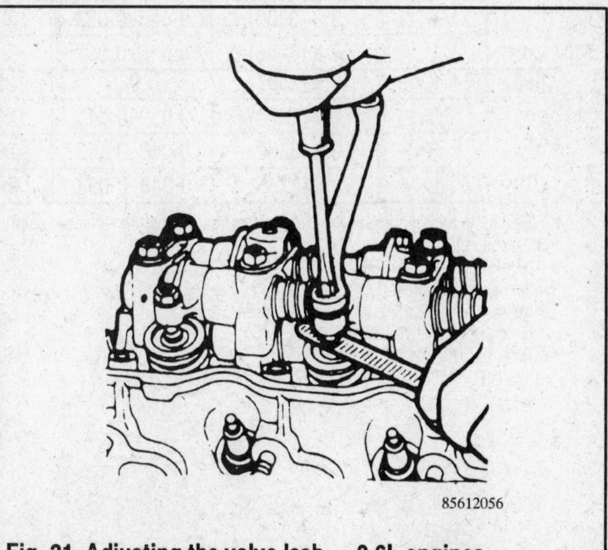

Fig. 31 Adjusting the valve lash — 2.6L engines

GASOLINE ENGINE TUNE-UP SPECIFICATIONS

Year	Engine ID/VIN	Engine Displacement Liters (cc)	Spark Plug Gap (in.)	Ignition Timing (deg.)		Fuel Pump (psi)	Idle Speed (rpm)		Valve Clearance	
				MT	AT		MT	AT	In.	Ex.
1984	C	2.2 (2212)	0.035	6B	6B	3-4	850	900	Hyd.	Hyd.
	G	2.6 (2556)	0.039-0.043	7B	7B	4.6-6.0	800	800	Hyd. ①	Hyd. ①
1985	C	2.2 (2212)	0.035	6B	6B	3-4	850	900	Hyd.	Hyd.
	G	2.6 (2556)	0.039-0.043	7B	7B	4.6-6.0	800	800	Hyd. ①	Hyd. ①
1986	C	2.2 (2212)	0.035	6B	6B	3-4	850	900	Hyd.	Hyd.
	G	2.6 (2556)	0.039-0.043	7B	7B	4.6-6.0	800	800	Hyd. ①	Hyd. ①
1987	C	2.2 (2212)	0.035	6B	6B	4.5-6.0	850	900	Hyd.	Hyd.
	G	2.6 (2556)	0.039-0.043	7B	7B	3-4	800	800	Hyd. ①	Hyd. ①
	K	2.5 (2507)	0.035	12B	12B	13.5-15.5	850	850	Hyd.	Hyd.
	3	3.0 (2972)	0.039-0.043	12B	12B	12-16	800	800	Hyd.	Hyd.
1988	K	2.5 (2507)	0.035	12B	12B	13.5-15.5	850	850	Hyd.	Hyd.
	3	3.0 (2972)	0.039-0.043	12B	12B	46-50	800	800	Hyd.	Hyd.
1989	K	2.5 (2507)	0.035-0.043	12B	12B	13.5-15.5	850	850	Hyd.	Hyd.
	J	2.5 (2507)	0.035-0.043	12B	12B	13.5-15.5	850	850	Hyd.	Hyd.
	3	3.0 (2972)	0.039-0.043	12B	12B	46-50	800	800	Hyd.	Hyd.
1990	K	2.5 (2507)	0.035-0.043	12B	12B	13.5-15.5	850	850	Hyd.	Hyd.
	3	3.0 (2972)	0.039-0.043	12B	12B	46-50	800	800	Hyd.	Hyd.
	R	3.3 (3300)	0.048-0.053	②	②	46-50	750	750	Hyd.	Hyd.
1991	K	2.5 (2507)	0.035	12B	12B	37-41	850	850	Hyd.	Hyd.
	3	3.0 (2972)	0.039-0.043	12B	12B	46-50	800	800	Hyd.	Hyd.
	R	3.3 (3300)	0.048-0.053	②	②	46-50	750	750	Hyd.	Hyd.
1992	K	2.5 (2507)	0.035	12B	12B	37-41	850	850	Hyd.	Hyd.
	3	3.0 (2972)	0.039-0.043	12B	12B	46-50	800	800	Hyd.	Hyd.
	R	3.3 (3300)	0.048-0.053	②	②	46-50	750	750	Hyd.	Hyd.
1993	K	2.5 (2507)	0.035	12B	12B	37-41	850	850	Hyd.	Hyd.
	3	3.0 (2972)	0.039-0.043	12B	12B	46-50	800	800	Hyd.	Hyd.
	R	3.3 (3300)	0.048-0.053	②	②	46-50	750	750	Hyd.	Hyd.
1994	K	2.5 (2507)	0.035	12B	12B	37-41	850	850	Hyd.	Hyd.
	3	3.0 (2972)	0.039-0.043	12B	12B	46-50	800	800	Hyd.	Hyd.
	R	3.3 (3300)	0.048-0.053	②	②	46-50	750	750	Hyd.	Hyd.
	L	3.8 (3785)	0.048-0.053	②	②	46-50	③	③	Hyd.	Hyd.
1995	K	2.5 (2507)	0.035	12B	12B	37-41	850	850	Hyd.	Hyd.
	3	3.0 (2972)	0.039-0.043	12B	12B	46-50	800	800	Hyd.	Hyd.
	R	3.3 (3300)	0.048-0.053	②	②	46-50	750	750	Hyd.	Hyd.
	L	3.8 (3785)	0.048-0.053	②	②	46-50	③	③	Hyd.	Hyd.

NOTE: The Vehicle Emission Control Information label often reflects specification changes made during production. The label figures must be used if they differ from those in this chart.

B—Before Top Dead Center

① Jet valve clearance: 0.010 in. (hot)

② Ignition timing cannot be adjusted; base engine timing is set at TDC during assembly

③ Refer to the Vehicle Emission Control Information (VECI) label for correct specification

85612C01

FIRING ORDERS

See Figures 32, 33, 34, 35 and 36

To avoid confusion, remove and tag the wires one at a time, for replacement.

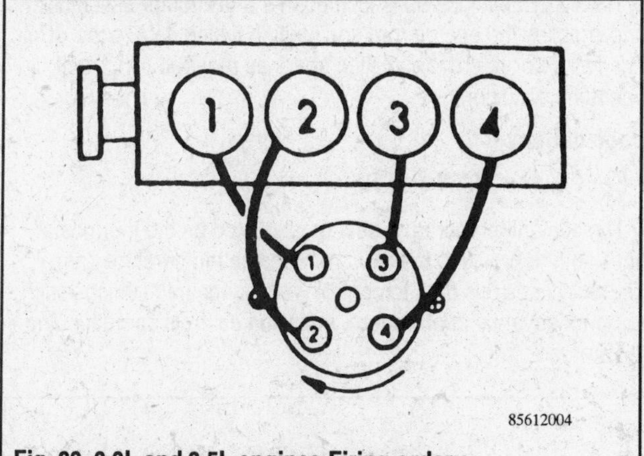

Fig. 32 2.2L and 2.5L engines Firing order: 1-3-4-2Distributor rotation: Clockwise

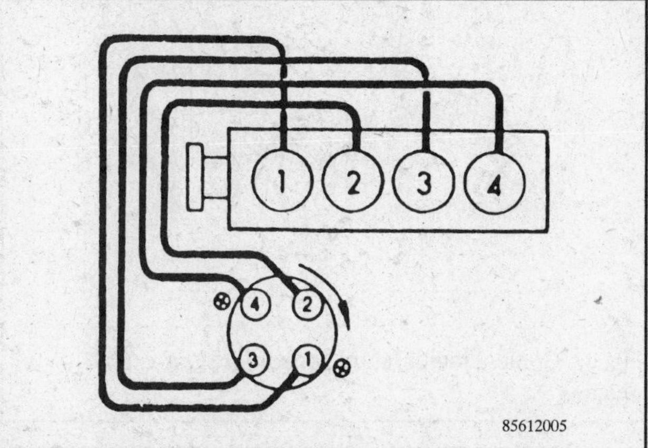

Fig. 33 2.6L engines Firing order: 1-3-4-2Distributor rotation: Clockwise

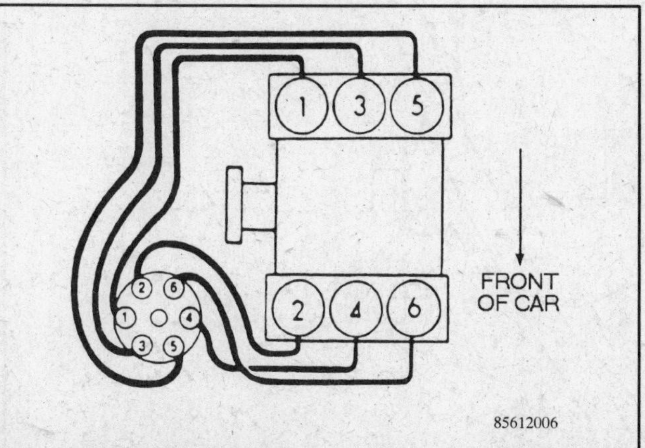

Fig. 34 3.0L engines Firing order: 1-2-3-4-5-6Distributor rotation: Counterclockwise

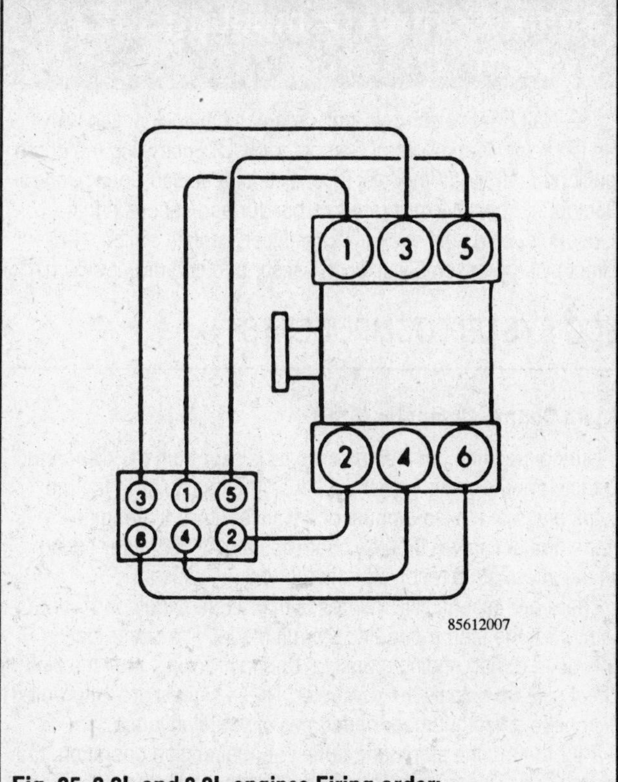

Fig. 35 3.3L and 3.8L engines Firing order: 1-2-3-4-5-6Distributorless Ignition System

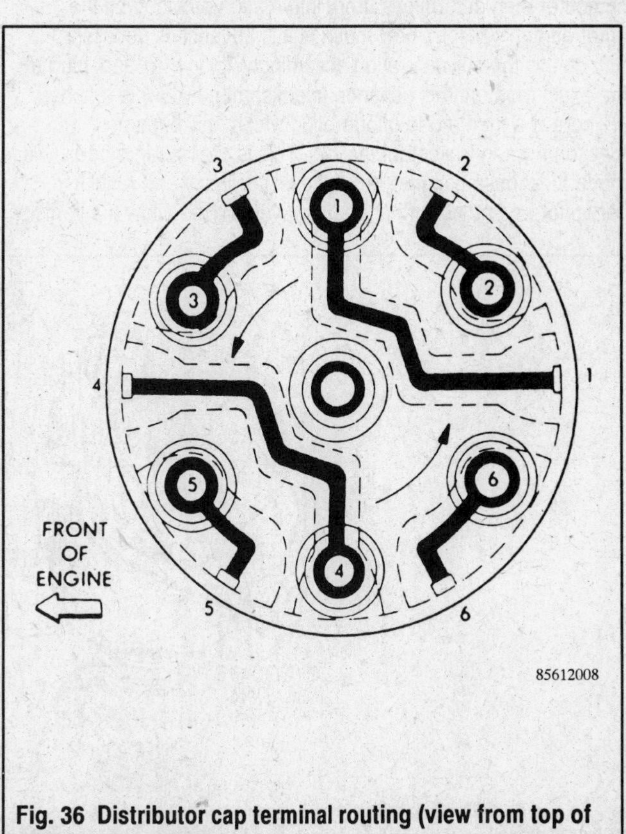

Fig. 36 Distributor cap terminal routing (view from top of cap) — 3.0L engines

CHRYSLER HALL EFFECT ELECTRONIC IGNITION

Spark Control Computer (SCC) System

The Hall Effect electronic ignition is used in conjunction with the Chrysler Spark Control Computer (SCC) controlling the entire ignition on 1984–87 models. It consists of a sealed Spark Control Computer, specially calibrated carburetor and various engine sensors, such as the vacuum transducer, coolant switch, Hall Effect pick-up assembly, oxygen sensor and carburetor switch.

SCC SYSTEM COMPONENTS

Spark Control Computer (SCC)

During cranking, an electrical signal is sent from the distributor to the computer. This signal will cause the computer to fire the spark plugs at a fixed amount of advance. Once the engine starts, the timing will then be controlled by the computer based on the information received from the various sensors.

There are essentially 2 modes of operation of the spark control computer: the start mode and the run mode. The start mode is only used during engine cranking. During cranking, only the Hall Effect pick-up signals the computer. These signals are interpreted to provide a fixed number of degrees of spark advance.

After the engine starts and during normal engine operation, the computer functions in the run mode. In this mode, the Hall Effect pick-up serves as only one of the signals to the computer. It is a reference signal of maximum possible spark advance. The computer then determines, from information provided by the other engine sensors, how much of this advance is necessary and delays the coil saturation accordingly, firing the spark plug at the exact moment this advance (crankshaft position) is reached.

There is a third mode of operation which only becomes functional when the computer fails. This is the limp-in mode. This mode functions on signals from the pick-up only and results in very poor engine performance. However, it does allow the vehicle to be driven to a repair shop. If a failure occurs in the pick-up assembly or the start mode of the computer, the engine will neither start nor run.

Hall Effect Pick-Up

The Hall Effect pick-up is located in the distributor assembly and supplies the engine rpm and ignition timing data to the SCC to advance or retard the ignition spark as required by current operating conditions.

Coolant Sensor

➧ See Figures 37, 38 and 39

The coolant temperature sensor is located on the thermostat housing and provides the SCC with engine temperature data. The SCC uses this data to control various engine functions such as spark advance, fuel mixture, emission controls operation and radiator fan.

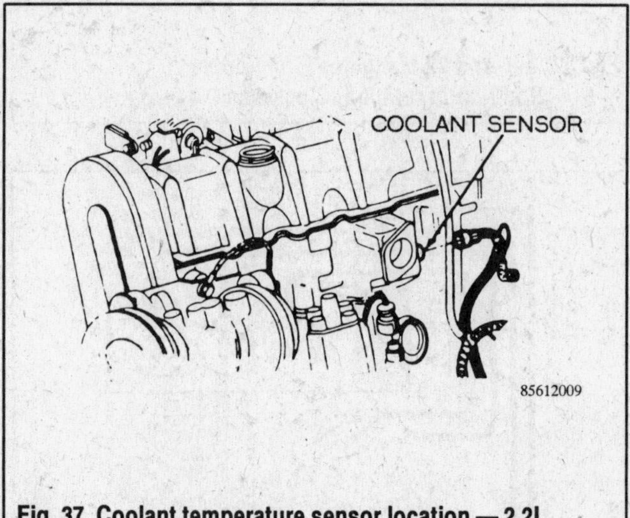

Fig. 37 Coolant temperature sensor location — 2.2L engines

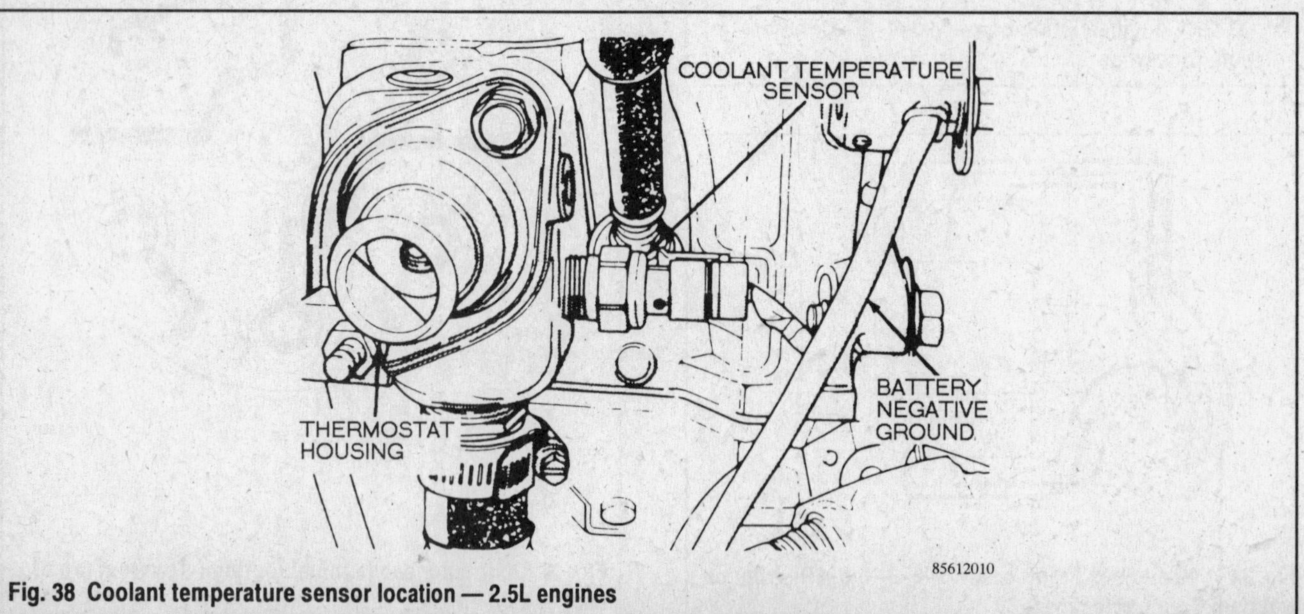

Fig. 38 Coolant temperature sensor location — 2.5L engines

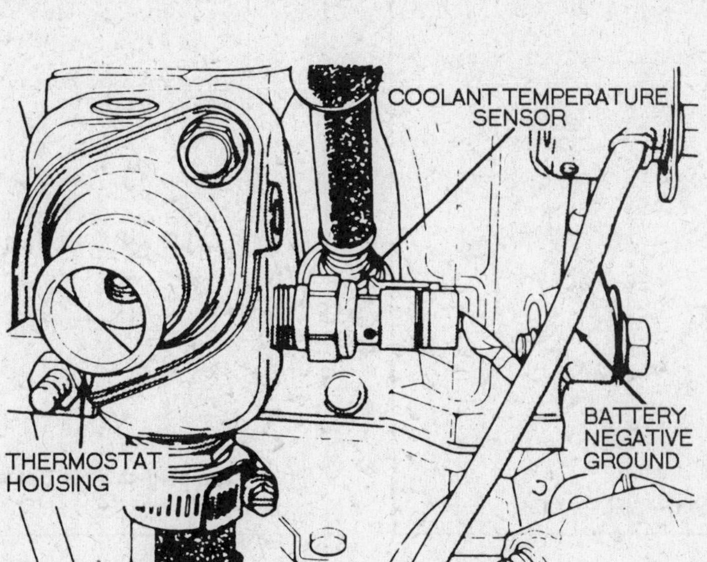

Fig. 39 Coolant temperature sensor location — 3.0L engines

Vacuum Sensor

➧ See Figure 40

The vacuum transducer is located on the Spark Control Computer (SCC) and informs the SCC as to the manifold vacuum during operation. The engine vacuum is one of the factors that will determine how the computer will advance/retard the ignition timing, and with the feedback carburetor, how the air/fuel ration will be changed.

Carburetor Switch

➧ See Figure 41

The carburetor switch is located on the left side of the carburetor; it provides the SCC with throttle open or throttle closed signal.

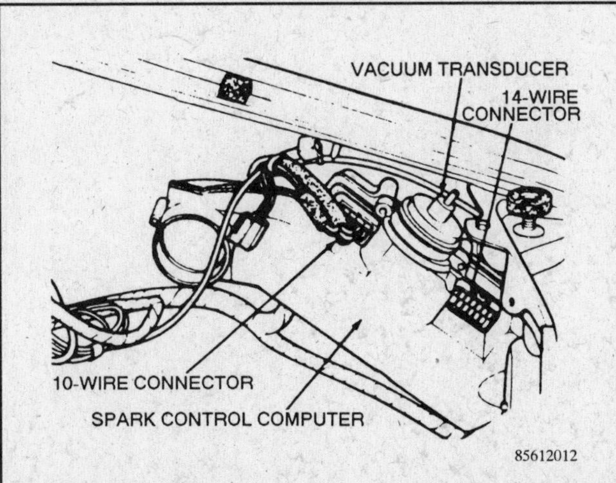

Fig. 40 Spark control vacuum transducer location — 2.2L engines

Oxygen Sensor

➧ See Figure 42

The oxygen sensor (used with feedback carburetors) is located in the exhaust manifold and signals the computer how much oxygen is present in the exhaust gases. Since this amount is proportional to rich and lean mixtures, the computer will adjust the air/fuel ration to a level which will maintain operating efficiency of the catalyst system and engine.

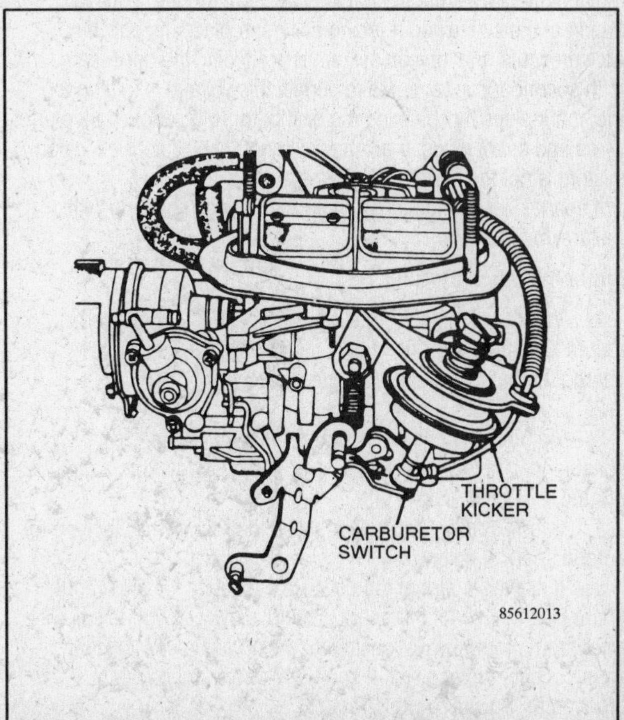

Fig. 41 Carburetor switch location — 2.2L engines

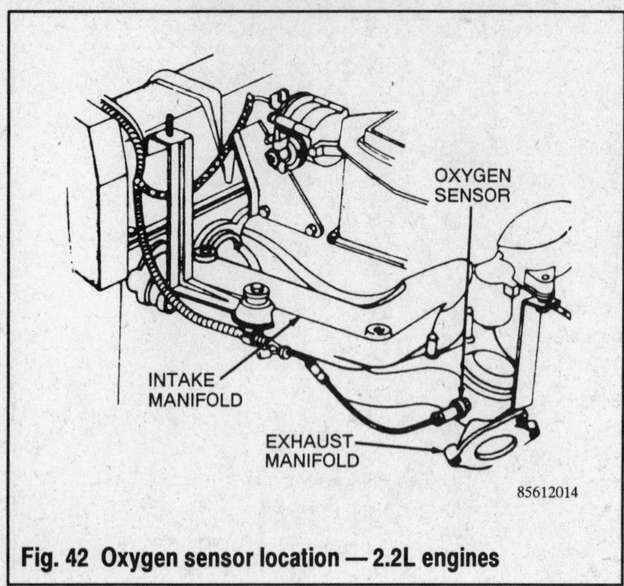

Fig. 42 Oxygen sensor location — 2.2L engines

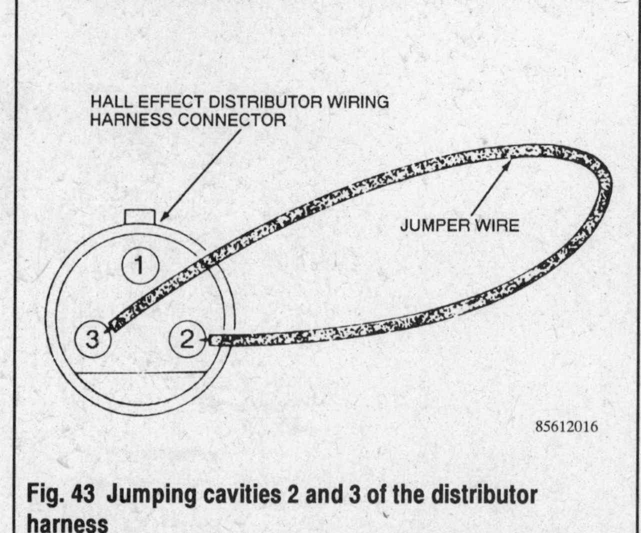

Fig. 43 Jumping cavities 2 and 3 of the distributor harness

SYSTEM DIAGNOSIS & TESTING

See Figures 43, 44 and 45

Apply the parking brake and block the wheels before performing any engine running tests, including idle or timing checks and adjustments.

Testing for Spark at Coil

Remove the coil secondary cable from the distributor cap. Using a suitable tool, hold the end of the cable about 1/4 in. (5mm) from a good engine ground. Crank the engine and look for a good, constant spark at the coil secondary wire. If spark is constant, have a helper continue to crank the engine while moving the coil secondary cable away from ground. Look for arcing at the coil tower. If arcing occurs, replace the coil. If no arcing occurs, the ignition system is producing the necessary high secondary voltage. Make certain this voltage is getting to the spark plugs by checking the distributor rotor, cap, spark plug wires and spark plugs. If all check in good condition, the ignition system is not the cause of the problem.

If spark is weak, not constant or not present, continue with Failure To Start test.

Ignition System Starting Test

1. With a voltmeter, measure voltage at the battery and record it. Battery specific gravity must be 12.20. If if is not, charge the battery to specification.
2. Turn ignition switch **ON**.
3. Remove the coil wire from the distributor cap. Using a suitable tool, hold wire about a 1/4 in. (5mm) away from a good ground.
4. Intermittently jump coil negative to ground while looking for a good spark at coil wire.
5. If there is spark at the coil wire it must be constant and bright blue in color. If the spark is good, slowly move the coil wire away from ground while looking for arcing at the coil tower. If arcing occurs replace coil. If spark is weak or not constant, proceed to "Failure to Start Test".

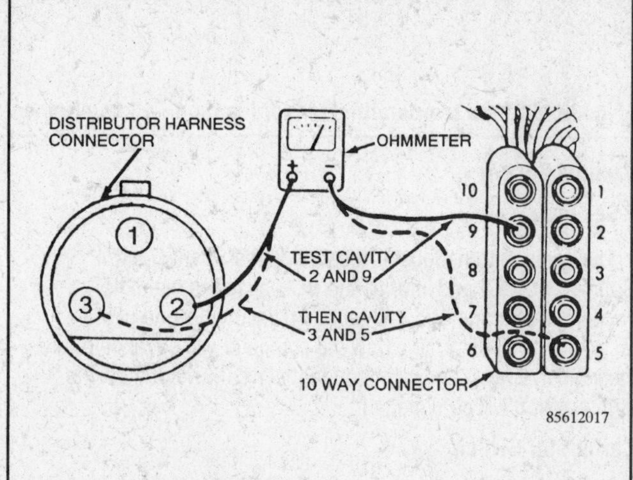

Fig. 44 Testing cavities 2 and 9, then cavities 3 and 5 for continuity

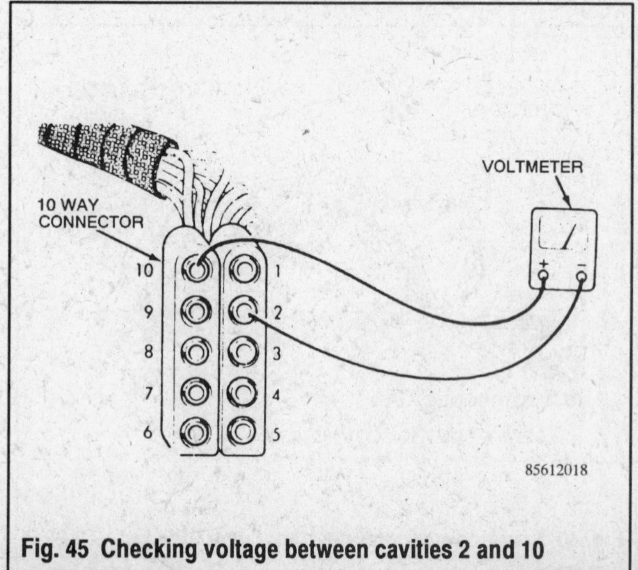

Fig. 45 Checking voltage between cavities 2 and 10

HALL EFFECT ELECTRONIC SPARK ADVANCE SYSTEM DIAGNOSIS

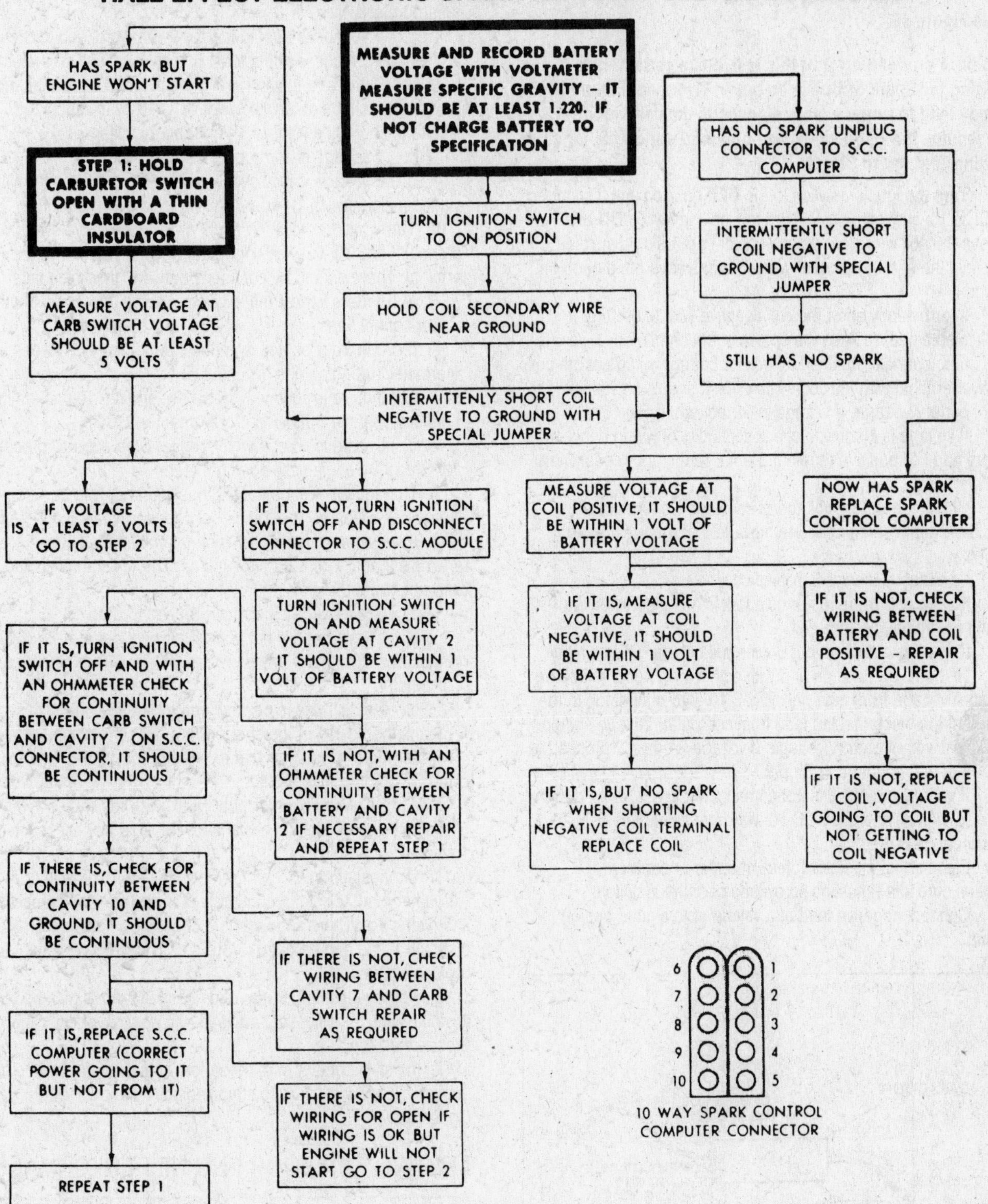

85612015

Failure to Start Test

See Figure 46

Before proceeding with this test, make certain that "Testing for Spark at Coil" has been performed. Failure to do so may lead to unnecessary diagnostic time and incorrect test results. If a good spark was obtained during the Ignition Starting Test, go to Step 8.

1. Turn the ignition switch to the **OFF** position and disconnect the SCC 10-way connector. Turn the ignition switch **ON** and remove the coil wire from the distributor cap. Using a suitable tool, hold the end of the wire $^1/_4$ in. (5mm) away from a good ground.
2. Intermittently short the coil negative wire to ground. If spark is obtained, replace the spark control computer.
3. If no spark is obtained, check for battery voltage at the coil positive terminal with ignition switch **ON**. It should be within 1 volt of battery voltage. If voltage is correct, go to Step 5.
4. If voltage is incorrect, check continuity of wiring between battery and coil positive terminal. Repair wiring and repeat Step 3.
5. Check for battery voltage at coil negative terminal, it should be within 1 volt of battery voltage. If it is correct go to Step 7.
6. If voltage is incorrect, replace coil.
7. If voltage is correct, but no spark is obtained when shorting negative terminal, replace coil.
8. If spark is obtained, but engine will not start, turn ignition switch to the **RUN**, position and with positive lead of a voltmeter, measure voltage from cavity 1 of SCC 10-way connector, to the ground of the disconnected lead from computer. Voltage should be within 1 volt of battery voltage. If voltage is correct, proceed to Step 10. If not, continue to Step 9.
9. If voltage in Step 8 is not correct, check wire for an open between the coil and the SCC 10-way connector. Repair wire and repeat Step 8.
10. Place a thin insulator (piece of paper or cardboard) between curb idle adjusting screw and carburetor switch.
11. Connect negative lead of a voltmeter to a good engine ground.

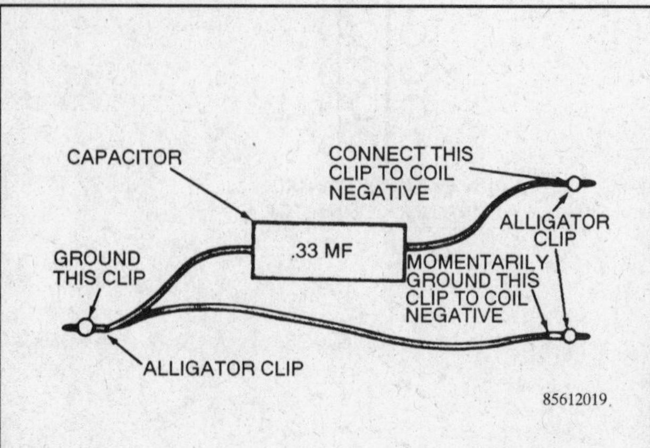

Fig. 46 Special jumper wire construction for grounding the coil

12. Turn ignition switch to **RUN** position and measure voltage at carburetor switch.
    a. If voltage is approximately 5 volts, proceed to Step 14.
    b. If voltage is not at least 5 volts, turn ignition switch to **OFF** position. Turn ignition switch back to **RUN** position and measure voltage at terminal 2 of SCC 10-way connector. Voltage should be within 1 volt of battery voltage.
    c. If voltage is correct, repeat Step 10.
    d. If voltage is incorrect, check wiring between terminal 2 and ignition switch for open, shorts or poor connections.
13. Turn ignition switch **OFF**, check for continuity between terminal 7 of SCC 10-way connector and carburetor switch terminal. There should be continuity between these 2 points.
    a. If there is no continuity, check wire for opens, shorts or poor connections.
    b. If there is continuity, check for continuity between terminal 10 and engine ground.
    c. If there is continuity between terminal 10 and engine ground, replace Spark Control Computer (SCC).
    d. If there is no continuity, repeat Step 13; only proceed to Step 14 if engine still does not start.
14. Turn ignition switch to **OFF** position and, with an ohm-meter, measure resistance between terminals 5 and 9 of SCC 10-way connector for run pick-up coil and between terminals 3 and 9 for start pick-up coil. The resistance should be between 150-900 ohms.
    a. If resistance is correct, proceed to Step 15.
    b. If resistance is not correct, disconnect pick-up coil leads from distributor. Measure resistance at lead going into distributor.
    c. If resistance is now between 150-900 ohms, this means there is an open, shorted, or poor connection between the distributor connector and terminals 5 and 9 or 3 and 9 of the SCC 10-way connector.
    d. Repair wire and repeat Step 14. If resistance is still out of specification, pick-up coil is bad. Replace pick-up coil and repeat Step 14.
15. Connect 1 lead of ohmmeter to an engine ground and, with other lead, check for continuity at each terminal lead going into distributor. There should be no continuity. Reconnect distributor lead and proceed to Step 16. If there is continuity, replace pick-up coil.
16. Remove distributor cap and check air gap of pick-up coil. If it is not within specification, adjust it. If it is within specification, proceed to Step 17.
17. Install distributor cap, reconnect all wiring and try to start engine. If engine still fails to start, replace Spark Control Computer.

TESTING FOR POOR ENGINE PERFORMANCE

Before performing test, make sure "Testing for Spark at Coil" has been carried out. Failure to do so may lead to unnecessary diagnostic time and incorrect test results.

Correct basic engine timing is essential for optimum vehicle performance and must be checked before any of the following testing procedures are performed. Refer to the individual vehicle section for ignition timing procedures and/or refer to the vehicle information label, located in the engine compartment.

Spark Control Computer System (SCC)

CARBURETOR SWITCH TEST

See Figure 47

Grounding carburetor switch lead wire will give a fixed air/fuel ratio.

1. With the ignition key **OFF**, unplug the 10-way dual connector from the computer.
2. With throttle completely closed, check continuity between cavity 7 of 10-way connector and a good ground. If there is no continuity, check wire and carburetor switch.
3. With throttle open, check continuity between cavity 7 of connector and a good ground. There should be no continuity.

COOLANT TEMPERATURE SENSOR TEST

See Figure 48

1. With the key in the **OFF** position, unplug the wire connector from the coolant sensor.
2. Connect 1 lead of ohmmeter to terminal 1 (common) of coolant sensor.

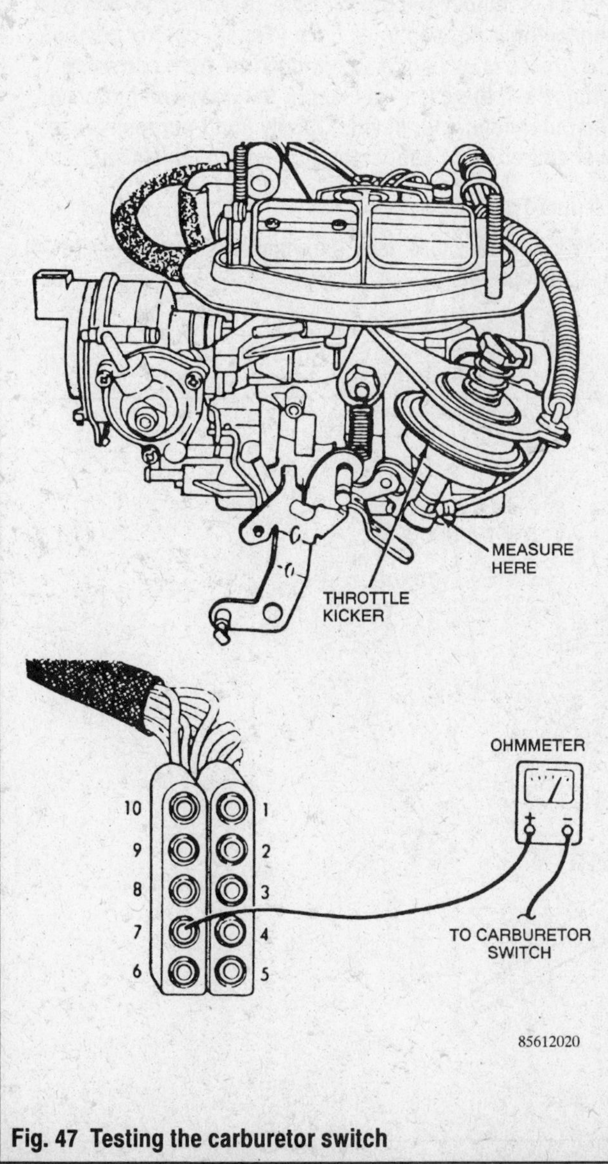

Fig. 47 Testing the carburetor switch

3. Connect other lead of ohmmeter to terminal 3 (fan control circuit).

Resistance between terminals 1 and 3 should be:

- Below 150°F (66°C): 20–200 ohms
- 150–200°F (66–93°C): 100–1500 ohms
- Above 200°F (93°C): 400–6000 ohms

4. Remove the ohmmeter lead from terminal 3.
5. Connect the ohmmeter lead to terminal 2 (SCC control circuit). Resistance between terminals 1 and 2 should be:

- 50–100°F (10–38°C): 3,300–36,000 ohms
- 140–245°F (60–118°C): 176–3,900 ohms

ELECTRONIC THROTTLE CONTROL SYSTEM

Incorporated within the spark control computer is the electronic throttle system. A solenoid, which regulates a vacuum dash-pot is energized when the air conditioner or electronic timers are activated. The 2 timers, incorporated within the ignition electronics, operate when the throttle is closed, plus a time delay of 2 seconds or after an engine start condition. To test the system:

1. Connect a tachometer to engine.
2. Start engine and run it until it reaches normal operating temperature.
3. Depress accelerator and release it. A higher than curb idle speed should be seen for a specified time.
4. On vehicles equipped with A/C, a slight decrease in idle speed will be noted when A/C is turned on; turning off the A/C will produce normal idle speed.

The A/C clutch will cycle on and off as the system is in operation. This should not be mistaken as part of the electronic control system.

5. As the A/C compressor clutch cycles on and off, the solenoid kicker plunger should extend and retract.
6. If the plunger does not move with the A/C clutch cycling or after a start-up, check the kicker system for vacuum leaks.
7. If the speed increases do not occur, disconnect the 6-way connector at carburetor.

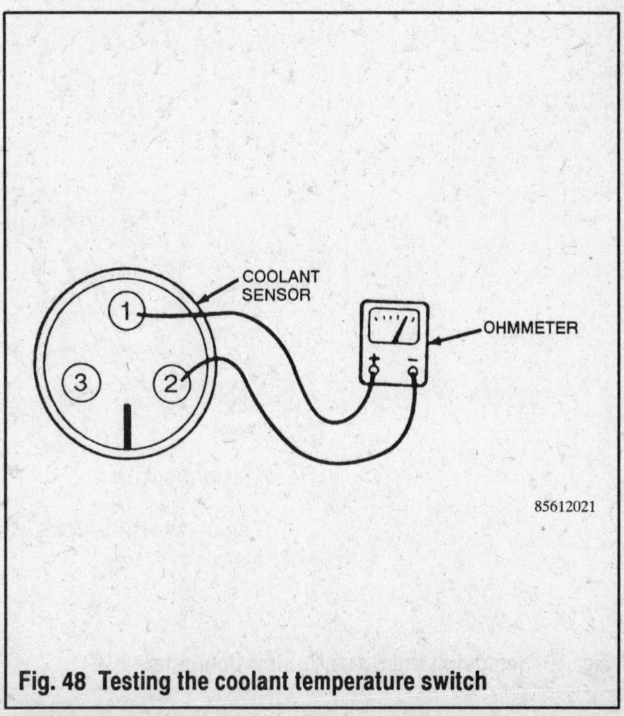

Fig. 48 Testing the coolant temperature switch

8. Check the solenoid with an ohmmeter by measuring resistance between the terminal that contains the black wire and ground. Resistance should be between 20–100 ohms. If not within specifications, replace the solenoid.

9. Start the vehicle and before time delay has timed out, measure the voltage across the vacuum solenoid terminals. The voltage should be within 2 volts of charging system voltage. If not within specifications, replace the computer.

10. Turning A/C on should also produce charging system voltage after time delay has timed out. If not, check wiring back to instrument panel for an open circuit.

SPARK ADVANCE OF SPARK CONTROL COMPUTER

Incorporated in the digital microprocessor electronics are some unique spark advance schedules, which will occur during cold and warm engine operation. These commands have been added to reduce engine emissions and improve driveability. Because they will be changing at different engine operating temperatures during the engine warm-up, all spark advance testing should be done with the engine at normal operating temperature.

1. Adjust the basic timing to specifications.
2. Have engine at normal operating temperature. The coolant temperature sensor must be connected and operating correctly.
3. Remove and plug the vacuum hose at the vacuum transducer.
4. Connect an auxiliary vacuum supply to the vacuum transducer; draw and hold vacuum to 16 in Hg. (54 kPa).
5. Start and raise engine speed to 2000 rpm. Wait 1 minute and check specifications.

➔ The use of a metal exhaust tube is recommended for this test. Using rubber hose may result in a fire due to high temperatures and a long test period.

6. The advance specifications are in addition to basic advance. If correct advance is not obtained, replace spark plug control computer.

Spark Control Computer (SCC) System — Component Replacement

REMOVAL & INSTALLATION

Spark Control Computer (SCC)

➧ See Figures 49, 50, 51, 52, 53, 54, 55 and 56

1. Disconnect the negative battery cable.
2. unplug the 10–way, 14–way connectors and outside air duct from SCC. Remove vacuum line from transducer.
3. Remove the 4 mounting screws that hold the computer in place.

To install:

4. Install a new computer and secure the mounting screws.
5. Reconnect the vacuum line to the transducer, making sure the vacuum line is not pinched. Engage the dual connectors and outside air duct to SCC unit.

➔ Do not remove the grease from 10–way or 14–way dual connector or connector cavities in spark control computer. The grease is used to prevent moisture from corroding terminals. If there isn't at least 1/8 in. grease on bottom of computer connector cavities, apply multi-purpose grease over entire end of connector plug before reinstalling.

Vacuum Transducer

If vacuum transducer fails, the complete computer unit (SCC) must be replaced.

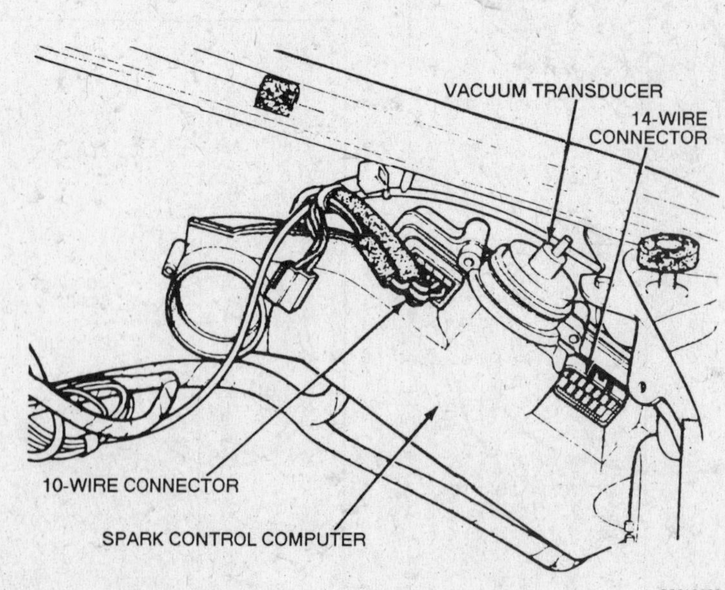

Fig. 49 Removing the Spark Control Computer (SCC)

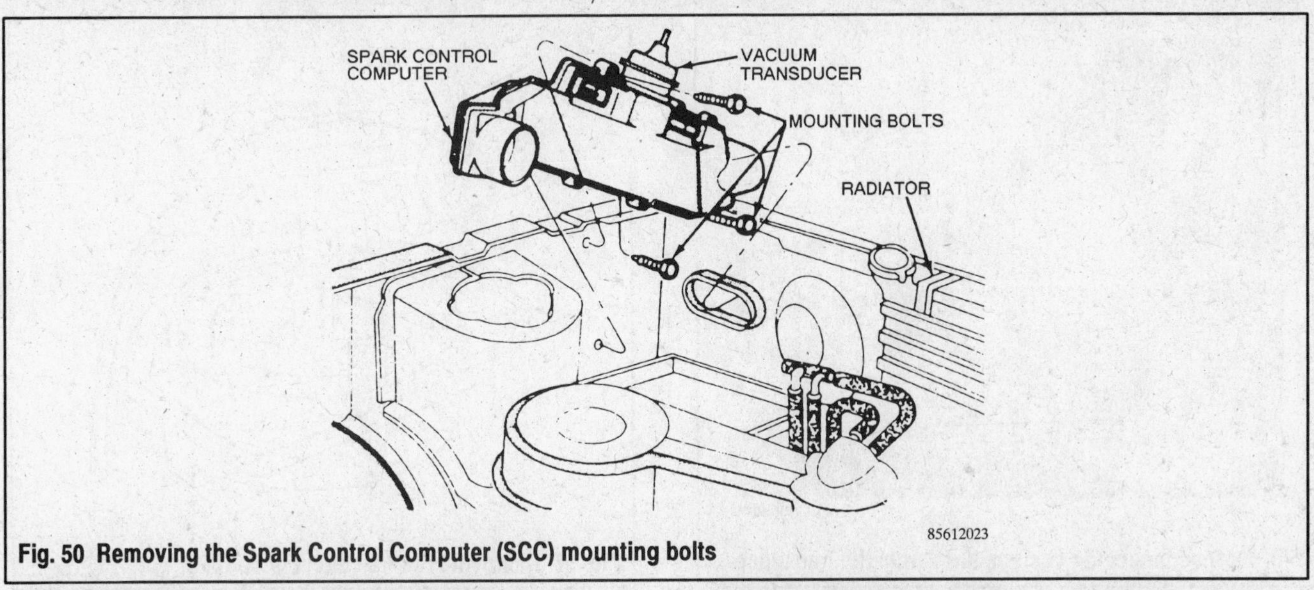

Fig. 50 Removing the Spark Control Computer (SCC) mounting bolts

Fig. 51 Disconnect the negative battery cable

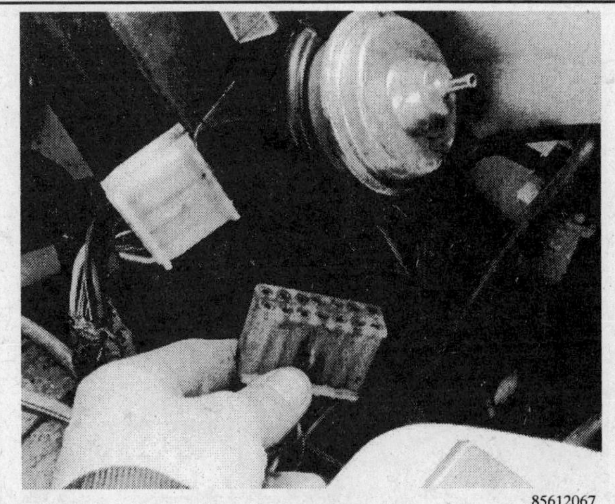

Fig. 53 Disconnect the 14-way connector from the controller assembly

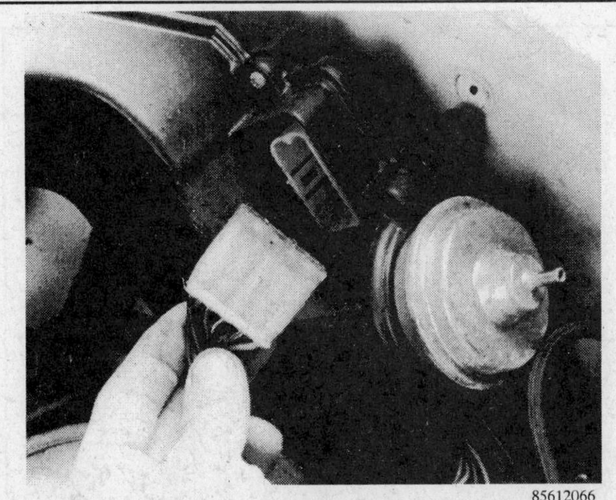

Fig. 52 Disconnect the 10-way connector from the controller assembly

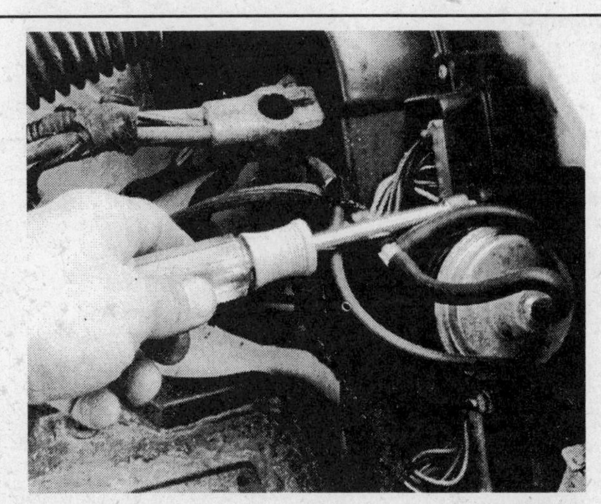

Fig. 54 Removing the bolts mounting the SCC to the inside of the fender

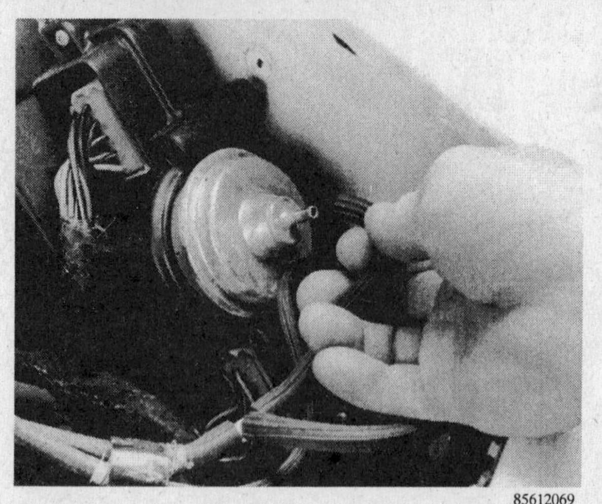
85612069

Fig. 55 Disconnect the vacuum lines from the transducer

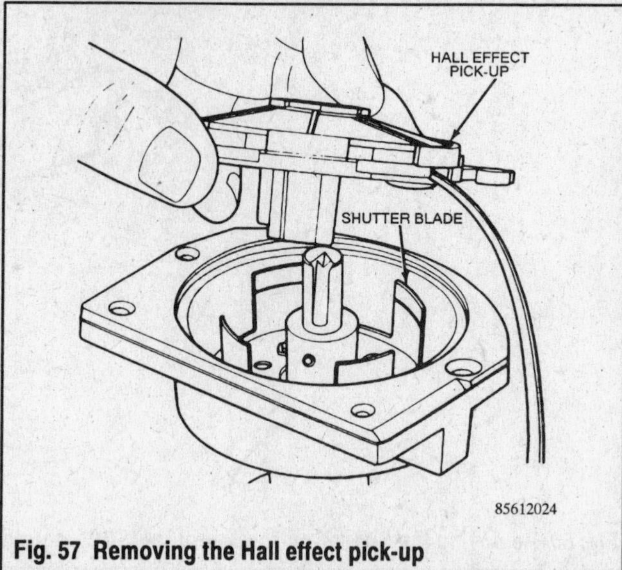

85612024

Fig. 57 Removing the Hall effect pick-up

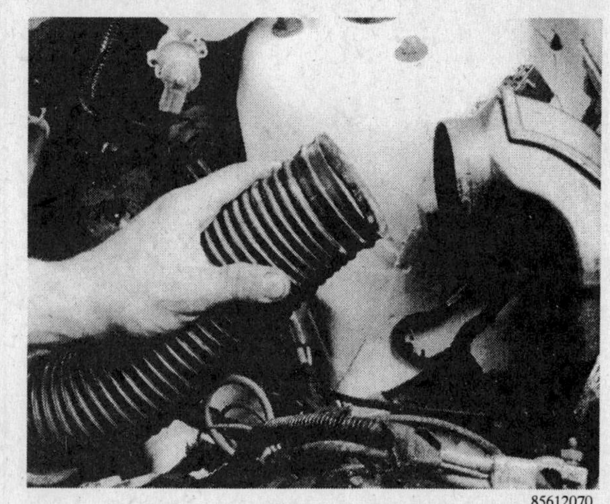
85612070

Fig. 56 Disconnect the outside air duct from the SCC

85612071

Fig. 58 Remove the distributor splash shield retaining bolts

Coolant Temperature Sensor

1. Unfasten the electrical connector from the sensor.
2. Remove the sensor from the engine. Some coolant may be lost from the system.

To install:

3. Install the new sensor and tighten to 20 ft lbs. (27 Nm).
4. Attach the electrical connector to the new sensor.
5. Replace any lost coolant.

Hall Effect Pick-Up

See Figures 57, 58, 59, 60, 61 and 62

1. Remove splash shield from distributor and remove distributor cap.
2. Pull straight up on rotor and remove it from shaft.
3. Remove Hall Effect pick-up assembly.

To install:

4. Install a new pick-up assembly onto distributor.

Hall Effect assembly wiring leads may be damaged if not properly reinstalled.

5. Install the distributor rotor.
6. Install the distributor cap and splash shield.

85612072

Fig. 59 Removing the distributor splash shield

Fig. 60 Removing the distributor cap with plug wires attached

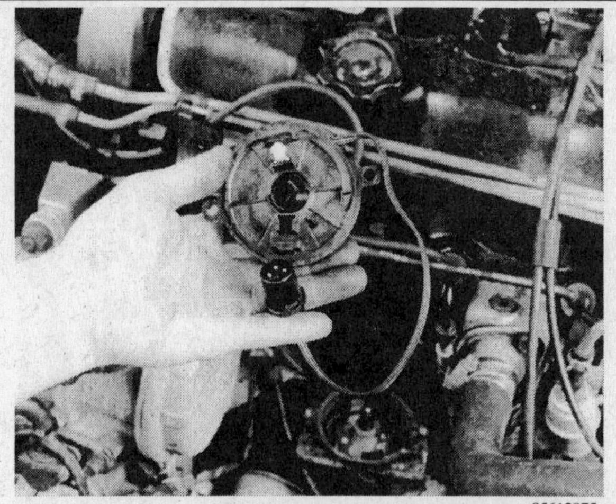

Fig. 62 Removing the Hall Effect pick-up assembly from the distributor

Fig. 61 After removing the distributor cap pull the rotor straight up and off the shaft

Distributor

➧ **See Figures 63, 64, 65, 66, 67, 68 and 69**

1. Disconnect the negative battery cable.
2. Disconnect the distributor pickup lead wires and vacuum hose(s), if equipped. Remove the splash shield, if equipped.
3. Unfasten the distributor cap retaining clips or screws and lift off the distributor cap with all ignition wires still connected. Remove the coil wire if necessary.
4. Matchmark the rotor to the distributor housing and the housing to the engine block.

➥ Do not crank the engine during this procedure. If the engine is cranked, the matchmark must be disregarded.

5. Remove the hold-down bolt and clamp.
6. Remove the distributor from the engine.
7. Remove and discard the O-ring.

To install:

8. Install a new distributor housing O-ring.

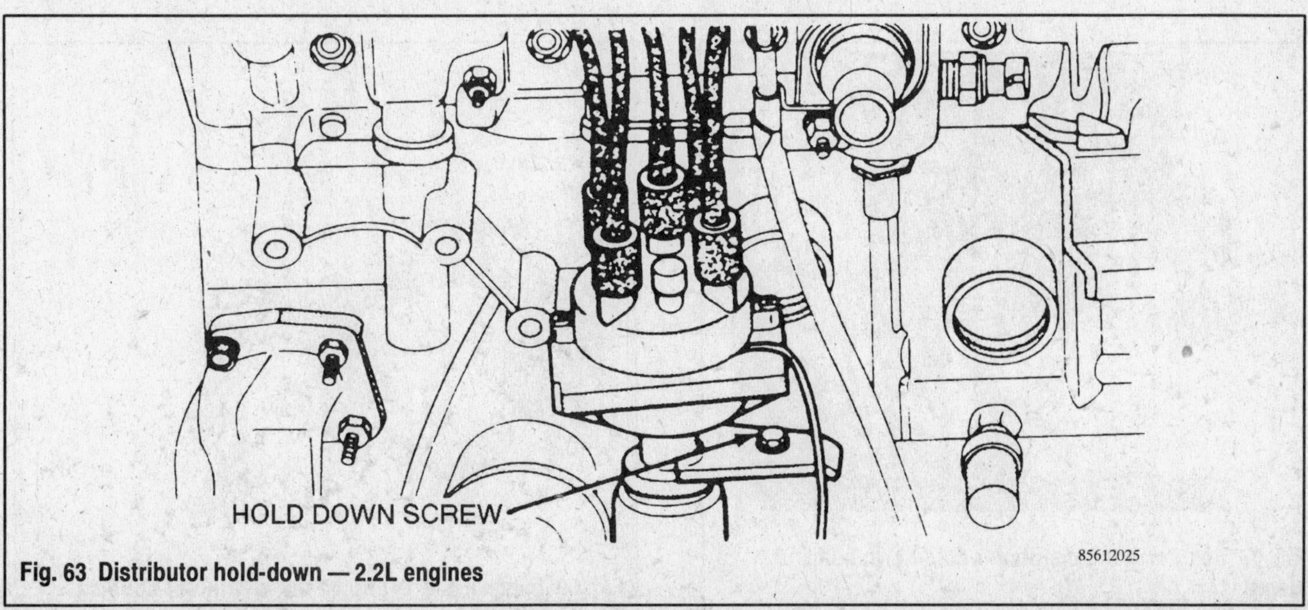

Fig. 63 Distributor hold-down — 2.2L engines

85612076

Fig. 64 Matchmark the rotor to the distributor housing

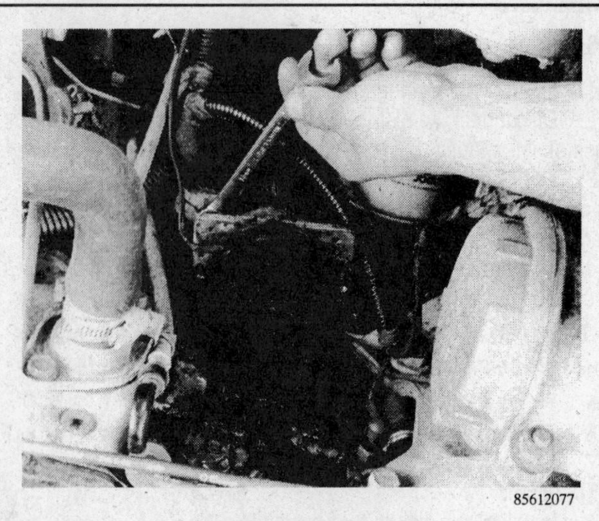

85612077

Fig. 65 Removing the distributor hold-down bolt

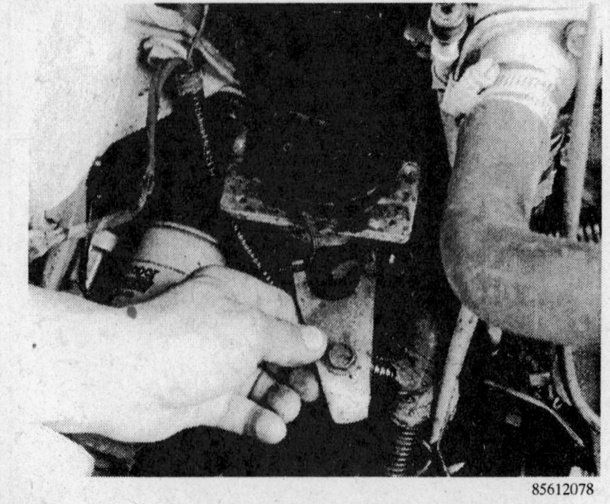

85612078

Fig. 66 Removing the distributor hold-down bolt and clamp

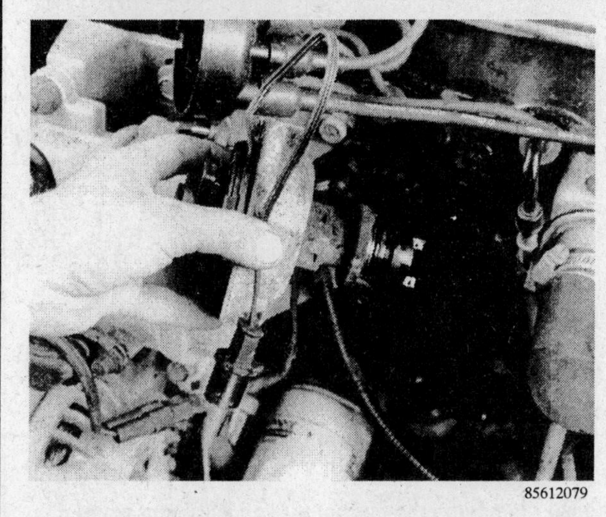

85612079

Fig. 67 Removing the distributor from the engine

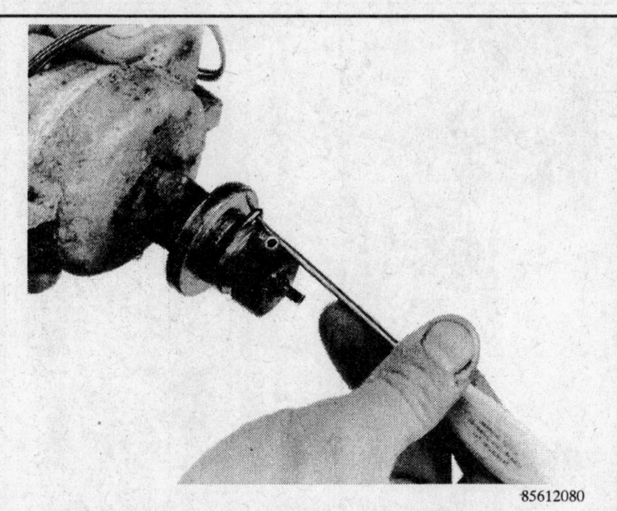

85612080

Fig. 68 Removing the distributor O-ring from the distributor housing

85612081

Fig. 69 Install a new O-ring on the distributor housing

9. Install the distributor in the engine so the rotor is lined up with the matchmark on the housing. Make sure the distributor is fully seated and that the distributor shaft is fully engaged.

10. If the engine has been cranked, position the engine so that the No. 1 piston is at TDC of the compression stroke and the mark on the vibration damper is lined up with **0** on the timing indicator. Then install the distributor so the rotor is aligned with the position of the No. 1 ignition wire on the distributor cap.

➔ There are distributor cap runners inside the cap on 3.0L engines. Make sure the rotor is pointing to where the No. 1 runner originates inside the cap and not where the No. 1 ignition wire plugs into the cap.

11. Install the hold-down clamp and snug the hold-down bolt. Connect the vacuum hose(s), if equipped.

12. Connect the distributor pickup lead wires. Install the splash shield, if equipped.

13. Install the distributor cap and snap the retaining clips into place or tighten the screws.

14. Connect the negative battery cable.

15. Adjust the ignition timing and tighten the hold-down bolt.

Ignition Coil

➧ See Figure 70

The ignition coil is designed to operate without an external ignition resistor. Inspect coil for external leaks and arcing. Test the primary and secondary circuit resistances, replacing any coil that does not meet the manufacturers specifications.

Every time an ignition coil is replaced because of a burned tower or carbon tracking, always replace the coil secondary wire.

Distributor Cap and Rotor

➧ See Figure 71

The distributor cap and rotor must be inspected for flash over, cracking, burning and/or worn terminals. Check the carbon button in cap for cracking. Light scale may be removed with a sharp knife. Heavy deposits on the cap terminal or the rotor, require replacement of the component.

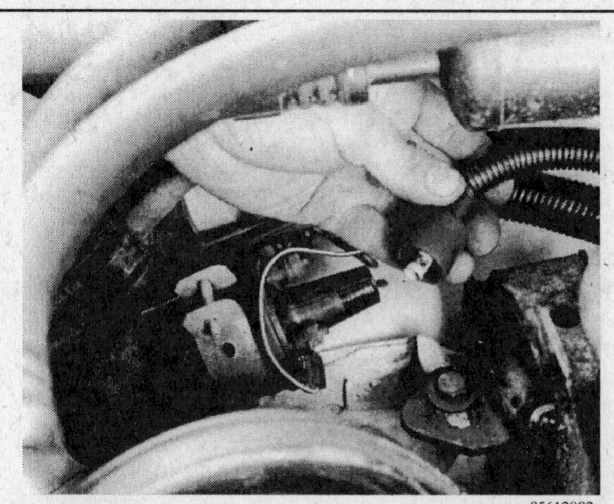

Fig. 70 Ignition coil with the secondary wire disconnected

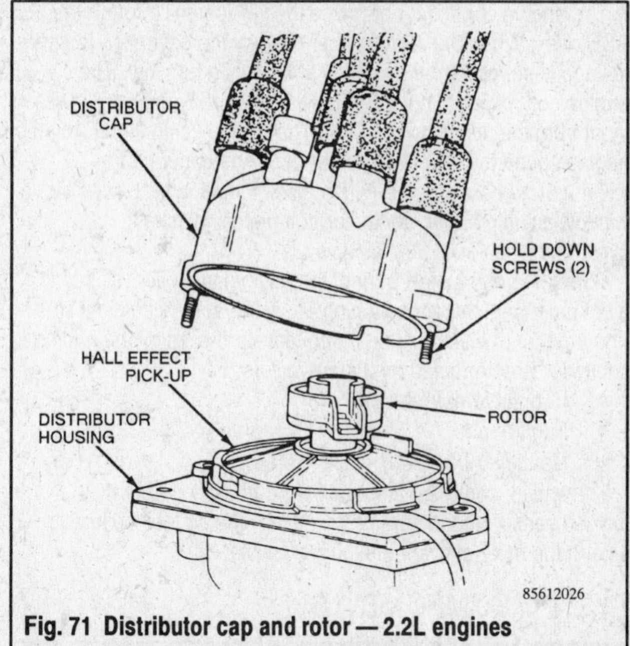

Fig. 71 Distributor cap and rotor — 2.2L engines

Single Module Engine Controller (SMEC) and Single Board Engine Controller (SBEC) Systems

1988–95 MODELS

General Information

The Hall Effect Pick-Up ignition system is used in conjunction with an engine controller, also referred to the Single Module Engine Controller (SMEC) for 1988–89, a Single Board Engine Controller (SBEC) for 1990–91 or a Single Board Engine Controller II (SBEC II) for 1992 and a Powertrain Control Module (PCM) for 1993–95. The SMEC, SBEC, SBEC II or PCM controls the entire ignition. The engine controller gives the capability of igniting the fuel mixture over all operating conditions, by delivering an infinite amount of variable electronic spark advance curves.

The Hall Effect Pick-Up ignition system consists of an engine controller (SMEC, SBEC, SBEC II and PCM)), a conventional but pointless distributor, a hall effect pick-up, an ignition coil, an Auto Shutdown (ASD) relay and primary and secondary ignition wiring.

SYSTEM OPERATION

A shutter, sometimes referred to as an interrupter, is attached to the distributor shaft. The shutter contains a set of blades, 1 for each cylinder. A switch plate is mounted to the distributor housing above the shutter. The switch plate contains the distributor pick-up (hall effect device) through which the shutter blades rotate. As the shutter blades pass through the pick-up, they interrupt the magnetic field. The hall effect device in the pick-up senses the change in the magnetic field and switches on and off, generating input signal (pulses) to the engine controller.

The engine controller energizes the ignition coil through the ASD relay. When the relay is energized by the controller, battery voltage is supplied to the ignition coil positive terminal. The engine controller will not energize the ASD relay until it receives input from the distributor pick-up. The engine controller calculates engine speed through the number of pulses generated.

On 2.5L turbocharged engines, one of the shutter blades has a window cut into it. The controller determines injector synchronization from that window.

During the crank-start period, the engine controller will provide a set amount of advanced timing to assure a quick efficient start. The amount of electronic spark advance provided by the engine controller is determined by 3 input factors:

- Coolant temperature
- Engine rpm
- Manifold Absolute Pressure (MAP)

The engine controller also receives information from the oxygen sensor and electronically adjusts the air fuel mixture to assure the most efficient fuel burn possible.

SYSTEM COMPONENTS

Engine Controller

The engine controller has a built in microprocessor which continuously monitor various engine sensors. The computer will then electronically advance or retard the ignition timing to provide even driveability during operation.

Hall Effect Pick-Up

The hall effect pick-up, located in the distributor, supplies the engine controller with engine rpm, fuel injection synchronization (turbocharged engines) and ignition timing information.

Manifold Absolute Pressure (MAP) Sensor

The MAP sensor, mounted under the hood, is a device which transmits information on manifold vacuum conditions and barometric pressure to the electronic controller. The MAP sensor data, along with data from other sensors, is used to determine proper air/fuel mixture.

Coolant Sensor

The coolant temperature sensor is located on the thermostat housing and provides the controller with engine temperature data. The controller uses this data to control various engine functions such as spark advance, fuel mixture, emission controls operation and radiator fan.

Auto Shutdown (ASD) Relay

The ASD relay is used basically as a fuel delivery safety factor. The ASD relay interrupts the power to the electrical fuel pump, fuel injectors and ignition coil if the ignition key is in **RUN** and there is no need for fuel delivery.

Detonation (Knock) Sensor

The detonation (knock) sensor, used on 2.5L turbocharged engines, is a device that generates a signal when spark knock occurs in the combustion chamber. The engine controller use this information to modify spark advance in order to eliminate detonation.

SMEC SYSTEM DIAGNOSIS & TESTING

➥ Apply the parking brake and block the wheels before performing any engine running tests, including idle or timing checks and adjustments.

Testing for Spark at Coil

Remove the coil secondary cable from the distributor cap. Using a suitable tool, hold end of cable about 1/4 in. (5mm) from good engine ground. Crank the engine and look for good, constant spark at the coil secondary wire. If the spark is constant, have a helper continue to crank the engine while moving the coil secondary cable away from ground. Look for arcing at the coil tower. If arcing occurs, replace the coil. If no arcing occurs, the ignition system is producing the necessary high secondary voltage. Make certain this voltage is getting to the spark plugs by checking the distributor rotor, cap, spark plug wires and spark plugs. If all check in good condition, the ignition system is not the cause of the problem.

If spark is weak, not constant or not present, continue with Failure To Start test.

Ignition System Starting Test

1. With a voltmeter, measure voltage at the battery and record it. Battery specific gravity must be 12.20. If if is not, charge the battery to specification.
2. Turn ignition switch **ON**.
3. Remove the coil wire from the distributor cap. Using a suitable tool, hold wire about a 1/4 in. (6mm) away from a good ground.
4. Intermittently jump coil negative to ground while looking for a good spark at coil wire.
5. If there is spark at the coil wire, it must be constant and bright blue in color. If the spark is good, slowly move the coil wire away from ground while looking for arcing at the coil tower. If arcing occurs replace the coil. If spark is weak or not constant, proceed to “Failure to Start Test”.

Failure To Start Test

➧ See Figures 72 and 73

➥ Apply parking brake and block wheels before performing any engine running tests, including idle or timing checks and adjustments.

1. Check battery voltage and determine that a minimum of 12.4 volts is available for operation of cranking and ignition systems.
2. Crank the engine for 5 seconds while monitoring voltage at the coil positive terminal. If voltage remains near 0 during entire period of cranking, please refer to Section 5 in this book for on-board diagnostic checks of SMEC and ASD relay.
3. If measured voltage is near battery voltage but drops to 0 after 1–2 seconds of cranking, please refer to Section 5 in this book for on-board diagnostic checks of distributor reference pick-up circuit to SMEC.
4. If measured voltage remains near battery voltage for entire 5 second cranking period, turn the key **OFF** and remove SMEC 14–way connector. Check the 14–way connector for any spread terminals.

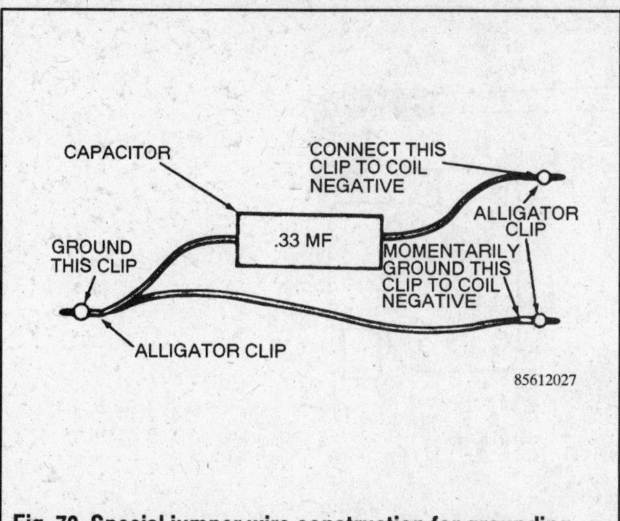

Fig. 72 Special jumper wire construction for grounding the coil

1 2 3 4 5 6 7
14 13 12 11 10 9 8
TERMINAL SIDE
85612028

Fig. 73 14-way electrical connector for the SMEC

5. Remove wire to coil positive terminal and connect regular jumper wire between coil positive terminal and battery positive terminal.
6. Using special jumper cable, momentarily ground terminal No. 12 of 14-way connector. A spark should be generated when ground is removed.
7. If spark is generated, replace the SMEC.
8. If no spark is seen, use special jumper to ground coil negative terminal directly.
9. If spark is produced, trace and repair open condition within wiring harness.
10. If no spark is produced, replace ignition coil.

COOLANT TEMPERATURE SENSOR TEST

1. With the key **OFF**, unplug the wire connector from the coolant temperature sensor.
2. Connect one lead of an ohmmeter to one terminal of sensor.
3. Connect the other ohmmeter lead to the other sensor terminal; ohmmeter should read: Coolant at operating temperature (200°F/93°C): Approximately 700–1000 ohms. Coolant at room temperature (70°F/21°C): Approximately 7,000–13,000 ohms.

SPARK ADVANCE OF SMEC SYSTEM

1. Adjust basic timing to specifications.
2. Have engine at normal operating temperature. The coolant temperature sensor must be connected and operating correctly.
3. Start and raise engine speed to 2000 rpm. Wait 1 minute and check specifications.

➥ The use of a metal exhaust tube is recommended for this test. Using rubber hose may result in a fire due to high temperatures and a long test period.

4. The advance specifications are in addition to basic advance. If correct advance is not obtained, SMEC must be replaced.

SBEC, SBEC II AND PCM SYSTEMS DIAGNOSIS & TESTING

➥ Apply the parking brake and block the wheels before performing any engine running tests, including idle or timing checks and adjustments.

Testing for Spark at Coil

2.5L AND 3.0L ENGINES

➧ See Figure 74

Remove the coil secondary cable from the distributor cap. Using a suitable tool, hold end of cable about $^1/_4$ in. (6mm) from a good engine ground. Crank engine and look for good, constant spark at the coil secondary wire. If spark is constant, have a helper continue to crank engine while moving the coil secondary cable away from ground. Look for arcing at the coil tower. If arcing occurs, replace the coil. If no arcing occurs, ignition system is producing the necessary high secondary voltage. Make certain this voltage is getting to spark plugs by checking the distributor rotor, cap, spark plug wires and spark plugs. If all check in good condition, ignition system is NOT cause of problem.

If the spark is weak, not constant or not present, continue with the Failure to Start test.

Failure to Start Test

2.5L AND 3.0L ENGINES

➧ See Figures 72, 75, 76 and 77

➥ Apply parking brake and block wheels before performing any engine running tests, including idle or timing checks and adjustments.

1. Check battery voltage and determine that a minimum of 12.4 volts is available for operation of cranking and ignition systems.
2. Crank the engine for 5 seconds while monitoring voltage at the coil positive terminal. If voltage remains near 0 during entire period of cranking, please refer to Section 5 in this book for on-board diagnostic checks of SBEC, SBEC II or PCM and auto shutdown relay.

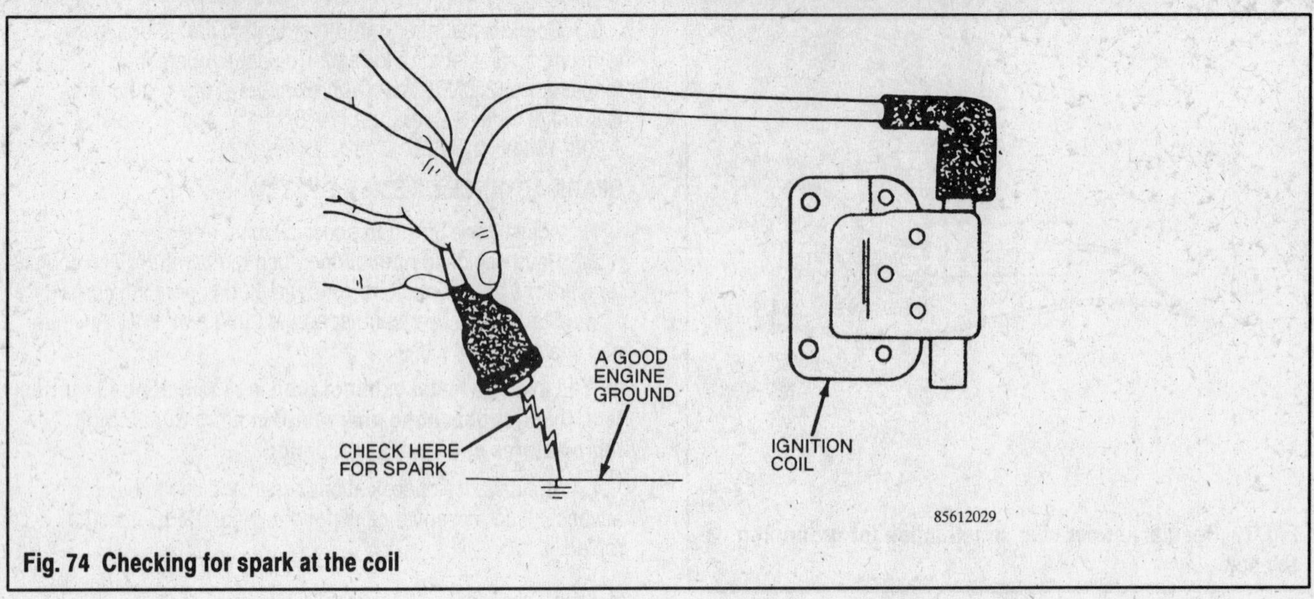

Fig. 74 Checking for spark at the coil

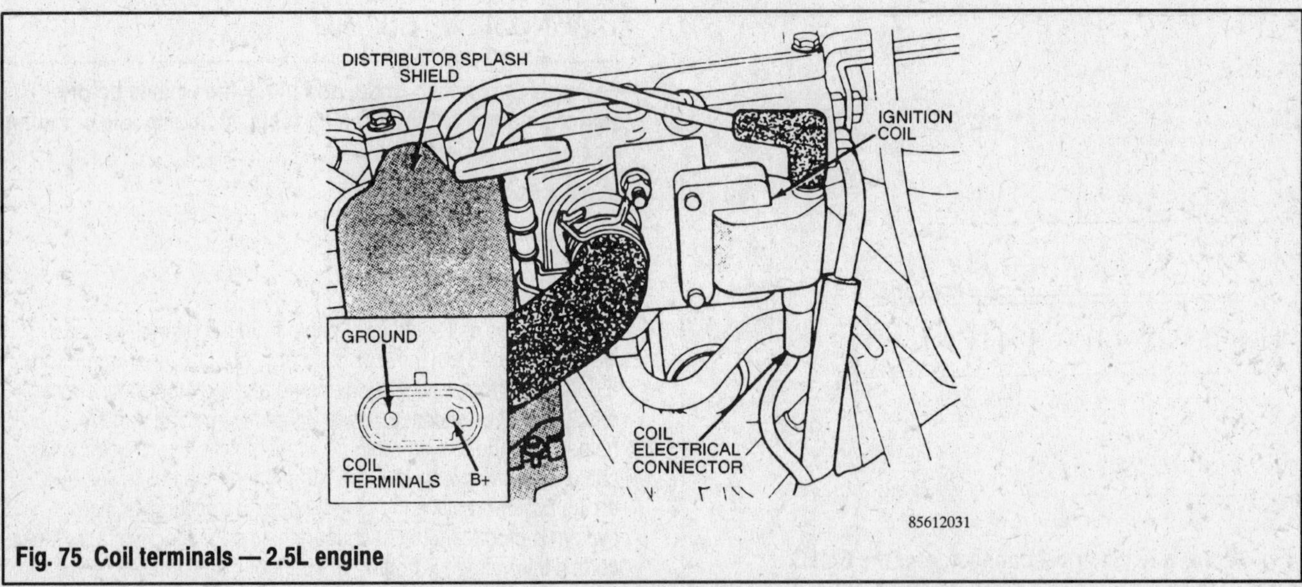

Fig. 75 Coil terminals — 2.5L engine

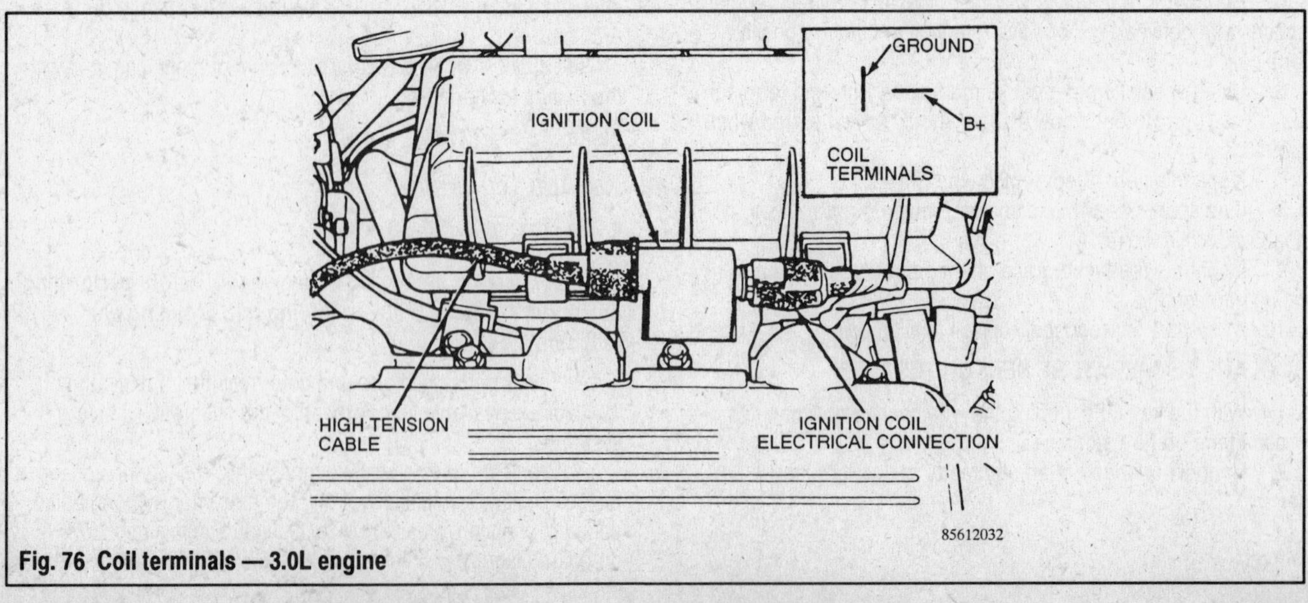

Fig. 76 Coil terminals — 3.0L engine

3. If measured voltage is near battery voltage but drops to 0 after 1-2 seconds of cranking, please refer to Section 5 in this book for on-board diagnostic checks of distributor reference pick-up circuit to SBEC, SBEC II or PCM.
4. If measured voltage remains near battery voltage for entire 5 second cranking period, turn key **OFF** and remove SBEC 60-way connector. Check 60-way connector for any spread terminals.
5. Remove wire to the coil positive terminal and connect regular jumper wire between coil positive terminal and battery positive terminal.
6. Using special jumper cable, momentarily ground terminal No. 19 of 60-way connector. A spark should be generated when ground is removed.
7. If spark is generated, replace the SBEC, SBEC II or PCM.
8. If no spark is seen, use special jumper to ground coil negative terminal directly.

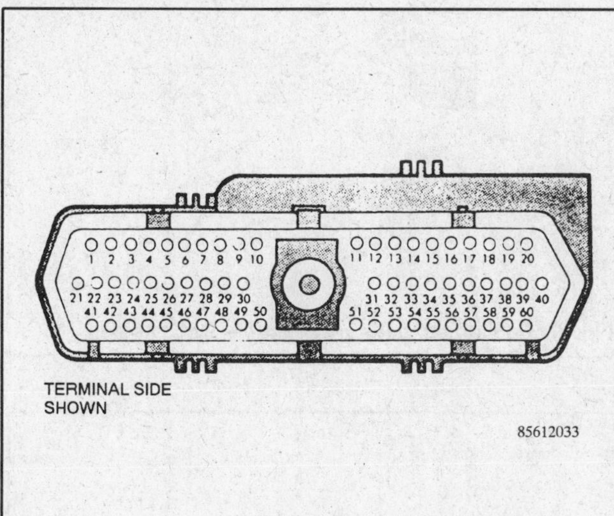

Fig. 77 60-way electrical connector engine controller

9. If spark is produced, trace and repair open condition within wiring harness.
10. If no spark is produced, replace ignition coil.

SMEC COMPONENT REMOVAL & INSTALLATION

Single Module Engine Control (SMEC) Unit

See Figure 78

1. Disconnect the negative battery cable.
2. Disconnect the air cleaner duct from the SMEC unit.
3. Carefully unplug the connectors from the unit.

Make sure there is at least an 1/8 in. (3mm) of grease in the connectors.

4. Install the connectors on the replacement unit.
5. Mount the unit in position and make sure the connectors are secure.
6. Install the air cleaner duct and connect the negative battery cable.

Hall Effect Pick-Up

See Figure 79

1. Disconnect the negative battery cable.
2. Remove the distributor cap and remove the rotor.
3. Remove the screws that retain the pick-up assembly. Disconnect the electrical lead from the pick-up.
4. Carefully remove the assembly from the distributor.

To install:

5. Install the new pick-up assembly and connect the electrical lead.
6. Install the retaining screws. Install the cap and rotor.
7. Connect the negative battery cable.

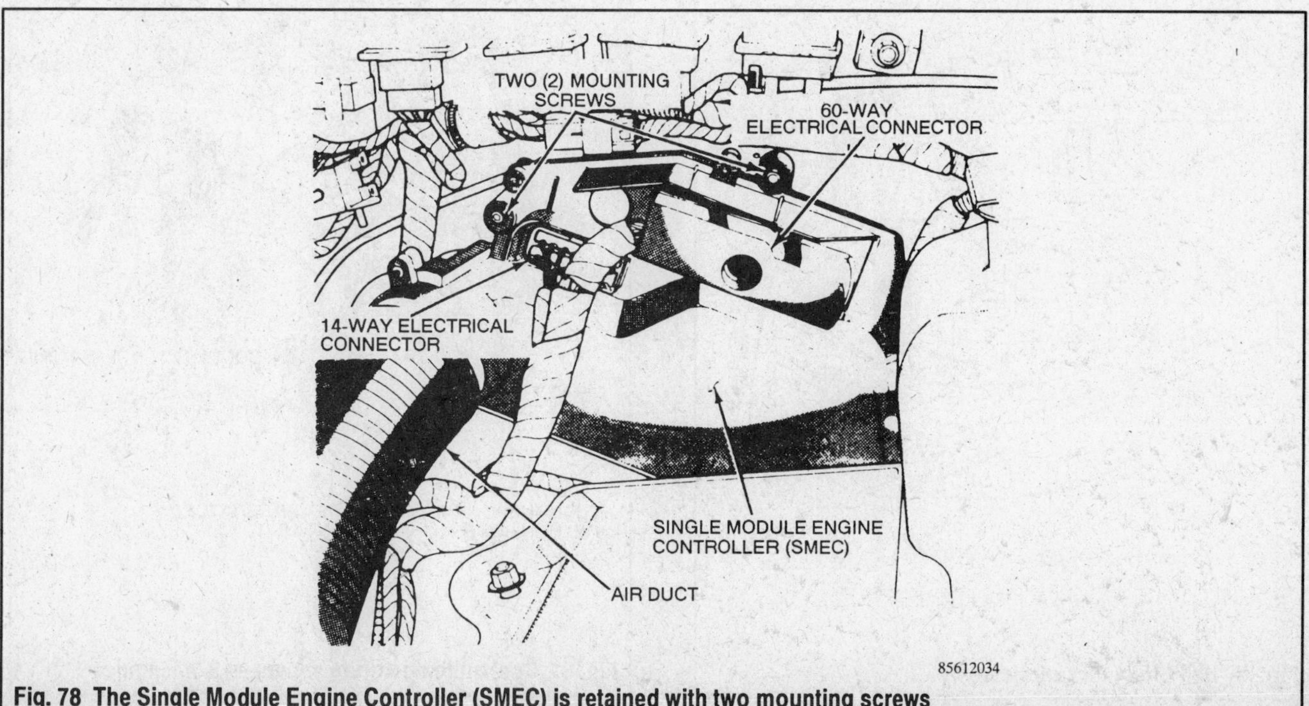

Fig. 78 The Single Module Engine Controller (SMEC) is retained with two mounting screws

Coolant Temperature Sensor

➧ See Figures 80 and 81

1. Detach the electrical connector from the sensor.
2. Remove the sensor from the engine. Some coolant may be lost from system.

To install:

3. Install new sensor and tighten to 20 ft lbs. (27 Nm). Attach the electrical connector.
4. Replace any lost coolant.

SBEC, SBEC II AND PCM COMPONENT REMOVAL & INSTALLATION

Single Board Engine Control (SBEC) Unit and Powertrain Control Module (PCM)

➧ See Figures 82 and 83

➥ **The SBEC/PCM is located behind the battery.**

1. Remove the battery.
2. Remove the air cleaner duct or air cleaner assembly.
3. Remove the battery.
4. Carefully unfasten the 60-way wiring connector from the PCM.
5. Remove the PCM.

To install:

6. Hold the SBEC/PCM in its original position, then install the retaining screws.
7. Tighten the screws until snug.

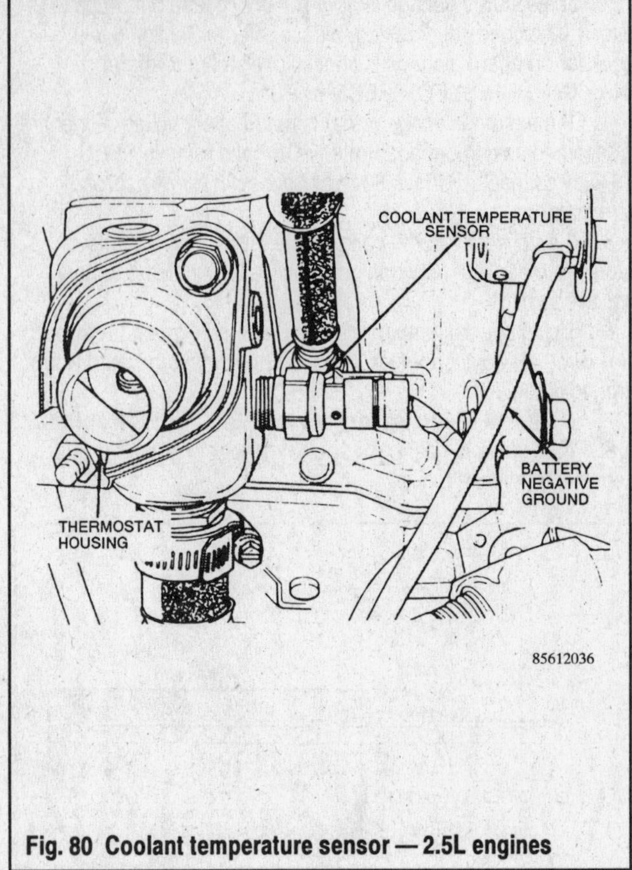

Fig. 80 Coolant temperature sensor — 2.5L engines

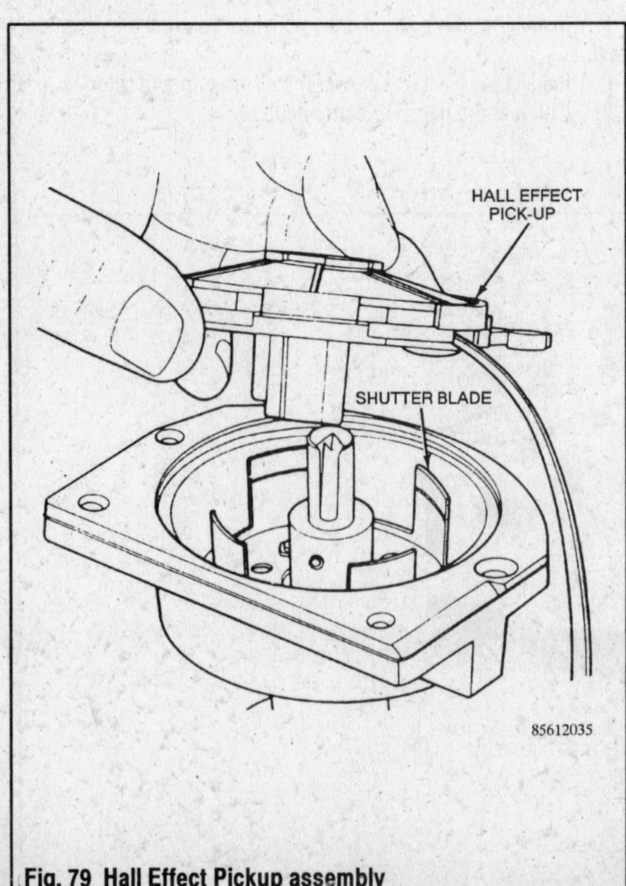

Fig. 79 Hall Effect Pickup assembly

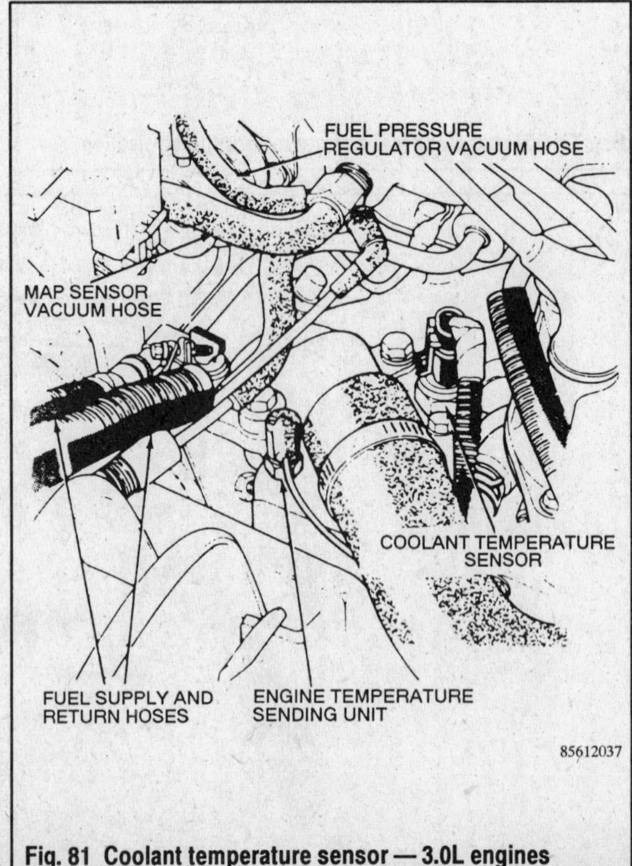

Fig. 81 Coolant temperature sensor — 3.0L engines

8. Attach the 60-way connector to the SBEC/PCM.
9. Install the battery tray and battery into the engine compartment.
10. Install the air cleaner duct.

Hall Effect Pick-Up

➧ See Figure 79

1. Disconnect the negative battery cable.
2. Remove the distributor cap and remove the rotor.
3. Remove the screws that retain the pick-up assembly. Disconnect the electrical lead from the pick-up.
4. Carefully remove the assembly from the distributor.

To install:

5. Install the new pick-up assembly and connect the electrical lead.
6. Install the retaining screws until snug.
7. Install the cap and rotor onto the distributor.
8. Connect the negative battery cable.

Coolant Temperature Sensor

➧ See Figures 84 and 85

1. Unfasten the electrical connector from the sensor.
2. Remove the sensor from the engine. Some coolant may be lost from system.

To install:

3. Install the new sensor and tighten to 20 ft. lbs. (27 Nm) for the 2.5L engine and to 60 inch lbs. (7 Nm) for the 3.0L engine.
4. Replace any lost coolant.

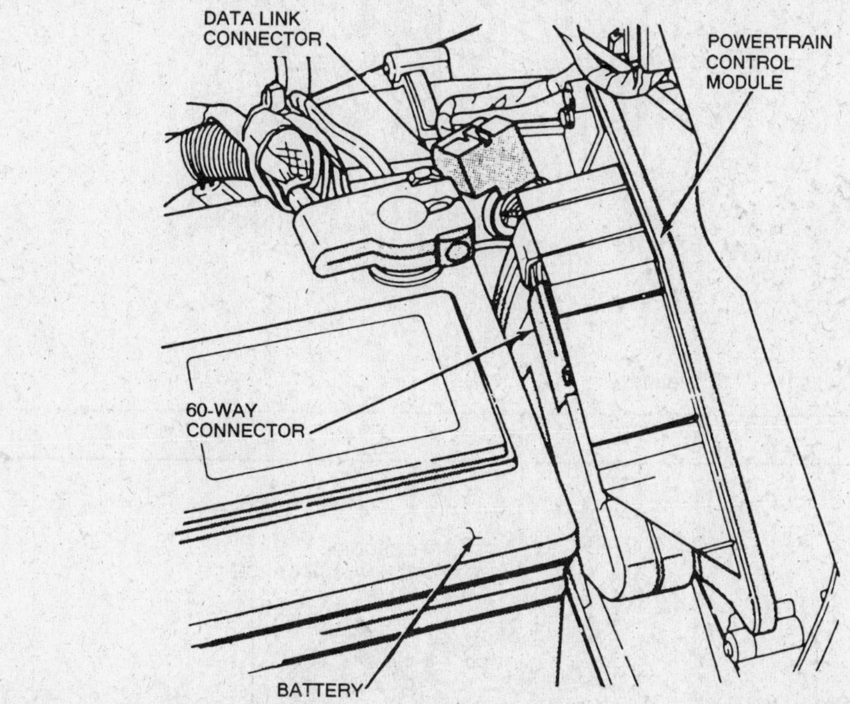

Fig. 82 The Single Board Engine Controller (SBEC), also referred to the Powertrain Control Module (PCM), is located behind the battery

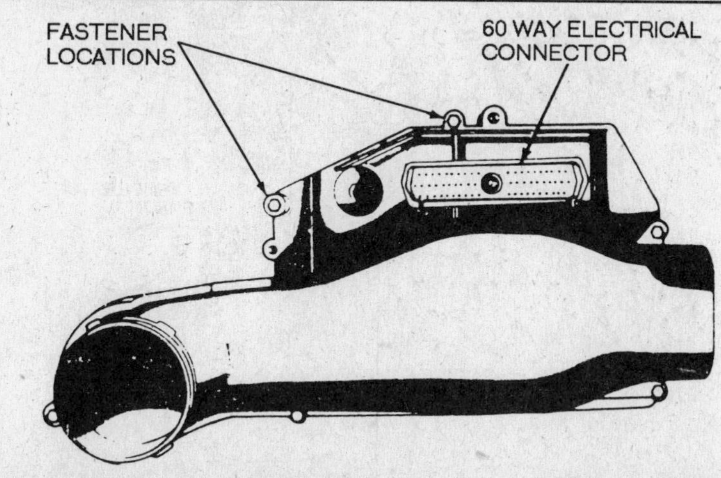

Fig. 83 The SBEC/PCM is retained with two mounting screws

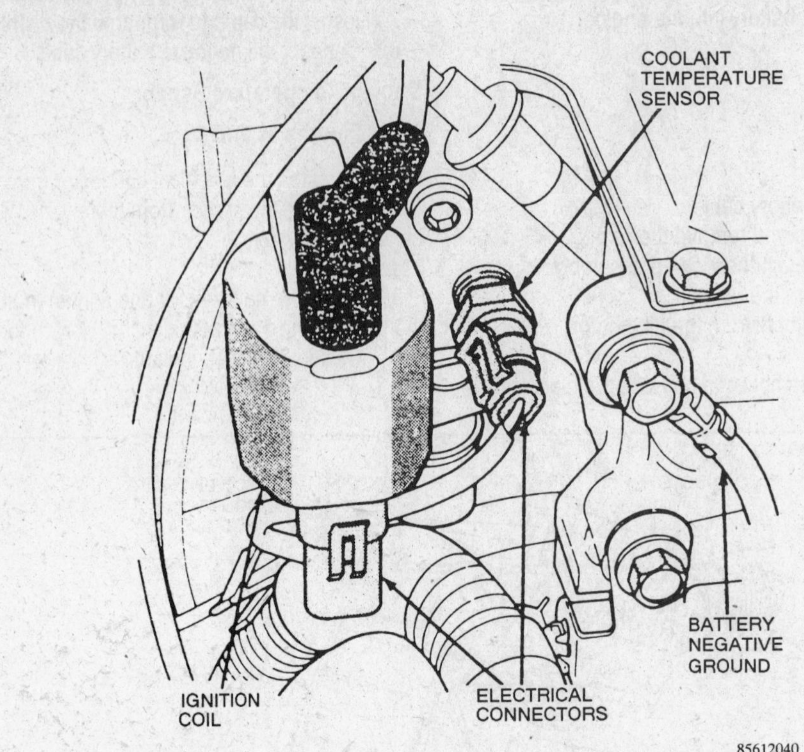

Fig. 84 Coolant temperature sensor — 2.5L engines

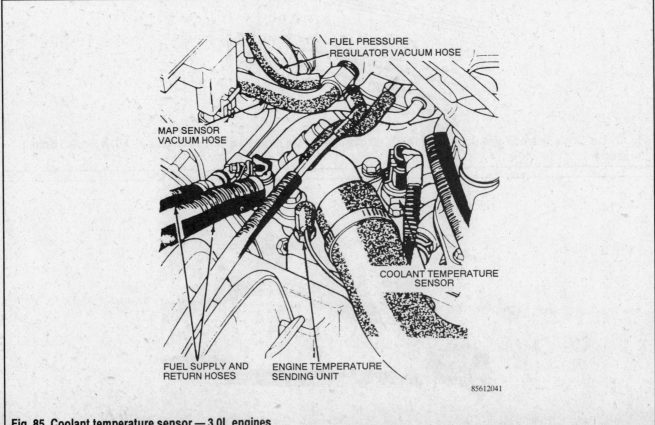

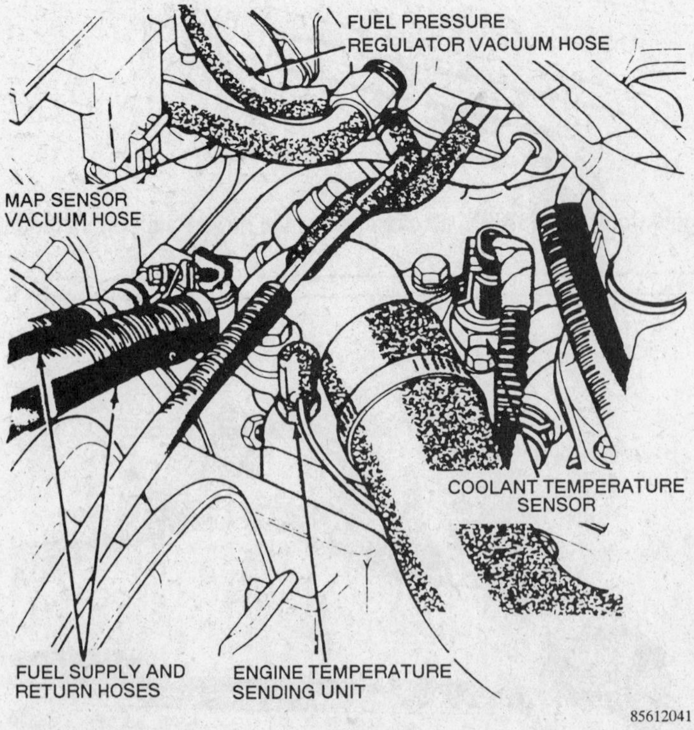

Fig. 85 Coolant temperature sensor — 3.0L engines

CHRYSLER OPTICAL DISTRIBUTOR SYSTEM

➧ **See Figure 86**

This ignition system was standard for vehicles equipped with the 3.0L engine in 1988–89. The system is similar to the SMEC system in operation except that it uses a different type of distributor. The computer receives its input from an optical distributor. The signals are used to control fuel injection, ignition timing and engine idle speed.

The timing member in the distributor is a thin disk, driven at half the speed of the engine, from the left camshaft. The disk has 2 sets of slots in it. The outer, high data rate slots, occur at 2 degrees of engine rotation. They are used for ignition timing at engine speed of up to 1200 rpm.

The inner, or low data rate set, contains 6 slots which are correlated to TDC of each cylinder. This is used to trigger the fuel injection system. This data set functions at engine speed over 1200 rpm. This set also controls the ignition timing.

Light emitting diodes and photo sensors are mounted in facing positions on opposite sides of the disk in the distributor. Masks over the LED's and the diodes focus the light beams onto the photo diodes. As each slot passes between the diodes, the light beam is turned on and off. This creates an alternating voltage in each photo diode, which is converted into on/off pulses by an integrated circuit within the distributor.

The distributor also delivers firing pulses from the coil to each of the cylinders through the cap and rotor.

Component Replacement and Testing

The replacement of components and their testing in the optical distributor system are the same as the SMEC system.

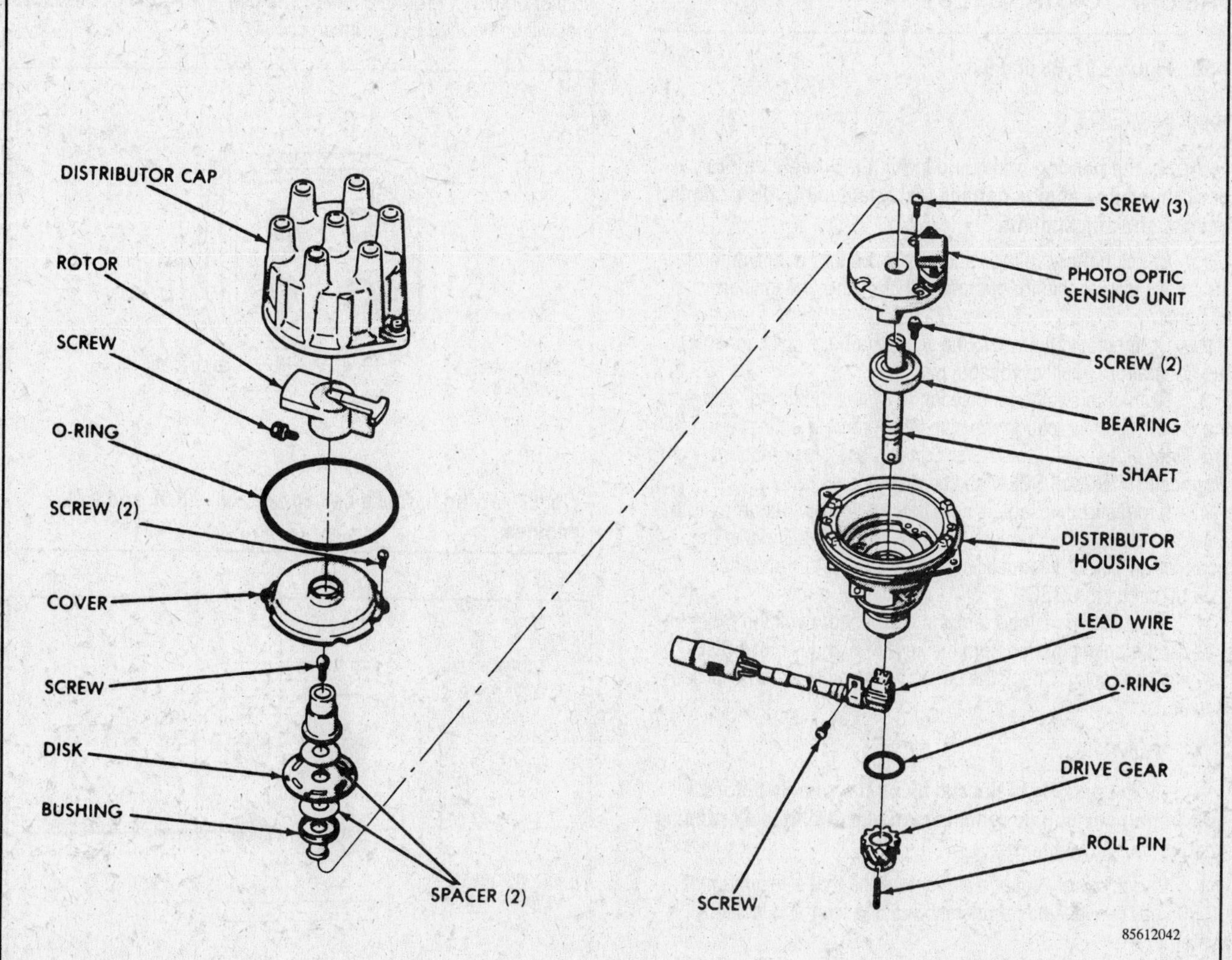

Fig. 86 Exploded view of the distributor used with the Chrysler Optical Distributor system — 1988–89 3.0L engines

DIRECT IGNITION SYSTEM (DIS)

General Information

Vehicles equipped with the 3.3L and 3.8L engines use a distributorless ignition system. The system has 3 main components, the coil, the camshaft reference sensor and the crankshaft timing sensor.

The Single Board Engine Controller (SBEC) receives its engine speed and crankshaft position signal from a sensor located in the transaxle housing. This crankshaft position sensor senses slots located around an extension on the torque converter drive plate. A camshaft sensor located in the timing case cover, supplies cylinder identification to the SBEC, by sensing slots located on the camshaft sprocket.

DIS System Diagnosis and Testing

FAILURE TO START TEST

See Figures 87, 88 and 89

1990-91 Models

Apply the parking brake and block the wheels before performing any engine running tests, including idle or timing checks and adjustments.

1. Check battery voltage and determine that a minimum of 12.4 volts is available for operation of cranking and ignition systems.
2. Connect a voltmeter to the wiring harness coil connector at the B+ (battery positive voltage) pin.
3. Crank the engine for 5 seconds while monitoring voltage at the B+ terminal. If voltage remains near 0 during entire period of cranking, please refer to Section 5 in this book for on-board diagnostic checks of SBEC and auto shutdown relay.
4. If measured voltage is near battery voltage but drops to 0 after 1-2 seconds of cranking, please refer to Section 5 in this book for on-board diagnostic checks of distributor reference pick-up circuit to SBEC.
5. If measured voltage remains near battery voltage for entire 5 second cranking period, turn the key **OFF** and remove SBEC 60-way connector. Check the 60-way connector for any spread terminals.

1992-95 Models

Apply the parking brake and block the wheels before performing any engine running tests, including idle or timing checks and adjustments.

1. Check battery voltage and determine that a minimum of 12.66 volts is available for operation of cranking and ignition systems.
2. Disconnect the harness connector from the coil pack.
3. Connect a test light to the coil connector at the B+ pin (battery positive voltage) and ground. The wire for the B+ terminal is dark green with a black tracer.
4. Turn the ignition key to the **ON** position. The test light should flash on and then off. Do not turn the key to the **OFF** position, leave it in the **ON** position. If the test light flashes momentarily, the PCM grounded the auto shutdown (ASD) relay. If the test light did not flash, the ASD relay did no energize. The cause is either the relay or the relay circuits.
5. Crank engine and if the test light momentarily flashes during cranking, the PCM is not receiving a crankshaft position sensor signal and the sensor and sensor circuits will have to be tested with the appropriate scan tool.
6. If the test light did not flash during cranking, unplug the crankshaft position sensor connector. Turn the ignition key to the **OFF** position. Turn the key to the **ON** position, and wait for the test light to momentarily flash once, then crank the engine. If the test light momentarily flashes, the crankshaft position sensor is shorted and must be replaced. If the light did not flash, the cause of the no-start is either the crankshaft position sensor/camshaft position sensor 8-volt supply circuit, or the camshaft position sensor output or ground circuits. The use of an appropriate scan tool will be needed to test these circuits.

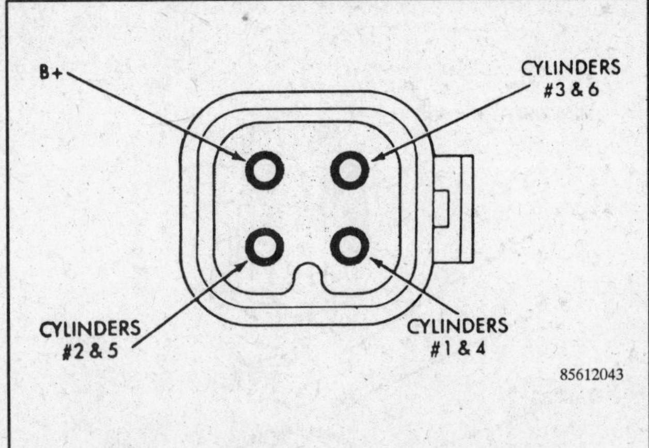

Fig. 87 Wiring harness coil connector — 3.3L and 3.8L engines

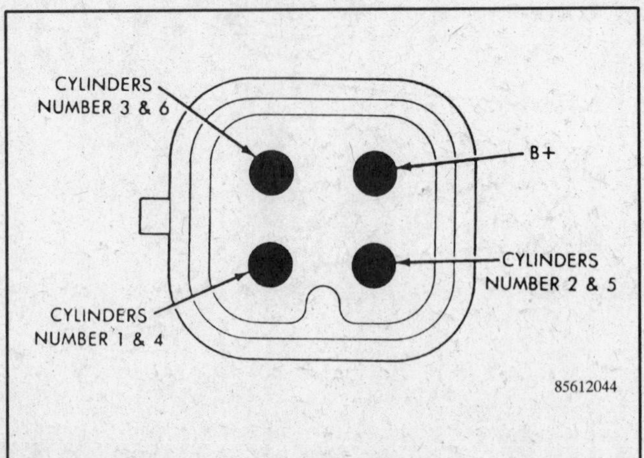

Fig. 88 Ignition coil terminal identification — 3.3L and 3.8L engines

SPARK AT COIL TEST

3.3L and 3.8L Engines

See Figure 90

Since their are 3 independent coils in the package, each coil must be checked individually. Remove the cable from the No. 2 spark plug. Insert a metal object into the spark plug boot and hold the end of the cable about 1/4 in. (6mm) from a good engine ground. Crank the engine and look for a spark at the cable. Repeat the above test for cylinders No. 4 and No. 6. If there is no spark during all 3 cylinder tests, proceed to the Failure To Start Test.

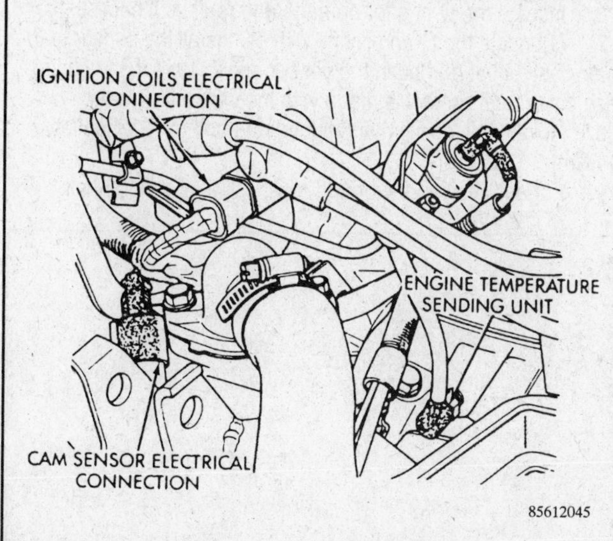

Fig. 89 Ignition coil electrical connection — 3.3L and 3.8L engines

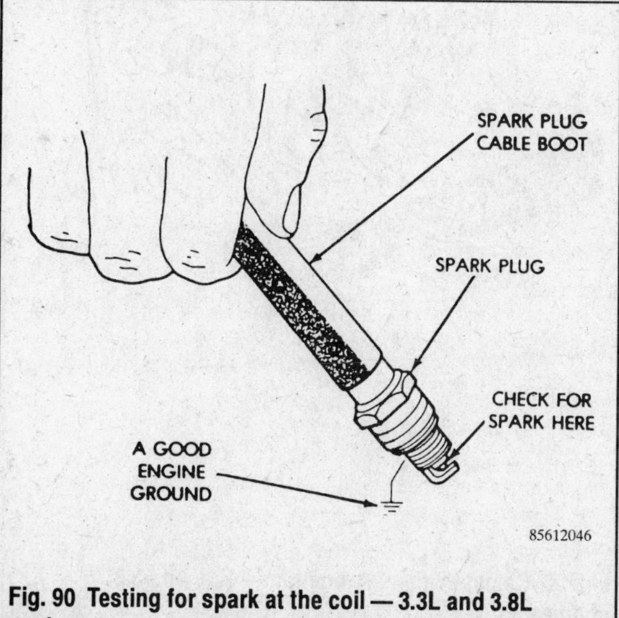

Fig. 90 Testing for spark at the coil — 3.3L and 3.8L engines

DIS System Component Replacement

REMOVAL & INSTALLATION

Ignition Coil

See Figure 91

1. Disconnect the negative battery cable.
2. Label and disconnect the spark plug wires from the coil.
3. Unfasten the electrical connector from the ignition coil.
4. Remove the coil fasteners.
5. Remove the coil from the ignition module.

To install:

6. Position the coil in place on the ignition module, then install the retaining fasteners. Tighten the retaining screws until snug.
7. Attach the electrical lead to the coil.
8. Install all spark plug wires to the coil towers.
9. Connect the negative battery cable.

Crankshaft Position Sensor

See Figures 92, 93 and 94

1. Disconnect the negative battery cable.
2. Unplug the sensor lead at the harness connector.
3. Remove the sensor retainer bolt.
4. Pull the sensor straight up and out of the transaxle housing.
5. If the removed sensor is being reinstalled, clean off the old spacer completely and attach a new spacer to the sensor. If a new spacer is not used, the sensor will not function properly. New sensors are equipped with a new spacer.

To install:

6. Install the sensor in the transaxle housing and push the sensor down until contact is made with the drive plate.
7. Hold in this position and install the retaining bolt. Torque to 105 inch lbs. (12 Nm).
8. Connect the sensor lead wire.

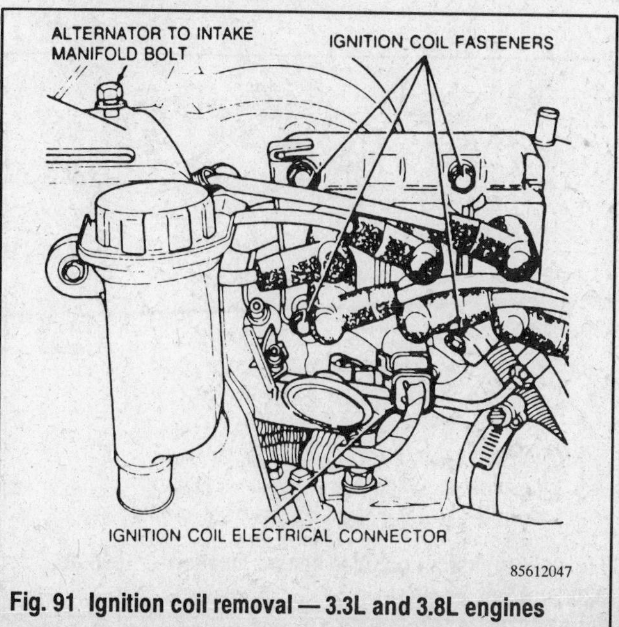

Fig. 91 Ignition coil removal — 3.3L and 3.8L engines

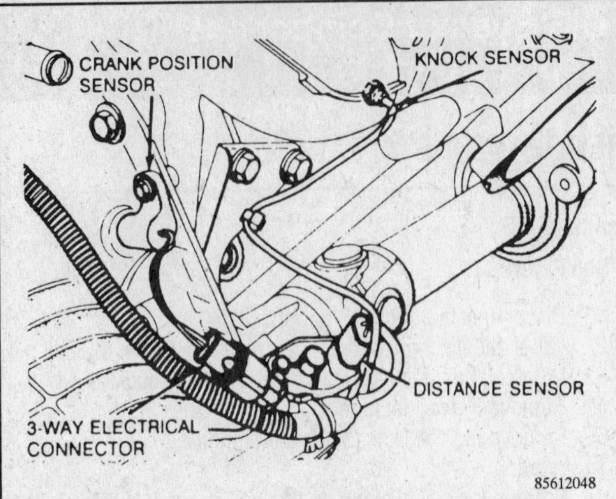

Fig. 92 Crankshaft position sensor location — 1990-91 3.3L engines

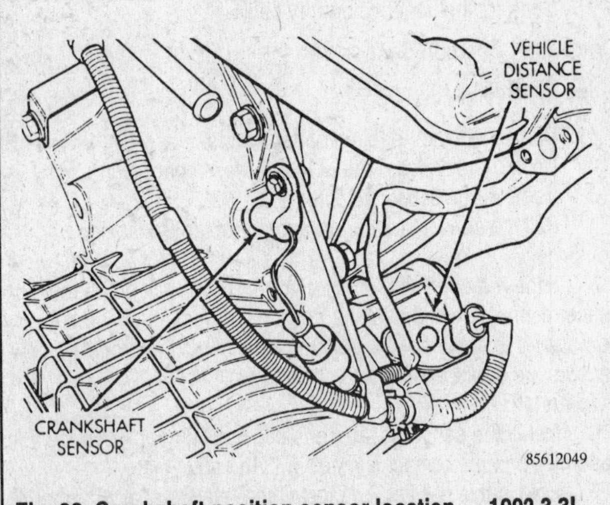

Fig. 93 Crankshaft position sensor location — 1992 3.3L engines

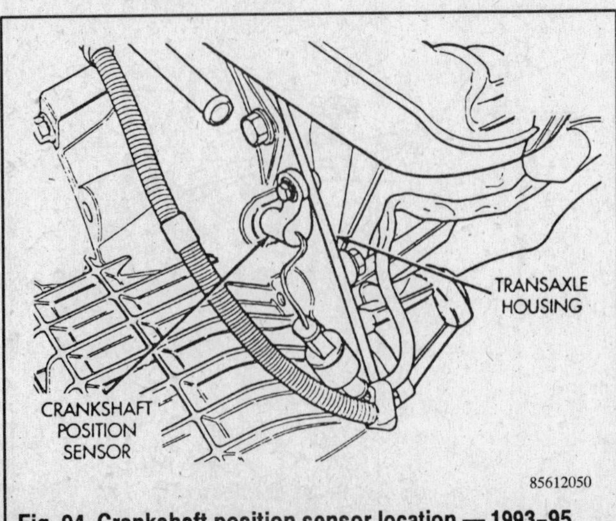

Fig. 94 Crankshaft position sensor location — 1993-95 3.3L and 3.8L engines

Camshaft Position Sensor

➧ **See Figure 95**

1. Disconnect the negative battery cable.
2. Unplug the sensor lead at the harness connector.
3. Loosen the sensor retaining bolt enough to allow the slot to slide past the bolt.
4. Pull the sensor (not by the wire) straight up and out of the chain case cover. Resistance may be high due to the presence of the rubber O-ring.
5. If the removed sensor is being reinstalled, clean off the old spacer completely and attach a new spacer to the sensor. If a new spacer is not used, the sensor will not function properly. New sensors are equipped with a new spacer.

To install:

6. Inspect the O-ring for damage and replace if necessary.
7. Lubricate the O-ring lightly with oil. Install the sensor to the chain case cover and push the sensor into its bore in the chain case cover until contact is made with the cam timing gear.
8. Hold in this position and tighten the bolt to 125 inch lbs. (14 Nm).
9. Engage the connector and route it away from the belt.

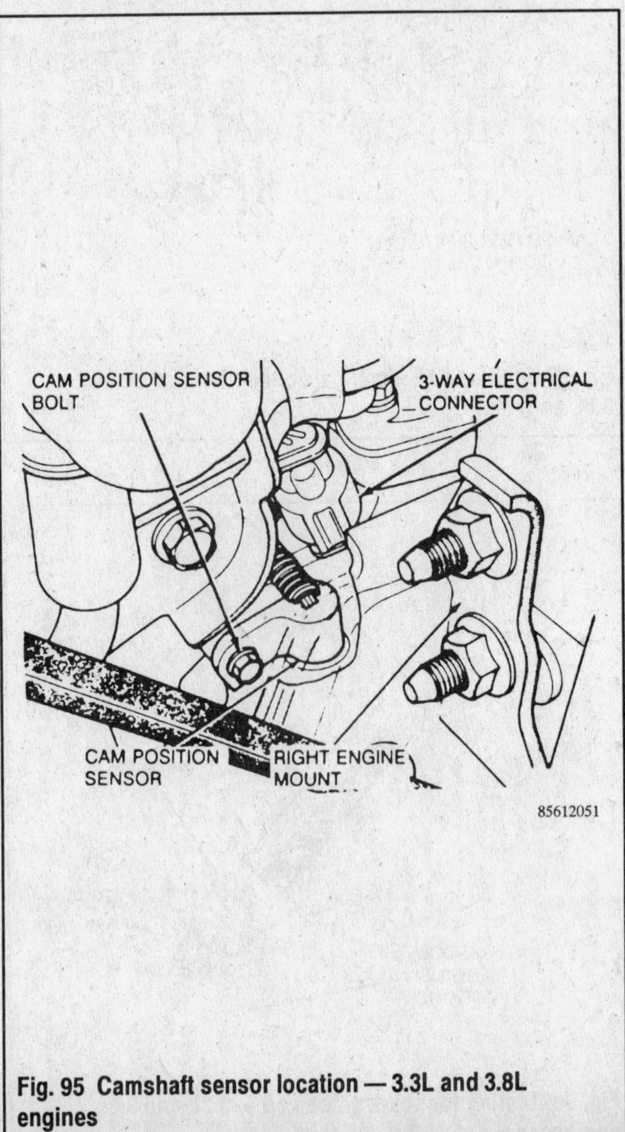

Fig. 95 Camshaft sensor location — 3.3L and 3.8L engines

BASIC ELECTRICAL THEORY
BATTERY, STARTING AND CHARGING SYSTEMS 3-4
UNDERSTANDING ELECTRICITY 3-2
ENGINE ELECTRICAL
ALTERNATOR 3-9
DISTRIBUTOR 3-8
DISTRIBUTOR CAP 3-8
DISTRIBUTOR ROTOR 3-8
IGNITION COIL 3-7
REGULATOR 3-13
STARTER 3-13
ENGINE MECHANICAL
AIR CONDITIONING CONDENSER 54
AUTOMATIC TRANSAXLE OIL COOLER 55
BALANCE SHAFTS 93
CAMSHAFT AND BEARINGS 89
CHECKING ENGINE COMPRESSION 3-19
COMBINATION MANIFOLD 49
CRANKSHAFT AND MAIN BEARINGS 105
CYLINDER HEAD 58
ELECTRIC COOLING FAN 54
ENGINE 3-28
ENGINE BLOCK HEATER 101
ENGINE OVERHAUL TIPS 3-17
EXHAUST MANIFOLD 47
FREEZE PLUGS 100
FRONT CRANKSHAFT SEAL RETAINER 104
FRONT TIMING COVER AND SEAL 75
INTAKE MANIFOLD 44
INTERMEDIATE SHAFT 93
OIL PAN 67
OIL PUMP 72
PISTONS AND CONNECTING RODS 96
RADIATOR 52
REAR MAIN SEAL 102
ROCKER (VALVE) COVER 3-35
ROCKER ARMS AND SHAFTS 38
SILENT SHAFTS 96
SOLID MOUNT COMPRESSOR BRACKET 3-34
THERMOSTAT 41
TIMING BELT/CHAIN 80
TIMING SPROCKETS/GEARS 87
TURBOCHARGER 52
VALVES 65
WATER PUMP 55
EXHAUST SYSTEM
EXHAUST (CONVERTER/RESONATOR) PIPE 107
MUFFLER 108
SAFETY PRECAUTIONS 107
TAIL PIPE 108
SPECIFICATIONS CHARTS
ADDITIONAL TORQUE SPECIFICATIONS 110
CAMSHAFT SPECIFICATIONS 3-22
CRANKSHAFT AND CONNECTING ROD SPECIFICATIONS 3-23
GENERAL ENGINE SPECIFICATIONS 3-20
PISTON AND RING SPECIFICATIONS 3-24
TORQUE SPECIFICATIONS 3-26
VALVE SPECIFICATIONS 3-21

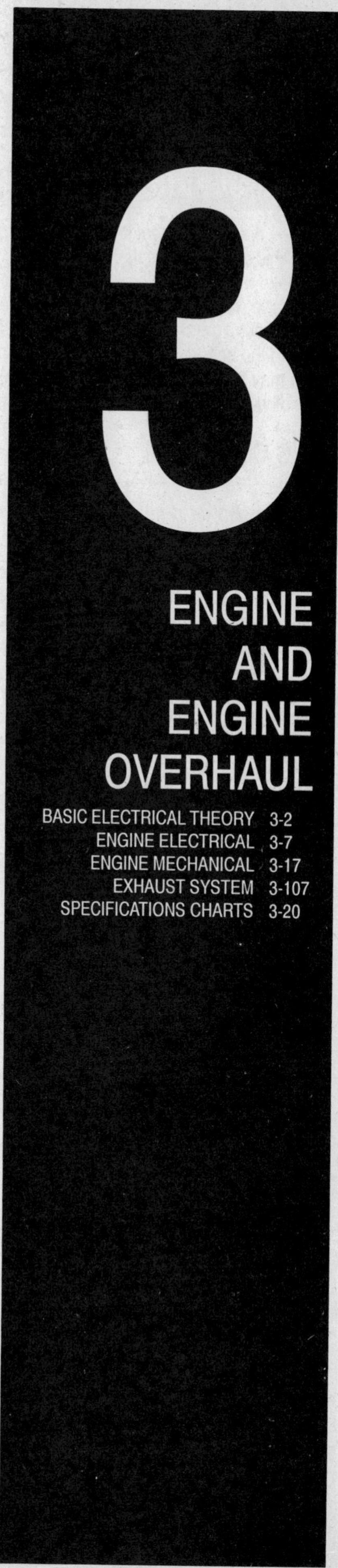

BASIC ELECTRICAL THEORY

Understanding Electricity

For any electrical system to operate, there must be a complete circuit. This simply means that the power flow from the battery must make a full circle. When an electrical component is operating, power flows from the battery to the components, passes through the component (load) causing it to function, and returns to the battery through the ground path of the circuit. This ground may be either another wire or a metal part of the vehicle (depending upon how the component is designed).

BASIC CIRCUITS

➧ See Figures 1 and 2

Perhaps the easiest way to visualize a circuit is to think of connecting a light bulb (with two wires attached to it) to the battery. If one of the two wires was attached to the negative post (-) of the battery and the other wire to the positive post (+), the circuit would be complete and the light bulb would illuminate. Electricity could follow a path from the battery to the bulb and back to the battery. It's not hard to see that with longer wires on our light bulb, it could be mounted anywhere on the vehicle. Further, one wire could be fitted with a switch so that the light could be turned on and off. Various other items could be added to our primitive circuit to make the light flash, become brighter or dimmer under certain conditions, or advise the user that it's burned out.

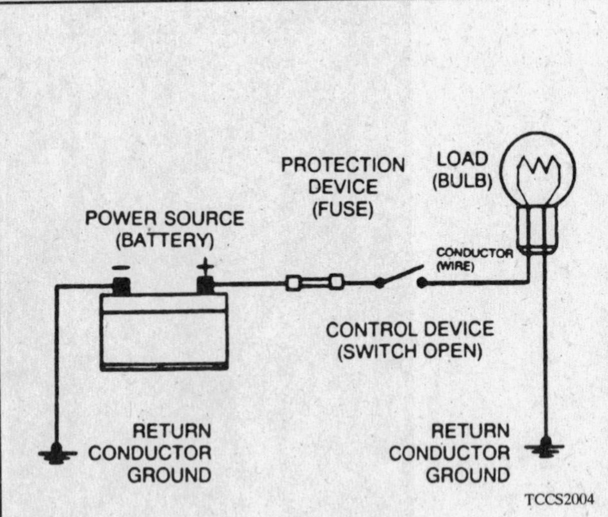

Fig. 1 Here is an example of a simple automotive circuit. When the switch is closed, power from the positive battery terminal flows through the fuse, then the switch and to the load (light bulb), the light illuminates and then, the circuit is completed through the return conductor and the vehicle ground. If the light did not work, the tests could be made with a voltmeter or test light at the battery, fuse, switch or bulb socket

Ground

Some automotive components are grounded through their mounting points. The electrical current runs through the chassis of the vehicle and returns to the battery through the ground (-) cable; if you look, you'll see that the battery ground cable connects between the battery and the body of the vehicle.

Load

Every complete circuit must include a "load" (something to use the electricity coming from the source). If you were to connect a wire between the two terminals of the battery (DON'T do this, but take out word for it) without the light bulb, the battery would attempt to deliver its entire power supply from one pole to another almost instantly. This is a short circuit. The electricity is taking a short cut to get to ground and is not being used by any load in the circuit. This sudden and uncontrolled electrical flow can cause great damage to other components in the circuit and can develop a tremendous amount of heat. A short in an automotive wiring harness can develop sufficient heat to melt the insulation on all the surrounding wires and reduce a multiple wire cable to one sad lump of plastic and copper. Two common causes of shorts are broken insulation (thereby exposing the wire to contact with surrounding metal surfaces or other wires) or a failed switch (the pins inside the switch come out of place and touch each other).

Switches and Relays

Some electrical components which require a large amount of current to operate also have a relay in their circuit. Since these circuits carry a large amount of current (amperage or amps), the thickness of the wire in the circuit (wire gauge) is also greater. If this large wire were connected from the load to the control switch on the dash, the switch would have to carry the high amperage load and the dash would be twice as large to accommodate wiring harnesses as thick as your wrist. To prevent these problems, a relay is used. The large wires in the circuit are connected from the battery to one side of the relay and from the opposite side of the relay to the load. The relay is normally open, preventing current from passing through the circuit. An additional, smaller wire is connected from the relay to the control switch for the circuit. When the control switch is turned on, it grounds the smaller wire to the relay and completes its circuit. The main switch inside the relay closes, sending power to the component without routing the main power through the inside of the vehicle. Some common circuits which may use relays are the horn, headlights, starter and rear window defogger systems.

Protective Devices

It is possible for larger surges of current to pass through the electrical system of your vehicle. If this surge of current were to reach the load in the circuit, it could burn it out or severely damage it. To prevent this, fuses, circuit breakers and/or fusible links are connected into the supply wires of the electrical system. These items are nothing more than a built-in weak spot in the system. It's much easier to go to a known location (the fusebox) to see why a circuit is inoperative than to dissect 15 feet of wiring under the dashboard, looking for what happened.

When an electrical current of excessive power passes through the fuse, the fuse blows (the conductor melts) and breaks the circuit, preventing the passage of current and protecting the components.

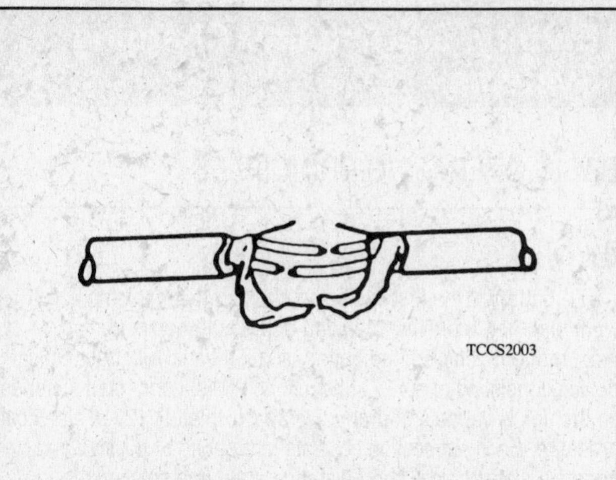

Fig. 2 Damaged insulation can allow wires to break (causing an open circuit) or touch (causing a short)

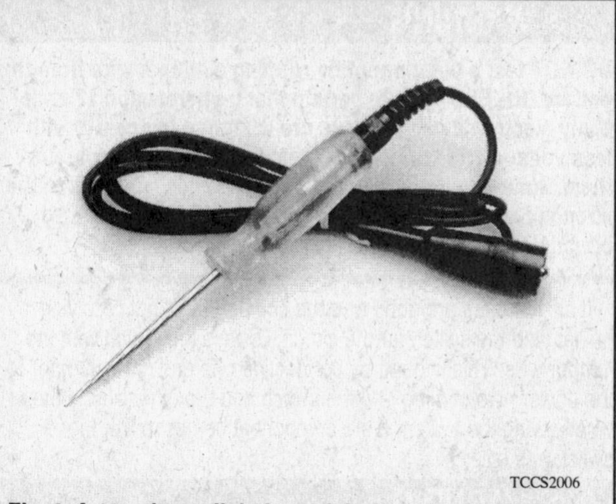

Fig. 3 A 12 volt test light is useful when checking parts of a circuit for power

A circuit breaker is basically a self repairing fuse. It will open the circuit in the same fashion as a fuse, but when either the short is removed or the surge subsides, the circuit breaker resets itself and does not need replacement.

A fuse link (fusible link or main link) is a wire that acts as a fuse. One of these is normally connected between the starter relay and the main wiring harness under the hood. Since the starter is usually the highest electrical draw on the vehicle, an internal short during starting could direct about 130 amps into the wrong places. Consider the damage potential of introducing this current into a system whose wiring is rated at 15 amps and you'll understand the need for protection. Since this link is very early in the electrical path, it's the first place to look if nothing on the vehicle works, but the battery seems to be charged and is properly connected.

TROUBLESHOOTING

➧ **See Figures 3, 4 and 5**

Electrical problems generally fall into one of three areas:

- The component that is not functioning is not receiving current.
- The component is receiving power but is not using it or is using it incorrectly (component failure).
- The component is improperly grounded.

The circuit can be can be checked with a test light and a jumper wire. The test light is a device that looks like a pointed screwdriver with a wire on one end and a bulb in its handle. A jumper wire is simply a piece of wire with alligator clips or special terminals on each end. If a component is not working, you must follow a systematic plan to determine which of the three causes is the villain.

1. Turn ON the switch that controls the item not working.

➝ **Some items only work when the ignition switch is turned ON.**

2. Disconnect the power supply wire from the component.
3. Attach the ground wire of a test light or a voltmeter to a good metal ground.

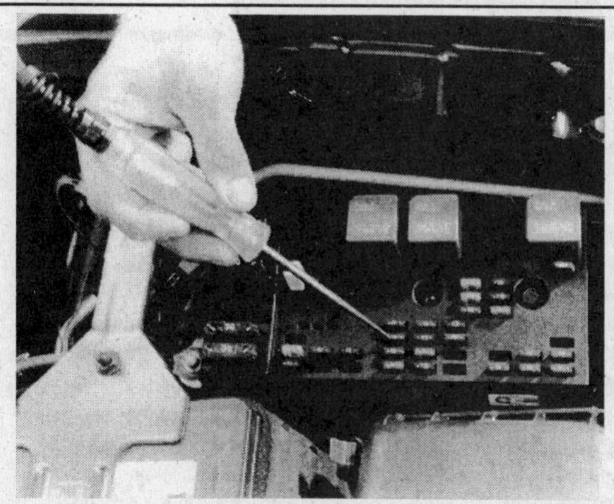

Fig. 4 Here, someone is checking a circuit by making sure there is power to the component's fuse

4. Touch the end probe of the test light (or the positive lead of the voltmeter) to the power wire; if there is current in the wire, the light in the test light will come on (or the voltmeter will indicate the amount of voltage). You have now established that current is getting to the component.
5. Turn the ignition or dash switch **OFF** and reconnect the wire to the component.

If there was no power, then the problem is between the battery and the component. This includes all the switches, fuses, relays and the battery itself. The next place to look is the fusebox; check carefully either by eye or by using the test light across the fuse clips. The easiest way to check is to simply replace the fuse. If the fuse is blown, and upon replacement, immediately blows again, there is a short between the fuse and the component. This is generally (not always) a sign of an internal short in the component. Disconnect the power wire at the component again and replace the fuse; if the fuse holds, the component is the problem.

✲✲WARNING

DO NOT test a component by running a jumper wire from the battery UNLESS you are certain that it operates on 12 volts. Many electronic components are designed to operate with less voltage and connecting them to 12 volts could destroy them. Jumper wires are best used to bypass a portion of the circuit (such as a stretch of wire or a switch) that DOES NOT contain a resistor and is suspected to be bad.

If all the fuses are good and the component is not receiving power, find the switch for the circuit. Bypass the switch with the jumper wire. This is done by connecting one end of the jumper to the power wire coming into the switch and the other end to the wire leaving the switch. If the component comes to life, the switch has failed.

✲✲WARNING

Never substitute the jumper for the component. The circuit needs the electrical load of the component. If you bypass it, you will cause a short circuit.

Checking the ground for any circuit can mean tracing wires to the body, cleaning connections or tightening mounting bolts for the component itself. If the jumper wire can be connected to the case of the component or the ground connector, you can ground the other end to a piece of clean, solid metal on the vehicle. Again, if the component starts working, you've found the problem.

A systematic search through the fuse, connectors, switches and the component itself will almost always yield an answer. Loose and/or corroded connectors, particularly in ground circuits, are becoming a larger problem in modern vehicles. The computers and on-board electronic (solid state) systems are highly sensitive to improper grounds and will change their function drastically if one occurs.

Remember that for any electrical circuit to work, ALL the connections must be clean and tight.

➦ **For more information on Understanding and Troubleshooting Electrical Systems, please refer to Section 6 of this manual.**

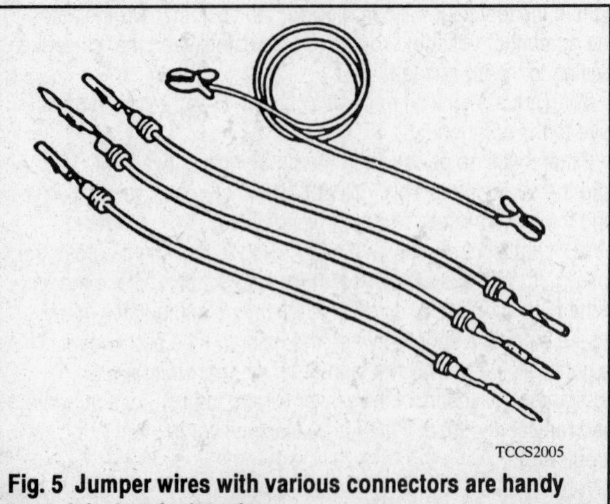

Fig. 5 Jumper wires with various connectors are handy for quick electrical testing

Battery, Starting and Charging Systems

BASIC OPERATING PRINCIPLES

Battery

The battery is the first link in the chain of mechanisms which work together to provide cranking of the automobile engine. In most modern vehicles, the battery is a lead/acid electrochemical device consisting of six 2v subsections (cells) connected in series so the unit is capable of producing approximately 12v of electrical pressure. Each subsection consists of a series of positive and negative plates held a short distance apart in a solution of sulfuric acid and water.

The two types of plates are of dissimilar metals. This sets-up a chemical reaction, and it is this reaction which produces current flow from the battery when its positive and negative terminals are connected to an electrical accessory such as a lamp or motor. The continued transfer of electrons would eventually convert the sulfuric acid to water, and make the two plates identical in chemical composition. As electrical energy is removed from the battery, its voltage output tends to drop. Thus, measuring battery voltage and battery electrolyte composition are two ways of checking the ability of the unit to supply power. During engine cranking, electrical energy is removed from the battery. However, if the charging circuit is in good condition and the operating conditions are normal, the power removed from the battery will be replaced by the alternator which will force electrons back through the battery, reversing the normal flow, and restoring the battery to its original chemical state.

Starting System

The battery and starting motor are linked by very heavy electrical cables designed to minimize resistance to the flow of current. Generally, the major power supply cable that leaves the battery goes directly to the starter, while other electrical system needs are supplied by a smaller cable. During starter operation, power flows from the battery to the starter and is grounded through the vehicle's frame/body or engine and the battery's negative ground strap.

The starter is a specially designed, direct current electric motor capable of producing a great amount of power for its size. One thing that allows the motor to produce a great deal of power is its tremendous rotating speed. It drives the engine through a tiny pinion gear (attached to the starter's armature), which drives the very large flywheel ring gear at a greatly reduced speed. Another factor allowing it to produce so much power is that only intermittent operation is required of it. Thus, little allowance for air circulation is necessary, and the windings can be built into a very small space.

The starter solenoid is a magnetic device which employs the small current supplied by the start circuit of the ignition switch. This magnetic action moves a plunger which mechanically engages the starter and closes the heavy switch connecting it to the battery. The starting switch circuit usually consists of the starting switch contained within the ignition switch, a neutral safety switch or clutch pedal switch, and the wiring necessary to connect these in series with the starter solenoid or relay.

The pinion, a small gear, is mounted to a one way drive clutch. This clutch is splined to the starter armature shaft. When the ignition switch is moved to the **START** position, the solenoid plunger slides the pinion toward the flywheel ring gear via a collar and spring. If the teeth on the pinion and flywheel match properly, the pinion will engage the flywheel immediately. If the gear teeth butt one another, the spring will be compressed and will force the gears to mesh as soon as the starter turns far enough to allow them to do so. As the solenoid plunger reaches the end of its travel, it closes the contacts that connect the battery and starter, then the engine is cranked.

As soon as the engine starts, the flywheel ring gear begins turning fast enough to drive the pinion at an extremely high rate of speed. At this point, the one-way clutch begins allowing the pinion to spin faster than the starter shaft so that the starter will not operate at excessive speed. When the ignition switch is released from the starter position, the solenoid is de-energized, and a spring pulls the gear out of mesh interrupting the current flow to the starter.

Some starters employ a separate relay, mounted away from the starter, to switch the motor and solenoid current on and off. The relay replaces the solenoid electrical switch, but does not eliminate the need for a solenoid mounted on the starter used to mechanically engage the starter drive gears. The relay is used to reduce the amount of current the starting switch must carry.

Charging System

The automobile charging system provides electrical power for operation of the vehicle's ignition system, starting system and all electrical accessories. The battery serves as an electrical surge or storage tank, storing (in chemical form) the energy originally produced by the engine driven generator. The system also provides a means of regulating output to protect the battery from being overcharged and to avoid excessive voltage to the accessories.

The storage battery is a chemical device incorporating parallel lead plates in a tank containing a sulfuric acid/water solution. Adjacent plates are slightly dissimilar, and the chemical reaction of the two dissimilar plates produces electrical energy when the battery is connected to a load such as the starter motor. The chemical reaction is reversible, so that when the generator is producing a voltage (electrical pressure) greater than that produced by the battery, electricity is forced into the battery, and the battery is returned to its fully charged state.

Newer automobiles use alternating current generators or alternators, because they are more efficient, can be rotated at higher speeds, and have fewer brush problems. In an alternator, the field usually rotates while all the current produced passes only through the stator winding. The brushes bear against continuous slip rings. This causes the current produced to periodically reverse the direction of its flow. Diodes (electrical one way valves) block the flow of current from traveling in the wrong direction. A series of diodes is wired together to permit the alternating flow of the stator to be rectified back to 12 volts DC for use by the vehicle's electrical system.

The voltage regulating function is performed by a regulator. The regulator is often built in to the alternator; this system is termed an integrated or internal regulator.

Troubleshooting Basic Charging System Problems

Problem	Cause	Solution
Noisy alternator	• Loose mountings • Loose drive pulley • Worn bearings • Brush noise • Internal circuits shorted (High pitched whine)	• Tighten mounting bolts • Tighten pulley • Replace alternator • Replace alternator • Replace alternator
Squeal when starting engine or accelerating	• Glazed or loose belt	• Replace or adjust belt
Indicator light remains on or ammeter indicates discharge (engine running)	• Broken belt • Broken or disconnected wires • Internal alternator problems • Defective voltage regulator	• Install belt • Repair or connect wiring • Replace alternator • Replace voltage regulator/alternator
Car light bulbs continually burn out—battery needs water continually	• Alternator/regulator overcharging	• Replace voltage regulator/alternator
Car lights flare on acceleration	• Battery low • Internal alternator/regulator problems	• Charge or replace battery • Replace alternator/regulator
Low voltage output (alternator light flickers continually or ammeter needle wanders)	• Loose or worn belt • Dirty or corroded connections • Internal alternator/regulator problems	• Replace or adjust belt • Clean or replace connections • Replace alternator/regulator

TCCS2C02

Troubleshooting Basic Starting System Problems

Problem	Cause	Solution
Starter motor rotates engine slowly	· Battery charge low or battery defective	· Charge or replace battery
	· Defective circuit between battery and starter motor	· Clean and tighten, or replace cables
	· Low load current	· Bench-test starter motor. Inspect for worn brushes and weak brush springs.
	· High load current	· Bench-test starter motor. Check engine for friction, drag or coolant in cylinders. Check ring gear-to-pinion gear clearance.
Starter motor will not rotate engine	· Battery charge low or battery defective	· Charge or replace battery
	· Faulty solenoid	· Check solenoid ground. Repair or replace as necessary.
	· Damaged drive pinion gear or ring gear	· Replace damaged gear(s)
	· Starter motor engagement weak	· Bench-test starter motor
	· Starter motor rotates slowly with high load current	· Inspect drive yoke pull-down and point gap, check for worn end bushings, check ring gear clearance
	· Engine seized	· Repair engine
Starter motor drive will not engage (solenoid known to be good)	· Defective contact point assembly	· Repair or replace contact point assembly
	· Inadequate contact point assembly ground	· Repair connection at ground screw
	· Defective hold-in coil	· Replace field winding assembly
Starter motor drive will not disengage	· Starter motor loose on flywheel housing	· Tighten mounting bolts
	· Worn drive end busing	· Replace bushing
	· Damaged ring gear teeth	· Replace ring gear or driveplate
	· Drive yoke return spring broken or missing	· Replace spring
Starter motor drive disengages prematurely	· Weak drive assembly thrust spring	· Replace drive mechanism
	· Hold-in coil defective	· Replace field winding assembly
Low load current	· Worn brushes	· Replace brushes
	· Weak brush springs	· Replace springs

TCCS2C01

ENGINE ELECTRICAL

Refer to Section 2 for further ignition system diagnosis and component replacement.

Ignition Coil

TESTING

All Models

See Figure 6

On models equipped with the 3.3L and 3.8L engines, the spark at the coil is tested in the same way as models with a distributor. But each of the coil's towers must be checked for spark.

1. Remove the coil wire from the distributor cap. Hold the end of the wire about 1/4 in. (6mm) away from a good engine ground point.
2. Have a helper crank the engine. Check for a spark between the coil wire end and the ground point.
3. If there is a spark, it must be constant and bright blue in color.
4. Continue to crank the engine. Slowly move the wire away from the ground point. If arching at the coil tower occurs, replace the coil.
5. If the spark is good and no arcing at the coil tower occurs, the ignition system is producing the necessary high secondary voltage.
6. Check to make sure that the voltage is getting to the spark plugs. Inspect the distributor cap, rotor, spark plug wires and spark plugs.
7. If all of the components check okay, the ignition system is probably not the reason why the engine does not start.
8. Check the fuel system and engine mechanical items, such as the timing belt.

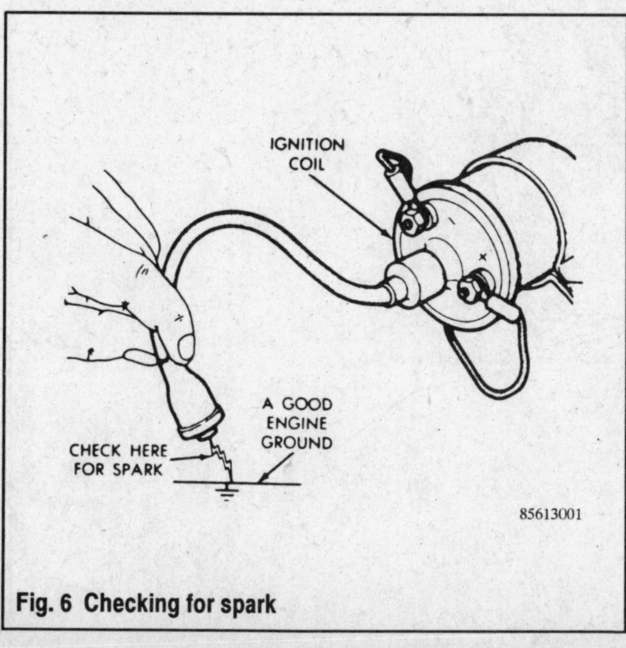

Fig. 6 Checking for spark

REMOVAL & INSTALLATION

Except 3.3L and 3.8L Engines

1. Disconnect the negative battery cable.
2. Remove the coil wire from the top of the coil.
3. Remove the wires from the top of the coil.
4. Remove the coil mounting bolt and remove the coil from the engine.

To install:

5. Mount the replacement coil in position.
6. Reconnect all of the wires.
7. Connect the battery cable.

3.3L and 3.8L Engines

See Figure 7

1. Disconnect the negative battery cable.
2. Remove the electrical connector from the coil assembly.
3. Tag and disconnect the spark plug wires from the coil assembly.
4. Remove the coil mounting bolts and remove the coil assembly from the engine.

To install:

5. Mount the coil in position and connect all of the wires.
6. Tighten the coil assembly mounting bolts to 105 inch lbs. (12 Nm).
7. Connect the negative battery cable.

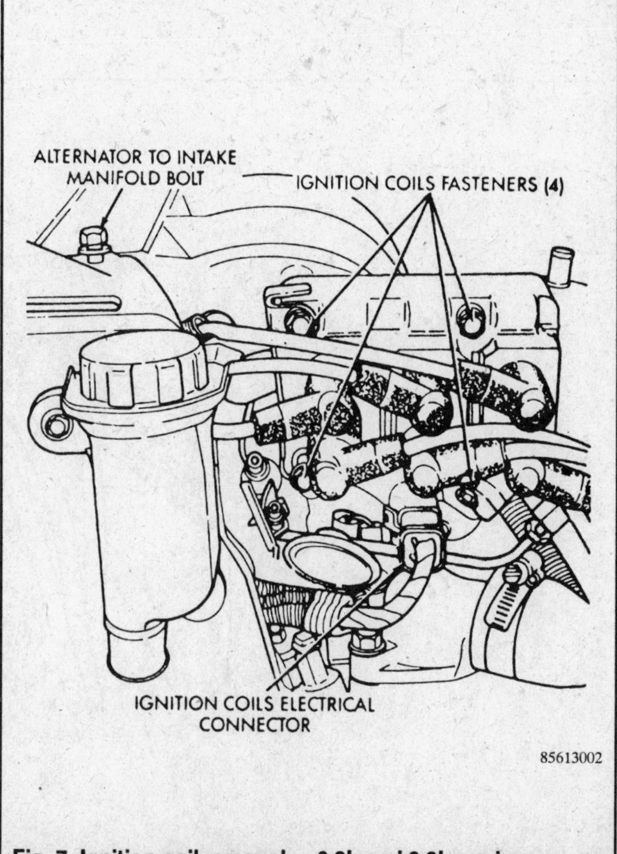

Fig. 7 Ignition coil removal — 3.3L and 3.8L engines

Distributor Cap

REMOVAL & INSTALLATION

1. Remove the splash shield retaining screws and the splash shield.
2. Loosen the distributor cap retaining screws.
3. Remove the distributor cap
4. Inspect the inside, of the cap, for spark flash over (burnt tracks on cap or terminals), center carbon button wear or cracking, and worn terminals. Replace the cap if any of these problems are present or suspected.

Light deposits on the terminals can be scraped cleaned with a knife, heavy deposits or scaling will require cap replacement.

Wash the cap with a solution of warm water and mild detergent, scrub with a soft brush and dry with a clean soft cloth to remove dirt and grease.

5. If cap replacement is necessary, take notice of the cap installed position in relationship to the distributor assembly.
6. Number each plug wire so that the correct wire goes on the proper cap terminal when replaced. This can be done with pieces of adhesive tape.

Do not pull plugs wires from distributor cap, they must first be released from inside of cap.

7. Position the replacement cap on the distributor assembly, and tighten the distributor cap retaining screws.
8. Push the wire terminals firmly to properly seat the wires into the cap.
9. Reinstall the splash shield.

Distributor Rotor

With the distributor cap removed, remove the rotor. Inspect the rotor for cracks, excessive wear or burn marks and sufficient spring tension of the spring to cap carbon button terminal. Clean light deposits, replace the rotor if scaled or burnt heavily. Clean the ground strap on the inner side of the shaft mount. Take care not to bend any of the shutter blades, if blades are bent replace the rotor.

Distributor

REMOVAL

See Figure 8

Although not absolutely necessary, it is probably easier (for reference reinstallation, especially if the engine is rotated after distributor removal) to bring the engine to No. 1 cylinder at TDC (top dead center) before removing the distributor.

1. Disconnect the distributor lead wires, and vacuum hose as necessary.
2. Remove the distributor cap.
3. Rotate the engine crankshaft (in the direction of normal rotation) until No. 1 cylinder is at Top Dead Center (TDC) on the compression stroke. Make a mark on the block to where the rotor points, for installation reference.
4. Remove the distributor hold-down bolt.
5. Carefully lift the distributor from the engine. The shaft will rotate slightly as the distributor is removed.

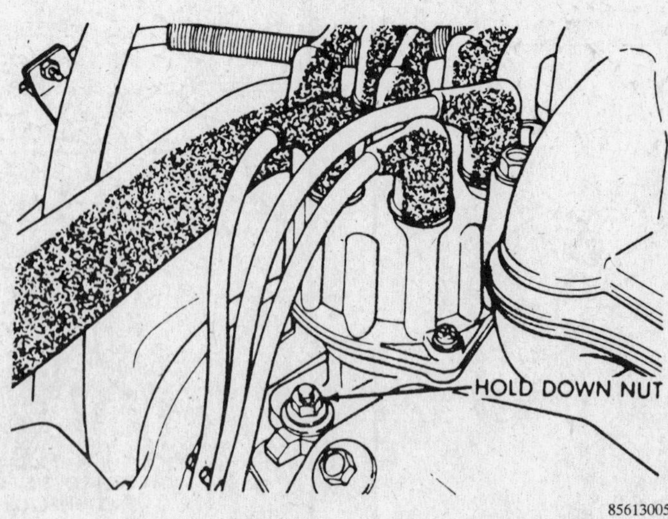

Fig. 8 Distributor hold-down — 3.0L engines

INSTALLATION

Engine Not Rotated

1. If the engine was not disturbed while the distributor was out, lower the distributor into the engine, engaging the gears and making sure that the gasket is properly seated in the block. The rotor should line up with the mark made before removal.
2. Install the distributor cap.
3. Tighten the hold-down bolt. Connect the wires and vacuum hose as necessary.
4. Check and, if necessary, adjust the ignition timing.

Engine Rotated

➥ The following procedure is to be used if the engine was rotated with the distributor removed.

1. If the engine has been cranked/turned while the distributor was removed, rotate the crankshaft until the number one piston is at TDC on the compression stroke. This will be indicated by the O mark on the flywheel (2.2L and 2.5L engines) aligned with the pointer on the clutch housing, or crank pulley (2.6L and 3.0L engines) aligned with the pointer on engine front cover.
2. Position the rotor just ahead of the No. 1 terminal of the cap and lower the distributor into the engine. With the distributor fully seated, the rotor should be directly under the No. 1 terminal.
3. Install the distributor cap.
4. Tighten the hold-down bolt. Connect the wires and vacuum hose as necessary.
5. Check and, if necessary, adjust the ignition timing.

Alternator

The alternator charging system is a negative (–) ground system which consists of an alternator, a regulator, a charge indicator, a storage battery and wiring connecting the components, and fuse link wire.

The alternator is belt-driven from the engine. Energy is supplied from the alternator/regulator system to the rotating field through 2 brushes to 2 slip-rings. The slip-rings are mounted on the rotor shaft and are connected to the field coil. This energy supplied to the rotating field from the battery is called excitation current and is used to initially energize the field to begin the generation of electricity. Once the alternator starts to generate electricity, the excitation current comes from its own output rather than the battery.

The alternator produces power in the form of alternating current. The alternating current is rectified by 6 diodes into direct current. The direct current is used to charge the battery and power the rest of the electrical system.

When the ignition key is turned **ON**, current flows from the battery, through the charging system indicator light on the instrument panel, to the voltage regulator, and to the alternator. Since the alternator is not producing any current, the alternator warning light comes on. When the engine is started, the alternator begins to produce current and turns the alternator light off. As the alternator turns and produces current, the current is divided in 2 ways: part to the battery to charge the battery and power the electrical components of the vehicle, and part is returned to the alternator to enable it to increase its output. In this situation, the alternator is receiving current from the battery and from itself. A voltage regulator is wired into the current supply to the alternator to prevent it from receiving too much current which would cause it to put out too much current. Conversely, if the voltage regulator does not allow the alternator to receive enough current, the battery will not be fully charged and will eventually go dead.

The battery is connected to the alternator at all times, whether the ignition key is turned **ON** or not. If the battery were shorted to ground, the alternator would also be shorted. This would damage the alternator. To prevent this, a fuse link is installed in the wiring between the battery and the alternator. If the battery is shorted, the fuse link is melted, protecting the alternator.

ALTERNATOR PRECAUTIONS

Some precautions should be taken when working on this, or any other, AC charging system.

- Never switch battery polarity.
- When installing a battery, always connect the grounded terminal first.
- Never disconnect the battery while the engine is running.
- If the molded connector is disengaged from the alternator, never ground the hot wire.
- Never run the alternator with the main output cable disconnected.
- Never electric weld around the truck without disconnecting the alternator.
- Never apply any voltage in excess of battery voltage while testing.
- Never jump a battery for starting purposes with more than 12 volts.

CHARGING SYSTEM TROUBLESHOOTING

There are many possible ways in which the charging system can malfunction. Often the source of a problem is difficult to diagnose, requiring special equipment and a good deal of experience. This is usually not the case, however, where the charging system fails completely and causes the dash board warning light to come on or the battery to become dead. To troubleshoot a complete system failure only 2 pieces of equipment are needed: a test light, to determine that current is reaching a certain point; and a current indicator (ammeter), to determine the direction of the current flow and its measurement in amps.

This test works under 3 assumptions:

- The battery is known to be good and fully charged.
- The alternator belt is in good condition and adjusted to the proper tension.
- All connections in the system are clean and tight.

➥ In order for the current indicator to give a valid reading, the vehicle must be equipped with battery cables which are of the same gauge size and quality as original equipment battery cables.

1. Turn off all electrical components on the vehicle. Make sure the doors of the vehicle are closed. If the vehicle is equipped with a clock, disconnect the clock by removing the lead wire from the rear of the clock. Disconnect the positive battery cable from the battery and connect the ground wire on a test light to the disconnected positive battery cable. Touch the probe end of the test light to the positive battery post. The test light should not light. If the test light does light, there is a short or open circuit on the vehicle.

2. Disconnect the voltage regulator wiring harness connector at the voltage regulator. Turn **ON** the ignition key. Connect the wire on a test light to a good ground (engine bolt). Touch the probe end of a test light to the ignition wire connector into the voltage regulator wiring connector. This wire corresponds to the **I** terminal on the regulator. If the test light goes on, the charging system warning light circuit is complete. If the test light does not come on and the warning light on the instrument panel is on, either the resistor wire, which is parallel with the warning light, or the wiring to the voltage regulator, is defective. If the test light does not come on and the warning light is not on, either the bulb is defective or the power supply wire form the battery through the ignition switch to the bulb has an open circuit. Connect the wiring harness to the regulator.

3. Examine the fuse link wire in the wiring harness from the starter relay to the alternator. If the insulation on the wire is cracked or split, the fuse link may be melted. Connect a test light to the fuse link by attaching the ground wire on the test light to an engine bolt and touching the probe end of the light to the bottom of the fuse link wire where it splices into the alternator output wire. If the bulb in the test light does not light, the fuse link is melted.

4. Start the engine and place a current indicator on the positive battery cable. Turn off all electrical accessories and make sure the doors are closed. If the charging system is working properly, the gauge will show a draw of less than 5 amps. If the system is not working properly, the gauge will show a draw of more than 5 amps. A charge moves the needle toward the battery, a draw moves the needle away from the battery. Turn the engine **OFF**.

5. Disconnect the wiring harness from the voltage regulator at the regulator at the regulator connector. Connect a male spade terminal (solderless connector) to each end of a jumper wire. Insert one end of the wire into the wiring harness connector which corresponds to the **A** terminal on the regulator. Insert the other end of the wire into the wiring harness connector which corresponds to the **F** terminal on the regulator. Position the connector with the jumper wire installed so that it cannot contact any metal surface under the hood. Position a current indicator gauge on the positive battery cable. Have an assistant start the engine. Observe the reading on the current indicator. Have your assistant slowly raise the speed of the engine to about 2000 rpm or until the current indicator needle stops moving, whichever comes first. Do not run the engine for more than a short period of time in this condition. If the wiring harness connector or jumper wire becomes excessively hot during this test, turn off the engine and check for a grounded wire in the regulator wiring harness. If the current indicator shows a charge of about 3 amps less than the output of the alternator, the alternator is working properly. If the previous tests showed a draw, the voltage regulator is defective. If the gauge does not show the proper charging rate, the alternator is defective.

REMOVAL & INSTALLATION

2.2L Engines

CHRYSLER ALTERNATOR

See Figures 9, 10, 11, 12 and 13

1. Disconnect the negative battery cable.
2. Label and disconnect the wiring (for easy installation).

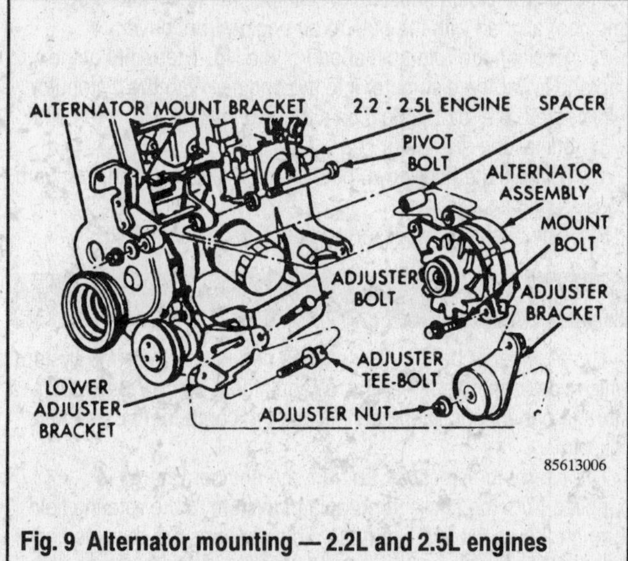

Fig. 9 Alternator mounting — 2.2L and 2.5L engines

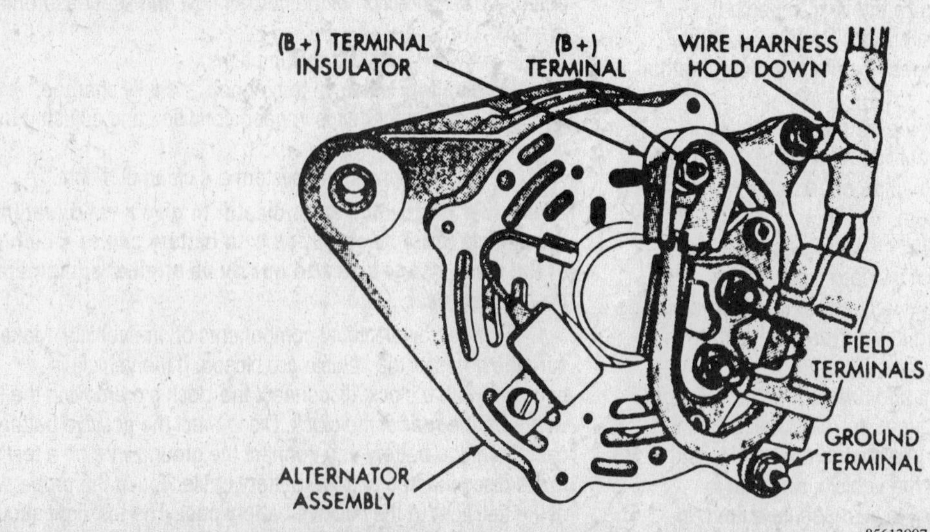

Fig. 10 Disconnecting alternator wiring — 2.2L and 2.5L engines

3. Remove the air conditioning compressor drive belt, if equipped.
4. Loosen the alternator adjusting bracket bolt and adjusting bolt. Remove the alternator belt.
5. Remove the bracket and mounting bolts.
6. Remove the pivot bolt and nut.
7. Lift the alternator from the vehicle.

→ When lifting the alternator out of the vehicle on some years with A/C, clearance may be restricted by the condenser cooling fan assembly or the A/C compressor and mounting bracket assembly, if so, removal of one of these items will be necessary.

To install:

8. Position the alternator against the engine.
9. Install the pivot bolt and nut.
10. Install the mounting bracket bolts, and adjusting bolt.
11. Install drive belts and adjust to specification.
12. Tighten all the mounting bolts and nuts.
13. Connect all alternator terminals.
14. Connect the negative battery cable.

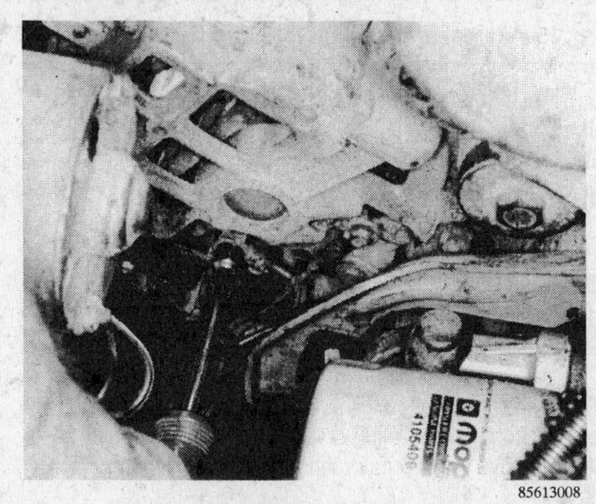
85613008

Fig. 11 Disconnecting alternator wiring

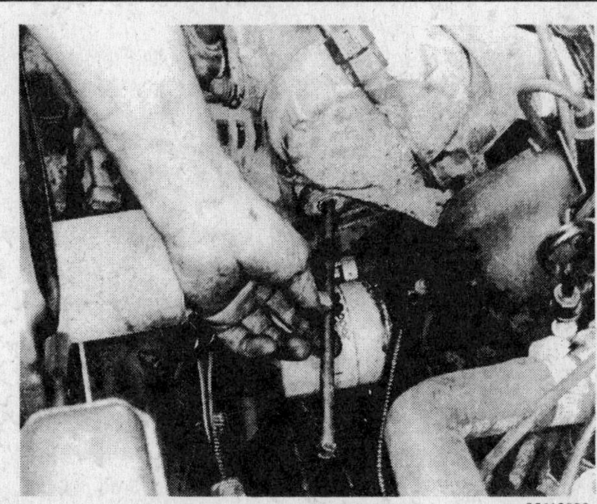
85613009

Fig. 12 Removing the pivot bolt and nut

85613010

Fig. 13 Removing the alternator from the vehicle

BOSCH ALTERNATOR

1. Disconnect the negative battery cable.
2. Disconnect the wiring and label for easy installation.
3. Remove the air conditioning compressor drive belt.
4. Loosen the alternator adjusting bracket locknut and adjusting screw. Remove the alternator belt.
5. Remove the bracket locknut and mounting bolt.
6. Remove the pivot bolt and nut.
7. Remove the alternator from the engine.

To install:

8. Position the alternator against the engine.
9. Install pivot bolt and nut.
10. Set the mounting bracket in place and install the bracket mounting bolt and locknut.
11. Install the drive belts and adjust to specification.
12. Tighten all the mounting bolts and nuts.
13. Connect all alternator terminals.
14. Connect the negative battery cable.

2.5L Engines

See Figures 9 and 10

→ 2.5L engines were equipped with either Chrysler or Bosch alternators.

1. Disconnect the negative battery cable.
2. Remove the drive belts.
3. Remove the adjusting bracket-to-engine mounting bolt.
4. Remove the adjusting locking bolt and nut, then remove the mounting bracket.
5. Position the alternator to gain access to the wiring.
6. Disconnect the wiring and label for easy installation.
7. Remove the pivot bolt, nut, and washers.
8. Remove the alternator assembly from the engine.

To install:

9. Position the alternator assembly against the engine.
10. Loosely install the pivot bolt, washers, and nut.
11. Attach all wiring connectors to the alternator.
12. Position the mounting bracket in place, then install engine mounting bolt.
13. Loosely install the adjusting locking bolt and nut.
14. Install the drive belts, and adjust to specification.

15. Tighten all mounting bolts and nuts.
16. Connect the negative battery cable.

2.6L Engines

➥ 2.6L engines were equipped with Mitsubishi alternators.

1. Disconnect the negative battery cable.
2. Disconnect the wiring and label for easy installation.
3. Remove the adjusting strap mounting bolt.
4. Remove the drive belts.
5. Remove the support mounting bolt and nut.
6. Remove the alternator assembly.

To install:

7. Position the alternator assembly against the engine, then install the support bolt.
8. Install the adjusting strap mounting bolt.
9. Install the alternator belts and adjust to specification.
10. Tighten all the support bolts and nuts.
11. Connect all of the wiring terminals to the alternator.
12. Connect the negative battery cable.

3.0L Engines

➧ See Figures 14 and 15

➥ The 3.0L engines were equipped with either the Nippondenso or Bosch alternators.

1. Disconnect the negative battery cable.
2. Install a $^1/_2$ in. breaker bar in the tensioner slot. Rotate counterclockwise to release belt tension and remove poly-V belt.
3. Remove the alternator mounting bolts (2).
4. Remove the wiring and remove alternator.

To install:

5. Position the alternator onto the engine, then install the wiring.
6. Set the alternator against the mounting bracket and install the mounting bolts.

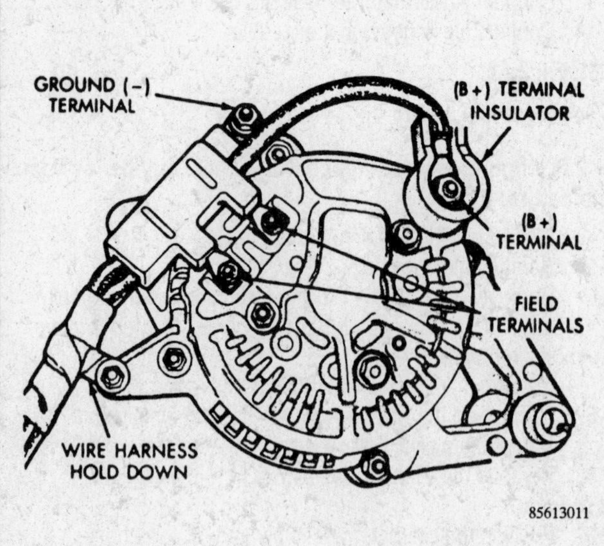

Fig. 14 Disconnecting the alternator wiring — 3.0L engines

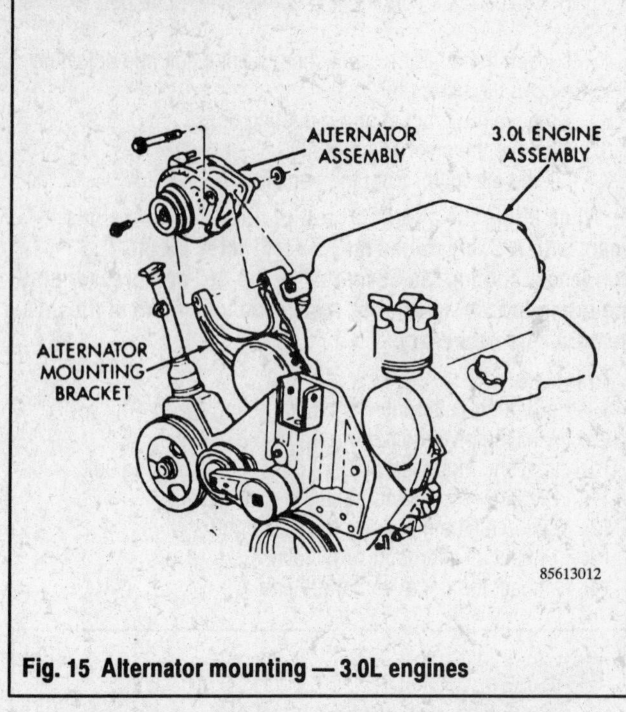

Fig. 15 Alternator mounting — 3.0L engines

7. Rotate the tensioner counterclockwise and install poly-V belt.
8. Connect the negative battery cable.

3.3L and 3.8L Engines

➥ The 3.3L and 3.8L engines were equipped with the Nippondenso alternators.

1. Disconnect the negative battery cable.
2. Remove the alternator drive belt, by relieving the tension on the dynamic tensioner.
3. Loosen the nut on the support bracket at the exhaust manifold, do not remove it.
4. Remove the alternator tensioner/power steering bracket bolt.
5. Remove the tensioner stud nut and remove the tensioner.
6. Remove the alternator mounting bolts.
7. Remove the power steering reservoir from the mounting bracket, do not disconnect the hoses, and position it out of the way.
8. Remove the alternator support bracket bolts. Remove the intake plenum to alternator bracket bolt and remove the alternator support bracket from the engine.
9. Remove the alternator from the engine and disconnect the electrical leads.

To install:

10. Install the alternator in position on the engine and connect the electrical leads.
11. Install the alternator support bracket, tighten the retaining bolts to 40 ft. lbs. (54 Nm).
12. Install the power steering reservoir on the mounting bracket.
13. Install the alternator mounting bolts, tighten the bolts to 40 ft. lbs. (54 Nm).
14. Install the tensioner and tensioner mounting stud. Install the retaining nut on the exhaust manifold.

15. Install the alternator belt, insert a 1/2 in. extension into the square hole in the tensioner and turn the tensioner. Tighten the tensioner bolt.
16. Connect the negative battery cable.

Regulator

REMOVAL & INSTALLATION

➡ All Bosch, Nippondenso, Mitsubishi, and Chrysler (late model) alternators have an integral electronic voltage regulator. Voltage regulator replacement on these models requires removal and disassembly of the alternator.

Chrysler Alternator (Early Model)

1. Disconnect the negative battery cable.
2. Remove the electrical connection from voltage regulator assembly.
3. Remove the mounting bolts and remove the regulator.
4. This regulator is not adjustable and must be replaced as a unit if found to be defective.

To install:

5. Clean any dirt or corrosion from the regulator mounting surface, including mounting holes.
6. Install the replacement electronic voltage regulator.
7. Secured the mounting screws.
8. Attach the voltage regulator wiring connector. Connect the negative battery cable.

Starter

➧ See Figures 16, 17 and 18

TEST PROCEDURES (ON VEHICLE)

➡ The battery is the heart of the electrical system. If the battery is not up to specification it will not deliver the necessary amperage for proper starter operation.

Starter Does Not Operate

****CAUTION**

Before performing this test, disconnect the coil wire from the distributor cap center tower and secure to a good engine ground. This will prevent the engine from starting.

1. Connect a voltmeter across the battery terminals and confirm that battery voltage (12.4 volts) is available for the ignition and cranking system.
2. Turn the headlights on.

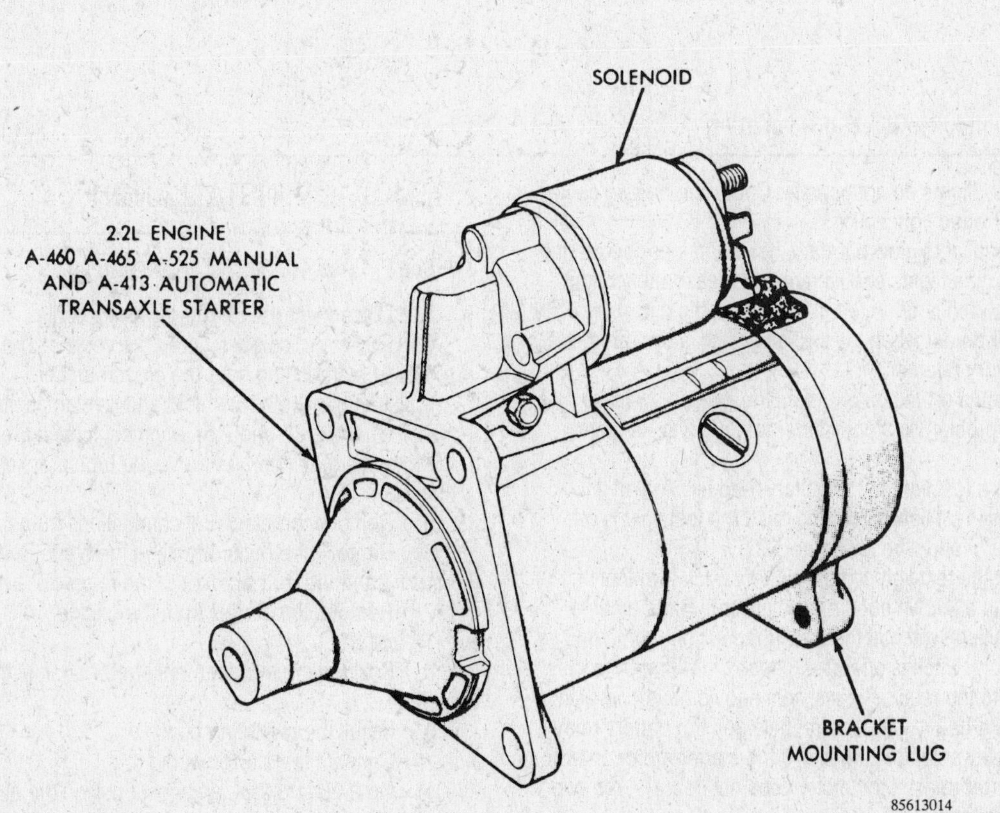

Fig. 16 Bosch direct drive starter

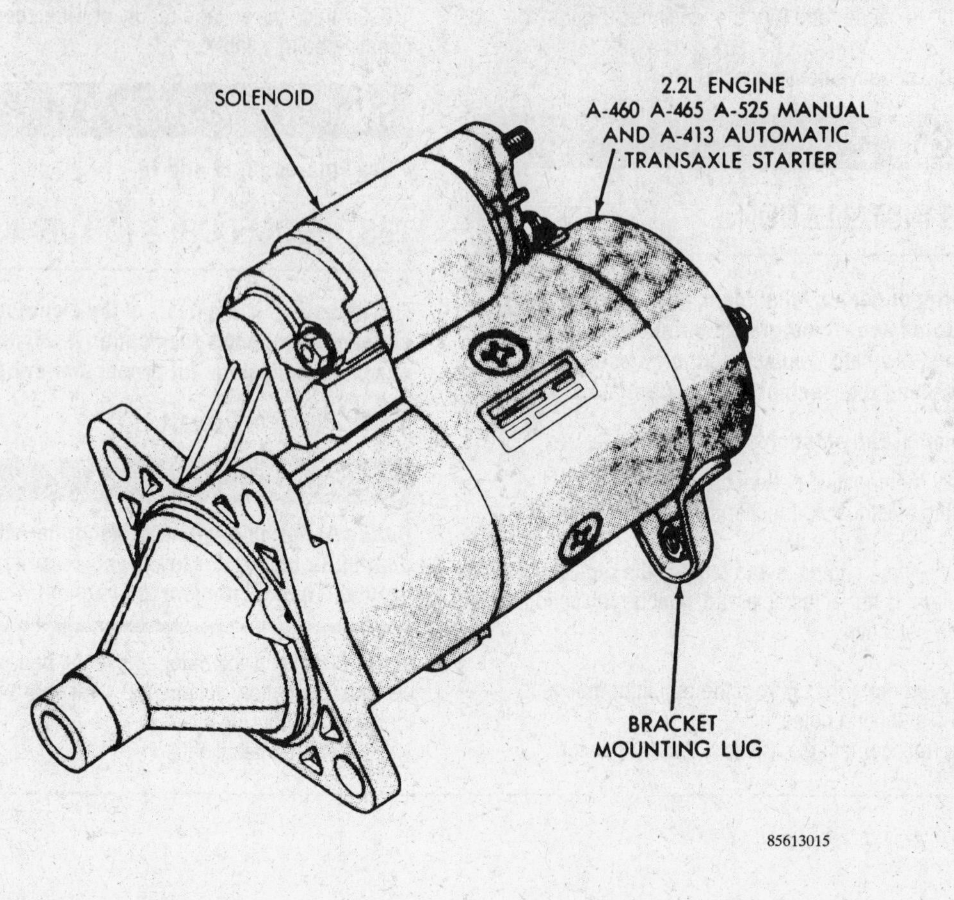

Fig. 17 Nippondenso direct drive starter

3. If the headlights do not operate. Check the battery cables for loose or corroded connection.
4. If the headlights glow normally, have a helper operate the ignition switch. Headlights should remained reasonably bright when ignition switch is operated. If the headlights dim considerably or go out when the ignition switch is operated, the problem is battery related.
5. If headlights remain bright when the ignition switch is operated. The problem is at the starter relay, wiring, or starter motor.
6. Connect a test light to the battery feed terminal of the starter relay. The test light should go on. If the test light is off, check the battery feed wire to starter relay.
7. Connect the test light to the ignition switch terminal of starter relay and a known good engine ground. Have a helper operate the ignition switch. If the test light does not come on when the ignition switch is operated, check the wiring from the ignition switch to the relay. The test light should have come on.
8. Connect a heavy jumper wire, between the battery relay feed and the relay solenoid terminal. If the starter motor operates replace the starter relay. If the motor does not operate, remove the starter for repairs.

REMOVAL & INSTALLATION

See Figures 19, 20, 21, 22, 23 and 24

1. Disconnect the negative battery cable.
2. Raise and safely support the vehicle. The starter can be removed by reaching over the crossmember.
3. Remove the heat shield and its clamps, if so equipped.
4. On the 2.2L and 2.5L engines, loosen the air pump tube at the exhaust manifold and move the tube bracket away from the starter.
5. Remove the electrical connections from the starter.
6. Remove the bolts attaching the starter to the flywheel housing and the rear bracket to the engine or transaxle.
7. Remove the starter from the engine.

To install:

8. Position the replacement starter against the mounting surface.
9. Install the mounting bolts.
10. Connect the starter wiring.
11. On 2.2L and 2.5L engines, position the air pump tube toward the starter, then connect the tube bracket to the exhaust manifold.
12. Install the heat shield and clamp.
13. Connect the negative battery cable.

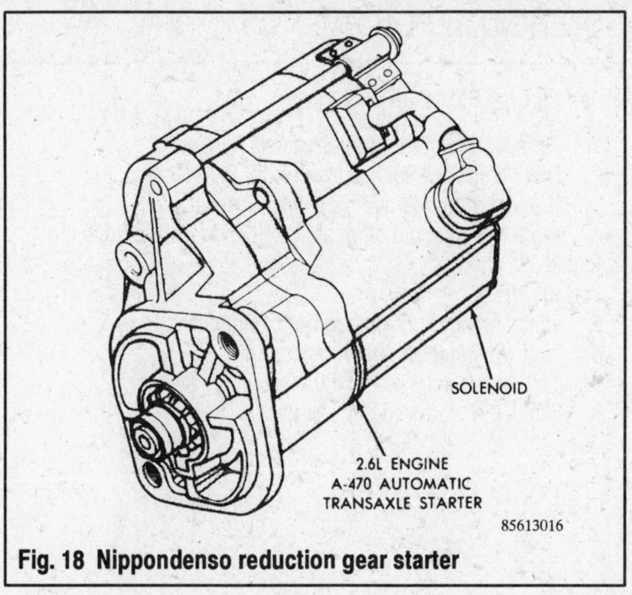

Fig. 18 Nippondenso reduction gear starter

Fig. 21 View of the starter motor with the heat shield removed while looking over the crossmember

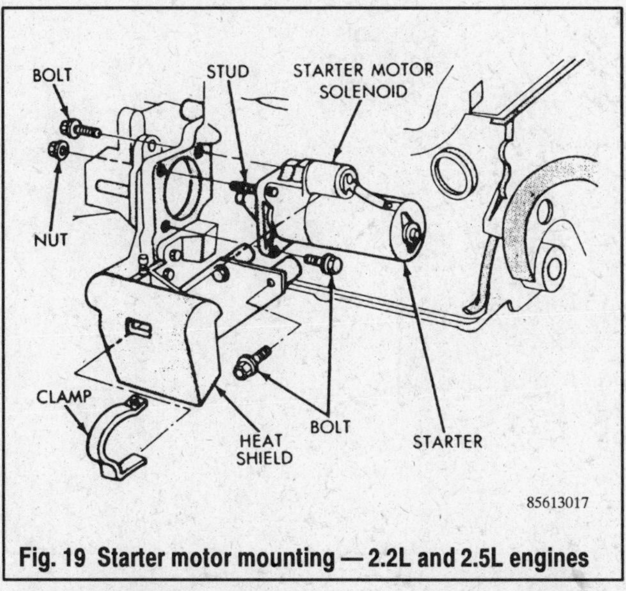

Fig. 19 Starter motor mounting — 2.2L and 2.5L engines

Fig. 22 Removing the starter motor mounting stud nut where the air pump tube bracket is also attached

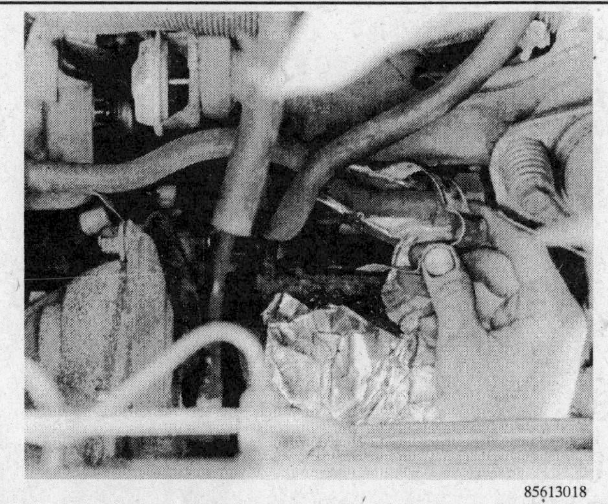

Fig. 20 Working from under the vehicle, disconnect the starter motor heat shield clamp

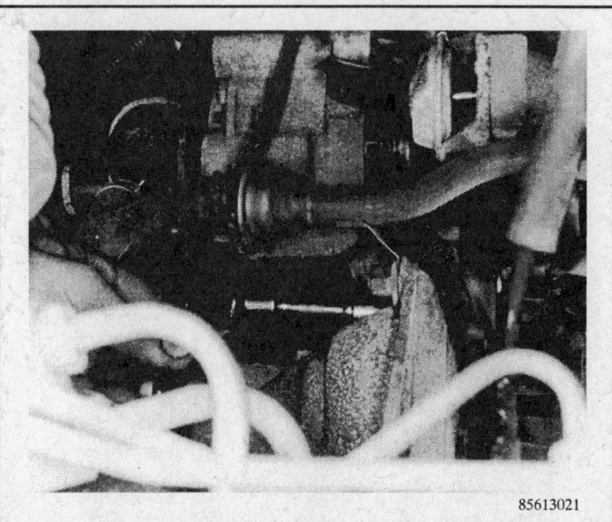

Fig. 23 Removing a starter motor mounting bolt

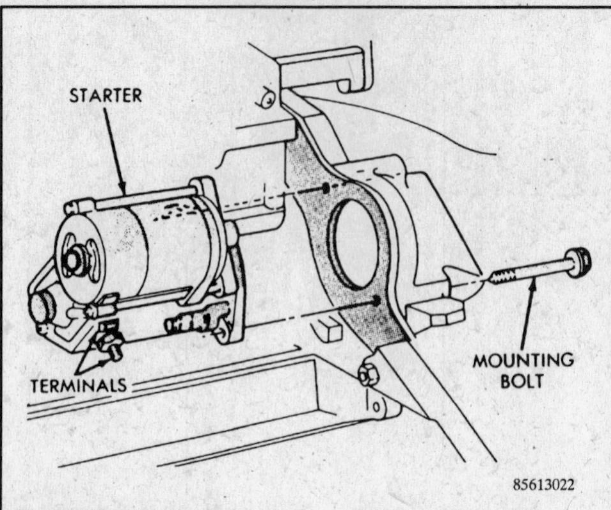

Fig. 24 Starter motor mounting — 2.6L engines with automatic transaxles

SOLENOID REPLACEMENT

See Figures 25, 26 and 27

1. Remove the starter as previously outlined.
2. Disconnect the field coil wire from the solenoid.
3. Remove the solenoid mounting screws.
4. Work the solenoid off of shift fork lever and remove the solenoid.

To install:

5. Install plunger on replacement solenoid.
6. Install plunger on shift fork lever.
7. Secure the solenoid with the mounting screws.
8. Install the starter motor assembly.

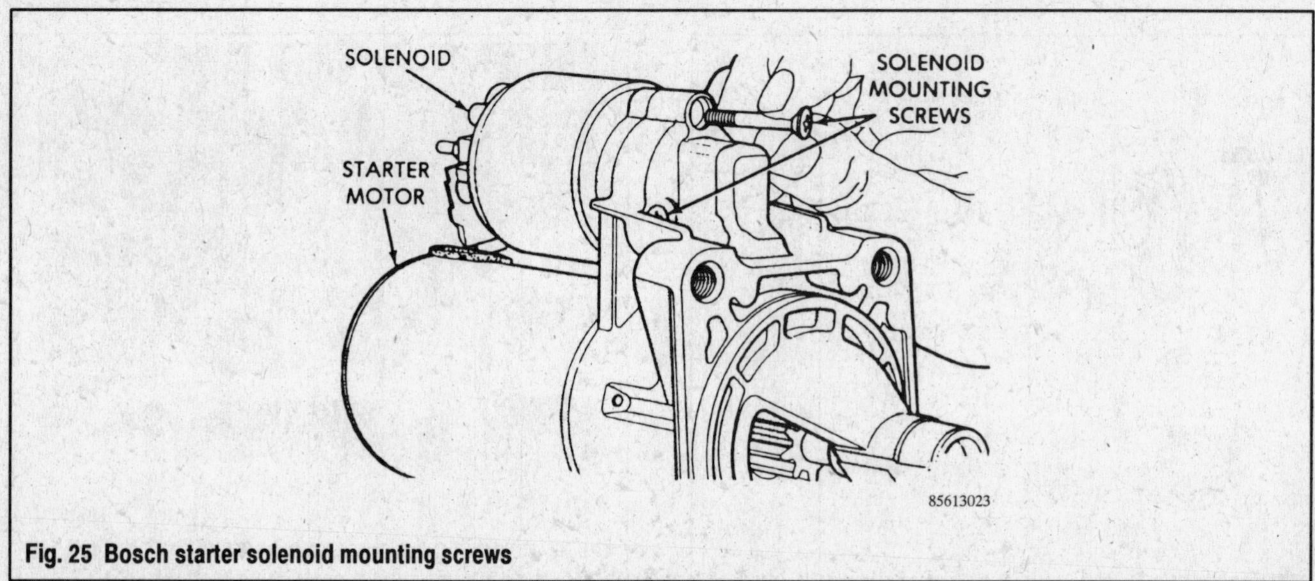

Fig. 25 Bosch starter solenoid mounting screws

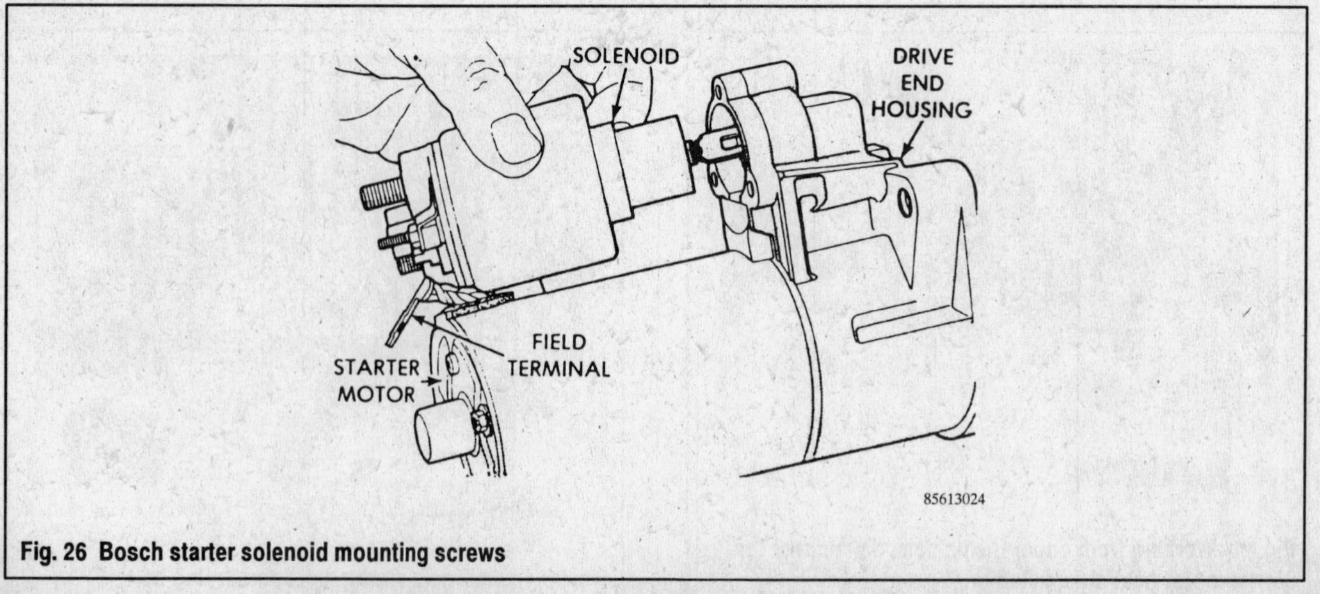

Fig. 26 Bosch starter solenoid mounting screws

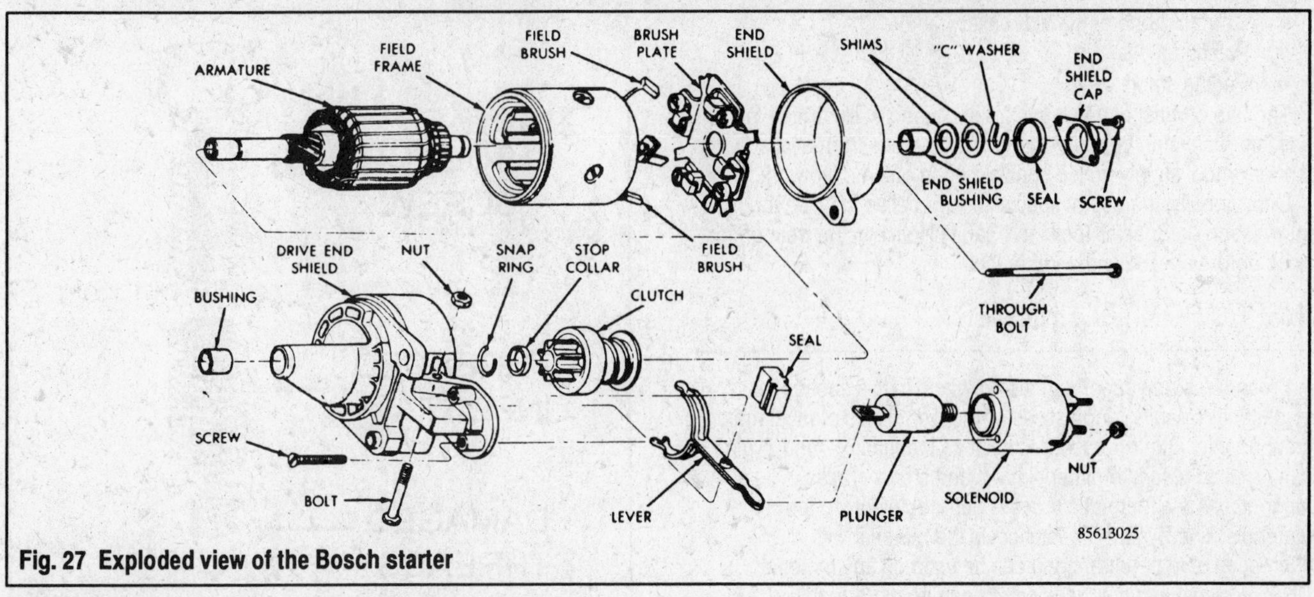

Fig. 27 Exploded view of the Bosch starter

STARTER GEAR & CLUTCH REPLACEMENT

➧ See Figure 28

1. Disconnect the negative battery cable.
2. Remove the starter from the vehicle.
3. Remove the 2 gear housing attaching screws from the starter.
4. Separate the gear housing from the solenoid housing. The pinion, pinion gear bearing and drive gear will all be loose between the 2 housings. The starter gear and clutch can also be removed at this time.

To install:

5. To reinstall the pinion gear and bearing, wipe clean with a rag and coat with light weight wheel bearing grease.
6. Place the bearing and gear over the shaft in the housing. Reinstall the starter gear and clutch if removed.
7. Install the housings and reinstall the retaining screws.
8. Install the starter in the vehicle, then connect the negative battery cable.

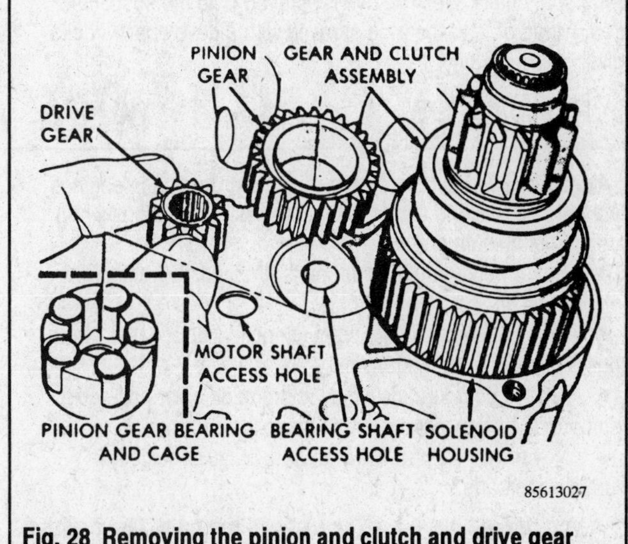

Fig. 28 Removing the pinion and clutch and drive gear

ENGINE MECHANICAL

Engine Overhaul Tips

Most engine overhaul procedures are fairly standard. In addition to specific parts replacement procedures and complete specifications for your individual engine, this section also is a guide to accept rebuilding procedures. Examples of standard rebuilding practice are shown and should be used along with specific details concerning your particular engine.

Competent and accurate machine shop services will ensure maximum performance, reliability and engine life.

In most instances it is more profitable for the do-it-yourself mechanic to remove, clean and inspect the component, buy the necessary parts and deliver these to a shop for actual machine work.

On the other hand, much of the rebuilding work (crankshaft, block, bearings, piston rods, and other components) is well within the scope of the do-it-yourself mechanic.

TOOLS

The tools required for an engine overhaul or parts replacement will depend on the depth of your involvement. With a few exceptions, they will be the tools found in a mechanic's tool kit (see "General Information and Maintenance"). More in-depth work will require any or all of the following:

- A dial indicator (reading in thousandths) mounted on a universal base
- Micrometers and telescope gauges
- Jaw and screw-type pullers
- Scraper
- Valve spring compressor
- Ring groove cleaner
- Piston ring expander and compressor
- Ridge reamer

- Cylinder hone or glaze breaker
- Plastigage®
- Engine stand

The use of most of these tools is explained or illustrated in this section. Many can be rented for a one-time use from a local parts jobber or tool supply house specializing in automotive work.

Occasionally, the use of special tools is called for. See the information on Special Tools and Safety Notice in the front of this book before substituting another tool.

INSPECTION TECHNIQUES

Procedures and specifications are given in this section for inspecting, cleaning and assessing the wear limits of most major components. Other procedures such as Magnaflux® and Zyglo® can be used to locate material flaws and stress cracks. Magnaflux® is a magnetic process applicable only to ferrous materials. The Zyglo® process coats the material with a fluorescent dye penetrant and can be used on any material Check for suspected surface cracks can be more readily made using spot check dye. The dye is sprayed onto the suspected area, wiped off and the area sprayed with a developer. Cracks will show up brightly.

OVERHAUL TIPS

Aluminum has become extremely popular for use in engines, due to its low weight. Observe the following precautions when handling aluminum parts:

- Never hot tank aluminum parts (the caustic hot tank solution will eat the aluminum.
- Remove all aluminum parts (identification tag, etc.) from engine parts prior to the tanking.
- Always coat threads lightly with engine oil or anti-seize compounds before installation, to prevent seizure.
- Never over-tighten bolts or spark plugs especially in aluminum threads.

➥ If you're not sure if a given part is aluminum, test it with a magnet. A magnet will not stick to aluminum.

Stripped threads in any component can be repaired using any of several commercial repair kits (Heli-Coil®, Microdot®, Keenserts®, etc.).

When assembling the engine, any parts that will be frictional contact must be prelubed to provide lubrication at initial start-up. Any product specifically formulated for this purpose can be used, but engine oil is not recommended as a prelube.

When semi-permanent (locked, but removable) installation of bolts or nuts is desired, threads should be cleaned and coated with Loctite® or other similar, commercial non-hardening sealant.

REPAIRING DAMAGED THREADS

➧ See Figures 29, 30, 31, 32 and 33

Several methods of repairing damaged threads are available. Heli-Coil® (shown here), Keenserts® and Microdot® are among the most widely used. All involve basically the same principle — drilling out stripped threads, tapping the hole and installing a prewound insert — making welding, plugging and oversize fasteners unnecessary.

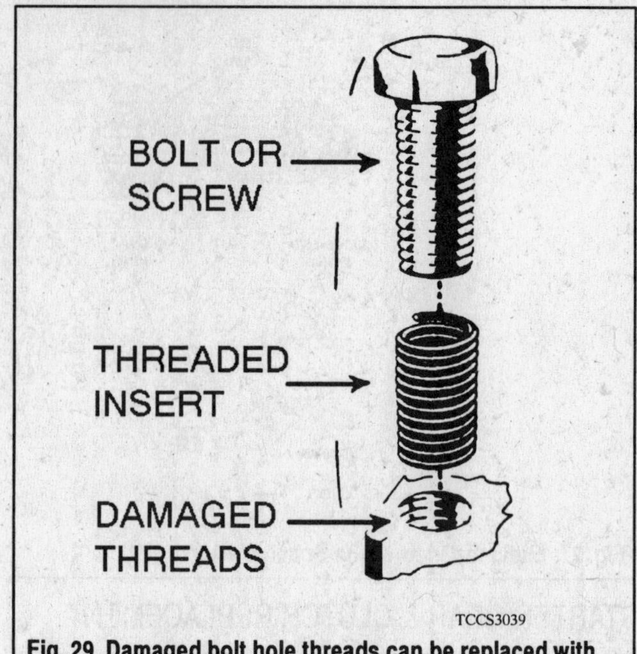

Fig. 29 Damaged bolt hole threads can be replaced with thread repair inserts

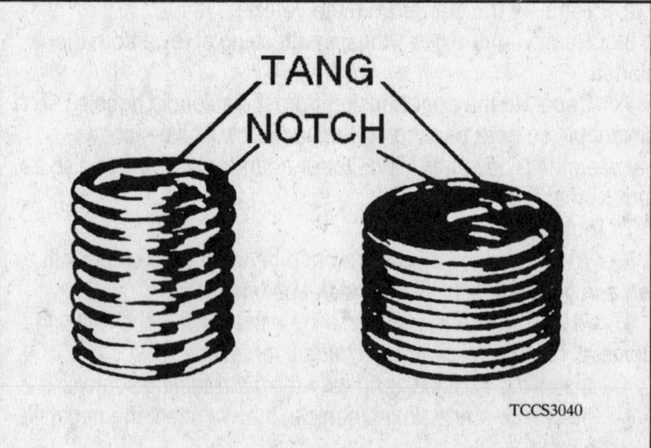

Fig. 30 Standard thread repair insert (left), and spark plug thread insert

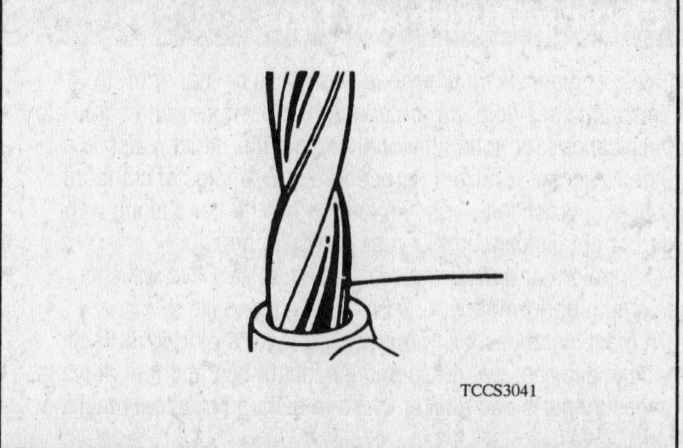

Fig. 31 Drill out the damaged threads with the specified size bit. Be sure to drill completely through the hole or to the bottom of a blind hole

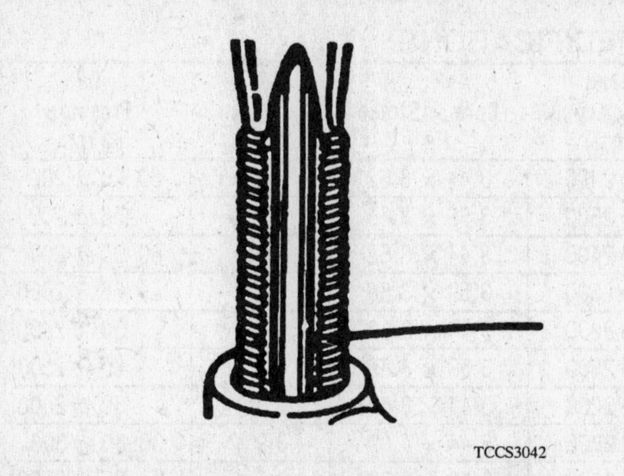

Fig. 32 Using the kit, tap the hole in order to receive the thread insert. Keep the tap well oiled and back it out frequently to avoid clogging the threads

Two types of thread repair inserts are usually supplied: a standard type for most inch coarse, inch fine, metric course and metric fine thread sizes and a spark lug type to fit most spark plug port sizes. Consult the individual tool manufacturer's catalog to determine exact applications. Typical thread repair kits will contain a selection of prewound threaded inserts, a tap (corresponding to the outside diameter threads of the insert) and an installation tool. Spark plug inserts usually differ because they require a tap equipped with pilot threads and a combined reamer/tap section. Most manufacturers also supply blister-packed thread repair inserts separately in addition to a master kit containing a variety of taps and inserts plus installation tools.

Before attempting to repair a threaded hole, remove any snapped, broken or damaged bolts or studs. Penetrating oil can be used to free frozen threads. The offending item can usually be removed with locking pliers or using a screw/stud extractor. After the hole is clear, the thread can be repaired, as shown in the series of accompanying illustrations and in the kit manufacturer's instructions.

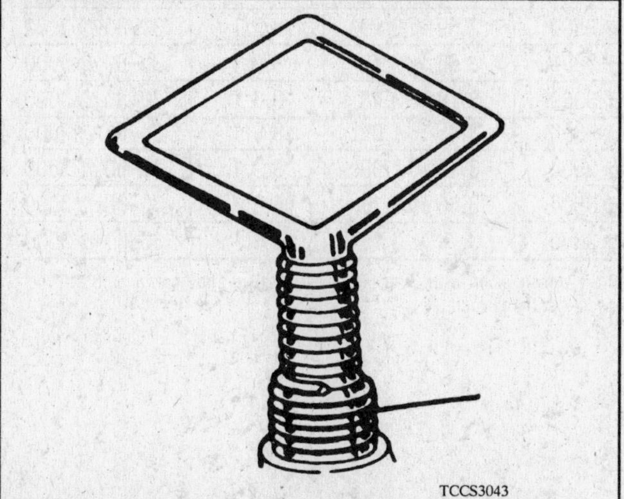

Fig. 33 Screw the insert onto the installer tool until the tang engages the slot. Thread the insert into the hole until it is $^1/_4$–$^1/_2$ turn below the top surface, then remove the tool and break off the tang using a punch

Checking Engine Compression

A noticeable lack of engine power, excessive oil consumption and/or poor fuel mileage measured over an extended period are all indicators of internal engine wear. Worn piston rings, scored or worn cylinder bores, blown head gaskets, sticking or burnt valves and worn valve seats are all possible culprits here. A check of each cylinder's compression will help you locate the problems.

As mentioned in the Tools and Equipment section, a screw-in type compression gauge is more accurate than the type you simply hold against the spark plug hole, although it takes slightly longer to use. It's worth it to obtain a more accurate reading. Follow the procedures below.

1. Warm up the engine to normal operating temperature.
2. Remove all spark plugs.
3. Disable the ignition system.
4. Fully open the throttle.
5. Screw the compression gauge into the No.1 spark plug hole until the fitting is snug.

➥ Be careful not to cross-thread the plug hole. On aluminum cylinder heads use extra care, as the threads in these heads are easily ruined.

6. Ask an assistant to depress the accelerator pedal fully on both carbureted and fuel injected trucks. Then, while you read the compression gauge, ask the assistant to crank the engine 2 or 3 times in short bursts using the ignition switch.
7. Read the compression gauge at the end of each series of cranks, and record the highest of these readings. Repeat this procedure for each of the engine's cylinders. Compare the highest reading of each cylinder to the compression pressures of the other cylinders.

Most engines should have at least 100 psi of compression. A cylinder's compression pressure is usually acceptable if it is not less than 80% of maximum. The difference between each cylinder should be no more than 12–14 psi.

8. If a cylinder is unusually low, pour a tablespoon of clean engine oil into the cylinder through the spark plug hole and repeat the compression test. If the compression comes up after adding the oil, it appears that the cylinder's piston rings or bore are damaged or worn. If the pressure remains low, the valves may not be seating properly (a valve job is needed), or the head gasket may be blown near that cylinder. If compression in any 2 adjacent cylinders is low, and if the addition of oil doesn't help the compression, there is probably leakage past the head gasket. Oil and coolant water in the combustion chamber can result from this problem. There may be evidence of water droplets on the engine dipstick when a head gasket has blown.

GENERAL ENGINE SPECIFICATIONS

Year	VIN	Engine No. Cyl. Liters	Fuel System Type	SAE Net Horsepower @ rpm	SAE Net Torque @ rpm (ft. lbs.)	Bore × Stroke (in.)	Com-pression Ratio	Oil Pressure @ rpm
1984	C	4-2.2L	2 bbl	84 @ 4800	111 @ 2400	3.44 × 3.62	8.5:1	60–90 @ 200
	G	4-2.6L	2 bbl	92 @ 4500	131 @ 2500	3.59 × 3.86	8.2:1	56 @ 2000
1985	C	4-2.2L	2 bbl	84 @ 4800	111 @ 2400	3.44 × 3.62	8.5:1	60–90 @ 200
	G	4-2.6L	2 bbl	92 @ 4500	131 @ 2500	3.59 × 3.86	8.2:1	56 @ 2000
1986	C	4-2.2L	2 bbl	96 @ 5200	119 @ 3200	3.44 × 3.62	9.5:1	50 @ 2000
	G	4-2.6L	2 bbl	101 @ 5600	140 @ 2800	3.59 × 3.86	8.7:1	85 @ 2500
1987	C	4-2.2L	2 bbl	96 @ 5200	119 @ 3200	3.44 × 3.62	9.5:1	50 @ 2000
	K	4-2.5L	EFI	100 @ 4800	135 @ 2800	3.44 × 4.09	8.9:1	30–80 @ 300
	G	4-2.6L	2 bbl	101 @ 5600	140 @ 2800	3.59 × 3.86	8.7:1	85 @ 2500
	3	6-3.0L	EFI	142 @ 5000	173 @ 2800	3.59 × 2.99	8.9:1	30–80 @ 300
1988	K	4-2.5L	EFI	100 @ 4800	135 @ 2800	3.44 × 4.09	8.9:1	30–80 @ 300
	3	6-3.0L	EFI	142 @ 5000	173 @ 2800	3.59 × 2.99	8.9:1	30–80 @ 300
1989	K	4-2.5L	EFI	100 @ 4800	135 @ 2800	3.44 × 4.09	8.9:1	30–80 @ 300
	J	4-2.5L	Turbo	150 @ 4800	180 @ 2000	3.44 × 4.09	7.8:1	30–80 @ 300
	3	6-3.0L	EFI	142 @ 5000	173 @ 2800	3.59 × 2.99	8.9:1	30–80 @ 300
1990	K	4-2.5L	EFI	100 @ 4800	135 @ 2800	3.44 × 4.09	8.9:1	30–80 @ 3000
	J	4-2.5L	Turbo	150 @ 4800	180 @ 2000	3.44 × 4.09	7.8:1	30–80 @ 3000
	3	6-3.0L	EFI	142 @ 5000	173 @ 2800	3.59 × 2.99	8.9:1	30–80 @ 3000
	R	6-3.3L	EFI	150 @ 4000	185 @ 3600	3.66 × 3.19	8.9:1	30–80 @ 3000
1991	K	4-2.5L	EFI	100 @ 4800	135 @ 2800	3.44 × 4.09	8.9:1	30–80 @ 3000
	3	6-3.0L	EFI	142 @ 5000	173 @ 2800	3.59 × 2.99	8.9:1	30–80 @ 3000
	R	6-3.3L	EFI	150 @ 4000	185 @ 3600	3.66 × 3.19	8.9:1	30–80 @ 3000
1992	K	4-2.5L	TFI	96 @ 4400	133 @ 2800	3.45 × 4.09	8.9:1	35–65 @ 2000
	3	6-3.0L	MFI	143 @ 5000	168 @ 2500	3.59 × 2.99	8.9:1	30–80 @ 3000
	R	6-3.3L	MFI	150 @ 4800	185 @ 3600	3.66 × 3.19	8.9:1	30–80 @ 3000
1993	K	4-2.5L	TFI	100 @ 4800	135 @ 2800	3.45 × 4.09	8.9:1	35–65 @ 2000
	3	6-3.0L	MFI	143 @ 5000	168 @ 2500	3.59 × 2.99	8.9:1	30–80 @ 3000
	R	6-3.3L	MFI	150 @ 4800	185 @ 3600	3.66 × 3.19	8.9:1	30–80 @ 3000
1994	K	4-2.5L	TFI	100 @ 4800	135 @ 2800	3.45 × 4.09	8.9:1	35–65 @ 2000
	3	6-3.0L	MFI	143 @ 5000	168 @ 2500	3.59 × 2.99	8.9:1	30–80 @ 3000
	R	6-3.3L	MFI	150 @ 4800	185 @ 3600	3.66 × 3.19	8.9:1	30–80 @ 3000
	L	6-3.8L	MFI	162 @ 4400	213 @ 3300	3.78 × 3.43	9.0:1	30–80 @ 3000
1995	K	4-2.5L	TFI	100 @ 4800	135 @ 2800	3.45 × 4.09	8.9:1	35–65 @ 2000
	3	6-3.0L	MFI	143 @ 5000	168 @ 2500	3.59 × 2.99	8.9:1	30–80 @ 3000
	R	6-3.3L	MFI	150 @ 4800	185 @ 3600	3.66 × 3.19	8.9:1	30–80 @ 3000
	L	6-3.8L	MFI	162 @ 4400	213 @ 3300	3.78 × 3.43	9.0:1	30–80 @ 3000

NOTE: Horsepower and torque are SAE net figures. They are measured at the rear of the transmission with all accessories installed and operating. Since the figures vary when a given engine is installed in different models, some are representative rather than exact.

85613C01

VALVE SPECIFICATIONS

Year	VIN	Engine No. Cyl. Liters	Seat Angle (deg.)	Face Angle (deg.)	Spring Test Pressure (lbs.)	Spring Installed Height (in.)	Stem-to-Guide Clearance (in.)		Stem Diameter (in.)	
							Intake	Exhaust	Intake	Exhaust
1984	C	4-2.2L	45	45	95	1.65	0.001-0.003	0.0030-0.0047	0.3124	0.3103
	G	4-2.6L	45	45	61	1.59	0.001-0.004	0.0020-0.0060	0.3150	0.3150
1985	C	4-2.2L	45	45	95	1.65	0.001-0.003	0.0030-0.0047	0.3124	0.3103
	G	4-2.6L	45	45	61	1.59	0.001-0.004	0.0020-0.0060	0.3150	0.3150
1986	C	4-2.2L	45	45	95	1.65	0.001-0.003	0.0030-0.0047	0.3124	0.3103
	G	4-2.6L	45	45	61	1.59	0.001-0.004	0.0020-0.0060	0.3150	0.3150
1987	C	4-2.2L	45	45	95	1.65	0.001-0.003	0.0030-0.0047	0.3124	0.3103
	K	4-2.5L	45	45	115	1.65	0.001-0.003	0.0030-0.0047	0.3124	0.3103
	G	4-2.6L	45	45	61	1.59	0.001-0.004	0.0020-0.0060	0.3150	0.3150
	3	6-3.0L	44.5	45.5	73	1.59	0.001-0.002	0.0020-0.0030	0.3130-0.3140	0.3120-0.3130
1988	K	4-2.5L	45	45	115	1.65	0.001-0.003	0.0030-0.0047	0.3124	0.3103
	3	6-3.0L	44.5	45.5	73	1.59	0.001-0.002	0.0020-0.0030	0.3130-0.3140	0.3120-0.3130
1989	K	4-2.5L	45	45	115	1.65	0.001-0.003	0.0030-0.0047	0.3124	0.3103
	J	4-2.5L	45	45	115	1.65	0.001-0.003	0.0030-0.0047	0.3124	0.3103
	3	6-3.0L	44.5	45.5	73	1.59	0.001-0.002	0.0020-0.0030	0.3130-0.3140	0.3120-0.3130
1990	K	4-2.5L	45	45	115	1.65	0.001-0.003	0.0030-0.0047	0.3124	0.3103
	J	4-2.5L	45	45	115	1.65	0.001-0.003	0.0030-0.0047	0.3124	0.3103
	3	6-3.0L	44.5	45.5	73	1.59	0.001-0.002	0.0020-0.0030	0.3130-0.3140	0.3120-0.3130
	R	6-3.3L	45	44.5	60	1.56				
1991	K	4-2.5L	45	45	115	1.65	0.001-0.003	0.0030-0.0047	0.3124	0.3103
	3	6-3.0L	44.5	45.5	73	1.59	0.001-0.002	0.0020-0.0030	0.3130-0.3140	0.3120-0.3130
	R	6-3.3L	45	44.5	60	1.56	0.002-0.016	0.0020-0.0160	0.3110-0.3120	0.3110-0.3120
1992	K	4-2.5L	45	45	115 @ 1.65	1.65	0.0009-0.0047	0.0030-0.0047	0.3124	0.3103
	3	6-3.0L	44.5	45.5	73 @ 1.59	1.59	0.001-0.002	0.0020-0.0030	0.3130-0.3140	0.3120-0.3130
	R	6-3.3L	45	44.5	95 @ 1.57	1.622-1.681	0.001-0.003	0.0020-0.0060	0.3120-0.3130	0.3110-0.3120
1993	K	4-2.5L	45	45	115 @ 1.65	1.65	0.0009-0.0047	0.0030-0.0047	0.3124	0.3103
	3	6-3.0L	44.5	45.5	73 @ 1.59	1.59	0.001-0.002	0.0020-0.0030	0.3130-0.3140	0.3120-0.3130
	R	6-3.3L	45	44.5	95 @ 1.57	1.622-1.681	0.001-0.003	0.0020-0.0060	0.3120-0.3130	0.3110-0.3120
1994	K	4-2.5L	45	45	115 @ 1.65	1.65	0.0009-0.0047	0.0030-0.0047	0.3124	0.3103
	3	6-3.0L	44.5	45.5	73 @ 1.59	1.59	0.001-0.002	0.0020-0.0030	0.3130-0.3140	0.3120-0.3130
	R	6-3.3L	45	44.5	95 @ 1.57	1.622-1.681	0.001-0.003	0.0020-0.0060	0.3120-0.3130	0.3110-0.3120
	L	6-3.8L	45	44.5	95 @ 1.57	1.622-1.681	0.001-0.003	0.0020-0.0060	0.3120-0.3130	0.3110-0.3120
1995	K	4-2.5L	45	45	115 @ 1.65	1.65	0.0009-0.0047	0.0030-0.0047	0.3124	0.3103
	3	6-3.0L	44.5	45.5	73 @ 1.59	1.59	0.001-0.002	0.0020-0.0030	0.3130-0.3140	0.3120-0.3130
	R	6-3.3L	45	44.5	95 @ 1.57	1.622-1.681	0.001-0.003	0.0020-0.0060	0.3120-0.3130	0.3110-0.3120
	L	6-3.8L	45	44.5	95 @ 1.57	1.622-1.681	0.001-0.003	0.0020-0.0060	0.3120-0.3130	0.3110-0.3120

85613C02

CAMSHAFT SPECIFICATIONS

Year	VIN	Engine No. Cyl. Liters	Journal Diameter (in.) 1	2	3	4	5	Bearing Clearance (in.)	Camshaft Endplay (in.)
1984	C	4-2.2L	1.375-1.376	1.375-1.376	1.375-1.376	1.375-1.376	1.375-1.376	0.002-0.004	0.005-0.013
	G	4-2.6L	—	—	—	—	—	0.002-0.008	0.004-0.008
1985	C	4-2.2L	1.375-1.376	1.375-1.376	1.375-1.376	1.375-1.376	1.375-1.376	0.002-0.004	0.005-0.013
	G	4-2.6L	—	—	—	—	—	0.002-0.008	0.004-0.008
1986	C	4-2.2L	1.375-1.376	1.375-1.376	1.375-1.376	1.375-1.376	1.375-1.376	0.002-0.004	0.005-0.013
	G	4-2.6L	—	—	—	—	—	0.002-0.008	0.004-0.008
1987	C	4-2.2L	1.375-1.376	1.375-1.376	1.375-1.376	1.375-1.376	1.375-1.376	0.002-0.004	0.005-0.013
	K	4-2.5L	1.375-1.376	1.375-1.376	1.375-1.376	1.375-1.376	1.375-1.376	0.002-0.004	0.005-0.020
	G	4-2.6L	—	—	—	—	—	0.002-0.008	0.004-0.008
	3	6-3.0L	—	—	—	—	—	—	—
1988	K	4-2.5L	1.375-1.376	1.375-1.376	1.375-1.376	1.375-1.376	1.375-1.376	0.002-0.004	0.005-0.020
	3	6-3.0L	—	—	—	—	—	—	—
1989	K	4-2.5L	1.375-1.376	1.375-1.376	1.375-1.376	1.375-1.376	1.375-1.376	0.002-0.004	0.005-0.020
	J	4-2.5L	1.375-1.376	1.375-1.376	1.375-1.376	1.375-1.376	1.375-1.376	0.002-0.004	0.005-0.020
	3	6-3.0L	—	—	—	—	—	—	—
1990	K	4-2.5L	1.375-1.376	1.375-1.376	1.375-1.376	1.375-1.376	1.375-1.376	0.002-0.004	0.005-0.020
	J	4-2.5L	1.375-1.376	1.375-1.376	1.375-1.376	1.375-1.376	1.375-1.376	0.002-0.004	0.005-0.020
	3	6-3.0L	—	—	—	—	—	—	—
	R	6-3.3L	1.997-1.999	1.980-1.982	1.965-1.96	1.949-1.952	—	0.001-0.005	0.005-0.012
1991	K	4-2.5L	1.375-1.376	1.375-1.376	1.375-1.376	1.375-1.376	1.375-1.376	0.002-0.004	0.005-0.020
	3	6-3.0L	—	—	—	—	—	—	—
	R	6-3.3L	1.997-1.999	1.980-1.982	1.965-1.96	1.949-1.952	—	0.001-0.005	0.005-0.012
1992	K	4-2.5L	1.375-1.376	1.375-1.376	1.375-1.376	1.375-1.376	1.375-1.376	0.002-0.004	0.005-0.013
	3	6-3.0L	NA	NA	NA	NA	NA	—	NA
	R	6-3.3L	1.997-1.999	1.980-1.982	1.965-1.96	1.949-1.952	—	0.001-0.005	0.005-0.012
1993	K	4-2.5L	1.375-1.376	1.375-1.376	1.375-1.376	1.375-1.376	1.375-1.376	0.002-0.004	0.005-0.013
	3	6-3.0L	NA	NA	NA	NA	NA	—	NA
	R	6-3.3L	1.997-1.999	1.980-1.982	1.965-1.96	1.949-1.952	—	0.001-0.005	0.005-0.012
1994	K	4-2.5L	1.375-1.376	1.375-1.376	1.375-1.376	1.375-1.376	1.375-1.376	0.002-0.004	0.005-0.013
	3	6-3.0L	NA	NA	NA	NA	NA	—	NA
	R	6-3.3L	1.997-1.999	1.980-1.982	1.965-1.96	1.949-1.952	—	0.001-0.005	0.005-0.012
	L	6-3.8L	1.997-1.999	1.980-1.982	1.965-1.96	1.949-1.952	—	0.001-0.005	0.005-0.012
1995	K	4-2.5L	1.375-1.376	1.375-1.376	1.375-1.376	1.375-1.376	1.375-1.376	0.002-0.004	0.005-0.013
	3	6-3.0L	NA	NA	NA	NA	NA	—	NA
	R	6-3.3L	1.997-1.999	1.980-1.982	1.965-1.96	1.949-1.952	—	0.001-0.005	0.005-0.012
	L	6-3.8L	1.997-1.999	1.980-1.982	1.965-1.96	1.949-1.952	—	0.001-0.005	0.005-0.012

85613C03

CRANKSHAFT AND CONNECTING ROD SPECIFICATIONS

Year	VIN	Engine No. Cyl. Liters	Crankshaft Main Brg. Journal Dia.	Crankshaft Main Brg. Oil Clearance	Crankshaft Shaft End-play	Crankshaft Thrust on No.	Connecting Rod Journal Diameter	Connecting Rod Oil Clearance	Connecting Rod Side Clearance
1984	C	4-2.2L	2.3630-2.3630	0.0003-0.0031	0.002-0.007	3	1.9680-1.9690	0.0008-0.0034	0.005-0.013
	G	4-2.6L	2.3622	0.0008-0.0028	0.002-0.007	3	2.0866	0.0008-0.0028	0.004-0.010
1985	C	4-2.2L	2.3630-2.3630	0.0003-0.0031	0.002-0.007	3	1.9680-1.9690	0.0008-0.0034	0.005-0.013
	G	4-2.6L	2.3622	0.0008-0.0028	0.002-0.007	3	2.0866	0.0008-0.0028	0.004-0.010
1986	C	4-2.2L	2.3630-2.3630	0.0003-0.0031	0.002-0.007	3	1.9680-1.9690	0.0008-0.0034	0.005-0.013
	G	4-2.6L	2.3622	0.0008-0.0028	0.002-0.007	3	2.0866	0.0008-0.0028	0.004-0.010
1987	C	4-2.2L	2.3630-2.3630	0.0003-0.0031	0.002-0.007	3	1.9680-1.9690	0.0008-0.0034	0.005-0.013
	K	4-2.5L	2.3630-2.3630	0.0003-0.0031	0.002-0.007	3	1.9680-1.9690	0.0008-0.0034	0.005-0.013
	G	4-2.6L	2.3622	0.0008-0.0028	0.002-0.007	3	2.0866	0.0008-0.0028	0.004-0.010
	3	6-3.0L	2.3610-2.3630	0.0006-0.0020	0.002-0.010	3	1.9680-1.9690	0.0008-0.0028	0.004-0.010
1988	K	4-2.5L	2.3630-2.3630	0.0003-0.0031	0.002-0.007	3	1.9680-1.9690	0.0008-0.0034	0.005-0.013
	3	6-3.0L	2.3610-2.3630	0.0006-0.0020	0.002-0.010	3	1.9680-1.9690	0.0008-0.0028	0.004-0.010
1989	K	4-2.5L	2.3630-2.3630	0.0003-0.0031	0.002-0.007	3	1.9680-1.9690	0.0008-0.0034	0.005-0.013
	J	4-2.5L	2.3630-2.3630	0.0003-0.0031	0.002-0.007	3	1.9680-1.9690	0.0008-0.0034	0.005-0.013
	3	6-3.0L	2.3610-2.3630	0.0006-0.0020	0.002-0.010	3	1.9680-1.9690	0.0008-0.0028	0.004-0.010
1990	K	4-2.5L	2.3630-2.3630	0.0003-0.0031	0.002-0.007	3	1.9680-1.9690	0.0008-0.0034	0.005-0.013
	J	4-2.5L	2.3630-2.3630	0.0003-0.0031	0.002-0.007	3	1.9680-1.9690	0.0008-0.0034	0.005-0.013
	3	6-3.0L	2.3610-2.3630	0.0006-0.0020	0.002-0.010	3	1.9680-1.9690	0.0008-0.0028	0.004-0.010
	R	6-3.3L	2.5190	0.0007-0.0022	0.001-0.007	2	2.2830	0.0008-0.0030	0.005-0.015
1991	K	4-2.5L	2.3630-2.3630	0.0003-0.0031	0.002-0.007	3	1.9680-1.9690	0.0008-0.0034	0.005-0.013
	3	6-3.0L	2.3610-2.3630	0.0006-0.0020	0.002-0.010	3	1.9680-1.9690	0.0008-0.0028	0.004-0.010
	R	6-3.3L	2.5190	0.0007-0.0022	0.001-0.007	2	2.2830	0.0008-0.0030	0.005-0.015
1992	K	4-2.5L	2.3620-2.3630	0.0004-0.0028	0.002-0.007	3	1.9680-1.9690	0.0008-0.0034	0.005-0.013
	3	6-3.0L	2.3610-2.3630	0.0006-0.0020	0.002-0.010	3	1.9680-1.9690	0.0008-0.0028	0.004-0.010
	R	6-3.3L	2.5190	0.0004-0.0028	0.003-0.009	2	2.2830	0.0008-0.0030	0.005-0.015
1993	K	4-2.5L	2.3620-2.3630	0.0004-0.0028	0.002-0.007	3	1.9680-1.9690	0.0008-0.0034	0.005-0.013
	3	6-3.0L	2.3610-2.3630	0.0006-0.0020	0.002-0.010	3	1.9680-1.9690	0.0008-0.0028	0.004-0.010
	R	6-3.3L	2.5190	0.0004-0.0028	0.003-0.009	2	2.2830	0.0008-0.0030	0.005-0.015
1994	K	4-2.5L	2.3620-2.3630	0.0004-0.0028	0.002-0.007	3	1.9680-1.9690	0.0008-0.0034	0.005-0.013
	3	6-3.0L	2.3610-2.3630	0.0006-0.0020	0.002-0.010	3	1.9680-1.9690	0.0008-0.0028	0.004-0.010
	R	6-3.3L	2.5190	0.0004-0.0028	0.003-0.009	2	2.2830	0.0008-0.0030	0.005-0.015
	L	6-3.8L	2.5190	0.0007-0.0030	0.004-0.012	2	2.2830	0.0007-0.0030	0.005-0.015
1995	K	4-2.5L	2.3620-2.3630	0.0004-0.0028	0.002-0.007	3	1.9680-1.9690	0.0008-0.0034	0.005-0.013
	3	6-3.0L	2.3610-2.3630	0.0006-0.0020	0.002-0.010	3	1.9680-1.9690	0.0008-0.0028	0.004-0.010
	R	6-3.3L	2.5190	0.0004-0.0028	0.003-0.009	2	2.2830	0.0008-0.0030	0.005-0.015
	L	6-3.8L	2.5190	0.0007-0.0030	0.004-0.012	2	2.2830	0.0007-0.0030	0.005-0.015

85613C04

PISTON AND RING SPECIFICATIONS

				Ring Gap			Ring Side Clearance		
Year	VIN	Engine No. Cyl. Liters	Piston Clearance	Top Compression	Bottom Compression	Oil Control	Top Compression	Bottom Compression	Oil Control
1984	C	4-2.2L	0.0005-0.0015	0.0110-0.0120	0.0110-0.0120	0.0160-0.0550	0.0016-0.0028	0.0008-0.0020	0.0008-0.0020
	G	4-2.6L	0.0008-0.0016	0.0100-0.0180	0.0100-0.0180	0.0078-0.0350	0.0015-0.0031	0.0015-0.0037	—
1985	C	4-2.2L	0.0005-0.0015	0.0110-0.0120	0.0110-0.0120	0.0160-0.0550	0.0016-0.0028	0.0008-0.0020	0.0008-0.0020
	G	4-2.6L	0.0008-0.0016	0.0100-0.0180	0.0100-0.0180	0.0078-0.0350	0.0015-0.0031	0.0015-0.0037	—
1986	C	4-2.2L	0.0005-0.0015	0.0110-0.0120	0.0110-0.0120	0.0160-0.0550	0.0016-0.0028	0.0008-0.0020	0.0008-0.0020
	G	4-2.6L	0.0008-0.0016	0.0100-0.0180	0.0100-0.0180	0.0078-0.0350	0.0015-0.0031	0.0015-0.0037	—
1987	C	4-2.2L	0.0005-0.0015	0.0110-0.0120	0.0110-0.0120	0.0160-0.0550	0.0016-0.0028	0.0008-0.0020	0.0008-0.0020
	K	4-2.5L	0.0005-0.0015	0.0110-0.0120	0.0100-0.0120	0.0160-0.0550	0.0016-0.0028	0.0008-0.0020	0.0008-0.0020
	G	4-2.6L	0.0005-0.0015	0.0110-0.0120	0.0100-0.0120	0.0160-0.0550	0.0016-0.0028	0.0008-0.0020	0.0008-0.0020
	3	6-3.0L	0.0008-0.0015	0.0120-0.0180	0.0100-0.0160	0.0120-0.0350	0.0020-0.0035	0.0008-0.0020	—
1988	K	4-2.5L	0.0005-0.0015	0.0110-0.0120	0.0100-0.0120	0.0160-0.0550	0.0016-0.0028	0.0008-0.0020	0.0008-0.0020
	3	6-3.0L	0.0008-0.0015	0.0120-0.0180	0.0100-0.0160	0.0120-0.0350	0.0020-0.0035	0.0008-0.0020	—
1989	K	4-2.5L	0.0005-0.0015	0.0110-0.0120	0.0100-0.0120	0.0160-0.0550	0.0016-0.0028	0.0008-0.0020	0.0008-0.0020
	J	4-2.5L	0.0006-0.0018	0.0100-0.0200	0.0080-0.0190	0.0150-0.0550	0.0016-0.0030	0.0016-0.0030	0.0002-0.0080
	3	6-3.0L	0.0008-0.0015	0.0120-0.0180	0.0100-0.0160	0.0120-0.0350	0.0020-0.0035	0.0008-0.0020	—
1990	K	4-2.5L	0.0005-0.0015	0.0110-0.0120	0.0100-0.0120	0.0160-0.0550	0.0016-0.0028	0.0008-0.0020	0.0008-0.0020
	J	4-2.5L	0.0006-0.0018	0.0100-0.0200	0.0080-0.0190	0.0150-0.0550	0.0016-0.0030	0.0016-0.0030	0.0002-0.0080
	3	6-3.0L	0.0008-0.0015	0.0120-0.0180	0.0100-0.0160	0.0120-0.0350	0.0020-0.0035	0.0008-0.0020	—
	R	6-3.3L	0.0009-0.0022	0.0120-0.0220	0.0120-0.0220	0.0100-0.0400	0.0012-0.0037	0.0012-0.0037	0.0005-0.0089
1991	K	4-2.5L	0.0005-0.0015	0.0110-0.0120	0.0100-0.0120	0.0160-0.0550	0.0016-0.0028	0.0008-0.0020	0.0008-0.0020
	3	6-3.0L	0.0008-0.0015	0.0120-0.0180	0.0100-0.0160	0.0120-0.0350	0.0020-0.0035	0.0008-0.0020	—
	R	6-3.3L	0.0009-0.0022	0.0120-0.0220	0.0120-0.0220	0.0100-0.0400	0.0012-0.0037	0.0012-0.0037	0.0005-0.0089

85613C05

PISTON AND RING SPECIFICATIONS

Year	VIN	Engine No. Cyl. Liters	Piston Clearance	Ring Gap Top Compression	Ring Gap Bottom Compression	Ring Gap Oil Control	Ring Side Clearance Top Compression	Ring Side Clearance Bottom Compression	Ring Side Clearance Oil Control
1992	K	4-2.5L	0.0005–0.0015	0.0110–0.0120	0.0100–0.0120	0.0160–0.0550	0.0016–0.0028	0.0008–0.0020	0.0008–0.0020
	3	6-3.0L	0.0008–0.0015	0.0120–0.0180	0.0100–0.0160	0.0120–0.0350	0.0020–0.0035	0.0008–0.0020	—
	R	6-3.3L	0.0009–0.0022	0.0120–0.0220	0.0120–0.0220	0.0100–0.0400	0.0012–0.0037	0.0012–0.0037	0.0005–0.0089
1993	K	4-2.5L	0.0005–0.0015	0.0110–0.0120	0.0100–0.0120	0.0160–0.0550	0.0016–0.0028	0.0008–0.0020	0.0008–0.0020
	3	6-3.0L	0.0008–0.0015	0.0120–0.0180	0.0100–0.0160	0.0120–0.0350	0.0020–0.0035	0.0008–0.0020	—
	R	6-3.3L	0.0009–0.0022	0.0120–0.0220	0.0120–0.0220	0.0100–0.0400	0.0012–0.0037	0.0012–0.0037	0.0005–0.0089
	L	6-3.8L	0.0009–0.0022	0.0120–0.0220	0.0120–0.0220	0.0100–0.0400	0.0012–0.0037	0.0012–0.0037	0.0005–0.0089
1994	K	4-2.5L	0.0005–0.0015	0.0110–0.0120	0.0100–0.0120	0.0160–0.0550	0.0016–0.0028	0.0008–0.0020	0.0008–0.0020
	3	6-3.0L	0.0008–0.0015	0.0120–0.0180	0.0100–0.0160	0.0120–0.0350	0.0020–0.0035	0.0008–0.0020	—
	R	6-3.3L	0.0009–0.0022	0.0120–0.0220	0.0120–0.0220	0.0100–0.0400	0.0012–0.0037	0.0012–0.0037	0.0005–0.0089
	L	6-3.8L	0.0009–0.0022	0.0120–0.0220	0.0120–0.0220	0.0100–0.0400	0.0012–0.0037	0.0012–0.0037	0.0005–0.0089
1995	K	4-2.5L	0.0005–0.0015	0.0110–0.0120	0.0100–0.0120	0.0160–0.0550	0.0016–0.0028	0.0008–0.0020	0.0008–0.0020
	3	6-3.0L	0.0008–0.0015	0.0120–0.0180	0.0100–0.0160	0.0120–0.0350	0.0020–0.0035	0.0008–0.0020	—
	R	6-3.3L	0.0009–0.0022	0.0120–0.0220	0.0120–0.0220	0.0100–0.0400	0.0012–0.0037	0.0012–0.0037	0.0005–0.0089
	L	6-3.8L	0.0009–0.0022	0.0120–0.0220	0.0120–0.0220	0.0100–0.0400	0.0012–0.0037	0.0012–0.0037	0.0005–0.0089

85613C11

TORQUE SPECIFICATIONS

All readings in ft. lbs.

Year	VIN	Engine No. Cyl. Liters	Cylinder Head	Main Bearing	Rod Bearing	Crankshaft Damper	Flywheel	Manifold Intake	Manifold Exhaust	Spark Plugs
1984	C	4-2.2L	①	30②	40②	50	70	17	17	26
	G	4-2.6L	70	58	34	87	70	13	13	NA
1985	C	4-2.2L	①	30②	40②	50	70	17	17	26
	G	4-2.6L	70	58	34	87	70	13	13	NA
1986	C	4-2.2L	①	30②	40②	50	70	17	17	26
	G	4-2.6L	70	58	34	87	70	13	13	NA
1987	C	4-2.2L	①	30②	40②	50	70	17	17	26
	K	4-2.5L	①	30②	40②	50	70	17	17	26
	G	4-2.6L	70	58	34	87	70	13	13	NA
	3	6-3.0L	70	60	38	110	70	17	17	20
1988	K	4-2.5L	①	30②	40②	50	70	17	17	26
	3	6-3.0L	70	60	38	110	70	17	17	20
1989	K	4-2.5L	①	30②	40②	50	70	17	17	26
	J	4-2.5L	①	30②	40②	50	70	17	17	26
	3	6-3.0L	70	60	38	110	70	17	17	20
1990	K	4-2.5L	①	30②	40②	50	70	17	17	26
	J	4-2.5L	①	30②	40②	50	70	17	17	26
	3	6-3.0L	70	60	38	110	70	17	17	20
	R	6-3.3L	③	30②	40②	40	70	17	17	26
1991	K	4-2.5L	①	30②	40②	50	70	17	17	26
	3	6-3.0L	80	60	38	110	70	17	17	20
	R	6-3.3L	③	30②	40②	40	70	17	17	26
1992	K	4-2.5L	①	30②	40②	50	70	17	17	26
	3	6-3.0L	80	60	38	110	70	17	17	20
	R	6-3.3L	③	30②	40②	40	70	17	17	26
1993	K	4-2.5L	①	30②	40②	50	70	17	17	26
	3	6-3.0L	80	60	38	110	70	17	17	20
	R	6-3.3L	③	30②	40②	40	70	17	17	26
1994	K	4-2.5L	①	30②	40②	50	70	17	17	26
	3	6-3.0L	80	60	38	110	70	17	17	20
	R	6-3.3L	③	30②	40②	40	70	17	17	26
	L	6-3.8L	③	30②	40②	40	70	17	17	20
1995	K	4-2.5L	①	30②	40②	50	70	17	17	26
	3	6-3.0L	80	60	38	110	70	17	17	20
	R	6-3.3L	③	30②	40②	40	70	17	17	26
	L	6-3.8L	③	30②	40②	40	70	17	17	20

① Tighten in 3 steps:
1st Step: 45 ft. lbs.
2nd Step: 65 ft. lbs.
3rd Step: 65 ft. lbs. plus additional 90 degree turn

② Plus an additional 90 degree turn

③ Tighten in 3 steps:
1st Step: 45 ft. lbs.
2nd Step: 65 ft. lbs.
3rd Step: 65 ft. lbs. plus additional 90 degree turn
Last, torque the small bolt in the rear of the head to 25 ft. lbs.

85613C06

Standard Torque Specifications and Fastener Markings

In the absence of specific torques, the following chart can be used as a guide to the maximum safe torque of a particular size/grade of fastener.

- There is no torque difference for fine or coarse threads.
- Torque values are based on clean, dry threads. Reduce the value by 10% if threads are oiled prior to assembly.
- The torque required for aluminum components or fasteners is considerably less.

U.S. Bolts

SAE Grade Number	1 or 2			5			6 or 7		
Number of lines always 2 less than the grade number.									
Bolt Size (Inches)—(Thread)	Maximum Torque			Maximum Torque			Maximum Torque		
	Ft./Lbs.	Kgm	Nm	Ft./Lbs.	Kgm	Nm	Ft./Lbs.	Kgm	Nm
¼—20	5	0.7	6.8	8	1.1	10.8	10	1.4	13.5
—28	6	0.8	8.1	10	1.4	13.6			
5/16—18	11	1.5	14.9	17	2.3	23.0	19	2.6	25.8
—24	13	1.8	17.6	19	2.6	25.7			
⅜—16	18	2.5	24.4	31	4.3	42.0	34	4.7	46.0
—24	20	2.75	27.1	35	4.8	47.5			
7/16—14	28	3.8	37.0	49	6.8	66.4	55	7.6	74.5
—20	30	4.2	40.7	55	7.6	74.5			
½—13	39	5.4	52.8	75	10.4	101.7	85	11.75	115.2
—20	41	5.7	55.6	85	11.7	115.2			
9/16—12	51	7.0	69.2	110	15.2	149.1	120	16.6	162.7
—18	55	7.6	74.5	120	16.6	162.7			
⅝—11	83	11.5	112.5	150	20.7	203.3	167	23.0	226.5
—18	95	13.1	128.8	170	23.5	230.5			
¾—10	105	14.5	142.3	270	37.3	366.0	280	38.7	379.6
—16	115	15.9	155.9	295	40.8	400.0			
⅞— 9	160	22.1	216.9	395	54.6	535.5	440	60.9	596.5
—14	175	24.2	237.2	435	60.1	589.7			
1— 8	236	32.5	318.6	590	81.6	799.9	660	91.3	894.8
—14	250	34.6	338.9	660	91.3	849.8			

Metric Bolts

Relative Strength Marking	4.6, 4.8			8.8		
Bolt Markings						
Bolt Size Thread Size x Pitch (mm)	Maximum Torque			Maximum Torque		
	Ft./Lbs.	Kgm	Nm	Ft./Lbs.	Kgm	Nm
6 x 1.0	2–3	.2–.4	3–4	3–6	.4–.8	5–8
8 x 1.25	6–8	.8–1	8–12	9–14	1.2–1.9	13–19
10 x 1.25	12–17	1.5–2.3	16–23	20–29	2.7–4.0	27–39
12 x 1.25	21–32	2.9–4.4	29–43	35–53	4.8–7.3	47–72
14 x 1.5	35–52	4.8–7.1	48–70	57–85	7.8–11.7	77–110
16 x 1.5	51–77	7.0–10.6	67–100	90–120	12.4–16.5	130–160
18 x 1.5	74–110	10.2–15.1	100–150	130–170	17.9–23.4	180–230
20 x 1.5	110–140	15.1–19.3	150–190	190–240	26.2–46.9	160–320
22 x 1.5	150–190	22.0–26.2	200–260	250–320	34.5–44.1	340–430
24 x 1.5	190–240	26.2–46.9	260–320	310–410	42.7–56.5	420–550

85613034

Engine

➧ See Figures 34, 35, 36, 37, 38, 39, 40, 41, 42, 43, 44 and 45

REMOVAL & INSTALLATION

Engine removal and installation procedures are similar on all models.

1. Disconnect the negative battery cable.
2. Scribe the hood hinge outlines on the hood, and remove the hood.
3. Drain the cooling system. Remove the radiator hoses from the radiator and engine connections.

✻✻CAUTION

When draining coolant, keep in mind that cats and dogs are attracted by ethylene glycol antifreeze, and are quite likely to drink any that is left in an uncovered container or in puddles on the ground. This will prove fatal in sufficient quantity. Always drain the coolant into a sealable container. Coolant should be reused unless it is contaminated or several years old.

4. Remove the radiator and fan assembly.
5. Remove the air conditioner compressor from the engine with the mounting brackets and hoses connected. Position the assembly to the side and secure out of the way.
6. Remove the power steering pump from the engine with mounting brackets and hoses connected. Position the assembly to the side and secure out of the way.
7. Remove all electrical connectors at the alternator, carburetor, injection unit and engine.
8. Unfasten the fuel line(s) from the engine. Disconnect the heater hoses from the engine. Remove the accelerator cable from the carburetor or throttle body.
9. Remove the alternator. Disconnect the clutch cable from the clutch lever, if equipped with a manual transaxle.
10. Remove the transaxle case lower cover.
11. On automatic transaxles, mark the flexplate-to-torque converter location. Remove the bolts that mount the converter to the flexplate. Attach a small C-clamp to the front bottom of the converter housing to prevent the converter from falling off of the transaxle.
12. Disconnect the starter motor wiring and remove the starter motor.
13. Disconnect the exhaust pipe from the exhaust manifold.

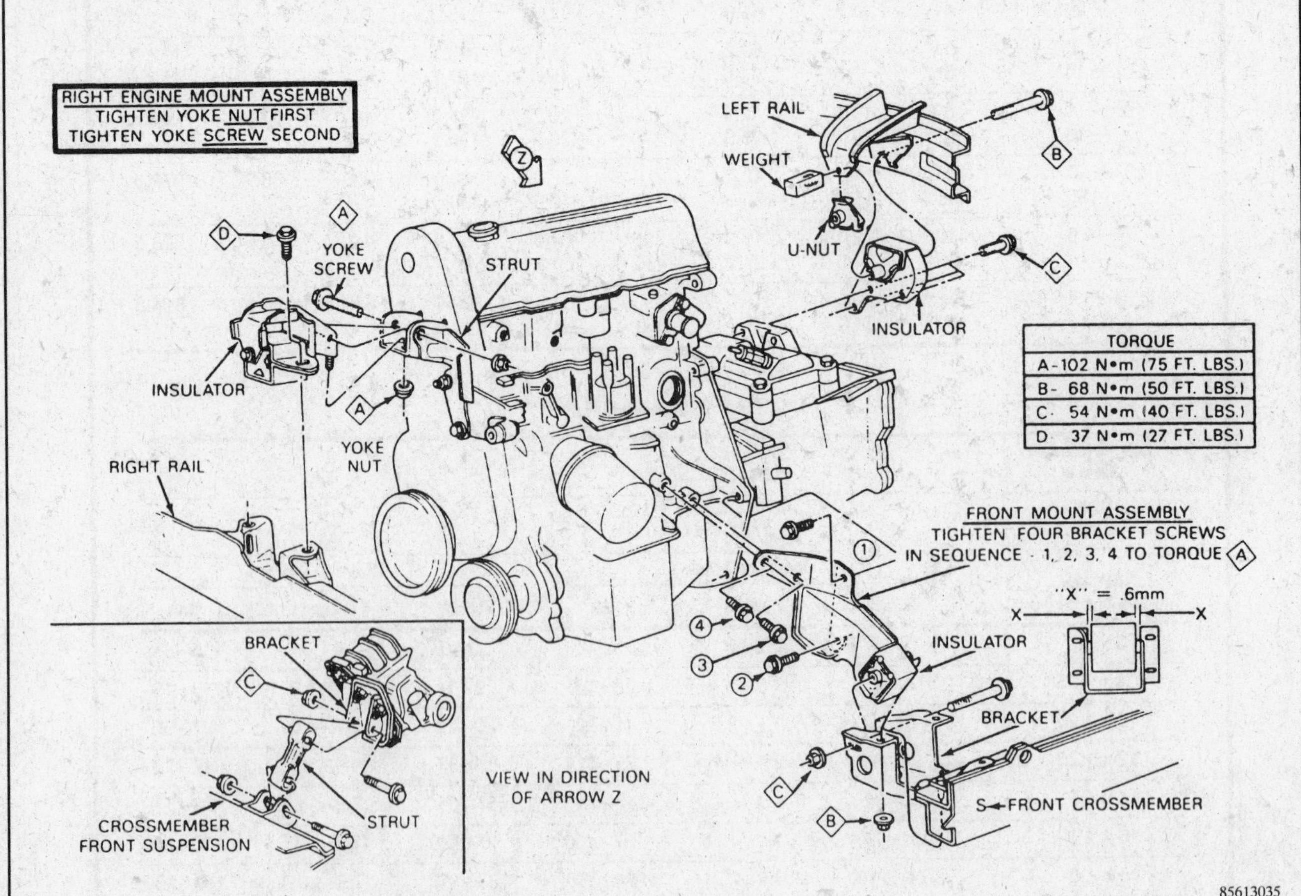

Fig. 34 Engine mounting — 1989-90 2.5L engines

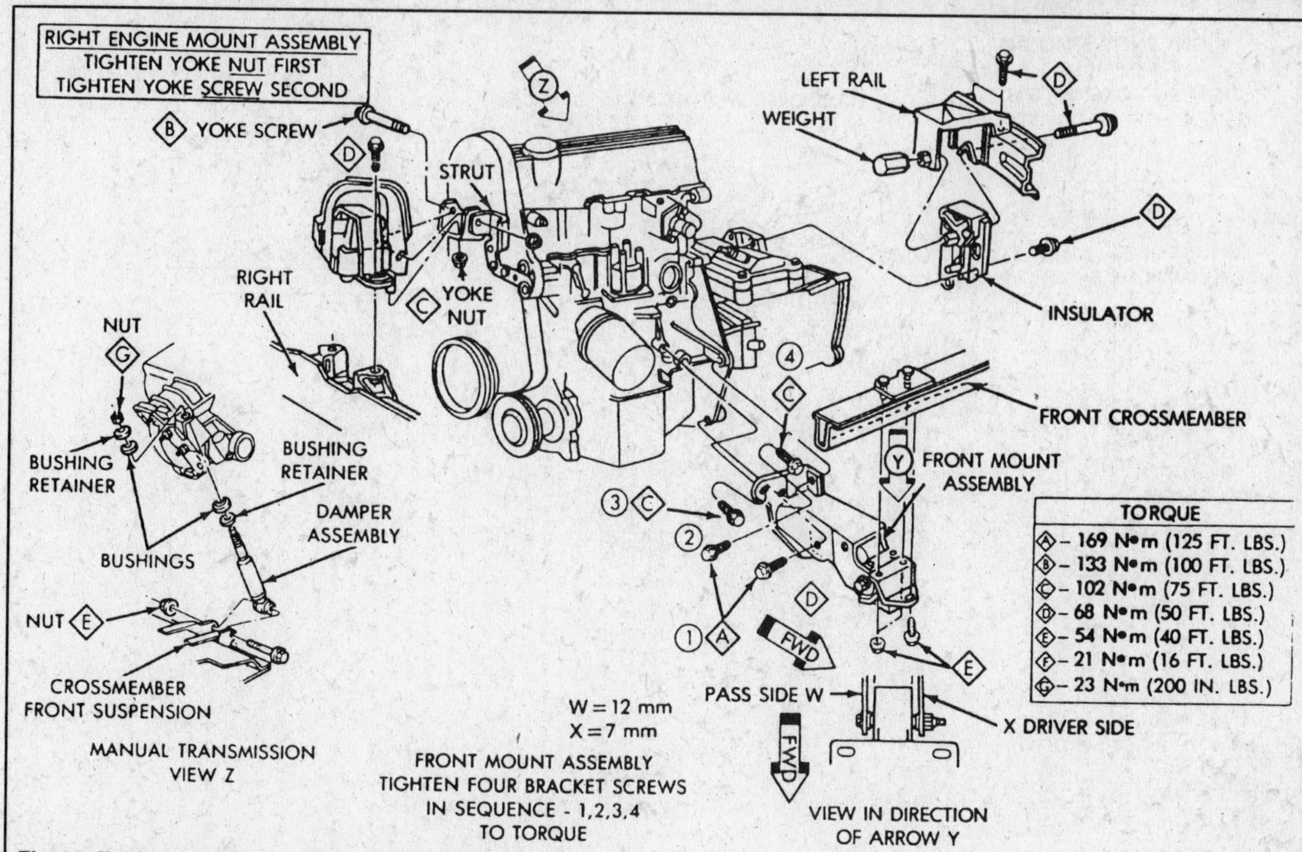

TORQUE
A – 169 N•m (125 FT. LBS.)
B – 133 N•m (100 FT. LBS.)
C – 102 N•m (75 FT. LBS.)
D – 68 N•m (50 FT. LBS.)
E – 54 N•m (40 FT. LBS.)
F – 21 N•m (16 FT. LBS.)
G – 23 N•m (200 IN. LBS.)

Fig. 35 Engine mounting — 1991–93 2.5L engines

85613036

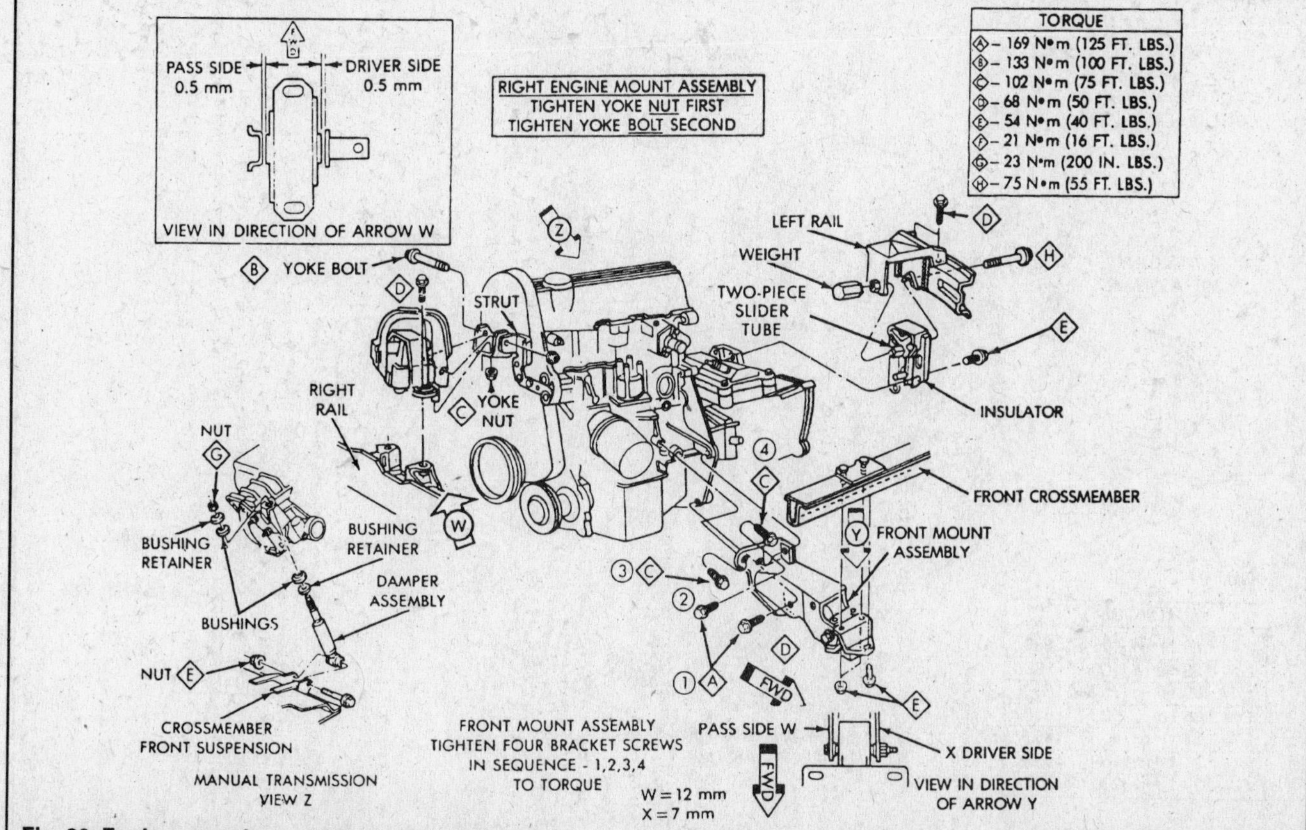

TORQUE
A – 169 N•m (125 FT. LBS.)
B – 133 N•m (100 FT. LBS.)
C – 102 N•m (75 FT. LBS.)
D – 68 N•m (50 FT. LBS.)
E – 54 N•m (40 FT. LBS.)
F – 21 N•m (16 FT. LBS.)
G – 23 N•m (200 IN. LBS.)
H – 75 N•m (55 FT. LBS.)

Fig. 36 Engine mounting — 1994–95 2.5L engines

85613037

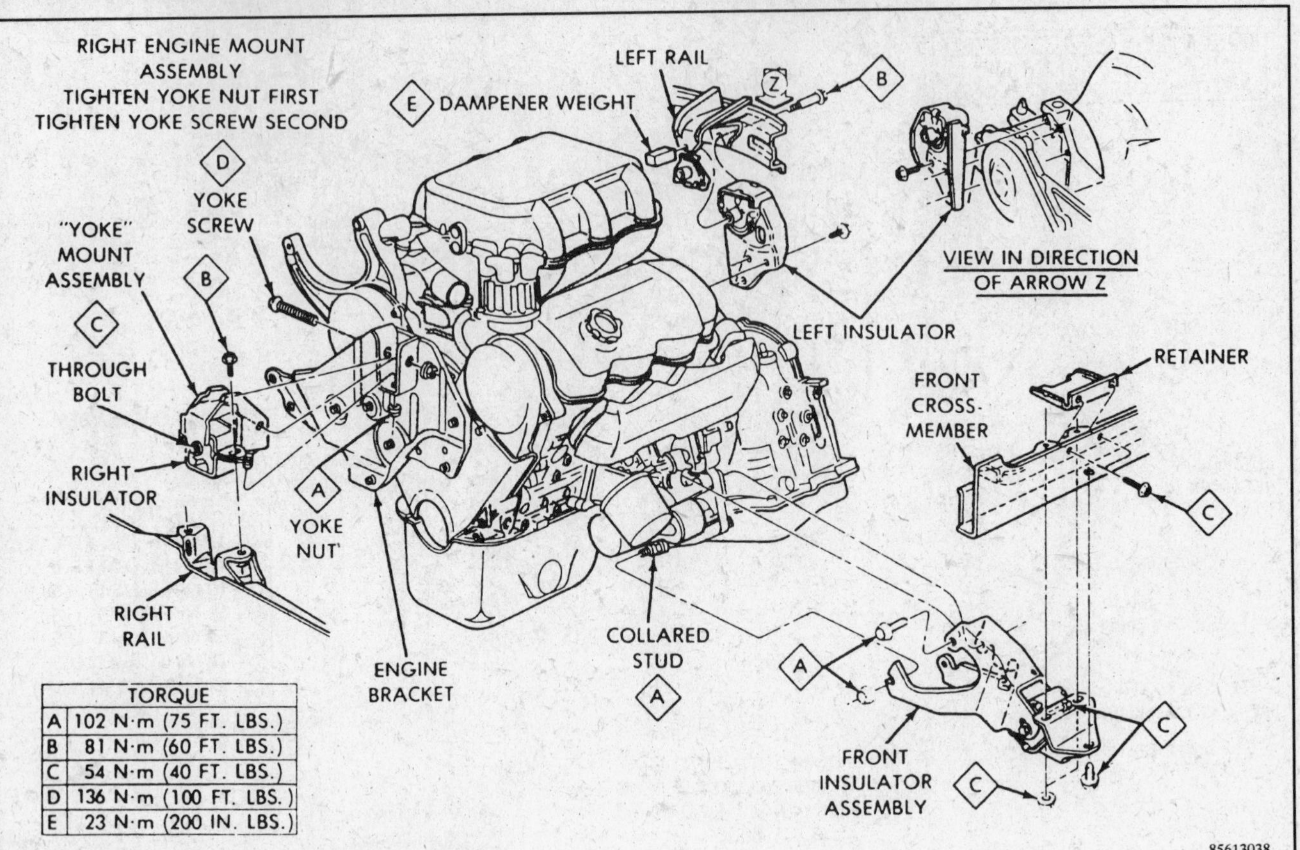
RIGHT ENGINE MOUNT ASSEMBLY
TIGHTEN YOKE NUT FIRST
TIGHTEN YOKE SCREW SECOND
D
YOKE SCREW
"YOKE" MOUNT ASSEMBLY
B
C
THROUGH BOLT
RIGHT INSULATOR
RIGHT RAIL
A
YOKE NUT'
E
DAMPENER WEIGHT
LEFT RAIL
Z
B
VIEW IN DIRECTION OF ARROW Z
LEFT INSULATOR
RETAINER
FRONT CROSS-MEMBER
C
ENGINE BRACKET
COLLARED STUD
A
A
FRONT INSULATOR ASSEMBLY
C
C
85613038

TORQUE	
A	102 N·m (75 FT. LBS.)
B	81 N·m (60 FT. LBS.)
C	54 N·m (40 FT. LBS.)
D	136 N·m (100 FT. LBS.)
E	23 N·m (200 IN. LBS.)

Fig. 37 Engine mounting — 1989-90 3.0L engines

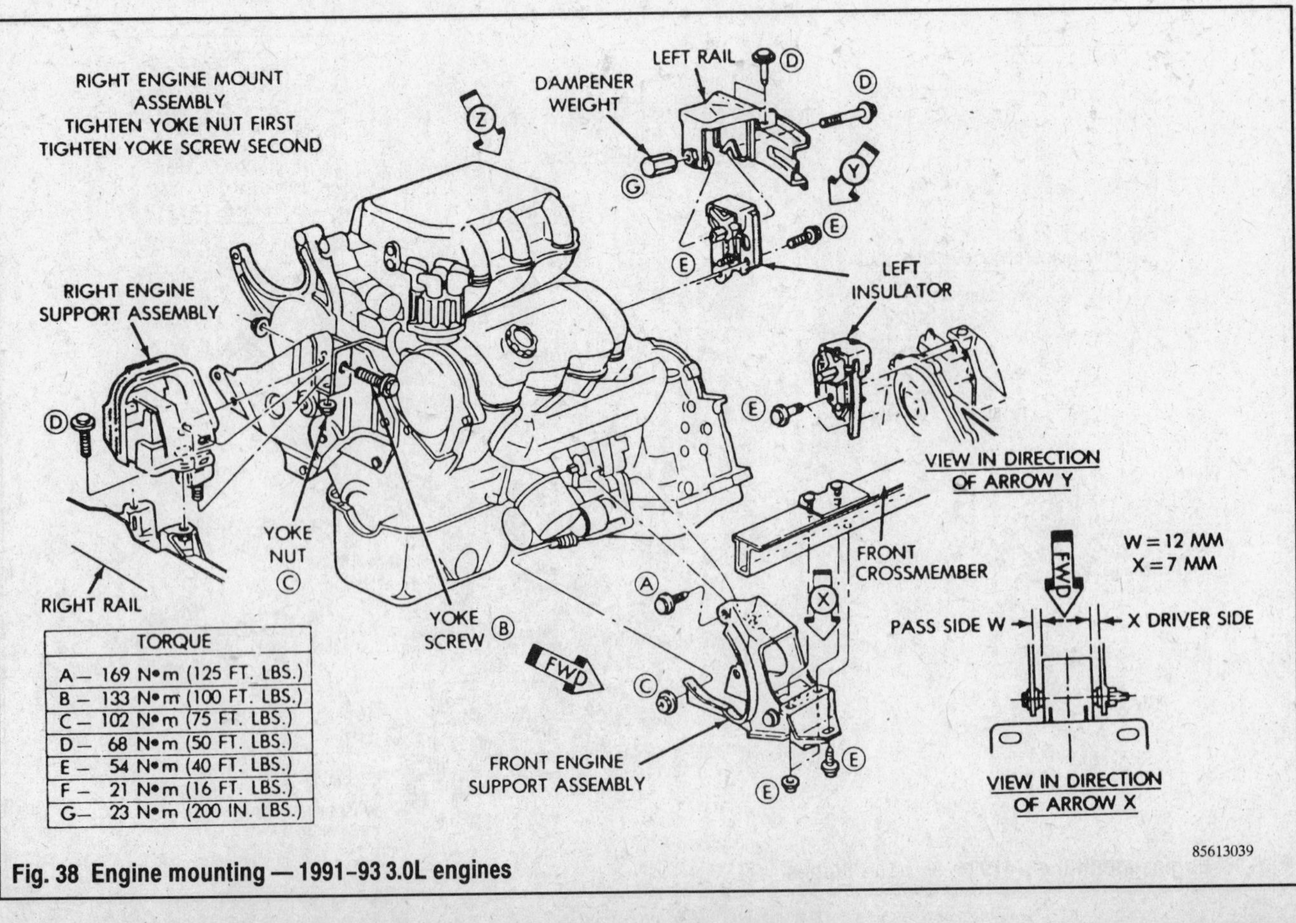
RIGHT ENGINE MOUNT ASSEMBLY
TIGHTEN YOKE NUT FIRST
TIGHTEN YOKE SCREW SECOND
Z
DAMPENER WEIGHT
LEFT RAIL
D
D
G
Y
E
E
LEFT INSULATOR
RIGHT ENGINE SUPPORT ASSEMBLY
D
E
VIEW IN DIRECTION OF ARROW Y
YOKE NUT
C
RIGHT RAIL
YOKE SCREW
B
FRONT CROSSMEMBER
FWD
W = 12 MM
X = 7 MM
PASS SIDE W
X DRIVER SIDE
A
X
FWD
C
FRONT ENGINE SUPPORT ASSEMBLY
E
E
VIEW IN DIRECTION OF ARROW X
85613039

TORQUE
A – 169 N•m (125 FT. LBS.)
B – 133 N•m (100 FT. LBS.)
C – 102 N•m (75 FT. LBS.)
D – 68 N•m (50 FT. LBS.)
E – 54 N•m (40 FT. LBS.)
F – 21 N•m (16 FT. LBS.)
G – 23 N•m (200 IN. LBS.)

Fig. 38 Engine mounting — 1991-93 3.0L engines

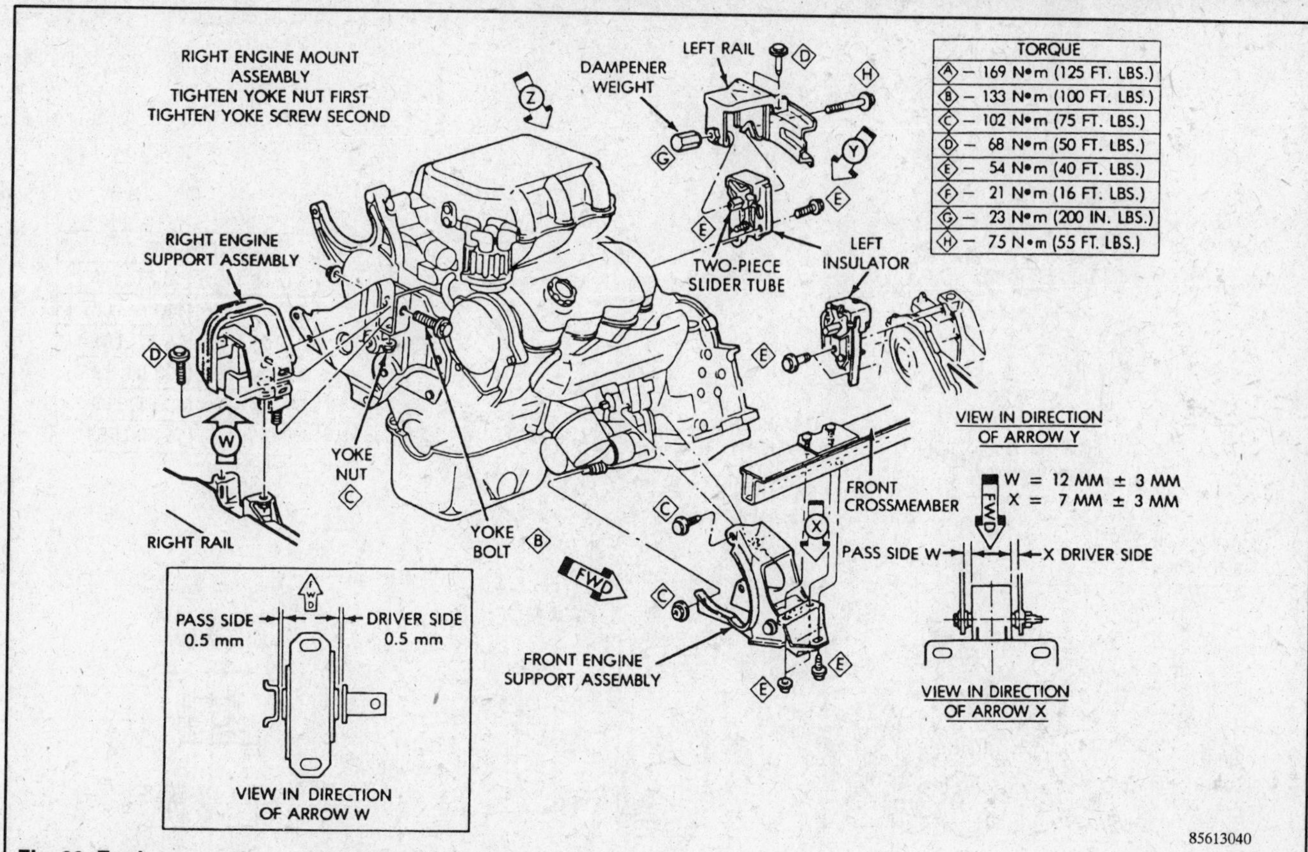

RIGHT ENGINE MOUNT ASSEMBLY
TIGHTEN YOKE NUT FIRST
TIGHTEN YOKE SCREW SECOND

TORQUE
A – 169 N•m (125 FT. LBS.)
B – 133 N•m (100 FT. LBS.)
C – 102 N•m (75 FT. LBS.)
D – 68 N•m (50 FT. LBS.)
E – 54 N•m (40 FT. LBS.)
F – 21 N•m (16 FT. LBS.)
G – 23 N•m (200 IN. LBS.)
H – 75 N•m (55 FT. LBS.)

LEFT RAIL
DAMPENER WEIGHT
RIGHT ENGINE SUPPORT ASSEMBLY
TWO-PIECE SLIDER TUBE
LEFT INSULATOR
YOKE NUT
YOKE BOLT
RIGHT RAIL
FRONT CROSSMEMBER
VIEW IN DIRECTION OF ARROW Y
W = 12 MM ± 3 MM
X = 7 MM ± 3 MM
PASS SIDE W
X DRIVER SIDE
VIEW IN DIRECTION OF ARROW X
FRONT ENGINE SUPPORT ASSEMBLY
PASS SIDE 0.5 mm
DRIVER SIDE 0.5 mm
VIEW IN DIRECTION OF ARROW W

85613040

Fig. 39 Engine mounting — 1994-95 3.0L engines

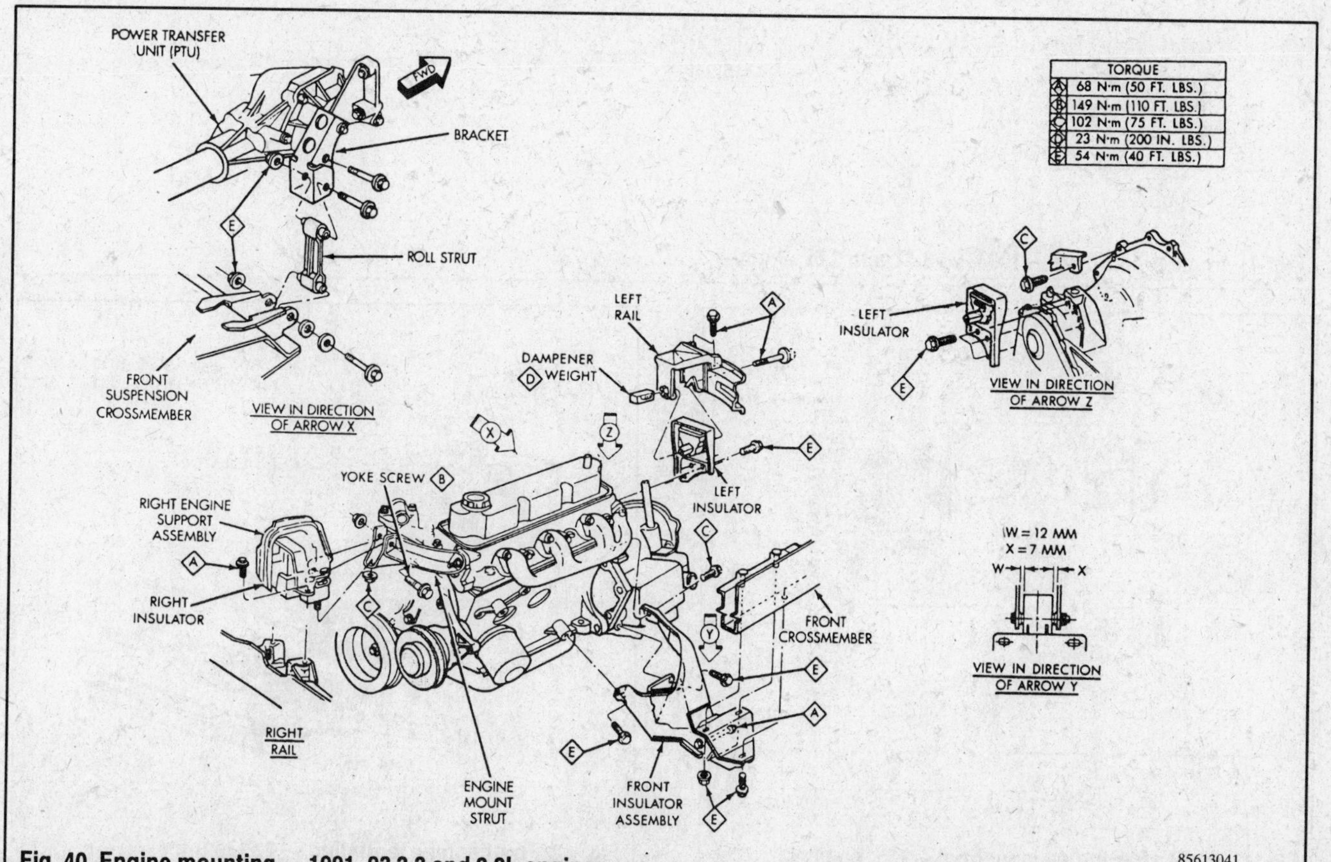

POWER TRANSFER UNIT (PTU)
BRACKET
ROLL STRUT
FRONT SUSPENSION CROSSMEMBER
VIEW IN DIRECTION OF ARROW X

TORQUE
A 68 N·m (50 FT. LBS.)
B 149 N·m (110 FT. LBS.)
C 102 N·m (75 FT. LBS.)
D 23 N·m (200 IN. LBS.)
E 54 N·m (40 FT. LBS.)

LEFT RAIL
DAMPENER WEIGHT
LEFT INSULATOR
VIEW IN DIRECTION OF ARROW Z
YOKE SCREW
RIGHT ENGINE SUPPORT ASSEMBLY
RIGHT INSULATOR
LEFT INSULATOR
W = 12 MM
X = 7 MM
FRONT CROSSMEMBER
VIEW IN DIRECTION OF ARROW Y
RIGHT RAIL
ENGINE MOUNT STRUT
FRONT INSULATOR ASSEMBLY

85613041

Fig. 40 Engine mounting — 1991-93 3.3 and 3.8L engines

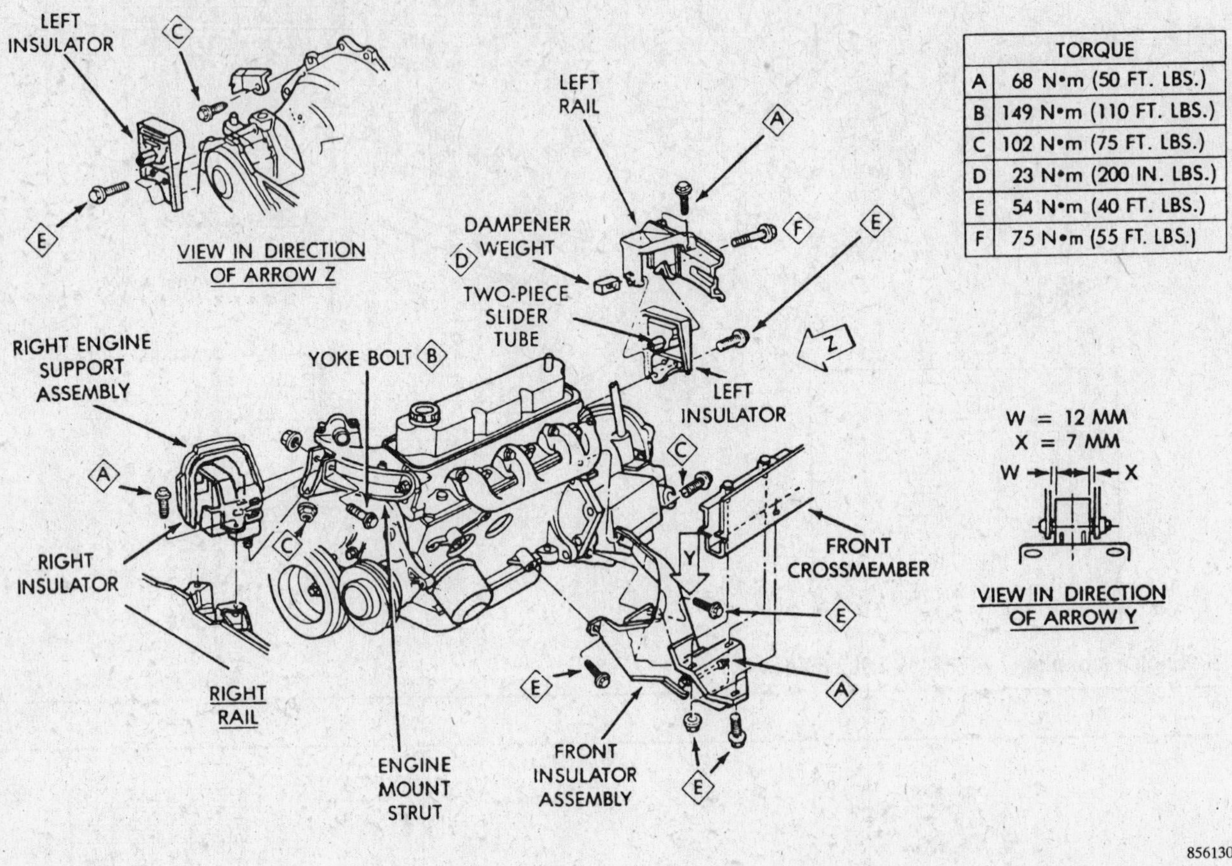

TORQUE	
A	68 N•m (50 FT. LBS.)
B	149 N•m (110 FT. LBS.)
C	102 N•m (75 FT. LBS.)
D	23 N•m (200 IN. LBS.)
E	54 N•m (40 FT. LBS.)
F	75 N•m (55 FT. LBS.)

W = 12 MM
X = 7 MM

85613042

Fig. 41 Engine mounting — 1994–95 3.3L and 3.8L engines

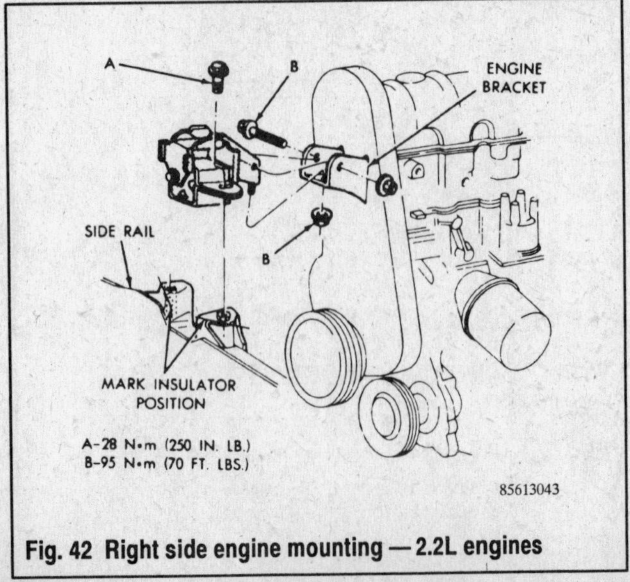

Fig. 42 Right side engine mounting — 2.2L engines

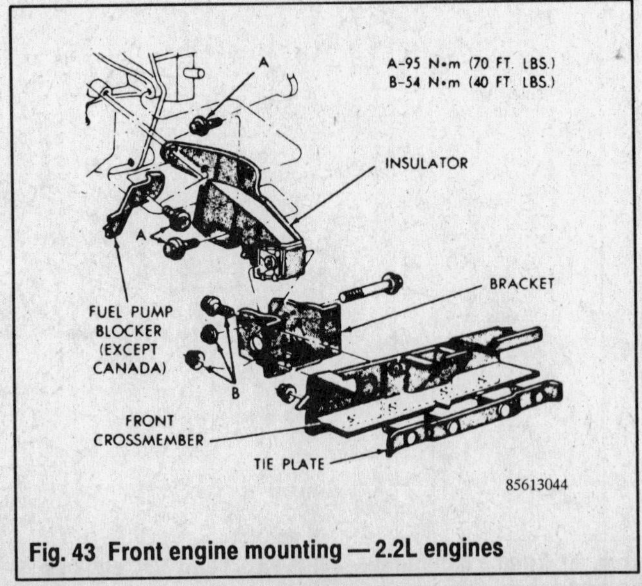

Fig. 43 Front engine mounting — 2.2L engines

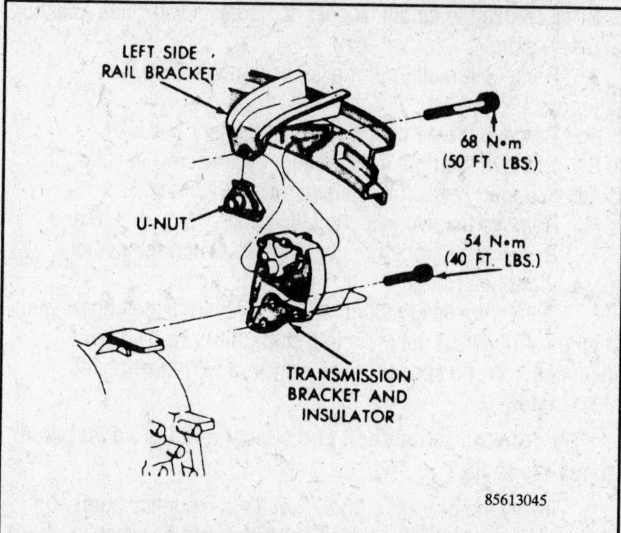

Fig. 44 Left side engine mounting — 2.2L engines

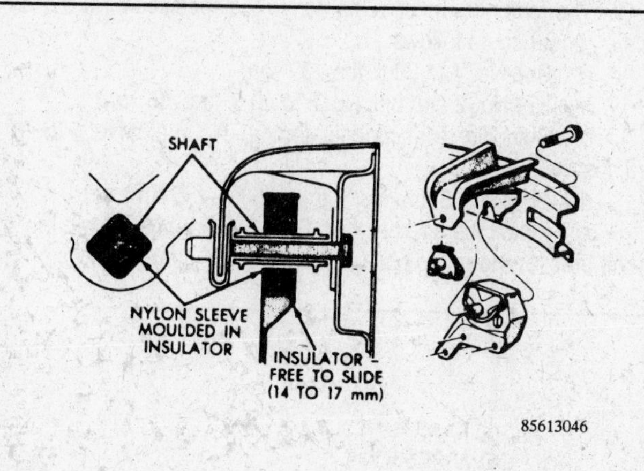

Fig. 45 Left side engine mount movement — 2.2L engines

14. If not done already for access, remove the right inner engine splash shield. Drain the engine oil and remove the oil filter. Disconnect the engine ground strap.

****CAUTION**

The EPA warns that prolonged contact with used engine oil may cause a number of skin disorders, including cancer! You should make every effort to minimize your exposure to used engine oil. Protective gloves should be worn when changing the oil. Wash your hands and any other exposed skin areas as soon as possible after exposure to used engine oil. Soap and water, or waterless hand cleaner should be used.

15. Attach a hoist to the engine.
16. Support the transaxle with a hydraulic floor jack. Apply slight upward pressure with the chain hoist and remove the through-bolt from the right (timing case cover) engine mount.

➥ If the complete engine mount is to be removed, mark the insulator position on the side rail to insure exact reinstallation location.

17. Remove the transaxle-to-cylinder block mounting bolts.
18. Remove the front engine mount through-bolt. Remove the manual transaxle anti-roll strut.
19. Remove the insulator through-bolt from the inside wheel house mount, or remove the insulator bracket-to-transaxle mounting bolt.
20. Raise the engine slowly with the hoist (transaxle supported). Separate the engine from the transaxle, then remove the engine.

To install:

21. With the hoist attached to the engine. Lower the engine into engine compartment.
22. Align the converter to the flexplate and the engine mounts. Install all mounting bolts loosely until all are in position, then tighten to 40 ft. lbs. (55 Nm).
23. Install the engine-to-transaxle mounting bolts. Tighten to 70 ft. lbs. (95 Nm) for the 2.2L, 2.5L and 3.0L engines and to 75 ft. lbs. (100 Nm) for the 3.3L and 3.8L engines.
24. Remove the engine hoist from the engine and transaxle support.
25. Secure the engine ground strap.
26. Install the inner splash shield.
27. Install the starter assembly.
28. Install the exhaust system to the exhaust manifolds.
29. On manual transaxle equipped vehicles, install the transaxle case lower cover. Connect the clutch cable.
30. For automatic transaxles, remove the C-clamp from the torque converter housing. Align flexplate and torque converter with the mark previously made, if applicable. Install the converter-to-flexplate mounting screws, then tighten to 40 ft. lbs. (55 Nm). Install the case lower cover.
31. Install the power steering pump.
32. Install the air conditioning compressor.
33. Install the alternator.
34. Connect all wiring to the engine accessories.
35. Install the radiator, fan and shroud assembly.
36. Connect all cooling system hoses, accelerator cable and fuel lines.
37. Install the engine oil filter. Fill the crankcase to proper oil level.
38. Fill the cooling system.
39. Adjust the accelerator and transaxle linkages.
40. Install the air cleaner and hoses.
41. Install the hood so that the scribe marks on the hood align with the hinges.
42. Connect the battery cables, positive cable first.
43. Start the engine and run until normal operation temperature is indicated. Adjust the carburetor and check for any fuel, coolant, oil and transaxle fluid leaks.

ENGINE/TRANSAXLE POSITIONING

The insulator on the frame rail (right side) and on the transaxle bracket (left side) are adjustable to allow right/left drive train adjustment in relation to the driveshaft distress, front end damage or insulator replacement.

1. Remove the load on the engine mounts by carefully supporting the weight of the engine/transaxle assembly on a floor jack. use a large block of wood to distribute the weight and protect the powertrain from damage.
2. Loosen the right engine mount insulator vertical mounting bolts and the front engine mount bracket-to-crossmember mounting nuts and bolts. The left insulator is sleeved to provide lateral movement.
3. Pry the engine/transaxle assembly to the left or right as required.
4. Tighten the right engine mount insulator vertical bolts to 20 ft. lbs. (29 Nm) for 1984–87 models, 27 ft. lbs. (37 Nm) for 1989–93 models and 50 ft. lbs. (68 Nm) for 1994–95 models. Tighten the center left engine mount insulator.

Solid Mount Compressor Bracket

REMOVAL & INSTALLATION

2.2L and 2.5 Engines

See Figure 46

When service procedures, such as timing belt removal, require solid mount bracket removal and installation, it is important that the bracket fasteners numbered 1 through 7 be removed and installed in sequence.

1. Remove the accessory drive belts.
2. Remove the air conditioner compressor with lines attached and set aside.
3. Remove the alternator pivot bolt and remove the alternator.
4. Remove the air conditioner compressor belt idler.
5. Remove the right engine mount yoke screw securing the isolator support bracket to the engine mount bracket.
6. Remove the five side mounting bolts No. 1, 4, 5, 6 and 7.
7. Remove the front mounting nut No. 2 and remove or loosen front bolt No. 3.
8. Rotate the solid mount bracket away from the engine and slide on stud (No. 2 nut mounting stud) until free. The front mounting bolt and spacer will be removed with the bracket.

To install:

The front mounting bolt and spacer need to be installed simultaneously.

9. Install the bracket on front No. 2 nut mounting stud) and slide the bracket over the timing belt cover into position.
10. Loosen the assembly bracket to engine fasteners No. 1 through 7.
11. The fasteners must be tighten to the specified torque and in the sequence as follows:
    a. Bolt No. 1 to 22 ft. lbs. (30 Nm).
    b. Nut No. 2 and bolt No. 3 to 40 ft. lbs. (55 Nm).
    c. Bolts No. 1 (second tightening), No. 4 and No. 5 to 40 ft. lbs. (55 Nm).
    d. Bolts No. 6 and No. 7 to 40 ft. lbs. (55 Nm).
    e. Install the alternator and compressor and tighten the compressor mounting bolts to 40 ft. lbs. (55 Nm).

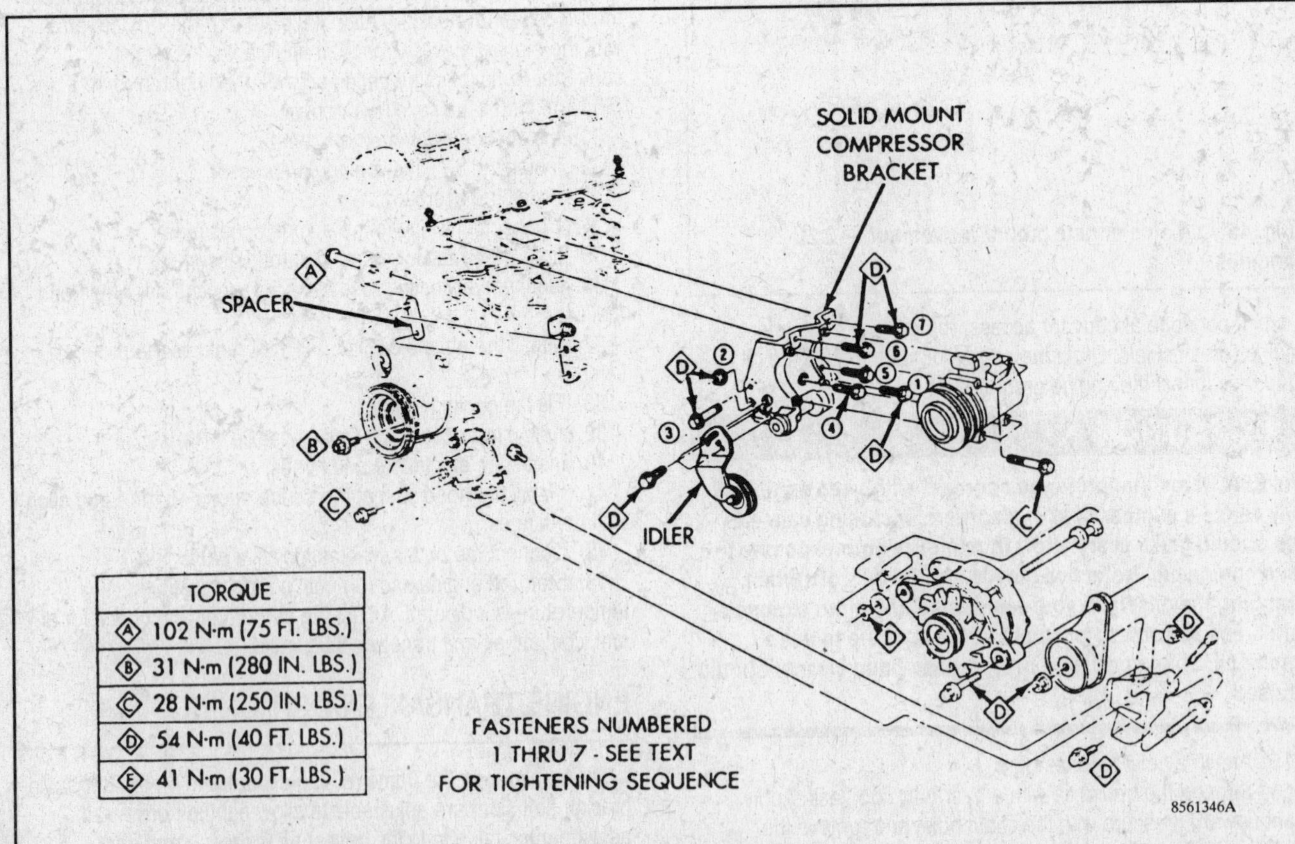

Fig. 46 Solid mount compressor bracket — 2.5L engines

Rocker (Valve) Cover

REMOVAL & INSTALLATION

2.2L Engines

See Figures 47, 48, 49, 50, 51, 52, 53, 54, 55 and 56

1. Disconnect the negative battery cable.
2. Remove the air cleaner assembly. Remove or relocate any hoses or cables that will interfere with rocker cover removal.
3. Depress the retaining clip that holds the PCV module in the rocker cover and turn the module counterclockwise to remove the module.
4. Remove the upper timing belt cover upper and lower retaining bolts.

As the timing belt cover is lifted up a few inches the inside plastic ear of the cover will sometimes get caught on the pulley. Use a suitable tool to pry the ear away as the cover is being removed.

5. Remove the upper cover from the engine.
6. At the other end of the valve cover, remove the air pump cover retaining bolts and remove the air pump pulley cover cover from the engine.
7. Carefully remove the rocker cover from the cylinder head.

To install:

8. Clean the cover and head mounting surfaces. Install the PCV module in rocker cover. Turn clockwise to install.

With the PCV module installed, the snorkel must point upward, toward the top of the valve cover. The snorkel should be free to rotate.

9. Apply RTV sealant to the rocker cover mounting rail, or install a new cover gasket if provided.
10. Install the rocker cover and tighten to 105 inch lbs. (12 Nm).
11. Install both front and rear belt covers.
12. Install the vacuum hoses and spark plug wires.
13. Install the air cleaner assembly.
14. Connect the battery cable.

85613048

Fig. 48 Rotate the PCV module counterclockwise to remove from the valve cover

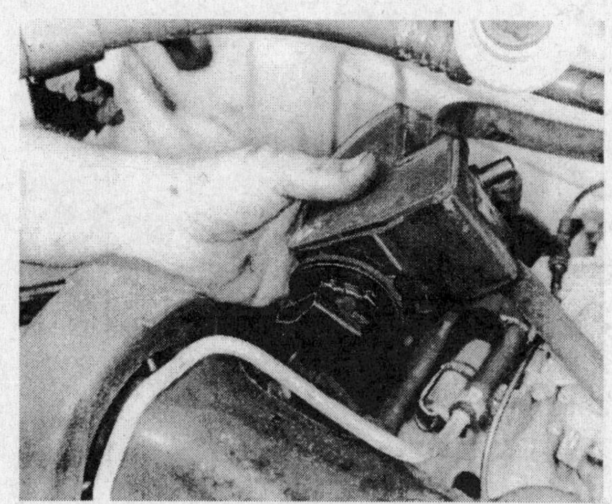
85613049

Fig. 49 The PCV module shown disconnected from the valve cover

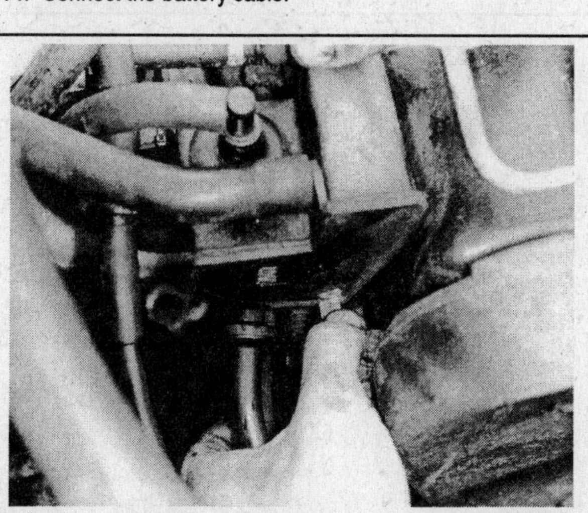
85613047

Fig. 47 Depress the retaining clip to release the PCV module

85613050

Fig. 50 Remove the upper timing cover/valve cover retaining bolts

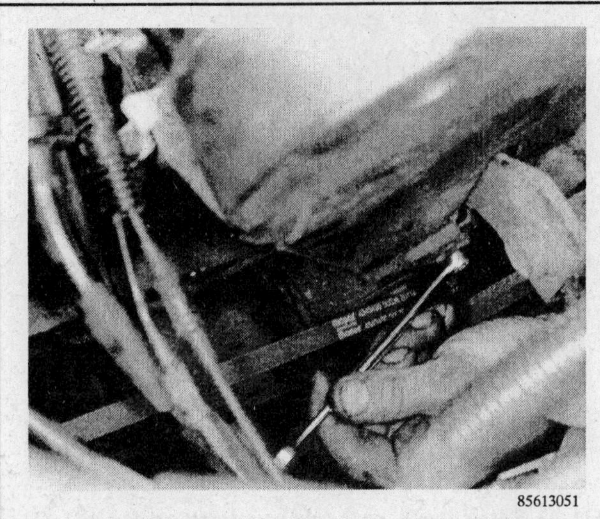

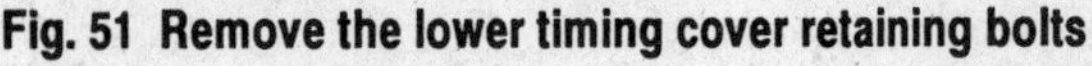
Fig. 51 Remove the lower timing cover retaining bolts

Fig. 54 After removing the air pump pulley cover retaining bolts, lift the cover from the engine

Fig. 52 Pry away the inner ear of the cover to free it from catching on the pulley and remove it

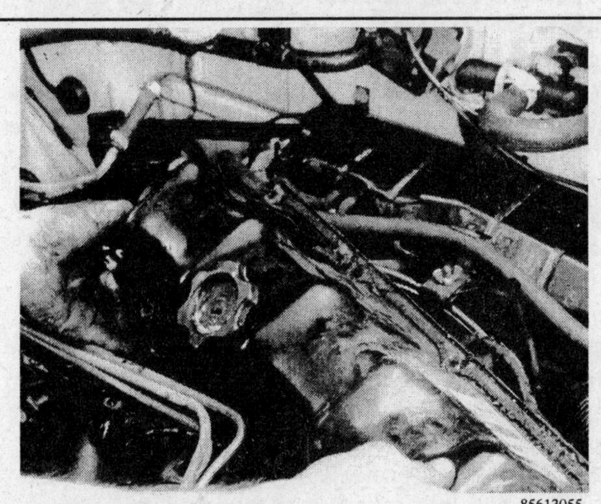

Fig. 55 Carefully lift the rocker cover from the cylinder head

Fig. 53 Remove the lower air pump pulley cover retaining bolts

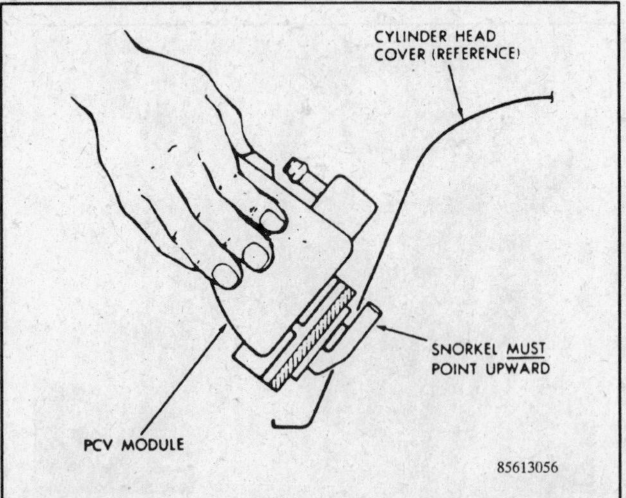

Fig. 56 Make sure the PCV module snorkel is positioned correctly during installation — 2.2L engine

2.5L Engines

➧ See Figure 57

A curtain aiding air/oil separation is located beneath the rocker cover on the cylinder head. The curtain is retained by rubber bumpers.

1. Disconnect the negative battery cable.
2. Remove the air cleaner assembly.
3. Remove any vacuum hoses necessary and relocate spark plug wires.
4. Remove the cover screws and remove the cover.
5. Remove the air/oil separation curtain.

To install:

6. Clean the cylinder head, curtain and cover mating surfaces before installation.
7. Install a gasket on the valve cover while pushing the tabs through slots in cover.
8. Install the curtain (manifold side first) with cutouts over cam towers and against cylinder head. Press opposite side into position below the cylinder head rail.
9. Install the cover and tighten to 105 inch lbs. (12 Nm).
10. Install the vacuum hoses and spark plug wires.
11. Install the air cleaner assembly.
12. Connect the battery cable.

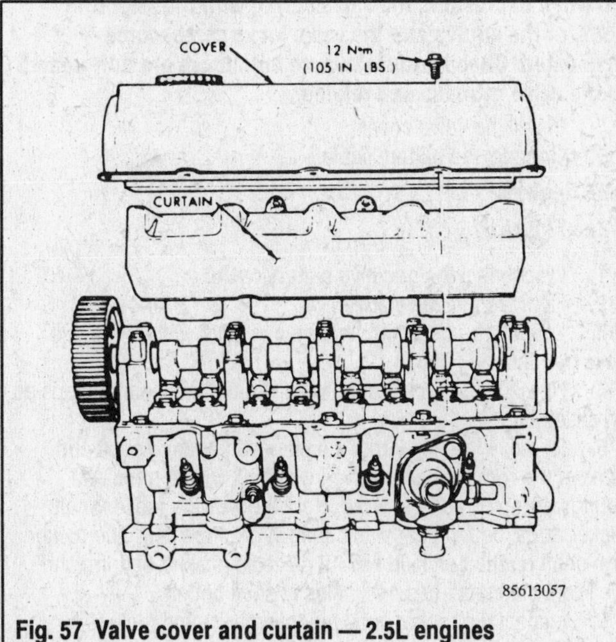

Fig. 57 Valve cover and curtain — 2.5L engines

2.6L Engines

➧ See Figure 58

1. Disconnect the negative battery cable.
2. Remove the air cleaner assembly. Remove or relocate any hoses or cables that will interfere with rocker cover removal.
3. Disconnect the hoses to the PCV tube.
4. Remove the cover mounting bolts and remove the rocker cover from the cylinder head. The water pump pulley belt shield is attached at rear of rocker cover.

To install:

5. Clean the cover and head mounting surfaces.
6. Apply RTV sealant to the top of the rubber cam seal and install the rocker cover.

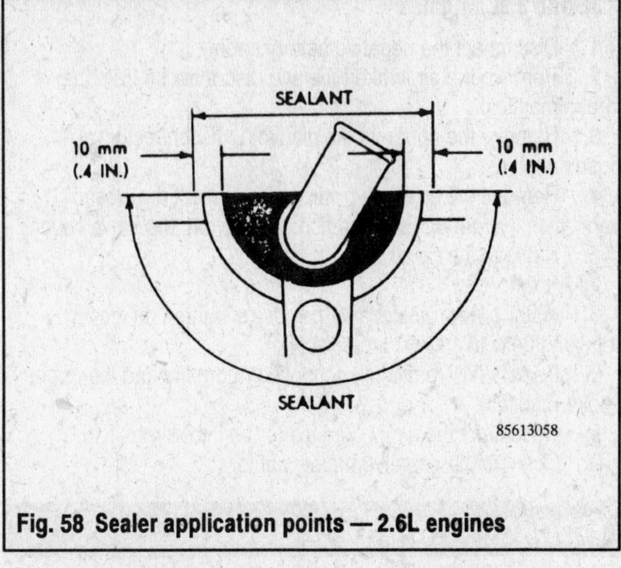

Fig. 58 Sealer application points — 2.6L engines

7. With rocker cover installed, apply RTV sealant to top of semi-circular packing.
8. Tighten the screws to 55 inch lbs. (6 Nm).
9. Install the vacuum hoses and spark plug wires.
10. Install the air cleaner assembly.
11. Connect the battery cable.

3.0L Engines

➧ See Figure 59

1. Disconnect the negative battery cable.
2. Remove the air cleaner assembly.
3. Remove any vacuum hoses necessary and relocate spark plug wires.
4. Remove the cover screws and remove cover.

To install:

5. Clean the cylinder head and cover mating surfaces before installation.
6. Install a new gasket. Apply RTV sealant to cover ends.
7. Install the cover and tighten to 68 inch lbs. (8 Nm).
8. Install the vacuum hoses and spark plug wires.
9. Install the air cleaner assembly.
10. Connect the battery cable.

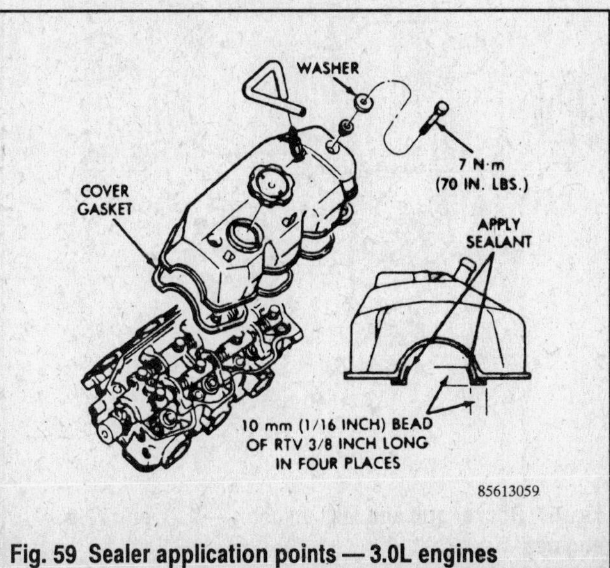

Fig. 59 Sealer application points — 3.0L engines

3.3L and 3.8L Engines

1. Disconnect the negative battery cable.
2. Remove the air intake tube and disconnect it from the intake manifold.
3. Remove the upper intake manifold, disconnecting any hoses or wires.
4. Remove the spark plug wires. Disconnect the closed ventilation system and evaporation control from the valve cover.
5. Remove the cover and gasket.

To install:

6. Install a new gasket and the cover. Tighten the cover retaining bolts to 102 inch lbs. (11 Nm).
7. Reinstall all ventilation control components and the upper intake manifold.
8. Reconnect the air intake tube to the intake manifold.
9. Connect the negative battery cable.

Rocker Arms and Shafts

REMOVAL & INSTALLATION

2.2L and 2.5L Engines

➧ See Figures 60 and 61

1. Disconnect the negative battery cable.
2. Remove the valve cover.
3. Rotate the camshaft until the lobe base is on the rocker arm that is to be removed.
4. Slightly depress the valve spring using Chrysler tool-4682 or the equivalent. Slide the rocker off the lash adjuster and valve tip and remove. Label the rocker arms for position identification. Proceed to the next rocker arm and repeat Steps 3 and 4.
5. Remove the lash adjuster, if servicing is necessary.

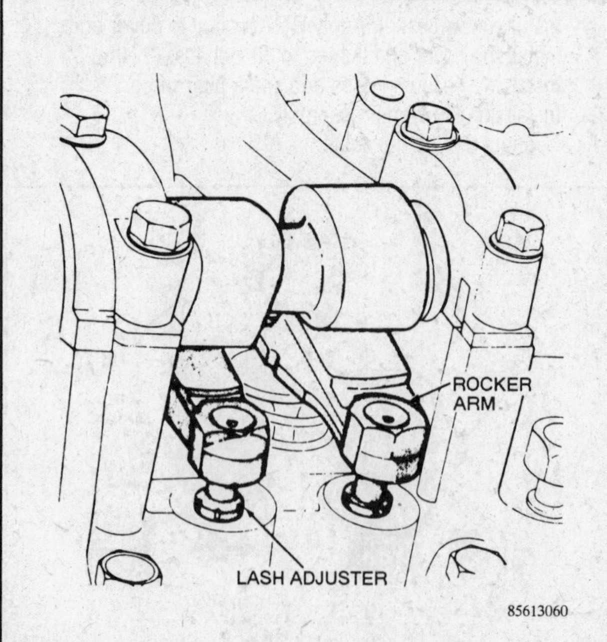

Fig. 60 Rocker arm and lash adjuster — 2.2L and 2.5L engines

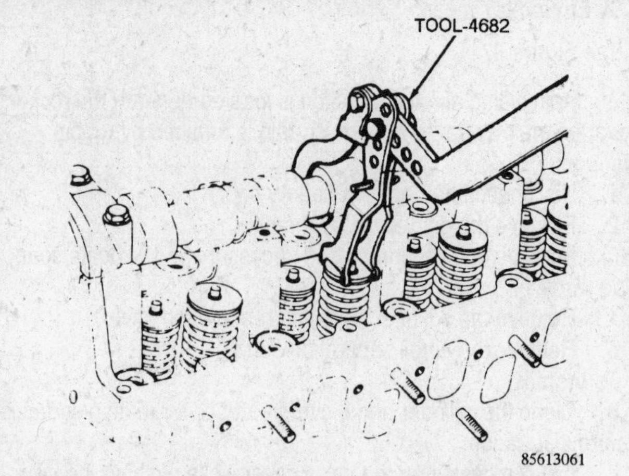

Fig. 61 Compressing a valve spring — 2.2L and 2.5L engines

To install:

6. If the lash adjuster was previously removed, partially fill with oil and install.
7. Rotate the camshaft until lobe base is in position with rocker arm. Slightly depress the valve spring using Chrysler tool 4682 or equivalent. Slide the rocker arm in position.

➥ When depressing the valve spring with Chrysler tool 4682, or the equivalent, the valve locks can become dislocated. Check and make sure both locks are fully seated in the valve grooves and retainer.

8. Install the valve cover.
9. Connect the battery cable.

2.6L Engines

➧ See Figure 62

1. Disconnect the negative battery cable.
2. Remove the valve cover.
3. Loosen the camshaft bearing cap bolts. Do not remove bolts from bearing cap.
4. Remove the rocker arm, rocker shafts and bearing caps as an assembly.
5. Remove the bolts from the camshaft bearing caps and remove the rocker shafts, waved washers, rocker arms and springs. Keep all parts in order. Note the way the rocker shaft, rocker arms, bearing caps and springs are mounted. The rocker arm shaft on the Left side has 12 oil holes at shaft bottom, and the Right side shaft has 4 oil holes at shaft bottom.
6. Inspect the rocker arms mounting area and rockers for damage. Replace if worn or heavily damaged.

To install:

7. Position the camshaft bearing caps with arrows pointing toward the timing chain and in numerical order.
8. Insert both shafts into the front bearing cap and install bolts to hold shafts in position.
9. Install the wave washers, rocker arms, bearing caps, and springs. Install bolts in the rear cap to retain assembly.
10. Place the assembly into position.
11. Tighten the camshaft bearing cap bolts in sequence to 10 Nm (85 inch lbs.) as followed:
    a. No. 3 Cap
    b. No. 2 Cap
    c. No. 4 Cap
    d. Front Cap
    e. Rear Cap

12. Repeat Step 12 and increase the torque to 175 inch lbs. (20 Nm).

13. Install the distributor drive gear, timing chain/camshaft sprocket, and sprocket bolt. Tighten the sprocket bolt to 40 ft. lbs. (55 Nm).

After servicing the rocker shaft assembly, Jet Valve Clearance (if used) and Intake/Exhaust Valve Clearance must be performed.

14. Install the water pump (upper shield) and valve cover.

15. Connect the battery cable.

3.0L Engines

See Figures 63, 64, 65 and 66

1. Disconnect the negative battery cable.
2. Remove the valve cover.
3. Loosen the camshaft bearing cap bolts. Do not remove the bolts from the bearing cap.
4. Remove the rocker arm, rocker shafts and bearing caps as an assembly.
5. Remove the bolts from the camshaft bearing caps and remove the rocker shafts and arms. Keep all parts in order. Note the way the rocker shaft, rocker arms, bearing caps and springs are mounted. The rocker arm shaft on the intake side has a 0.12 in. (3mm) diameter oil passage hole from the cylinder head. The exhaust side does not have this oil passage.
6. Inspect the rocker arm mounting area and rocker for damage. Replace if worn or heavily damaged.

To install:

7. Identify No. 1 bearing cap, (No. 1 and No. 4 caps are similar). Install the rocker shafts into the bearing cap with notches in proper position. Insert the attaching bolts to retain assemble.
8. Install the rocker arms, springs and bearing caps on shafts in numerical sequence.
9. Align the camshaft bearing caps with arrows (depending on cylinder bank).
10. Install the bolts in No. 4 cap to retain assembly.
11. Apply sealant at bearing cap ends.
12. Install the rocker arm shaft assembly.

Make sure the arrow mark on the bearing caps and the arrow mark on the cylinder heads are in the same direction. The direction of arrow marks on the front and rear assemblies are opposite to each other.

13. Tighten the bearing caps bolts to 85 inch lbs. (10 Nm) in the following sequence:
    a. No. 3 Cap
    b. No. 2 Cap
    c. No. 1 Cap
    d. No. 4 Cap
14. Repeat Step 13, but increase the torque value to 180 inch lbs. (20 Nm).
15. Install the valve cover.
16. Connect the battery cable.

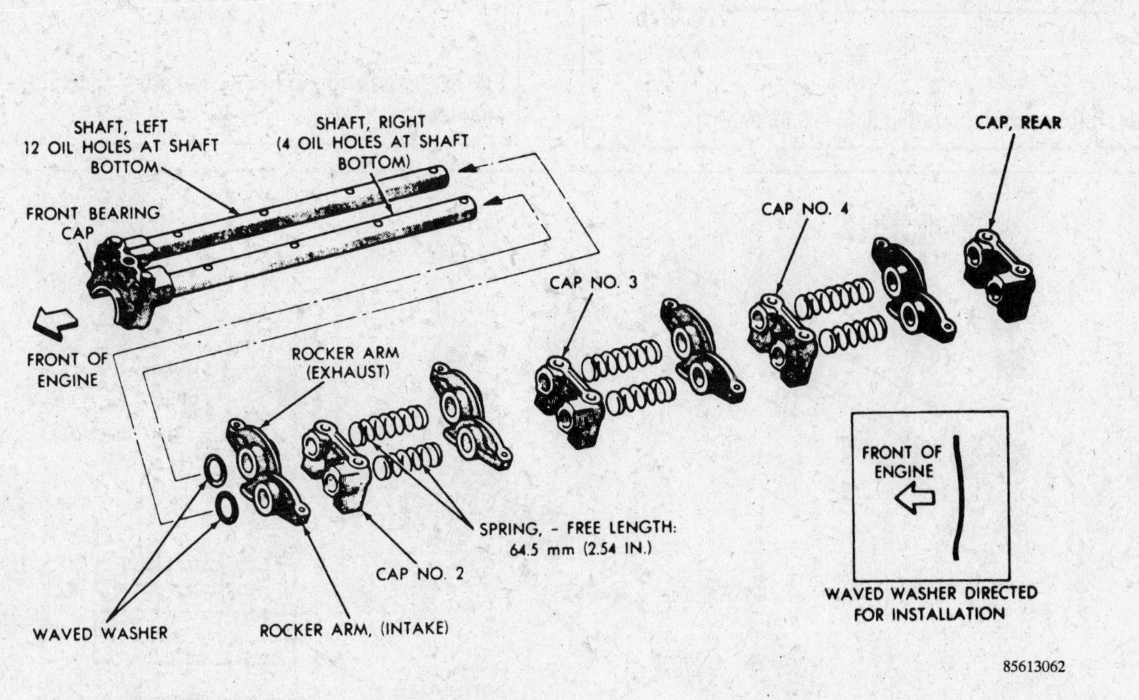

Fig. 62 Rocker arm and shaft assemblies — 2.6L engines

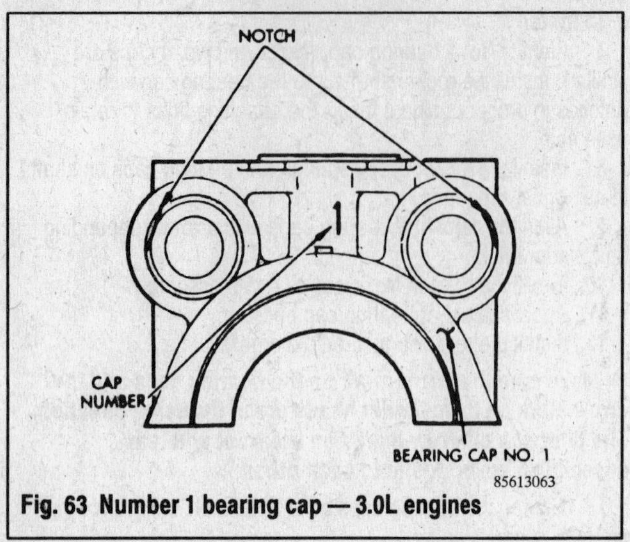

Fig. 63 Number 1 bearing cap — 3.0L engines

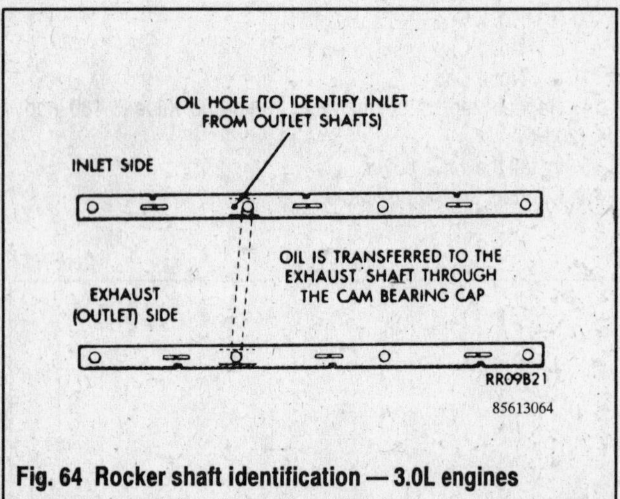

Fig. 64 Rocker shaft identification — 3.0L engines

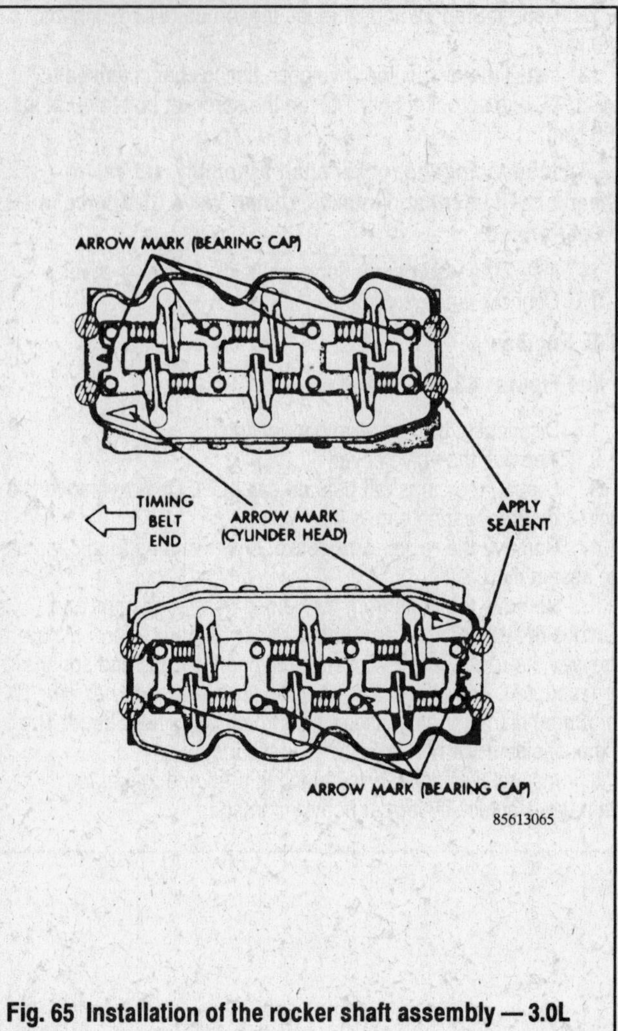

Fig. 65 Installation of the rocker shaft assembly — 3.0L engines

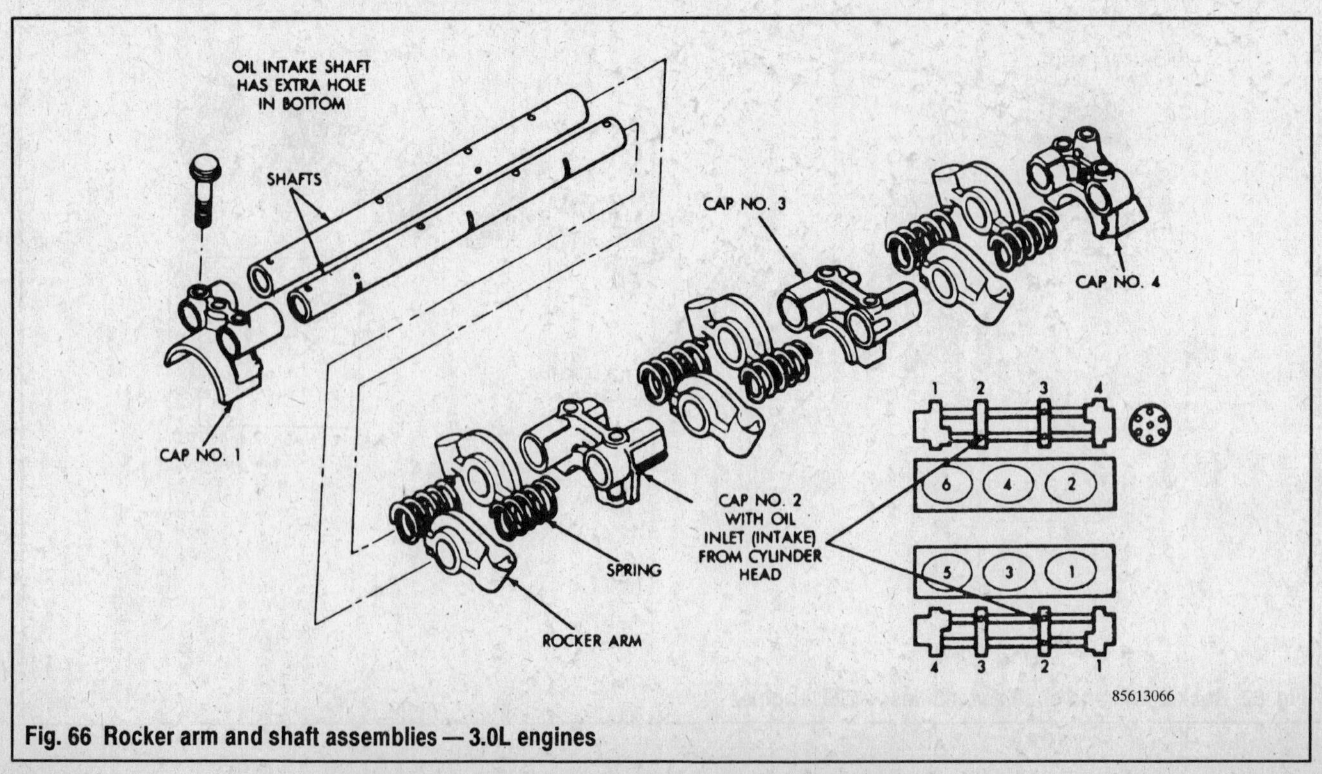

Fig. 66 Rocker arm and shaft assemblies — 3.0L engines

3.3L and 3.8L Engines

➧ See Figures 67 and 68

1. Disconnect the negative battery cable.
2. Remove the upper intake manifold assembly.
3. Remove the rocker arm cover.
4. Remove the 4 rocker shaft retaining bolts and retainers.
5. Remove the rocker arms and shaft assembly.
6. If you are disassembling the rocker shaft, be sure to install the rocker arms in their original locations.

To install:

7. Install the rocker arm and shaft assembly, using the 4 retainers. Tighten the retaining bolts to 21 ft. lbs. (28 Nm).

➥ The rocker arm shaft should be torqued down slowly, starting with the center bolts. After installation, allow 20 minutes for tappet bleed down, before engine operation.

8. Install the rocker cover.
9. Install the crankcase ventilation components and connect the spark plug wires.
10. Install the upper intake manifold assembly.
11. Connect the negative battery cable.

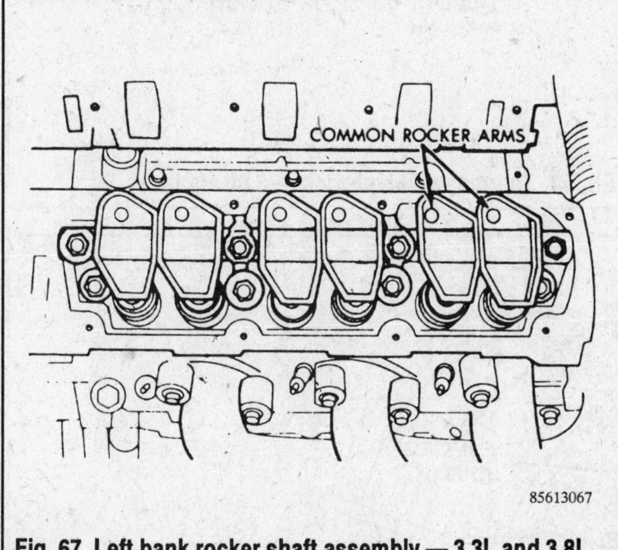

Fig. 67 Left bank rocker shaft assembly — 3.3L and 3.8L engines

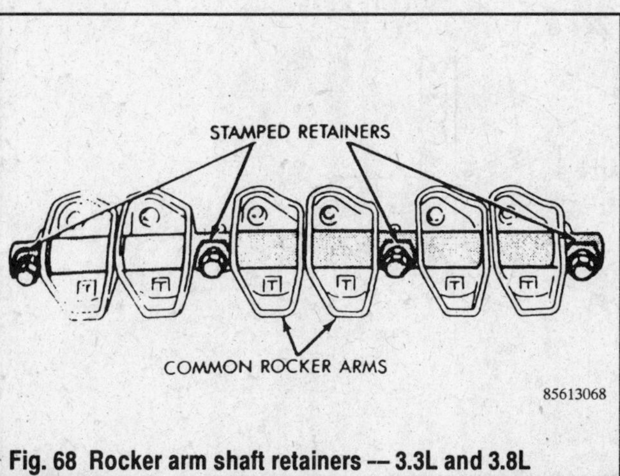

Fig. 68 Rocker arm shaft retainers — 3.3L and 3.8L engines

Thermostat

REMOVAL & INSTALLATION

➧ See Figures 69, 70, 71, 72, 73, 74, 75 and 76

The thermostat is located in a water box at the side of the engine (facing grille) 2.2L and 2.5L engines. The thermostat on 2.6L, 3.0L, 3.3L and 3.8L engines is located in a water box at the timing belt end of the intake manifold.

1. Drain the cooling system to a level below the thermostat.

****CAUTION**

When draining coolant, keep in mind that cats and dogs are attracted by ethylene glycol antifreeze, and are quite likely to drink any that is left in an uncovered container or in puddles on the ground. This will prove fatal in sufficient quantity. Always drain the coolant into a sealable container. Coolant should be reused unless it is contaminated or several years old.

2. Remove the hoses from the thermostat housing.
3. Remove the thermostat housing.
4. Remove the thermostat and discard the gasket. Clean the gasket surfaces thoroughly.

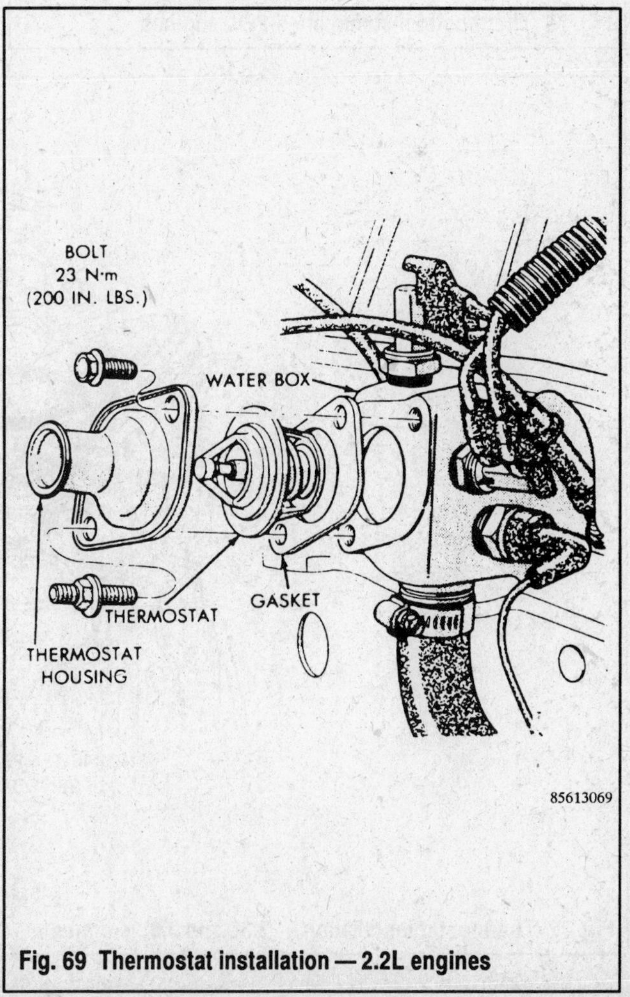

Fig. 69 Thermostat installation — 2.2L engines

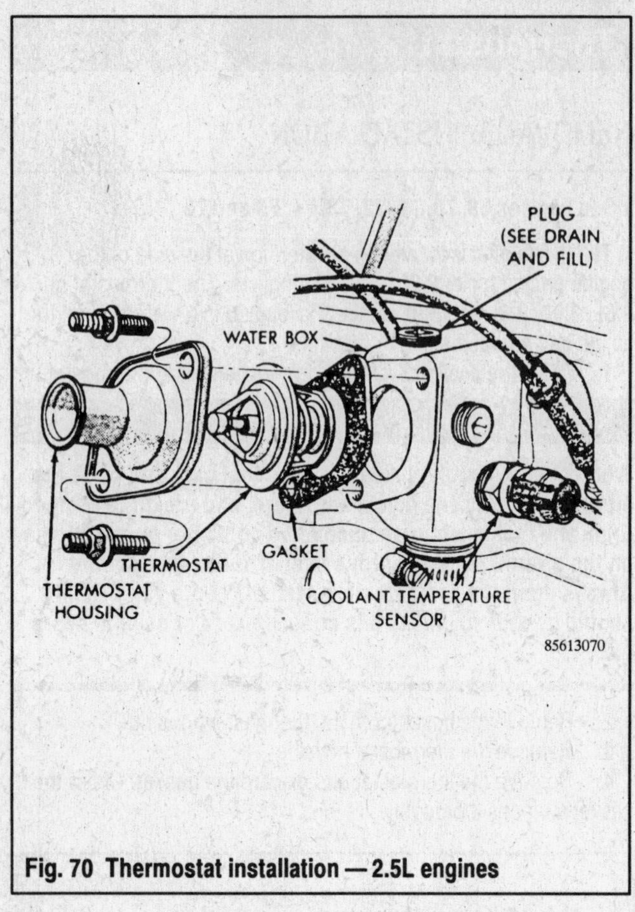

Fig. 70 Thermostat installation — 2.5L engines

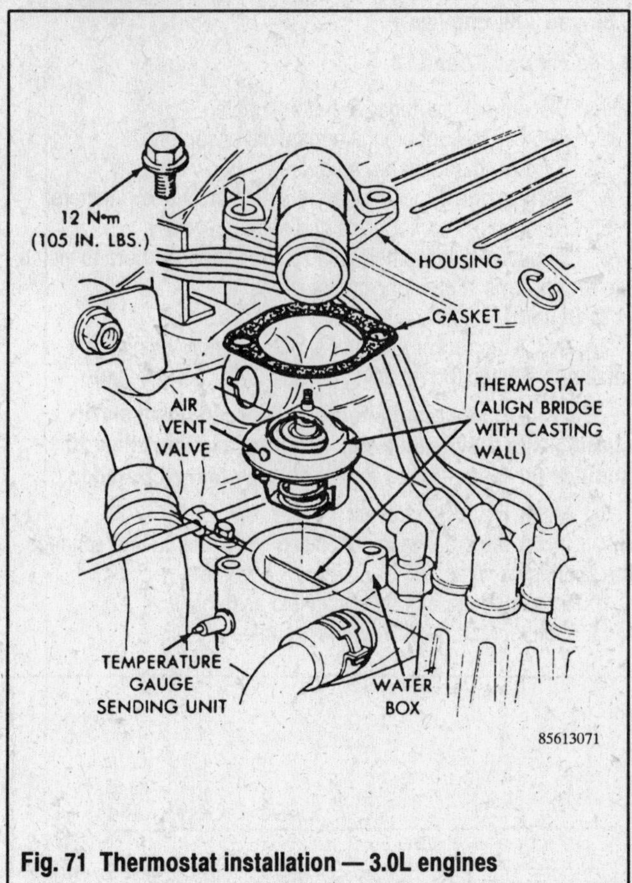

Fig. 71 Thermostat installation — 3.0L engines

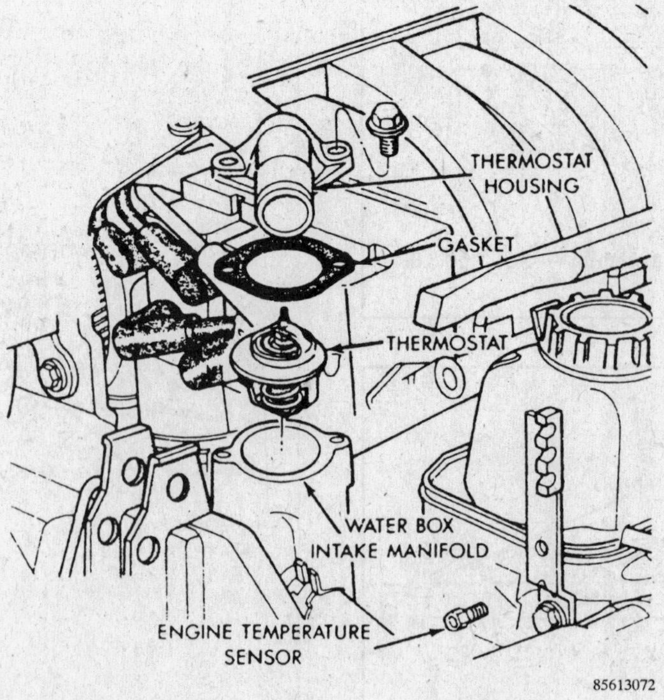

Fig. 72 Thermostat installation — 3.3L and 3.8L engines

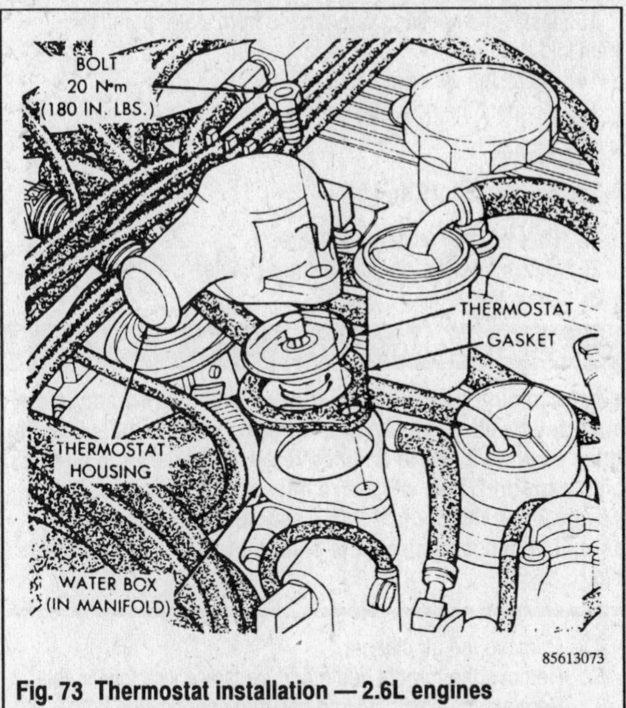

Fig. 73 Thermostat installation — 2.6L engines

Fig. 74 Removing a thermostat housing to water box retaining bolt

The thermostat is located in a water box at the side of the engine (facing grille) 2.2L and 2.5L engines. The thermostat on 2.6L, 3.0L, 3.3L and 3.8L engines is located in a water box at the timing belt end of the intake manifold.

1. Drain the cooling system to a level below the thermostat.

✱✱CAUTION

When draining coolant, keep in mind that cats and dogs are attracted by ethylene glycol antifreeze, and are quite likely to drink any that is left in an uncovered container or in puddles on the ground. This will prove fatal in sufficient quantity. Always drain the coolant into a sealable container. Coolant should be reused unless it is contaminated or several years old.

Fig. 75 Removing the thermostat housing

Fig. 76 Removing the thermostat from the water box

2. Remove the hoses from the thermostat housing.
3. Remove the thermostat housing.
4. Remove the thermostat and discard the gasket. Clean the gasket surfaces thoroughly.
5. Install a new gasket on water box housing 2.2L and 2.5L engines. Center the thermostat in the water box on gasket surface. Install the thermostat housing on gasket. Make sure thermostat sits in its recess of the housing. Tighten bolts to 15 ft. lbs. (20 Nm).
6. On 2.6L engine position gasket on water box. Center thermostat in water box and attached housing. Tighten the bolts to 15 ft. lbs. (20 Nm).
7. On 3.0L, 3.3L and 3.8L engines position thermostat in water box pocket. Make sure thermostat flange in seated properly in flange groove of the water box. Position the new gasket on water box and install housing. Tighten the bolts to 15 ft. lbs. (20 Nm).
8. Connect the radiator hose to the thermostat housing. Tighten the hose clamp to 35 inch lbs. (4 Nm).
9. Fill the cooling system.

Intake Manifold

REMOVAL & INSTALLATION

2.6L Engines

➧ See Figure 77

1. Disconnect the negative battery cable.
2. Drain the cooling system and disconnect the hoses from the water pump to the intake manifold.

✻✻CAUTION

When draining coolant, keep in mind that cats and dogs are attracted by ethylene glycol antifreeze, and are quite likely to drink any that is left in an uncovered container or in puddles on the ground. This will prove fatal in sufficient quantity. Always drain the coolant into a sealable container. Coolant should be reused unless it is contaminated or several years old.

3. Disconnect the carburetor air horn adapter and move to one side.
4. Disconnect the vacuum hoses and throttle linkage from the carburetor.
5. Disconnect the fuel inlet line at the fuel filter.
6. Remove the fuel filter and fuel pump, then move to one side.
7. Remove the intake manifold retaining nuts and washers, then remove the manifold.
8. Remove old gasket. Clean cylinder head and manifold gasket surface. Check for cracks or warpage. Install a new gasket on cylinder head.

To install:

9. Install the manifold onto cylinder head. Install the washers and nuts. Refer to the torque specification chart for the proper tightening values.
10. Install the fuel pump and filter.
11. Install the carburetor air horn.
12. Install the throttle control cable.

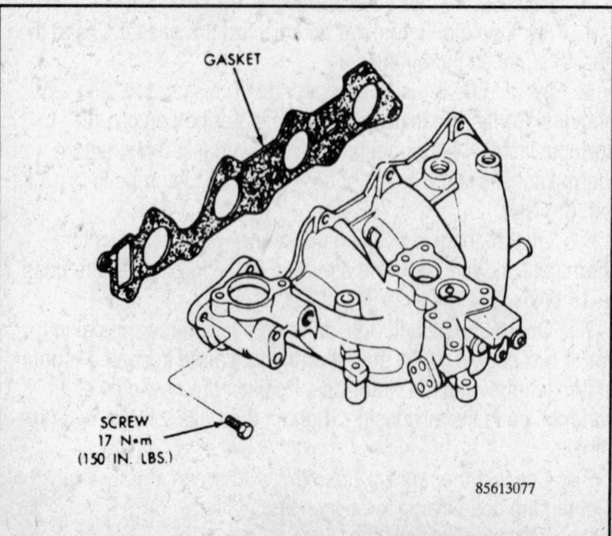

Fig. 77 Intake manifold assembly — 2.6L engines

13. Install the cooling system hose from water pump to manifold.
14. Install the vacuum hoses.
15. Connect the negative battery cable.

3.0L Engines

➧ See Figures 78, 79 and 85

1. Release fuel system pressure.
2. Disconnect the negative battery cable.
3. Drain the cooling system.

✻✻CAUTION

When draining coolant, keep in mind that cats and dogs are attracted by ethylene glycol antifreeze, and are quite likely to drink any that is left in an uncovered container or in puddles on the ground. This will prove fatal in sufficient quantity. Always drain the coolant into a sealable container. Coolant should be reused unless it is contaminated or several years old.

4. Remove the air cleaner.
5. Remove the throttle cable and transaxle kickdown cable.
6. Remove the electrical and vacuum connections from throttle body.
7. Remove the air intake hose from air cleaner to throttle body.
8. Remove the EGR tube to intake plenum.
9. Remove the electrical connection from charge temperature and coolant temperature sensors.
10. Remove the vacuum connection from the pressure regulator and remove the air intake connection from the manifold.
11. Remove fuel hoses to fuel rail connection.
12. Remove the air intake plenum to manifold bolts (usually 8), then remove the air intake plenum and gasket.

✻✻WARNING

Whenever the air intake plenum is removed, cover the intake manifold properly to avoid objects from entering cylinder head.

13. Disconnect the fuel injector wiring harness from the engine wiring harness.
14. Remove the pressure regulator attaching bolts and remove pressure regulator from rail.
15. Remove the fuel rail attaching bolts and remove fuel rail.
16. Remove the radiator hose from thermostat housing and heater hose from pipe.
17. Remove the intake manifold attaching nuts and washers and remove intake manifold.
18. Clean the gasket material from cylinder head and manifold gasket surface. Check for cracks or damaged mounting surfaces.

To install:

19. Install a new gasket on the intake surface of the cylinder head and install the intake manifold.
20. Install the intake manifold washers and nuts, then tighten them in the sequence shown in the illustration. Refer to the torque specification chart for the proper torque values.
21. Clean the injectors and lubricate the injector O-rings with a drop of clean engine oil.

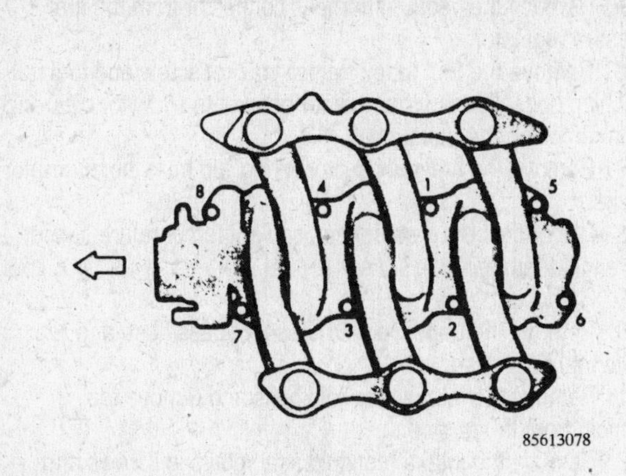

Fig. 78 Intake manifold tightening sequence — 3.0L engines

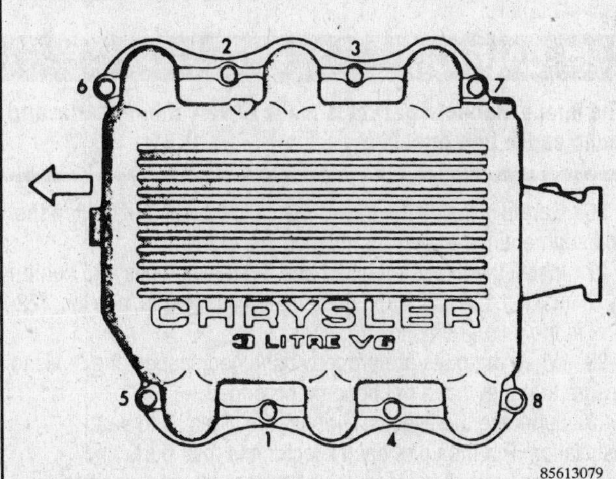

Fig. 79 Intake plenum tightening sequence — 3.0L engines

22. Place the tip of each injector into their ports. Push assembly into place until the injectors are seated in their ports.
23. Install rail attaching bolts and tighten to 115 inch lbs. (13 Nm).
24. Install pressure regulator to rail. Install pressure regulator mounting bolts and tighten to 95 inch lbs. (11 Nm).
25. Install fuel supply and return tube hold-down bolt and vacuum crossover tube hold-down bolt. Tighten to 95 inch lbs. (11 Nm).
26. Tighten fuel pressure regulator hose clamps to 10 inch lbs. (1 Nm).
27. Connect injector wiring harness to engine wiring harness.
28. Connect vacuum harness to fuel rail and pressure regulator.
29. Remove covering from intake manifold.
30. Position the intake manifold gasket, beaded side up, on the intake manifold.
31. Put the air intake plenum in place. Install attaching bolts and tighten in sequence to 115 inch lbs. (13 Nm).
32. Connect the fuel line to fuel rail. Tighten clamps to 10 inch lbs. (1 Nm).
33. Connect the vacuum hoses to intake plenum.
34. Engage the electrical connection to coolant temperature sensor and charge temperature sensor.
35. Connect the EGR tube flange to intake plenum and tighten to 15 ft. lbs. (20 Nm).
36. Connect the throttle body vacuum hoses and electrical connections.
37. Install the throttle cable and transaxle kickdown linkage.
38. Install the radiator and heater hose. Fill the cooling system.
39. Connect the negative battery cable.

3.3L and 3.8L Engines

➧ See Figures 80, 81, 82 and 83

1. Disconnect the negative battery cable.
2. Relieve the fuel pressure as outlined in Section 1.
3. Drain the cooling system.
4. Remove the air cleaner-to-throttle body hose assembly.
5. Disconnect the throttle cable and remove the wiring harness from the bracket.
6. Remove AIS motor and TPS wiring connectors from the throttle body.
7. Remove the vacuum hose harness from the throttle body.
8. Remove the PCV and brake booster hoses from the air intake plenum.
9. Disconnect the charge temperature sensor electrical connector. Remove the vacuum harness connectors from the intake plenum.
10. Remove the cylinder head to the intake plenum strut.
11. Disengage the MAP sensor and oxygen sensor connectors. Remove the engine mounted ground strap.
12. Remove the fuel hoses from the fuel rail and plug them.
13. Remove the DIS coils and the alternator bracket to intake manifold bolt.
14. Remove the upper intake manifold attaching bolts and remove the upper manifold.

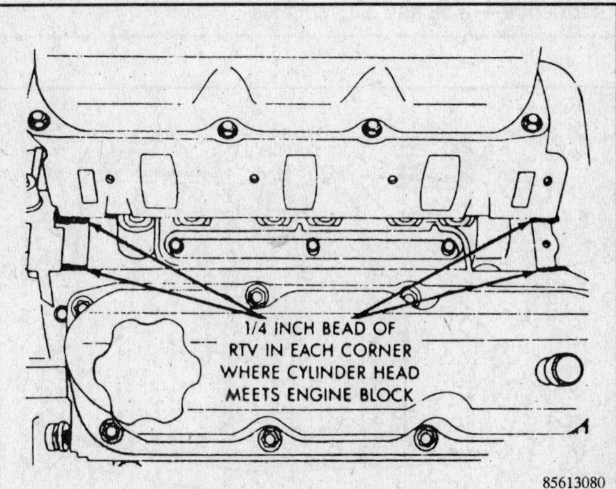

Fig. 80 Intake manifold gasket sealing — 3.3L and 3.8L engines

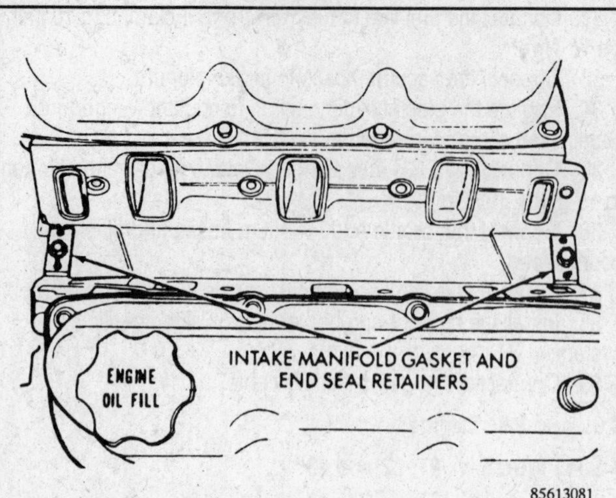

Fig. 81 Intake manifold gasket retainers — 3.3L and 3.8L engines

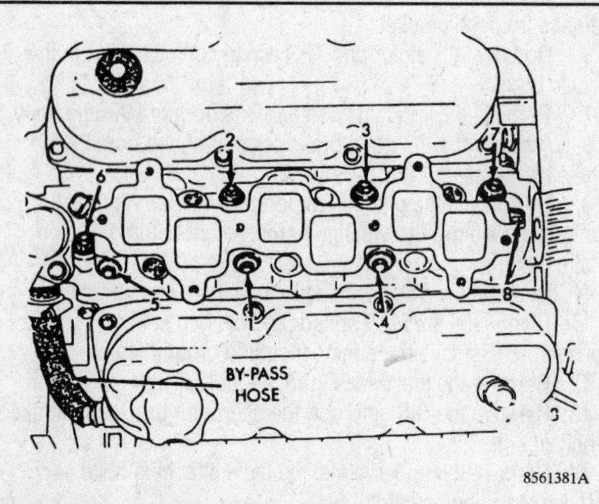

Fig. 82 Lower intake manifold tightening sequence — 3.3L and 3.8L engines

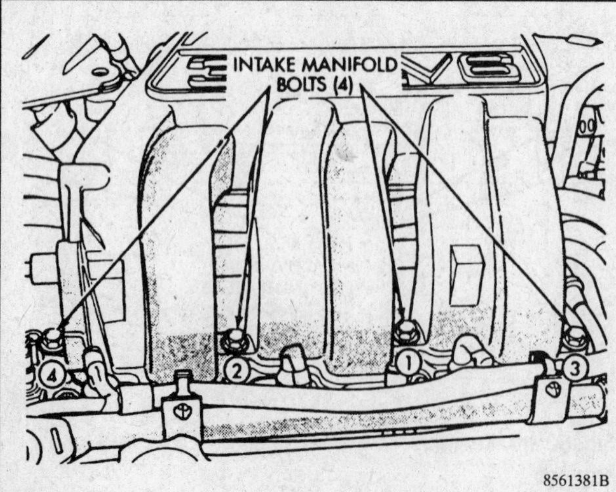

Fig. 83 Upper intake manifold tightening sequence — 3.3L and 3.8L engines

15. Remove the vacuum harness connector from the fuel pressure regulator.
16. Remove the fuel tube retainer bracket screw and fuel rail attaching bolts. Spread the retainer bracket to allow for clearance when removing the fuel tube.
17. Remove the fuel rail injector wiring clip from the alternator bracket.
18. Disconnect the cam sensor, coolant temperature sensor and engine temperature sensor.
19. Remove the fuel rail.
20. Remove the upper radiator hose, bypass hose and rear intake manifold hose.
21. Remove the intake manifold bolts and remove the manifold from the engine.
22. Remove the intake manifold seal retaining screws and remove the manifold gasket.
23. Clean out clogged end water passages and fuel runners.

To install:

24. Clean and dry all gasket mating surfaces.
25. Place a drop of silicone sealant (approximately 1/4 in. or 6mm in diameter) onto each of the 4 manifold-to-cylinder head gasket corners.

****CAUTION**

The intake manifold gasket is made of very thin material and could cause personal injury.

26. Carefully install the intake manifold gasket and tighten the end seal retainer screws to 105 inch lbs. (12 Nm).
27. Install the intake manifold and 8 retaining bolts and tighten to 10 inch lbs. (1 Nm). Then tighten the bolts to 200 inch lbs. (22 Nm) in the sequence shown.
28. When the bolts are properly tightened, inspect the seals to ensure that they have not become dislodged.
29. Lubricate the injector O-rings with clean oil to ease installation. Put the tip of each injector into their ports and position the fuel rail in place. Install the rail mounting bolts and tighten to 200 inch lbs. (22 Nm).
30. Connect the cam sensor, coolant temperature sensor and engine temperature sensor.
31. Install the fuel injector harness wiring clip to the alternator bracket.
32. Install the vacuum harness to the pressure regulator.
33. Install the upper intake manifold with a new gasket. Install the bolts only finger-tight. Install the alternator bracket-to-intake manifold bolt and the cylinder head-to-intake manifold strut and bolts. Tighten the intake manifold mounting bolts to 21 ft. lbs. (28 Nm) starting from the middle and working outward in the sequence shown. Tighten the bracket and strut bolts to 40 ft. lbs. (55 Nm).
34. Install or connect all items that were removed or disconnected from the intake manifold and throttle body.
35. Connect the fuel hoses to the rail. Push the fittings in until they click in place.
36. Install the air cleaner assembly.
37. Connect the negative battery cable. Turn the ignition key **ON** and **OFF** several times. This will pressurize the fuel system. Check for leaks.

Exhaust Manifold

REMOVAL & INSTALLATION

2.6L Engines

➧ See Figure 84

1. Disconnect the negative battery cable.
2. Remove the air cleaner assembly.
3. Remove the belt from the power steering pump.
4. Raise the vehicle and make sure it is supported safely.
5. Remove the exhaust pipe from the manifold.
6. Disconnect the air injection tube assembly from the exhaust manifold and lower the vehicle.
7. Remove the power steering pump assembly and move to one side.
8. Remove the heat cowl from the exhaust manifold.
9. Remove the exhaust manifold retaining nuts and remove the assembly from the vehicle.
10. Remove the carburetor air heater from the manifold.
11. Separate the exhaust manifold from the catalytic converter by removing the retaining screws.

To install:

12. Clean gasket material from cylinder head and exhaust manifold gasket surfaces. Check mating surfaces for cracks or distortion.
13. Install a new gasket between the exhaust manifold and catalytic converter. Install mounting screws and tighten to 32 Nm (24 ft. lbs.).
14. Install the carburetor air heater on manifold and tighten to 80 inch lbs. (9 Nm).
15. Lightly coat the new exhaust manifold gasket with sealant (P/N 3419115) or equivalent on cylinder head side.
16. Install the exhaust manifold and mounting nuts. Refer to the torque specification chart in this section for the proper tightening value.
17. Install the heat cowl onto the manifold, then tighten the bolts to 80 inch lbs. (9 Nm).
18. Install the air cleaner support bracket.

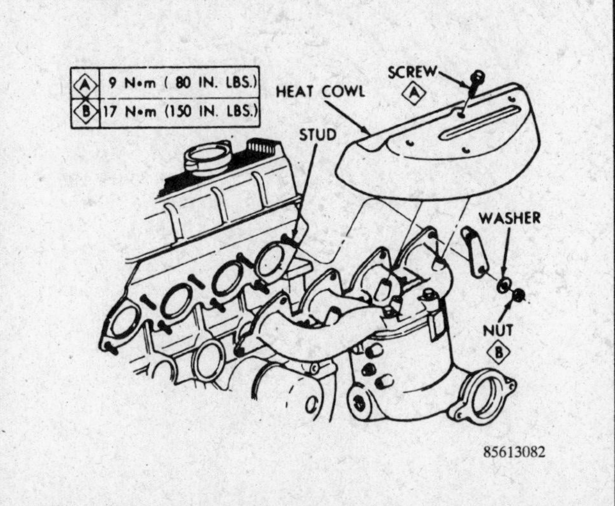

Fig. 84 Exhaust manifold — 2.6L engines

19. Install the power steering pump assembly.
20. Install the air injection tube assembly to air pump.
21. Raise the vehicle and install air injection tube assembly to exhaust manifold.
22. Install the exhaust pipe to manifold.
23. Lower the vehicle and install power steering belt.
24. Fill the cooling system.
25. Install the air cleaner assembly.
26. Connect the negative battery cable.

3.0L Engines

➧ See Figure 85

1. Disconnect the negative battery cable.
2. Raise vehicle and support properly.
3. Disconnect the exhaust pipe from rear (cowl side) exhaust manifold at articulated joint.
4. Remove the EGR tube from the rear manifold and disconnect oxygen sensor lead.
5. Remove the attaching bolts from crossover pipe to manifold.
6. Remove the attaching nuts which retained manifold to cylinder head and remove manifold.
7. Lower the vehicle and remove bolt securing front heat shield to front exhaust manifold.
8. Remove the bolts retaining crossover pipe to front exhaust manifold and nuts retaining manifold to cylinder head. Remove manifold assembly.

To install:

9. Clean all gasket material from cylinder the head and exhaust manifold gasket surfaces. Check mating surfaces for cracks or distortion.
10. Install the new gasket with the numbers 1-3-5 stamped on the top on the rear bank. The gasket with the numbers 2-4-6 must be installed on the front bank (radiator side).
11. Install rear exhaust manifold and tighten attaching nuts to 15 ft. lbs. (20 Nm).
12. Install exhaust pipe to manifold and tighten shoulder bolts to 20 ft. lbs. (27 Nm).
13. Install crossover pipe to manifold and tighten bolts to 69 Nm (51 ft. lbs.).
14. Install oxygen sensor lead and EGR tube.
15. Install front exhaust manifold and attach exhaust crossover.
16. Install front manifold heat shield and tighten bolts to 10 ft. lbs. (14 Nm).
17. Connect the negative battery cable.

3.3L and 3.8L Engines

1. Disconnect the negative battery cable.
2. If removing the rear manifold, raise the vehicle and support safely. Disconnect the exhaust pipe at the articulated joint from the rear exhaust manifold.
3. Separate the EGR tube from the rear manifold and disconnect the oxygen sensor wire.
4. Remove the alternator/power steering support strut.
5. Remove the bolts attaching the crossover pipe to the manifold.
6. Remove the bolts attaching the manifold to the head and remove the manifold.
7. If removing the front manifold, remove the heat shield, bolts attaching the crossover pipe to the manifold and the nuts attaching the manifold to the head.

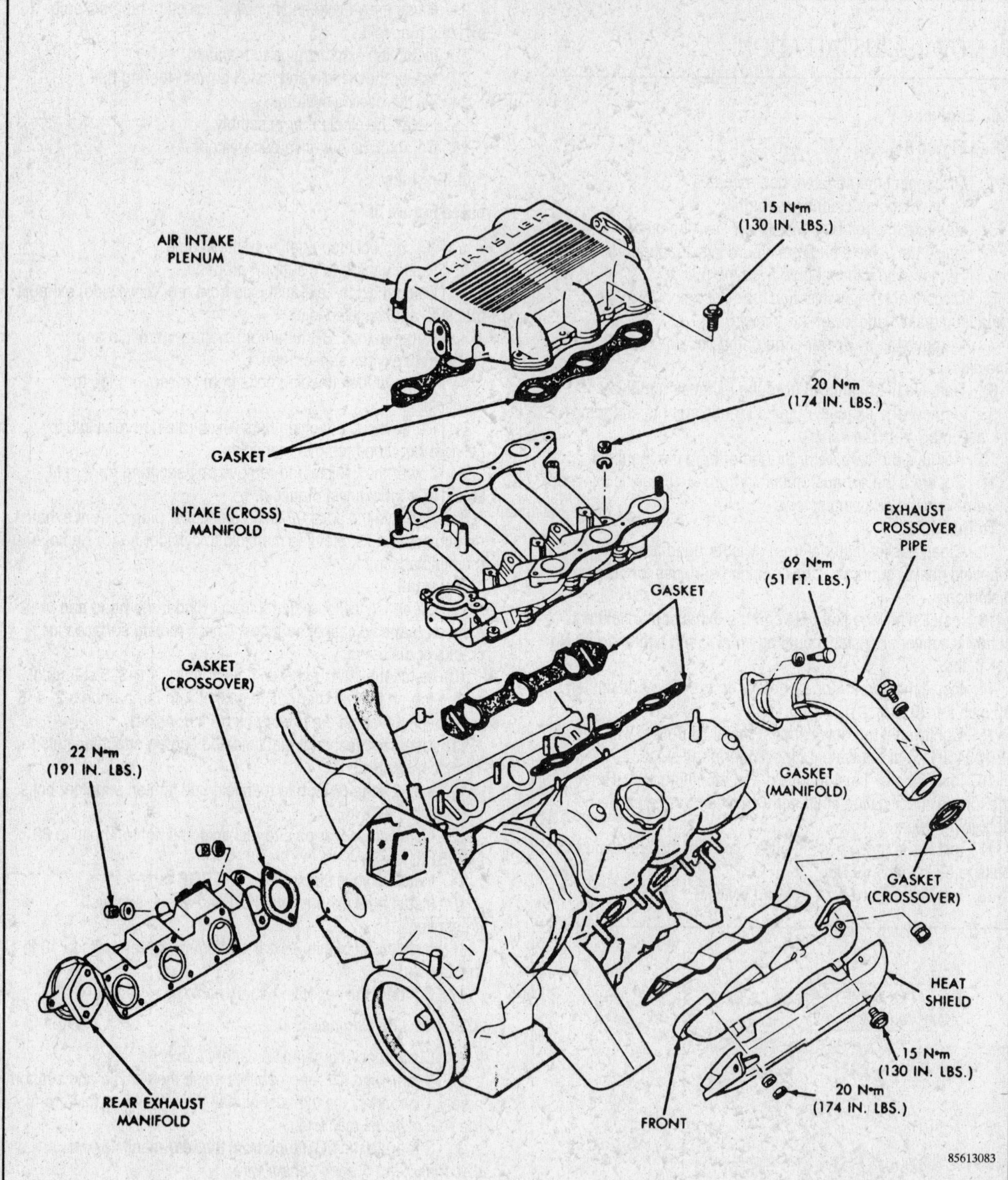

Fig. 85 Manifold assemblies — 3.0L engines

8. Remove the manifold from the engine.
9. The installation is the reverse of the removal procedure. Tighten all exhaust manifold attaching bolts to 17 ft. lbs. (23 Nm).
10. Start the engine and check for exhaust leaks.

Combination Manifold

REMOVAL & INSTALLATION

2.2L and 2.5L Engines

WITHOUT TURBOCHARGER

See Figures 86, 87, 88, 89, 90, 91 and 92

When removing the combination manifold some bolts are easier accessed from under the vehicle by reaching over the crossmember, others are accessed from under the hood. You will need an assortment of extensions and universals to remove the various bolts and nuts.

1. Disconnect the battery negative cable.
2. Drain the cooling system.

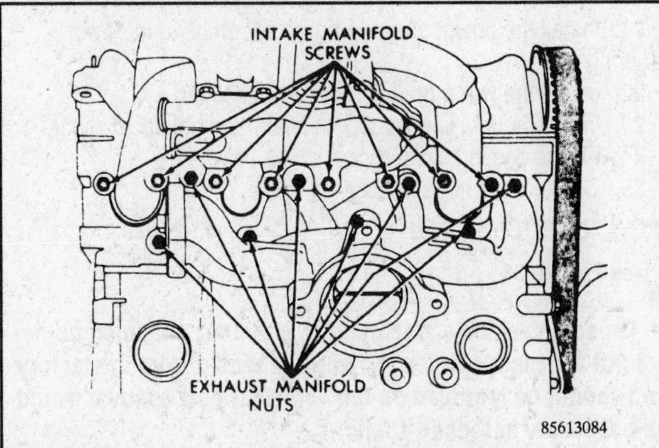

Fig. 86 Intake and exhaust manifold attaching bolts — 2.2L and 2.5L engines without turbocharger

Fig. 87 Disconnecting the throttle linkage bracket (carburetor removed for viewing purposes)

Fig. 88 Without disconnecting the hoses, remove the power steering pump and lay it aside

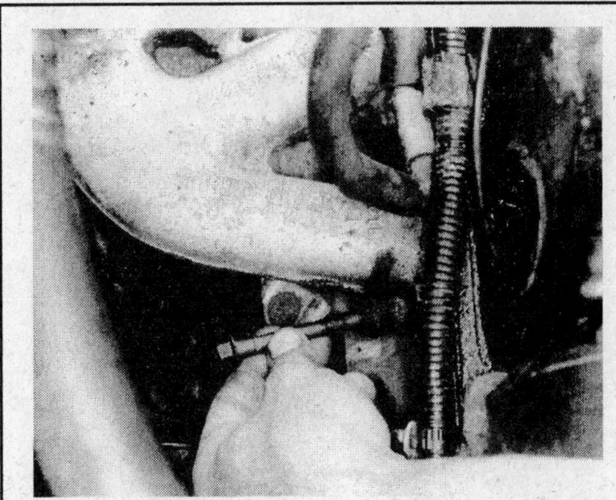

Fig. 89 Remove the intake manifold retaining bolts

Fig. 90 Removing the intake manifold from the engine

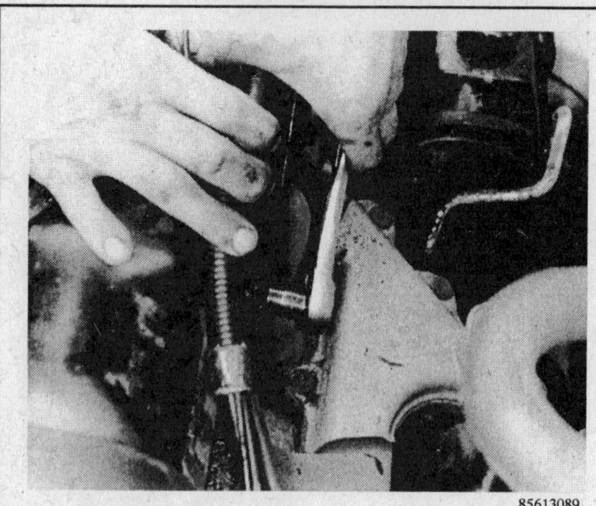

85613089

Fig. 91 Remove the exhaust manifold retaining bolts

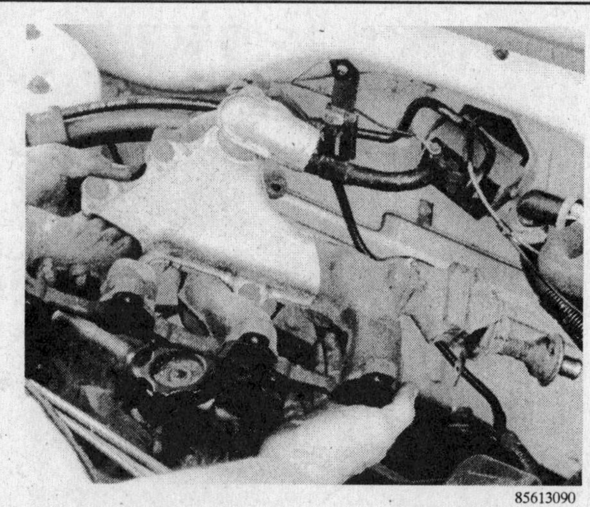

85613090

Fig. 92 Removing the exhaust manifold from the engine

****CAUTION**

When draining coolant, keep in mind that cats and dogs are attracted by ethylene glycol antifreeze, and are quite likely to drink any that is left in an uncovered container or in puddles on the ground. This will prove fatal in sufficient quantity. Always drain the coolant into a sealable container. Coolant should be reused unless it is contaminated or several years old.

3. Remove the air cleaner, disconnect all vacuum lines, electrical wiring and fuel lines from carburetor and intake manifold.
4. Remove the throttle linkage.
5. Remove the water hoses from water crossover.
6. Raise the vehicle and remove exhaust pipe from manifold.
7. Remove power steering pump and set aside.
8. Remove intake manifold support bracket and EGR tube.
9. On Canadian cars remove (4) air injection tube bolts and injection tube assembly.
10. Remove the intake manifold retaining screws.
11. Lower vehicle and remove the intake manifold.
12. Remove exhaust manifold retaining nuts and remove exhaust manifold.

To install:

13. Clean gasket surface of both manifold and cylinder block surface.
14. Install a new gasket on exhaust and intake manifold. Coat manifold with Sealer (P/N 3419115) or equivalent on manifold side.
15. Position the exhaust manifold against cylinder block and install nuts. Tighten nuts from center while alternating outward in both direction. Refer to the torque specification chart in this section for the proper tightening values.
16. Position the intake manifold against the cylinder head.
17. From beneath the vehicle tighten intake manifold screws. Start at the center while alternating outward in both directions. Refer to the torque specification chart in this section for the proper tightening values.
18. Install the exhaust pipe to the exhaust manifold.
19. On Canadian vehicles, install air injection tube assembly.
20. Install the intake manifold support bracket and EGR tube.
21. Install the power steering pump assembly and power steering belt.
22. Install the water hoses to water crossover.
23. Install the fuel lines, vacuum lines, and electrical wiring.
24. Fill the cooling system.
25. Connect the negative battery cable.

WITH TURBOCHARGER

See Figure 93

➜ On some vehicles, some of the manifold attaching bolts are not accessible or are too heavily sealed from the factory and cannot be removed on the vehicle. Head removal would be necessary in these situations.

1. Disconnect the negative battery cable. Drain the cooling system. Raise and safely support the vehicle.
2. Disconnect the accelerator linkage, throttle body electrical connector and vacuum hoses.
3. Relocate the fuel rail assembly. Remove the bracket-to-intake manifold screws and the bracket to heat shield clips. Lift and secure the fuel rail (with injectors, wiring harness and fuel lines intact) up and out of the way.
4. Disconnect the turbocharger oil feed line at the oil sending unit Tee fitting.
5. Disconnect the upper radiator hose from the thermostat housing.
6. Remove the cylinder head, manifolds and turbocharger as an assembly.
7. With the assembly on a workbench, loosen the upper turbocharger discharge hose end clamp.

➜ Do not disturb the center deswirler retaining clamp.

8. Remove the throttle body-to-intake manifold screws and throttle body assembly. Disconnect the turbocharger coolant return tube from the water box. Disconnect the retaining bracket on the cylinder head.
9. Remove the heat shield-to-intake manifold screws and the heat shield.

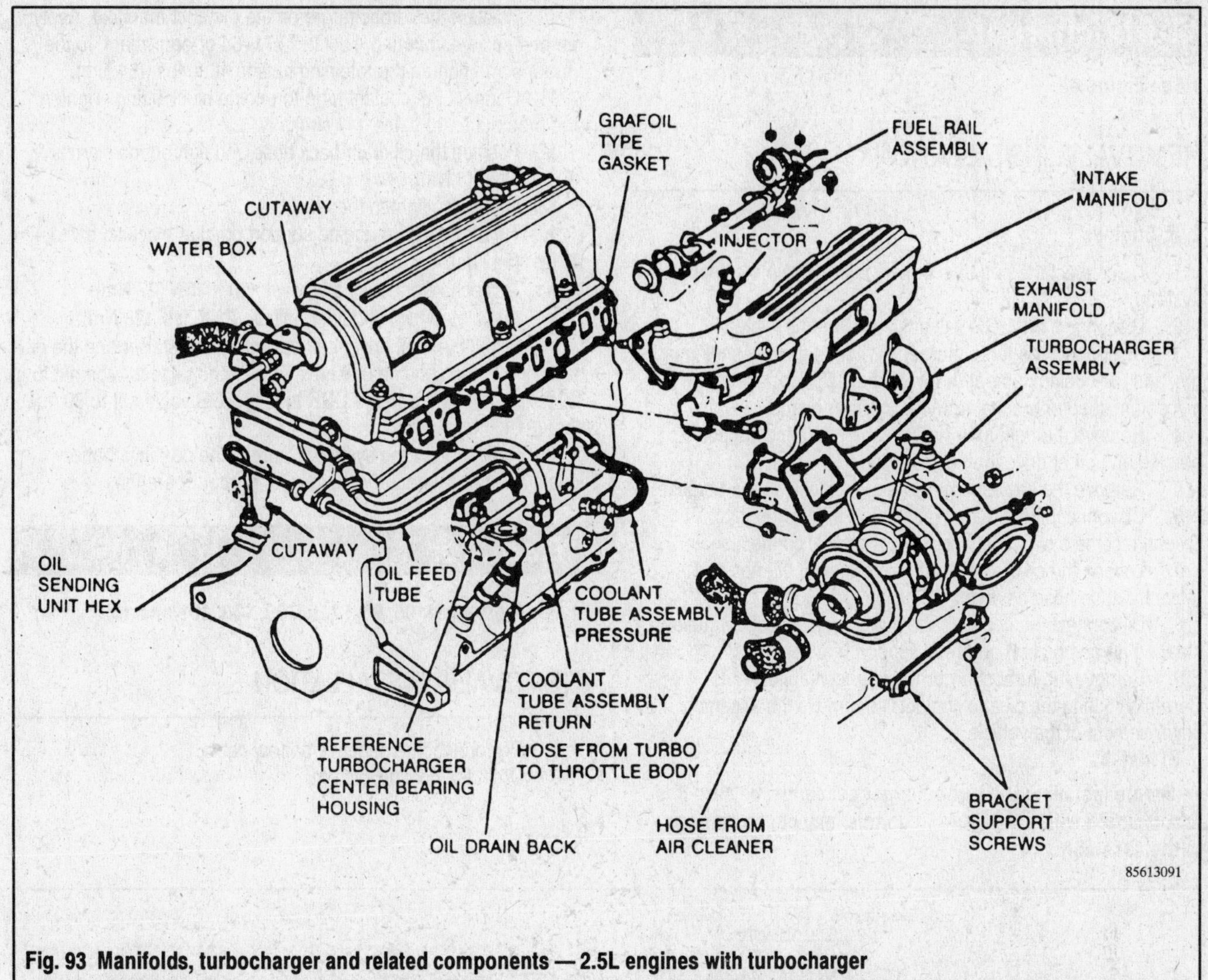

Fig. 93 Manifolds, turbocharger and related components — 2.5L engines with turbocharger

10. Remove the turbocharger-to-exhaust manifold nuts and the turbocharger assembly.
11. Remove the intake manifold bolts and the intake manifold.
12. Remove the exhaust manifold nuts and the exhaust manifold.

To install:

13. Place a new 2-sided Grafoil type intake/exhaust manifold gasket; do not use sealant.
14. Position the exhaust manifold on the cylinder head. Apply anti-seize compound to threads, install and tighten the retaining nuts, starting at center and progressing outward in both directions, to 17 ft. lbs. (23 Nm). Repeat this procedure until all nuts are at 17 ft. lbs. (23 Nm).
15. Position the intake manifold on the cylinder head. Install and tighten the retaining screws, starting at center and progressing outward in both directions, to 19 ft. lbs. (26 Nm). Repeat this procedure until all screws are at 19 ft. lbs. (26 Nm).
16. Connect the turbocharger outlet to the intake manifold inlet tube. Position the turbocharger on the exhaust manifold. Apply anti-seize compound to threads and tighten the nuts to 30 ft. lbs. (41 Nm). Tighten the connector tube clamps to 30 inch lbs. (41 Nm).
17. Install the tube support bracket to the cylinder head.
18. Install the heat shield on the intake manifold. Tighten the screws to 105 inch lbs. (12 Nm).
19. Install the throttle body air horn into the turbocharger inlet tube. Install and tighten the throttle body to intake manifold screws to 21 ft. lbs. (28 Nm). Tighten the tube clamp to 30 inch lbs. (3 Nm).
20. Install the cylinder head/manifolds/turbocharger assembly on the engine.
21. Reconnect the turbocharger oil feed line to the oil sending unit Tee fitting and bearing housing, if disconnected. Tighten the tube nuts to 10 ft. lbs. (14 Nm).
22. Install the air cleaner assembly. Connect the vacuum lines and accelerator cables.
23. Reposition the fuel rail. Install and tighten the bracket screws to 21 ft. lbs. (28 Nm). Install the air shield to bracket clips.
24. Connect the turbocharger inlet coolant tube to the engine block. Tighten the tube nut to 30 ft. lbs. (41 Nm). Install the tube support bracket.
25. Install the turbocharger housing to engine block support bracket and the screws hand-tight. Tighten the block screw 1st to 40 ft. lbs. (54 Nm). Tighten the screw to the turbocharger housing to 20 ft. lbs. (27 Nm).
26. Reposition the drain back hose connector and tighten the hose clamps. Reconnect the exhaust pin at the EGR valve.
27. Lower the vehicle. Connect the battery cable and fill the cooling system.

Turbocharger

See Figure 93

REMOVAL & INSTALLATION

2.5L Engines

1. Disconnect the negative battery cable. Drain the cooling system.
2. Disconnect the EGR valve tube at the EGR valve.
3. Disconnect the turbocharger oil feed at the oil sending unit hex and the coolant tube at the water box. Disconnect the oil/coolant support bracket from the cylinder head.
4. Remove the right intermediate shaft, bearing support bracket and outer driveshaft assemblies.
5. Remove the turbocharger-to-engine block support bracket.
6. Disconnect the exhaust pipe at the articulated joint. Disconnect the oxygen sensor at the electrical connection.
7. Loosen the oil drain-back tube connector clamps and move the tube hose down on the nipple.
8. Disconnect the coolant tube nut at the block outlet (below steering pump bracket) and tube support bracket.
9. Remove the turbocharger-to-exhaust manifold nuts. Carefully routing the oil and coolant lines, move the assembly down and out of the vehicle.

To Install:

Before installing the turbocharger assembly, be sure it is first charged with oil. Failure to do this may cause damage to the assembly.

10. Position the turbocharger on the exhaust manifold. Apply an anti-seize compound, Loctite® 771-64 or equivalent, to the threads and tighten the retaining nuts to 40 ft. lbs. (54 Nm).
11. Connect the coolant tube-to-engine block fitting. Tighten the tube nut to 30 ft. lbs. (41 Nm).
12. Position the oil drain-back hose and tighten the clamps to 30 inch lbs. (3 Nm).
13. Install and tighten the:
    - Turbocharger-to-engine support bracket block screw to 40 ft. lbs. (54 Nm).
    - Turbocharger housing screw to 20 ft. lbs. (27 Nm).
    - Articulated joint shoulder bolts to 21 ft. lbs. (28 Nm).
14. Install the right driveshaft assembly, the starter and the oil feed line at the sending unit hex. Tighten the oil feed tube nut to 10 ft. lbs. (14 Nm) and the EGR tube to EGR valve nut to 60 ft. lbs. (81 Nm).
15. Refill the cooling system. Connect the negative battery cable and check the turbocharger for proper operation.

Radiator

See Figures 94, 95, 96, 97, 98, 99, 100, 101 and 102

REMOVAL & INSTALLATION

1. Disconnect the negative battery cable.
2. Drain the cooling system.

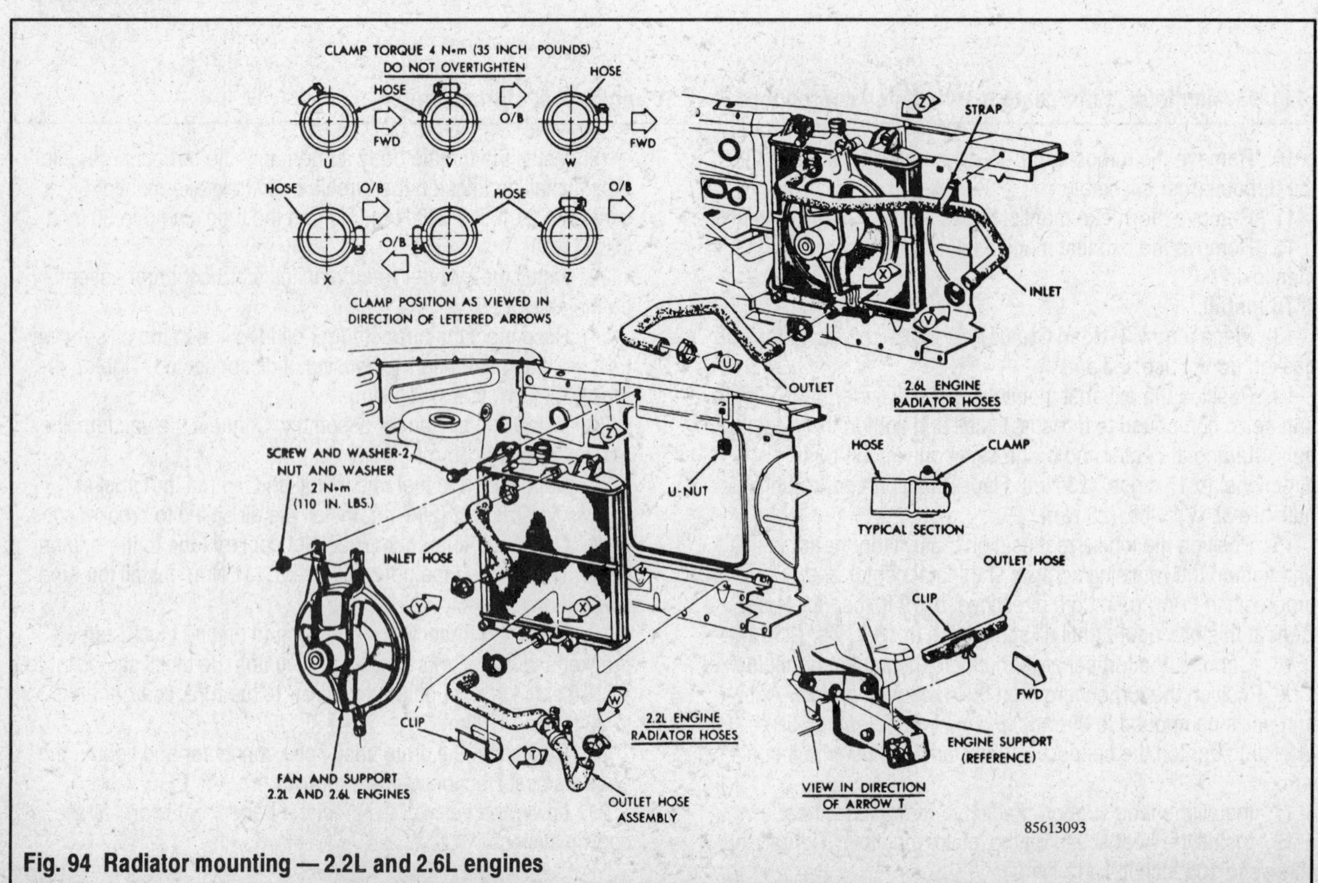

Fig. 94 Radiator mounting — 2.2L and 2.6L engines

85613094

Fig. 95 Unscrew the upper radiator hose clamp at the radiator — 1987 2.2L engine shown

85613095

Fig. 96 Disconnect the upper radiator hose from the radiator — 1987 2.2L engine shown

85613096

Fig. 97 Disconnect the radiator fan electrical connector — 1987 2.2L engine shown

85613097

Fig. 98 Remove the radiator fan assembly-to-radiator attaching bolts.

85613098

Fig. 99 Remove the radiator fan assembly from the vehicle — 1987 2.2L engine shown

85613099

Fig. 100 Disconnect the radiator overflow hose from the radiator — 1987 2.2L engine shown

85613100

Fig. 101 Remove the radiator retaining bolts — 1987 2.2L engine shown

85613101

Fig. 102 Removing the radiator with the fan assembly attached from the vehicle — 1987 2.2L engine shown

CAUTION

When draining coolant, keep in mind that cats and dogs are attracted by ethylene glycol antifreeze, and are quite likely to drink any that is left in an uncovered container or in puddles on the ground. This will prove fatal in sufficient quantity. Always drain the coolant into a sealable container. Coolant should be reused unless it is contaminated or several years old.

3. Remove the upper and lower hoses along with the coolant recovery tank tube to filler neck.
4. Disconnect the wiring harness from fan motor.
5. Remove the upper mounting bolts from fan assembly.
6. Lift fan assembly from bottom ring retaining clip.
7. Remove the radiator upper mounting bolts and carefully lift radiator from engine compartment.
8. Carefully slide the radiator into place while aligning radiator with holes in radiator support seat.
9. Install the upper radiator mounting bolts and tighten to 105 inch lbs. (12 Nm).
10. Install the lower radiator hose and tighten to 35 inch lbs. (4 Nm).
11. Carefully install the fan assembly while aligning lower fan support into retaining clip.
12. Attach washers and nuts to upper fan support.
13. Engage the fan electrical connector.
14. Install the upper radiator hose and tighten clamp to 35 inch lbs. (4 Nm).
15. Fill the cooling system.

Air Conditioning Condenser

See Figure 103

REMOVAL & INSTALLATION

1. Disconnect the negative battery cable.
2. Properly discharge the air conditioning system.
3. Remove the headlight bezels in order to gain access to the grille. Remove the grille assembly. A hidden screw fastens the grille to the center vertical support.
4. Remove the refrigerant lines attaching nut and separate the lines from the condenser sealing plate. Discard the gasket.
5. Cover the exposed ends of the lines to minimize contamination.
6. Remove the bolts that attach the condenser to the radiator support.
7. Remove the condenser from the vehicle.

To install:

8. Position the condenser and install the bolts.
9. Coat the new gasket with wax-free refrigerant oil and install. Connect the lines to the condenser sealing plate and tighten the nut.
10. Install the grille assembly.
11. Evacuate and recharge the air conditioning system. Add 1 oz. of refrigerant oil during the recharge.
12. Connect the negative battery cable and check the entire climate control system for proper operation and leaks.

Electric Cooling Fan

CAUTION

Make sure the key is in the OFF position when checking the electric cooling fan. If not, the fan could turn ON at any time, causing serious personal injury.

TESTING

1. Unplug the fan connector.
2. Using a jumper wire, connect the female terminal of the fan connector to the negative battery terminal.
3. The fan should turn on when the male terminal is connected to the positive battery terminal.
4. If not, the fan is defective and should be replaced.

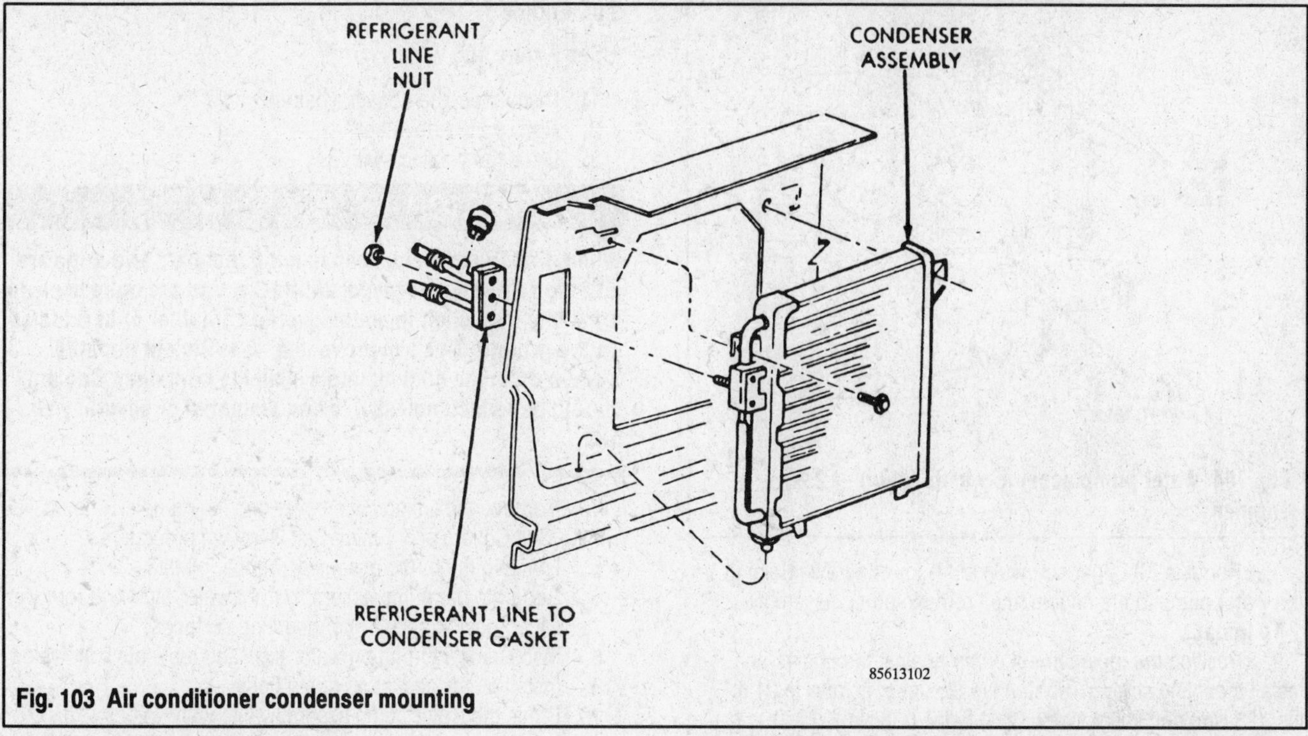

Fig. 103 Air conditioner condenser mounting

REMOVAL & INSTALLATION

See Figures 97, 98 and 99

1. Disconnect the negative battery cable.
2. Unplug the connector.
3. Remove the mounting screws.
4. Remove the fan assembly from the vehicle.
5. The installation is the reverse of the removal procedure.
6. Connect the negative battery cable and check the fan for proper operation.

Automatic Transaxle Oil Cooler

REMOVAL & INSTALLATION

The transaxle oil cooler used on these models are externally mounted ahead of the radiator. This is considered an oil-to-air type system.

1. Remove the electrical cooling fan assembly and remove the radiator. For more details, refer to the radiator removal procedures found earlier in this section.
2. Loosen the clamps retaining the hoses from the transaxle cooler lines.
3. Place an oil drain pan under the hoses and remove hoses from the cooler assembly.
4. Remove (2) screws retaining the cooler assembly to support and remove cooler assembly.

To install:

5. If reusing the cooler assembly, reverse flush the cooler.
6. Position the cooler assembly against its support.
7. Install the cooler mounting bolts and tighten to 35 inch lbs. (4 Nm).
8. Install hoses from the cooler lines to cooler assembly and tighten clamps to 16 inch lbs. (2 Nm).
9. Install the radiator and cooling fan assembly. Refer to the radiator procedures outlined earlier in this section.

Water Pump

REMOVAL & INSTALLATION

2.2L and 2.5L Engines

See Figure 104

1. Disconnect the negative battery cable.
2. Drain the cooling system.

****CAUTION**

When draining coolant, keep in mind that cats and dogs are attracted by ethylene glycol antifreeze, and are quite likely to drink any that is left in an uncovered container or in puddles on the ground. This will prove fatal in sufficient quantity. Always drain the coolant into a sealable container. Coolant should be reused unless it is contaminated or several years old.

Jack up the front of the vehicle, support on jackstands and remove the lower splash shield to access the water pump and drive belts.

3. Remove the drive belts. (Refer to Section 1).
4. Remove the upper radiator hose.
5. Without discharging the system, remove the air conditioning compressor from the engine mount and set to one side. If necessary remove the compressor mount (4 bolts) to gain access to the water pump retaining bolts.
6. Remove the alternator and move to one side.
7. Disconnect the lower radiator hose and heater hose.

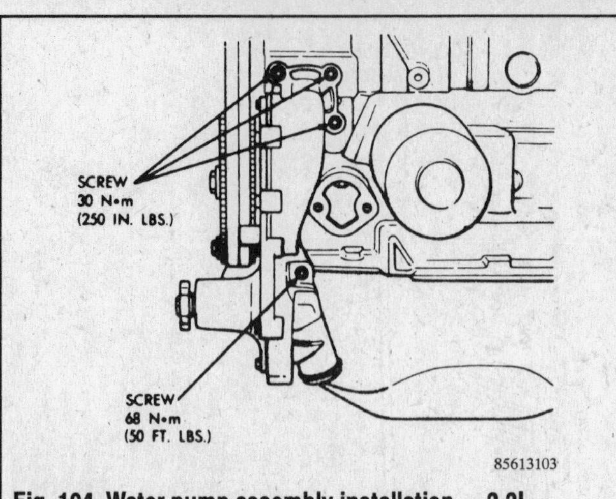

Fig. 104 Water pump assembly installation — 2.2L engines

8. Remove (3) upper screws and (1) lower screw retaining the water pump to the engine, then remove pump assembly.

To install:

9. Position the replacement pump against the engine and install mounting screws. Tighten the (3) upper screws to 21 ft. lbs. (28 Nm) and lower screw to 50 ft. lbs. (68 Nm).
10. Install heater hose and lower radiator hose. Tighten the clamps to 16 inch lbs. (2 Nm).
11. Install air conditioning compressor and alternator.
12. Install the drive belts and adjust to specification.
13. Fill the cooling system.
14. Connect the negative battery cable.

2.6L Engine

See Figure 105

1. Drain the cooling system.

****CAUTION**

When draining coolant, keep in mind that cats and dogs are attracted by ethylene glycol antifreeze, and are quite likely to drink any that is left in an uncovered container or in puddles on the ground. This will prove fatal in sufficient quantity. Always drain the coolant into a sealable container. Coolant should be reused unless it is contaminated or several years old.

2. Remove the radiator hose, by-pass hose and heater hose from the water pump.
3. Remove the drive pulley shield.
4. Remove the locking screw and pivot screws.
5. Remove the drive belt and water pump from the engine.
6. Install a new O-ring gasket in O-ring groove of pump body assembly to cylinder block.
7. Position the water pump assembly against the engine and install pivot screws and locking screw finger-tight.
8. Install the water pump drive belt and adjust to specification. New belts should have 0.31 in. (8mm) deflection, used belts should have 0.35 in. (9mm) deflection.
9. Install drive belt pulley cover.
10. Install the radiator hose, by-pass hose and heater hose.
11. Fill the cooling system.

3.0L Engine

See Figure 106

1. Disconnect the negative battery cable.
2. Remove the drive belts.
3. Drain the cooling system.

****CAUTION**

When draining coolant, keep in mind that cats and dogs are attracted by ethylene glycol antifreeze, and are quite likely to drink any that is left in an uncovered container or in puddles on the ground. This will prove fatal in sufficient quantity. Always drain the coolant into a sealable container. Coolant should be reused unless it is contaminated or several years old.

4. Remove the timing case cover and timing belt. Refer to Timing Belt Covers and Timing Belt Removal procedures.
5. Remove the pump assembly mounting bolts.
6. Separate the pump assembly from water pipe and remove.
7. Clean gasket and O-ring mounting surfaces.
8. Install a new O-ring on water pipe and lubricate with water.
9. Install a new gasket on pump body.
10. Press the water pump assembly into water pipe.
11. Install pump mounting bolts and tighten to 27 Nm (20 ft. lbs.).
12. Install timing belt and cover. Refer to Timing Belt procedures.
13. Install drive belts.
14. Fill the cooling system.

3.3L and 3.8L Engines

See Figure 107

1. Disconnect the negative battery cable.
2. Drain the cooling system.
3. Remove the serpentine belt.
4. Raise the vehicle and support safely. Remove the right front tire and wheel assembly and lower fender shield.
5. Remove the water pump pulley.
6. Remove the 5 mounting screws and remove the pump from the engine.
7. Discard the O-ring.

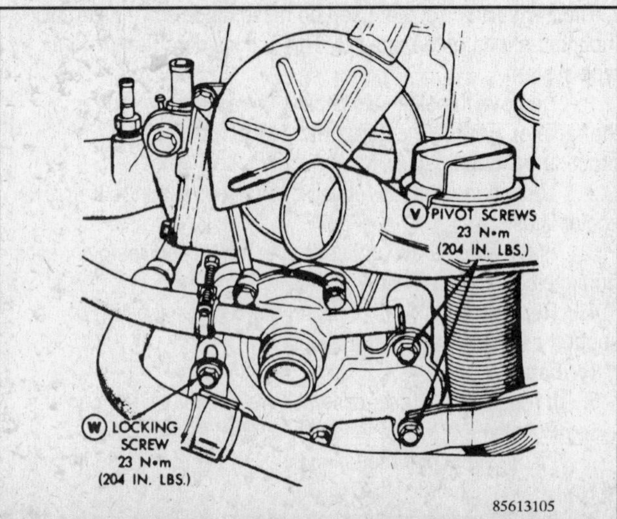

Fig. 105 Water pump mounting — 2.6L engines

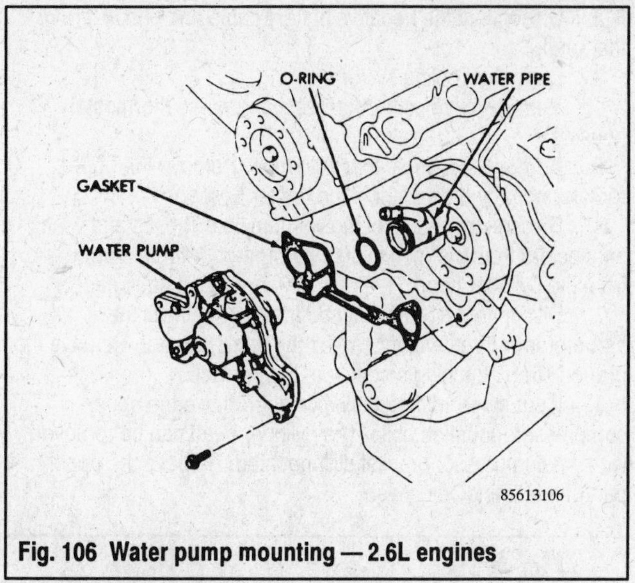

Fig. 106 Water pump mounting — 2.6L engines

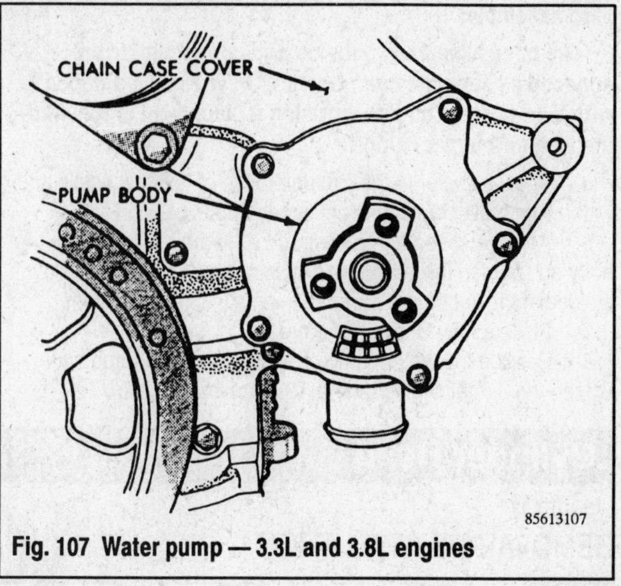

Fig. 107 Water pump — 3.3L and 3.8L engines

To install:

8. Using a new O-ring, install the pump to the engine. Tighten the mounting bolts to 21 ft. lbs. (30 Nm).
9. Install the water pump pulley.
10. Install the fender shield and tire and wheel assembly. Lower the vehicle.
11. Install the serpentine belt.
12. Remove the engine temperature sending unit. Fill the radiator with coolant until the coolant comes out the sending unit hole. Install the sending unit and continue to fill the radiator.
13. Connect the negative battery cable, run the vehicle until the thermostat opens, fill the radiator completely and check for leaks.
14. Once the vehicle has cooled, recheck the coolant level.

OVERHAUL

2.2L and 2.5L Engines

➧ See Figure 108

1. Remove the 3 screws holding the pulley to the water pump.
2. Remove the 9 screws holding the water pump to the body. Because of the gasket seal a chisel is required to separate the pump from the body.
3. Clean the gasket surfaces on the pump and the body.
4. Remove and discard the O-ring gasket and clean the O-ring groove.

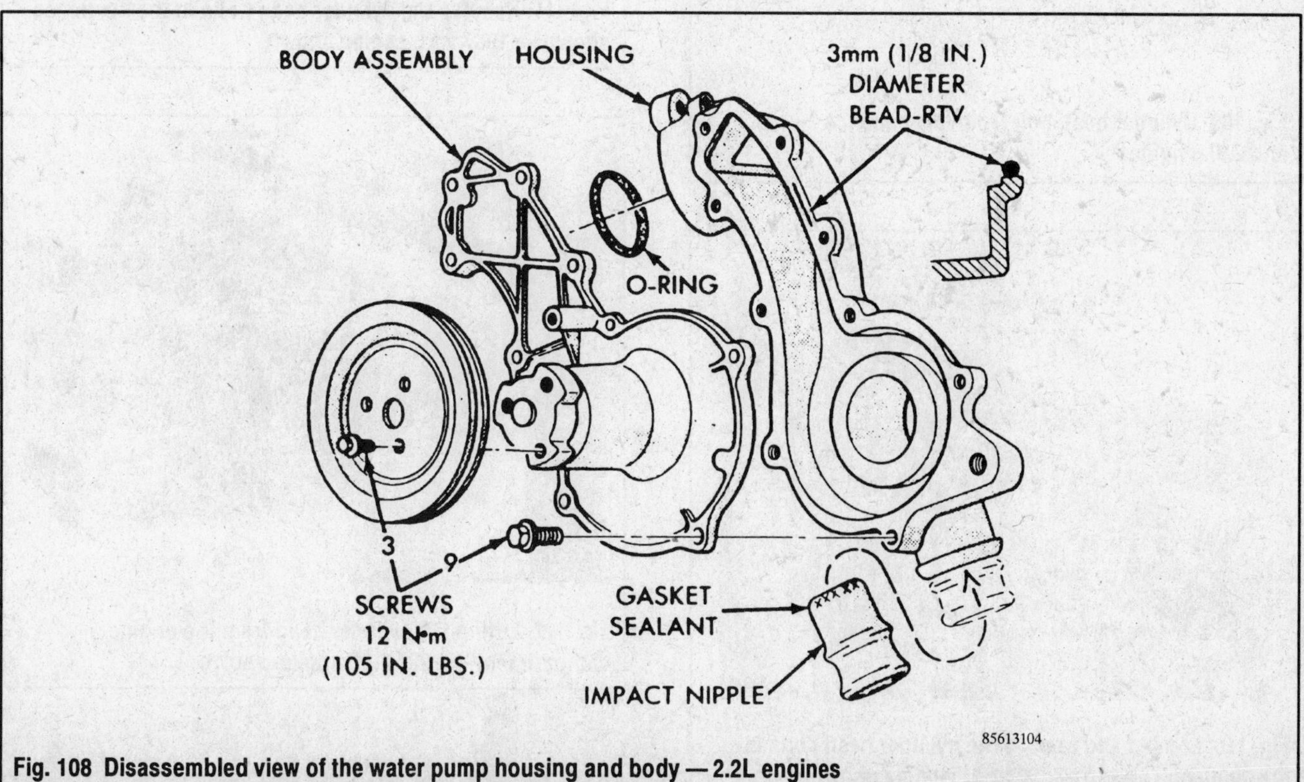

Fig. 108 Disassembled view of the water pump housing and body — 2.2L engines

To assemble:

➥ The body assembly, housing and impact nipple are serviced as separate components. On vehicles equipped with a carbureted engine, housing replacement is required. Install a new impact nipple.

5. Apply a sealer to the circumference of the new nipple and with a light mallet tap the nipple into the housing.
6. Apply RTV sealant to the body. Assemble the pump to the body and tighten the screws to 105 inch lbs. (12 Nm) and allow the sealant to set before filling and pressurizing the system.
7. Place a new O-ring in the groove.
8. Position the water pump pulley to the water pump and tighten the 3 retaining screws to 105 inch lbs. (12 Nm).

Cylinder Head

REMOVAL & INSTALLATION

2.2L and 2.5L Engines

➧ See Figures 109, 110, 111, 112, 113, 114, 115 and 116

1. Relieve the fuel pressure if equipped with fuel injection.

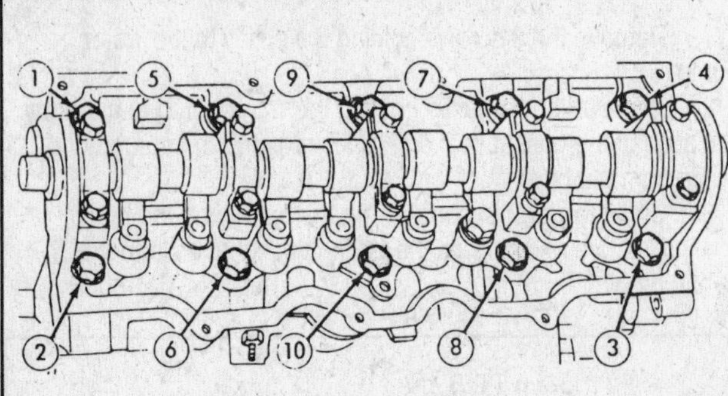

Fig. 109 Cylinder head bolt removal sequence — 2.2L and 2.5L engines

Fig. 110 Loosen and remove the cylinder head bolts in the sequence shown — 1987 2.2L engine shown

2. Disconnect the negative battery cable and unbolt it from the head.
3. Drain the cooling system.
4. Remove the dipstick bracket nut from the thermostat housing.
5. Remove the air cleaner assembly. Remove the upper radiator hose and disconnect the heater hoses.
6. Disconnect and label the vacuum lines, hoses and wiring connectors from the manifold(s), carburetor or throttle body and from the cylinder head. Remove the air pump, if equipped.
7. Disconnect all linkages and the fuel line from the carburetor or throttle body. Unbolt the cable bracket. Remove the ground strap attaching screw from the fire wall.
8. If equipped with air conditioning, remove the upper compressor mounting bolts. The cylinder head can be removed with the compressor bracket still mounted. Remove the upper part of the timing belt cover.

Fig. 111 Remove the cylinder head bolts in the sequence shown — 1987 2.2L engine shown

Fig. 112 Lifting the cylinder head from the engine compartment — 1987 2.2L engine shown

Fig. 113 Remove the cylinder head gasket — 1987 2.2L engine shown

Fig. 114 Clean the gasket mating surfaces — 1987 2.2L engine shown

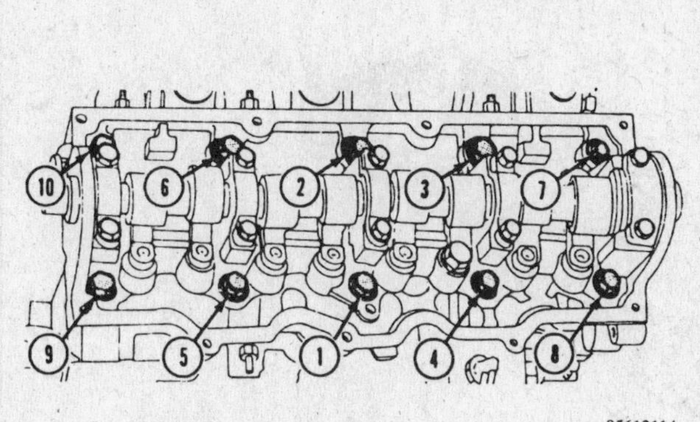

Fig. 115 Cylinder head bolt tightening sequence — 2.2L and 2.5L engines

9. Raise the vehicle and support safely. Disconnect the converter from the exhaust manifold. Disconnect the water hose and oil drain from the turbocharger, if equipped.

10. Rotate the engine by hand, until the timing marks align (No. 1 piston at TDC). Lower the vehicle.

11. With the timing marks aligned, remove the camshaft sprocket. The camshaft sprocket can be suspended to keep the timing intact. Remove the spark plug wires from the spark plugs.

12. Remove the valve cover and curtain, if equipped. Remove the cylinder head bolts and washers, starting from the middle and working outward.

13. Remove the cylinder head from the engine.

Before disassembling or repairing any part of the cylinder head assembly, identify factory installed oversized components. To do so, look for the tops of the bearing caps painted green and O/SJ stamped rearward of the oil gallery plug on the rear of the head. In addition, the barrel of the camshaft is painted green and O/SJ is stamped onto the rear end of the camshaft. Installing standard sized parts in an head equipped with oversized parts — or visa versa — will cause severe engine damage.

To install:

14. Clean the cylinder head gasket mating surfaces.

15. Using new gaskets and seals, install the head to the engine. Using new head bolts assembled with the old washers, tighten the cylinder head bolts in sequence, to 45 ft. lbs. (61 Nm). Repeating the sequence, tighten the bolts to 65 ft. lbs. (88 Nm). With the bolts at 65 ft. lbs. (88 Nm), turn each bolt an additional $^1/_4$ turn (90°).

Head bolt diameter for 1986-91 vehicles is 11mm. These bolts are identified with the number 11 on the head of the bolt. The 10mm bolts used on previous vehicles will thread into an 11mm bolt hole, but will permanently damage the engine block. Make sure the correct bolts are being used.

16. Install the timing belt.

17. Install or connect all items that were removed or disconnected during the removal procedures.

18. Refill the cooling system. Connect the negative battery cable. Start the engine and check for leaks.

2.6L Engines

See Figures 117 and 118

1. Disconnect the negative battery cable and unbolt if from the head.

2. Drain the cooling system. Remove the upper radiator hose and disconnect the heater hoses. Remove the air cleaner assembly.

3. Remove the dipstick bracket bolt from the thermostat housing.

4. Remove the carburetor to valve cover bracket. Remove the valve cover. Remove and plug the fuel lines to the carburetor.

5. Matchmark the distributor gear to its drive gear and remove the distributor. Remove the camshaft bolt and remove the distributor drive gear. Remove the camshaft gear with the chain installed from the camshaft and allow to rest on the holder just below it. This will not upset the valve timing. Do not crank the engine until the distributor has been reinstalled or the timing will be lost and timing components could be damaged.

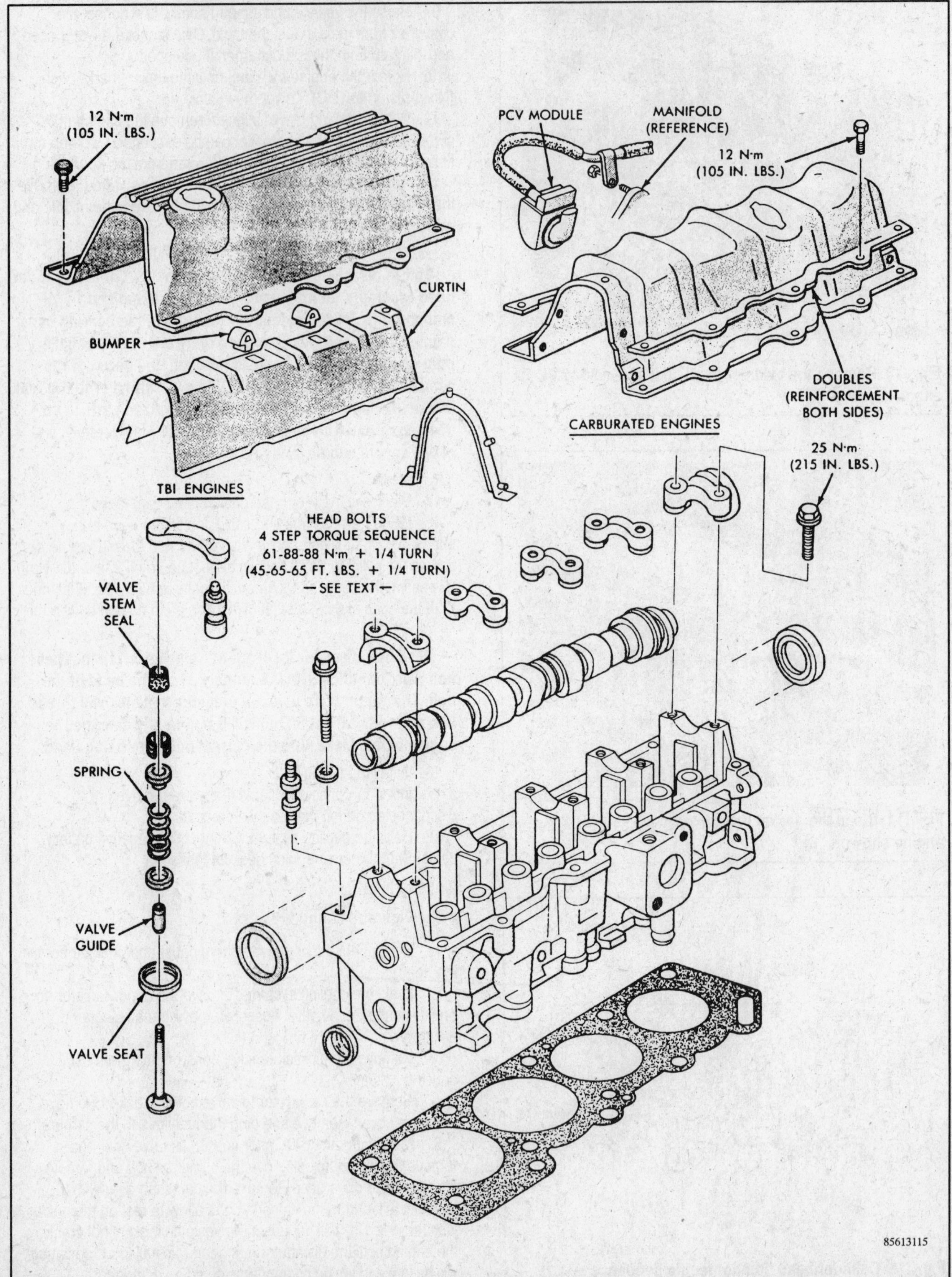

Fig. 116 Exploded view of the cylinder head assembly — 2.2L and 2.5L engines

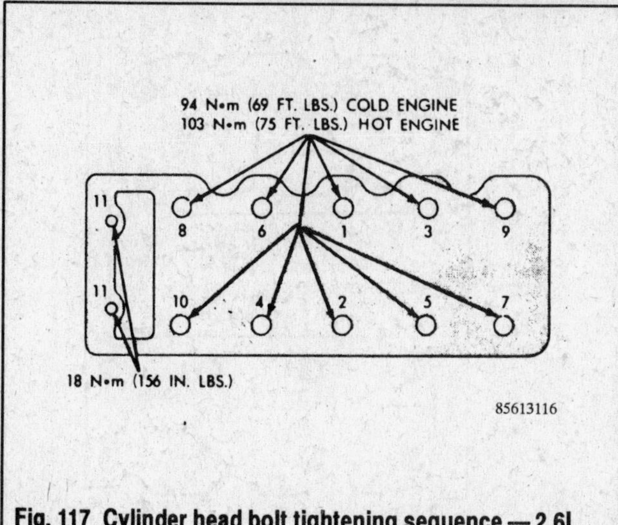

Fig. 117 Cylinder head bolt tightening sequence — 2.6L engines

6. Remove the water pump drive pulley retaining bolt and remove the pulley from the camshaft.

7. Disconnect and label the vacuum lines, hoses and wiring connectors from the manifold(s), carburetor and cylinder head. Since some of the vacuum lines from the carburetor connect to a solenoid pack on the right side inner fender, unbolt the solenoids from the fender with the vacuum lines attached and fold the assembly over the carburetor.

8. Disconnect all the linkages and the fuel line from the carburetor. Remove the ground strap attaching screw from the fire wall. Unbolt the power steering pump from the bracket and position to the side.

9. Raise the vehicle and support safely. Disconnect the vacuum hoses from the source below the carburetor and disconnect the air feeder tubes.

10. Remove the exhaust pipe from the exhaust manifold. Lower the vehicle.

11. Remove the small end bolts from the head first, then remove the remaining head bolts, starting from the outside and working inward.

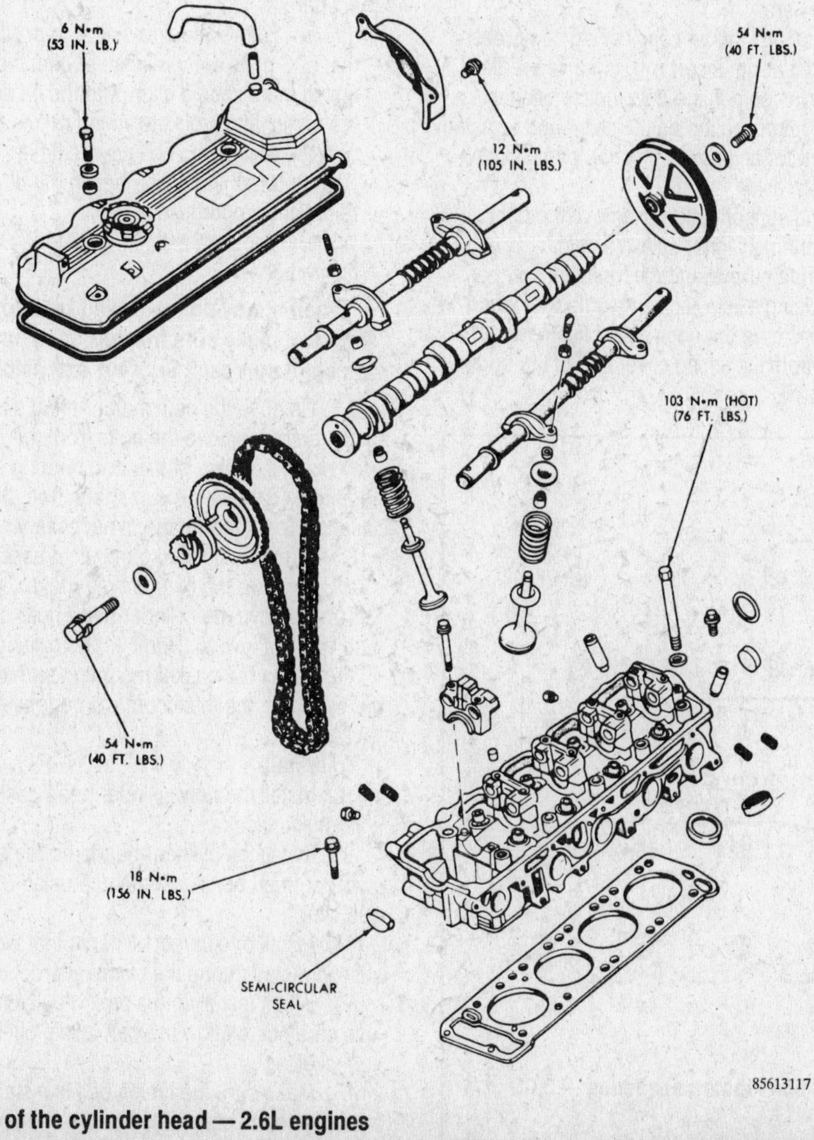

Fig. 118 Exploded view of the cylinder head — 2.6L engines

12. Remove the cylinder head from the engine.
13. Clean the cylinder head gasket mating surfaces.

To install:

14. Install a new head gasket to the block and install all head bolts and washers. Tighten the bolts in sequence to 34 ft. lbs. (40 Nm). Repeat the sequence increasing the tighten to 69 ft. lbs. (94 Nm). Tighten the small end bolts to 13 ft. lbs. (18 Nm).
15. Install the camshaft gear with the timing chain. If the timing will not allow for gear installation, reach into the case with a long, thin tool and push the rubber foot into the oil pump to allow for more chain movement. Install the distributor drive gear, bolt and washer. Tighten the bolt to 40 ft. lbs. (54 Nm). Install the distributor, aligning the matchmarks.
16. Install or connect all items that were removed or disconnected during the removal procedure.
17. Refill the cooling system. Connect the negative battery cable. Start the engine and check for leaks. Adjust the timing as required.

3.0L Engines

See Figures 119, 120 and 121

1. Relieve the fuel pressure. Disconnect the negative battery cable. Drain the cooling system.
2. Remove the drive belt and the air conditioning compressor from its mount and support it aside. Insert a $^1/_2$ in. drive breaker bar into the square hole of the serpentine drive belt tensioner, rotate it counterclockwise (to reduce the belt tension) and remove the belt. Remove the alternator and power steering pump from the brackets and move them aside.
3. Raise the vehicle and support safely. Remove the right front wheel assembly and the right inner splash shield.
4. Remove the crankshaft pulleys and the torsional damper.
5. Lower the vehicle. Using a floor jack and a block of wood positioned under the oil pan, raise the engine slightly. Remove the engine mount bracket from the timing cover end of the engine and the timing belt covers.

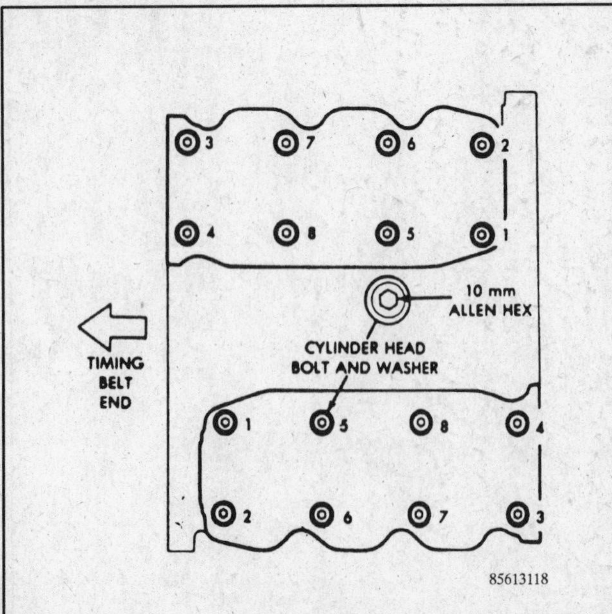

Fig. 119 Cylinder head bolt loosing sequence — 3.0L engines

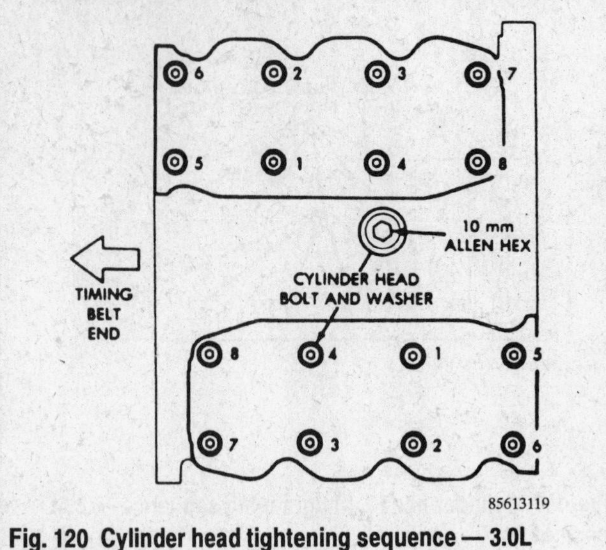

Fig. 120 Cylinder head tightening sequence — 3.0L engines

6. To remove the timing belt, perform the following procedures:
   a. Rotate the crankshaft to position the No. 1 cylinder on the TDC of its compression stroke; the crankshaft sprocket timing mark should align with the oil pan timing indicator and the camshaft sprockets timing marks (triangles) should align with the rear timing belt covers timing marks.
   b. Mark the timing belt in the direction of rotation for reinstallation purposes.
   c. Loosen the timing belt tensioner and remove the timing belt.

When removing the timing belt from the camshaft sprocket, make sure the belt does not slip off of the other camshaft sprocket. Support extension.

7. Remove the camshaft bearing assembly to cylinder head bolts (do not remove the bolts from the assembly). Remove the rocker arms, rocker shafts and bearing caps as an assembly, as required. Remove the camshafts from the cylinder head and inspect them for damage, if necessary.
8. Remove the intake manifold assembly.
9. Remove the exhaust manifold.
10. Remove the cylinder head bolts starting from the outside and working inward. Remove the cylinder head from the engine.
11. Clean the gasket mounting surfaces and check the heads for warpage; the maximum warpage allowed is 0.008 in. (0.20mm).

To install:

12. Install the new cylinder head gaskets over the dowels on the engine block.
13. Install the cylinder heads on the engine and tighten the cylinder head bolts in sequence using 3 even steps, to 70 ft. lbs. (95 Nm).
14. Install or connect all items that were removed or disconnected during the removal procedure.
15. When installing the timing belt over the camshaft sprocket, use care not to allow the belt to slip off the opposite camshaft sprocket.
16. Make sure the timing belt is installed on the camshaft sprocket in the same position as when removed.

17. Refill the cooling system. Connect the negative battery cable.

18. Start the engine and check for leaks. Adjust the timing as required.

3.3L and 3.8L Engines

See Figures 122, 123 and 124

1. Relieve the fuel pressure. Disconnect the negative battery cable. Drain the cooling system.
2. Remove the intake manifold with throttle body.
3. Disconnect the coil wires, sending unit wire, heater hoses and bypass hose.
4. Remove the closed ventilation system, evaporation control system and cylinder head cover.
5. Remove the exhaust manifold.
6. Remove the rocker arm and shaft assemblies. Remove the pushrods and identify them in ensure installation in their original positions.
7. Remove the head bolts and remove the cylinder head from the block.

To install:

8. Clean the gasket mounting surfaces and install a new head gasket to the block.
9. Install the head to the block. Before installing the head bolts, inspect them for stretching. Hold a straight edge up to the threads. If the threads are not all on line, the bolt is stretched and should be replaced.
10. Tighten the bolts in sequence to 45 ft. lbs. (61 Nm). Repeat the sequence and tighten the bolts to 65 ft. lbs. (88 Nm). With the bolts at 65 ft. lbs. (88 Nm), turn each bolt an additional $^1/_4$ turn (90°).
11. Tighten the lone head bolt to 25 ft. lbs. (33 Nm) after the other 8 bolts have been properly tightened.
12. Install the pushrods, rocker arms and shafts and tighten the bolts to 21 ft. lbs. (12 Nm).
13. Place a drop of silicone sealer onto each of the 4 manifold-to-cylinder head gasket corners.

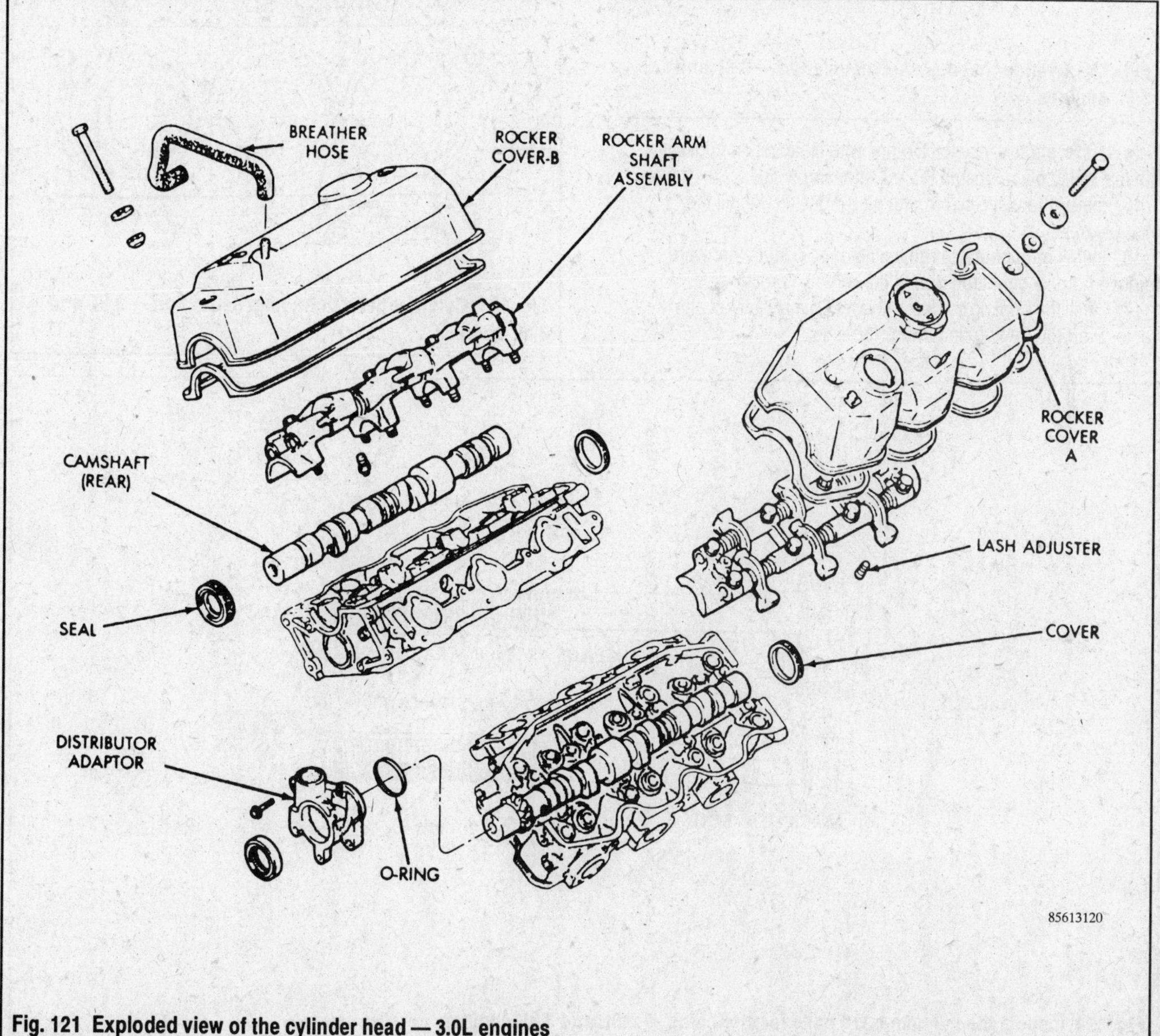

Fig. 121 Exploded view of the cylinder head — 3.0L engines

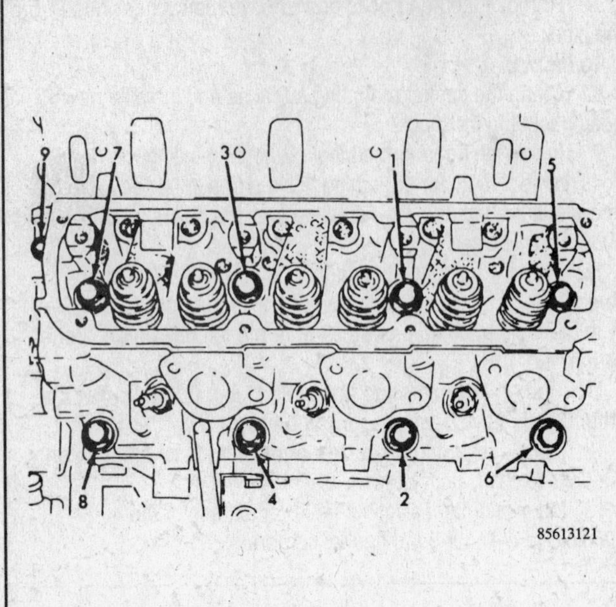

Fig. 122 Cylinder head gasket installation — 3.3L and 3.8L engines

14. Lubricate the injector O-rings with clean oil and position the fuel rail in place. Install the rail retaining bolts.

15. Install the valve cover with a new gasket. Install the exhaust manifold.

16. Install or connect all remaining components that were removed or disconnected during the removal procedures.

17. Refill the cooling system. Connect the negative battery cable. Start the engine and check for leaks.

✽✽CAUTION

The intake manifold gasket is composed of very thin and sharp metal. Handle this gasket with care or damage to the gasket or personal injury could result.

18. Install the intake manifold gasket and tighten the end retainers to 105 inch lbs. (12 Nm).

19. Install the intake manifold and tighten the bolts in sequence to 10 inch lbs. (1 Nm). Repeat the sequence increasing the torque to 17 ft. lbs. (23 Nm) and recheck each bolt for 17 ft. lbs. (23 Nm) of torque. After the bolts are tightened, inspect the seals to ensure that they have not become dislodged.

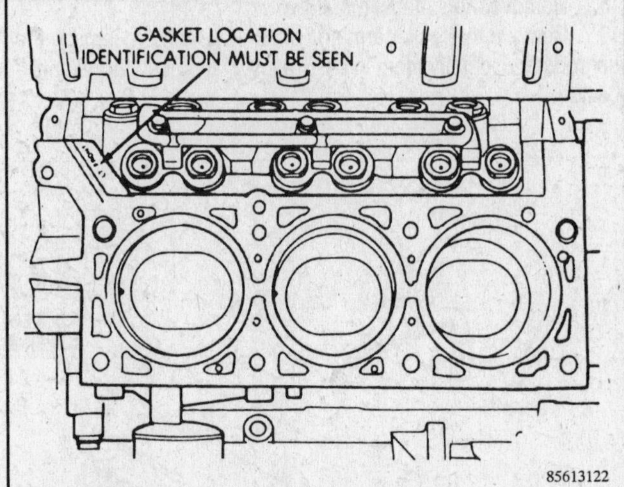

Fig. 123 Cylinder head tightening sequence — 3.3L and 3.8L engines

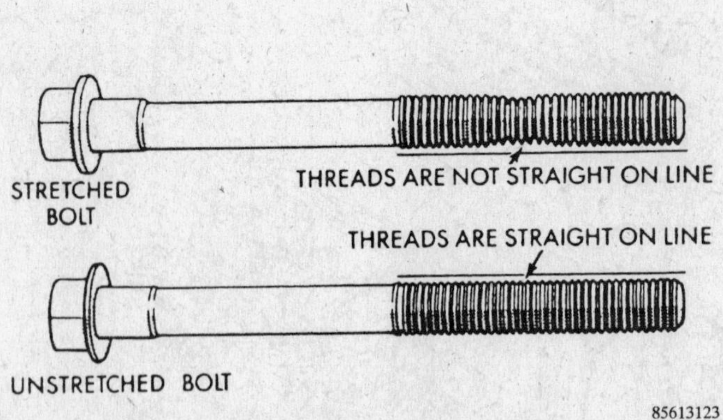

Fig. 124 Inspect the cylinder head bolts for stretching — 3.3L and 3.8L engines

CLEANING & INSPECTION

➧ See Figure 125

1. Turn the cylinder head over so that the mounting surface is facing up and support evenly on wooden blocks.
2. Use a scraper and remove all of the gasket material and carbon stuck to the head mounting surface and engine block. Mount a wire carbon removal brush in an electric drill and clean away the carbon on the valve heads and head combustion chambers.

➥ When scraping or decarbonizing the cylinder head, take care not to damage or nick the gasket mounting surface or combustion chamber.

3. Clean cylinder head oil passages.
4. After cleaning check cylinder head for cracks or damage.
5. Check cylinder head flatness. Flatness must be within 0.004 in. (0.1mm).

RESURFACING

➧ See Figures 126 and 127

If the cylinder head is warped, resurfacing by a automotive machine shop will be required. After cleaning the gasket surface, place a straight-edge across the mounting surface of the head, diagonally from one end to the other. Using a feeler gauge, determine the clearance at the center and along the length between the head and straight-edge.

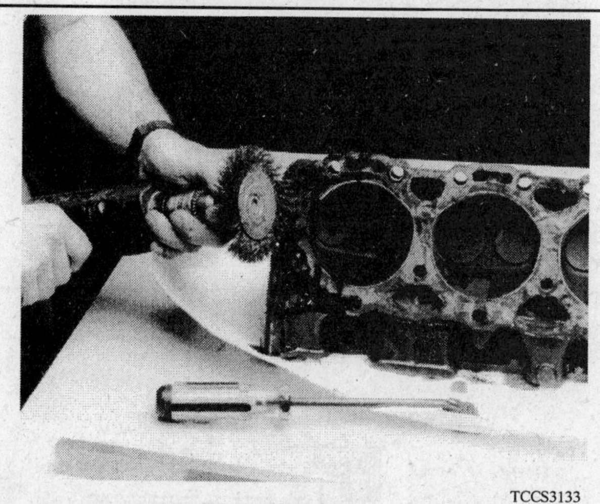

TCCS3133

Fig. 125 An electric drill equipped with a wire wheel will expedite complete gasket material

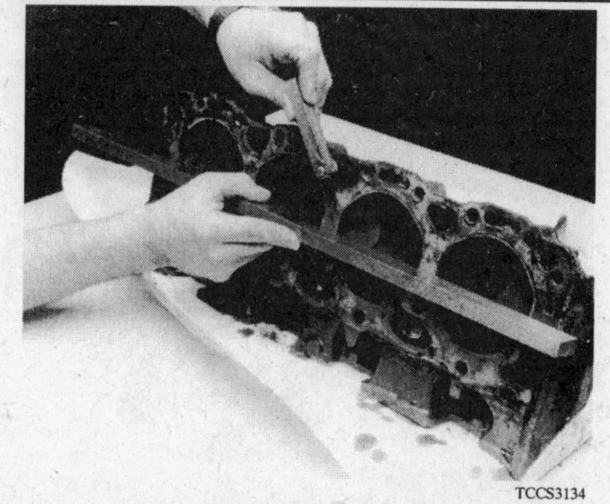

TCCS3134

Fig. 126 Check the cylinder head for warpage along the center using a straightedge and a feeler gauge

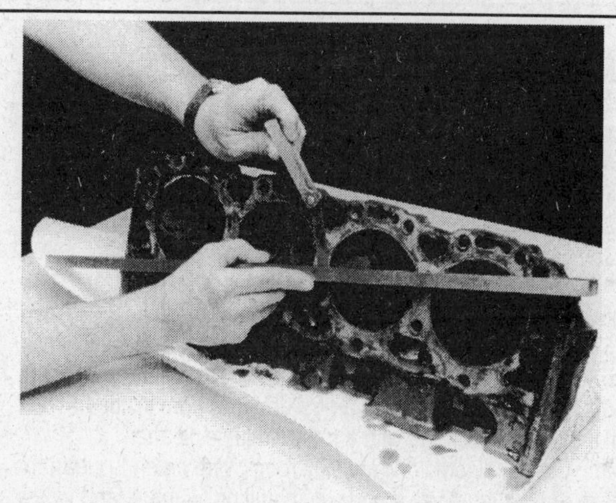

TCCS3135

Fig. 127 Be sure to check for warpage across the cylinder head at both diagonals

Valves

➧ See Figure 128

REMOVAL

➥ The following procedures to be performed with cylinder head removed from engine.

1. Compress the valve springs using Tool C-3422A or equivalent. Do not mix the removed parts. Place the parts from each valve in a separate container, numbered and identified for the valve and cylinder.
2. Remove the valve retaining locks, valve spring retainers, valve stem seal, valve springs and valve spring seats from the valve stem.

➥ Before removing valve assembly remove any burrs from valve stem lock grooves to prevent damage to valve guides.

3. Remove the valve assembly.

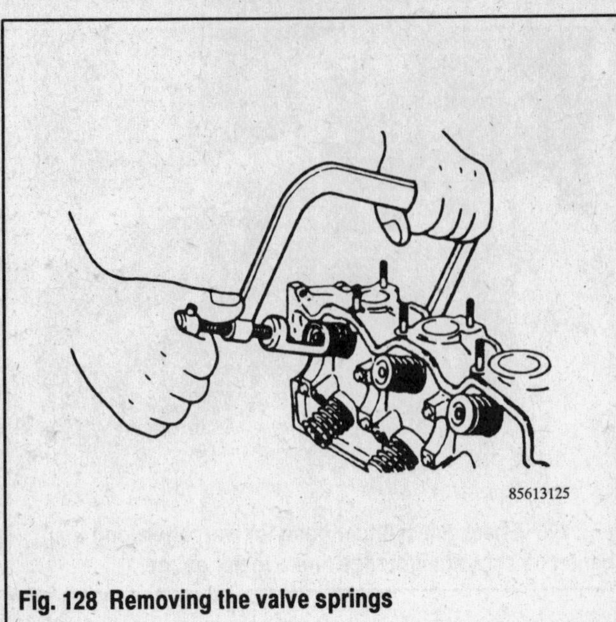

Fig. 128 Removing the valve springs

INSPECTION

➧ See Figure 129

1. Clean valves thoroughly.
2. Check valve stem tip for pitting or depression.
3. Check for ridge wear on valve stem area.
4. Inspect valve (with Prussian blue) for even contact between valve face and cylinder head valve seat.
5. Gently remove valve stem seals with a pliers or screwdriver by prying side-to-side. Do not reused old seals.
6. Remove carbon and varnish deposits from inside of valve guides of cylinder head with a suitable guide cleaner.
7. Use an electric drill and soft rotary wire brush to clean the intake and exhaust valve ports, combustion chamber and valve seats. In some cases, the carbon build-up will have to be chipped away. Use a blunt pointed drift for carbon chipping, be careful around valve seat areas.

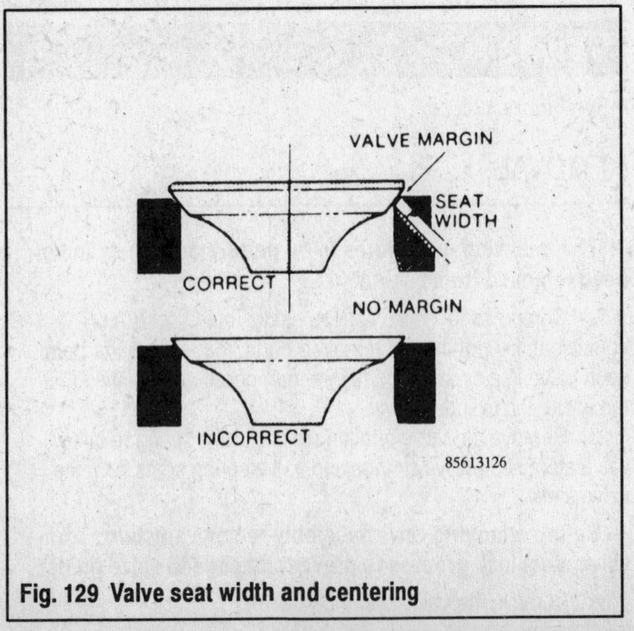

Fig. 129 Valve seat width and centering

➜ When using a wire brush to clean carbon on the valve ports, valves, etc., be sure the deposits are actually removed, rather then burnished.

8. Wash and clean all valve spring, locks, retainers and other related components in safe solvent. Remember to keep parts from each valve separate.

➜ If valve guide replacement is necessary, or valve or seat refacing is necessary, the job must be handled by a qualified machine shop. If a valve seat is damaged, burnt or loose, the seat may be resurfaced or replaced as necessary. The automotive machine shop can handle the job for you.

CHECKING VALVE SPRINGS

➧ See Figures 130, 131 and 132

Place the valve spring on a flat surface next to a carpenters square. Measure the height of the spring, and rotate the spring against the edge of the square to measure distortion. If the spring height varies (by comparison) by more than $^{1}/_{16}$ in. (1.58mm) or if the distortion exceeds $^{1}/_{16}$ in. (1.58mm), replace the spring.

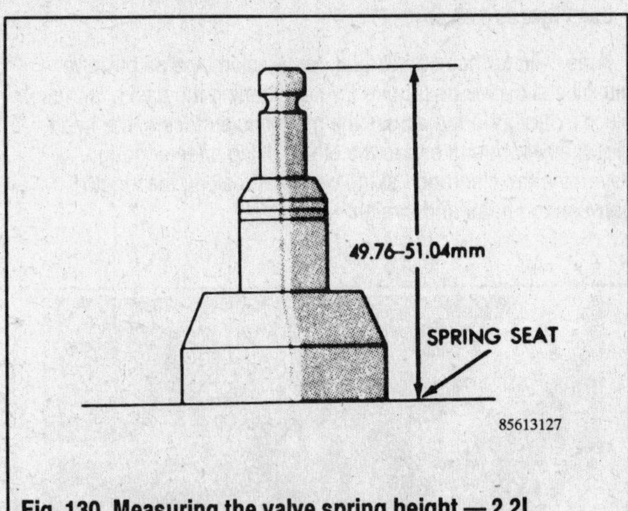

Fig. 130 Measuring the valve spring height — 2.2L engine shown

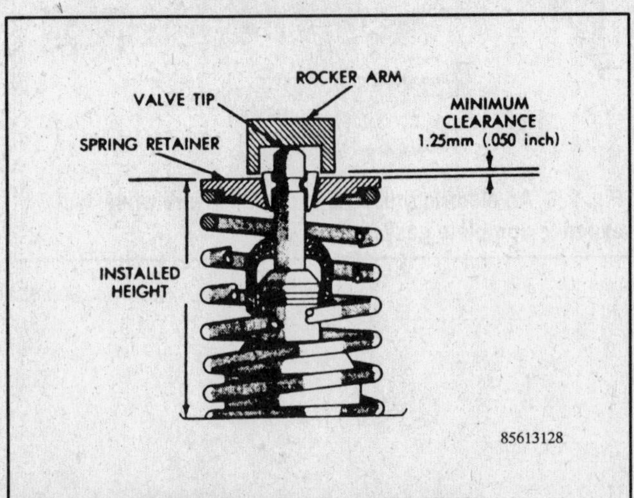

Fig. 131 Checking the valve spring installed height — 2.2L engine

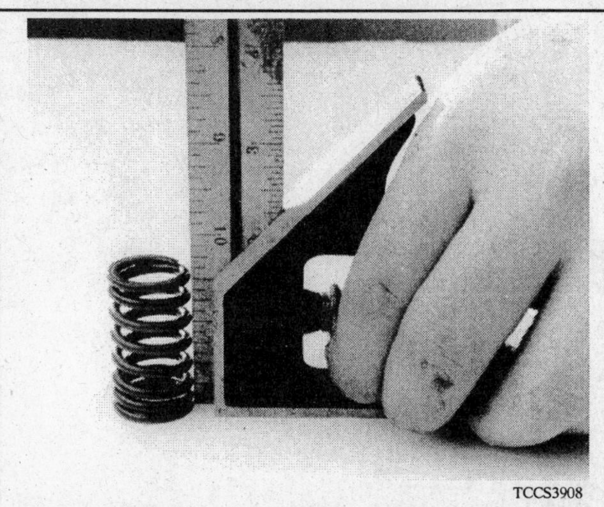
TCCS3908

Fig. 132 Check the valve spring for squareness on a flat surface; a carpenter's square can be used

Have the valve springs tested for spring pressure at the installed and compressed (installed height minus valve lift) height using a valve spring tester. Springs should be within one pound, plus or minus of each other. Replace the springs as necessary.

INSTALLATION

➧ See Figure 133

1. Coat valve stems with lubrication oil and install in cylinder head.
2. Install a new valve stem seal on the valve. The valve stem seal should be install firmly and squarely over the valve guide.' The lower edge of the seal should rest on the valve guide boss.
3. Install the valve spring seat, valve spring, and retainer.
4. Using Tool C-3422A, or equivalent, compress the valve spring only far enough to install the retainer locks. Install the retainer locks and make certain that the locks are in their correct location before removing the valve compressor.
5. Repeat Steps 1-4 on the remaining valves.

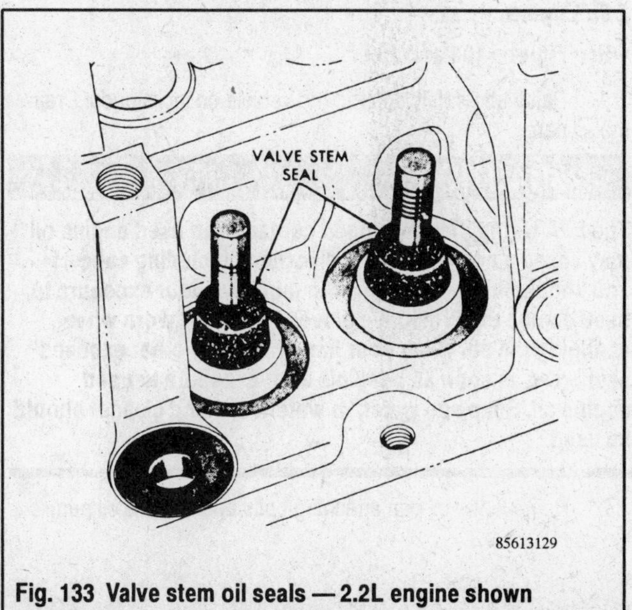

85613129

Fig. 133 Valve stem oil seals — 2.2L engine shown

Oil Pan

REMOVAL & INSTALLATION

2.2L Engines

➧ See Figures 134, 135, 136, 137 and 138

1. Raise and safely support the vehicle on jackstands. Drain the oil pan.

✻✻CAUTION

The EPA warns that prolonged contact with used engine oil may cause a number of skin disorders, including cancer! You should make every effort to minimize your exposure to used engine oil. Protective gloves should be worn when changing the oil. Wash your hands and any other exposed skin areas as soon as possible after exposure to used engine oil. Soap and water, or waterless hand cleaner should be used.

2. Remove the oil pan attaching bolts and remove oil pan.

To install:

3. Clean the oil pan and engine block gasket surfaces thoroughly.
4. Apply RTV sealant to oil pan side rails.
5. Install new oil pan seals and install oil pan. Tighten the pan screws to 15 ft. lbs. (20 Nm).
6. Refill the crankcase, start the engine and check for leaks.

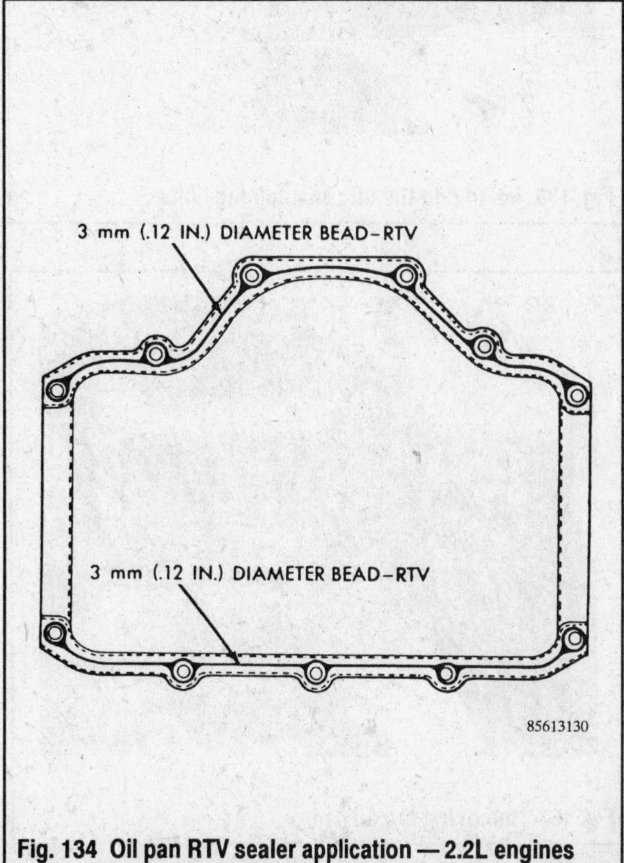

85613130

Fig. 134 Oil pan RTV sealer application — 2.2L engines

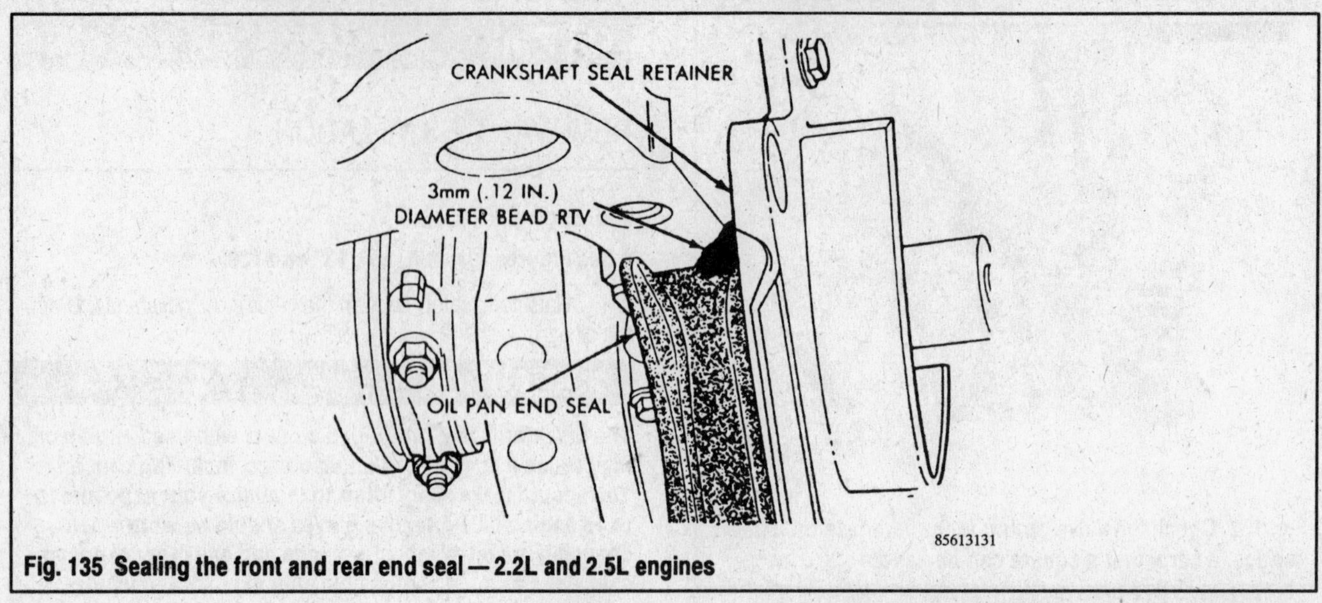

Fig. 135 Sealing the front and rear end seal — 2.2L and 2.5L engines

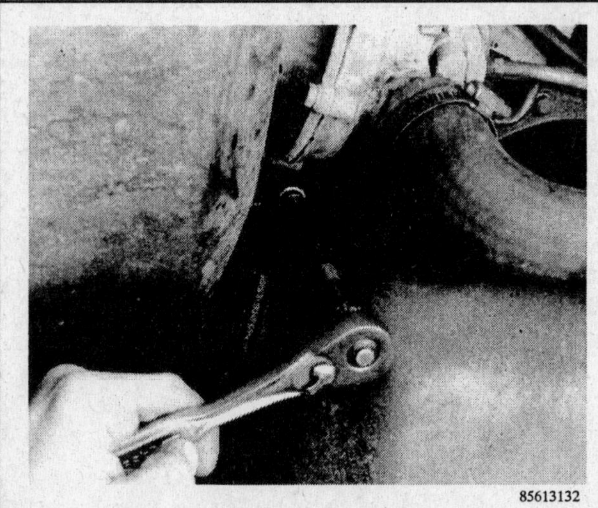

Fig. 136 Removing the oil pan retaining bolts

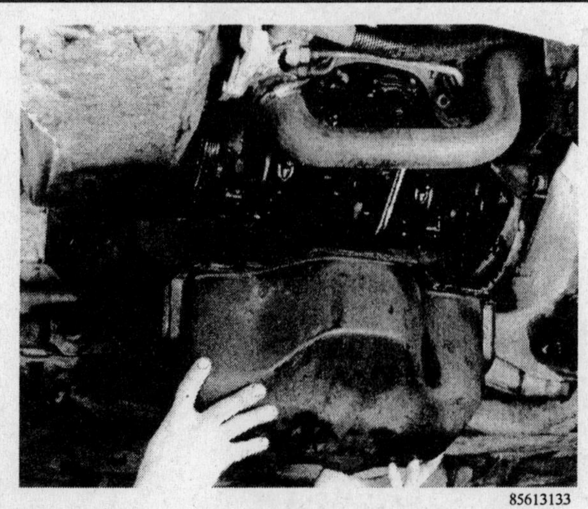

Fig. 137 Removing the oil pan

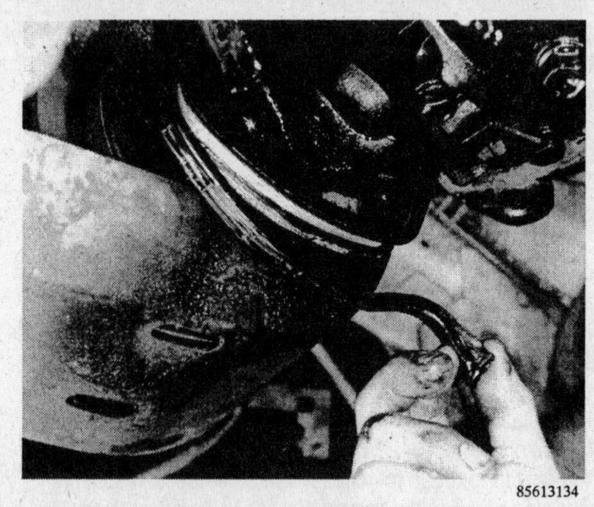

Fig. 138 Removing one of the end seals

2.5L Engines

➧ See Figures 135 and 139

1. Raise and safely support the vehicle on jackstands. Drain the oil pan.

****CAUTION**

The EPA warns that prolonged contact with used engine oil may cause a number of skin disorders, including cancer! You should make every effort to minimize your exposure to used engine oil. Protective gloves should be worn when changing the oil. Wash your hands and any other exposed skin areas as soon as possible after exposure to used engine oil. Soap and water, or waterless hand cleaner should be used.

2. Remove the oil pan attaching bolts and remove oil pan.

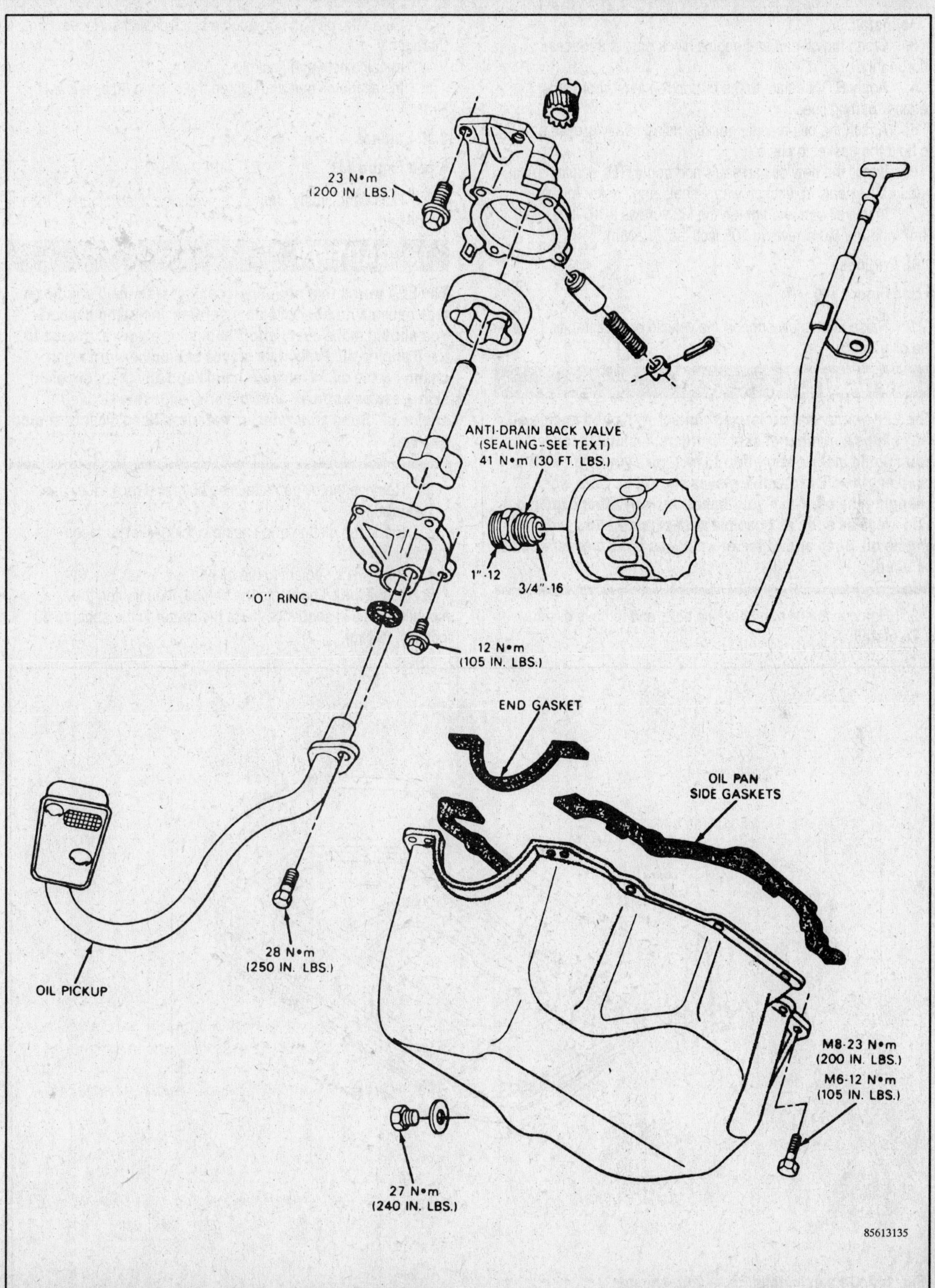

Fig. 139 Engine lubrication components — 2.5L engines

To install:

3. Clean the oil pan and engine block gasket surfaces thoroughly.
4. Apply RTV sealant to the oil pan rail at the front seal retainer parting line.
5. Attach the oil pan side gaskets using heavy grease or RTV to hold the gasket in place.
6. Install the new oil pan seals and apply RTV sealant to the ends of the seals at junction where seals and gasket meets.
7. Install oil pan and tighten the M8 screws to 15 ft. lbs. (20 Nm), and the M6 screws to 105 inch lbs. (12 Nm).

2.6L Engines

See Figure 140

1. Raise and safely support the vehicle on jackstands. Drain the oil pan.

****CAUTION**

The EPA warns that prolonged contact with used engine oil may cause a number of skin disorders, including cancer! You should make every effort to minimize your exposure to used engine oil. Protective gloves should be worn when changing the oil. Wash your hands and any other exposed skin areas as soon as possible after exposure to used engine oil. Soap and water, or waterless hand cleaner should be used.

2. Remove the oil pan attaching bolts and remove oil pan.

To install:

3. Clean the oil pan and engine block gasket surfaces thoroughly.
4. Install a new pan gasket.
5. Install the oil pan and tighten the bolts to 60 inch lbs. (7 Nm).

3.0L Engines

See Figure 141

1. Raise and safely support the vehicle on jackstands. Drain the oil pan.

****CAUTION**

The EPA warns that prolonged contact with used engine oil may cause a number of skin disorders, including cancer! You should make every effort to minimize your exposure to used engine oil. Protective gloves should be worn when changing the oil. Wash your hands and any other exposed skin areas as soon as possible after exposure to used engine oil. Soap and water, or waterless hand cleaner should be used.

2. Remove the oil pan attaching bolts and remove oil pan.

To install:

3. Clean the oil pan and engine block gasket surfaces thoroughly.
4. Apply RTV sealant to the oil pan.
5. Install the oil pan onto the engine, then tighten the mounting bolts in sequence (from the center to the ends) to 50 inch lbs. (6 Nm).

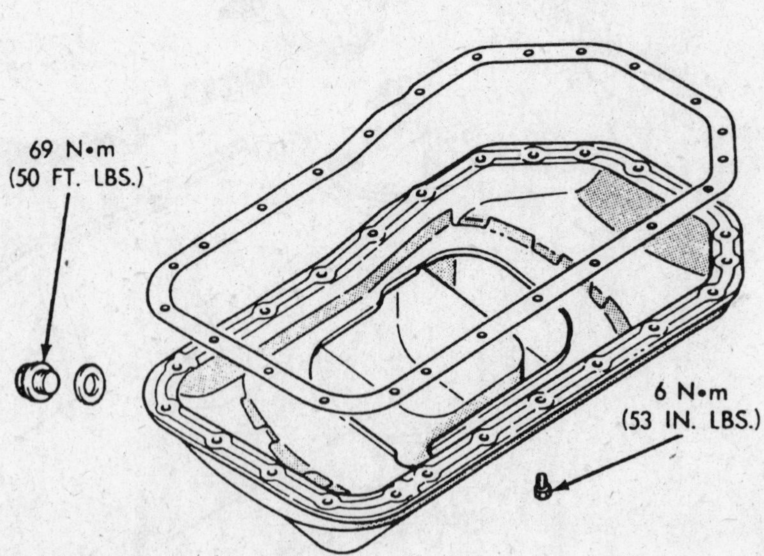

Fig. 140 Oil pan installation — 2.6L engines

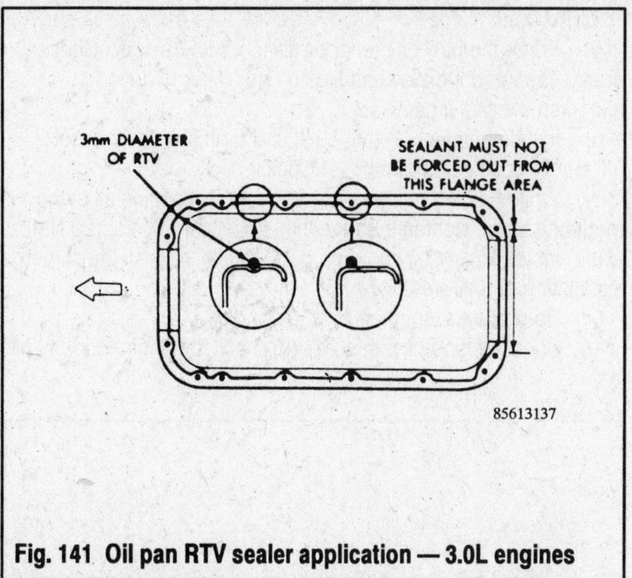

Fig. 141 Oil pan RTV sealer application — 3.0L engines

3.3L and 3.8L Engines

See Figures 142 and 143

1. Disconnect the negative battery cable.
2. Raise the vehicle and support safely.
3. Remove the torque converter bolt access cover, if equipped.
4. Drain the engine oil.
5. Remove the oil pan retaining screws and remove the oil pan and gasket.

To install:

6. Thoroughly clean and dry all sealing surfaces, bolts and bolt holes.
7. Apply silicone sealer to the chain cover to block mating seam and the rear main seal retainer to block seam, if equipped.
8. Install a new pan gasket or apply silicone sealer to the sealing surface of the pan and install to the engine.
9. Install the retaining screws and tighten to 17 ft. lbs. (23 Nm).
10. Install the torque converter bolt access cover, if equipped.
11. Lower the vehicle.
12. Install the dipstick. Fill the engine with the proper amount of oil.
13. Connect the negative battery cable and check for leaks.

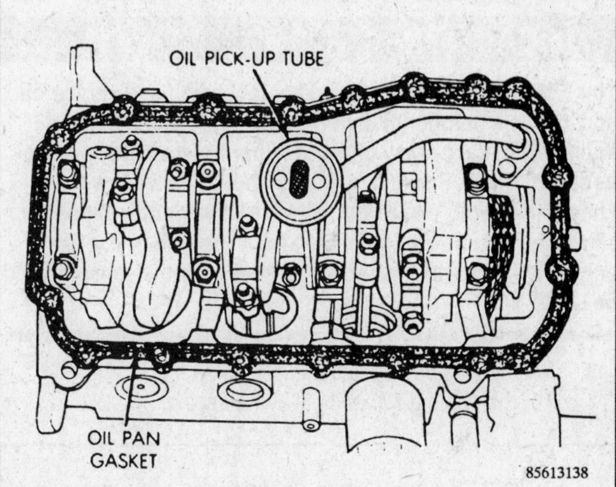

Fig. 142 Oil pan gasket installation — 3.3L and 3.8L engines

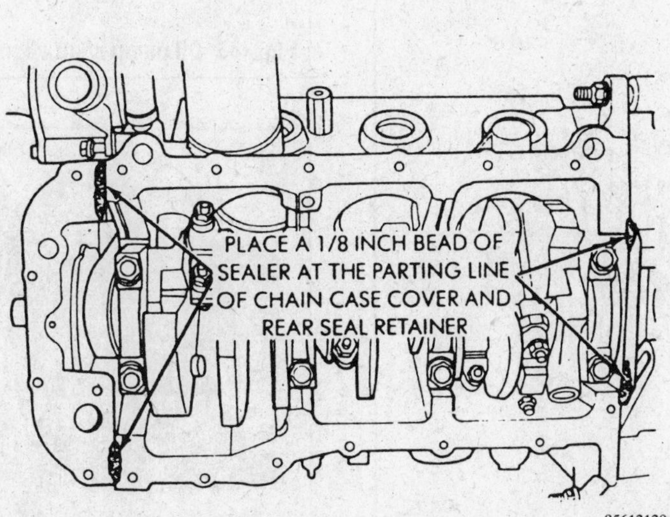

Fig. 143 Oil pan sealing — 3.3L and 3.8L engines

Oil Pump

REMOVAL & INSTALLATION

2.2L and 2.5L Engines

See Figures 144, 145, 146 and 147

1. Raise and safely support the vehicle.
2. Drain the oil and remove engine oil pan. For more details, refer to the oil pan removal procedure earlier in this section.

****CAUTION**

The EPA warns that prolonged contact with used engine oil may cause a number of skin disorders, including cancer! You should make every effort to minimize your exposure to used engine oil. Protective gloves should be worn when changing the oil. Wash your hands and any other exposed skin areas as soon as possible after exposure to used engine oil. Soap and water, or waterless hand cleaner should be used.

3. Remove the pump mounting bolts.
4. Pull the pump down and out of the engine.

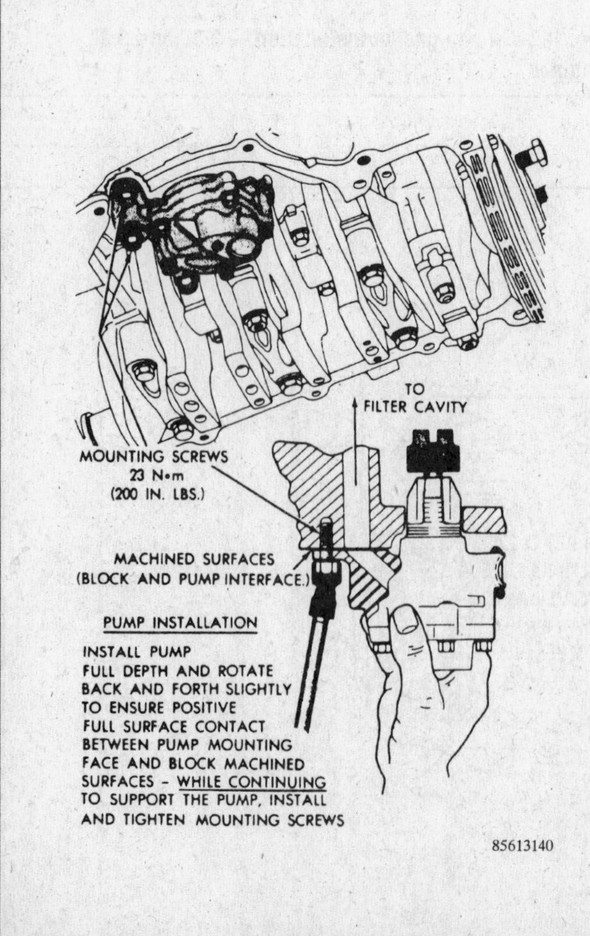

Fig. 144 Oil pump application — 2.2L and 2.5L engines

To install:

5. Prime the new oil pump, by filling it with fresh oil. Check crankshaft/intermediate shaft timing and oil pump drive alignment. Adjust if necessary.
6. Install pump and rotate back and forth slightly to ensure full surface contact of pump and block.
7. While holding pump in fully seated position, install pump mounting bolts. Tighten the mounting bolts to 15 ft. lbs. (20 Nm).
8. Install engine oil pan. For more details, refer to the oil pan installation procedures.
9. Refill crankcase, then start the engine.
10. Check engine oil pressure and check the engine for any oil leaks.

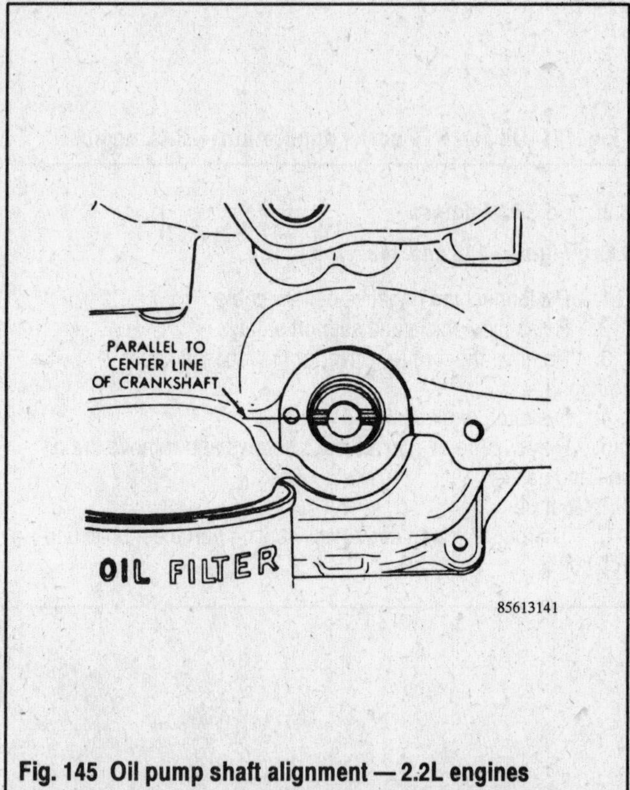

Fig. 145 Oil pump shaft alignment — 2.2L engines

Fig. 146 Oil pump pick-up tube and screen

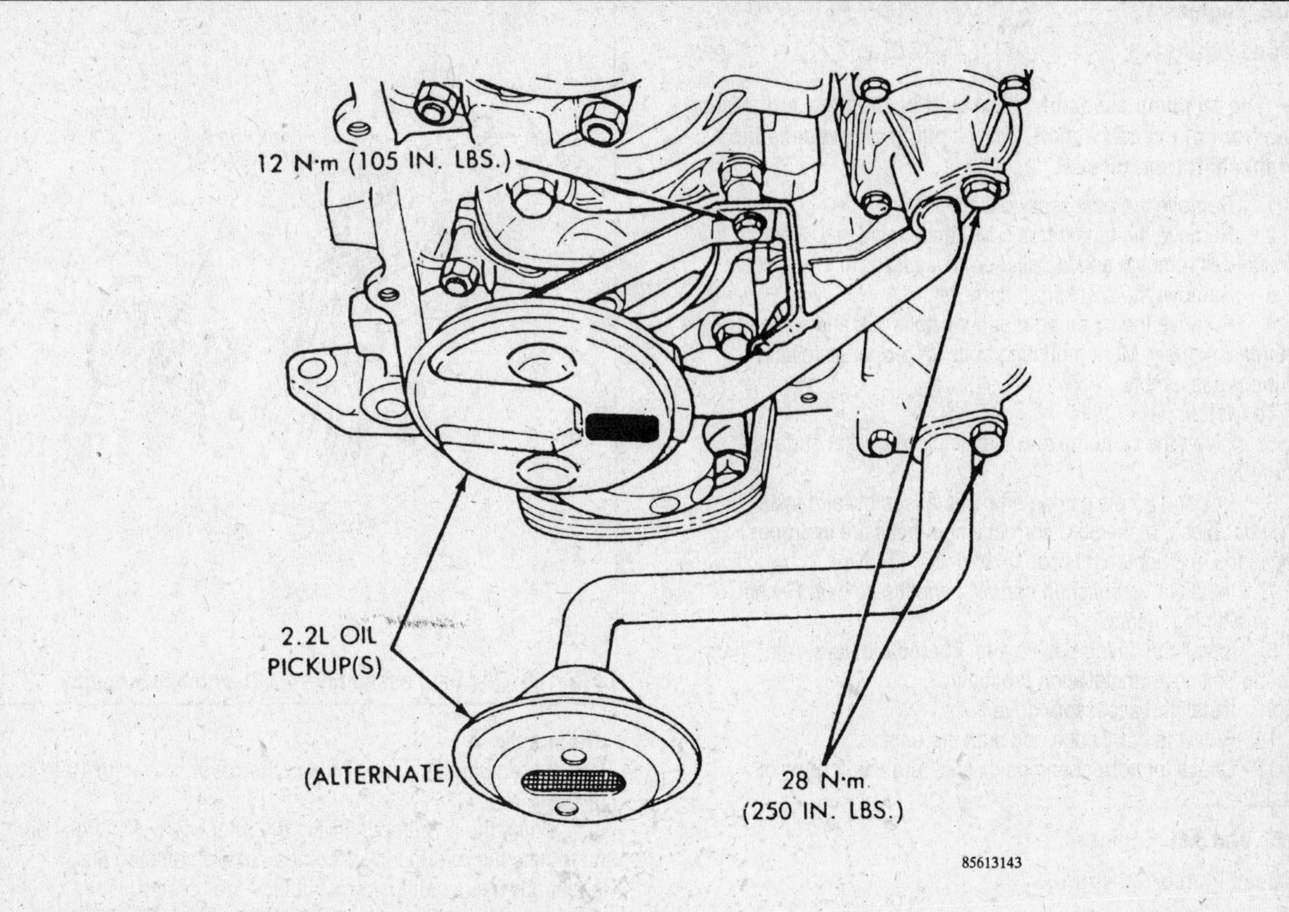

12 N·m (105 IN. LBS.)
2.2L OIL PICKUP(S)
(ALTERNATE)
28 N·m (250 IN. LBS.)
85613143

Fig. 147 Oil pump pick-up tube and screen — 2.2L engines

2.6L Engines

➧ **See Figure 148**

1. Remove the accessory drive belts.
2. Remove the timing chain case cover. Refer to the Front Timing Cover and Seal procedure later in this section.
3. Remove the silent shaft chain assembly and timing chain assembly. For more details, refer to the timing chain removal procedures.
4. Remove the silent shaft bolt (it's the bolt directly above the silent chain sprocket).
5. Remove the oil pump bolts and pull the pump housing straight forward. Remove the gaskets and the oil pump backing plate.

To install:

6. Clean gasket from mounting surfaces.
7. Install new gaskets/seals, align mating marks of the oil pump gears, refill the pump with oil, and install the pump assembly.
8. Install oil pump silent shaft sprocket and sprocket bolt. Tighten sprocket bolt to 25 ft. lbs. (34 Nm).
9. Install timing chain and silent shaft chain assembly. Refer to the timing chain installation procedure earlier in this section.
10. Install the timing chain case cover. Refer to the Front Timing Cover and Seal procedure later in this section.
11. Install the accessory drive belts.
12. Reconnect the battery negative cable.
13. Start the engine, then check for correct engine oil pressure and for any oil leakage.

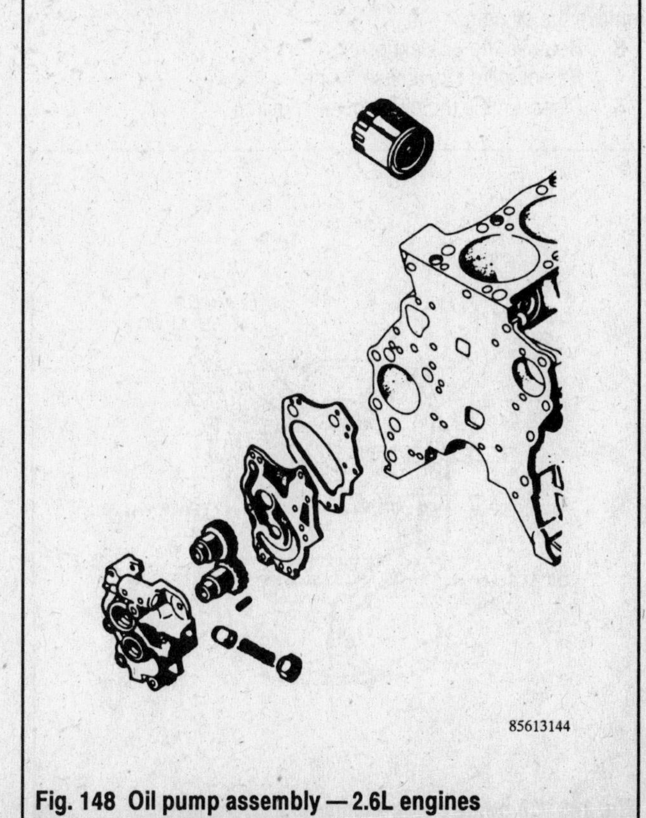

Fig. 148 Oil pump assembly — 2.6L engines

3.0L Engines

See Figure 149

The oil pump assembly used on this engine is mounted at the front of the crankshaft. The oil pump also retains the crankshaft front oil seal.

1. Remove the accessory drive belts.
2. Remove the timing belt cover and timing belt. Refer to the timing belt removal and installation procedures in this section.
3. Remove the crankshaft sprocket.
4. Remove the oil pump mounting bolts (5), and remove oil pump assembly. Mark mounting bolts for proper installation during reassembly.

To install:

5. Clean the oil pump and engine block gasket surfaces thoroughly.
6. Position a new gasket on pump assembly and install on cylinder block. Make sure correct length bolts are in proper locations and tighten all bolts to 10 ft. lbs. (14 Nm).
7. Install the crankshaft sprocket and timing belt. Recheck engine timing marks.
8. Install the timing belt covers. For more details, refer to the timing belt cover installation procedures.
9. Install the accessory drive belts.
10. Refill the crankcase and start the engine.
11. Check for correct engine oil pressure and for any oil leakage.

3.3L and 3.8L Engines

See Figures 150 and 151

1. Disconnect the negative battery cable. Remove the dipstick.
2. Raise the vehicle and support safely. Drain the oil and remove the oil pan.
3. Remove the oil pickup.
4. Remove the chain case cover.
5. Disassemble the oil pump as required.

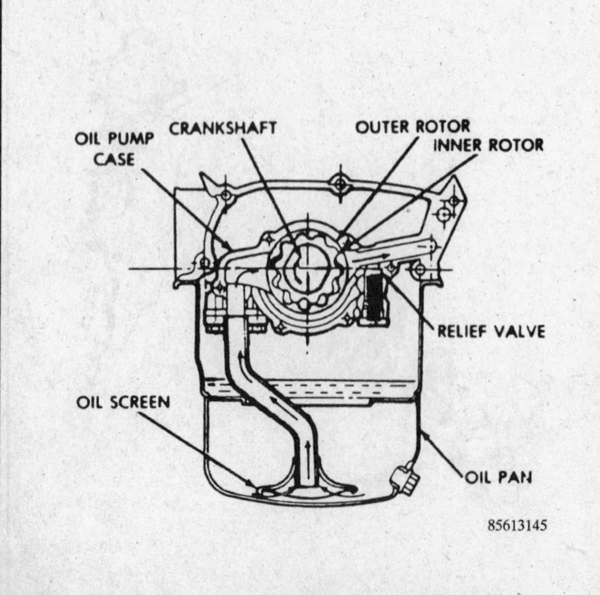

Fig. 149 Oil pump components — 3.0L engines

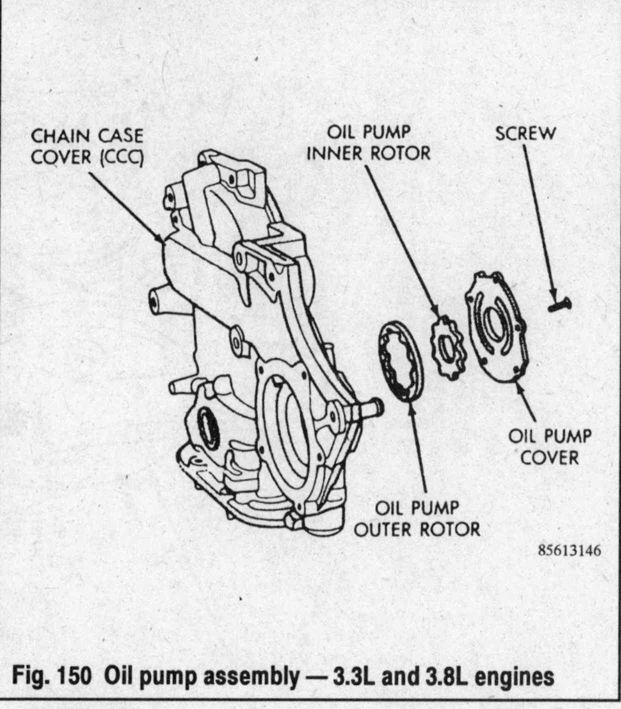

Fig. 150 Oil pump assembly — 3.3L and 3.8L engines

To install:

6. Assemble the pump. Tighten the cover screws to 10 ft. lbs. (14 Nm).
7. Prime the oil pump by filling the rotor cavity with fresh oil and turning the rotors until oil comes out the pressure port. Repeat a few times until no air bubbles are present.
8. Install the chain case cover.
9. Clean out the oil pickup or replace as required. Replace the oil pickup O-ring and install the pickup to the pump.
10. Install the oil pan.
11. Install the dipstick. Fill the engine with the proper amount of oil.
12. Connect the negative battery cable and check the oil pressure. Check for any oil leaks.

INSPECTION

2.2L and 2.5L Engines

1. Remove the cover from the oil pump.
2. Check end-play of the inner rotor using a feeler gauge and a straight edge placed across the pump body. The specification is 0.001–0.004 in. (0.03–0.09mm).
3. Measure the clearance between the inner and outer rotors. The maximum clearance is 0.008 in. (0.20mm).
4. Measure the clearance between the outer rotor and the pump body. The maximum clearance is 0.014 in. (0.35mm).
5. The minimum thickness of the outer rotor is 0.944 in. (23.96mm). The minimum diameter of the outer rotor is 2.77 in. (62.70mm). The minimum thickness of the inner rotor is 0.943 in. (23.95mm).
6. Check the cover for warpage. The maximum allowable is 0.003 in. (0.076mm).
7. Check the pressure relief valve for damage. The spring's free length specification is 1.95 in. (49.50mm).
8. Assemble the outer rotor with the larger chamfered edge in the pump body. Tighten the cover screws to 10 ft. lbs. (14 Nm).

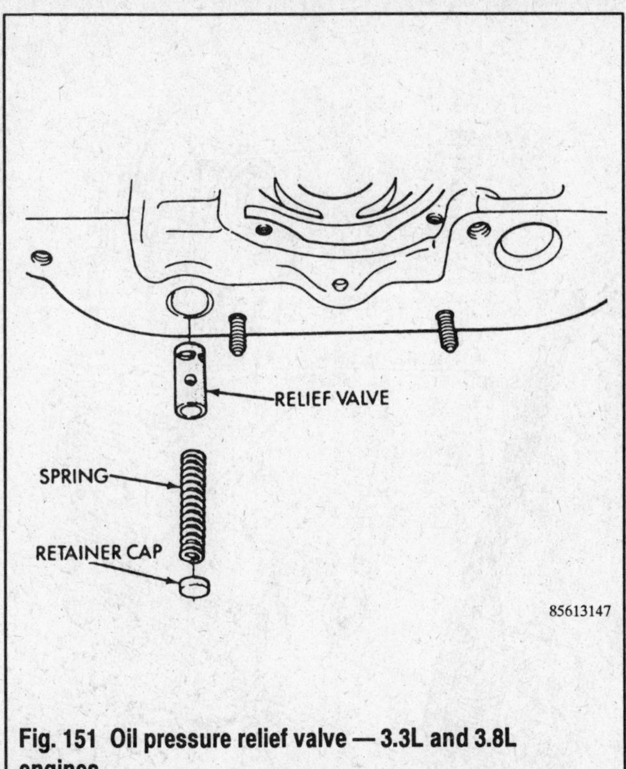

Fig. 151 Oil pressure relief valve — 3.3L and 3.8L engines

2.6L Engines

1. Remove the cover from the oil pump.
2. Measure the clearance between the gears and their bearings. The specification for both is 0.0008–0.0020 in. (0.02–0.05mm).
3. Check the clearance between the gears and the housing. The specification for both gears is 0.004–0.006 in. (0.11–0.15mm).
4. Check end-play of the gears using a feeler gauge and a straight edge placed across the pump body. The specification for both is 0.002–0.004 in. (0.04–0.11mm).
5. Check the pressure relief valve for damage. The spring's free length specification is 1.85 in. (47.00mm).
6. If the gears were removed from the body, install them with the mating aligned. If they are not aligned properly, the silent shaft will be out of time.
7. Tighten the cover screws to 13 ft. lbs. (18 Nm).

3.0L Engines

1. Remove the rear cover.
2. Remove the pump rotors and inspect the case for excessive wear.
3. Measure the diameter of the inner rotor hub that sits in the case. Measure the inside diameter of the inner rotor hub bore. Subtract the first measurement from the second; if the result is over 0.006 in. (0.15mm), replace the oil pump assembly.
4. Measure the clearance between the outer rotor and the case. The specification is 0.004–0.007 in. (0.10–0.18mm).
5. Check the side clearance of the rotors using a feeler gauge and a straight edge placed across the case. The specification is 0.0015–0.0035 in. (0.04–0.09mm).
6. Check the relief plunger and spring for damage and breakage.
7. Install the rear cover to the case.

3.3L and 3.8L Engines

1. Thoroughly clean and dry all parts. The mating surface of the chain case cover should be smooth. Replace the pump cover if it is scratched or grooved.
2. Lay a straight edge across the pump cover surface. If a 0.076mm feeler gauge can be inserted between the cover and the straight edge, the cover should be replaced.
3. The maximum thickness of the outer rotor is 0.301 in. (7.63mm). The minimum diameter of the outer rotor is 3.14 in. (79.78mm). The minimum thickness of the inner rotor is 0.301 in. (7.64m).
4. Install the outer rotor onto the chain case cover, press to one side and measure the clearance between the rotor and case. If the measurement exceeds 0.022 in. (56mm) and the rotor is good, replace the chain case cover.
5. Install the inner rotor to the chain case cover and measure the clearance between the rotors. If the clearance exceeds 0.008 in. (0.203mm), replace both rotors.
6. Place a straight edge over the chain case cover between bolt holes. If a 0.004 in. (0.102mm) thick feeler gauge can be inserted under the straight edge, replace the pump assembly.
7. Inspect the relief valve plunger for scoring and freedom of movement. Small marks may be removed with 400-grit wet or dry sandpaper.
8. The relief valve spring should have a free length of 1.95 in. (49.5mm).
9. Assemble the pump using new parts where necessary.

Front Timing Cover and Seal

REMOVAL & INSTALLATION

2.2L and 2.5L Engines

➧ See Figures 152, 153, 154, 155, 156, 157, 158 and 159

1. Remove the accessory drive belts.
2. Support the vehicle on jackstands and remove the right inner splash shield.
3. Loosen and remove the 3 water pump pulley mounting screws and remove the pulley.
4. Remove the 4 crankshaft pulley retaining screws.
5. Remove the nuts at upper portion of timing cover and screws from lower portion and remove both halves of cover.

To install:

6. Install the cover. Secure the upper section to cylinder head with nuts and lower section to cylinder block with screws.
7. Install the crankshaft pulley and tighten the bolt to 20 ft. lbs. (27 Nm).
8. Lower the vehicle.
9. Install the water pump pulley, then tighten the mounting bolts to 105 inch lbs. (12 Nm).
10. Install the accessory drive belts.

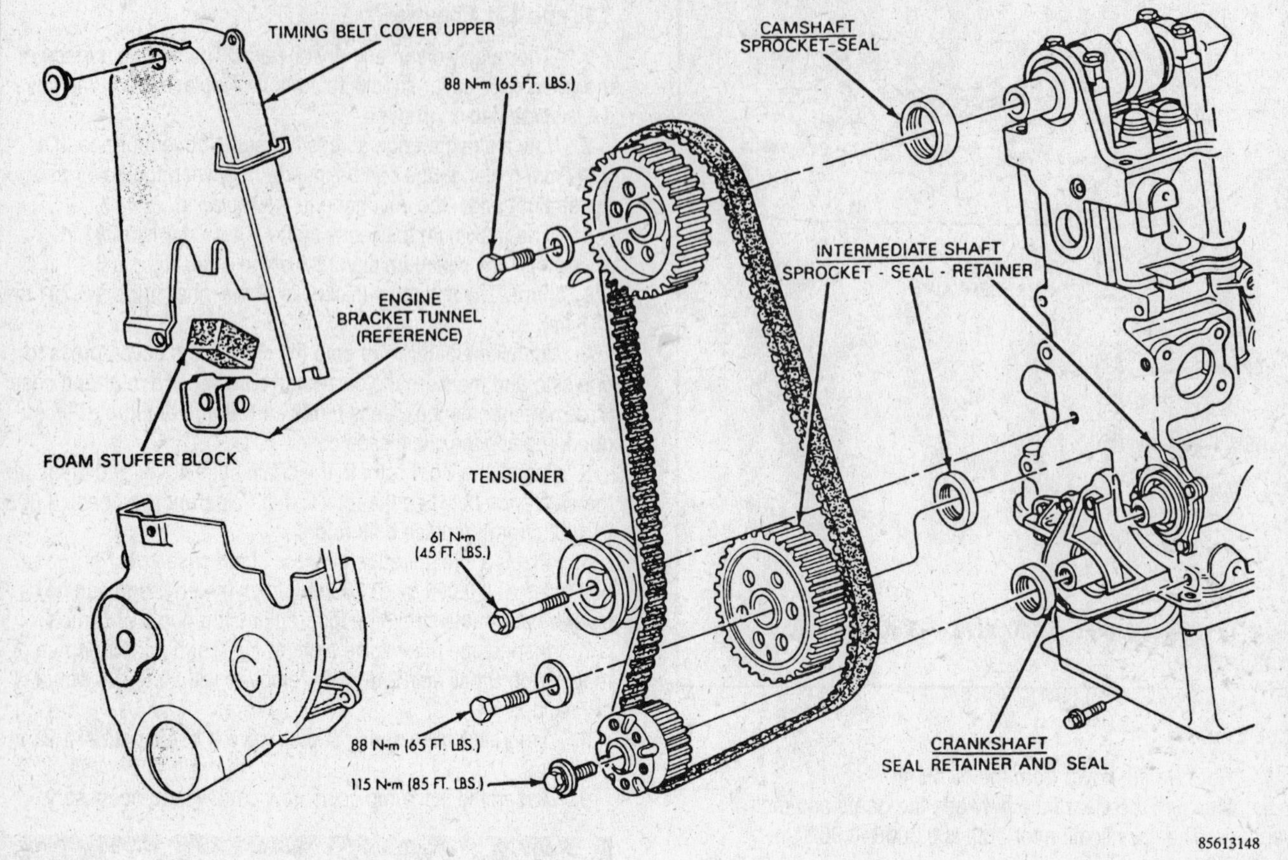

Fig. 152 Timing system and seals — 2.2L and 2.5L engines

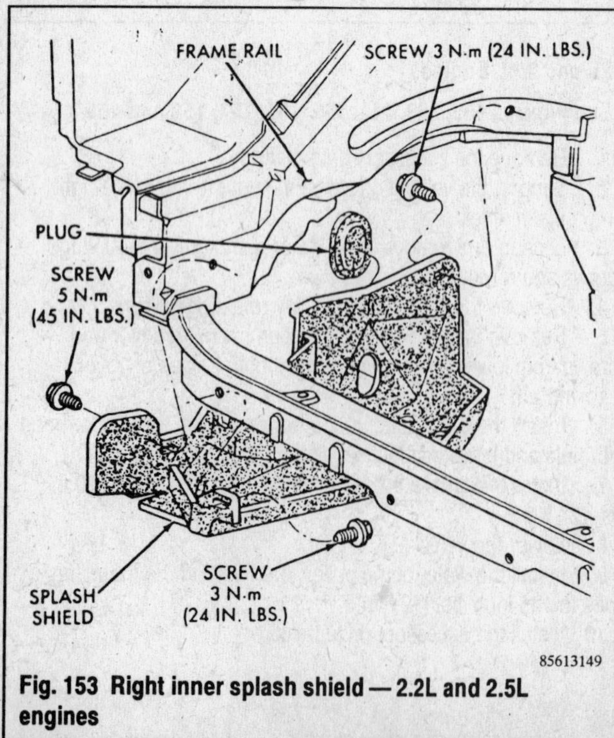

Fig. 153 Right inner splash shield — 2.2L and 2.5L engines

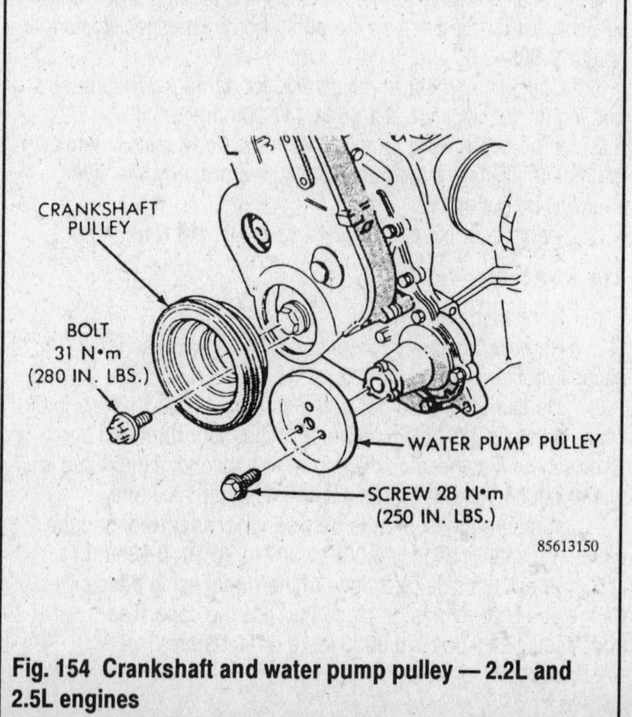

Fig. 154 Crankshaft and water pump pulley — 2.2L and 2.5L engines

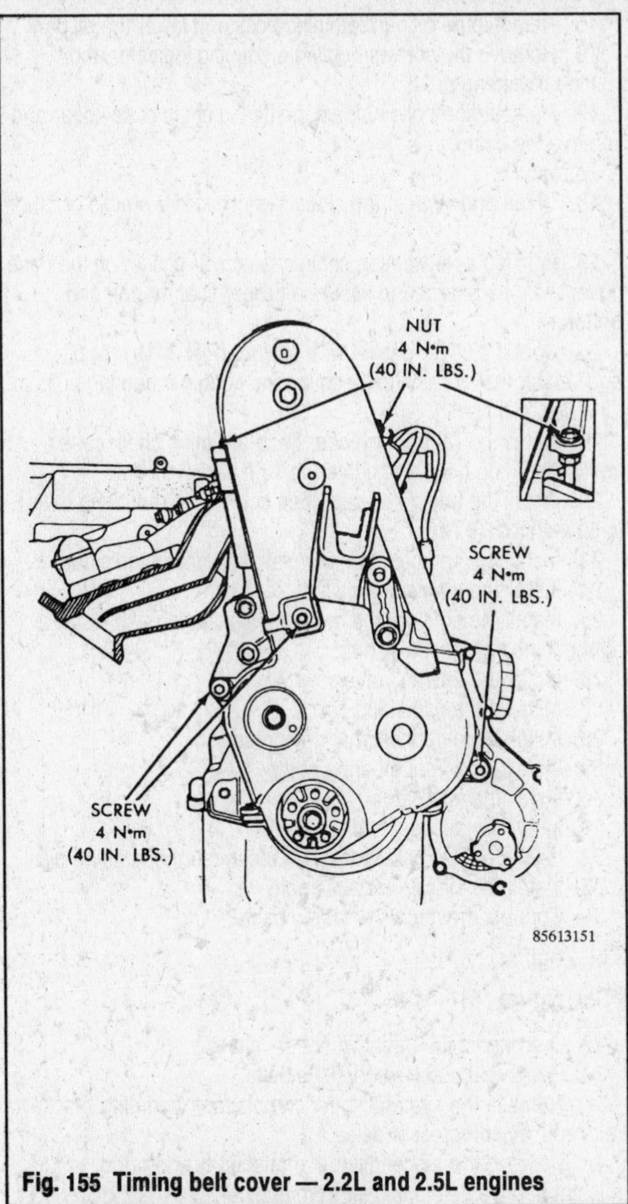

Fig. 155 Timing belt cover — 2.2L and 2.5L engines

Fig. 157 Remove the 4 crankshaft pulley retaining screws and remove the pulley

Fig. 158 After removing the upper cover remove the lower cover retaining screws

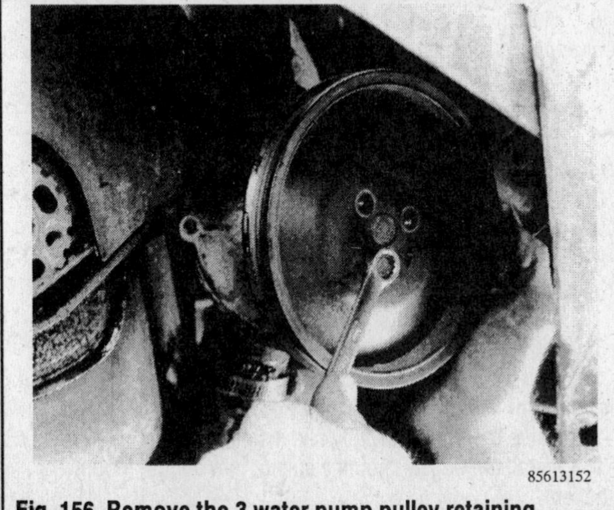

Fig. 156 Remove the 3 water pump pulley retaining screws and remove the pulley

Fig. 159 Removing the lower cover

2.6L Engines

➧ See Figure 160

1. Disconnect the negative battery cable.
2. Remove the air cleaner assembly.
3. Remove the accessory drive belts.
4. Remove the alternator mounting bolts and remove alternator.
5. Remove the power steering mounting bolts and set power steering pump aside.
6. Remove the air conditioner compressor mounting bolts and set compressor aside.
7. Support the vehicle on jackstands and remove right inner splash shield.
8. Drain the engine oil.

****CAUTION**

The EPA warns that prolonged contact with used engine oil may cause a number of skin disorders, including cancer! You should make every effort to minimize your exposure to used engine oil. Protective gloves should be worn when changing the oil. Wash your hands and any other exposed skin areas as soon as possible after exposure to used engine oil. Soap and water, or waterless hand cleaner should be used.

9. Remove the crankshaft pulley.
10. Lower the vehicle and place a jack under the engine with a piece of wood between jack and lifting point.
11. Raise the jack until contact is made with the engine. Relieve pressure by jacking slightly and remove the center bolt from the right engine mount. Remove right engine mount.
12. Remove the engine oil dipstick.
13. Remove the engine valve cover. Refer to Rocker Cover removal procedures earlier in this section.
14. Remove the front (2) cylinder head to timing chain cover bolts.

➥ **Do not loosen any other cylinder head bolts.**

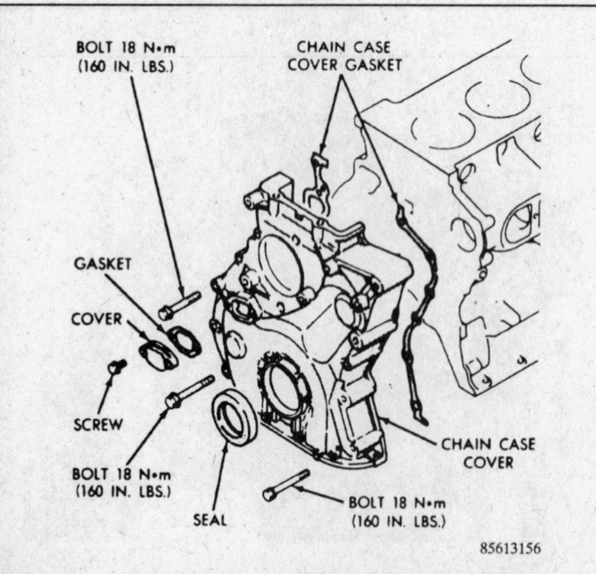

Fig. 160 Timing case cover assembly — 2.6L engines

15. Remove the oil pan retaining bolts and lower the oil pan.
16. Remove the screws holding the timing indicator and engine mounting plate.
17. Remove the bolts holding the timing chain case cover and remove the cover.

To install:

18. Clean and inspect the chain case cover for cracks or other damage.
19. Position a new timing chain case cover gasket on the case cover. Trim as required to assure a proper fit at the top and bottom.
20. Coat the cover gasket with sealant (P/N 3419115) or equivalent. Install chain case cover and tighten mounting bolts to 13 ft. lbs. (18 Nm).
21. Install the (2) front cylinder head-to-timing chain case cover mounting bolts and tighten to 13 ft. lbs. (18 Nm).
22. Install the engine oil pan, then tighten the mounting bolts to 53 inch lbs. (6 Nm).
23. Install the engine mounting plate and timing indicator.
24. Install the crankshaft pulley.
25. Install the right engine mount, lower engine and install right engine mount center bolt.
26. Install the engine valve cover.
27. Install the engine oil dipstick.
28. Install the air conditioner compressor.
29. Install the power steering pump.
30. Install the alternator.
31. Install the accessory drive belts.
32. Fill the engine crankcase with recommended engine oil.
33. Install the air cleaner assembly.
34. Connect the negative battery cable.

3.0L Engines

➧ See Figure 161

1. Disconnect the negative battery cable.
2. Remove the accessory drive belts.
3. Remove the air conditioner compressor mounting bracket bolts and lay compressor aside.
4. Remove the air conditioner mounting bracket and adjustable drive belt tensioner from engine.
5. Remove the steering pump/alternator belt tensioner mounting bolt and remove belt tensioner.
6. Remove the power steering pump mounting bracket bolts, rear support locknut and set power steering pump aside.
7. Raise the vehicle and support on jackstands.
8. Remove the right inner splash shield.
9. Remove the crankshaft drive pulley bolt, drive pulley and torsional damper.
10. Lower the vehicle and place a floor jack under the engine. Separate engine mount insulator from engine mount bracket.
11. Raise the engine slightly and remove engine mount bracket.
12. Remove the timing belt covers.

To install:

13. Install the timing belt covers and tighten all screws to 10 ft. lbs. (14 Nm).
14. Raise the engine slightly and install engine mount bracket.
15. Install the engine mount insulator into engine mount bracket.

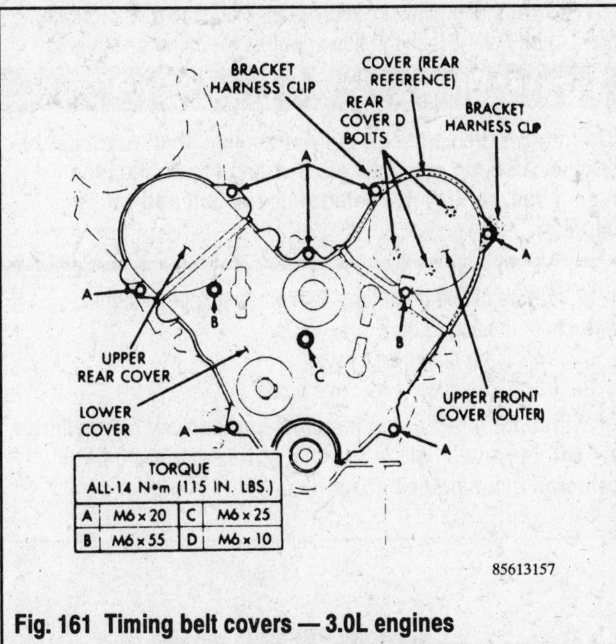

Fig. 161 Timing belt covers — 3.0L engines

16. Install the torsional damper, drive pulley and drive pulley bolt. Tighten bolt to 150 ft. lbs. (205 Nm). Install the right inner splash shield.
17. Install the power steering mounting bracket and install the power steering pump.
18. Install the steering pump/alternator belt tensioner.
19. Install the air conditioner adjustable drive belt tensioner and mounting bracket.
20. Install the air conditioner compressor.
21. Install the accessory drive belts.
22. Connect the negative battery cable.

3.3L and 3.8L Engines

See Figures 162 and 163

1. Disconnect the negative battery cable. Drain the cooling system.
2. Support the engine with a suitable engine support device and remove the right side motor mount.
3. Raise the vehicle and support safely. Drain the engine oil and remove the oil pan.
4. Remove the right wheel and tire assembly, then remove the splash shield.
5. Remove the drive belt.
6. Unbolt the air conditioning compressor and position it to the side. Remove the compressor mounting bracket.
7. Remove the crankshaft pulley bolt and remove the pulley using a suitable puller.
8. Remove the idler pulley from the engine bracket and remove the bracket.
9. Remove the cam sensor from the timing chain cover.
10. Unbolt and remove the cover from the engine. Make sure the oil pump inner rotor does not fall out. Remove the 3 O-rings from the coolant passages and the oil pump outlet.

To install:

11. Thoroughly clean and dry the gasket mating surfaces. Install new O-rings to the block.
12. Remove the crankshaft oil seal from the cover. The seal must be removed from the cover when installing to ensure proper oil pump engagement.
13. Using a new gasket, install the chain case cover to the engine.
14. Make certain that the oil pump is engaged onto the crankshaft before proceeding, or severe engine damage will result. Install the attaching bolts and tighten to 20 ft. lbs. (27 Nm).
15. Use tool C-4992 (or equivalent) to install the crankshaft oil seal. Install the crankshaft pulley using a 5.9 in. suitable bolt and thrust bearing and washer plate L-4524 (or equivalent). Make sure the pulley bottoms out on the crankshaft seal diameter. Install the bolt and tighten to 40 ft. lbs. (54 Nm).
16. Install the engine bracket and tighten the bolts to 40 ft. lbs. (54 Nm). Install the idler pulley to the engine bracket.
17. To install the cam sensor, first clean off the old spacer from the sensor face completely. Inspect the O-ring for damage and replace if necessary. A new spacer must be attached to the cam sensor, prior to installation; if a new spacer is not used, engine performance will be affected. Oil the O-ring lightly and push the sensor in to its bore in the timing case cover until contact is made with the cam timing gear. Hold in this position and tighten it to 9 ft. lbs. (12 Nm).
18. Install the air conditioning compressor and bracket.
19. Install the drive belt.
20. Install the inner splash shield, then install the wheel and tire assembly.
21. Install the oil pan with a new gasket.
22. Install the motor mount.
23. Remove the engine temperature sensor and fill the cooling system until the level reaches the vacant sensor hole. Install the sensor and continue to fill the radiator. Fill the engine with the proper amount of oil.
24. Connect the negative battery cable and check for leaks.

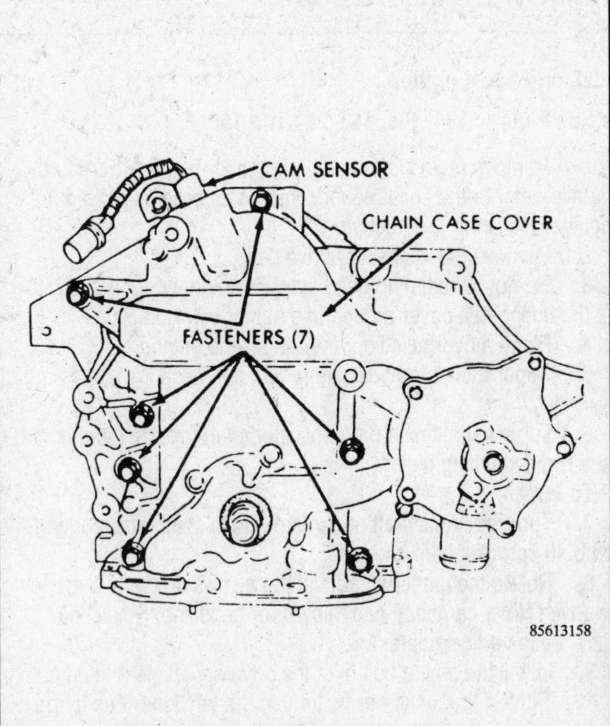

Fig. 162 Timing chain case cover retaining bolts — 3.3L and 3.8L engines

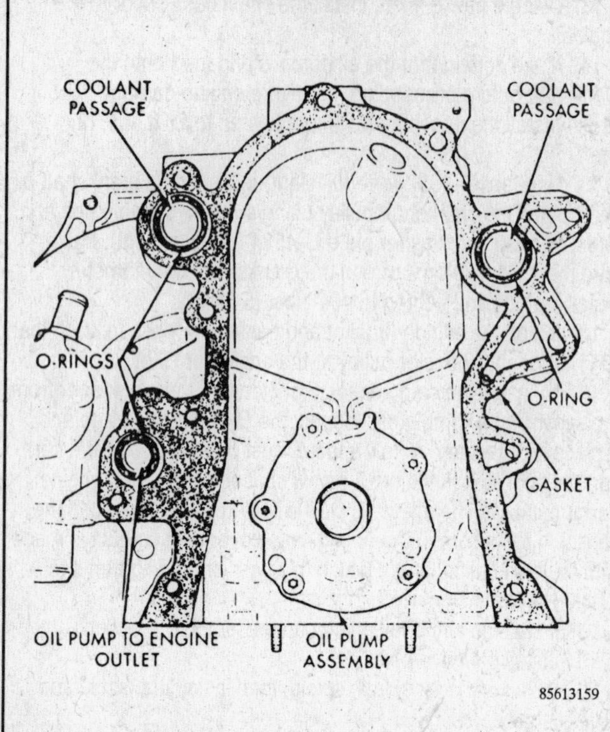

Fig. 163 Timing chain case cover gaskets and O-rings — 3.3L and 3.8L engines

Timing Belt/Chain

REMOVAL & INSTALLATION

2.2L and 2.5L Engines

➧ See Figures 164, 165, 166, 167 and 168

1. Remove the solid mount compressor bracket. For more details, refer to the solid mount compressor bracket procedure outlined earlier in this section.
2. Remove the accessory drive belts.
3. Remove the timing belt cover. For more information, refer to the timing belt cover procedures earlier in this section.
4. Place a hydraulic floor jack under the engine.
5. Separate the right engine mount and raise the engine slightly.
6. Loosen the timing belt tensioner screw, rotate the hex nut, and remove timing belt.

To install:

7. Turn the crankshaft and intermediate shaft until markings on both sprockets are aligned.
8. Rotate the camshaft so that the arrows on the hub are in line with No. 1 camshaft cap to cylinder head line. Small hole must be in vertical center line.
9. Install the timing belt over the drive sprockets and adjust.
10. Tighten the tensioner by turning the tensioner hex to the right. Tension should be correct when the belt can be twisted 90° with the thumb and forefinger, midway between the camshaft and intermediate sprocket.
11. Turn the engine clockwise from TDC 2 revolutions with crankshaft bolt. Check the timing marks for correct alignment.

✻✻WARNING

Do not use the camshaft or intermediate shaft to rotate the engine. Also, do not allow oil or solvent to contact the timing belt, as they will deteriorate the belt and cause slipping.

12. Tighten locknut on tensioner while holding weighted wrench in position to 45 ft. lbs. (61 Nm).
13. Install the timing belt cover.
14. Install the accessory drive belts.

➝ With timing belt cover installed and number one cylinder at TDC, the small hole in the cam sprocket should be centered in timing belt cover hole.

Fig. 164 Loosening the timing belt tensioner screw

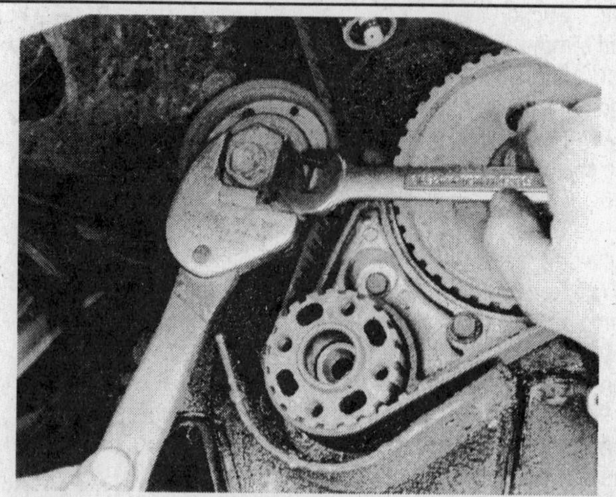

Fig. 165 Loosen the belt tensioner screw, then rotate the hex nut to release the tension. During installation, rotate this hex nut to increase belt tension, then tighten the screw

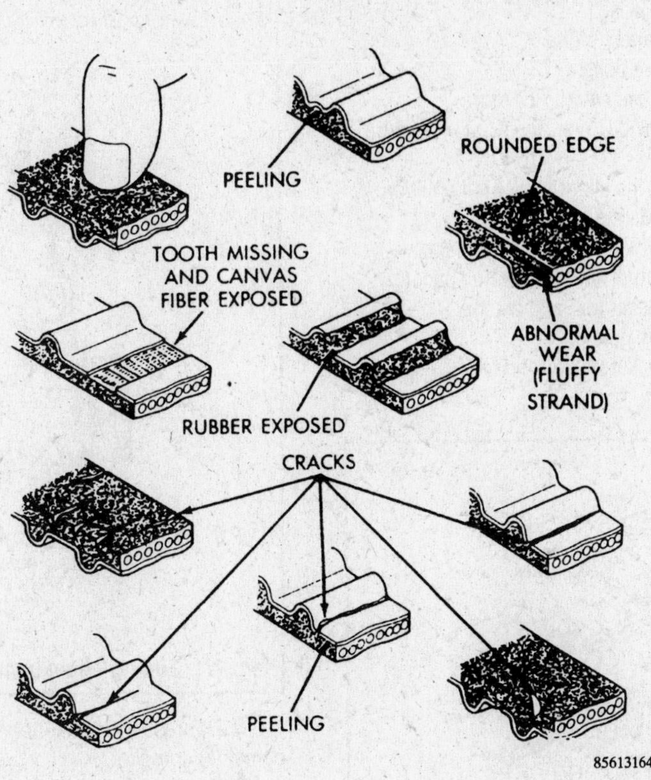

Fig. 166 Timing belt inspection

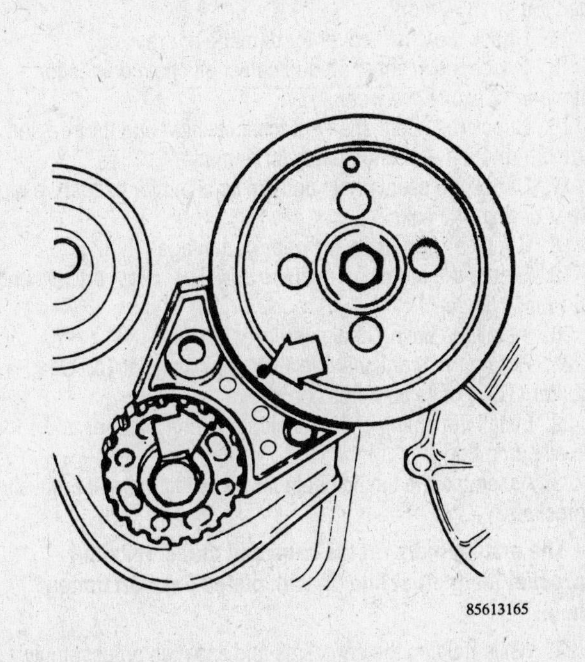

Fig. 167 Crankshaft and intermediate shaft timing mark alignment — 2.2L and 2.5L engines

Fig. 168 Camshaft sprocket timing alignment — 2.2L and 2.5L engines

2.6L Engines

➧ See Figures 169, 170, 171, 172, 173, 174 and 175

1. Disconnect the negative battery cable.
2. Remove the accessory drive belts.
3. Remove the timing chain case cover. For more information, refer to the Front Timing Cover and Seal procedure, earlier in this section.
4. Remove the bolts securing the silent shaft chain guides. Mark all parts for proper location during assembly.
5. Remove the sprocket bolts, silent shaft drive chain, crankshaft/silent sprocket, silent shaft sprockets and spacer.
6. Remove the camshaft sprocket bolt and washer.
7. Remove the distributor drive gear.
8. Remove the camshaft sprocket holder and timing chain guides.

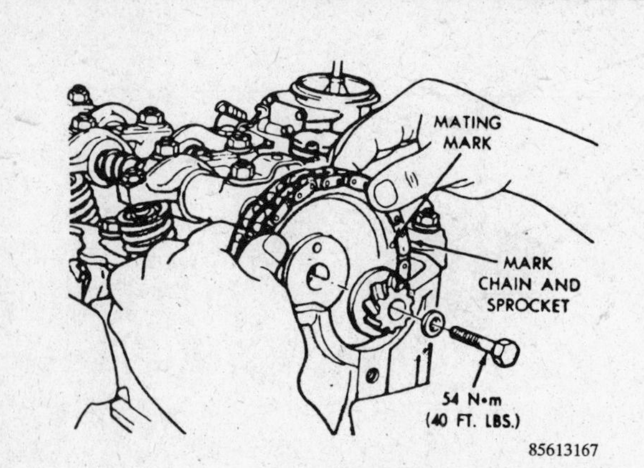

Fig. 169 Mark the chain and sprockets and remove the bolt, washer distributor drive gear and sprocket — 2.6L engines

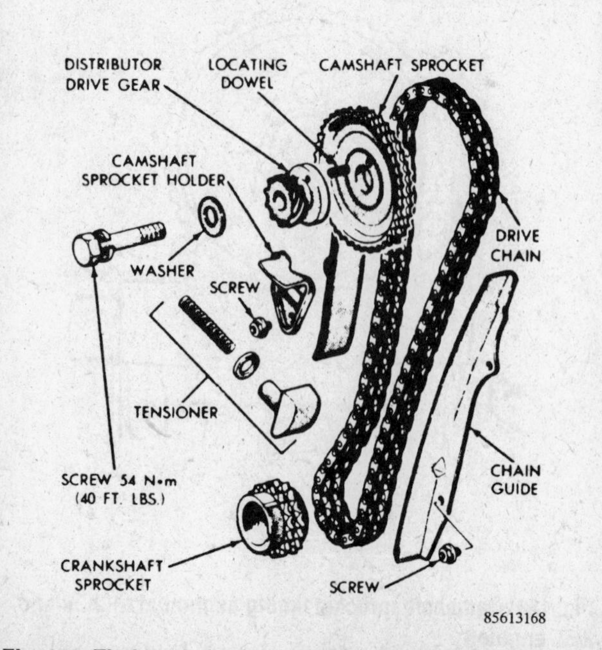

Fig. 170 Timing chain components — 2.6L engines

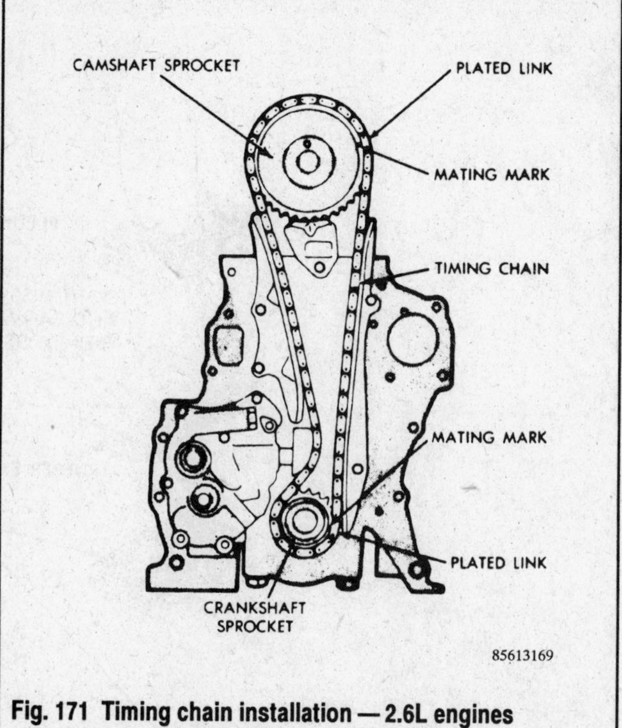

Fig. 171 Timing chain installation — 2.6L engines

9. Depress the tensioner and remove the timing chain and camshaft sprocket.
10. Remove the crankshaft sprocket.
11. Remove the tensioner shoe, washer and spring.

To install:

12. Clean and inspect all parts.
13. Check the tensioner shoe for wear or damage and tensioner spring for deterioration. The spring free-length should be 2.59 in. (65.7mm).
14. Check the chain cover for damage or cracks.
15. Check the silent shaft and camshaft chain guides for damage or excessive wear.
16. Check the silent shaft sprocket cushion ring for free and smooth rotation and ring guides for damage.
17. Check the silent chain and timing chain for excessive play, wear or damage links.
18. Check all sprockets for wear or damage teeth.
19. Rotate the camshaft until the dowel pin is at vertical center line with cylinder.
20. Install the timing chain sprocket holders.
21. Rotate the crankshaft until No. 1 piston is at Top Dead Center (TDC) of its compression stroke.
22. Install the timing chain tensioner spring, washer and shoe on oil pump body.
23. Assemble the timing chain on the camshaft and crankshaft sprockets.

➥ The mating mark on the camshaft and crankshaft sprocket teeth must line up with plated links on timing chain.

24. While holding the sprockets and chain as an assembly, install the crankshaft sprocket to key way of crankshaft and camshaft sprocket to dowel pin of camshaft.
25. Install the distributor drive gear, camshaft sprocket bolt and washer, and tighten bolt to 40 ft. lbs. (54 Nm).
26. Install the silent shaft chain drive sprocket on crankshaft.

27. Assemble the silent shaft chain to oil pump sprocket and to silent shaft sprocket.

➔ The timing marks on the sprockets teeth must line up with plated links on of silent shaft chain.

28. While holding the parts as an assembly, align the crankshaft sprocket plated link with the punch mark on the sprocket. With the chain installed on crankshaft sprocket, install the oil pump sprocket and silent chain sprocket on their respective shafts.

29. Install the oil pump and silent shaft sprocket bolts and tighten to 25 ft. lbs. (34 Nm).

30. Loosely install the 3 silent shaft chain guides and adjust silent shaft chain tension as follows.

   a. Tighten chain guide **A** mounting screws.
   b. Tighten chain guide **C** mounting screws.
   c. Slightly rotate the oil pump and silent shaft sprockets to remove any slack in the silent shaft chain.
   d. Adjust the position of chain guide **B** so that when the chain is pulled inward, the clearance between chain guide **B** and the chain links will be 0.039–0.138 in. (1.0–3.5mm). Tighten chain guide **B** mounting screws.

31. Install a new timing case cover gasket and install the timing case cover.

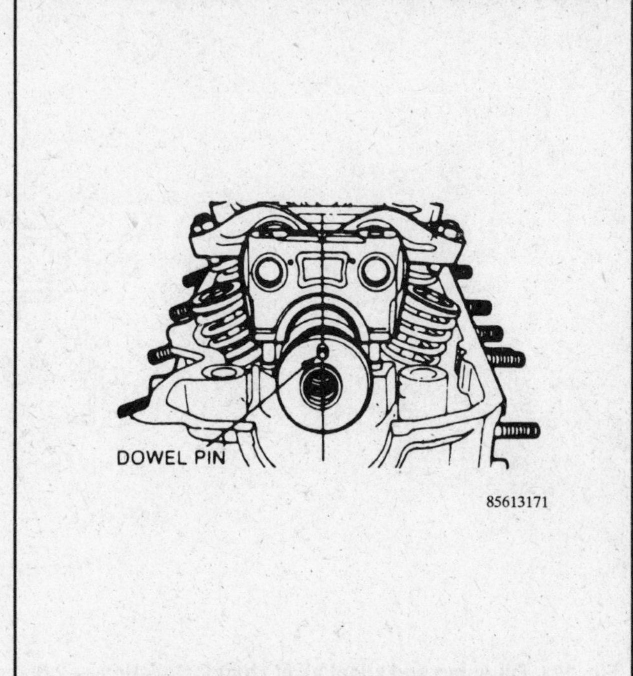

Fig. 172 Dowel pin set at 12 o'clock — 2.6L engines

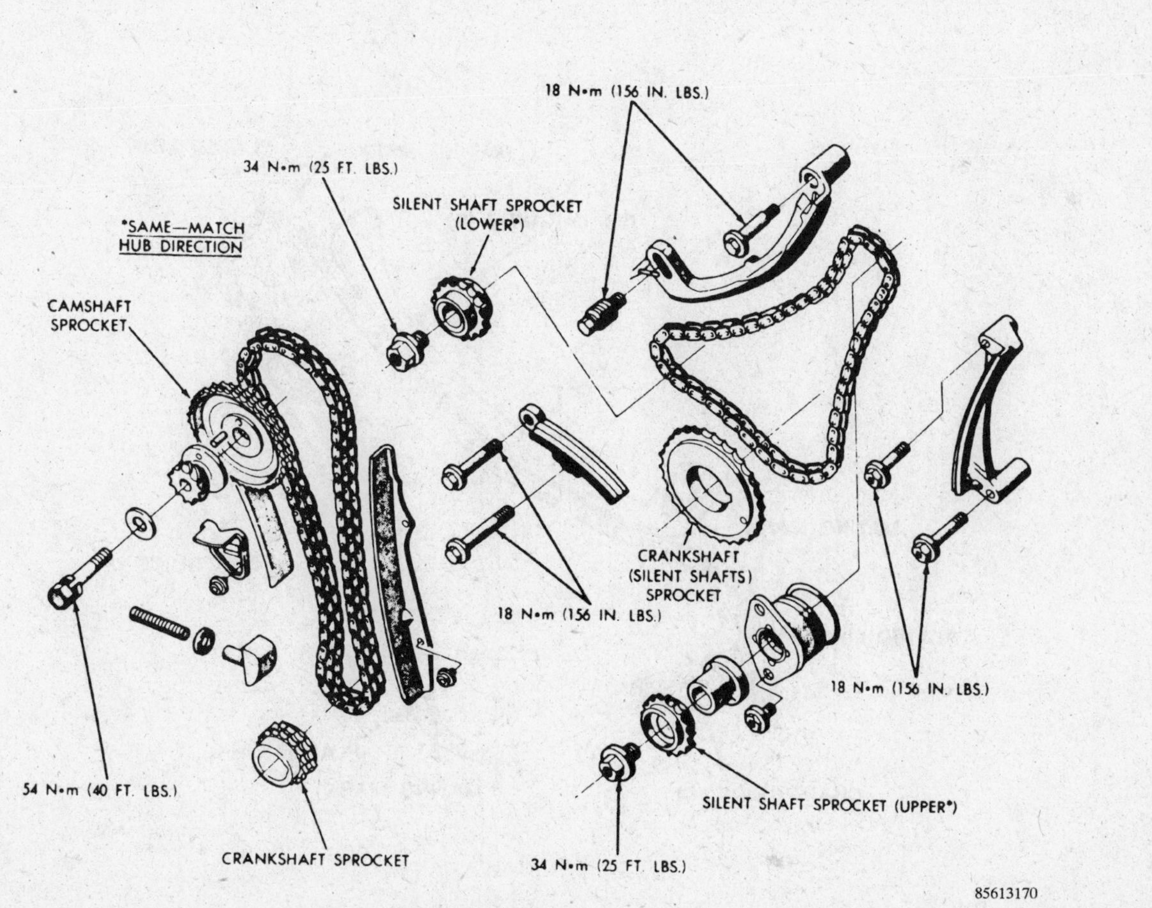

Fig. 173 Timing/silent shaft chain and drive components — 2.6L engines

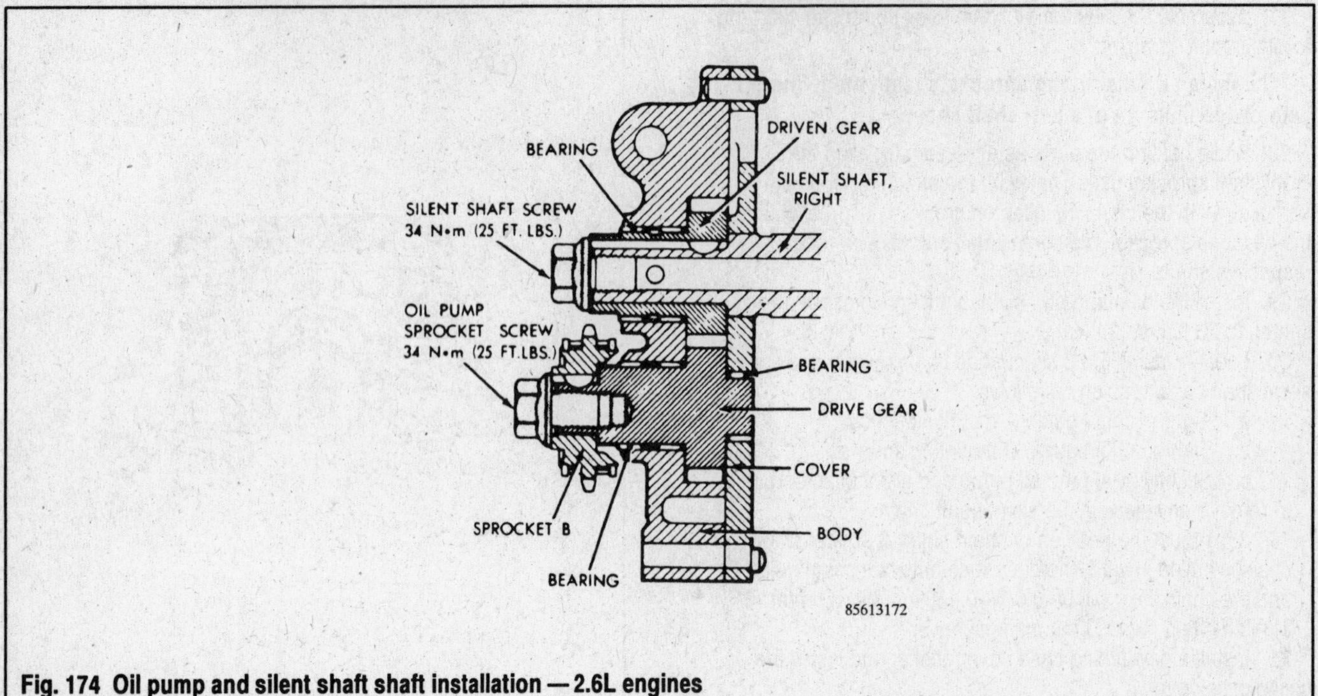

Fig. 174 Oil pump and silent shaft shaft installation — 2.6L engines

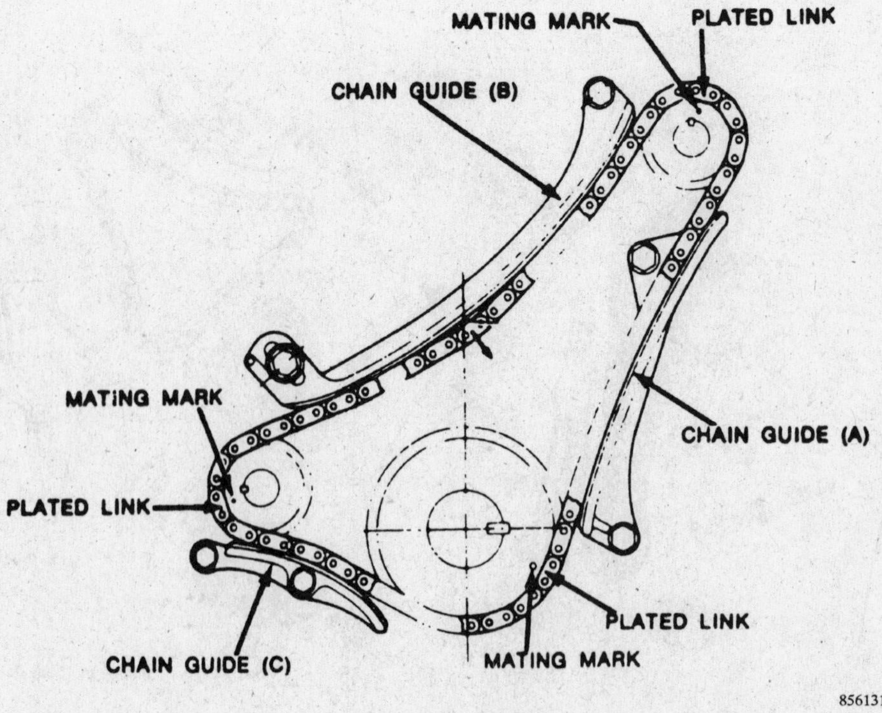

Fig. 175 Timing mark alignment for the silent shaft timing chain installation — 2.6L engines

SILENT SHAFT CHAIN ADJUSTMENT

➧ See Figure 176

If necessary, the silent shaft chain adjustment may be performed without removing the timing chain case cover. Proceed as follows:

1. Remove the access cover from the timing case cover.
2. Through the access hole loosen special bolt **B**.
3. Using your finger only, push on the boss to apply tension.
4. While applying tension, tighten special bolt **B** to 13 ft. lbs. (18 Nm).
5. Install the access cover to the timing chain case cover.

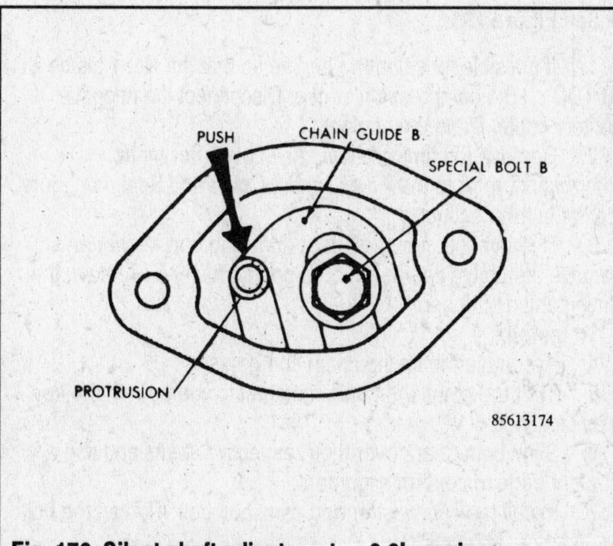

Fig. 176 Silent shaft adjustment — 2.6L engines

3.0L Engines

➧ See Figures 177, 178, 179 and 180

➥ The timing belt can be inspected by removing the upper (front outer) timing cover.

1. Disconnect the negative battery cable.
2. Remove the accessory drive belts.
3. Remove the timing belt covers.
4. Identify the timing belt running direction to avoid reversal during installation.
5. Loosen timing belt tensioner bolt and remove timing belt.
6. Remove the crankshaft sprocket flange.

To install:

7. Rotate the crankshaft sprocket until timing mark on crankshaft sprocket is lined up with the oil pump timing mark at 1 o'clock position.
8. Rotate the (inner) camshaft sprocket until mark on (inner) camshaft sprocket is lined up with the timing mark on alternator bracket.
9. Rotate the (outer) camshaft sprocket (radiator side) until mark on the sprocket is lined up with the timing mark on the timing belt inner cover. Refer to timing belt illustration.
10. Install the timing belt on the crankshaft sprocket while maintaining pressure on the tensioner side.
11. Position the timing belt over the camshaft sprocket (radiator side). Next, position the belt under the water pump pulley, then over the (inner) sprocket and finally over the tensioner.
12. Apply rotating force in the opposite direction to the camshaft sprocket (radiator side) to create tension on the timing belt tension side.

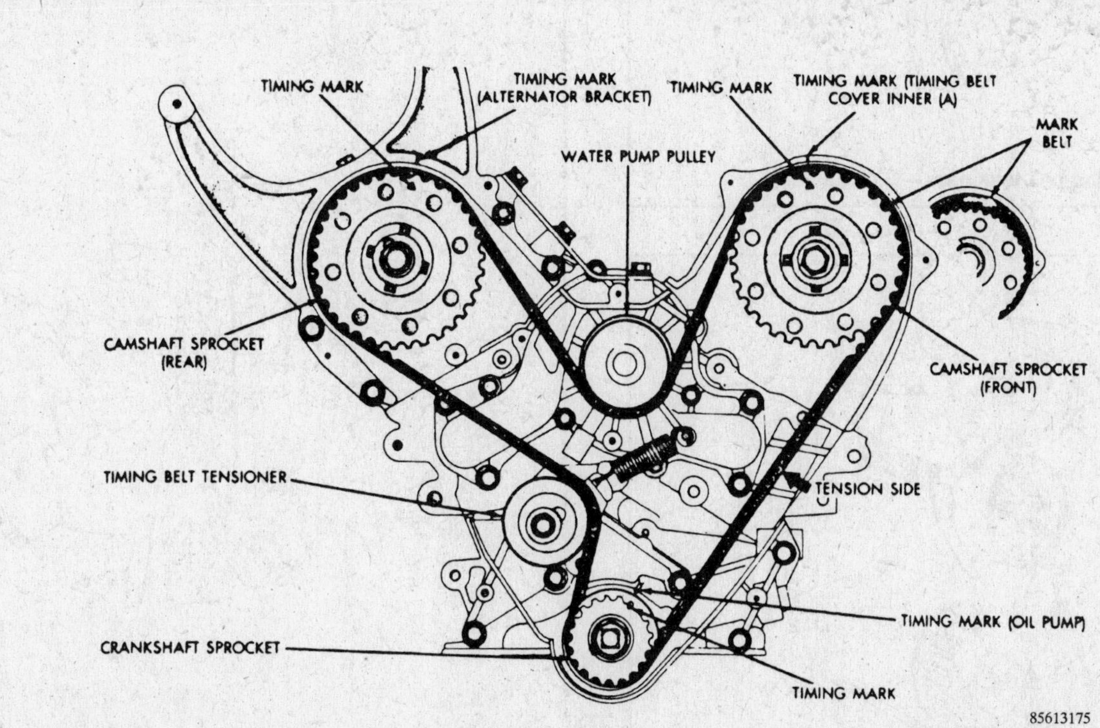

Fig. 177 Sprocket timing for belt installation — 3.0L engines

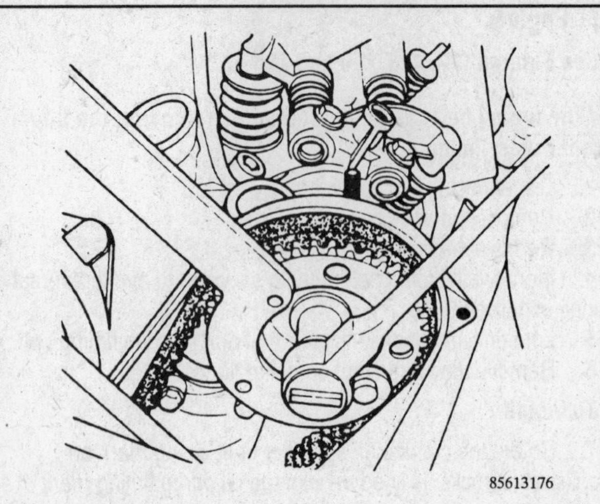

Fig. 178 Secure the sprocket when removing or installing the nut — 3.0L engines

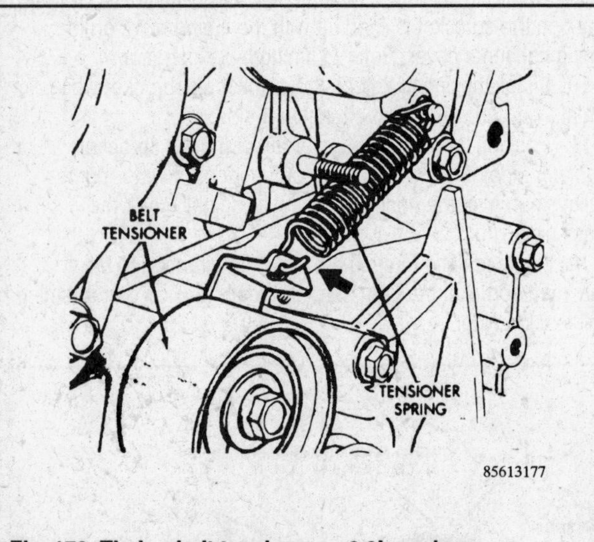

Fig. 179 Timing belt tensioner — 3.0L engines

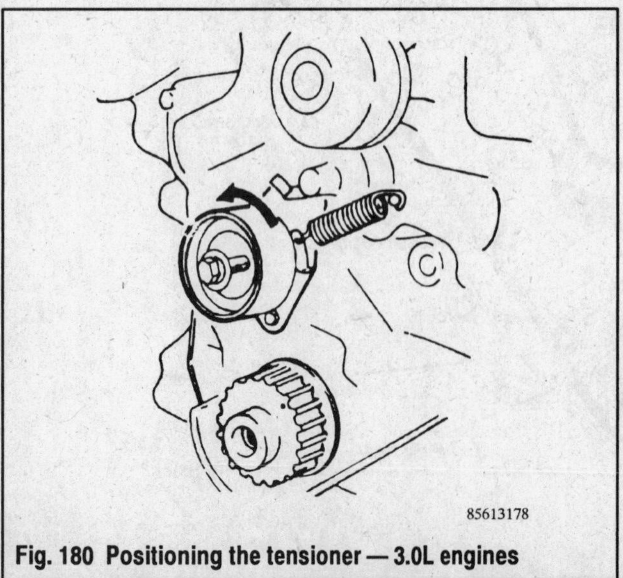

Fig. 180 Positioning the tensioner — 3.0L engines

13. Rotate the crankshaft in a clockwise direction and recheck engine timing marks.
14. Install the crankshaft sprocket flange.
15. Loosen the tensioner bolt and allow tensioner spring to tension the belt.
16. Again rotate the crankshaft in a clockwise direction (2) full turns. Recheck the engine timing. Tighten the tensioner bolt to 23 ft. lbs. (31 Nm).
17. Install the timing covers.
18. Install the accessory drive belts.
19. Connect battery negative cable.

3.3L and 3.8L Engines

➧ See Figure 181

1. If possible, position the engine so that the No. 1 piston is at TDC on the compression stroke. Disconnect the negative battery cable. Drain the coolant.
2. Remove the timing chain case cover. For more information, refer to the Front Timing Cover and Seal procedure, earlier in this section.
3. Remove the camshaft gear attaching cup washer and remove the timing chain with both gears attached. Remove the timing chain snubber.

To install:

4. Assemble the timing chain and gears.
5. Turn the crankshaft and camshaft to line up with the key way locations of the gears.
6. Slide both gears over their respective shafts and use a straight edge to confirm alignment.
7. Install the cup washer and camshaft bolt. Tighten the bolt to 35 ft. lbs. (47 Nm).

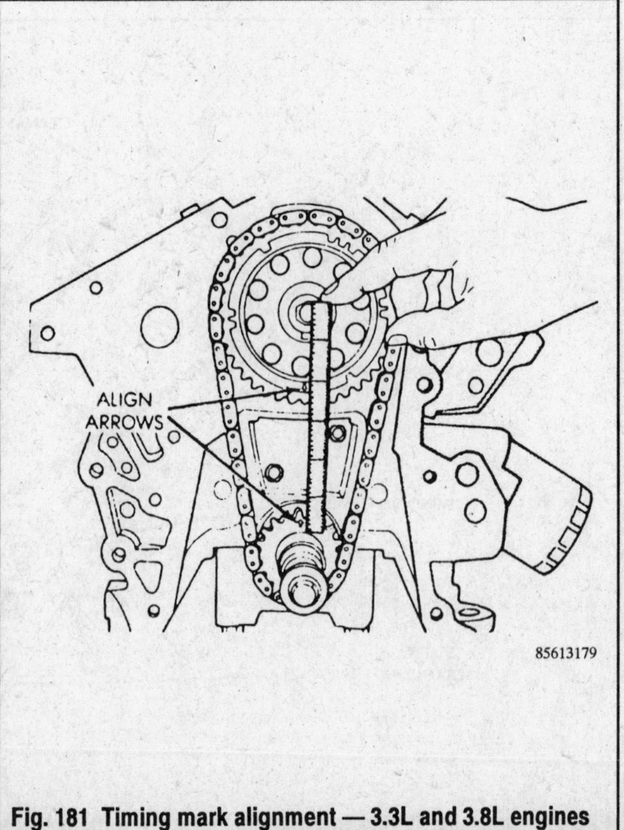

Fig. 181 Timing mark alignment — 3.3L and 3.8L engines

8. Check camshaft end-play. The specification with a new plate is 0.002–0.006 in. (0.051–0.052mm) and 0.002–0.010 in. (0.51–0.254mm) with a used plate. Replace the thrust plate if not within specifications.
9. Install the timing chain snubber.
10. Thoroughly clean and dry the gasket mating surfaces.
11. Install new O-rings to the block.
12. Remove the crankshaft oil seal from the cover. The seal must be removed from the cover when installing to ensure proper oil pump engagement.
13. Using a new gasket, install the chain case cover to the engine.
14. Make certain that the oil pump is engaged onto the crankshaft before proceeding, or severe engine damage will result. Install the attaching bolts and tighten to 20 ft. lbs. (27 Nm).
15. Use tool C-4992, or equivalent, to install the crankshaft oil seal. Install the crankshaft pulley using a 5.9 in. suitable bolt and thrust bearing and washer plate L-4524, or equivalent. Make sure the pulley bottoms out on the crankshaft seal diameter. Install the bolt and tighten to 40 ft. lbs. (54 Nm).
16. Install all other parts removed during the chain case cover removal procedure and fill the engine with oil.
17. Connect the negative battery cable, road test the vehicle and check for leaks.

Timing Sprockets/Gears

REMOVAL & INSTALLATION

2.2L and 2.5L Engines

➧ See Figures 182, 183, 184, 185, 186, 187 and 188

1. Remove the drive belts, timing belt cover and timing belt. For more details, refer to the timing belt cover and timing belt removal procedures earlier in this section.
2. Remove the crankshaft sprocket bolt.
3. Remove the crankshaft sprocket using Tool C-4685 and Tool L-4524, or equivalent puller. If crankshaft seal removal is necessary, remove with Tool C-4679 (2.2L) or Tool C-4991 (2.5L), or an equivalent tool.
4. Clean the crankshaft seal surface with 400 grit paper.
5. Lightly coat the seal (Steel case seal) outer surface with Loctite Stud N' Bearing Mount (P/N 4057987) or equivalent. A soap and water solution is recommended to lubricate (Rubber Coated Case Seal) outer surface.
6. Lightly lubricate the seal lip with engine oil.

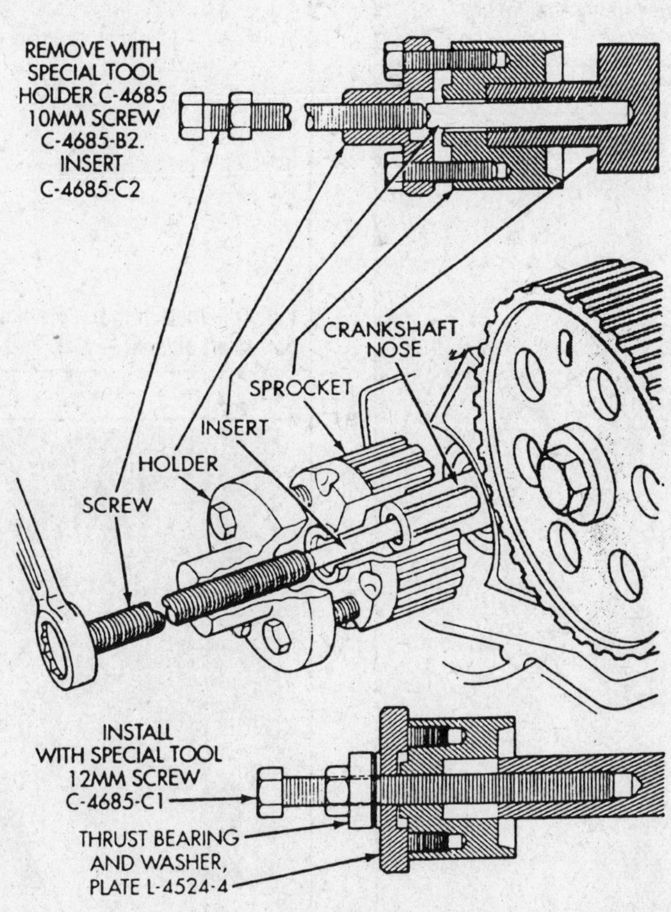

Fig. 182 Removing crankshaft sprocket — 2.2L and 2.5L engines

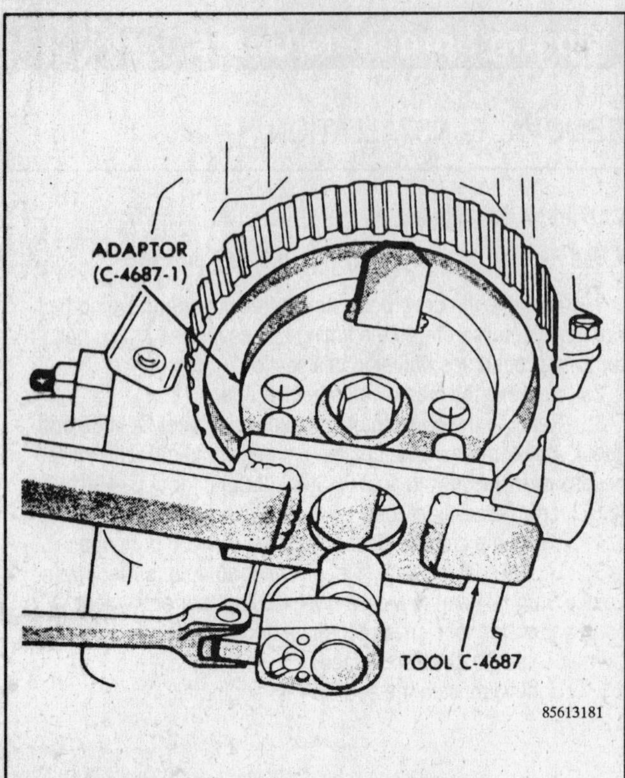

Fig. 183 Removing or installing the camshaft or intermediate shaft sprocket screw using the special tools — 2.2L and 2.5L engines

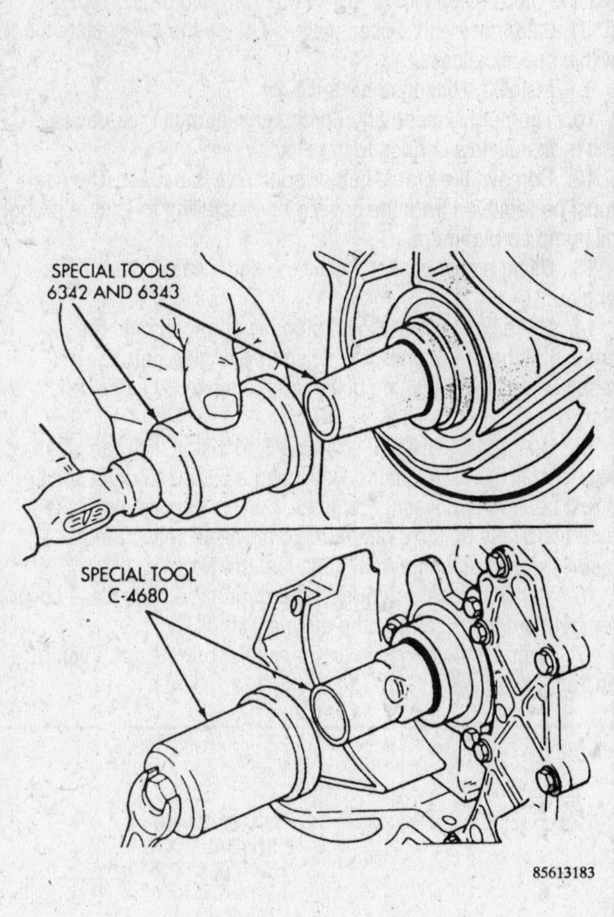

Fig. 185 Installing the crankshaft, intermediate shaft and camshaft oil seal — 2.2L and 2.5L engines

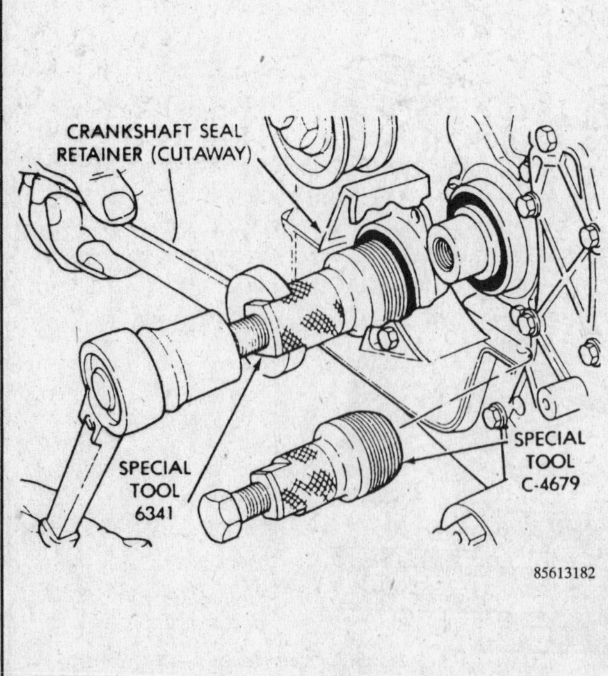

Fig. 184 Removing of the crankshaft, intermediate shaft and camshaft oil seal — 2.2L and 2.5L engines

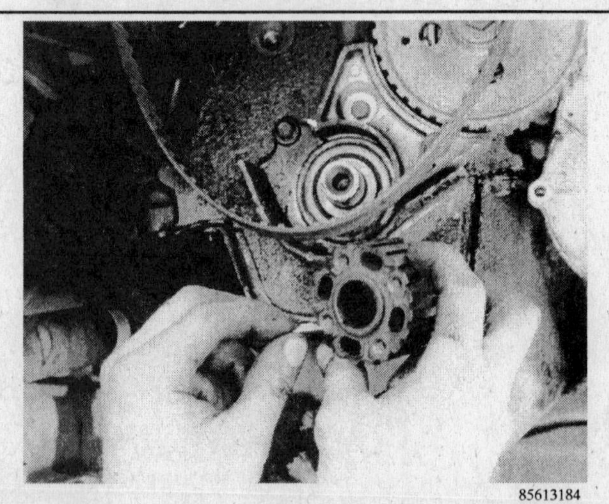

Fig. 186 The crankshaft sprocket and key removed from the shaft

85613185

Fig. 187 Using a strap wrench to the remove the intermediate shaft sprocket

85613186

Fig. 188 The intermediate shaft sprocket shown removed from the shaft

7. Install seal with Tool No. C-4680 (2.2L) or Tool No. C-4992 (2.5L).
8. Install the sprocket and install sprocket bolt.
9. Install the camshaft and intermediate shaft sprockets with Tool C-4687 and Tool C-4687-1 or a similar tool such as a strap wrench.
10. Install the timing belt and timing belt cover.
11. Install the accessory drive belts.

2.6L Engine

Refer to the Timing Chain procedure earlier in this section.

3.0L, 3.3L and 3.8L Engines

Refer to the Timing Belt (3.0L) and Timing Chain (3.3L and 3.8L) procedures earlier in this section.

Camshaft and Bearings

REMOVAL & INSTALLATION

2.2L and 2.5L Engines

See Figures 189, 190, 191, 192, 193, 194, 195, 196, 197, 198 and 199

The following procedure is written for engines still in the vehicle.

1. Disconnect the negative battery cable. Relieve the fuel pressure, if equipped with fuel injection.

Removal of the camshaft requires removal of the camshaft sprocket. To maintain proper engine timing, the timing belt can be left indexed on the sprockets and suspended under light pressure. This will prevent the belt from coming off and maintain timing.

2. Turn the crankshaft so the No. 1 piston is at the TDC of the compression stroke. Remove the upper timing belt cover. Remove the air pump pulley, if equipped.
3. Remove the bolt and the camshaft sprocket, then suspend it tightly so the belt does not lose tension. If it does, the belt timing will have to be reset.
4. Remove the valve cover.
5. Remove the air pump belt from the pulley.
6. If the rocker arms are being reused, mark them for installation identification and loosen the camshaft bearing bolts, evenly and gradually.
7. Using a soft mallet, rap the rear of the camshaft a few times to break the bearing caps loose.
8. Remove the bolts, bearing caps and the camshaft with seals.

Before replacing the camshaft, identify factory installed oversized components. To do so, look for the tops of the bearing caps painted green and O/SJ stamped rearward of the oil gallery plug on the rear of the head. In addition, the barrel of the camshaft is painted green and O/SJ is stamped onto the rear end of the camshaft. Installing standard sized parts in an head equipped with oversized parts-or vice versa-will cause severe engine damage.

9. Check the oil passages for blockage and the parts for damage. Clean all mating surfaces.

To Install:

10. Transfer the sprocket key to the new camshaft. New rocker arms and a new camshaft sprocket bolt are normally included with the camshaft package. Install the rocker arms, lubricate the camshaft and install with end seals installed.
11. Place the bearing caps with No. 1 at the timing belt end and No. 5 at the transaxle end. The camshaft bearing caps are numbered and have arrows facing forward. Tighten the camshaft bearing bolts evenly and gradually to 18 ft. lbs. (24 Nm).

Apply RTV silicone gasket material to the No. 1 and 5 bearing caps. Install the bearing caps before the seals are installed.

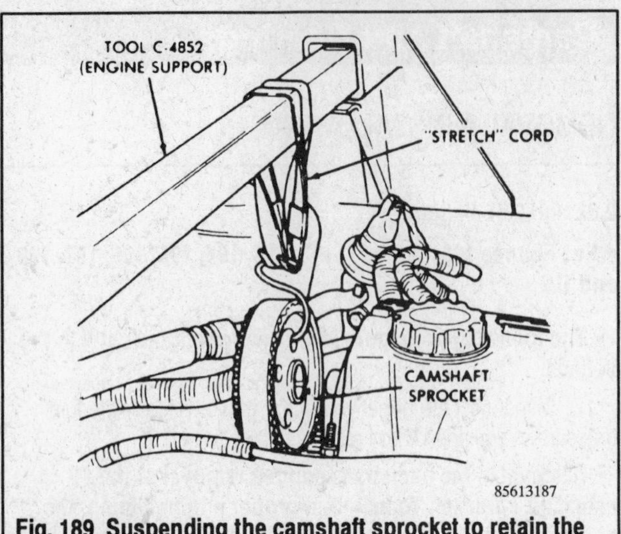

Fig. 189 Suspending the camshaft sprocket to retain the engine timing — 2.2L and 2.5L engines

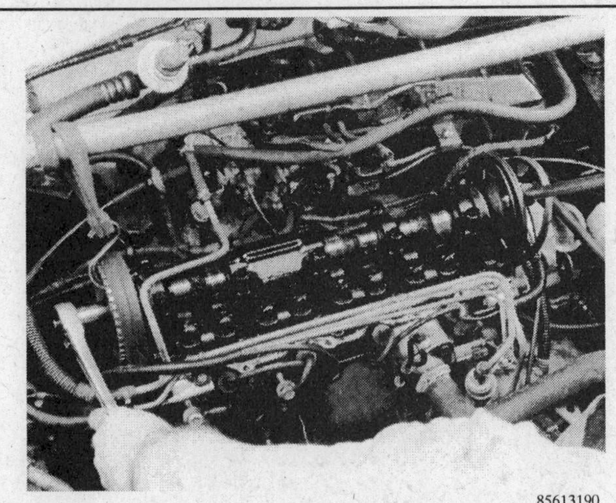

Fig. 192 Place a wrench on both ends of the camshaft and remove the camshaft sprocket leaving it suspended

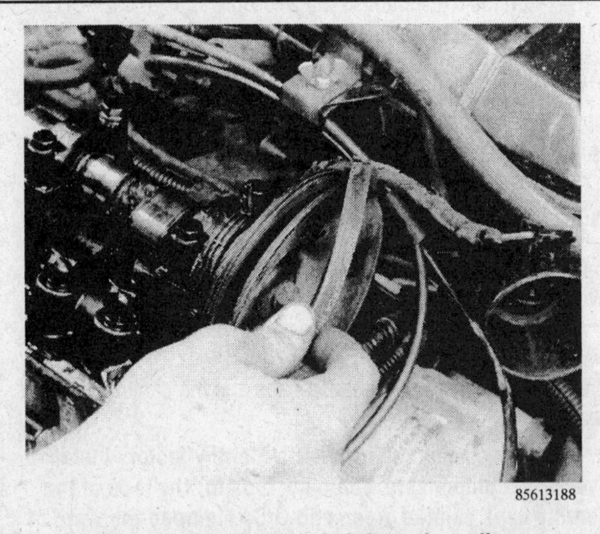

Fig. 190 Remove the air pump belt from the pulley

Fig. 193 Removing the oil shield

Fig. 191 Suspending the camshaft sprocket to retain timing before removing it from the camshaft

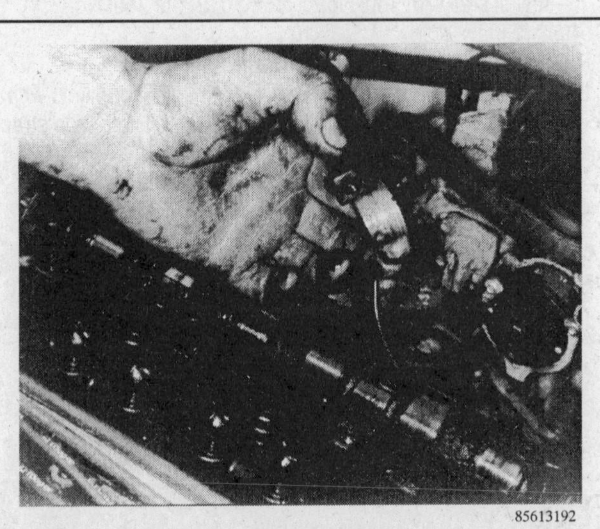

Fig. 194 Removing the bearing caps

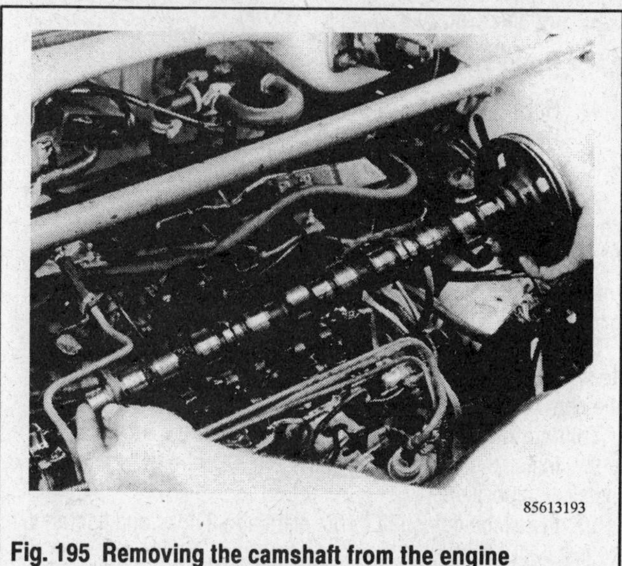
Fig. 195 Removing the camshaft from the engine

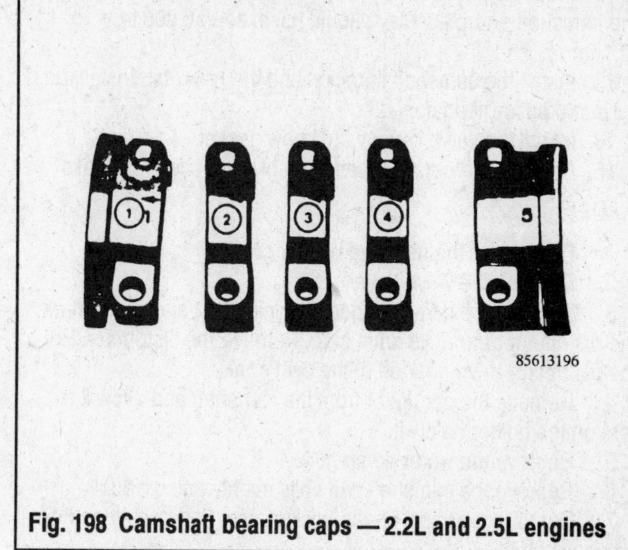
Fig. 198 Camshaft bearing caps — 2.2L and 2.5L engines

Fig. 196 Removing the seal from the end of the camshaft

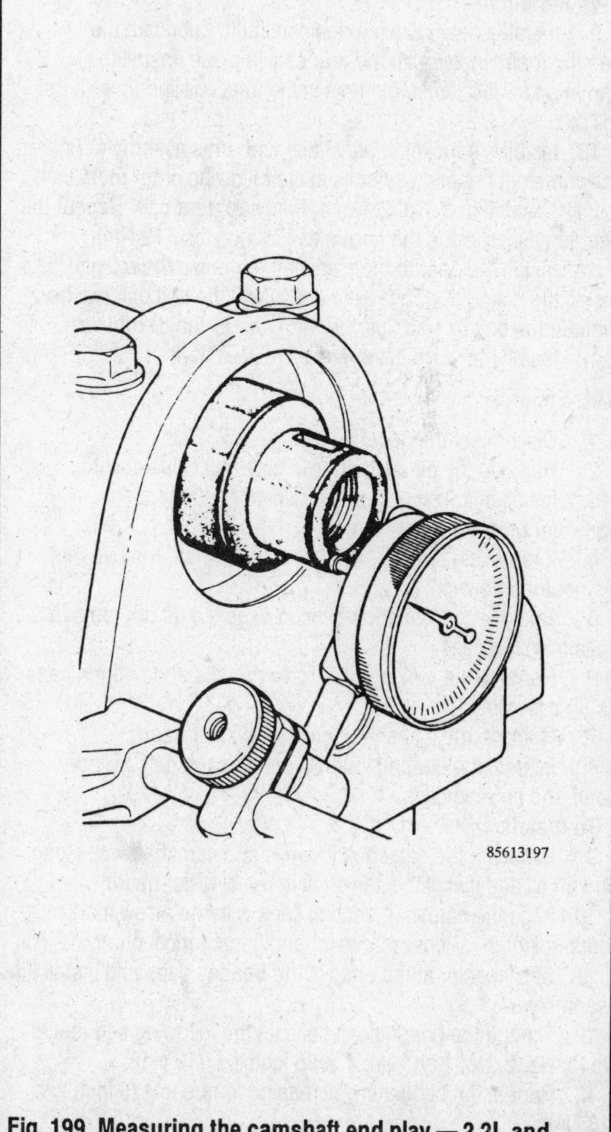
Fig. 199 Measuring the camshaft end play — 2.2L and 2.5L engines

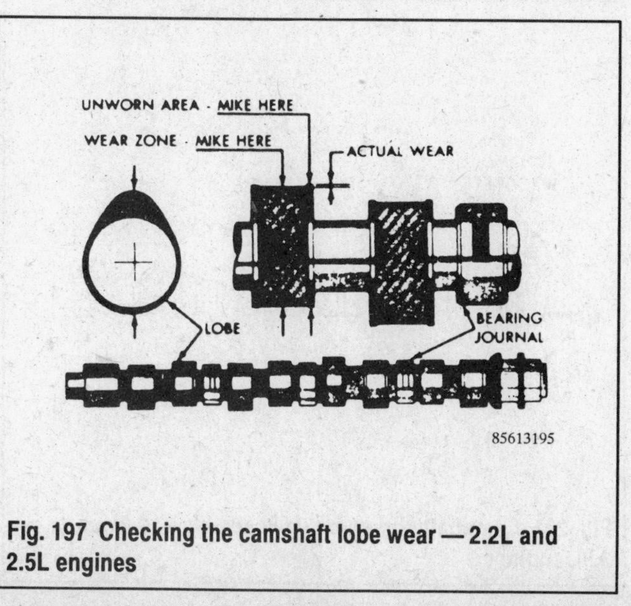

Fig. 197 Checking the camshaft lobe wear — 2.2L and 2.5L engines

12. Mount a dial indicator to the front of the engine and check the camshaft end-play. Play should not exceed 0.006 in. (0.15mm).
13. Install the camshaft sprocket and the new bolt. Install the air pump pulley, if equipped.
14. Install the valve cover with a new gasket.
15. Connect the negative battery cable and check for leaks.

2.6L Engines

1. Disconnect the negative battery cable.
2. Remove the valve cover.
3. Remove the camshaft gear retaining bolt and matchmark the distributor gear to its drive gear. Remove the distributor. Pry the distributor drive gear off of the cam gear.
4. Remove the cam gear from the camshaft and allow it to rest on the holder below it.
5. Remove the water pump pulley.
6. Remove the camshaft cap bolts evenly and gradually.
7. Remove the caps, shafts, rocker arms and bolts together as an assembly.
8. Remove the camshaft with the rear seal from the engine.

To install:

9. Install a new roll pin to the camshaft. Lubricate the camshaft and install with the rear seal in place. Install the camshaft in position so the hole in the gear will line up with the roll pin.
10. Install the rocker caps, shafts and arms assembly. Tighten the camshaft bearing cap bolts in the following order to 85 inch lbs. (10 Nm): No. 3, No. 2, No. 4, front cap, rear cap. Repeat the sequence increasing the torque to 175 inch lbs. (19 Nm).
11. Install the gear to the camshaft engaging the roll pin. Install the distributor drive gear and install the bolt and washer. Tighten the bolt to 40 ft. lbs. (54 Nm). Install the distributor.
12. Install the valve cover and all related parts.

3.0L Engines

1. Disconnect the negative battery cable.
2. Remove the air cleaner assembly and valve covers.
3. Install auto lash adjuster retainers MD998443, or equivalent, on the rocker arms.
4. If removing the right side (front) camshaft, remove the distributor extension.
5. Remove the camshaft bearing caps but do not remove the bolts from the caps.
6. Remove the rocker arms, rocker shafts and bearing caps, as an assembly.
7. Remove the camshaft from the cylinder head.
8. Inspect the bearing journals on the camshaft, cylinder head and bearing caps.

To Install:

9. Lubricate the camshaft journals and camshaft with clean engine oil and install the camshaft in the cylinder head.
10. Align the camshaft bearing caps with the arrow mark (depending on cylinder numbers) and in numerical order.
11. Apply sealer at the ends of the bearing caps and install the assembly.
12. Tighten the bearing cap bolts, in the following sequence: No. 3, No. 2, No. 1 and No. 4 to 85 inch lbs. (10 Nm).
13. Repeat the sequence, increasing torque to 175 inch lbs. (18 Nm).
14. Install the distributor extension, if it was removed.
15. Install the valve cover and all related components.

3.3L and 3.8L Engines

➧ See Figures 200 and 201

1. Relieve the fuel system pressure.
2. Disconnect the negative battery cable.
3. Remove the engine from the vehicle.
4. Remove the intake manifold, cylinder heads, timing chain cover and timing chain from the engine.
5. Remove the rocker arm and shaft assemblies.
6. Label and remove the pushrod and lifters.
7. Remove the camshaft thrust plate.
8. Install a long bolt into the front of the camshaft to facilitate its removal. Remove the camshaft being careful not to damage the cam bearings with the cam lobes.

To install:

9. Install the camshaft to within 2 in. (51mm) of its final installation position.
10. Install the camshaft thrust plate and 2 bolts and tighten to 10 ft. lbs. (12 Nm).

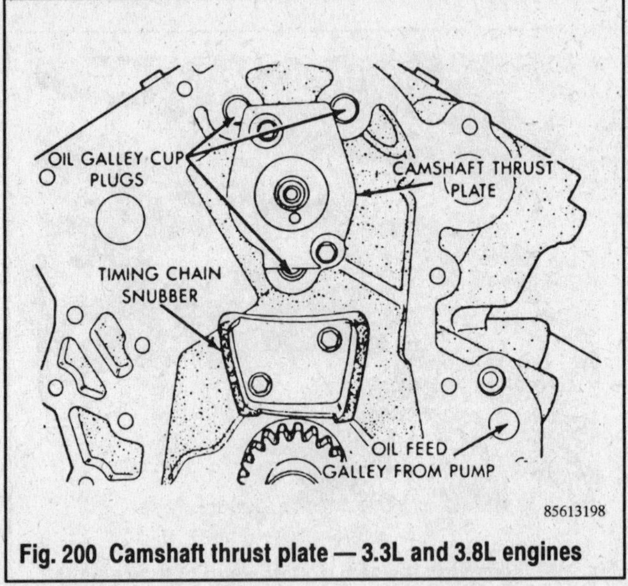

Fig. 200 Camshaft thrust plate — 3.3L and 3.8L engines

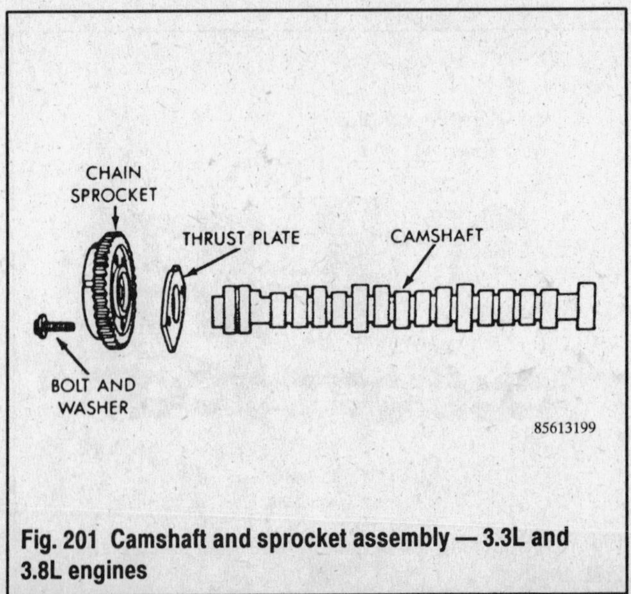

Fig. 201 Camshaft and sprocket assembly — 3.3L and 3.8L engines

11. Place both camshaft and crankshaft gears on the bench with the timing marks on the exact imaginary center line through both gear bores as they are installed on the engine. Place the timing chain around both sprockets.

12. Turn the crankshaft and camshaft so the keys line up with the key ways in the gears when the timing marks are in proper position.

13. Slide both gears over their respective shafts and use a straight edge to check timing mark alignment.

14. Measure camshaft end-play. If not within specifications, replace the thrust plate.

15. If the camshaft was not replaced, lubricate and install the lifters in their original locations. If the camshaft was replaced, new lifters must be used.

16. Install the pushrods and rocker shaft assemblies.

17. Install the timing chain cover, cylinder heads and intake manifold.

18. Install the engine in the vehicle.

19. When everything is bolted in place, change the engine oil and replace the oil filter.

➡ If the camshaft or lifters have been replaced, add 1 pint (0.47 L) of Mopar crankcase conditioner, or equivalent when replenishing the oil to aid in break in. This mixture should be left in the engine for a minimum of 500 miles (800 km) and drained at the next normal oil change.

20. Fill the radiator with coolant.

21. Connect the negative battery cable, set all adjustments to specifications and check for leaks.

INSPECTION

1. Inspect the camshaft bearing journals for wear or damage.
2. Inspect the cylinder head and check oil return holes.
3. Check the tooth surface of the distributor drive gear teeth of the right camshaft for wear or damage.
4. Check both camshaft surfaces for wear or damage.
5. Remove the distributor drive adaptor seal.
6. Check camshaft lobe height and replace if out of limit. Standard value is 1.61 in. (41mm).

Intermediate Shaft

REMOVAL & INSTALLATION

2.2L and 2.5L Engines

➧ See Figures 187 and 203

➡ The following procedure is to be performed with the engine removed from the vehicle.

1. Remove the distributor assembly.
2. Remove the fuel pump.
3. Remove timing case cover and timing belt.
4. Remove the intermediate shaft sprocket.
5. Remove the intermediate shaft retainer screws and remove retainer.
6. Remove the intermediate shaft and inspect journals and bushing.

To install:

7. When installing the shaft, lubricate the fuel pump eccentric and distributor drive gear. Install the intermediate shaft.
8. Inspect the shaft seal in retainer. Replace if necessary.
9. Lightly lubricate the seal lip with engine oil.
10. Install the intermediate shaft retainer assembly and retainer screws. Tighten the retainer screws to 105 inch lbs. (12 Nm). On the 2.5L engines, apply anaerobic (Form-in-Place) gasket material to retainer sealing surface before installing.
11. Install the intermediate shaft sprocket.
12. Make sure all timing marks are properly aligned.
13. Install the timing belt and adjust.
14. Install the timing belt cover.
15. Install the fuel pump.
16. Install the distributor.

Balance Shafts

➧ See Figures 202, 203, 204, 205, 206 and 207

The 2.5L engine is equipped with 2 balance shafts located in a housing attached to the lower crankcase. These shafts are driven by a chain and 2 gears from the crankshaft at 2 times crankshaft speed. This counterbalances certain engine reciprocating masses.

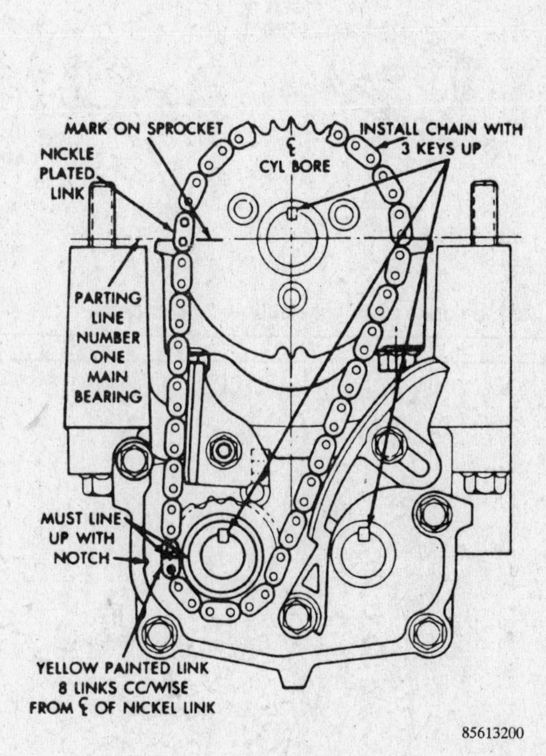

Fig. 202 Balance shaft timing — 2.5L engines

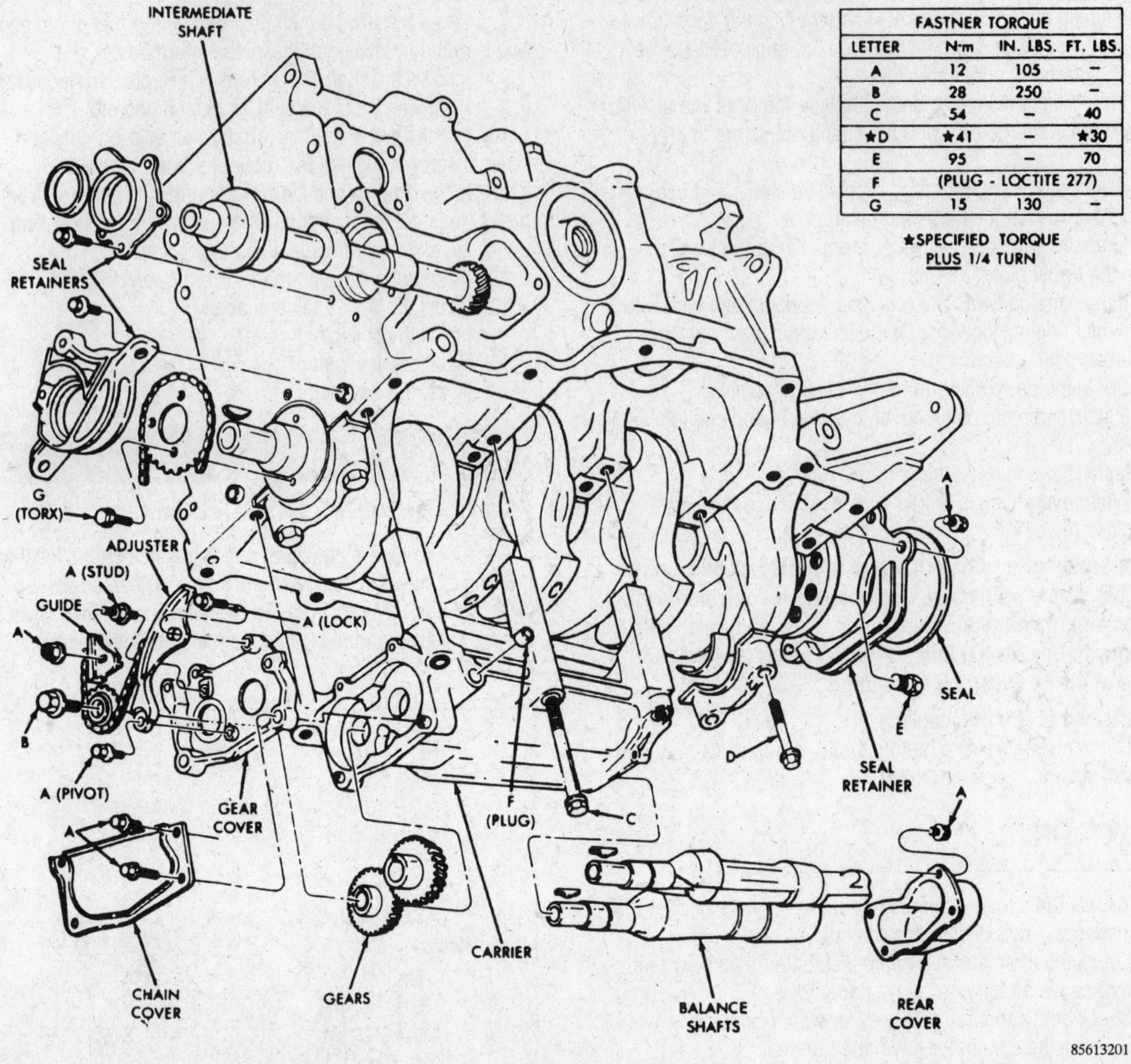

FASTNER TORQUE			
LETTER	N·m	IN. LBS.	FT. LBS.
A	12	105	–
B	28	250	–
C	54	–	40
★D	★41	–	★30
E	95	–	70
F	(PLUG - LOCTITE 277)		
G	15	130	–

★SPECIFIED TORQUE PLUS 1/4 TURN

85613201

Fig. 203 Balance shaft assembly — 2.5L engines

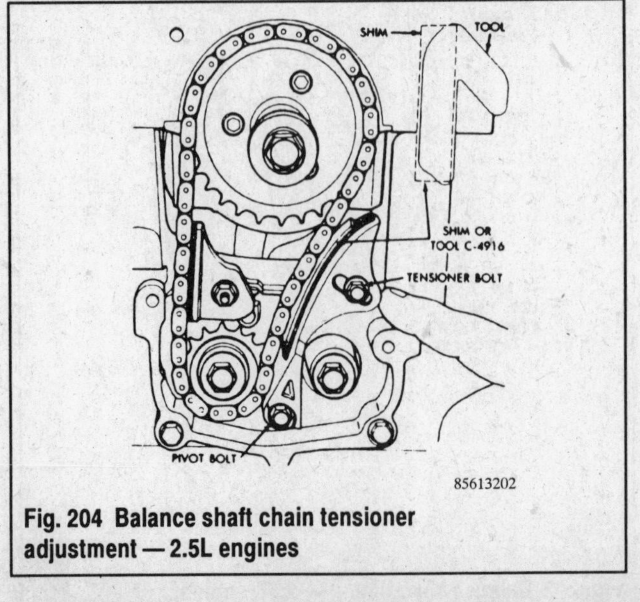

Fig. 204 Balance shaft chain tensioner adjustment — 2.5L engines

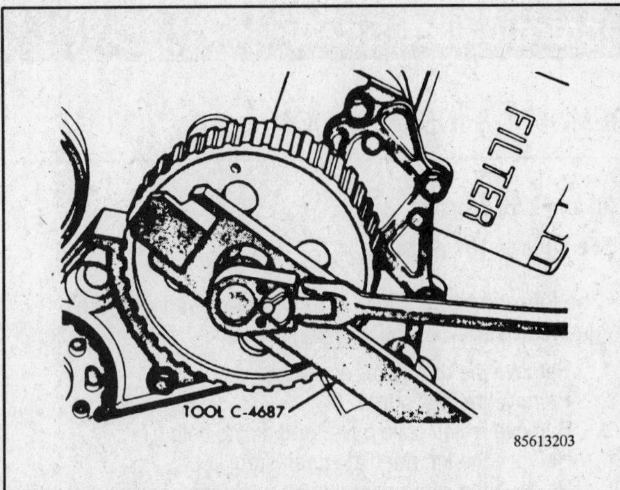

Fig. 205 Removing the intermediate shaft sprocket using the special tools — 2.5L engines

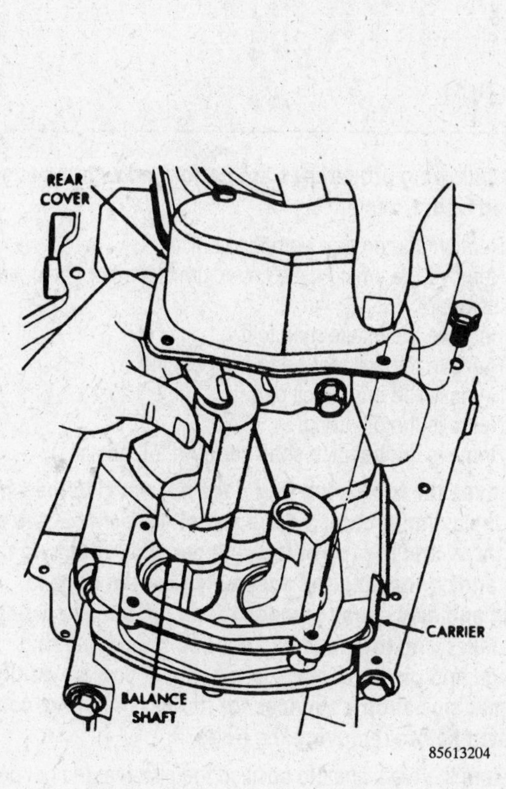

Fig. 206 Balance shaft removal and installation — 2.5L engines

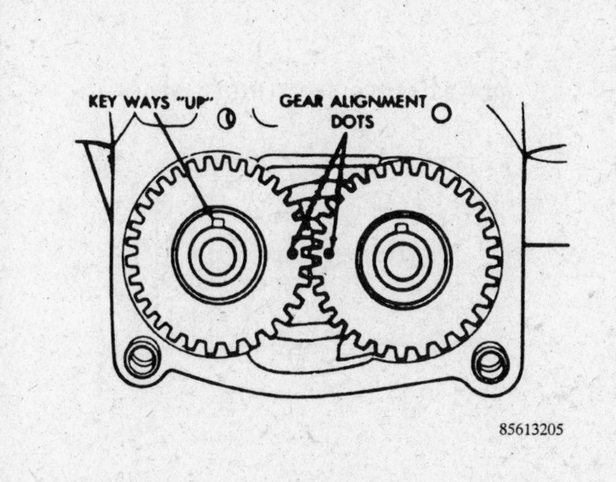

Fig. 207 Balance shaft gear timing — 2.5L engines

REMOVAL & INSTALLATION

1. Remove the engine from the vehicle.
2. Remove the timing case cover, timing belt and sprockets.
3. Remove the engine oil pan.
4. Remove the front crankshaft seal retainer.
5. Remove the balance shafts chain cover.
6. Remove the chain guide and tensioner.
7. Remove the balance shafts sprocket retaining screws and crankshaft chain sprocket Torx® screws. Remove the chain and sprocket assembly.
8. Remove the balance shafts carrier front gear cover retaining double ended stud. Remove the cover and balance shafts gears.
9. Remove the carrier rear cover and balance shafts.
10. To separate the carrier, remove the 6 crankcase-to-carrier attaching bolts and remove carrier.
11. Take notice of all parts to avoid interchanging.

To install:

12. Install both shafts into carrier the assembly from rear of carrier.
13. Install the rear cover.
14. Install the balance shafts drive and driven gears to shafts.
15. Position the carrier assembly on crankcase, then tighten the 6 crankcase-to-carrier bolts to 40 ft. lbs. (55 Nm).
16. Crankshaft-to-balance shaft timing must be established. Rotate both balance shafts until the key ways are in the Up position.
17. Install the short hub drive gear on balance shaft driving shaft.
18. Install the long hub gear on the driven shaft.
19. With both gears on the balance shafts and key ways Up, the timing marks should be meshed.
20. Align the balance shaft carrier cover with the carrier housing dowel pin and install double ended stud. Tighten to 105 inch lbs. (12 Nm).
21. Install the crankshaft sprocket and tighten sprocket Torx® screw to 11 ft. lbs. (15 Nm).
22. Turn the crankshaft until number one cylinder is at TDC. The timing marks on the chain sprocket should line up with the parting line on the left side of number one main bearing cap.
23. Install the chain over the crankshaft sprocket so the nickel plated link of the chain is over the timing mark on the crankshaft sprocket.
24. Install the balance shaft sprocket into the timing chain so that the timing mark on the sprocket (yellow dot) mates with the yellow painted link on the chain.
25. With the balance shaft key way in 12 o'clock position slide the balance shaft sprocket on the nose of the balance shaft. The balance shaft may have to be pushed in slightly to allow for clearance.

➥ The timing mark on the sprocket, the painted link, and the arrow on the side of the gear cover should line up if the balance shafts are timed correctly.

26. Install the balance shaft bolt, then tighten it to 21 ft. lbs. (28 Nm). Place a wooden block between the crankcase and crankshaft counterbalance to prevent crankshaft from turning.
27. Proper balance shaft timing chain tension must be established.

28. Place a shim 0.039 in. (1mm) thick by 2.75 in. (70mm) long between the chain and tensioner.

29. Apply firm hand pressure behind the adjustment slot and tighten adjustment bolt first, followed by the pivot screw to 105 inch lbs. (12 Nm). Remove the shim.

30. Install the chain guide making sure the tab on the guide fits into slot on the gear cover. Install the nut and washer, then tighten them to 105 inch lbs. (12 Nm).

31. Install the chain cover, then tighten the screws to 105 inch lbs. (12 Nm).

32. Apply a 1/16 in. (1.5mm) diameter bead of RTV gasket material to retainer sealing surface. Install retainer assembly.

33. Install the crankshaft sprocket and timing belt. For more details, refer to the timing belt adjustment procedure in this section.

34. Install the timing cover.

Silent Shafts

The 2.6L engine uses 2 counter shafts (silent shafts) in the cylinder block to reduce engine noise and vibration.

REMOVAL & INSTALLATION

➥ The following procedures to be performed with engine removed from vehicle.

1. Remove the timing chain case cover. For more information, refer to the Front Timing Cover and Seal procedure in this section.
2. Remove the silent shaft chain assembly and timing chain assembly, by referring to the timing chain procedure in this section.
3. Remove the silent shaft bolt (it's the bolt directly above the silent chain sprocket).
4. Remove the oil pump bolts and pull the pump housing straight forward. Remove the gaskets and the oil pump backing plate.
5. Remove the right silent shaft.
6. Remove the left silent shaft thrust plate by screwing two 8mm screws into tapped holes in thrust plate. Remove the left silent shaft.

To install:

7. Install both silent shafts into cylinder block. Be careful not to damage inner bearings.
8. Install the left silent shaft thrust plate on the left silent shaft using a new O-ring.
9. Install the oil pump. For more details, refer to the oil pump installation procedure in this section.
10. Install the timing chain and silent chain assembly, by referring to the timing chain installation procedure.
11. Install the timing chain case cover, as described in the Front Timing Cover and Seal procedure.

SILENT SHAFT CLEARANCE

1. Outer diameter-to-outer bearing clearance: 0.0008–0.0023 in. (0.02–0.06mm).
2. Inner diameter-to-inner bearing clearance: 0.0020–0.0035 in. (0.05–0.09mm).

Pistons and Connecting Rods

➧ See Figures 208, 209, 210, 211, 212, 213, 214, 215, 216, 217 and 218

REMOVAL

➥ The following procedures are performed with the engine removed from vehicle.

1. Remove the engine from the vehicle.
2. Remove the timing case cover, timing belt or chain, and sprockets/gears.
3. Remove the intake manifold.
4. Remove the cylinder head from engine.
5. Remove the engine oil pan.
6. Remove the oil pump.
7. Remove the balance shaft carrier (2.5L engines).

➥ Because the top piston ring does not travel to the very top of the cylinder bore, a ridge is built up between the end of the travel and the top of the cylinder walls. Pushing the piston and connecting rod assembly past the ridge is difficult and may cause damage to the piston. If new rings are installed and the ridge has not been removed, ring breakage and piston damage can occur. If you are going to use a machine shop's services for honing or boring, consult with them before removing the ridge.

8. Turn the crankshaft to position the piston at the bottom of the cylinder bore. Cover the top of the piston with a rag. Install a ridge reamer in the bore and follow the manufacturer's instructions to remove the ridge. Use caution, avoid cutting too deeply. Remove the rag and cuttings from the top of the piston. Remove the ridge from all cylinders.
9. Turn the crankshaft until the connecting rod is at the bottom of travel.
10. Number all connecting rod caps if not already labeled to aid during assembly. Remove connecting rod bearing cap nuts and remove caps. Keep all parts separated.

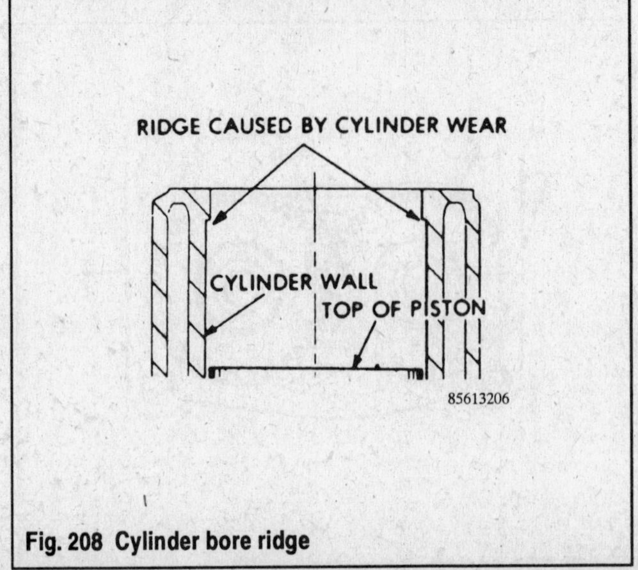

Fig. 208 Cylinder bore ridge

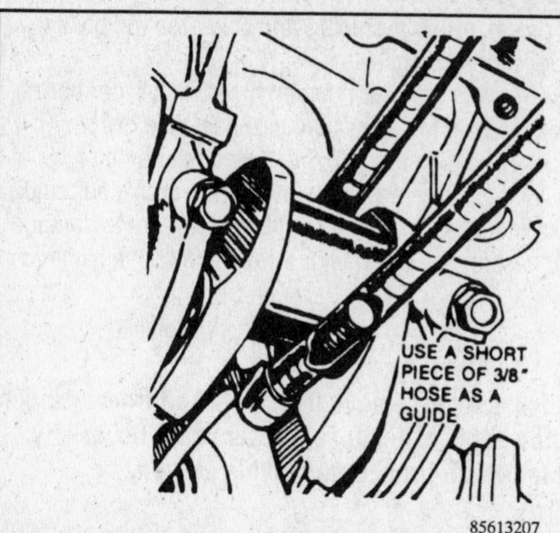

Fig. 209 Use lengths of rubber tubing to protect the crankshaft journal and cylinder linings during piston and rod removal and installation

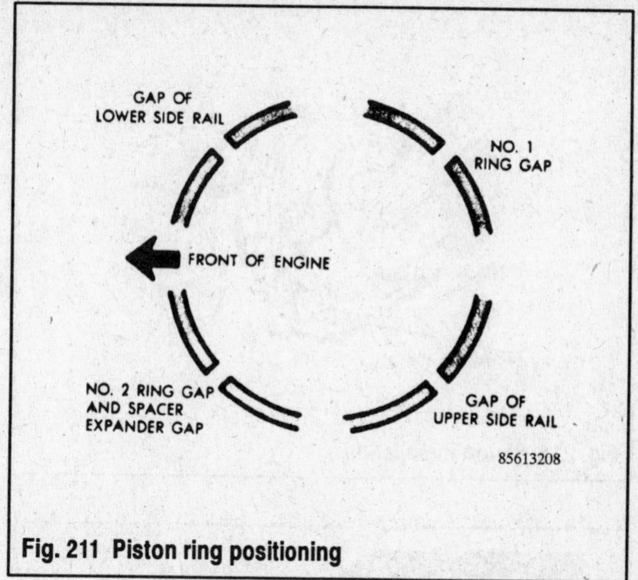

Fig. 211 Piston ring positioning

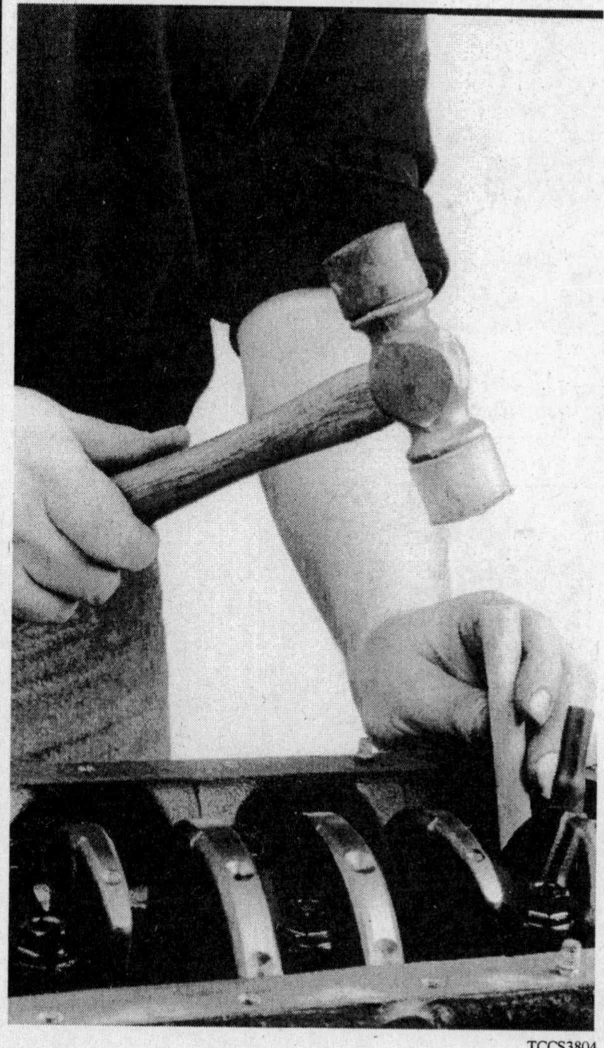

Fig. 210 Carefully tap the piston out of the bore using a wooden dowel

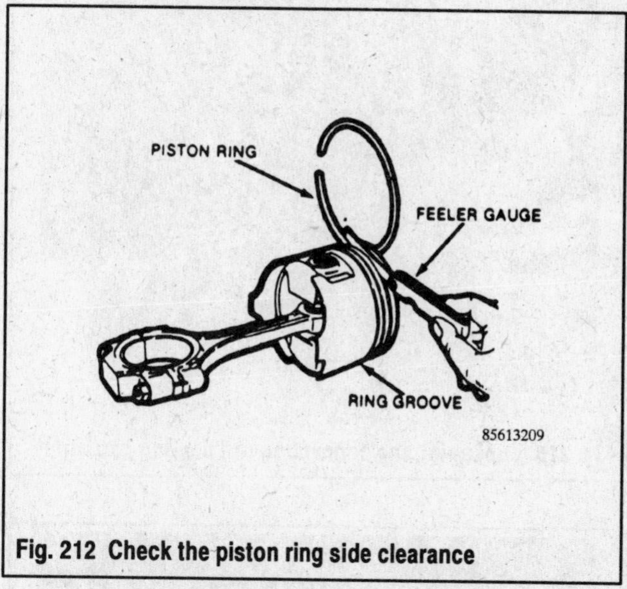

Fig. 212 Check the piston ring side clearance

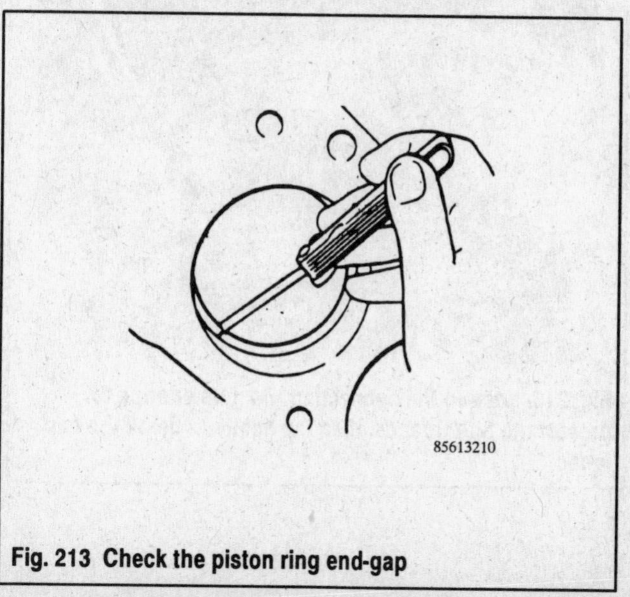

Fig. 213 Check the piston ring end-gap

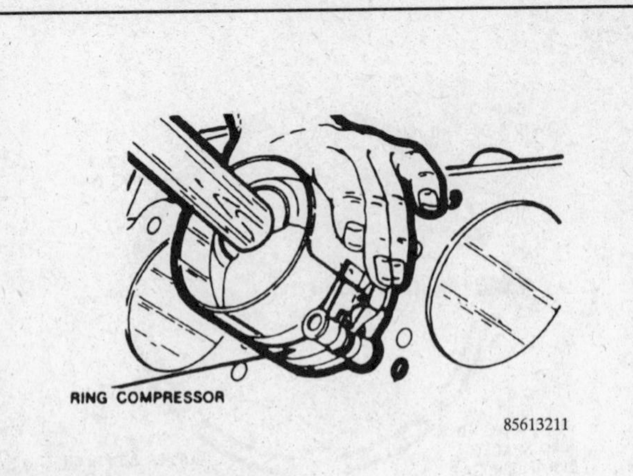

Fig. 214 Piston installation

11. Take 2 pieces of rubber tubing and cover the rod bolts to prevent cylinder wall scoring.

12. Before removing the piston assembly from cylinder bore scribe a mark indicating front position, or take notice of manufacturer identification mark. Using a wooden hammer handle, carefully tap piston assembly away from crankshaft and remove from cylinder block. Care should be taken not to damage crankshaft connecting rod journals or threads on connecting rod cap bolts.

13. Remove all the pistons from cylinder block in similar fashion.

➥ It is not necessary to remove the crankshaft from cylinder block for piston service. If crankshaft service is necessary, refer to the crankshaft procedures in this section.

Fig. 215 Loosening the connecting rod bearing cap nuts

Fig. 217 The connecting rod bearing cap and bearing removed from the connecting rod

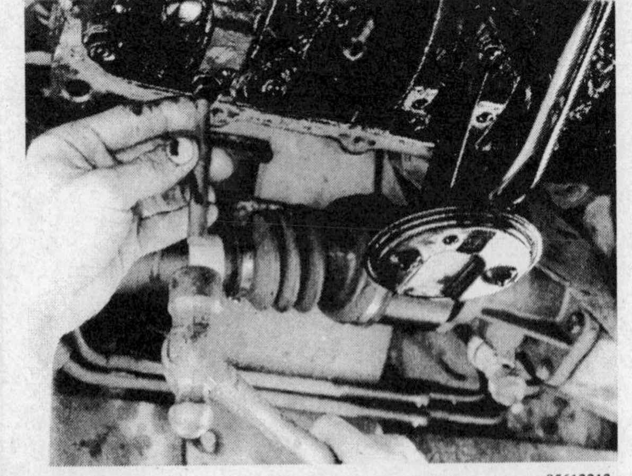

Fig. 216 Loosen the connecting rod nuts enough to protect the bolt threads, then tap lightly to break the cap loose

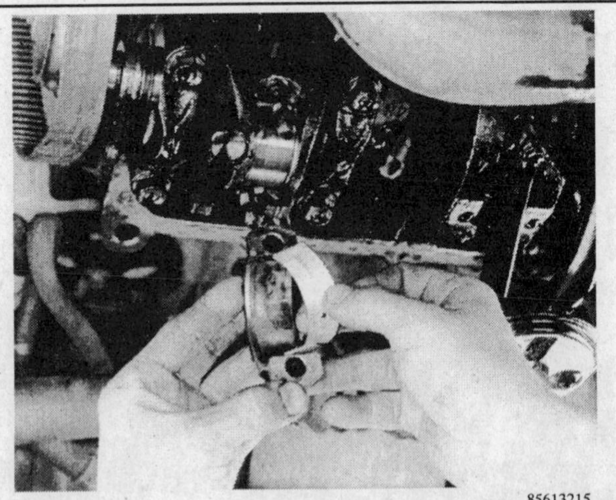

Fig. 218 Removing the bearing from the connecting rod bearing cap

CLEANING & INSPECTION

See Figures 219, 220, 221, 222 and 223

1. Use a piston ring expander and remove the rings from the piston.
2. Clean the ring grooves using an appropriate cleaning tool, exercise care to avoid cutting too deeply.
3. Clean all varnish and carbon from the piston with a safe solvent. Do not use a wire brush or caustic solution on the pistons.
4. Inspect the pistons for scuffing, scoring, cracks, pitting or excessive ring groove wear. If wear is evident, the piston must be replaced.
5. Have the piston and connecting rod assembly checked by a machine shop for correct alignment, piston pin wear and piston diameter. If the piston has collapsed it will have to be replaced or knurled to restore original diameter. Connecting rod bushing replacement, piston pin fitting and piston changing can be handled by the machine shop.
6. Check the cylinder bore diameter and cylinder bore for wear using a telescoping gauge at 3 different levels. Cylinder bore out of round: 0.0020 in. (0.05mm) maximum. Cylinder bore taper: 0.005 in. (0.13mm) maximum. Refer to the general engine specification chart for the cylinder bore specification.
7. Check piston dimensions. Measure approximately 0.078 in. (2mm) above the bottom of the piston skirt and across the thrust face. Refer to the piston and ring specification chart for the piston diameter.
8. After recording cylinder bore measurement and piston diameter, subtract the low reading. The difference is the piston-to-cylinder wall clearance: 0.0008–0.0016 in. (0.02–0.04mm).
9. Check piston ring gap using a piston to position the ring at least 0.62 in. (16mm) from the bottom of cylinder bore. Measure clearance using a feeler gauge. Refer to the piston and rings specification chart.
10. Check the ring-to-piston ring groove clearance using a feeler gauge.

85943208

Fig. 220 Clean the piston grooves using a ring groove cleaner

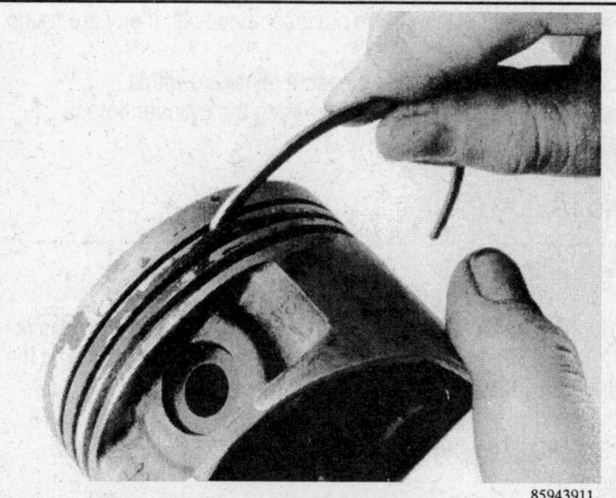

85943911

Fig. 221 You can use a piece of an old ring to clean the ring grooves, be careful the ring is sharp

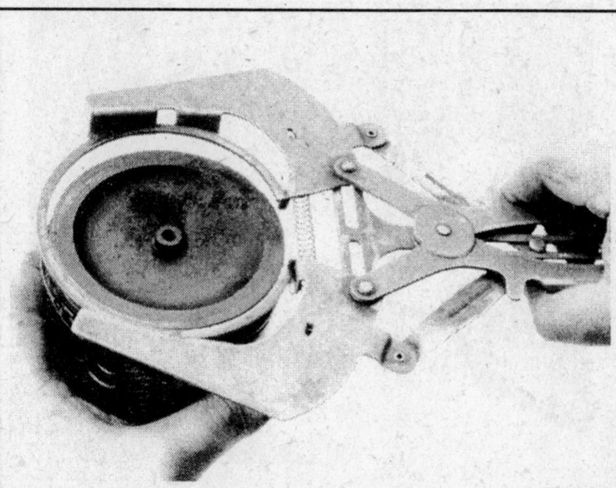

85943211

Fig. 219 Use a ring expander tool to remove the piston rings

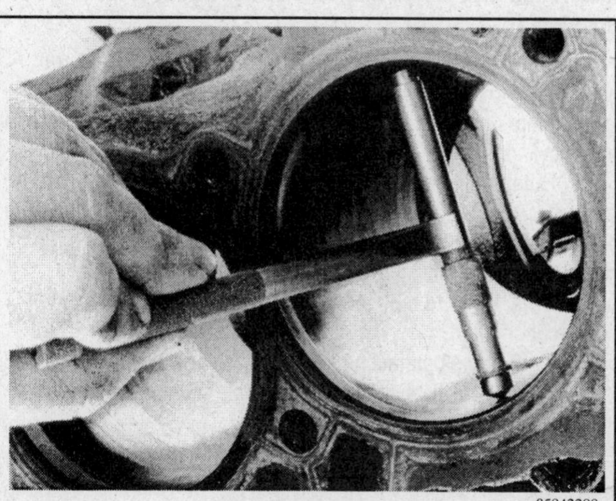

85943209

Fig. 222 An telescoping gauge may be used to measure the cylinder bore diameter

85943210

Fig. 223 Measure the piston's outer diameter using a micrometer

TCCS3914

Fig. 224 Installing the piston into the block using a ring compressor and the handle of a hammer

11. Check the ring groove by rolling the new piston ring around the groove to check for burrs or carbon deposits. If any are found, remove with a fine file.
12. If all clearances and measurements are within specifications, honing or glaze breaking the cylinder bore is all that is required.

INSTALLATION

➧ See Figure 224

1. Start with the oil ring expander in the lower oil ring groove.
2. Install one oil rail at bottom of the oil ring expander and the other at top. The oil rails must be spaced 180° apart from each other.
3. Using the ring expander install the intermediate piston ring.
4. Install the upper piston ring using the ring expander.

➝ Generally marks on the upper and intermediate piston rings must point toward the crown of piston. Consult the illustration with piston ring set instruction sheet for ring positioning.

5. Install a ring compressor, then insert the piston and rod assembly into the engine with the mark previously made, or the labeled mark on the piston head, toward the timing belt/chain end of the cylinder block.
6. Rotate the crankshaft so that the connecting rod journal is on center of cylinder bore. Install a new connecting rod bearing in connecting rod and cap. Check the connecting rod bearing oil clearance using Plastigage®. Follow the manufacturer procedures. Refer to the crankshaft and connecting rod specification chart.
7. Tighten the connecting rod cap nuts to specification. Refer to the torque specification chart later in this section for the proper torque values.
8. Install the remaining piston and rod assemblies.
9. Using a feeler gauge, check connecting rod side clearance.
10. On 2.5L engines, install the balance shaft carrier.
11. Install the oil pump and pick-up.
12. Install the cylinder head.
13. Install the intake manifold.
14. Install the timing chain or belt and the sprockets or gears.
15. Install the timing case cover.
16. Install the engine oil pan.
17. Install the engine in the vehicle.

Freeze Plugs

REMOVAL & INSTALLATION

➧ See Figures 225 and 226

Freeze plugs can be removed with the engine in or out of the vehicle.

Using a blunt tool, such as a drift and hammer, strike the bottom edge of the plug. With the plug rotated, grasp it firmly with pliers and remove it. Do not drive the plug into the block as coolant flow restriction would occur.

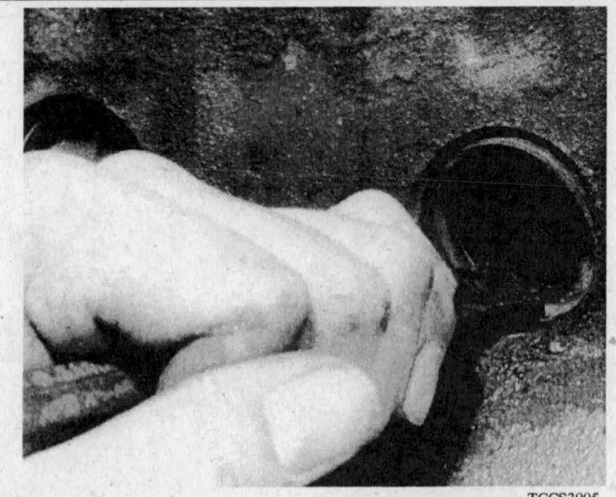
TCCS3905

Fig. 225 Using a punch and hammer, the freeze plug can be loosened in the block

Fig. 226 Once the freeze plug has been loosened, it can be removed from the block

When installing the replacement plug, thoroughly clean the plug bore, removing any old sealant. Coat the new plug with Loctite® Stud Mount, or equivalent. Position the plug on the block and drive it into the block so that the sharp edge is at least 0.020 in. (0.5mm) inside the chamfer. Check the plug for leaks after cooling system refilling.

Engine Block Heater

➧ See Figure 227

REMOVAL & INSTALLATION

1. Disconnect the negative battery cable.
2. Drain the cooling system, including the engine block.
3. Detach the power cord plug from the block heater assembly.
4. Loosen the screw in the center of the heater and pull the heater from the block.

To install:

5. Clean the heater hole in the block and the heater seat.
6. Insert the heater with the element loop facing upward.
7. Tighten the heater retaining screw securely.
8. Refill the cooling system and pressurize the cooling system with a radiator pressure tool. Check for leaks before operating block heater.
9. Connect the negative battery cable.

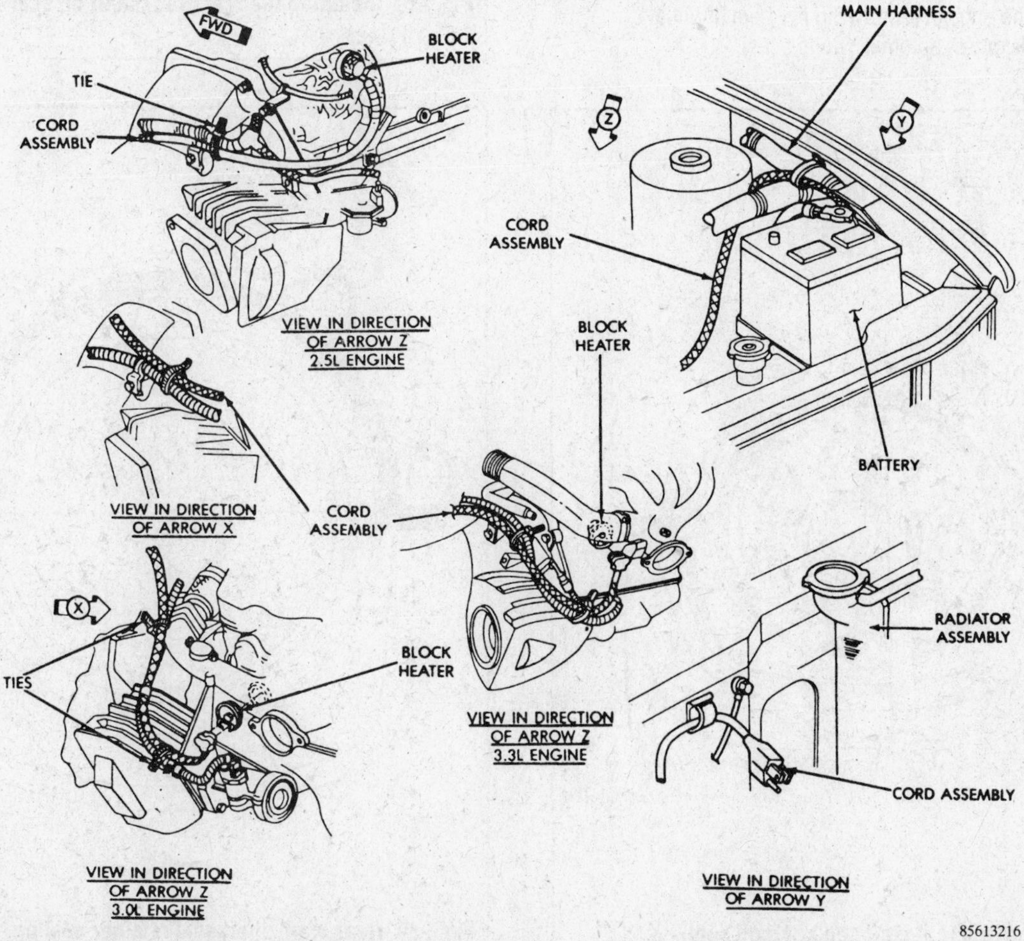

85613216

Fig. 227 Engine block heater system components

Rear Main Seal

REMOVAL & INSTALLATION

2.2L and 2.5L Engines

See Figures 228, 229 and 230

1. With the engine removed from the vehicle, or the transaxle removed from the engine, remove the flywheel (manual transaxles) or the flexplate (automatic transaxles).
2. Pry out rear crankshaft oil seal from seal retainer. Be careful not to nick of damage crankshaft sealing surface or seal retainer.

To install:

3. Place Tool C-4681, or equivalent, on the crankshaft.
4. Lubricate the outer diameter with Loctite Stud N' Bearing Mount (PN. 4057987) or equivalent.
5. Lightly lubricate the seal lip with engine oil, then tap it into place with a plastic or soft faced hammer.
6. Install the flywheel/flexplate and tighten bolts to 70 ft. lbs. (95 Nm).

2.6L Engines

See Figure 231

1. With the engine removed from the vehicle, or the transaxle removed from the engine, remove the flywheel (manual transaxles) or flexplate (automatic transaxles).

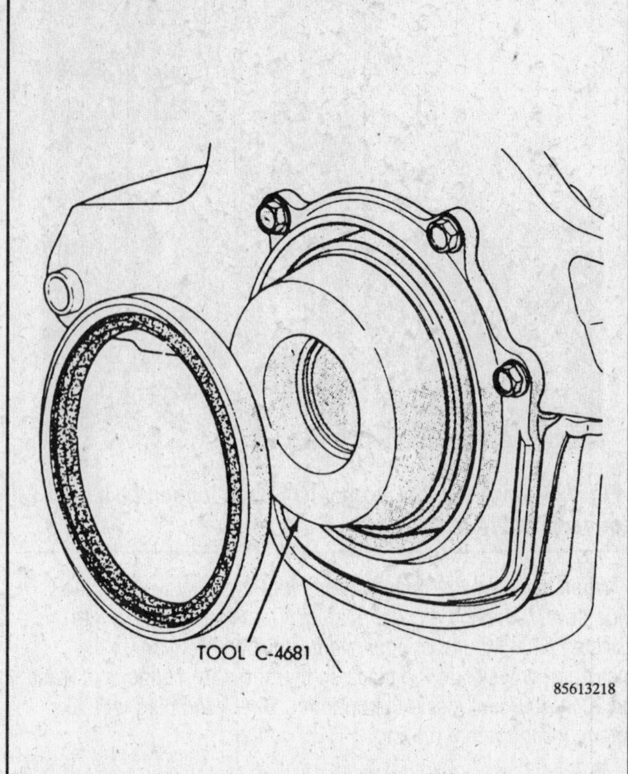

Fig. 229 Installing the rear crankshaft oil seal — 2.2L and 2.5L engines

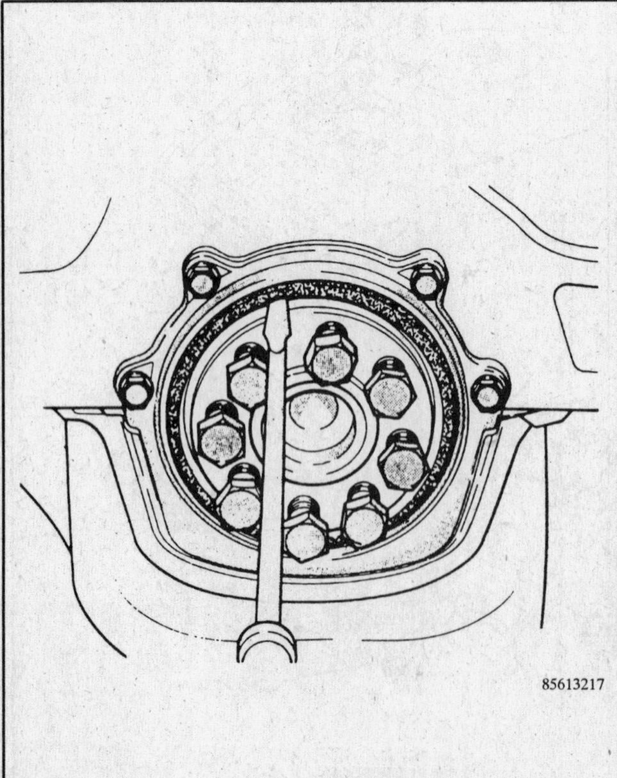

Fig. 228 Removing the rear crankshaft oil seal — 2.2L and 2.5L engines

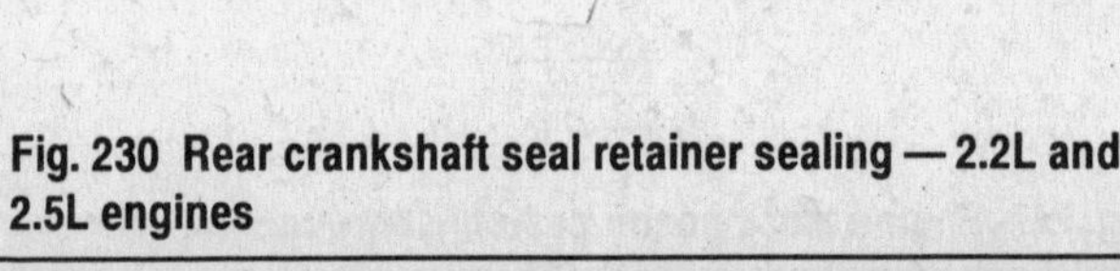

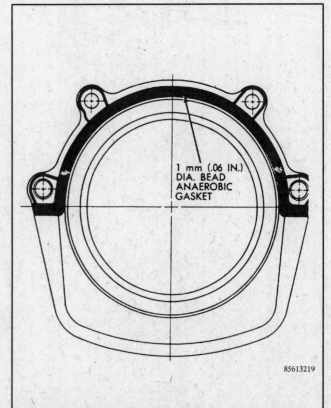

Fig. 230 Rear crankshaft seal retainer sealing — 2.2L and 2.5L engines

2. Remove the rear crankshaft seal retainer.
3. Remove the separator from the retainer, then remove the seal.

To install:

4. Clean all old gasket material from the retainer and engine block surface.
5. Install a new gasket on the retainer.
6. Lightly lubricate the new seal lip with engine oil and install the separator making sure the oil hole is at the bottom of separator.
7. Install flywheel tighten bolts to 70 ft. lbs. (95 Nm).

3.0L, 3.3L and 3.8L Engines

See Figures 232 and 233

1. With the engine removed from the vehicle, or the transaxle removed from the engine, remove the flywheel (manual transaxles) or the flexplate (automatic transaxles).
2. Pry out the rear crankshaft oil seal from the seal retainer. Be careful not to nick or damage the crankshaft sealing surface or seal retainer.

To install:

3. Lightly lubricate the new seal lip with engine oil and install seal in retainer housing using Tool MD998718, or the equivalent.
4. Install the flywheel/flexplate, then tighten the mounting bolts to 70 ft. lbs. (95 Nm).

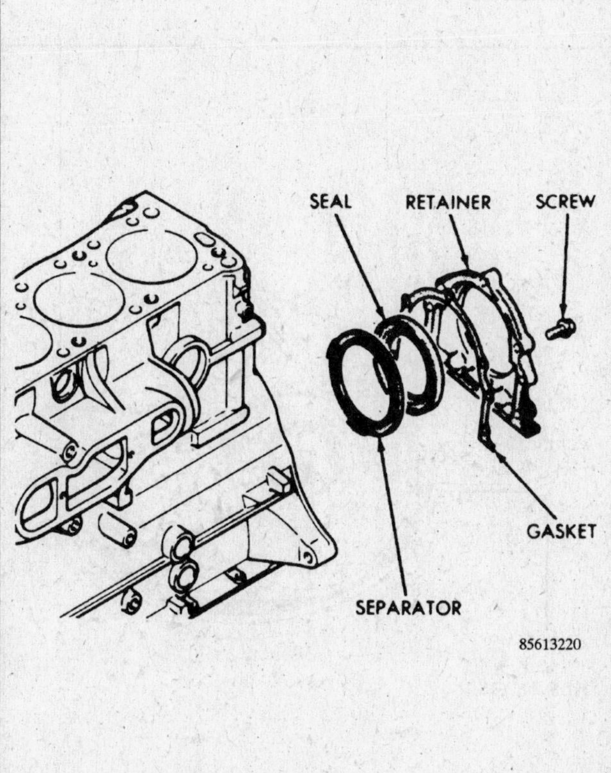

Fig. 231 Rear main oil seal installation — 2.6L engines

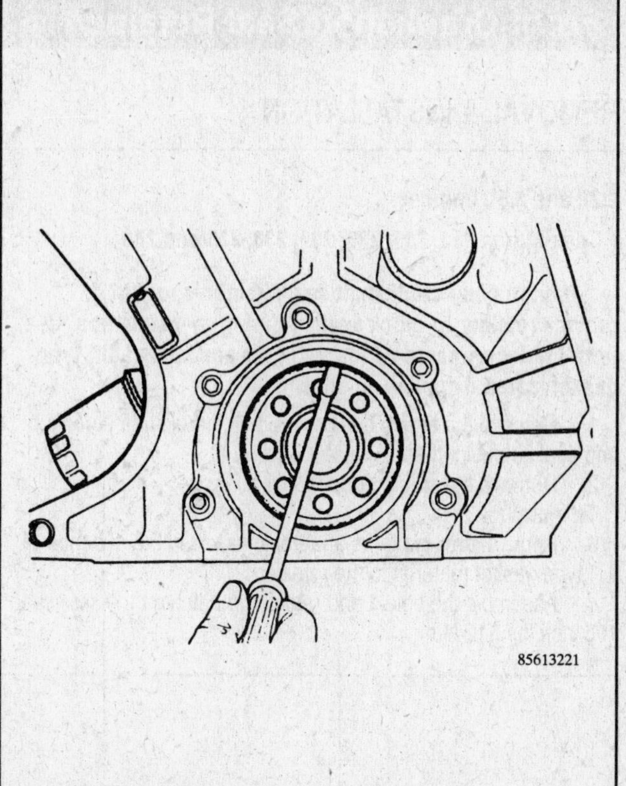

Fig. 232 Removing the rear crankshaft oil seal — 3.3L and 3.8L engines

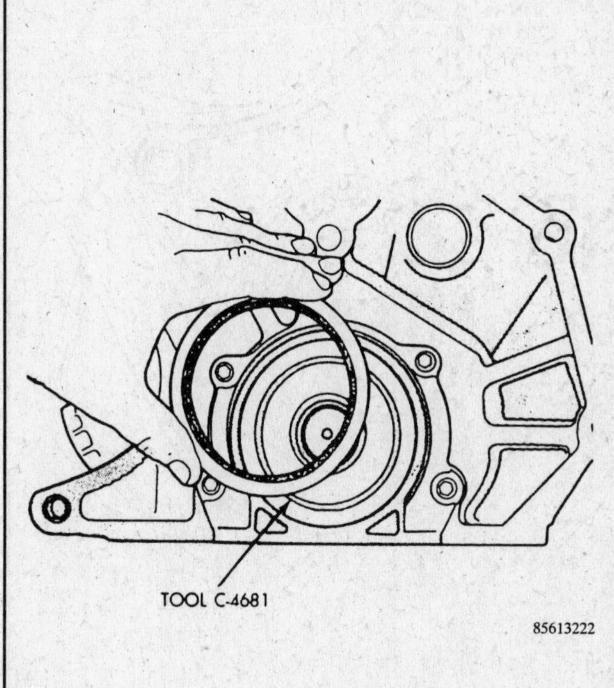

Fig. 233 Installing the rear crankshaft oil seal — 3.3L and 3.8L engines

Front Crankshaft Seal Retainer

REMOVAL & INSTALLATION

2.2L and 2.5L Engines

➧ See Figures 234, 235, 236, 237, 238, 239 and 240

➥ When the rear crankshaft seal retainer is required, provide retainer-to-block sealing during re-installation. Use form-in-place, anaerobic (cures in the absence of air) type gasket material applied as shown.

1. Remove the timing belt covers, belt, crankshaft sprocket and seal as outlined earlier in this section.
2. Remove the shield and retainer screws.

To install:

3. Apply a form-in-place, anaerobic (cures in the absence of air) type gasket material to the retainer.
4. Assemble the shield and retainer and tighten the screws to 105 inch lbs. (12 Nm).

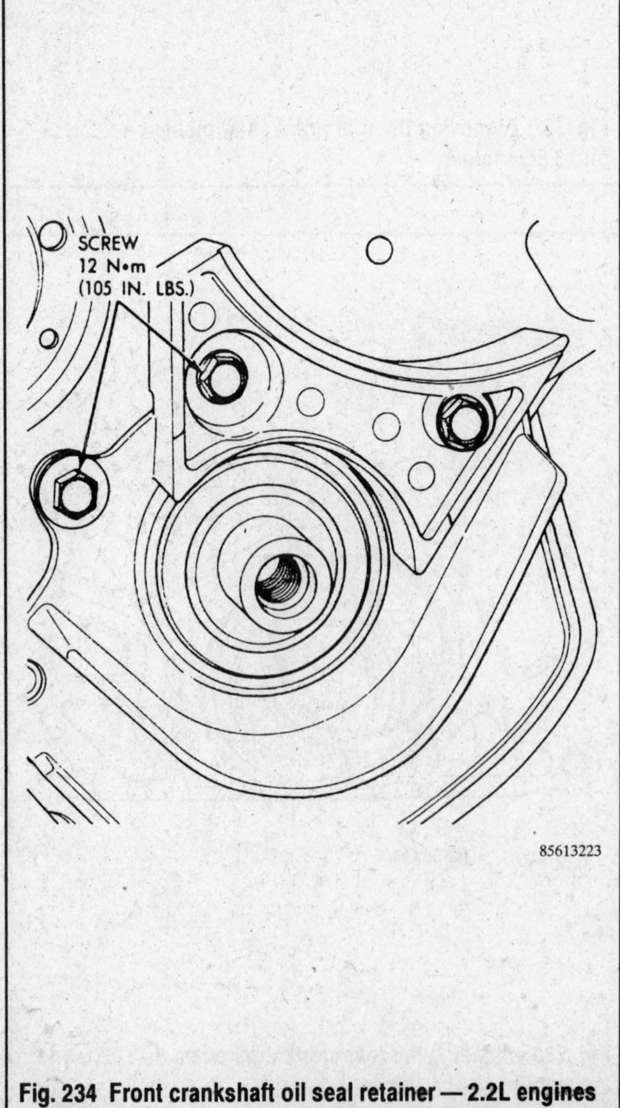

Fig. 234 Front crankshaft oil seal retainer — 2.2L engines

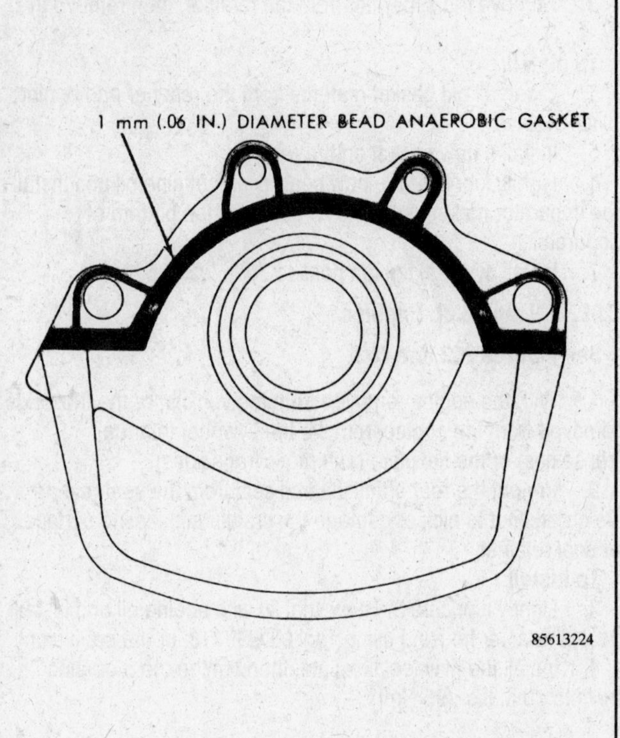

Fig. 235 Front crankshaft oil seal retainer sealing — 2.2L engines

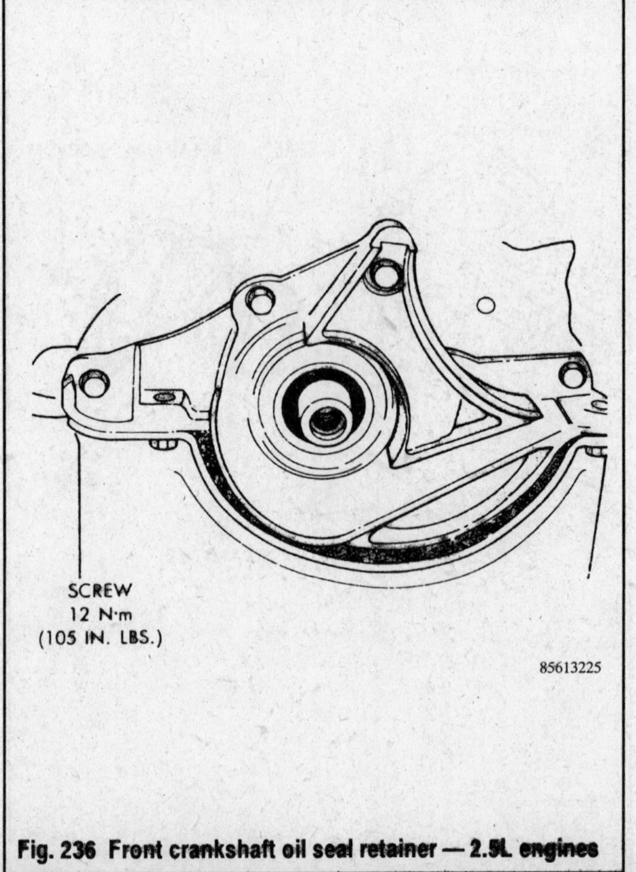

Fig. 236 Front crankshaft oil seal retainer — 2.5L engines

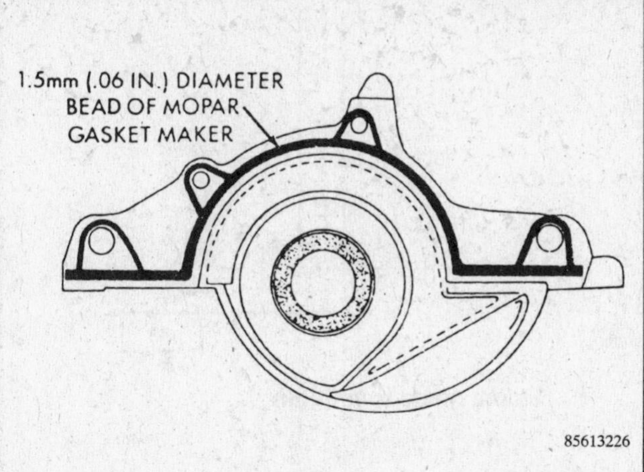

Fig. 237 Front crankshaft oil seal retainer sealing — 2.5L engines

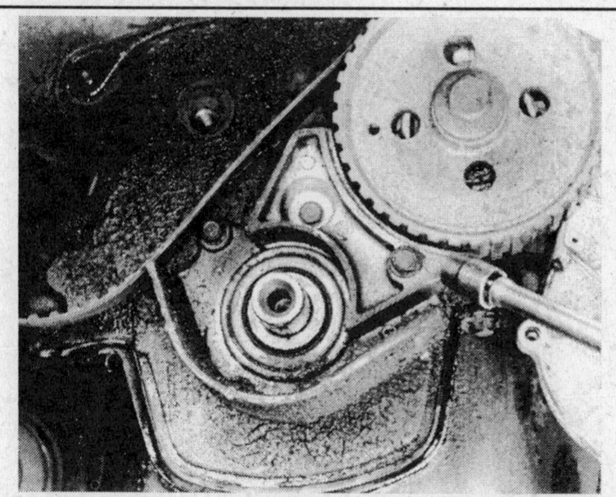

Fig. 238 Removing the snow guard retaining bolts from the front crankshaft oil seal retainer

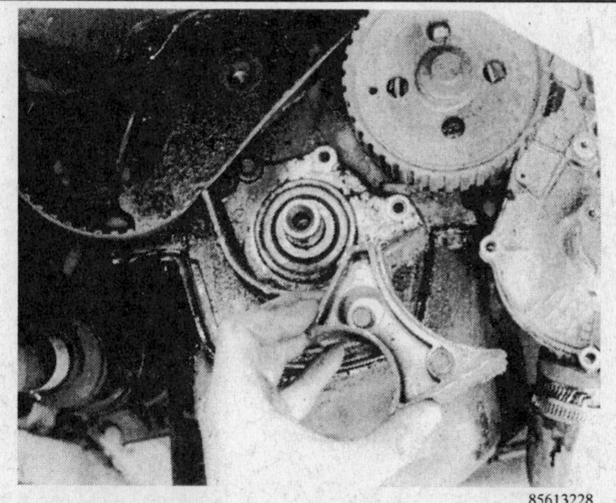

Fig. 239 Removing the snow guard from the front crankshaft oil seal retainer

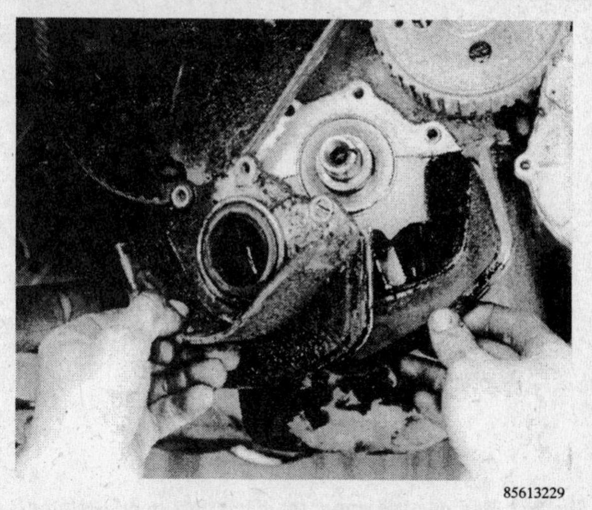

Fig. 240 Removing the front crankshaft oil seal retainer

Crankshaft and Main Bearings

➧ See Figures 241, 242 and 243

Although, crankshaft service can be performed without removing the engine from the vehicle, it is far easier to work on the engine after it has been removed from the vehicle.

REMOVAL & INSTALLATION

1. Remove the engine from vehicle. For more details, refer to the engine removal procedure.
2. Remove the timing case cover, timing belt or chain and sprockets.
3. Remove the flywheel.
4. Remove the engine oil pan.
5. Remove the front crankshaft seal retainer, if applicable. On 3.0L, 3.3L and 3.8L engines, the front crankshaft seal is located in the oil pump assembly.
6. Remove the oil pump assembly on the 3.0L, 3.3L and 3.8L engines.
7. On 2.5L engines, remove the balance shaft carrier assembly.
8. Remove the rear crankshaft oil seal retainer bolts and remove retainer.
9. Before removing the crankshaft, check the crankshaft end-play as follows:
   a. Position a small prybar between a main bearing cap and crankshaft. Move the crankshaft all the way to the rear of its travel.
   b. Position a feeler gauge between the thrust bearing and crankshaft machined surface to determine end-play. Refer to the crankshaft and connecting rod specification chart.
10. Use the following procedure if only crankshaft removal is necessary. If other engine repairs are being performed, complete engine disassembly will be required.
11. Number all connecting rod caps (if not already labeled) to aid during assembly. Remove the connecting rod bearing caps nuts and remove caps.

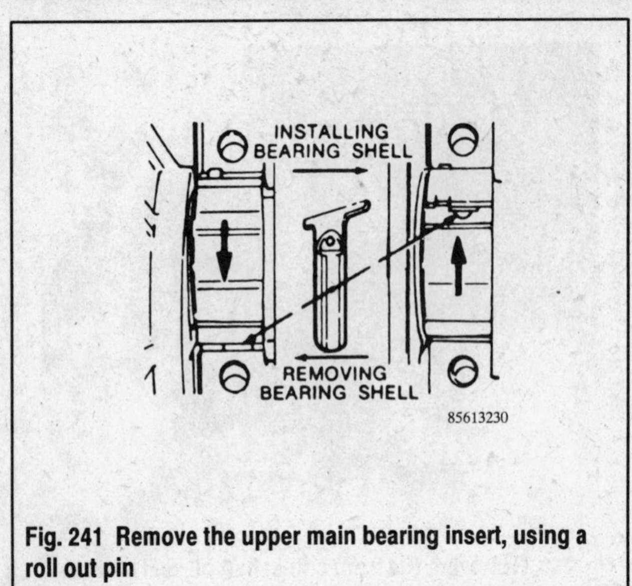

Fig. 241 Remove the upper main bearing insert, using a roll out pin

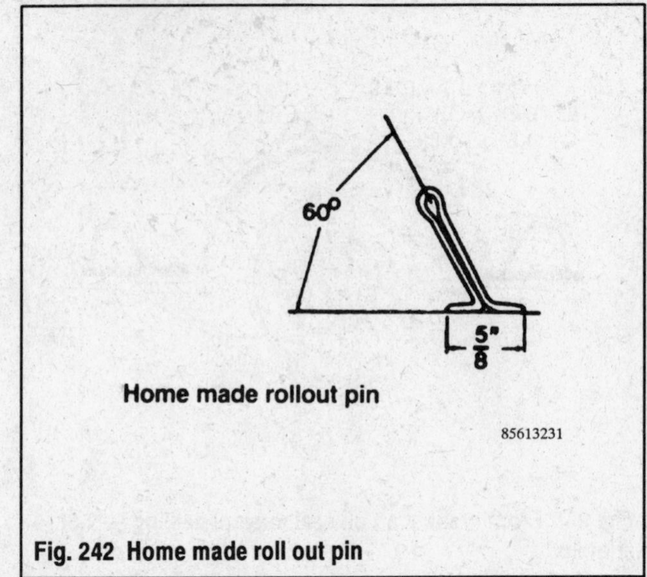

Fig. 242 Home made roll out pin

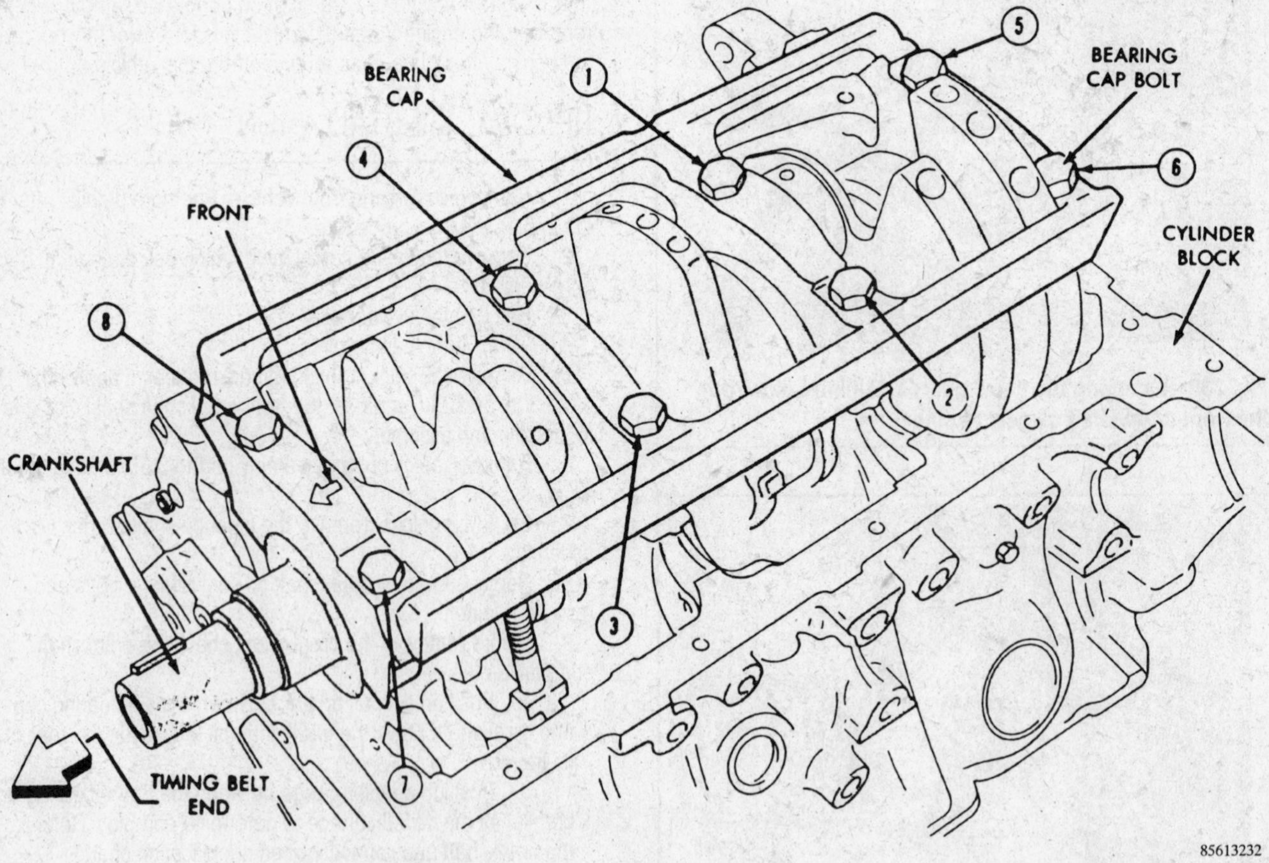

Fig. 243 Installing the crankshaft mono-block main bearing. Tighten the bolts in the sequence shown — 3.0L engines

12. Use 2 pieces of rubber tubing to cover the rod bolts to prevent crankshaft scoring.
13. Tap the piston assembly lightly away from crankshaft. Care should be taken not to damage the connecting rod journals or the threads on the rod cap bolts.
14. Remove the main bearing cap bolts and remove caps. Remove crankshaft.

To install:

15. Install the main bearing shells with the lubrication groove in the cylinder block. Make certain the oil holes are in alignment, and bearing tabs seat in block.
16. Install the thrust bearing into the applicable journal.
17. Oil the bearings and journals with clean, new engine oil, then set the crankshaft into the engine block.
18. Install the lower main bearing shells (without oil grooves) in the lower bearing caps.
19. Check the main or connecting bearing oil clearance as follows:
    a. Wipe oil from bearing shells.
    b. Cut a piece of Plastigage® to the same length as width of the bearing and place it in parallel with the journal.
    c. Install the bearing cap and tighten to specification.

Do not rotate crankshaft or the Plastigage® will be smeared.

    d. Carefully remove the bearing cap and measure the width of the Plastigage® at the widest part using the scale printed on the Plastigage® package. Refer to the crankshaft and connecting rod specification chart for the maximum allowable oil clearance values.

20. Install all main bearing caps with arrows toward the timing chain end of cylinder block.
21. Dip the bolts in fresh, clean engine oil and install the bolts finger-tight. Alternately tighten each bolt to the figure listed in the torque specification chart in this section.
22. Position the connecting rods with new bearing shells against crankshaft. Install lower caps.
23. Before installing the nuts oil the threads. Install the nut on each bolt finger-tight, then alternately tighten each nut to specification. Refer to the torque specification chart later in this section for the proper torque values.
24. On 2.5L engine, install balance shaft carrier assembly.
25. Install the front and rear crankshaft oil seal retainer assembly. Apply a $^{1}/_{16}$ in. (1.5mm) diameter bead of RTV gasket material to the retainers' sealing surfaces.
26. Install the timing sprockets, timing belt/chain and timing case cover. Refer to the applicable procedures earlier in this section.
27. Install the engine oil pan. Refer to Oil Pan Installation procedures.
28. Install the flywheel. Refer to the torque specifications chart at the end of this section.

CLEANING & INSPECTION

1. Inspect the main and connecting rod bearings replace if necessary.
2. Clean the crankshaft oil passages. Check the crankshaft main journals and connecting rod journals for wear or damage.

EXHAUST SYSTEM

See Figures 244, 245 and 246

Safety Precautions

For a number of reasons, exhaust system work can be one of the most dangerous types of work you can do on your vehicle. Always observe the following precautions:

- Support the vehicle extra securely. Not only will you often be working directly under it, but you'll frequently be using a lot of force, say, heavy hammer blows, to dislodge rusted parts. This can cause a vehicle that's improperly supported to shift and possibly fall.
- Wear goggles. Exhaust system parts are always rusty. Metal chips can be dislodged, even when you're only turning rusted bolts. Attempting to pry pipes apart with a chisel makes the chips fly even more frequently.
- If you're using a cutting torch, keep it a great distance from either the fuel tank or lines. Stop what you're doing and feel the temperature of the fuel bearing pipes on the tank frequently. Even slight heat can expand and/or vaporize fuel, resulting in accumulated vapor, or even a liquid leak, near your torch.
- Watch where your hammer blows fall and make sure you hit squarely. You could easily tap a brake or fuel line when you hit an exhaust system part with a glancing blow. Inspect all lines and hoses in the area where you've been working.

CAUTION

Be very careful when working on or near the catalytic converter. External temperatures can reach 1,500°F (816°C) and more, causing severe burns. Removal or installation should be performed only on a cold exhaust system.

A number of special exhaust system tools can be rented from auto supply houses or local stores that rent special equipment. A common one is a tail pipe expander, designed to enable you to join pipes of identical diameter.

It may also be quite helpful to use solvents designed to loosen rusted bolts or flanges. Soaking rusted parts the night before you do the job can speed the work of freeing rusted parts considerably. Remember that these solvents are often flammable. Apply only to parts after they are cool!

Exhaust (Converter/Resonator) Pipe

REMOVAL & INSTALLATION

1. Raise the vehicle and properly support on jackstands.

⁂CAUTION

Be very careful when working on or near the catalytic converter! External temperatures can reach 1500°F (816°C) and more, causing severe burns! Removal or installation should be performed only on a cold exhaust system.

2. Apply penetrating oil to clamp bolts, nuts and connecting points of system to be remove.
3. Remove the nuts and clamp assembly from exhaust pipe to muffler connecting point.
4. Remove the shoulder bolts, springs and nuts attaching exhaust pipe to exhaust manifold.
5. Remove the exhaust pipe/converter assembly from muffler.

To install:

6. Clean the exhaust manifold to exhaust pipe/converter assembly gasket mating surfaces and the end of muffler with a wire brush.
7. Install the exhaust pipe/converter assembly or resonator into muffler. Make certain the key on the converter or resonator pipe bottomed in slot of muffler.
8. Install a new gasket on the exhaust pipe and position exhaust pipe into exhaust manifold. Install springs, shoulder bolts and nuts. Tighten the nuts to 21 ft. lbs. (28 Nm).
9. Align the parts, then install a new clamp assembly at the exhaust pipe and muffler connecting point. Tighten the clamps nuts to 23 ft. lbs. (31 Nm).

Tail Pipe

REMOVAL & INSTALLATION

1. Raise the vehicle and properly support on jackstands.
2. Apply penetrating oil to the clamp bolts, nuts and connecting points of the section of the system to be removed.
3. Remove the support saddle type clamp assembly from the tail pipe-to-muffler connecting point.
4. Remove the U-nut and shoulder bolts from the tail pipe mid-point and rear tail pipe bracket.
5. When removing the tail pipe, raise the rear of vehicle enough to provide clearance between pipe and rear axle parts.
6. Remove the tail pipe from muffler.

To install:

7. Clean the muffler mating surface with a wire brush.
8. Replace broken or worn insulators, supports or attaching parts.
9. Loosely assemble the tail pipe to muffler, mid-point support and tail pipe bracket. Make certain slot in tail pipe is keyed with key in muffler.
10. Align parts and install support saddle type clamp tighten nuts to 28 ft. lbs. (38 Nm).

Muffler

REMOVAL & INSTALLATION

1. Raise the vehicle and properly support on jackstands.
2. Apply penetrating oil to clamp bolts, nuts and connecting points of system to be removed.
3. Disconnect the tail pipe from the muffler assembly. Refer to the tail pipe removal procedure earlier in this section.
4. Remove nuts and clamp from exhaust pipe and muffler connection and remove the muffler.

To install:

5. Clean the exhaust pipe and tail pipe mating surfaces with a wire brush.
6. Replace broken or worn insulators, supports or attaching parts.
7. Loosely assemble the muffler to exhaust pipe and tail pipe. Make certain keys are bottomed in slots of muffler and pipes.
8. Align parts and install support saddle type clamp between tail pipe and muffler connecting point. Tighten nuts to 28 ft. lbs. (38 Nm).
9. Install clamp assembly and nuts at exhaust pipe and muffler connecting point and tighten to 25 ft. lbs. (34 Nm).

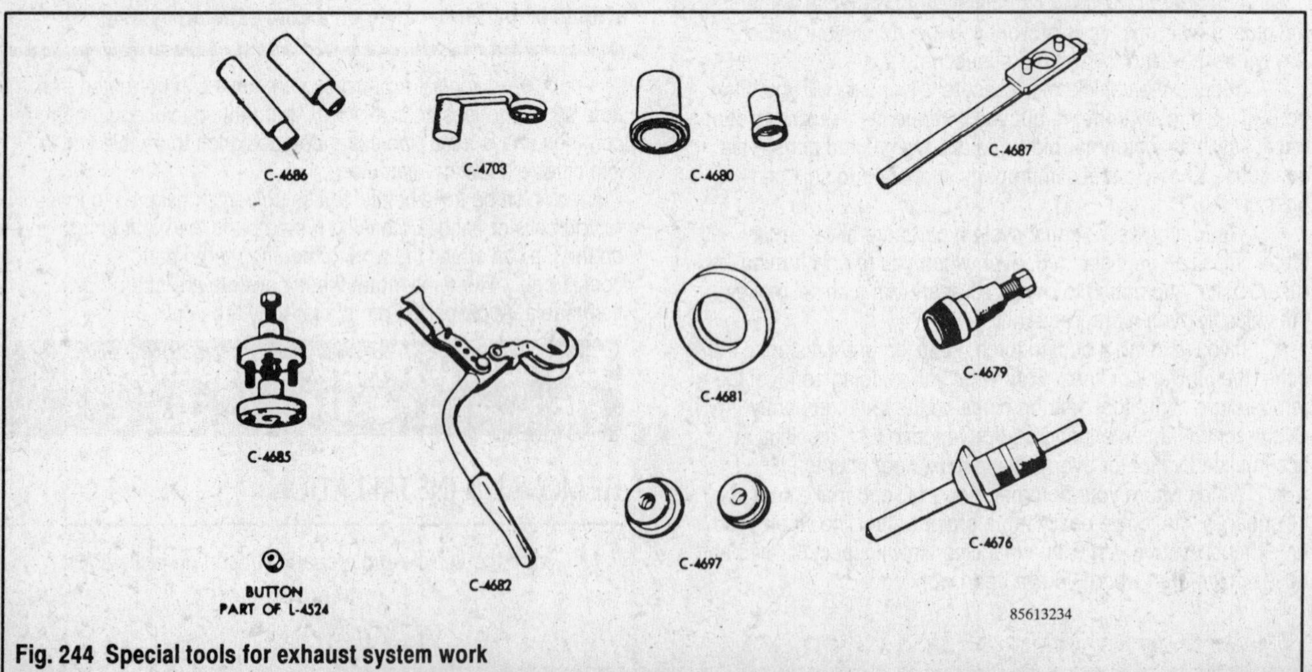

Fig. 244 Special tools for exhaust system work

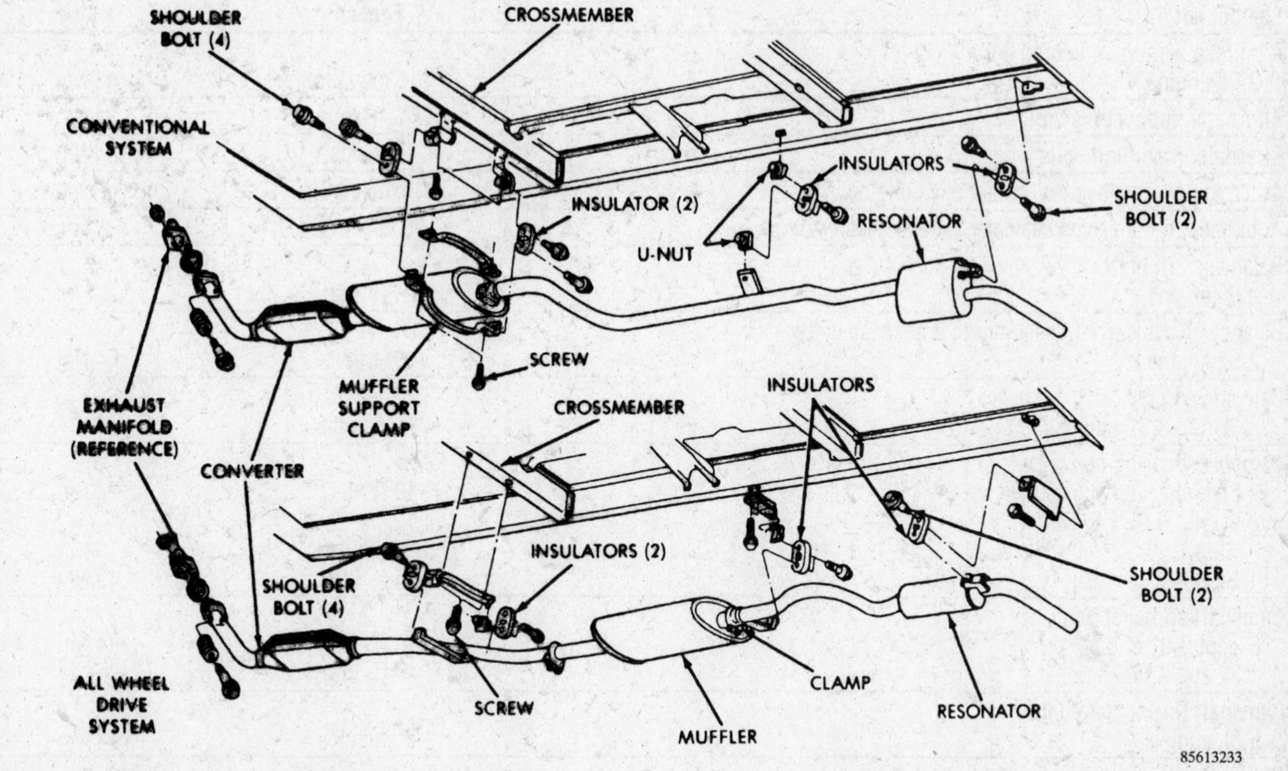

Fig. 245 Exhaust system components

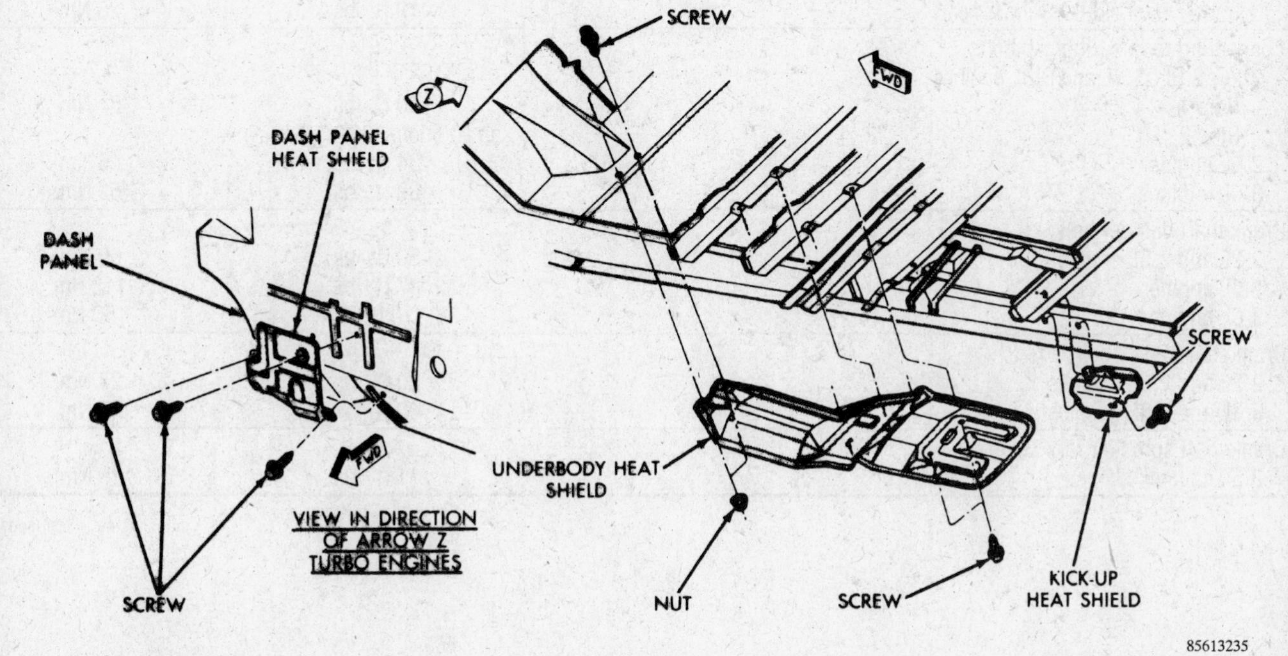

Fig. 246 Exhaust system heat shield mounting

TORQUE SPECIFICATIONS

Component	English	Metric
Air intake plenum attaching bolts		
3.0L engine	115 inch lbs.	13 Nm
Alternator support bracket	40 ft. lbs.	54 Nm
Alternator mounting bolts	40 ft. lbs.	54 Nm
Automatic transmission oil cooler mounting bolts	35 inch lbs.	4 Nm
Automatic transmission oil cooler lines-to-cooler clamps	16 inch lbs.	2 Nm
Balance shaft bolt		
2.5L engine	21 ft. lbs.	29 Nm
Balance shafts carrier assembly-to-crankcase bolts		
2.5L engine	40 ft. lbs.	54 Nm
Cam sensor bolt		
3.3L and 3.8L engines	105 inch lbs.	12 Nm
Camshaft bearing cap bolts		
2.2L and 2.5L engines	18 ft. lbs.	24 Nm
2.6L and 3.0L engines		
Step 1	85 inch lbs.	10 Nm
Step 2	15 ft. lbs.	19 Nm
Camshaft sprocket bolt		
Except 3.3L engine	40 ft. lbs.	54 Nm
3.3L and 3.8L engines	40 ft. lbs.	54 Nm
Camshaft thrust plate bolts		
3.3L engine	105 inch lbs.	12 Nm
Carburetor air heater-to-manifold		
2.6L engine	80 inch lbs.	9 Nm
Catalytic converter-to-manifold		
3.0L engine	24 ft. lbs.	32 Nm
Combination Manifold		
2.2L and 2.5L engines		
Exhaust manifold-to-cylinder head	17 ft. lbs.	23 Nm
Intake manifold-to-cylinder head	19 ft. lbs.	26 Nm
Connecting rod bearing cap bolts		
2.2L, 2.5L, 3.3L and 3.8L engines		
Step 1	40 ft. lbs.	54 Nm
Step 2	an additional 90° (1/4) turn	
2.6L engine	34 ft. lbs.	46 Nm
3.0L engine	38 ft. lbs.	52 Nm
Crankshaft damper bolt		
2.2L and 2.5L engines	50 ft. lbs.	68 Nm
2.6L engine	87 ft. lbs.	118 Nm
3.0L engine	110 ft. lbs.	150 Nm
Crankshaft pulley bolt		
2.2L and 2.5L engines	20 ft. lbs.	27 Nm
3.3L and 3.8L engines	40 ft. lbs.	54 Nm
Crankshaft sprocket Torx® screws		
2.5L engine	11 ft. lbs.	15 Nm

85613C07

TORQUE SPECIFICATIONS

Component	English	Metric
Cylinder Head		
2.2L and 2.5L engines		
Step 1	45 ft. lbs.	61 Nm
Step 2	65 ft. lbs.	88 Nm
Step 3	additional 90° (1/4) turn	
2.6L engine		
Step 1	34 ft. lbs.	40 Nm
Step 2	69 ft. lbs.	94 Nm
3.0L engine		
Step 1	30 ft. lbs.	41 Nm
Step 2	50 ft. lbs.	68 Nm
Step 3	70 ft. lbs.	95 Nm
3.3L and 3.8L engines		
8 shorter bolts first		
Step 1	45 ft. lbs.	61 Nm
Step 2	65 ft. lbs.	88 Nm
Step 3	65 ft. lbs.	88 Nm
Step 4	an additional 90° (1/4) turn	
2 longer bolts next	25 ft. lbs.	33 Nm
Distributor drive gear bolt		
2.6L engine	40 ft. lbs.	54 Nm
EGR tube flange-to-intake plenum		
3.0L engine	15 ft. lbs.	20 Nm
Engine-to-transaxle mounting bolts	70 ft. lbs.	95 Nm
Exhaust crossover pipe-to-manifold		
3.0L engine	51 ft. lbs.	69 Nm
Exhaust Manifold		
All exc. 2.6L engine	17 ft. lbs.	23 Nm
2.6L engine	13 ft. lbs.	18 Nm
Exhaust pipe-to-manifold		
3.0L engine	20 ft. lbs.	27 Nm
Exhaust pipe-to-exhaust manifold nuts	21 ft. lbs.	29 Nm
Exhaust pipe-to-muffler clamp nuts	23 ft. lbs.	31 Nm
Exhaust system saddle type clamp nuts	28 ft. lbs.	38 Nm
Flywheel/flex plate bolts		
All engines	70 ft. lbs.	95 Nm
Front engine mount	40 ft. lbs.	54 Nm
Fuel line-to-fuel rail clamps		
3.0L engine	10 inch lbs.	1 Nm
Fuel pressure regulator hose clamps		
3.0L engine	10 inch lbs.	1 Nm
Fuel pressure regulator mounting bolts		
3.0L engine	95 inch lbs.	11 Nm
Fuel rail bracket screws		
2.2L and 2.5L engines	21 ft. lbs.	28 Nm
Fuel supply and return tube holddown bolt		
3.0L engine	95 inch lbs.	11 Nm
Heat shield-to-manifold		
2.6L engine	80 inch lbs.	9 Nm
3.0L engine	10 ft. lbs.	14 Nm
Idler pulley-to-engine bracket bolts		
3.3L engine	40 ft. lbs.	54 Nm
Ignition coil mounting bolts	105 inch lbs.	12 Nm
Injector rail attaching bolts		
3.0L engine	115 inch lbs.	13 Nm

85613C08

TORQUE SPECIFICATIONS

Component	English	Metric
Intake Manifold		
2.2L and 2.5L engines	17 ft. lbs.	23 Nm
2.6L engine	13 ft. lbs.	18 Nm
3.0L engine	17 ft. lbs.	23 Nm
3.3L and 3.8L engines		
Step 1	10 inch lbs.	1 Nm
Step 2	17 ft. lbs.	23 Nm
Step 3	17 ft. lbs.	23 Nm
Intake manifold and retainers		
3.3L and 3.8L engines	105 inch lbs.	12 Nm
Intermediate shaft retainer screws		
2.2L and 2.5L engines	105 inch lbs.	12 Nm
Main bearing cap bolts		
2.2L, 2.5L, 3.3L and 3.8L engines		
Step 1	30 ft. lbs.	41 Nm
Step 2	an additional 90° (1/4) turn	
2.6L engine	58 ft. lbs.	79 Nm
3.0L engine	60 ft. lbs.	82 Nm
Oil Pan		
2.2L engine	15 ft. lbs.	21 Nm
2.5L engine		
M8 screws	15 ft. lbs.	21 Nm
M6 screws	105 inch lbs.	12 Nm
2.6L engine		
Oil pan-to-block	60 inch lbs.	7 Nm
Oil pan-to-timing case	53 inch lbs.	6 Nm
3.0L engine	50 inch lbs.	6 Nm
3.3L and 3.8L engines	105 inch lbs.	12 Nm
Oil Pump attaching bolts		
2.2L and 2.5L engines	15 ft. lbs.	21 Nm
3.0L engine	10 ft. lbs.	14 Nm
Oil pump cover screws		
3.3L and 3.8L engines	105 inch lbs.	12 Nm
Oil pump sprocket bolt		
2.6L engine	25 ft. lbs.	34 Nm
Radiator mounting bolts	105 inch lbs.	12 Nm
Radiator hose-to-thermostat housing	35 inch lbs.	4 Nm
Radiator hose-to-radiator clamps	to 35 inch lbs.	4 Nm
Right engine mount	20 ft. lbs.	27 Nm
Rocker arm and shaft assembly bolts		
3.3L and 3.8L engines	21 ft. lbs.	28 Nm
Rocker (Valve) Cover		
2.2L engine	105 inch lbs.	12 Nm
2.5L engine	105 inch lbs.	12 Nm
2.6L engine	55 inch lbs.	6 Nm
3.0L engine	68 inch lbs.	7 Nm
3.3L and 3.8L engines	105 inch lbs.	12 Nm
Silent shaft chain tensioner bolt		
2.6L engine	13 ft. lbs.	18 Nm
Thermostat housing		
All engines	15 ft. lbs.	20 Nm
Throttle body-to-intake manifold screws		
2.2L and 2.5L engines	21 ft. lbs.	28 Nm
Timing belt cover screws		
3.0L engine	10 ft. lbs.	14 Nm

85613C09

TORQUE SPECIFICATIONS

Component	English	Metric
Timing belt tensioner lock nut		
2.2L and 2.5L engines	45 ft. lbs.	61 Nm
3.0L engine	23 ft. lbs.	31 Nm
Timing chain case cover		
2.6L engine	13 ft. lbs.	18 Nm
Timing chain cover screws		
2.5L engine	105 inch lbs.	12 Nm
3.3L and 3.8L engines		
M8x1.25 bolt	20 ft. lbs.	27 Nm
M10x1.50 bolt	40 ft. lbs.	54 Nm
Timing chain guide nut		
2.5L engine	105 inch lbs.	12 Nm
Timing chain tensioner adjustment and pivot bolts		
2.5L engine	105 inch lbs.	12 Nm
Torque converter-to-flex plate bolts	40 ft. lbs.	54 Nm
Turbocharger-to-exhaust manifold	40 ft. lbs.	54 Nm
Turbocharger articulated joint shoulder bolts	21 ft. lbs.	28 Nm
Turbocharger connector tube clamps	30 inch lbs.	41 Nm
Turbocharger inlet tube-to-throttle body tube clamp	30 inch lbs.	3 Nm
Turbocharger inlet coolant tube-to-engine block	30 ft. lbs.	41 Nm
Turbocharger mounting screws		
Block screw	40 ft. lbs.	54 Nm
Housing screw	20 ft. lbs.	27 Nm
Turbocharger oil feed line nuts	10 ft. lbs.	14 Nm
Turbocharger oil drain-back hose clamps	30 inch lbs.	3 Nm
Turbocharger outlet-to-exhaust manifold nuts	30 ft. lbs.	41 Nm
Upper intake manifold bolts		
3.3L and 3.8L engines	21 ft. lbs.	28 Nm
Upper intake manifold bracket and strut bolts		
3.3L and 3.8L engines	40 ft. lbs.	54 Nm
Water Pump		
2.2L and 2.5L engines		
3 upper bolts	20 ft. lbs.	27 Nm
1 lower bolt	50 ft. lbs.	68 Nm
2.6L and 3.0L engines	20 ft. lbs.	27 Nm
3.3L and 3.8L engines	105 inch lbs.	12 Nm
Water pump pulley screws		
2.2L and 2.5L engine	105 inch lbs.	12 Nm

85613C10

USING A VACUUM GAUGE

White needle = steady needle ***Dark needle = drifting needle***

The vacuum gauge is one of the most useful and easy-to-use diagnostic tools. It is inexpensive, easy to hook up, and provides valuable information about the condition of your engine.

Indication: Normal engine in good condition

Gauge reading: Steady, from 17–22 in./Hg.

Indication: Sticking valve or ignition miss

Gauge reading: Needle fluctuates from 15–20 in./Hg. at idle

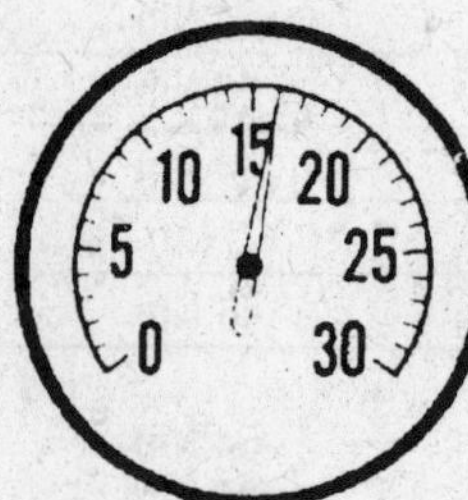

Indication: Late ignition or valve timing, low compression, stuck throttle valve, leaking carburetor or manifold gasket.

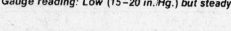

Gauge reading: Low (15–20 in./Hg.) but steady

Indication: Improper carburetor adjustment, or minor intake leak at carburetor or manifold

NOTE: Bad fuel injector O-rings may also cause this reading.

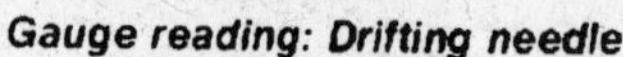

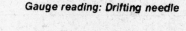

Gauge reading: Drifting needle

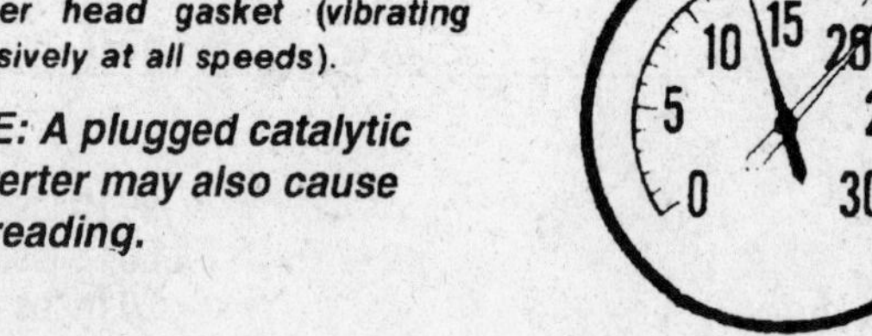

Indication: Weak valve springs, worn valve stem guides, or leaky cylinder head gasket (vibrating excessively at all speeds).

NOTE: A plugged catalytic converter may also cause this reading.

Gauge reading: Needle fluctuates as engine speed increases

Indication: Burnt valve or improper valve clearance. The needle will drop when the defective valve operates.

Gauge reading: Steady needle, but drops regularly

Indication: Choked muffler or obstruction in system. Speed up the engine. Choked muffler will exhibit a slow drop of vacuum to zero.

Gauge reading: Gradual drop in reading at idle

Indication: Worn valve guides

Gauge reading: Needle vibrates excessively at idle, but steadies as engine speed increases

TCCS3C01

Troubleshooting Engine Mechanical Problems

Problem	Cause	Solution
External oil leaks	• Cylinder head cover RTV sealant broken or improperly seated	• Replace sealant; inspect cylinder head cover sealant flange and cylinder head sealant surface for distortion and cracks
	• Oil filler cap leaking or missing	• Replace cap
	• Oil filter gasket broken or improperly seated	• Replace oil filter
	• Oil pan side gasket broken, improperly seated or opening in RTV sealant	• Replace gasket or repair opening in sealant; inspect oil pan gasket flange for distortion
	• Oil pan front oil seal broken or improperly seated	• Replace seal; inspect timing case cover and oil pan seal flange for distortion
	• Oil pan rear oil seal broken or improperly seated	• Replace seal; inspect oil pan rear oil seal flange; inspect rear main bearing cap for cracks, plugged oil return channels, or distortion in seal groove
	• Timing case cover oil seal broken or improperly seated	• Replace seal
	• Excess oil pressure because of restricted PCV valve	• Replace PCV valve
	• Oil pan drain plug loose or has stripped threads	• Repair as necessary and tighten
	• Rear oil gallery plug loose	• Use appropriate sealant on gallery plug and tighten
	• Rear camshaft plug loose or improperly seated	• Seat camshaft plug or replace and seal, as necessary
Excessive oil consumption	• Oil level too high	• Drain oil to specified level
	• Oil with wrong viscosity being used	• Replace with specified oil
	• PCV valve stuck closed	• Replace PCV valve
	• Valve stem oil deflectors (or seals) are damaged, missing, or incorrect type	• Replace valve stem oil deflectors
	• Valve stems or valve guides worn	• Measure stem-to-guide clearance and repair as necessary
	• Poorly fitted or missing valve cover baffles	• Replace valve cover
	• Piston rings broken or missing	• Replace broken or missing rings
	• Scuffed piston	• Replace piston
	• Incorrect piston ring gap	• Measure ring gap, repair as necessary
	• Piston rings sticking or excessively loose in grooves	• Measure ring side clearance, repair as necessary
	• Compression rings installed upside down	• Repair as necessary
	• Cylinder walls worn, scored, or glazed	• Repair as necessary

TCCS3C02

Troubleshooting Engine Mechanical Problems

Problem	Cause	Solution
Excessive oil consumption (cont.)	• Piston ring gaps not properly staggered	• Repair as necessary
	• Excessive main or connecting rod bearing clearance	• Measure bearing clearance, repair as necessary
No oil pressure	• Low oil level	• Add oil to correct level
	• Oil pressure gauge, warning lamp or sending unit inaccurate	• Replace oil pressure gauge or warning lamp
	• Oil pump malfunction	• Replace oil pump
	• Oil pressure relief valve sticking	• Remove and inspect oil pressure relief valve assembly
	• Oil passages on pressure side of pump obstructed	• Inspect oil passages for obstruction
	• Oil pickup screen or tube obstructed	• Inspect oil pickup for obstruction
	• Loose oil inlet tube	• Tighten or seal inlet tube
Low oil pressure	• Low oil level	• Add oil to correct level
	• Inaccurate gauge, warning lamp or sending unit	• Replace oil pressure gauge or warning lamp
	• Oil excessively thin because of dilution, poor quality, or improper grade	• Drain and refill crankcase with recommended oil
	• Excessive oil temperature	• Correct cause of overheating engine
	• Oil pressure relief spring weak or sticking	• Remove and inspect oil pressure relief valve assembly
	• Oil inlet tube and screen assembly has restriction or air leak	• Remove and inspect oil inlet tube and screen assembly. (Fill inlet tube with lacquer thinner to locate leaks.)
	• Excessive oil pump clearance	• Measure clearances
	• Excessive main, rod, or camshaft bearing clearance	• Measure bearing clearances, repair as necessary
High oil pressure	• Improper oil viscosity	• Drain and refill crankcase with correct viscosity oil
	• Oil pressure gauge or sending unit inaccurate	• Replace oil pressure gauge
	• Oil pressure relief valve sticking closed	• Remove and inspect oil pressure relief valve assembly
Main bearing noise	• Insufficient oil supply	• Inspect for low oil level and low oil pressure
	• Main bearing clearance excessive	• Measure main bearing clearance, repair as necessary
	• Bearing insert missing	• Replace missing insert
	• Crankshaft end-play excessive	• Measure end-play, repair as necessary
	• Improperly tightened main bearing cap bolts	• Tighten bolts with specified torque
	• Loose flywheel or drive plate	• Tighten flywheel or drive plate attaching bolts
	• Loose or damaged vibration damper	• Repair as necessary

TCCS3C03

Troubleshooting Engine Mechanical Problems

Problem	Cause	Solution
Connecting rod bearing noise	• Insufficient oil supply	• Inspect for low oil level and low oil pressure
	• Carbon build-up on piston	• Remove carbon from piston crown
	• Bearing clearance excessive or bearing missing	• Measure clearance, repair as necessary
	• Crankshaft connecting rod journal out-of-round	• Measure journal dimensions, repair or replace as necessary
	• Misaligned connecting rod or cap	• Repair as necessary
	• Connecting rod bolts tightened improperly	• Tighten bolts with specified torque
Piston noise	• Piston-to-cylinder wall clearance excessive (scuffed piston)	• Measure clearance and examine piston
	• Cylinder walls excessively tapered or out-of-round	• Measure cylinder wall dimensions, rebore cylinder
	• Piston ring broken	• Replace all rings on piston
	• Loose or seized piston pin	• Measure piston-to-pin clearance, repair as necessary
	• Connecting rods misaligned	• Measure rod alignment, straighten or replace
	• Piston ring side clearance excessively loose or tight	• Measure ring side clearance, repair as necessary
	• Carbon build-up on piston is excessive	• Remove carbon from piston
Valve actuating component noise	• Insufficient oil supply	• Check for: (a) Low oil level (b) Low oil pressure (c) Wrong hydraulic tappets (d) Restricted oil gallery (e) Excessive tappet to bore clearance
	• Rocker arms or pivots worn	• Replace worn rocker arms or pivots
	• Foreign objects or chips in hydraulic tappets	• Clean tappets
	• Excessive tappet leak-down	• Replace valve tappet
	• Tappet face worn	• Replace tappet; inspect corresponding cam lobe for wear
	• Broken or cocked valve springs	• Properly seat cocked springs; replace broken springs
	• Stem-to-guide clearance excessive	• Measure stem-to-guide clearance, repair as required
	• Valve bent	• Replace valve
	• Loose rocker arms	• Check and repair as necessary
	• Valve seat runout excessive	• Regrind valve seat/valves
	• Missing valve lock	• Install valve lock
	• Excessive engine oil	• Correct oil level

TCCS3C04

Troubleshooting Engine Performance

Problem	Cause	Solution
Hard starting (engine cranks normally)	• Faulty engine control system component	• Repair or replace as necessary
	• Faulty fuel pump	• Replace fuel pump
	• Faulty fuel system component	• Repair or replace as necessary
	• Faulty ignition coil	• Test and replace as necessary
	• Improper spark plug gap	• Adjust gap
	• Incorrect ignition timing	• Adjust timing
	• Incorrect valve timing	• Check valve timing; repair as necessary
Rough idle or stalling	• Incorrect curb or fast idle speed	• Adjust curb or fast idle speed (If possible)
	• Incorrect ignition timing	• Adjust timing to specification
	• Improper feedback system operation	• Refer to Chapter 4
	• Faulty EGR valve operation	• Test EGR system and replace as necessary
	• Faulty PCV valve air flow	• Test PCV valve and replace as necessary
	• Faulty TAC vacuum motor or valve	• Repair as necessary
	• Air leak into manifold vacuum	• Inspect manifold vacuum connections and repair as necessary
	• Faulty distributor rotor or cap	• Replace rotor or cap (Distributor systems only)
	• Improperly seated valves	• Test cylinder compression, repair as necessary
	• Incorrect ignition wiring	• Inspect wiring and correct as necessary
	• Faulty ignition coil	• Test coil and replace as necessary
	• Restricted air vent or idle passages	• Clean passages
	• Restricted air cleaner	• Clean or replace air cleaner filter element
Faulty low-speed operation	• Restricted idle air vents and passages	• Clean air vents and passages
	• Restricted air cleaner	• Clean or replace air cleaner filter element
	• Faulty spark plugs	• Clean or replace spark plugs
	• Dirty, corroded, or loose ignition secondary circuit wire connections	• Clean or tighten secondary circuit wire connections
	• Improper feedback system operation	• Refer to Chapter 4
	• Faulty ignition coil high voltage wire	• Replace ignition coil high voltage wire (Distributor systems only)
	• Faulty distributor cap	• Replace cap (Distributor systems only)
Faulty acceleration	• Incorrect ignition timing	• Adjust timing
	• Faulty fuel system component	• Repair or replace as necessary
	• Faulty spark plug(s)	• Clean or replace spark plug(s)
	• Improperly seated valves	• Test cylinder compression, repair as necessary
	• Faulty ignition coil	• Test coil and replace as necessary

TCCS3C05

Troubleshooting Engine Performance

Problem	Cause	Solution
Faulty acceleration (cont.)	• Improper feedback system operation	• Refer to Chapter 4
Faulty high speed operation	• Incorrect ignition timing	• Adjust timing (if possible)
	• Faulty advance mechanism	• Check advance mechanism and repair as necessary (Distributor systems only)
	• Low fuel pump volume	• Replace fuel pump
	• Wrong spark plug air gap or wrong plug	• Adjust air gap or install correct plug
	• Partially restricted exhaust manifold, exhaust pipe, catalytic converter, muffler, or tailpipe	• Eliminate restriction
	• Restricted vacuum passages	• Clean passages
	• Restricted air cleaner	• Cleaner or replace filter element as necessary
	• Faulty distributor rotor or cap	• Replace rotor or cap (Distributor systems only)
	• Faulty ignition coil	• Test coil and replace as necessary
	• Improperly seated valve(s)	• Test cylinder compression, repair as necessary
	• Faulty valve spring(s)	• Inspect and test valve spring tension, replace as necessary
	• Incorrect valve timing	• Check valve timing and repair as necessary
	• Intake manifold restricted	• Remove restriction or replace manifold
	• Worn distributor shaft	• Replace shaft (Distributor systems only)
	• Improper feedback system operation	• Refer to Chapter 4
Misfire at all speeds	• Faulty spark plug(s)	• Clean or relace spark plug(s)
	• Faulty spark plug wire(s)	• Replace as necessary
	• Faulty distributor cap or rotor	• Replace cap or rotor (Distributor systems only)
	• Faulty ignition coil	• Test coil and replace as necessary
	• Primary ignition circuit shorted or open intermittently	• Troubleshoot primary circuit and repair as necessary
	• Improperly seated valve(s)	• Test cylinder compression, repair as necessary
	• Faulty hydraulic tappet(s)	• Clean or replace tappet(s)
	• Improper feedback system operation	• Refer to Chapter 4
	• Faulty valve spring(s)	• Inspect and test valve spring tension, repair as necessary
	• Worn camshaft lobes	• Replace camshaft
	• Air leak into manifold	• Check manifold vacuum and repair as necessary
	• Fuel pump volume or pressure low	• Replace fuel pump
	• Blown cylinder head gasket	• Replace gasket
	• Intake or exhaust manifold passage(s) restricted	• Pass chain through passage(s) and repair as necessary
Power not up to normal	• Incorrect ignition timing	• Adjust timing
	• Faulty distributor rotor	• Replace rotor (Distributor systems only)

TCCS3C06

Troubleshooting Engine Performance

Problem	Cause	Solution
Power not up to normal (cont.)	• Incorrect spark plug gap	• Adjust gap
	• Faulty fuel pump	• Replace fuel pump
	• Faulty fuel pump	• Replace fuel pump
	• Incorrect valve timing	• Check valve timing and repair as necessary
	• Faulty ignition coil	• Test coil and replace as necessary
	• Faulty ignition wires	• Test wires and replace as necessary
	• Improperly seated valves	• Test cylinder compression and repair as necessary
	• Blown cylinder head gasket	• Replace gasket
	• Leaking piston rings	• Test compression and repair as necessary
	• Improper feedback system operation	• Refer to Chapter 4
Intake backfire	• Improper ignition timing	• Adjust timing
	• Defective EGR component	• Repair as necessary
	• Defective TAC vacuum motor or valve	• Repair as necessary
Exhaust backfire	• Air leak into manifold vacuum	• Check manifold vacuum and repair as necessary
	• Faulty air injection diverter valve	• Test diverter valve and replace as necessary
	• Exhaust leak	• Locate and eliminate leak
Ping or spark knock	• Incorrect ignition timing	• Adjust timing
	• Distributor advance malfunction	• Inspect advance mechanism and repair as necessary (Distributor systems only)
	• Excessive combustion chamber deposits	• Remove with combustion chamber cleaner
	• Air leak into manifold vacuum	• Check manifold vacuum and repair as necessary
	• Excessively high compression	• Test compression and repair as necessary
	• Fuel octane rating excessively low	• Try alternate fuel source
	• Sharp edges in combustion chamber	• Grind smooth
	• EGR valve not functioning properly	• Test EGR system and replace as necessary
Surging (at cruising to top speeds)	• Low fuel pump pressure or volume	• Replace fuel pump
	• Improper PCV valve air flow	• Test PCV valve and replace as necessary
	• Air leak into manifold vacuum	• Check manifold vacuum and repair as necessary
	• Incorrect spark advance	• Test and replace as necessary
	• Restricted fuel filter	• Replace fuel filter
	• Restricted air cleaner	• Clean or replace air cleaner filter element
	• EGR valve not functioning properly	• Test EGR system and replace as necessary
	• Improper feedback system operation	• Refer to Chapter 4

TCCS3C07

AIR POLLUTION
AUTOMOTIVE POLLUTANTS 4-2
INDUSTRIAL POLLUTANTS 4-2
NATURAL POLLUTANTS 4-2
AUTOMOTIVE EMISSIONS
CRANKCASE EMISSIONS 4-5
EVAPORATIVE EMISSIONS 4-5
EXHAUST GASES 4-3
CHRYSLER SELF-DIAGNOSTIC SYSTEM
GENERAL INFORMATION 4-17
ACTUATOR TEST MODE (ATM) CODES 4-18
CHECK ENGINE LIGHT 4-18
ENGINE RUNNING TEST CODES 4-18
ENTERING SELF-DIAGNOSTICS 4-18
EXITING THE DIAGNOSTIC TEST 4-19
FAULT CODES 4-18
INDICATOR CODES 4-18
EMISSION CONTROLS 4-5
AIR INJECTION SYSTEM 4-13
CRANKCASE VENTILATION SYSTEM 4-6
DUAL AIR ASPIRATOR SYSTEM 4-16
ELECTRIC CHOKE ASSEMBLY 4-17
ELECTRONIC FEEDBACK CARBURETOR (EFC) SYSTEM 4-16
EMISSION MAINTENANCE LIGHT 4-17
EVAPORATIVE EMISSION CONTROLS 4-6
EXHAUST EMISSION CONTROLS 4-8
EXHAUST GAS RECIRCULATION (EGR) SYSTEM 4-10
OXYGEN FEEDBACK SOLENOID 4-17
OXYGEN SENSOR 4-16
PULSE AIR FEEDER SYSTEM 4-15
VEHICLE EMISSION CONTROL INFORMATION LABEL 4-5
TROUBLE CODES 4-20
VACUUM DIAGRAMS 4-37

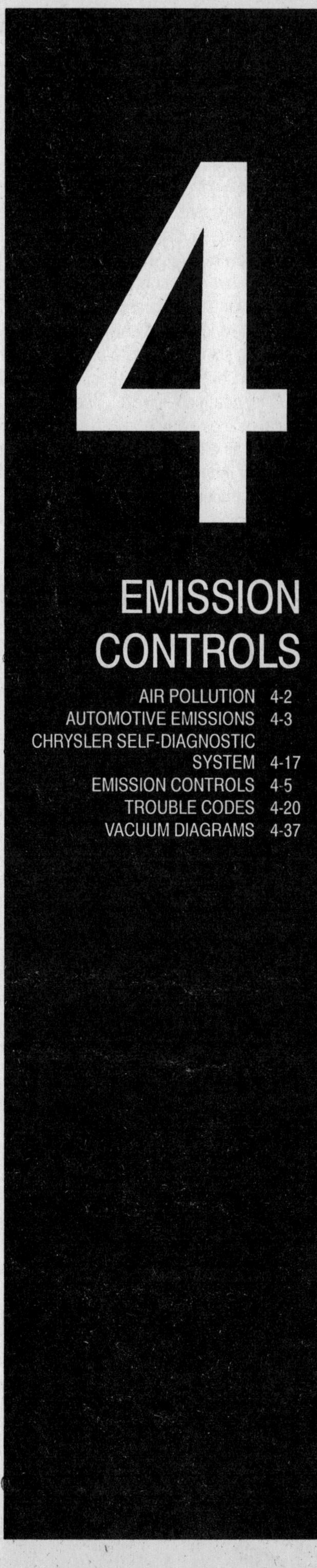

AIR POLLUTION

The earth's atmosphere, at or near sea level, consists of approximately 78 percent nitrogen, 21 percent oxygen and 1 percent other gases. If it were possible to remain in this state, 100 percent clean air would be the result. However, many varied sources allow other gases and particulates to mix with the clean air, causing our atmosphere to become unclean or polluted.

Certain of these pollutants are visible while others are invisible, with each having the capability of causing distress to the eyes, ears, throat, skin and respiratory system. Should these pollutants become concentrated in a specific area and under certain conditions, death could result due to the displacement or chemical change of the oxygen content in the air. These pollutants can also cause great damage to the environment and to the many man made objects that are exposed to the elements.

To better understand the causes of air pollution, the pollutants can be categorized into 3 separate types, natural, industrial and automotive.

Natural Pollutants

Natural pollution has been present on earth since before man appeared and continues to be a factor when discussing air pollution, although it causes only a small percentage of the overall pollution problem. It is the direct result of decaying organic matter, wind born smoke and particulates from such natural events as plain and forest fires (ignited by heat or lightning), volcanic ash, sand and dust which can spread over a large area of the countryside.

Such a phenomenon of natural pollution has been seen in the form of volcanic eruptions, with the resulting plume of smoke, steam and volcanic ash blotting out the sun's rays as it spreads and rises higher into the atmosphere. As it travels into the atmosphere the upper air currents catch and carry the smoke and ash, while condensing the steam back into water vapor. As the water vapor, smoke and ash travel on their journey, the smoke dissipates into the atmosphere while the ash and moisture settle back to earth in a trail hundreds of miles long. In some cases, lives are lost and millions of dollars of property damage result.

Industrial Pollutants

Industrial pollution is caused primarily by industrial processes, the burning of coal, oil and natural gas, which in turn produce smoke and fumes. Because the burning fuels contain large amounts of sulfur, the principal ingredients of smoke and fumes are sulfur dioxide and particulate matter. This type of pollutant occurs most severely during still, damp and cool weather, such as at night. Even in its less severe form, this pollutant is not confined to just cities. Because of air movements, the pollutants move for miles over the surrounding countryside, leaving in its path a barren and unhealthy environment for all living things.

Working with Federal, State and Local mandated regulations and by carefully monitoring emissions, big business has greatly reduced the amount of pollutant introduced from its industrial sources, striving to obtain an acceptable level. Because of the mandated industrial emission clean up, many land areas and streams in and around the cities that were formerly barren of vegetation and life, have now begun to move back in the direction of nature's intended balance.

Automotive Pollutants

The third major source of air pollution is automotive emissions. The emissions from the internal combustion engines were not an appreciable problem years ago because of the small number of registered vehicles and the nation's small highway system. However, during the early 1950's, the trend of the American people was to move from the cities to the surrounding suburbs. This caused an immediate problem in transportation because the majority of suburbs were not afforded mass transit conveniences. This lack of transportation created an attractive market for the automobile manufacturers, which resulted in a dramatic increase in the number of vehicles produced and sold, along with a marked increase in highway construction between cities and the suburbs. Multi-vehicle families emerged with a growing emphasis placed on an individual vehicle per family member. As the increase in vehicle ownership and usage occurred, so did pollutant levels in and around the cities, as suburbanites drove daily to their businesses and employment, returning at the end of the day to their homes in the suburbs.

It was noted that a smoke and fog type haze was being formed and at times, remained in suspension over the cities, taking time to dissipate. At first this "smog," derived from the words "smoke" and "fog," was thought to result from industrial pollution but it was determined that automobile emissions shared the blame. It was discovered that when normal automobile emissions were exposed to sunlight for a period of time, complex chemical reactions would take place.

It is now known that smog is a photo chemical layer which develops when certain oxides of nitrogen (NOx) and unburned hydrocarbons (HC) from automobile emissions are exposed to sunlight. Pollution was more severe when smog would become stagnant over an area in which a warm layer of air settled over the top of the cooler air mass, trapping and holding the cooler mass at ground level. The trapped cooler air would keep the emissions from being dispersed and diluted through normal air flows. This type of air stagnation was given the name "Temperature Inversion."

TEMPERATURE INVERSION

In normal weather situations, surface air is warmed by heat radiating from the earth's surface and the sun's rays. This causes it to rise upward, into the atmosphere. Upon rising it will cool through a convection type heat exchange with the cooler upper air. As warm air rises, the surface pollutants are carried upward and dissipated into the atmosphere.

When a temperature inversion occurs, we find the higher air is no longer cooler, but is warmer than the surface air, causing the cooler surface air to become trapped. This warm air blanket can extend from above ground level to a few hundred or even a few thousand feet into the air. As the surface air is trapped, so are the pollutants, causing a severe smog condition. Should this stagnant air mass extend to a few thousand feet high, enough air movement with the inversion takes place to allow the smog layer to rise above ground level but the pollutants still cannot dissipate. This inversion can remain for days over an area, with the smog level only rising or lowering from ground level to a few hundred feet high. Meanwhile, the pollutant levels increase, causing eye irritation, respiratory problems, reduced visibility, plant damage and in some cases, even disease.

This inversion phenomenon was first noted in the Los Angeles, California area. The city lies in terrain resembling a basin and with certain weather conditions, a cold air mass is held in the basin while a warmer air mass covers it like a lid.

Because this type of condition was first documented as prevalent in the Los Angeles area, this type of trapped pollution was named Los Angeles Smog, although it occurs in other areas where a large concentration of automobiles are used and the air remains stagnant for any length of time.

HEAT TRANSFER

Consider the internal combustion engine as a machine in which raw materials must be placed so a finished product comes out. As in any machine operation, a certain amount of wasted material is formed. When we relate this to the internal combustion engine, we find that through the input of air and fuel, we obtain power during the combustion process to drive the vehicle. The by-product or waste of this power is, in part, heat and exhaust gases with which we must dispose.

The heat from the combustion process can rise to over 4000°F (2204°C). The dissipation of this heat is controlled by a ram air effect, the use of cooling fans to cause air flow and a liquid coolant solution surrounding the combustion area to transfer the heat of combustion through the cylinder walls and into the coolant. The coolant is then directed to a thin-finned, multi-tubed radiator, from which the excess heat is transferred to the atmosphere by 1 of the 3 heat transfer methods, conduction, convection or radiation.

The cooling of the combustion area is an important part in the control of exhaust emissions. To understand the behavior of the combustion and transfer of its heat, consider the air/fuel charge. It is ignited and the flame front burns progressively across the combustion chamber until the burning charge reaches the cylinder walls. Some of the fuel in contact with the walls is not hot enough to burn, thereby snuffing out or quenching the combustion process. This leaves unburned fuel in the combustion chamber. This unburned fuel is then forced out of the cylinder and into the exhaust system, along with the exhaust gases.

Many attempts have been made to minimize the amount of unburned fuel in the combustion chambers due to quenching, by increasing the coolant temperature and lessening the contact area of the coolant around the combustion area. However, design limitations within the combustion chambers prevent the complete burning of the air/fuel charge, so a certain amount of the unburned fuel is still expelled into the exhaust system, regardless of modifications to the engine.

AUTOMOTIVE EMISSIONS

Before emission controls were mandated on internal combustion engines, other sources of engine pollutants were discovered along with the exhaust emissions. It was determined that engine combustion exhaust produced approximately 60 percent of the total emission pollutants, fuel evaporation from the fuel tank and carburetor vents produced 20 percent, with the final 20 percent being produced through the crankcase as a by-product of the combustion process.

Exhaust Gases

The exhaust gases emitted into the atmosphere are a combination of burned and unburned fuel. To understand the exhaust emission and its composition, we must review some basic chemistry.

When the air/fuel mixture is introduced into the engine, we are mixing air, composed of nitrogen (78 percent), oxygen (21 percent) and other gases (1 percent) with the fuel, which is 100 percent hydrocarbons (HC), in a semi-controlled ratio. As the combustion process is accomplished, power is produced to move the vehicle while the heat of combustion is transferred to the cooling system. The exhaust gases are then composed of nitrogen, a diatomic gas (N_2), the same as was introduced in the engine, carbon dioxide (CO_2), the same gas that is used in beverage carbonation, and water vapor (H_2O). The nitrogen (N_2), for the most part, passes through the engine unchanged, while the oxygen (O_2) reacts (burns) with the hydrocarbons (HC) and produces the carbon dioxide (CO_2) and the water vapors (H_2O). If this chemical process would be the only process to take place, the exhaust emissions would be harmless. However, during the combustion process, other compounds are formed which are considered dangerous. These pollutants are hydrocarbons (HC), carbon monoxide (CO), oxides of nitrogen (NOx) oxides of sulfur (SOx) and engine particulates.

HYDROCARBONS

Hydrocarbons (HC) are essentially fuel which was not burned during the combustion process or which has escaped into the atmosphere through fuel evaporation. The main sources of incomplete combustion are rich air/fuel mixtures, low engine temperatures and improper spark timing. The main sources of hydrocarbon emission through fuel evaporation on most vehicles used to be the vehicle's fuel tank and carburetor float bowl.

To reduce combustion hydrocarbon emission, engine modifications were made to minimize dead space and surface area in the combustion chamber. In addition, the air/fuel mixture was made more lean through the improved control which feedback carburetion and fuel injection offers and by the addition of external controls to aid in further combustion of the hydrocarbons outside the engine. Two such methods were the addition of air injection systems, to inject fresh air into the exhaust manifolds and the installation of catalytic converters, units that are able to burn traces of hydrocarbons without affecting the internal combustion process or fuel economy.

To control hydrocarbon emissions through fuel evaporation, modifications were made to the fuel tank to allow storage of the fuel vapors during periods of engine shut-down. Modifications were also made to the air intake system so that at specific times during engine operation, these vapors may be purged and burned by blending them with the air/fuel mixture.

CARBON MONOXIDE

Carbon monoxide is formed when not enough oxygen is present during the combustion process to convert carbon (C) to carbon dioxide (CO_2). An increase in the carbon monoxide (CO) emission is normally accompanied by an increase in the hydrocarbon (HC) emission because of the lack of oxygen to completely burn all of the fuel mixture.

Carbon monoxide (CO) also increases the rate at which the photo chemical smog is formed by speeding up the conversion of nitric oxide (NO) to nitrogen dioxide (NO_2). To accomplish this, carbon monoxide (CO) combines with oxygen (O_2) and nitric oxide (NO) to produce carbon dioxide (CO_2) and nitrogen dioxide (NO_2). ($CO + O_2 + NO = CO_2 + NO_2$).

The dangers of carbon monoxide, which is an odorless and colorless toxic gas are many. When carbon monoxide is inhaled into the lungs and passed into the blood stream, oxygen is replaced by the carbon monoxide in the red blood cells, causing a reduction in the amount of oxygen supplied to the many parts of the body. This lack of oxygen causes headaches, lack of coordination, reduced mental alertness and, should the carbon monoxide concentration be high enough, death could result.

NITROGEN

Normally, nitrogen is an inert gas. When heated to approximately 2500°F (1371°C) through the combustion process, this gas becomes active and causes an increase in the nitric oxide (NO) emission.

Oxides of nitrogen (NOx) are composed of approximately 97–98 percent nitric oxide (NO). Nitric oxide is a colorless gas but when it is passed into the atmosphere, it combines with oxygen and forms nitrogen dioxide (NO_2). The nitrogen dioxide then combines with chemically active hydrocarbons (HC) and when in the presence of sunlight, causes the formation of photo-chemical smog.

Ozone

To further complicate matters, some of the nitrogen dioxide (NO_2) is broken apart by the sunlight to form nitric oxide and oxygen. (NO_2 + sunlight = NO + O). This single atom of oxygen then combines with diatomic (meaning 2 atoms) oxygen (O_2) to form ozone (O_3). Ozone is one of the smells associated with smog. It has a pungent and offensive odor, irritates the eyes and lung tissues, affects the growth of plant life and causes rapid deterioration of rubber products. Ozone can be formed by sunlight as well as electrical discharge into the air.

The most common discharge area on the automobile engine is the secondary ignition electrical system, especially when inferior quality spark plug cables are used. As the surge of high voltage is routed through the secondary cable, the circuit builds up an electrical field around the wire, which acts upon the oxygen in the surrounding air to form the ozone. The faint glow along the cable with the engine running that may be visible on a dark night, is called the "corona discharge." It is the result of the electrical field passing from a high along the cable, to a low in the surrounding air, which forms the ozone gas. The combination of corona and ozone has been a major cause of cable deterioration. Recently, different and better quality insulating materials have lengthened the life of the electrical cables.

Although ozone at ground level can be harmful, ozone is beneficial to the earth's inhabitants. By having a concentrated ozone layer called the "ozonosphere," between 10 and 20 miles (16–32 km) up in the atmosphere, much of the ultra violet radiation from the sun's rays are absorbed and screened. If this ozone layer were not present, much of the earth's surface would be burned, dried and unfit for human life.

OXIDES OF SULFUR

Oxides of sulfur (SOx) were initially ignored in the exhaust system emissions, since the sulfur content of gasoline as a fuel is less than $^1/_{10}$ of 1 percent. Because of this small amount, it was felt that it contributed very little to the overall pollution problem. However, because of the difficulty in solving the sulfur emissions in industrial pollutions and the introduction of catalytic converter to the automobile exhaust systems, a change was mandated. The automobile exhaust system, when equipped with a catalytic converter, changes the sulfur dioxide (SO_2) into the sulfur trioxide (SO_3).

When this combines with water vapors (H_2O), a sulfuric acid mist (H_2SO_4) is formed and is a very difficult pollutant to handle since it is extremely corrosive. This sulfuric acid mist that is formed, is the same mist that rises from the vents of an automobile battery when an active chemical reaction takes place within the battery cells.

When a large concentration of vehicles equipped with catalytic converters are operating in an area, this acid mist may rise and be distributed over a large ground area causing land, plant, crop, paint and building damage.

PARTICULATE MATTER

A certain amount of particulate matter is present in the burning of any fuel, with carbon constituting the largest percentage of the particulates. In gasoline, the remaining particulates are the burned remains of the various other compounds used in its manufacture. When a gasoline engine is in good internal condition, the particulate emissions are low but as the engine wears internally, the particulate emissions increase. By visually inspecting the tail pipe emissions, a determination can be made as to where an engine defect may exist. An engine with light gray or blue smoke emitting from the tail pipe normally indicates an increase in the oil consumption through burning due to internal engine wear. Black smoke would indicate a defective fuel delivery system, causing the engine to operate in a rich mode. Regardless of the color of the smoke, the internal part of the engine or the fuel delivery system should be repaired to prevent excess particulate emissions.

Diesel and turbine engines emit a darkened plume of smoke from the exhaust system because of the type of fuel used. Emission control regulations are mandated for this type of emission and more stringent measures are being used to prevent excess emission of the particulate matter. Electronic components are being introduced to control the injection of the fuel at precisely the proper time of piston travel, to achieve the optimum in fuel ignition and fuel usage. Other particulate after-burning components are being tested to achieve a cleaner emission.

Good grades of engine lubricating oils should be used, which meet the manufacturers specification. Cut-rate oils can contribute to the particulate emission problem because of their low flash or ignition temperature point. Such oils burn prematurely during the combustion process causing emission of particulate matter.

The cooling system is an important factor in the reduction of particulate matter. The optimum combustion will occur, with the cooling system operating at a temperature specified by the manufacturer. The cooling system must be maintained in the same manner as the engine oiling system, as each system is required to perform properly in order for the engine to operate efficiently for a long time.

Crankcase Emissions

Crankcase emissions are made up of water, acids, unburned fuel, oil fumes and particulates. These emissions are classified as hydrocarbons (HC) and are formed by the small amount of unburned, compressed air/fuel mixture entering the crankcase from the combustion area (between the cylinder walls and piston rings) during the compression and power strokes. The head of the compression and combustion help to form the remaining crankcase emissions.

Since the first engines, crankcase emissions were allowed into the atmosphere through a road draft tube, mounted on the lower side of the engine block. Fresh air came in through an open oil filler cap or breather. The air passed through the crankcase mixing with blow-by gases. The motion of the vehicle and the air blowing past the open end of the road draft tube caused a low pressure area (vacuum) at the end of the tube. Crankcase emissions were simply drawn out of the road draft tube into the air.

To control the crankcase emission, the road draft tube was deleted. A hose and/or tubing was routed from the crankcase to the intake manifold so the blow-by emission could be burned with the air/fuel mixture. However, it was found that intake manifold vacuum, used to draw the crankcase emissions into the manifold, would vary in strength at the wrong time and not allow the proper emission flow. A regulating valve was needed to control the flow of air through the crankcase.

Testing, showed the removal of the blow-by gases from the crankcase as quickly as possible, was most important to the longevity of the engine. Should large accumulations of blow-by gases remain and condense, dilution of the engine oil would occur to form water, soots, resins, acids and lead salts, resulting in the formation of sludge and varnishes. This condensation of the blow-by gases occurs more frequently on vehicles used in numerous starting and stopping conditions, excessive idling and when the engine is not allowed to attain normal operating temperature through short runs.

Evaporative Emissions

Gasoline fuel is a major source of pollution, before and after it is burned in the automobile engine. From the time the fuel is refined, stored, pumped and transported, again stored until it is pumped into the fuel tank of the vehicle, the gasoline gives off unburned hydrocarbons (HC) into the atmosphere. Through the redesign of storage areas and venting systems, the pollution factor was diminished, but not eliminated, from the refinery standpoint. However, the automobile still remained the primary source of vaporized, unburned hydrocarbon (HC) emissions.

Fuel pumped from an underground storage tank is cool but when exposed to a warmer ambient temperature, will expand. Before controls were mandated, an owner might fill the fuel tank with fuel from an underground storage tank and park the vehicle for some time in warm area, such as a parking lot. As the fuel would warm, it would expand and should no provisions or area be provided for the expansion, the fuel would spill out of the filler neck and onto the ground, causing hydrocarbon (HC) pollution and creating a severe fire hazard. To correct this condition, the vehicle manufacturers added overflow plumbing and/or gasoline tanks with built in expansion areas or domes.

However, this did not control the fuel vapor emission from the fuel tank. It was determined that most of the fuel evaporation occurred when the vehicle was stationary and the engine not operating. Most vehicles carry 5–25 gallons (19–95 liters) of gasoline. Should a large concentration of vehicles be parked in one area, such as a large parking lot, excessive fuel vapor emissions would take place, increasing as the temperature increases.

To prevent the vapor emission from escaping into the atmosphere, the fuel systems were designed to trap the vapors while the vehicle is stationary, by sealing the system from the atmosphere. A storage system is used to collect and hold the fuel vapors from the carburetor (if equipped) and the fuel tank when the engine is not operating. When the engine is started, the storage system is then purged of the fuel vapors, which are drawn into the engine and burned with the air/fuel mixture.

EMISSION CONTROLS

Vehicle Emission Control Information Label

➧ See Figures 1 and 2

All vehicles described in this manual are equipped with a Vehicle Emission Control Information (VECI) label. The VECI label is located in the engine compartment and is permanently attached. No attempt should be made to remove the VECI label. The VECI label contains specific information for the vehicle to which it is attached. If the specifications on the VECI label differ from the information contained in this manual, those shown on the label should be followed.

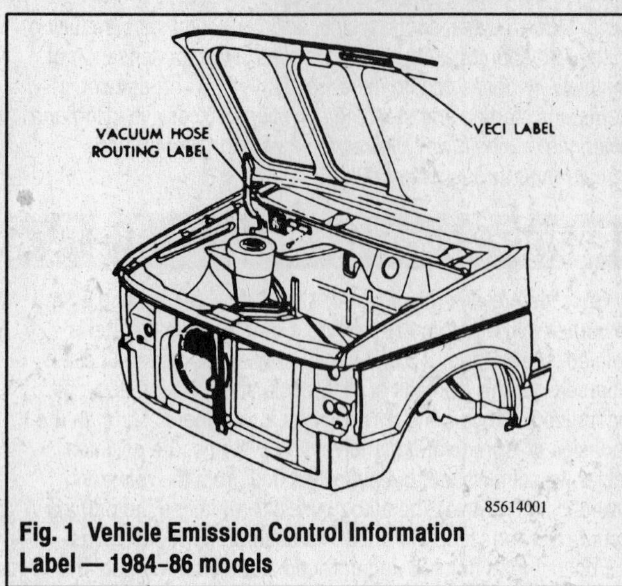

Fig. 1 Vehicle Emission Control Information Label — 1984-86 models

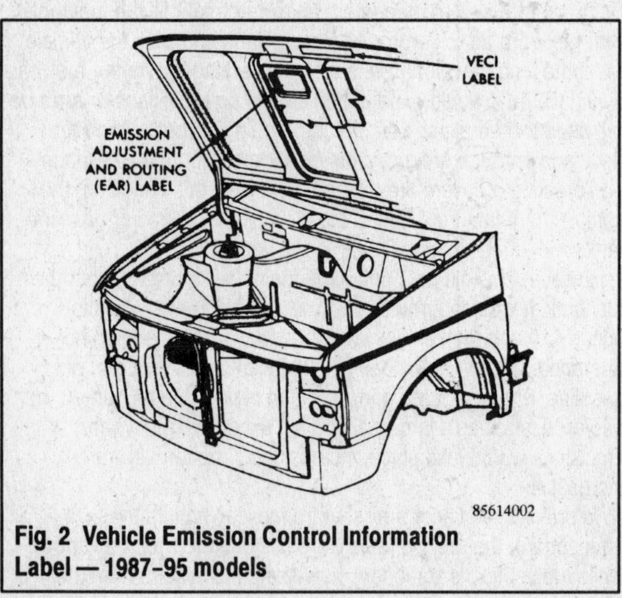

Fig. 2 Vehicle Emission Control Information Label — 1987-95 models

Crankcase Ventilation System

The Positive Crankcase Ventilation (PCV) system is described, and servicing procedures are detailed, in Section 1 of this manual.

Evaporative Emission Controls

The evaporative emission control system prevents gasoline vapor emissions from the fuel system from entering the atmosphere.

Evaporating fuel from the gas tank or carburetor, passes through vent hoses and tubes to a charcoal canister where they are temporarily stored until they can be drawn into the intake manifold and burned when the engine is running.

CHARCOAL CANISTER

➧ See Figures 3, 4 and 5

The charcoal canister is a sealed, maintenance-free unit which stores fuel vapors from the fuel tank and carburetor bowl. Although all carburetor bowls are vented internally, some models do not required venting to the canister. In cases where the carburetor is not vented to the canister, the bowl vent port on the canister will be capped. If the canister becomes damaged, replacement with a new unit is required. The hoses connecting the canister are of fuel resistant construction. Use only fuel resistant hoses if replacement is necessary.

DAMPING CANISTER

Some models are equipped with a damping canister that is connected in series with the charcoal canister. The damping canister cushions the effect of a sudden release of fuel rich vapors when the purge valve is signaled to open. The rich vapors are held momentarily and then gradually fed into the intake manifold to be burned.

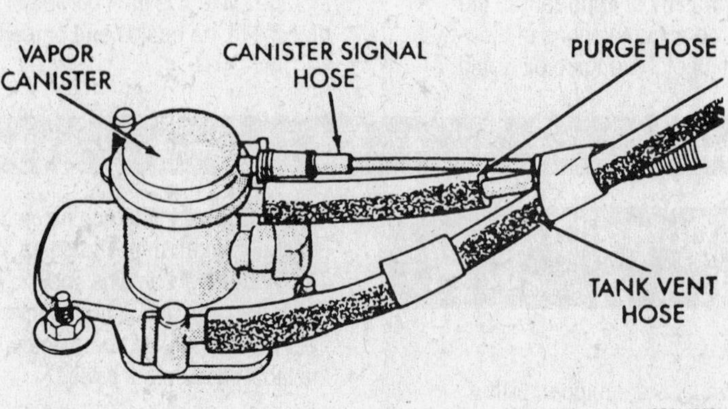

Fig. 3 Evaporative canister — 2.5L engines

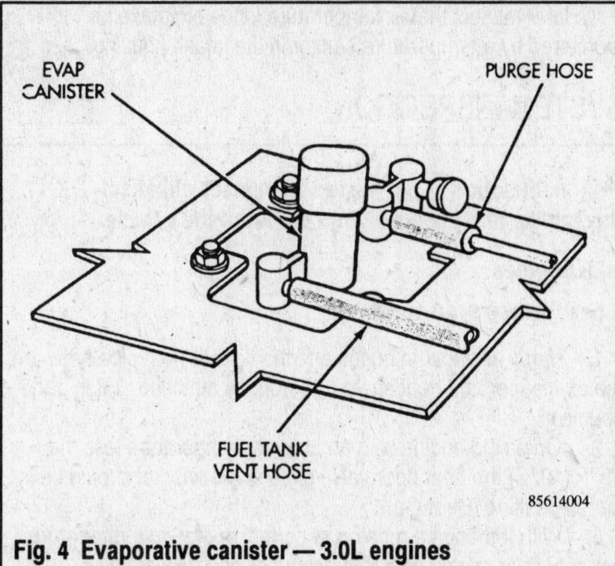

Fig. 4 Evaporative canister — 3.0L engines

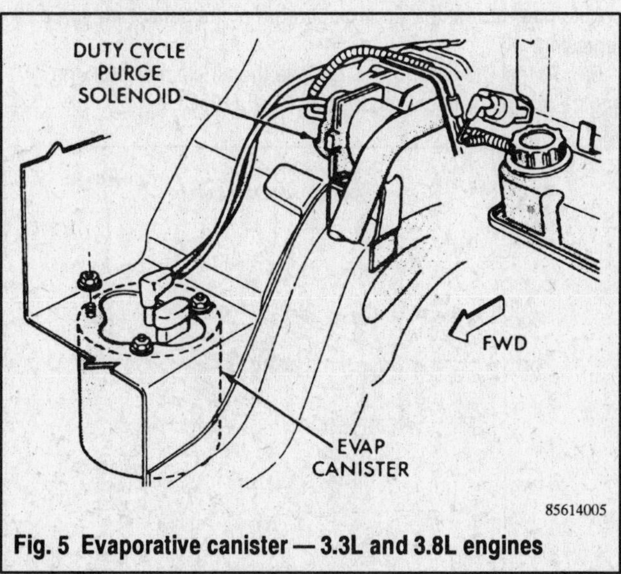

Fig. 5 Evaporative canister — 3.3L and 3.8L engines

CANISTER PURGE SOLENOID

➧ See Figure 6

All engines, except 1994–95 vehicles equipped with 3.0L, 3.3L and 3.8L engines, are equipped with a canister purge solenoid which is connected in series with the charcoal canister. The canister purge solenoid is electrically operated by the engine computer (SMEC, SBEC, SBEC II or PCM), which grounds the solenoid when the engine temperature is below 151°F (66°C). This prevents vacuum from reaching the charcoal canister. When the engine reaches operating temperature the SMEC de-energizes the solenoid and allows purge vapors from the canister to pass through the throttle body.

DUTY CYCLE CANISTER PURGE SOLENOID

➧ See Figure 7

All 1994–95 vehicles equipped with 3.0L, 3.3L and 3.8L engines are equipped with a duty cycle EVAP canister purge solenoid. The duty cycle EVAP canister purge solenoid regulates the rate of vapor flow from the EVAP canister to the throttle body and is controlled by the Powertrain Control Module (PCM).

ROLL OVER VALVE

All vehicles must pass a full 360° roll over test without allowing fuel leakage. To keep fuel from leaking when the vehicle is inverted, fuel and vapor flow controls are needed for all fuel tank connections. A roll over valve is mounted in the top of the fuel tank to prevent leakage if the vehicle is involved in a roll over.

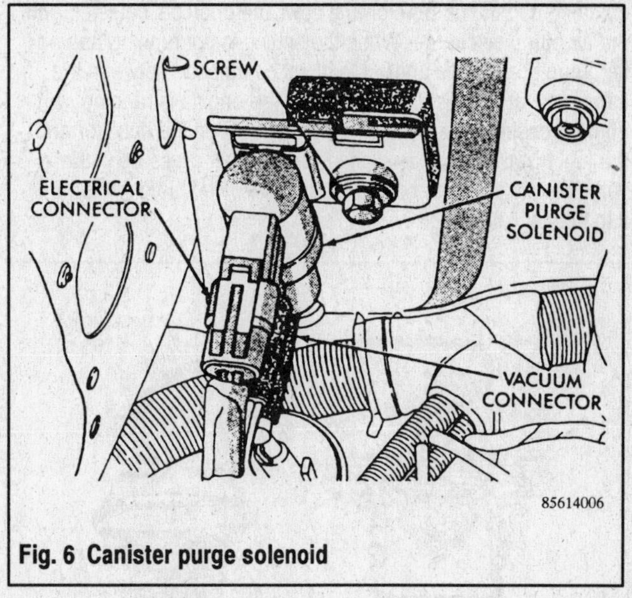

Fig. 6 Canister purge solenoid

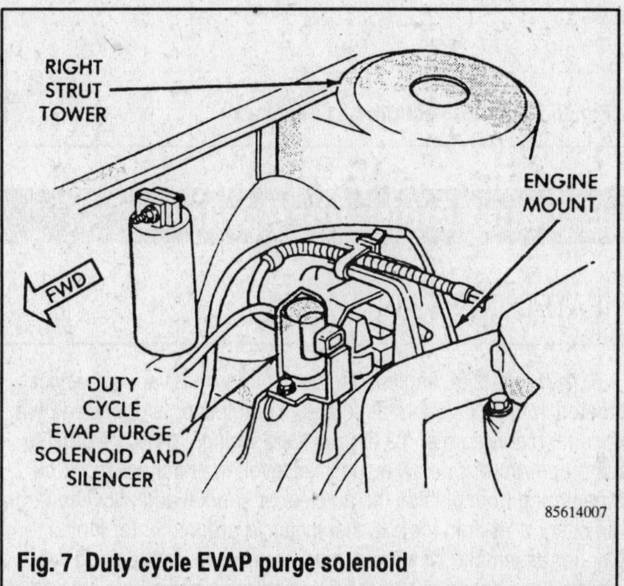

Fig. 7 Duty cycle EVAP purge solenoid

GAS TANK FILLER CAP

➧ See Figure 8

The fuel tank is covered and sealed with a specially engineered pressure/vacuum relief gas cap. The built-in relief valve is a safety feature, and allows pressure to be relieved without separating the cap from the filler tube while eliminating excessive tank pressure. If a replacement cap is required, a similar cap must be installed in order for the system to remain effective.

➥ Always remove the gas tank cap to release pressure whenever the fuel system requires servicing.

BOWL VENT VALVE

The bowl vent valve (carburetor equipped models) is connected to the carburetor fuel bowl, the charcoal canister, and the air pump discharge. When the engine is not running and no air pump pressure is applied, a direct connection between the carburetor and canister exists. When the engine is running, air pump pressure closes the connection between the canister and the fuel bowl. When the engine is shut off, air pressure in the valve bleeds down and the fuel bowl is allowed to vent vapors into the canister.

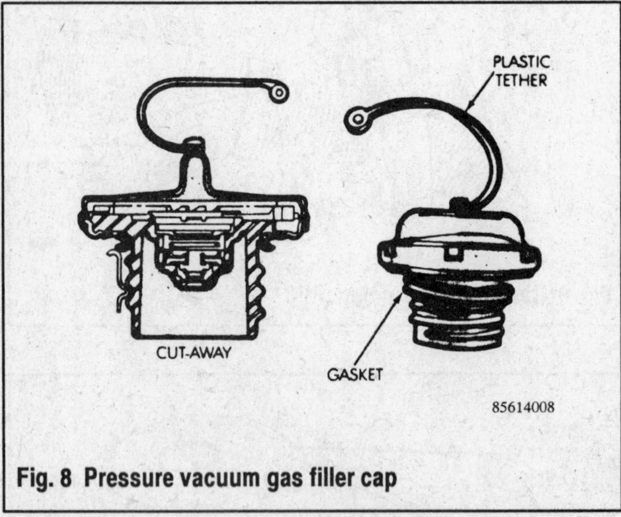

Fig. 8 Pressure vacuum gas filler cap

Exhaust Emission Controls

HEATED INLET AIR SYSTEM

All 2.2L and 2.5L engines are equipped with a vacuum device located in the air cleaner air intake. A small door is operated by a vacuum diaphragm and a thermostatic spring. When the outside air temperature is below a specified level, the door will block off air entering from outside the air cleaner snorkel and allow heated air, channeled from the exhaust manifold area, to enter the air cleaner assembly. With the engine warmed up and running the thermostatic spring allows the heat control door to draw outside air through the air cleaner snorkel.

On later models the air temperature in the air intake is monitored by a temperature sensor in the intake housing.

SYSTEM INSPECTION

➥ A malfunction in the heated air system will affect driveability and the emissions output of the vehicle.

2.2L Engines

➧ See Figures 9, 10 and 11

1. Verify all vacuum hoses and the flexible heat pipe between the air cleaner and heat stove are properly attached and in good condition.
2. On a cold engine with an ambient temperature less than 65°F (19°C) the heat door valve plate in the snorkel should be in the up position (Heat On).
3. With the engine running at normal operating temperature, the heat door should be in the down position (Heat Off).
4. If the heat door valve plate does not respond to hot and cold temperatures, the door diaphragm or the sensor may need replacing.
5. To test the diaphragm, remove the air cleaner from the engine and allow it to cool down to 65°F (19°C).

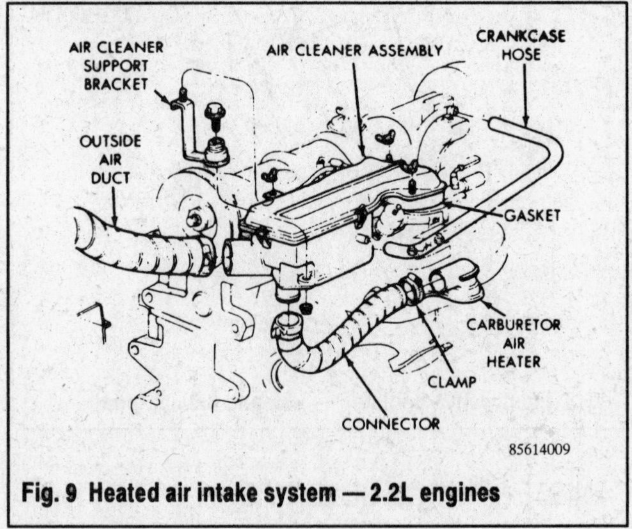

Fig. 9 Heated air intake system — 2.2L engines

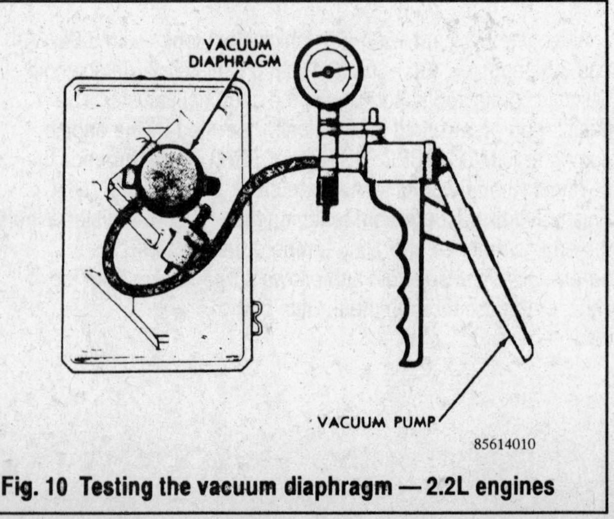

Fig. 10 Testing the vacuum diaphragm — 2.2L engines

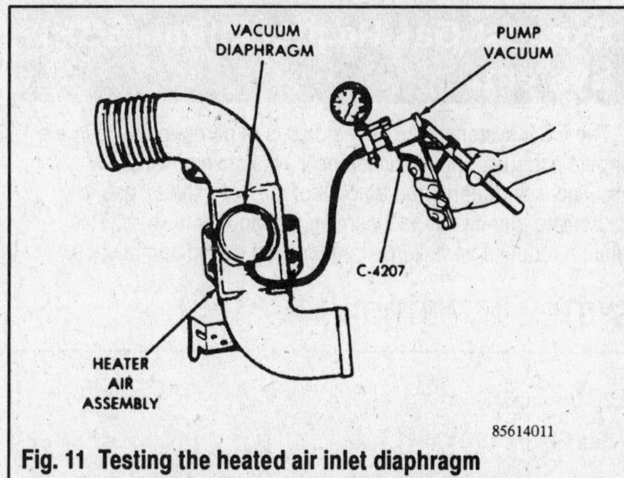

Fig. 11 Testing the heated air inlet diaphragm

6. Connect a hand-operated vacuum pump to the vacuum diaphragm and apply 20 in. Hg (68 kPa) of vacuum. The diaphragm should not leak down more than 10 in. Hg (34 kPa) in 5 minutes. The control door should not lift from the bottom of the snorkel at less than 2 in. Hg (7 kPa) and be in the full up position with no more than 4 in. Hg (14 kPa) of vacuum. If the vacuum test proves the diaphragm defective, replace the air cleaner.

7. If the vacuum test shows the diaphragm in proper working condition, replace the sensor.

8. Label the vacuum hoses at the sensor to aid during reassembly. Disconnect the vacuum hoses, remove the retaining clips with a prytool and discard. Remove the sensor and mounting gasket.

9. Position the new gasket on the sensor and install sensor. Support the sensor on the outer diameter, and install the retaining clips.

10. Reconnect vacuum hoses.

2.5L Engines

➧ See Figure 12

1. Verify all vacuum hoses and the flexible heat pipe between the air cleaner and heat stove are properly attached and in good condition.

2. On a cold engine with an ambient temperature less than 115°F (46°C) the heat door valve plate in the snorkel should be in the up position (Heat On).

3. With the engine running at normal operating temperature, the heat door should be in the down position (Heat Off).

4. If the heat door valve plate does not respond to hot and cold temperatures, the door diaphragm or the sensor may need replacing.

5. To test the diaphragm, remove the air cleaner from the engine and allow it to cool down to 115°F (46°C).

6. Connect a hand-operated vacuum pump to the sensor and apply 20 in. Hg (68 kPa) of vacuum. The door valve should be in the up position (Heat On).

7. If the door does not raise to "Heat On" position, test the vacuum diaphragm for proper operation.

8. Apply 20 in. Hg (68 kPa) of vacuum with a hand operated vacuum pump to the vacuum diaphragm. The diaphragm should not leak down more than 10 in. Hg (34 kPa) in 5 minutes. The control door should not lift from the bottom of the snorkel at less than 2 in. Hg (7 kPa) of vacuum and be in the full up position with no more than 4 in. Hg (14 kPa) of vacuum. If the vacuum test proves the diaphragm defective, replace the air cleaner.

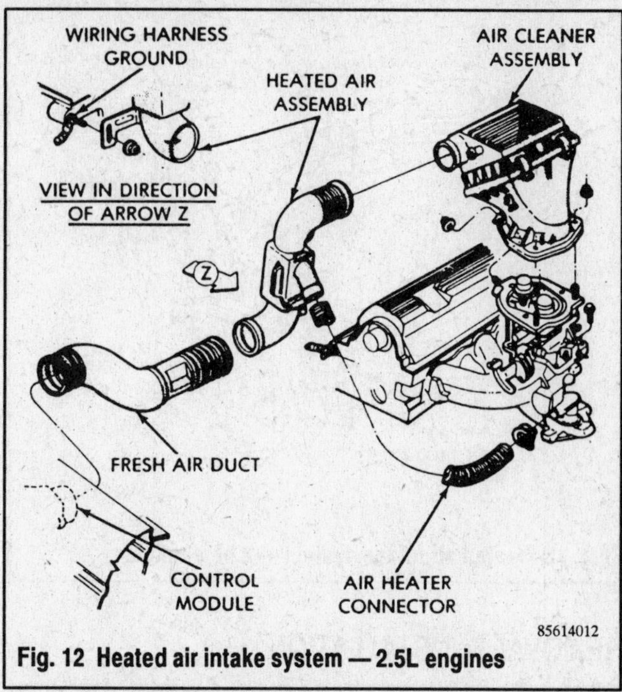

Fig. 12 Heated air intake system — 2.5L engines

9. If the vacuum test shows the diaphragm in proper working condition, replace the sensor.

10. Label the vacuum hoses at the sensor to aid during assembly. Disconnect the vacuum hoses, remove the retaining clips with a prytool and discard. Remove the sensor and mounting gasket.

11. Position the new gasket on the sensor and install sensor. Support the sensor on the outer diameter, and install the retaining clips.

12. Connect the vacuum hoses.

2.6L Engines

➧ See Figure 13

1. Verify all vacuum hoses and the flexible heat pipe between the air cleaner and heat stove are properly attached and in good condition.

2. On a cold engine with an ambient temperature less than 84°F (30°C) the heat door valve plate in the snorkel should be in the up position (Heat On).

3. With the engine running at normal operating temperature, the heat door should be in the down position (Heat Off).

4. If the heat door valve plate does not respond to hot and cold temperatures, the door diaphragm or the sensor may need replacing.

5. To test the diaphragm, remove the air cleaner from the engine and allow it to cool down to 84°F (30°C).

6. Connect a hand-operated vacuum pump to the sensor and apply 15 in. Hg (51 kPa) of vacuum. The valve should be in the up position (Heat On).

7. If the door does not raise to Heat On position, test the vacuum motor for proper operation.

8. Apply 10 in. Hg (34 kPa) of vacuum to the vacuum motor with a hand-operated vacuum pump, if the valve does not remain in the full up position, replace the air cleaner body assembly.

9. If the door performed adequately with vacuum applied to the motor, replace the sensor.

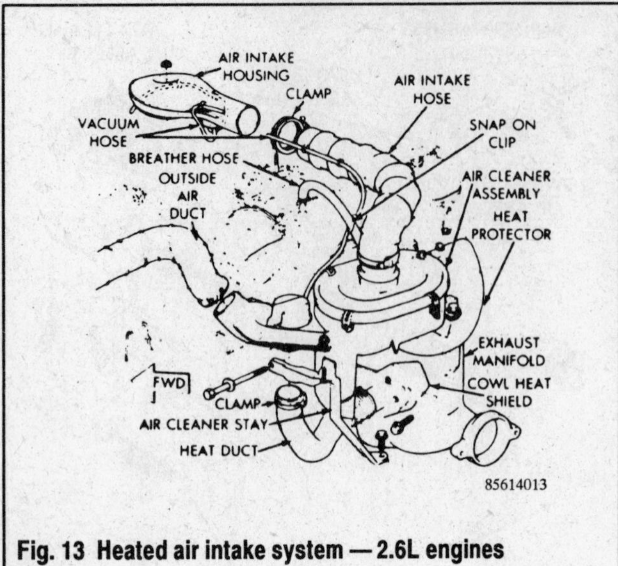

Fig. 13 Heated air intake system — 2.6L engines

REMOVAL & INSTALLATION

Heated Air Temperature Sensor

➧ See Figure 14

➥ **The heated air temperature sensor is located in the air cleaner housing and can be removed with the air filter removed from the housing.**

1. Remove the top of the air cleaner housing, this can be done by releasing the clips.
2. Remove the air filter.
3. Disconnect the vacuum lines from the sensor.
4. Remove the sensor from the housing by prying it carefully out.

To install:

5. Install the new sensor in position using a new gasket. Make sure the sensor is firmly seated.
6. Reconnect the vacuum lines to the sensor and reinstall the air filter.

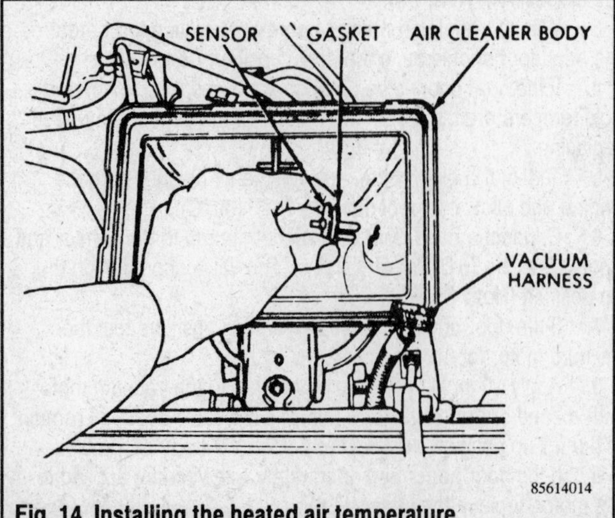

Fig. 14 Installing the heated air temperature sensor — 2.5L engines

Exhaust Gas Recirculation (EGR) System

The EGR system reduces the oxides of nitrogen (NOx) in the engine exhaust. The reduction of NOx is accomplished by allowing a predetermined amount of the hot exhaust gas to recirculate and dilute the incoming fuel and air mixture. This dilution reduces peak flame temperature during combustion.

SYSTEM INSPECTION

2.2L Engines

➧ See Figure 15

The components of the EGR system on the 2.2L engine are; a Coolant Controlled Exhaust Gas Recirculation/Coolant Vacuum Switch Cold Closed (CVSCC) unit mounted in the thermostat housing, an EGR valve, and a EGR tube.

The CVSCC prevents vacuum from being supplied to the EGR system or other systems until the coolant temperature reaches a certain level. When a certain temperature is reached the CVSCC opens and vacuum is supplied as necessary. To assure proper operation test the system as follows:

1. Inspect all passages and moving parts for free movement.
2. Inspect all hoses. If any are hardened, cracked or have faulty connections, replacement is necessary.
3. Allow the engine to reach normal operating temperature. Locate the EGR valve at the end of the intake manifold. Allow the engine to idle for about a minute, then abruptly accelerate to about 2000 rpm, but not over 3000 rpm. Visible movement of the EGR valve stem should be noticed. Movement of the stem indicates the valve is operating normally. If no movement is noticed. Remove the EGR valve and inspect it for deposits and wear.
4. If deposits around the poppet and seat are more than a film, apply some heat control solvent to the area to help soften the deposits. Apply vacuum to the valve with a hand-operated vacuum pump. When the valve opens, scrape away the deposits from the poppet and seat. If the valve poppet does not open when vacuum is applied, replace the valve. If the stem or seat is worn replace the valve.
5. If the EGR valve is functioning properly, check the CVSCC.
6. Check condition of vacuum hoses at the CVSCC and make certain they are properly routed (see vacuum hose underhood sticker).
7. Check engine coolant level.
8. Disconnect the vacuum hoses and remove the valve from the thermostat housing. Place the valve in an ice bath below 40°F (4.4°C) so that the threaded portion is covered. Attach a vacuum pump to the lower connection on the valve (the one connected to the vacuum hose showing a yellow stripe). Apply 10 in. Hg (34 kPa) of vacuum. Pressure should drop no more than 1 in. Hg. (6.895 kPa) in one minute. If the vacuum drops more, replace the CVSCC.

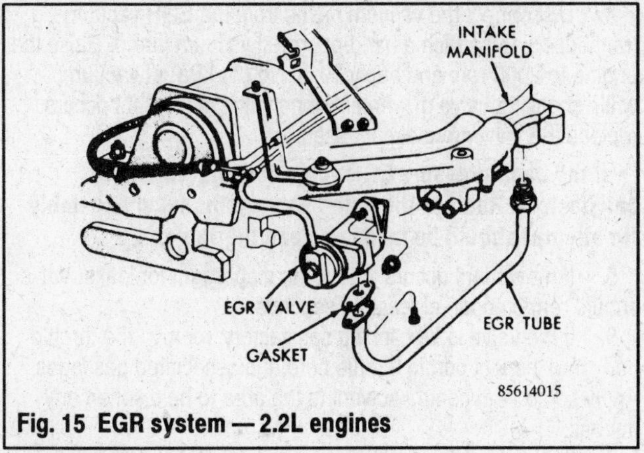

Fig. 15 EGR system — 2.2L engines

2.6L Engines

➧ See Figure 16

With this system exhaust gases are partially recirculated from an exhaust port in the cylinder head into a port at the intake manifold below the carburetor. EGR flow is controlled by thermo-valves, and a combination of a Dual EGR valve and Sub-EGR valve.

The dual EGR valve consists of a primary and secondary valve, which are controlled by different carburetor vacuum circuits in response to the throttle opening. EGR flow is halted at idle and wide open throttle operation. The primary valve controls the EGR flow at narrow throttle openings, while the secondary valve allows flow into the intake mixture at wider throttle openings. Vacuum to the dual EGR valve is controlled by thermo-valves.

A carburetor mounted Sub-EGR valve is directly opened and closed by the throttle linkage in order to closely modulate the EGR flow controlled by the EGR control valve, in response to the throttle opening.

Two thermo-valves connected to the EGR system, sense coolant temperature changes and open and close accordingly to control the vacuum flow to the EGR system. **Test the system as follows:**

1. Check the vacuum hose for good condition and proper routing (see vacuum hose under hood sticker).
2. Engine must be cold. Cold start the engine and allow to idle.
3. Check to make sure that the fast idle does not cause the secondary EGR valve to operate. If the secondary EGR valve operates at cold start fast idle, replace the secondary EGR valve thermo-valve.
4. Run the engine until the operating temperature exceeds 149°F (65°C). The secondary EGR valve should now be in operation. If if it does not operate, inspect the EGR valve or thermo-valve.
5. Disconnect the green stripped vacuum hose from the carburetor. Connect a hand vacuum pump to the hose and apply 6 in. Hg (20 kPa) of vacuum while opening the sub EGR valve by hand. If the idle speed becomes unstable, the secondary valve is operating properly. If the idle speed remains the same, replace the secondary EGR valve and thermo valve.
6. Engage the green striped hose to the carburetor. Disconnect the yellow striped hose from the carburetor and connect it to the hand vacuum pump. Hold the sub-EGR valve opened and apply 6 in. Hg (20 kPa) of vacuum.
7. If the idle speed becomes unstable, the primary EGR valve is operating properly. If the idle speed remains unchanged, replace the primary EGR valve and thermo valve.

2.5L, 3.0L, 3.3L and 3.8L Engines

➧ See Figures 17, 18, 19, 20 and 21

The EGR system on these engines, is a back-pressure type. A back-pressure transducer measures the amount of exhaust gas back-pressure on the exhaust side of the EGR valve and varies the strength of the vacuum signal applied to the EGR valve. The transducer uses this back-pressure signal to provide the correct amount of exhaust gas recirculation under all conditions.

This utilizes an intake manifold mounted EGR valve and Electric EGR Transducer (EET). An EGR tube carries the exhaust gases from the intake manifold to the exhaust manifold. The EGR systems are solenoid controlled, using a manifold vacuum signal from the throttle body. The EGR solenoid is part of the EET. These systems do not allow EGR at idle. EGR systems operate at all temperatures above 60°F (16°C).

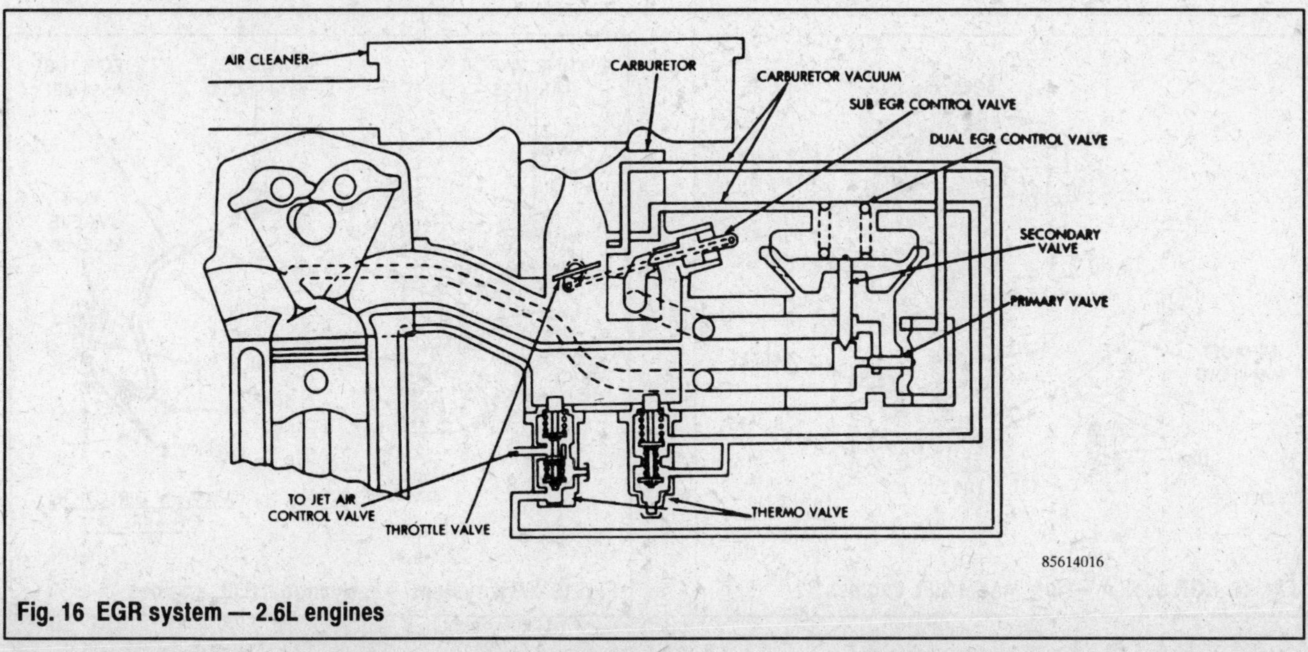

Fig. 16 EGR system — 2.6L engines

1989–92 California vehicles, and all 1993–95 vehicles with EGR, have an on-board diagnostic system and a solenoid in series with the vacuum line to the EGR valve. The engine controller monitors EGR system performance and energizes or de-energizes the solenoid based on engine/driving conditions. If the system malfunctions the engine controller will turn on the Check Engine light and a fault code will be stored in the diagnostic system. **Test the system as follows:**

1. Inspect all passages and moving parts for free movement.
2. Inspect all hoses. If any are hardened, cracked or have faulty connection, replacement is necessary.
3. Warm the engine to normal operating temperature. Allow the engine to idle for about a minute, then abruptly accelerate to about 2000 rpm, but not over 3000 rpm. Visible movement of the groove on EGR valve stem should be noticed. Movement of the stem indicates the valve is operating normally. If no movement is noticed.
4. Disconnect the vacuum hoses from the EGR vacuum transducer, and attach a hand-operated vacuum pump. Raise the engine to 2000 rpm and apply 10 in. Hg (34 kPa) of vacuum, while checking valve movement. If no valve movement occurs, replace the valve/transducer assembly.

➥ If the back-pressure EGR valve does not function satisfactory. Replace the entire Valve/Transducer assembly. No attempt should be made to clean the valve.

5. If movement occurs, check the diaphragm for leaks. Valve should remain open at least 30 seconds.
6. If the valve is functioning satisfactory, remove the throttle body and inspect port in throttle bore and associated passages. Apply some heat control solvent to the area to help soften any deposit.
7. Install the throttle body and recheck EGR operation.

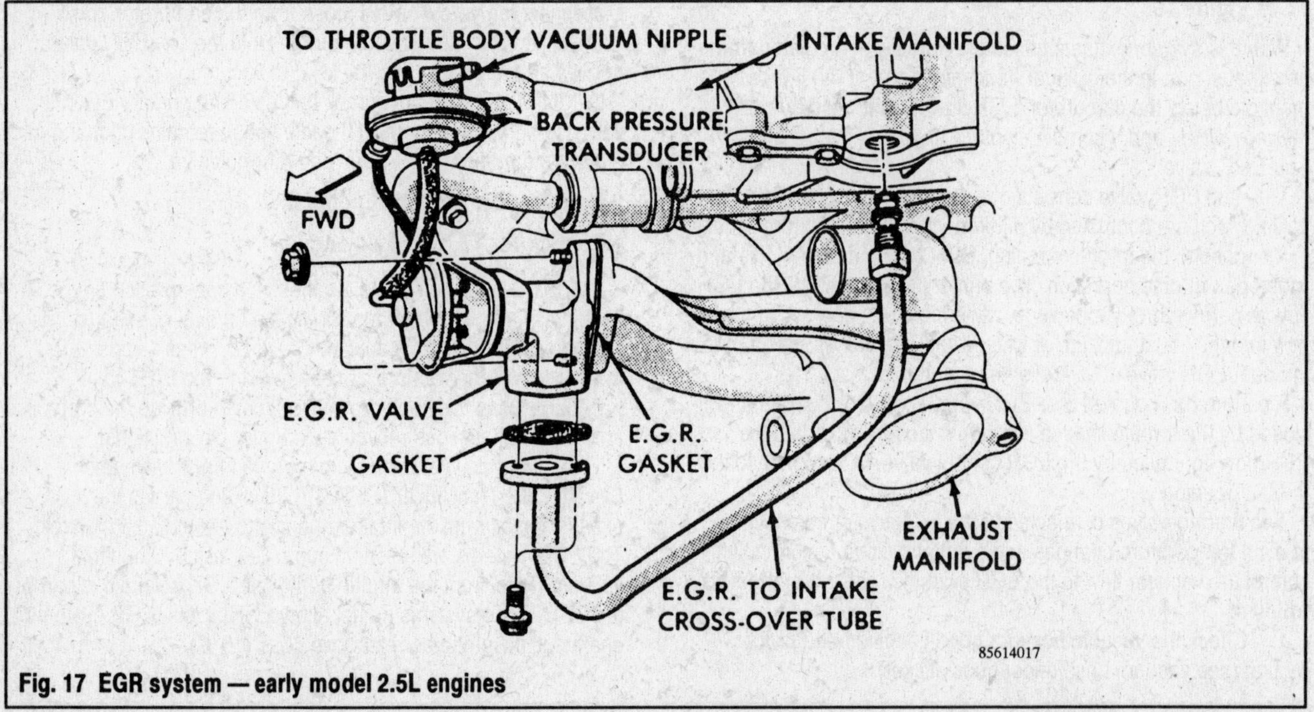

Fig. 17 EGR system — early model 2.5L engines

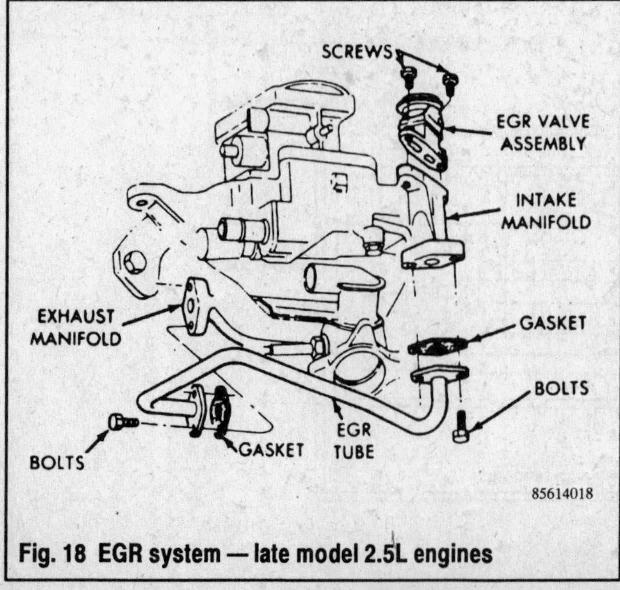

Fig. 18 EGR system — late model 2.5L engines

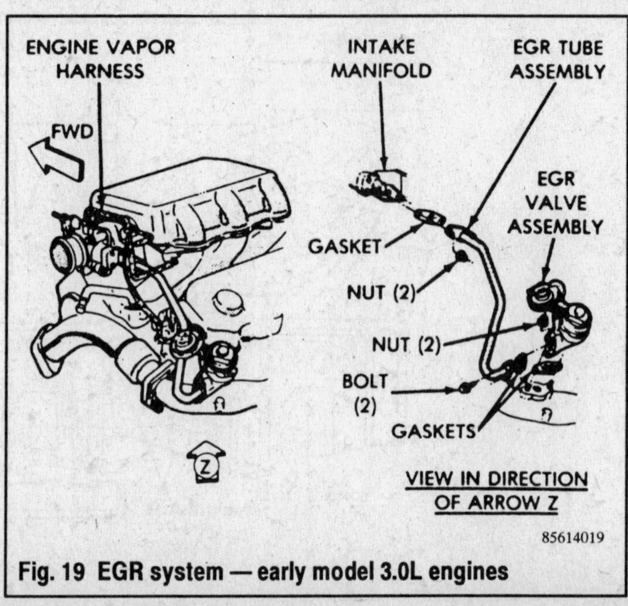

Fig. 19 EGR system — early model 3.0L engines

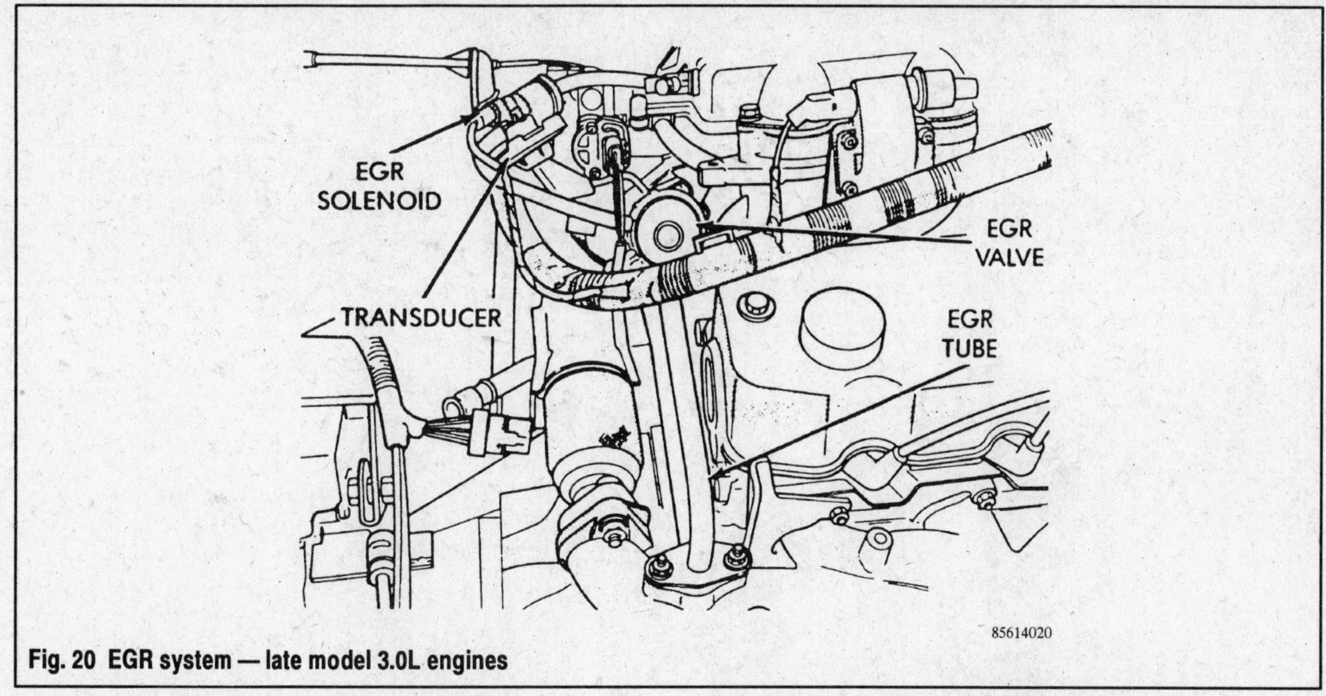

Fig. 20 EGR system — late model 3.0L engines

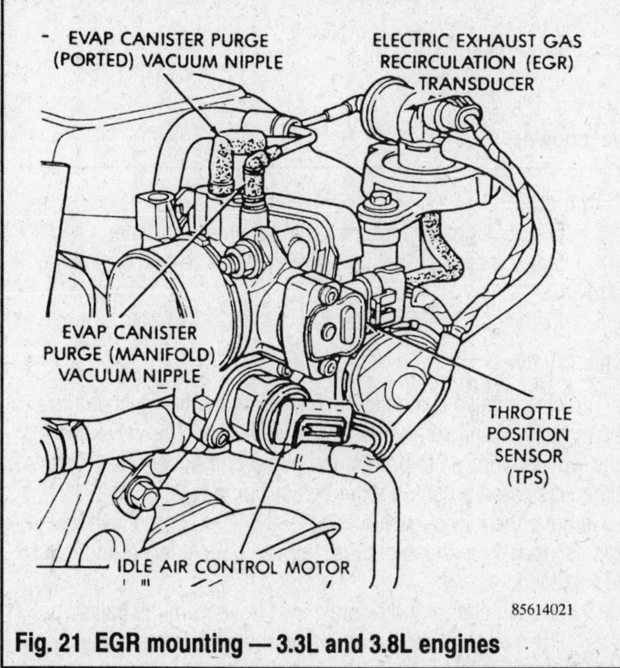

Fig. 21 EGR mounting — 3.3L and 3.8L engines

Air Injection System

See Figure 22

2.2L engines are equipped with an air injection system. This system is designed to supply a controlled amount of air to the exhaust gases, through exhaust ports, aiding in the oxidation of the gases and reduction of carbon monoxide and hydrocarbons to an appreciable level.

During engine warm-up air is injected into the base of the exhaust manifold. After the engine warms up, the air flow is switched (by a Coolant Vacuum Switch Cold Open or by a vacuum solenoid) to the 3-way catalytic converter where it further aids in the reduction of carbon monoxide and hydrocarbons in the exhaust system.

The system consists of a belt driven air pump, hoses, a switch/relief valve and a check valve to prevent the components within the system separate from high temperature exhaust gases.

No repairs are possible on any of the air injection system components. All replacement parts must be serviced as a unit.

REMOVAL & INSTALLATION

Coolant Vacuum Switch Cold Open

1. Locate the switch on the thermostat housing.
2. Label the hoses before removing. Remove hoses.
3. Remove the vacuum switch from housing.

To install:

4. Install a new vacuum switch and connect the vacuum hoses. (See under hood vacuum hose routing label).

Air Pump

See Figures 23, 24 and 25

The air injection system is not completely noiseless. Do not assume the air pump is defective because it squeals. If the system creates excessive noise, remove the drive belt and operate the engine. If the noise ceases, check all hose connections for proper tightening. Replace pump, if necessary.

1. Remove all hoses and vacuum lines from the air pump and diverter valve or switch/relief valve (depending on how equipped).
2. Remove the air pump drive pulley shield.
3. Remove the air pump pivot bolt and remove air pump belt.
4. Remove the remaining mounting bolts and remove pump.
5. Remove the diverter valve or switch/relief valve from pump.

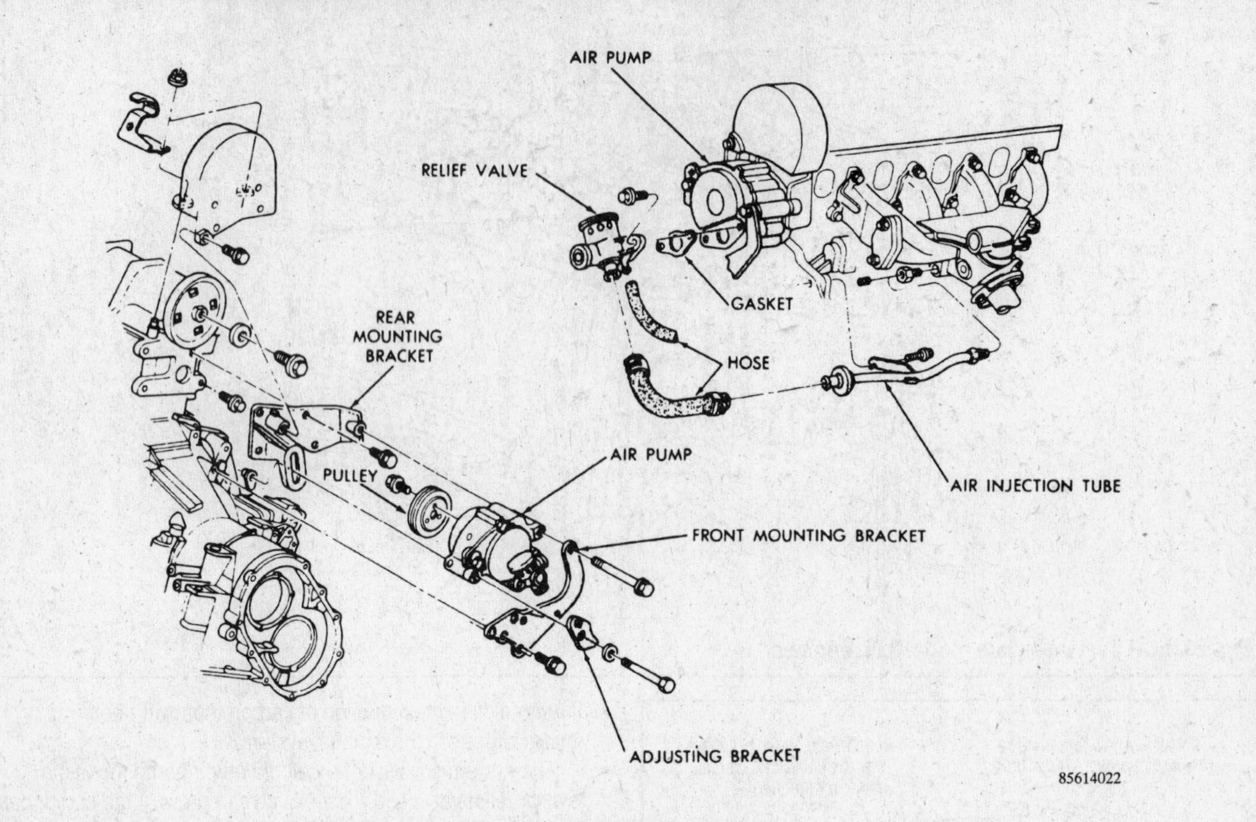

Fig. 22 Air injection system — 2.2L engines (Federal/Canadian model shown)

To install:

6. Clean all gasket material from valve and pump mounting surface.
7. Install the diverter valve or switch/relief valve using a new gasket, to the new pump.
8. Install the pump on the engine and loosely install pivot bolt.
9. Install the drive belt and tighten pivot bolt.
10. Install the air pump drive pulley shield.
11. Install all hoses and vacuum lines.

Switch/Relief Valve

If vacuum is applied to the valve and air injection is not upstream, or if air injection is in both upstream and downstream, the valve is faulty and must be replaced.

1. Remove all air hoses and vacuum hoses.
2. Remove the valve-to-pump mounting bolts, and remove valve.

To install:

3. Clean all gasket material from mounting surfaces.
4. Install the new valve to the pump with a new gasket.
5. Secure the valve with mounting bolts, tighten bolts to 125 inch lbs. (14 Nm).
6. Reinstall all air hoses and vacuum hoses.

Relief Valve

The purpose of this valve is to control air pump pressure during high engine speeds. If the pump discharge pressure exceeds 9 psi (62 kPa) the valve will open and vent the excess pressure to the atmosphere.

1. Remove the air hoses from the valve.
2. Remove the valve mounting screws and remove valve.

To install:

3. Clean all gasket material from mounting surfaces.
4. Install a new gasket on valve and secure with mounting screws.
5. Reconnect the air hoses.

Check Valve

The check valve is located in the injection tube which leads to the exhaust manifold and converter assembly. The valve has a one-way diaphragm to protect the pump and hoses from high exhaust system pressure if the belt or pump fails.

Remove the air hose from check valve inlet tube. If exhaust gas escapes from the inlet tube, the valve have failed and must be replaced.

1. Loosen clamp and remove inlet hose from the valve.
2. Remove the tube nut retaining the tube to the exhaust manifold or catalyst.
3. Loosen the starter motor mounting bolt and remove injection tube from engine.
4. Remove the catalytic converter injection tube mounting screws from catalytic converter flange and remove injection tube.

To install:

5. Position the injection tube to catalytic converter flange and secured with mounting screws.
6. Install the injection tube into fitting in exhaust manifold and bracket at starter motor.
7. Connect hoses to the check valve.

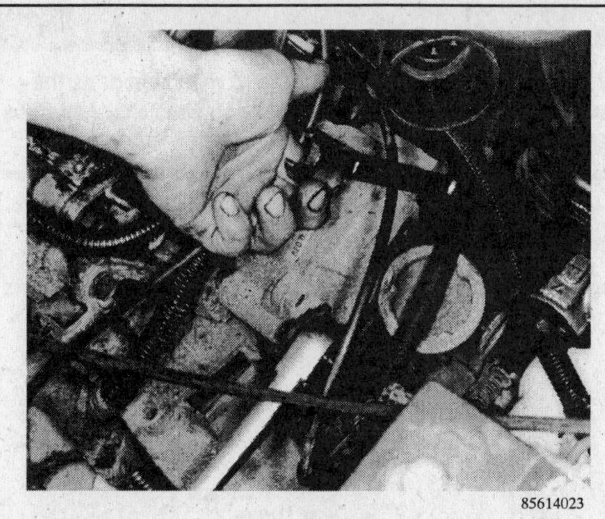

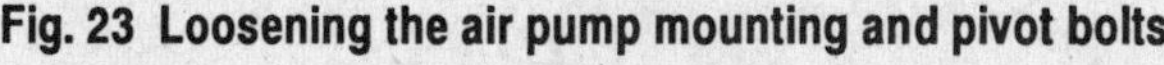

Fig. 23 Loosening the air pump mounting and pivot bolts

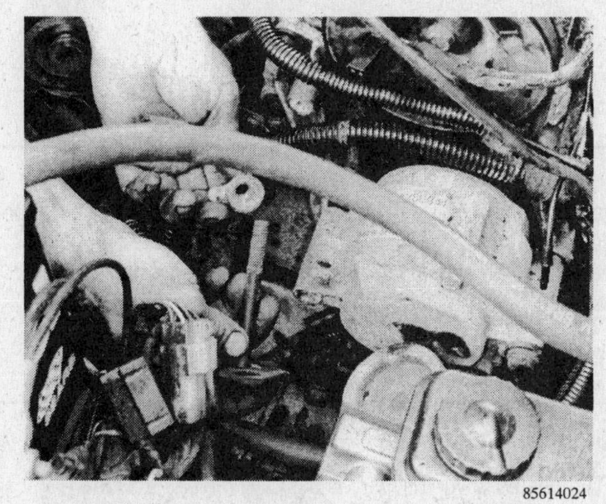

Fig. 24 Removing a mounting bolt from the air pump

Fig. 25 Removing the air pump and belt from the engine — 1987 2.2L engine shown

Pulse Air Feeder System

➧ **See Figure 26**

2.6L engines use a pulse air feeder system to promote oxidation of exhaust emissions in the rear catalytic converter. The system consists of a main reed valve and sub-reed valve. The main reed valve is controlled by a diaphragm, which is activated by pressure pulses from the crankcase. The sub-reed valve is activated by pulsation in the exhaust system between the front and rear converters.

1. Remove the air duct from the right side of the radiator.
2. Remove the carburetor protector shield.
3. Remove the engine oil dipstick and tube.
4. Remove the pulse air feeder mounting bolts.
5. Raise and support the front of the vehicle on jackstands. Disconnect the pulse air feeder hoses and remove the feeder.

To install:

6. Install the hoses on the pulse air feeder.
7. Lower the vehicle and tighten feeder mounting bolts.
8. Check O-ring on lower end of the dipstick tube. Replace if damaged.
9. Install carburetor protector shield.
10. Install the air deflector onto the radiator.

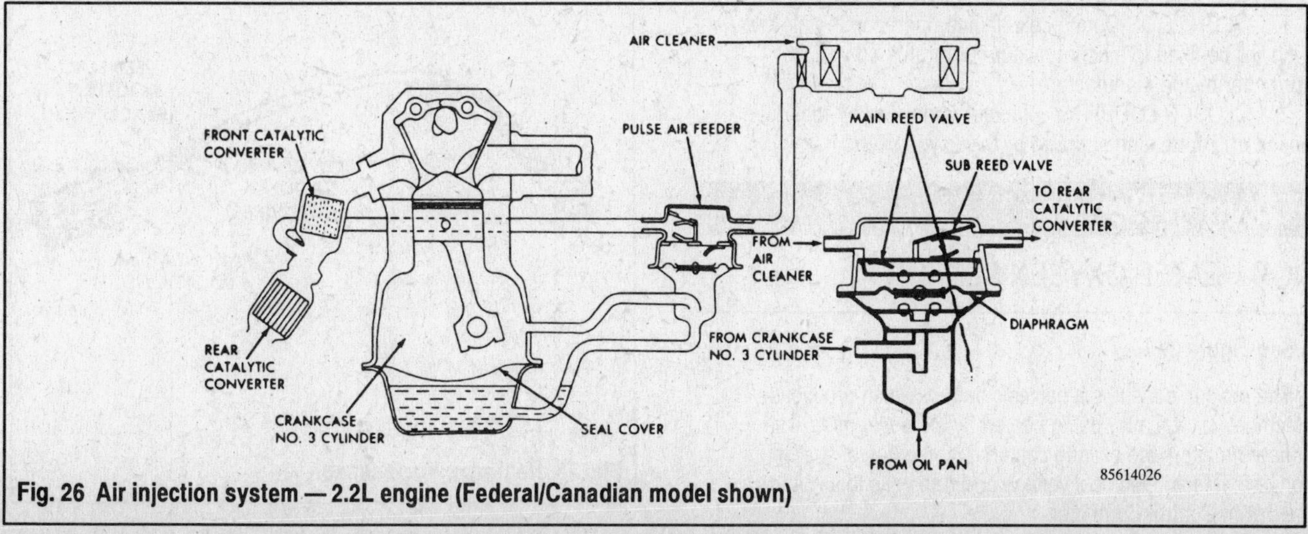

Fig. 26 Air injection system — 2.2L engine (Federal/Canadian model shown)

Dual Air Aspirator System

2.6L engines use an air aspirator system which aids in reducing carbon monoxide (CO) and hydrocarbon emissions. The system uses pulsating exhaust pressure to draw fresh air from the air cleaner assembly. Failure of the aspirator valve will result in excess noise.

SYSTEM TEST

1. Check the aspirator tube/exhaust manifold assembly joint and hoses. If aspirator tube/exhaust manifold joint is leaking, retighten to 50 ft. lbs. (68 Nm). If hoses are hardened, replace as necessary.
2. Disconnect the inlet hose from aspirator valve.
3. With engine at idle, the negative (vacuum) exhaust pulses should be felt at the valve inlet.
4. If hot exhaust gases escape from the aspirator inlet, replace the valve.

REMOVAL & INSTALLATION

1. Remove the air inlet hose from aspirator valve.
2. Remove screws from aspirator bracket, and remove tube assembly from engine.

To install:

3. Install tube and tighten nuts to 40 ft. lbs. (54 Nm).
4. Install tube bracket assembly and tighten to 21 ft. lbs. (28 Nm).
5. Connect the air hose to valve and air cleaner nipple; install clamps.

Electronic Feedback Carburetor (EFC) System

Some models are equipped with an Electronic Feedback Carburetor (EFC) System which is designed to convert Hydrocarbons(HC), Carbon Monoxide (CO) and Oxides of Nitrogen (NOx) into harmless substances. An exhaust gas oxygen sensor generates an electronic signal which is used by the Spark Control Computer to precisely control the air-fuel mixture ratio to the carburetor.

There are two operating modes in the EFC system:

1. OPEN LOOP-During cold engine operation the air-fuel ratio will be fixed to a richer mixture programmed into the computer by the manufacture.
2. CLOSED LOOP-The computer varies the air-fuel ratio based on information supplied by the oxygen sensor.

Oxygen Sensor

NON-HEATED OXYGEN SENSOR

➧ See Figure 27

The oxygen sensor is a galvanic battery which produces electrical voltage after being heated by exhaust gases. The sensor monitors the oxygen content in the exhaust stream, converts it to an electrical voltage and transmits this voltage to the Spark Control Computer.

****WARNING**

Use care when working around the oxygen sensor as the exhaust manifold may be extremely hot. The sensor must be removed using Tool C-4907, or the equivalent.

When the sensor is removed, the exhaust manifold threads must be cleaned with an 18mm x 1.5 x 6E tap.

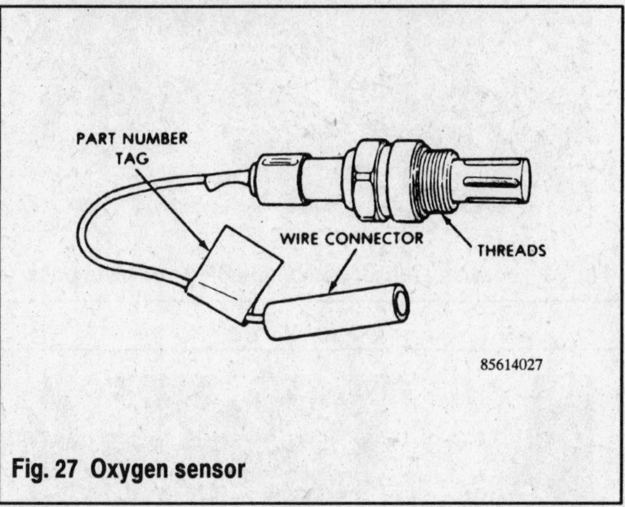

Fig. 27 Oxygen sensor

If the sensor is to be reinstalled, the sensor threads must be coated with an anti-seize compound such as Loctite® 771-64, or equivalent. New sensors are coated with compound on the threads and no additional compound is required. The sensor should be tightened to 20 ft. lbs. (27 Nm).

HEATED OXYGEN SENSOR

➧ See Figure 28

The heated oxygen sensor is basically the same as the standard oxygen sensor, except that it is internally heated for faster switching during engine operation. Replacement of the heated oxygen sensor is the same as the standard sensor.

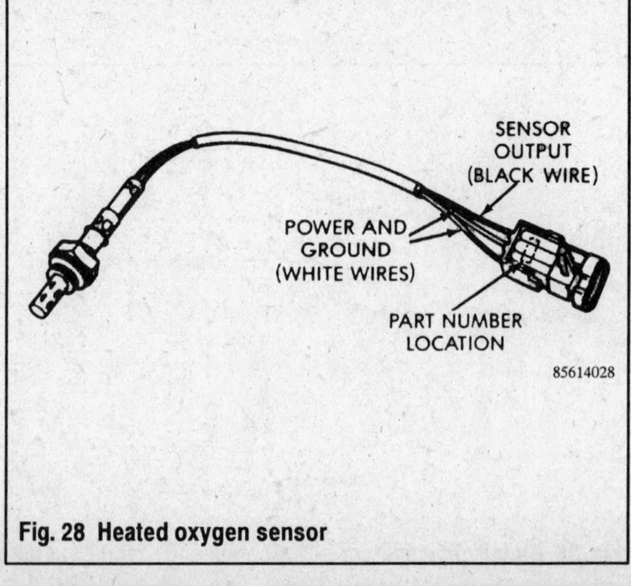

Fig. 28 Heated oxygen sensor

Oxygen Feedback Solenoid

See Figure 29

In addition to the oxygen sensor, the EFC uses an Oxygen Feedback Solenoid. Its purpose is to regulate the air/fuel ratio of the feedback carburetor, along with a conventional fixed main metering jet, in response to the electrical signal generated by the Spark Control Computer.

With the feedback solenoid de-energized, the main metering orifice is fully uncovered and the richest condition exists within the carburetor.

With the feedback solenoid energized, the solenoid pushrod seals the main metering orifice. This position offers the leanest condition within the carburetor.

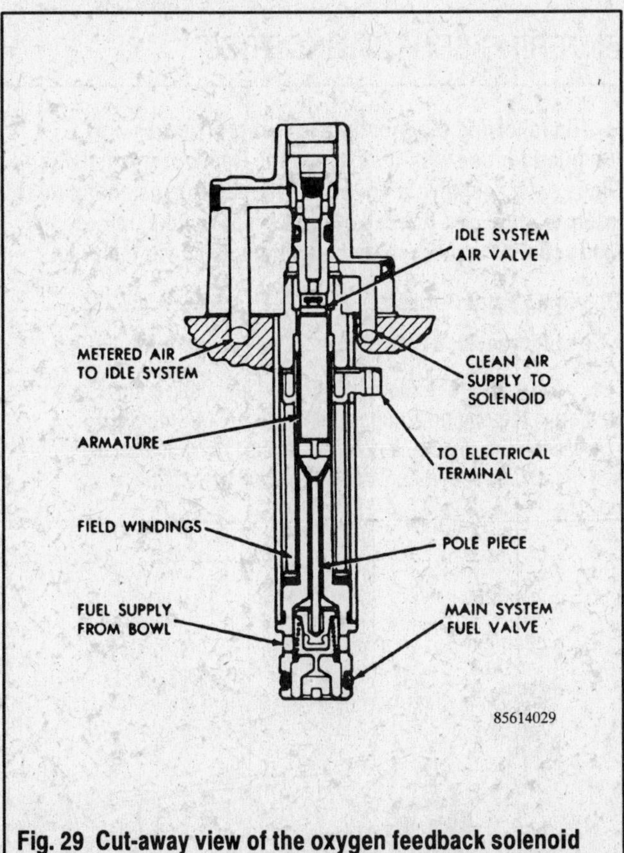

Fig. 29 Cut-away view of the oxygen feedback solenoid

Electric Choke Assembly

The electric choke system is a heater and switch assembly sealed within the choke housing. When the engine is running and the engine oil pressure is 4 psi (27 kPa) or above, the contacts in the oil pressure switch closes and feed current to the automatic choke system to open the choke and keep it open.

The choke assembly must never be immersed in fluid as damage to the internal switch and heater assembly will result.

TESTING

1. Disconnect the electrical lead from choke heater assembly.
2. Connect direct battery voltage to choke heater connection.
3. The choke valve should reach the open position within five minutes.

****WARNING**

Operation of any type should be avoided if there is a loss of choke power. This condition causes a very rich mixture to burn and results in abnormally high exhaust system temperatures, which may cause damage to the catalytic converter or other underbody parts of the vehicle.

Emission Maintenance Light

All models have an Emission Maintenance Reminder (EMR) lamp, this lamp is illuminated when the ignition key is turned **ON**. The lamp is connected with the engine controller, which records the vehicle mileage and stores it into memory every 8 miles (13 km). At the time the mileage is stored, the controller checks for the 60,000 (96,000 km), 82,500 (132,000 km) and 120,000 mile (192,000 km) trip points. When the current mileage matches one of these mileages, the EMR lamp is illuminated.

When the EMR lamp is illuminated, some of the emission components are supposed to be changed. These components are: EGR valve, EGR tube and PCV valve at 60,000 miles (96,000 km) and 120,000 miles (192,000 km). At 82,500 miles (132,000 km) the oxygen sensor must also be replaced. The EMR lamp can then be reset using an appropriate DRB tester or equivalent.

CHRYSLER SELF-DIAGNOSTIC SYSTEM

General Information

The Chrysler fuel injection systems combine electronic spark advance and fuel control. At the center of these systems is a digital, pre-programmed computer, known as a Single Module Engine Controller (SMEC) for 1987–89, a Single Board Engine Controller (SBEC) for 1990–91, a Single Board Engine Controller II (SBEC II) for 1992 and a Powertrain Control Module (PCM) for 1993–95. The SMEC, SBEC, SBEC II or PCM regulates ignition timing, air-fuel ratio, emission control devices, cooling fan, charging system idle speed and speed control. It has the ability to update and revise its commands to meet changing operating conditions.

Various sensors provide the input necessary for controller to correctly regulate fuel flow at the injectors. These include the Manifold Absolute Pressure (MAP), Throttle Position Sensor (TPS), oxygen sensor, coolant temperature sensor, charge temperature sensor, and vehicle speed sensors.

In addition to the sensors, various switches are used to provide important information to the controller. These include the neutral safety switch, air conditioning clutch switch, brake switch and speed control switch. These signals cause the SMEC, SBEC, SBEC II or PCM to change either the fuel flow at the injectors or the ignition timing or both.

The SMEC, SBEC, SBEC II or PCM , are designed to test their own input and output circuits, If a fault is found in a major system, this information is stored in the SMEC, SBEC, SBEC II or PCM for eventual display to the technician. Information on this fault can be displayed to the technician by means of the instrument panel CHECK ENGINE light or by connecting a diagnostic read-out tester and reading a numbered display code, which directly relates to a general fault. Some inputs and outputs are checked continuously and others are checked under certain conditions. If the problem is repaired or no longer exists, the The SMEC, SBEC, SBEC II or PCM cancels the fault code after 50–100 key ON/OFF cycles.

When a fault code is detected, it appears as either a flash of the CHECK ENGINE light on the instrument panel or by watching the Diagnostic Readout Box II (DRB II). This indicates that an abnormal signal in the system has been recognized by the SMEC, SBEC, SBEC II or PCM . Fault codes do indicate the presence of a failure but they don't identify the failed component directly.

FAULT CODES

Fault codes are 2 digit numbers that tell the technician which circuit is bad. Fault codes do indicate the presence of a failure but they don't identify the failed component directly. Therefore a fault code and a result are not always the reason for the problem.

INDICATOR CODES

Indicator codes are 2 digit numbers that tell the technician if particular sequences or conditions have occurred. Such a condition where the indicator code will be displayed is at the beginning or the end of a diagnostic test. Indicator codes will not generate a CHECK ENGINE light or engine running test code.

ACTUATOR TEST MODE (ATM) CODES

ATM test codes are 2 digit numbers that identify the various circuits used by the technician during the diagnosis procedure.

ENGINE RUNNING TEST CODES

Engine running test codes are 2 digit numbers. The codes are used to access sensor readouts while the engine is running and place the engine in particular operating conditions for diagnosis.

CHECK ENGINE LIGHT

The CHECK ENGINE light has 2 modes of operation: diagnostic mode and switch test mode.

If a DRB II diagnostic tester is not available, the PCM/SMEC/SBEC can show the technician fault codes by flashing the CHECK ENGINE light on the instrument panel in the diagnostic mode. In the switch test mode, after all codes are displayed, switch function can be confirmed. The light will turn on and off when a switch is turned **ON** and **OFF**.

Even though the light can be used as a diagnostic tool, it cannot do the following:

1. Once the light starts to display fault codes, it cannot be stopped. If the technician loses count, he must start the test procedure again.
2. The light cannot display all of the codes or any blank displays.
3. The light cannot tell the technician if the oxygen feed-back system is lean or rich and if the idle motor and detonation systems are operational.
4. The light cannot perform the actuation test mode, sensor test mode or engine running test mode.

➜ Be advised that the CHECK ENGINE light can only perform a limited amount of functions and is not to be used as a substitute for a diagnostic tester. All diagnostic procedures described herein are intended for use with a Diagnostic Readout Box II (DRB II) or equivalent tool.

ENTERING SELF-DIAGNOSTICS

➜ The following diagnostic and test procedures are intended for use with the Diagnostic Readout Box II (DRB II). Since each available diagnostic readout box may differ in its interpretation and display of the sensor results, refer to the instructional procedure that accompanies each tester unit.

Obtaining Fault Codes

➧ See Figures 30, 31 and 32

1. Connect the readout box to the diagnostic connector located in the engine compartment near PCM/SMEC/SBEC.
2. Start the engine, if possible, cycle the transaxle selector and the A/C switch, if applicable. Shut off the engine.

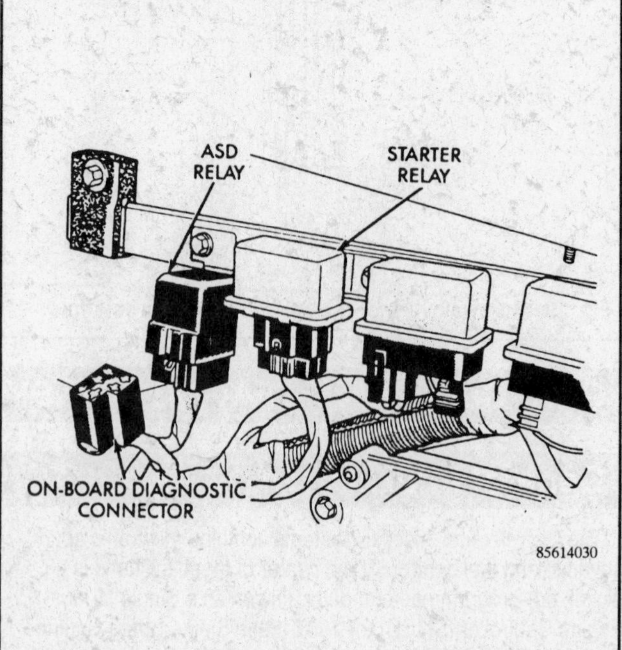

Fig. 30 Engine diagnostic connector location — 1987–90 models

3. On 1988 models, turn the ignition switch **ON, OFF, ON, OFF, ON** within 5 seconds. On 1989-95 models, simply turn the ignition switch **ON** to access the read fault code data. Record all the fault code messages displayed on the readout box.

4. Observe the CHECK ENGINE light on the instrument panel. The light should illuminate for 3 seconds and then go out.

EXITING THE DIAGNOSTIC TEST

By turning the ignition switch to the **OFF** position, the test mode system is exited. With a Diagnostic Readout Box attached to the system and the ATM control button not pressed, the computer will continue to cycle the selected circuits for 5 minutes and then automatically shut the system down.

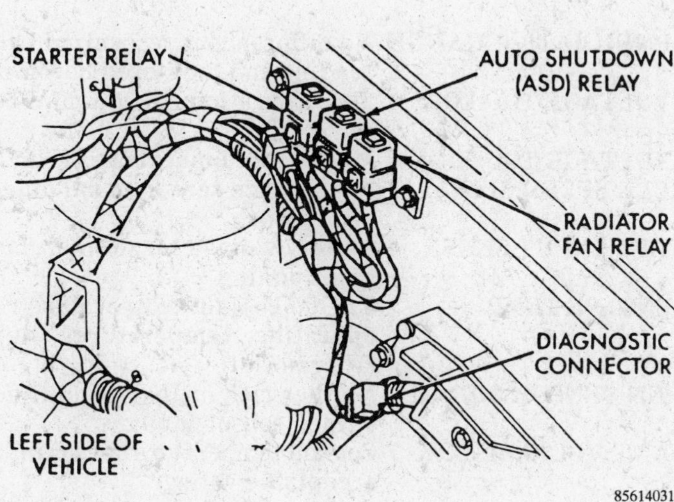

Fig. 31 Engine diagnostic connector location — 1991-93 models

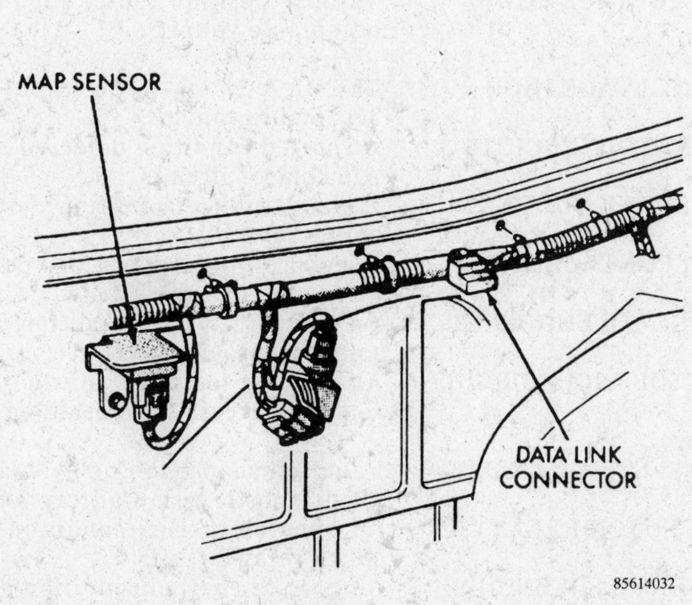

Fig. 32 Engine diagnostic connector location — 1994-95 models

TROUBLE CODES

CHECK ENGINE LAMP FAULT CODE	DRB II DISPLAY	DESCRIPTION OF FAULT CONDITION
11	IGN REFERENCE SIGNAL	No distributor reference signal detected during engine cranking.
12	No. of Key-ons since last fault or since faults were erased.	Direct battery input to controller disconnected within the last 50-100 ignition key-ons.
13†**	MAP PNEUMATIC SIGNAL	No variation in MAP sensor signal is detected.
	or	
	MAP PNEUMATIC CHANGE	No difference is recognized between the engine MAP reading and the stored barometric pressure reading.
14†**	MAP VOLTAGE TOO LOW	MAP sensor input below minimum acceptable voltage.
	or	
	MAP VOLTAGE TOO HIGH	MAP sensor input above maximum acceptable voltage.
15**	VEHICLE SPEED SIGNAL	No distance sensor signal detected during road load conditions.
16†**	BATTERY INPUT SENSE	Battery voltage sense input not detected during engine running.
17	LOW ENGINE TEMP	Engine coolant temperature remains below normal operating temperatures during vehicle travel (Thermostat).
21**	OXYGEN SENSOR SIGNAL	Neither rich or lean condition is detected from the oxygen sensor input.
22†**	COOLANT VOLTAGE LOW	Coolant temperature sensor input below the minimum acceptable voltage.
	or	
	COOLANT VOLTAGE HIGH	Coolant temperature sensor input above the maximum acceptable voltage.
23	T/B TEMP VOLTAGE LOW	Throttle body temperature sensor input below the minimum acceptable voltage.
	or	
	T/B TEMP VOLTAGE HI	Throttle body temperature sensor input above the maximum acceptable voltage.
24†**	TPS VOLTAGE LOW	Throttle position sensor input below the minimum acceptable voltage.
	or	
	TPS VOLTAGE HIGH	Throttle position sensor input above the maximum acceptable voltage.
25**	AIS MOTOR CIRCUITS	A shorted condition detected in one or more of the AIS control circuits.
26	INJ 1 PEAK CURRENT	High resistance condition detected in the injector output circuit.
27	INJ 1 CONTROL CKT	Injector output driver stage does not respond properly to the control signal.
31**	PURGE SOLENOID CKT	An open or shorted condition detected in the purge solenoid circuit.
32**	EGR SOLENOID CIRCUIT	An open or shorted condition detected in the EGR solenoid circuit. (California emissions only)
	or	
	EGR SYSTEM FAILURE	Required change in Fuel/Air ratio not detected during diagnostic test. (California emissions only)
33	A/C CLUTCH RELAY CKT	An open or shorted condition detected in the A/C clutch relay circuit.
34	S/C SERVO SOLENOIDS	An open or shorted condition detected in the speed control vacuum or vent solenoid circuits.

85614C01

Fig. 33 Fault Code Identification — 1987-89 models with TBI

CHECK ENGINE LAMP FAULT CODE	DRB II DISPLAY	DESCRIPTION OF FAULT CONDITION
35	RADIATOR FAN RELAY	An open or shorted condition detected in the radiator fan relay circuit.
41	CHARGING SYSTEM CKT	Output driver stage for alternator field does not respond properly to the voltage regulator control signal.
42	ASD RELAY CIRCUIT	An open or shorted condition detected in the auto shutdown relay circuit.
43	IGNITION CONTROL CKT	Output driver stage for ignition coil does not respond properly to the dwell control signal.
44	FJ2 VOLTAGE SENSE	No FJ2 voltage present at the logic board during controller operation.
46**	BATTERY VOLTAGE HIGH	Battery voltage sense input above target charging voltage during engine operation.
47	BATTERY VOLTAGE LOW	Battery voltage sense input below target charging voltage during engine operation.
51**	AIR FUEL AT LIMIT	Oxygen sensor signal input indicates lean fuel/air ratio condition during engine operation.
52**	AIR FUEL AT LIMIT	Oxygen sensor signal input indicates rich fuel/air ratio condition during engine operation.
	or	
	EXCESSIVE LEANING	Adaptive fuel value leaned excessively due to a sustained rich condition.
53	INTERNAL SELF-TEST	Internal engine controller fault condition detected.
55		Completion of fault code display on the CHECK ENGINE lamp.
62	EMR MILEAGE ACCUM	Unsuccessful attempt to update EMR mileage in the controller EEPROM.
63	EEPROM WRITE DENIED	Unsuccessful attempt to write to an EEPROM location by the controller.
	FAULT CODE ERROR	An unrecognized fault ID received by DRB II.

†Check Engine Lamp On
**Check Engine Lamp On (California Only)

85614C02

Fig. 34 Fault Code Identification — 1987–89 models with TBI (continued)

CHECK ENGINE LAMP FAULT CODE	DRB II DISPLAY	DESCRIPTION OF FAULT CONDITION
11	IGN REFERENCE SIGNAL	No distributor reference signal detected during engine cranking.
12	No. of Key-ons since last fault or since faults were erased.	Direct battery input to controller disconnected within the last 50-100 ignition key-ons.
13†**	MAP PNEUMATIC SIGNAL	No variation in MAP sensor signal is detected.
	or	
	MAP PNEUMATIC CHANGE	No difference is recognized between the engine MAP reading and the stored barometric pressure reading.
14†**	MAP VOLTAGE TOO LOW	MAP sensor input below minimum acceptable voltage.
	or	
	MAP VOLTAGE TOO HIGH	MAP sensor input above maximum acceptable voltage.
15**	VEHICLE SPEED SIGNAL	No distance sensor signal detected during road load conditions.
16†**	BATTERY INPUT SENSE	Battery voltage sense input not detected during engine running.
17	LOW ENGINE TEMP	Engine coolant temperature remains below normal operating temperatures during vehicle travel (Thermostat).
21**	OXYGEN SENSOR SIGNAL	Neither rich or lean condition is detected from the oxygen sensor input.
22†**	COOLANT VOLTAGE LOW	Coolant temperature sensor input below the minimum acceptable voltage.
	or	
	COOLANT VOLTAGE HIGH	Coolant temperature sensor input above the maximum acceptable voltage.
24	TPS VOLTAGE LOW	Throttle position sensor input below the minimum acceptable voltage.
	or	
	TPS VOLTAGE HIGH	Throttle position sensor input above the maximum acceptable voltage.
25	AIS MOTOR CIRCUITS	A shorted condition detected in one or more of the AIS control circuits.
26†**	INJ 1 PEAK CURRENT	High resistance condition detected in the INJ 1 injector bank circuit.
	or	
	INJ 2 PEAK CURRENT	High resistance condition detected in the INJ 2 injector bank circuit.
	or	
	INJ 3 PEAK CURRENT	High resistance condition detected in the INJ 3 injector bank circuit.
27†**	INJ 1 CONTROL CKT	INJ 1 injector bank output driver stage does not respond properly to the control signal.
	or	
	INJ 2 CONTROL CKT	INJ 2 injector bank output driver stage does not respond properly to the control signal.
	or	
	INJ 3 CONTROL CKT	INJ 3 injector bank output driver stage does not respond properly to the control signal.
31**	PURGE SOLENOID CKT	An open or shorted condition detected in the purge solenoid circuit.

85614C03

Fig. 35 Fault Code Identification — 1987-89 models with MFI

CHECK ENGINE LAMP FAULT CODE	DRB II DISPLAY	DESCRIPTION OF FAULT CONDITION
33	A/C CLUTCH RELAY CKT	An open or shorted condition detected in the A/C clutch relay circuit.
34	S/C SERVO SOLENOIDS	An open or shorted condition detected in the speed control vacuum or vent solenoid circuits.
35	RADIATOR FAN RELAY	An open or shorted condition detected in the radiator fan relay circuit.
41	CHARGING SYSTEM CKT	Output driver stage for alternator field does not respond properly to the voltage regulator control signal.
42	ASD RELAY CIRCUIT	An open or shorted condition detected in the auto shutdown relay circuit.
	or	
	Z1 VOLTAGE SENSE	No Z1 voltage sensed when the auto shutdown relay is energized.
43	IGNITION CONTROL CKT	Output driver stage for ignition coil does not respond properly to the dwell control signal.
44	FJ2 VOLTAGE SENSE	No FJ2 voltage present at the logic board during controller operation. (S-body only)
46†**	BATTERY VOLTAGE HIGH	Battery voltage sense input above target charging voltage during engine operation.
47	BATTERY VOLTAGE LOW	Battery voltage sense input below target charging voltage during engine operation.
51	AIR FUEL AT LIMIT	Oxygen sensor signal input indicates lean fuel/air ratio condition during engine operation.
52	AIR FUEL AT LIMIT	Oxygen sensor signal input indicates rich fuel/air ratio condition during engine operation.
53	INTERNAL SELF-TEST	Internal engine controller fault condition detected.
54†**	SYNC PICK-UP SIGNAL	No high data rate signal detected during engine rotation.
55		Completion of fault code display on the CHECK ENGINE lamp.
62	EMR MILEAGE ACCUM	Unsuccessful attempt to update EMR mileage in the controller EEPROM.
63	EEPROM WRITE DENIED	Unsuccessful attempt to write to an EEPROM location by the controller.
	FAULT CODE ERROR	An unrecognized fault ID received by DRB II.

†Check Engine Lamp On
**Check Engine Lamp On (California Only)

85614C04

Fig. 36 Fault Code Identification — 1987–89 models with MFI (continued)

Fault Code	DRB II Display	Description of Fault Code
11	No Reference Signal During Cranking	No distributor reference signal detected during engine cranking.
13+**	Slow Change in Idle MAP Signal or No Change in MAP from Start to Run	No variation in MAP Sensor signal is detected. No difference is recognized between the engine MAP reading and the barometric pressure reading at start-up.
14+**	MAP Voltage Too Low or MAP Voltage Too High	MAP sensor input below minimum acceptable voltage. MAP sensor input above maximum acceptable voltage.
15**	No Vehicle Speed Signal	No distance sensor signal detected during road load conditions.
17	Engine Is Cold Too Long	Engine coolant temperature remains below normal operating temperatures during vehicle travel (Thermostat).
21**	O2 Signal Stays at Center or O2 Signal Shorted to Voltage	Neither rich or lean condition is detected from the oxygen sensor input. Oxygen sensor input voltage maintained above normal operating range.
22+**	Coolant Sensor Voltage Too High or Coolant Sensor Voltage Too Low	Coolant temperature sensor input above the maximum acceptable voltage. Coolant temperature sensor input below the minimum acceptable voltage.

85614C05

Fig. 37 Fault Code Identification — 1990–91 models with TBI

Fault Code	DRB II Display	Description of Fault Code
24+**	Throttle Position Sensor Voltage High or Throttle Position Sensor Voltage Low	Throttle position sensor input above the maximum acceptable voltage. Throttle position sensor input below the minimum acceptable voltage.
25**	Automatic Idle Speed Motor Circuits	A shorted condition detected in one or more of the AIS control circuits.
27	Injector #1 Control Circuit	Injector #1 output driver does not respond properly to the control signal.
31**	Purge Solenoid Circuit	An open or shorted condition detected in the purge solenoid circuit.
32**	EGR Solenoid Circuit or EGR System Failure	An open or shorted condition detected in the EGR solenoid circuit. (All except Federal with Auto Trans.) Required change in Fuel/Air ratio not detected during diagnostic test. (California only)
33	A/C Clutch Relay Circuit	An open or shorted condition detected in the A/C clutch relay circuit.
34	Speed Control Solenoid Circuits	An open or shorted condition detected in the speed control vacuum or vent solenoid circuits.
35	Radiator Fan Relay Circuit	An open or shorted condition detected in the radiator fan relay circuit.
37	Torque Converter Unlock Solenoid CKT	An open or shorted condition detected in the torque converter part throttle unlock solenoid circuit. (automatic transmission only)

85614C06

Fig. 38 Fault Code Identification — 1990–91 models with TBI (continued)

Fault Code	DRB II Display	Description of Fault Code
41+**	Alternator Field Not Switching Properly	An open or shorted condition detected in the alternator field control circuit.
42	Auto Shutdown Relay Control Circuit	An open or shorted condition detected in the auto shutdown relay circuit.
46+**	Charging System Voltage Too High	Battery voltage sense input above target charging voltage during engine operation.
47+**	Charging System Voltage Too Low	Battery voltage sense input below target charging voltage during engine operation and no significant change in voltage detected during active test of alternator output.
51**	O2 Signal Stays Below Center (Lean)	Oxygen sensor signal input indicates lean fuel/air ratio condition during engine operation.
52**	O2 Signal Stays Above Center (Rich)	Oxygen sensor signal input indicates rich fuel/air ratio condition during engine operation.
53	Internal Controller Failure	Internal engine controller fault condition detected.
62	Controller Failure EMR Miles Not Stored	Unsuccessful attempt to update EMR mileage in the controller EEPROM.
63	Controller Failure EEPROM Write Denied	Unsuccessful attempt to write to an EEPROM location by the controller.
55	N/A	Completion of fault code display on CHECK ENGINE lamp.

+ Check Engine Lamp On
** Check Engine Lamp On (California Only)

85614C07

Fig. 39 Fault Code Identification — 1990–91 models with TBI (continued)

Fault Code	DRB II Display	Description of Fault Code
11	No Reference Signal During Cranking	No ignition reference signal detected during engine cranking.
13+**	Slow Change in Idle MAP Signal	No variation in MAP Sensor signal is detected.
	or	
	No Change in MAP from Start to Run	No difference is recognized between the engine MAP reading and the barometric pressure reading at start-up.
14+**	MAP Voltage Too Low	MAP sensor input below minimum acceptable voltage.
	or	
	MAP Voltage Too High	MAP sensor input above maximum acceptable voltage.
15**	No Vehicle Speed Signal	No distance sensor signal detected during road load conditions.
17	Engine Is Cold Too Long	Engine coolant temperature remains below normal operating temperatures during vehicle travel (Thermostat).
21**	O2 Signal Stays at Center	Neither rich or lean condition is detected from the oxygen sensor input.
	or	
	O2 Signal Shorted to Voltage	Oxygen sensor input voltage maintained above normal operating range.
22+**	Coolant Sensor Voltage Too High	Coolant temperature sensor input above the maximum acceptable voltage.
	or	
	Coolant Sensor Voltage Too Low	Coolant temperature sensor input below the minimum acceptable voltage.

85614C08

Fig. 40 Fault Code Identification — 1990–91 models with MFI

Fault Code	DRB II Display	Description of Fault Code
24+**	Throttle Position Sensor Voltage High or Throttle Position Sensor Voltage Low	Throttle position sensor input above the maximum acceptable voltage. Throttle position sensor input below the minimum acceptable voltage.
25**	Automatic Idle Speed Motor Circuits	A shorted condition detected in one or more of the AIS control circuits.
26+**	Injector #1 Peak Current Not Reached or Injector #2 Peak Current Not Reached or Injector #3 Peak Current Not Reached	High resistance condition detected in the INJ 1 injector bank circuit. High resistance condition detected in the INJ 2 injector bank circuit. High resistance condition detected in the INJ 3 injector bank circuit.
27+**	Injector #1 Control Circuit or Injector #2 Control Circuit or Injector #3 Control Circuit	Injector #1 output driver does not respond properly to the control signal. Injector #2 output driver does not respond properly to the control signal. Injector #3 output driver does not respond properly to the control signal.
31**	Purge Solenoid Circuit	An open or shorted condition detected in the purge solenoid circuit.

85614C09

Fig. 41 Fault Code Identification — 1990–91 models with MFI (continued)

Fault Code	DRB II Display	Description
11	No reference Signal During Cranking	No distributor reference signal detected during engine cranking.
13+••	No change in MAP from start to run	No difference recognized between the engine MAP reading and the barometric (atmospheric) pressure reading at start-up.
14+••	MAP voltage too low or MAP voltage too High	MAP sensor input below minimum acceptable voltage. MAP sensor input above maximum acceptable voltage.
15••	No vehicle speed signal	No vehicle distance (speed) sensor signal detected during road load conditions.
17	Engine is cold too long	Engine coolant temperature remains below normal operating temperatures during vehicle travel (thermostat).
21••	O_2 signal stays at center or O_2 signal shorted to voltage	Neither rich or lean condition detected from the oxygen sensor input. Oxygen sensor input voltage maintained above the normal operating range.
22+••	Coolant sensor voltage too high or Coolant sensor voltage too low	Coolant temperature sensor input above the maximum acceptable voltage. Coolant temperature sensor input below the minimum acceptable voltage.
24+••	Throttle position sensor voltage high or Throttle position sensor voltage low	Throttle position sensor input above the maximum acceptable voltage. Throttle position sensor input below the minimum acceptable voltage.
25••	Automatic idle speed motor circuits	A shorted condition detected in one or more of the AIS control circuits.
27	Injector control circuit (DRB II)	Injector output driver does not respond properly to the control signal (DRB II specifies the injector by cylinder number).
31••	Purge solenoid circuit	An open or shorted condition detected in the purge solenoid circuit.
33	A/C clutch relay circuit	An open or shorted condition detected in the A/C clutch relay circuit.
34	Speed control solenoid circuits	An open or shorted condition detected in the speed control vacuum or vent solenoid circuits.

+ Check Engine Lamp On
•• Check Engine Lamp On (California Only)

85614C10

Fig. 42 Fault Code Identification — 1992-93 models with TBI

Fault Code	DRB II Display	Description
35	Radiator fan relay circuits	An open or shorted condition detected in the radiator fan circuit
37	Torque convertor unlock solenoid CKT	An open or shorted condition detected in the torque convertor part throttle unlock solenoid circuit (automatic transmission).
41+**	Alternator field not switching properly	An open or shorted condition detected in the alternator field control circuit.
42	Auto shutdown relay control circuit	An open or shorted condition detected in the auto shutdown relay circuit.
44	Battery temp voltage	An open or shorted condition exists in the coolant temperature sensor circuit or a problem exists in the engine controller's battery temperature voltage circuit.
46+**	Charging system voltage too high	Battery voltage sense input above target charging voltage during engine operation.
47+**	Charging system voltage too low	Battery voltage sense input below target charging during engine operation. Also, no significant change detected in battery voltage during active test of alternator output.
51**	O_2 signal stays below center (lean)	Oxygen sensor signal input indicates lean air/fuel ratio condition during engine operation.
52**	O_2 signal stays above center (rich)	Oxygen sensor signal input indicates rich air/fuel ratio condition during engine operation.
53	Internal controller	Engine controller internal fault condition detected.
62	Controller Failure EMR miles not stored	Unsuccessful attempt to update EMR milage in the controller EEPROM.
63	Controller Failure EEPROM write denied	Unsuccessful attempt to write to an EEPROM location by the engine controller.
55	N/A	Completion of fault code display on Check Engine lamp.

+ Check Engine Lamp On
** Check Engine Lamp On (California Only)

85614C11

Fig. 43 Fault Code Identification — 1992–93 models with TBI (continued)

Fault Code	DRB II Display	Description
11	No reference Signal During Cranking	No distributor reference signal detected during engine cranking.
13+**	No change in MAP from start to run	No difference recognized between the engine MAP reading and the barometric (atmospheric) pressure reading at start-up.
14+**	MAP voltage too low	MAP sensor input below minimum acceptable voltage.
	or	
	MAP voltage too High	MAP sensor input above maximum acceptable voltage.
15**	No vehicle speed signal	No vehicle distance (speed) sensor signal detected during road load conditions.
17	Engine is cold too long	Engine coolant temperature remains below normal operating temperatures during vehicle travel (thermostat).
21**	O_2 signal stays at center	Neither rich or lean condition detected from the oxygen sensor input.
	or	
	O_2 signal shorted to voltage	Oxygen sensor input voltage maintained above the normal operating range.
22+**	Coolant sensor voltage too high	Coolant temperature sensor input above the maximum acceptable voltage.
	or	
	Coolant sensor voltage too low	Coolant temperature sensor input below the minimum acceptable voltage.
24+**	Throttle position sensor voltage high	Throttle position sensor input above the maximum acceptable voltage.
	or	
	Throttle position sensor voltage low	Throttle position sensor input below the minimum acceptable voltage.
25**	Automatic idle speed motor circuits	A shorted condition detected in one or more of the AIS control circuits.
27	Injector control circuit (DRB II)	Injector output driver does not respond properly to the control signal (DRB II specifies the injector by cylinder number).
31**	Purge solenoid circuit	An open or shorted condition detected in the purge solenoid circuit.
33	A/C clutch relay circuit	An open or shorted condition detected in the A/C clutch relay circuit.
34	Speed control solenoid circuits	An open or shorted condition detected in the speed control vacuum or vent solenoid circuits.

+ Check Engine Lamp On
** Check Engine Lamp On (California Only)

85614C12

Fig. 44 Fault Code Identification — 1992–93 models with MFI

Fault Code	DRB II Display	Description
35	Radiator fan relay circuits	An open or shorted condition detected in the radiator fan circuit
41+••	Alternator field not switching properly	An open or shorted condition detected in the alternator field control circuit.
42	Auto shutdown relay control circuit	An open or shorted condition detected in the auto shutdown relay circuit.
43+••	Ignition coil #1 primary circuit or Ignition coil #2 primary circuit or Ignition coil #3 primary circuit	Peak primary circuit current not achieved with maximum dwell time. Peak primary circuit current not achieved with maximum dwell time. Peak primary circuit current not achieved with maximum dwell time.
44	Battery temp voltage	An open or shorted condition exists in the coolant temperature sensor circuit or a problem exists in the engine controller's battery temperature voltage circuit.
46+••	Charging system voltage too high	Battery voltage sense input above target charging voltage during engine operation.
47+••	Charging system voltage too low	Battery voltage sense input below target charging during engine operation. Also, no significant change detected in battery voltage during active test of alternator output.
51••	O_2 signal stays below center (lean)	Oxygen sensor signal input indicates lean air/fuel ratio condition during engine operation.
52••	O_2 signal stays above center (rich)	Oxygen sensor signal input indicates rich air/fuel ratio condition during engine operation.
53	Internal controller	Engine controller internal fault condition detected.
54+••	No sync pick-up signal	No fuel sync signal detected during engine rotation.
62	Controller Failure EMR miles not stored	Unsuccessful attempt to update EMR milage in the controller EEPROM.
63	Controller Failure EEPROM write denied	Unsuccessful attempt to write to an EEPROM location by the engine controller.
55	N/A	Completion of fault code display on Check Engine lamp.

\+ Check Engine Lamp On
•• Check Engine Lamp On (California Only)

85614C13

Fig. 45 Fault Code Identification — 1992–93 models with MFI (continued)

Diagnostic Trouble Code	DRB Scan Tool Display	Description of Diagnostic Trouble Code
11*	No Crank Reference Signal at PCM	No crank reference signal detected during engine cranking.
12*	Battery Disconnect	Direct battery input to PCM was disconnected within the last 50 Key-on cycles.
13**	No Change in MAP From Start to Run	No difference recognized between the engine MAP reading and the barometric (atmospheric) pressure reading at start-up.
	or	
	Slow Change in Idle MAP Signal	MAP output change is slower and/or smaller than expected.
14**	MAP Sensor Voltage Too Low	MAP sensor input below minimum acceptable voltage.
	or	
	MAP Sensor Voltage Too High	MAP sensor input above maximum acceptable voltage.
15**	No Vehicle Speed Sensor Signal	No vehicle distance (speed) sensor signal detected during road load conditions.
17*	Engine is Cold Too Long	Engine coolant temperature remains below normal operating temperatures during vehicle travel (thermostat).
21**	O2S Stays at Center	Neither rich or lean condition detected from the oxygen sensor input.
	or	
	O2S Shorted to Voltage	Oxygen sensor input voltage maintained above the normal operating range.
22**	ECT Sensor Voltage Too High	Engine coolant temperature sensor input above maximum acceptable voltage.
	or	
	ECT Sensor Voltage Too Low	Engine coolant temperature sensor input below minimum acceptable voltage.
24**	Throttle Position Sensor Voltage High	Throttle position sensor input above the maximum acceptable voltage.
	or	
	Throttle Position Sensor Voltage Low	Throttle position sensor input below the minimum acceptable voltage.
25**	Idle Air Control Motor Circuits	A shorted condition detected in one or more of the IAC motor control circuits.
27**	Injector Control Circuit	Injector output driver does not respond properly to the control signal.
31**	EVAP Solenoid Circuit	An open or shorted condition detected in the EVAP purge solenoid circuit.
33*	A/C Clutch Relay	An open or shorted condition detected in the A/C clutch relay circuit.

* Check Engine Lamp will not illuminate at all times if this Diagnostic Trouble Code was recorded. Cycle Ignition key as described in manual and observe code flashed by Check Engine lamp.

** Check Engine Lamp will illuminate during engine operation if this Diagnostic Trouble Code was recorded.

85614C14

Fig. 46 Fault Code Identification — 1994–95 models with TBI

Diagnostic Trouble Code	DRB Scan Tool Display	Description of Diagnostic Trouble Code
34*	Speed Control Solenoid Circuits	An open or shorted condition detected in the speed control vacuum or vent solenoid circuits.
35*	Low Speed Fan CTRL Relay Circuits	An open or shorted condition detected in the radiator fan low speed relay circuit.
	or	
	High Speed Fan CTRL Relay Circuits	An open or shorted condition detected in the radiator fan high speed relay circuit.
37*	Torque Convertor Clutch Solenoid CKT	An open or shorted condition detected in the torque convertor clutch solenoid circuit.
41*	Generator Field Not Switching Properly	An open or shorted condition detected in the generator field control circuit.
42*	Auto Shutdown Relay Control Circuit	An open or shorted condition detected in the automatic shut down relay circuit.
	or	
	No ASD Relay Output Voltage at PCM	PCM did not detect ASD sense signal after grounding the ASD relay.
46**	Charging System Voltage Too High	Battery voltage sense input above target charging voltage during engine operation.
47**	Charging System Voltage Too Low	Battery voltage sense input below target charging during engine operation. Also, no significant change detected in battery voltage during active test of generator output.
51**	O2S Signal Stays Below Center (Lean)	Oxygen sensor signal input indicates lean air/fuel ratio condition during engine operation.
52**	O2S Signal Stays Above Center (Rich)	Oxygen sensor signal input indicates rich air/fuel ratio condition during engine operation.
53*	Internal Controller Failure	Powertrain Control Module internal fault condition detected.
62*	PCM Failure SRI Mile Not Stored	Unsuccessful attempt to update SRI Milage.
63*	PCM Failure EEPROM Write Denied	Unsuccessful attempt to write to an EEPROM location by the Powertrain Control Module.
55	N/A	Completion of fault code display on Malfunction Indicator Lamp (Check Engine lamp).

* Check Engine Lamp will not illuminate at all times if this Diagnostic Trouble Code was recorded. Cycle Ignition key as described in manual and observe code flashed by Check Engine lamp.

** Check Engine Lamp will illuminate during engine operation if this Diagnostic Trouble Code was recorded.

85614C15

Fig. 47 Fault Code Identification — 1994-95 models with TBI (continued)

Diagnostic Trouble Code	DRB Scan Tool Display	Description of Diagnostic Trouble Code
34*	Speed Control Solenoid Circuits	An open or shorted condition detected in the speed control vacuum or vent solenoid circuits.
35*	Low Speed Fan CTRL Relay Circuits or High Speed Fan CTRL Relay Circuits	An open or shorted condition detected in the radiator fan low speed relay circuit. An open or shorted condition detected in the radiator fan high speed relay circuit.
37*	Torque Convertor Clutch Solenoid CKT	An open or shorted condition detected in the torque convertor clutch solenoid circuit.
41*	Generator Field Not Switching Properly	An open or shorted condition detected in the generator field control circuit.
42*	Auto Shutdown Relay Control Circuit or No ASD Relay Output Voltage at PCM	An open or shorted condition detected in the automatic shut down relay circuit. PCM did not detect ASD sense signal after grounding the ASD relay.
46**	Charging System Voltage Too High	Battery voltage sense input above target charging voltage during engine operation.
47**	Charging System Voltage Too Low	Battery voltage sense input below target charging during engine operation. Also, no significant change detected in battery voltage during active test of generator output.
51**	O2S Signal Stays Below Center (Lean)	Oxygen sensor signal input indicates lean air/fuel ratio condition during engine operation.
52**	O2S Signal Stays Above Center (Rich)	Oxygen sensor signal input indicates rich air/fuel ratio condition during engine operation.
53*	Internal Controller Failure	Powertrain Control Module internal fault condition detected.
54*	No Cam Sync Signal at PCM	No fuel sync signal detected during engine rotation.
62*	PCM Failure SRI Mile Not Stored	Unsuccessful attempt to update SRI Milage.
63*	PCM Failure EEPROM Write Denied	Unsuccessful attempt to write to an EEPROM location by the Powertrain Control Module.
55	N/A	Completion of fault code display on Malfunction Indicator Lamp (Check Engine lamp).

* Check Engine Lamp will not illuminate at all times if this Diagnostic Trouble Code was recorded. Cycle Ignition key as described in manual and observe code flashed by Check Engine lamp.

** Check Engine Lamp will illuminate during engine operation if this Diagnostic Trouble Code was recorded.

85614C16

Fig. 48 Fault Code Identification — 1994–95 models with MFI

Diagnostic Trouble Code	DRB Scan Tool Display	Description of Diagnostic Trouble Code
11*	No Crank Reference Signal at PCM	No crank reference signal detected during engine cranking.
12*	Battery Disconnect	Direct battery input to PCM was disconnected within the last 50 Key-on cycles.
13**	No Change in MAP From Start to Run	No difference recognized between the engine MAP reading and the barometric (atmospheric) pressure reading at start-up.
14**	MAP Sensor Voltage Too Low	MAP sensor input below minimum acceptable voltage.
	or	
	MAP Sensor Voltage Too High	MAP sensor input above maximum acceptable voltage.
15**	No Vehicle Speed Sensor Signal	No vehicle distance (speed) sensor signal detected during road load conditions.
17*	Engine is Cold Too Long	Engine coolant temperature remains below normal operating temperatures during vehicle travel (thermostat).
21**	O2S Stays at Center	Neither rich or lean condition detected from the oxygen sensor input.
	or	
	O2S Shorted to Voltage	Oxygen sensor input voltage maintained above the normal operating range.
22**	ECT Sensor Voltage Too High	Engine coolant temperature sensor input above maximum acceptable voltage.
	or	
	ECT Sensor Voltage Too Low	Engine coolant temperature sensor input below minimum acceptable voltage.
24**	Throttle Position Sensor Voltage High	Throttle position sensor input above the maximum acceptable voltage.
	or	
	Throttle Position Sensor Voltage Low	Throttle position sensor input below the minimum acceptable voltage.
25**	Idle Air Control Motor Circuits	A shorted condition detected in one or more of the IAC motor control circuits.
27**	Injector Control Circuit	Injector output driver does not respond properly to the control signal. DRB scan tool specifies which injector.
31**	EVAP Solenoid Circuit	An open or shorted condition detected in the duty cycle EVAP purge solenoid circuit.
32**	EGR Solenoid Circuit	An open or shorted condition detected in the EGR transducer solenoid circuit.
	or	
	EGR System Failure	Required change in air/fuel ratio not detected during diagnostic test.
33*	A/C Clutch Relay	An open or shorted condition detected in the A/C clutch relay circuit.

* Check Engine Lamp will not illuminate at all times if this Diagnostic Trouble Code was recorded. Cycle Ignition key as described in manual and observe code flashed by Check Engine lamp.

** Check Engine Lamp will illuminate during engine operation if this Diagnostic Trouble Code was recorded.

85614C17

Fig. 49 Fault Code Identification — 1994-95 models with MFI (continued)

VACUUM DIAGRAMS

Following is a listing of vacuum diagrams for most of the engine and emissions package combinations covered by this manual. Because vacuum circuits will vary based on various engine and vehicle options, always refer first to the vehicle emission control information label, if present. Should the label be missing, or should the vehicle be equipped with a different engine from the vehicle's original equipment, refer to the diagrams below for the same or similar configuration.

If you wish to obtain a replacement emissions label, most manufacturers make the labels available for purchase. The labels can usually be ordered from a local dealer.

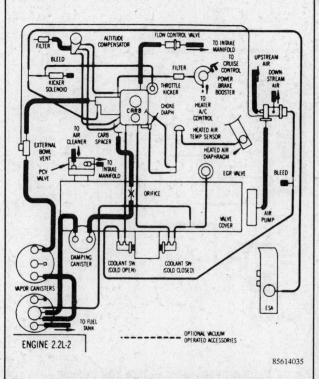

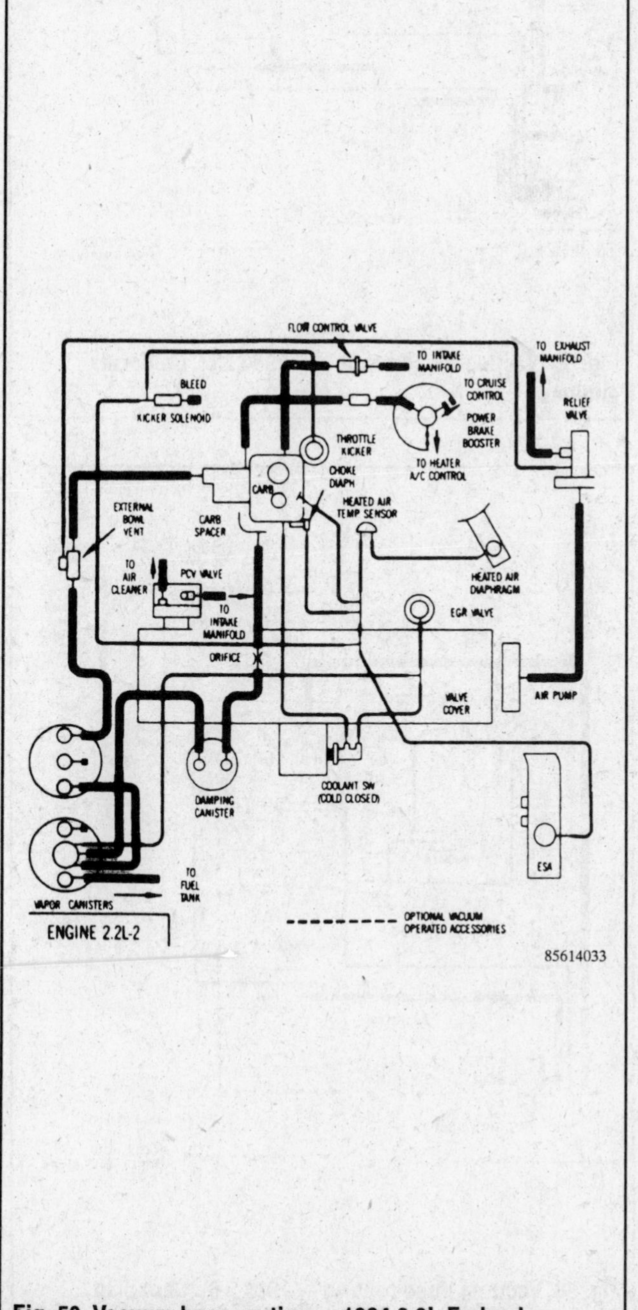

Fig. 50 Vacuum hose routing — 1984 2.2L Federal engines

Fig. 51 Vacuum hose routing — 1984 2.2L California engines

Fig. 52 Vacuum hose routing — 1984 2.2L Altitude engines

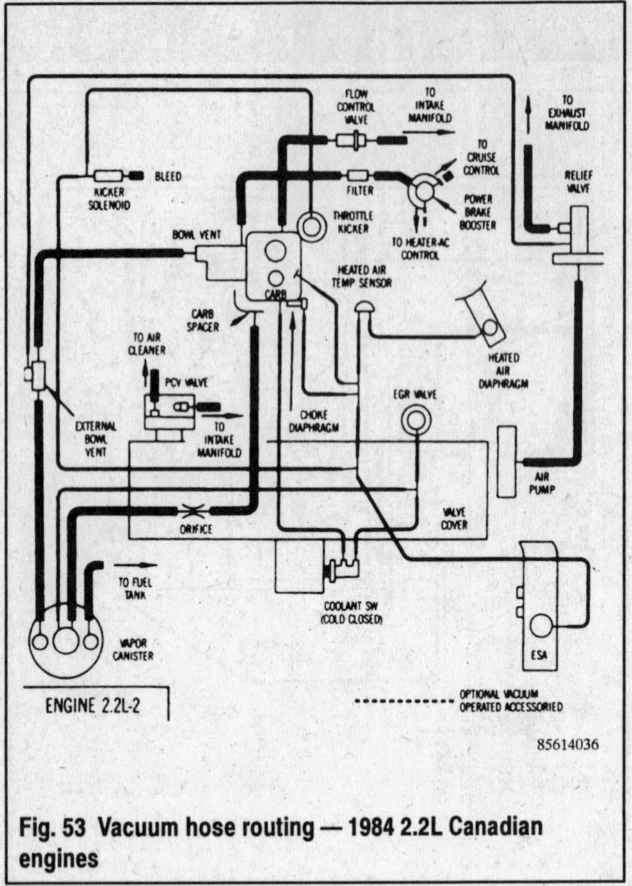

Fig. 53 Vacuum hose routing — 1984 2.2L Canadian engines

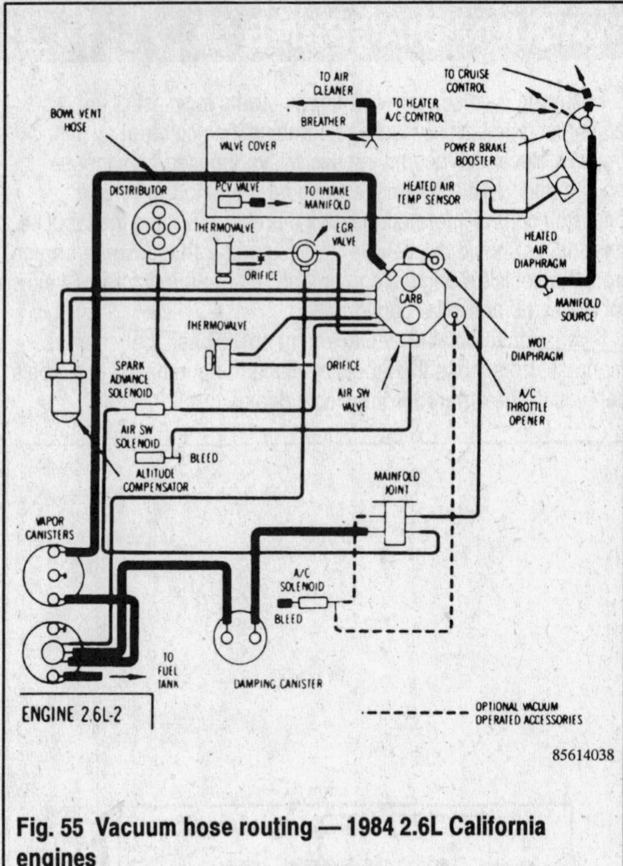

Fig. 55 Vacuum hose routing — 1984 2.6L California engines

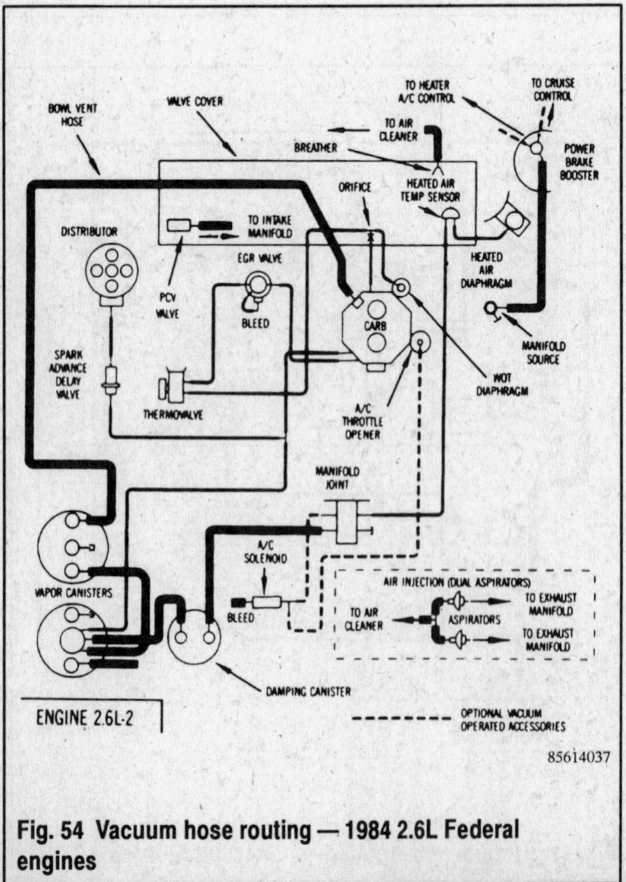

Fig. 54 Vacuum hose routing — 1984 2.6L Federal engines

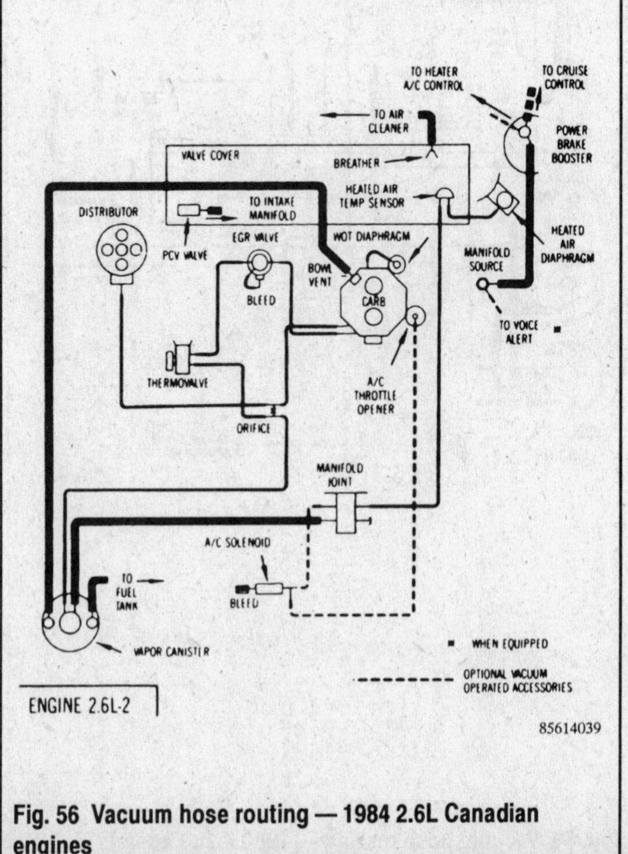

Fig. 56 Vacuum hose routing — 1984 2.6L Canadian engines

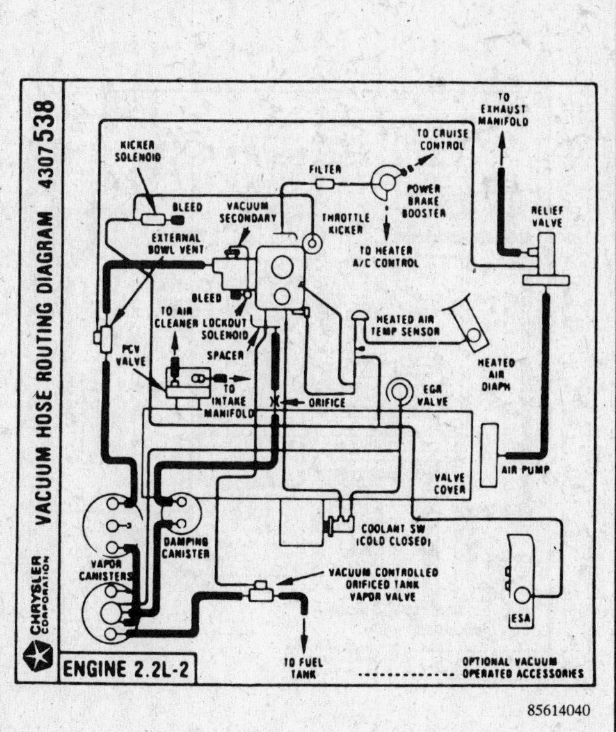

Fig. 57 Vacuum hose routing — 1985 2.2L Federal engines

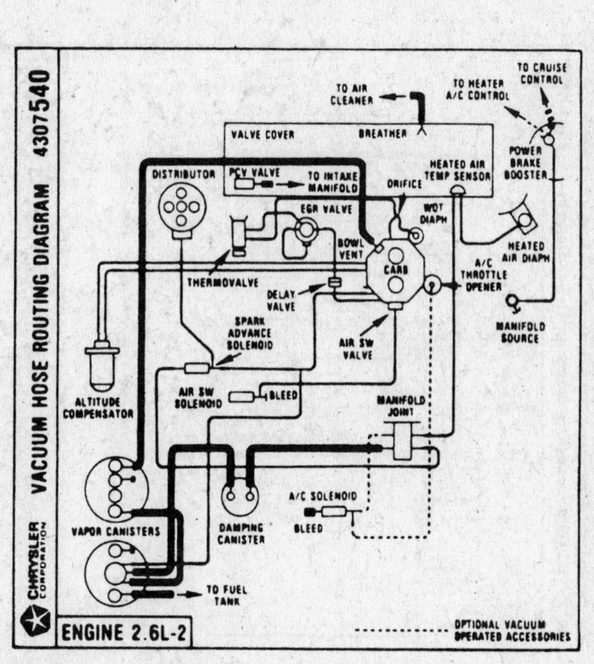

Fig. 59 Vacuum hose routing — 1985 2.6L Altitude engines

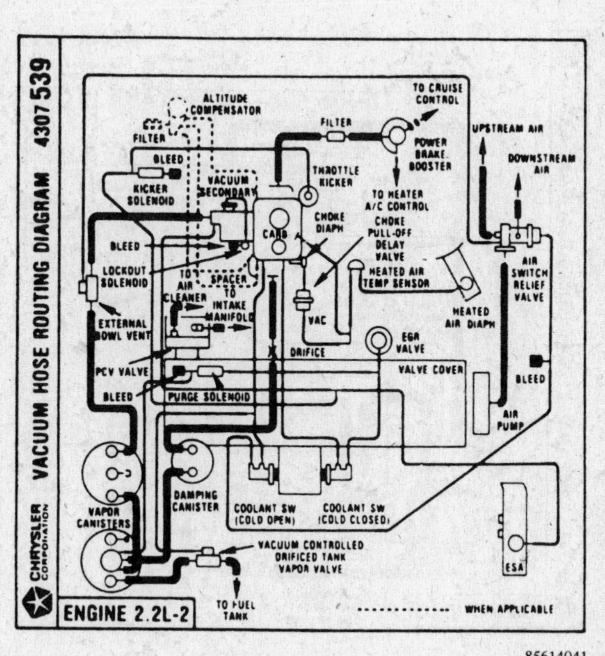

Fig. 58 Vacuum hose routing — 1985 2.2L California engines

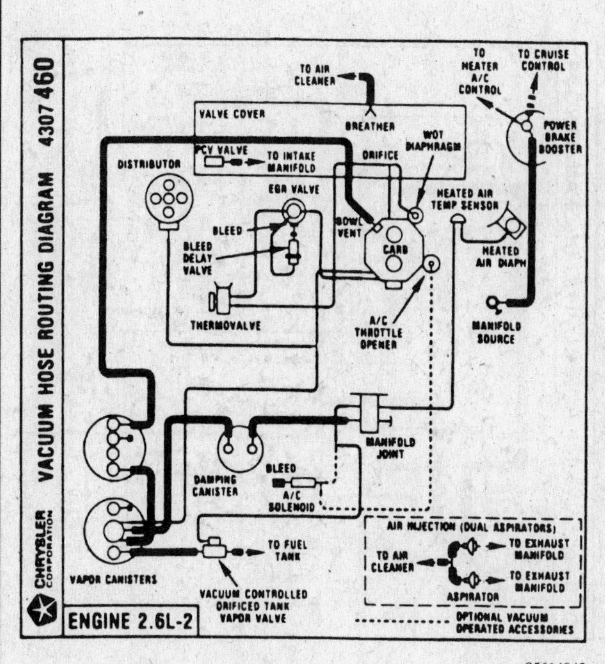

Fig. 60 Vacuum hose routing — 1985 2.6L Federal engines

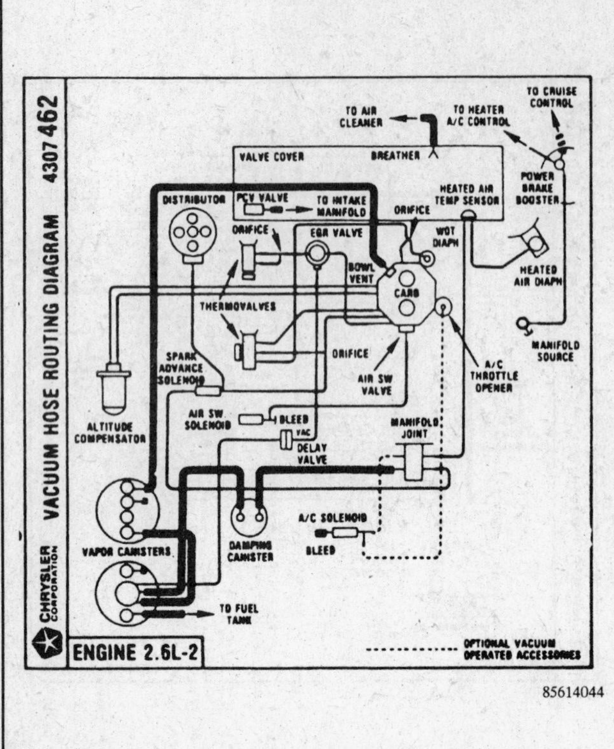
85614044

Fig. 61 Vacuum hose routing — 1985 2.6L California engines

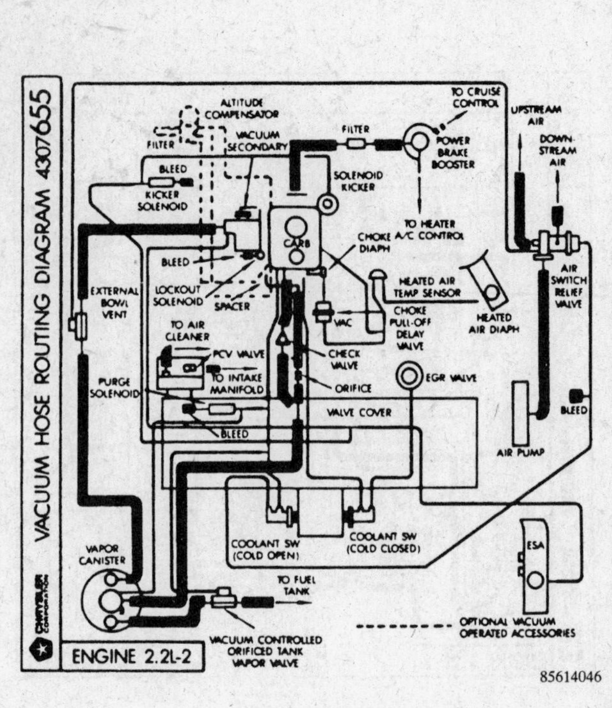
85614046

Fig. 63 Vacuum hose routing — 1986 2.2L California engines

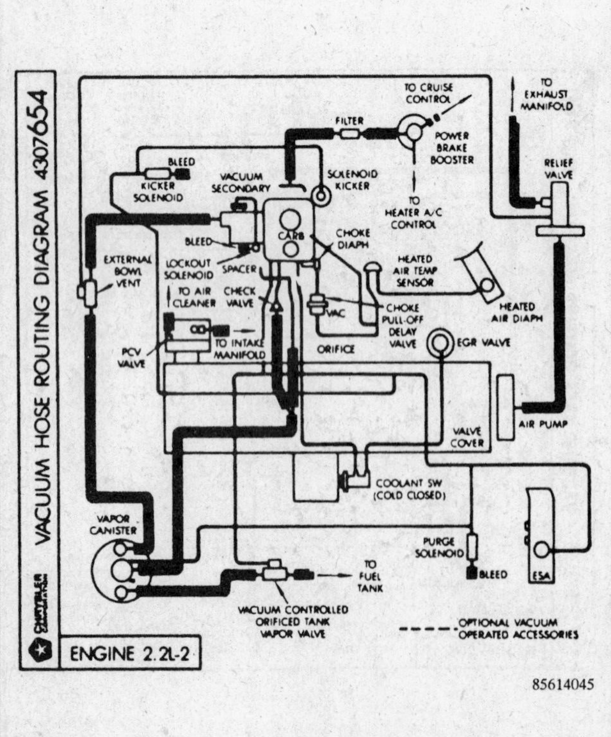
85614045

Fig. 62 Vacuum hose routing — 1986 2.2L Federal engines

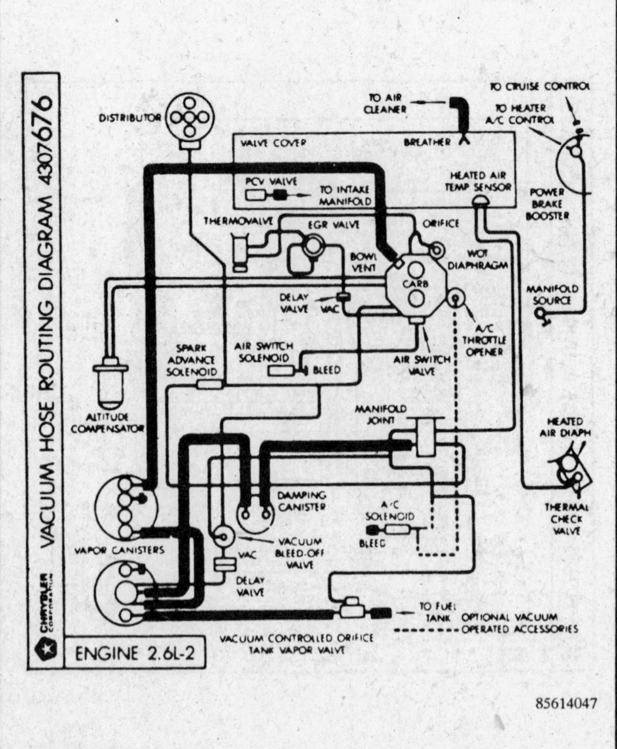
85614047

Fig. 64 Vacuum hose routing — 1986 2.6L Altitude engines

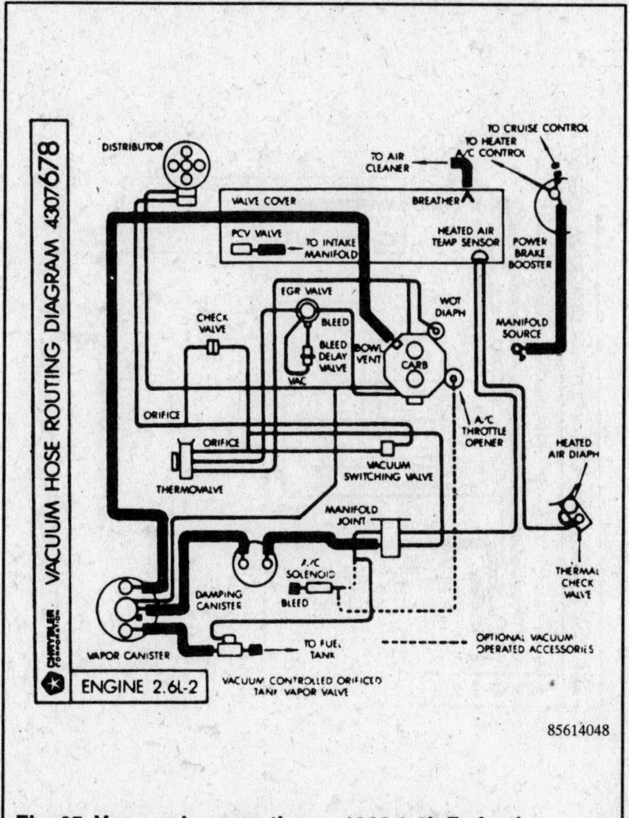

85614048

Fig. 65 Vacuum hose routing — 1986 2.6L Federal engines

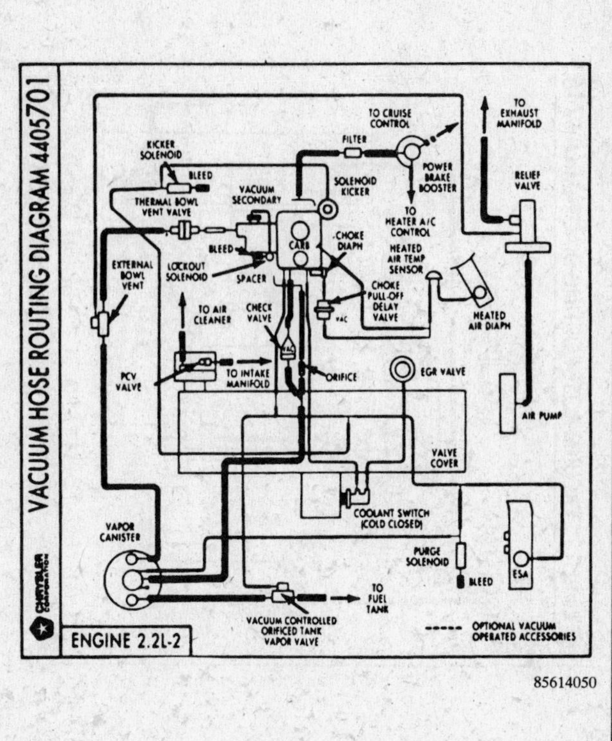

85614050

Fig. 67 Vacuum hose routing — 1987 2.2L Federal engines

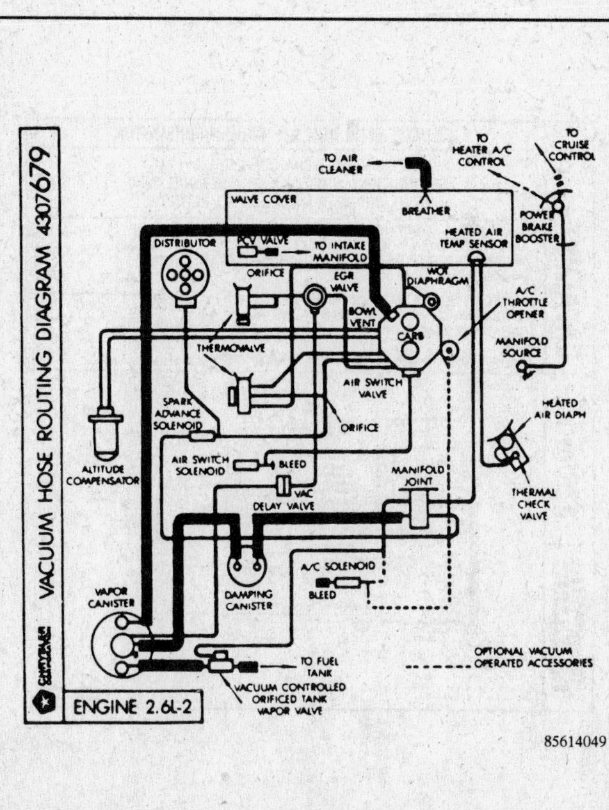

85614049

Fig. 66 Vacuum hose routing — 1986 2.6L California engines

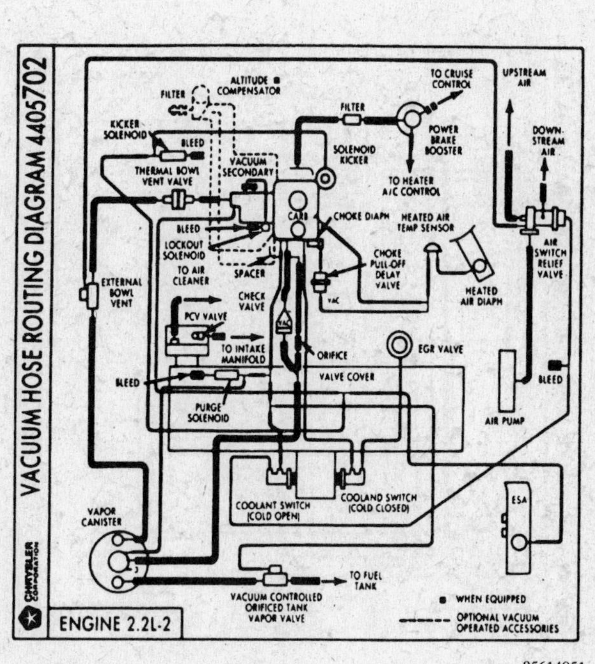

85614051

Fig. 68 Vacuum hose routing — 1987 2.2L California engines

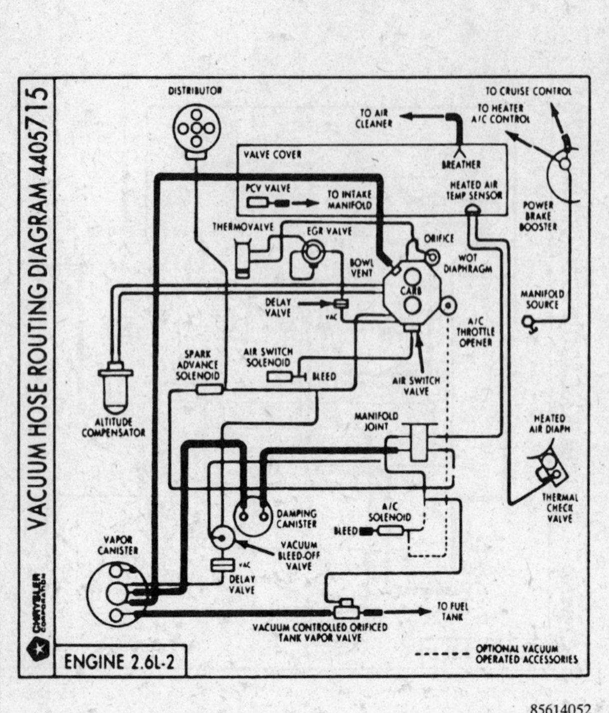

Fig. 69 Vacuum hose routing — 1987 2.6L Federal engines

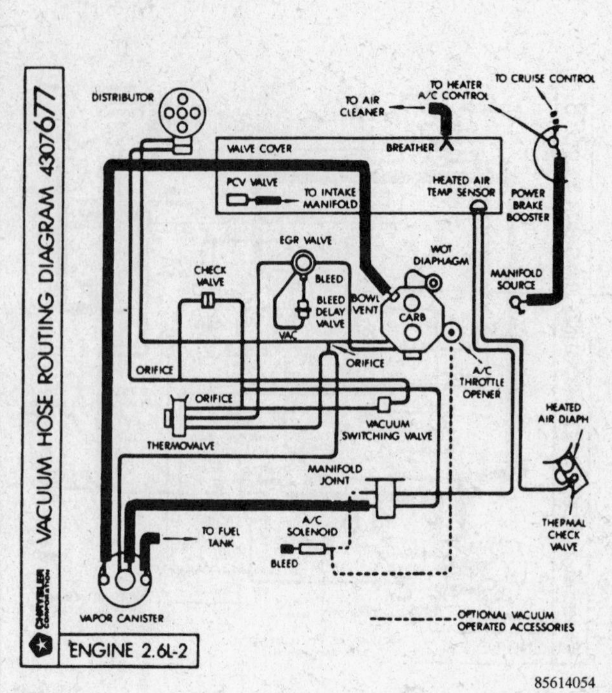

Fig. 71 Vacuum hose routing — 1987 2.6L Canadian engines

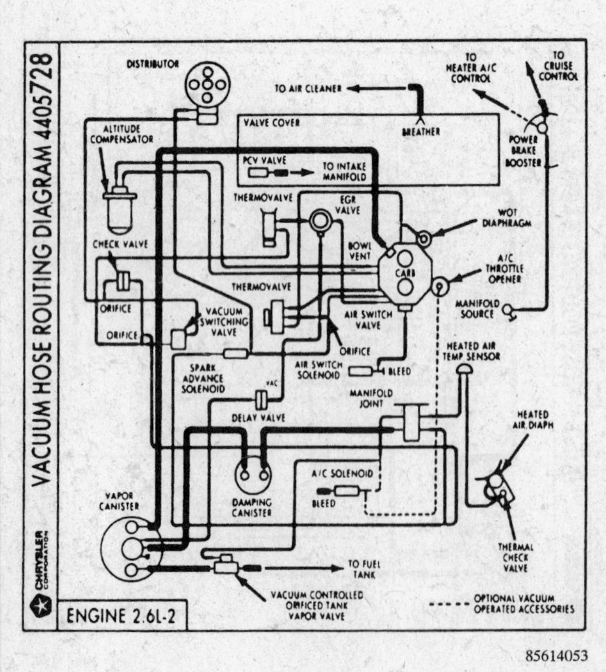

Fig. 70 Vacuum hose routing — 1987 2.6L California engines

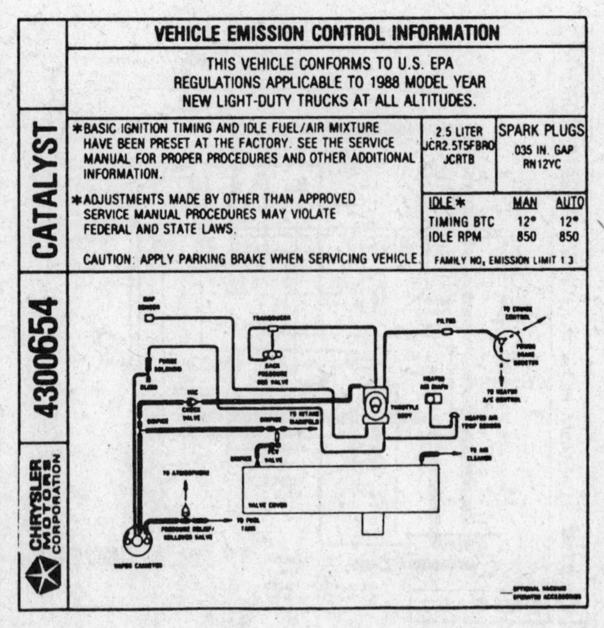
VEHICLE EMISSION CONTROL INFORMATION

THIS VEHICLE CONFORMS TO U.S. EPA REGULATIONS APPLICABLE TO 1988 MODEL YEAR NEW LIGHT-DUTY TRUCKS AT ALL ALTITUDES.

CATALYST

✱BASIC IGNITION TIMING AND IDLE FUEL/AIR MIXTURE HAVE BEEN PRESET AT THE FACTORY. SEE THE SERVICE MANUAL FOR PROPER PROCEDURES AND OTHER ADDITIONAL INFORMATION.

✱ADJUSTMENTS MADE BY OTHER THAN APPROVED SERVICE MANUAL PROCEDURES MAY VIOLATE FEDERAL AND STATE LAWS.

CAUTION: APPLY PARKING BRAKE WHEN SERVICING VEHICLE

2.5 LITER JCR2.5T5FBR0 JCRTB	SPARK PLUGS .035 IN. GAP RN12YC

IDLE ✱	MAN	AUTO
TIMING BTC	12°	12°
IDLE RPM	850	850

FAMILY NO. EMISSION LIMIT 1 3

4300654

CHRYSLER MOTORS CORPORATION

85614055

Fig. 72 Vacuum hose routing — 1988 2.5L Federal and Altitude engines

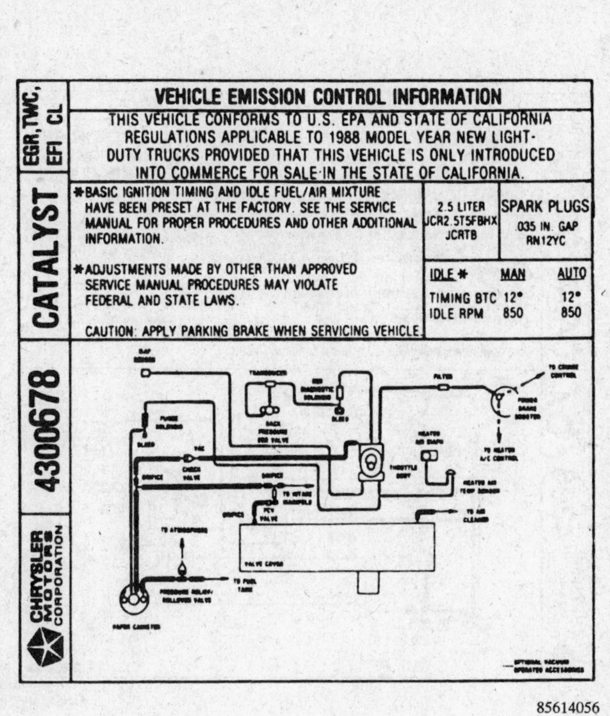

Fig. 73 Vacuum hose routing — 1988 2.5L California engines

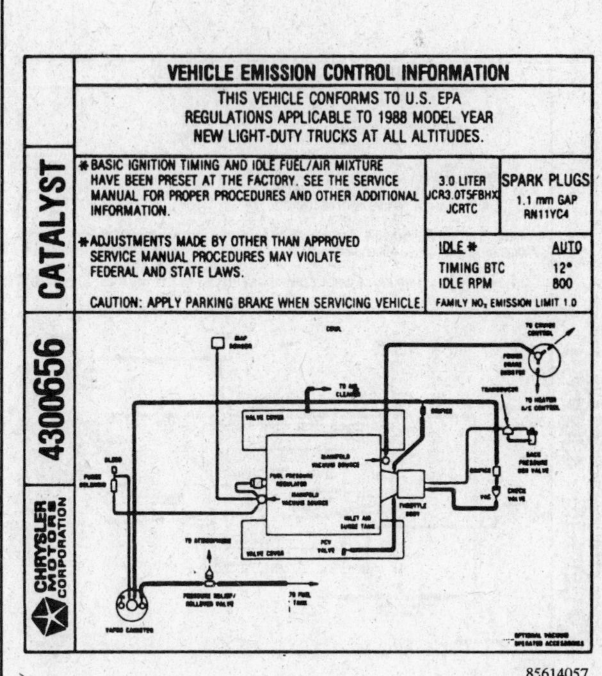

Fig. 75 Vacuum hose routing — 1988 3.0L Federal and Altitude engines

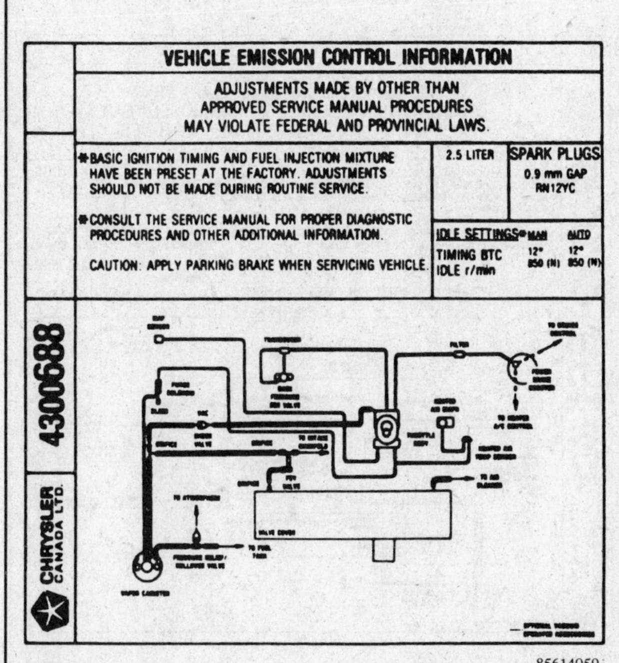

Fig. 74 Vacuum hose routing — 1988 2.5L Canadian engines

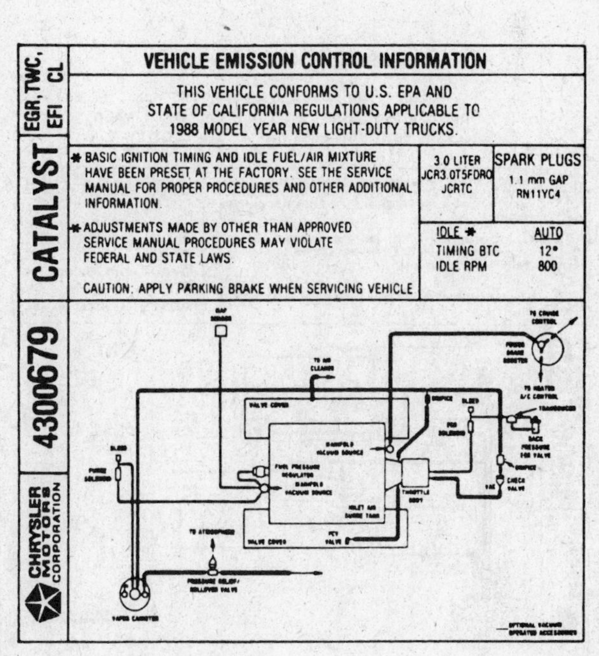

Fig. 76 Vacuum hose routing — 1988 3.0L California engines

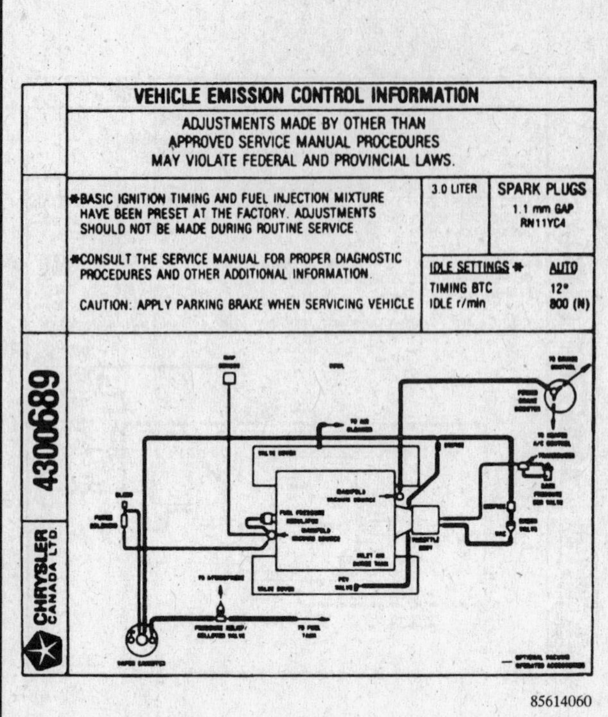

85614060

Fig. 77 Vacuum hose routing — 1988 3.0L Canadian engines

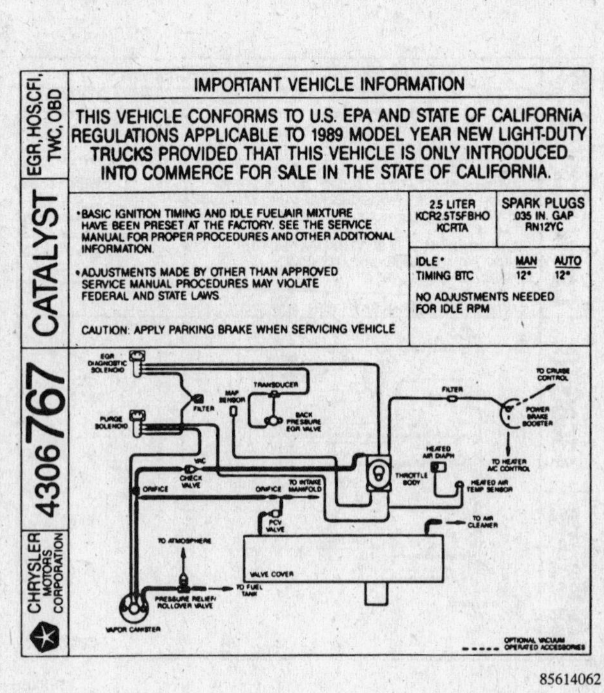

85614062

Fig. 79 Vacuum hose routing — 1989 2.5L California engines

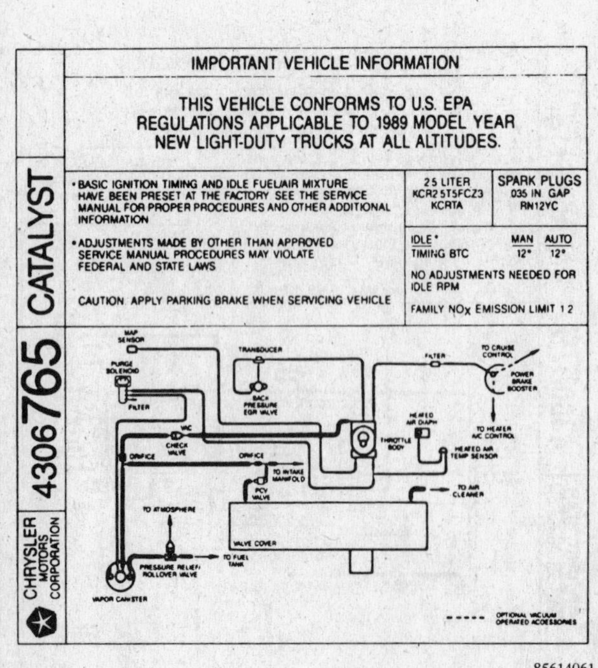

85614061

Fig. 78 Vacuum hose routing — 1989 2.5L Federal, Altitude and Canadian engines

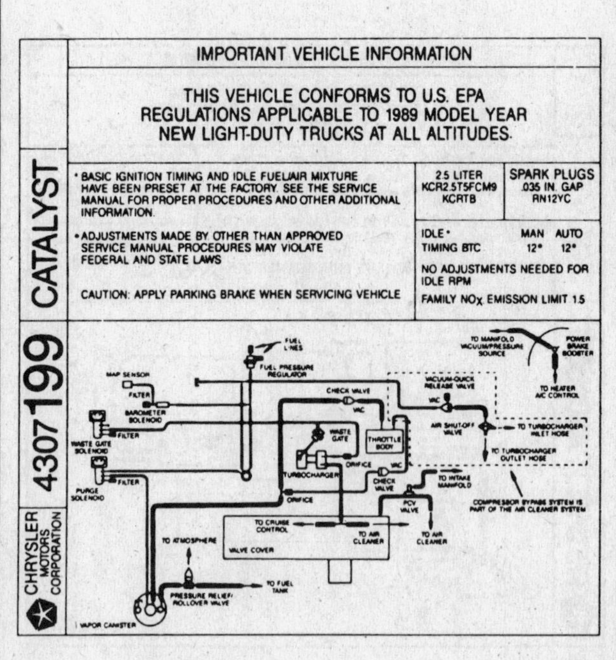

85614063

Fig. 80 Vacuum hose routing — 1989 2.5L turbocharged engines

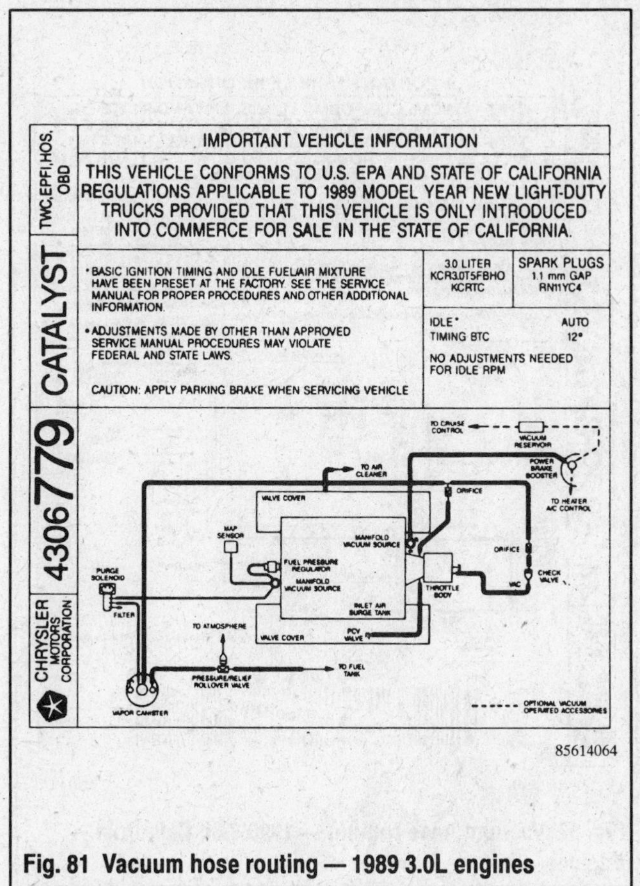

Fig. 81 Vacuum hose routing — 1989 3.0L engines

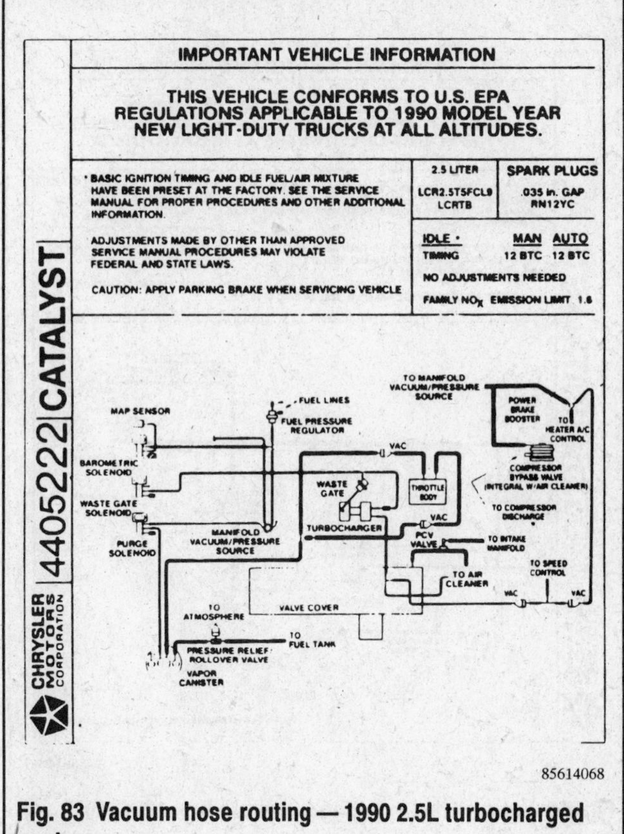

Fig. 83 Vacuum hose routing — 1990 2.5L turbocharged engines

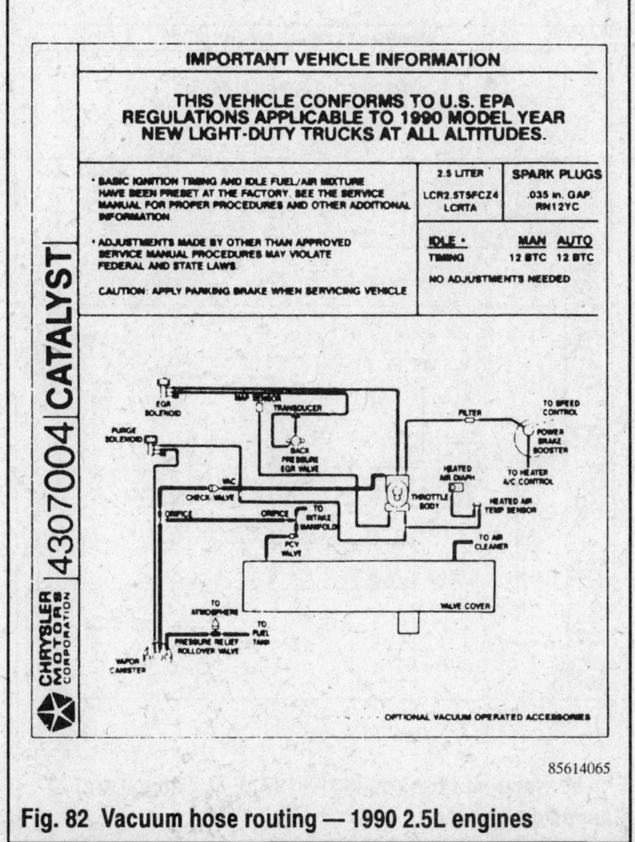

Fig. 82 Vacuum hose routing — 1990 2.5L engines

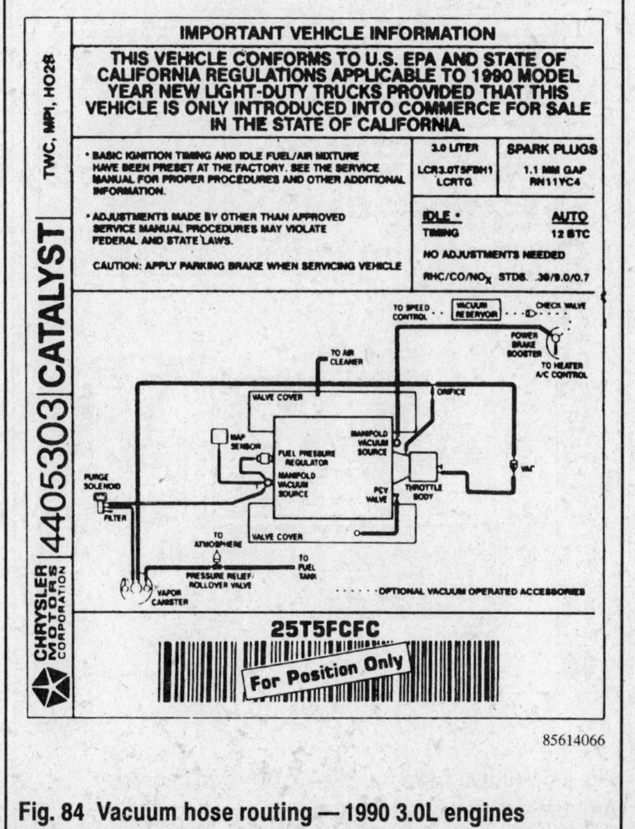

Fig. 84 Vacuum hose routing — 1990 3.0L engines

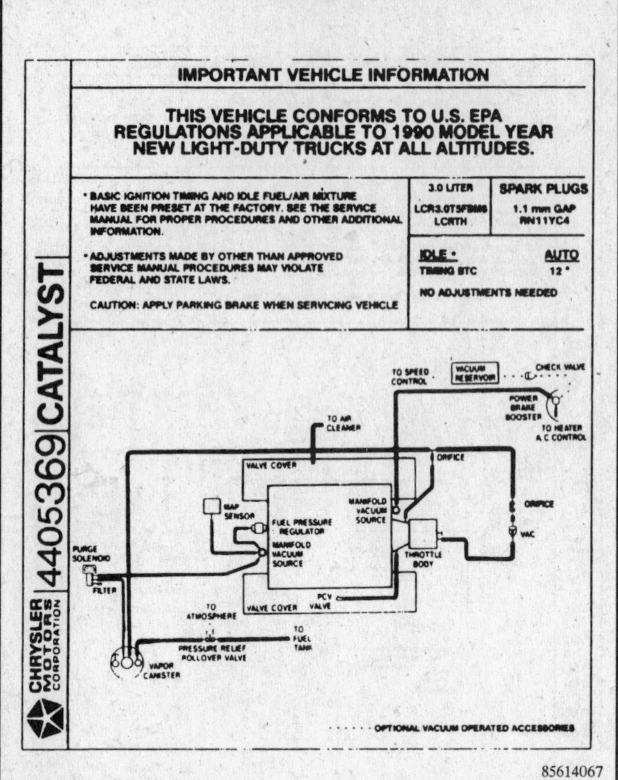

Fig. 85 Vacuum hose routing (continued) — 1990 3.0L engines

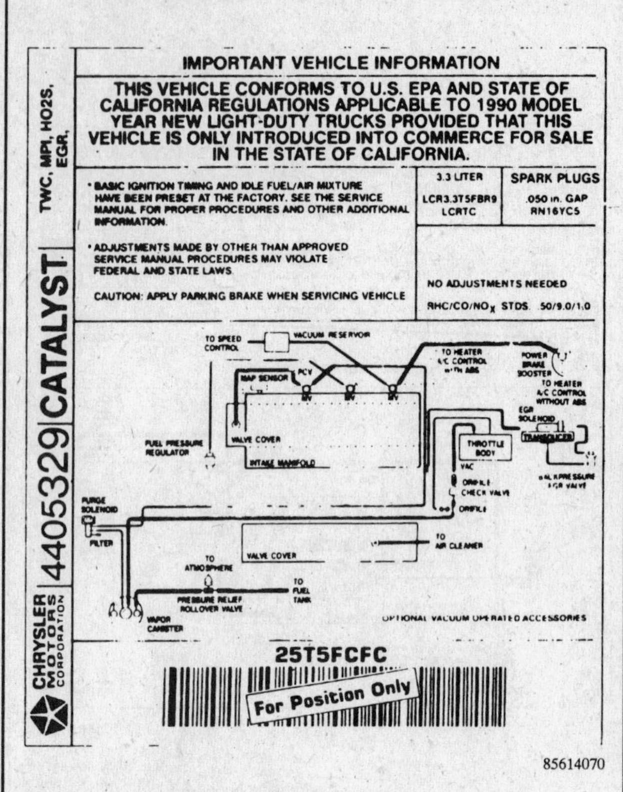

Fig. 87 Vacuum hose routing — 1990 3.3L California engines

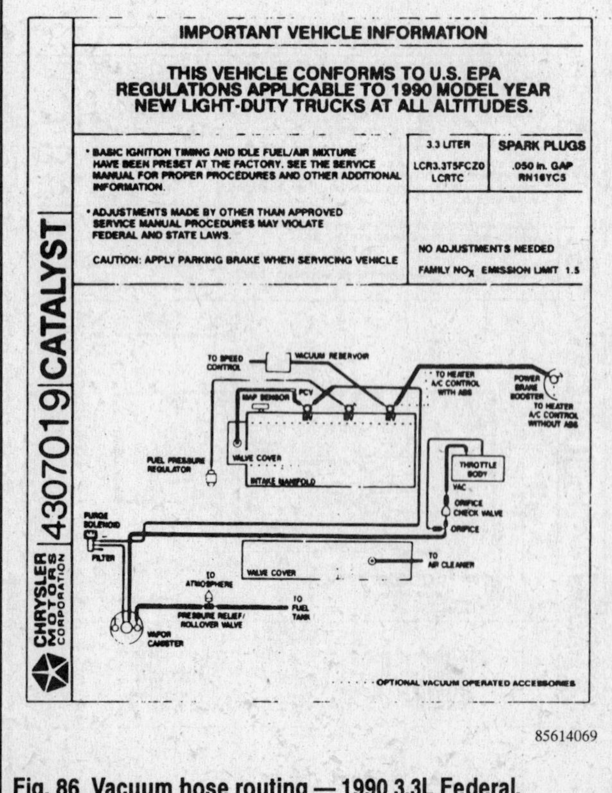

Fig. 86 Vacuum hose routing — 1990 3.3L Federal, Altitude and Canadian engines

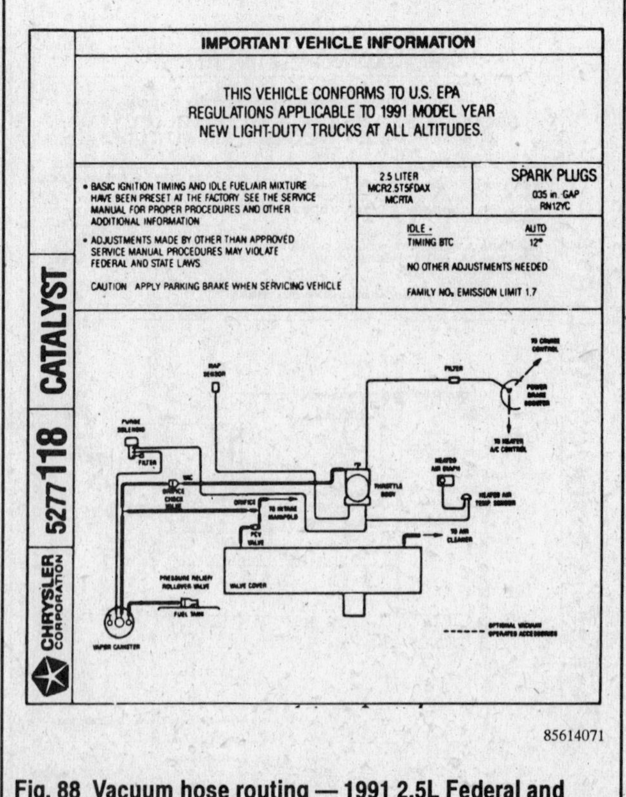

Fig. 88 Vacuum hose routing — 1991 2.5L Federal and Canadian engines

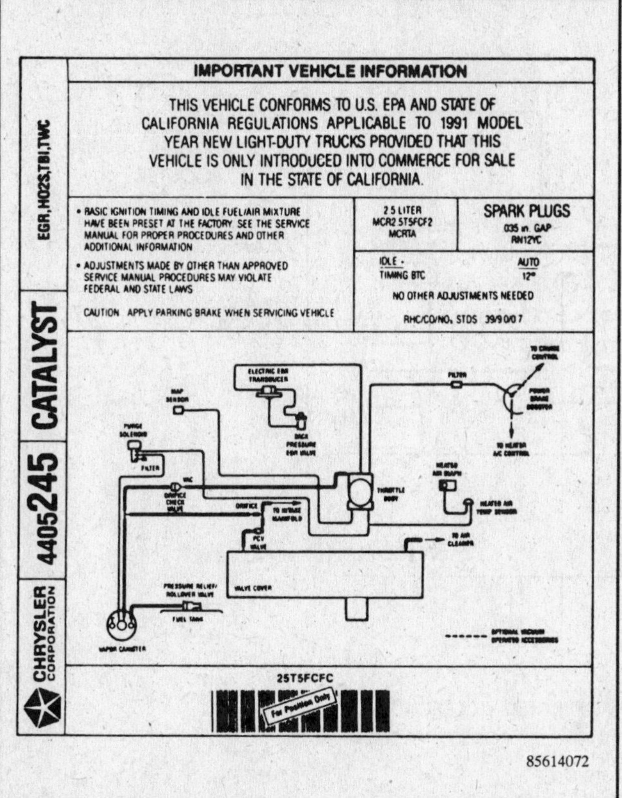

85614072

Fig. 89 Vacuum hose routing — 1991 2.5L California engines

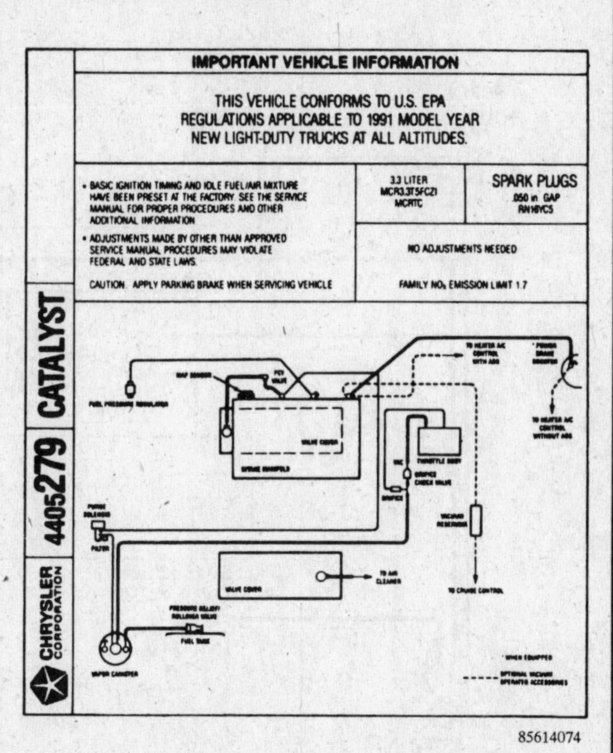

85614074

Fig. 91 Vacuum hose routing — 1991 3.3L engines (front wheel drive models)

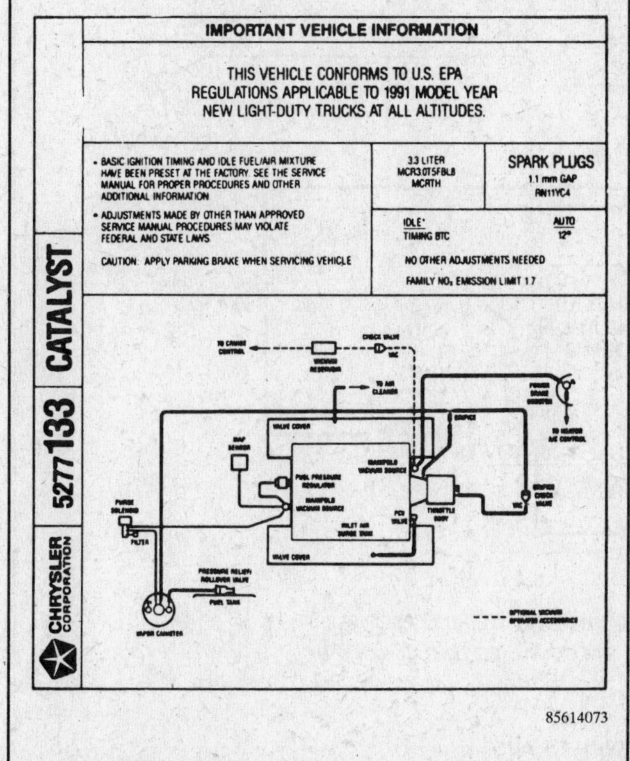

85614073

Fig. 90 Vacuum hose routing — 1991 3.0L engines

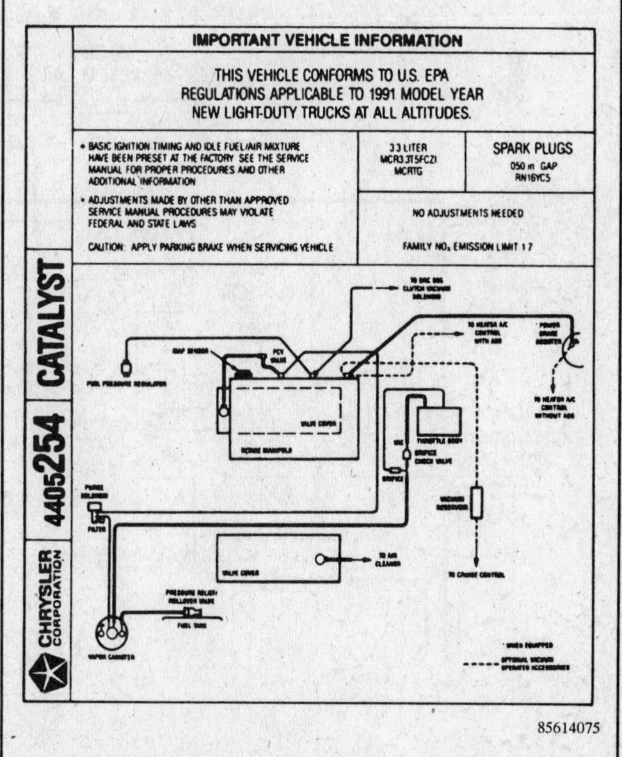

85614075

Fig. 92 Vacuum hose routing — 1991 3.3L engines (all wheel drive models)

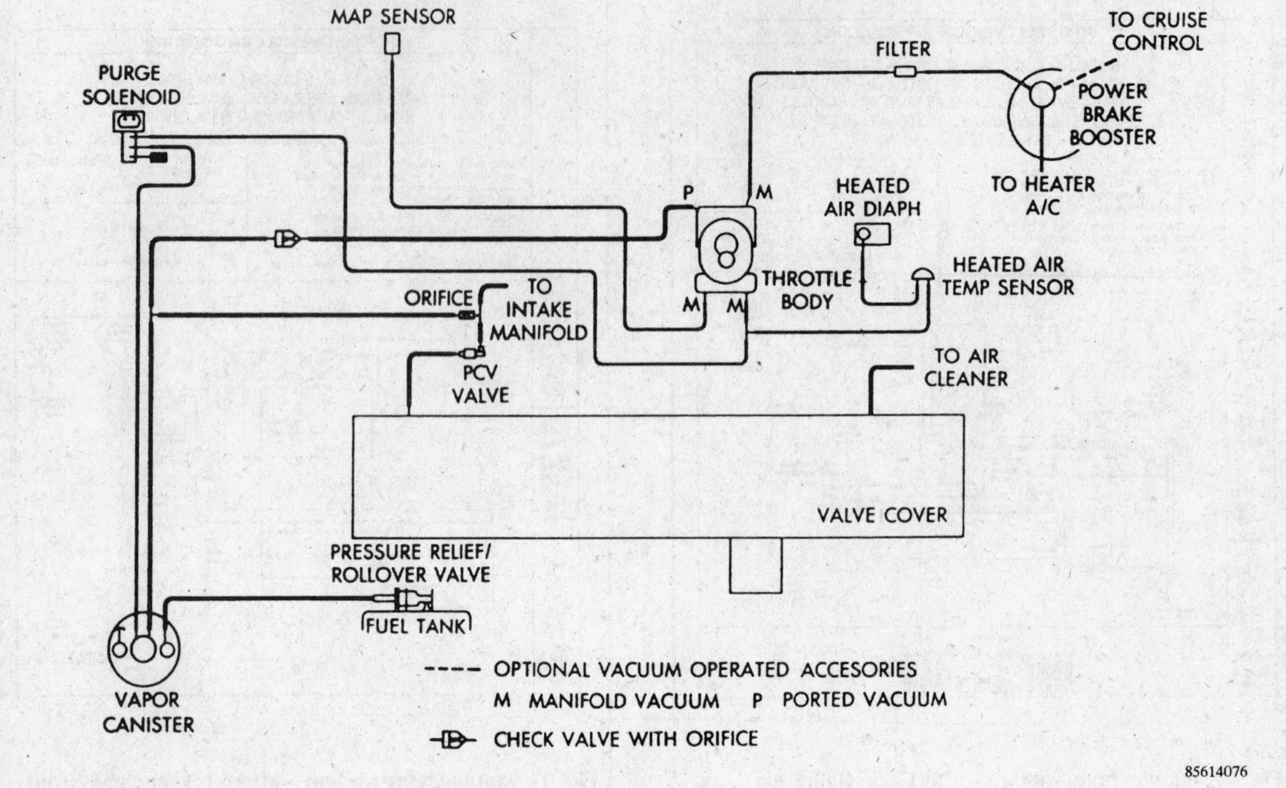

MAP SENSOR
TO CRUISE CONTROL
FILTER
PURGE SOLENOID
POWER BRAKE BOOSTER
P
M
HEATED AIR DIAPH
TO HEATER A/C
HEATED AIR TEMP SENSOR
THROTTLE BODY
M
M
ORIFICE
TO INTAKE MANIFOLD
PCV VALVE
TO AIR CLEANER
VALVE COVER
PRESSURE RELIEF/ ROLLOVER VALVE
FUEL TANK
VAPOR CANISTER
---- OPTIONAL VACUUM OPERATED ACCESORIES
M MANIFOLD VACUUM P PORTED VACUUM
CHECK VALVE WITH ORIFICE
85614076

Fig. 93 Vacuum hose routing — 1992 2.5L engines

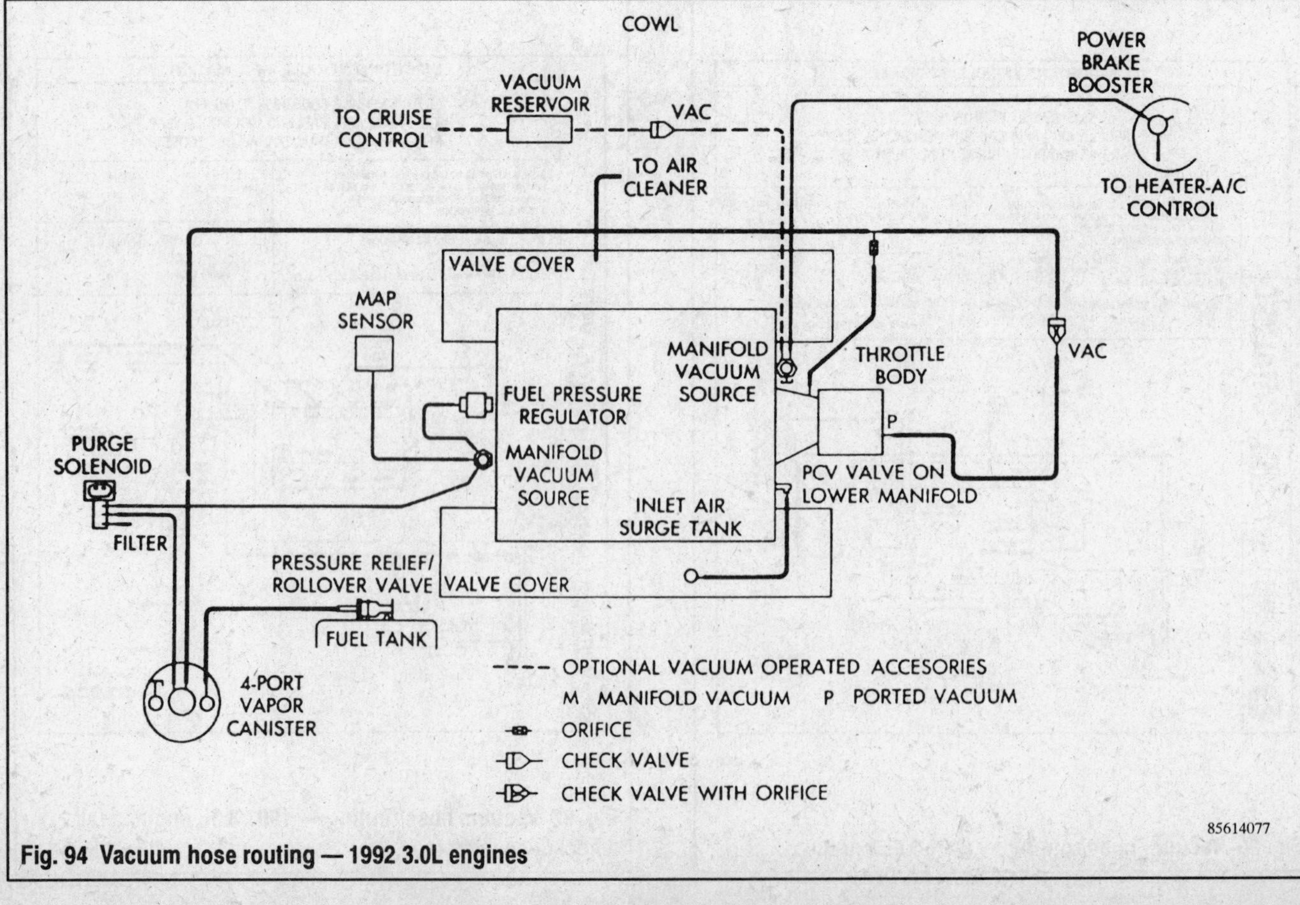

COWL
POWER BRAKE BOOSTER
VACUUM RESERVOIR
TO CRUISE CONTROL
VAC
TO AIR CLEANER
TO HEATER-A/C CONTROL
VALVE COVER
MAP SENSOR
MANIFOLD VACUUM SOURCE
THROTTLE BODY
VAC
FUEL PRESSURE REGULATOR
P
PURGE SOLENOID
MANIFOLD VACUUM SOURCE
PCV VALVE ON LOWER MANIFOLD
INLET AIR SURGE TANK
FILTER
PRESSURE RELIEF/ ROLLOVER VALVE
VALVE COVER
FUEL TANK
4-PORT VAPOR CANISTER
---- OPTIONAL VACUUM OPERATED ACCESORIES
M MANIFOLD VACUUM P PORTED VACUUM
ORIFICE
CHECK VALVE
CHECK VALVE WITH ORIFICE
85614077

Fig. 94 Vacuum hose routing — 1992 3.0L engines

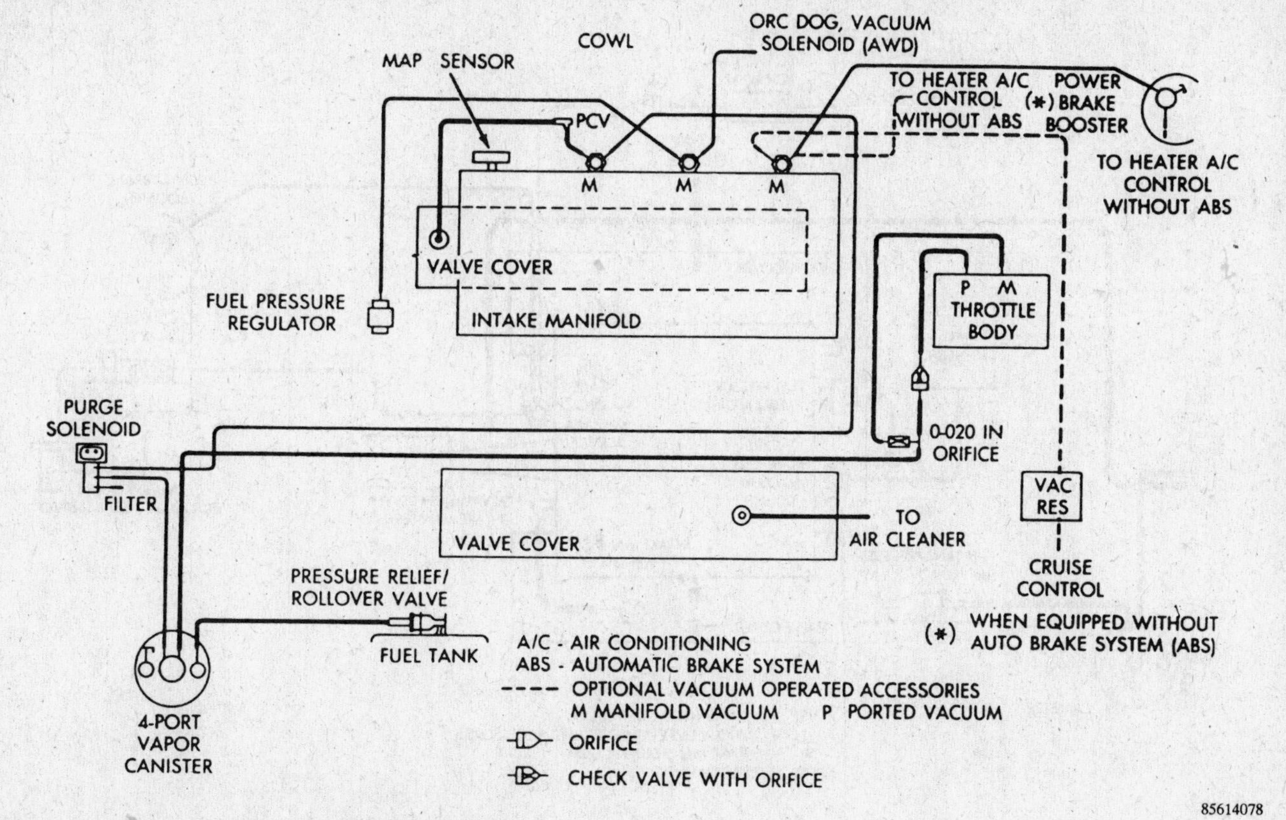

MAP SENSOR
COWL
ORC DOG, VACUUM SOLENOID (AWD)
TO HEATER A/C CONTROL WITHOUT ABS
(*) POWER BRAKE BOOSTER
TO HEATER A/C CONTROL WITHOUT ABS
PCV
M M M
VALVE COVER
FUEL PRESSURE REGULATOR
INTAKE MANIFOLD
P M
THROTTLE BODY
PURGE SOLENOID
FILTER
0-020 IN ORIFICE
VAC RES
VALVE COVER
TO AIR CLEANER
CRUISE CONTROL
PRESSURE RELIEF/ ROLLOVER VALVE
FUEL TANK
4-PORT VAPOR CANISTER

A/C - AIR CONDITIONING
ABS - AUTOMATIC BRAKE SYSTEM
---- OPTIONAL VACUUM OPERATED ACCESSORIES
M MANIFOLD VACUUM P PORTED VACUUM
ORIFICE
CHECK VALVE WITH ORIFICE
(*) WHEN EQUIPPED WITHOUT AUTO BRAKE SYSTEM (ABS)

85614078

Fig. 95 Vacuum hose routing — 1992 3.3L engines

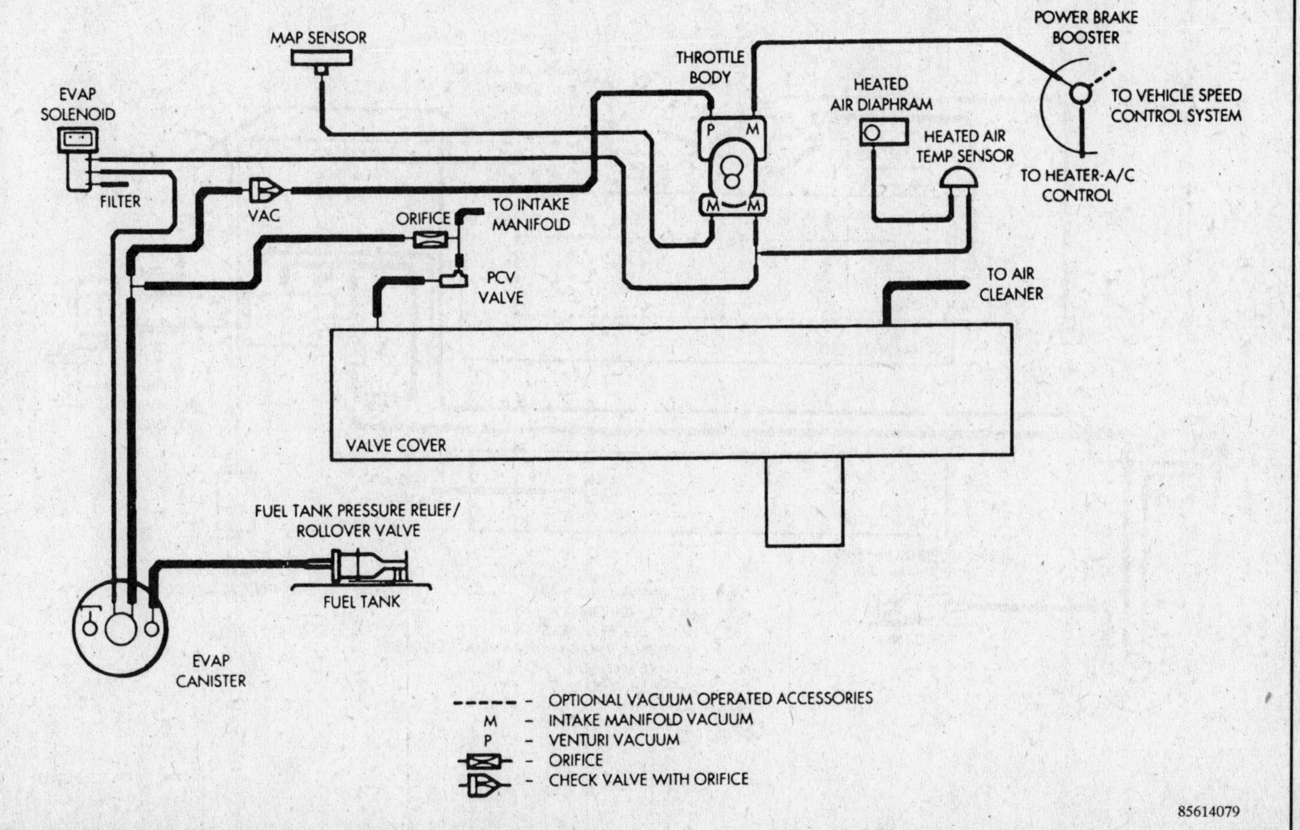

MAP SENSOR
EVAP SOLENOID
FILTER
THROTTLE BODY
P M
M M
POWER BRAKE BOOSTER
HEATED AIR DIAPHRAM
HEATED AIR TEMP SENSOR
TO VEHICLE SPEED CONTROL SYSTEM
TO HEATER-A/C CONTROL
VAC
ORIFICE
TO INTAKE MANIFOLD
PCV VALVE
TO AIR CLEANER
VALVE COVER
FUEL TANK PRESSURE RELIEF/ ROLLOVER VALVE
FUEL TANK
EVAP CANISTER

----- - OPTIONAL VACUUM OPERATED ACCESSORIES
M - INTAKE MANIFOLD VACUUM
P - VENTURI VACUUM
- ORIFICE
- CHECK VALVE WITH ORIFICE

85614079

Fig. 96 Vacuum hose routing — 1993–95 2.5L engines

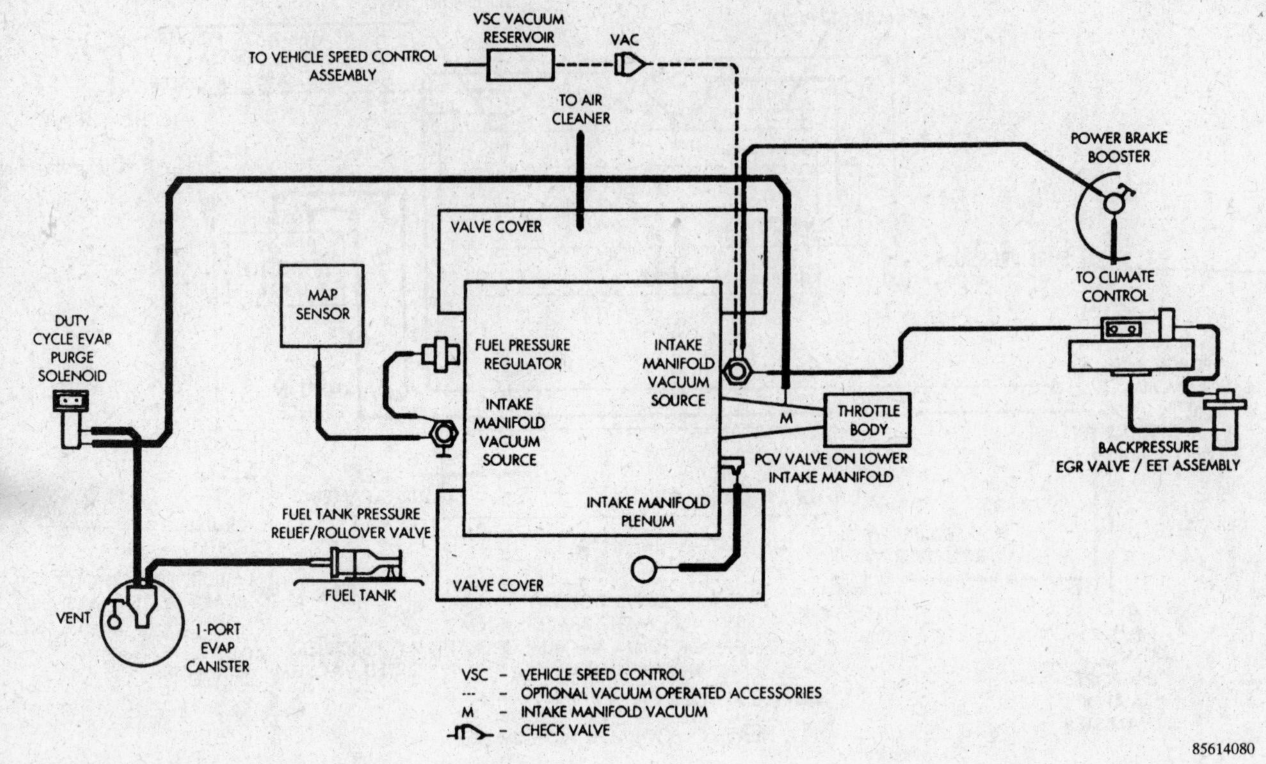

Fig. 97 Vacuum hose routing — 1993–95 3.0L engines

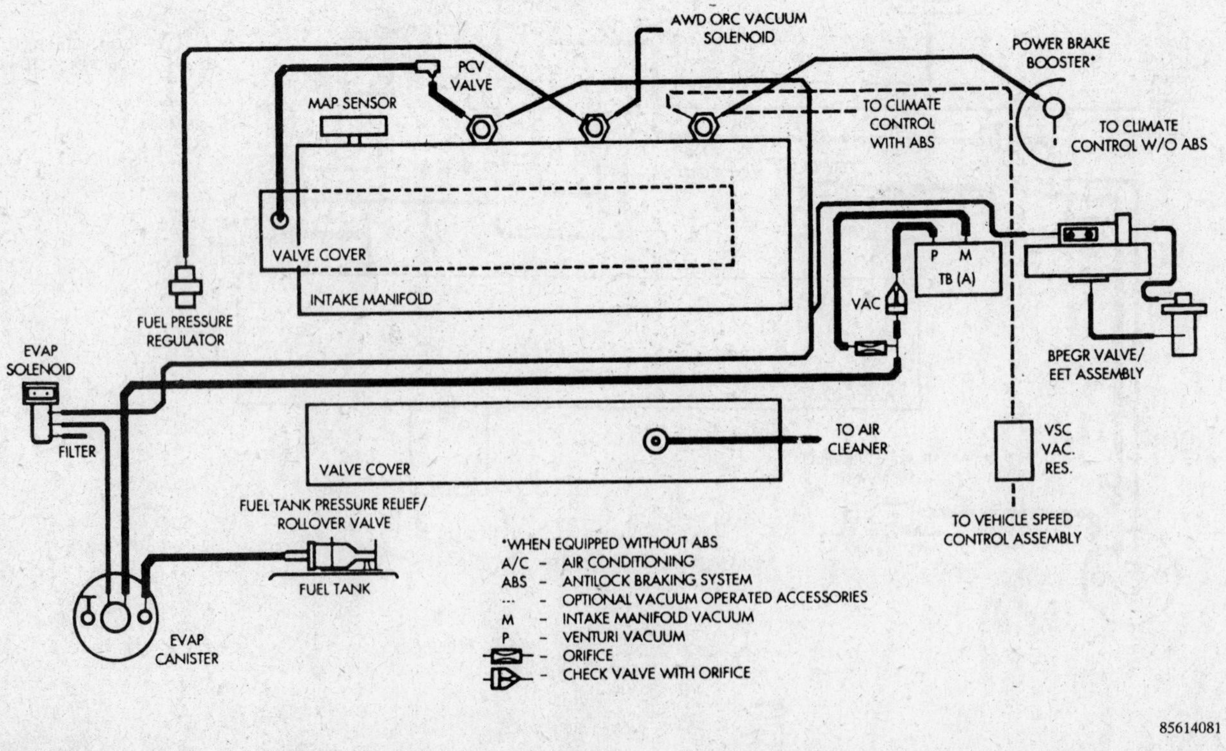

Fig. 98 Vacuum hose routing — 1993–95 3.3L and 3.8L engines

BASIC FUEL SYSTEM DIAGNOSIS 5-2
CARBURETED FUEL SYSTEM
CARBURETOR 5-3
MECHANICAL FUEL PUMP 5-2
CHRYSLER MULTI-POINT ELECTRONIC FUEL INJECTION
AUTOMATIC IDLE SPEED (AIS) MOTOR 5-15
CHECK ENGINE LIGHT 5-12
DIAGNOSIS AND TESTING 5-13
FUEL INJECTOR RAIL ASSEMBLY 5-16
FUEL INJECTORS 5-21
FUEL PRESSURE DAMPENER 5-23
FUEL PRESSURE REGULATOR 5-21
FUEL PRESSURE TEST 5-13
FUEL SYSTEM PRESSURE RELEASE PROCEDURE 5-13
GENERAL INFORMATION 5-12
HEATED OXYGEN SENSOR 5-23
POWERTRAIN CONTROL MODULE (PCM) 5-23
THROTTLE BODY 5-14
THROTTLE POSITION SENSOR (TPS) 5-15
WASTEGATE CALIBRATION 5-14
CHRYSLER SINGLE POINT FUEL INJECTION SYSTEM
AUTOMATIC IDLE SPEED (AIS) MOTOR ASSEMBLY 5-29
FUEL FITTINGS 5-26
FUEL INJECTOR 5-27
FUEL PRESSURE REGULATOR 5-26
GENERAL INFORMATION 5-24
THROTTLE BODY 5-25
THROTTLE BODY TEMPERATURE SENSOR 5-28
THROTTLE POSITION SENSOR (TPS) 5-28
FUEL TANK 5-29
SPECIFICATIONS CHARTS
TORQUE SPECIFICATIONS 5-30

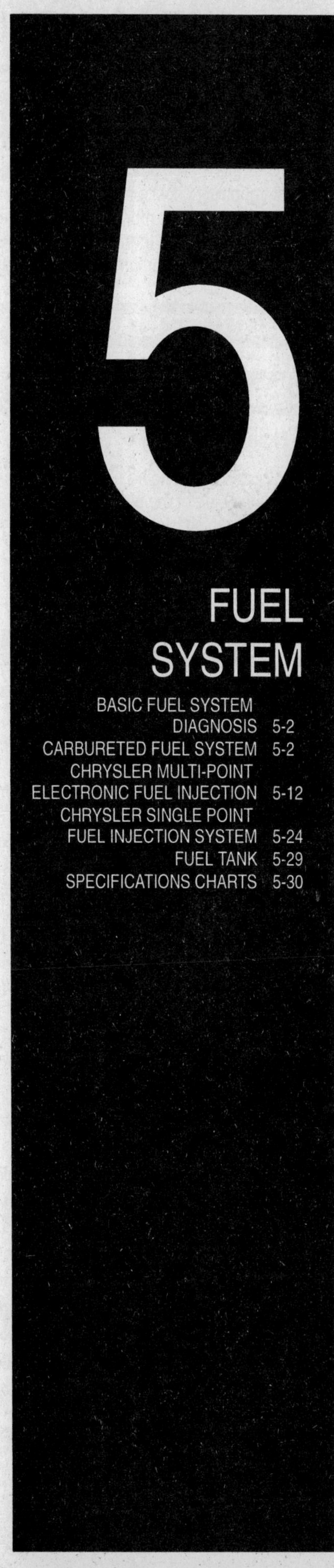

5

FUEL SYSTEM

BASIC FUEL SYSTEM DIAGNOSIS 5-2
CARBURETED FUEL SYSTEM 5-2
CHRYSLER MULTI-POINT ELECTRONIC FUEL INJECTION 5-12
CHRYSLER SINGLE POINT FUEL INJECTION SYSTEM 5-24
FUEL TANK 5-29
SPECIFICATIONS CHARTS 5-30

BASIC FUEL SYSTEM DIAGNOSIS

When there is a problem starting or driving a vehicle, two of the most important checks involve the ignition and the fuel systems. The questions most mechanics attempt to answer first, "is there spark?" and "is there fuel?" will often lead to solving most basic problems. For ignition system diagnosis and testing, please refer to the information on engine electrical components and ignition systems found earlier in this manual. If the ignition system checks out (there is spark), then you must determine if the fuel system is operating properly (is there fuel?).

CARBURETED FUEL SYSTEM

Mechanical Fuel Pump

➧ See Figures 1, 2, 3 and 4

The 2.2L and 2.6L engine use a mechanical type fuel pump located on the side of the engine. The fuel pump is driven by an eccentric cam which is cast on the accessory drive shaft.

REMOVAL & INSTALLATION

****CAUTION**

Do not smoke when working around gasoline, cleaning solvent or other flammable substances.

1. Remove the oil filter.
2. Disconnect the fuel lines from the pump.
3. Plug the lines to prevent fuel leakage.
4. Remove the fuel pump blocker strut from front engine mount-to-blocker assembly.
5. Remove the fuel pump mounting bolts.

To install:

6. Clean all gasket material from engine block mounting surface and spacer block.
7. Assemble the new gaskets and spacer block to fuel pump.
8. Install the fuel pump mounting bolts in pump mounting flange.
9. Position the pump assembly on engine block and tighten bolts alternately to 21 ft. lbs. (28 Nm).
10. Connect the fuel lines to the pump.
11. Position the fuel pump blocker strut on blocker assembly and front engine mount. Tighten assembly.
12. Install the oil filter. Check and adjust oil level.
13. Start the engine and check fuel fittings for leaks.

TESTING

****CAUTION**

Never smoke when working around gasoline! Avoid all sources of sparks or ignition. Gasoline vapors are EXTREMELY volatile!

Volume Test

The fuel pump should supply 1 qt. (0.946 l) of fuel in 1 minute or less at idle.

Pressure Test

1. Insert a T-fitting in the fuel line at the carburetor.
2. Connect a six inch piece of hose between the T-fitting and a pressure gauge. A longer piece of hose will result in an inaccurate reading.
3. Disconnect the inlet line to the carburetor at the fuel pump and vent the pump. Failure to vent the pump will result in low pressure reading. Reconnect the fuel line.
4. Connect a tachometer to the engine. Start the engine and allow to idle. The pressure gauge should show a constant 4.5–6 psi (31–41 kPa) reading. When the engine is turned **OFF**, the pressure should slowly drop to zero. An instant drop to zero indicates a leaky diaphragm or weak spring. If pressure is too high, the main spring is too strong or the air vent is plugged.
5. Proceed with the vacuum test.

Vacuum Test

1. Remove the inlet and outlet fuel lines from the pump.
2. Plug the fuel line to the carburetor to prevent fuel leakage.
3. Connect a vacuum gauge to the fuel pump inlet fitting.
4. Using the starter motor, turn the engine over several times and observe the vacuum gauge. The fuel pump should develop a minimum of 11 in. Hg (37 kPa) of vacuum.
5. If the vacuum readings are below specification, replace the pump.

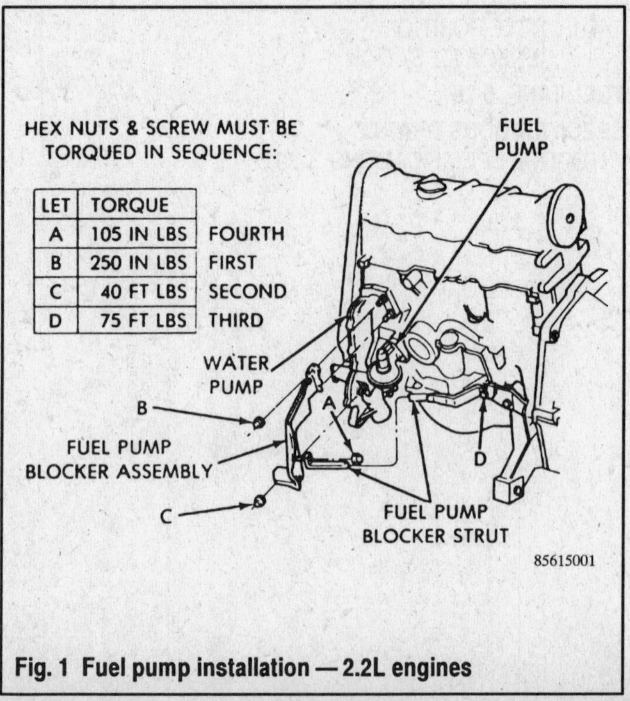

Fig. 1 Fuel pump installation — 2.2L engines

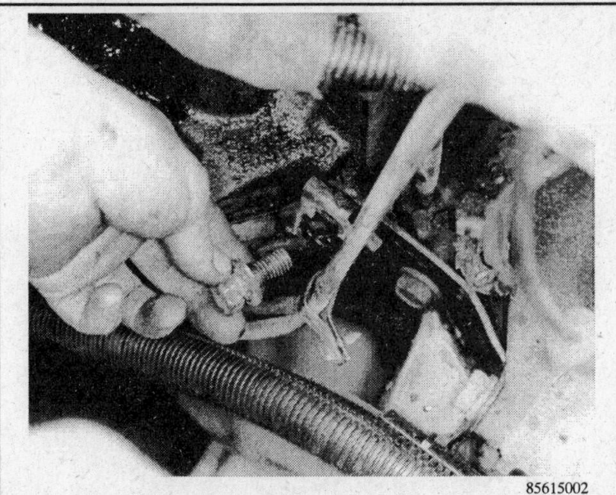
85615002

Fig. 2 Removing the fuel pump blocker strut retaining bolt

85615004

Fig. 4 The fuel pump removed from the engine. Oil filter removed for illustration purposes

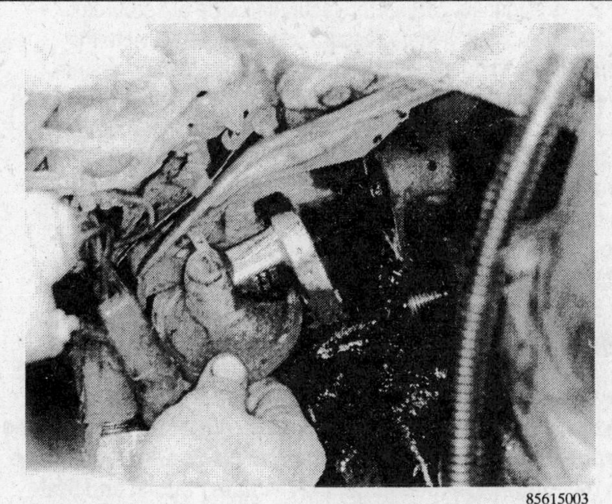
85615003

Fig. 3 Removing the fuel pump blocker strut

Carburetor

ADJUSTMENTS

Holley Carburetor

IDLE SPEED/SOLENOID KICKER CHECK

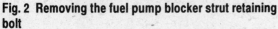

See Figure 5

Vehicles equipped with the 2.2L engine and air conditioning are equipped with a solenoid kicker.

1. Start engine and run until operating temperature is reached.
2. Turn air conditioning switch **ON** and set temperature control lever to the coldest position.
3. Notice the kicker solenoid for in and out movement as the compressor cycles on and off. If no movement occurred, check the kicker system for vacuum leaks. Check the operation of the vacuum solenoid. If no problems are found, replace the kicker.

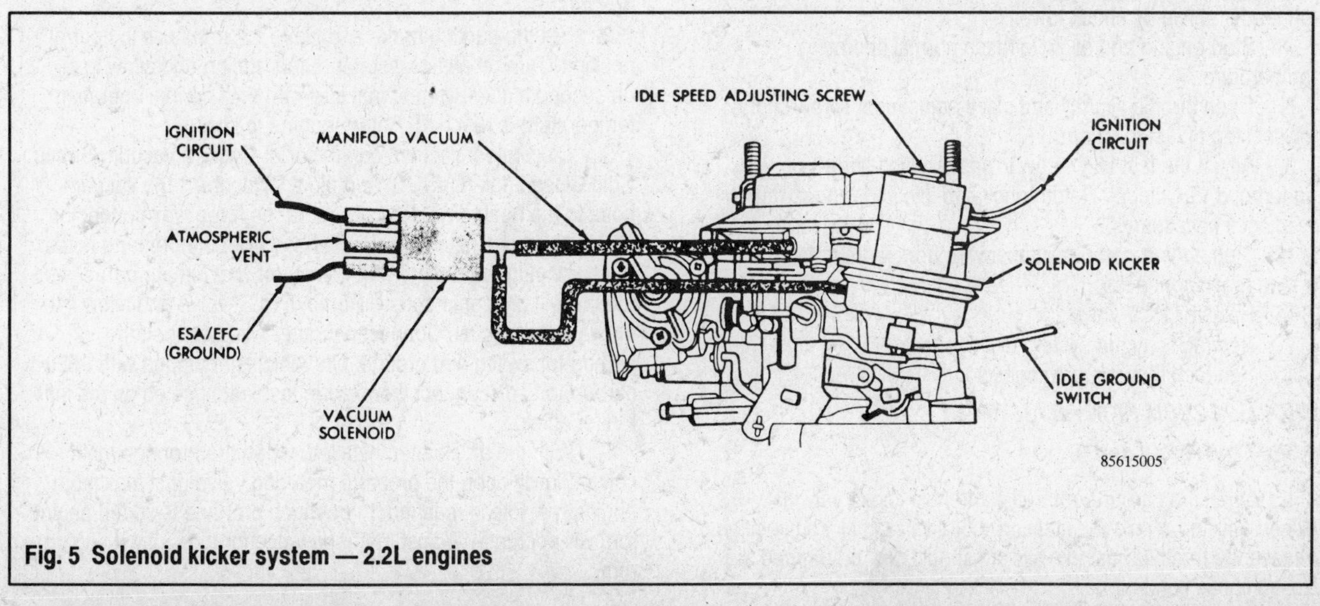

Fig. 5 Solenoid kicker system — 2.2L engines

4. If the kicker solenoid functions properly, turn off the air conditioning switch and shut engine **OFF**.

SOLENOID KICKER ADJUSTMENT

1. Check ignition timing and adjust if necessary.
2. Disconnect and plug vacuum connector at the Coolant Vacuum Switch Cold Closed unit (CVSCC).
3. Unplug connector at cooling fan and jumper harness so fan will run continuously.
4. Remove the PCV valve and allow it to draw under hood air.
5. Connect a tachometer to the engine.
6. Ground the carburetor switch with a jumper wire.
7. Disconnect the oxygen system test lead located on the left fender shield on vehicles equipped with 6520 carburetors.
8. Start the engine and run until normal operating temperature is reached.
9. Adjust idle speed screw to specification given on the underhood label.
10. Reconnect PCV valve, oxygen connector and CVSCC vacuum connector.
11. Remove the jumper from carburetor switch.
12. Remove the jumper from radiator fan and reconnect harness.

➥ After Steps 10, 11 and 12 are completed, the idle speed may change slightly. This is normal and engine speed should not be readjusted.

FAST IDLE ADJUSTMENT

➧ See Figure 6

Before adjusting the fast idle, check and adjust the ignition timing.

1. Disconnect the electrical harness at the radiator fan and install a jumper wire so the fan will run continuously.
2. Remove the PCV valve and allow it to draw under hood air.
3. Disconnect and plug the vacuum connector at the Coolant Vacuum Switch Cold Closed unit (CVSCC).
4. Install a tachometer.
5. Ground the carburetor switch with a jumper wire.
6. Disconnect oxygen system test connector located on the left fender shield by shock tower.
7. Start engine and allow to reach normal operating temperature.
8. Open throttle slightly and place adjustment screw on the lowest step of fast idle cam.
9. Adjust the fast idle screw to specification shown on underhood VECI label. Return engine to idle and repeat Step 8, readjust if necessary.
10. Stop engine, remove jumper wire from radiator fan harness and reattach connector.
11. Reinstall PCV valve.
12. Reattach oxygen system test connector.
13. Reattach the vacuum connector at CVSCC.

CHOKE VACUUM KICK ADJUSTMENT

➧ See Figures 7, 8 and 9

1. Open the carburetor throttle and hold choke valve in closed position. While maintaining choke valve in closed position, release the throttle. Fast idle system should now be trapped at closed choke condition.

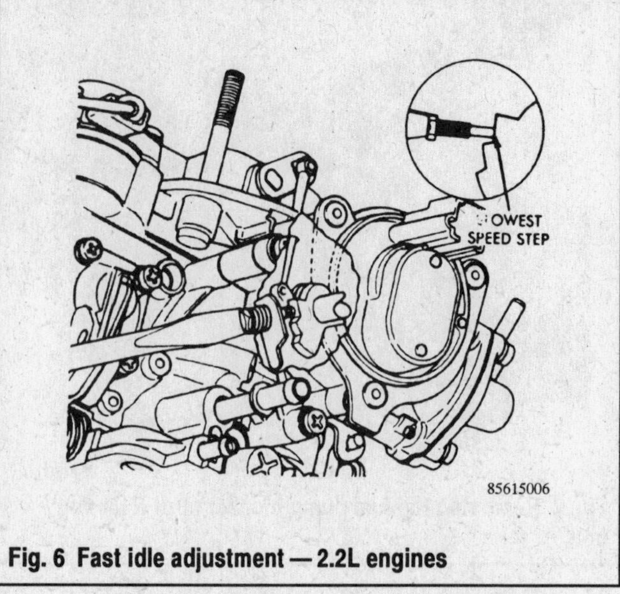

Fig. 6 Fast idle adjustment — 2.2L engines

2. Disconnect carburetor vacuum source at carburetor.
3. Using light finger pressure, close choke valve to the smallest opening possible without disturbing linkage system.
4. Using the proper size drill or gauge, insert between choke valve and air horn wall at primary throttle end of carburetor. For more information, refer to the choke vacuum kick specification chart.
5. Using an Allen head screw in center of diaphragm housing, adjust by turning clockwise or counterclockwise to obtain correct setting.
6. Reconnect vacuum hose to carburetor vacuum source.

MIXTURE ADJUSTMENT (PROPANE ASSISTED)

➥ The following procedures require the use of a propane cylinder, vacuum hose and a special control valve to provide proper enrichment. Any adjustments made other than those in the following procedures, may violate Federal and State Laws.

1. Remove the mixture adjustment concealment plug. For more details, refer to Steps 18–20 in the carburetor disassembly procedure.
2. Set the parking brake and place the transaxle in neutral position. Turn off all accessories. Start engine and allow to idle on second highest step of fast idle cam until normal operating temperature is reached. Return engine to idle.
3. Disconnect vacuum connector at Coolant Vacuum Switch Cold Closed unit (CVSCC) and plug. Disconnect the vacuum hose to the heated air door sensor at the three way connector, and in its place, install the supply hose from the propane bottle.
4. Unplug the radiator fan connector and jumper harness so the fan will run continuously. Remove PCV valve and allow it to draw underhood air. Connect a jumper wire between the carburetor switch and ground. On vehicles equipped with 6520 carburetors, disconnect the oxygen test lead located on the left fender shield.
5. With the air cleaner installed. Open the propane main valve. Slowly open the propane metering valve until maximum engine rpm idle is reached. If too much propane is added engine rpm will decrease. Adjust metering valve for the highest engine rpm.

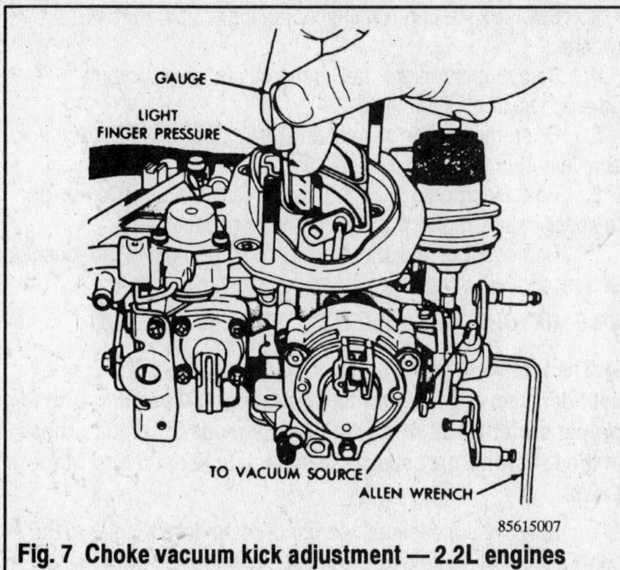

Fig. 7 Choke vacuum kick adjustment — 2.2L engines

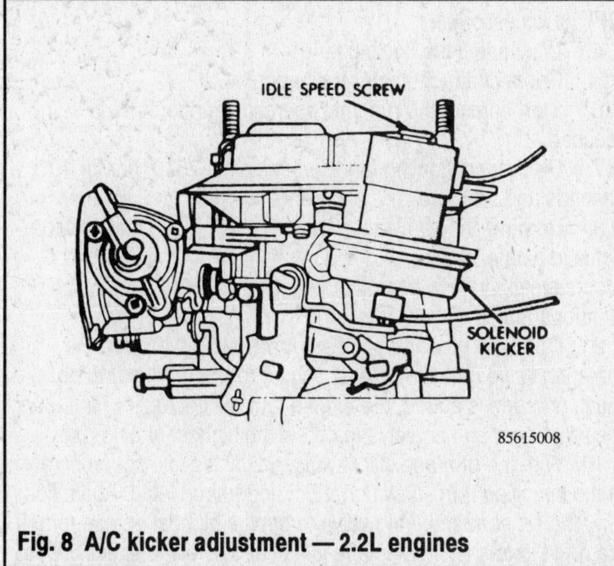

Fig. 8 A/C kicker adjustment — 2.2L engines

Vacuum Kick Specifications

Carb Number	Setting
4288460	.07 in.
4288461	.07 in.
4288262	.07 in.
4288263	.07 in.
4288456	.08 in.
4288458	.08 in.
4288459	.08 in.

85615009

Fig. 9 Vacuum kick adjustment specifications — 2.2L engines

6. With the propane still flowing, adjust the idle speed screw on top of the solenoid to obtain specified rpm on underhood label. Again adjust the propane metering valve to get the highest engine rpm. If the maximum rpm changes, readjust the idle speed screw to the specified propane rpm.
7. Shut off the propane main valve and allow the engine to stabilize. With the air cleaner still in place, slowly adjust the mixture screws to obtain the specified set rpm. Pause for a few seconds after each adjustment to allow engine speed to stabilized.
8. Again turn on the propane main valve and adjust the metering valve to obtain the highest engine rpm. If the maximum speed differs more than 25 rpm, repeat Steps 5-8.
9. Shut off both valves on propane cylinder. Disconnect the propane vacuum supply hose and connect the vacuum hose to the heated air door sensor at the three way connector.
10. Install concealment plug. Proceed with fast idle adjustment starting at Step 7.

ANTI-DIESELING ADJUSTMENT

➝ Always check and adjust ignition timing before any idle speed adjustment is performed.

1. Warm engine to normal operating temperature. Place transaxle in neutral position and set parking brake.
2. Turn **OFF** all accessories. Jumper wire between carburetor switch and ground.
3. Remove the RED wire from the 6-Way connector (carburetor side).
4. Adjust the throttle stop speed screw to obtain 700 rpm.
5. Reconnect RED wire and remove jumper from carburetor switch.

Mikuni Carburetor

IDLE SPEED ADJUSTMENT

➧ See Figure 10

1. Check and adjust ignition timing.
2. Set the parking brake and place transaxle in neutral. Turn off all accessories.
3. Disconnect the radiator fan.
4. Connect a tachometer to the engine.

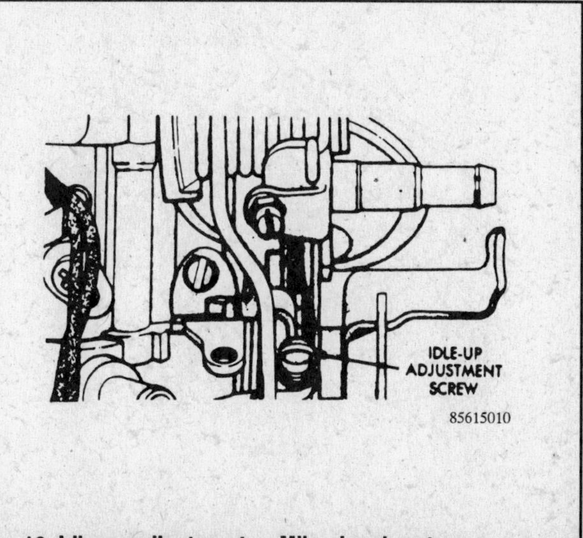

Fig. 10 Idle up adjustment — Mikuni carburetors

5. Start engine and run until operating temperature is reached.

6. Disconnect cooling fan. Run engine at 2500 rpm for 10 seconds and return to idle.

7. Wait 2 minutes and record rpm. If rpm differs from VECI under hood specification label, turn idle speed adjusting screw until specification is obtained.

8. On air condition models, set the temperature lever to the coldest position and turn air conditioning switch **ON**. With the air conditioning running, set the engine speed to 900 rpm using the idle-up adjustment screw.

9. Shut engine **OFF**. Connect the cooling fan and remove tachometer.

FAST IDLE ADJUSTMENT

See Figures 11 and 12

1. Connect a tachometer to the engine. Check and adjust ignition timing.

2. Set the parking brake and place transaxle in neutral. Turn **OFF** all accessories.

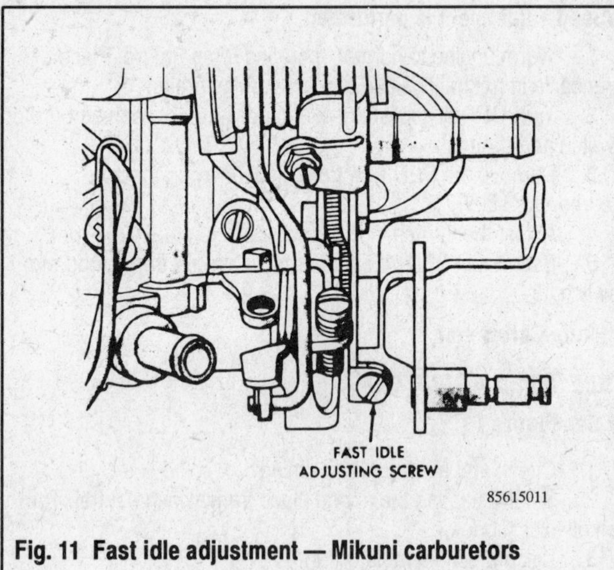

Fig. 11 Fast idle adjustment — Mikuni carburetors

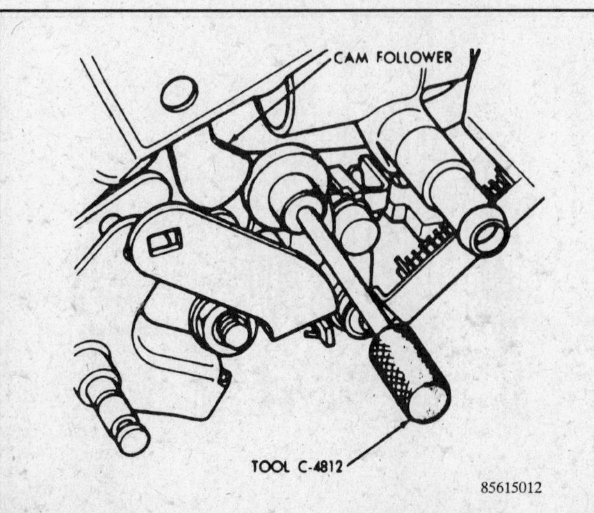

Fig. 12 Installing tool C-4812 — Mikuni carburetors

3. Start engine and run until operating temperature is reached.

4. Disconnect radiator fan. Remove and plug vacuum advance hose at distributor.

5. Open the throttle slightly and install Tool C-4812 (or the equivalent) on the cam follower pin.

6. Release throttle lever and adjust fast idle adjusting screw to specification shown on VECI under hood label.

7. Remove tool and shut engine **OFF**. Reconnect fan, unplug and reconnect vacuum hose, and remove tachometer.

IDLE MIXTURE ADJUSTMENT (PROPANE ASSISTED)

The following procedures require the use of a propane cylinder, vacuum hose and a special control valve to provide proper enrichment. Any adjustments made other than those in the following procedures, may violate Federal and State Laws.

1. Remove concealment plug. For more details, refer to the concealment plug removal procedure later in this section.

2. Check and adjust ignition timing.

3. Set the parking brake and place transaxle in neutral. Turn **OFF** all accessories.

4. Disconnect the cooling fan.

5. Connect a tachometer to the engine.

6. Start engine and run until operating temperature is reached.

7. Disconnect cooling fan. Run engine at 2500 rpm for 10 seconds and return to idle. Allow engine to idle for 2 minutes.

8. Remove the air cleaner fresh air duct. Place the propane bottle in a safe location and in an upright position. Insert the propane supply hose approximately 4 in. (10cm) into the air cleaner snorkel.

9. Open the propane bottle main valve. Slowly open the metering valve until the highest engine rpm is reached. If too much propane is added, the engine rpm will decrease. Fine tune the propane metering valve to obtain the highest engine rpm.

10. With the propane still flowing, adjust the idle speed screw to the specified rpm shown on VECI underhood label. Again fine tune the propane metering valve to get the highest engine rpm. If the rpm increases, readjust the idle speed screw to specification.

11. Shut **OFF** the propane main valve and allow the engine speed to stabilize. Slowly adjust the carburetor mixture screws to obtain the specified idle rpm. Pause between each adjustment to allow engine speed to stabilize.

12. Again turn **ON** the propane main valve, fine tune the metering valve to get the highest engine rpm. If the rpm changes, repeat Steps 8–10.

13. Shut **OFF** the propane main valve and metering valve. Remove the propane supply hose. Install the air cleaner fresh air duct. Install the concealment plug and impact plate.

CONCEALMENT PLUG REMOVAL

1. Remove the impact plate, if used.

2. Remove the vacuum connector from High Altitude Compensator (HAC) fitting on carburetor, if used.

3. With an $^{1}/_{8}$ in. (3mm) long, $^{1}/_{4}$ in. (6mm) diameter drill bit, drill out concealment plug at location show.

4. Remove the concealment plug.

REMOVAL & INSTALLATION

2.2L Engines

➧ See Figures 13, 14, 15, 16, 17, 18, 19, 20, 21, 22, 23 and 24

****CAUTION**

Never remove a carburetor from an engine that has just been road tested. Allow the engine to cool down to prevent accidental fuel ignition or personal injury.

1. Disconnect the negative battery cable.
2. Remove the air cleaner.
3. Remove the fuel tank filler cap to relieve fuel system pressure.
4. Disconnect all carburetor electrical wiring.

****CAUTION**

Never smoke when working around gasoline! Avoid all sources of sparks or ignition. Gasoline vapors are EXTREMELY volatile!

5. Disconnect the carburetor inlet line and block off line to prevent fuel leakage.
6. Disconnect the throttle linkage. Label and remove all vacuum hoses.
7. Remove the carburetor mounting nuts and remove carburetor.

To install:

8. Inspect the mating surfaces of the carburetor and isolator for nicks, burrs, dirt or other damage. It is not necessary to disturb the isolator to intake manifold mounting screws, unless the isolator is damaged.
9. Carefully install carburetor on engine. Install nuts evenly and tighten them to 17 ft. lbs. (22 Nm). Make certain throttle plates and choke plate opens and closes properly when operated.
10. Connect the throttle linkage and fuel inlet line.
11. Connect the vacuum hoses.
12. Connect the negative battery cable.
13. Install the air cleaner and adjust the carburetor.

2.6L Engines

****CAUTION**

Never remove a carburetor from an engine that has just been road tested. Allow the engine to cool down to prevent accidental fuel ignition or personal injury.

1. Disconnect the negative battery cable.
2. Remove the air cleaner.
3. Remove the fuel tank filler cap to relieve fuel system pressure.
4. Disconnect the carburetor protector and all carburetor electrical wiring.
5. Drain the cooling system. Label and remove the vacuum hoses and coolant hoses at carburetor.

****CAUTION**

When draining coolant, keep in mind that cats and dogs are attracted by ethylene glycol antifreeze, and are quite likely to drink any that is left in an uncovered container or in puddles on the ground. This will prove fatal in sufficient quantity. Always drain the coolant into a sealable container. Coolant should be reused unless it is contaminated or several years old.

6. Disconnect the carburetor inlet line and block off line to prevent fuel leakage.

****CAUTION**

Never smoke when working around gasoline! Avoid all sources of sparks or ignition. Gasoline vapors are EXTREMELY volatile!

7. Disconnect the throttle linkage.
8. Remove the carburetor mounting bolts and nuts and remove carburetor.

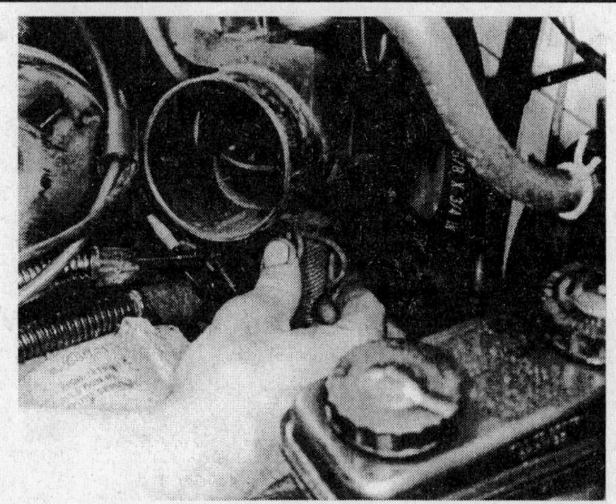

85615013

Fig. 13 After disconnecting the air intake duct, disconnect the air heat tube to the air cleaner

85615014

Fig. 14 Disconnecting the breather hose to the air cleaner — 2.2L engines

85615016

Fig. 15 Disconnecting the breather hose to the air cleaner — 2.2L engines

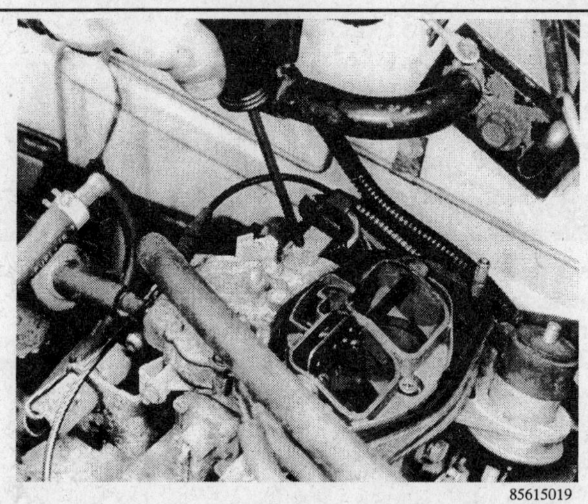

85615019

Fig. 18 Disconnect the wiring harness and vacuum tube retaining bracket — 2.2L engines

85615017

Fig. 16 Disconnect the carburetor inlet line — 2.2L engines

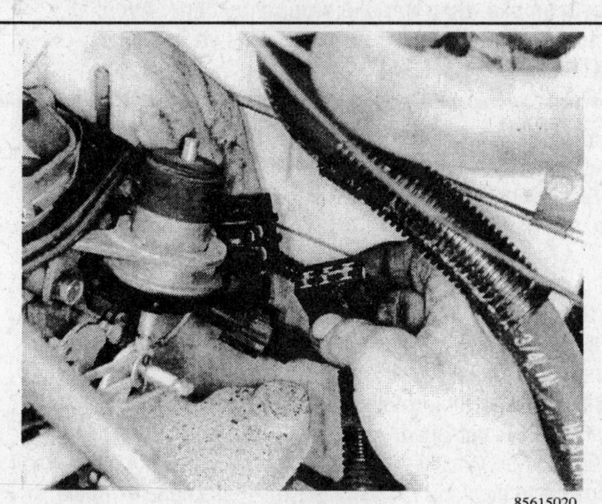

85615020

Fig. 19 Unplug the main wiring harness connector — 2.2L engines

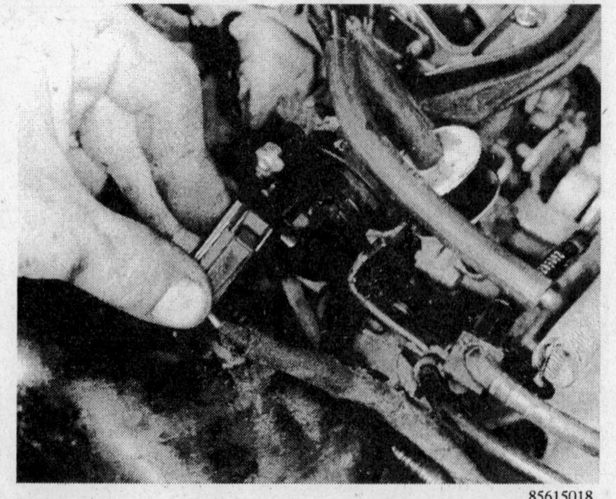

85615018

Fig. 17 Detach the electrical connector to the electric choke — 2.2L engines

85615021

Fig. 20 Disconnect the throttle linkage from the carburetor — 2.2L engines

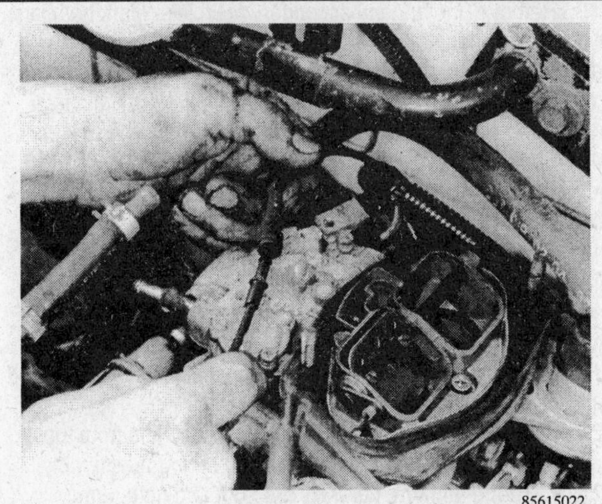
85615022

Fig. 21 Disconnect the vacuum tube — 2.2L engines

85615023

Fig. 22 Removing the carburetor mounting nuts — 2.2L engines

85615024

Fig. 23 Removing the carburetor mounting nuts (continued) — 2.2L engines

85615025

Fig. 24 Removing the carburetor assembly from the manifold — 2.2L engines

To install:

9. Inspect the mating surfaces of the carburetor and intake manifold for nicks, burrs, dirt or other damage.
10. Install a new gasket on intake manifold.
11. Carefully install the carburetor on the engine. Install mounting bolts and nuts. Tighten evenly to 12 ft. lbs. (17 Nm). Make certain throttle plates and choke plate opens and closes properly when operated.
12. Connect the throttle linkage, fuel line and electrical connectors.
13. Install and tighten carburetor protector.
14. Fill the cooling system.
15. Connect the negative battery cable.
16. Install the air cleaner and adjust the carburetor.

DISASSEMBLY

Holley Model 5220/6520

1. Remove the carburetor from the engine as described in carburetor removal procedure.
2. Using a small prytool disconnect and remove choke valve operating rod and seal.
3. Remove the idle stop solenoid mounting screws and remove solenoid.
4. Remove the oxygen solenoid retaining screws and carefully remove the sensor.
5. Remove the retaining clip securing the vacuum diaphragm control rod, remove the vacuum diaphragm mounting screws and remove vacuum diaphragm assembly.
6. Make a mark, for proper alignment during assembly, on the air conditioning wide open throttle cut-out switch, and remove switch and wiring assembly.
7. Remove the (5) air horn screws and separate the air horn from carburetor body.
8. Invert the air horn and remove the float pin, float and inlet needle.
9. Remove the fuel inlet needle and seat.
10. Notice the size and position of the secondary main metering jets, and remove jets.

11. Notice the size and position of the primary main metering jets, and remove jets.

12. Using a small prytool remove the secondary high speed bleed and secondary main well tube. Note the size and position so it can be reinstalled in its proper location.

13. Remove the primary high speed bleed and primary main well tube. Note the size and position so it can be reinstalled in its proper location.

14. Remove the pump discharge nozzle retaining screw, nozzle and gasket. Invert the carburetor and remove the pump discharge weight ball and check ball. (Both are the same size).

15. Remove the accelerator pump cover retaining screws, cover, pump diaphragm and spring.

16. Remove the choke diaphragm retaining screws and remove cover and spring.

17. Rotate the choke shaft and lever assembly counterclockwise. Rotate choke diaphragm assembly clockwise and remove from housing. Remove end of lower screw from housing. If the choke diaphragm need replacement, the diaphragm cover must also be replaced.

18. To remove concealment plug, center punch at a point $^1/_4$ in. (6mm) from the end of the mixture screw housing.

19. Drill through the outer housing with a $^1/_8$ in. diameter drill bit.

20. Pry out the concealment plug and save for reinstallation.

21. Remove the idle mixture screws from carburetor body.

Mikuni Carburetor

2.6L engines are equipped with a downdraft type two barrel carburetor, which can be identified with its black resin compound main body. The automatic choke is a thermowax type which is controlled by engine coolant temperature.

This carburetor also features a diaphragm type accelerator pump, bowl vent, fuel cut-off solenoid, Air Switching Valve (ASV), sub-EGR valve, Coasting Air Valve (CAV), Jet Air Control Valve (JACV) and a High Altitude Compensation (HAC) system. (California only).

1. Grind head from screws of choke cover. Gently tap the remaining screw portions using a hammer and a pointed punch in a counterclockwise direction until screws are removed.

2. Take notice of the painted punch mark and scribed lines on choke pinion plate. During reassembly, these marks must be aligned.

3. Remove the E-clip from the throttle opener link. Remove the throttle opener mounting screws and set aside.

4. Remove the ground wire from the fuel cut-off solenoid, remove solenoid mounting screws, and remove solenoid.

5. Remove the throttle return spring and damper spring.

6. Remove the choke unloader E-clip from its link and remove choke unloader.

7. Remove vacuum hose and link from vacuum chamber. Remove vacuum chamber mounting screws and remove vacuum chamber.

8. Remove accelerator rod link from throttle lever.

9. Remove the air horn mounting screws (6) and carefully separate air horn from carburetor body.

10. Slide out float pivot pin and remove float assembly. Remove air horn gasket.

11. Unscrew needle/seat retainer, remove needle/seat, O-ring and screen.

12. Remove the primary and secondary venturi and O-rings. Mark both venturi for proper location during reassembly.

13. Remove primary and secondary main jets. Mark both jets for proper location during reassembly.

14. Remove primary and secondary pedestals and gaskets.

15. Remove bowl vent solenoid mounting screws, solenoid, bowl vent assembly, seal and gasket.

16. Remove the Coasting Air Valve (CAV) mounting screws and remove valve assembly from air horn. (California and Altitude models).

17. Remove enrichment valve mounting screws and remove enrichment valve assembly.

18. Remove Air Switching Valve (ASV) mounting screws and remove air switching valve assembly from air horn.

19. Remove the primary and secondary pilot jet set screw and lock. Remove pilot jet set assembly.

20. Remove primary and secondary air bleed jets from top of air horn. Mark both jets for proper location during reassembly.

21. Invert the air horn, carefully drop out and note pump weight, check ball and hex nut.

22. Remove accelerator pump mounting screws and remove pump cover, diaphragm, spring, pump body and gasket.

23. Remove jet air control valve mounting screws and remove JACV cover, spring, retainer and diaphragm seal.

24. Remove E-clip from sub-EGR lever. The sub-EGR valve is under pressure by a steel ball and spring. Care should be used when removing lever to prevent accidental lost of spring or ball. Carefully slide the pin from lever and sub-EGR valve. Remove the steel ball, spring, sub-EGR valve and boot seal.

CLEANING AND INSPECTION

Efficient carburetion depends greatly on careful cleaning and inspection during overhaul, since dirt, gum, water, or varnish in or on the carburetor parts are often responsible for poor performance. There are many commercial carburetor cleaning solvent which can give satisfactory results.

➥ Avoid placing any seals, O-rings, float, choke and vacuum diaphragm in cleaning solvent. Such components can be damaged if immersed in cleaning solvent. Clean the external surfaces of these parts with a clean, lint-free cloth or brush.

Soak carburetor parts in cleaning solvent, but do not leave parts in solvent any longer than necessary to loosen deposits. Remove parts and rinse with clean hot water. Blow out all passages and jets with compressed air. Blow dry all parts.

Inspect the following:

1. Check the float needle and seat for wear. If wear is found, replace the needle/seat assembly.

2. Check the float pin for wear and the float for damage, replace if necessary.

3. Check the throttle and choke shaft bores for wear or an out-of-round condition. Damage or wear to the throttle arm, shaft, or shaft bore will often require replacement of the throttle body. These parts require a close tolerance fit. Wear on these parts may allow air leakage, which could affect starting and idling.

4. Inspect the idle mixture adjusting needles for burrs or grooves, any such condition requires replacement of the needle, since you will not be able to obtain a satisfactory idle.

5. Check the bowl cover with a straight edge for warped surfaces .

ASSEMBLY

Holley Model 5220/6520

1. Install the choke shaft, while rotating counterclockwise. Install the diaphragm with a clockwise motion. Position spring and cover over diaphragm, and install retaining screws. Be certain fast idle link has been properly installed.
2. Install the accelerator pump spring, diaphragm cover and screws.

****CAUTION**

Never smoke when working around gasoline! Avoid all sources of sparks or ignition. Gasoline vapors are EXTREMELY volatile!

3. Install the accelerator pump discharge check ball in discharge passage. Check the accelerator pump and seat operation before complete reassembling as follows:
    a. Fill the fuel bowl with clean fuel.
    b. Hold the discharge check ball down with a small brass rod and operate the pump plunger by hand. If the check ball and seat is leaking, no resistance will be felt when the plunger is operated. If the valve is leaking, use the old ball and carefully stake the ball using a suitable drift punch. Avoid damaging the bore containing the pump weight.
    c. After staking the old ball, remove and replace with the new ball. Recheck for leaks.
4. Install a new gasket, discharge nozzle and nozzle retaining screw.
5. Install the primary main well tube and primary high speed bleed.
6. Install the secondary main well tube and secondary high speed bleed.
7. Install the primary main metering (smaller size number) jet.
8. Install the secondary main metering (larger size number) jet.
9. Install the needle and seat assembly with a new gasket.
10. Invert the air horn and install float, inlet needle and float lever pin. Reset "dry float setting" and "float drop.", according to the following adjustment procedures.
11. Install a new gasket on air horn, and install choke rod seal and choke rod.
12. Carefully position the air horn on carburetor body.
13. Install a new retainer on choke shaft lever and fast idle cam pick-up lever and connect choke rod.
14. Install air horn retaining screws and tighten to 30 inch lbs. (3 Nm).
15. Install idle stop solenoid, and reinstall anti-rattle spring.
16. Install the air conditioning wide open throttle cut-out switch and align it with mark previously made. The switch must be positioned so that the air conditioning clutch circuit is open 10° before wide open throttle position.
17. Install the oxygen solenoid gasket on air horn. Install new O-ring seal on oxygen solenoid. Coat the new O-ring seal with petroleum jelly and install solenoid in carburetor body. Tighten solenoid mounting screws and secure wiring and clamps.
18. Install the vacuum solenoid.
19. Install the vacuum control valve.

SETTING THE FLOAT

1. Invert the air horn. With gasket removed, insert a 0.480 in. (12.2mm) gauge or drill between air horn and float.
2. To obtain proper dry float level bend adjusting tang with a small prytool.

FLOAT DROP

➧ **See Figures 25 and 26**

1. With the air horn upright, check float drop with a depth gauge.
2. To obtain proper float drop adjustment, hold float assembly securely with one hand. Using a small prytool, carefully bend adjusting tang to obtain a float drop of 1.87 in. (47.6mm).

Mikuni Carburetor

1. Install the sub-EGR valve to throttle valve and check for proper operation.
2. Assemble the Jet Air Control Valve (JACV) to throttle body and secure with mounting screws.

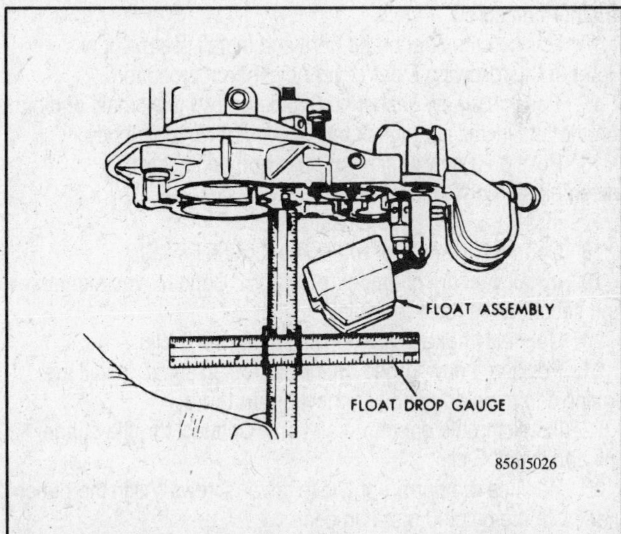

Fig. 25 Measuring the float drop — 2.2L engine shown

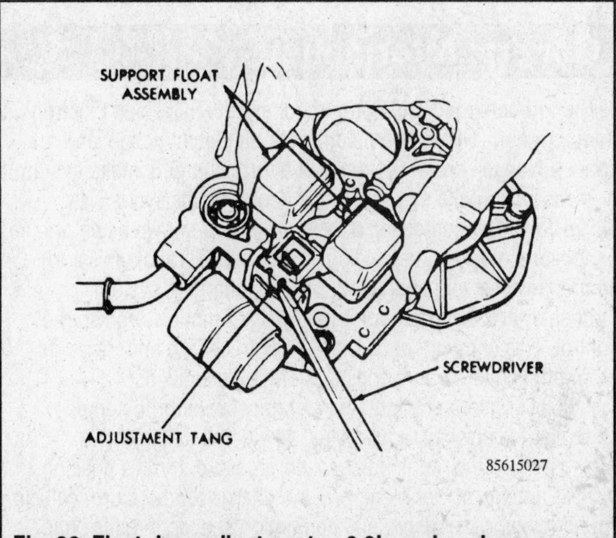

Fig. 26 Float drop adjustment — 2.2L engine shown

3. Assemble the accelerator pump to throttle body and secure with mounting screws.
4. Install the primary and secondary air bleed jets. The secondary air bleed jet has the largest number.
5. Position new O-ring seals on primary and secondary pilot jet side. Slide assembly into place and install lock and screw.
6. Assemble the Air Switching Valve (ASV) to air horn and secure with mounting screws.
7. Assemble the enrichment valve to air horn.
8. Assemble the coasting air valve to air horn.
9. Position a new O-ring and gasket on bowl vent assembly and install on air horn.
10. Position a new gasket on air horn and install primary and secondary pedestals.
11. Install primary and secondary main jets in their pedestals. The secondary main jet has the largest number.
12. Position new O-rings on both primary and secondary venturi. Install primary and secondary venturi and retainers.
13. Position a new O-ring on needle seat. Install a new screen on needle seat. Install shim and needle seat into air horn. Install retainer and screw.
14. Position the float on air horn and install float pivot pin. Refer to the following Float Level Adjustment procedure.
15. Position a new gasket on throttle body. Install main body to throttle and install nut, check ball and weight in main body.
16. Position a new gasket on main body and carefully assemble air horn to main body.
17. Install vacuum hoses to air horn.
18. Connect accelerator rod link to throttle lever.
19. Install vacuum chamber to air horn. Connect vacuum hose and secondary throttle lever link.
20. Connect choke unloader link and install E-clip.
21. Position a new O-ring on fuel cut-off solenoid. Install the solenoid to main body and connect ground wire.
22. Install throttle opener to air horn. Connect throttle opener link and install E-clip.
23. Replace tamper-proof choke cover screws. Align the punch mark with the painted mark on gear.
24. Install the choke cover and peen over screws. Tighten the remaining screw using a pointed punch and a small hammer.
25. Install the choke water hose and clamp.

FLOAT LEVEL ADJUSTMENT

See Figure 27

1. Remove air horn from carburetor main body.
2. Remove air horn gasket and invert air horn.
3. Using a gauge measure the distance from bottom of float to air horn surface. The distance should be 0.78 in. (20mm) ± 0.039 in. (1mm). If distance is not within specification, the shim under the needle and seat must be changed. Shim pack MD606952 or equivalent has three shims: 0.3mm, 0.4mm, or 0.5mm. Adding or removing one shim will change the float level three its thickness.

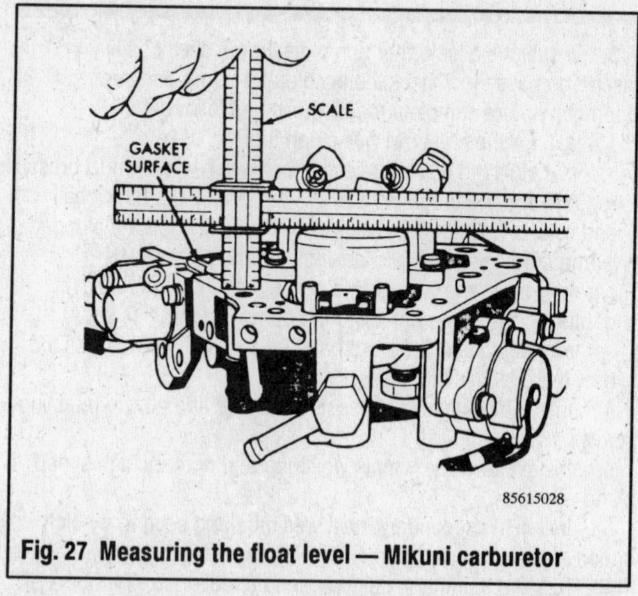

Fig. 27 Measuring the float level — Mikuni carburetor

CHRYSLER MULTI-POINT ELECTRONIC FUEL INJECTION

General Information

The turbocharged and non-turbocharged Multi-Point Electronic Fuel Injection (MPI) system combines an electronic fuel and spark advance control system with a turbocharged intake system or cross type intake system. At the center of this system is a digital computer containing a microprocessor known as an engine controller that regulates ignition timing, air/fuel ratio, emission control devices, idle speed, cooling fan, charging system, turbocharger waste gate (on turbocharged models) and speed control. This component has the ability to update and revise its programming to meet changing operating conditions.

Various sensors provide the input necessary for the engine controller to correctly regulate fuel flow at the fuel injectors. These include the manifold absolute pressure, throttle position, oxygen sensor, coolant temperature, charge temperature, vehicle speed (distance) sensors and detonation sensor. In addition to the sensors, various switches also provide important information. These include the neutral-safety, air conditioning clutch switch, brake switch and speed control switch.

Check Engine Light

The check engine light comes on each time the ignition key is turned **ON** and stays on for a few seconds as a bulb test. If the engine controller receives an incorrect signal or no signal from either the coolant temperature sensor, charge temperature sensor, manifold absolute pressure sensor, throttle position sensor, battery voltage sensor input or emission related system on California vehicles the check engine light on the instrument panel is illuminated.

This is a warning that the engine controller has gone into Limp In Mode in an attempt to keep the system operational. Cycle the ignition switch **ON**, **OFF**, **ON**, **OFF**, **ON**, within 5 seconds and any fault codes stored in the memory will be displayed. For more details on fault codes, please refer to Section 4.

Limp In Mode is the attempt by the engine controller to compensate for the failure of certain components by substituting information from other sources.

Diagnosis and Testing

➥ **For Self-Diagnostic System and Accessing Trouble Code Memory, see the diagnostic procedures in Section 4. These procedures require an extensive knowledge of electronic fuel injection systems, use extreme care when performing any of these procedures.**

The engine controller computer (known as the SMEC, SBEC, SBEC II or PCM) has been programmed to monitor several different circuits of the fuel injection system. This monitoring is called On Board Diagnosis. If a problem is sensed with a monitored circuit, often enough to indicate an actual problem, its fault code is stored in the computer for eventual display to the service technician. If the problem is repaired or ceases to exist, the engine controller cancels the fault code after 50–100 ignition key **ON/OFF** cycles.

Fault codes are 2 digit numbers that identify which circuit is bad. In most cases, they DO NOT identify which component is bad in a circuit. When a fault code appears it indicates that the engine controller has recognized an abnormal signal in the system. Fault codes indicate the results of a failure but do not always identify the failed component directly.

Fuel System Pressure Release Procedure

1987–92 MODELS

2.5L, 3.0L and 3.3L Engines

1. Loosen the gas cap to release tank pressure.
2. Disconnect injector wiring harness from the engine or main harness.
3. Connect a jumper to ground terminal No. 1 of the injector harness to engine ground.
4. Connect a jumper to the positive terminal No. 2 of the injector harness and momentarily touch the positive terminal of the battery for no longer than 5 seconds. This releases the system pressure. Remove the jumper wires.

1993–95 MODELS

3.0L Engines

1. Loosen the gas cap to release tank pressure.
2. Disconnect the fuel rail electrical harness from the engine harness.
3. Connect one end of a jumper wire to the A142 circuit terminal of the fuel rail harness connector.
4. Connect the other end of the jumper wire to a good ground source.
5. Momentarily ground one of the injectors by connecting the other end of the jumper wire to an injector terminal in the harness connector. Repeat the procedure for 2 or 3 injectors.

3.3L and 3.8L Engines

1. Disconnect the negative battery cable.
2. Loosen the gas cap to release tank pressure.
3. Remove the protective cap from the fuel pressure test port on the fuel rail.
4. Place the open end of fuel pressure release hose, tool No. C-4799-1 (or equivalent), into an approved gasoline container. Connect the other end of hose C-4799-1 to the fuel pressure test port. Fuel pressure will bleed off through the hose into the gasoline container.

➥ **Fuel gauge C-4799-A contains hose C-4799-1**

Fuel Pressure Test

2.5L TURBOCHARGED ENGINES

1. Release fuel system pressure.
2. Remove the protective cover from the service valve on the fuel rail.
3. Connect a suitable fuel pressure gauge to fuel rail service valve.
4. Using the DRB II tester, or equivalent, with the key in the **RUN** position, use "Actuate Outputs Test-Auto Shutdown Relay" this will activate the fuel pump for 1.5 seconds to pressurize the system.
5. If the gauge reads 53-57 psi (365–393 kPa), fuel pressure is correct and no further testing is necessary. Remove all test equipment.
6. If pressure is not correct, record the pressure and continue with the test procedure.
7. If the fuel pressure is below specifications, install the fuel pressure gauge in the fuel supply line, between the fuel tank and fuel filter at the rear of the vehicle.
8. Repeat the test. If pressure is 5 psi (34 kPa) higher than recorded pressure replace the fuel filter. If no change in pressure is observed, gently squeeze the return hose. If the pressure increases replace the pressure regulator. If no change is observed check for a defective fuel pump or plugged filter sock.

➥ **The test (Step 9) should be performed when the fuel tank is at least $^1/_2$–$^3/_4$ full.**

9. If the fuel pressure is above specifications, remove the fuel return line hose from the chassis line at fuel tank and connect a 3 ft. (91cm) piece of fuel hose to the return line. Position the other end in a suitable container (2 gallons or more). Repeat test and, if pressure is now correct, check in-tank return hose for kinking.
10. Replace the fuel tank assembly if the in-tank reservoir check valve or the aspirator jet is blocked.
11. If the pressure is still above specifications, remove fuel return hose from fuel pressure regulator. Connect a suitable hose to the fuel pressure regulator nipple and place the other in a suitable container. Repeat the test. If pressure is now correct, check for restricted fuel line. If no change is observed, replace fuel pressure regulator.

3.0L, 3.3L AND 3.8L ENGINES

1. Release fuel system pressure.
2. Disconnect the fuel supply hose from the engine fuel line assembly. Connect a suitable fuel pressure gauge between fuel supply hose and engine fuel line assembly.
3. Using the DRB II tester, or equivalent, with the key in the **RUN** position, use "Actuate Outputs Test-Auto Shutdown Relay" this will activate the fuel pump for 1.5 seconds to pressurize the system.
4. If the gauge reads 46–50 psi (317–345 kPa) fuel pressure is correct and no further testing is necessary. Remove all test equipment.
5. If pressure is not correct, record the pressure and continue with the test procedure.
6. If the fuel pressure is below specifications, install the fuel pressure gauge in the fuel supply line, between the fuel tank and fuel filter at the rear of the vehicle.
7. Repeat the test. If pressure is 5 psi (34 kPa) higher than recorded pressure replace the fuel filter. If no change in pressure is observed, gently squeeze the return hose. If the pressure increases replace the pressure regulator. If no change is observed check for a defective fuel pump or plugged filter sock.

The test (Step 8) should be performed when fuel tank is at least 1/2–3/4 full.

8. If the fuel pressure is above specifications, remove the fuel return line hose from the chassis line at fuel tank and connect a 3 ft. (91cm) piece of fuel hose to the return line. Position the other end in suitable container (2 gallons/7.5 liters or more). Repeat test and, if pressure is now correct, check in-tank return hose for kinking.
9. Replace the fuel tank assembly if the in-tank reservoir check valve or the aspirator jet is blocked.
10. If the pressure is still above specifications, remove fuel return hose from fuel pressure regulator. Connect a suitable hose to the fuel return line and place the other end in a suitable container. Repeat the test. If the pressure is now correct, check for restricted fuel line. If no change has occurred, replace the fuel pressure regulator.

Wastegate Calibration

INSPECTION

2.5L Turbocharged Engines

1. Disconnect the vacuum hose from the wastegate diaphragm.
2. Connect a cooling system pressure tester or equivalent to the wastegate diaphragm.
3. Slowly apply pressure while watching the actuator rod.
4. If the wastegate actuator rod moves more than 0.015 in. (0.381mm) before 2–4 psi (13–27 kPa), (4 psi — 27 kPa on Turbo II) or does not move after 5 psi (34 kPa) is applied the wastegate is faulty.
5. Service faulty component as necessary.

Throttle Body

REMOVAL & INSTALLATION

See Figures 28, 29 and 30

When servicing the fuel portion of the throttle body, it will be necessary to bleed fuel pressure before opening any hoses; refer to Fuel Pressure Release procedure. Always reassemble throttle body components with new O-rings and seals where applicable. Use care when removing fuel hoses to prevent damage to hose or hose nipple. Always use new hose clamps of the correct type when reassembling and tighten hose clamps to 10 inch lbs. (1.12 Nm).

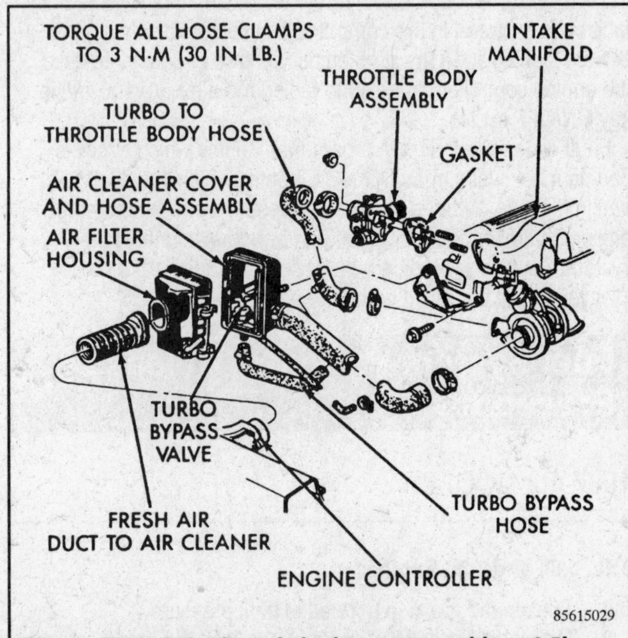

Fig. 28 Throttle body and air cleaner assembly — 2.5L turbocharged engines

1. Drain engine coolant, if necessary, and release fuel pressure. Disconnect negative battery cable.
2. Remove air cleaner-to-throttle body screws (or nuts), loosen hose clamp and remove air cleaner adaptor.

When removing accelerator cable, note position or adjustment for correct installation.

3. Remove accelerator, speed control and transaxle kick-down cables and return spring.
4. Remove throttle cable bracket from throttle body.
5. Disengage all necessary electrical connector(s).
6. Disconnect vacuum hoses from throttle body.
7. Loosen throttle body-to-turbocharger hose clamp, if so equipped.
8. Remove throttle body-to-intake manifold or adapter screws (or nuts). Always note position of retaining bolts as some may be different in length.
9. Remove throttle body and gasket.
10. Reverse the above procedure for installation.

If fuel system hoses are to be replaced, only hoses marked EFI/EFM may be used.

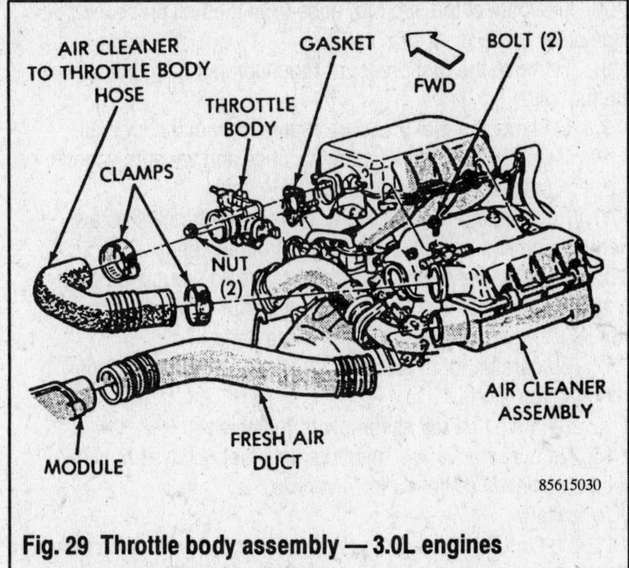

Fig. 29 Throttle body assembly — 3.0L engines

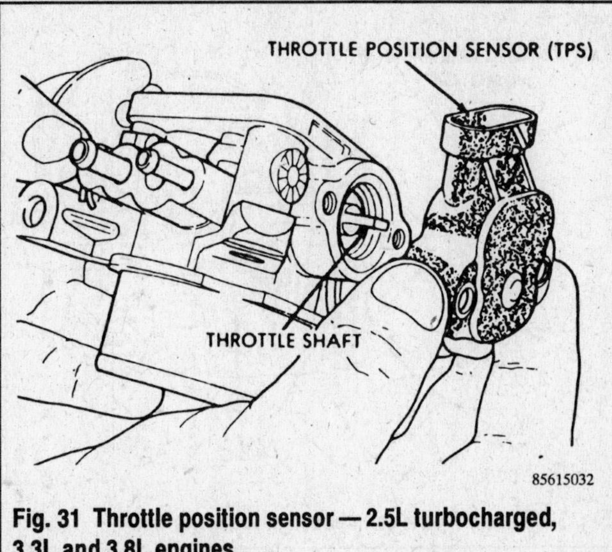

Fig. 31 Throttle position sensor — 2.5L turbocharged, 3.3L and 3.8L engines

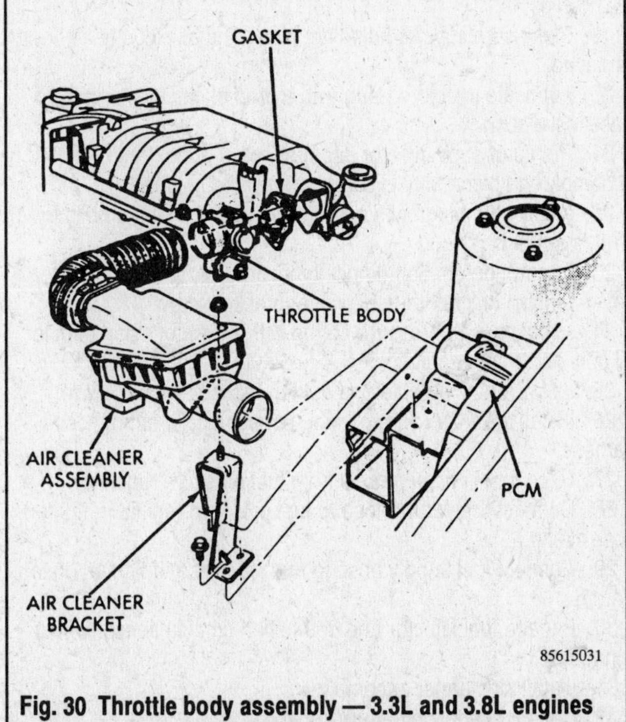

Fig. 30 Throttle body assembly — 3.3L and 3.8L engines

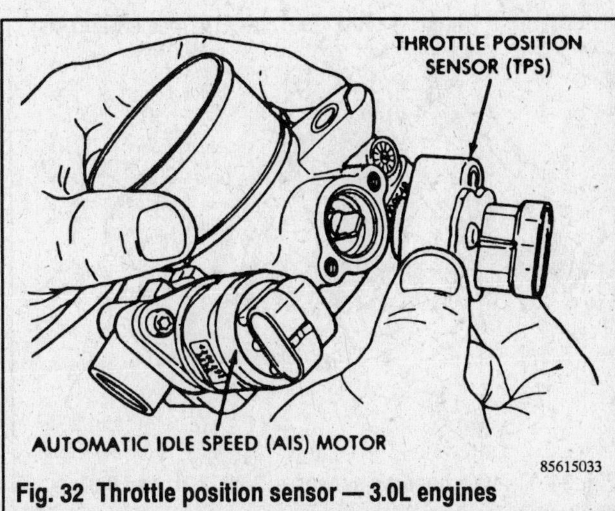

Fig. 32 Throttle position sensor — 3.0L engines

Throttle Position Sensor (TPS)

REMOVAL & INSTALLATION

See Figures 31 and 32

1. Disconnect negative battery cable and 3-way throttle position sensor wiring connector.
2. Remove 2 screws, mounting throttle position sensor to throttle body.
3. Lift throttle position sensor off throttle shaft.
4. To install, reverse removal procedure and tighten screws to 17 inch lbs. (2 Nm).

Automatic Idle Speed (AIS) Motor

REMOVAL & INSTALLATION

See Figures 33 and 34

1. Disconnect negative battery cable and 4-way AIS motor wiring connector.
2. Remove 2 screws that mount AIS motor to throttle body.
3. Remove AIS motor from throttle body. Make certain that the O-ring is on the AIS motor.

To install:

4. Place new O-ring on AIS motor. If pintle measures more than 1 in. (25.4mm), it must be retracted by using the AIS Motor Test in the Actuate Outputs mode of the DRB II. (Battery must be reconnected for this operation.)
5. Carefully place AIS motor into throttle body.
6. Install 2 mounting screws and tighten to 17 inch lbs. (2 Nm).
7. Connect 4-way wiring connector to AIS motor and reconnect negative battery cable.

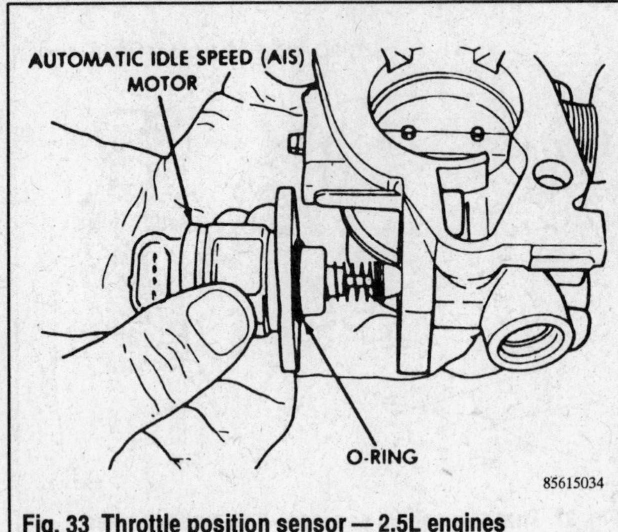

Fig. 33 Throttle position sensor — 2.5L engines

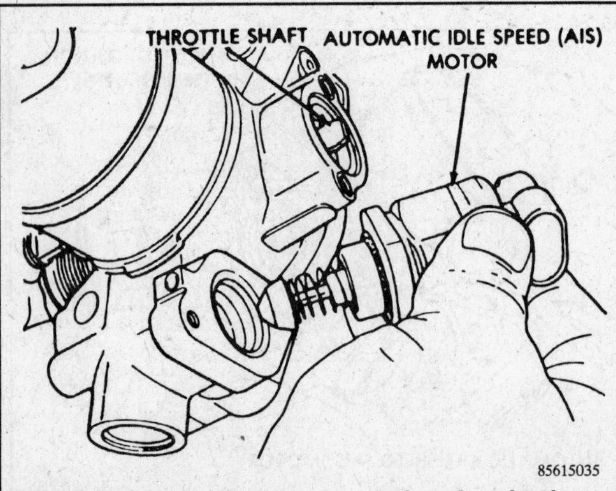

Fig. 34 Throttle position sensor — 3.0L, 3.3L and 3.8L engines

Fuel Injector Rail Assembly

REMOVAL & INSTALLATION

2.5L Turbocharged Engines

➧ See Figures 28, 35, 36, 37, 38 and 39

1. Perform fuel system pressure release procedure.
2. Disconnect negative battery cable.
3. Remove air cleaner assembly.
4. Disconnect detonation (knock) sensor and fuel injector wiring connectors.
5. Loosen fuel supply hose clamp at fuel rail inlet and remove hose. Wrap a shop towel around hose to absorb any fuel spillage which may occur when removing.
6. Loosen fuel return hose clamp at the fuel pressure regulator and remove the hose. Wrap a shop towel around the hose to absorb any fuel spillage, which may occur when removing the hose.
7. Disconnect the vacuum hose from the fuel pressure regulator.
8. Remove the fuel pressure regulator mounting bolts from the fuel rail.
9. Remove the fuel pressure regulator from the fuel rail.
10. Remove the PCV vacuum harness and vacuum vapor harness from the intake manifold.
11. Remove the fuel rail to the valve cover bracket screw. Remove the knock sensor connector from the sensor.
12. Remove the fuel rail to intake manifold mounting bolts.
13. Remove fuel rail and injector assembly by pulling rail so that injectors come straight out of there ports.
14. Be careful not to damage rubber injector O-ring upon removal from ports.
15. Remove fuel rail assembly from vehicle.
16. Do not remove fuel injectors until fuel rail assembly has been completely removed from vehicle.

To install:

17. Be sure injectors are seated into receiver cup, with lockring in place.
18. Install injector wiring harness to injectors and fasten into wiring clips.
19. Make sure injector holes are clean and all plugs have been removed.
20. Lubricate injector O-ring with a drop of clean engine oil to ease installation.
21. Put tip of each injector into respective ports. Push assembly into place until injectors are seated in ports.
22. Install attaching bolts and ground eyelet. Tighten bolts to 21 ft. lbs. (28 Nm).
23. Engage detonation (knock) sensor wire connector to sensor. Install fuel rail-to-valve cover bracket screw.
24. Lubricate fuel pressure O-ring with a drop of clean engine oil and install into receiver cup on fuel rail.
25. Install attaching nuts and tighten to 65 inch lbs. (7 Nm).
26. Install the PCV system hose harness and vacuum hose harness.
27. Reconnect vacuum hose from fuel pressure regulator.
28. Connect fuel return hose to fuel pressure regulator; tighten hose clamp.
29. Connect fuel supply hose to fuel rail inlet and tighten hose clamp.
30. Engage fuel injector and detonation (knock) sensor wiring connector.
31. Install air cleaner assembly.
32. Connect negative battery cable.
33. Check the system for leaks.

3.0L Engines

➧ See Figures 40 and 41

1. Perform fuel system pressure release procedure.
2. Disconnect negative battery cable.
3. Remove air cleaner-to-throttle body hose.
4. Remove throttle cable and transaxle kickdown linkage.
5. Remove Automatic Idle Speed (AIS) motor and Throttle Position Sensor (TPS) wiring connectors from throttle body.
6. Remove vacuum hose harness from throttle body.
7. Remove PCV and brake booster hoses from air intake plenum.

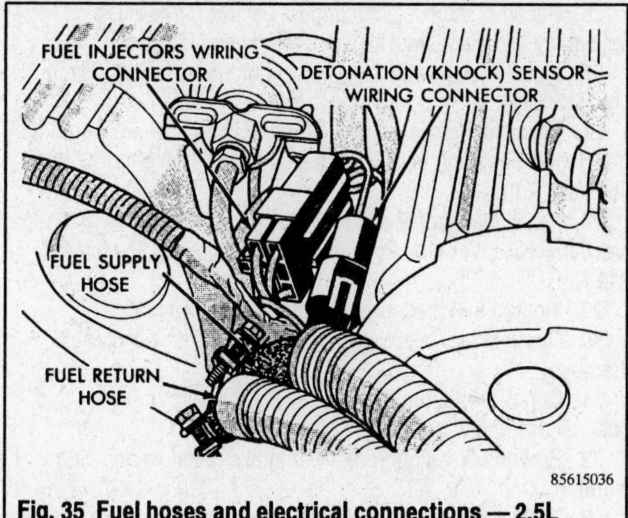

Fig. 35 Fuel hoses and electrical connections — 2.5L engines

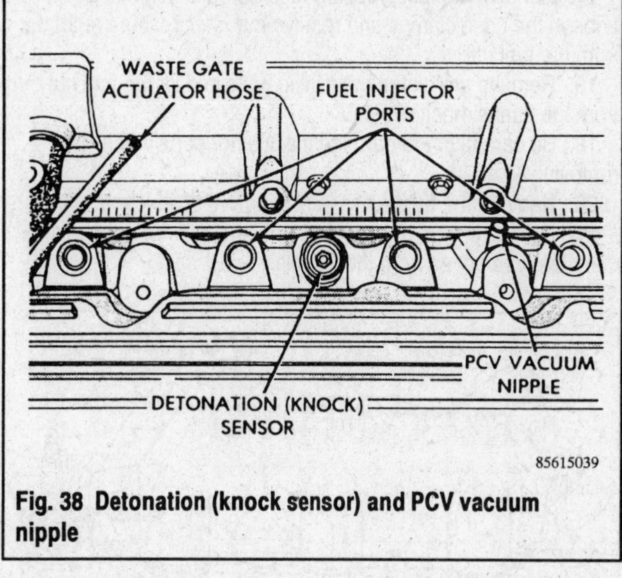

Fig. 38 Detonation (knock sensor) and PCV vacuum nipple

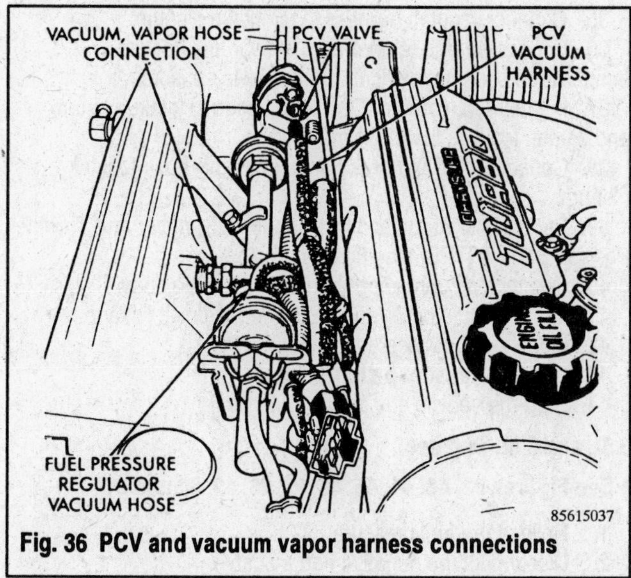

Fig. 36 PCV and vacuum vapor harness connections

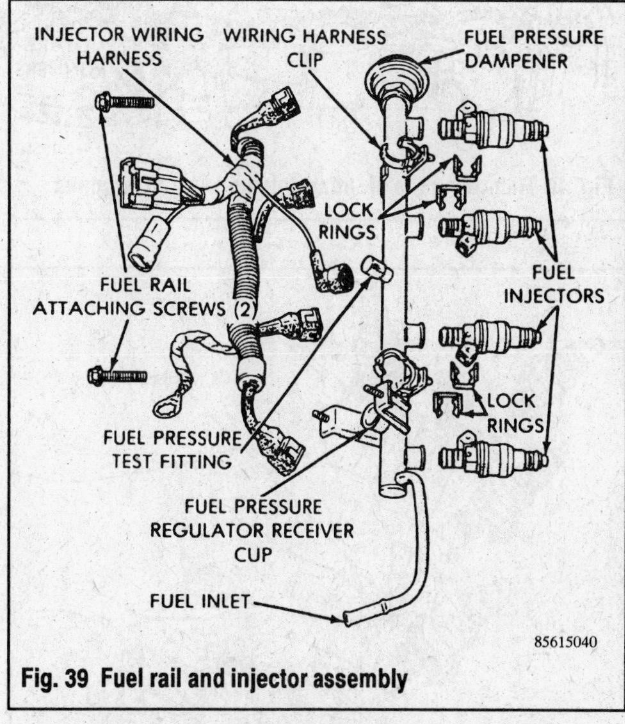

Fig. 39 Fuel rail and injector assembly

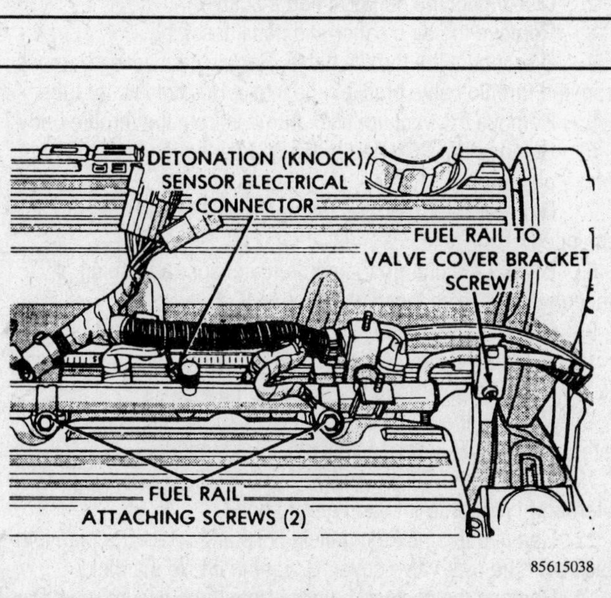

Fig. 37 Fuel hoses and electrical connections

8. If equipped, remove EGR tube flange from intake plenum.
9. Remove wiring connectors from charge temperature sensor and coolant temperature sensor.
10. Remove vacuum connections from air intake plenum vacuum connector.
11. Remove fuel hoses from fuel rail. Wrap a shop towel around hose to absorb any fuel spillage which may occur when removing.
12. Remove fasteners from air intake plenum to intake manifold.
13. Remove air intake plenum.
14. Cover intake manifold with suitable cover when servicing.
15. Remove vacuum hoses from fuel rail and fuel pressure regulator.
16. Disconnect fuel injector wiring harness from engine wiring harness.

17. Remove the fuel pressure regulator attaching bolts. Loosen the hose clamps and remove the fuel pressure regulator from the fuel rail.
18. Remove the fuel rail attaching bolts and lift the fuel rail from the intake manifold.
19. Be careful not to damage the injector ports when removing.
20. Remove the fuel rail assembly from the vehicle.
21. Do not remove the injectors until the fuel rail has been completely removed from the vehicle.

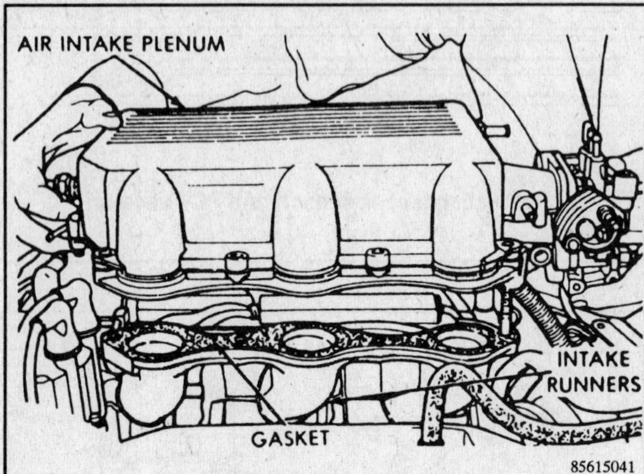

Fig. 40 Removing the air intake plenum — 3.0L engines

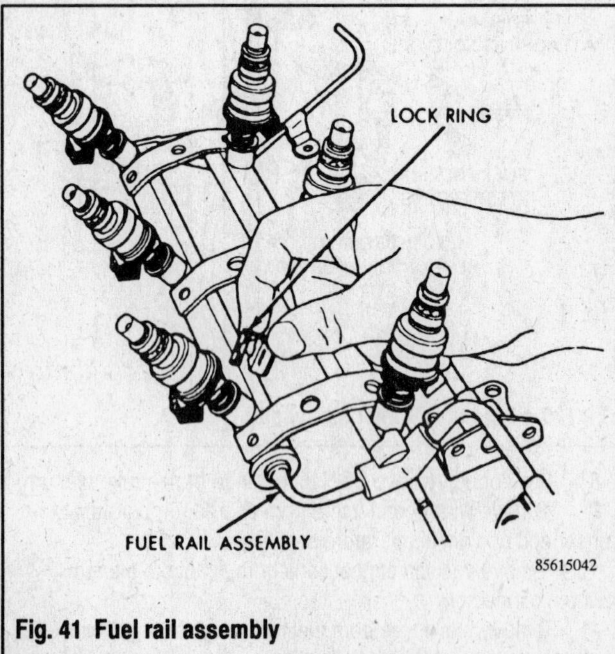

Fig. 41 Fuel rail assembly

To install:

22. Make sure the injectors are completely seated with the lockring in place.
23. Make sure the injector holes are clean and that all plugs have been removed.
24. Lubricate injector O-ring with a drop of clean engine oil to ease installation.
25. Put tip of each injector into respective ports. Push assembly into place until injectors are seated in ports.
26. Install fuel rail attaching bolts. Tighten bolts to 115 inch lbs. (13 Nm).
27. Install fuel pressure regulator and hose assembly onto fuel rail. Install attaching bolts to intake manifold. Tighten to 77 inch lbs. (8.7 Nm).
28. Install fuel supply and return tube hold-down bolt and vacuum crossover tube hold-down bolt. Tighten to 95 inch lbs. (11 Nm).
29. Tighten fuel pressure regulator hose clamps.
30. Connect fuel injector wiring harness to engine wiring harness.
31. Connect vacuum harness to fuel pressure regulator and fuel rail assembly.
32. Remove covering from lower intake manifold and clean surface.
33. Place intake manifold gaskets, with beaded sealer up, on lower manifold. Put air intake in place. Install attaching fasteners and tighten to 115 inch lbs. (13 Nm).
34. Connect fuel line to fuel rail and tighten.
35. Connect vacuum harness to air intake plenum.
36. Engage charge temperature sensor and coolant temperature sensor electrical connectors to sensors.
37. If equipped, connect EGR tube flange to intake plenum and tighten to 16 ft. lbs. (22 Nm).
38. Connect PCV and brake booster supply hose to intake plenum.
39. Engage the Automatic Idle Speed (AIS) motor and Throttle Position Sensor (TPS) electrical connectors.
40. Connect vacuum vapor harness to throttle body.
41. Install throttle cable and transaxle kickdown linkage.
42. Install air inlet hose assembly.
43. Connect negative battery cable.
44. Start the vehicle and check for leaks.

3.3L and 3.8L Engines

➧ See Figures 42, 43, 44, 45, 46, 47, 48, 49, 50 and 51

1. Relieve the fuel pressure.
2. Disconnect the negative battery cable.
3. Remove the air cleaner and hose assembly.
4. Disconnect the throttle cable. Remove the wiring harness from the throttle cable bracket and intake manifold water tube.
5. Remove the vacuum hose harness from the throttle body.
6. Remove the PCV and brake booster hoses from the air intake plenum.
7. Remove the EGR tube flange from the intake plenum, if equipped.
8. Unplug the charge temperature sensor and unplug all vacuum hoses from the intake plenum.
9. Remove the cylinder head-to-intake plenum strut.
10. Disengage the MAP sensor and oxygen sensor connector. Remove the engine mounted ground strap.
11. Release the fuel hose quick-disconnect fittings and remove the hoses from the fuel rail. Plug the hoses.
12. Remove the Direct Ignition System (DIS) coils and the alternator bracket-to-intake manifold bolt.
13. Remove the intake manifold bolts and rotate the manifold back over the rear valve cover. Cover the intake manifold.
14. Remove the vacuum harness from the pressure regulator.

15. Remove the fuel tube retainer bracket screw and the fuel rail attaching bolts. Spread the retainer bracket to allow for clearance when removing the fuel tube.
16. Remove the fuel rail injector wiring clip from the alternator bracket.
17. Disconnect the camshaft sensor, coolant temperature sensor and engine temperature sensor.
18. Remove the fuel rail.
19. Position the fuel rail on a work bench, so that the injectors are easy to get at.
20. Remove the small connector retaining clip and unplug the injector. Remove the injector clip from the fuel rail and injector. Pull the injector straight off of the rail.

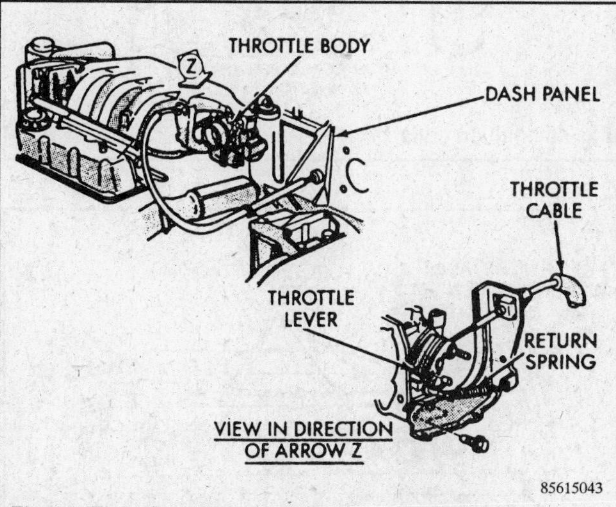

Fig. 42 Throttle cable attachment — 3.3L and 3.8L engines

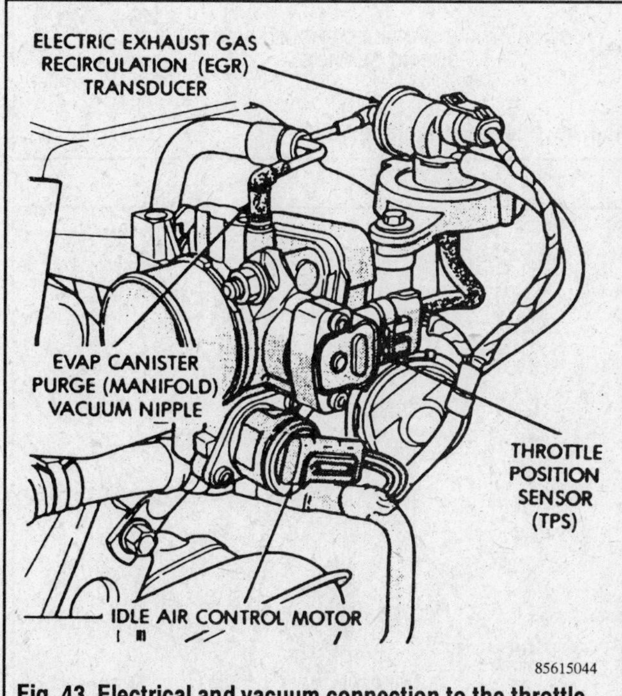

Fig. 43 Electrical and vacuum connection to the throttle body

To install:

21. Lubricate the rubber O-ring with clean oil and install to the rail receiver cap. Install the injector clip to the slot in the injector, plug in the connector and install the connector clip.
22. Install the fuel rail.
23. Connect the camshaft sensor, coolant temperature sensor and engine temperature sensor.
24. Install the fuel rail injector wiring clip to the alternator bracket.
25. Install the fuel rail attaching bolts and fuel tube retainer bracket screw.
26. Install the vacuum harness to the pressure regulator.
27. Install the intake manifold with a new gasket. Install the bolts only finger-tight. Install the alternator bracket-to-intake manifold bolt and the cylinder head-to-intake manifold strut and bolts. Tighten the intake manifold mounting bolts to 21 ft. lbs. (28 Nm) starting from the middle and working outward. Tighten the bracket and strut bolts to 40 ft. lbs. (54 Nm).
28. Install or connect all items that were removed or disconnected from the intake manifold and throttle body.
29. Connect the fuel hoses to the rail. Push the fittings in until they click in place.
30. Install the air cleaner assembly.
31. Connect the negative battery cable and check for leaks using the DRB II or equivalent to activate the fuel pump.

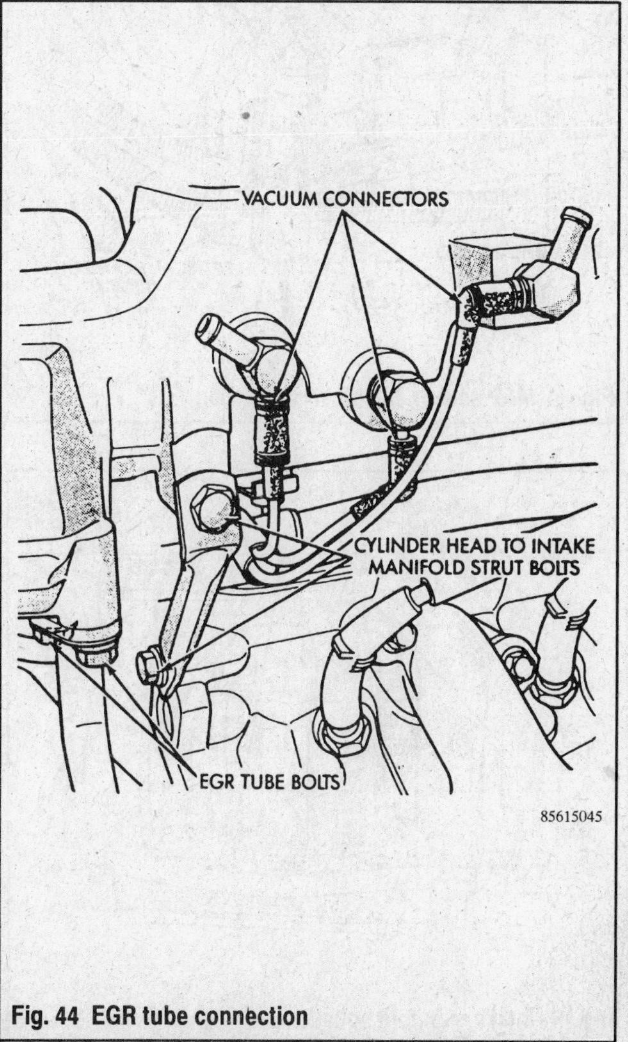

Fig. 44 EGR tube connection

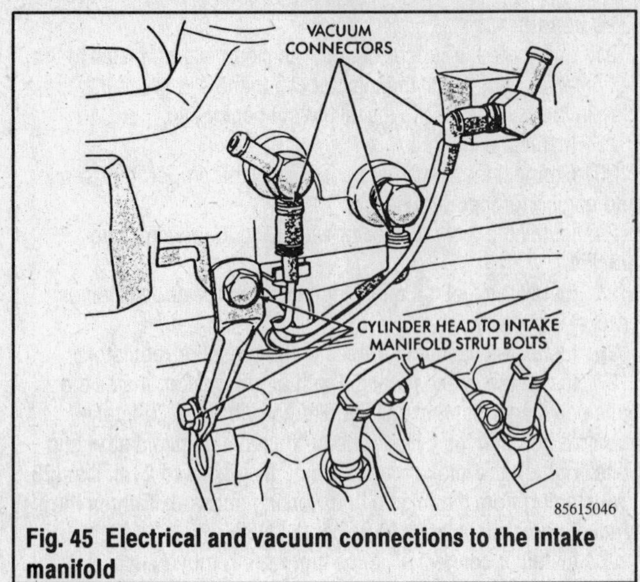

Fig. 45 Electrical and vacuum connections to the intake manifold

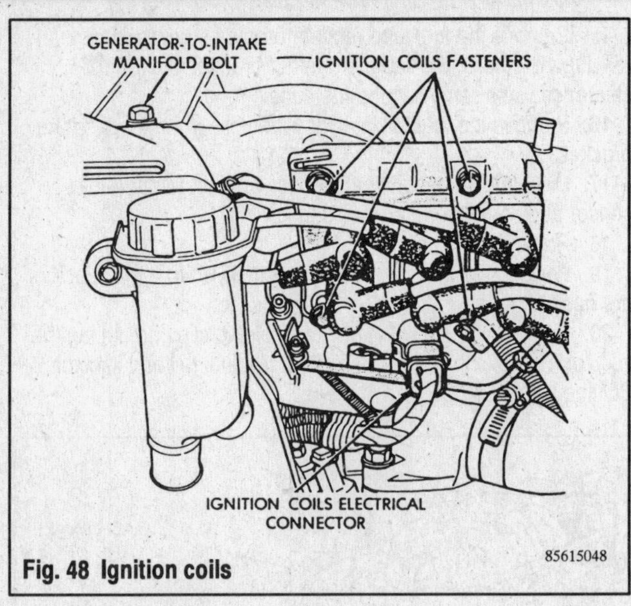

Fig. 48 Ignition coils

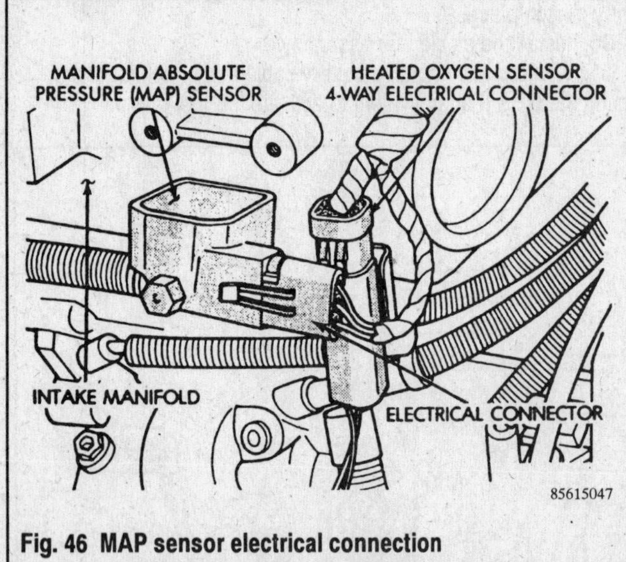

Fig. 46 MAP sensor electrical connection

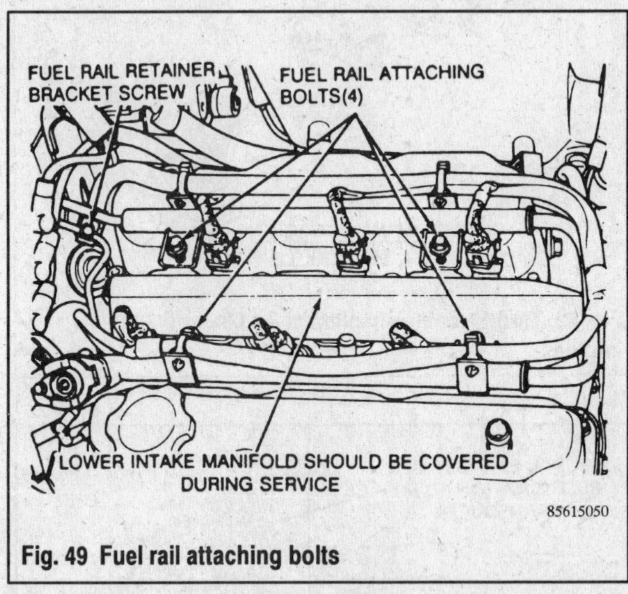

Fig. 49 Fuel rail attaching bolts

Fig. 47 Intake manifold bolts

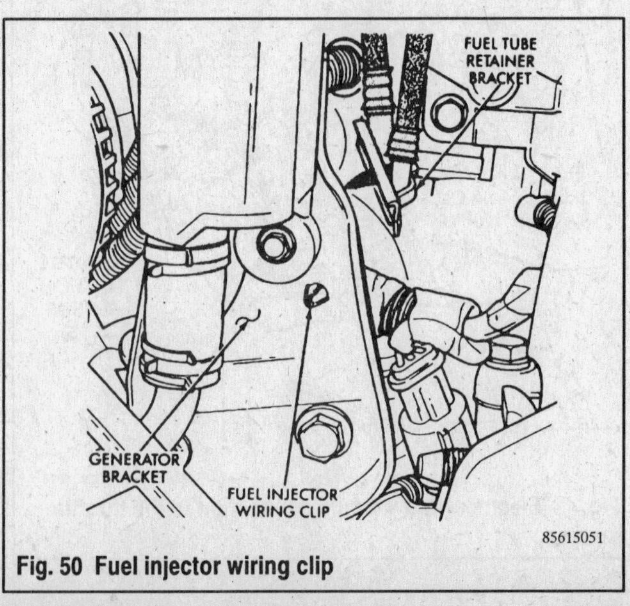

Fig. 50 Fuel injector wiring clip

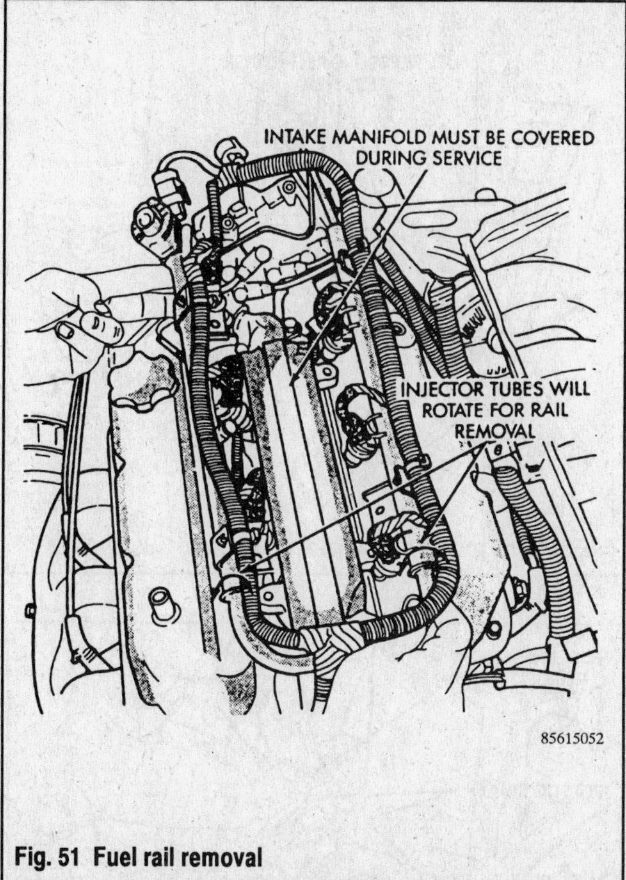

Fig. 51 Fuel rail removal

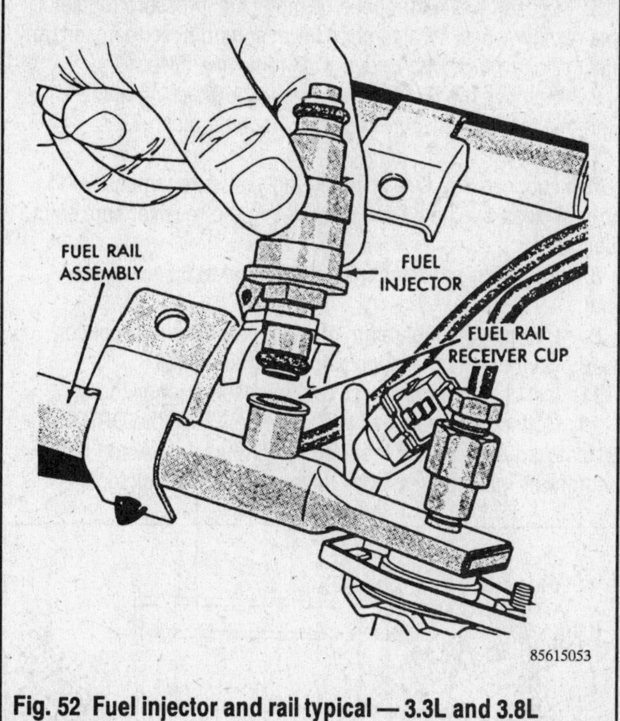

Fig. 52 Fuel injector and rail typical — 3.3L and 3.8L engines

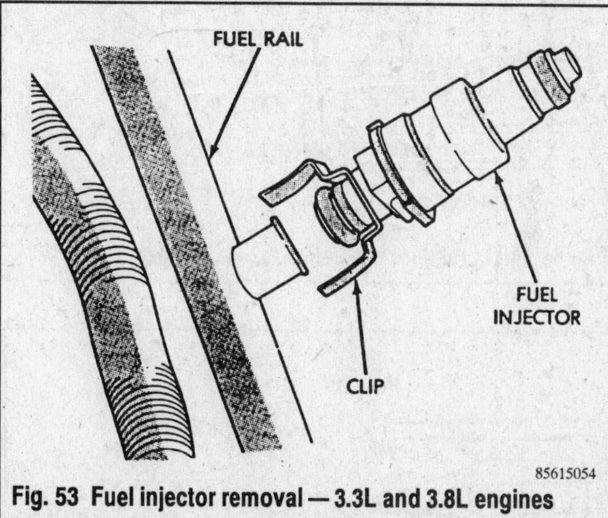

Fig. 53 Fuel injector removal — 3.3L and 3.8L engines

Fuel Injectors

REMOVAL & INSTALLATION

See Figures 39, 41, 52 and 53

1. Remove the fuel rail as described earlier in this section.
2. Disconnect injector wiring connector from injector.
3. Position fuel rail assembly so that fuel injectors are easily accessible.
4. Remove injector clip off fuel rail and injector. Pull injector straight out of fuel rail receiver cup.
5. Check injector O-ring for damage. If O-ring is damaged, it must be replaced. If injector is to be reused, a protective cap must be installed on injector tip to prevent damage while injector is out for service.
6. Repeat for the remaining injectors.

To install:

7. Before installing an injector, the rubber O-ring must be lubricated with a drop of clean engine oil to aid in installation.
8. Install injector top end into fuel rail receiver cup. Be careful not to damage O-ring during installation.
9. Install injector clip by sliding open end into top slot of injector and onto receiver cup ridge into side slots of clip.
10. Repeat the installation steps for the remaining injectors.

Fuel Pressure Regulator

REMOVAL & INSTALLATION

See Figures 54, 55, 56, 57 and 58

1. Perform fuel system pressure release procedure.
2. Disconnect negative battery cable.
3. Remove vacuum hose from fuel pressure regulator.
4. Loosen fuel supply hose clamp at fuel rail inlet and remove hose. Wrap a shop towel around hose to absorb any fuel spillage which may occur when removing hose.

5. Loosen fuel return hose clamp at fuel pressure regulator and remove hose. Wrap a shop towel around hose to absorb any fuel spillage which may occur when removing hose.

6. Remove the fuel pressure regulator attaching nuts. Remove the fuel pressure regulator from the fuel rail.

To install:

7. Lubricate the O-ring for the fuel pressure regulator with a drop of clean engine oil and install it into the receiver cup, on the fuel rail.

8. Install the attaching nuts and tighten to 65 inch lbs. (7 Nm).

9. Connect the fuel return hose to the pressure regulator.

10. Connect the fuel supply hose to the fuel rail.

11. Install the vacuum hose to the pressure regulator.

12. Connect the negative battery cable. Using the DRB II tester or equivalent, use the Actuate Outputs Test-Auto Shutdown Relay to pressurize the system and check for leaks.

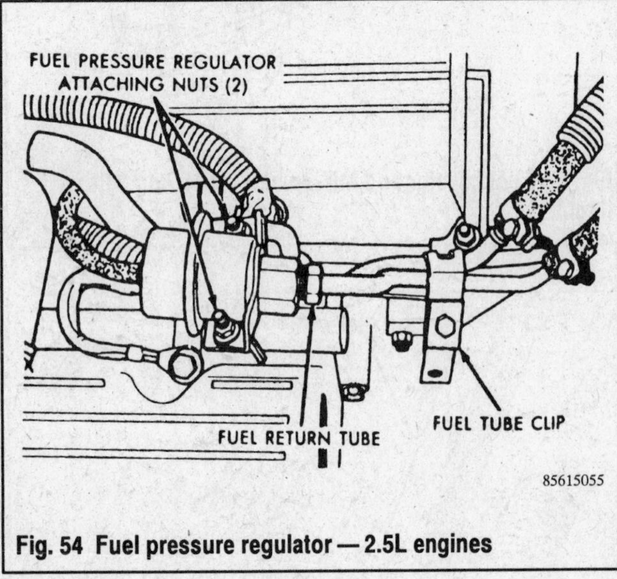

Fig. 54 Fuel pressure regulator — 2.5L engines

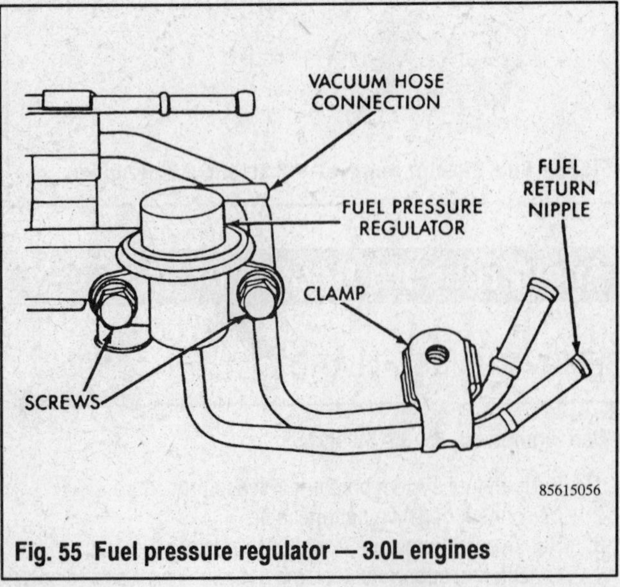

Fig. 55 Fuel pressure regulator — 3.0L engines

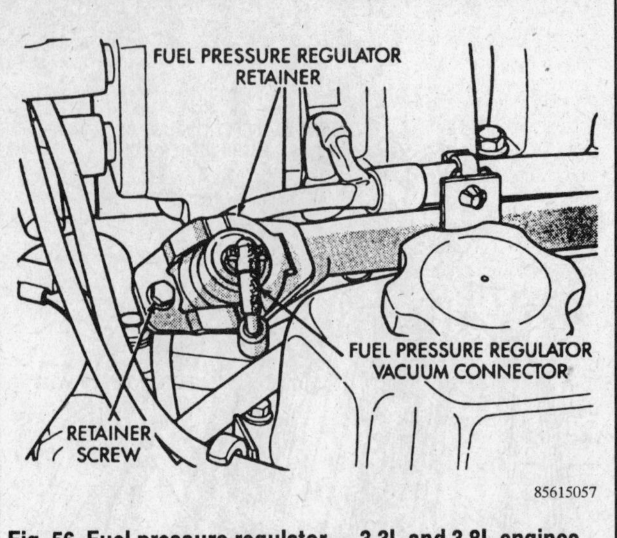

Fig. 56 Fuel pressure regulator — 3.3L and 3.8L engines

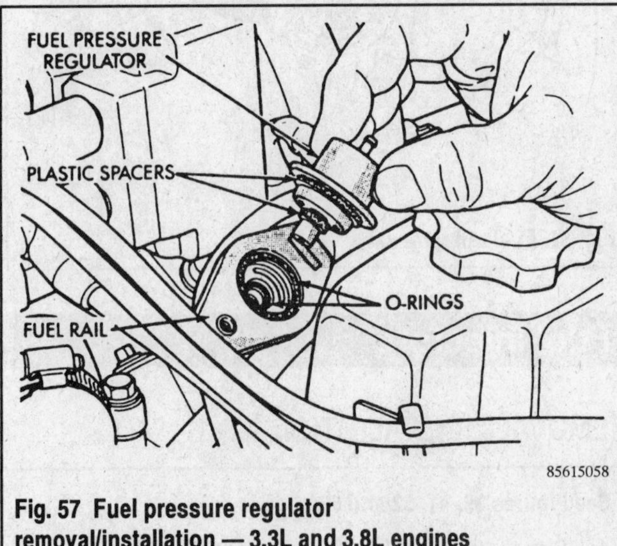

Fig. 57 Fuel pressure regulator removal/installation — 3.3L and 3.8L engines

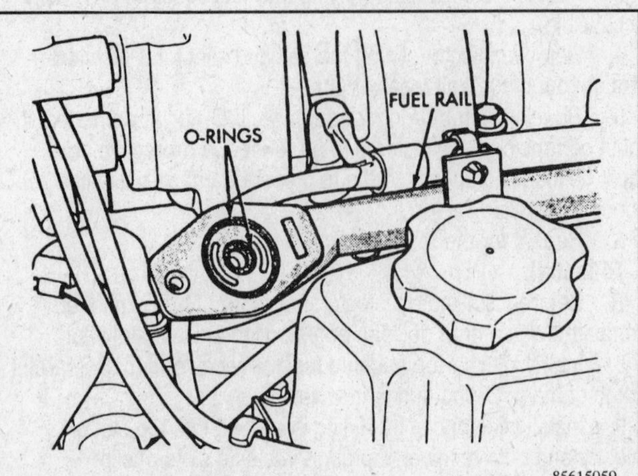

Fig. 58 Fuel pressure regulator O-rings — 3.3L and 3.8L engines

Fuel Pressure Dampener

REMOVAL & INSTALLATION

➧ See Figure 59

1. Perform fuel system pressure release procedure.
2. Remove PCV system hose assembly from intake manifold and valve cover.
3. Place a shop towel under fuel pressure dampener to absorb any fuel spillage.
4. Using 2 open end wrenches, 1 on the flats of fuel rail and the other on fuel pressure dampener, remove fuel pressure dampener and copper washer.

To install:

5. Place a new copper washer on fuel rail and install fuel pressure dampener tighten to 30 ft. lbs. (41 Nm) using a wrench to hold fuel rail while tightening fuel pressure dampener.
6. Connect fuel injector wiring harness; reinstall PCV system hose assembly.
7. Using the DRB II tester (or equivalent) use the Actuate Outputs Test — Auto Shutdown Relay to pressurize system to check for leaks.

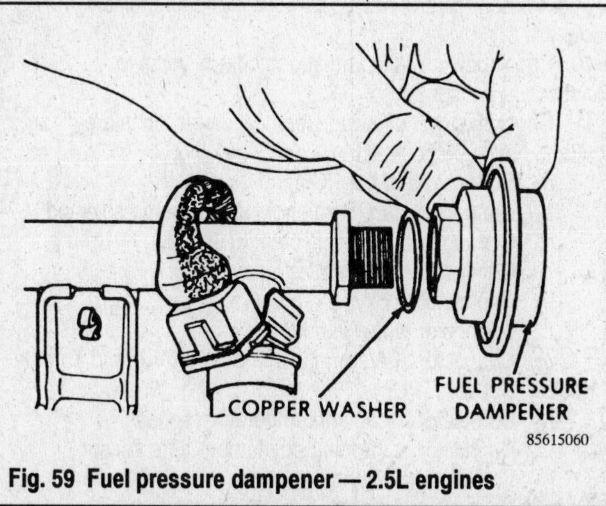

Fig. 59 Fuel pressure dampener — 2.5L engines

Powertrain Control Module (PCM)

REMOVAL & INSTALLATION

➧ See Figure 60

➥ **Refer to Section 4 for more information on the PCM (also referred to as the SBEC, SMEC and SBEC II)**

1. Remove the air cleaner duct from the PCM.
2. Remove the battery.
3. Remove 2 module mounting screws. Remove the 14 and 60-way wiring connectors from the module and remove the module.
4. Reverse the above procedure for installation.

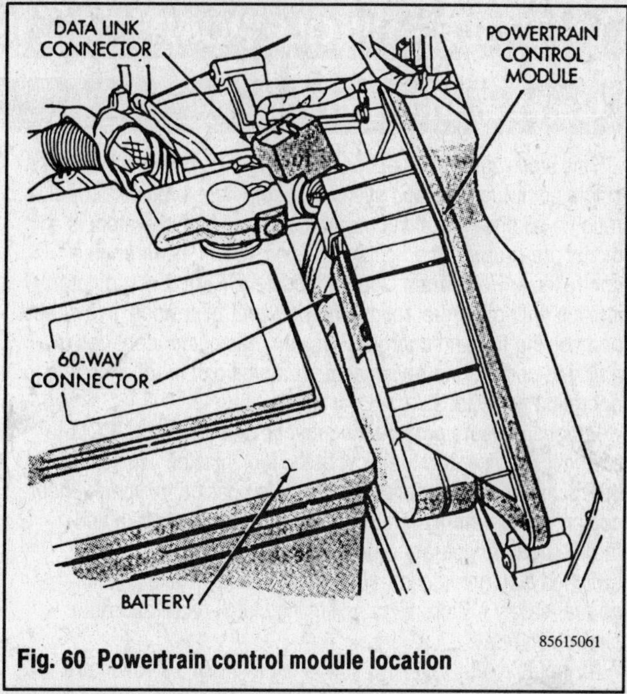

Fig. 60 Powertrain control module location

Heated Oxygen Sensor

REMOVAL & INSTALLATION

➧ See Figure 61

Removing the oxygen sensor from the exhaust manifold may be difficult, if the sensor was overtightened during installation. Use tool C-4907 or equivalent, to remove the sensor. The threads in the exhaust manifold must be cleaned with an 18mm **X** 1.5mm **X** 6E tap. If the same sensor is to be reinstalled, the threads must be coated with an anti-seize compound such as Loctite® 771-64 or equivalent. New sensors are packaged with anti-seize compound on the threads and no additional compound is required. Sensors must be tightened to 20 ft. lbs. (27 Nm).

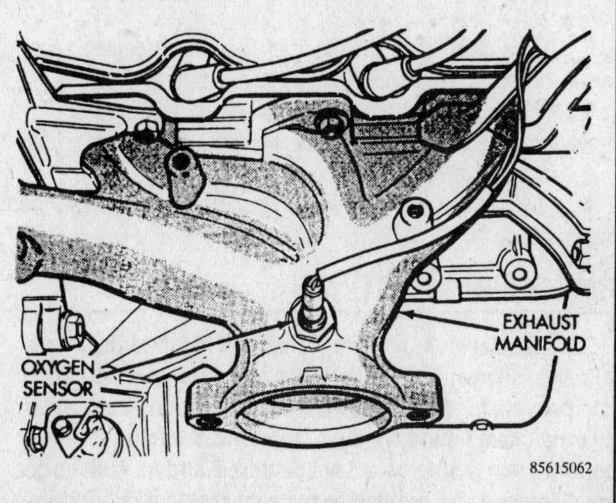

Fig. 61 Typical oxygen sensor location — 3.0L engine shown

CHRYSLER SINGLE POINT FUEL INJECTION SYSTEM

General Information

This electronic fuel injection system is a computer regulated single point fuel injection system that provides precise air/fuel ratio for all driving conditions. At the center of this system is a digital pre-programmed computer also known as an engine controller or Powertrain Control Module (PCM), that regulates ignition timing, air/fuel ratio, emission control devices, idle speed and cooling fan and charging system. This component has the ability to update and revise its programming to meet changing operating conditions.

Various sensors provide the input necessary for the PCM to correctly regulate the fuel flow at the fuel injector. These include the manifold absolute pressure, throttle position, oxygen sensor, coolant temperature, vehicle speed (distance) sensors and throttle body temperature. In addition to the sensors, various switches also provide important information. These include the neutral-safety switch, air conditioning clutch relay, and auto shut-down relay.

All inputs to the PCM are converted into signals which are used by the computer. Based on these inputs, air/fuel ratio, ignition timing or other controlled outputs are adjusted accordingly.

The PCM tests many of its own input and output circuits. If a fault is found in a major system this information is stored in the memory. Information on this fault can be displayed to a technician by means of the instrument panel check engine light or by connecting a diagnostic read out and reading a numbered display code which directly relates to a specific fault.

SERVICE PRECAUTIONS

When working around any part of the fuel system, take precautionary steps to prevent possible fire and/or explosion:

- Disconnect the negative battery terminal, except when testing with battery voltage is required.
- Whenever possible, use a flashlight instead of a drop light to inspect fuel system components or connections.
- Keep all open flames and smoking material out of the area and make sure there is adequate ventilation to remove fuel vapors.
- Use a clean shop cloth to catch fuel when opening a fuel system. Dispose of gasoline-soaked rags properly.
- Relieve the fuel system pressure before any service procedures are attempted that require disconnecting a fuel line.
- Use eye protection.
- Always keep a dry chemical (class B) fire extinguisher near the area.

DIAGNOSIS & TESTING

➔ Mechanical malfunctions are more difficult to diagnose with the EFI system. The PCM has been programmed to compensate for some mechanical malfunctions such as incorrect cam timing, vacuum leaks, etc. If engine performance problems are encountered, and no fault codes are displayed, the problem may be mechanical rather than electronic. Refer to Section 4 for additional information on accessing and reading diagnostic codes

VISUAL INSPECTION

A visual inspection for loose, disconnected or misrouted wires and hoses should be made before attempting to diagnose or service the fuel injection system. A visual check will help spot these faults and save unnecessary test and diagnostic time. A thorough visual inspection will include the following checks:

1. Check that vacuum connections on rear and/or front of throttle body are secure and not leaking.
2. Check that vacuum connection(s) at EGR and/or purge solenoid is secure and not leaking.
3. Check that hoses are securely attached to vapor canister.
4. Check that hose from PCV valve is securely attached to the intake manifold vacuum port.
5. Check that hoses are attached to back-pressure transducer.
6. Check that alternator wiring and belt are correctly installed and tight.
7. Check that heated air door vacuum connection is connected and not leaking.
8. Check vacuum connections at MAP sensor.
9. Check that hose and wiring connections at the fuel pump are tight and wires are making contact with the terminals on pump.
10. Check power brake and speed control vacuum connections are tight.
11. Check that the following electrical connections are clean, tight and have good contact:
    a. Connectors to the PCM
    b. Connector at EGR solenoid and/or purge solenoid
    c. Connector at speed (distance) sensor
    d. Connector at cooling fan relay
    e. Connector to oxygen sensor
    f. Connector at fuel injector(s)
    g. Connector at Automatic Idle Speed (AIS) and Throttle Position Sensor (TPS)
    h. Connector at coolant temperature sensor
    i. Connector at throttle body temperature sensor
    j. Connector to distributor
    k. Connectors for engine-to-main harness
    l. Connectors for all relays
    m. Connector to neutral safety switch (automatic only)
    n. All ignition cables are in order and seated
    o. Ground straps to engine and dash panel
    p. Connection to battery

FUEL SYSTEM PRESSURE TEST

1987–91 Models

✱✱CAUTION

Fuel system pressure must be released as previously described each time a fuel hose is to be disconnected. Take precautions to avoid the risk of fire.

1. Remove fuel intake hose from throttle body and connect fuel system pressure testers C-3292, and C-4749, or equivalent, between fuel filter hose and throttle body.
2. Start engine and read gauge. Pressure should be 14.5 psi (100 kPa).

➥ ATM tester C-4805 (or equivalent) can be used. With ignition in RUN, depress ATM button. This activate the fuel pump and pressure system

3. If fuel pressure is below specifications:
   a. Install tester between fuel filter hose and fuel line.
   b. Start engine. If pressure is now correct, replace fuel filter. If no change is observed, gently squeeze return hose. If pressure increases, replace pressure regulator. If no change is observed, problem is either a plugged pump filter sock or defective fuel pump.
4. If pressure is above specifications:
   a. Remove fuel return hose from throttle body. Connect a substitute hose and place other end of hose in clean container.
   b. Start engine. If pressure is now correct, check for restricted fuel return line. If no change is observed, replace fuel regulator.

1991-95 Models

✱✱CAUTION

Fuel system pressure must be released as previously described each time a fuel hose is to be disconnected. Take precautions to avoid the risk of fire.

1. Release the fuel system pressure as outlined below.
2. Remove the fuel supply hose quick connector from the chassis lines (at the engine).
3. Connect fuel pressure Gauge C-4799 (or equivalent) to the Fuel Pressure Test Adapter 6539. Install the adapter between the fuel supply hose and the chassis fuel line assembly.

✱✱CAUTION

When using the ASD Fuel System Test, the ASD relay and fuel pump relay remain energized for 7 minutes, until the test is stopped, or until the ignition switch is turned to the OFF position.

4. Place the ignition key to the **ON** position. Using the DRB II scan tool, access the ASD Fuel System Test. The ASD Fuel System Test will activate the fuel pump and pressurize the system. If the gauge reads 39 psi (269 kPa), further testing is not required. If the pressure is not correct, record the pressure and remove the gauge.
5. If the fuel pressure reading was below specifications, proceed to next step.
6. Perform the fuel pressure release procedure.
7. Remove the fuel supply hose quick connector from the chassis lines (at the engine).
8. Connect fuel pressure Gauge C-4799 and Fuel Pressure Adapter 6433 (or equivalents) in the fuel supply fuel line between the fuel tank and the fuel filter.
9. Using the DRB II scan tool, with the ignition key in the **ON** position, repeat the ASD Fuel System Test.
10. If the pressure is at least 5 psi (34 kPa) higher than the reading recorded earlier, replace the fuel filter.
11. If no change is observed, gently squeeze the return hose. If the gauge reading does not change when the return hose is squeezed, the problem is either a plugged inlet strainer or defective fuel pump.
12. If the fuel pressure reading was above specifications in Step 4, proceed to next step.
13. Perform the fuel pressure release procedure.
14. Connect fuel pressure Gauge C-4799 and Fuel Pressure Adapter 6433 (or equivalents) in the fuel supply fuel line between the fuel tank and the fuel filter.
15. Remove the fuel return hose from the fuel pump at the fuel tank. Connect the Fuel Pressure Test Adapter 6541 to the return line. Place the other end of adapter 6541 into an approved gasoline container (minimum 2 gallon/7.5 liters size). All return fuel will flow into the container.
16. Using the DRB II scan tool (or equivalent), with the ignition key in the **ON** position, repeat the ASD Fuel System Test.
17. If the pressure is now correct, replace the fuel pump assembly.
18. If the pressure is still above specifications, remove the fuel return hose from the chassis fuel tubes at engine.
19. Connect the Fuel Pressure Test Adapter 6541 to the return line. Place the other end of adapter 6541 into an approved gasoline container. Repeat the test. If pressure is now correct, check for a restricted fuel return line. If no change is observed, replace the fuel pressure regulator.

FUEL SYSTEM PRESSURE RELEASE

✱✱CAUTION

The fuel injection system is under a constant pressure of approximately 14.5 psi (100 kPa). Before servicing any part of the fuel injection system, the system pressure must be released. Use a clean shop towel to catch any fuel spray and take precautions to avoid the risk of fire.

1. Loosen gas cap to release tank pressure.
2. Remove wiring harness connector from injector.
3. Ground 1 terminal of the injector harness.
4. Connect jumper wire to positive second terminal of the harness and touch battery positive post for no longer than 10 seconds. This releases system pressure.
5. Remove jumper wire and continue fuel system service.

Throttle Body

REMOVAL & INSTALLATION

➧ See Figure 62

1. Remove air cleaner.
2. Perform fuel system pressure release.
3. Disconnect negative battery cable.
4. Disengage vacuum hoses and electrical connectors.
5. Remove throttle cable and, if so equipped, speed control and transaxle kickdown cables.
6. Remove return spring.
7. Remove fuel intake and return hoses.
8. Remove throttle body mounting screws and lift throttle body from vehicle.

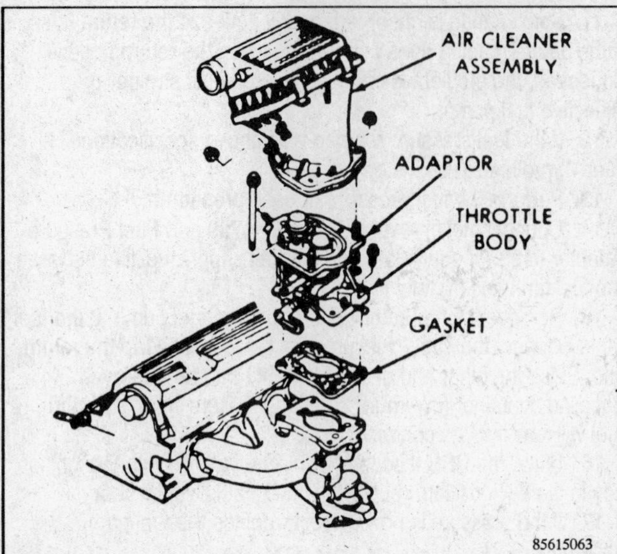

Fig. 62 Throttle body and air cleaner assembly, 2.5L engine

To install:

9. When installing throttle body, use a new gasket. Install throttle body and tighten mounting screws to 15 ft. lbs. (20 Nm).
10. Install fuel intake and return hoses using new original equipment type clamps.
11. Install return spring.
12. Install throttle cable and, if so equipped, install kickdown and speed control cables.
13. Install wiring connectors and vacuum hoses.
14. Install air cleaner.
15. Reconnect negative battery cable.

Fuel Fittings

REMOVAL & INSTALLATION

See Figures 63 and 64

1. Remove air cleaner assembly.
2. Perform fuel system pressure release.
3. Disconnect negative battery cable.
4. On 1991-95 models, loosen the fuel tube clamp on the valve cover.
5. On 1987-90 models, loosen fuel intake and return hose clamps. On 1991-95 models remove the fuel tubes from the quick-disconnect fittings. Wrap a shop towel around each hose, twist and pull off each hose.
6. Remove each fitting and note inlet diameter. Remove copper washers.

To install:

7. Replace copper washers with new washers.
8. Install fuel fittings in proper ports and tighten to 15 ft. lbs. (20 Nm).
9. On 1987-90 models, using new original equipment type hose clamps, install fuel return and supply hoses.
10. On 1991-95 models, Lubricate the ends of the fuel tubes with 30 weight oil. Insert the tubes into the quick-disconnect fittings and pull to make sure they are securely locked.

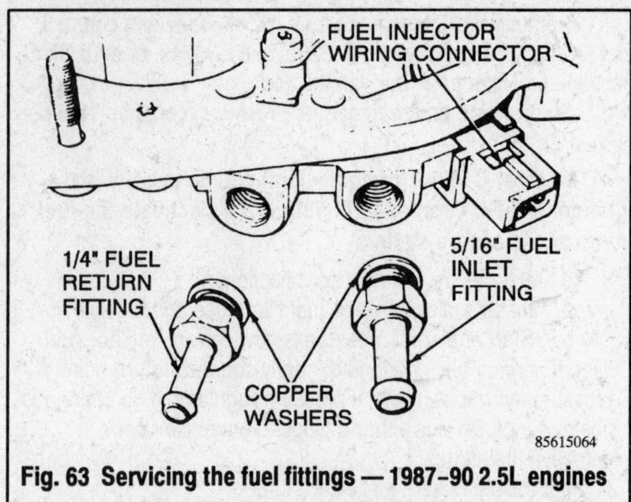

Fig. 63 Servicing the fuel fittings — 1987-90 2.5L engines

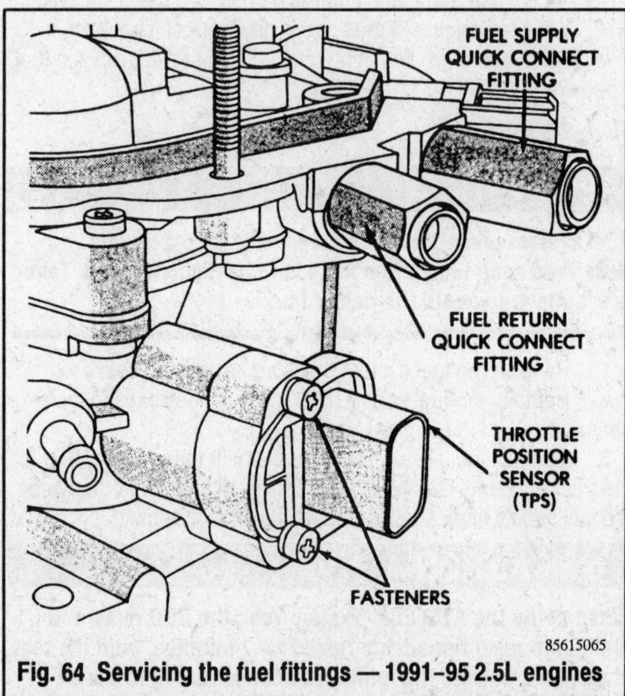

Fig. 64 Servicing the fuel fittings — 1991-95 2.5L engines

11. On 1991-95 models, tighten the fuel tube clamp on the valve cover.
12. Reconnect negative battery cable.
13. Test for leaks using ATM tester C-4805 or equivalent. With ignition in the **RUN** position depress ATM button. This will activate pump and pressurize the system. Check for leaks.
14. Reinstall the air cleaner assembly.

Fuel Pressure Regulator

REMOVAL & INSTALLATION

See Figure 65

1. Remove air cleaner assembly.
2. Perform fuel system pressure release.
3. Disconnect negative battery cable.

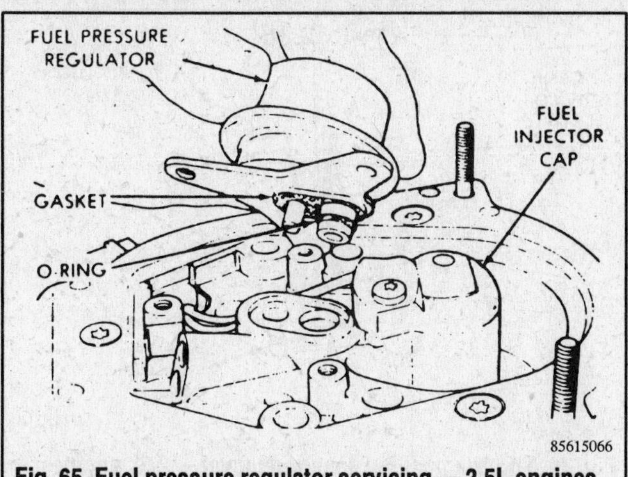

Fig. 65 Fuel pressure regulator servicing — 2.5L engines

4. Remove 3 screws attaching pressure regulator to throttle body. Place a shop towel around inlet chamber to contain any fuel remaining in the system.
5. Pull pressure regulator from throttle body.
6. Carefully remove O-ring from pressure regulator and remove gasket.

To install:

7. Place a new gasket on pressure regulator and carefully install new O-ring.
8. Position pressure regulator on throttle body press: into place.
9. Install 3 screws and tighten to 40 inch lbs. (5 Nm).
10. Connect negative battery cable.
11. Test for leaks using ATM tester C-4805 (or equivalent). With ignition in the **RUN** position depress ATM button. This will activate pump and pressurize the system. Check for leaks.
12. Reinstall the air cleaner assembly.

Fuel Injector

REMOVAL & INSTALLATION

➧ **See Figures 66, 67, 68, 69 and 70**

1. Remove air cleaner assembly.
2. Perform fuel system pressure release.
3. Disconnect negative battery cable.
4. Remove the fuel pressure regulator.
5. Remove the Torx® screw holding down injector cap.
6. With 2 small pry tools, lift cap off injector using slots provided.
7. Using a small pry tool placed in hole in front of electrical connector, gently pry injector from pod.
8. Make sure injector lower O-ring has been removed from pod.

To install:

9. Place a new lower O-ring on injector and a new O-ring on injector cap. The injector will have upper O-ring already installed.
10. Put injector cap on injector. (Injector and cap are keyed). Cap should sit on injector without interference. Apply a light coating of castor oil or petroleum jelly on O-rings. Place assembly in pod.
11. Rotate cap and injector to line up attachment hole.
12. Push down on cap until it contacts injector pod.
13. Install Torx® screw and tighten to 35-45 inch lbs. (4-5 Nm).
14. Install fuel pressure regulator.
15. Connect negative battery cable.
16. Test for leaks using ATM tester C-4805 or equivalent. With ignition in the **RUN** position depress ATM button. This will activate pump and pressurize the system. Check for leaks.
17. Reinstall air cleaner assembly.

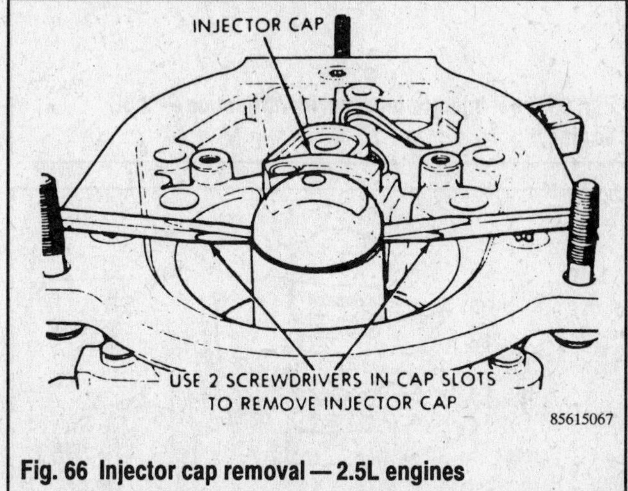

Fig. 66 Injector cap removal — 2.5L engines

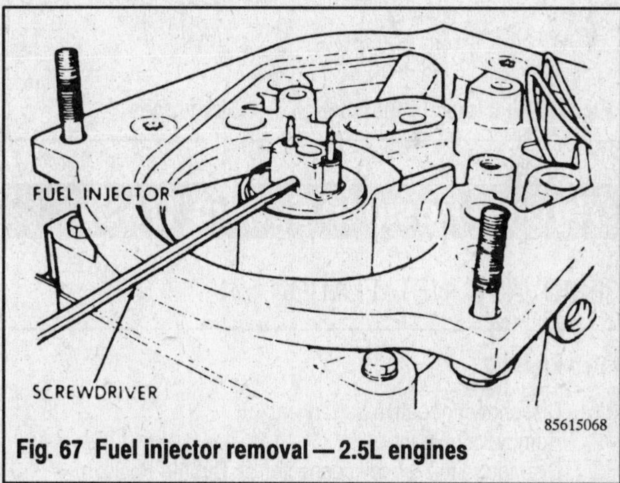

Fig. 67 Fuel injector removal — 2.5L engines

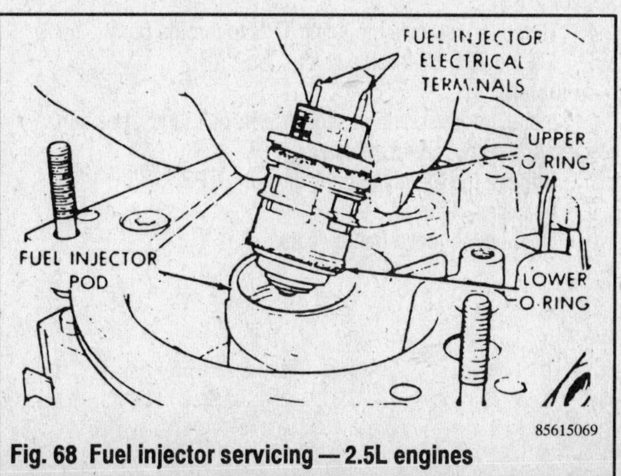

Fig. 68 Fuel injector servicing — 2.5L engines

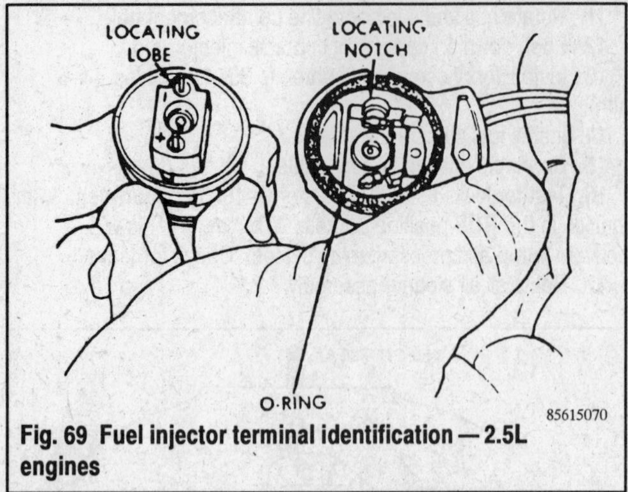

Fig. 69 Fuel injector terminal identification — 2.5L engines

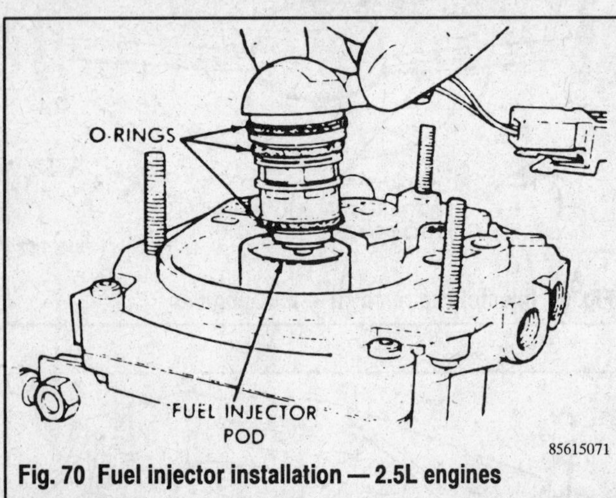

Fig. 70 Fuel injector installation — 2.5L engines

Throttle Position Sensor (TPS)

REMOVAL & INSTALLATION

See Figure 71

1. Disconnect negative battery cable.
2. Remove air cleaner.
3. Disengage the 3-way connector at Throttle Position Sensor (TPS).
4. Remove 2 screws mounting TPS to throttle body.
5. Lift the TPS off throttle shaft.

To install:

6. Install throttle position sensor to throttle body, position connector toward rear of vehicle.
7. Engage the 3-way connector at the TPS.
8. Install air cleaner.
9. Connect negative battery cable.

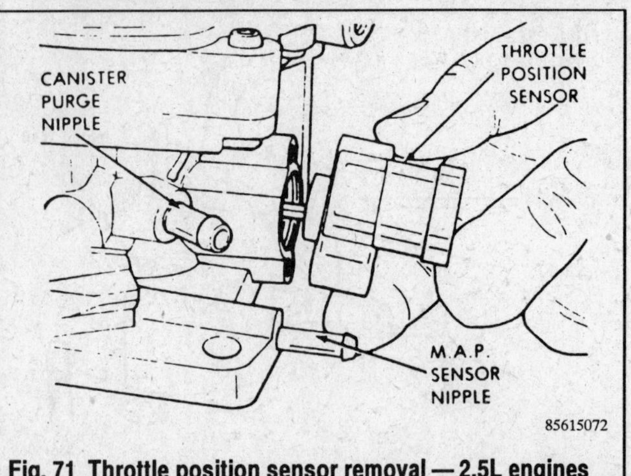

Fig. 71 Throttle position sensor removal — 2.5L engines

Throttle Body Temperature Sensor

REMOVAL & INSTALLATION

See Figure 72

1. Remove air cleaner.
2. Disconnect throttle cables from throttle body linkage.
3. Remove 2 screws from throttle cable bracket and lay bracket aside.
4. Disengage wiring connector.
5. Using a wrench, remove the sensor from the throttle body.

To install:

6. Apply heat transfer compound to the tip portion of the new sensor.
7. Install and tighten to 100 inch lbs. (11 Nm).
8. Engage wiring connector.
9. Install throttle cable bracket with 2 screws.
10. Connect throttle cables to throttle body linkage and install clips.
11. Install air cleaner.

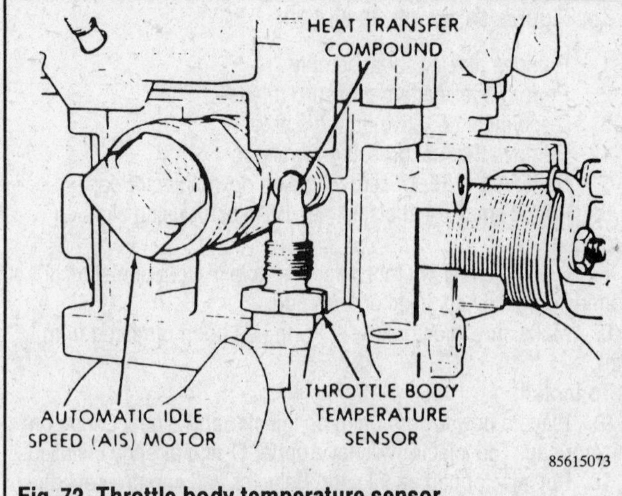

Fig. 72 Throttle body temperature sensor removal — 1988-90 2.5L engine shown

Automatic Idle Speed (AIS) Motor Assembly

➥ The Automatic Idle Speed (AIS) motor is sometimes referred to as the Idle Air Control Motor (IACM).

REMOVAL & INSTALLATION

➧ See Figure 73

1. Remove air cleaner.
2. Disconnect negative battery cable.
3. Disconnect 4 pin connector on AIS.
4. Remove temperature sensor from throttle body housing.
5. Remove 2 Torx® head screws.
6. Remove AIS from throttle body housing, making sure that O-ring is with AIS.

To install:

7. Be sure that pintle is in the retracted position. If pintle measures more than 1 in. (25mm), it must be retracted by using ATM test code No. 03. (battery must be connected for this operation.)
8. Install new O-ring on AIS.
9. Install AIS into housing making sure O-ring is in place.
10. Install 2 Torx® head screws.
11. Connect 4 pin connector to AIS.
12. Install temperature sending unit into throttle body housing.
13. Connect negative battery cable.

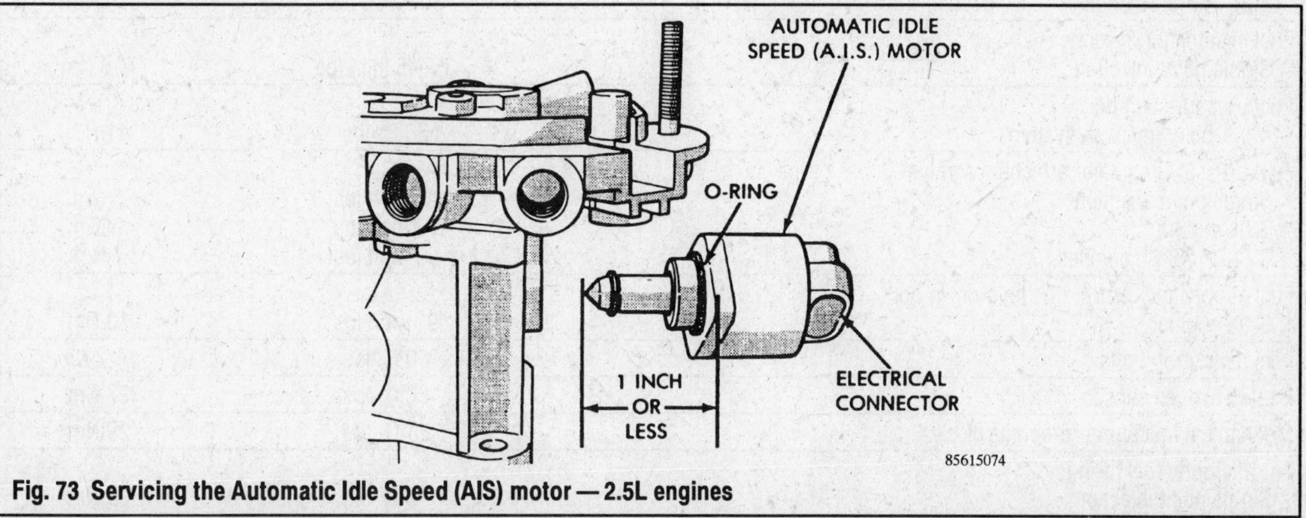

Fig. 73 Servicing the Automatic Idle Speed (AIS) motor — 2.5L engines

FUEL TANK

REMOVAL & INSTALLATION

➥ All Wheel Drive vehicles, have a fuel tank that is made of plastic. Care should be taken to avoid damaging this tank. The fuel tank in AWD vehicles is mounted at the side of the vehicle instead of the rear.

1. Release the fuel system pressure. Refer to fuel system pressure release procedure in this section.

✻✻CAUTION

Never smoke when working around gasoline! Avoid all sources of sparks or ignition. Gasoline vapors are EXTREMELY volatile!

2. Disconnect battery negative cable.
3. Raise the vehicle and support properly.
4. Remove drain tube rubber cap on left rail and connect a siphon hose to drain tube. Drain fuel into a safe gasoline container.
5. Remove screws supporting filler tube to inner and outer quarter panel.
6. Disconnect wiring and lines from the tank.
7. Position a transaxle jack to support the fuel tank and remove the bolts from fuel tank straps.
8. Lower tank slightly, and carefully work filler tube from tank.
9. Lower tank, disconnect vapor separator roll over valve hose and remove the fuel tank and insulator pad from vehicle.

To install:

10. Support the fuel tank with a transaxle jack. Connect the vapor separator roll over valve hose and position insulator pad on fuel tank.

➥ Be certain vapor vent hose is clipped to the tank and not pinched between tank and floor pan during installation.

11. Raise tank into position and carefully work filler tube into tank.
12. Install straps and tighten bolts to 40 ft. lbs. (54 Nm). Remove transaxle jack.
13. Engage lines, drain tube cap and wiring connector, use new hose clamps.
14. Install and tighten filler tube to inner and outer quarter panel. On some models be sure to install the gasket between the filler tube and the inner quarter panel, before installing the mounting screws.
15. Replace cap on drain tube using a new hose clamp.
16. Fill the fuel tank, install the cap, connect battery cable and check operation.

TORQUE SPECIFICATIONS

Component	English	Metric
AIS Motor		
Multi-Point Fuel Injection	17 inch lbs.	2 Nm
Carburetor air horn retaining screws	30 inch lbs.	3 Nm
Carburetor mounting nuts		
2.2L engine	17 ft. lbs.	23 Nm
2.6L engine	13 ft. lbs.	17 Nm
EGR tube flange-to-intake plenum		
3.0L engine	200 inch lbs.	22 Nm
Fuel injector rail assembly		
2.5L turbo engines	21 ft. lbs.	28 Nm
3.0L engine	10 ft. lbs.	13 Nm
3.3L and 3.8L engines	200 inch lbs.	25 Nm
Fuel injector Torx® screws		
Single point injection	35–45 inch lbs.	4–5 Nm
Fuel pressure damper		
Multi-point injection systems	30 ft. lbs.	41 Nm
Fuel pressure regulator attaching screws		
Single point injection	40 inch lbs.	5 Nm
3.0L engine	77 inch lbs.	9 Nm
3.3L and 3.8L engines	65 inch lbs.	7 Nm
Fuel supply and return tube hold-down bolt		
3.0L engine	95 inch lbs.	10 Nm
Fuel tank strap bolts	40 ft. lbs.	54.2 Nm
Heated oxygen sensor	20 ft. lbs.	27 Nm
Mechanical fuel pump-to-engine block	21 ft. lbs.	28 Nm
Throttle body fuel fittings		
Single point injection	15 ft. lbs.	20 Nm
Throttle body mounting screws		
Single point injection	175 inch lbs.	20 Nm
Throttle position sensor		
Multi-Point Fuel Injection	17 inch lbs.	2 Nm
Throttle body temperature sensor		
Single point injection	100 inch lbs.	11 Nm
Vacuum crossover tube hold-down bolt		
3.0L engine	95 inch lbs.	10 Nm

85615C01

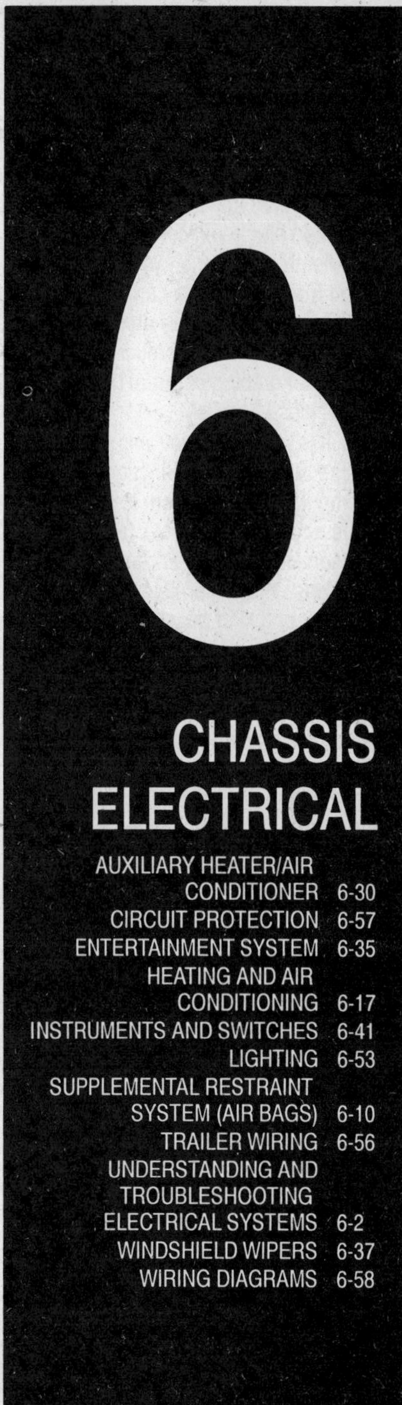

AUXILIARY HEATER/AIR CONDITIONER
- BLOWER MOTOR 6-31
- BLOWER MOTOR RESISTOR 6-31
- EVAPORATOR 6-31
- EXPANSION VALVE 6-30
- HEATER CORE 6-31
- REFRIGERANT LINES 6-31

CIRCUIT PROTECTION
- FUSE BLOCK 6-57
- FUSIBLE LINKS 6-57

ENTERTAINMENT SYSTEM
- ANTENNA 6-36
- RADIO 6-35

HEATING AND AIR CONDITIONING
- AIR CONDITIONING COMPRESSOR 6-17
- BLOWER MOTOR 6-22
- BLOWER MOTOR RESISTOR 6-23
- CLIMATE CONTROL HEAD 6-27
- EXPANSION VALVE (H-VALVE) 6-29
- FILTER/DRIER 6-28
- HEATER CORE AND EVAPORATOR 6-23
- HEATER/AIR CONDITIONING CONTROL CABLES 6-28
- HEATER/EVAPORATOR UNIT 6-20

INSTRUMENTS AND SWITCHES
- CLUSTER LAMP BULBS 6-45
- CLUSTER LAMP SOCKETS 6-45
- FORWARD CONSOLE 6-49
- FUEL GAUGE 6-43
- HEADLAMP DIMMER SWITCH 6-52
- HEADLAMP SWITCH 6-52
- INSTRUMENT CLUSTER ASSEMBLY 6-41
- INSTRUMENT PANEL ASSEMBLY 6-47
- LOWER INSTRUMENT PANEL 6-45
- OIL PRESSURE GAUGE 6-44
- PRINTED CIRCUIT BOARD 6-44
- TEMPERATURE GAUGE 6-44
- UPPER INSTRUMENT PANEL 6-47
- VOLTMETER 6-43
- WINDSHIELD WIPER SWITCH 6-50

LIGHTING
- HEADLIGHTS 6-53
- SIGNAL AND MARKER LIGHTS 6-55

SUPPLEMENTAL RESTRAINT SYSTEM (AIR BAGS)
- AIR BAG CONTROL MODULE (ACM) 6-15
- AIR BAG SYSTEM CHECK 6-14
- CLOCKSPRING 6-15
- DRIVER AIR BAG MODULE 6-14
- GENERAL INFORMATION 6-10
- PASSENGER AIR BAG MODULE 6-14
- SERVICE PRECAUTIONS 6-13
- STEERING COLUMN SWITCHES 6-16

TRAILER WIRING 6-56

UNDERSTANDING AND TROUBLESHOOTING ELECTRICAL SYSTEMS
- ADD-ON ELECTRICAL EQUIPMENT 6-10
- SAFETY PRECAUTIONS 6-2
- TROUBLESHOOTING 6-3
- UNDERSTANDING BASIC ELECTRICITY 6-2
- WIRING HARNESSES 6-7

WINDSHIELD WIPERS
- LIFTGATE WIPER MOTOR 6-40
- WINDSHIELD WIPER LINKAGE 6-40
- WINDSHIELD WIPER MOTOR 6-39
- WIPER ARM (LIFTGATE) 6-39
- WIPER ARM (WINDSHIELD) 6-37
- WIPER BLADE 6-37

WIRING DIAGRAMS 6-58

UNDERSTANDING AND TROUBLESHOOTING ELECTRICAL SYSTEMS

Over the years import and domestic manufacturers have incorporated electronic control systems into their production lines. In fact, electronic control systems are so prevalent that all new cars and trucks built today are equipped with at least one on-board computer. These electronic components (with no moving parts) should theoretically last the life of the vehicle, provided that nothing external happens to damage the circuits or memory chips.

While it is true that electronic components should never wear out, in the real world malfunctions do occur. It is also true that any computer-based system is extremely sensitive to electrical voltages and cannot tolerate careless or haphazard testing/service procedures. An inexperienced individual can literally cause major damage looking for a minor problem by using the wrong kind of test equipment or connecting test leads/connectors with the ignition switch **ON**. When selecting test equipment, make sure the manufacturer's instructions state that the tester is compatible with whatever type of system is being serviced. Read all instructions carefully and double check all test points before installing probes or making any test connections.

The following section outlines basic diagnosis techniques for dealing with automotive electrical systems. Along with a general explanation of the various types of test equipment available to aid in servicing modern automotive systems, basic repair techniques for wiring harnesses and connectors are also given. Read the basic information before attempting any repairs or testing. This will provide the background of information necessary to avoid the most common and obvious mistakes that can cost both time and money. Although the replacement and testing procedures are simple in themselves, the systems are not, and unless one has a thorough understanding of all components and their function within a particular system, the logical test sequence these systems demand cannot be followed. Minor malfunctions can make a big difference, so it is important to know how each component affects the operation of the overall system in order to find the ultimate cause of a problem without replacing good components unnecessarily. It is not enough to use the correct test equipment; the test equipment must be used correctly.

Safety Precautions

**CAUTION

Whenever working on or around any electrical or electronic systems, always observe these general precautions to prevent the possibility of personal injury or damage to electronic components.

- Never install or remove battery cables with the key **ON** or the engine running. Jumper cables should be connected with the key **OFF** to avoid power surges that can damage electronic control units. Engines equipped with computer controlled systems should avoid both giving and getting jump starts due to the possibility of serious damage to components from arcing in the engine compartment if connections are made with the ignition **ON**.
- Always remove the battery cables before charging the battery. Never use a high output charger on an installed battery or attempt to use any type of "hot shot" (24 volt) starting aid.
- Exercise care when inserting test probes into connectors to insure good contact without damaging the connector or spreading the pins. Always probe connectors from the rear (wire) side, NOT the pin side, to avoid accidental shorting of terminals during test procedures.
- Never remove or attach wiring harness connectors with the ignition switch **ON**, especially to an electronic control unit.
- Do not drop any components during service procedures and never apply 12 volts directly to any component (like a solenoid or relay) unless instructed specifically to do so. Some component electrical windings are designed to safely handle only 4 or 5 volts and can be destroyed in seconds if 12 volts are applied directly to the connector.
- Remove the electronic control unit if the vehicle is to be placed in an environment where temperatures exceed approximately 176°F (80°C), such as a paint spray booth or when arc/gas welding near the control unit location.

Understanding Basic Electricity

Understanding the basic theory of electricity makes electrical troubleshooting much easier. Several gauges are used in electrical troubleshooting to see inside the circuit being tested. Without a basic understanding, it will be difficult to understand testing procedures.

THE WATER ANALOGY

Electricity is the flow of electrons — hypothetical particles thought to constitute the basic stuff of electricity. Many people have been taught electrical theory using an analogy with water. In a comparison with water flowing in a pipe, the electrons would be the water. As the flow of water can be measured, the flow of electricity can be measured. The unit of measurement is amperes, frequently abbreviated amps. An ammeter will measure the actual amount of current flowing in the circuit.

Just as the water pressure is measured in units such as pounds per square inch, electrical pressure is measured in volts. When a voltmeter's two probes are placed on two live portions of an electrical circuit with different electrical pressures, current will flow through the voltmeter and produce a reading which indicates the difference in electrical pressure between the two parts of the circuit.

While increasing the voltage in a circuit will increase the flow of current, the actual flow depends not only on voltage, but on the resistance of the circuit. The standard unit for measuring circuit resistance is an ohm, measured by an ohmmeter. The ohmmeter is somewhat similar to an ammeter, but incorporates its own source of power so that a standard voltage is always present.

CIRCUITS

An actual electric circuit consists of four basic parts. These are: the power source, such as a generator or battery; a hot wire, which conducts the electricity under a relatively high voltage to the component supplied by the circuit; the load, such as a lamp, motor, resistor or relay coil; and the ground wire, which carries the current back to the source under very low voltage. In such a circuit the bulk of the resistance exists between the point where the hot wire is connected to the load, and the point where the load is grounded. In an automobile, the vehicle's frame or body, which is made of steel, is used as a part of the ground circuit for many of the electrical devices.

Remember that, in electrical testing, the voltmeter is connected in parallel with the circuit being tested (without disconnecting any wires) and measures the difference in voltage between the locations of the two probes; that the ammeter is connected in series with the load (the circuit is separated at one point and the ammeter inserted so it becomes a part of the circuit); and the ohmmeter is self-powered, so that all the power in the circuit should be off and the portion of the circuit to be measured contacted at either end by one of the probes of the meter.

For any electrical system to operate, it must make a complete circuit. This simply means that the power flow from the battery must make a complete circle. When an electrical component is operating, power flows from the battery to the component, passes through the component causing it to perform it to function (such as lighting a light bulb) and then returns to the battery through the ground of the circuit. This ground is usually (but not always) the metal part of the vehicle on which the electrical component is mounted.

Perhaps the easiest way to visualize this is to think of connecting a light bulb with two wires attached to it to your vehicle's battery. The battery in your vehicle has two posts (negative and positive). If one of the two wires attached to the light bulb was attached to the negative post of the battery and the other wire was attached to the positive post of the battery, you would have a complete circuit. Current from the battery would flow out one post, through the wire attached to it and then to the light bulb, where it would pass through causing it to light. It would then leave the light bulb, travel through the other wire, and return to the other post of the battery.

AUTOMOTIVE CIRCUITS

The normal automotive circuit differs from this simple example in two ways. First, instead of having a return wire from the bulb to the battery, the light bulb return the current to the battery through the chassis of the vehicle. Since the negative battery cable is attached to the chassis and the chassis is made of electrically conductive metal, the chassis of the vehicle can serve as a ground wire to complete the circuit. Secondly, most automotive circuits contain switches to turn components on and off.

Some electrical components which require a large amount of current to operate also have a relay in their circuit. Since these circuits carry a large amount of current, the thickness of the wire in the circuit (gauge size) is also greater. If this large wire were connected from the component to the control switch on the instrument panel, and then back to the component, a voltage drop would occur in the circuit. To prevent this potential drop in voltage, an electromagnetic switch (relay) is used. The large wires in the circuit are connected from the vehicle battery to one side of the relay, and from the opposite side of the relay to the component. The relay is normally open, preventing current from passing through the circuit. An additional, smaller wire is connected from the relay to the control switch for the circuit. When the control switch is turned on, it grounds the smaller wire from the relay and completes the circuit.

SHORT CIRCUITS

If you were to disconnect the light bulb (from the previous example of a light-bulb being connected to the battery by two wires) from the wires and touch the two wires together (please take our word for this; don't try it), the result will be a shower of sparks. A similar thing happens (on a smaller scale) when the power supply wire to a component or the electrical component itself becomes grounded before the normal ground connection for the circuit. To prevent damage to the system, the fuse for the circuit blows to interrupt the circuit — protecting the components from damage. Because grounding a wire from a power source makes a complete circuit — less the required component to use the power — the phenomenon is called a short circuit. The most common causes of short circuits are: the rubber insulation on a wire breaking or rubbing through to expose the current carrying core of the wire to a metal part of the car, or a shorted switch.

Some electrical systems on the vehicle are protected by a circuit breaker which is, basically, a self-repairing fuse. When either of the described events takes place in a system which is protected by a circuit breaker, the circuit breaker opens the circuit the same way a fuse does. However, when either the short is removed from the circuit or the surge subsides, the circuit breaker resets itself and does not have to be replaced as a fuse does.

Troubleshooting

When diagnosing a specific problem, organized troubleshooting is a must. The complexity of a modern automobile demands that you approach any problem in a logical, organized manner. There are certain troubleshooting techniques that are standard:

1. Establish when the problem occurs. Does the problem appear only under certain conditions? Were there any noises, odors, or other unusual symptoms?
2. Isolate the problem area. To do this, make some simple tests and observations; then eliminate the systems that are working properly. Check for obvious problems such as broken wires, dirty connections or split/disconnected vacuum hoses. Always check the obvious before assuming something complicated is the cause.
3. Test for problems systematically to determine the cause once the problem area is isolated. Are all the components functioning properly? Is there power going to electrical switches and motors? Is there vacuum at vacuum switches and/or actuators? Is there a mechanical problem such as bent linkage or loose mounting screws? Performing careful, systematic checks will often turn up most causes on the first inspection without wasting time checking components that have little or no relationship to the problem.
4. Test all repairs after the work is done to make sure that the problem is fixed. Some causes can be traced to more than one component, so a careful verification of repair work is important in order to pick up additional malfunctions that may cause a problem to reappear or a different problem to arise. A blown fuse, for example, is a simple problem that may require more than another fuse to repair. If you don't look for a problem that caused a fuse to blow, a shorted wire (for example) may go undetected.

Experience has shown that most problems tend to be the result of a fairly simple and obvious cause, such as loose or corroded connectors or air leaks in the intake system. This makes careful inspection of components during testing essential to quick and accurate troubleshooting.

BASIC TROUBLESHOOTING THEORY

Electrical problems generally fall into one of three areas:

- The component that is not functioning is not receiving current.
- The component itself is not functioning.
- The component is not properly grounded.

Problems that fall into the first category are by far the most complicated. It is the current supply system to the component which contains all the switches, relay, fuses, etc.

The electrical system can be checked with a test light and a jumper wire. A test light is a device that looks like a pointed screwdriver with a wire attached to it. It has a light bulb in its handle. A jumper wire is a piece of insulated wire with an alligator clip attached to each end.

If a light bulb is not working, you must follow a systematic plan to determine which of the three causes is the villain.

1. Turn on the switch that controls the inoperable bulb.
2. Disconnect the power supply wire from the bulb.
3. Attach the ground wire to the test light to a good metal ground.
4. Touch the probe end of the test light to the end of the power supply wire that was disconnected from the bulb. If the bulb is receiving current, the test light will go on.

➡ If the bulb is one which works only when the ignition key is turned on (turn signal), make sure the key is turned on.

If the test light does not go on, then the problem is in the circuit between the battery and the bulb. As mentioned before, this includes all the switches, fuses, and relays in the system. Turn to a wiring diagram and find the bulb on the diagram. Follow the wire that runs back to the battery. The problem is an open circuit between the battery and the bulb. If the fuse is blown and, when replaced, immediately blows again, there is a short circuit in the system which must be located and repaired. If there is a switch in the system, bypass it with a jumper wire. This is done by connecting one end of the jumper wire to the power supply wire into the switch and the other end of the jumper wire to the wire coming out of the switch. If the test light illuminates with the jumper wire installed, the switch or whatever was bypassed is defective.

➡ Never substitute the jumper wire for the bulb, as the bulb is the component required to use the power from the power source.

5. If the bulb in the test light goes on, then the current is getting to the bulb that is not working in the car. This eliminates the first of the three possible causes. Connect the power supply wire and connect a jumper wire from the bulb to a good metal ground. Do this with the switch which controls the bulb works with jumper wire installed, then it has a bad ground. This is usually caused by the metal area on which the bulb mounts to the vehicle being coated with some type of foreign matter.
6. If neither test located the source of the trouble, then the light bulb itself is defective.

The above test procedure can be applied to any of the components of the chassis electrical system by substituting the component that is not working for the light bulb. Remember that for any electrical system to work, all connections must be clean and tight.

TEST EQUIPMENT

➡ Pinpointing the exact cause of trouble in an electrical system can sometimes only be accomplished by the use of special test equipment. The following describes different types of commonly used test equipment and explains how to use them in diagnosis. In addition to the information covered below, the tool manufacturer's instructions booklet (provided with the tester) should be read and clearly understood before attempting any test procedures.

Jumper Wires

Jumper wires are simple, yet extremely valuable, pieces of test equipment. They are basically test wires which are used to bypass sections of a circuit. The simplest type of jumper wire is a length of multi-strand wire with an alligator clip at each end. Jumper wires are usually fabricated from lengths of standard automotive wire and whatever type of connector (alligator clip, spade connector or pin connector) that is required for the particular vehicle being tested. The well equipped tool box will have several different styles of jumper wires in several different lengths. Some jumper wires are made with three or more terminals coming from a common splice for special purpose testing. In cramped, hard-to-reach areas it is advisable to have insulated boots over the jumper wire terminals in order to prevent accidental grounding, sparks, and possible fire, especially when testing fuel system components.

Jumper wires are used primarily to locate open electrical circuits, on either the ground (−) side of the circuit or on the hot (+) side. If an electrical component fails to operate, connect the jumper wire between the component and a good ground. If the component operates only with the jumper installed, the ground circuit is open. If the ground circuit is good, but the component does not operate, the circuit between the power feed and component may be open. By moving the jumper wire successively back from the lamp toward the power source, you can isolate the area of the circuit where the open is located. When the component stops functioning, or the power is cut off, the open is in the segment of wire between the jumper and the point previously tested.

You can sometimes connect the jumper wire directly from the battery to the hot terminal of the component, but first make sure the component uses 12 volts in operation. Some electrical components, such as fuel injectors, are designed to operate on about 4 volts and running 12 volts directly to the injector terminals can cause damage.

By inserting an in-line fuse holder between a set of test leads, a fused jumper wire can be used for bypassing open circuits. Use a 5 amp fuse to provide protection against voltage spikes. When in doubt, use a voltmeter to check the voltage input to the component and measure how much voltage is normally being applied.

****CAUTION**

Never use jumpers made from wire that is of lighter gauge than that which is used in the circuit under test. If the jumper wire is of too small a gauge, it may overheat and possibly melt. Never use jumpers to bypass high resistance loads in a circuit. Bypassing resistances, in effect, creates a short circuit. This may, in turn, cause damage and fire. Jumper wires should only be used to bypass lengths of wire.

Unpowered Test Lights

The 12 volt test light is used to check circuits and components while electrical current is flowing through them. It is used for voltage and ground tests. Twelve volt test lights come in different styles but all have three main parts; a ground clip, a probe, and a light. The most commonly used 12 volt test lights have pick-type probes. To use a 12 volt test light, connect the ground clip to a good ground and probe wherever necessary with the pick. The pick should be sharp so that it can be probed into tight spaces.

****CAUTION**

Do not use a test light to probe electronic ignition spark plug or coil wires. Never use a pick-type test light to probe wiring on computer controlled systems unless specifically instructed to do so. Any wire insulation that is pierced by the test light probe should be taped and sealed with silicone after testing.

Like the jumper wire, the 12 volt test light is used to isolate opens in circuits. But, whereas the jumper wire is used to bypass the open to operate the load, the 12 volt test light is used to locate the presence of voltage in a circuit. If the test light glows, you know that there is power up to that point; if the 12 volt test light does not glow when its probe is inserted into the wire or connector, you know that there is an open circuit (no power). Move the test light in successive steps back toward the power source until the light in the handle does glow. When it glows, the open is between the probe and point which was probed previously.

➔ The test light does not detect that 12 volts (or any particular amount of voltage) is present; it only detects that some voltage is present. It is advisable before using the test light to touch its terminals across the battery posts to make sure the light is operating properly.

Self-Powered Test Lights

The self-powered test light usually contains a 1.5 volt penlight battery. One type of self-powered test light is similar in design to the 12 volt unit. This type has both the battery and the light in the handle, along with a pick-type probe tip. The second type has the light toward the open tip, so that the light illuminates the contact point. The self-powered test light is a dual purpose piece of test equipment. It can be used to test for either open or short circuits when power is isolated from the circuit (continuity test). A powered test light should not be used on any computer controlled system or component unless specifically instructed to do so. Many engine sensors can be destroyed by even this small amount of voltage applied directly to the terminals.

Voltmeters

A voltmeter is used to measure voltage at any point in a circuit, or to measure the voltage drop across any part of a circuit. It can also be used to check continuity in a wire or circuit by indicating current flow from one end to the other. Analog voltmeters usually have various scales on the meter dial and a selector switch to allow the selection of different voltages. The voltmeter has a positive and a negative lead. To avoid damage to the meter, always connect the negative lead to the negative (-) side of the circuit (to ground or nearest the ground side of the circuit) and connect the positive lead to the positive (+) side of the circuit (to the power source or the nearest power source). Note that the negative voltmeter lead will always be black and that the positive voltmeter will always be some color other than black (usually red).

Depending on how the voltmeter is connected into the circuit, it has several uses. A voltmeter can be connected either in parallel or in series with a circuit and it has a very high resistance to current flow. When connected in parallel, only a small amount of current will flow through the voltmeter current path; the rest will flow through the normal circuit current path and the circuit will work normally. When the voltmeter is connected in series with a circuit, only a small amount of current can flow through the circuit. The circuit will not work properly, but the voltmeter reading will show if the circuit is complete or not.

Ohmmeters

The ohmmeter is designed to read resistance (which is measured in ohms or Ω) in a circuit or component. Although there are several different styles of ohmmeters, all analog meters will usually have a selector switch which permits the measurement of different ranges of resistance (usually the selector switch allows the multiplication of the meter reading by 10, 100, 1000, and 10,000). A calibration knob allows the meter to be set at zero for accurate measurement. Since all ohmmeters are powered by an internal battery, the ohmmeter can be used as a self-powered test light. When the ohmmeter is connected, current from the ohmmeter flows through the circuit or component being tested. Since the ohmmeter's internal resistance and voltage are known values, the amount of current flow through the meter depends on the resistance of the circuit or component being tested.

The ohmmeter can be used to perform a continuity test for opens or shorts (either by observation of the meter needle or as a self-powered test light), and to read actual resistance in a circuit. It should be noted that the ohmmeter is used to check the resistance of a component or wire while there is no voltage applied to the circuit. Current flow from an outside voltage source (such as the vehicle battery) can damage the ohmmeter, so the circuit or component should be isolated from the vehicle electrical system before any testing is done. Since the ohmmeter uses its own voltage source, either lead can be connected to any test point.

➔ When checking diodes or other solid state components, the ohmmeter leads can only be connected one way in order to measure current flow in a single direction. Make sure the positive (+) and negative (-) terminal connections are as described in the test procedures to verify the one-way diode operation.

In using the meter for making continuity checks, do not be concerned with the actual resistance readings. Zero resistance, or any ohm reading, indicates continuity in the circuit. Infinite resistance indicates an open in the circuit. A high resistance reading where there should be none indicates a problem in the circuit. Checks for short circuits are made in the same manner as checks for open circuits except that the circuit must be isolated from both power and normal ground. Infinite resistance indicates no continuity to ground, while zero resistance indicates a dead short to ground.

Ammeters

An ammeter measures the amount of current flowing through a circuit in units called amperes or amps. Amperes are units of electron flow which indicate how fast the electrons are flowing through the circuit. Since Ohms Law dictates that current flow in a circuit is equal to the circuit voltage divided by the total circuit resistance, increasing voltage also increases the current level (amps). Likewise, any decrease in resistance will increase the amount of amps in a circuit. At normal operating voltage, most circuits have a characteristic amount of amperes, called "current draw" which can be measured using an ammeter. By referring to a specified current draw rating, measuring the amperes, and comparing the two values, one can determine what is happening within the circuit to aid in diagnosis. An open circuit, for example, will not allow any current to flow so the ammeter reading will be zero. More current flows through a heavily loaded circuit or when the charging system is operating.

An ammeter is always connected in series with the circuit being tested. All of the current that normally flows through the circuit must also flow through the ammeter; if there is any other path for the current to follow, the ammeter reading will not be accurate. The ammeter itself has very little resistance to current flow and therefore will not affect the circuit, but it will measure current draw only when the circuit is closed and electricity is flowing. Excessive current draw can blow fuses and drain the battery, while a reduced current draw can cause motors to run slowly, lights to dim and other components to not operate properly. The ammeter can help diagnose these conditions by locating the cause of the high or low reading.

Multimeters

Different combinations of test meters can be built into a single unit designed for specific tests. Some of the more common combination test devices are known as Volt/Amp testers, Tach/Dwell meters, or Digital Multimeters. The Volt/Amp tester is used for charging system, starting system or battery tests and consists of a voltmeter, an ammeter and a variable resistance carbon pile. The voltmeter will usually have at least two ranges for use with 6, 12 and/or 24 volt systems. The ammeter also has more than one range for testing various levels of battery loads and starter current draw. The carbon pile can be adjusted to offer different amounts of resistance. The Volt/Amp tester has heavy leads to carry large amounts of current and many later models have an inductive ammeter pickup that clamps around the wire to simplify test connections. On some models, the ammeter also has a zero-center scale to allow testing of charging and starting systems without switching leads or polarity. A digital multimeter is a voltmeter, ammeter and ohmmeter combined in an instrument which gives a digital readout. These are often used when testing solid state circuits because of their high input impedance (usually 10 megohms or more).

The tach/dwell meter that combines a tachometer and a dwell (cam angle) meter is a specialized kind of voltmeter. The tachometer scale is marked to show engine speed in rpm and the dwell scale is marked to show degrees of distributor shaft rotation. In most electronic ignition systems, dwell is determined by the control unit, but the dwell meter can also be used to check the duty cycle (operation) of some electronic engine control systems. Some tach/dwell meters are powered by an internal battery, while others take their power from the vehicle battery in use. The battery powered testers usually require calibration (much like an ohmmeter) before testing.

TESTING

Open Circuits

To use the self-powered test light or a multimeter to check for open circuits, first isolate the circuit from the vehicle's 12 volt power source by disconnecting the battery or wiring harness connector. Connect the test light or ohmmeter ground clip to a good ground and probe sections of the circuit sequentially with the test light. (start from either end of the circuit). If the light is out/or there is infinite resistance, the open is between the probe and the circuit ground. If the light is on/or the meter shows continuity, the open is between the probe and end of the circuit toward the power source.

Short Circuits

By isolating the circuit both from power and from ground, and using a self-powered test light or multimeter, you can check for shorts to ground in the circuit. Isolate the circuit from power and ground. Connect the test light or ohmmeter ground clip to a good ground and probe any easy-to-reach test point in the circuit. If the light comes on or there is continuity, there is a short somewhere in the circuit. To isolate the short, probe a test point at either end of the isolated circuit (the light should be on/there should be continuity). Leave the test light probe engaged and open connectors, switches, remove parts, etc., sequentially, until the light goes out/continuity is broken. When the light goes out, the short is between the last circuit component opened and the previous circuit opened.

➔ **The battery in the test light and does not provide much current. A weak battery may not provide enough power to illuminate the test light even when a complete circuit is made (especially if there are high resistances in the circuit). Always make sure that the test battery is strong. To check the battery, briefly touch the ground clip to the probe; if the light glows brightly the battery is strong enough for testing. Never use a self-powered test light to perform checks for opens or shorts when power is applied to the electrical system under test. The 12 volt vehicle power will quickly burn out the light bulb in the test light.**

Available Voltage Measurement

Set the voltmeter selector switch to the 20V position and connect the meter negative lead to the negative post of the battery. Connect the positive meter lead to the positive post of the battery and turn the ignition switch **ON** to provide a load. Read the voltage on the meter or digital display. A well charged battery should register over 12 volts. If the meter reads below 11.5 volts, the battery power may be insufficient to operate the electrical system properly. This test determines voltage available from the battery and should be the first step in any electrical trouble diagnosis procedure. Many electrical problems, especially on computer controlled systems, can be caused by a low state of charge in the battery. Excessive corrosion at the battery cable terminals can cause a poor contact that will prevent proper charging and full battery current flow.

Normal battery voltage is 12 volts when fully charged. When the battery is supplying current to one or more circuits it is said to be "under load." When everything is off the electrical system is under a "no-load" condition. A fully charged battery may show about 12.5 volts at no load; will drop to 12 volts under medium load; and will drop even lower under heavy load. If the battery is partially discharged the voltage decrease under heavy load may be excessive, even though the battery shows 12 volts or more at no load. When allowed to discharge further, the battery's available voltage under load will decrease more severely. For this reason, it is important that the battery be fully charged during all testing procedures to avoid errors in diagnosis and incorrect test results.

Voltage Drop

When current flows through a resistance, the voltage beyond the resistance is reduced (the larger the current, the greater the reduction in voltage). When no current is flowing, there is no voltage drop because there is no current flow. All points in the circuit which are connected to the power source are at the same voltage as the power source. The total voltage drop always equals the total source voltage. In a long circuit with many connectors, a series of small, unwanted voltage drops due to corrosion at the connectors can add up to a total loss of voltage which impairs the operation of the normal loads in the circuit. The maximum allowable voltage drop under load is critical, especially if there is more than one high resistance problem in a circuit because all voltage drops are cumulative. A small drop is normal due to the resistance of the conductors.

INDIRECT COMPUTATION OF VOLTAGE DROPS

1. Set the voltmeter selector switch to the 20 volt position.
2. Connect the meter negative lead to a good ground.
3. While operating the circuit, probe all loads in the circuit with the positive meter lead and observe the voltage readings. A drop should be noticed after the first load. But, there should be little or no voltage drop before the first load.

DIRECT MEASUREMENT OF VOLTAGE DROPS

1. Set the voltmeter switch to the 20 volt position.
2. Connect the voltmeter negative lead to the ground side of the load to be measured.
3. Connect the positive lead to the positive side of the resistance or load to be measured.
4. Read the voltage drop directly on the 20 volt scale.

Too high a voltage indicates too high a resistance. If, for example, a blower motor runs too slowly, you can determine if perhaps there is too high a resistance in the resistor pack. By taking voltage drop readings in all parts of the circuit, you can isolate the problem. Too low a voltage drop indicates too low a resistance. Take the blower motor for example again. If a blower motor runs too fast in the MED and/or LOW position, the problem might be isolated in the resistor pack by taking voltage drop readings in all parts of the circuit to locate a possibly shorted resistor.

HIGH RESISTANCE TESTING

1. Set the voltmeter selector switch to the 4 volt position.
2. Connect the voltmeter positive lead to the positive post of the battery.
3. Turn on the headlights and heater blower to provide a load.
4. Probe various points in the circuit with the negative voltmeter lead.
5. Read the voltage drop on the 4 volt scale. Some average maximum allowable voltage drops are:

- FUSE PANEL: 0.7 volts
- IGNITION SWITCH: 0.5 volts
- HEADLIGHT SWITCH: 0.7 volts
- IGNITION COIL (+): 0.5 volts
- ANY OTHER LOAD: 1.3 volts

➜ **Voltage drops are all measured while a load is operating; without current flow, there will be no voltage drop.**

Resistance Measurement

The batteries in an ohmmeter will weaken with age and temperature, so the ohmmeter must be calibrated or "zeroed" before taking measurements. To zero the meter, place the selector switch in its lowest range and touch the two ohmmeter leads together. Turn the calibration knob until the meter needle is exactly on zero.

➜ **All analog (needle) type ohmmeters must be zeroed before use, but some digital ohmmeter models are automatically calibrated when the switch is turned on. Self-calibrating digital ohmmeters do not have an adjusting knob, but its a good idea to check for a zero readout before use by touching the leads together. All computer controlled systems require the use of a digital ohmmeter with at least 10 megohms impedance for testing. Before any test procedures are attempted, make sure the ohmmeter used is compatible with the electrical system or damage to the on-board computer could result.**

To measure resistance, first isolate the circuit from the vehicle power source by disconnecting the battery cables or the harness connector. Make sure the key is **OFF** when disconnecting any components or the battery. Where necessary, also isolate at least one side of the circuit to be checked in order to avoid reading parallel resistances. Parallel circuit resistances will always give a lower reading than the actual resistance of either of the branches. When measuring the resistance of parallel circuits, the total resistance will always be lower than the smallest resistance in the circuit. Connect the meter leads to both sides of the circuit (wire or component) and read the actual measured ohms on the meter scale. Make sure the selector switch is set to the proper ohm scale for the circuit being tested to avoid misreading the ohmmeter test value.

****WARNING**

Never use an ohmmeter with power applied to the circuit. Like the self-powered test light, the ohmmeter is designed to operate on its own power supply. The normal 12 volt automotive electrical system current could damage the meter!

Wiring Harnesses

The average automobile contains about 1/2 mile of wiring, with hundreds of individual connections. To protect the many wires from damage and to keep them from becoming a confusing tangle, they are organized into bundles, enclosed in plastic or taped together and called wiring harnesses. Different harnesses serve different parts of the vehicle. Individual wires are color coded to help trace them through a harness where sections are hidden from view.

Automotive wiring or circuit conductors can be in any one of three forms:

1. Single strand wire
2. Multi-strand wire
3. Printed circuitry

Single strand wire has a solid metal core and is usually used inside such components as alternators, motors, relays and other devices. Multi-strand wire has a core made of many small strands of wire twisted together into a single conductor. Most of the wiring in an automotive electrical system is made up of multi-strand wire, either as a single conductor or grouped together in a harness. All wiring is color coded on the insulator, either as a solid color or as a colored wire with an identification stripe. A printed circuit is a thin film of copper or other conductor that is printed on an insulator backing. Occasionally, a printed circuit is sandwiched between two sheets of plastic for more protection and flexibility. A complete printed circuit, consisting of conductors, insulating material and connectors for lamps or other components is called a printed circuit board. Printed circuitry is used in place of individual wires or harnesses in places where space is limited, such as behind instrument panels.

Since automotive electrical systems are very sensitive to changes in resistance, the selection of properly sized wires is critical when systems are repaired. A loose or corroded connection or a replacement wire that is too small for the circuit will add extra resistance and an additional voltage drop to the circuit. A ten percent voltage drop can result in slow or erratic motor operation, for example, even though the circuit is complete. The wire gauge number is an expression of the cross-section area of the conductor. The most common system for expressing wire size is the American Wire Gauge (AWG) system.

Gauge numbers are assigned to conductors of various cross-section areas. As gauge number increases, area decreases and the conductor becomes smaller. A 5 gauge conductor is smaller than a 1 gauge conductor and a 10 gauge is smaller than a 5 gauge. As the cross-section area of a conductor decreases, resistance increases and so does the gauge number. A conductor with a higher gauge number will carry less current than a conductor with a lower gauge number.

➜ Gauge wire size refers to the size of the conductor, not the size of the complete wire. It is possible to have two wires of the same gauge with different diameters because one may have thicker insulation than the other.

12 volt automotive electrical systems generally use 10, 12, 14, 16 and 18 gauge wire. Main power distribution circuits and larger accessories usually use 10 and 12 gauge wire. Battery cables are usually 4 or 6 gauge, although 1 and 2 gauge wires are occasionally used. Wire length must also be considered when making repairs to a circuit. As conductor length increases, so does resistance. An 18 gauge wire, for example, can carry a 10 amp load for 10 feet without excessive voltage drop; however if a 15 foot wire is required for the same 10 amp load, it must be a 16 gauge wire.

An electrical schematic shows the electrical current paths when a circuit is operating properly. It is essential to understand how a circuit works before trying to figure out why it doesn't. Schematics break the entire electrical system down into individual circuits and show only one particular circuit. In a schematic, no attempt is made to represent wiring and components as they physically appear on the vehicle; switches and other components are shown as simply as possible. Face views of harness connectors show the cavity or terminal locations in all multi-pin connectors to help locate test points.

If you need to backprobe a connector while it is on the component, the order of the terminals must be mentally reversed. The wire color code can help in this situation, as well as a keyway, lock tab or other reference mark.

WIRING REPAIR

Soldering is a quick, efficient method of joining metals permanently. Everyone who has the occasion to make wiring repairs should know how to solder. Electrical connections that are soldered are far less likely to come apart and will conduct electricity much better than connections that are only "pig-tailed" together. The most popular (and preferred) method of soldering is with an electrical soldering gun. Soldering irons are available in many sizes and wattage ratings. Irons with higher wattage ratings deliver higher temperatures and recover lost heat faster. A small soldering iron rated for no more than 50 watts is recommended, especially on electrical systems where excess heat can damage the components being soldered.

There are three ingredients necessary for successful soldering; proper flux, good solder and sufficient heat. A soldering flux is necessary to clean the metal of tarnish, prepare it for soldering and to enable the solder to spread into tiny crevices. When soldering, always use a rosin core solder which is non-corrosive and will not attract moisture once the job is finished. Other types of flux (acid core) will leave a residue that will attract moisture and cause the wires to corrode. Tin is a unique metal with a low melting point. In a molten state, it dissolves and alloys easily with many metals. Solder is made by mixing tin with lead. The most common proportions are 40/60, 50/50 and 60/40, with the percentage of tin listed first. Low priced solders usually contain less tin, making them very difficult for a beginner to use because more heat is required to melt the solder. A common solder is 40/60 which is well suited for all-around general use, but 60/40 melts easier and is preferred for electrical work.

Soldering Techniques

Successful soldering requires that the metals to be joined be heated to a temperature that will melt the solder, usually 360–460°F (182–238°C). Contrary to popular belief, the purpose of the soldering iron is not to melt the solder itself, but to heat the parts being soldered to a temperature high enough to melt the solder when it is touched to the work. Melting flux-cored solder on the soldering iron will usually destroy the effectiveness of the flux.

➜ Soldering tips are made of copper for good heat conductivity, but must be "tinned" regularly for quick transference of heat to the project and to prevent the solder from sticking to the iron. To "tin" the iron, simply heat it and touch the flux-cored solder to the tip; the solder will flow over the hot tip. Wipe the excess off with a clean rag, but be careful as the iron will be hot.

After some use, the tip may become pitted. If so, simply dress the tip smooth with a smooth file and "tin" the tip again. Flux-cored solder will remove oxides but rust, bits of insulation and oil or grease must be removed with a wire brush or emery cloth. For maximum strength in soldered parts, the joint must start off clean and tight. Weak joints will result in gaps too wide for the solder to bridge.

If a separate soldering flux is used, it should be brushed or swabbed on only those areas that are to be soldered. Most solders contain a core of flux and separate fluxing is unnecessary. Hold the work to be soldered firmly. It is best to solder on a wooden board, because a metal vise will only rob the piece to be soldered of heat and make it difficult to melt the solder. Hold the soldering tip with the broadest face against the work to be soldered. Apply solder under the tip close to the work, using enough solder to give a heavy film between the iron and the piece being soldered, while moving slowly and making sure the solder melts properly. Keep the work level or the solder will run to the lowest part and favor the thicker parts, because these require more heat to melt the solder. If the soldering tip overheats (the solder coating on the face of the tip burns up), it should be retinned. Once the soldering is completed, let the soldered joint stand until cool. Tape and seal all soldered wire splices after the repair has cooled.

Wire Harness Connectors

Most connectors in the engine compartment or that are otherwise exposed to the elements are protected against moisture and dirt which could create oxidation and deposits on the terminals.

These special connectors are weather-proof. All repairs require the use of a special terminal and the tool required to service it. This tool is used to remove the pin and sleeve terminals. If removal is attempted with an ordinary pick, there is a good chance that the terminal will be bent or deformed. Unlike standard blade type terminals, these weather-proof terminals cannot be straightened once they are bent. Make certain that the connectors are properly seated and all of the sealing rings are in place when connecting leads. On some models, a hinge-type flap provides a backup or secondary locking feature for the terminals. Most secondary locks are used to improve connector reliability by retaining the terminals if the small terminal lock tangs are not positioned properly.

Molded-on connectors require complete replacement of the connection. This means splicing a new connector assembly into the harness. All splices should be soldered to insure proper contact. Use care when probing the connections or replacing terminals in them as it is possible to short between opposite terminals. If this happens to the wrong terminal pair, it is possible to damage certain components. Always use jumper wires between connectors for circuit checking and never probe through weatherproof seals.

Open circuits are often difficult to locate by sight because corrosion or terminal misalignment are hidden by the connectors. Merely wiggling a connector on a sensor or in the wiring harness may correct the open circuit condition. This should always be considered when an open circuit or a failed sensor is indicated. Intermittent problems may also be caused by oxidized or loose connections. When using a circuit tester for diagnosis, always probe connections from the wire side. Be careful not to damage sealed connectors with test probes.

All wiring harnesses should be replaced with identical parts, using the same gauge wire and connectors. When signal wires are spliced into a harness, use wire with high temperature insulation only. It is seldom necessary to replace a complete harness. If replacement is necessary, pay close attention to insure proper harness routing. Secure the harness with suitable plastic wire clamps to prevent vibrations from causing the harness to wear in spots or contact any hot components.

➥ Weatherproof connectors cannot be replaced with standard connectors. Instructions are provided with replacement connector and terminal packages. Some wire harnesses have mounting indicators (usually pieces of colored tape) to mark where the harness is to be secured.

In making wiring repairs, its important that you always replace damaged wires with wiring of the same gauge as the wire being replaced. The heavier the wire, the smaller the gauge number. Wires are color-coded to aid in identification and whenever possible the same color coded wire should be used for replacement. A wire stripping and crimping tool is necessary to install solderless terminal connectors. Test all crimps by pulling on the wires; it should not be possible to pull the wires out of a good crimp.

Wires which are open, exposed or otherwise damaged are repaired by simple splicing. Where possible, if the wiring harness is accessible and the damaged place in the wire can be located, it is best to open the harness and check for all possible damage. In an inaccessible harness, the wire must be bypassed with a new insert, usually taped to the outside of the old harness.

When replacing fusible links, be sure to use fusible link wire, NOT ordinary automotive wire. Make sure the fusible segment is of the same gauge and construction as the one being replaced and double the stripped end when crimping the terminal connector for a good contact. The melted (open) fusible link segment of the wiring harness should be cut off as close to the harness as possible, then a new segment spliced in as described. In the case of a damaged fusible link that feeds two harness wires, the harness connections should be replaced with two fusible link wires so that each circuit will have its own separate protection.

➥ Most of the problems caused in the wiring harness are due to bad ground connections. Always check all vehicle ground connections for corrosion or looseness before performing any power feed checks to eliminate the chance of a bad ground affecting the circuit.

Hard-Shell Connectors

Unlike molded connectors, the terminal contacts in hard-shell connectors can be replaced. Weatherproof hard-shell connectors with the leads molded into the shell have non-replaceable terminal ends. Replacement usually involves the use of a special terminal removal tool that depresses the locking tangs (barbs) on the connector terminal and allows the connector to be removed from the rear of the shell. The connector shell should be replaced if it shows any evidence of burning, melting, cracks, or breaks. Replace individual terminals that are burnt, corroded, distorted or loose.

➥ The insulation crimp must be tight to prevent the insulation from sliding back on the wire when the wire is pulled. The insulation must be visibly compressed under the

crimp tabs, and the ends of the crimp should be turned in for a firm grip on the insulation.

The wire crimp must be made with all wire strands inside the crimp. The terminal must be fully compressed on the wire strands with the ends of the crimp tabs turned in to make a firm grip on the wire. Check all connections with an ohmmeter to insure a good contact. There should be no measurable resistance between the wire and the terminal when connected.

Add-On Electrical Equipment

The electrical system in your vehicle is designed to perform under reasonable operating conditions without interference between components. Before any additional electrical equipment is installed, it is recommended that you consult your dealer or a reputable repair facility that is familiar with the vehicle and its systems.

If the vehicle is equipped with mobile radio equipment and/or mobile telephone, it may have an effect upon the operation of any on-board computer control modules. Radio Frequency Interference (RFI) from the communications system can be picked up by the vehicle's wiring harnesses and conducted into the control module, giving it the wrong messages at the wrong time. Although well shielded against RFI, the computer should be further protected by taking the following measures:

- Install the antenna as far as possible from the control module. For instance, if the module is located behind the center console area, then the antenna should be mounted at the rear of the vehicle.
- Keep the antenna wiring a minimum of eight inches away from any wiring running to control modules and from the module itself. NEVER wind the antenna wire around any other wiring.
- Mount the equipment as far from the control module as possible. Be very careful during installation not to drill through any wires or short a wire harness with a mounting screw.
- Insure that the electrical feed wire(s) to the equipment are properly and tightly connected. Loose connectors can cause interference.
- Make certain that the equipment is properly grounded to the vehicle. Poor grounding can damage expensive equipment.

SUPPLEMENTAL RESTRAINT SYSTEM (AIR BAGS)

General Information

AIR BAG MODULE

➧ See Figures 1 and 2

The air bag module is the most visible part of the system. It contains the air bag cushion and its supporting components. The air bag module contains a housing to which the cushion and inflator are attached and sealed.

The inflator assembly is mounted to the back of the module housing. When supplied with the proper electrical signal the inflator assembly will produce a gas and discharges it directly into the cushion. A protective cover is fitted to the front of the air bag module and forms a decorative cover in the center of the steering wheel. The air bag module is mounted directly to the steering wheel.

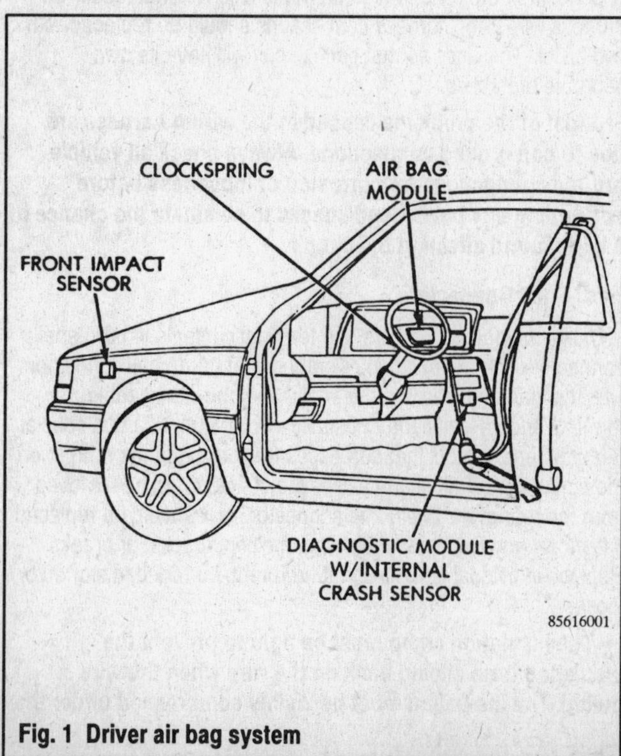

Fig. 1 Driver air bag system

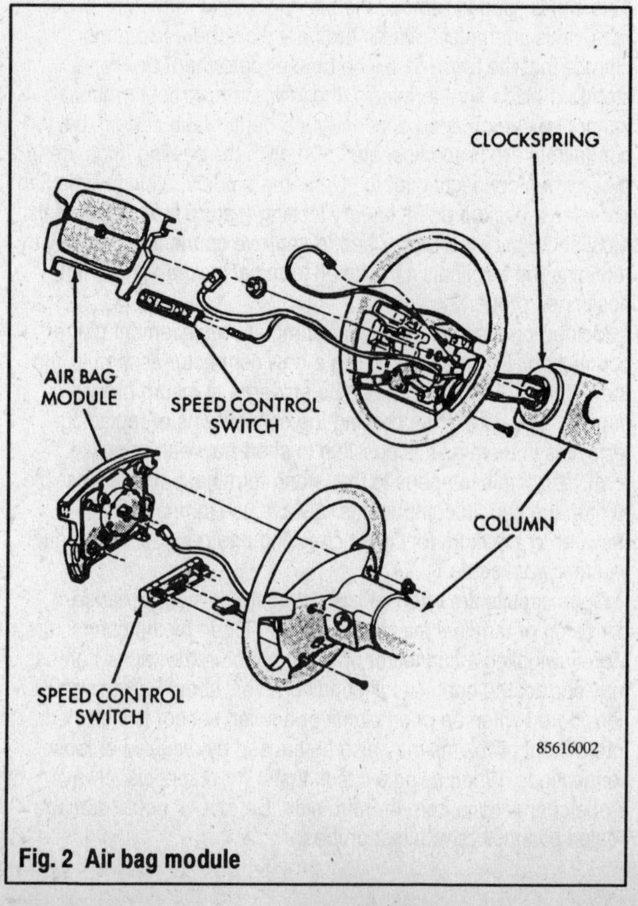

Fig. 2 Air bag module

FRONT IMPACT SENSORS

➧ **See Figures 3 and 4**

The driver air bag system is a safety device designed to reduce the risk of fatality or serious injury, caused by a frontal impact of the vehicle.

The impact sensors provide verification of the direction and severity of the impact. Three impact sensors are used. One is called a safing sensor. It is located inside the diagnostic module which is mounted on the floor pan, just forward of the center console. The other two sensors are mounted on the upper crossmember of the radiator closure panel on the left and right side of the vehicle under the hood.

The impact sensors are threshold sensitive switches that complete an electrical circuit when an impact provides a sufficient G force to close the switch. The sensors are calibrated for the specific vehicle and react to the severity and direction of the impact.

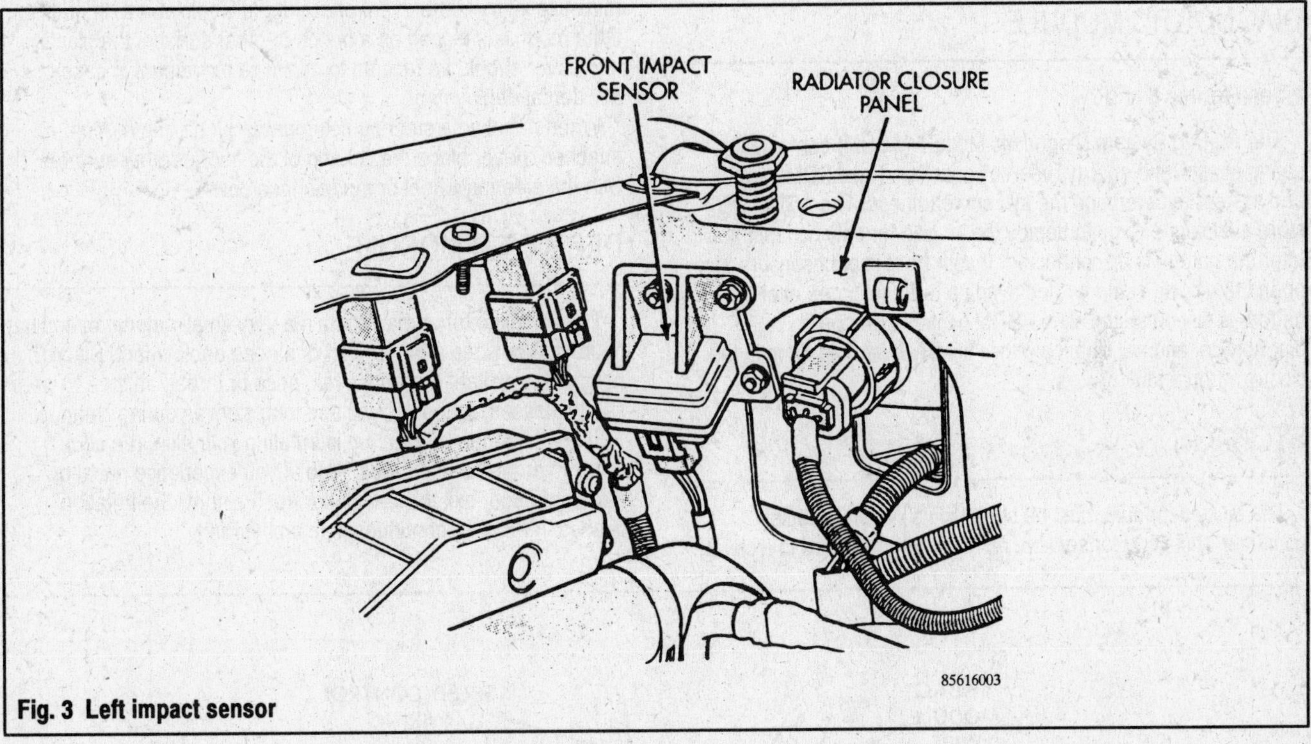

Fig. 3 Left impact sensor

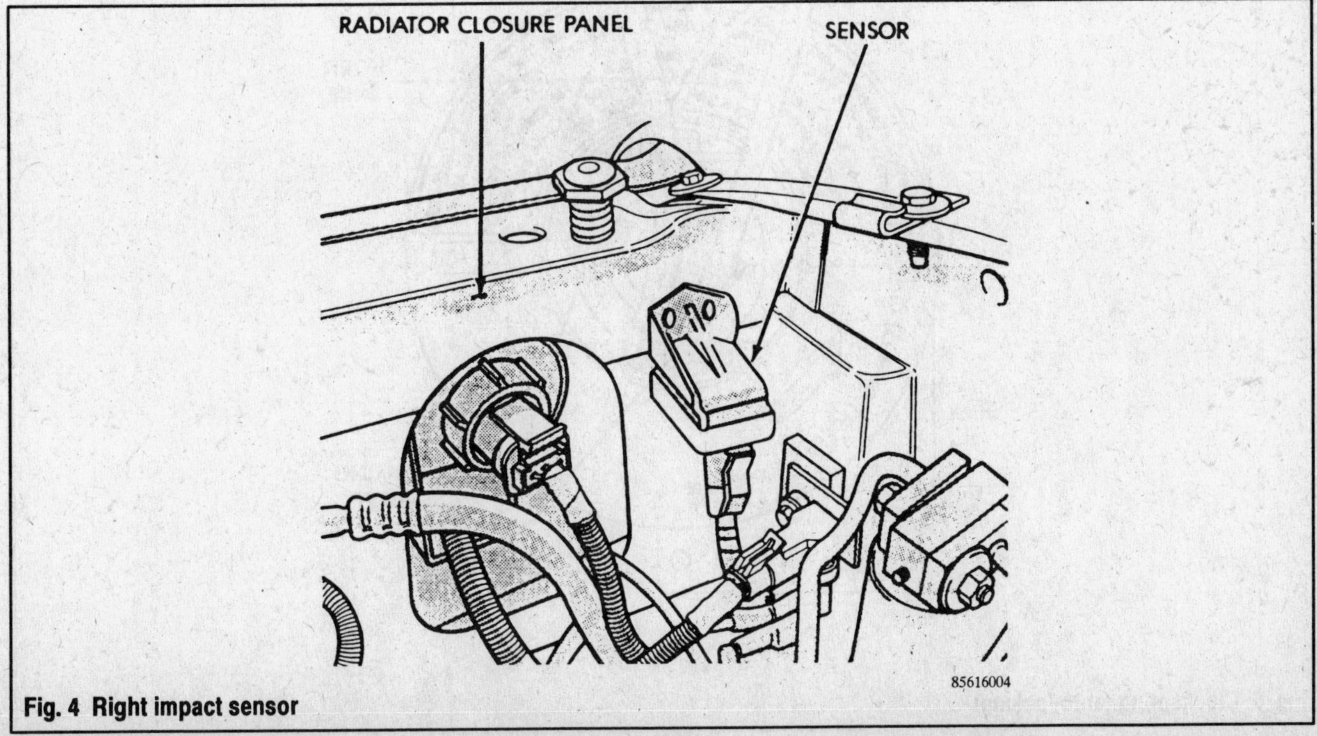

Fig. 4 Right impact sensor

CLOCKSPRING

➧ See Figure 5

The clockspring is mounted on the steering column behind the steering wheel, and is used to maintain a continuous electrical circuit between the wiring harness and the driver's air bag module. This assembly consists of a flat ribbon-like electrically conductive tape which winds and unwinds with the steering wheel rotation.

DIAGNOSTIC MODULE

➧ See Figures 6 and 7

The Air Bag System Diagnostic Module (ASDM) contains the safing sensor and energy reserve capacitor. The ASDM monitors and system to determine the system readiness. The ASDM will store sufficient energy to deploy the air bag for only two minutes after the battery is disconnected. If both front impact sensors are open the air bag could be deployed up to 9.5 minutes after the battery is disconnected. The ASDM contains on-board diagnostics, and will illuminate the AIR BAG warning lamp in the cluster when a fault occurs.

STORAGE

The air bag module must be stored in its original special container until used for service. Also, it must be stored in a clean, dry environment, away from sources of extreme heat, sparks, and sources of high electrical energy. Always place or store the module on a surface with the trim cover facing up to minimize movement in case of accidental deployment.

HANDLING A LIVE MODULE

At no time should any source of electricity be permitted near the inflator on the back of the module. When carrying a live module, the trim cover should be pointed away from the body to minimize injury in the event of accidental deployment. In addition, if the module is placed on a bench or other surface, the plastic trim cover should be face up to minimize movement in case of accidental deployment.

When handling a steering column with an air bag module attached, never place the column of the floor or other surface with the steering wheel or module face down.

DEPLOYED MODULE

The vehicle interior may contain a very small amount of sodium hydroxide powder, a by-product of air bag deployment. Since this powder can irritate the skin, eyes, nose or throat, be sure to wear safety glasses, rubber gloves and long sleeves during cleanup.

If you find that the cleanup is irritating your skin, run cool water over the affected area. Also, if you experience nasal or throat irritation, exit the vehicle for fresh air until the irritation ceases. If irritation continues, see a physician.

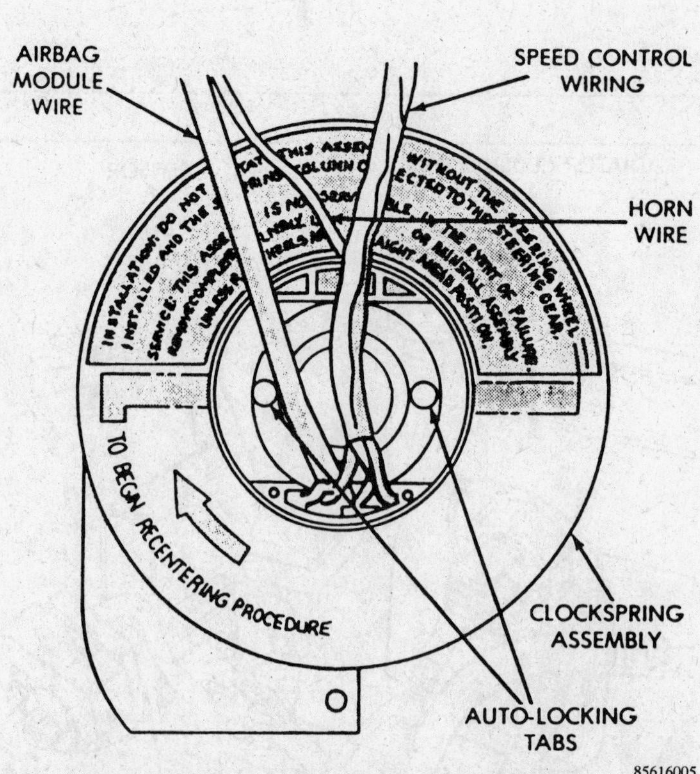

Fig. 5 Clockspring (auto-locking)

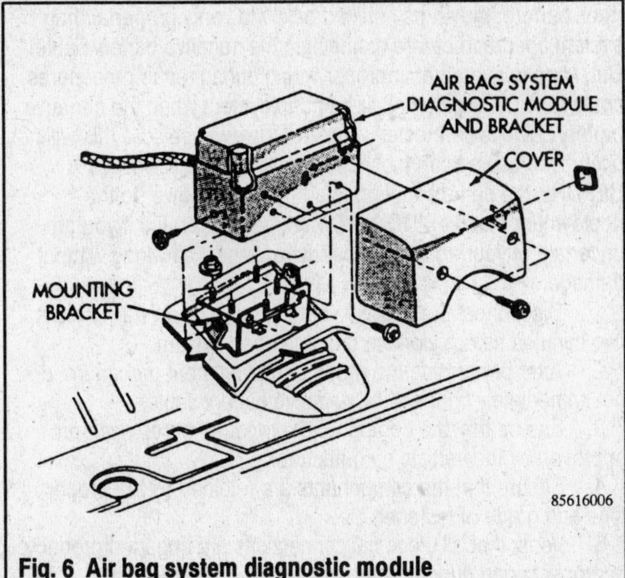

Fig. 6 Air bag system diagnostic module

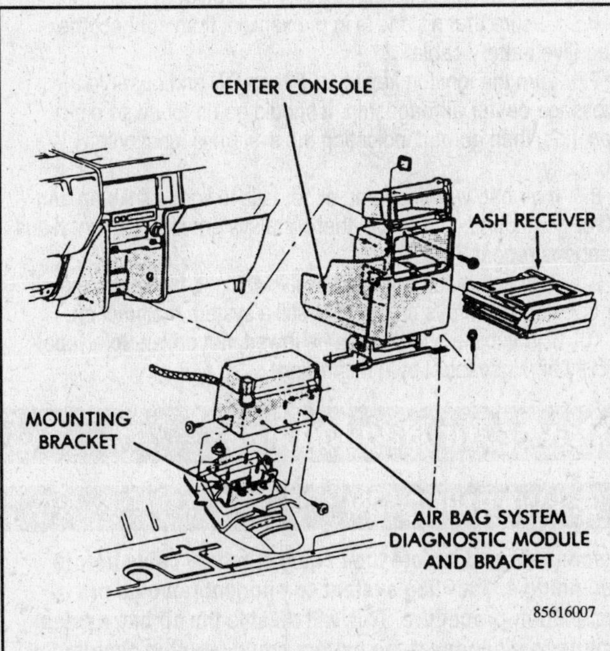

Fig. 7 Air bag system diagnostic module with center console

Clean-Up Procedure

◆ See Figure 8

Begin the clean-up by putting tape over the two air bag exhaust vents so that no additional powder will find its way into the vehicle interior. Then remove the air bag and air bag module from the vehicle.

Use a vacuum cleaner to remove any residual powder from the vehicle interior. Work from the outside in so that you avoid kneeling or sitting in a uncleaned area.

Be sure to vacuum the heater and A/C outlets as well. In fact it's a good idea to run the blower on low and to vacuum up any powder expelled from the plenum. You may need to vacuum the interior of the car a second time to recover all of the powder.

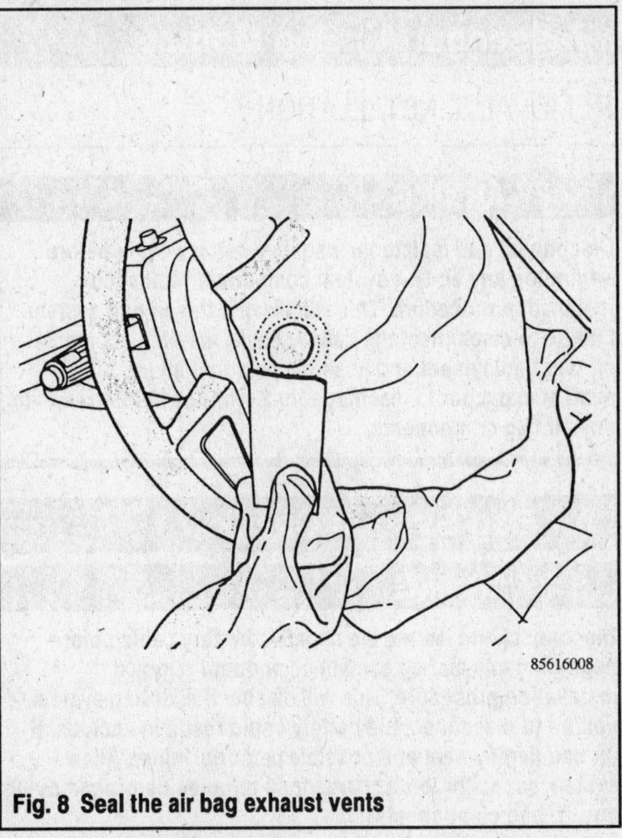

Fig. 8 Seal the air bag exhaust vents

Service Of a Deployed Air Bag

After an air bag has been deployed, the air bag module and clockspring must be replaced because they cannot be reused. Other air bag system components are replaced if damaged.

Service Precautions

This system is a sensitive, complex electromechanical unit. Before attempting to diagnose, remove or install the air bag system components, you must first disconnect and isolate the negative (ground) battery cable. Failure to do so could result in accidental deployment and possible personal injury.

When an undeployed air bag assembly is to be removed from the steering wheel, disconnect battery ground cable and isolate. Allow system capacitor to discharge for two (2) minutes, then begin air bag system component removal.

If the Air Bag Module Assembly is defective and non-deployed, refer to Chrysler Motors current return list for proper handling procedures.

****WARNING**

Replace air bag system components with Chrysler Mopar specified replacement parts. Substitute parts may visually appear interchangeable, but internal differences may result in inferior occupant protection.The fasteners, screws, and bolts, originally used for the air bag components, have special coatings and are specifically designed for the air bag system. They must never be replaced with any substitutes. Anytime a new fastener is needed, replace with the correct fasteners provided in the service package or fasteners listed in the Chrysler parts books.

Passenger Air Bag Module

REMOVAL & INSTALLATION

****WARNING**

Disconnect and isolate the negative battery cable before beginning any air bag system component removal or installation procedure. This will disable the air bag system. Failure to disconnect the battery could result in accidental air bag deployment and possible personal injury. Allow system capacitor to discharge for 2 minutes before removing any air bag components.

Air Bag System Check

****WARNING**

Disconnect and isolate the negative battery cable before beginning any air bag system component removal or installation procedure. This will disable the air bag system. Failure to disconnect the battery could result in accidental air bag deployment and possible personal injury. Allow system capacitor to discharge for 2 minutes before removing any air bag components.

WITH A SCAN TOOL

The use of a DRB scan tool is required to ENSURE proper air bag system operation. If you have a DRB scan tool perform the test outlined below and follow the tool manufactures procedure to verify that there are no faults codes stored which would affect air bag operation

1. Disconnect the negative battery cable and isolate.
2. Remove forward console or cover as necessary.
3. Connect a scan tool to the ACM data link 6-way connector, located at right of steering column.
4. Turn the ignition key to **ON** position. Exit vehicle with DRB. Use the latest version of the proper cartridge.
5. After checking that no one is inside the vehicle, connect the negative battery cable.
6. Using the DRB, read and record active diagnostic data.
7. Read and record any stored diagnostic codes.
8. Correct any problems found in Steps 6 and 7.
9. Erase stored diagnostic codes if there are no active diagnostic codes. If problems remain, diagnostic codes will not erase.
10. Turn the ignition key to **OFF** then **ON** and observe the message center air bag lamp. It should go on for six to eight seconds, then go out; indicating system is functioning normally.
11. If air bag warning lamp either fails to light, blinks on and off or goes on and stays on, there is a system malfunction.

WITHOUT A SCAN TOOL

The use of a scan tool is required to ENSURE proper air bag system operation. If you do not have a DRB, or equivalent scan tool, perform the steps outlined below to verify proper air bag system operation before connecting the negative battery cable. But, keep in mind that improper wiring during repair procedures could result in accidental air bag deployment when the negative battery cable is connected. The ONLY way to be sure this will not occur is to use a scan tool to perform system diagnostics BEFORE the battery is connected (returning power to the deployment module). DO NOT proceed with repairs if you are uncertain of your ability to properly reconnect all wiring without damage.

1. Disconnect the negative battery cable, then wait at least two minutes before working on the air bag system.
2. After performing the repair or replacement procedure, do not immediately connect the negative battery cable.
3. Ensure that the component(s) repaired or replaced are approved by the vehicle manufacturer.
4. Ensure that the components are retained by the proper type and grade of fastener.
5. Verify that all electrical connections are engaged properly. Improper wiring during repair procedures could result in accidental air bag deployment when the negative battery cable is engaged, resulting in personal injury or even death.
6. Ensure that no one is in the vehicle, then connect the negative battery cable.
7. Turn the ignition key to **OFF** then **ON** and observe the message center air bag lamp. It should go on for six to eight seconds, then go out; indicating the system is functioning normally.
8. If air bag warning lamp either fails to light, blinks on and off or goes on and stays on, there is a system malfunction. If this happens repeat Steps 3-7.
9. If air bag warning lamp still fails to light, blinks on and off or goes on and stays on, there is still a system malfunction.
10. The vehicle should then be towed, not driven, to a repair facility and inspected by a technician.

Driver Air Bag Module

****WARNING**

Disconnect and isolate the negative battery cable before beginning any air bag system component removal or installation procedure. This will disable the air bag system. Failure to disconnect the battery could result in accidental air bag deployment and possible personal injury. Allow system capacitor to discharge for 2 minutes before removing any air bag components.

REMOVAL & INSTALLATION

When removing a deployed module, rubber gloves, eye protection and long sleeve shirt should be worn, as there may be deposits on the surface which could irritate the skin and eyes.

1. Disconnect the negative battery cable and isolate.
2. Wait two minutes for the reserve capacitor to discharge before removing a non-deployed module.
3. Remove four nuts attaching air bag module to steering wheel.
4. Lift module and disengage the electrical connector from the rear of the module.

5. Remove module.

6. When replacing a deployed module, the clockspring must also be replaced. Refer to Clockspring Removal and Installation for proper procedure.

To install:

7. Connect clockspring squib connector to the module, by pressing straight in on the connector. Push connector past the secondary latching fingers until it is FULLY SEATED into the module squib.

8. Install four nuts and tighten to 80–100 inch lbs. (9–11 Nm).

9. Perform the Air Bag System Check procedures outlined in this section before connecting the negative battery cable.

Undeployed Modules

➥ Before performing repair procedures on any air bag system component, refer to the Air Bag Systems Check procedures outlined in this section

1. Disconnect and isolate the negative battery cable.
2. Disconnect glove box door check straps and allow door to open fully.
3. Remove the four screws attaching the module to the bracket.
4. Using a large flat tipped screwdriver by hand, pry module up to unsnap door from the trim pad and lift away from snaps. The access hole for the screwdriver is located at the center of the module mounting bracket.
5. Hold on to the door and raise module from opening. Rest module on trim pad and disconnect the two connectors and remove module. Use a shop towel to protect trim pad before placing module on it.
6. For installation, reverse above procedures. Tighten module attaching screws to 50 inch lbs. (6 Nm).
7. Perform the Air Bag System Check procedures outlined in this section before connecting the negative battery cable.

Deployed Modules

✲✲CAUTION

When removing a deployed module, rubber gloves, eye protection and a long-sleeved shirt should be worn. There may be deposits on the surface which could irritate the skin and eyes.

➥ Before performing repair procedures on any air bag system component, refer to the Air Bag Systems Check procedures outlined in this section

1. Disconnect and isolate the negative battery cable.
2. Roll/fold air bag towards instrument panel.
3. Close door over folded air bag and tape door closed.
4. Refer to Clean-up Procedure above.
5. Disconnect glove box door check straps and allow door to open fully.
6. Remove the four screws attaching the module to the bracket.
7. Using a large flat tipped screwdriver or by hand, pry module up to unsnap door from the trim pad and lift away from snaps. The access hole for the screwdriver is located at the center of the module mounting bracket.
8. Hold on to the door and raise module from opening. Rest module on trim pad and disconnect the two connectors and remove module. Use a shop towel to protect trim pad before placing module on it.
9. Check trim pad for any cracking or surface marks and replace as necessary.
10. For installation, reverse above procedures. Check door for fit and finish while tightening module screws. Tighten module attaching screws to 50 inch lbs. (6 Nm).
11. Perform the Air bag System Check procedures outlined in this section before connecting the negative battery cable.

Air Bag Control Module (ACM)

✲✲WARNING

Disconnect and isolate the negative battery cable before beginning any air bag system component removal or installation procedure. This will disable the air bag system. Failure to disconnect the battery could result in accidental air bag deployment and possible personal injury. Allow system capacitor to discharge for 2 minutes before removing any air bag components.

REMOVAL & INSTALLATION

➥ Before performing repair procedures on any air bag system component, refer to the Air Bag Systems Check procedures outlined in this section

1. Disconnect the negative battery cable and isolate cable.
2. Remove the two screws attaching lower console to instrument panel support brackets.
3. Slide cup holder out.
4. Remove the two upper console attaching screws behind the cup holder.
5. Slide console rearward and up to remove.
6. Disconnect wiring at ACM and remove module.
7. Remove the four ACM mounting screws.
8. Slide the ACM off the mounting bracket toward the drive side and remove module.

✲✲WARNING

Because of special loads put on the air bag system during an impact, make sure to use only fasteners specially designed for this system.

9. For installation, reverse above procedures. Attach module and bracket with screws and tighten to 95 inch lbs. (11 Nm).
10. Perform the Air Bag System Check procedures outlined in this section before connecting the negative battery cable.

Clockspring

✲✲WARNING

Disconnect and isolate the negative battery cable before beginning any air bag system component removal or installation procedure. This will disable the air bag system. Failure to disconnect the battery could result in accidental air bag deployment and possible personal injury. Allow system capacitor to discharge for 2 minutes before removing any air bag components.

REMOVAL & INSTALLATION

➛ Before performing repair procedures on any air bag system component, refer to the Air Bag Systems Check procedures outlined in this section

1. Place the front wheels in the straight-ahead position before starting the repair.
2. Disconnect the negative battery cable and isolate.
3. Wait two minutes for the reserve capacitor to discharge before removing non deployed module.
4. Remove the air bag module.
5. Remove speed control switch and connector, if equipped.
6. Disconnect horn terminals.
7. Remove the steering wheel.
8. Remove upper and lower steering column shrouds to gain access to clockspring wiring.
9. Disengage the 2-way connector between the clockspring and the instrument panel wiring harness on top of the fuse block.
10. To remove, pull clockspring assembly from the steering column by lifting locating fingers as necessary. The clockspring cannot be repaired and must be replaced if faulty.

To install:

11. Snap clockspring onto the steering column. If the clockspring is not properly positioned, follow the clockspring centering procedure before installing steering wheel.
12. Connect the clockspring to the instrument panel harness, ensure wiring locator clips are properly seated on wiring trough. Ensure harness locking tabs are properly engaged.
13. Install steering column shrouds. Be sure air bag wire is inside of shrouds.
14. Front wheels should still be in the straight-ahead position. Install steering wheel, ensure the flats on hub align with clockspring. Pull the horn lead through the smaller upper hole. Pull the air bag and speed control leads through the larger bottom hole. Ensure leads are not pinched under the steering wheel.
15. Connect the horn lead wire, then the air bag lead wire to the air bag module.
16. Install the air bag module and tighten nuts to 80–100 inch lb. (9–11 Nm).
17. If equipped, install vehicle speed control switch and connector or cover.
18. Perform the Air Bag System Check procedures outlined in this section before connecting the negative battery cable.

CLOCKSPRING CENTERING PROCEDURE

****WARNING**

Disconnect and isolate the negative battery cable before beginning any air bag system component removal or installation procedure. This will disable the air bag system. Failure to disconnect the battery could result in accidental air bag deployment and possible personal injury. Allow system capacitor to discharge for 2 minutes before removing any air bag components.

➛ Before performing repair procedures on any air bag system component, refer to the Air Bag Systems Check procedures outlined in this section

1. Place front wheels in the straight-ahead position.

****WARNING**

If the rotating tape within the clockspring is not positioned properly with the steering wheel and the front wheels, the clockspring may fail during use. The following procedure MUST BE USED to center the clockspring if it is not known to be properly positioned, or if the front wheels were moved from the straight-ahead position.

2. Disconnect the negative battery cable.
3. Wait two minutes for the reserve capacitor to discharge before removing non deployed module.
4. Refer to Steering Wheel procedures for removal of air bag module and steering wheel.
5. Depress the two plastic locking pins to disengage locking mechanism.
6. Keeping locking mechanism disengaged, rotate the clockspring rotor in the CLOCKWISE DIRECTION to the end of travel. Do not apply excessive torque.
7. From the end of travel, rotate the rotor two full turns and a half in the counterclockwise direction. The horn wire should end up at the top and the squib wire at the bottom. Engage clockspring locking mechanism.
8. Refer to drivers airbag module in this section for installation of the air bag module and steering wheel.
9. Perform the Air Bag System Check procedures outlined in this section before connecting the negative battery cable.

Steering Column Switches

REMOVAL & INSTALLATION

➛ Before performing repair procedures on any air bag system component, refer to the Air Bag Systems Check procedures outlined in this section

This procedure covers the removal and installation of the steering wheel and clockspring. Once the steering wheel and clockspring have been removed, refer to the appropriate section of this service manual for switch replacement.

****WARNING**

Disconnect and isolate the negative battery cable before beginning any air bag system component removal or installation procedure. This will disable the air bag system. Failure to disconnect the battery could result in accidental air bag deployment and possible personal injury. Allow system capacitor to discharge for 2 minutes before removing any air bag components.

1. Place front wheels in the straight-ahead position.
2. Disconnect the negative battery cable and isolate.

3. Wait two minutes for the reserve capacitor to discharge before removing non deployed module.
4. Remove four nuts attaching air bag module from the back side of steering wheel.
5. Lift module and disconnect connector from rear of module.
6. Remove vehicle speed control switch and connector if so equipped or cover.
7. Remove steering wheel.
8. Unsnap clockspring and remove it.
9. Refer to the appropriate section for switch replacement.

To install:

10. Snap clockspring on to steering column. Assure the 4-way connector is still seated.
11. Install steering wheel.
12. Install vehicle speed control switch and connector or cover.
13. Attach the clockspring wiring connector to the module.
14. Install the four nuts to the module, then tighten them to 80-100 inch lbs. (9 to 11 Nm).
15. Perform the Air Bag System Check procedures outlined in this section before connecting the negative battery cable.

HEATING AND AIR CONDITIONING

Service such as blower motor and heater core replacement on 1984-87 models, requires the removal of the Heater/Evaporator unit from the vehicle. Two persons will be required for this operation.

Air Conditioning Compressor

REMOVAL & INSTALLATION

➧ See Figures 9, 10, 11, 12, 13, 14, 15 and 16

➥ Be sure to consult the laws in your area before servicing the air conditioning system. In most areas, it is illegal to perform repairs involving refrigerant unless the work is done by a certified technician. Also, it is quite likely that you will not be able to purchase refrigerant without proof of certification.

1. Disconnect the negative battery cable.
2. Have the system discharged by a qualified professional mechanic using an approved recovery/recycling machine.
3. Remove the compressor drive belt(s). Disconnect the compressor lead.
4. Raise and safely support the vehicle, if necessary. Remove the refrigerant lines from the compressor and discard the gaskets. Cover the exposed ends of the lines to minimize contamination.
5. Remove the compressor mounting nuts and bolts.
6. Lift the compressor off of its mounting studs and remove from the engine compartment.

To install:

7. Install the compressor, then tighten all mounting nuts and bolts.
8. Coat the new gaskets with wax-free refrigerant oil and install. Connect the refrigerant lines to the compressor and tighten the bolts.
9. Install the drive belt(s) and adjust to specification. Connect the electrical lead.
10. Have the system evacuated and recharged by a qualified professional mechanic, utilizing the proper equipment.
11. Connect the negative battery cable, then check the entire climate control system for proper operation and leaks.

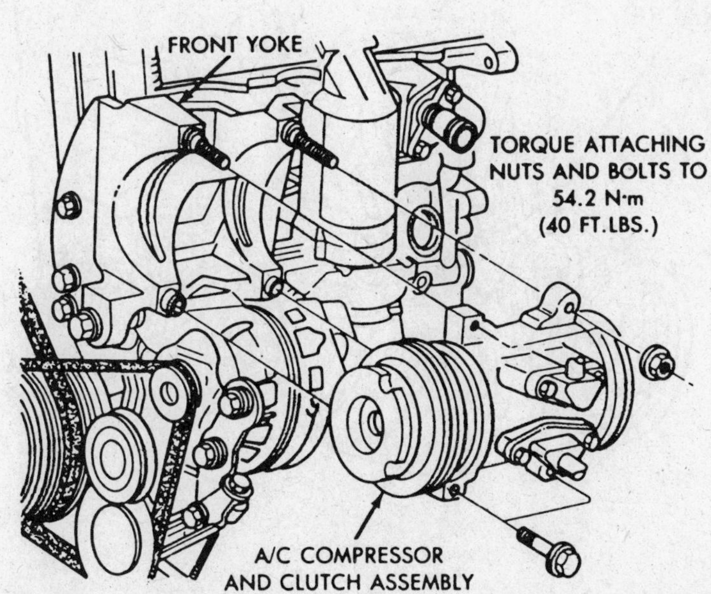

Fig. 9 Air conditioner compressor installation — 2.2L and 2.5L engines

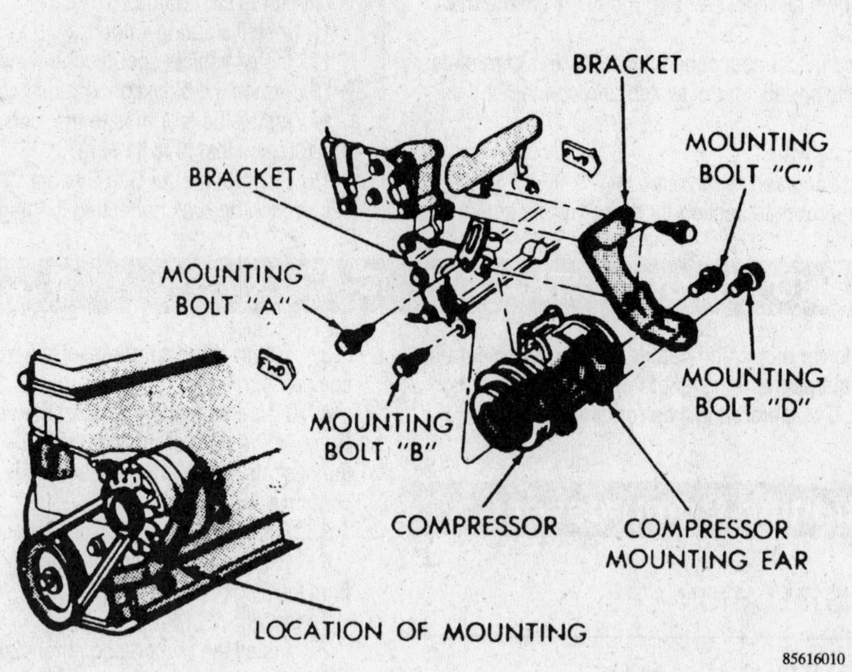

Fig. 10 Air conditioner compressor installation — 2.6L engines

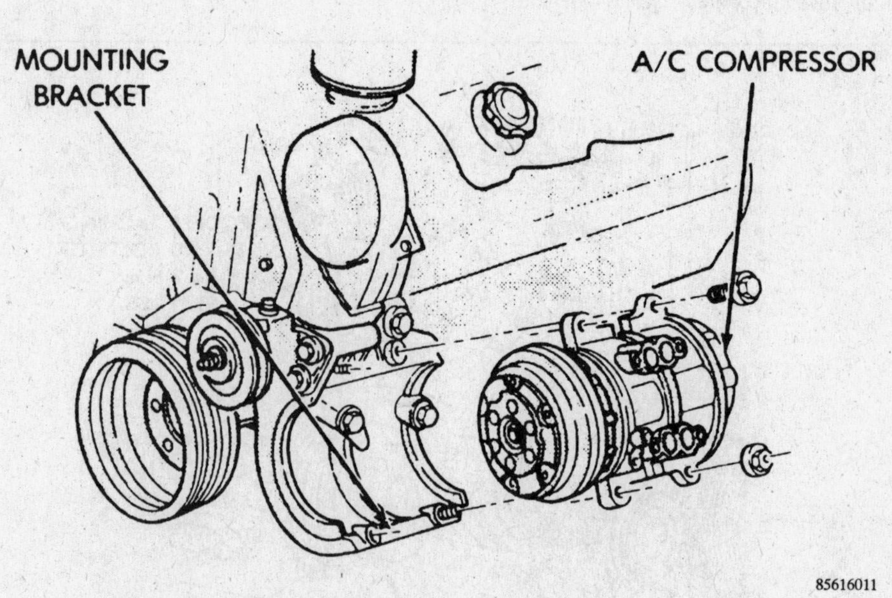

Fig. 11 Air conditioner compressor installation — 3.0L engines

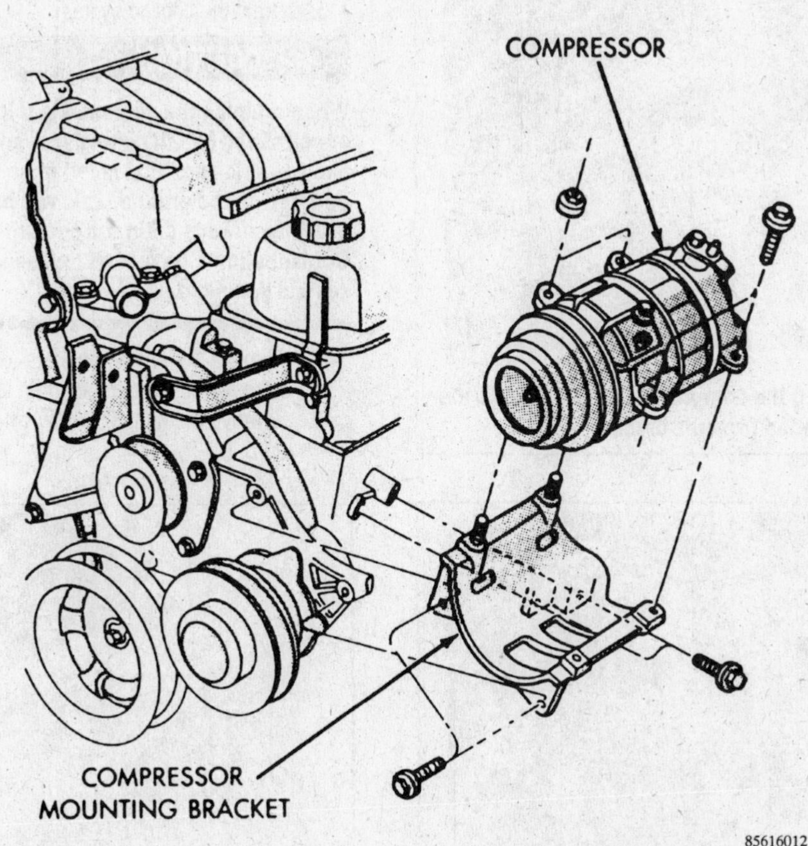

Fig. 12 Air conditioner compressor installation — 3.3L and 3.8L engines

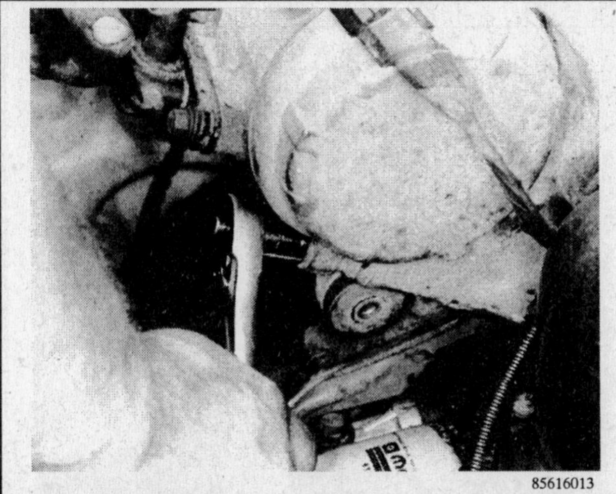

Fig. 13 Removing the air conditioner compressor lower mounting bolts

Fig. 14 Removing the upper compressor mounting nuts

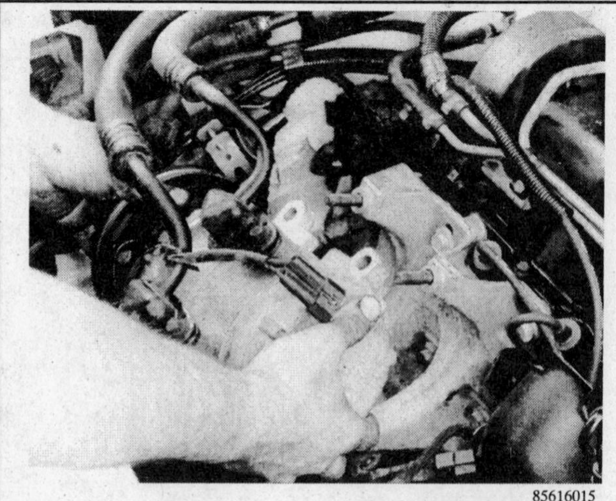

85616015

Fig. 15 After removing the compressor bolts and nuts the compressor may be lifted from the bracket

85616016

Fig. 16 If necessary, remove the air conditioner compressor mounting bracket

Heater/Evaporator Unit

REMOVAL & INSTALLATION

1984–87 Models

➧ See Figures 17, 18, 19, 20, 21, 22, 23 and 24

✱✱CAUTION

The air conditioning system contains refrigerant under high pressure. Severe personal injury may result from improper service procedures. If the knowledge and necessary equipment are not on hand, have the system serviced by a qualified mechanic who will service the refrigerant system completely.

1. Disconnect the negative battery cable. Have the system discharged by a qualified professional mechanic using an approved recovery/recycling machine.
2. Block the vehicle wheels and apply the parking brake.
3. Drain the cooling system.

✱✱CAUTION

When draining the coolant, keep in mind that cats and dogs are attracted by ethylene glycol antifreeze, and are quite likely to drink any that is left in an uncovered container or in puddles on the ground. This will prove fatal in sufficient quantity. Always drain the coolant into a sealable container. Coolant should be reused unless it is contaminated or several years old.

4. Remove the passenger side lower instrument panel.
5. Remove the steering column lower cover.
6. Remove the right side cowl and sill trim.

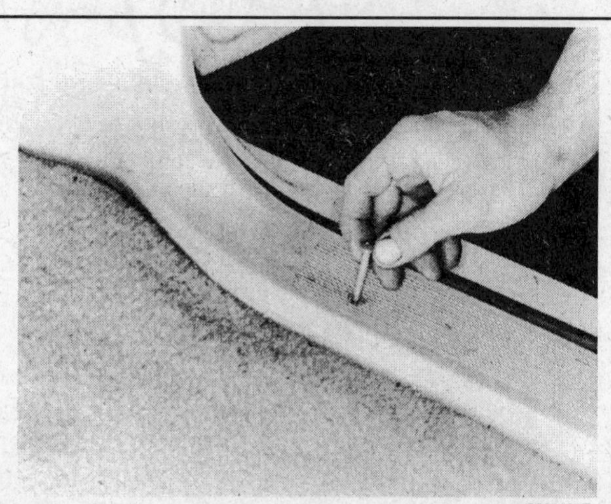

85616017

Fig. 17 Removing the passenger side cowl and sill trim panel lower retaining screws — 1987 Voyager shown

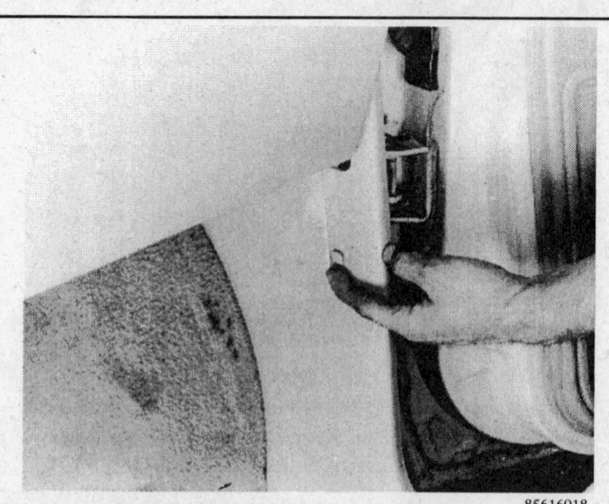

85616018

Fig. 18 Remove the screw hole cover plugs from the upper cowl and sill trim panel

85616019

Fig. 19 Remove the screws from the upper cowl and sill trim panel

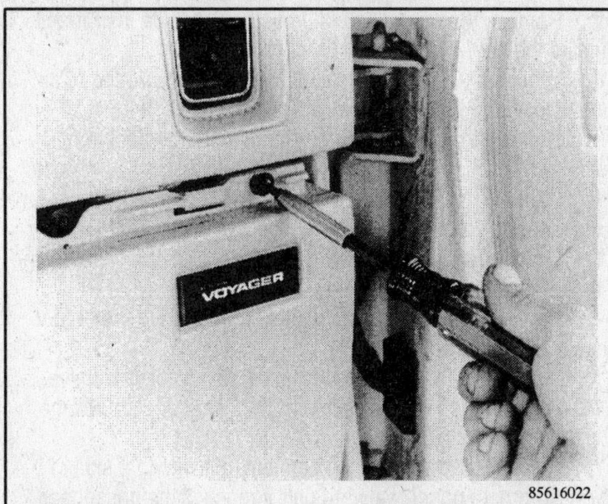

85616022

Fig. 22 Removing the passenger side lower dash panel retaining screws

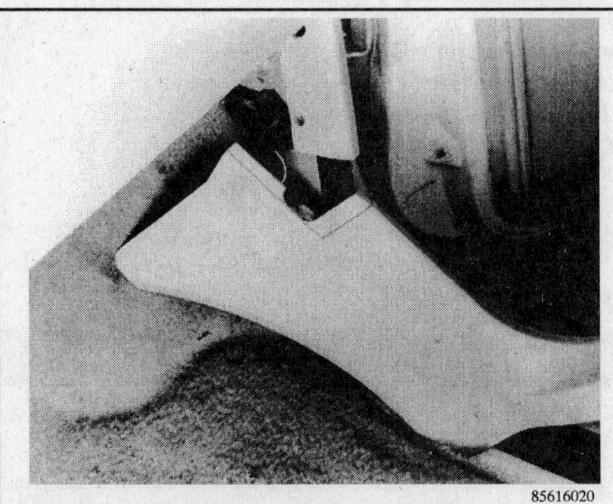
85616020

Fig. 20 Removing the passenger side cowl and sill trim panel

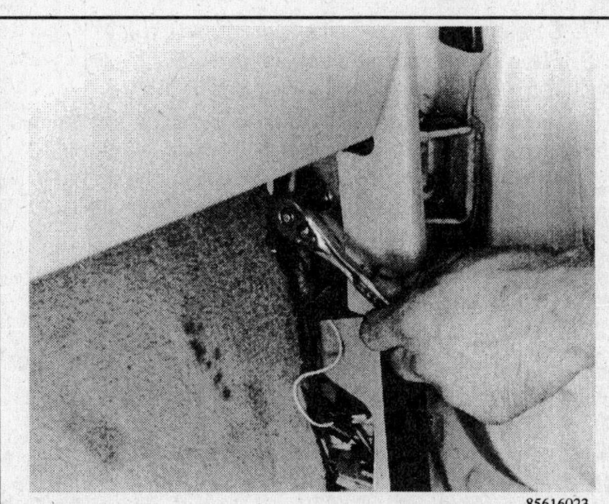
85616023

Fig. 23 Removing the passenger side lower dash panel mounting bolt

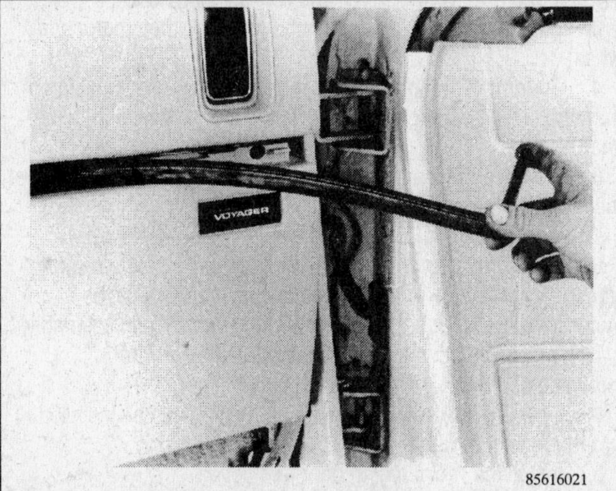

85616021

Fig. 21 Slide out the trim strip to access the passenger side lower dash panel retaining screws

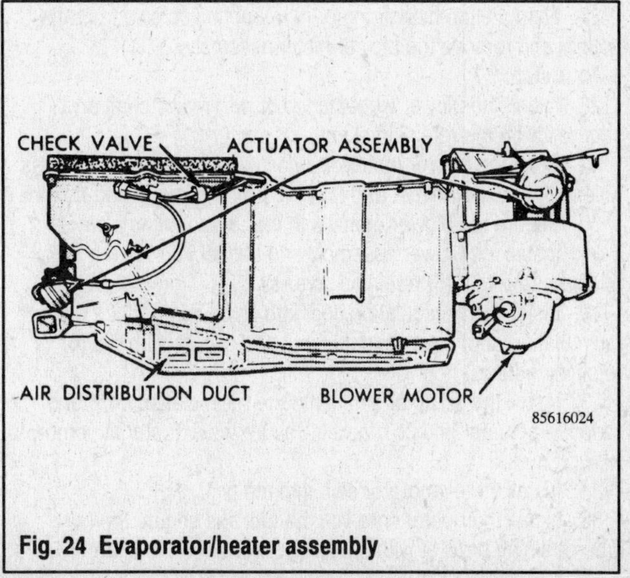

Fig. 24 Evaporator/heater assembly

7. Remove the mounting bolt from the right side instrument panel to the right cowl.
8. Loosen the (2) brackets supporting the lower edge to air conditioning and heater unit housing.
9. Remove the mid-reinforcement instrument panel trim molding.
10. Remove the attaching screws from the right side to center of the steering column.
11. From the engine compartment, disconnect the vacuum line at brake booster and water valve.
12. Remove the hoses from the heater core. Plug the heater tubes.
13. Disconnect the air conditioning plumbing at the H-valve.
14. Remove the (4) nuts from engine compartment package mounting studs.
15. From the passenger compartment, pull the right side of lower instrument panel rearward until it reaches the passenger seat. Disengage the electrical connectors and temperature control cable.
16. Remove the hangar strap from the unit assembly and bend rearward.
17. Carefully remove the unit assembly from the vehicle.
18. Place the heater/evaporator unit assembly on a work bench.
19. Remove the vacuum harness attaching screw and remove the harness through the access hole in the cover.
20. Remove the (13) attaching screws from the cover and remove the cover. The temperature control door will come out with the cover.
21. Remove the retaining bracket screws and the remove heater core assembly.
22. Remove the evaporator core assembly.
23. Disconnect the actuator linkage from the recirculation door and remove the vacuum line. Remove the actuator retaining screws and remove the actuator.
24. Remove the (4) attaching screws from the recirculation door cover to evaporator/heater assembly. Lift the cover from the unit and remove the recirculation door from its housing.
25. Remove the (5) attaching screws from the blower assembly sound helmet.
26. Remove the retaining clamp from the blower wheel hub and slide the blower wheel from the blower motor shaft.
27. Remove the blower motor (3) mounting screws from the helmet and remove the blower motor assembly.

To install:

28. Install the blower wheel to the blower motor shaft and secure it with the retaining clamp.
29. Feed the blower motor electrical wires through the access hole in the sound helmet and lower the blower motor into helmet.
30. Secure the blower motor with the (3) mounting screws.
31. Install the blower assembly and helmet into the fan scroll and secure it with (5) retaining screws.
32. Install the recirculation door into its housing. Place the recirculation door cover onto the unit and secure with the (4) retaining screws.
33. Install the actuator shaft onto the recirculation door and slide the actuator into its bracket. Secure the actuator assembly with (2) nuts.
34. Install the evaporator core into the unit.
35. Install the heater core into the unit and secure the core tube retaining bracket with attaching screws.
36. Install the unit cover and secure with (13) attaching screws.
37. Install the vacuum harness through the access hole in the cover and secure the vacuum harness.
38. Place the heater/evaporator assembly into the vehicle and position it against the dash panel.
39. Install the hangar strap.
40. Connect the temperature control cable, vacuum and electrical connectors.
41. Install the (4) retaining nuts to the unit mounting studs from the engine compartment.
42. Connect the air conditioning plumbing to the H-valve.
43. Connect the vacuum line at the brake booster and water valve.
44. Install the attaching screws from the right side to the center of the steering column.
45. Install the mid-reinforcement instrument panel trim molding.
46. Tighten the (2) brackets supporting the lower edge to the heater/evaporator unit housing.
47. Install the mounting bolt from the right side of the instrument panel to the right cowl.
48. Install the right side cowl and sill trim.
49. Install the steering column lower cover.
50. Install the passenger side lower instrument panel
51. Connect the heater hoses to heater core in the engine compartment.
52. Connect the negative battery cable.
53. Fill the cooling system.
54. Have the system evacuated and recharged by a qualified professional mechanic, utilizing the proper equipment.

Blower Motor

REMOVAL & INSTALLATION

1984–87 Models

1. Remove the heater/evaporator unit from the vehicle.
2. Remove the 4 screws retaining the recirculation cover to the unit and remove the cover and recirculating door.
3. Remove the blower assembly, sound helmet, motor and wheel.
4. To remove the blower wheel, remove the retaining clamp from the blower wheel hub and slide the blower wheel from the shaft.
5. Remove the 3 screws in the helmet and remove the blower motor and wires.

To install:

6. Install the blower wheel to the shaft and install the spring clip. Inspect the blower mounting plate seal and repair, as necessary. Apply rubber adhesive to the seal to aid in assembly.
7. Install the blower into the helmet and install the 3 mounting screws.
8. The entire blower assembly and helmet can be installed into the fan scroll with the 5 screws.
9. Install the recirculating door and cover.

1988–91 Models

1. Disconnect the negative battery cable.

2. Locate and disengage the 2-way connector at the blower motor lead under the instrument panel on the passenger side of the vehicle. The wire connector insulator may be wrapped with a foam silencer material.

3. Remove the 5 blower motor screws attaching the the motor to the A/C-heater unit.

4. Allow the blower assembly to drop downward to clear the instrument panel.

5. Install in reverse of removal.

1992-95 Models

1. Disconnect the negative battery cable.
2. Remove the lower right instrument panel assembly.
3. Remove the blower motor screws attaching the the motor to the A/C-heater unit.
4. Allow the blower assembly to drop downward to clear the instrument panel.
5. Install in reverse of removal.

Blower Motor Resistor

REMOVAL & INSTALLATION

➧ **See Figure 25**

➥ **The resistor block is located at the left rear corner of the engine compartment on Caravan, Voyager and Town & Country.**

1. Remove the glovebox, if necessary. Locate the resistor block and disconnect the wire harness.
2. Remove the attaching screws and remove the resistor from the housing.
3. Make sure there is no contact between any of the coils before installing.
4. The installation is the reverse of the removal procedure. Make sure the foam seal is in good condition.
5. Perform the Air Bag System Check procedures outlined in this section before connecting the negative battery cable.
6. Connect the negative battery cable and check the blower system for proper operation.

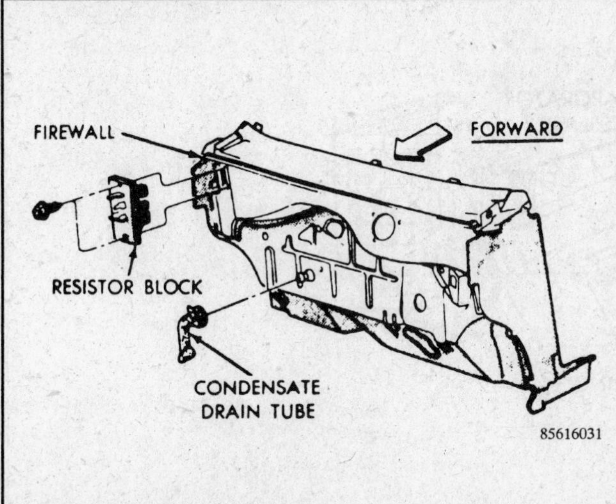

Fig. 25 Resister block removal and installation

Heater Core and Evaporator

➧ **See Figures 26, 27, 28, 29, 30 and 31**

REMOVAL & INSTALLATION

1984-90 Models

1. Have the system discharged by a qualified professional mechanic using an approved recovery/recycling machine.
2. Disconnect the negative battery cable, then drain the cooling system.
3. Remove the lower steering column cover.
4. Remove the lower reinforcement under the steering column, right side cowl and sill trim. Remove the bolt holding the right side instrument panel to the right cowl.
5. Loosen the 2 brackets supporting the lower edge of the heater housing. Remove the instrument panel trim covering and reinforcement. Remove the retaining screws from the right side of the steering column.
6. Disconnect the vacuum lines at the brake booster and water valve.
7. Clamp off the heater hoses at the heater core and remove them from the heater core tubes. Plug the ends to prevent leakage.
8. Disconnect the H-valve at the water valve and remove it. Remove the retaining nuts at the package tray mounting studs. Remove the drain tube.
9. Disconnect the blower motor wiring and temperature control cable. Disconnect the vacuum harness at the top of the heater unit.
10. Remove the retaining nuts from the package mounting studs at the firewall. Disconnect the hanger strap from the package and rotate it aside.
11. Pull the right side of the instrument panel out as far as possible. Fold the carpeting and insulation back to provide a little more working room and to prevent spillage from staining the carpeting.
12. Remove the entire housing assembly from the dash panel and remove it from the vehicle.
13. To disassemble the housing assembly, remove the vacuum diaphragm and retaining screws from the cover and remove the cover.
14. Remove the retaining screw from the heater core and/or evaporator and remove from the housing assembly.

To install:

15. Remove the temperature control door from the unit and clean the unit out with solvent. Lubricate the lower pivot rod and its well and install. Wrap the heater core and/or evaporator with foam tape and place in position. Secure with the screws.
16. Assemble the unit, making sure all vacuum tubes are properly routed.
17. Install the assembly to the vehicle and connect the vacuum harness. Install the nuts to the firewall and install the condensation tube. Fold the carpeting back into position.
18. Connect the hanger strap from the package and rotate it aside. Install the 2 brackets supporting the lower edge of the heater housing. Connect the blower motor wiring, resistor wiring and the temperature control cable.

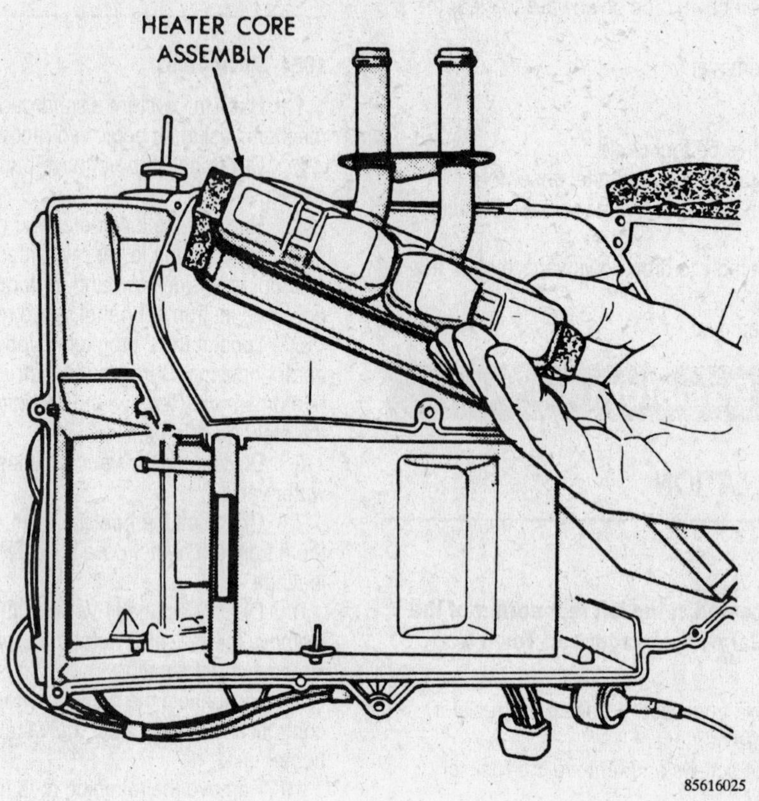

Fig. 26 Removing and installing the heater core assembly

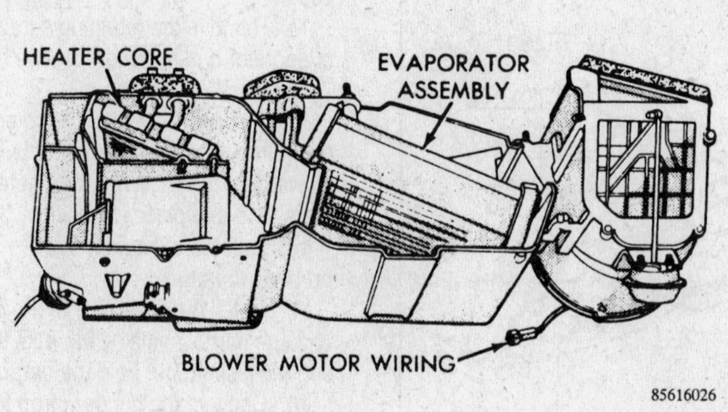

Fig. 27 Heater/evaporator assembly components

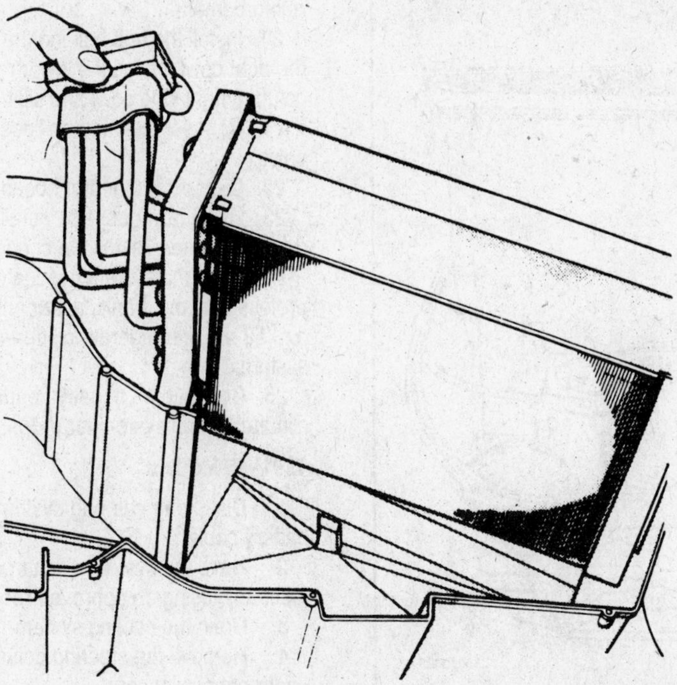

85616027

Fig. 28 Removing or installing the actuator and linkage on the blower housing

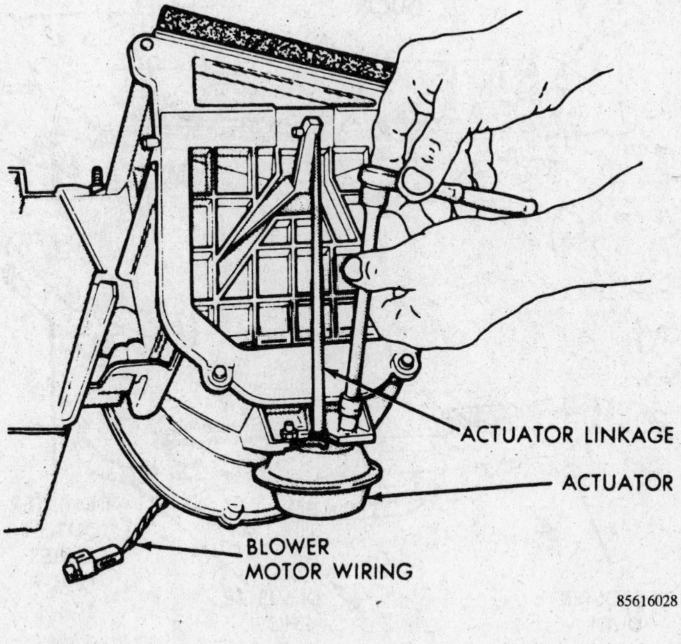

Fig. 29 Removing or installing the evaporator

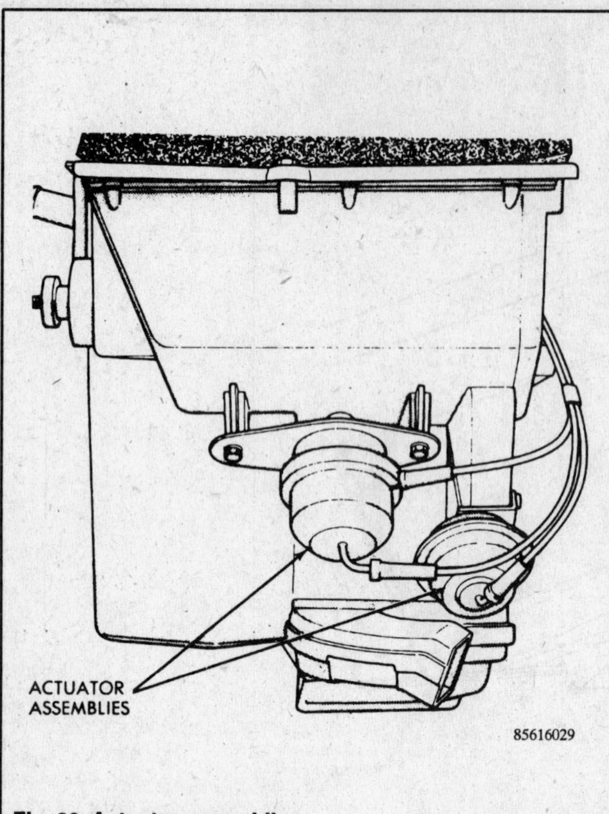

Fig. 30 Actuator assemblies

19. Install the retaining screws from the right side to the steering column. Install the instrument panel trim covering and reinforcement.
20. Install the bolt holding the right side instrument panel to the right cowl. Install the lower reinforcement under the steering column, right side cowl and sill trim.
21. Connect the vacuum lines at the brake booster and water valve.
22. Connect the heater hoses to the core tubes.
23. Using new gaskets, install the H-valve and connect the refrigerant lines. Install the condensation tube.
24. Have the system evacuated and recharged by a qualified professional mechanic, utilizing the proper equipment. Add 2 fl. oz. (59 ml) of refrigerant oil during the recharge. Fill the cooling system.
25. Connect the negative battery cable and check the entire climate control system for proper operation and leaks.

1991–95 Models

1. Disable the air bag system by disconnecting the negative battery cable.
2. Have the system discharged by a qualified professional mechanic using an approved recovery/recycling machine.
3. Drain the cooling system.
4. Remove the steering column cover and left and right side under panel silencers.
5. Remove the center bezel by unclipping it from the instrument panel.

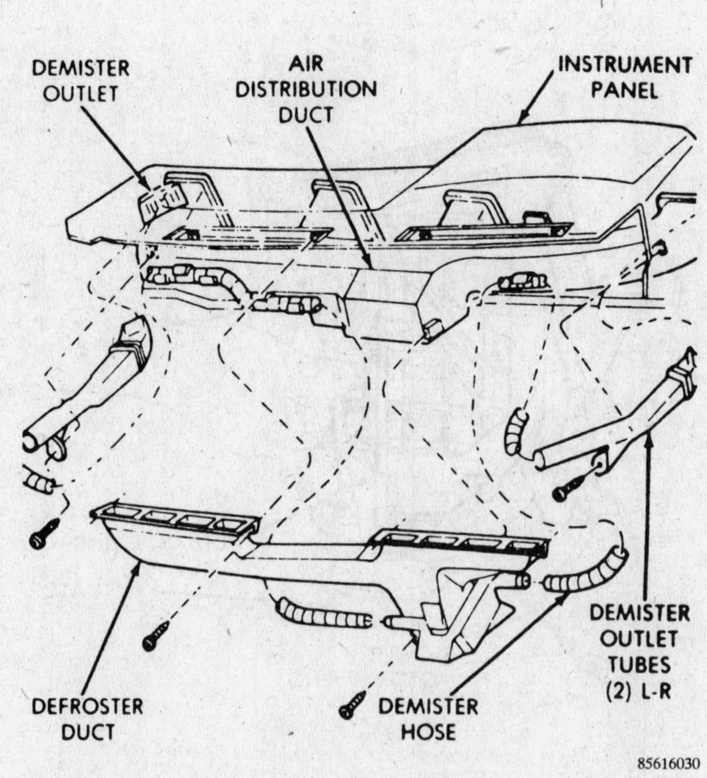

Fig. 31 Instrument panel ventilation ducts and hoses

6. Remove the accessory switch carrier and the heater/air conditioning control head.
7. Remove storage bin and lower right instrument panel.
8. Disconnect the blower motor lead under the right side of the instrument panel.
9. Remove the right side 40-way connector wiring bracket.
10. Remove the lower right reinforcement, body computer bracket and mid-to-lower reinforcement as an assembly.
11. Disconnect the vacuum lines at the brake booster and water valve.
12. Clamp off the heater hoses near the heater core and remove the hoses from the core tubes. Plug the hose ends and the core tubes to prevent spillage of coolant.
13. If equipped with air conditioning, remove the H-valve and condensation tube.
14. Disconnect the temperature control cable and vacuum harness at the connection at the top of the unit.
15. Remove the retaining nuts from the package mounting studs at the firewall. Disconnect the hanger strap from the package and rotate it aside.

To install:

16. Remove the temperature control door from the unit and clean the unit out with solvent. Lubricate the lower pivot rod and its well and install. Wrap the heater core and/or evaporator with foam tape and place in position. Secure with the screws.
17. Assemble the unit, making sure all vacuum tubes are properly routed.
18. Install the assembly to the vehicle and connect the vacuum harness. Install the nuts to the firewall and install the condensation tube. Fold the carpeting back into position.
19. Connect the hanger strap from the package and rotate it aside. Install the 2 brackets supporting the lower edge of the heater housing. Connect the blower motor wiring, resistor wiring and the temperature control cable.
20. Install the retaining screws from the right side to the steering column. Install the instrument panel trim covering and reinforcement.
21. Assemble the unit, making sure all vacuum tubes are properly routed.
22. Install the assembly to the vehicle and connect the vacuum harness. Install the nuts to the firewall and install the condensation tube. Fold the carpeting back into position.
23. Connect the hanger strap from the package and rotate it aside. Connect the blower motor wiring and temperature control cable.
24. Install the lower right reinforcement, body computer bracket and mid-to-lower reinforcement as an assembly.
25. Install the right side 40-way connector wiring bracket.
26. Install the lower right instrument panel and storage bin.
27. Install the heater/air conditioning control head and accessory switch carrier.
28. Install the center bezel to the instrument panel.
29. Install the under panel silencers and steering column cover.
30. Install the vacuum lines at the brake booster and water valve.
31. Connect the heater hoses to the core tubes.
32. Using new gaskets, install the H-valve and connect the refrigerant lines. Install the condensation tube.
33. Have the system evacuated and recharged by a qualified professional mechanic, utilizing the proper equipment. Add 2 fl. oz. (59 ml) of refrigerant oil during the recharge. Fill the cooling system.
34. Perform the Air Bag System Check procedures outlined in this section before connecting the negative battery cable.
35. Connect the negative battery cable and check the entire climate control system for proper operation and leaks.

Climate Control Head

REMOVAL & INSTALLATION

➧ See Figure 32

1. Disconnect the negative battery cable.
2. Remove the necessary bezel(s) in order to gain access to the control head.
3. Remove the screws that fasten the control head to the instrument panel.
4. Pull the unit out and unplug the electrical and vacuum connectors. Disconnect the temperature control cable by pushing the flag in and pulling the end from its seat.
5. Remove the control head from the instrument panel.
6. The installation is the reverse of the removal proceed that fasten the control head to the instrument panel.

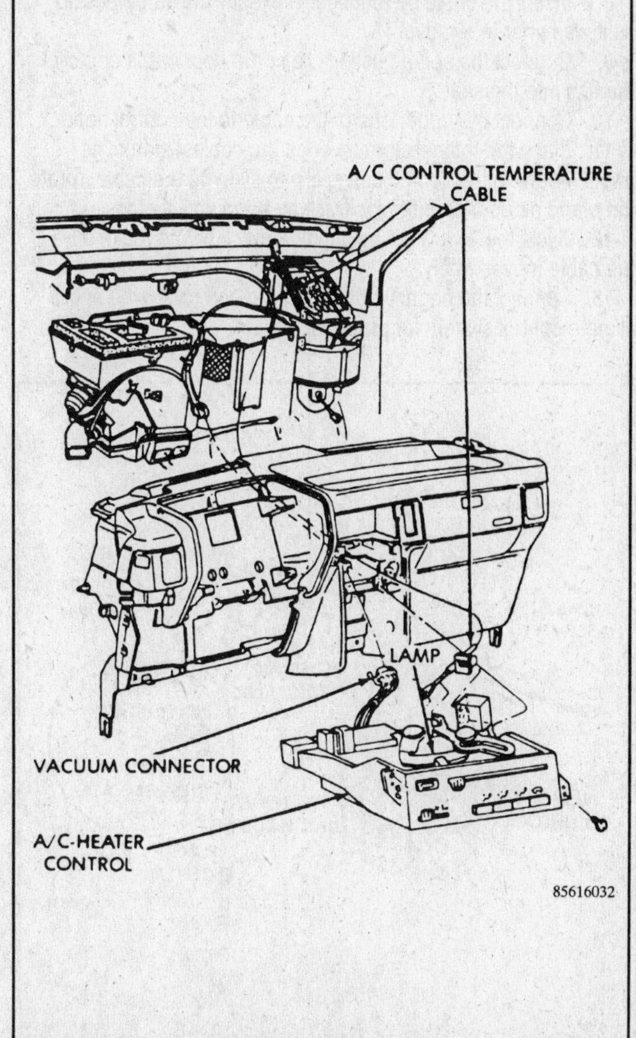

Fig. 32 Air conditioning and heater control head removal

Heater/Air Conditioning Control Cables

REMOVAL & INSTALLATION

See Figure 33

1. Disconnect the negative battery cable.
2. Remove the necessary bezel(s) in order to gain access to the control head.
3. Remove the screws that fasten the control head to the instrument panel.
4. Pull the unit out and disconnect the temperature control cable by pushing the flag in and pulling the end from its seat.
5. The temperature control cable end is located at the bottom of the heater/air conditioning housing. Disconnect the cable end by pushing the flag in and pulling the end from its seat.
6. Disconnect the self-adjusting clip from the blend air or mode door crank.
7. Take note of the cable's routing and remove them from the vehicle.

To install:

8. Install the cable by routing it in exactly the same position as it was prior to removal.
9. Connect the self-adjusting clip to the door crank and click the flag into the seat.
10. Connect the upper end of the cable to the control head.
11. Place the temperature lever on the coolest side of its travel. Allowing the self-adjusting clip to slide on the cable, rotate the blend air door counterclockwise by hand until it stops.
12. Cycle the lever back and forth a few times to make sure the cable moves freely.
13. Connect the negative battery cable and check the entire climate control system for proper operation.

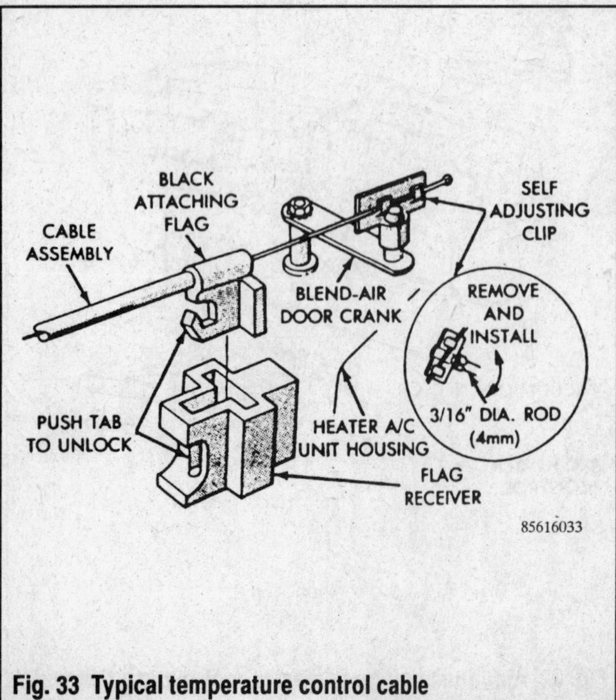

Fig. 33 Typical temperature control cable

Filter/Drier

REMOVAL & INSTALLATION

See Figure 34

1. Have the system discharged by a qualified professional mechanic using an approved recovery/recycling machine.
2. Disconnect the negative battery cable.
3. On 1992–95 vehicles, remove the vehicle jack.
4. Remove the nuts that fasten the refrigerant lines to sides of the receiver/drier assembly.
5. Remove the refrigerant lines from the receiver/drier and discard the gaskets. Cover the exposed ends of the lines to minimize contamination.
6. Remove the mounting strap bolts and remove the receiver/drier from the engine compartment.

To install:

7. Transfer the mounting strap to the new receiver/drier.
8. Coat the new gaskets with wax-free refrigerant oil and install. Connect the refrigerant lines to the receiver/drier and tighten the nuts.
9. Have the system evacuated and recharged by a qualified professional mechanic, utilizing the proper equipment. Add 1 fl. oz. (29 ml) of refrigerant oil during the recharge. Check for leaks.

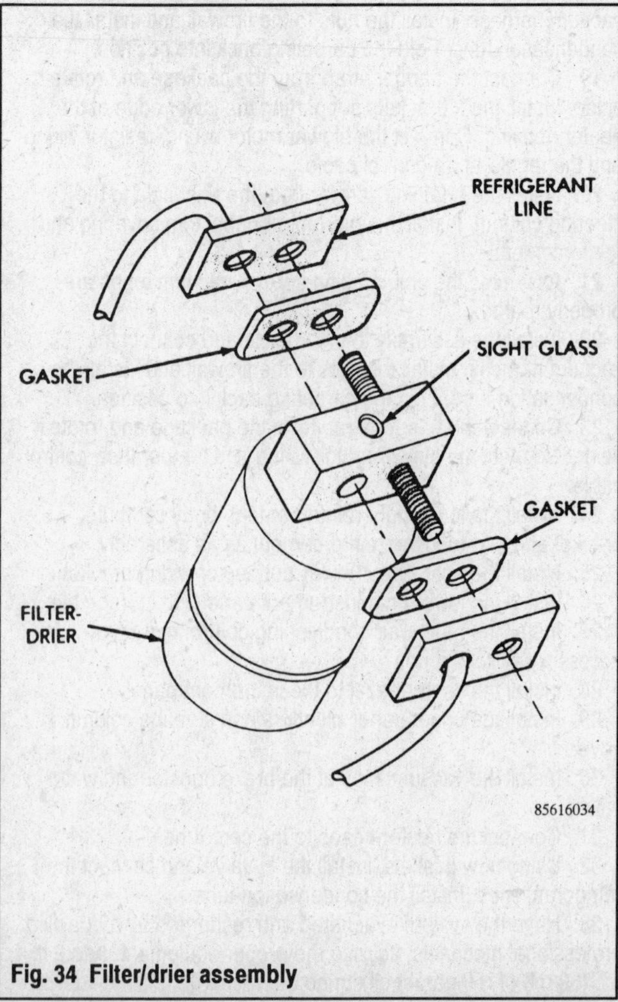

Fig. 34 Filter/drier assembly

Expansion Valve (H-Valve)

TESTING

1. Connect a manifold gauge set or charging station to the air conditioning system. Verify adequate refrigerant level.
2. Disconnect and plug the vacuum hose at the water control valve.
3. Disconnect the low pressure or differential pressure cut off switch connector and jump the wires inside the boot.
4. Close all doors, windows and vents to the passenger compartment.
5. Set controls to **MAX A/C**, full heat and high blower speed.
6. Start the engine and hold the idle speed at 1000 rpm. After the engine has reached normal operating temperature, allow the passenger compartment to heat up to create the need for maximum refrigerant flow into the evaporator.
7. The discharge (high pressure) gauge should read 140–240 psi (965–1655 kPa) and suction (low pressure) gauge should read 20–30 psi (138–207 kPa), providing the refrigerant charge is sufficient.
8. If the suction side is within specifications, freeze the expansion valve control head using a very cold substance (liquid CO2 or dry ice) for 30 seconds:
    a. If equipped with a silver H-valve used with fixed displacement compressor, the suction side pressure should drop to 15 in. Hg (50 kPa) vacuum. If not, the expansion valve is stuck open and should be replaced.
    b. If equipped with a black H-valve used with variable displacement compressor, the discharge pressure should drop about 15 percent. If not, the expansion valve is stuck open and should be replaced.
9. Allow the expansion valve to thaw. As it thaws, the pressures should stabilize to the values in Step 7. If not, replace the expansion valve.
10. Once the test is complete, put the vacuum line and connector back in the original locations, and perform the overall performance test.

REMOVAL & INSTALLATION

1984–91 Models

➧ See Figure 35

1. Have the system discharged by a qualified professional mechanic using an approved recovery/recycling machine.
2. Disconnect the negative battery cable.
3. Disconnect the low or differential pressure cut off switch.
4. Remove the attaching bolt at the center of the refrigerant plumbing sealing plate.
5. Pull the refrigerant lines assembly away from the expansion valve. Cover the exposed ends of the lines to minimize contamination.
6. Remove the 2 Torx® screws that mount the expansion valve to the evaporator sealing plate.
7. Remove the valve and discard the gaskets.

To install:

8. Transfer the low pressure cutoff switch to the new valve, if necessary.

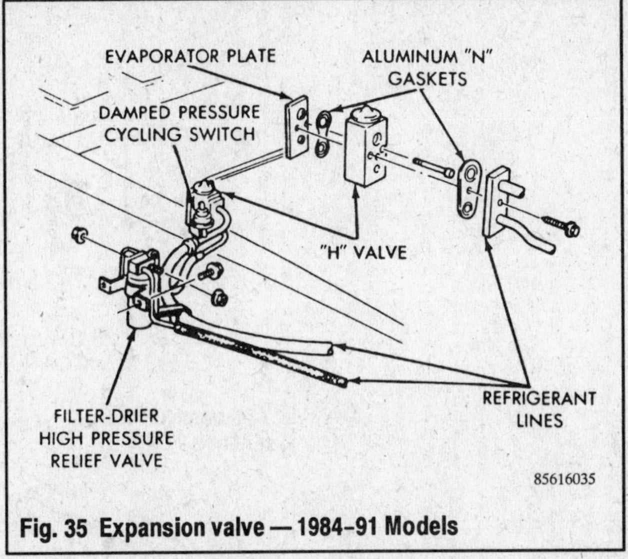

Fig. 35 Expansion valve — 1984–91 Models

9. Coat the new "figure-8" gasket with wax-free refrigerant oil and install to the evaporator sealing plate.
10. Install the expansion valve and torque the Torx® screws to 100 inch lbs. (11 Nm).
11. Lubricate the remaining gasket and install with the blower motor lead under the right side of the instrument panel.
12. Connect the refrigerant lines and sealing plate, tighten to 17 ft. lbs. (23 Nm).
13. Connect the electrical leads and connect the negative battery cable.
14. Have the system evacuated and recharged by a qualified professional mechanic, utilizing the proper equipment.

1991–95 Models

➧ See Figure 36

1. Have the system discharged by a qualified professional mechanic using an approved recovery/recycling machine.
2. Disconnect the negative battery cable.
3. Disconnect the boot-type wire connector from pressure cut off switch.
4. Disconnect the 3-pin connector from the ECCS.
5. Remove the attaching bolt at the center of the refrigerant plumbing sealing plate.
6. Pull the refrigerant lines assembly away from the expansion valve. Cover the exposed ends of the lines to minimize contamination.
7. Remove the 2 screws that mount the expansion valve to the evaporator sealing plate.
8. Remove the valve and discard the gaskets.

To install:

9. Remove and replace the aluminum gasket on the evaporator sealing plate.
10. Carefully hold the expansion valve sealing plate and torque the 2 screws to 100 inch lbs. (11 Nm).
11. Remove and replace the aluminum gasket on the refrigerant line sealing plate.
12. Connect the refrigerant lines and sealing plate, tighten to 17 ft. lbs. (23 Nm).
13. Connect the electrical leads and connect the negative battery cable.
14. Have the system evacuated and recharged by a qualified professional mechanic, utilizing the proper equipment.

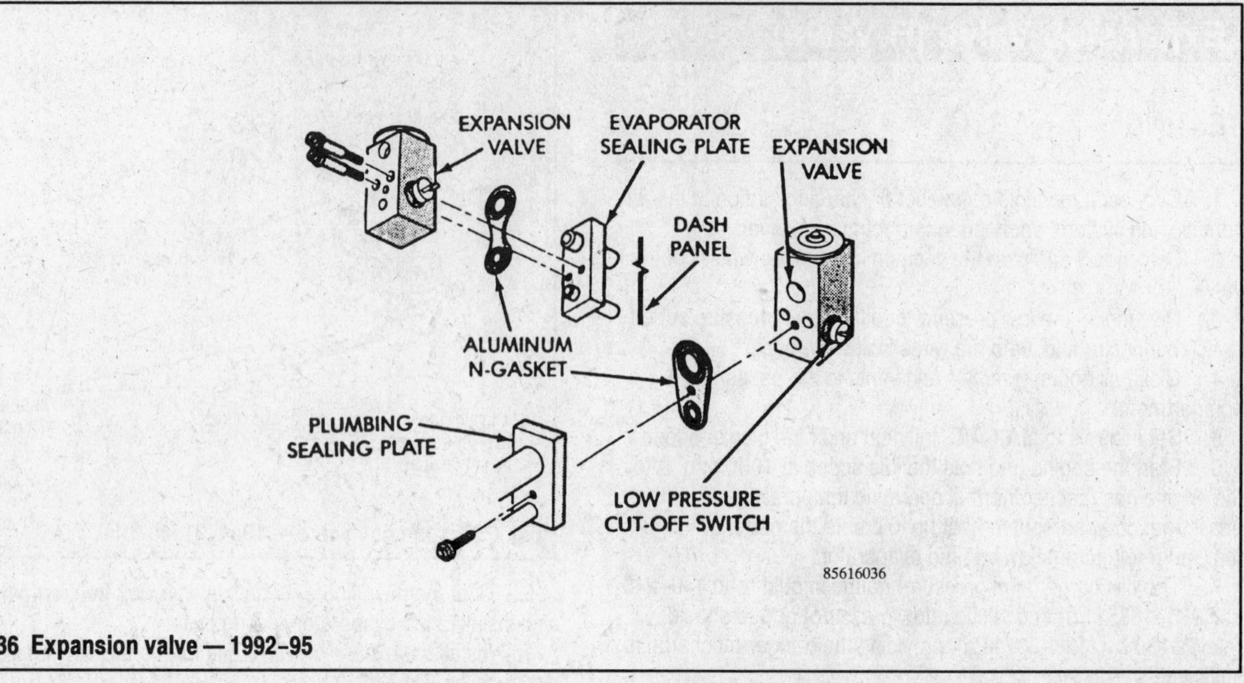

Fig. 36 Expansion valve — 1992–95

AUXILIARY HEATER/AIR CONDITIONER

➧ See Figure 37

Expansion Valve

REMOVAL & INSTALLATION

1. Have the system discharged by a qualified professional mechanic using an approved recovery/recycling machine.
2. Disconnect the negative battery cable.
3. Remove the middle bench, if equipped. Remove the interior left lower quarter trim panel.
4. Remove the 7 screws that attach the air distribution duct to the floor and unit. Pull the distribution duct straight up to remove.
5. Remove the 6 screws from the top surface of the unit and remove the unit cover.
6. Remove the bolt that secures the refrigerant lines to the evaporator sealing plate and separate the parts. Discard the gasket. Cover the exposed ends of the lines to minimize contamination.
7. Pull the evaporator and expansion valve straight up in order to clear the extension tube pilots and remove from the vehicle. Cover the exposed ends of the lines to minimize contamination.
8. Remove the Torx® screws and remove the expansion valve from the evaporator. Discard the gasket.

To install:

9. Remove and replace the aluminum gasket on the evaporator sealing plate.
10. Carefully hold the expansion valve sealing plate and torque the 2 screws to 100 inch lbs. (11 Nm).
11. Remove and replace the aluminum gasket on the refrigerant line sealing plate.
12. Connect the refrigerant lines and sealing plate, tighten to 17 ft. lbs. (23 Nm).
13. Install the unit cover and air distribution duct.
14. Install the interior trim cover and middle bench.
15. Have the system evacuated and recharged by a qualified professional mechanic, utilizing the proper equipment.
16. Connect the negative battery cable and check the entire climate control system for proper operation and leaks.

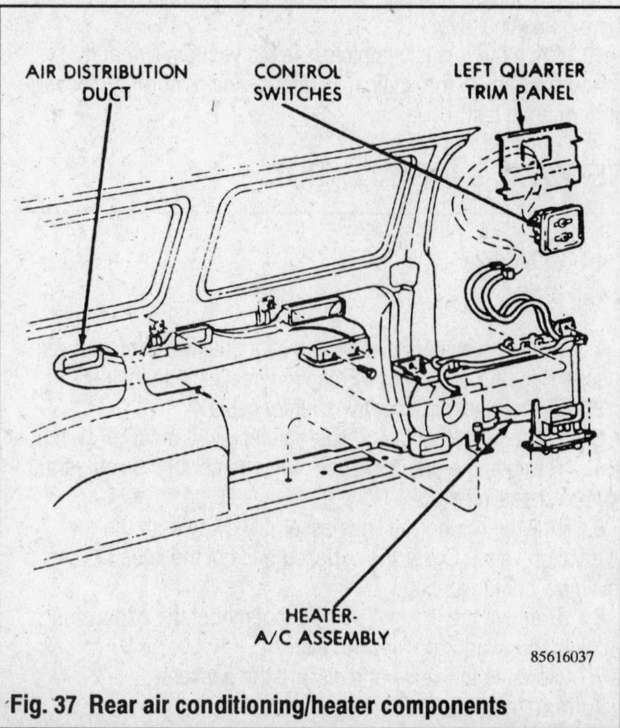

Fig. 37 Rear air conditioning/heater components

Blower Motor

REMOVAL & INSTALLATION

1. Disconnect the negative battery cable.
2. Remove the middle bench, if equipped. Remove the left lower quarter trim panel.
3. Remove 1 blower scroll cover to floor screw and 7 scroll to unit screws.
4. Remove the blower relay.
5. Rotate the blower scroll cover from under the unit.
6. Remove the fan from the blower motor, remove the 3 motor attaching screws and remove the motor from the unit.
7. The installation is the reverse of the removal procedure.
8. Connect the negative battery cable and check the blower motor for proper operation.

Blower Motor Resistor

REMOVAL & INSTALLATION

1. Disconnect the negative battery cable.
2. Remove the middle bench, if equipped. Remove the left lower quarter trim panel.
3. Disconnect the wiring harness from the resistor.
4. Remove the screws that attach the resistor to the rear unit and remove the resistor.
5. The installation is the reverse of the removal procedure.
6. Connect the negative battery cable and check for proper operation.

Heater Core

REMOVAL & INSTALLATION

1. Disconnect the negative battery cable. Pinch off the hoses to the rear heater core.
2. Raise the vehicle and support safely. Disconnect the underbody heater hoses from the rear heater core tubes.
3. Remove the middle bench, if equipped. Remove the interior left lower quarter trim panel.
4. Remove the 7 screws that attach the air distribution duct to the floor and unit. Pull the distribution duct straight up to remove.
5. Remove the 6 screws from the top surface of the unit and remove the unit cover.
6. Pull the heater core straight up and out of the unit.
7. The installation is the reverse of the removal procedure.
8. Connect the negative battery cable and check for leaks.

Evaporator

REMOVAL & INSTALLATION

1. Have the system discharged by a qualified professional mechanic using an approved recovery/recycling machine.
2. Disconnect the negative battery cable.
3. Remove the unit cover and duct.
4. Remove the middle bench, if equipped. Remove the interior left lower quarter trim panel.
5. Remove the 7 screws that attach the air distribution duct to the floor and unit. Pull the distribution duct straight up to remove.
6. Remove the 6 screws from the top surface of the unit and remove the unit cover.
7. Pull the evaporator and expansion valve straight up in order to clear the extension tube pilots and remove from the vehicle. Cover the exposed ends of the lines to minimize contamination.
8. Remove the Torx® screws and remove the expansion valve from the evaporator. Discard the gasket.

To install:

9. Lubricate the gasket with wax-free refrigerant oil and assemble the expansion valve and evaporator.
10. Lubricate the gasket with wax-free refrigerant oil and install the evaporator and expansion valve assembly to the refrigerant lines and install the bolt.
11. Install the unit cover and air distribution duct.
12. Install the interior trim cover and middle bench.
13. Have the system evacuated and recharged by a qualified professional mechanic, utilizing the proper equipment. If the evaporator was replaced, measure the amount of oil that was in the original evaporator and add that amount during the recharge.
14. Connect the negative battery cable and check the entire climate control system for proper operation and leaks.

Refrigerant Lines

REMOVAL & INSTALLATION

➧ **See Figures 38 and 39**

1. Have the system discharged by a qualified professional mechanic using an approved recovery/recycling machine.
2. Disconnect the negative battery cable.
3. Raise the vehicle and support safely.
4. Remove the nuts or bolts that attach the refrigerant line sealing plates to the adjoining components. If the lines are connected with flare nuts, use a back-up wrench when disassembling. Cover the exposed ends of the lines to minimize contamination.
5. Remove the support mount.
6. Remove the lines and discard the gaskets or O-rings.

To install:

7. Coat the new gaskets or O-rings with wax-free refrigerant oil and install. Connect the refrigerant lines to the adjoining components and tighten the nuts or bolts.
8. Install the support mount.
9. Have the system evacuated and recharged by a qualified professional mechanic, utilizing the proper equipment.
10. Connect the negative battery cable and check the entire climate control system for proper operation and leaks.

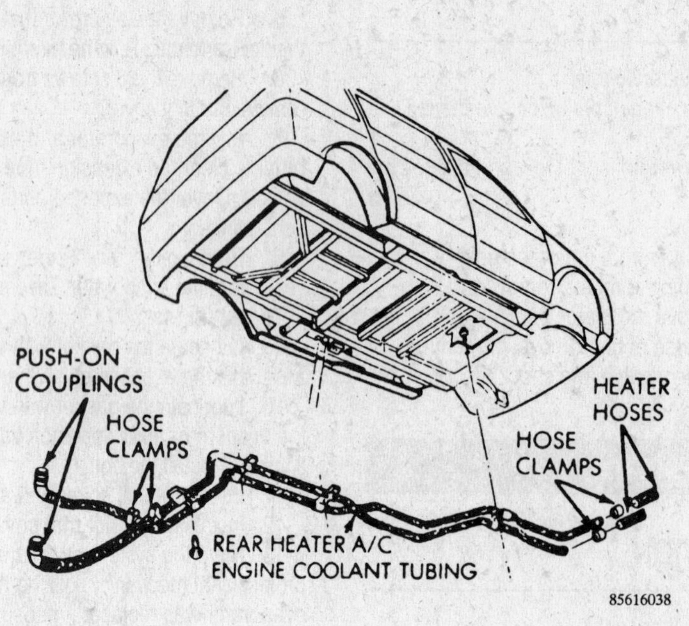

Fig. 38 Rear heater assembly, underbody hose routing

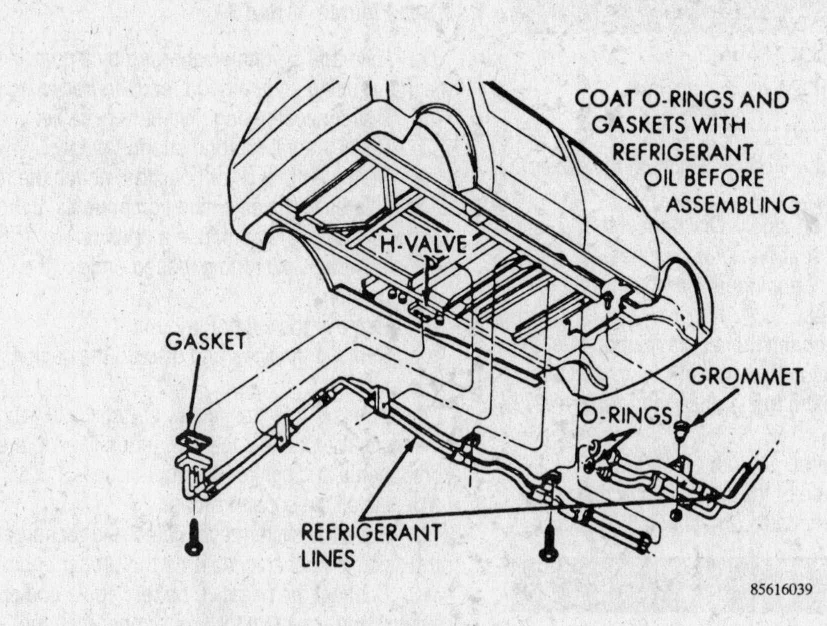

Fig. 39 Rear air conditioner assembly underbody line routing

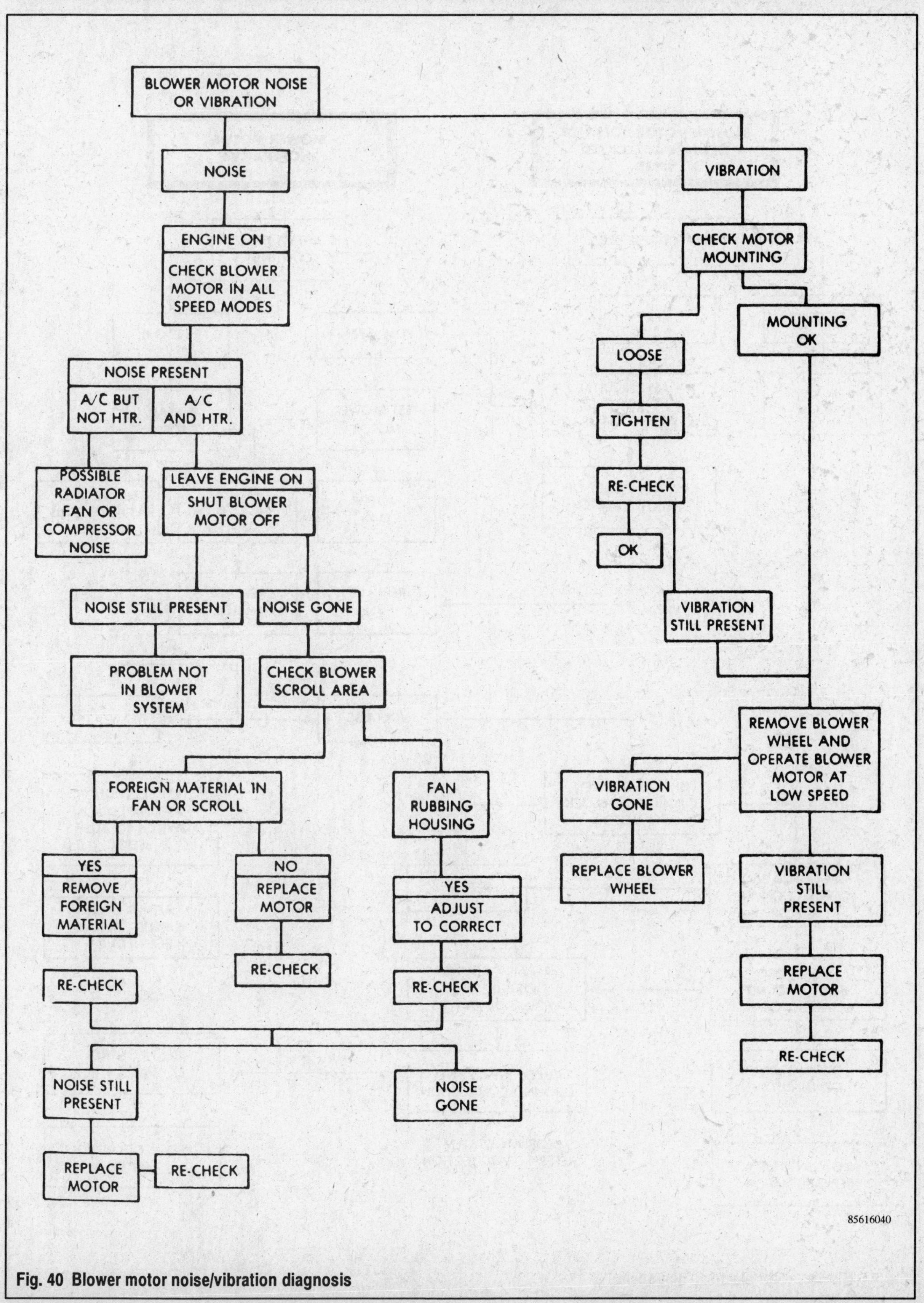

Fig. 40 Blower motor noise/vibration diagnosis

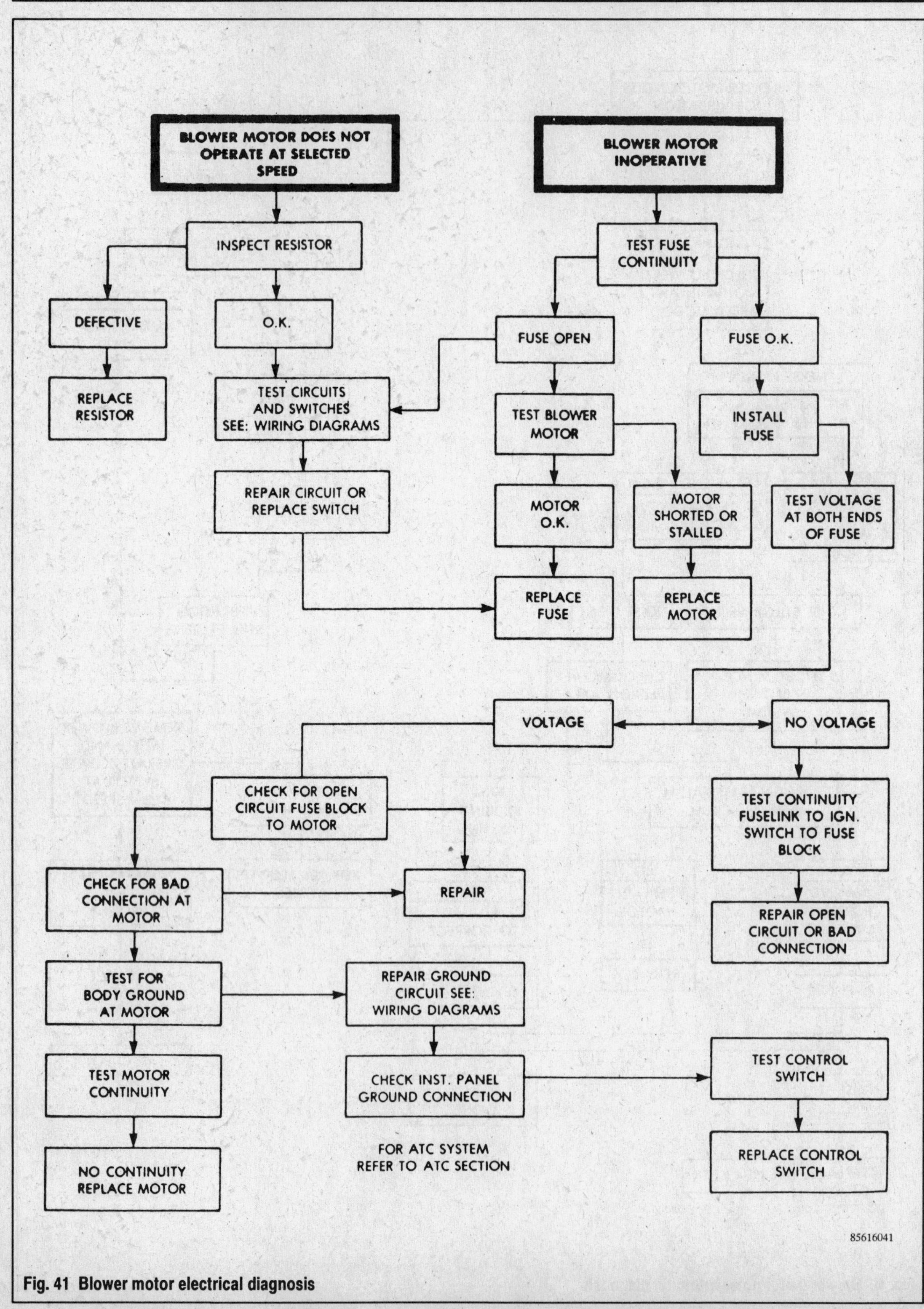

Fig. 41 Blower motor electrical diagnosis

ENTERTAINMENT SYSTEM

Radio

REMOVAL & INSTALLATION

See Figures 42, 43, 44, 45, 46, 47, 48, 49 and 50

1. Disconnect the negative battery cable.
2. Remove the control knobs by pulling them from the mounting stalks.
3. Remove the three (3) screws from the top of the radio trim bezel.
4. Remove the ash tray to gain access to the trim bezel lower screws.
5. Remove the two (2) screws from the lower portion of the trim bezel.
6. Pull outward on the left side of bezel to unsnap the mounting clips. Remove the bezel.
7. Remove the radio to instrument panel retaining screws.
8. Pull the radio through the front of the instrument panel and unplug the wiring harness, ground strap and antenna plug.

To install:

9. Connect the radio wiring harness, ground strap and antenna lead.
10. Position the radio into the instrument panel and install the retaining screws.
11. Install the trim bezel and secure it with the lower and upper retaining screws. Install the ash tray.

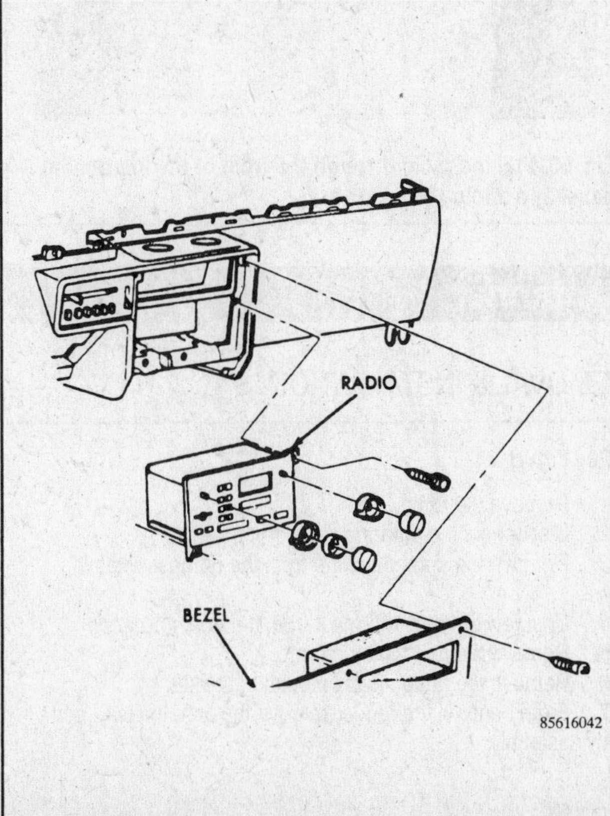

Fig. 42 Radio assembly removal

Fig. 43 Pull the radio control knobs off of the shafts — 1987 Voyager shown

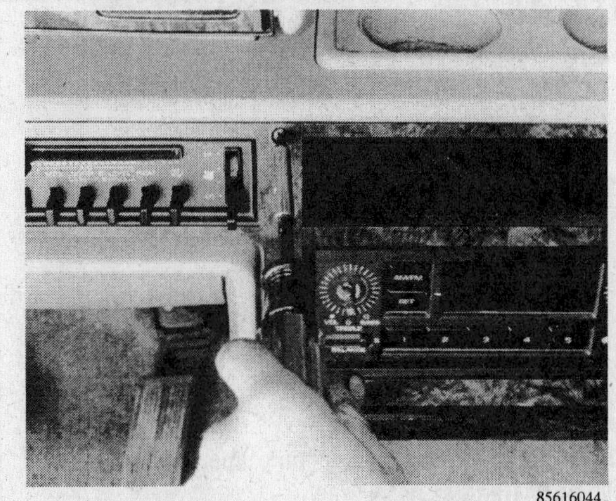

Fig. 44 Removing the trim bezel 3 upper retaining screws

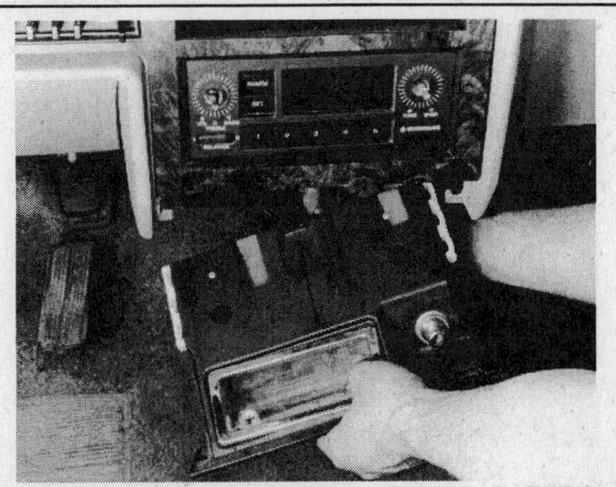

Fig. 45 Remove the ash tray to gain access to the lower trim bezel retaining screws

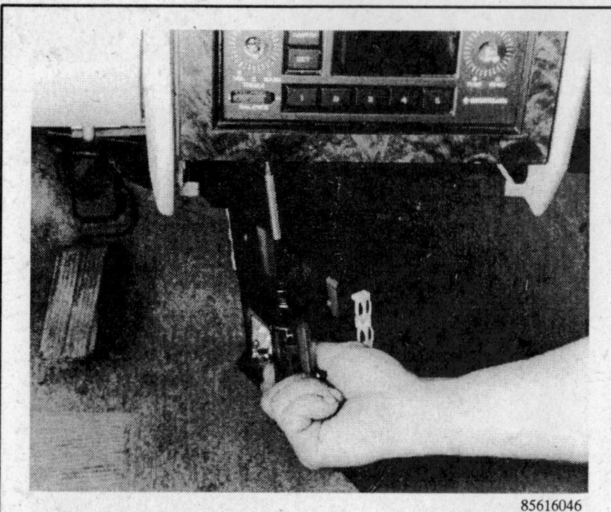

85616046

Fig. 46 Remove the 2 lower trim bezel retaining screws

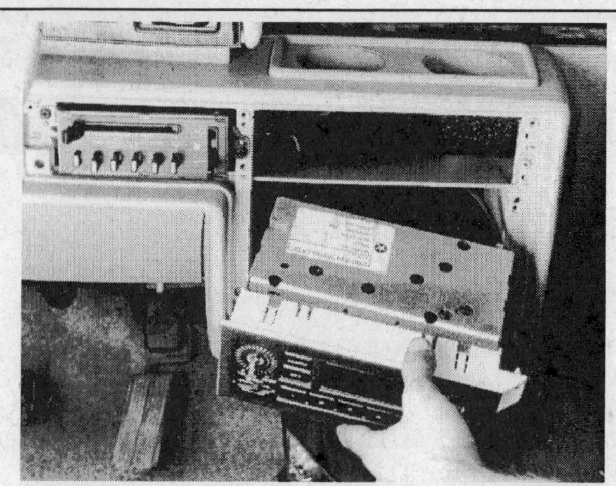

85616049

Fig. 49 After removing the radio-to-instrument panel retaining screws, the radio can be pulled from the dash panel

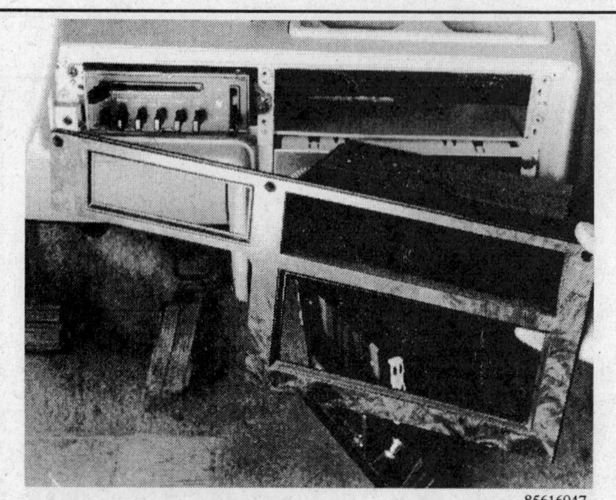

85616047

Fig. 47 Unsnap from the mounting clips and remove the trim bezel from the dash panel

85616050

Fig. 50 Pull the radio through the front of the instrument panel and unplug the wiring

85616048

Fig. 48 Removing the radio to instrument panel retaining screws

Antenna

REMOVAL & INSTALLATION

➧ See Figure 51

1. Remove the radio.
2. Disconnect the antenna cable from the radio.
3. Remove the antenna cable from the harness retaining clips.
4. Unscrew the antenna mast from the upper adapter.
5. Remove the cap mounting nut.
6. Remove the adapter and mounting gasket.
7. From beneath the fender remove the antenna lead and body assembly.

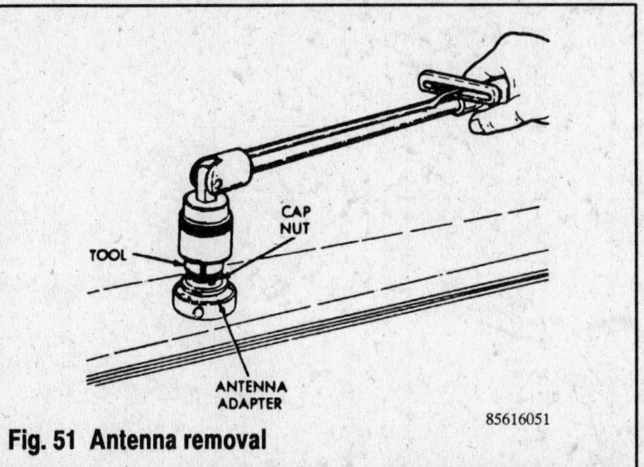

Fig. 51 Antenna removal

To install:

8. Install the new antenna body and cable assembly from under fender.
9. Install the adapter gasket, adapter and cap nut.
10. Install the antenna cable through harness mounting clips and install the cable into radio receiver.
11. Install the radio into the instrument panel.

WINDSHIELD WIPERS

See Figure 55

Wiper Blade

Refer to Section 1 for the removal and installation procedure.

Wiper Arm (Windshield)

REMOVAL & INSTALLATION

See Figures 52, 53, 54, 55, 56 and 57

1. Remove the head cover from the wiper arm base.
2. Remove the arm to pivot attaching nut.
3. Remove the wiper arm from pivot using a rocking motion.

To install:

4. With the wiper motor in Park position, position the arm on the pivot shaft. Choose a point where the tip of the left wiper arm is approximately 2–3 in. (51–76mm) above the windshield cowl top, and the right arm 1.0–1.5 in. (25–38mm) above the windshield cowl top.
5. Install the attaching nut and tighten to 120 inch lbs. (13 Nm).
6. Install the pivot head cover on the wiper arm.

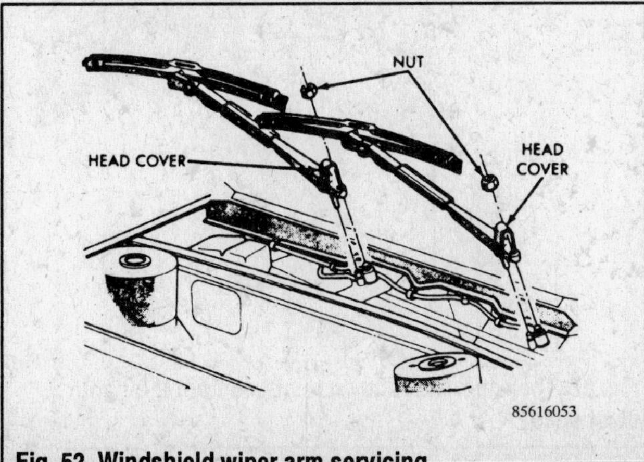

Fig. 52 Windshield wiper arm servicing

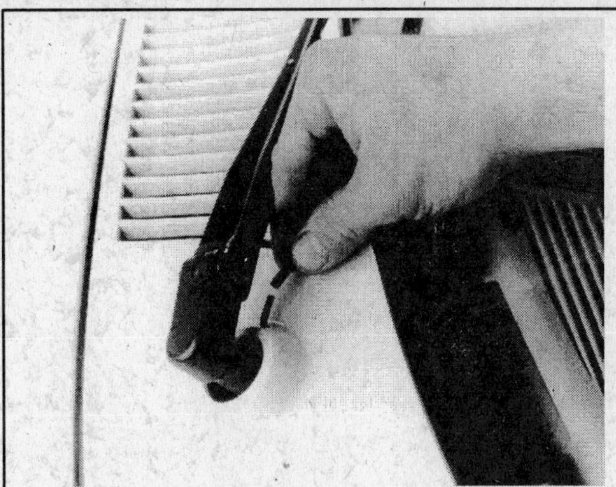

Fig. 53 Disconnecting the washer hose from the connector — 1987 Voyager shown

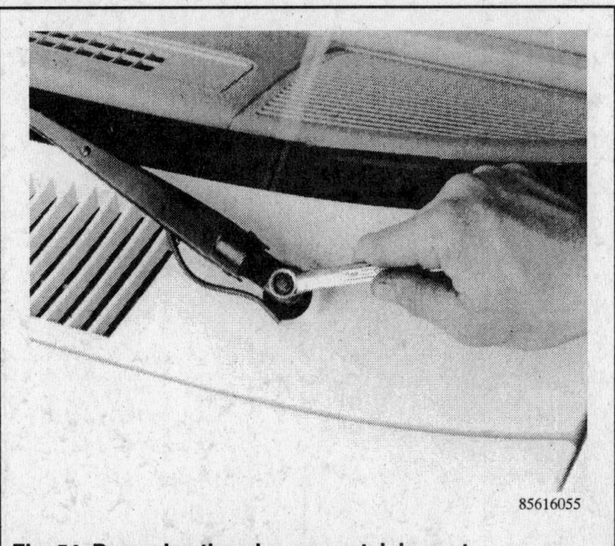

Fig. 54 Removing the wiper arm retaining nut

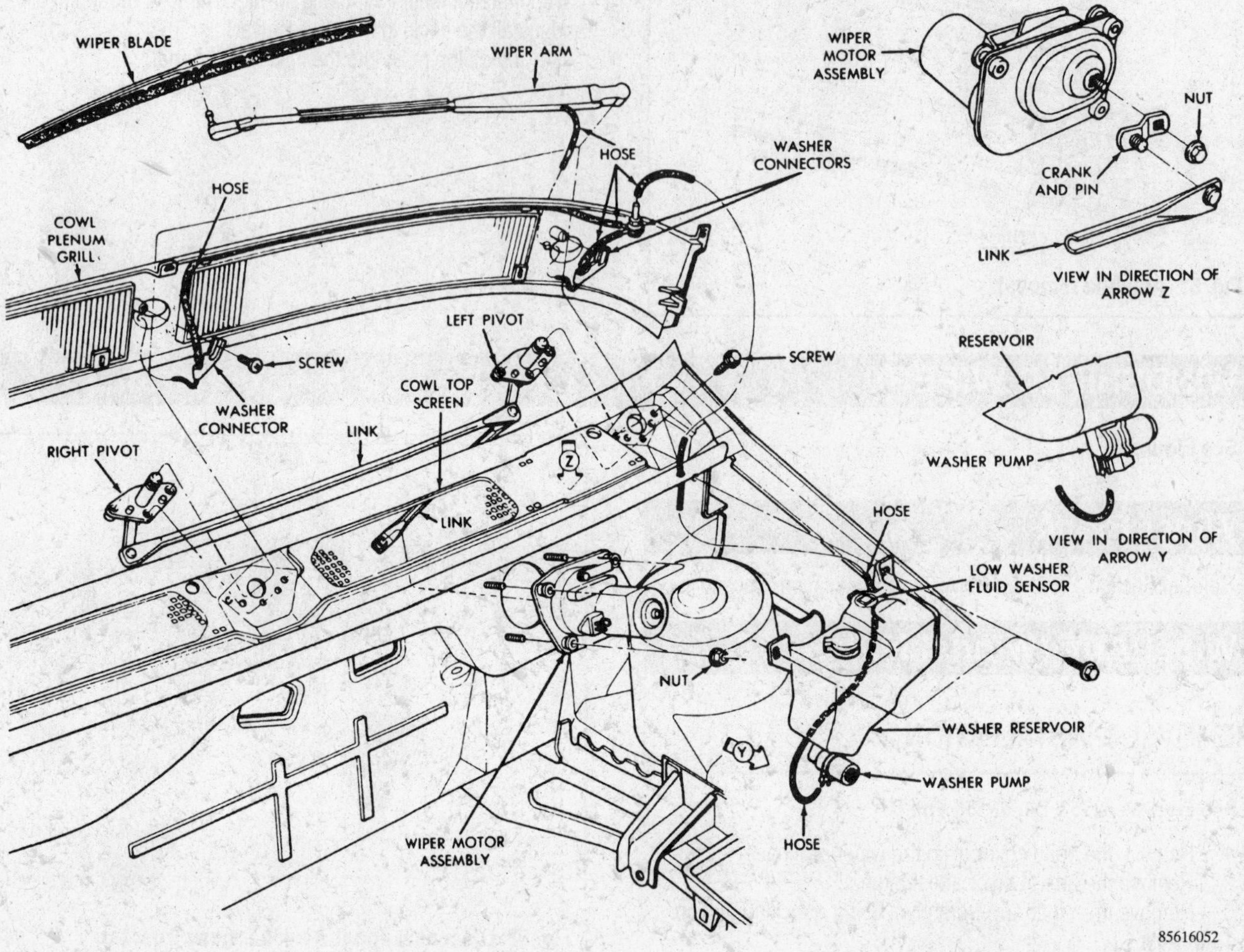

WIPER BLADE
WIPER ARM
WIPER MOTOR ASSEMBLY
NUT
HOSE
WASHER CONNECTORS
CRANK AND PIN
HOSE
COWL PLENUM GRILL
LINK
VIEW IN DIRECTION OF ARROW Z
LEFT PIVOT
RESERVOIR
SCREW
SCREW
COWL TOP SCREEN
WASHER CONNECTOR
LINK
RIGHT PIVOT
WASHER PUMP
LINK
HOSE
VIEW IN DIRECTION OF ARROW Y
LOW WASHER FLUID SENSOR
NUT
WASHER RESERVOIR
WASHER PUMP
WIPER MOTOR ASSEMBLY
HOSE
85616052

Fig. 55 Windshield wiper motor and linkage assemblies

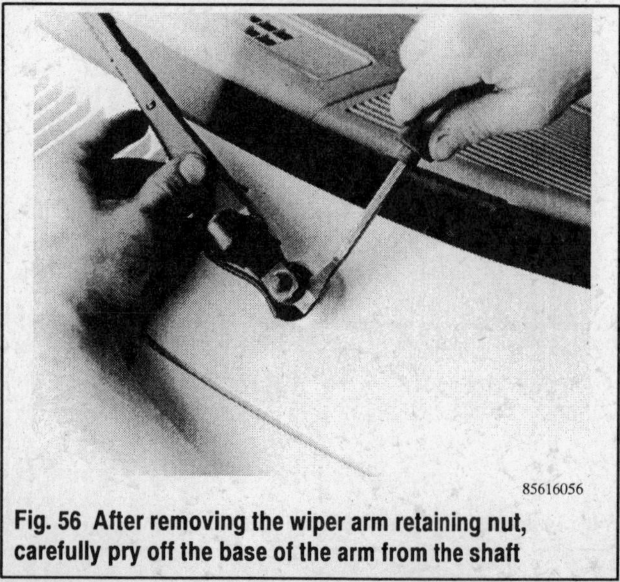

85616056

Fig. 56 After removing the wiper arm retaining nut, carefully pry off the base of the arm from the shaft

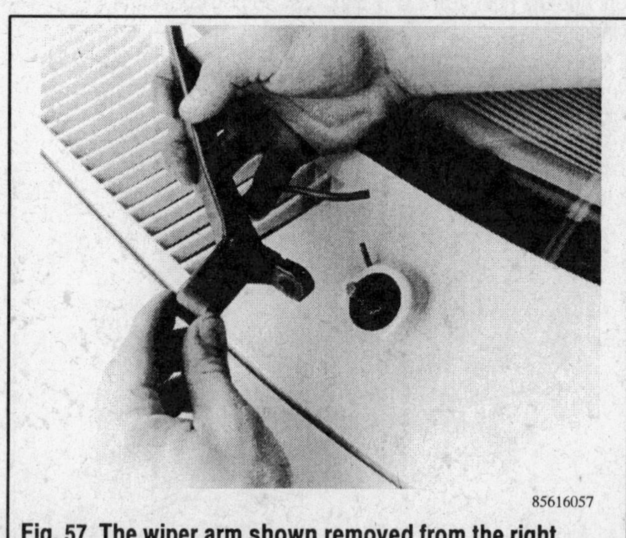

85616057

Fig. 57 The wiper arm shown removed from the right pivot shaft

Wiper Arm (Liftgate)

REMOVAL & INSTALLATION

➧ **See Figure 58**

1. Insert Tool C-3982, or the equivalent, between the wiper arm and wiper motor output shaft.

➥ The use of screwdrivers or prying tools may damaged the spring clip in the base of the arm, while trying to release the arm. Damage of the spring clip will result in the arm coming off the shaft regardless of how carefully it is installed.

2. Lift the arm and remove it from motor output shaft.

To install:

3. With the wiper motor in the Park position, position the arm on the motor output shaft. Choose a point where the tip of blade is about 1.5 in. (38mm) parallel with the bottom lower edge of liftgate glass.
4. Push the wiper arm onto the motor shaft.

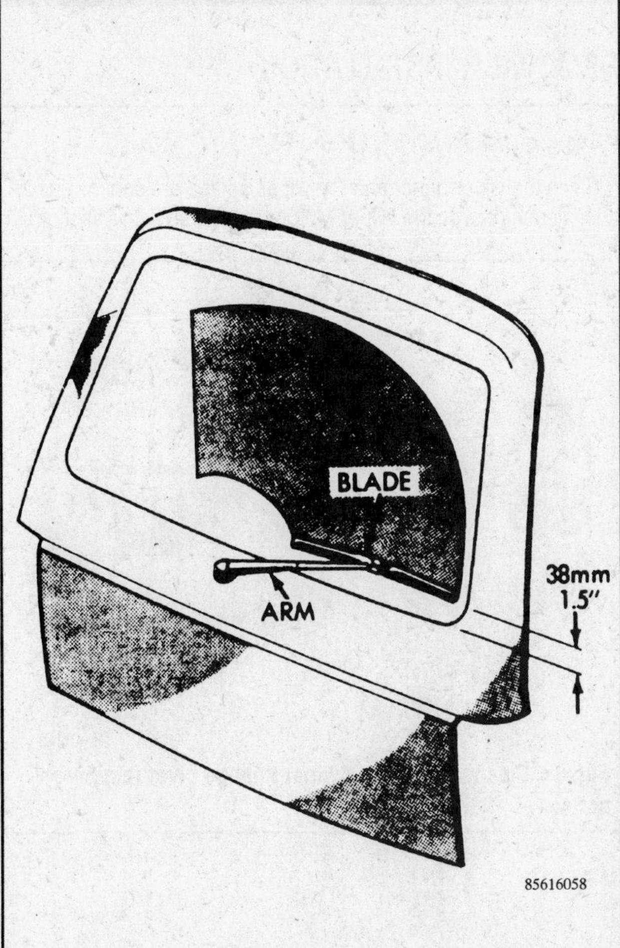

Fig. 58 Liftgate wiper arm installation — 1984-91 models, (for 1992-95 models the measurement is 3.5 in. 89mm)

Windshield Wiper Motor

REMOVAL & INSTALLATION

➧ **See Figures 59, 60, 61 and 62**

Both the motor and wiper linkage are serviced as a unit.

1. Disconnect the negative battery cable. Remove the wiper arm and blade assemblies. Refer to the windshield wiper arm removal and installation procedure in this section.
2. Open the hood, then remove the cowl plenum grille and plastic screen.
3. Remove the hoses from the turret connector. Remove the pivot mounting screws.
4. Disengage the motor wiring connector from the motor.
5. Remove the retaining nut from the wiper motor shaft-to-linkage drive crank, then separate the drive crank from the wiper motor shaft.
6. Remove the wiper motor assembly mounting screws and nuts, then remove the wiper motor.

To install:

7. Position the wiper motor against it's mounting surface, then secure in position with the mounting screws and nuts.
8. Connect the wiring harness.
9. Install the linkage drive crank onto the wiper motor shaft and secure it with the retaining nut. Torque the nut to 95 inch lbs. (11 Nm).
10. Install the cowl plenum grille plastic screen.
11. Connect hoses to turret connector.
12. Install the cowl plenum grille. Connect the negative battery cable. Close the hood.
13. Install the windshield wiper arm and blade assemblies.

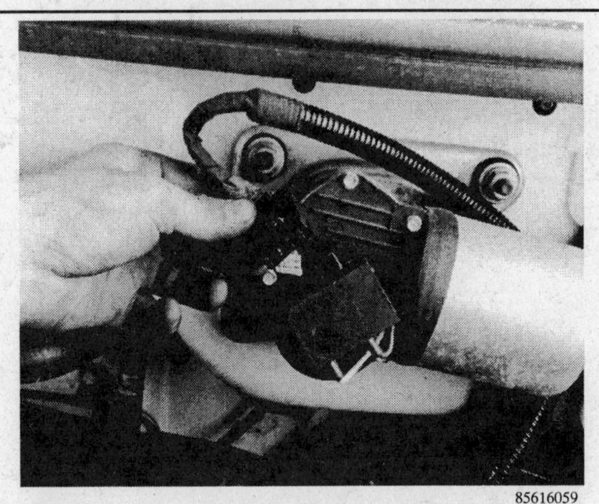

Fig. 59 Remove the wiper motor harness connector — 1987 Voyager shown

85616060

Fig. 60 Removing the wiper motor mounting screws

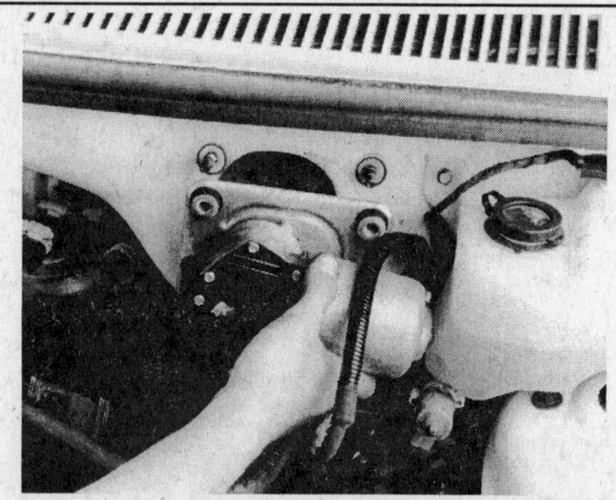

85616061

Fig. 61 After removing the 3 mounting bolts, pull the wiper motor away enough to expose the linkage

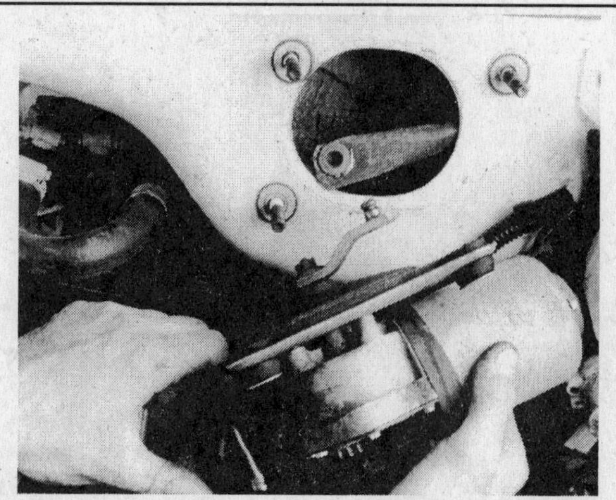

85616062

Fig. 62 Disconnect the arm from the linkage and remove the wiper motor

Liftgate Wiper Motor

REMOVAL & INSTALLATION

1. Disconnect the negative battery cable. Remove the wiper arm and blade assembly.
2. Open the liftgate and remove the trim panel.
3. Remove the four (4) mounting screws from liftgate wiper motor and bracket assembly.
4. Unfasten the electrical harness connector, then remove the liftgate motor.

To install:

5. Install the liftgate wiper motor and bracket assembly. Secure it with the mounting screws.
6. Connect the wiring harness to the wiper motor.
7. Install the liftgate trim panel and secure it with the mounting screws.
8. Install the liftgate wiper arm and blade assembly.

Windshield Wiper Linkage

REMOVAL & INSTALLATION

See Figures 59, 60, 61, 62 and 63

Since the wiper motor and the wiper linkage are serviced as a unit, please refer to the Wiper Motor procedures in this section.

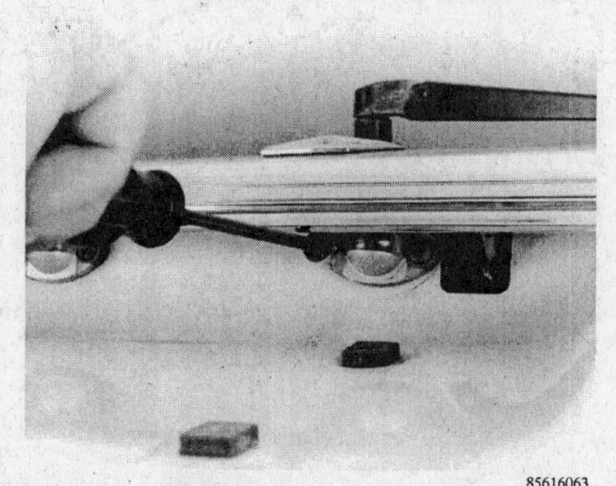

85616063

Fig. 63 Disconnecting the wiper linkage pivot retaining screws — 1987 Voyager shown

INSTRUMENTS AND SWITCHES

Instrument Cluster Assembly

✲✲WARNING

Before servicing the instrument cluster or components, disconnect the negative battery cable.

REMOVAL & INSTALLATION

1984-90 Models

➧ **See Figures 64 and 65**

1. Disconnect the negative battery cable.
2. Remove the cluster assembly bezel mounting (7) screws and remove the cluster bezel.
3. On vehicles equipped with an automatic transaxle, remove the steering column lower cover.
4. Disconnect the shift indicator wire.
5. Remove the cluster assembly retaining screws.
6. Remove the cluster assembly retaining screws.
7. Carefully pull the cluster assembly from the panel and disconnect the speedometer cable.
8. Remove the cluster assembly wiring harness.
9. Remove the cluster assembly past the right side of the steering column.

To install:

10. Position the cluster assembly to the dash from the right side of the steering column.
11. Connect the cluster wiring.
12. Connect the speedometer cable.
13. Install the cluster assembly and retaining screws.
14. On models equipped with an automatic transaxle, place the selector lever in **Drive (D)** position.
15. Connect the shift indicator wire to the steering column shift housing. Route the wire on the outside of slotted flange.
16. On models equipped with an automatic transaxle, place the shift lever in **Park (P)** position to make the indicator self-adjust.
17. Connect the shift indicator wire.
18. Install the steering column lower cover.
19. Install the cluster assembly bezel. Secure the bezel with the retaining screws.

➜ The instruments can be serviced after removing the instrument cluster mask/lens. Do not completely remove the cluster assembly if only instrument service or cluster bulb replacement is necessary.

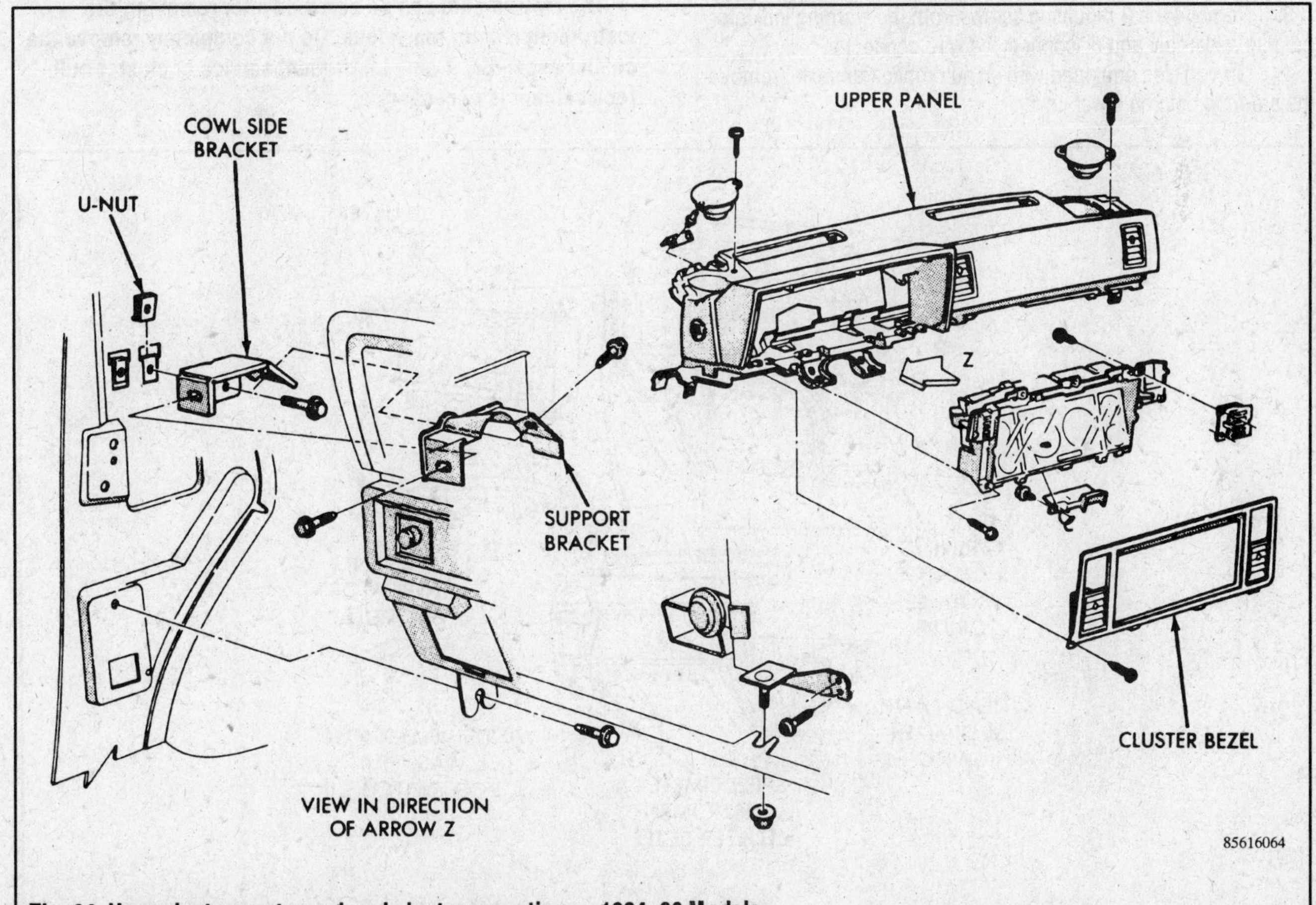

Fig. 64 Upper instrument panel and cluster mounting — 1984-90 Models

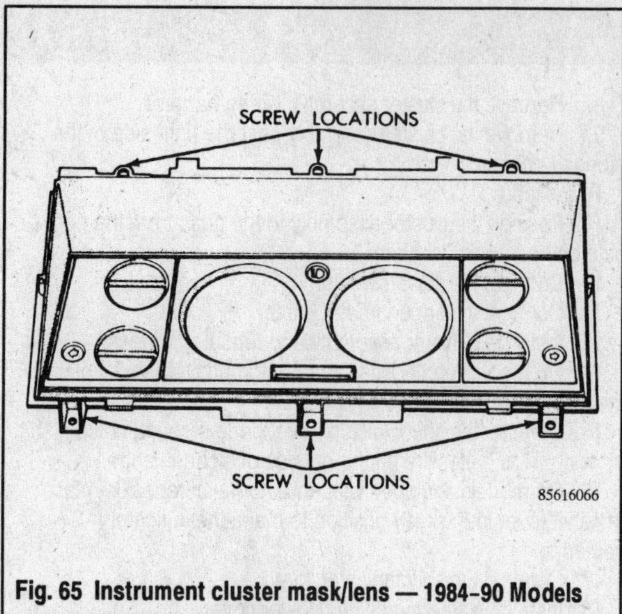

Fig. 65 Instrument cluster mask/lens — 1984-90 Models

1991-95 Models

➧ **See Figures 66, 67 and 68**

1. Disable the air bag system by disconnecting the negative battery cable.
2. Remove the warning indicator grille by prying up with a flat bladed tool.
3. Remove the 3 mounting screws from the warning indicator module assembly and disconnect the wire connector.
4. On vehicles equipped with an automatic transaxle, remove the steering column lower cover.
5. On vehicles equipped with an automatic transaxle, set the parking brake and shift gear selector into low.
6. Remove the cluster assembly bezel mounting screws and remove the cluster bezel.
7. Disconnect the shift indicator wire.
8. Remove the cluster assembly retaining screws.
9. Carefully rotate the cluster and disengage the connector, to access the PRNDL attaching screws.
10. Remove the 2 screws attaching the PRNDL to the cluster.
11. Remove the cluster assembly wiring harness.

To install:

12. Reverse the removal procedure.
13. Connect the cluster wiring.
14. Connect the speedometer cable.
15. Install the cluster assembly and retaining screws.
16. On models equipped with an automatic transaxle, place the selector lever in **Drive (D)** position.
17. Connect the shift indicator wire to the steering column shift housing. Route the wire on the outside of slotted flange.
18. On models equipped with an automatic transaxle, place the shift lever in **Park (P)** position to make the indicator self-adjust.
19. Connect the shift indicator wire.
20. Install the steering column lower cover.
21. Install the cluster assembly bezel. Secure the bezel with the retaining screws.
22. Perform the Air Bag System Check procedures outlined in this section before connecting the negative battery cable.

➥ The instruments can be serviced after removing the instrument cluster mask/lens. Do not completely remove the cluster assembly if only instrument service or cluster bulb replacement is necessary.

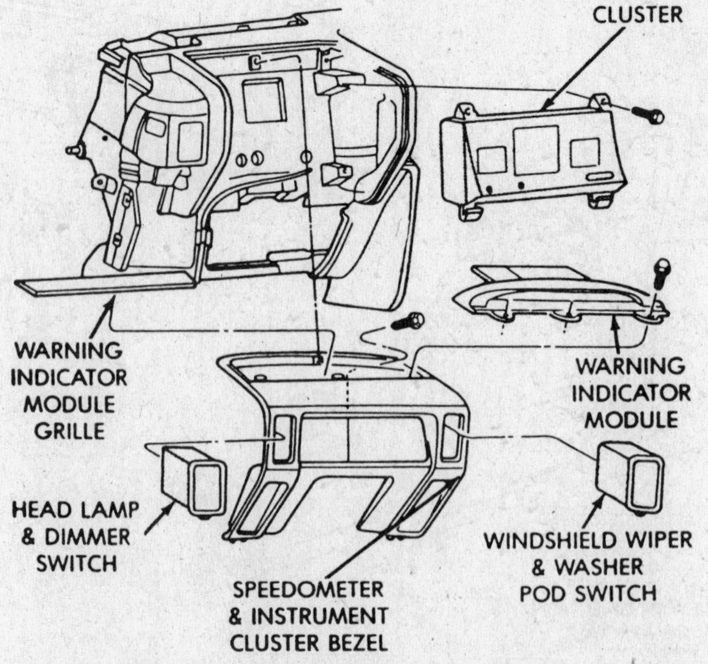

Fig. 66 Instrument panel and cluster mounting — 1991-95 Models

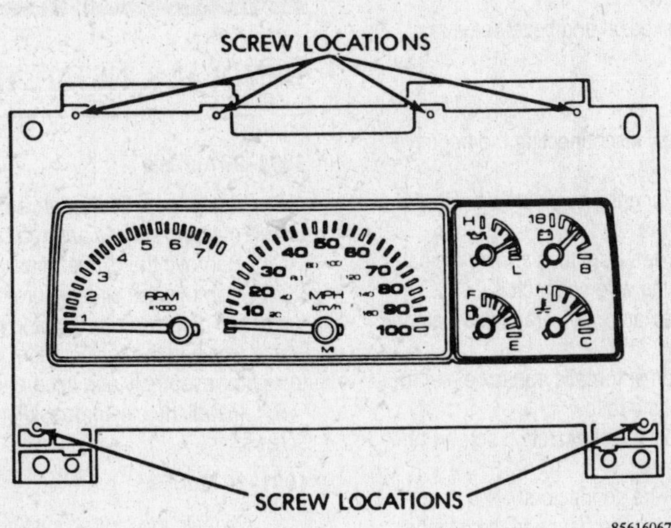

Fig. 67 Instrument cluster mask/lens

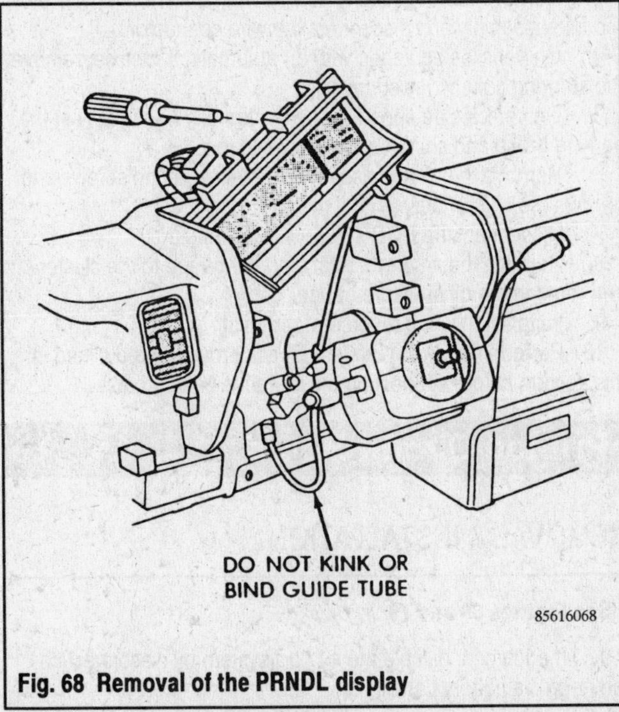

Fig. 68 Removal of the PRNDL display

To install:

4. Position the replacement gauge to the cluster assembly and secure it with attaching screws.
5. Install the cluster mask/lens, bezel and bezel retaining screws.

1991–95 Models

1. Disable the air bag system by disconnecting the negative battery cable.
2. Remove the warning indicator grille by prying up with a flat-bladed tool.
3. Remove the 3 mounting screws from the warning indicator module assembly and disengage the wire connector.
4. On vehicles equipped with an automatic transaxle, remove the steering column lower cover.
5. On vehicles equipped with an automatic transaxle, set the parking brake and shift gear selector into low.
6. Remove the cluster assembly bezel mounting screws and remove the cluster bezel.
7. Disengage the POD switch wire connectors.
8. Remove the 4 screws attaching the gauge to the cluster and remove the fuel gauge.
9. Installation is the reverse of removal.
10. Perform the Air Bag System Check procedures outlined in this section before connecting the negative battery cable.

Fuel Gauge

REMOVAL & INSTALLATION

1984–90 Models

1. Disconnect the negative battery cable. Unfasten the cluster bezel retaining screws and remove the cluster bezel.
2. Remove the cluster mask/lens.
3. Remove the fuel gauge attaching screws to cluster assembly and remove the fuel gauge.

Voltmeter

REMOVAL & INSTALLATION

1984–90 Models

1. Disconnect the negative battery cable. Remove the cluster bezel retaining screws and remove the cluster bezel.
2. Remove the cluster mask/lens.
3. Remove the voltmeter attaching screws to cluster assembly and remove the voltmeter.

4. Position the replacement voltmeter to cluster assembly and secure with the attaching screws.
5. Install the cluster mask/lens, bezel and bezel retaining screws.

1991-95 Models

1. Disable the air bag system by disconnecting the negative battery cable.
2. Remove the warning indicator grille by prying up with a flat-bladed tool.
3. Remove the 3 mounting screws from the warning indicator module assembly and disconnect the wire connector.
4. On vehicles equipped with an automatic transaxle, remove the steering column lower cover.
5. On vehicles equipped with an automatic transaxle, set the parking brake and shift gear selector into low.
6. Remove the cluster assembly bezel mounting screws and remove the cluster bezel.
7. Disengage the POD switch wire connectors.
8. Remove the 4 screws attaching the gauge to the cluster and remove the voltmeter.
9. Installation is the reverse of removal.
10. Perform the Air Bg System Check procedures outlined in this section before connecting the negative battery cable.

Temperature Gauge

REMOVAL & INSTALLATION

1984-90 Models

1. Disconnect the negative battery cable. Remove the cluster bezel retaining screws and remove the cluster bezel.
2. Remove the cluster mask/lens.
3. Remove the temperature/oil pressure gauge attaching screws to cluster assembly and remove the temperature gauge.
4. Position the replacement temperature/oil pressure gauge to cluster assembly and secure with the attaching screws.
5. Install the cluster mask/lens, bezel and bezel retaining screws.

1991-95 Models

1. Disable the air bag system by disconnecting the negative battery cable.
2. Remove the warning indicator grille by prying up with a flat-bladed tool.
3. Remove the 3 mounting screws from the warning indicator module assembly and disconnect the wire connector.
4. On vehicles equipped with an automatic transaxle, remove the steering column lower cover.
5. On vehicles equipped with an automatic transaxle, set the parking brake and shift gear selector into low.
6. Remove the cluster assembly bezel mounting screws and remove the cluster bezel.
7. Disengage the POD switch wire connectors.
8. Remove the 4 screws attaching the gauge to the cluster and remove the temperature gauge.
9. Installation is the reverse of removal.
10. Perform the Air Bg System Check procedures outlined in this section before connecting the negative battery cable.

Oil Pressure Gauge

REMOVAL & INSTALLATION

1984-90 Models

1. Disconnect the negative battery cable. Remove the cluster bezel retaining screws and remove the cluster bezel.
2. Remove the cluster mask/lens.
3. Remove the oil pressure/temperature gauge attaching screws to cluster assembly and remove the temperature gauge.
4. Position the replacement oil pressure/temperature gauge to cluster assembly and secure with the attaching screws.
5. Install the cluster mask/lens, bezel and bezel retaining screws.

1991-95 Models

1. Disable the air bag system by disconnecting the negative battery cable.
2. Remove the warning indicator grille by prying up with a flat-bladed tool.
3. Remove the 3 mounting screws from the warning indicator module assembly and disconnect the wire connector.
4. On vehicles equipped with an automatic transaxle, remove the steering column lower cover.
5. On vehicles equipped with an automatic transaxle, set the parking brake and shift gear selector into low.
6. Remove the cluster assembly bezel mounting screws and remove the cluster bezel.
7. Disconnect the POD switch wire connectors.
8. Remove the 4 screws attaching the gauge to the cluster and remove the oil pressure gauge.
9. Installation is the reverse of removal.
10. Perform the Air Bg System Check procedures outlined in this section before connecting the negative battery cable.

Printed Circuit Board

REMOVAL & INSTALLATION

➧ **See Figures 69 and 70**

1. If equipped, disable the air bag system by disconnecting the negative battery cable.

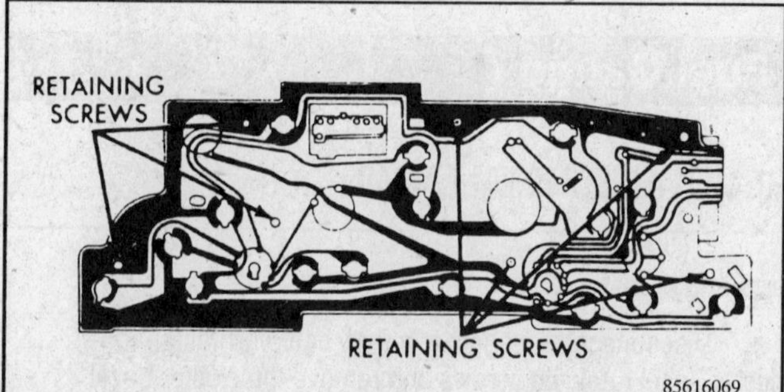

Fig. 69 Printed circuit board retaining screws — 1984-90 models

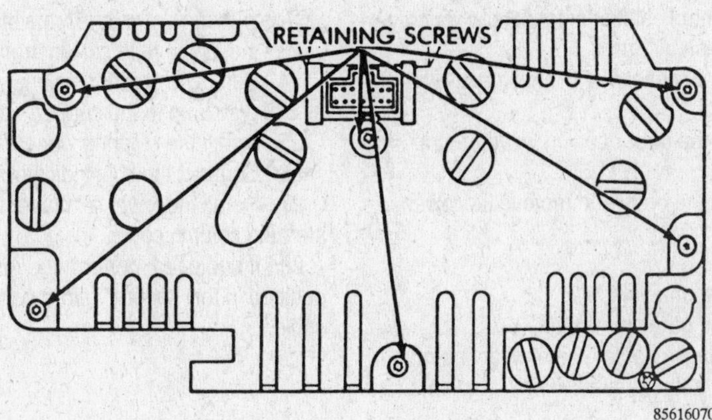

Fig. 70 Printed circuit board retaining screws — 1991-95 models

2. Remove the instrument cluster from the instrument panel.
3. Remove the circuit board retaining screws.
4. Remove the lamp sockets, by twisting them out.
5. Carefully remove the circuit board.

To install:

6. Install the new circuit board in position and install the lamp sockets.
7. If equipped, perform the Air Bag System Check procedures outlined in this section before connecting the negative battery cable.

Cluster Lamp Bulbs

REMOVAL & INSTALLATION

1. If equipped, disable the air bag system by disconnecting the negative battery cable.
2. Unfasten the cluster bezel retaining screws and remove the cluster bezel.
3. Remove the cluster mask/lens.
4. Remove the gauge assembly in front of blown bulbs and replace the bulbs.

To install:

5. Install the gauge to the cluster assembly.
6. Install the cluster mask/lens, bezel and bezel retaining screws.
7. If equipped, perform the Air Bag System Check procedures outlined in this section before connecting the negative battery cable.

Cluster Lamp Sockets

REMOVAL & INSTALLATION

All cluster lamp sockets are twist out sockets and are removed from the rear of the instrument cluster. Refer to the instrument cluster removal and installation procedure earlier in this section.

Lower Instrument Panel

REMOVAL & INSTALLATION

1984-90 Models

➧ See Figure 71

✱✱CAUTION

Before servicing the lower instrument panel, chock the wheels. Servicing the steering column may cause an automatic transaxle to come out of the Park (P) position. Always release the parking brake before the release cable is disconnected. Disconnecting the parking brake cable without releasing the parking brake may cause personal injury.

1. If equipped, disable the air bag system by disconnecting the negative battery cable.
2. Block the vehicle wheels and release the parking brake. Disconnect the negative battery cable.
3. Remove the steering column lower left cover.
4. Remove the side cowl and the sill molding.
5. Remove the instrument panel silencer and reinforcement.
6. Loosen the bolt in the side cowl, but do not remove the bolt.
7. On vehicles equipped with an automatic transaxle, place the gear selector into the **Neutral (N)** position and disconnect the shift indicator cable.
8. Remove the steering wheel.
9. Remove the (5) nuts securing the steering column to the support bracket.
10. Lower the steering column. Use a cover to protect the steering column and the front seat.
11. Remove the right side instrument panel trim molding.
12. Remove the (9) screws securing the lower panel to the upper panel and mid-reinforcement.

13. Lower the instrument panel approximately six inches.
14. Disconnect the park brake release cable, heater attachment or air conditioning control cables, antenna and wiring connectors from the radio and fresh air ducts.
15. Disengage the electrical connections and label them with tape for identification.
16. Pry the A-pillar garnish off the door opening weather-strip at the panel bolt.
17. Pull the weather-strip from the body and remove the lower panel from the vehicle.

To install:

18. Position the lower panel into the vehicle.
19. Install the weather-strip and garnish molding.
20. Connect the park brake release cable, heater attachment or air conditioning control cables, antenna and wiring connectors to the radio and fresh air ducts.
21. Engage all electrical connections.
22. Secure the lower instrument panel to upper panel and mid-reinforcement with (9) retaining screws.
23. Install the right side instrument panel trim molding.
24. Raise the steering column and install the (5) nuts securing steering column to the support bracket.
25. Install the steering wheel.
26. Connect the shift indicator cable.
27. Install the lower reinforcement, silencer and the lower left steering column cover.
28. If equipped, perform the Air bag System Check procedures outlined in this section before connecting the negative battery cable.

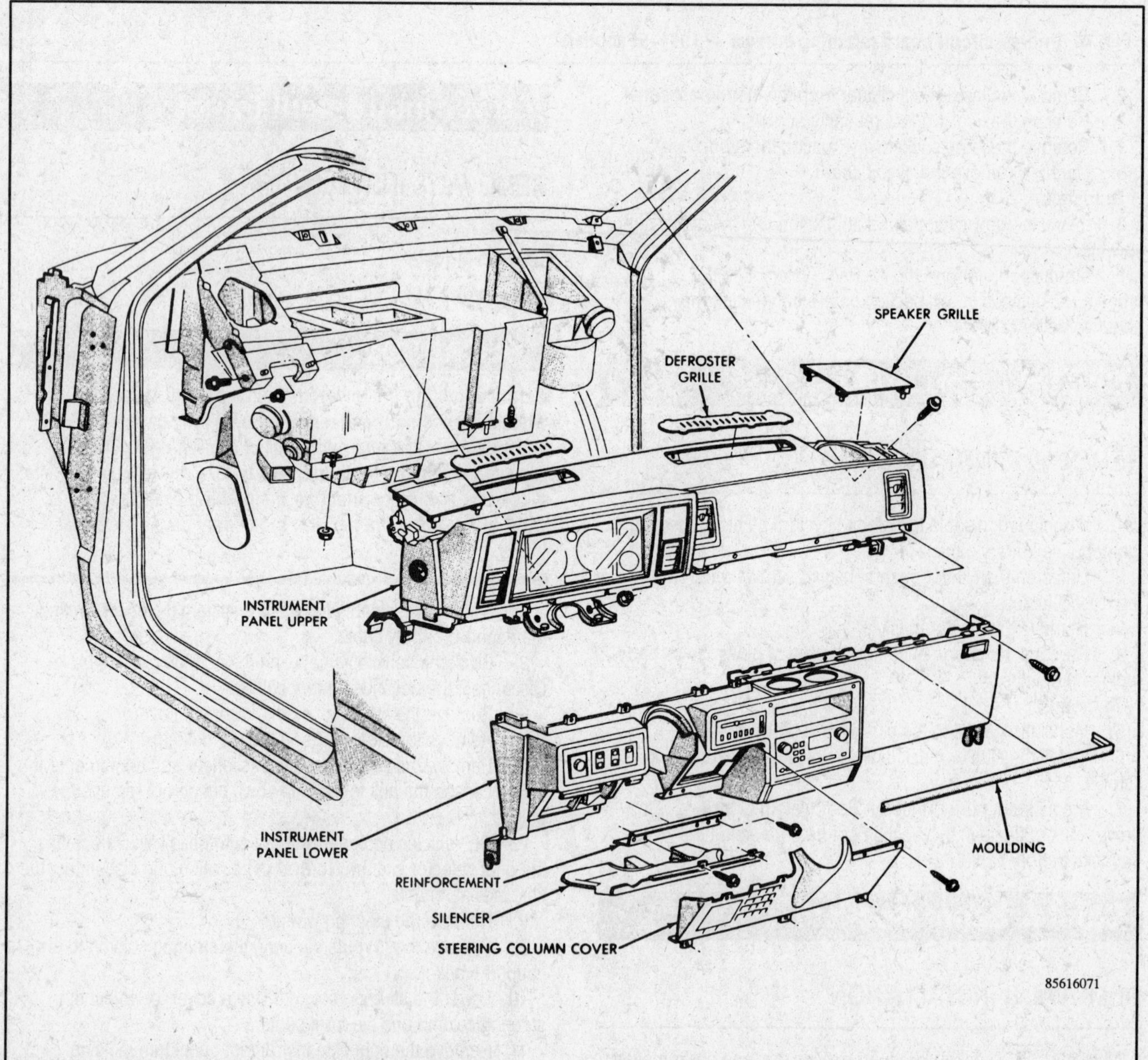

Fig. 71 Instrument panel assembly — 1984–90 models

Upper Instrument Panel

REMOVAL & INSTALLATION

➧ See Figure 71

1984–90 Models

1. If equipped, disable the air bag system by disconnecting the negative battery cable.
2. Separate the lower instrument panel from the upper half (see Steps 1 through 12 of the Lower Instrument Panel procedure).
3. Disconnect the speedometer cable from the engine compartment.
4. Remove (2) nuts at the steering column floating bracket.
5. Disconnect the gear shift selector indicator wire.
6. Disengage the electrical connector at the radio speakers.
7. Remove the radio speaker and defroster grilles.
8. Remove the (2) mounting screws from each side cowl bracket.
9. Remove the (4) upper panel attaching screws from the defroster duct slots and the (2) screws next to the radio speakers.
10. Pull the panel and disconnect the speedometer cable from the speedometer.
11. Remove upper instrument panel from vehicle.

To install:

12. Position the upper instrument panel into the vehicle.
13. Connect the speedometer cable.
14. Install the (6) upper panel attaching screws.
15. Install the cowl bracket retaining screws.
16. Install the radio speaker and defroster grilles.
17. Connect the radio speaker wiring.
18. Connect the gear shift selector indicator wire.
19. Install the retaining nuts at the steering column floating bracket.
20. Connect the speedometer cable in the engine compartment.
21. Install the lower panel to the upper.
22. If equipped, perform the Air bag System Check procedures outlined in this section before connecting the negative battery cable.

Instrument Panel Assembly

REMOVAL & INSTALLATION

1991 Models

➧ See Figures 72 and 73

****CAUTION**

Before servicing the lower instrument panel, chock the wheels. Servicing the steering column may cause an automatic transaxle to come out of the Park (P) position. Always release the parking brake before the release cable is disconnected. Disconnecting the parking brake cable without releasing the parking brake may cause personal injury.

1. Block the vehicle wheels and release the parking brake. Disconnect the negative battery cable.
2. Remove the steering column lower left cover.
3. Disconnect the PRNDL display at the column.
4. Remove the steering column.
5. Remove the lower right instrument panel silencer.
6. Remove the forward console if necessary.
7. Remove the instrument panel speaker grilles.
8. Remove the A-pillar intermediate and sill scuff garnish mouldings.
9. Unfasten the hood release mechanism from the side cowl.
10. Unfasten the parking brake handle bracket.
11. Disconnect the parking brake light switch, parking brake switch and bulk head wiring connectors.
12. Under the hood disconnect the ABS connector and resistor block. Unseat the grommet at the dash panel and feed the wiring back into the passenger compartment.
13. Remove the 2 nuts securing the instrument panel at the steering column support brace.
14. Loosen the instrument panel roll up bolts.
15. Remove the screws securing the instrument panel at the left cowl side ramp bracket.
16. Remove the 6 screws securing the instrument panel at the fence line.
17. Lift upward on the instrument panel to clear the roll up ramp. Roll the instrument panel back and hang it from the short position of the roll up hook.
18. With the instrument panel hanging in this position, disconnect the left and right side body wiring connections, vacuum lines and cables.
19. Remove the instrument panel from the vehicle.
20. To install, reverse the removal steps.

1992–95 Models

➧ See Figures 72, 73 and 74

****CAUTION**

Before servicing the lower instrument panel, chock the wheels. Servicing the steering column may cause an automatic transaxle to come out of the Park (P) position. Always release the parking brake before the release cable is disconnected. Disconnecting the parking brake cable without releasing the parking brake may cause personal injury.

1. Disable the air bag system by disconnecting the negative battery cable.
2. Block the vehicle wheels and release the parking brake.
3. Disconnect the negative battery cable.
4. Remove the instrument panel cluster bezel.
5. Remove the lower right instrument panel.
6. Remove the lower left instrument panel silencer.
7. Remove the steering column lower left cover.
8. Remove the premium console or module cover.
9. Remove the lower left reinforcement.
10. Remove the floor braces.
11. Remove the steering column.
12. Remove the lower right instrument panel silencer.
13. Remove the premium console or module cover.
14. Remove the A-pillar intermediate and sill scuff garnish mouldings.

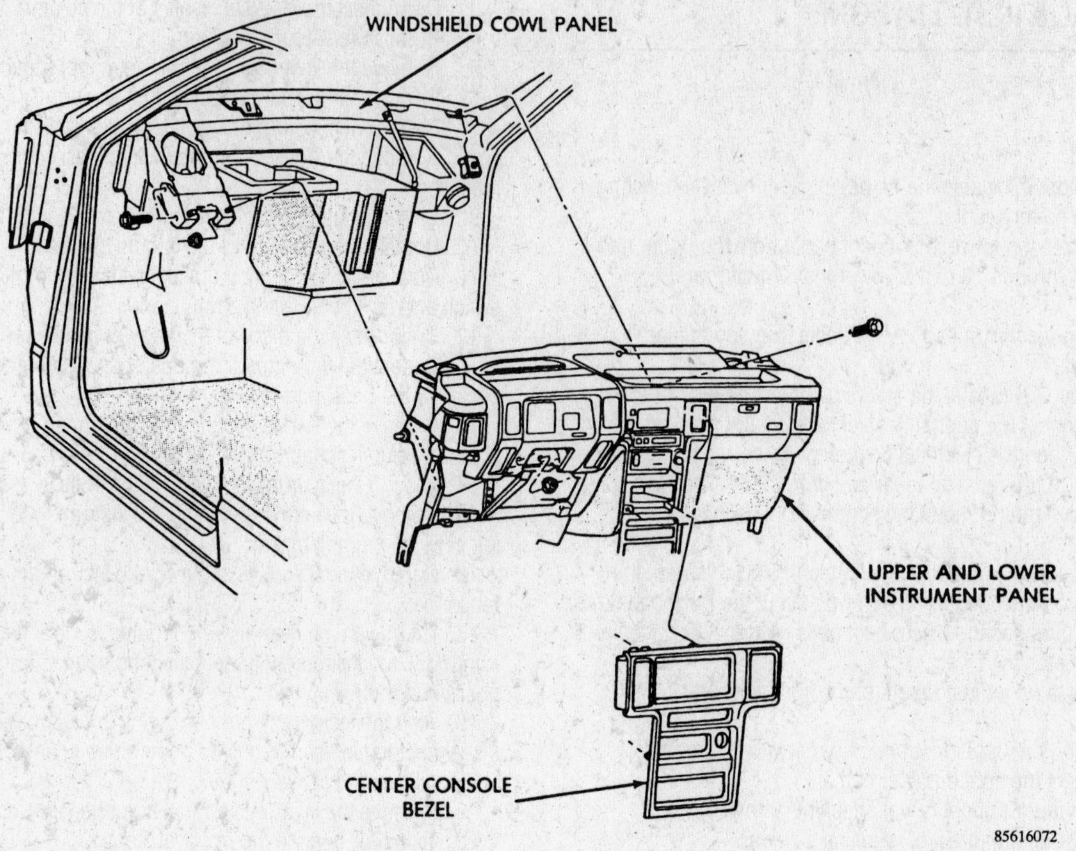

WINDSHIELD COWL PANEL

UPPER AND LOWER INSTRUMENT PANEL

CENTER CONSOLE BEZEL

85616072

Fig. 72 Instrument panel assembly — 1991-93 models

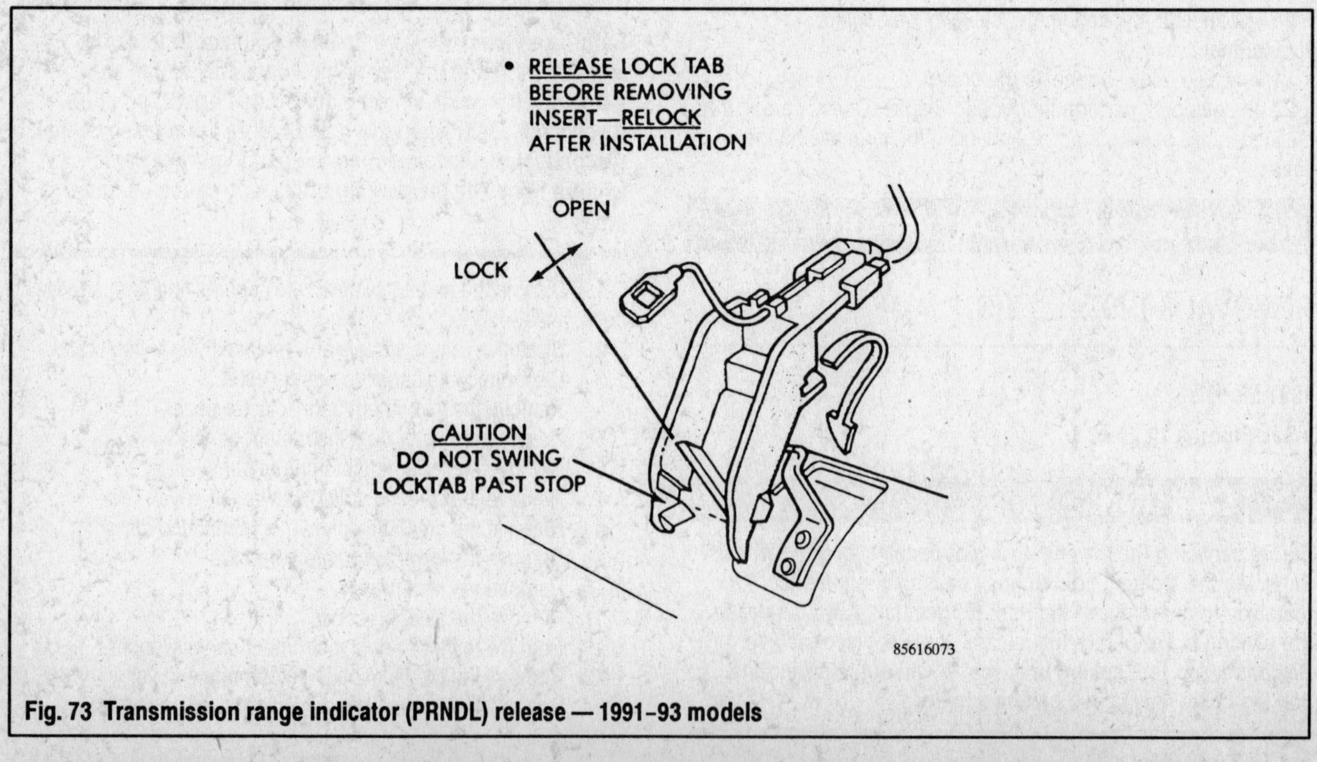

Fig. 73 Transmission range indicator (PRNDL) release — 1991-93 models

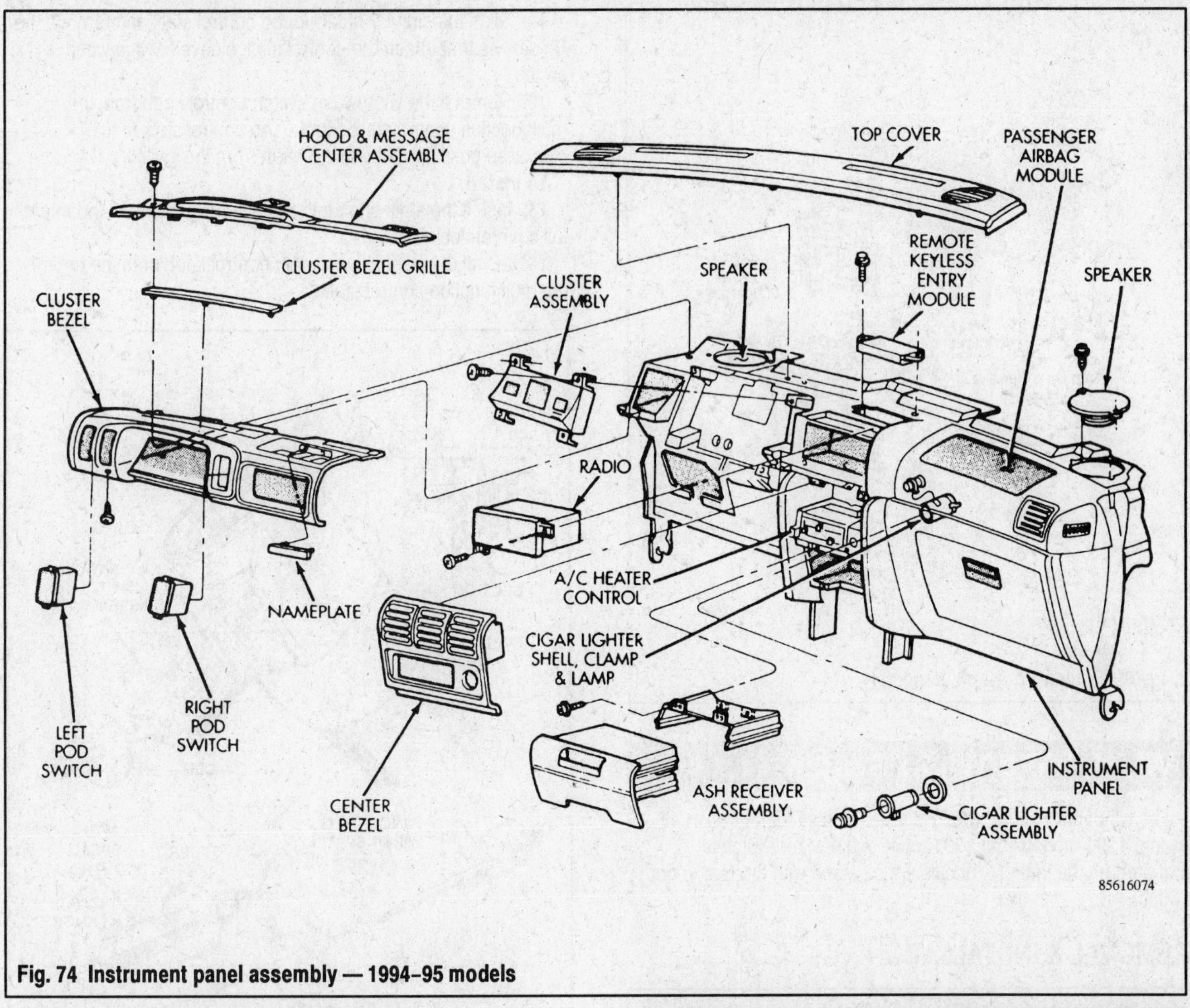

Fig. 74 Instrument panel assembly — 1994-95 models

15. Unfasten the hood release mechanism from the side cowl.
16. Unfasten the parking brake handle bracket.
17. Disengage the parking brake light switch, parking brake switch and bulk head wiring connectors.
18. Under the hood disengage the ABS connector and resistor block. Unseat the grommet at the dash panel and feed the wiring back into the passenger compartment.
19. Remove the 2 nuts securing the instrument panel at the steering column support brace.
20. Loosen the instrument panel roll-up bolts.
21. Remove the screws securing the instrument panel at the left cowl side ramp bracket.
22. Remove the 6 screws securing the instrument panel at the fence line.
23. Lift upward on the instrument panel to clear the roll-up ramp. Roll the instrument panel back and hang it from the short position of the roll-up hook.
24. With the instrument panel hanging in this position, disconnect the left and right side body wiring connections, vacuum lines and cables.
25. Remove the instrument panel from the vehicle.
26. To install, reverse the above removal steps.
27. Perform the Air Bag System Check procedures outlined in this section before connecting the negative battery cable.

Forward Console

REMOVAL & INSTALLATION

➧ See Figure 75

1. Remove the cigarette lighter and ash receiver.
2. Remove the retaining screws securing the forward console to the upper mounting bracket.
3. Remove the retaining screws securing the forward console to the lower bracket.
4. Pull the console rearward and disengage the cigarette lighter and illumination electrical wiring connectors.
5. Remove the forward console from vehicle.

To install:

6. Position the forward console into the vehicle.
7. Engage the cigarette lighter and illumination wiring connectors.
8. Install the console lower bracket retaining screws.
9. Install the console upper bracket retaining screws.
10. Install the cigarette lighter and ash receiver.

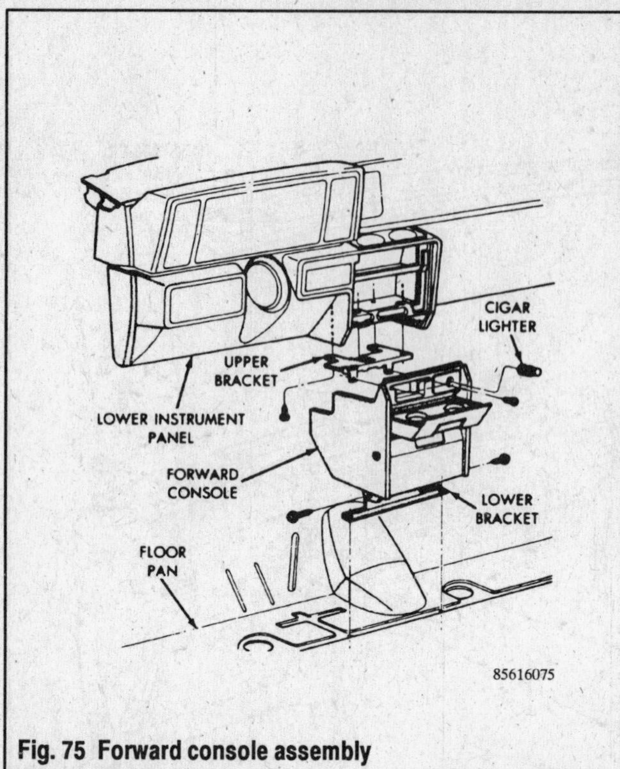

Fig. 75 Forward console assembly

Windshield Wiper Switch

The windshield wiper switch is a stalk mounted control on all except 1991 models. On 1991 models, the wiper switch is mounted on the instrument cluster pod along with the rear wiper switch.

REMOVAL & INSTALLATION

1984–90 Models

STANDARD STEERING COLUMN

➧ See Figures 76 and 77

1. Disconnect the negative battery cable.
2. Remove the steering wheel horn pad assembly.
3. Remove the lower steering column cover, silencer and reinforcement.
4. Remove the wiper switch wiring harness from the steering column retainer.
5. Remove the wash/wipe switch cover. Rotate the cover upward.
6. Disengage the wipe/wash seven terminal electrical connector.
7. Disengage the intermittent the wipe switch electrical connector or speed control electrical connector, if equipped.
8. Unlock the steering column and turn the wheel so that the access hole provided in the wheel base is in the 9 o'clock position.
9. Reach through the access hole using a small screwdriver and loosen the turn signal lever mounting screw.
10. Remove the wipe/wash switch assembly the from steering column.
11. Slide the circular hider up the control stalk and remove the (2) screws that attach the control stalk sleeve to wipe/wash switch.
12. Remove the wipe/wash switch control knob from the multifunction control stalk. Rotate the control stalk to full clockwise position and pull the shaft from the switch.

To install:

13. Install the stalk shaft into the wash/wipe switch and rotate full counterclockwise.
14. Install the wash/wipe switch control knob onto the end of the multifunction control stalk.

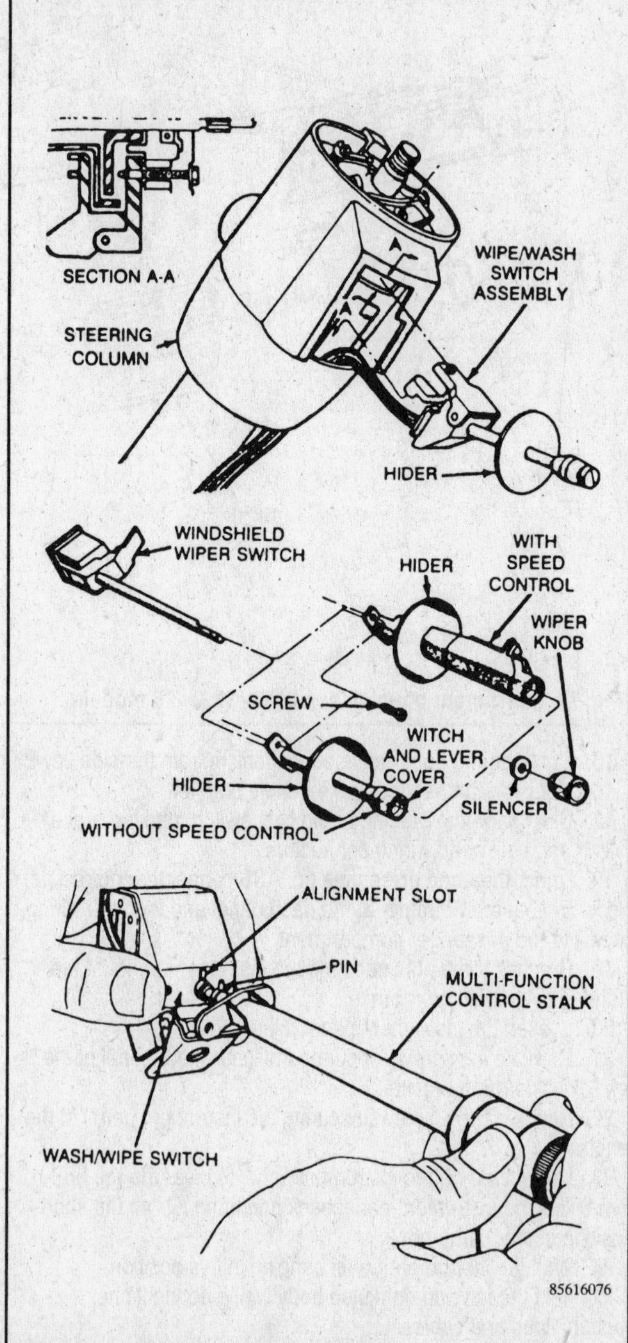

Fig. 76 Removing the wiper switch on the standard steering column — 1984–90 models

15. Install (2) retaining screws that secure the wipe/wash switch to the control stalk sleeve.

16. Install the wipe/wash switch assembly to the steering column.

17. Install and tighten the turn signal lever screw (through the access hole).

18. Engage the wipe/wash seven terminal electrical connector.

19. Engage the intermittent wipe switch electrical connector or speed control electrical connector, if equipped.

20. Install the wash/wipe switch cover.

21. Secure the wiring harness into the steering column retainer.

22. Install the reinforcement, silencer and lower steering column cover.

23. Install the steering wheel horn pad assembly.

24. Connect the negative batter cable.

TILT STEERING COLUMN

See Figure 77

1. Disconnect the negative battery cable.

2. Remove the horn cover pad from the steering wheel. Remove steering column cover. Remove the steering wheel nut.

3. Remove the steering wheel using puller C-3428B, or equivalent.

4. Carefully remove the plastic cover from the locking plate. Install locking plate depressing tool C-4156 or equivalent onto the steering shaft. Depress the locking plate and remove the retaining ring from the mounting groove using a small screwdriver. To avoid difficulty when removing the retaining ring, the full load of the upper bearing spring should not be relieved. Remove the locking plate, canceling cam, and upper bearing spring.

5. Remove the switch stalk actuator screw and arm.

6. Remove the hazard warning knob.

7. Disengage the wipe/wash seven terminal electrical connector.

8. Disengage the intermittent wipe switch electrical connector or speed control electrical connector, if equipped.

9. Remove the turn signal switch (3) retaining screws.

10. Tape the connectors at end of the wiring to prevent snagging when removing. Place the shift bowl in low (1st) position. Remove the switch and wiring.

11. Remove the ignition key lamp located next to the hazard warning knob.

12. Insert a thin screwdriver into the lock release slot next to the lock cylinder mounting and depress the spring latch at the bottom of the slot. Remove the lock cylinder.

13. Insert a straightened paper clip or similar piece of wire with a hook bent on one end into the exposed loop of the wedge spring of key buzzer switch. Pull on the clip to remove both spring and switch.

If the wedge spring is dropped, it could fall into steering column, requiring complete disassembly of the column.

14. Remove the column housing cover (3) screws and remove the housing cover.

15. Use a punch, and tap the wiper switch pivot pin from the lock housing. Use tape to hold the dimmer switch rod in place.

16. Remove the wipe/wash switch assembly.

17. Slide the circular hider up the control stalk and remove the (2) screws that attach the control stalk sleeve to the wipe/wash switch.

18. Remove the wipe/wash switch control knob from the multifunction control stalk. Rotate the control stalk to full clockwise position and pull the shaft from the switch.

To install:

19. Install the stalk shaft into the wash/wipe switch and rotate full counterclockwise.

20. Install the wash/wipe switch control knob on the end of the multifunction control stalk.

21. Install the (2) retaining screws that secure the wipe/wash switch to the control stalk sleeve.

22. Install the wipe/wash switch assembly to the steering column.

23. Install the wiper switch pivot pin.

24. Install the housing cover and secure with retaining screws.

25. Install the lock cylinder.

26. Assemble the wedge spring to key buzzer and install the key buzzer switch.

27. Install the ignition key lamp.

28. With the shift bowl in low (1st) position, install the turn signal switch and secure with retaining screws.

29. Engage the wipe/wash seven terminal electrical connector.

30. Engage the intermittent wipe switch electrical connector or speed control electrical connector, if equipped.

31. Secure the wiring harness in retainer.

32. Install the hazard warning knob.

33. Install the switch stalk actuator screw and arm.

34. Install the locking plate, canceling cam, and upper bearing spring. Install the locking plate. Depress the locking plate with tool C-4156, or equivalent, and install the retaining ring in groove of steering shaft. Install the plastic cover on locking plate.

35. Install the reinforcement, silencer and lower steering column cover.

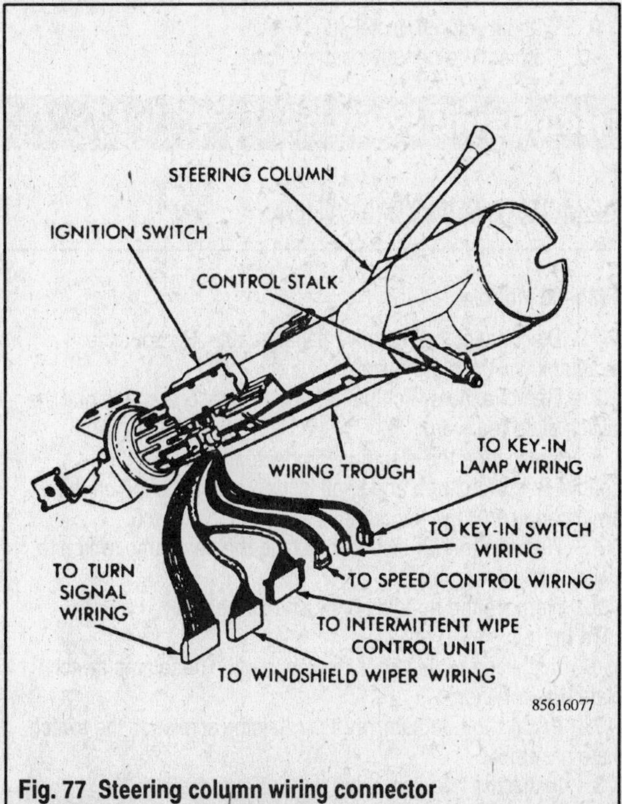

Fig. 77 Steering column wiring connector identification — 1984–90 models

36. Install the steering wheel and steering shaft nut.
37. Install the horn contact, horn pad and install the horn pad retaining screws.
38. Connect the negative battery cable.

1991 Models

POD MOUNTED

1. Disconnect the negative battery cable.
2. Remove the cluster bezel retaining screws.
3. Tilt the steering column down, if equipped.
4. Pull the cluster bezel out enough to gain access to the switch retaining tabs.
5. Release the tabs and pull the switch from the cluster.

To install:

6. Install the switch in position and seat it firmly. Install the cluster bezel retaining screws.
7. Connect the negative battery cable.

1992–95 Models

1. Disconnect the negative battery cable.
2. With tilt column, remove the tilt lever.
3. Remove both upper and lower steering column covers.
4. Remove the multi-function switch tamper proof mounting screws.
5. Pull the switch away from the column and loosen the connector screw. The screw will remain in the connector.
6. Remove the wiring connector from the multi-function switch.

To install:

7. Install the wiring connector to the switch and tighten the connector retaining screw to 17 inch lbs. (2 Nm).
8. Mount the multi-function switch to the column and tighten the retaining screws to 17 inch lbs. (2 Nm).
9. With tilt column, install the tilt lever.
10. Connect the negative battery cable.

Headlamp Switch

REMOVAL & INSTALLATION

1984–90 Models

1. Disconnect the negative battery cable. Remove the headlamp switch plate bezel.
2. Remove the switch plate (4) retaining screws and pull the switch plate rearward.
3. Disengage the electrical connectors. Remove the headlamp switch knob and shaft by depressing button on the switch body. Pull the knob and shaft out of the switch.
4. Remove the (2) screws retaining the headlamp switch to switch plate assembly.
5. Remove the headlamp switch retainer.

To install:

6. Install the replacement switch into the headlamp switch plate with retainer.
7. Install the headlamp switch retaining screws to the switch plate assembly.
8. Install the headlamp switch knob and shaft.
9. Engage the electrical connectors.
10. Secure the headlamp switch plate with (4) attaching screws.
11. Install the headlamp switch plate bezel.

1991 Models

On the 1991 models, the headlight switch is removed in the same manner as the windshield wiper switch. Refer to the windshield wiper switch removal procedure on these models.

1992–95 Models

On these models, the left POD switch consists of the headlamp, parking lamp and hazard switches.

1. To remove the left POD switch, place a tool fabricated from a metal rod, shown in the illustration, in the hole right of the switch in the cluster bezel below the POD switch.
2. Move the tool to the lower tab and depress. Pull the switch out to free the lower tab.
3. Move the tool upward along the right side of the switch to place on the top tab. Pull down on the tab and pull the switch out of the bezel.
4. Disengage the wire connector.

To install:

5. Engage the wire connector and push the switch into position until the tab locks in place.

Headlamp Dimmer Switch

REMOVAL & INSTALLATION

➜ On 1991–95 models, the headlight dimmer switch is part of the turn signal, wiper (multi-function switch). Refer to the wiper switch removal and installation procedure outlined earlier in this Section

1984–90 Models

1. Remove the lower left steering column cover.
2. Tape the actuator control rod to prevent the rod from falling out.
3. Remove the dimmer switch retaining screws.
4. Unfasten the switch electrical connector, then remove the switch.

To install:

5. Install a new switch, then attach the electrical connector.
6. Position the actuator control rod into the dimmer switch and secure the switch onto the steering column.
7. Remove the tape from the actuator control rod.
8. Install the lower left steering column cover.

ADJUSTMENT

1984–90 Models

1. Loosen the dimmer switch retaining screws.
2. Insert a 24mm diameter drill bit or pin in the adjusting pin hole. Push the switch lightly against the control rod to remove free play. Tighten the switch retaining screws while maintaining light pressure on the dimmer switch.
3. Remove the drill bit or pin.

LIGHTING

Headlights

REMOVAL & INSTALLATION

Sealed Beam

➧ See Figure 78

1. Remove the headlight bezel retaining screws and remove the bezel.
2. Remove the headlamp retaining ring screws and remove the retaining ring. Do not disturb the headlamp adjusting crews.
3. Pull the sealed beam forward, then unfasten the electrical connector.

To install:

4. Install the replacement beam and connect the electrical connector.
5. Install the retaining ring.
6. Install the headlight bezel.

Aerodynamic Headlamp

➧ See Figures 79, 80, 81, 82, 83, 84, 85, 86, 87 and 88

➥ DO NOT handle elements with your bare hands, always handle with a clean cloth. Oil from your hands will cause the element to fail.

1. From the engine compartment, remove the three wire connector behind the headlamp assembly.
2. Rotate the bulb retaining ring counterclockwise and remove the retaining ring and lamp bulb.

To install:

3. Install the replacement bulb and retaining ring assembly. Rotate the ring clockwise.
4. Attach the three wire connector.

85616081

Fig. 79 Removing the headlamp assembly bezel attaching screws — 1987 Voyager shown

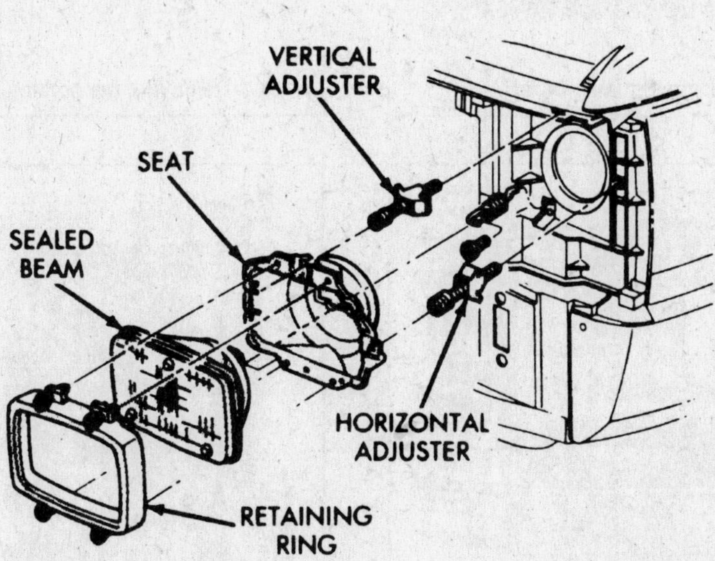

Fig. 78 Sealed beam replacement

85616082

Fig. 80 Removing the headlamp assembly bezel attaching screws

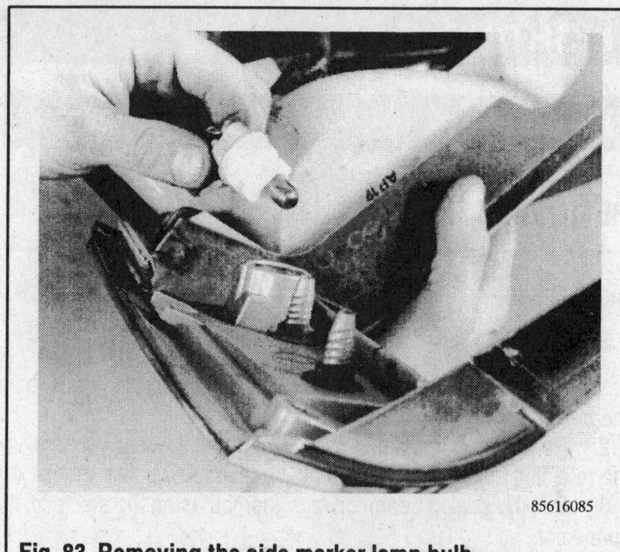

85616085

Fig. 83 Removing the side marker lamp bulb

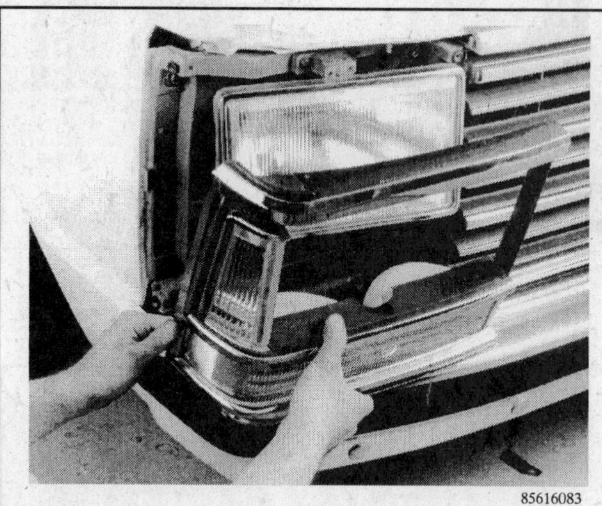

85616083

Fig. 81 Removing the headlamp retaining bezel

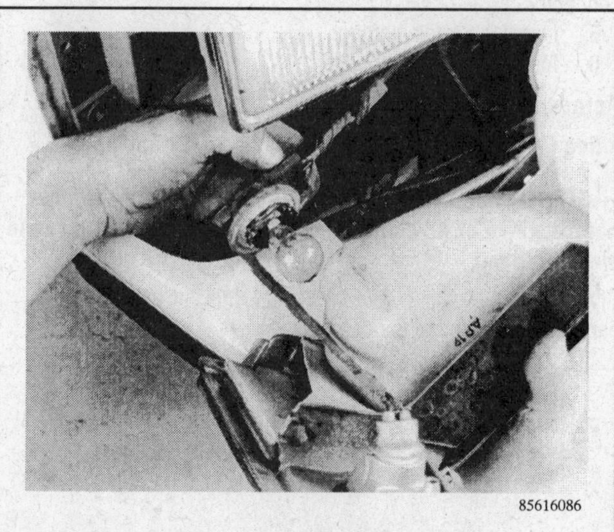

85616086

Fig. 84 Removing the parking lamp bulb

85616084

Fig. 82 Removing the headlamp retaining bezel

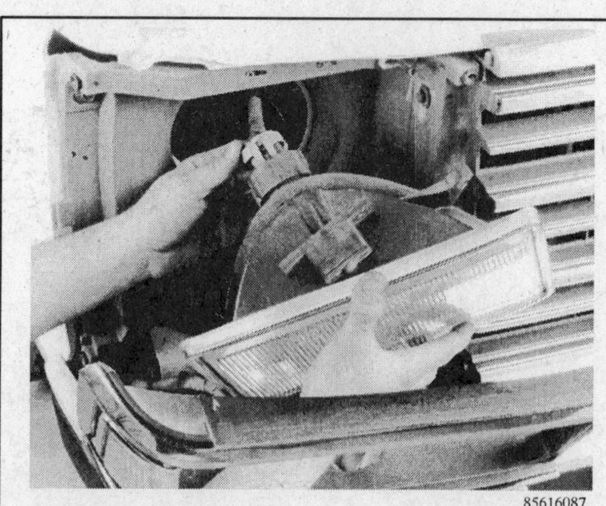

85616087

Fig. 85 Disconnecting the wire connector from the back of the headlamp assembly

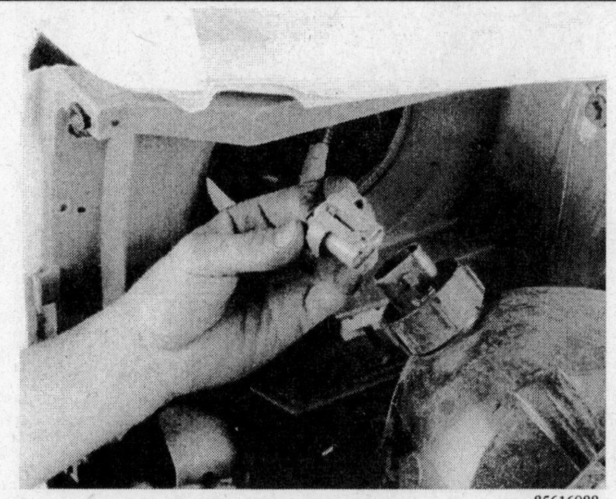

85616088

Fig. 86 Removing the wire connector from the back of the headlamp assembly

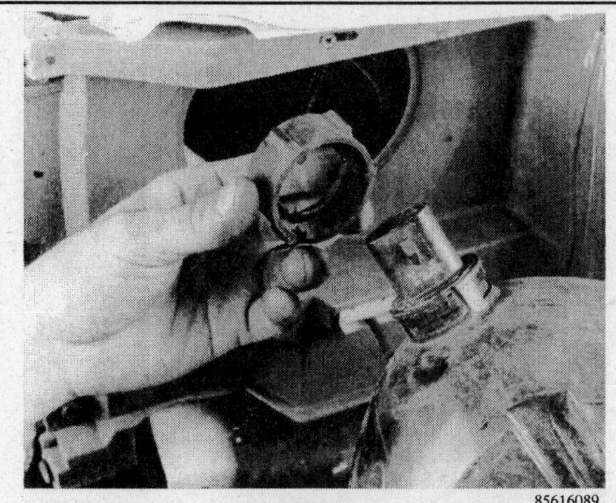

85616089

Fig. 87 Rotate counterclockwise and remove the ring from the back of the headlamp assembly

85616090

Fig. 88 Removing the bulb from the back of the headlamp assembly

Signal and Marker Lights

REMOVAL & INSTALLATION

Front Park, Turn Signal and Side Marker

➧ See Figures 81, 82, 83 and 84

1. Remove the headlamp bezel retaining screws and remove the bezel.
2. Twist the bulb from the lamp socket.

To install:

3. Install the replacement bulb and twist into position.
4. Install the headlamp bezel and retaining screws.

Rear Tail, Stop, Turn Signal, Back Up, Side Marker and License Lamps

➧ See Figures 89, 90, 91, 92, 93 and 94

1. To replace the bulb, remove (4) attaching screws.

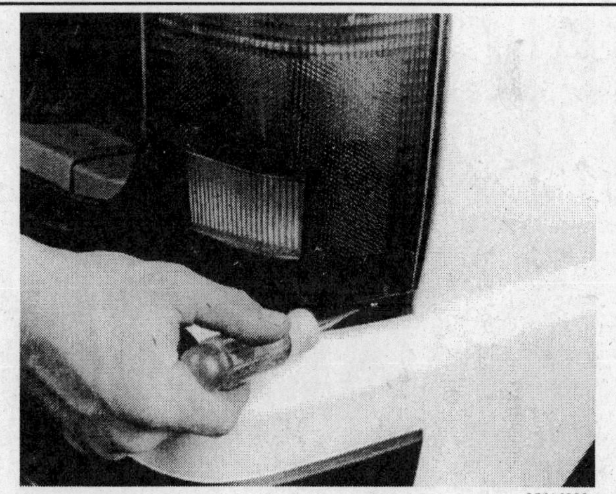

85616093

Fig. 89 Removing the rear tail lamp assembly lower retaining screw

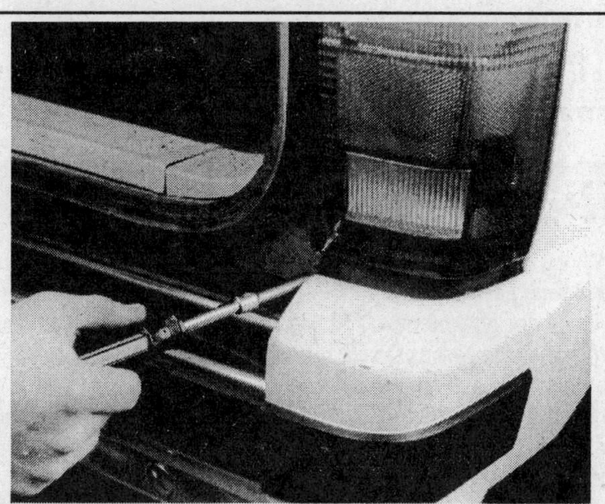

85616094

Fig. 90 Removing the rear tail lamp assembly lower retaining screw

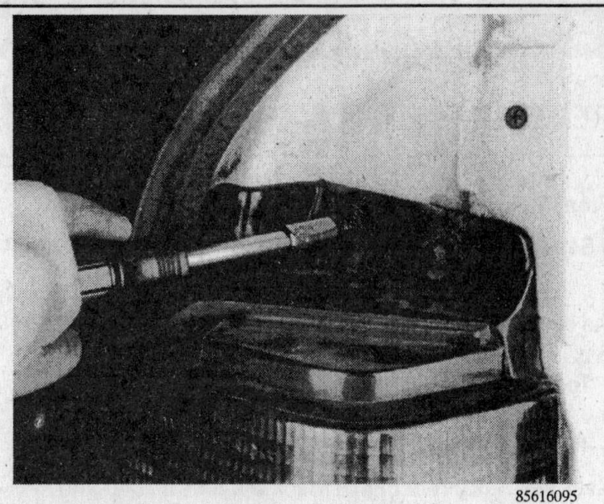

Fig. 91 Removing the rear tail lamp assembly upper retaining screw

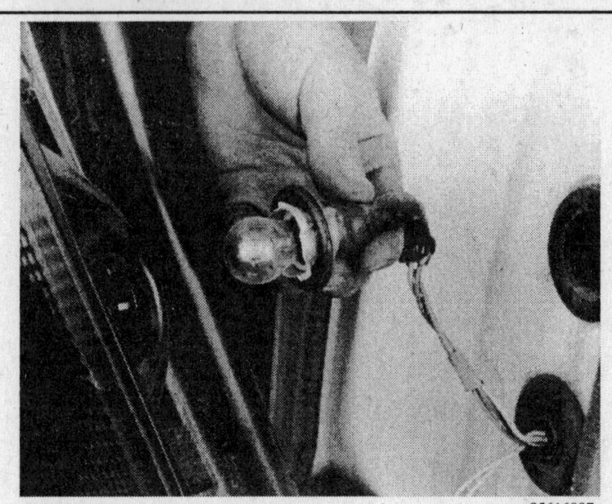

Fig. 93 Removing the rear tail lamp bulb and socket assembly

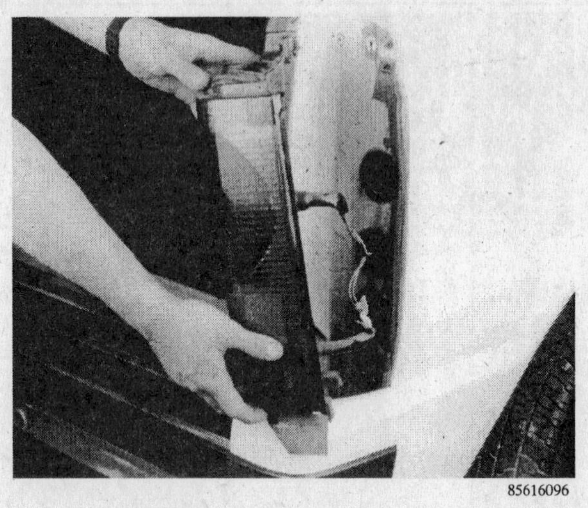

Fig. 92 Removing the rear tail lamp assembly

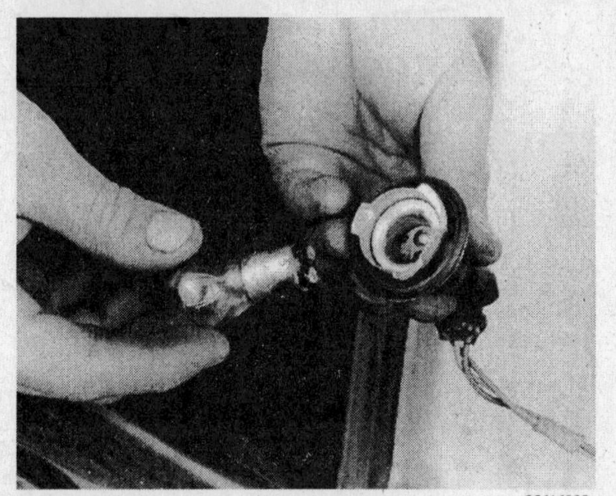

Fig. 94 The rear tail lamp bulb removed from the socket

2. Pull out the lamp assembly. Twist the socket from the lamp and replace the bulb.

To install:

3. Install the replacement bulb and twist the socket into the lamp assembly.
4. Position the lamp assembly in place and secure with (4) attaching screws.

TRAILER WIRING

Wiring the truck for towing is fairly easy. There are a number of good wiring kits available and these should be used, rather than trying to design your own. All trailers will need brake lights and turn signals as well as tail lights and side marker lights. Most states require extra marker lights for overly wide trailers. Also, most states have recently required back-up lights for trailers, and most trailer manufacturers have been building trailers with back-up lights for several years.

Additionally, some Class I, most Class II and just about all Class III trailers will have electric brakes.

Add to this number an accessories wire, to operate trailer internal equipment or to charge the trailer's battery, and you can have as many as seven wires in the harness.

Determine the equipment on your trailer and buy the wiring kit necessary. The kit will contain all the wires needed, plus a plug adapter set which included the female plug, mounted on the bumper or hitch, and the male plug, wired into, or plugged into the trailer harness.

When installing the kit, follow the manufacturer's instructions. The color coding of the wires is standard throughout the industry.

One point to note, some domestic vehicles, and most imported vehicles, have separate turn signals. On most domestic vehicles, the brake lights and rear turn signals operate with the same bulb. For those vehicles with separate turn signals, you can purchase an isolation unit so that the brake lights won't blink whenever the turn signals are operated, or, you can go to your local electronics supply house and buy four diodes to wire in series with the brake and turn signal bulbs. Diodes will isolate the brake and turn signals. The choice is yours. The isolation units are simple and quick to install, but far more expensive than the diodes. The diodes, however, require more work to install properly, since they require the cutting of each bulb's wire and soldering in place of the diode.

One final point, the best kits are those with a spring loaded cover on the vehicle mounted socket. This cover prevents dirt and moisture from corroding the terminals. Never let the vehicle socket hang loosely. Always mount it securely to the bumper or hitch.

CIRCUIT PROTECTION

Fuse Block

➧ See Figure 95

The fuse block and relay bank is located on the driver's side under the lower instrument panel. The fuse block contains fuses for various circuits as well as circuit breakers, horn relay, ignition lamp thermal time delay, and the turn signal flasher. The hazard warning flasher is mounted into a bracket below the fuse block. The individual fuse and relay locations can be found in the wiring diagrams at the end of this section.

Fusible Links

The main wiring harnesses are equipped with fusible links to protect against harness damage should a short circuit develop.

Never replace a fusible link with standard wire. Only fusible link wire of the correct gauge with hypalon insulation should be used.

When a fusible link blows, it is very important to locate and repair the short. Do not just replace the link to correct the problem.

Always disconnect negative battery cable when servicing the electrical system.

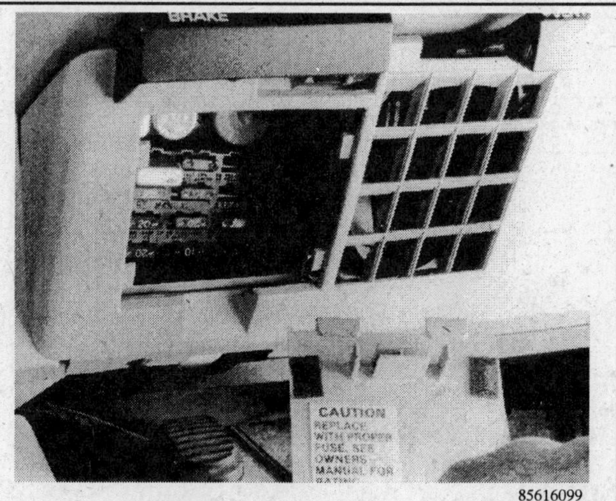

85616099

Fig. 95 The fuse box is located under a cover at the lower left instrument panel — 1987 Voyager shown

REPLACEMENT

1. Disconnect the negative battery cable.
2. Cut off the remaining portion of the blown fusible link flush with the multiple connection insulator. Take care not to cut any of the other fusible links.
3. Carefully remove about 1 in. (25mm) of insulation from the main harness wire at a point one inch away from the connection insulator.
4. Remove 1 in. (25mm) of insulation from the replacement fusible link wire and wrap the exposed area around the main harness wire at the point where the insulation was removed.
5. Heat the splice with a high temperature soldering gun and apply resin type solder until it runs freely. Remove the soldering gun and confirm that a "bright" solder joint has been made. Resolder if "cold" (dull) joint.
6. Cut the other end of the fusible link off at a point just behind the small single wire insulator. Strip one inch of insulation from fusible link and connection wires. Wrap and solder.
7. After the connections have cooled, wrap the splices with at least three layers of electrical tape.

WIRING DIAGRAMS

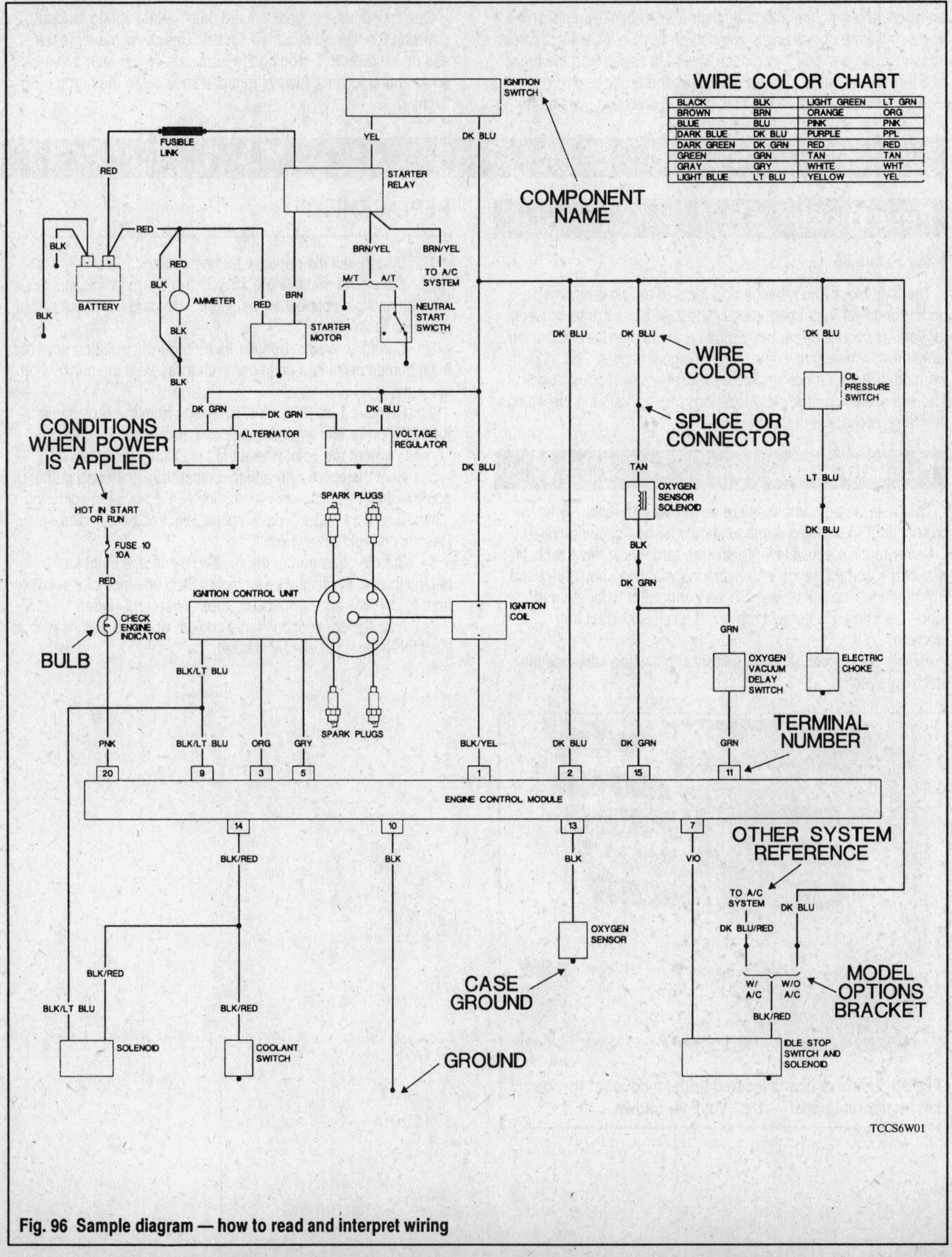

WIRE COLOR CHART

BLACK	BLK	LIGHT GREEN	LT GRN
BROWN	BRN	ORANGE	ORG
BLUE	BLU	PINK	PNK
DARK BLUE	DK BLU	PURPLE	PPL
DARK GREEN	DK GRN	RED	RED
GREEN	GRN	TAN	TAN
GRAY	GRY	WHITE	WHT
LIGHT BLUE	LT BLU	YELLOW	YEL

Fig. 96 Sample diagram — how to read and interpret wiring

WIRING DIAGRAM SYMBOLS

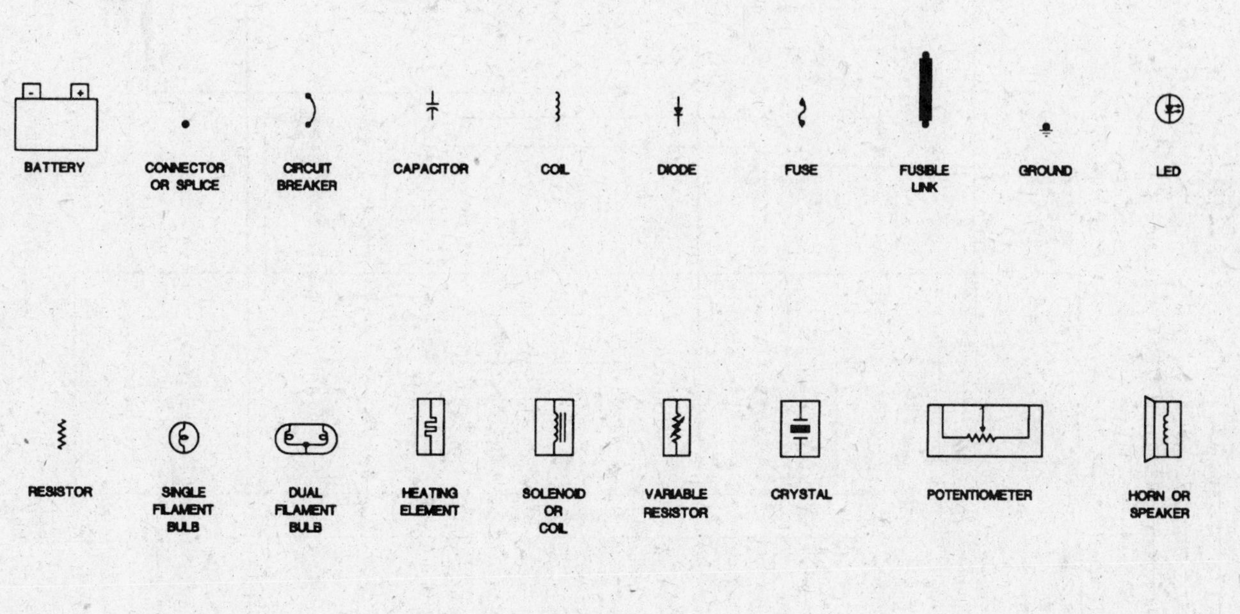

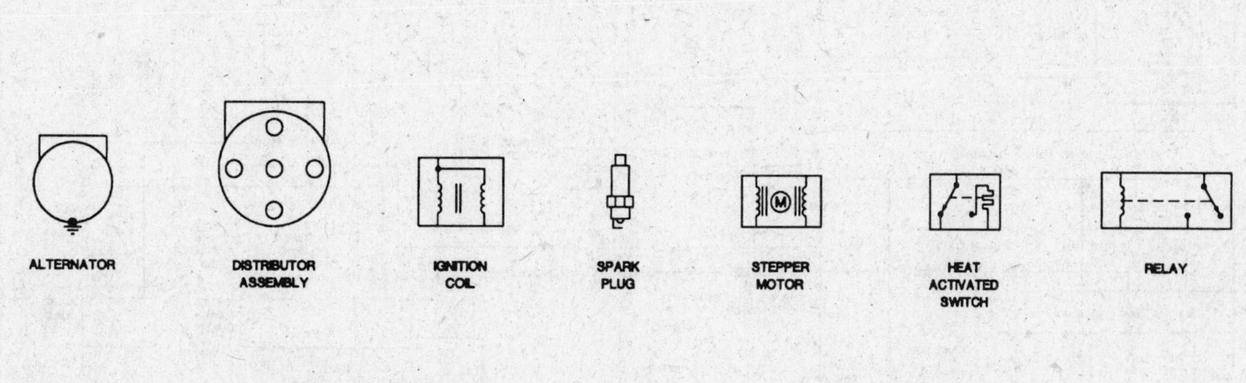

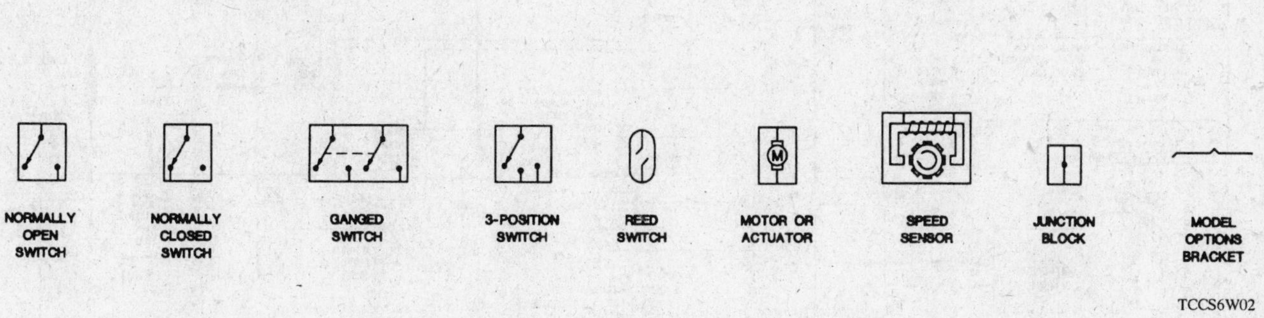

TCCS6W02

Fig. 97 Common wiring diagram symbols

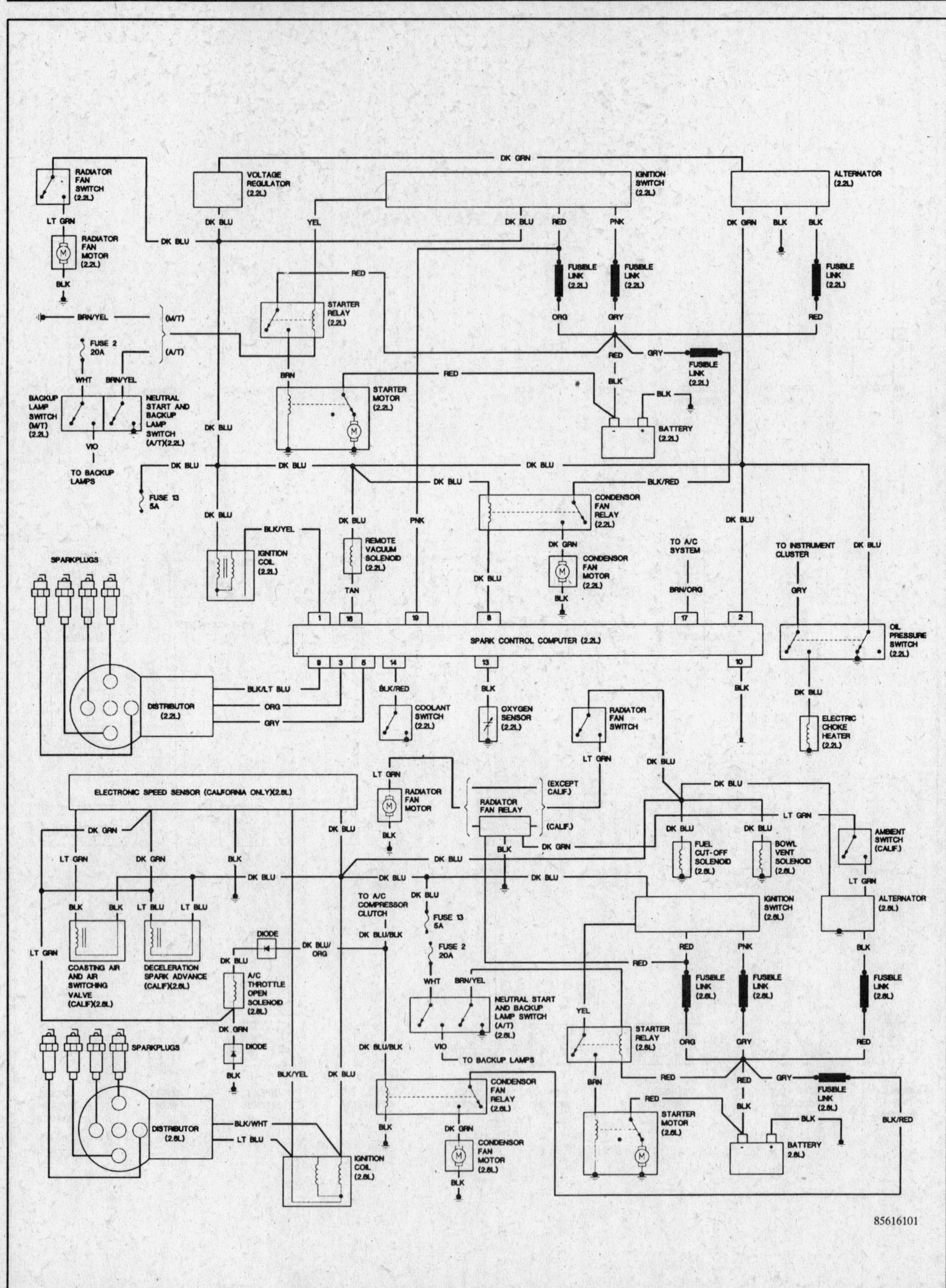

Fig. 98 Engine wiring schematic — 1984 Caravan/Voyager with 2.2L and 2.6L engines

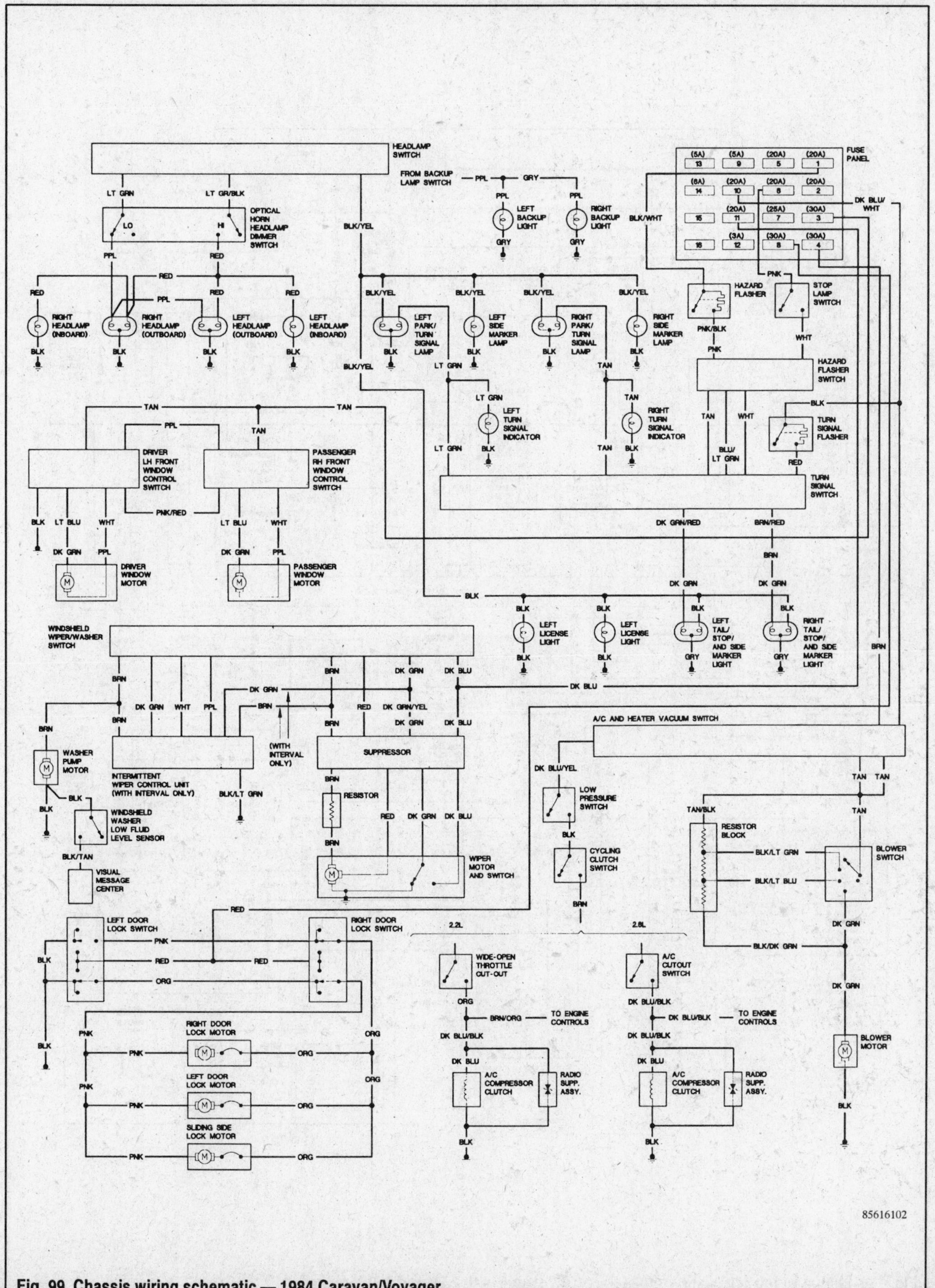

85616102

Fig. 99 Chassis wiring schematic — 1984 Caravan/Voyager

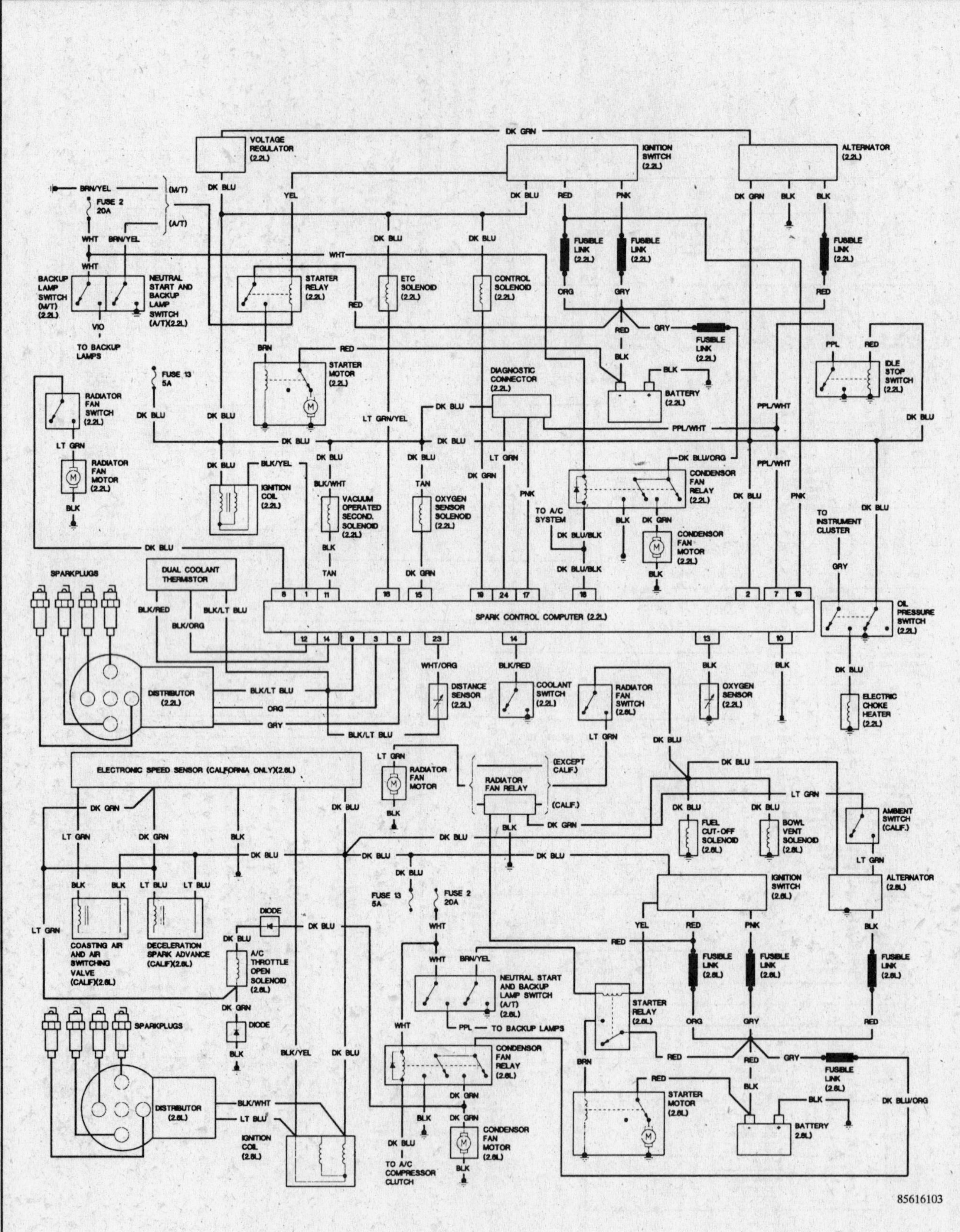

Fig. 100 Engine wiring schematic — 1985 Caravan/Voyager with 2.2L and 2.6L engines

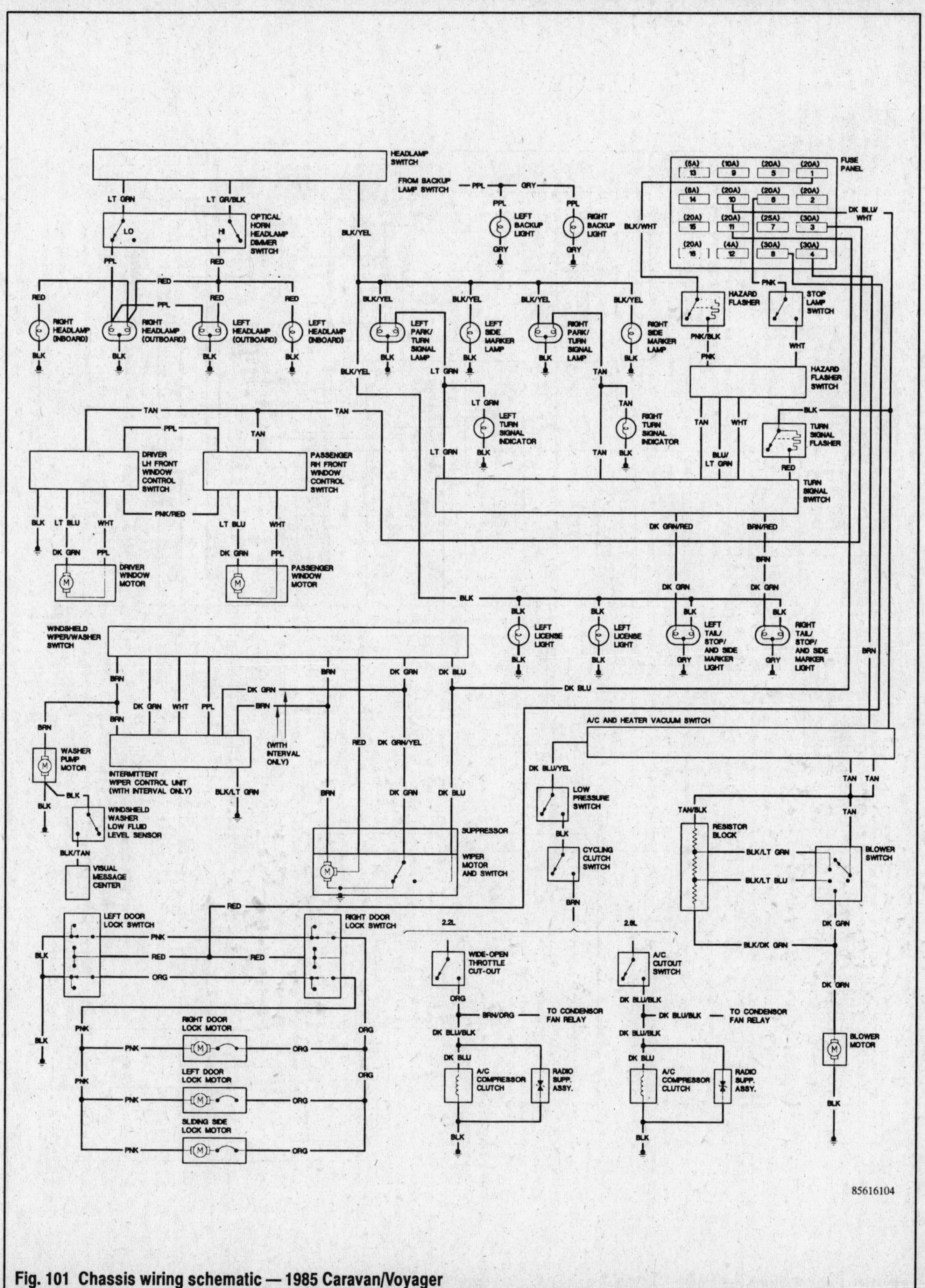

Fig. 101 Chassis wiring schematic — 1985 Caravan/Voyager

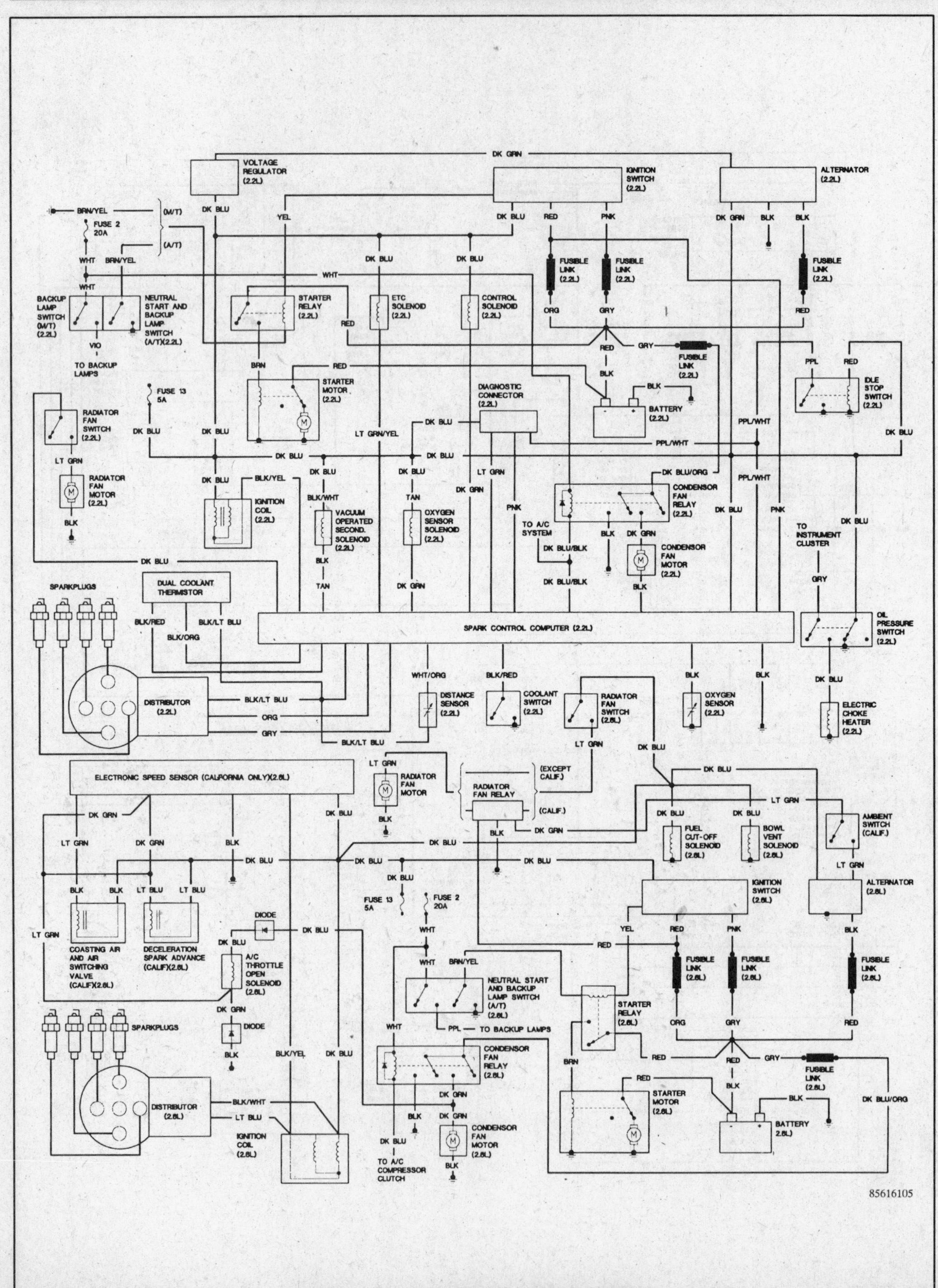

Fig. 102 Engine wiring schematic — 1986 Caravan/Voyager with 2.2L and 2.6L engines

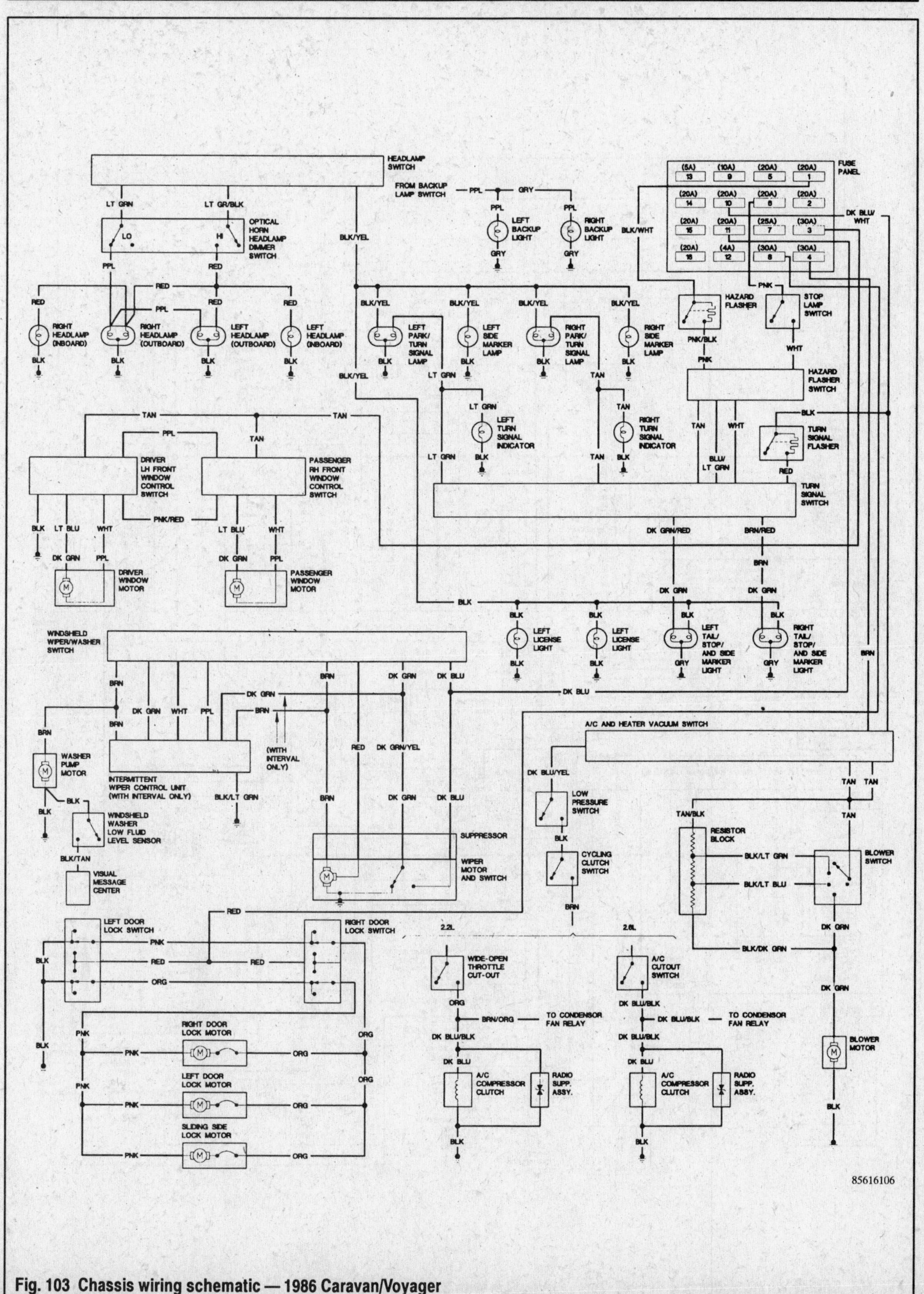

Fig. 103 Chassis wiring schematic — 1986 Caravan/Voyager

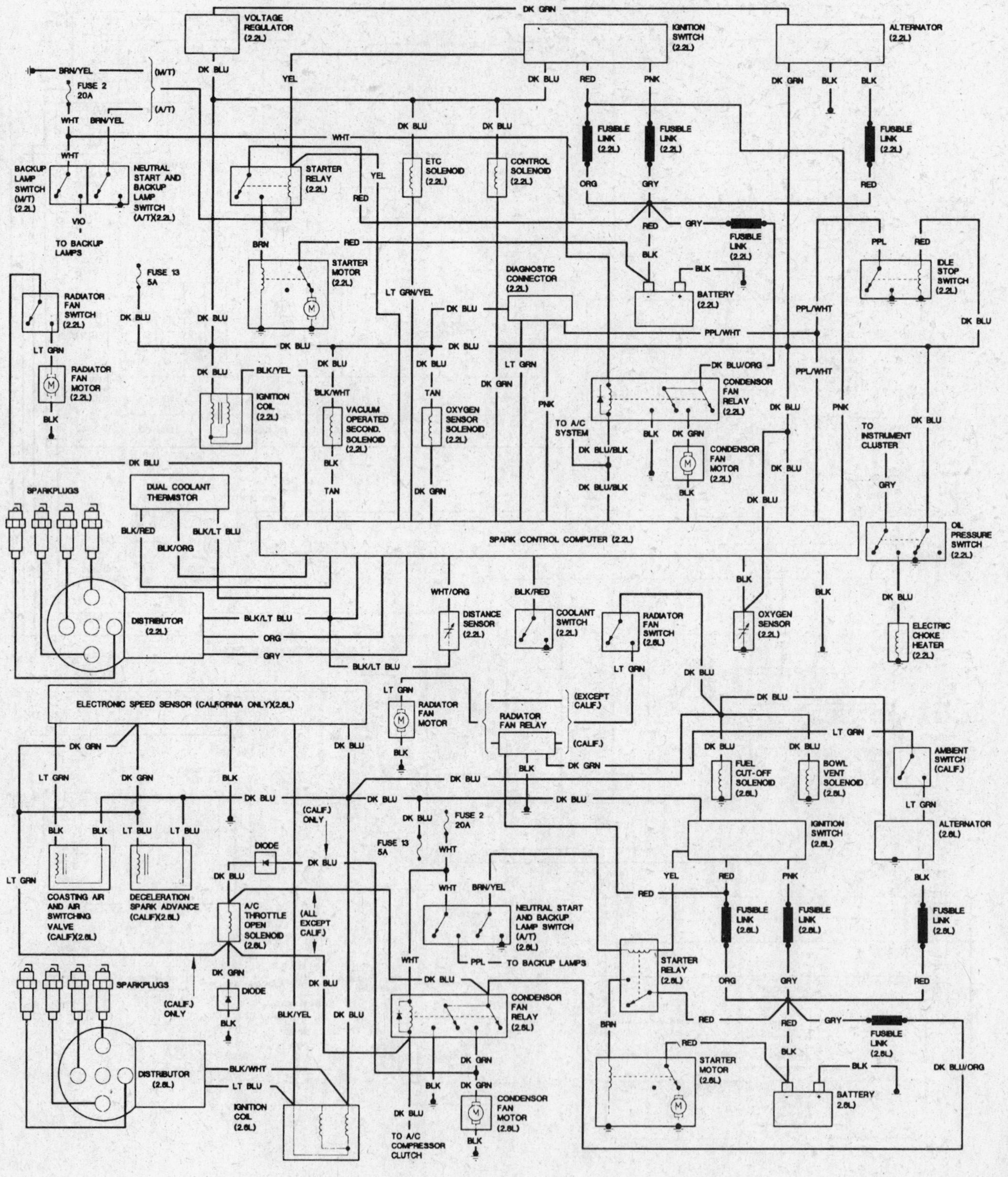

85616107

Fig. 104 Engine wiring schematic — 1987 Caravan/Voyager with 2.2L and 2.6L engines

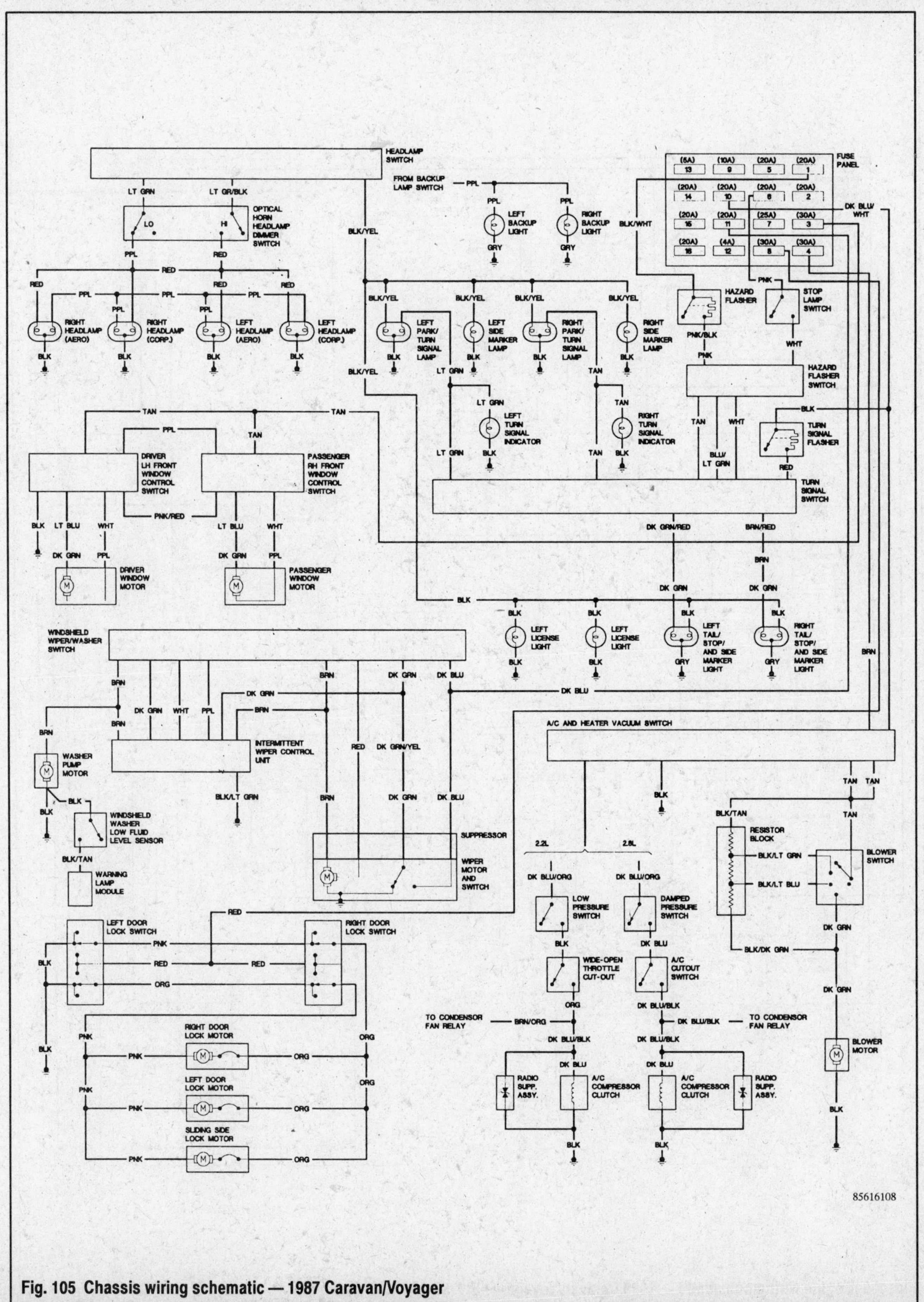

Fig. 105 Chassis wiring schematic — 1987 Caravan/Voyager

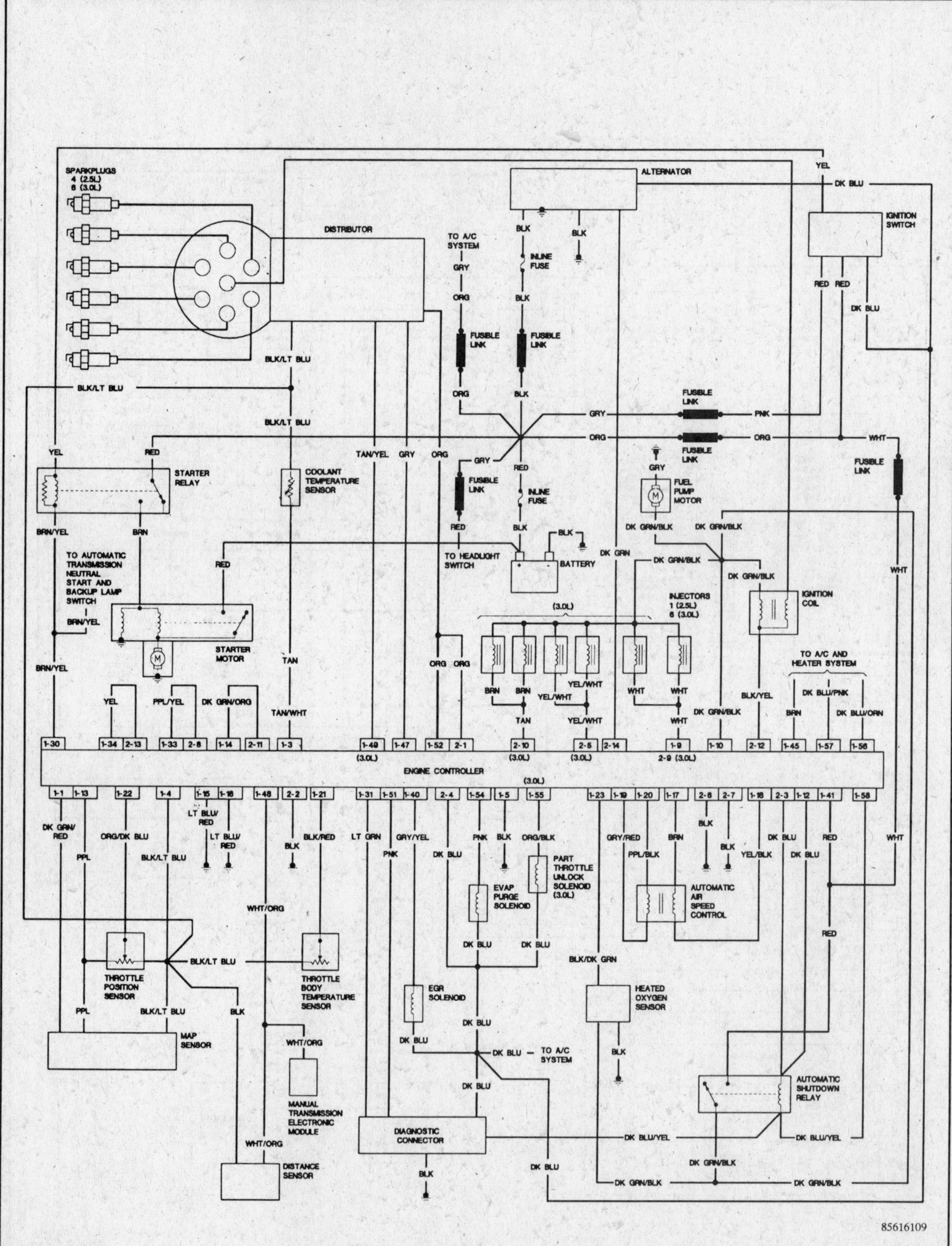

Fig. 106 Engine wiring schematic — 1988 Caravan/Voyager with 2.5L and 3.0L engines

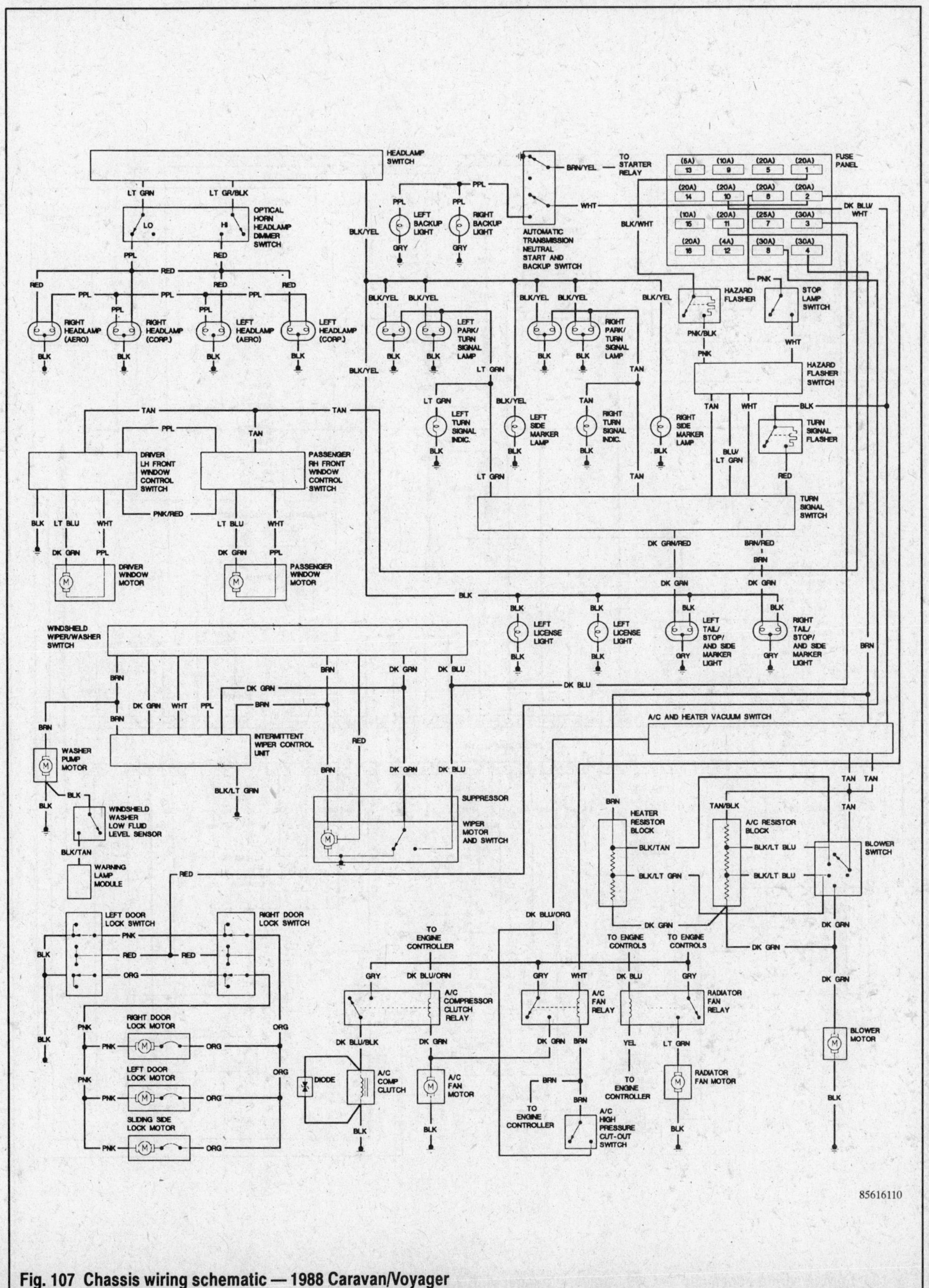

Fig. 107 Chassis wiring schematic — 1988 Caravan/Voyager

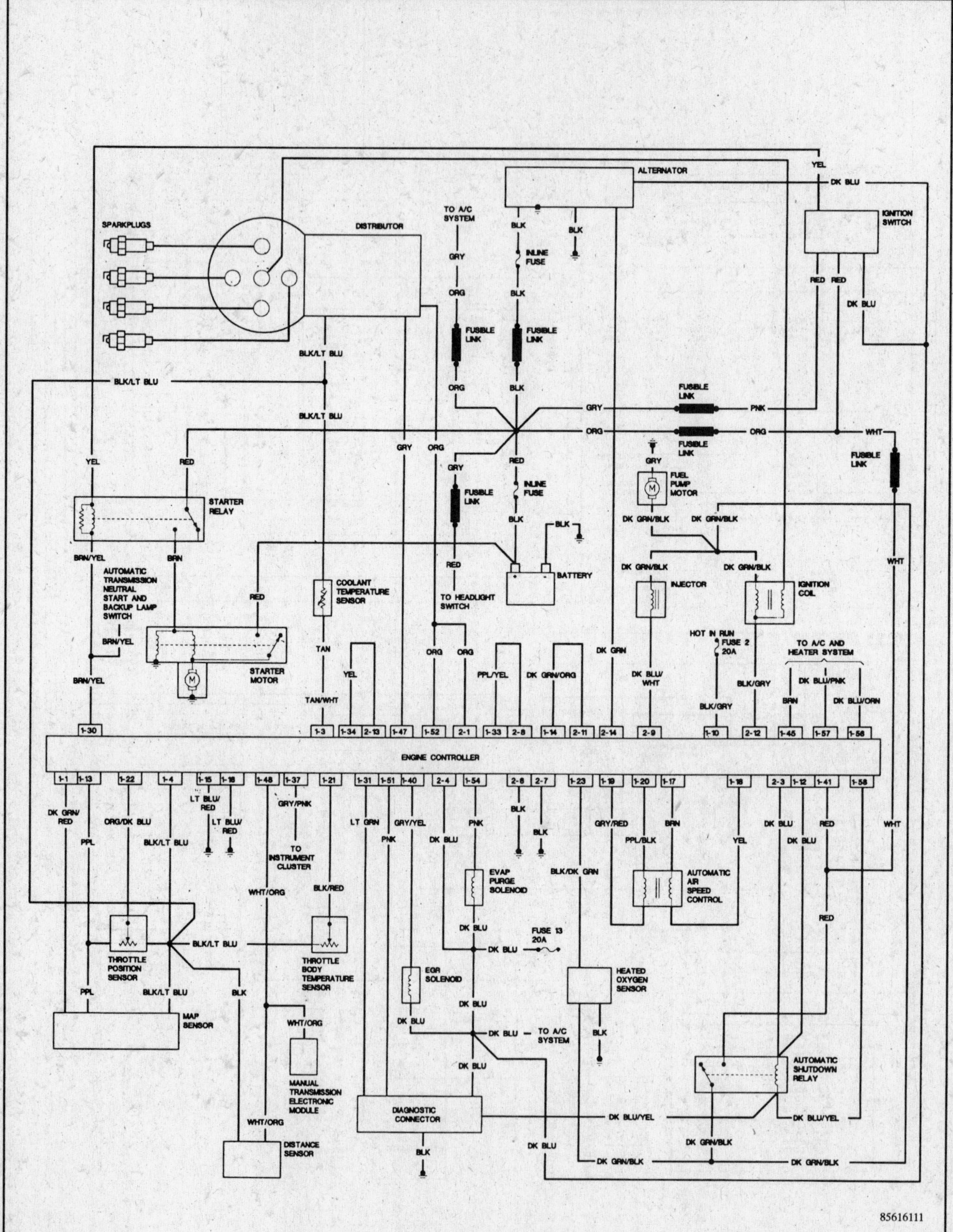

Fig. 108 Engine wiring schematic — 1989 Caravan/Voyager with 2.5L engine

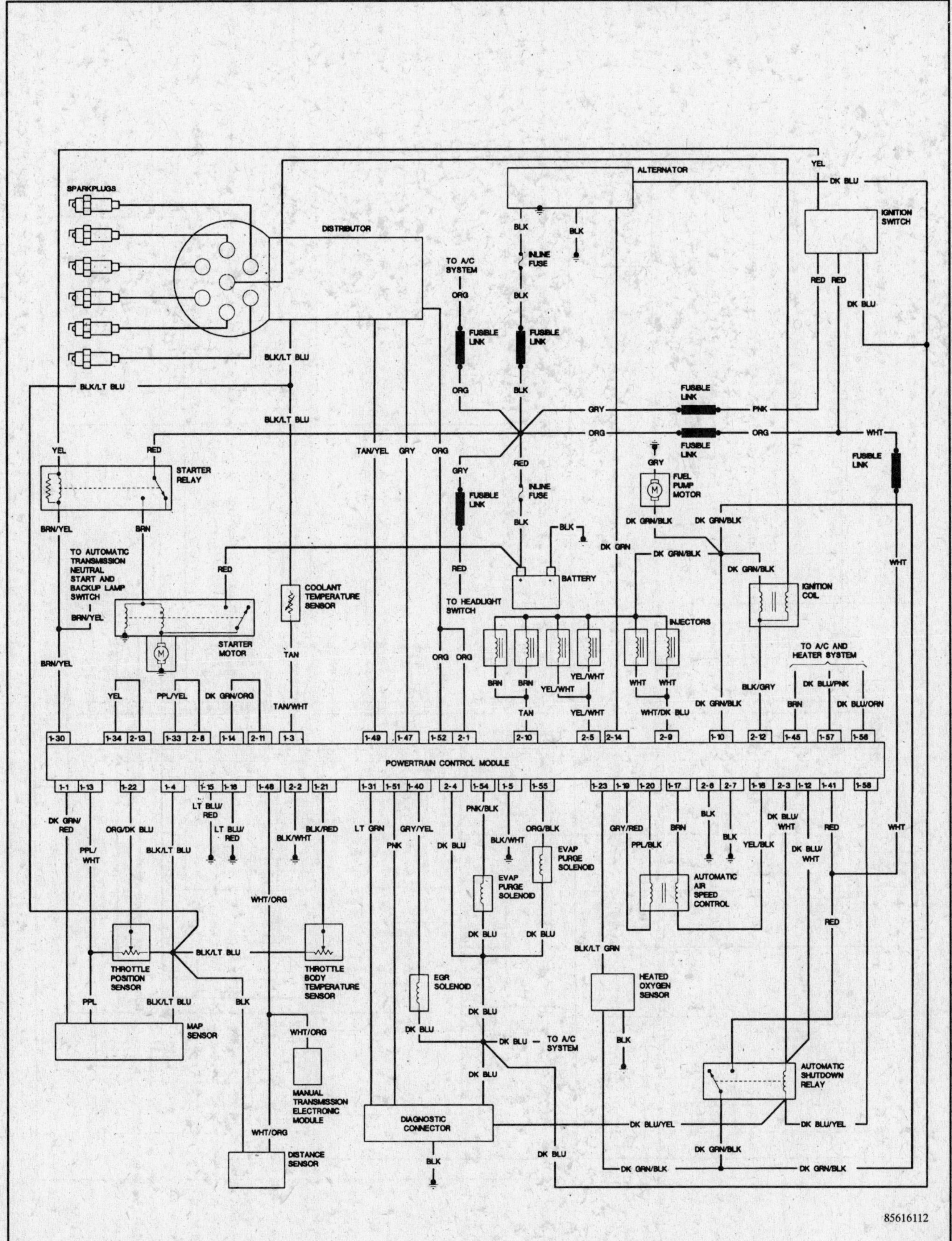

Fig. 109 Engine wiring schematic — 1989 Caravan/Voyager with 3.0L engine

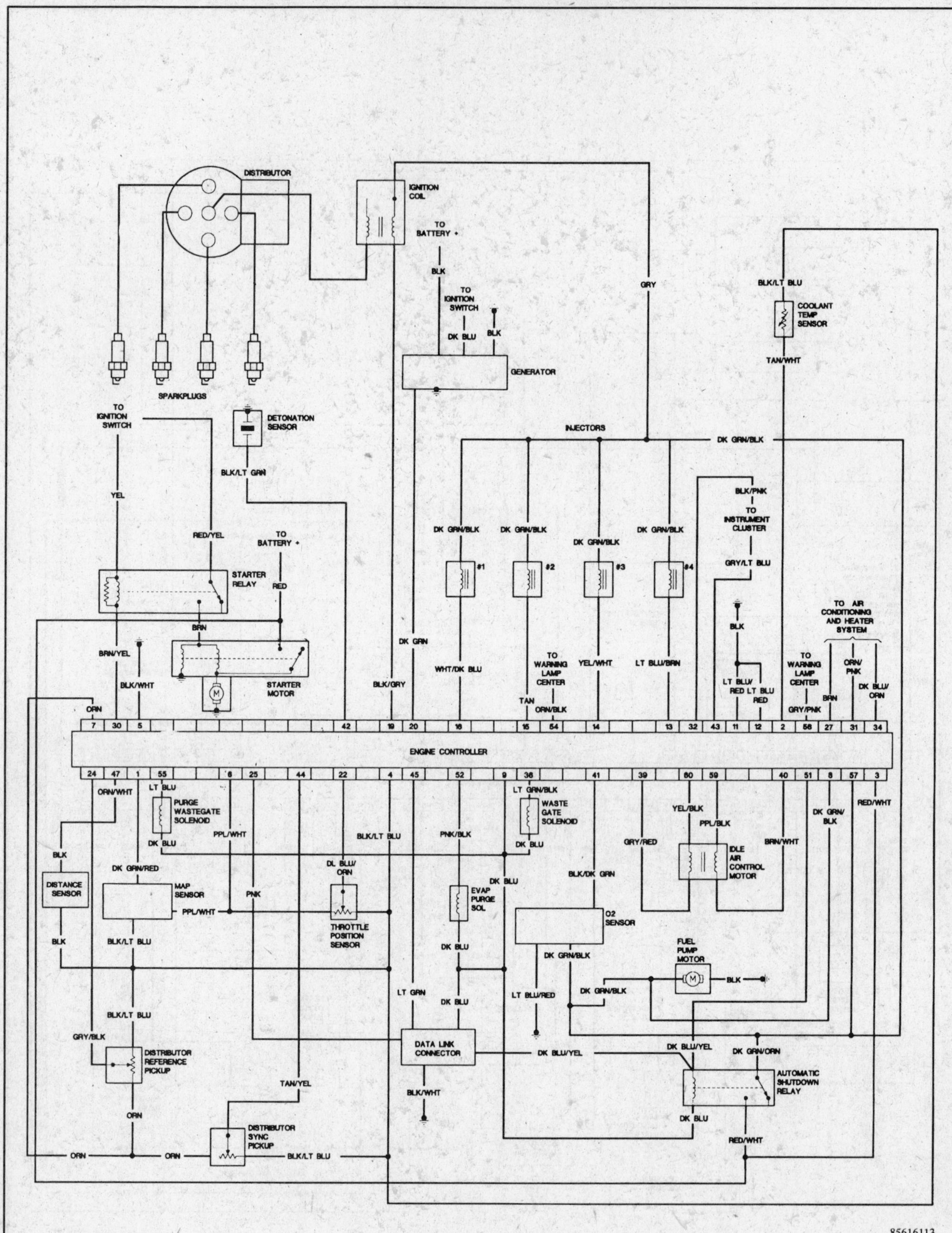

Fig. 110 Engine wiring schematic — 1989 Chrysler Town & Country, Caravan and Voyager with 2.5L turbocharged engine

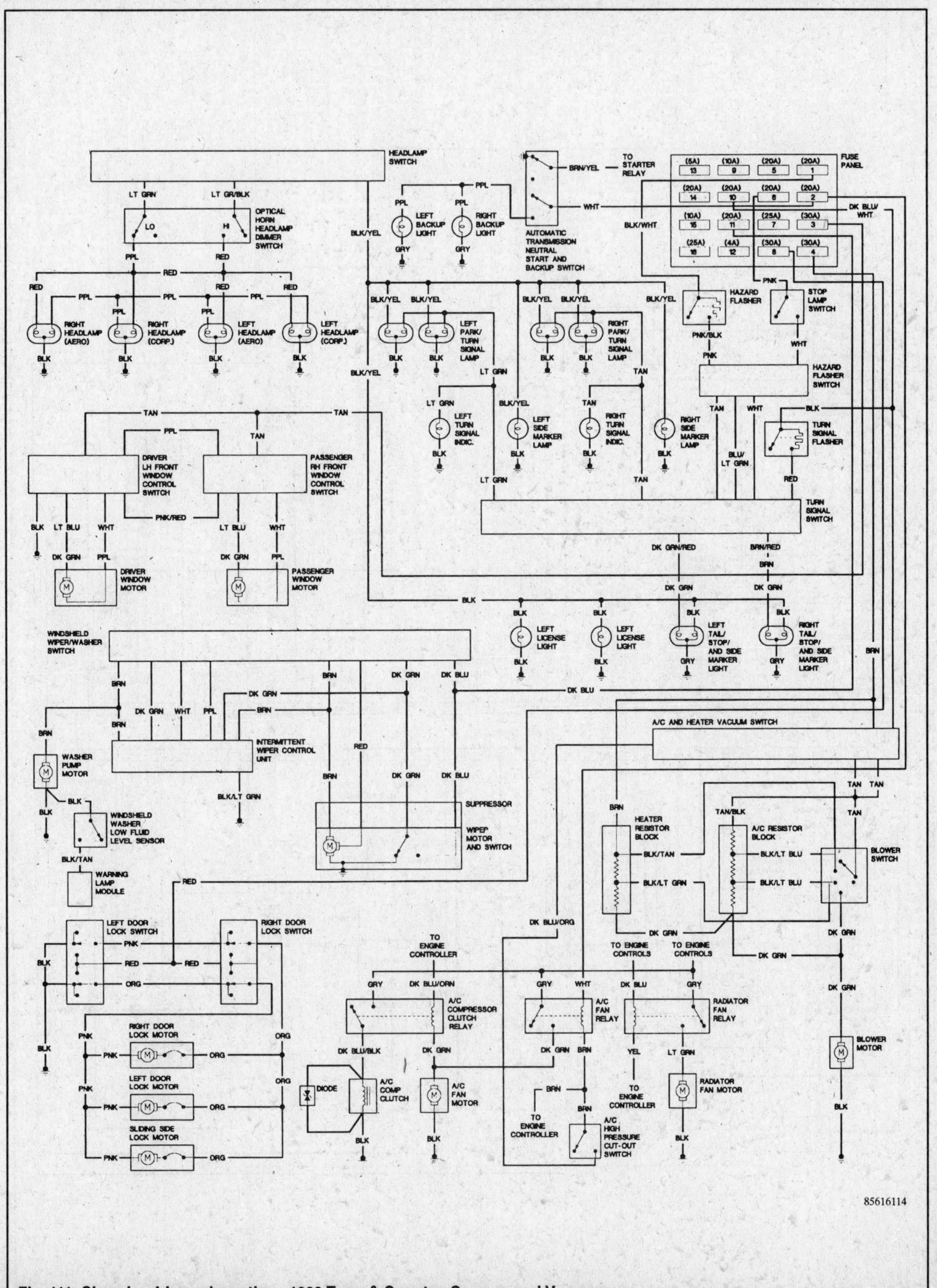

Fig. 111 Chassis wiring schematic — 1989 Town & Country, Caravan and Voyager

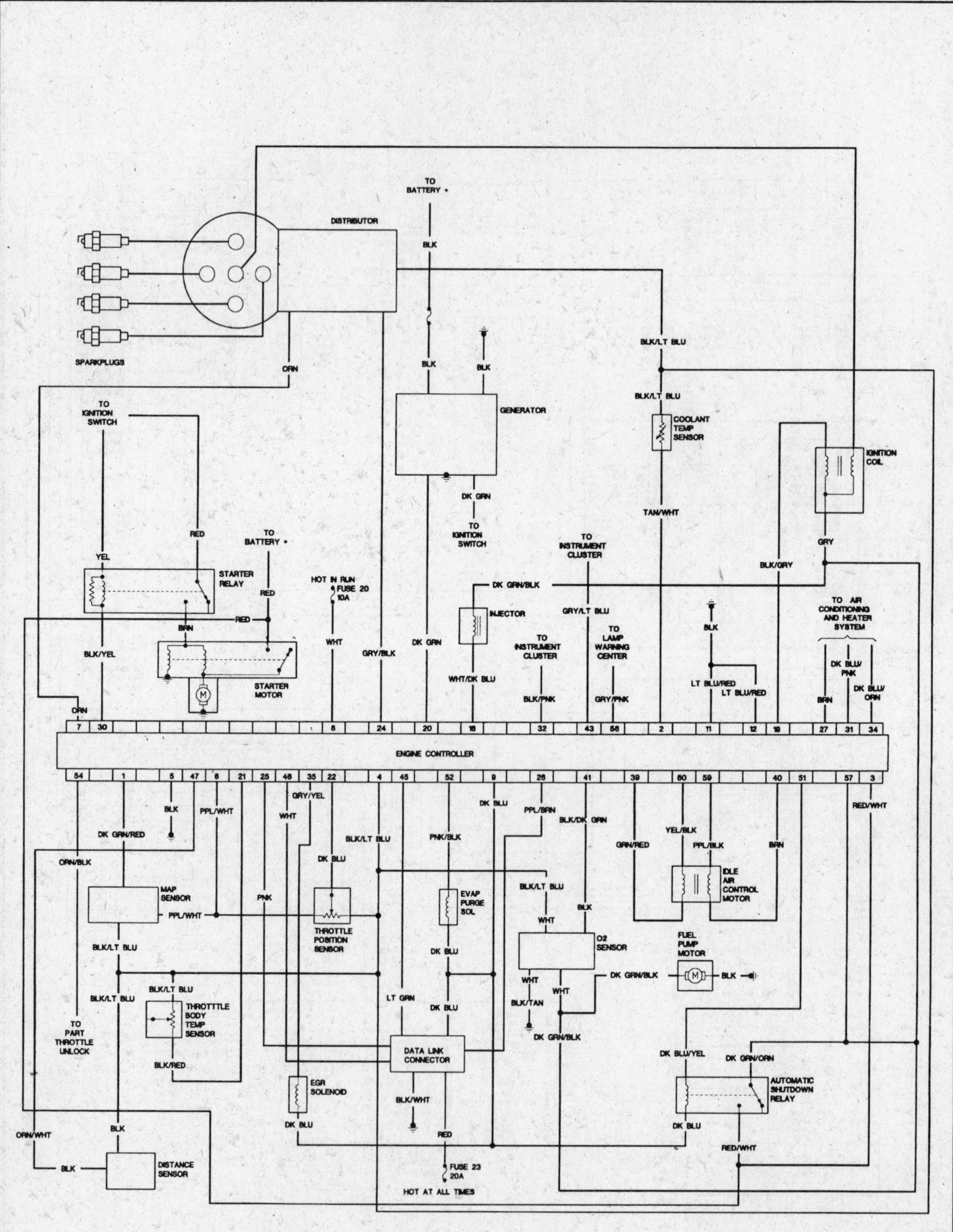

Fig. 112 Engine wiring schematic — 1990 Chrysler Town & Country, Caravan and Voyager with 2.5L engine

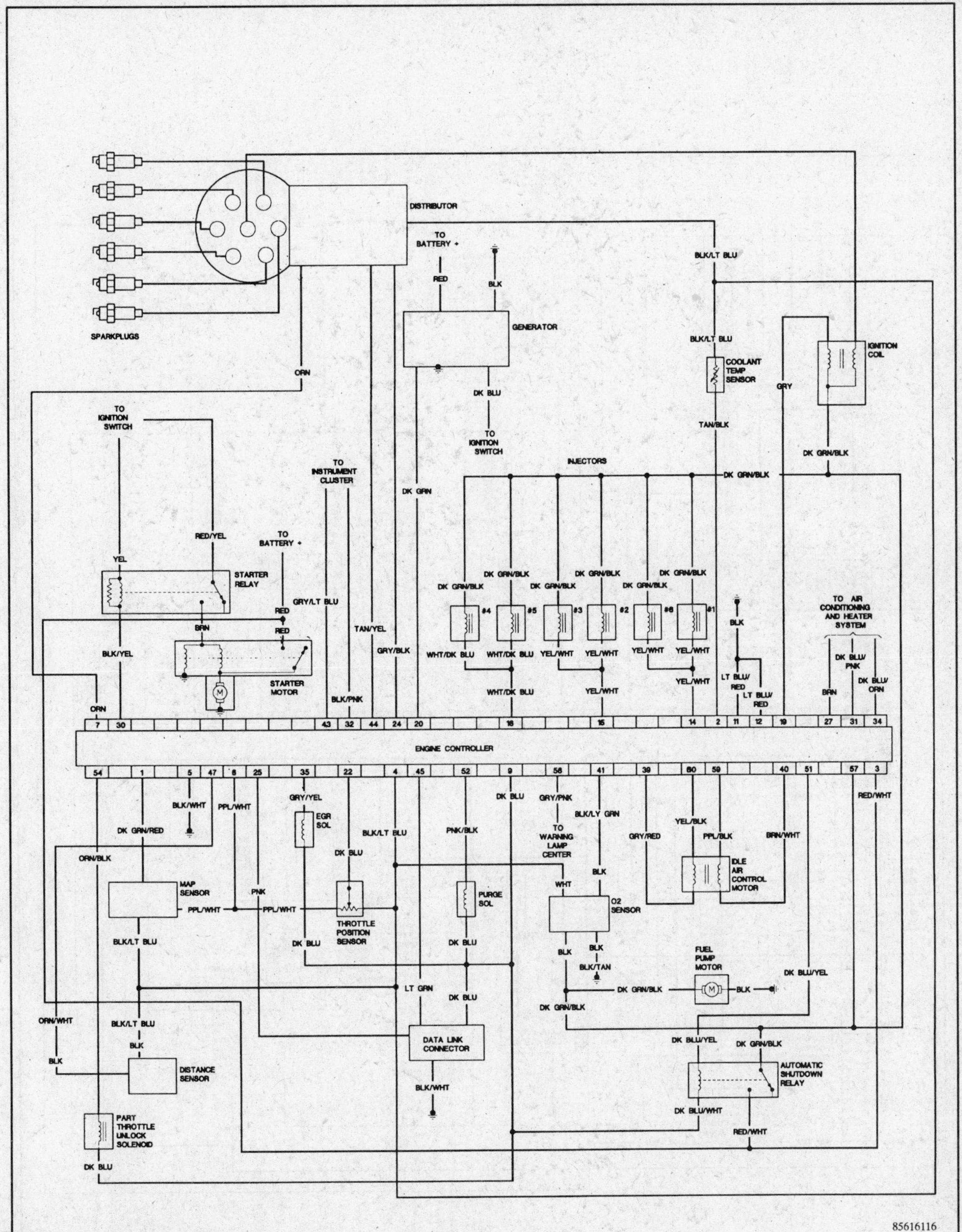

Fig. 113 Engine wiring schematic — 1990 Chrysler Town & Country, Caravan and Voyager with 3.0L engine

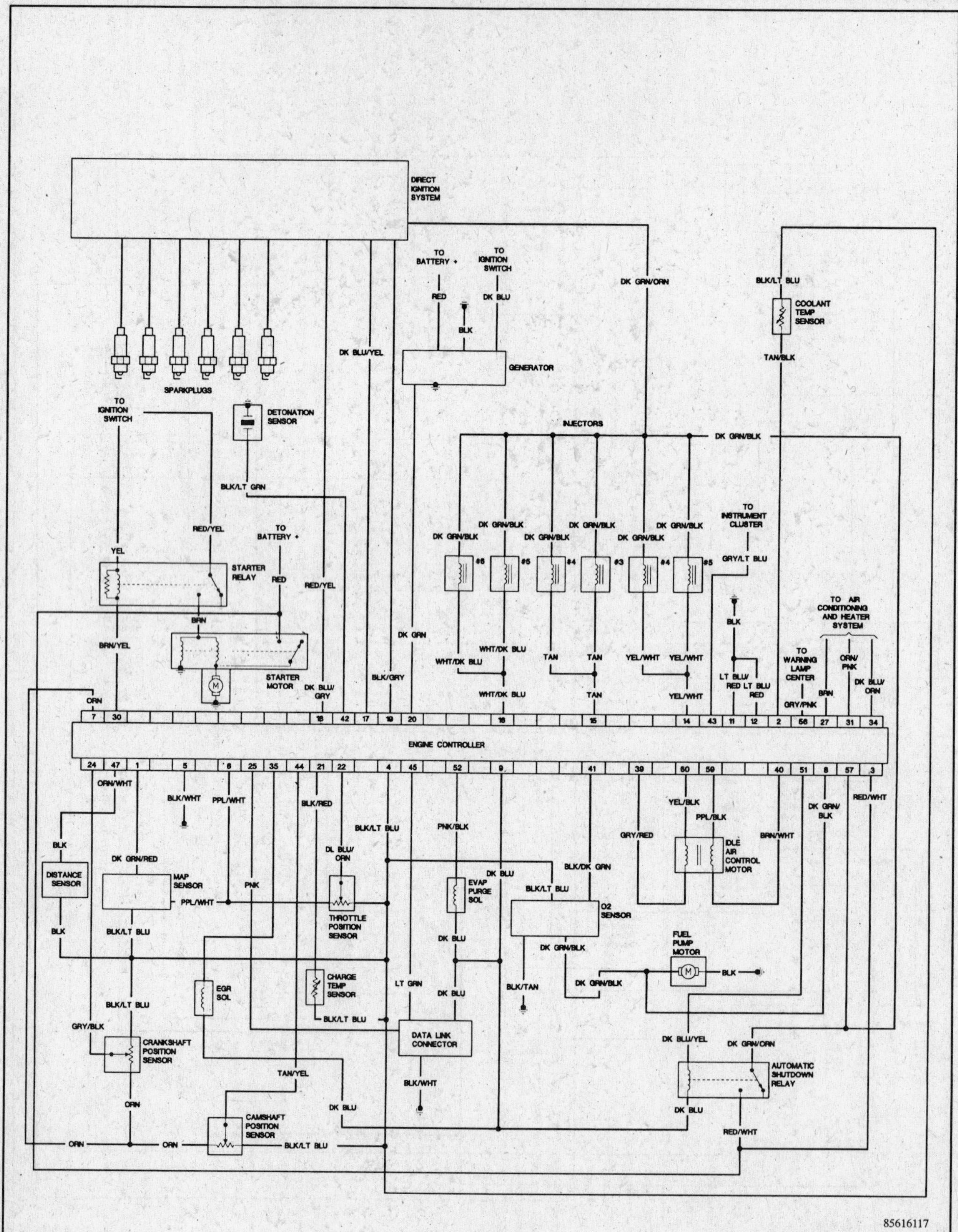

Fig. 114 Engine wiring schematic — 1990 Chrysler Town & Country, Caravan and Voyager with 3.3L engine

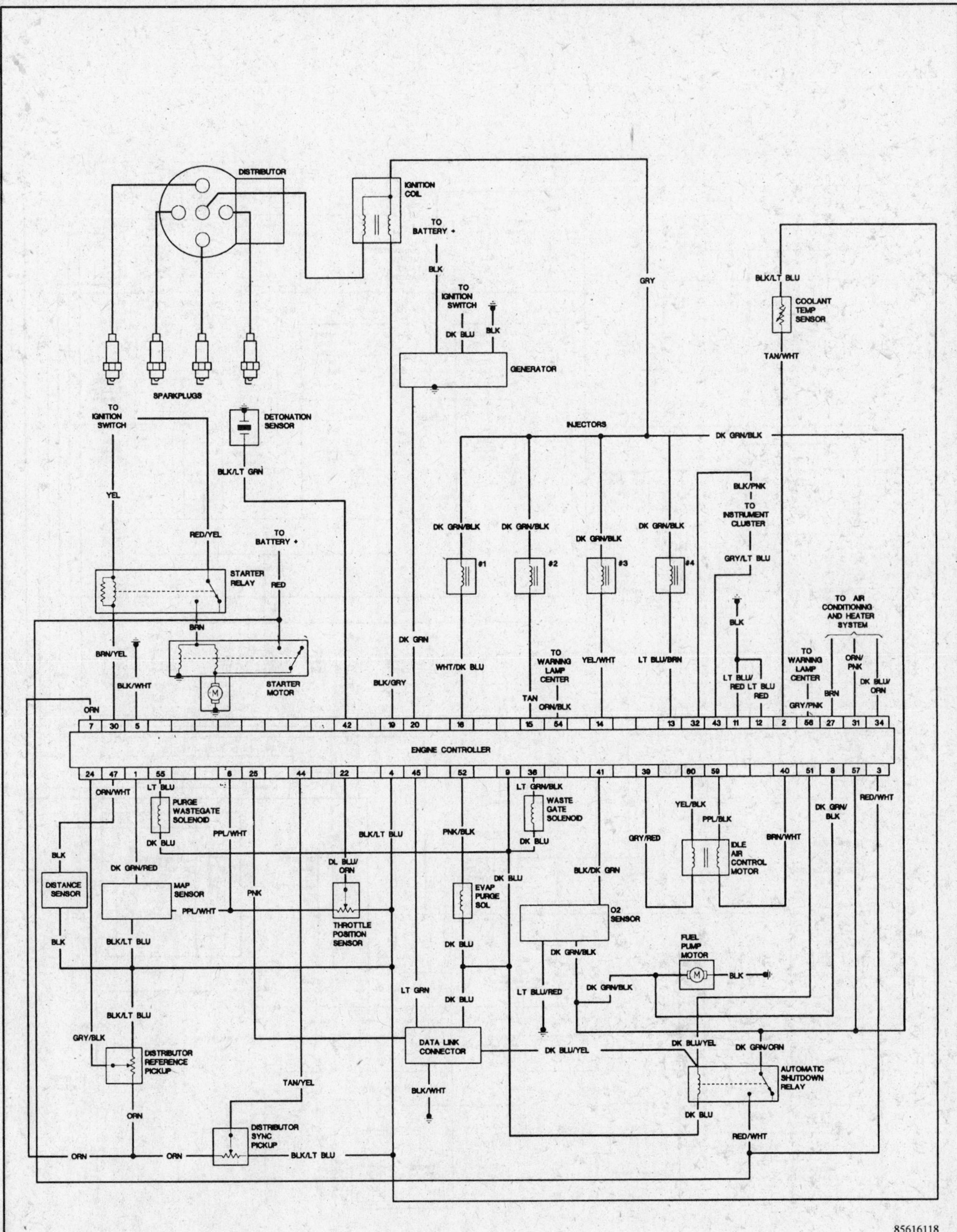

Fig. 115 Engine wiring schematic — 1990 Chrysler Town & Country, Caravan and Voyager with 2.5L turbocharged engine

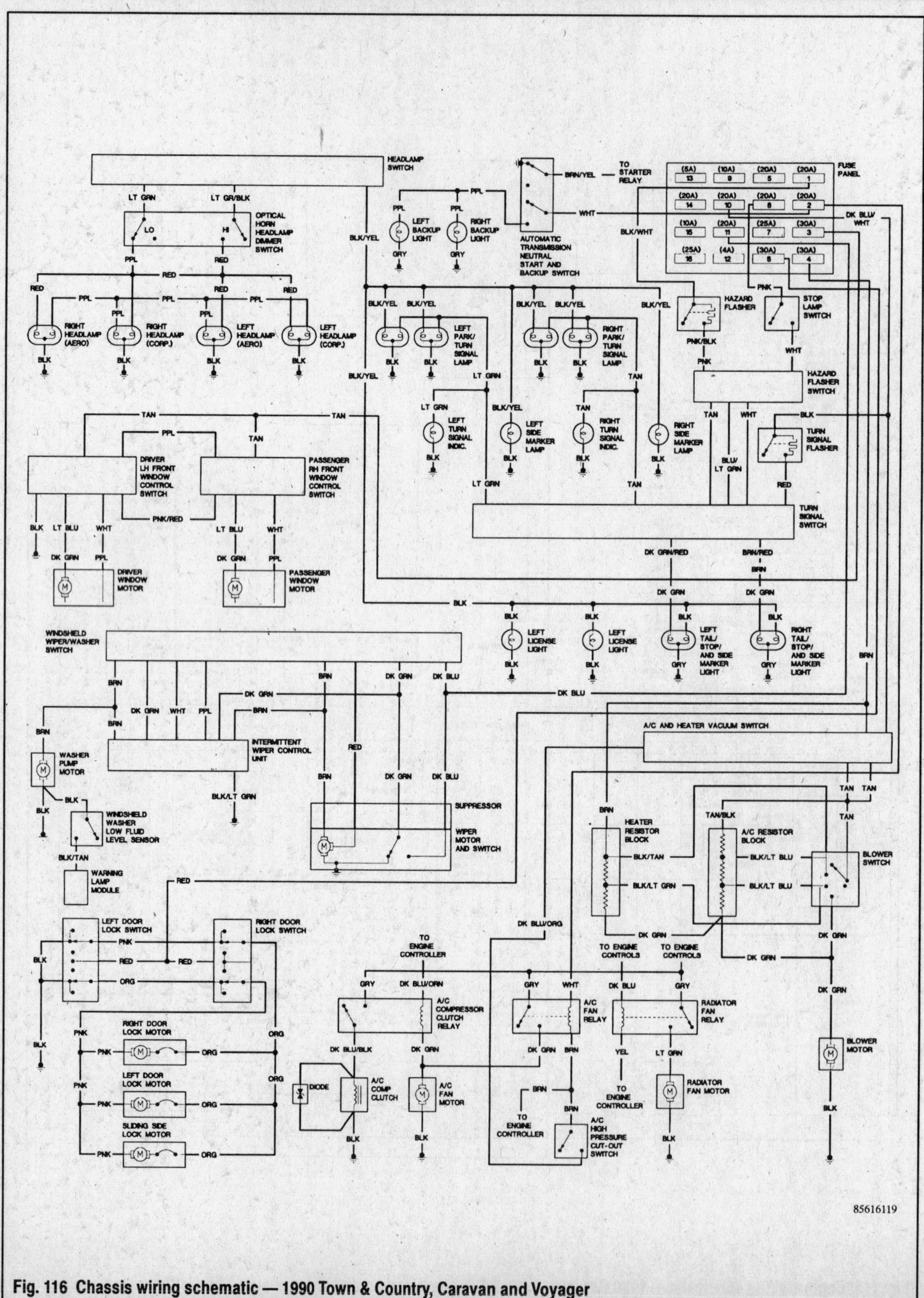

Fig. 116 Chassis wiring schematic — 1990 Town & Country, Caravan and Voyager

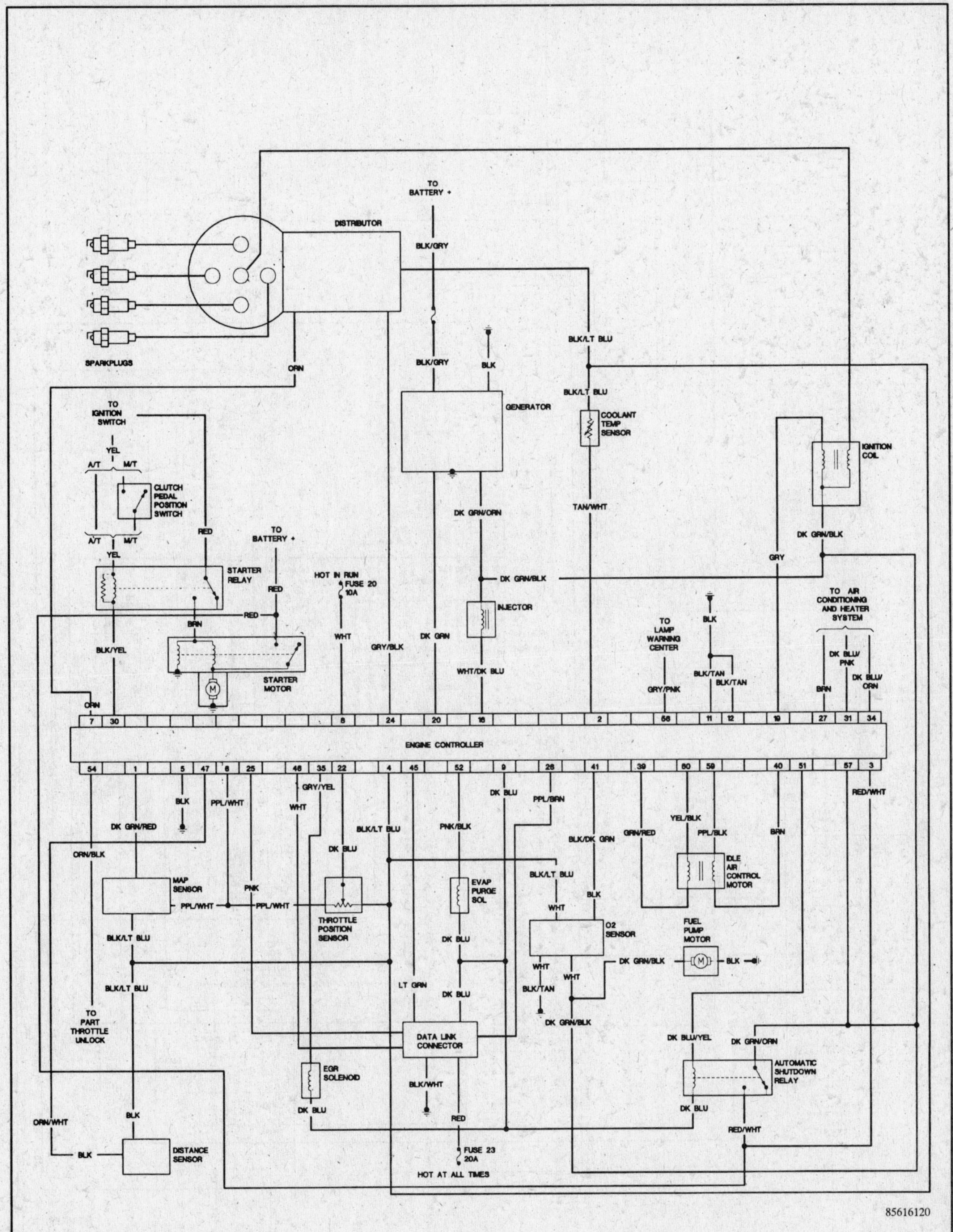

Fig. 117 Engine wiring schematic — 1991 Town & Country, Caravan and Voyager with 2.5L engine

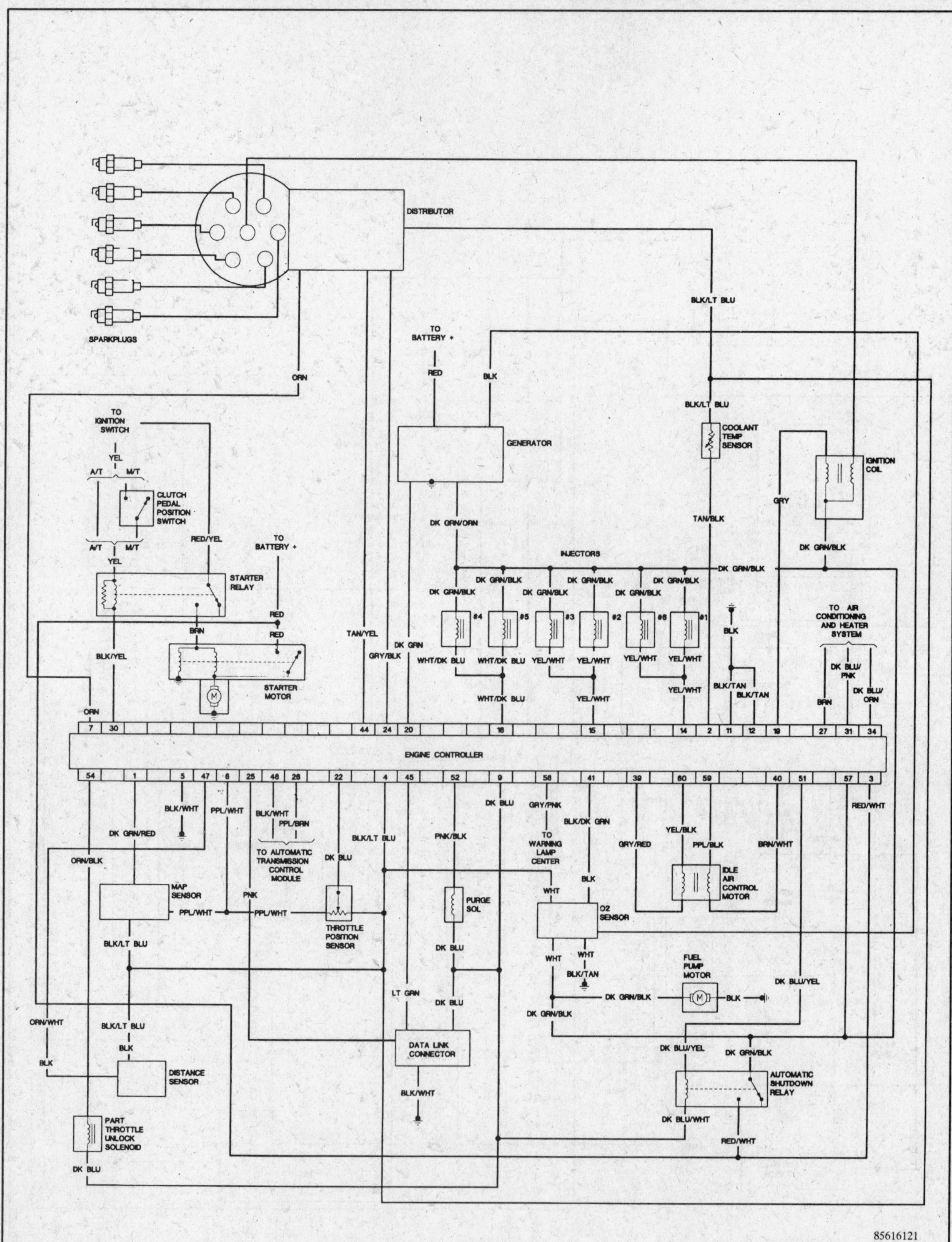

Fig. 118 Engine wiring schematic — 1991 Town & Country, Caravan and Voyager with 3.0L engine

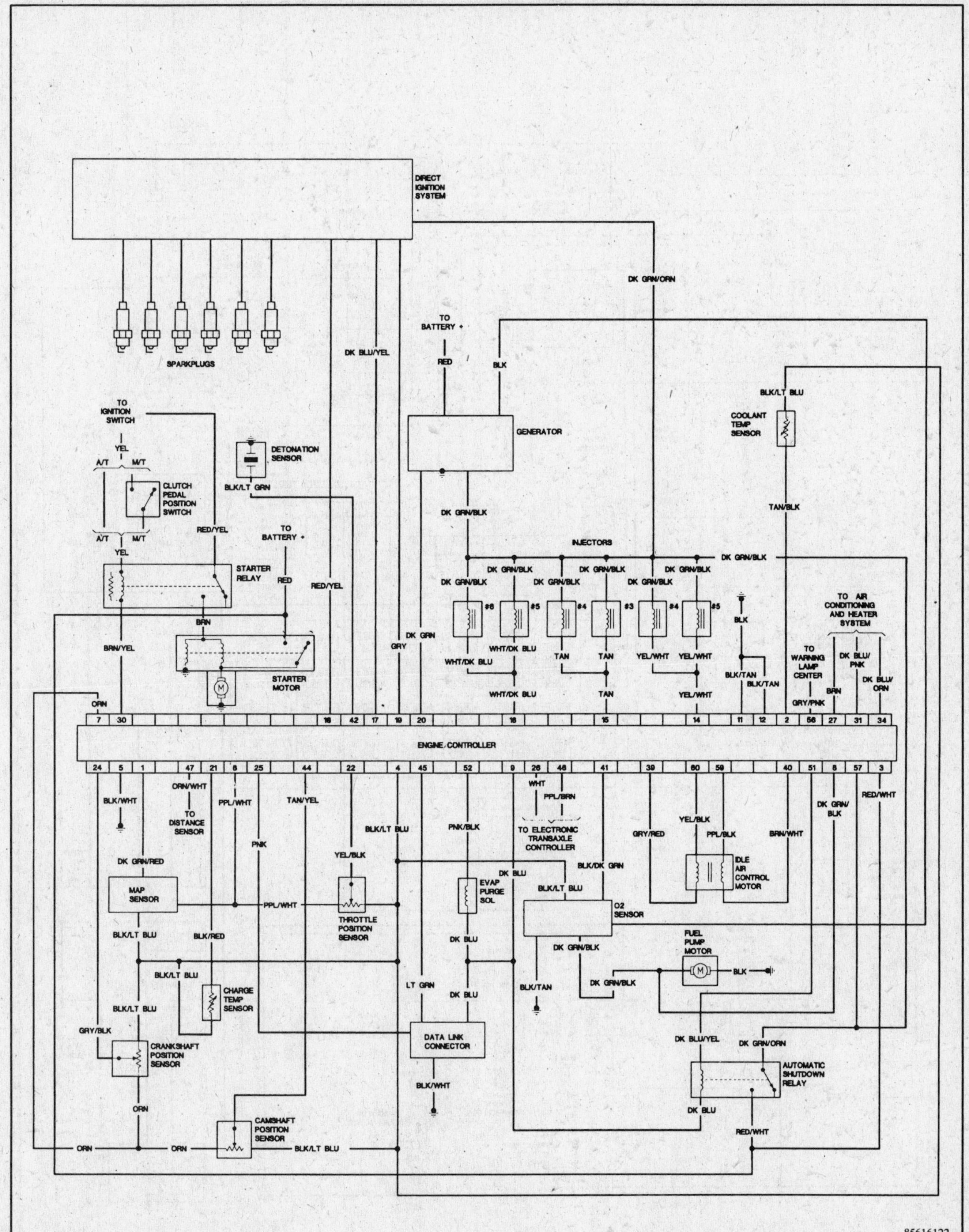

85616122

Fig. 119 Engine wiring schematic — 1991 Town & Country, Caravan and Voyager with 3.3L engine

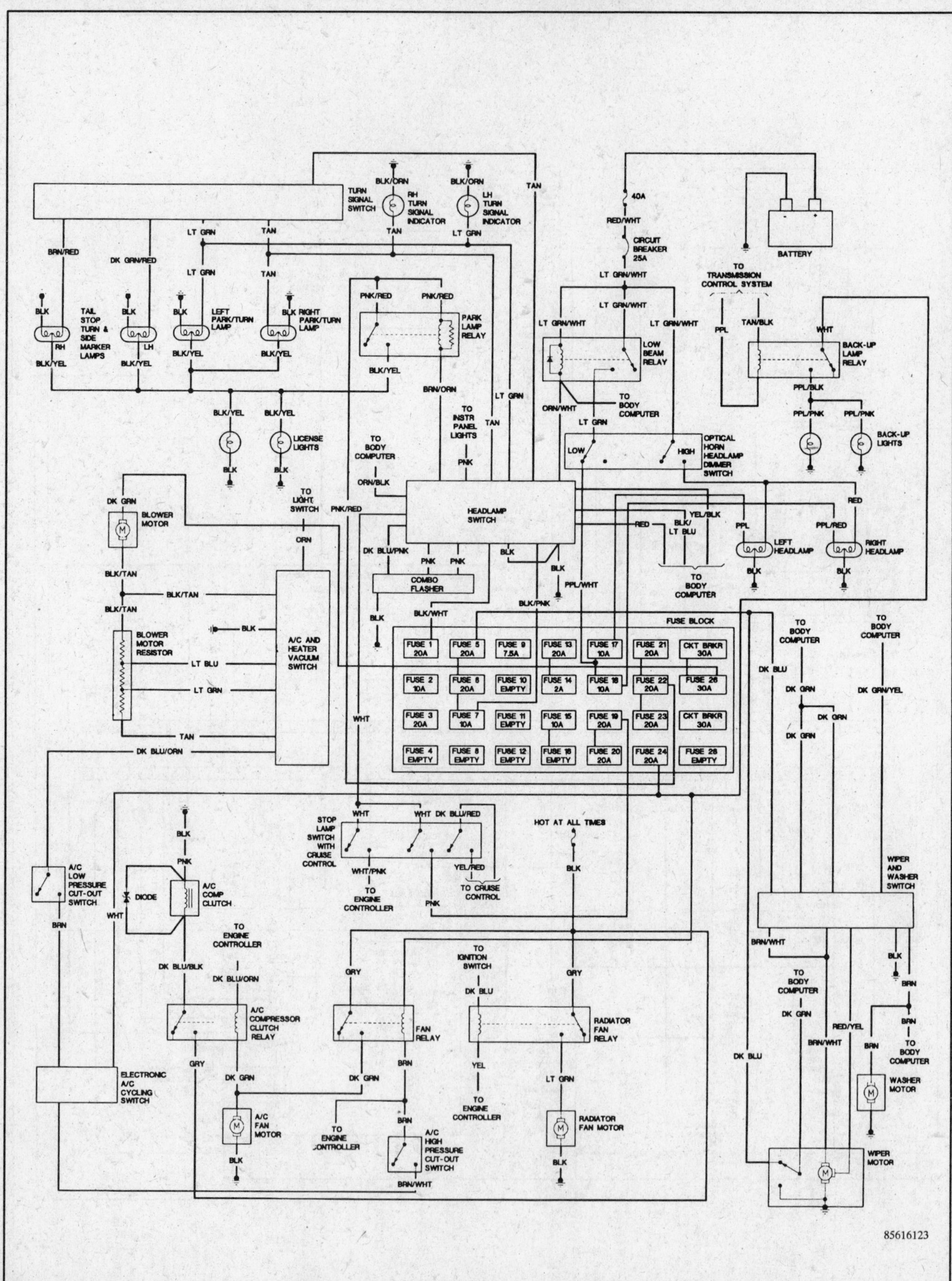

Fig. 120 Chassis wiring schematic — 1991 Town & Country, Caravan and Voyager

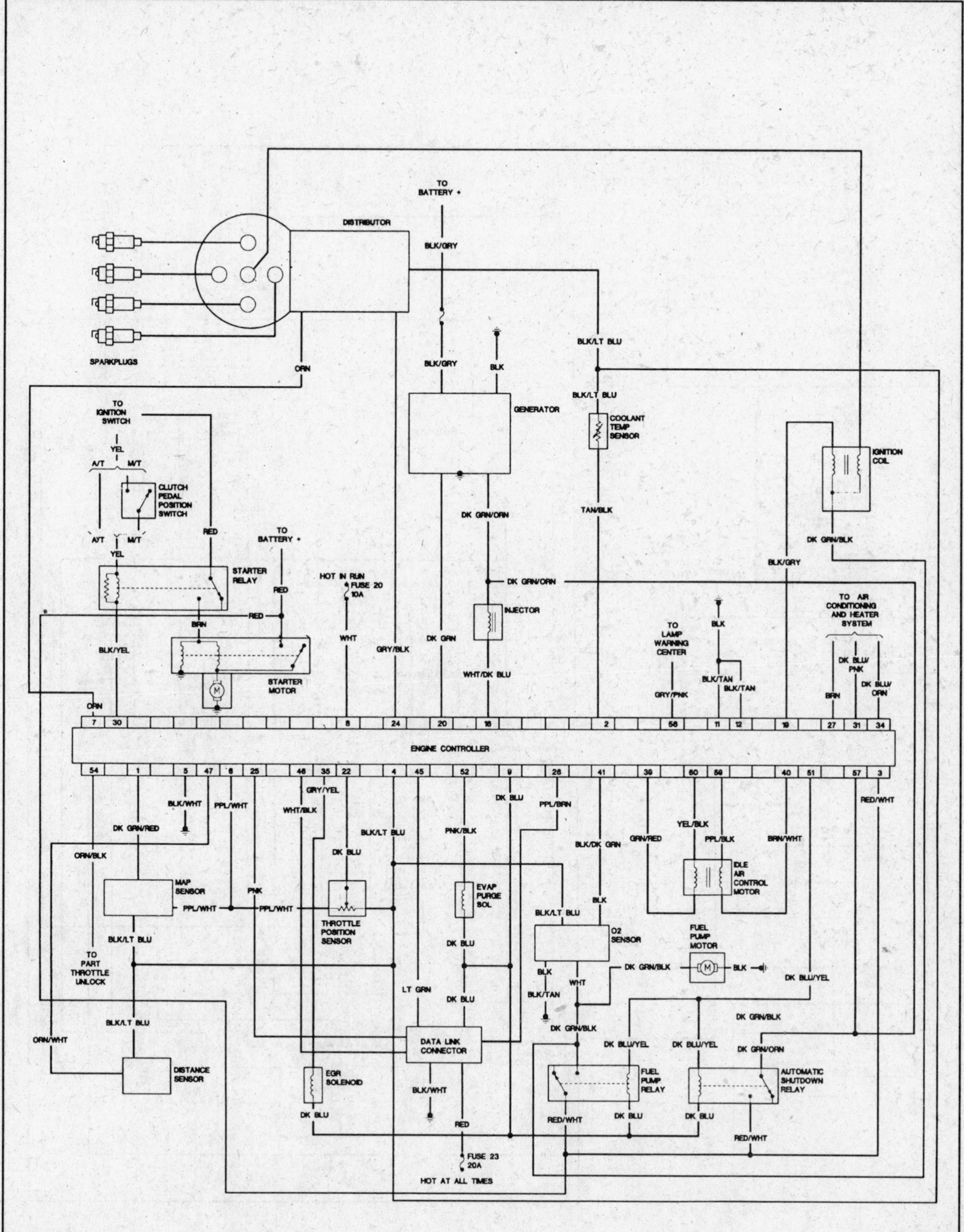

Fig. 121 Engine wiring schematic — 1992 Town & Country, Caravan and Voyager with 2.5L engine

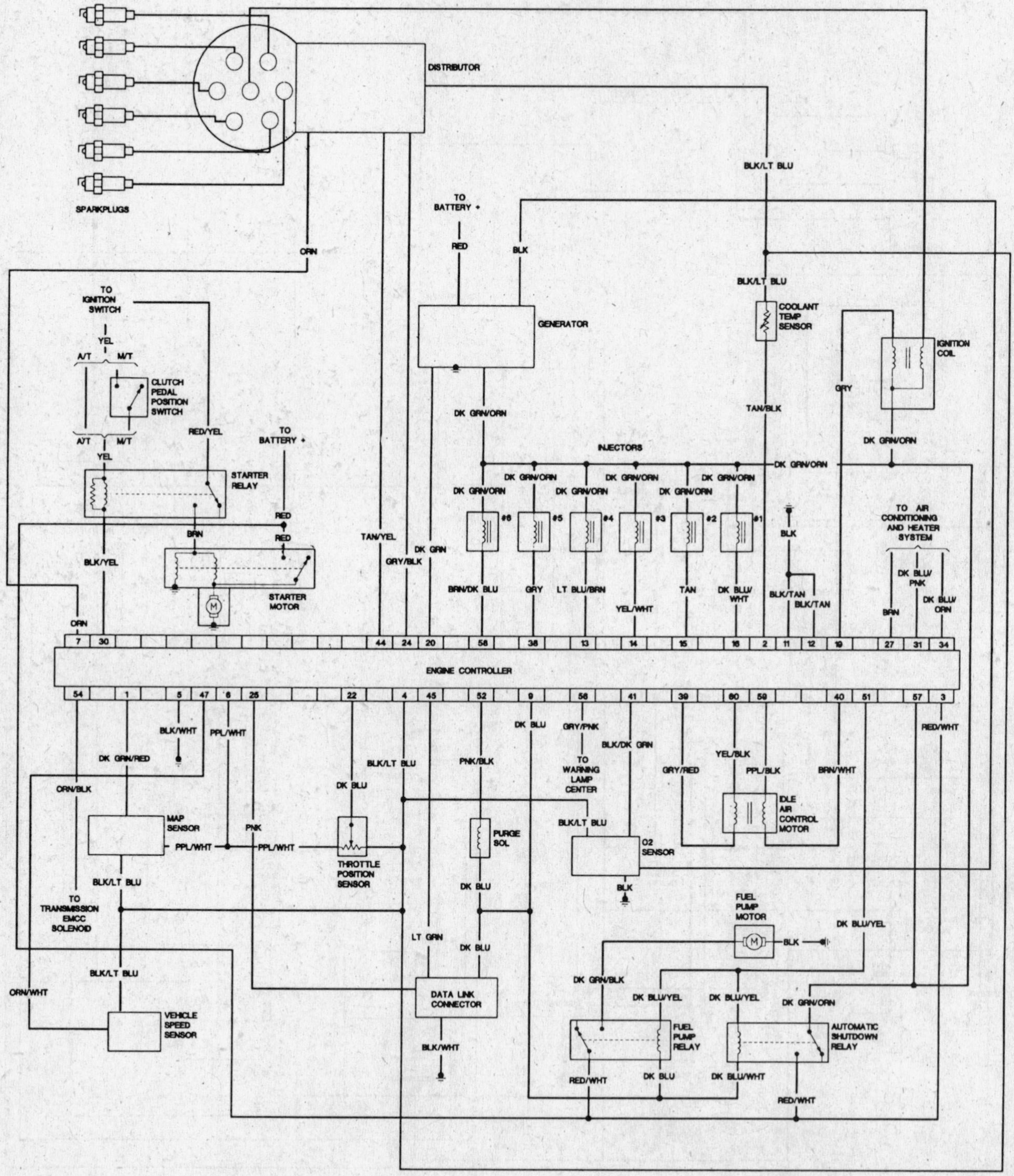

SPARKPLUGS
DISTRIBUTOR
BLK/LT BLU
TO BATTERY +
RED
BLK
ORN
TO IGNITION SWITCH
YEL
A/T M/T
CLUTCH PEDAL POSITION SWITCH
RED/YEL
TO BATTERY +
A/T M/T
YEL
STARTER RELAY
RED
BRN
RED
BLK/YEL
STARTER MOTOR
GENERATOR
DK GRN/ORN
TAN/YEL
DK GRN
GRY/BLK
BLK/LT BLU
COOLANT TEMP SENSOR
TAN/BLK
IGNITION COIL
GRY
DK GRN/ORN
INJECTORS
DK GRN/ORN
DK GRN/ORN DK GRN/ORN DK GRN/ORN DK GRN/ORN DK GRN/ORN DK GRN/ORN
#6 #5 #4 #3 #2 #1
BLK
TO AIR CONDITIONING AND HEATER SYSTEM
BRN/DK BLU GRY LT BLU/BRN YEL/WHT TAN DK BLU/WHT
BLK/TAN BLK/TAN
DK BLU/PNK
BRN
DK BLU/ORN
ORN
7 30 44 24 20 58 38 13 14 15 16 2 11 12 19 27 31 34
ENGINE CONTROLLER
54 1 5 47 6 25 22 4 45 52 9 56 41 39 60 59 40 51 57 3
BLK/WHT
PPL/WHT
DK GRN/RED
ORN/BLK
DK BLU
GRY/PNK
RED/WHT
BLK/DK GRN
TO WARNING LAMP CENTER
YEL/BLK
GRY/RED
PPL/BLK
BRN/WHT
BLK/LT BLU
PNK/BLK
DK BLU
MAP SENSOR
PPL/WHT
PNK
PPL/WHT
THROTTLE POSITION SENSOR
PURGE SOL
BLK/LT BLU
O2 SENSOR
IDLE AIR CONTROL MOTOR
BLK
BLK/LT BLU
TO TRANSMISSION EMCC SOLENOID
DK BLU
FUEL PUMP MOTOR
BLK
DK BLU/YEL
LT GRN
DK BLU
BLK/LT BLU
ORN/WHT
DATA LINK CONNECTOR
DK GRN/BLK
DK BLU/YEL
DK BLU/YEL
DK GRN/ORN
VEHICLE SPEED SENSOR
BLK/WHT
FUEL PUMP RELAY
AUTOMATIC SHUTDOWN RELAY
RED/WHT
DK BLU
DK BLU/WHT
RED/WHT
85616125

Fig. 122 Engine wiring schematic — 1992 Town & Country, Caravan and Voyager with 3.0L engine

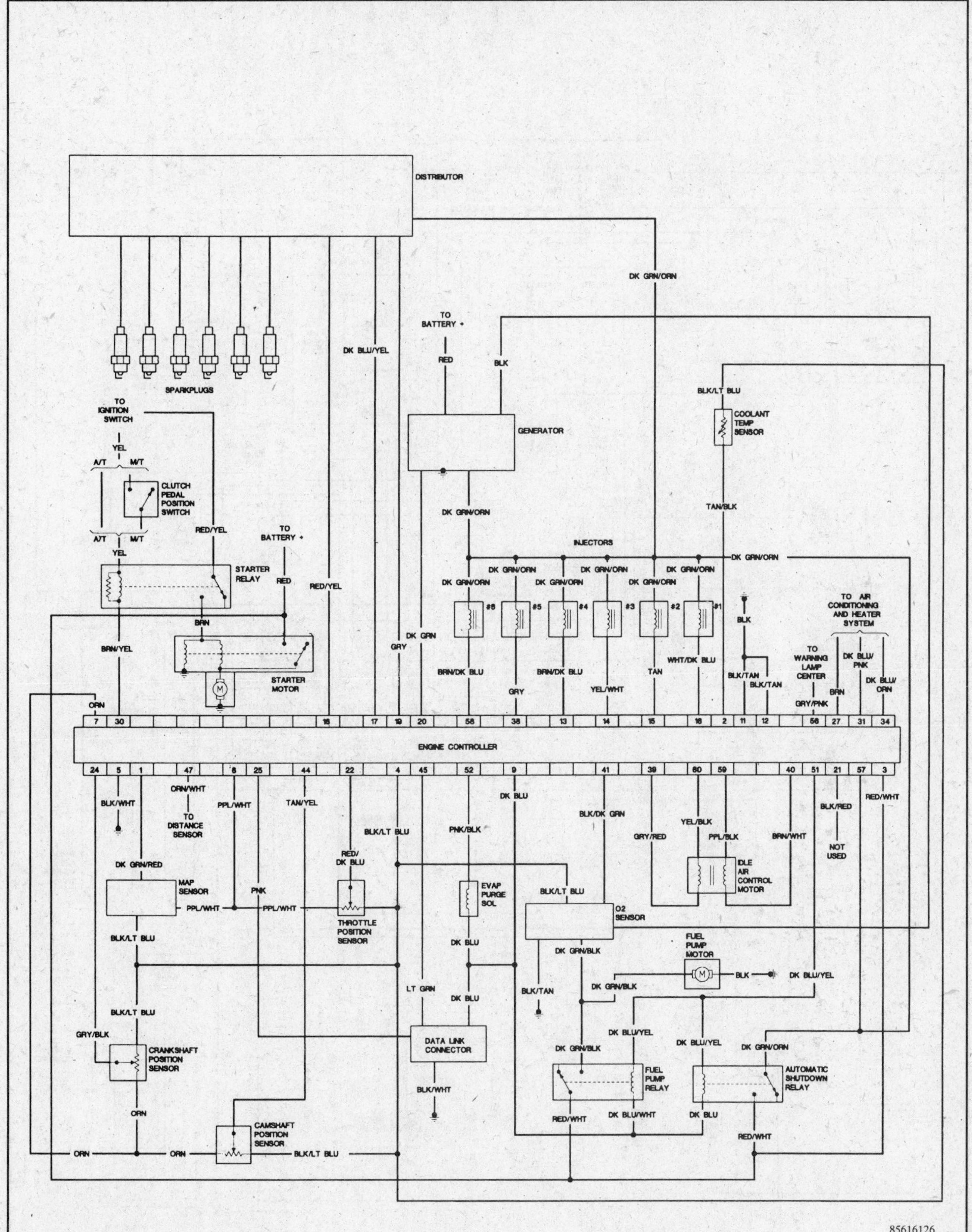

Fig. 123 Engine wiring schematic — 1992 Town & Country, Caravan and Voyager with 3.3L engine

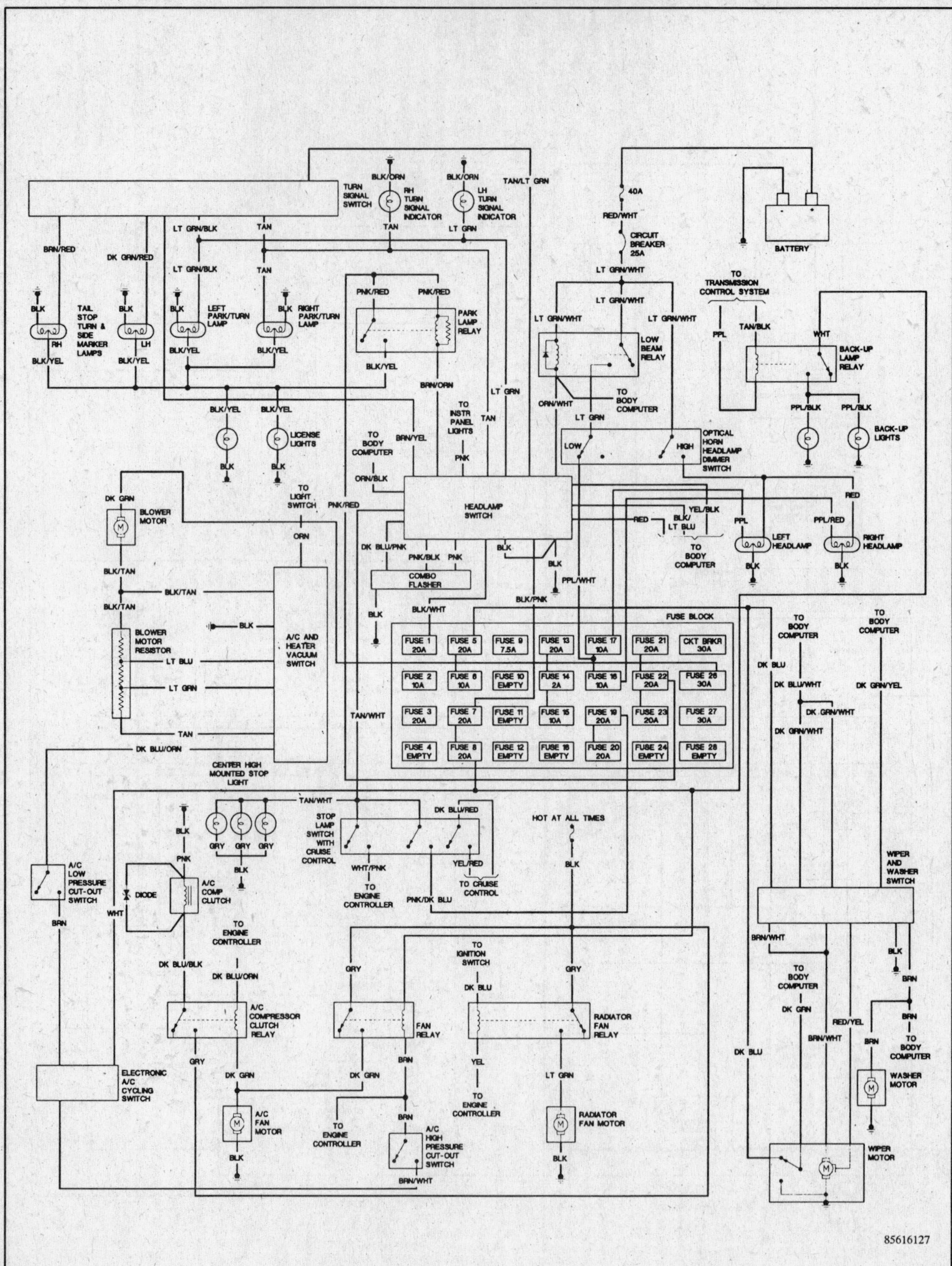

Fig. 124 Chassis wiring schematic — 1992 Town & Country, Caravan and Voyager

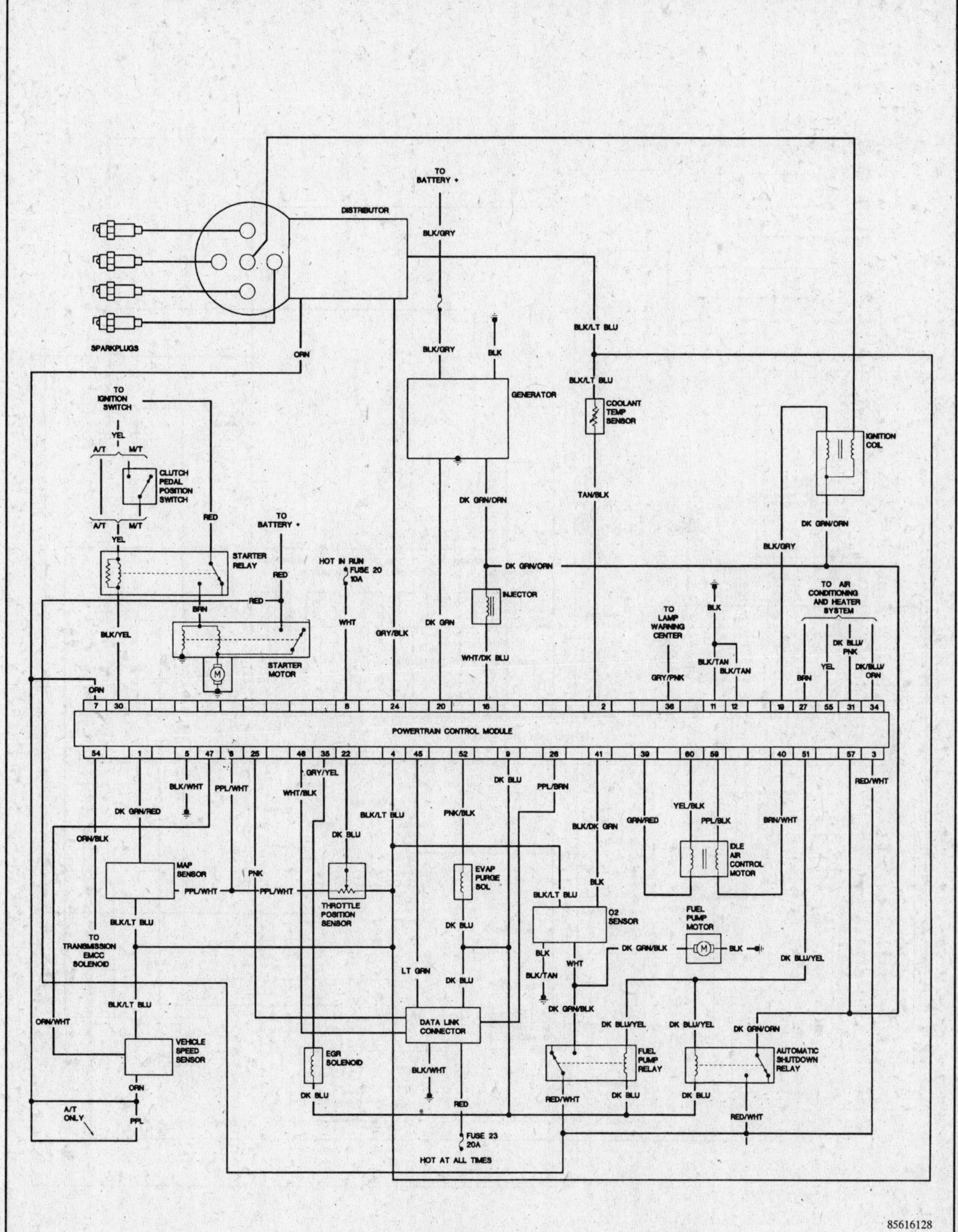

Fig. 125 Engine wiring schematic — 1993 Town & Country, Caravan and Voyager with 2.5L engine

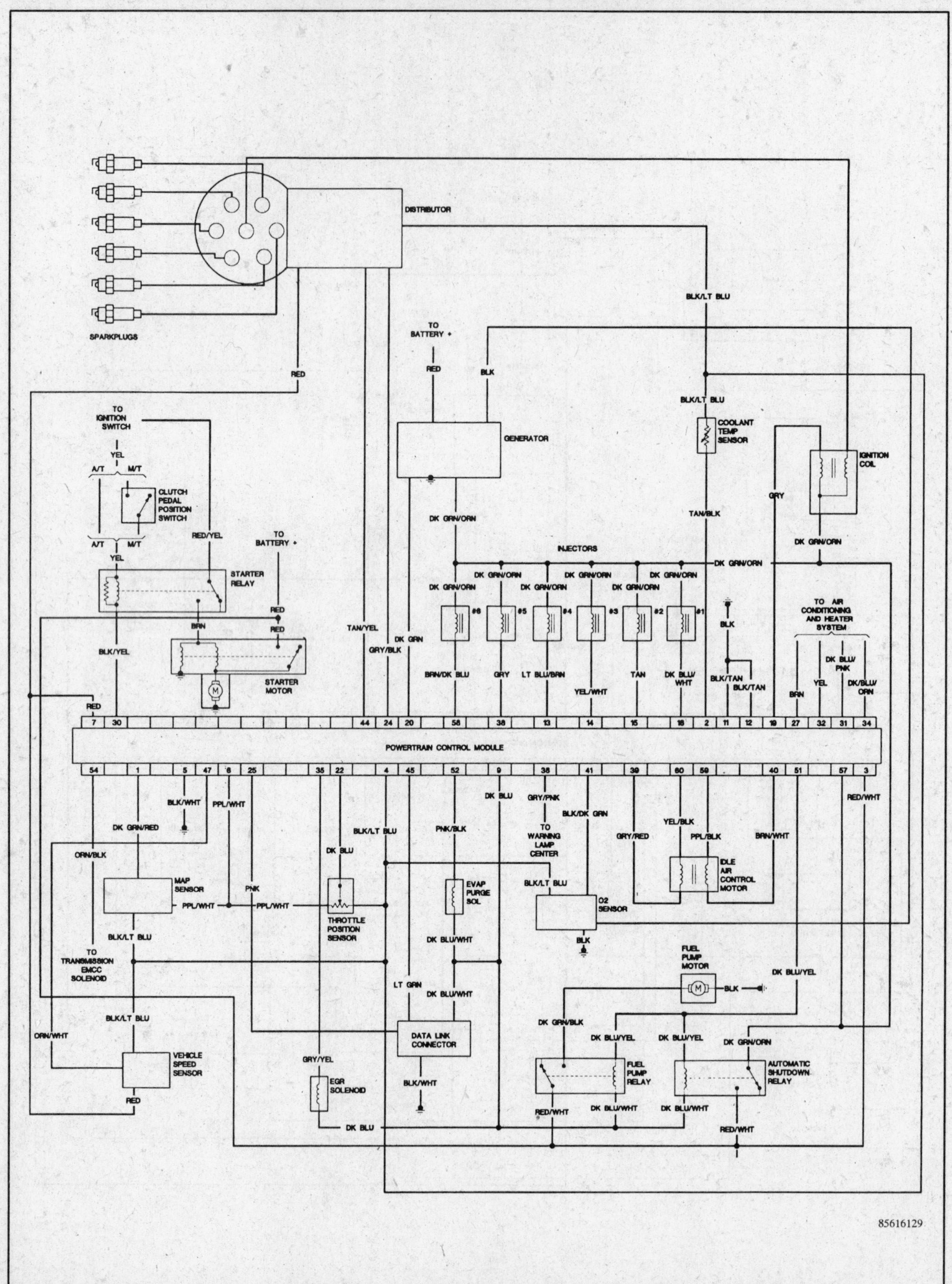

Fig. 126 Engine wiring schematic — 1993 Town & Country, Caravan and Voyager with 3.0L engine

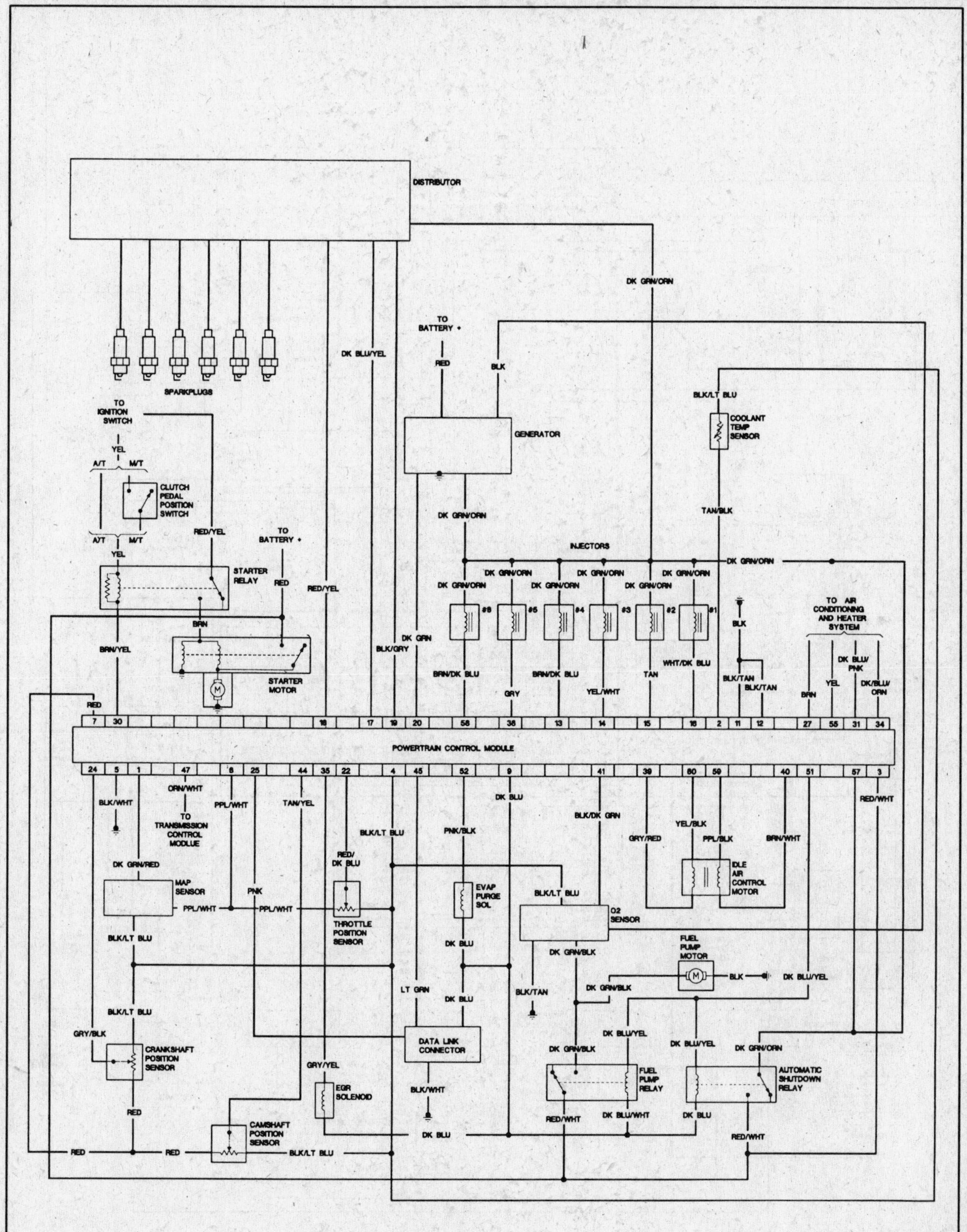

Fig. 127 Engine wiring schematic — 1993 Town & Country, Caravan and Voyager with 3.3L engine

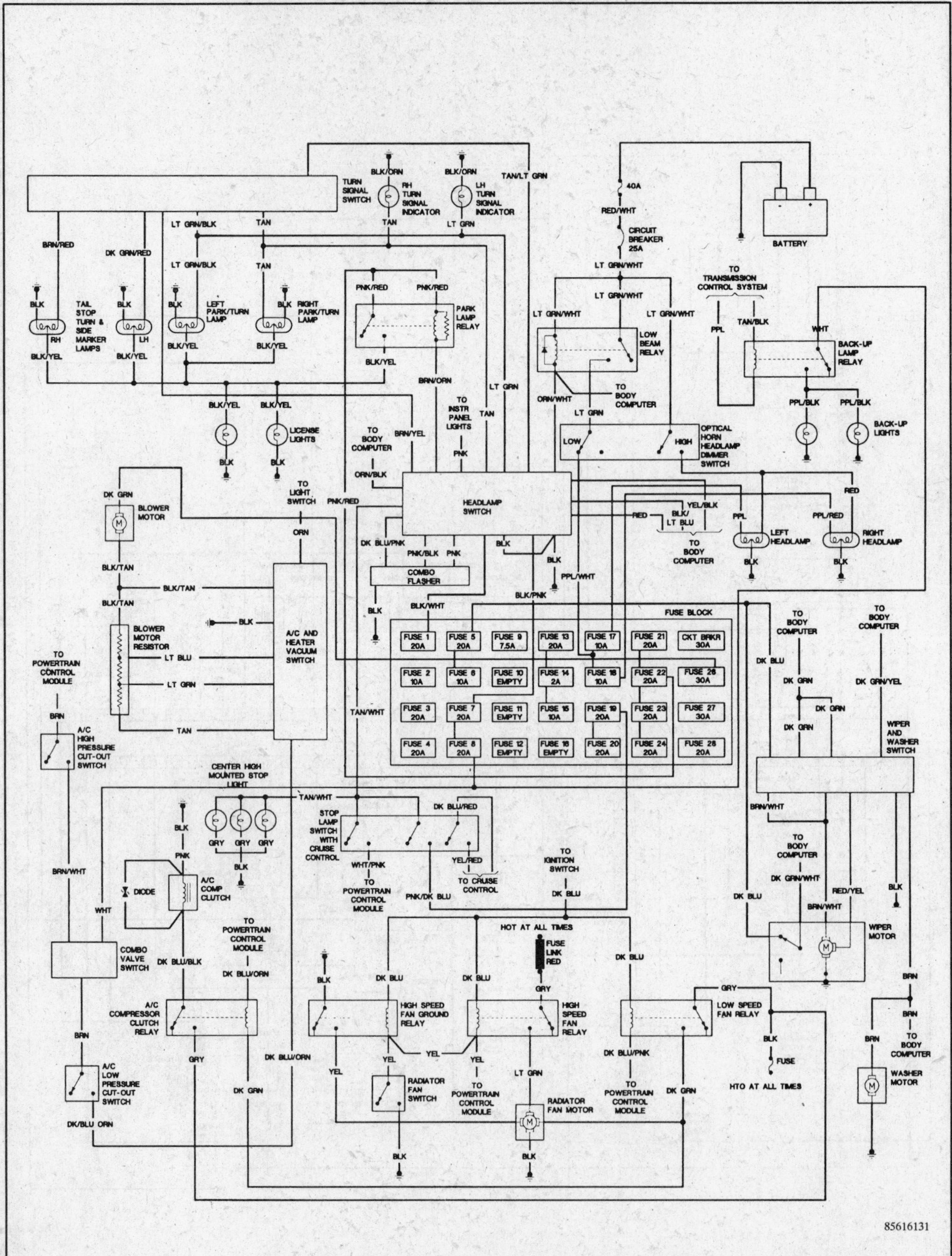

Fig. 128 Chassis wiring schematic — 1993 Town & Country, Caravan and Voyager

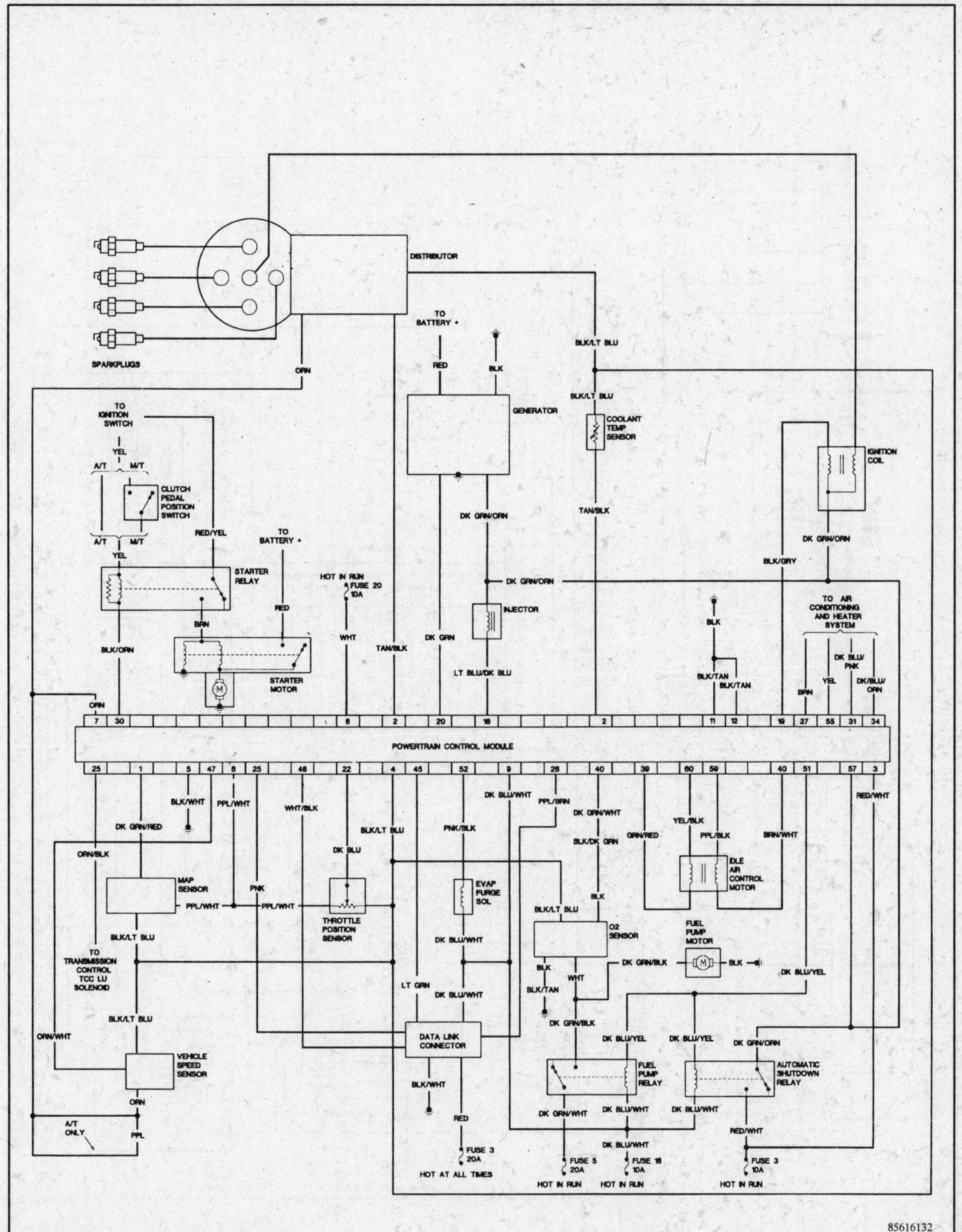

Fig. 129 Engine wiring schematic — 1994–95 Town & Country, Caravan and Voyager with 2.5L engine

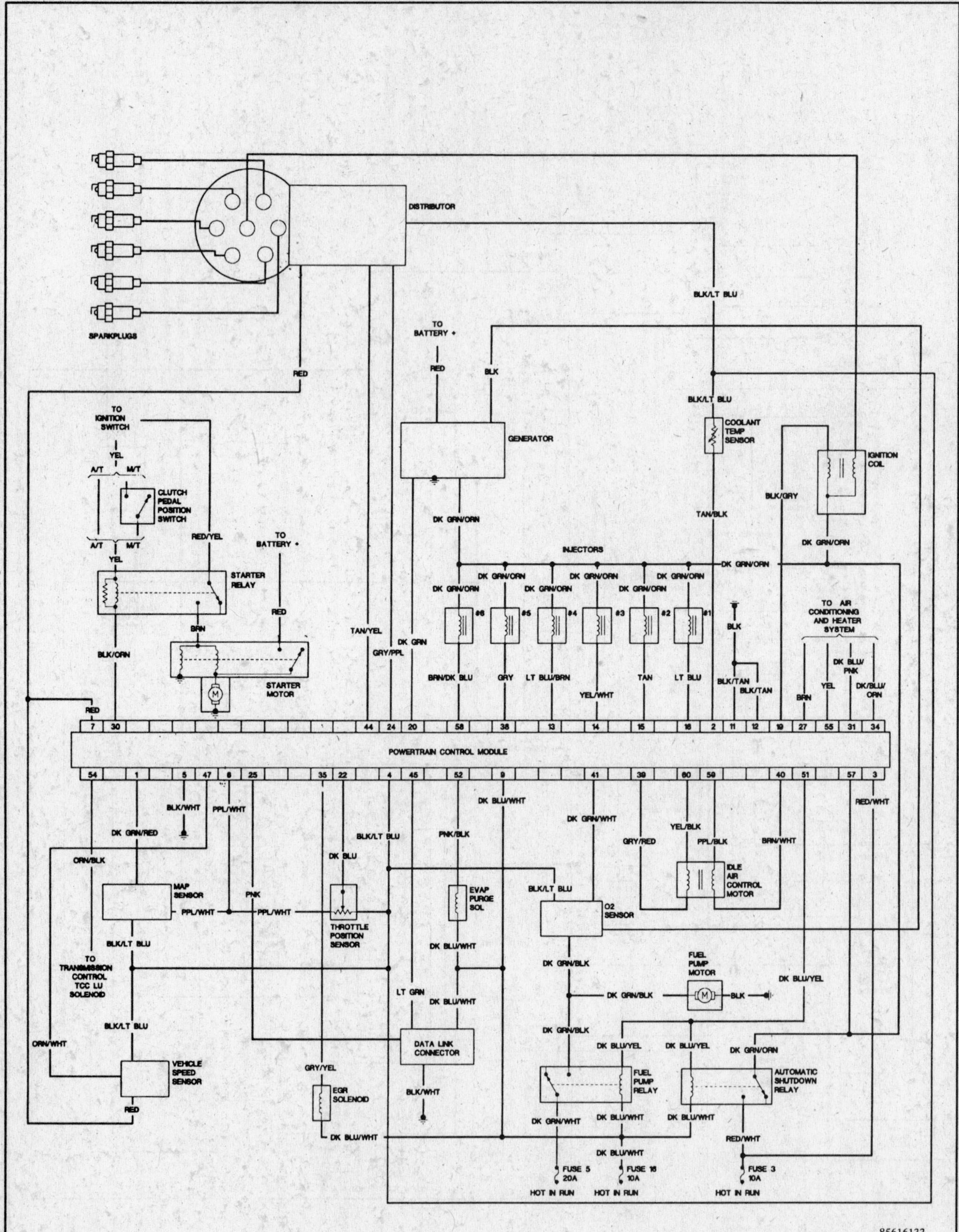

Fig. 130 Engine wiring schematic — 1994–95 Town & Country, Caravan and Voyager with 3.0L engine

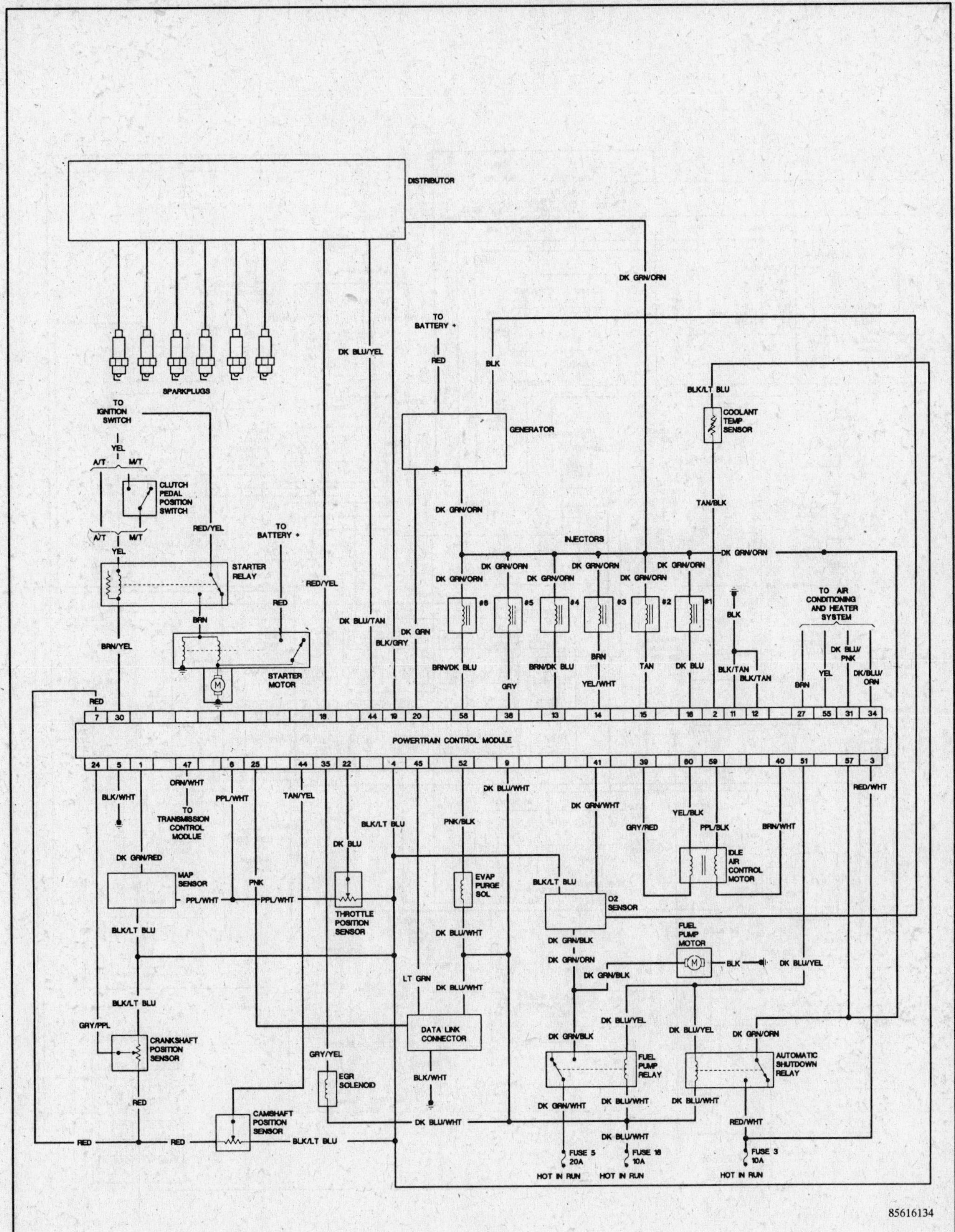

Fig. 131 Engine wiring schematic — 1994–95 Town & Country, Caravan and Voyager with 3.3L and 3.8L engines

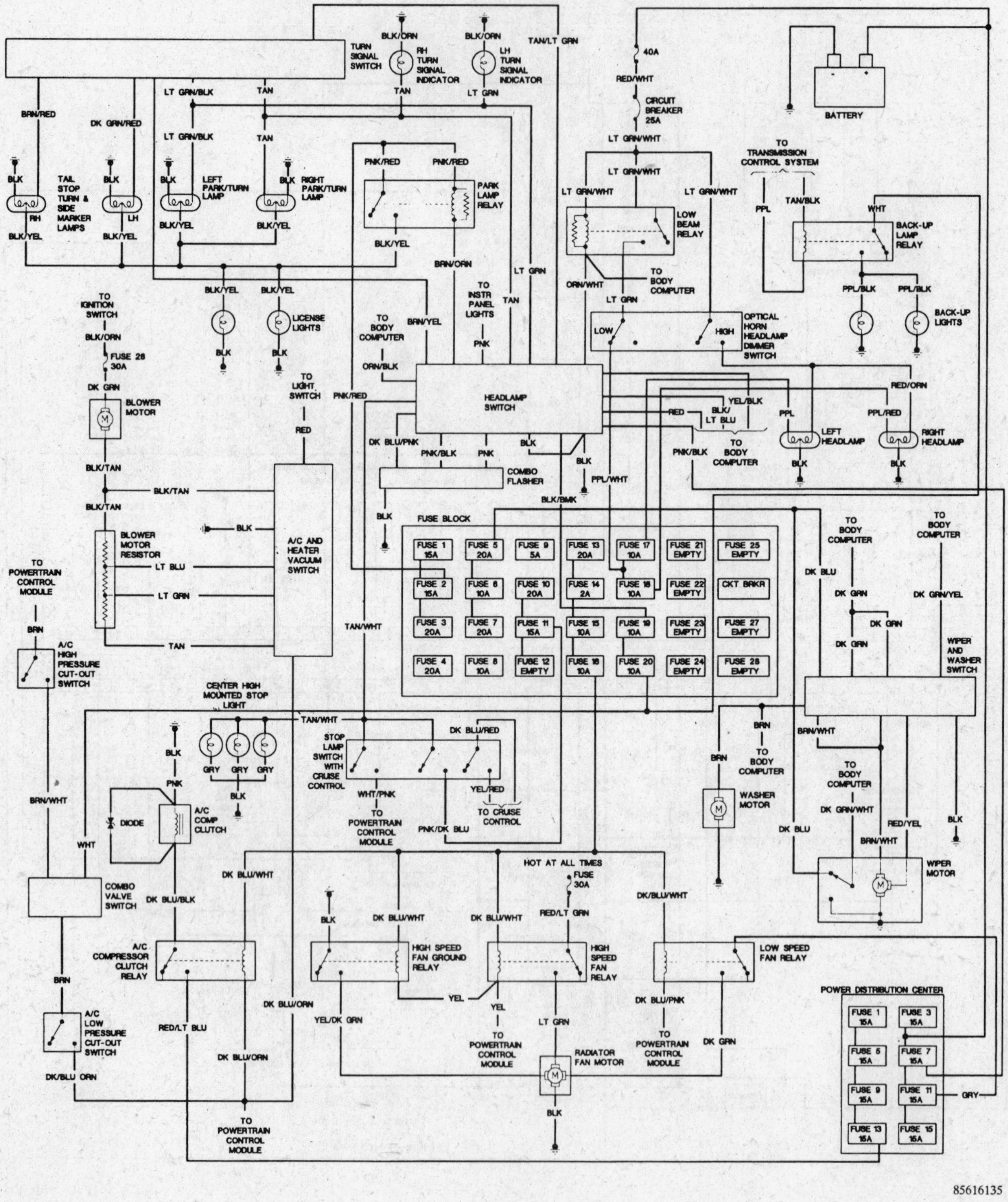

85616135

Fig. 132 Chassis wiring schematic — 1994-95 Town & Country, Caravan and Voyager

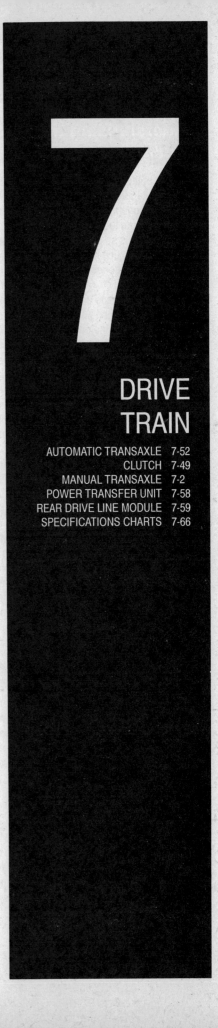

AUTOMATIC TRANSAXLE
ADJUSTMENTS 7-55
FLUID PAN AND FILTER 7-53
NEUTRAL STARTING/BACK-UP LIGHT SWITCH 7-56
TRANSAXLE ASSEMBLY 7-57
UNDERSTANDING AUTOMATIC TRANSAXLES 7-52
CLUTCH
CLUTCH PEDAL 7-50
DRIVEN DISC AND PRESSURE PLATE 7-49
UNDERSTANDING THE CLUTCH 7-49
MANUAL TRANSAXLE
4–SPEED TRANSAXLE OVERHAUL 7-8
5–SPEED TRANSAXLE OVERHAUL 7-15
ADJUSTMENTS 7-2
HALFSHAFTS 7-39
IDENTIFICATION 7-2
TRANSAXLE ASSEMBLY 7-6
UNDERSTANDING THE MANUAL TRANSAXLE 7-2
POWER TRANSFER UNIT
IDENTIFICATION 7-58
REAR DRIVE LINE MODULE
DIFFERENTIAL SIDE GEARS 7-63
DRIVE PINION 7-61
IDENTIFICATION 7-59
REAR DRIVE LINE ASSEMBLY MODULE 7-59
REAR HALFSHAFT 7-60
TORQUE TUBE 7-63
SPECIFICATIONS CHARTS
TORQUE SPECIFICATIONS 7-66

7

DRIVE TRAIN

AUTOMATIC TRANSAXLE 7-52
CLUTCH 7-49
MANUAL TRANSAXLE 7-2
POWER TRANSFER UNIT 7-58
REAR DRIVE LINE MODULE 7-59
SPECIFICATIONS CHARTS 7-66

MANUAL TRANSAXLE

Understanding the Manual Transaxle

Because of the way an internal combustion engine breathes, it can produce torque, or twisting force, only within a narrow speed range. Most modern, overhead valve pushrod engines must turn at about 2500 rpm to produce their peak torque. By 4500 rpm they are producing so little torque that continued increases in engine speed produce no power increases. The torque peak on overhead camshaft engines is generally much higher, but much narrower.

The manual transaxle and clutch are employed to vary the relationship between engine speed and the speed of the wheels so that adequate engine power can be produced under all circumstances. The clutch allows engine torque to be applied to the transaxle input shaft gradually, due to mechanical slippage. Consequently, the vehicle may be started smoothly from a full stop. The transaxle changes the ratio between the rotating speeds of the engine and the wheels by the use of gears. The gear ratios allow full engine power to be applied to the wheels during acceleration at low speeds and at highway/passing speeds.

In a front wheel drive transaxle, power is usually transmitted from the input shaft to a mainshaft or output shaft located slightly beneath and to the side of the input shaft. The gears of the mainshaft mesh with gears on the input shaft, allowing power to be carried from one to the other. All forward gears are in constant mesh and are free from rotating with the shaft unless the synchronizer and clutch is engaged. Shifting from one gear to the next causes one of the gears to be freed from rotating with the shaft and locks another to it. Gears are locked and unlocked by internal dog clutches which slide between the center of the gear and the shaft. The forward gears employ synchronizers; friction members which smoothly bring gear and shaft to the same speed before the toothed dog clutches are engaged.

Identification

Seven manual transaxles, built by Chrysler, are used; a 4-speed, A-460 and six 5-speeds; A-465, A-520, A-523, A-525, A-555 and A-568. All of these transaxles are based on the same design and components, therefore servicing each is almost identical. The transmission and differential are contained together in a single die-cast aluminum case. All of the transmissions are fully synchronized in all gears. Dexron®II automatic transmission/transaxle type fluid (models through 1987) or 5W-30 motor oil (1988 and later models) is used for lubrication. Please refer to Section 1 for additional lubrication information. The transaxle model, build date and final drive ratio are stamped on a tag that is attached to the top of the transaxle. Always give the tag information when ordering parts for the unit.

Adjustments

SHIFT LINKAGE

See Figures 1, 2, 3, 4, 5, 6, 7, 8, 9, 10, 11, 12, 13, 14 and 15

If a hard shifting situation is experienced, determine if the cables are binding and need replacement, or if a linkage adjustment is necessary. Disconnect both cables at the transaxle and move the selector through the various positions. If the selector moves freely an adjustment may be all that is necessary; if not, cable replacement might be indicated.

1. Working over the left front fender, unscrew the lock pin from the transaxle selector shaft housing.
2. Reverse the lock pin so that the long end faces down and insert into the same threaded hole it was removed from. Push the selector shaft into the selector housing while inserting the pin. A hole in the selector shaft will align with the lock pin, allowing the pin to be threaded into the housing. This will lock the selector shaft into the neutral position.
3. From inside the vehicle, remove the gearshift knob by pulling straight up.
4. Remove the reverse pull up ring by first removing the retaining nut and then pull the ring up and off of the lever.
5. Remove the shift lever boot.
6. Remove the console.
7. For models built through 1987: fabricate two adjusting lock pins out of a $^{1}/_{16}$ in. (1.6mm) diameter rod. Total length of the pins should be 5 in. (127mm) with a hook shaped on one end.
8. Loosen the selector and cross-over cable end adjusting/retainer bolts. Be sure the transaxle end of the cables are connected.
9. Install one adjusting lock pin on the side of the lever bracket in hole provided while moving lever slightly to help alignment.
10. Install the other lock pin at the rear of the lever bracket (cross-over cable). Be sure that both cable end pieces are free to move.
11. After pins are inserted, the cable ends will be positioned to the correct adjustment point. Tighten the adjustment/retainer bolts to 55 inch lbs. (6 Nm).
12. On models built in late 1986 and later: loosen the selector and crossover cable adjusting screws. Remove the adjusting screw tool and attached spacer block from the shifter support.
13. Install the adjusting screw tool through the attached spacer, and screw the tool into the base of the shifter tower base.
14. Tighten the adjusting screw tool to 20 inch lbs. (2 Nm).
15. Tighten the selector/crossover cable retaining screws to 70 inch lbs. (8 Nm). Proper torque on the selector/crossover cable bracket is very important for proper operation.
16. Remove the adjusting screw tool and attach it to the bracket.

17. Check the gearshift cables for proper connection to the transaxle.

18. Install the console and remainder of the removed parts.

19. Remove the selector housing lock pin at the transaxle and install it in the reversed position (see Step 1). Tighten the lock pin to 105 inch lbs. (12 Nm), then check the gear shift operation.

BACK-UP LIGHT SWITCH

The back-up light switch is located at the upper left side of the transaxle case. The switch is screwed into the transaxle and serviced by replacement. No adjustment is possible.

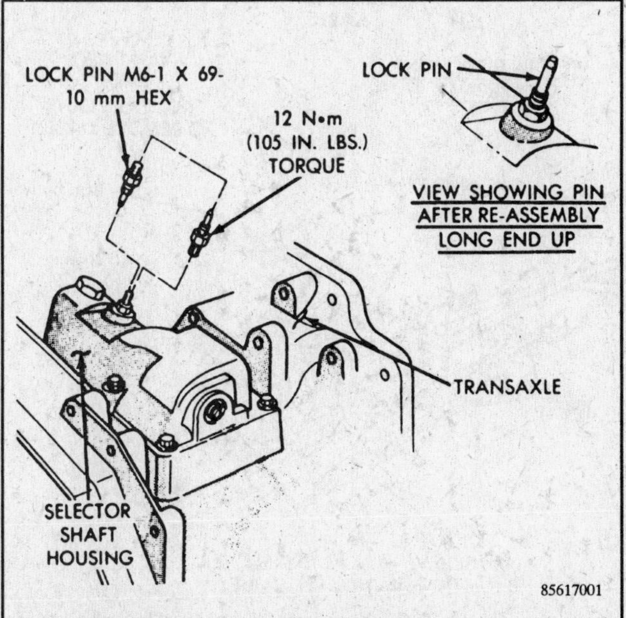

Fig. 1 Transaxle pinned in the neutral position to adjust gearshift linkage — 1984-90 models

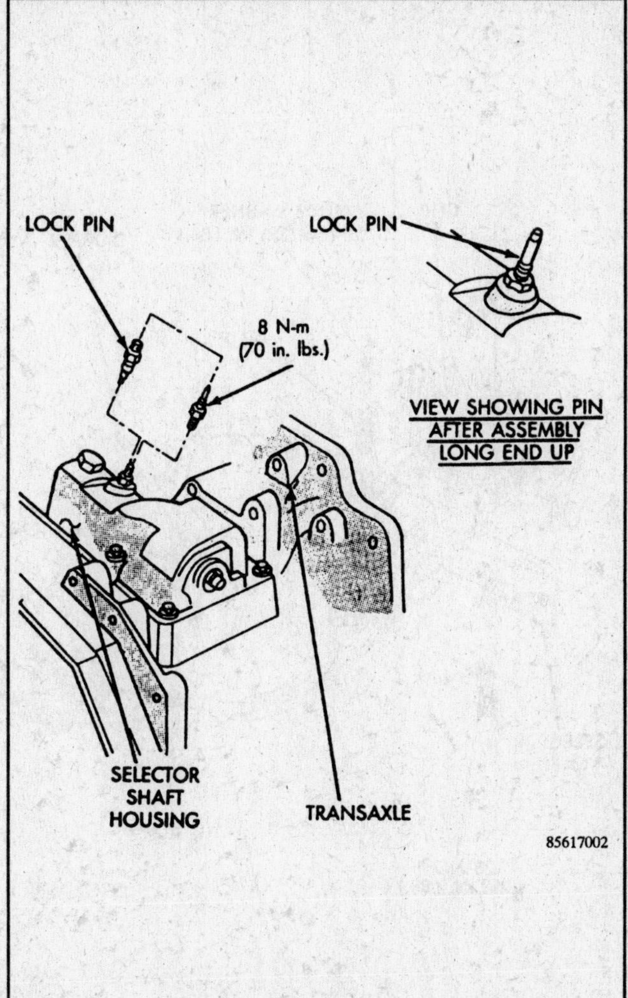

Fig. 2 Transaxle pinned in the neutral position to adjust gearshift linkage — 1992-95 models

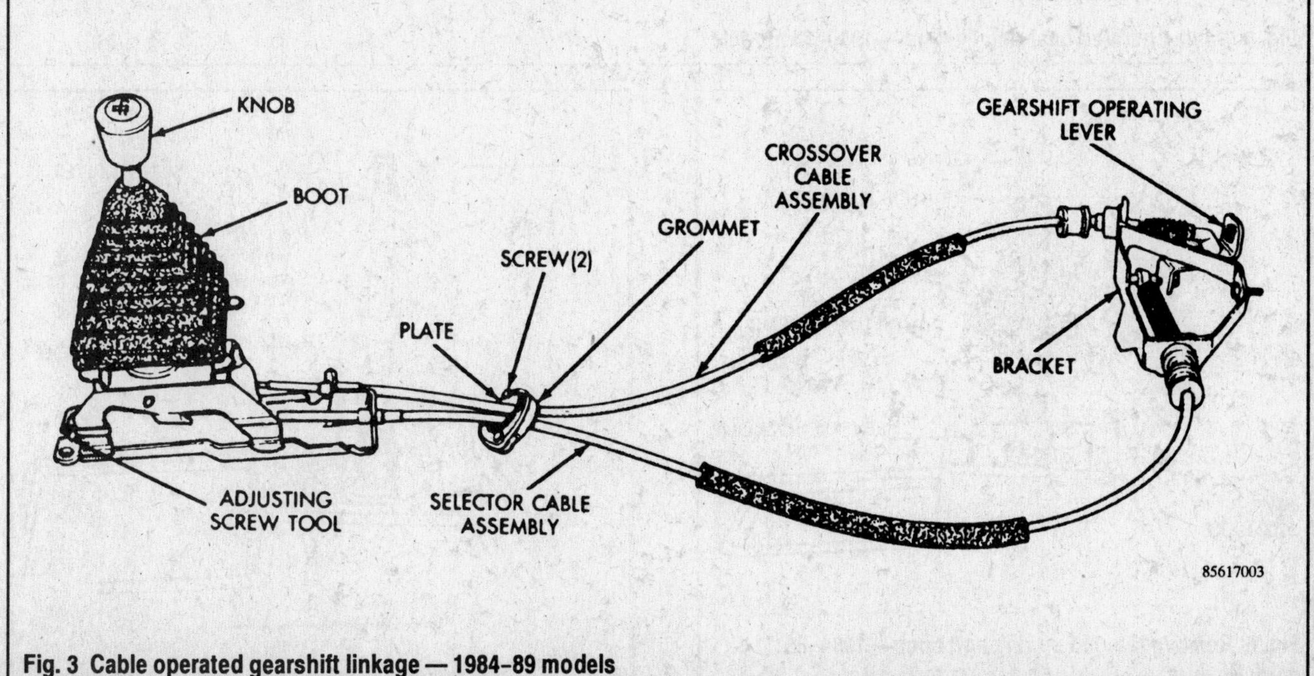

Fig. 3 Cable operated gearshift linkage — 1984-89 models

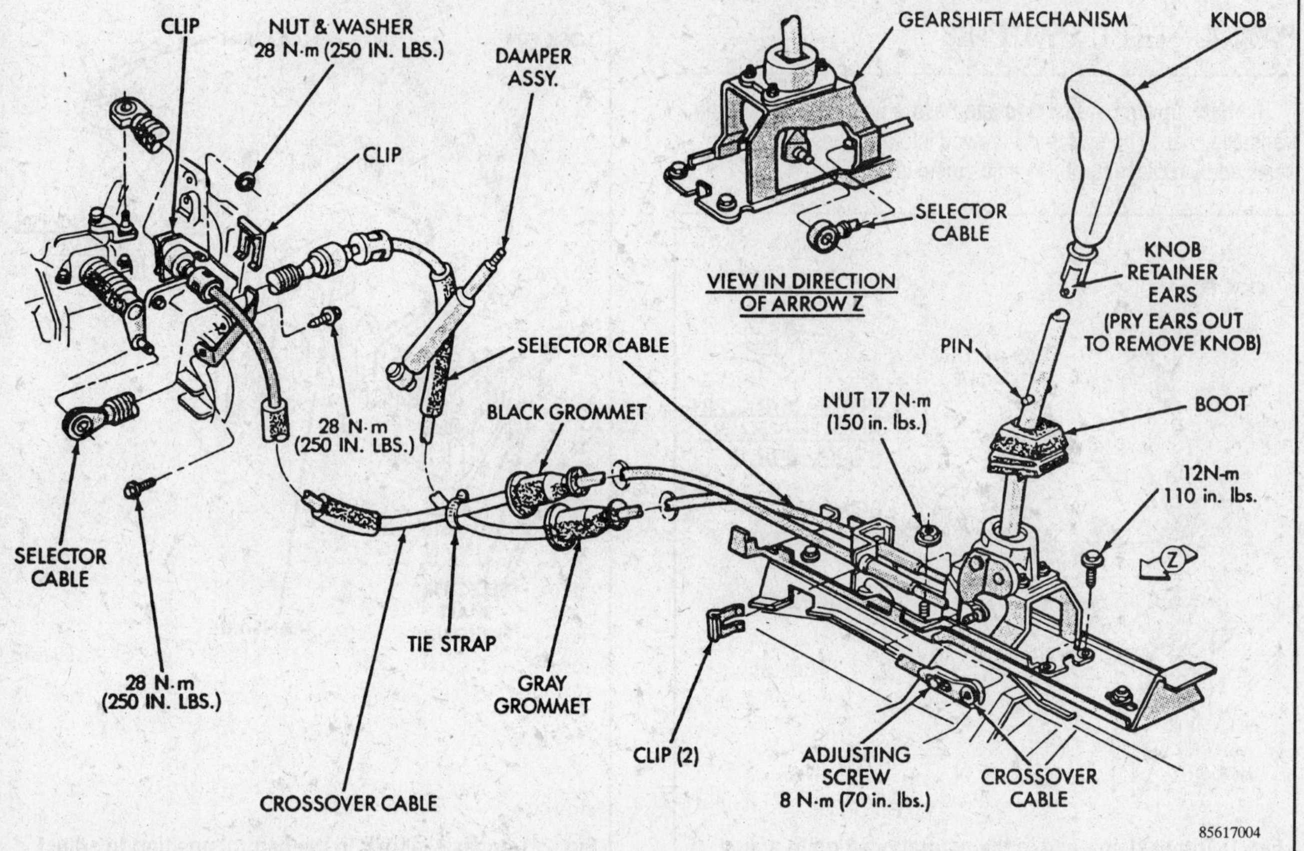

Fig. 4 Cable operated gearshift linkage — 1990-95 models

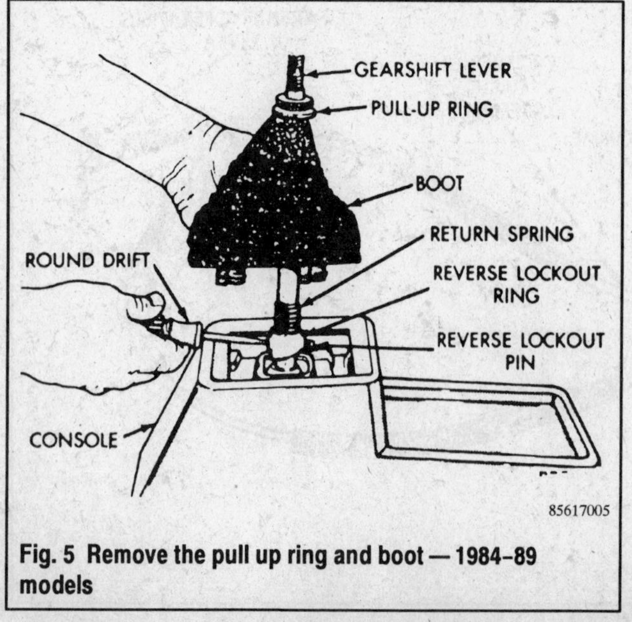

Fig. 5 Remove the pull up ring and boot — 1984-89 models

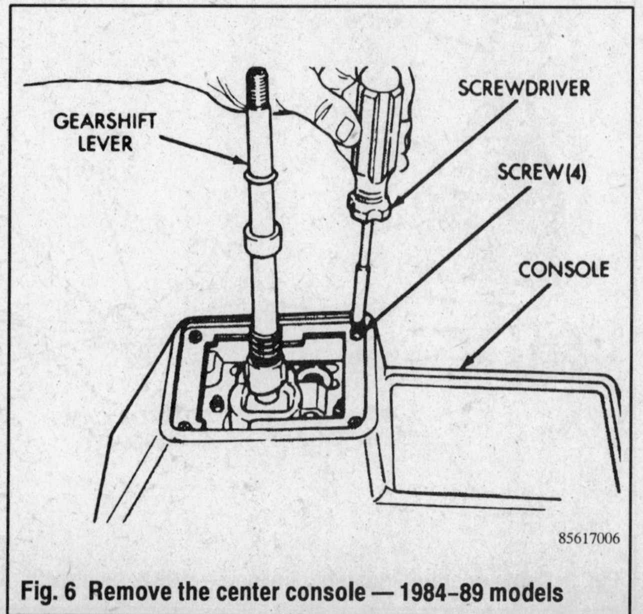

Fig. 6 Remove the center console — 1984-89 models

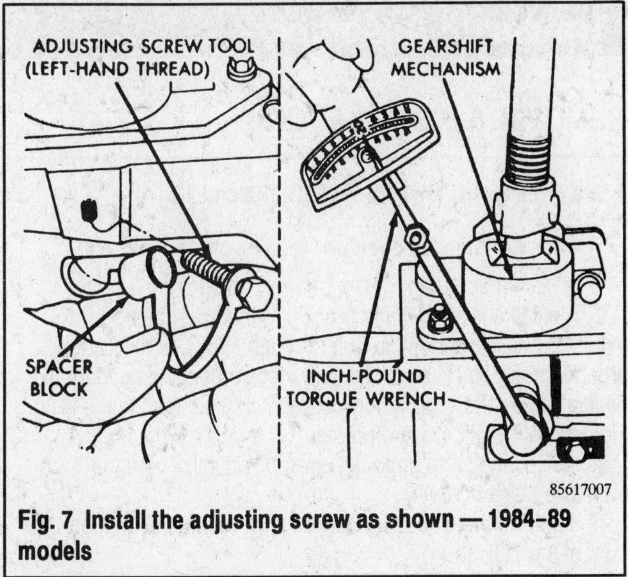

Fig. 7 Install the adjusting screw as shown — 1984-89 models

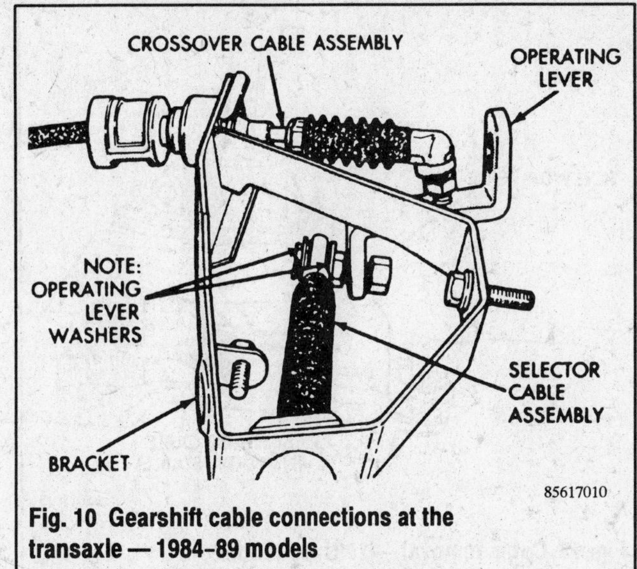

Fig. 10 Gearshift cable connections at the transaxle — 1984-89 models

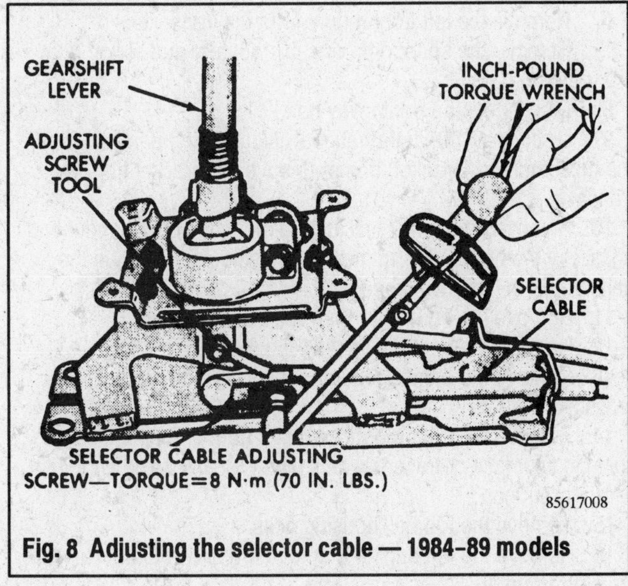

Fig. 8 Adjusting the selector cable — 1984-89 models

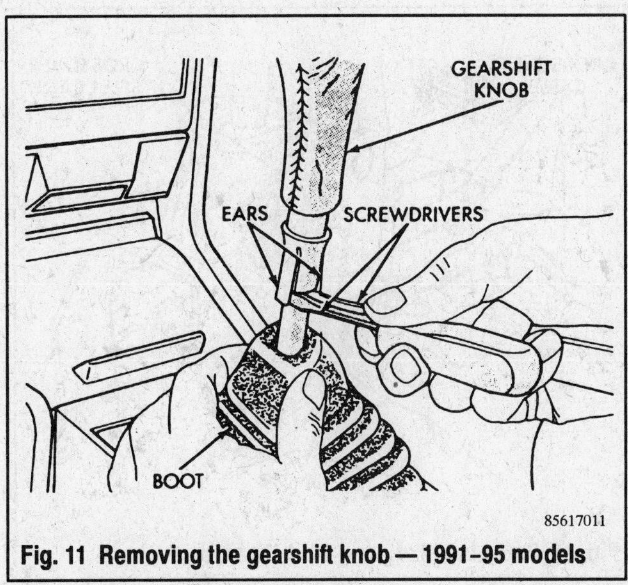

Fig. 11 Removing the gearshift knob — 1991-95 models

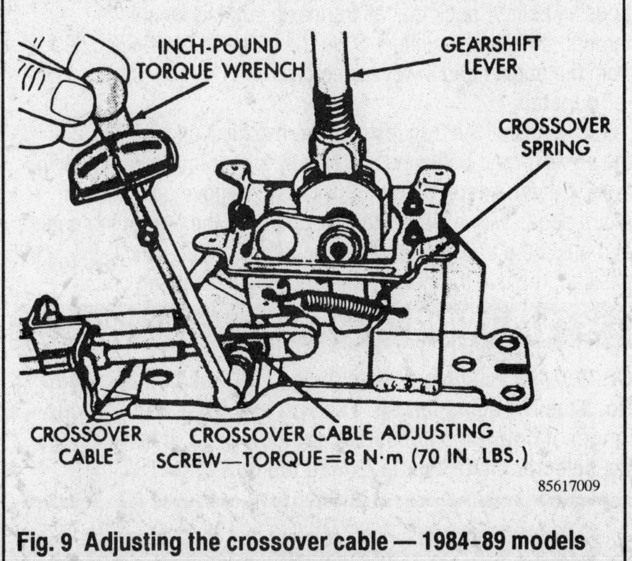

Fig. 9 Adjusting the crossover cable — 1984-89 models

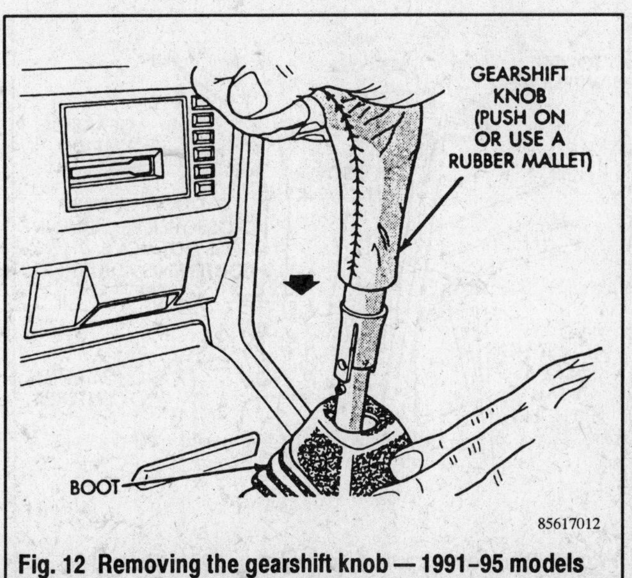

Fig. 12 Removing the gearshift knob — 1991-95 models

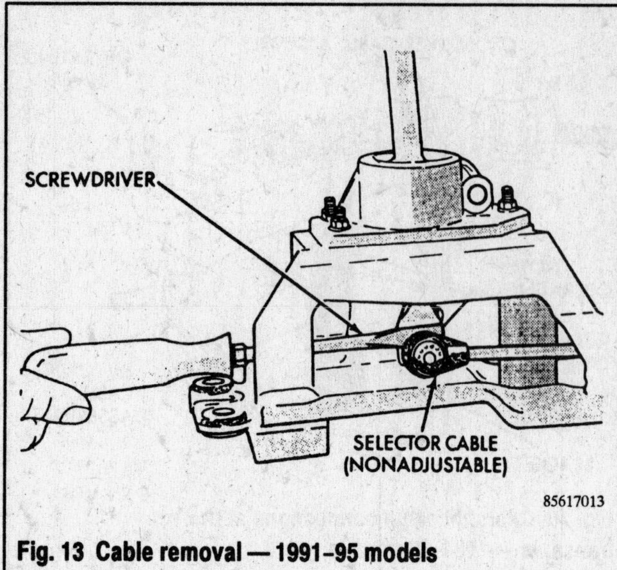

Fig. 13 Cable removal — 1991-95 models

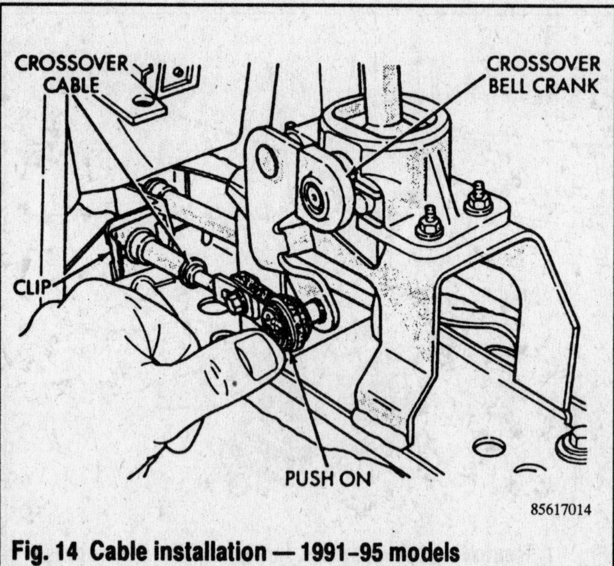

Fig. 14 Cable installation — 1991-95 models

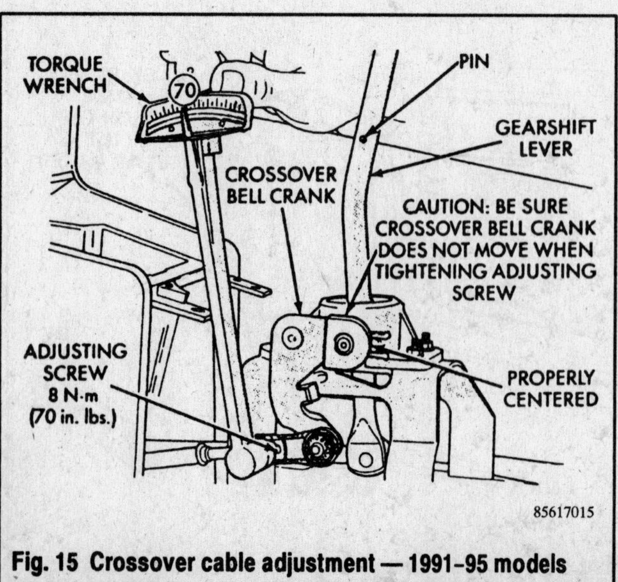

Fig. 15 Crossover cable adjustment — 1991-95 models

Transaxle Assembly

REMOVAL & INSTALLATION

See Figures 16, 17, 18, 19, 20, 21, 22 and 23

Transaxle removal does not require engine removal.

1. Disconnect the negative battery cable from the battery.
2. Install a sling or lifting bracket to the No. 4 cylinder exhaust manifold mounting bolt (through 1987), or the battery ground strap bolt (1988 and later). Place an engine support device across the engine compartment and connect to the sling. Tighten until slight upward pressure is applied to the engine.
3. Disconnect the gearshift operating control from the transaxle selector lever.
4. Loosen the wheel lug nuts slightly. Raise and support the front of the vehicle.
5. Remove both front wheel and tire assemblies. Remove the left front engine splash shield. Drain the fluid from the transaxle.
6. Remove the left front mount from the transaxle.
7. Remove the speedometer cable adapter and pinion from the transaxle.
8. Disconnect the front sway bar.
9. Disconnect the anti-rotational link (anti-hop damper) from the crossmember bracket, do not remove the bracket from the transaxle.
10. Remove both lower ball joint-to-steering knuckle mounting bolts. Pry the ball joint from the steering knuckle. Remove the halfshaft from the drive wheel hub.
11. Remove the halfshafts from the differential.
12. Remove the back-up light switch connector.
13. Remove the engine mount bracket from the front crossover.
14. Remove the front mount insulator through-bolt. Place a suitable floor jack or transaxle jack under the transaxle and raise to gently support.
15. Remove the top bell housing bolts.
16. Remove the left engine mount at rear cover plate. Remove the starter motor.
17. Secure the transaxle to the jack and remove the lower bell housing bolts. Check that all transaxle support mounts or through-bolts are removed. Slide the jack and transaxle away from the engine and lower assembly.

To install:

18. To install the transaxle; make two locating pins which are the same thread bolts and are slightly longer than the mounting bolts. Cut the heads off with a hacksaw, remove any burrs or sharp edges with a file. Install the bolts into the rear of the engine and guide the transaxle over them. After the transaxle is in position, remove the guide bolts and install mounting bolts.

****WARNING**

On 1992-93 vehicles, the bolts used for position No. 1 and No. 3 are the same length. The bolt in the No. 2 position is longer. If bolt No. 2 is used in position No. 3, it can damage the selector shaft housing when the bolt is seated.

19. Raise the transaxle into position and slide it over the locating pins. Install the top bell housing bolts.

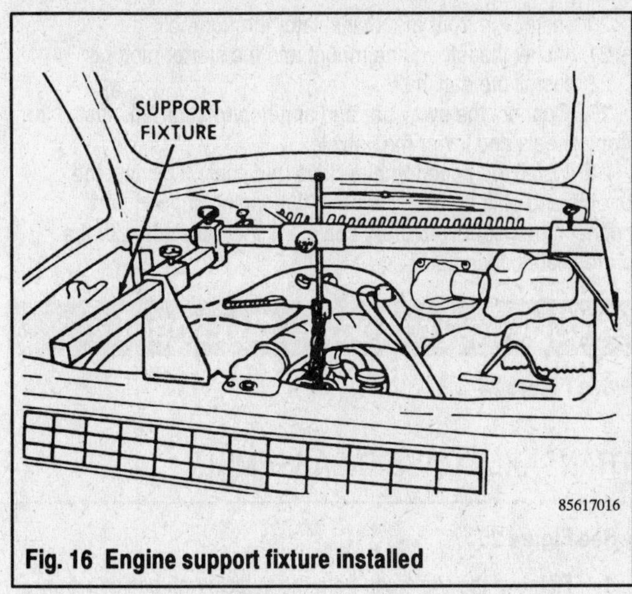

Fig. 16 Engine support fixture installed

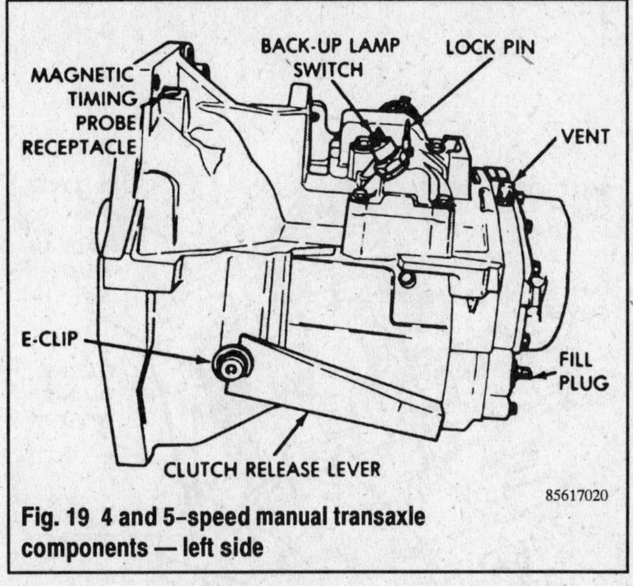

Fig. 19 4 and 5-speed manual transaxle components — left side

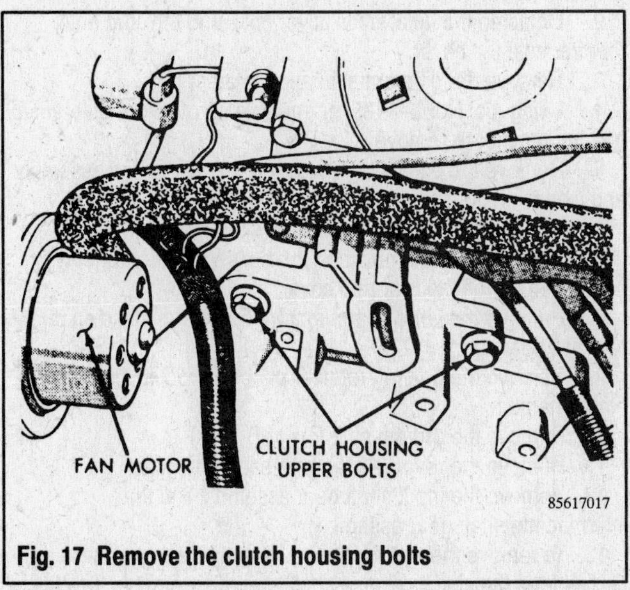

Fig. 17 Remove the clutch housing bolts

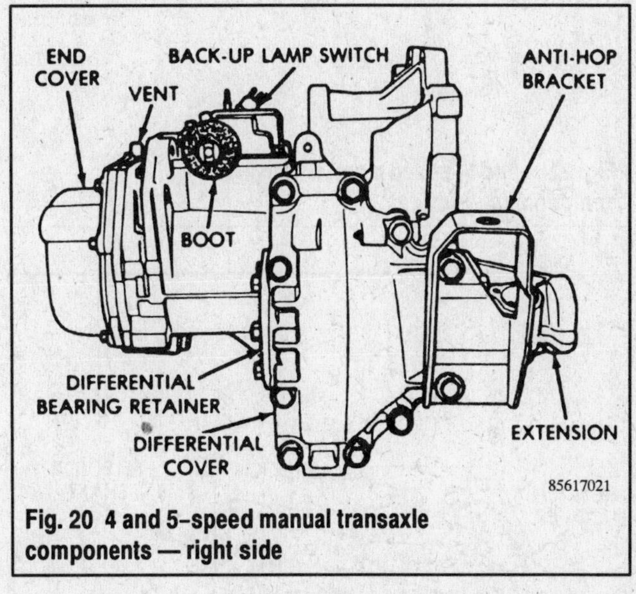

Fig. 20 4 and 5-speed manual transaxle components — right side

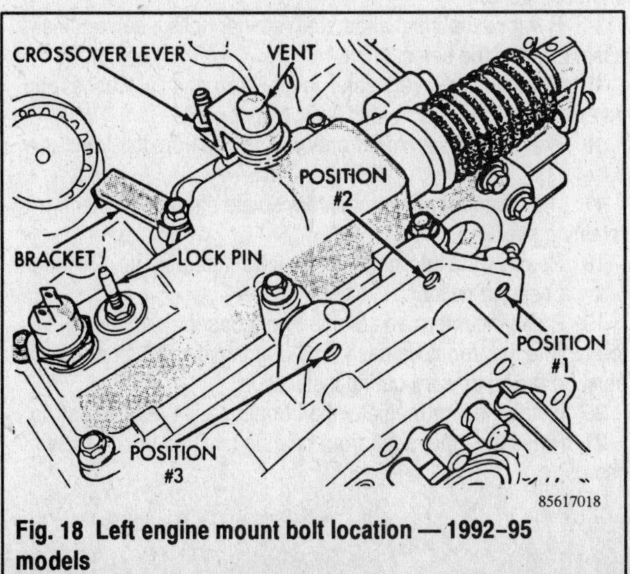

Fig. 18 Left engine mount bolt location — 1992–95 models

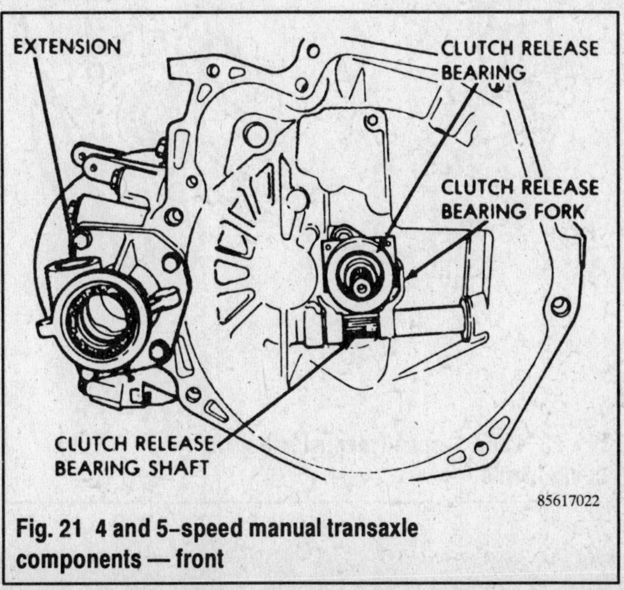

Fig. 21 4 and 5-speed manual transaxle components — front

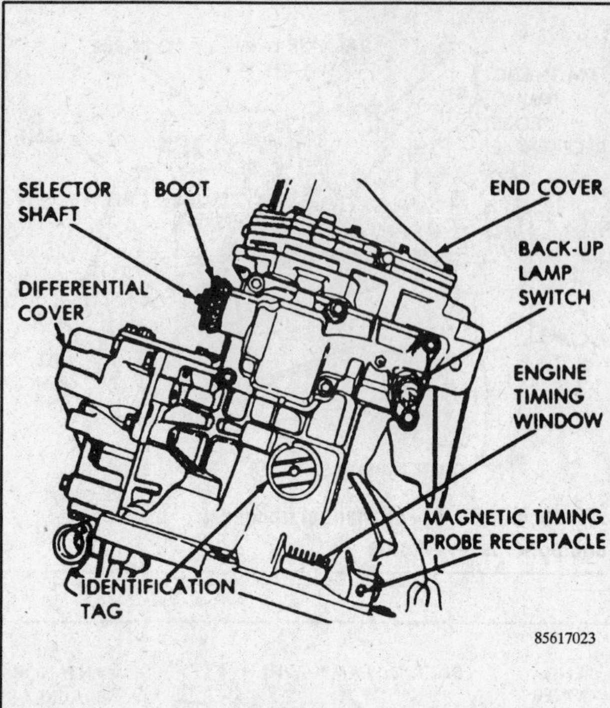

Fig. 22 4 and 5-speed manual transaxle components — top

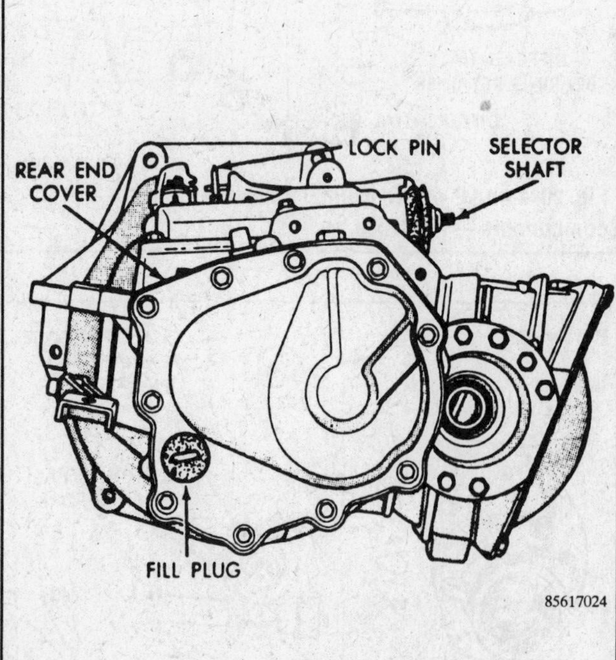

Fig. 23 4 and 5-speed manual transaxle components — rear

20. Install the front mount insulator through-bolt.
21. Install the left engine mount and the starter motor.
22. Install the halfshafts.
23. Connect the sway bar and anti-hop/rotation link. Install the front wheels and lower the vehicle.
24. Install the speedometer drive and cable. Connect the throttle and shift linkage. Remove the engine support and connect the negative battery cable. Fill the transaxle with the correct lubrication fluid.

4-Speed Transaxle Overhaul

➧ See Figure 24

TRANSAXLE CASE DISASSEMBLY

➧ See Figure 25

1. Remove the transaxle from the vehicle and position it on suitable holding fixture.
2. Unfasten the differential cover bolts and the stud nuts, then remove the cover.
3. Remove the differential bearing retainer bolts.
4. Using tool No. L-4435, or equivalent, rotate the differential bearing retainer to remove it.
5. Remove the extension housing bolts, differential assembly and extension housing.
6. Unbolt and remove the selector shaft housing.
7. Remove the stud nuts and the bolts from the rear end cover then pry off the rear end cover.
8. Remove the large snapring from the intermediate shaft rear ball bearing.
9. Remove the bearing retainer plate by tapping it with a plastic hammer.
10. Remove the 3rd/4th shift fork rail.
11. Remove the reverse idler gear shaft and gear.
12. Remove the input shaft gear assembly and the intermediate shaft gear assembly.
13. To remove the clutch release bearing, disengage the E-clips from the clutch release shaft, then disassemble the clutch shaft components.
14. Remove the input shaft seal retainer bolts, seal, retainer assembly and the select shim.
15. Remove the reverse shift lever E-clip and flat washer and disassemble the reverse shift lever components.
16. Press the input shaft front bearing cup from the transaxle case.
17. Unbolt and remove the intermediate shaft front bearing retaining strap.
18. Remove the intermediate shaft front bearing and oil feeder using a bearing puller.
19. Press the intermediate shaft front bearing with the oil feeder into the transaxle case. The bearing identification letters must be facing upward during installation.
20. Install the intermediate shaft front bearing retaining strap.
21. Press the input shaft front bearing cup into the transaxle case.

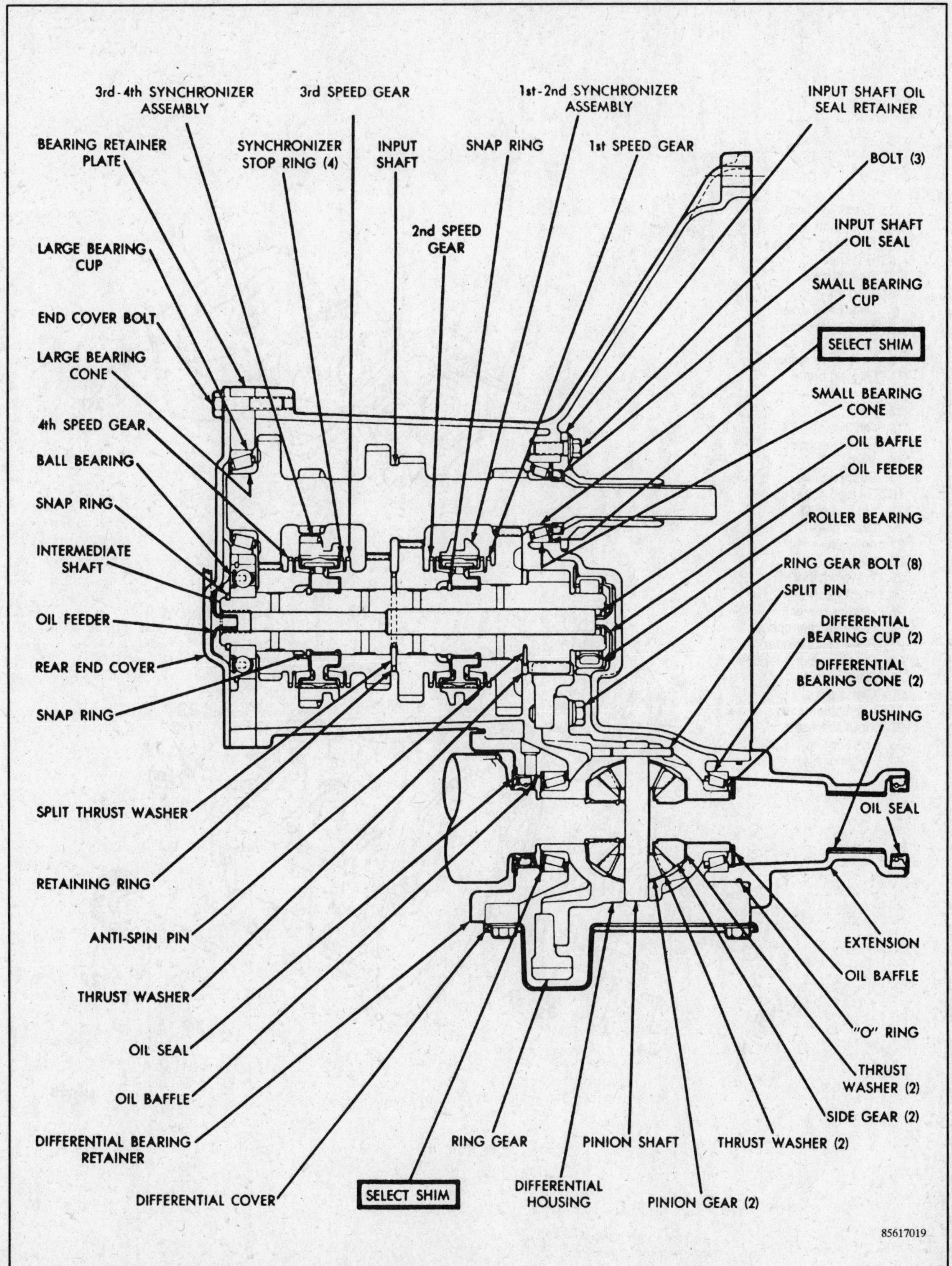

Fig. 24 4-speed manual transaxle component identification

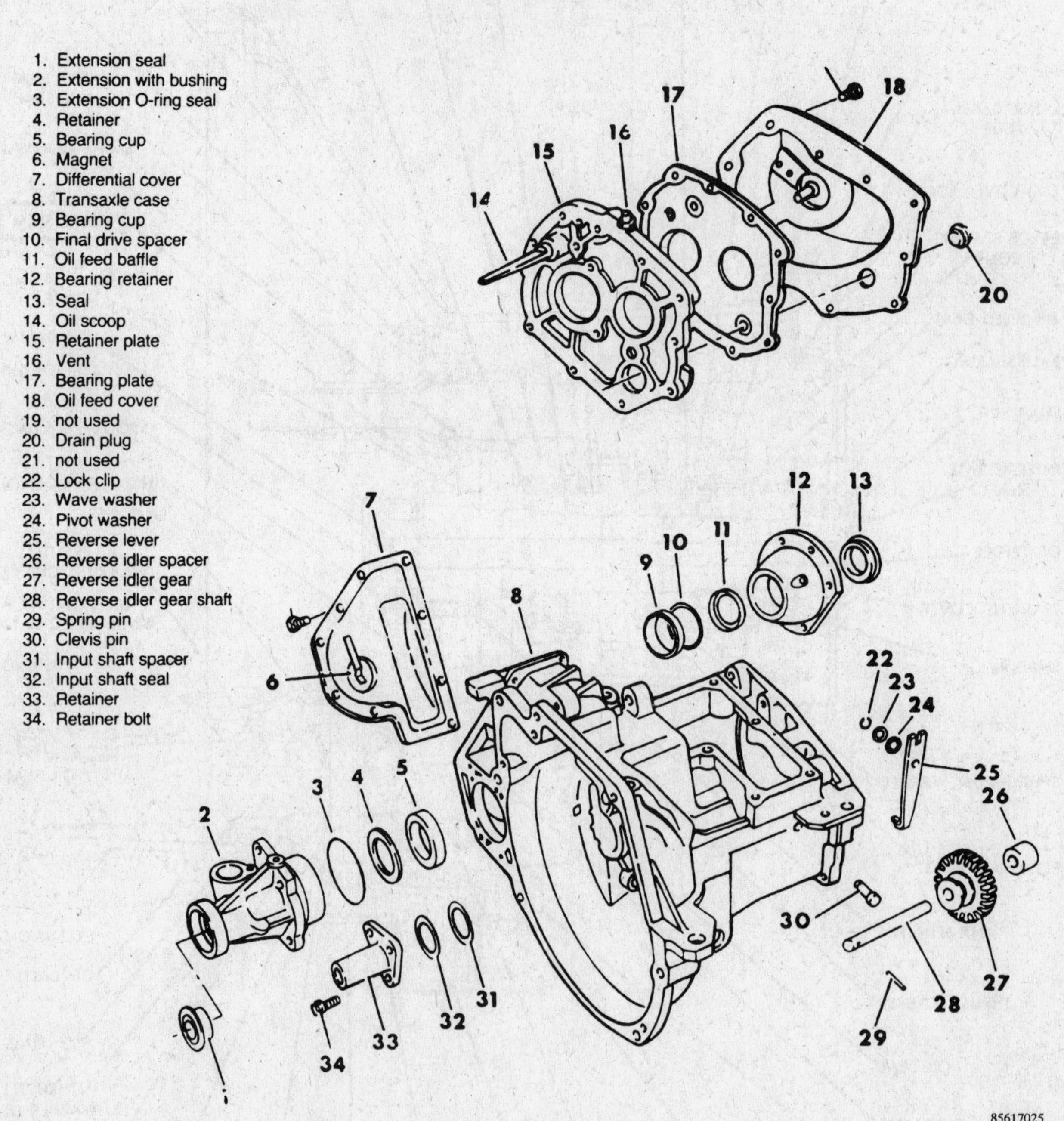
1. Extension seal
2. Extension with bushing
3. Extension O-ring seal
4. Retainer
5. Bearing cup
6. Magnet
7. Differential cover
8. Transaxle case
9. Bearing cup
10. Final drive spacer
11. Oil feed baffle
12. Bearing retainer
13. Seal
14. Oil scoop
15. Retainer plate
16. Vent
17. Bearing plate
18. Oil feed cover
19. not used
20. Drain plug
21. not used
22. Lock clip
23. Wave washer
24. Pivot washer
25. Reverse lever
26. Reverse idler spacer
27. Reverse idler gear
28. Reverse idler gear shaft
29. Spring pin
30. Clevis pin
31. Input shaft spacer
32. Input shaft seal
33. Retainer
34. Retainer bolt
85617025

Fig. 25 4-speed manual transaxle case components

INTERMEDIATE SHAFT

See Figure 26

The 1st/2nd, the 3rd/4th shift forks are interchangeable, however, the synchronizer stop rings are not. The 1st and 2nd synchronizer stop rings have a larger diameter than the other stop rings.

1. Remove the intermediate shaft rear bearing snapring.
2. Remove the intermediate shaft rear bearing with a bearing puller.
3. Remove the 3rd/4th synchronizer hub snapring.
4. Matchmark then remove the 3rd/4th synchronizer hub and the 3rd speed gear using a puller.

To install:

5. Install the 1st speed gear thrust washer, gear, stop ring and 1-2 synchronizer assembly
6. Install the 1-2 synchronizer snapring.
7. Install the 2nd speed gear and stop ring.
8. Install the retaining ring and split thrust washer. Install the 3rd speed gear and the 3-4 synchronizer. Install the hub snapring.
9. Install the intermediate shaft rear bearing and retaining snapring.
10. Install the intermediate shaft front bearing.

Pay attention to the following when servicing the intermediate shaft: when assembling the intermediate shaft, make sure the speed gears turn freely and have a minimum of 0.076mm end-play. When installing the 1st speed gear thrust washer make sure the chamfered edge is facing the pinion gear. When installing the 1st/2nd synchronizer make sure the relief faces the 2nd speed gear. Use an arbor press to install the intermediate shaft rear bearing, the 3rd/4th synchronizer hub and the 3rd speed gear. When installing the 3-4 synchronizer hub and 3rd speed gear, index the snapring 90° to the split washer. During the installation of synchronizer ring assemblies, make sure that all the matchmarks are aligned.

SELECTOR SHAFT HOUSING

1. Disengage the snapring from the selector shaft boot and remove the boot.
2. Pry the shaft oil seal from the selector shaft housing.
3. With a small prybar positioned against the gearshift selector, compress the crossover and push the E-clip from the selector shaft. Remove the E-clip to release the selector shaft.
4. Withdraw the selector shaft from the selector housing.
5. Unfasten the plate stop retaining bolts and remove the stop.
6. Disassemble the selector shaft housing components.

To assemble:

7. Assemble the selector shaft housing components in the reverse order of removal. Use a new back-up lamp switch gasket if needed.
8. Install the plate stop with the retaining bolts.
9. Insert the selector shaft into the housing.
10. Compress the gearshift selector and install the E-clip.
11. Clean the bore and drive a new oil seal into the housing using the proper tool.
12. Place the boot onto the shaft and retain with the snapring.

DIFFERENTIAL BEARING RETAINER

1. Pry the oil seal from the retainer.
2. Remove the retainer cup with a puller. Be careful not to damage the oil baffle and the select shim .
3. Remove the oil baffle and the select shim from the retainer cup.

To assemble:

4. Drive the oil baffle and select shim into the retainer cup using the proper tool.
5. Drive the retainer cup into the retainer using the proper tool.
6. Drive in a new retainer oil seal.

EXTENSION HOUSING

1. Pry the oil seal from the extension housing.
2. Pull the extension cup from the extension housing using the proper tool.
3. Remove the O-ring and oil baffle from the housing.

To assemble:

4. Install a new O-ring into the groove on the outside of the housing.
5. Press the oil baffle in the housing using the proper tool.
6. Press the bearing cup into the extension housing using the proper tool.
7. Install a new housing oil seal.

INPUT SHAFT

1. Remove the input shaft rear and front bearing cones using a suitable puller.
2. Mount the bearing retainer plate on wood blocks and press the input shaft rear bearing cup from the plate.

To install:

3. Before pressing in the bearing cup, bolt the support plate onto the retainer plate.
4. With the support plate in place, press the bearing cup into the retainer plate.
5. Press the front and rear bearing cones onto the input shaft using the proper tool.

Bearing End-Play Adjustment

Shim thickness calculation and end-play adjustment need only be done if any of the following parts are replaced: transaxle case, input shaft seal retainer, bearing retainer plate, rear end cover, input shaft or input shaft bearings.

If any of the above components were replaced, use the following procedure to adjust the bearing preload and proper bearing turning torque.

1. Select a gauging shim which will give 0.001-0.010 in. (0.025-0.250mm) of end-play.

Measure the original shim from the input shaft seal retainer and select a shim 0.010 in. (0.25mm) thinner than the original for the gauging shim.

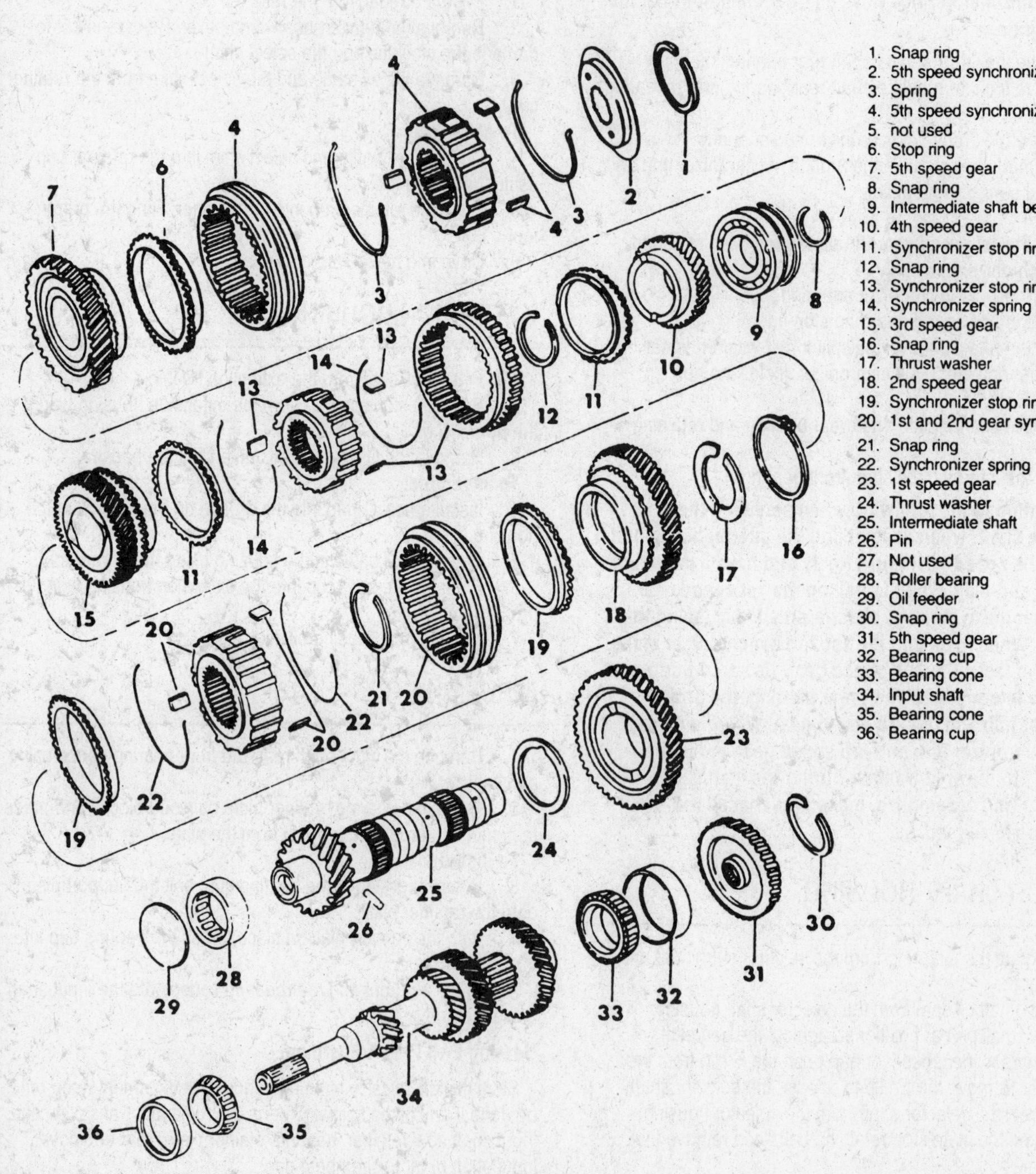
1. Snap ring
2. 5th speed synchronizer retainer
3. Spring
4. 5th speed synchronizer
5. not used
6. Stop ring
7. 5th speed gear
8. Snap ring
9. Intermediate shaft bearing
10. 4th speed gear
11. Synchronizer stop ring
12. Snap ring
13. Synchronizer stop ring
14. Synchronizer spring
15. 3rd speed gear
16. Snap ring
17. Thrust washer
18. 2nd speed gear
19. Synchronizer stop ring
20. 1st and 2nd gear synchronizer
21. Snap ring
22. Synchronizer spring
23. 1st speed gear
24. Thrust washer
25. Intermediate shaft
26. Pin
27. Not used
28. Roller bearing
29. Oil feeder
30. Snap ring
31. 5th speed gear
32. Bearing cup
33. Bearing cone
34. Input shaft
35. Bearing cone
36. Bearing cup
85617026

Fig. 26 4-speed manual transaxle gear train

2. Install the gauging shim on the bearing cup and the input shaft seal retainer.

3. Alternately tighten the input shaft seal retainer bolts until the retainer is bottomed against the case. Tighten the bolts to 21 ft. lbs. (28 Nm).

The input shaft seal retainer is used to draw the input shaft front bearing cup the proper distance into the case bore.

4. Oil the input shaft bearings with A.T.F. (1984–87 models) or SAE 5W-30 engine oil (1988 models) and install the input shaft in the case.

5. Install the bearing retainer plate with the input shaft rear bearing cup pressed in and the end cover installed. Tighten all bolts and nuts to 21 ft. lbs. (28 Nm).

6. Position the dial indicator to check the input shaft end-play. Apply moderate load, by hand, to the input shaft splines. Push toward the rear while rotating the input shaft back and forth a number of times and to settle out the bearings. Zero the dial indicator. Pull the input shaft toward the front while rotating the input shaft back and forth a number of times to settle out the bearings. Record the end-play.

7. The shim required for proper bearing preload is the total of the gauging shim thickness, plus end-play, plus (constant) preload of 0.0019–0.0029 in. (0.050–0.076mm). Combine shims if necessary, to obtain a shim within 0.0016 in. (0.04mm) of the required shim.

8. Remove the input shaft seal retainer and gauging shim. Install the shim(s) selected in Step 6 and install the input shaft seal retainer with a 1/8 in. (3mm) bead of RTV sealant.

Keep RTV sealant out of the oil slot.

9. Tighten the input shaft seal retainer bolts to 21 ft. lbs. (28 Nm).

The input shaft seal retainer is used to draw the input shaft front bearing cup the proper distance into the case bore.

10. Using special tool L-4508, or equivalent, and an inch lb. torque wrench, check the input shaft turning torque. The turning torque should be 1–5 inch lbs. (0.1–0.5 Nm) for new bearings or a minimum of 1 inch lb. (0.1 Nm) for used bearings. If the turning torque is too high, install a 0.0016 in. (0.04mm) thinner shim. If the turning torque is too low, install a 0.0016 in. (0.04mm) thicker shim.

11. Check the input shaft turning torque. Repeat Step 9 until the proper bearing turning torque is obtained.

DIFFERENTIAL

See Figure 27

1. Remove the bearing cone from the differential case.

2. Remove the ring gear bolts and separate the gear from the differential case. The ring gear bolts are epoxy patch type bolts and not to be reused.

3. Using a steel punch and hammer, knock the pinion shaft split pin from the ring gear and differential case.

4. Withdraw the pinion shaft(s) from the differential case.

5. Rotate the side gears to align them with the case opening and remove the thrust washers, side gears and pinion gears.

Shim thickness calculation and bearing preload adjustment need only be done if any of the following parts are replaced: transaxle case, input shaft seal retainer, bearing retainer plate, rear end cover, input shaft or input shaft bearings. If any of the those components were replaced, refer to the appropriate section to adjust the bearing preload, proper bearing turning torque or side gear end-play.

6. In their original order, install the side gears, pinion gears and pinion gear washers.

7. Insert the pinion shaft(s) into the differential case making sure that the hole in the shaft is aligned with the roll pin opening in the case.

8. Insert the pinion shaft roll pin(s) into the notched opening(s) on the side of the differential case and drive them into place.

9. Connect the ring gear to the differential case using new bolts. Tighten the bolts in a crisscross pattern to the proper specification.

10. Attach special tool L-4410, or equivalent, to a suitable extension handle and press the bearing cone onto the differential case.

11. Refer to the appropriate section to check and adjust the bearing preload, if necessary.

Bearing Preload Adjustment Procedure

1. Remove the bearing cup and existing shim from the differential bearing retainer.

2. Select a gauging shim which will give 0.001–0.010 in. (0.025–0.250mm) end-play.

Measure the original shim from the differential bearing retainer and select a shim 0.015 in. (0.38mm) thinner than the original for the gauging shim.

3. Install the gauging shim in the differential bearing retainer and press in the bearing cup. Installation of the oil baffle is not necessary when checking differential assembly end-play.

4. Lubricate the differential bearings with A.T.F. (1984–87 models) or SAE 5W-30 engine oil (1988–89 models) and install the differential assembly in the transaxle case.

5. Inspect the extension housing for damage and replace it as necessary.

6. Position the transaxle with the bell housing facing down on the workbench and secure with C-clamps. Position the dial indicator.

7. Apply a medium load to the ring gear, by hand, in the downward direction while rolling the differential assembly back and forth a number of times to settle the bearings. Zero the dial indicator. To obtain end-play readings, apply a medium load upward by hand while rolling the differential assembly back and forth a number of times to settle out the bearings. Record the end-play.

8. The shim required for proper bearing preload is the total of the gauging shim thickness, plus end-play, plus (constant) preload of 0.010 in. (0.25mm). Combine shims if necessary, to obtain a shim within 0.002 in. (0.05mm) of the shim(s).

9. Remove the differential bearing retainer.

10. Remove the bearing cup and gauging shim. Properly install the oil baffle making sure the oil baffle is not damaged.

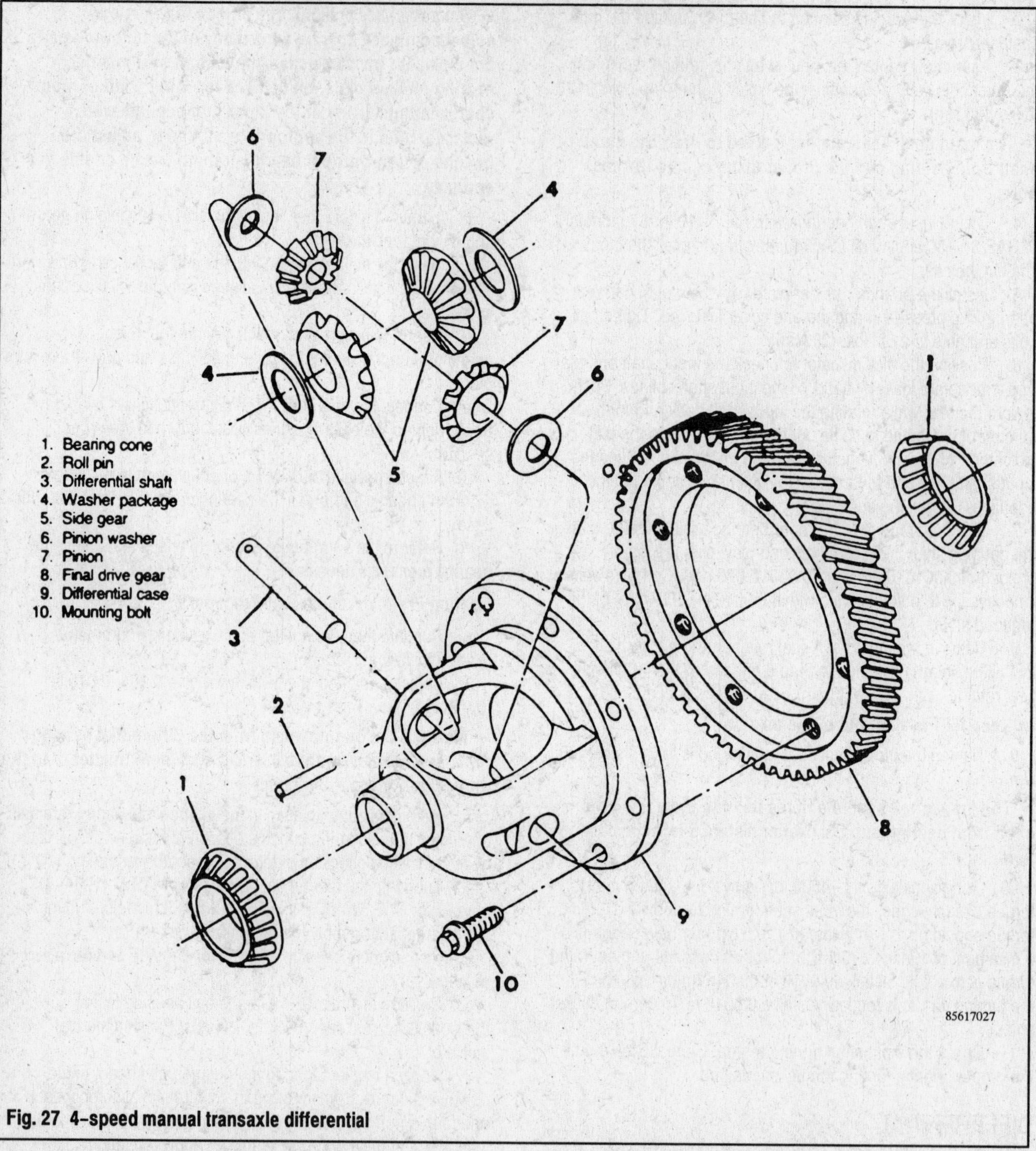

Fig. 27 4-speed manual transaxle differential

11. Install the shim(s) selected in Step 8 and press the bearing cup into the differential bearing retainer.

12. Using a 1/8 in. (3mm) bead of RTV sealant for gaskets, install the differential bearing retainer and extension housing. Tighten the bolts to 21 ft. lbs. (28 Nm).

13. Using an appropriate tool and an inch lb. torque wrench, check the turning torque of the differential assembly. The turning torque should be 9–14 inch lbs. (1.0–1.5 Nm) for new bearings or a minimum of 6 inch lbs. (0.7 Nm) for used bearings. If the turning torque is too low, install a 0.002 in. (0.05mm) thicker shim.

14. Check the turning torque. Repeat Step 11 until the proper turning torque is obtained.

TRANSAXLE CASE ASSEMBLY

1. Engage the reverse shift lever components to the transaxle case and lock it in place with the E-clip.

2. Clean the input shaft bore and press in a new oil seal with special tool C-4674, or equivalent. Place the select shim into the retainer race and bolt the input shaft seal retainer onto the transaxle case. The drain hole on the retainer sleeve must be facing downward.

3. Assemble the clutch release shaft components in the reverse order of disassembly and secure the release lever with the E-clip. Insert the release shaft spline end through the bushing and engage it with the release shaft fork. Install the E-clip on the shaft groove to secure the shaft.
4. Install the shift fork and shift fork pads onto the intermediate shaft gear set.
5. Install the intermediate and input shaft gear sets.
6. Install the reverse idler gear (with plastic stop) so that the roll pin on the end of the gear shaft aligns with the roll pin notch in the transaxle case. Lock the gear and engage the reverse shift lever. Make sure the plastic stop is firmly seated on the gear.
7. Install the 3-4 shift fork rail into the locating hole above the intermediate shaft assembly.
8. Remove all the excess sealant from the bearing retainer plate and run an $^1/_8$ in. (3mm) bead of RTV around the plate's seating surface. Keep the RTV away from the bolt holes. Align the locating dowel on the plate with the dowel on the transaxle case and install by tapping the plate with a rubber mallet. Install the intermediate shaft rear bearing snapring once the plate is in place.
9. Clean the excess sealant from the end cover and make sure the oil feeder hole is clear. Run a bead of RTV around the cover's seating surface and place the cover on the bearing retainer plate. Install the end cover bolts and tighten to specification.
10. Clean the excess sealant from the selector shaft housing. If the back-up light switch was removed, install the switch with a new gasket. Run a $^1/_8$ in. (3mm) bead of RTV sealant around the cover's seating surface and install the housing with the housing bolts. Tighten the bolts to specification.
11. Connect the differential to the extension housing. Use a new extension housing O-ring seal. Attach the housing with the housing bolts and tighten the bolts to specification.
12. Seal the differential bearing retainer with RTV and tighten the retainer with special tool L-4435, or equivalent spanner wrench.
13. Install the differential bearing retainer bolts and tighten them to specification.
14. If the magnet was removed from the differential cover, install it at this time. Clean the excess sealant from the differential cover and run a $^1/_8$ in. (3mm) bead of RTV around the cover's seating surface. Install the differential cover with the cover bolts. Tighten the bolts to specification.
15. Remove the transaxle from the holding fixture and install it in the vehicle.

5-Speed Transaxle Overhaul

TRANSAXLE DISASSEMBLY

Differential

➧ See Figures 28, 29, 30, 31, 32, 33, 34, 35, 36 and 37

1. Remove the transaxle from the vehicle and position it on suitable holding fixture.
2. Remove the extension outer bolts.
3. Remove the differential retainer outer bolts.
4. Remove the differential assembly.

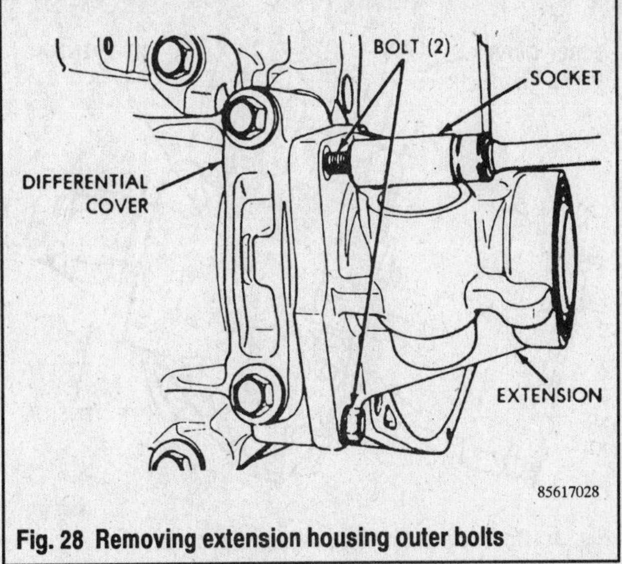

Fig. 28 Removing extension housing outer bolts

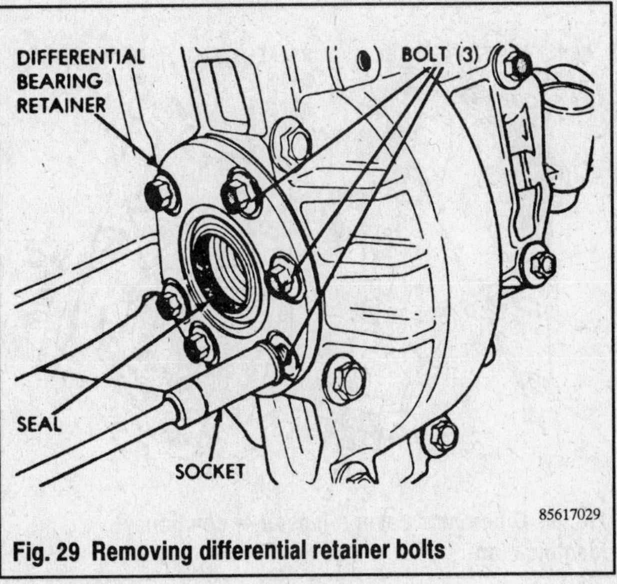

Fig. 29 Removing differential retainer bolts

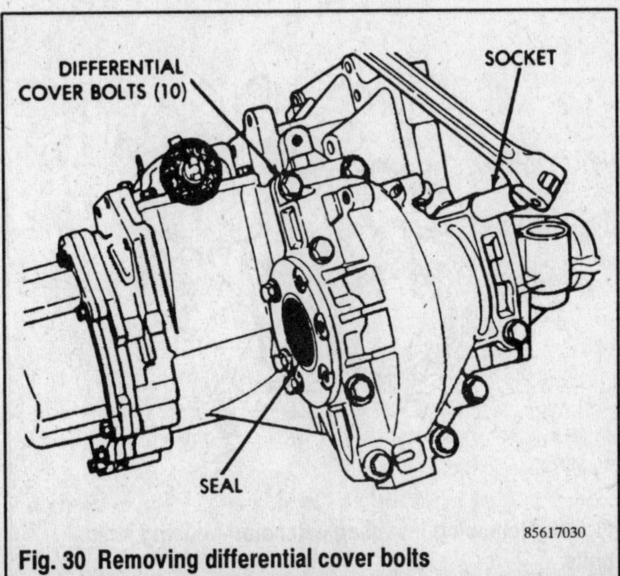

Fig. 30 Removing differential cover bolts

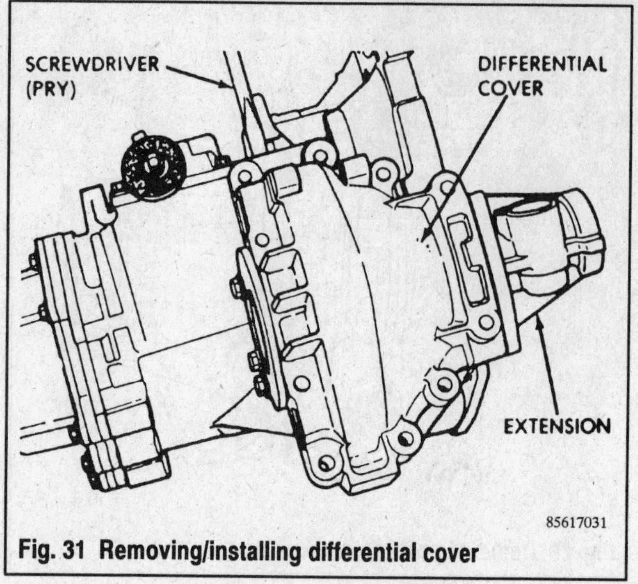

Fig. 31 Removing/installing differential cover

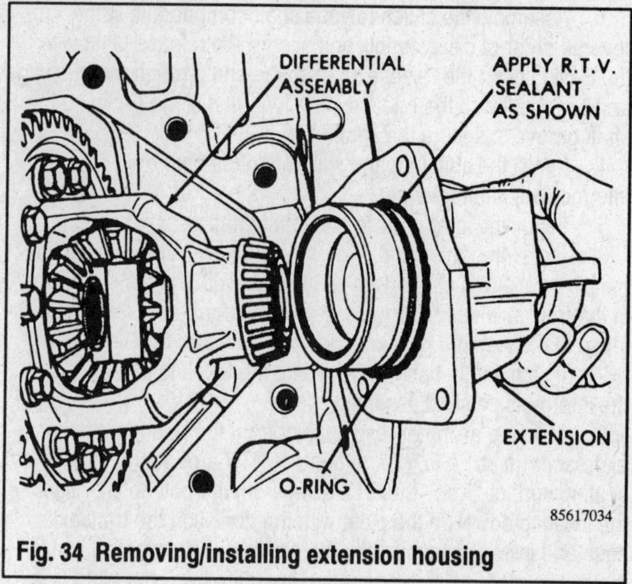

Fig. 34 Removing/installing extension housing

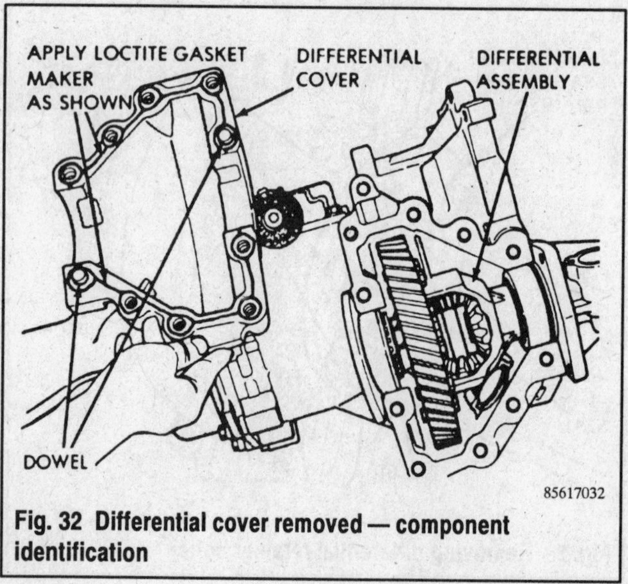

Fig. 32 Differential cover removed — component identification

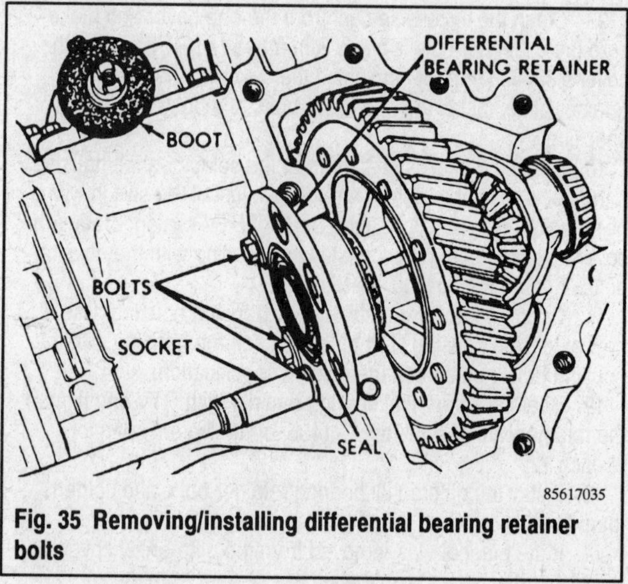

Fig. 35 Removing/installing differential bearing retainer bolts

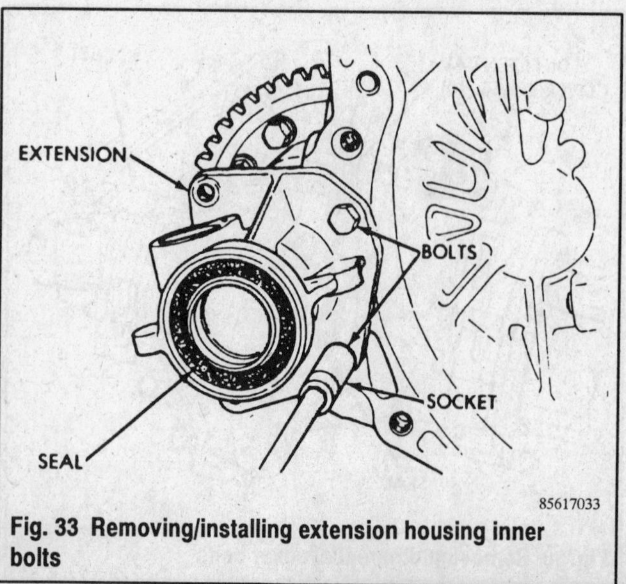

Fig. 33 Removing/installing extension housing inner bolts

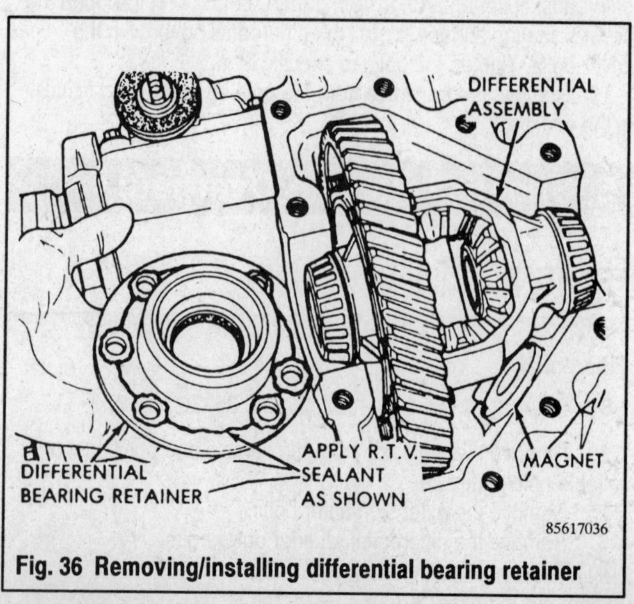

Fig. 36 Removing/installing differential bearing retainer

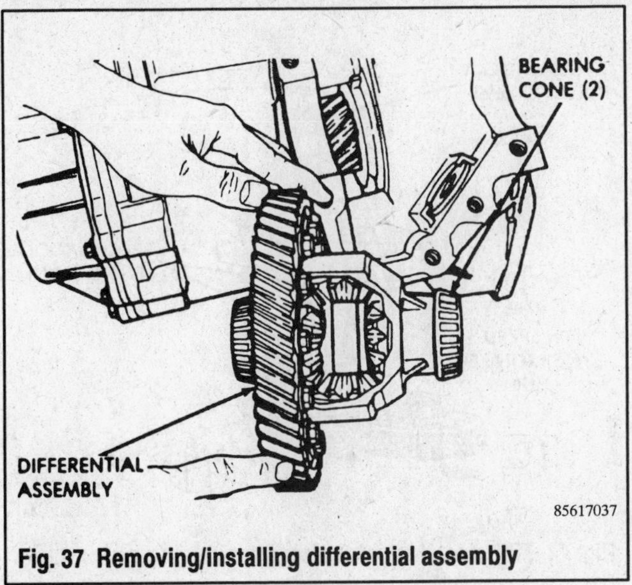

Fig. 37 Removing/installing differential assembly

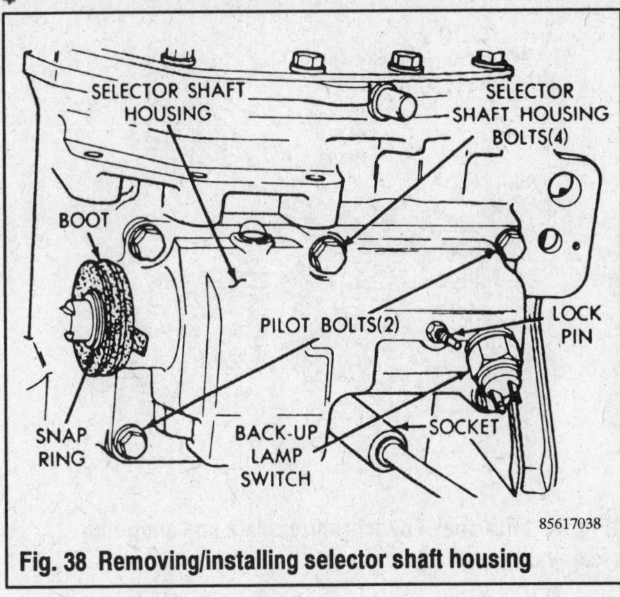

Fig. 38 Removing/installing selector shaft housing

Transaxle

➧ See Figures 38, 39, 40, 41, 42, 43, 44, 45, 46, 47, 48, 49, 50, 51, 52, 53, 54, 55, 56, 57, 58 and 59

1. Remove the differential cover bolts and gently pry the cover from the extension.
2. Unfasten the extension housing bolts then separate the differential assembly and extension housing. Remove the O-ring seal and clean the RTV from extension housing. Discard the O-ring seal.
3. Unbolt and remove the differential retainer.
4. Unfasten the selector shaft housing assembly bolts and remove the selector shaft housing.
5. Unbolt and remove the rear end cover.
6. Remove the snapring from the 5th speed synchronizer strut retainer plate.
7. Unscrew the 5th speed shift fork set screw. Lift the 5th speed synchronizer sleeve and shift fork off the synchronizer hub. Retrieve the (3) winged struts and top synchronizer spring.
8. Use a puller to remove the 5th speed synchronizer hub. Retrieve the remaining synchronizer spring.
9. Slide the 5th speed gear off the intermediate shaft.
10. Using holding tool 6252, or equivalent, remove the input shaft 5th speed gear nut. This nut is not to be reused.
11. Remove the remaining bearing support plate bolts. Gently pry off the bearing support plate.
12. Remove the large snapring from the intermediate shaft rear ball bearing. Then, gently tap the lower surface of the bearing retainer plate with a plastic hammer to free it and lift it off the transaxle case. Clean the RTV sealer from both surfaces.
13. Unscrew the 5th speed shifter guide pin. Do the same with the 1st/2nd shift fork setscrew. Withdraw the 1st/2nd, 3rd/4th shift fork rail.
14. Slide out the reverse idler gear shaft, gear, and plastic stop.
15. Rotate the 3rd/4th shift fork to the left, and the 5th gear shifter to the right. Pull out the 5th speed shift rail. Pull out the input shaft and intermediate shaft assemblies.

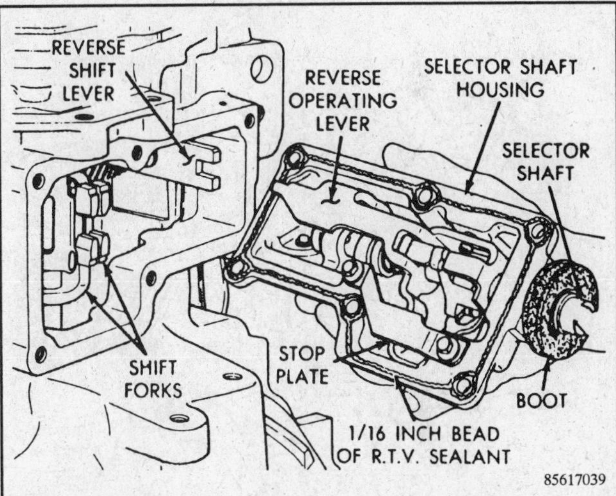

Fig. 39 Select or shaft housing removed — component identification

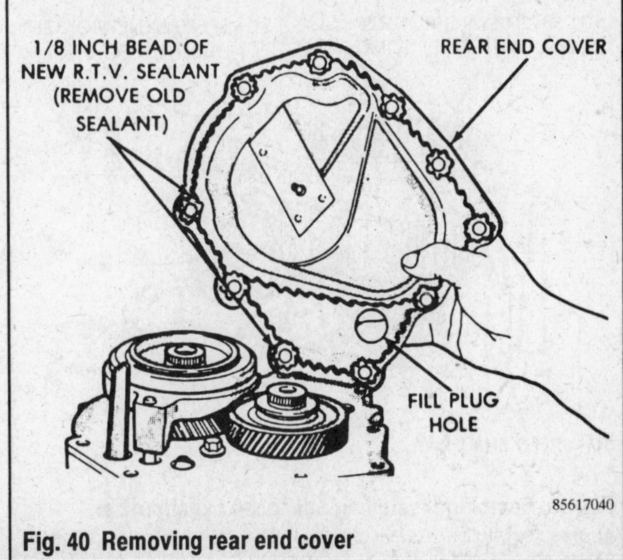

Fig. 40 Removing rear end cover

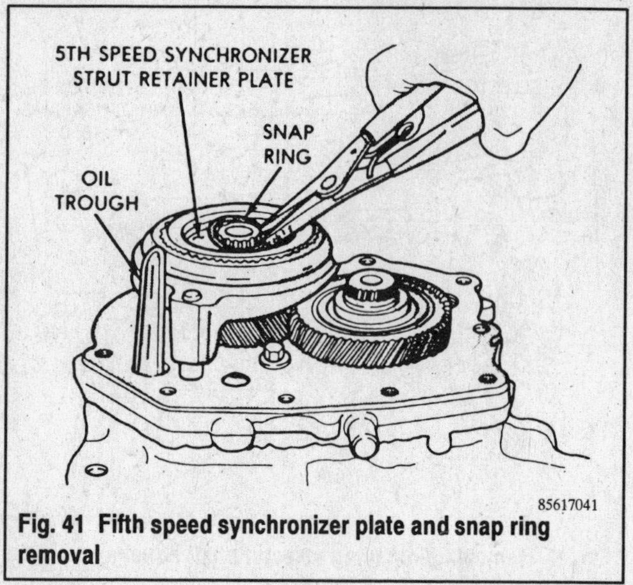

Fig. 41 Fifth speed synchronizer plate and snap ring removal

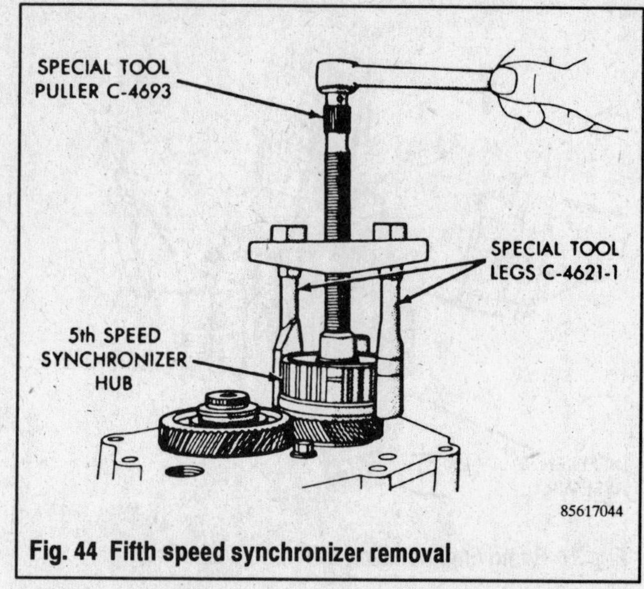

Fig. 44 Fifth speed synchronizer removal

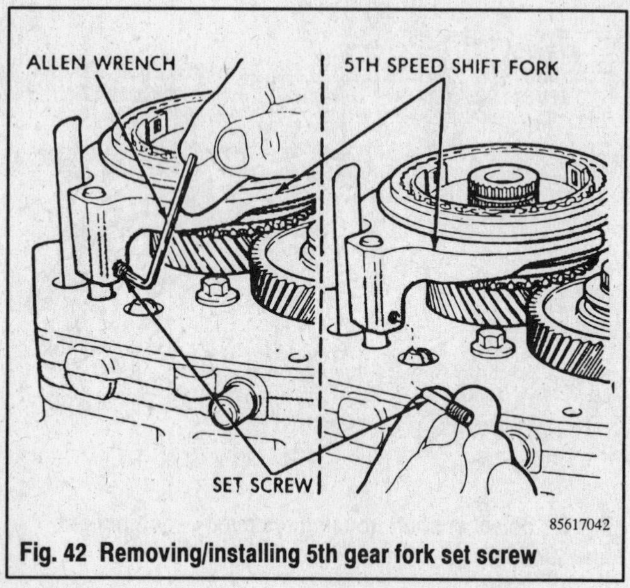

Fig. 42 Removing/installing 5th gear fork set screw

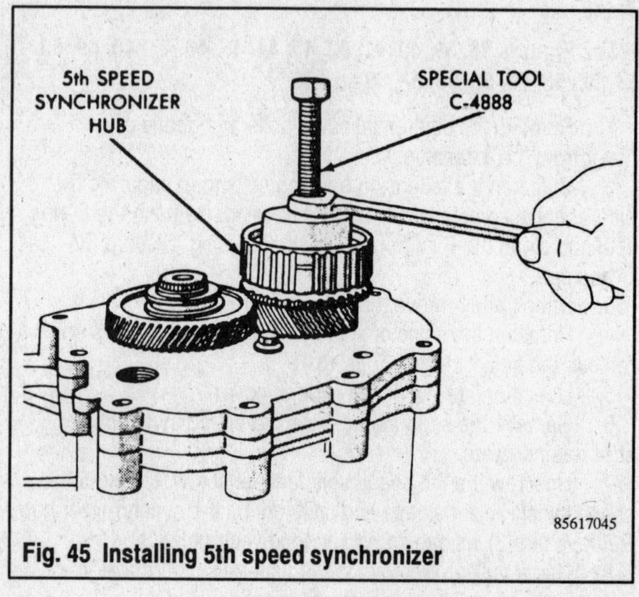

Fig. 45 Installing 5th speed synchronizer

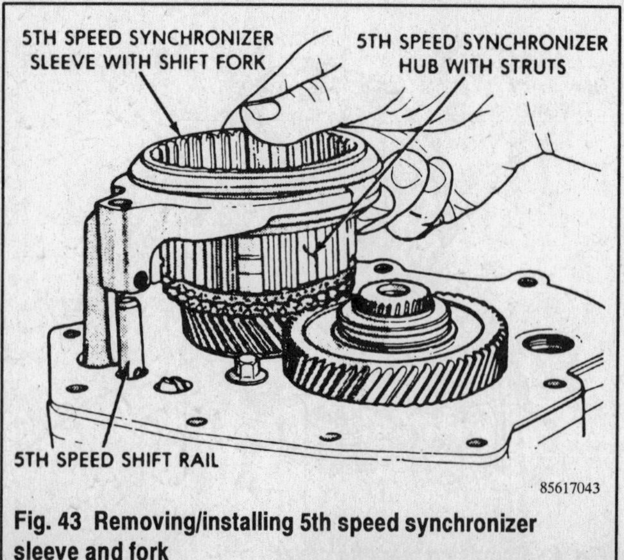

Fig. 43 Removing/installing 5th speed synchronizer sleeve and fork

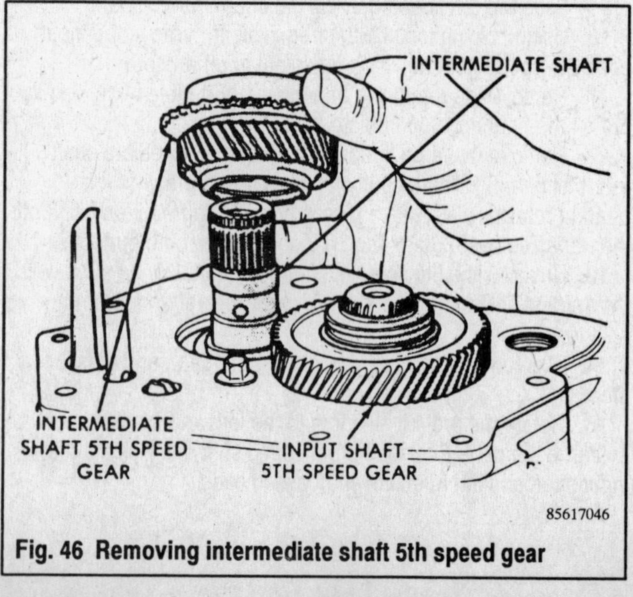

Fig. 46 Removing intermediate shaft 5th speed gear

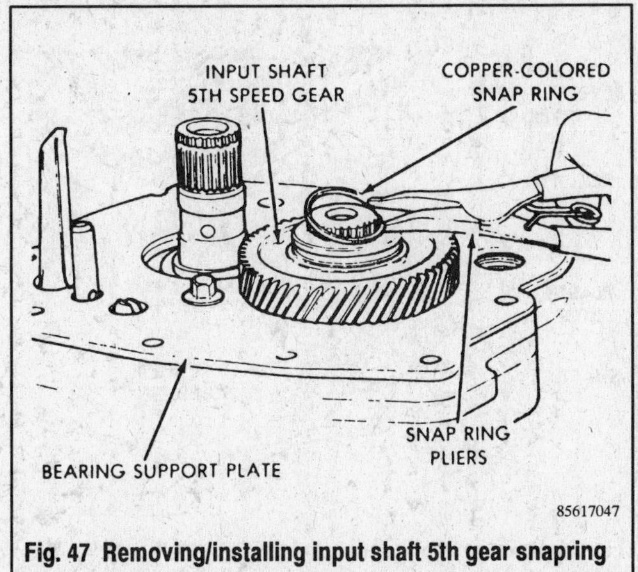

Fig. 47 Removing/installing input shaft 5th gear snapring

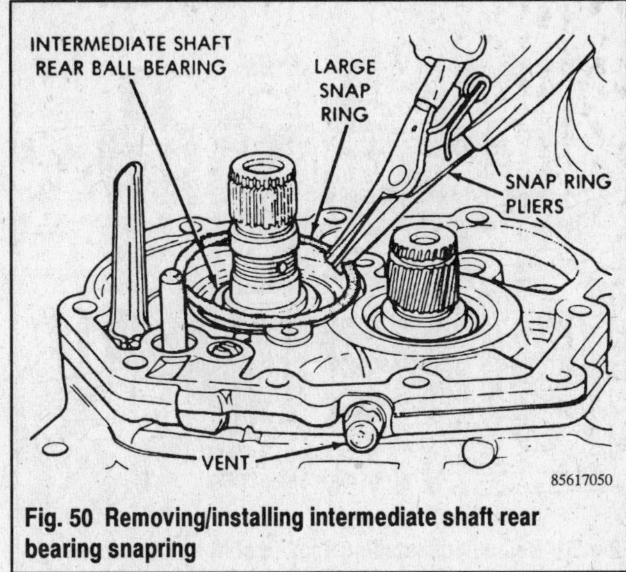

Fig. 50 Removing/installing intermediate shaft rear bearing snapring

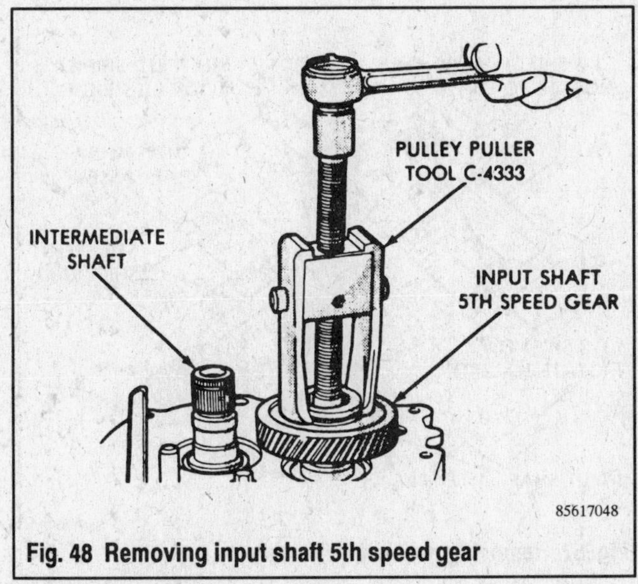

Fig. 48 Removing input shaft 5th speed gear

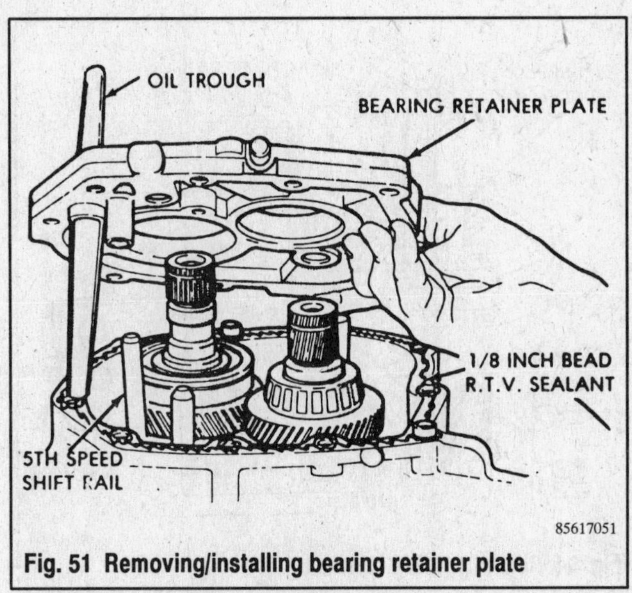

Fig. 51 Removing/installing bearing retainer plate

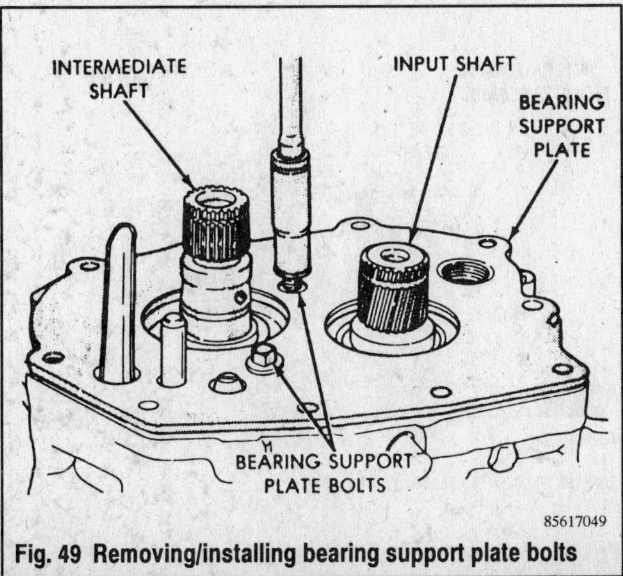

Fig. 49 Removing/installing bearing support plate bolts

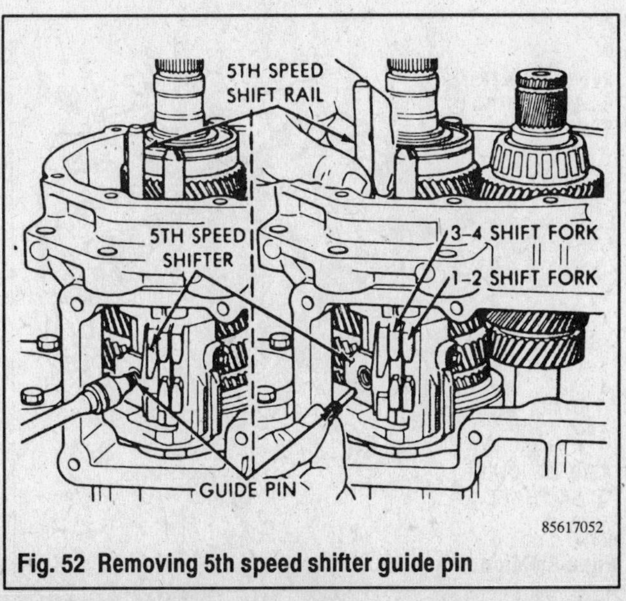

Fig. 52 Removing 5th speed shifter guide pin

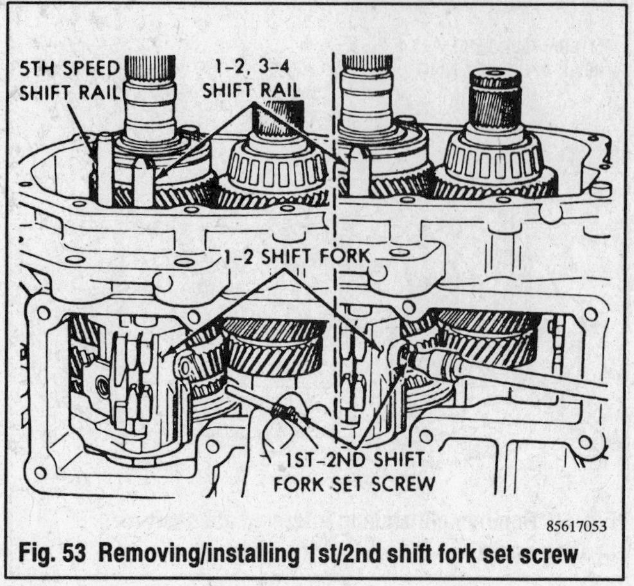

Fig. 53 Removing/installing 1st/2nd shift fork set screw

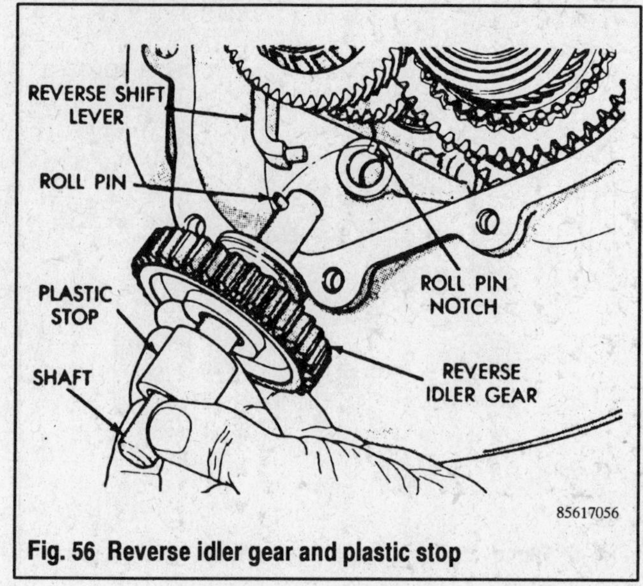

Fig. 56 Reverse idler gear and plastic stop

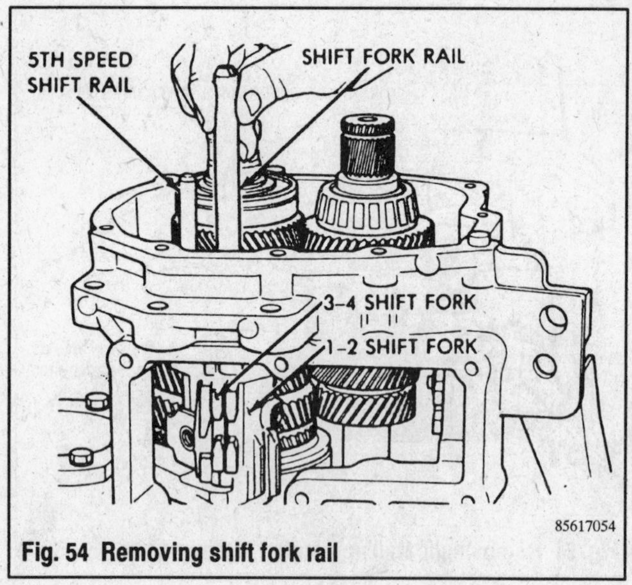

Fig. 54 Removing shift fork rail

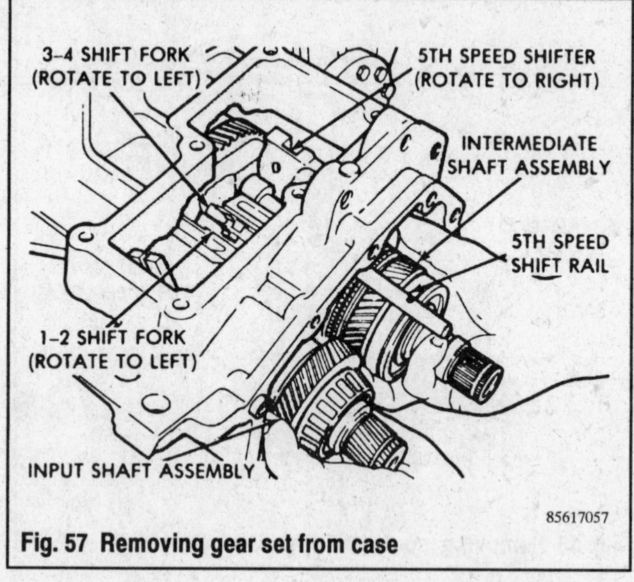

Fig. 57 Removing gear set from case

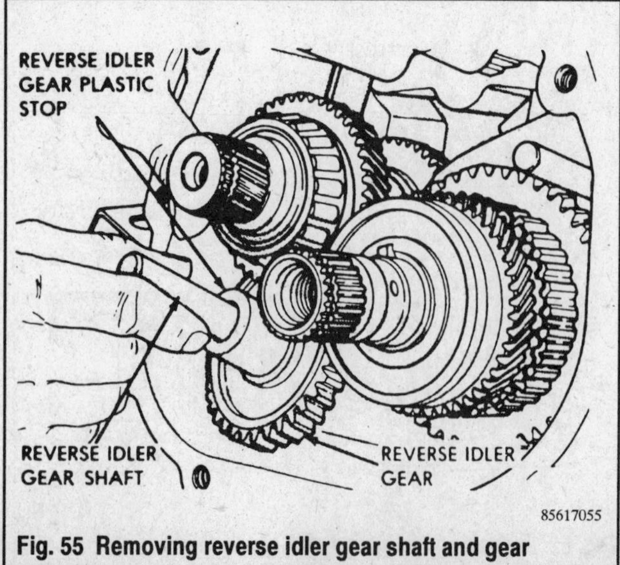

Fig. 55 Removing reverse idler gear shaft and gear

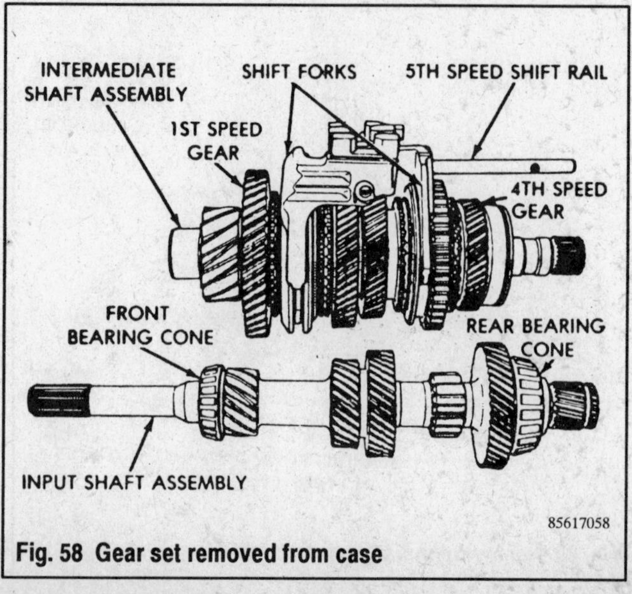

Fig. 58 Gear set removed from case

Clutch Release Bearing

➧ See Figures 60 and 61

1. Remove the 1st/2nd, 3rd/4th, and 5th speed shift forks.
2. To remove the clutch release bearing, disengage the E-clips from the clutch release shaft, then disassemble the clutch shaft components.

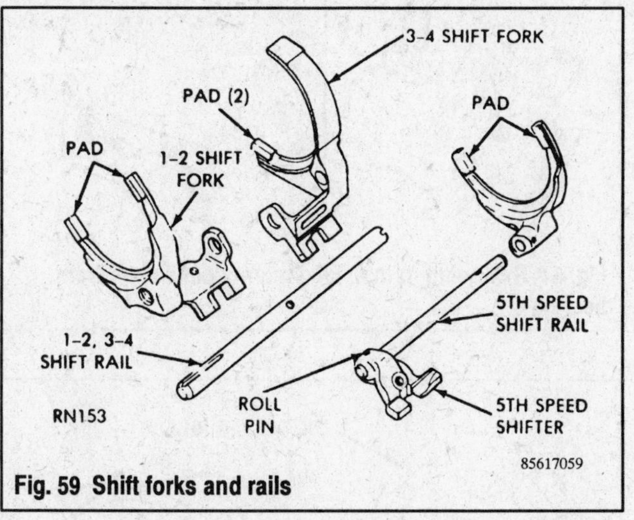

Fig. 59 Shift forks and rails

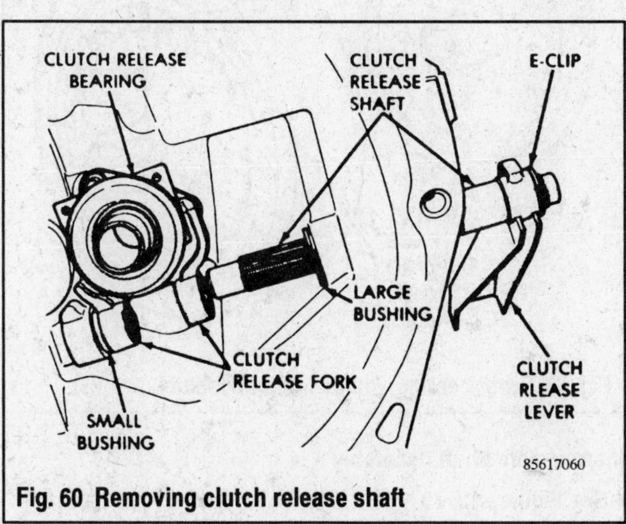

Fig. 60 Removing clutch release shaft

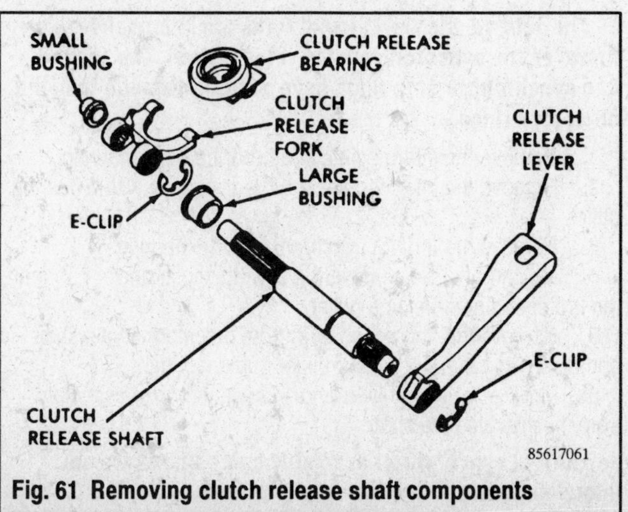

Fig. 61 Removing clutch release shaft components

Input Shaft Oil Seal

➧ See Figures 62, 63, 64 and 65

1. Remove the input shaft seal retainer bolts, seal, retainer assembly and the select shim.

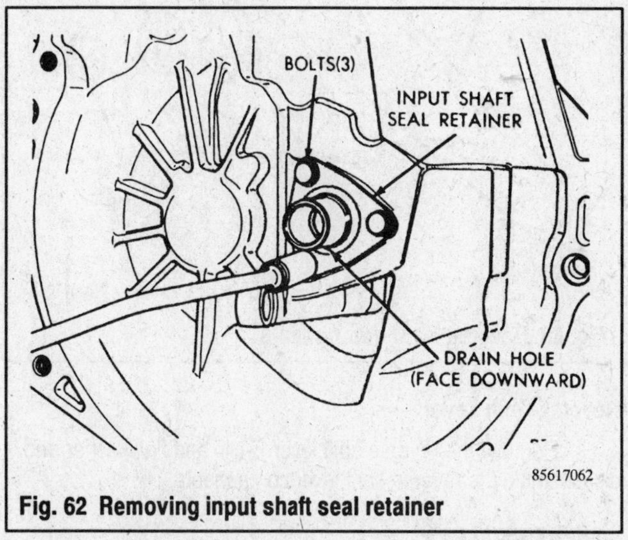

Fig. 62 Removing input shaft seal retainer

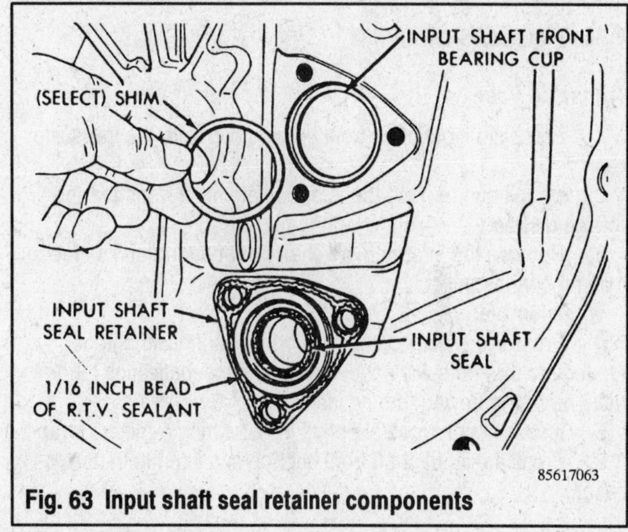

Fig. 63 Input shaft seal retainer components

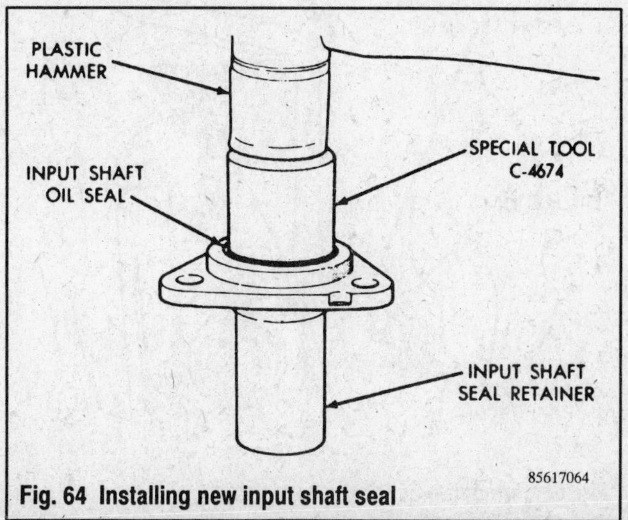

Fig. 64 Installing new input shaft seal

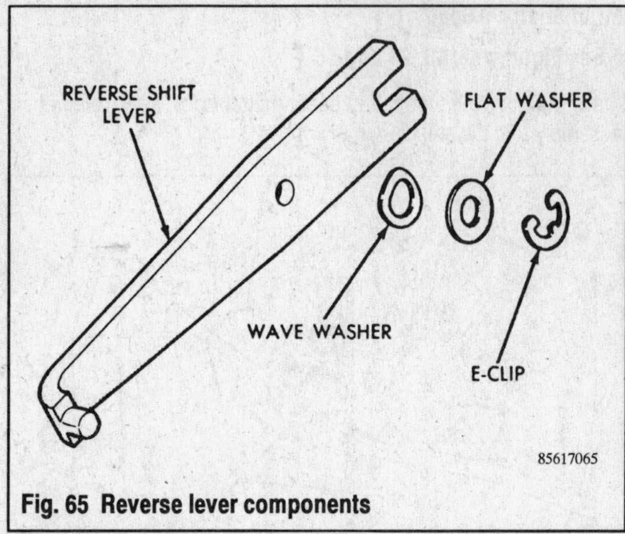

Fig. 65 Reverse lever components

Reverse Shift Lever

1. Remove the reverse shift lever E-clip and flat washer and disassemble the reverse shift lever components.

SUBASSEMBLY

See Figures 66, 67 and 68

Transaxle Case

1. Press the input shaft front bearing cup from the transaxle case.
2. Unbolt and remove the intermediate shaft front bearing retaining strap.
3. Remove the intermediate shaft front bearing and oil feeder using a bearing puller.

To assemble:

4. Press the intermediate shaft front bearing with the oil feeder into the transaxle case. The bearing identification letters must be facing upward during installation.
5. Install the intermediate shaft front bearing retaining strap.
6. Press the input shaft front bearing cup into the transaxle case.

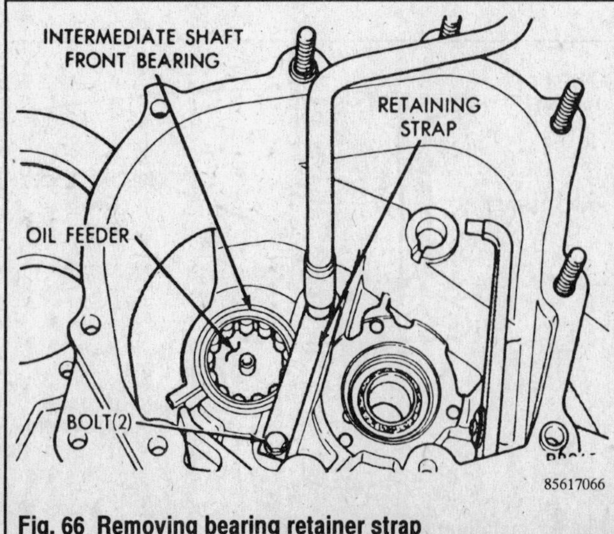

Fig. 66 Removing bearing retainer strap

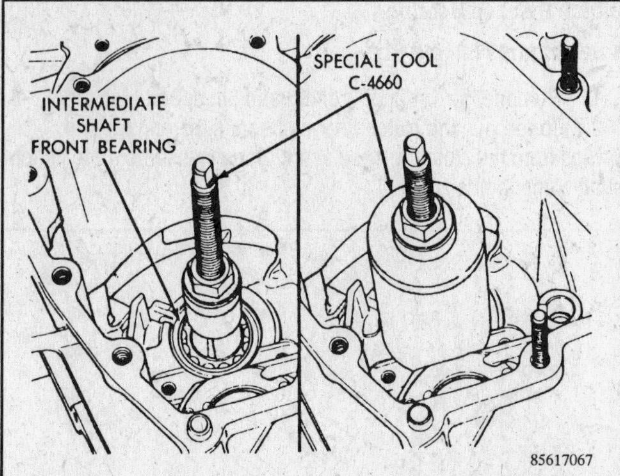

Fig. 67 Removing or installing intermediate shaft front bearing

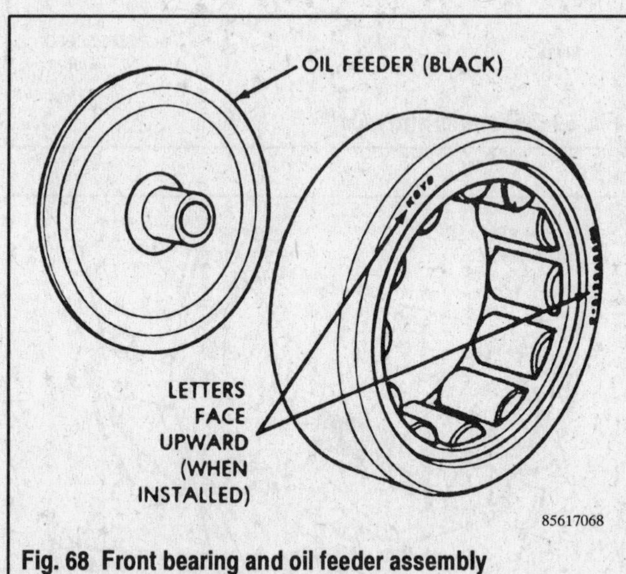

Fig. 68 Front bearing and oil feeder assembly

Intermediate Shaft Assembly

See Figures 69, 70, 71, 72, 73, 74, 75, 76, 77, 78, 79, 80, 81, 82, 83, 84 and 85

The 1st/2nd, the 3rd/4th shift forks are interchangeable, however, the synchronizer stop rings are not. The 1st and 2nd synchronizer stop rings have a larger diameter than the other stop rings.

1. Remove the intermediate shaft rear bearing snapring.
2. Remove the intermediate shaft rear bearing with a bearing puller.
3. Remove the 3rd/4th synchronizer hub snapring.
4. Matchmark then remove the 3rd/4th synchronizer hub and the 3rd speed gear using a puller.
5. Remove the 2nd speed gear from the intermediate shaft and disengage the 1-2 synchronizer hub snapring.
6. Pull the 1st speed gear and 1-2 synchronizer assembly from the intermediate shaft.

The 1-2 synchronizer assembly components are not interchangeable with other synchronizers.

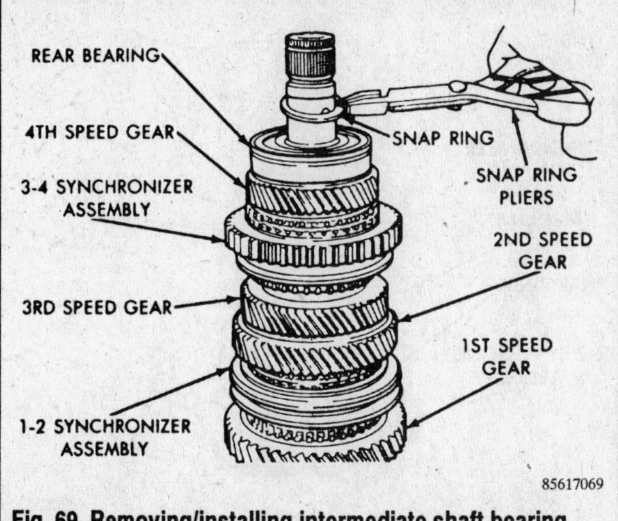

Fig. 69 Removing/installing intermediate shaft bearing snapring

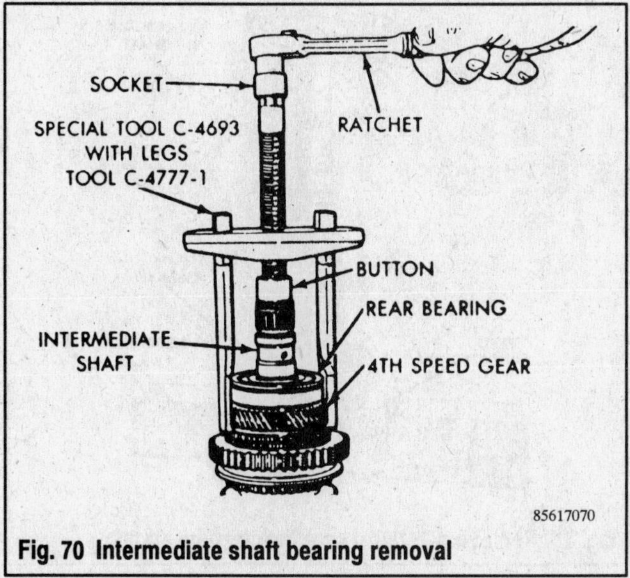

Fig. 70 Intermediate shaft bearing removal

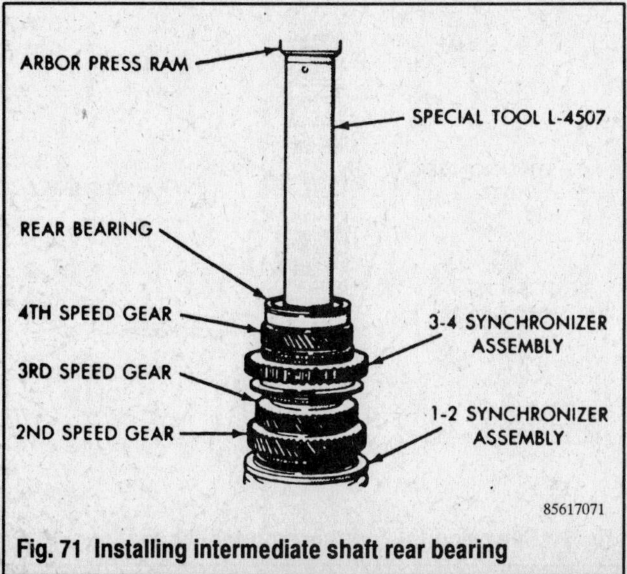

Fig. 71 Installing intermediate shaft rear bearing

To assemble:

7. Install the 1st speed gear thrust washer, 1st speed gear, stop ring and 1-2 synchronizer assembly
8. Install the 1-2 synchronizer snapring.
9. Install the 2nd speed gear and stop ring.
10. Install the retaining ring and split thrust washer. Install the 3rd speed gear and the 3-4 synchronizer. Engage the hub snapring.
11. Install the intermediate shaft rear bearing and retaining snapring.
12. Install the intermediate shaft front bearing.

→ Pay attention to the following when servicing the intermediate shaft: when assembling the intermediate shaft, make sure the speed gears turn freely and have a minimum of 0.003 in. (0.076mm) end-play. When installing the 1st speed gear thrust washer make sure the chamfered edge is facing the pinion gear. When installing the 1st/2nd synchronizer make sure the relief faces the 2nd speed gear. Use an arbor press to install the intermediate shaft rear bearing, the 3rd/4th synchronizer hub and the 3rd speed gear. When installing the 3-4 synchronizer hub and 3rd speed gear, index the snapring 90° to the split washer. During the installation of synchronizer ring assemblies, make sure that all he matchmarks are aligned.

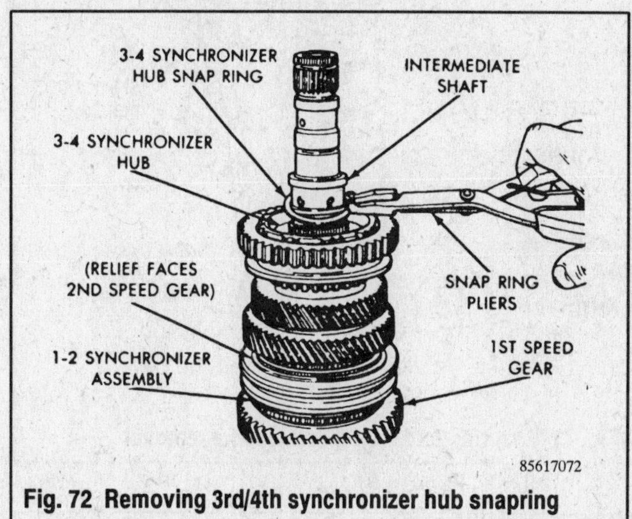

Fig. 72 Removing 3rd/4th synchronizer hub snapring

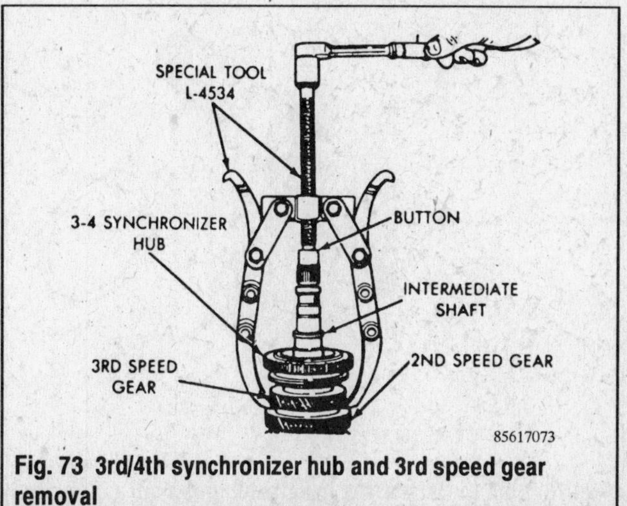

Fig. 73 3rd/4th synchronizer hub and 3rd speed gear removal

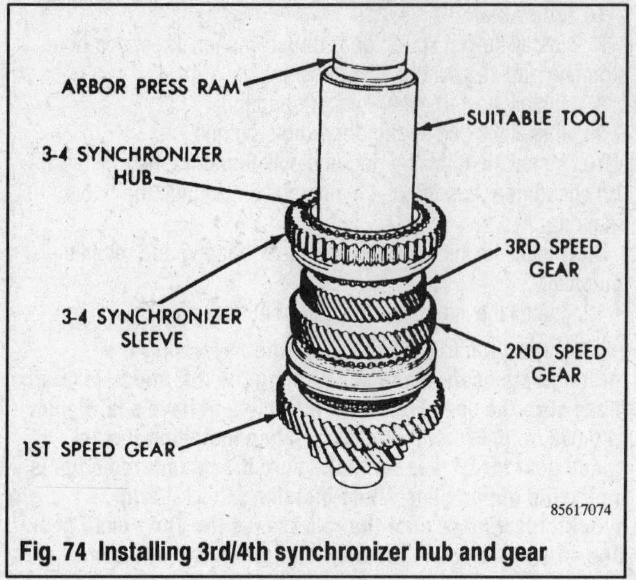

Fig. 74 Installing 3rd/4th synchronizer hub and gear

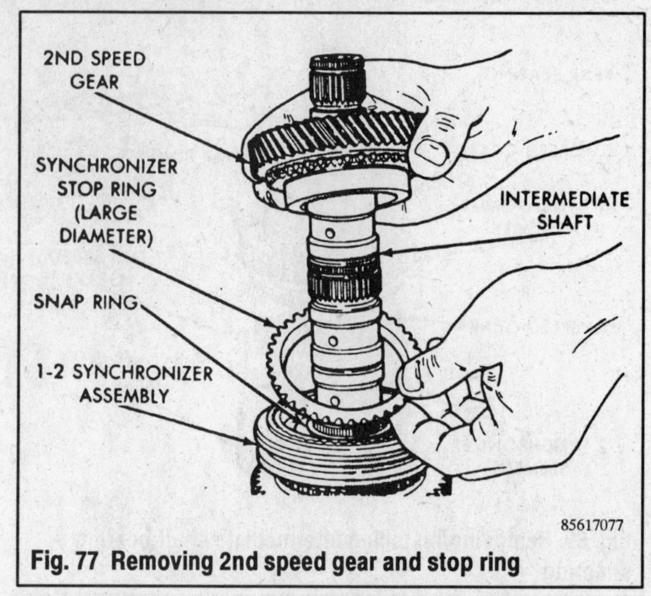

Fig. 77 Removing 2nd speed gear and stop ring

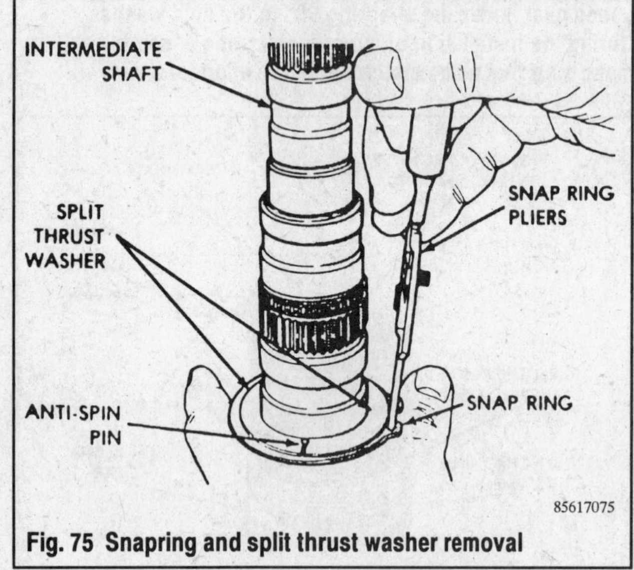

Fig. 75 Snapring and split thrust washer removal

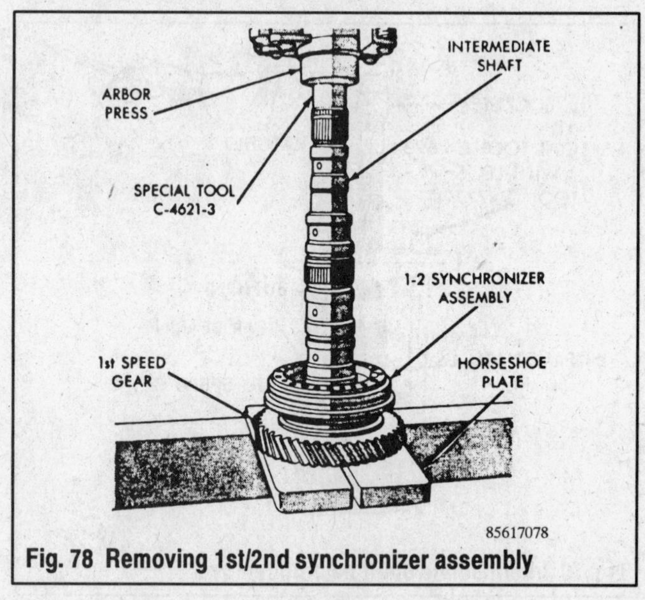

Fig. 78 Removing 1st/2nd synchronizer assembly

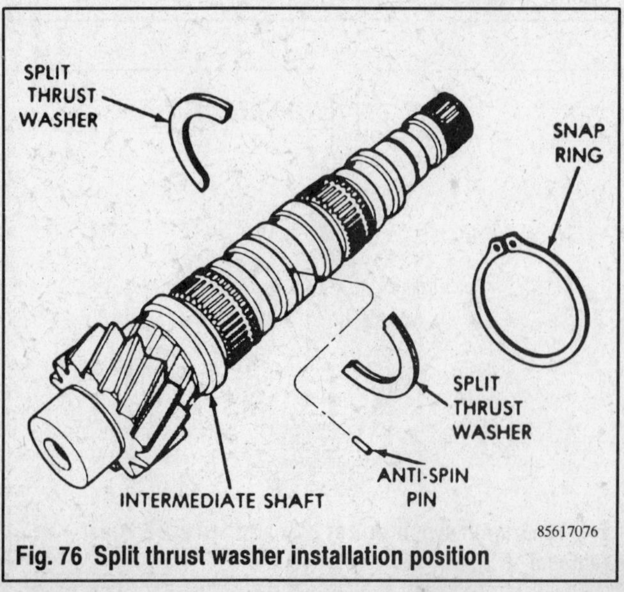

Fig. 76 Split thrust washer installation position

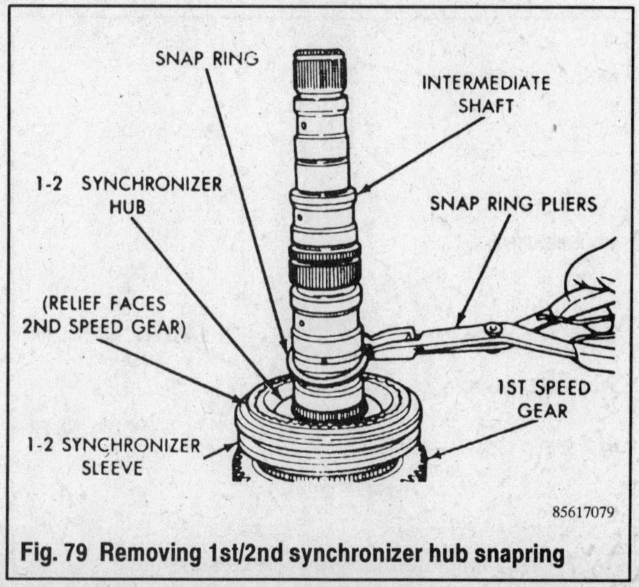

Fig. 79 Removing 1st/2nd synchronizer hub snapring

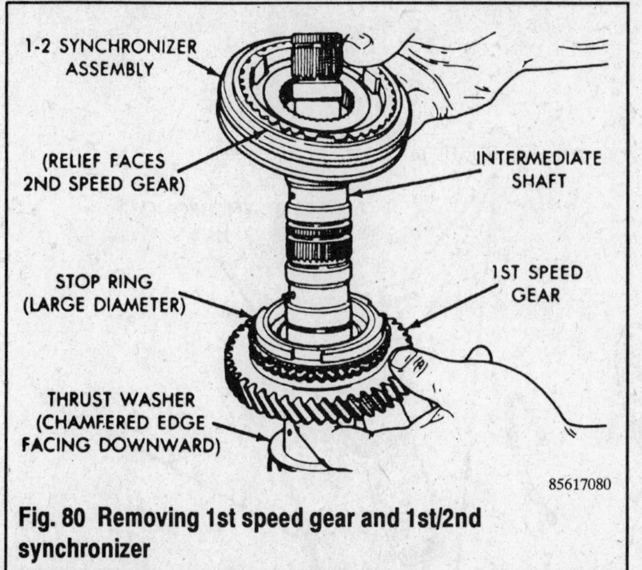

Fig. 80 Removing 1st speed gear and 1st/2nd synchronizer

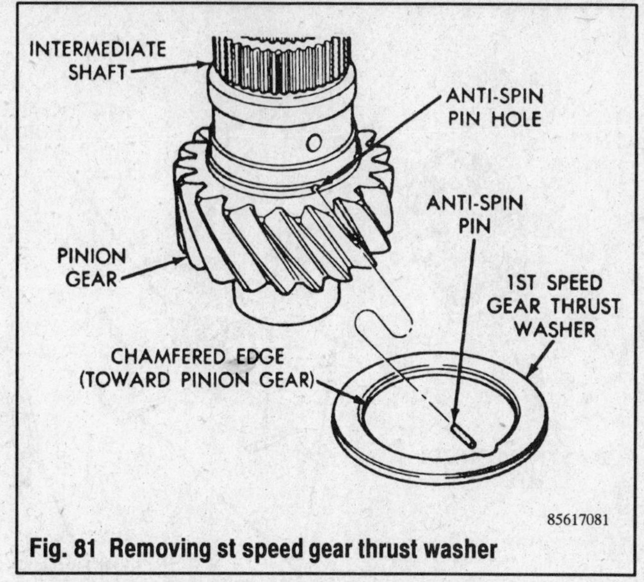

Fig. 81 Removing st speed gear thrust washer

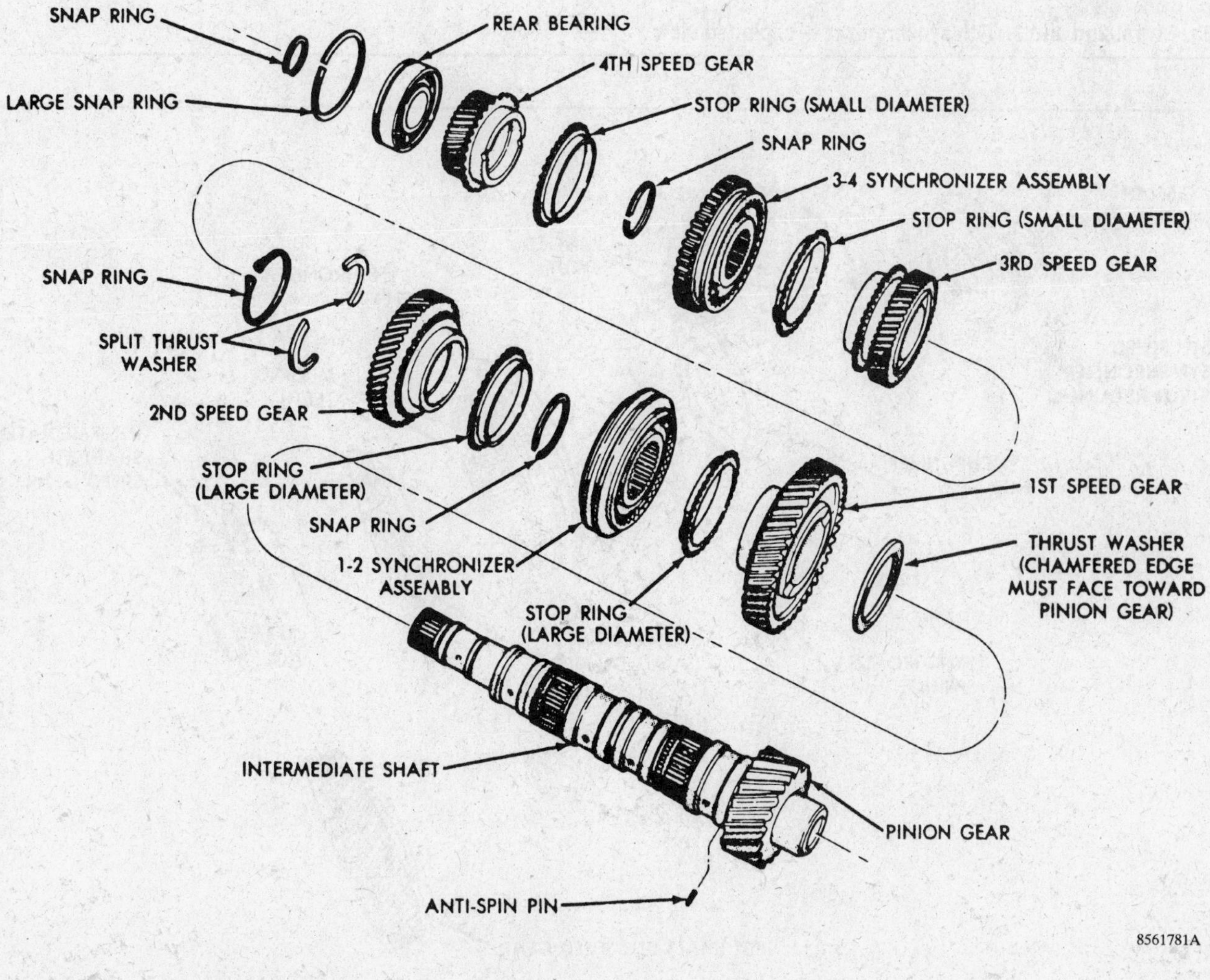

Fig. 82 Intermediate shaft — exploded view

WINGED STRUT (3)
3-4 SYNCHRONIZER HUB
WINGED STRUT (3)
1-2 SYNCHRONIZER HUB
SYNCHRONIZER SPRING
3-4 SYNCHRONIZER SLEEVE
SYNCHRONIZER SPRINGS (2)
1-2 SYNCHRONIZER SLEEVE
SYNCHRONIZER SPRING
85617082

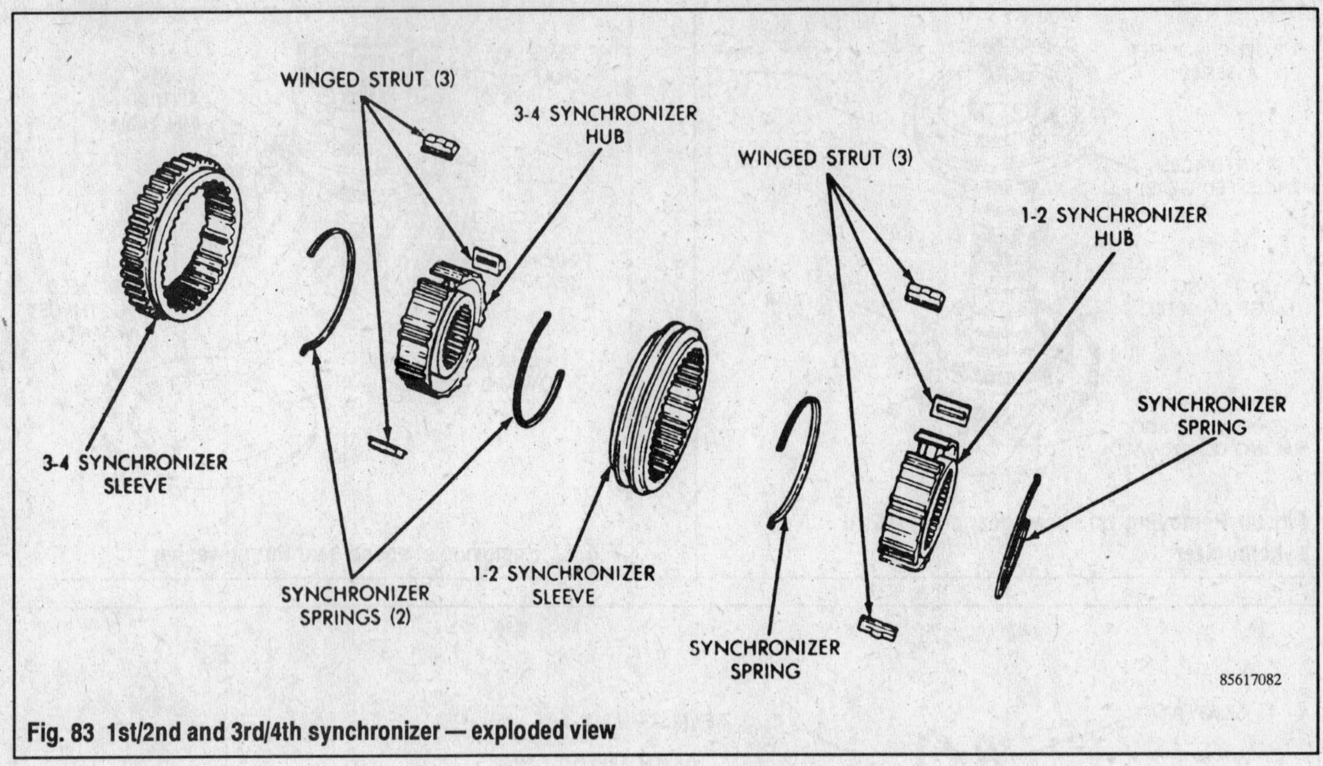

Fig. 83 1st/2nd and 3rd/4th synchronizer — exploded view

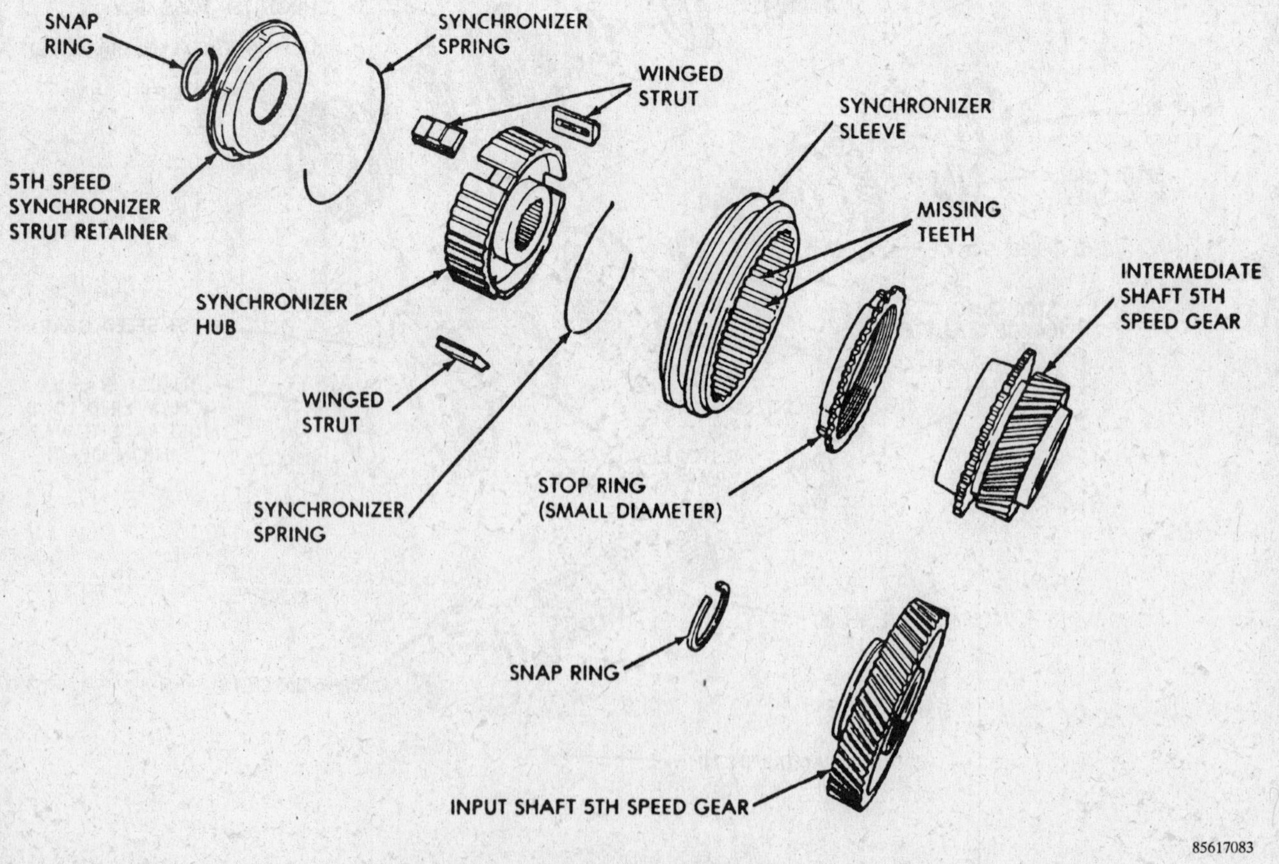

SNAP RING
SYNCHRONIZER SPRING
WINGED STRUT
SYNCHRONIZER SLEEVE
5TH SPEED SYNCHRONIZER STRUT RETAINER
MISSING TEETH
INTERMEDIATE SHAFT 5TH SPEED GEAR
SYNCHRONIZER HUB
WINGED STRUT
SYNCHRONIZER SPRING
STOP RING (SMALL DIAMETER)
SNAP RING
INPUT SHAFT 5TH SPEED GEAR
85617083

Fig. 84 5th speed synchronizer assembly — exploded view

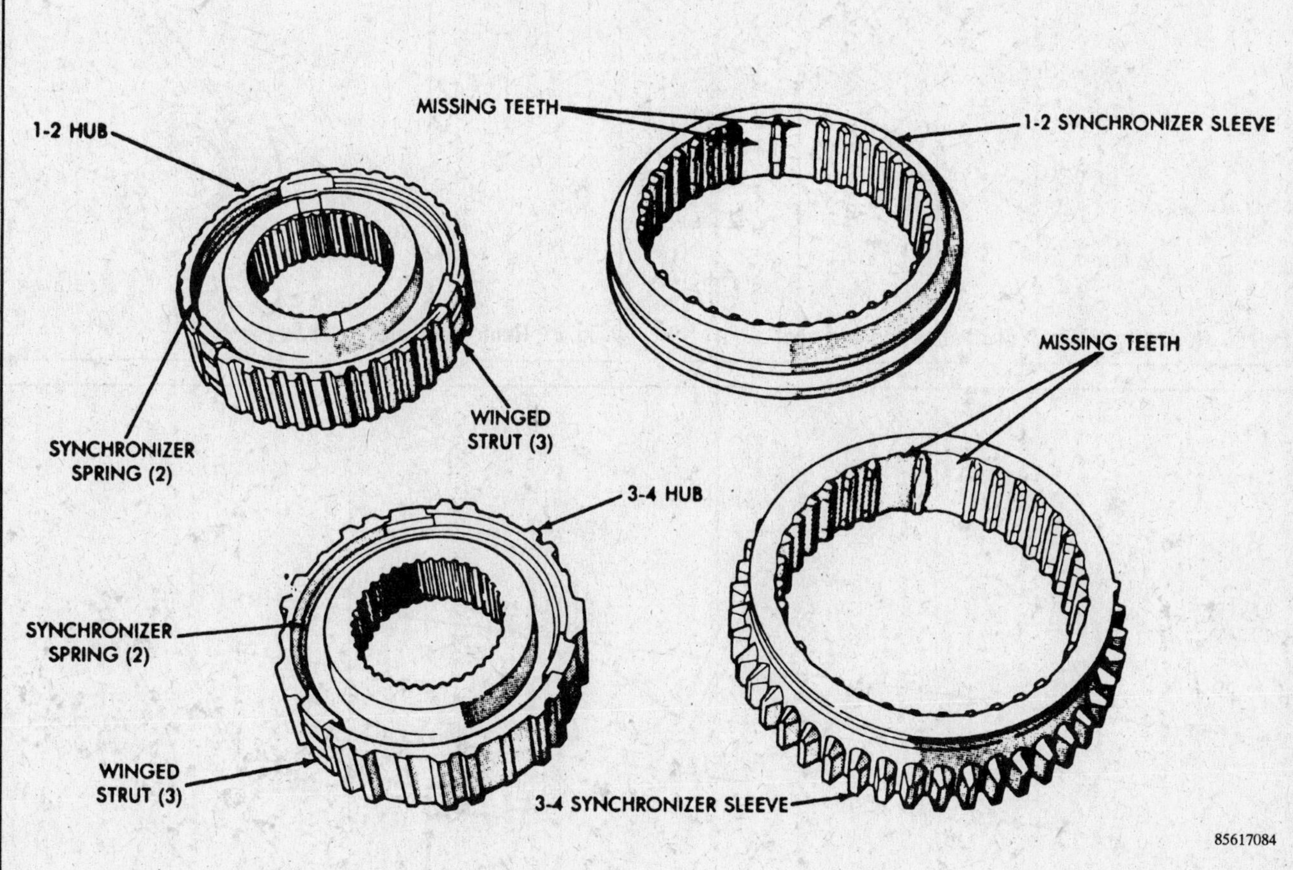

Fig. 85 Synchronizer sleeves — identification

Selector Shaft Housing

➧ See Figures 86, 87, 88, 89 and 90

1. Disengage the snapring from the selector shaft boot and remove the boot.
2. Pry the shaft oil seal from the selector shaft housing.
3. With a small prybar positioned against the gearshift selector, compress the crossover and 5th speed load spring and push the E-clip from the selector shaft. Disengage the E-clip to release the selector shaft.
4. Withdraw the selector shaft from the selector housing.
5. Unfasten the plate stop retaining bolts and remove the stop.
6. Disassemble the selector shaft housing components.

To assemble:

7. Assemble the selector shaft housing components in the reverse order of removal. Use a new back-up lamp switch gasket if needed.
8. Install the plate stop with the retaining bolts.
9. Insert the selector shaft into the housing.
10. Compress the gearshift selector and install the E-clip.
11. Clean the bore and drive a new oil seal into the housing using the proper tool.
12. Place the boot onto the shaft and retain with the snapring.

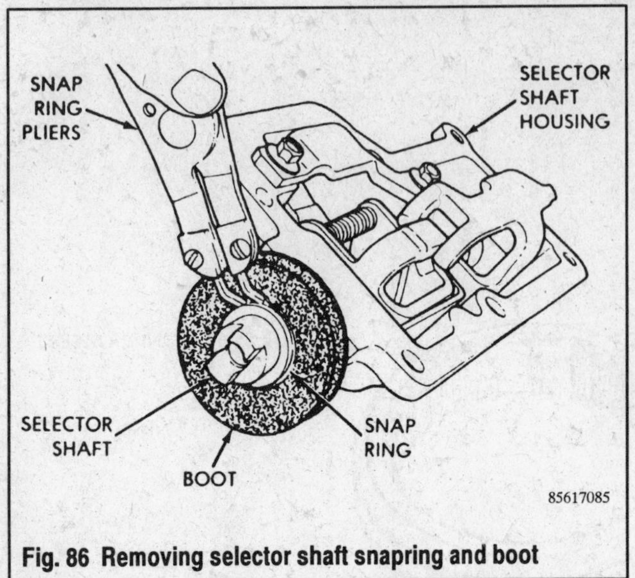

Fig. 86 Removing selector shaft snapring and boot

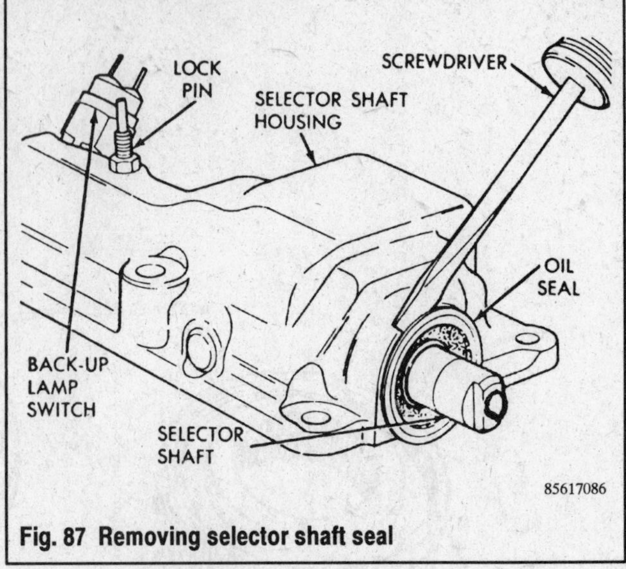

Fig. 87 Removing selector shaft seal

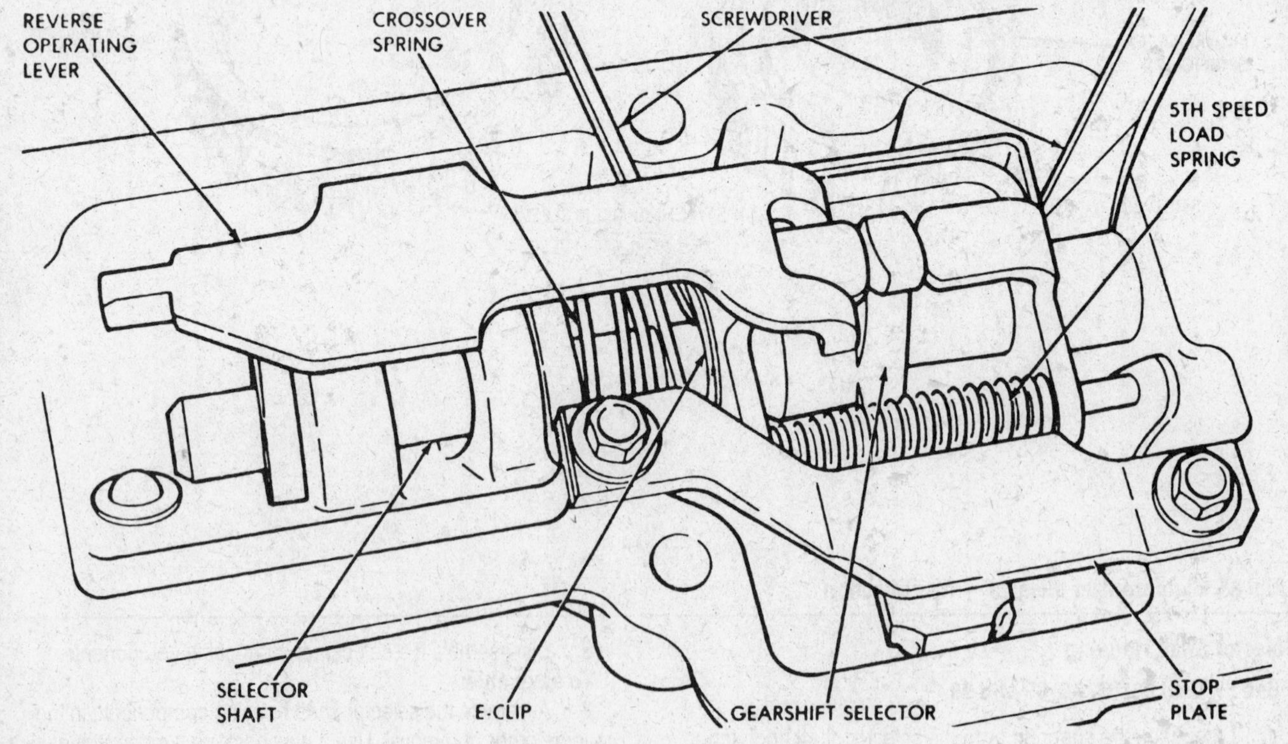

Fig. 88 Removing/installing selector shaft E-clip

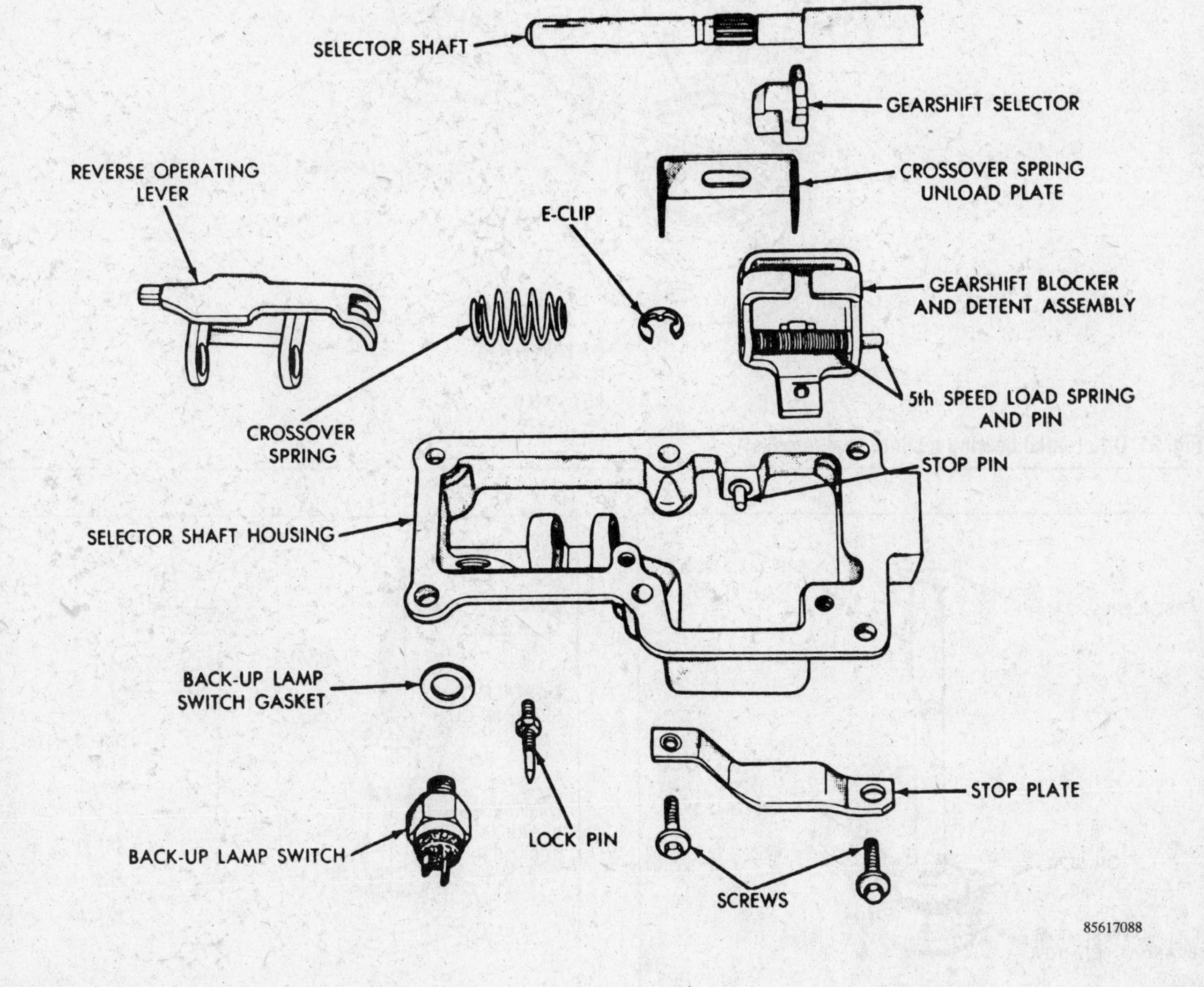

Fig. 89 Selector shaft housing components

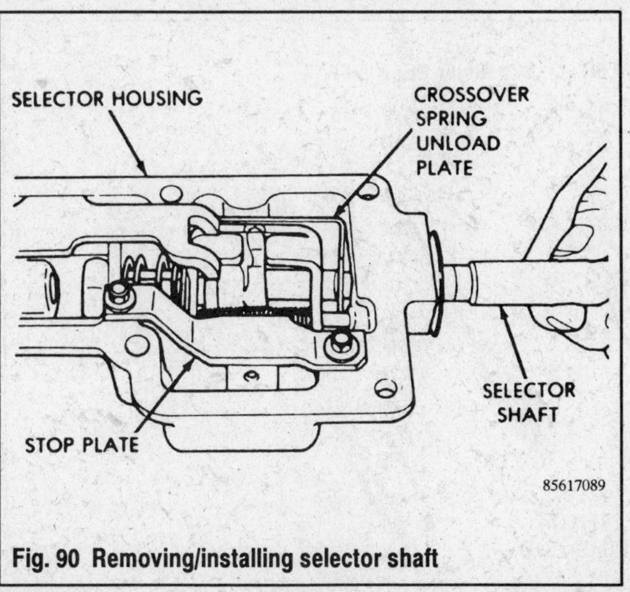

Fig. 90 Removing/installing selector shaft

Differential Bearing Retainer

➧ See Figures 91, 92, 93, 94 and 95

1. Pry the oil seal from the retainer.
2. Remove the retainer cup with a puller. Be careful not to damage the oil baffle and the select shim .
3. Remove the oil baffle and the select shim from the retainer cup.

To assemble:

4. Drive the oil baffle and select shim into the retainer cup using the proper tool.
5. Drive the retainer cup into the retainer using the proper tool.
6. Drive in a new retainer oil seal.

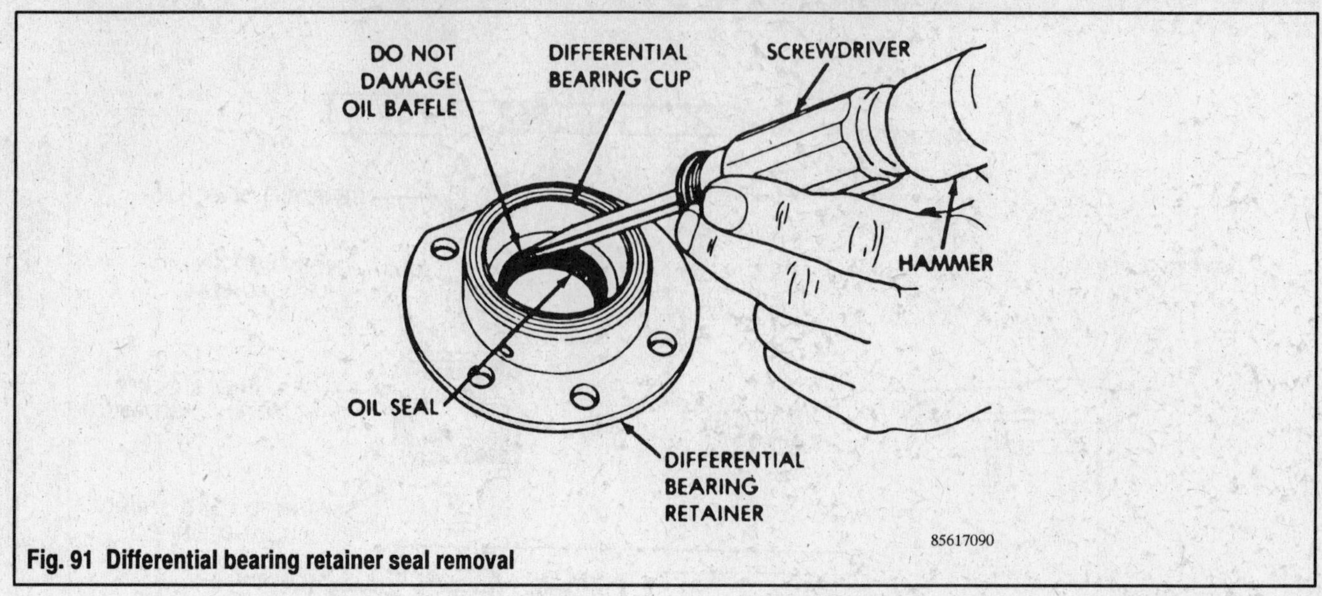

Fig. 91 Differential bearing retainer seal removal

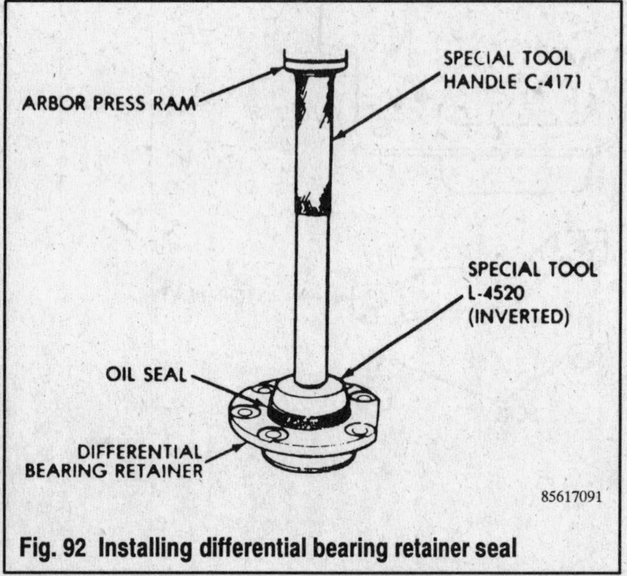

Fig. 92 Installing differential bearing retainer seal

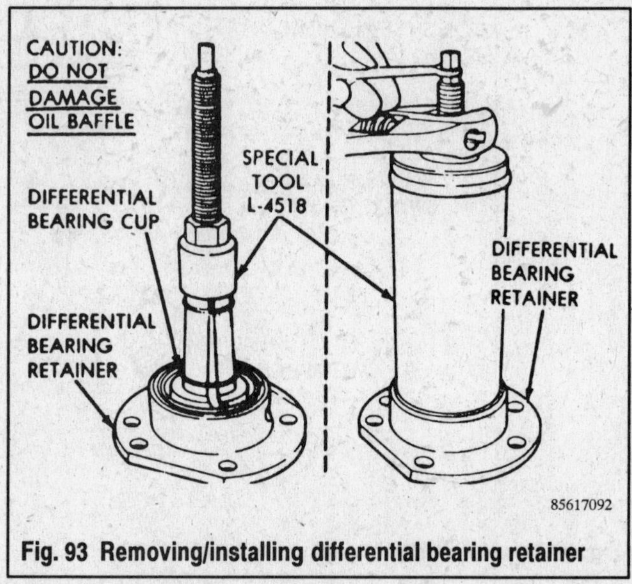

Fig. 93 Removing/installing differential bearing retainer

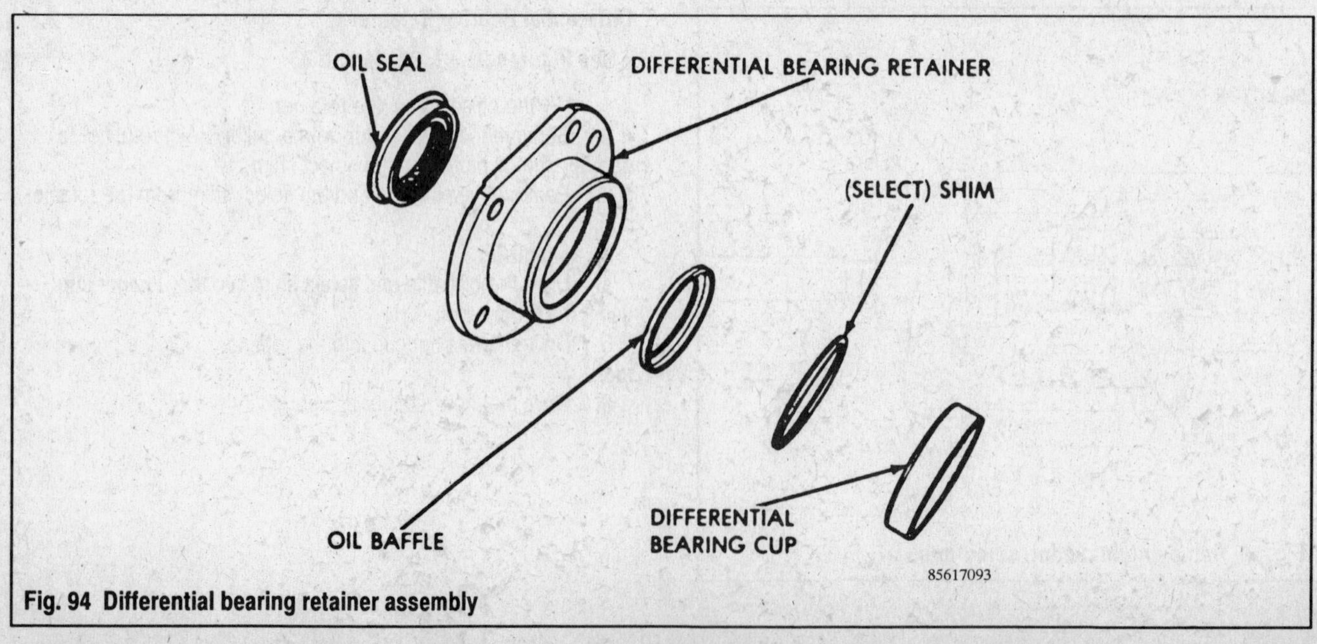

Fig. 94 Differential bearing retainer assembly

EXTENSION HOUSING

➧ See Figures 96, 97, 98, 99, 100

1. Pry the oil seal from the extension housing.
2. Pull the extension cup from the extension housing using the proper tool.
3. Remove the O-ring and oil baffle from the housing.

To assemble:

4. Install a new O-ring into the groove on the outside of the housing.
5. Press the oil baffle in the housing using the proper tool.
6. Press the bearing cup into the extension housing using the proper tool.
7. Install a new housing oil seal.

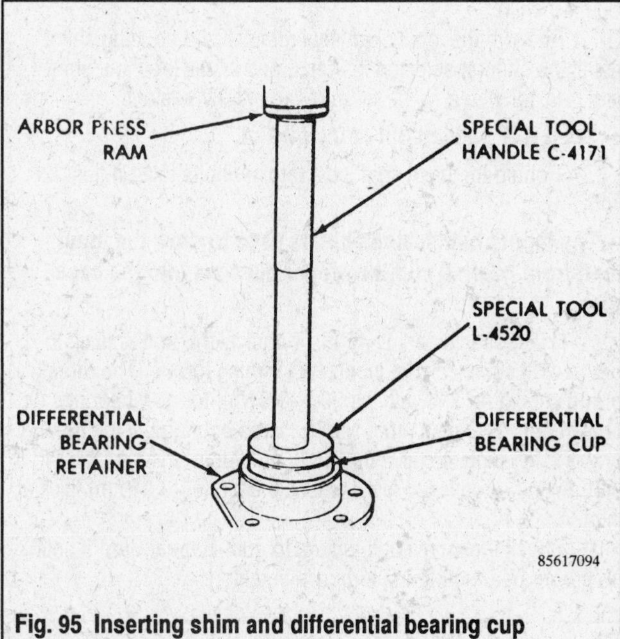

Fig. 95 Inserting shim and differential bearing cup

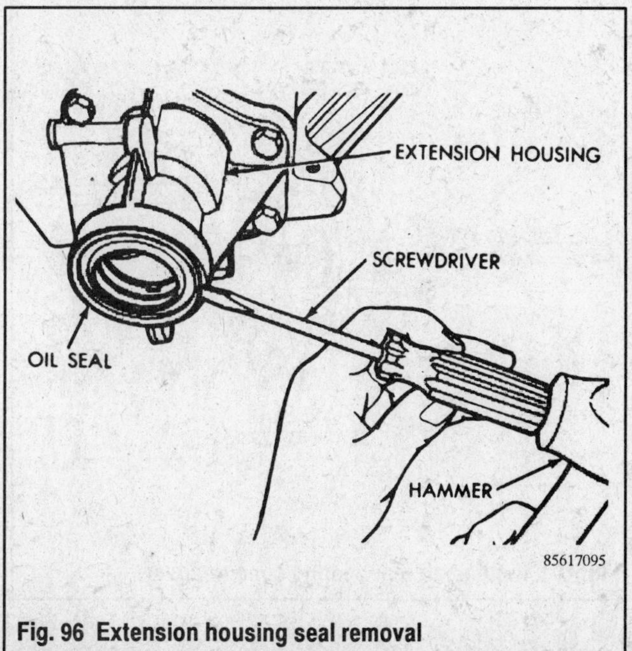

Fig. 96 Extension housing seal removal

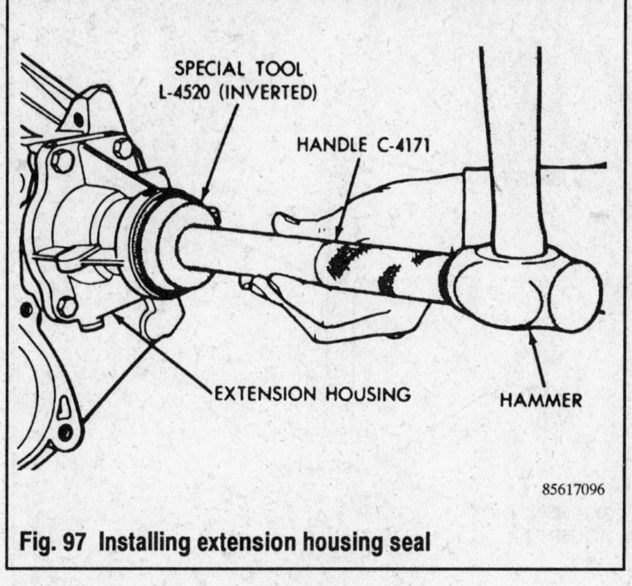

Fig. 97 Installing extension housing seal

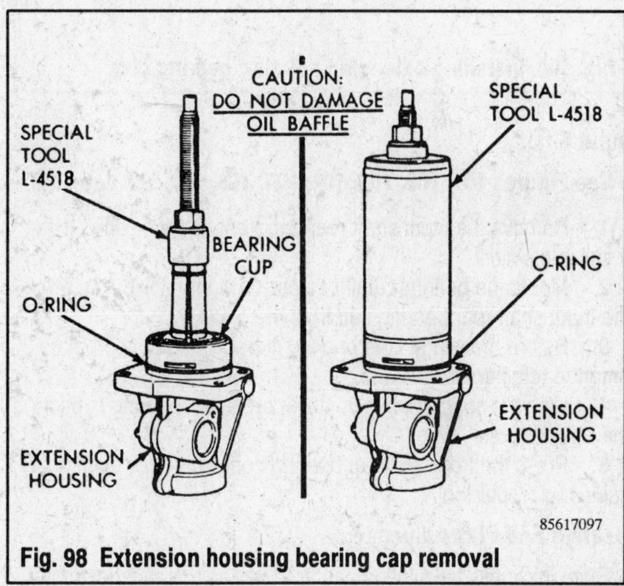

Fig. 98 Extension housing bearing cap removal

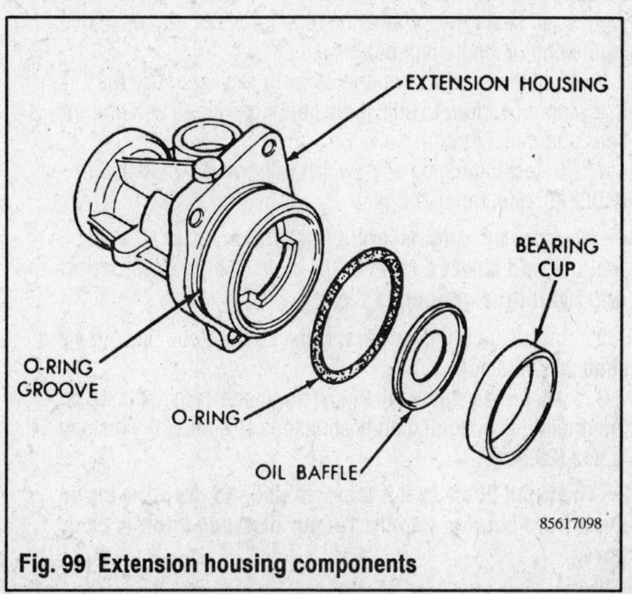

Fig. 99 Extension housing components

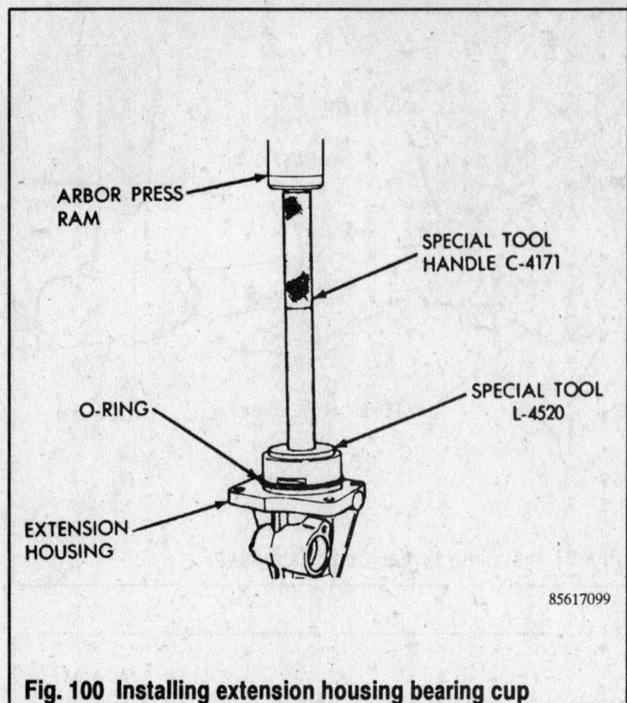

Fig. 100 Installing extension housing bearing cup

Input Shaft

See Figures 101, 102, 103, 104, 105, 106, 107, 108 and 109

1. Remove the input shaft rear and front bearing cones using a suitable puller.
2. Mount the bearing retainer plate on wood blocks and press the input shaft rear bearing cup from the plate.
3. Before pressing in the bearing cup, bolt the support plate onto the retainer plate.
4. With the support plate in place, press the bearing cup into the retainer plate.
5. Press the front and rear bearing cones onto the input shaft using the proper tool.

Bearing End-Play Adjustment

Shim thickness calculation and end-play adjustment need only be done if any of the following parts are replaced: transaxle case, input shaft seal retainer, bearing retainer plate, rear end cover, input shaft or input shaft bearings.

If any of the above components were replaced, use the following procedure to adjust the bearing preload and proper bearing turning torque.

1. Select a gauging shim which will give 0.001–0.010 in. (0.025–0.250mm) of end-play.

Measure the original shim from the input shaft seal retainer and select a shim 0.010 in. (0.25mm) thinner than the original for the gauging shim.

2. Install the gauging shim on the bearing cup and the input shaft seal retainer.
3. Alternately tighten the input shaft seal retainer bolts until the retainer is bottomed against the case. Tighten the bolts to 21 ft. lbs. (28 Nm).

The input shaft seal retainer is used to draw the input shaft front bearing cup the proper distance into the case bore.

4. Oil the input shaft bearings with A.T.F. (1984–87 models) or SAE 5W–30 engine oil (1988–91 models) and install the input shaft in the case. Install the bearing retainer plate with the input shaft rear bearing cup pressed in and the support plate installed. Tighten all bolts and nuts to 21 ft. lbs. (28 Nm).
5. Position the dial indicator to check the input shaft end-play. Apply moderate load, by hand, to the input shaft splines. Push toward the rear while rotating the input shaft back and forth a number of times and to settle out the bearings. Zero the dial indicator. Pull the input shaft toward the front while rotating the input shaft back and forth a number of times to settle out the bearings. Record the end-play.
6. The shim required for proper bearing preload is the total of the gauging shim thickness, plus end-play, plus (constant) preload of 0.002–0.003 in. (0.050–0.076mm). Combine shims, if necessary, to obtain a shim within 0.0016 in. (0.04mm) of the required shim.
7. Remove the input shaft seal retainer and gauging shim. Install the shim(s) selected in Step 6 and install the input shaft seal retainer with a $^1/_8$ in. (3mm) bead of RTV sealant.

Keep RTV sealant out of the oil slot.

8. Tighten the input shaft seal retainer bolts to 21 ft. lbs. (28 Nm).

The input shaft seal retainer is used to draw the input shaft front bearing cup the proper distance into the case bore.

9. Using special tool L–4508, or equivalent, and an inch lb. torque wrench, check the input shaft turning torque. The turning torque should be 1–5 inch lbs. (0.1–0.6 Nm) for new bearings or a minimum of 1 inch lb. (0.1 Nm) for used bearings. If the turning torque is too high, install a 0.0016 in. (0.04mm) thinner shim. If the turning torque is too low, install a 0.0016 in. (0.04mm) thicker shim.
10. Check the input shaft turning torque. Repeat Step 9 until the proper bearing turning torque is obtained.

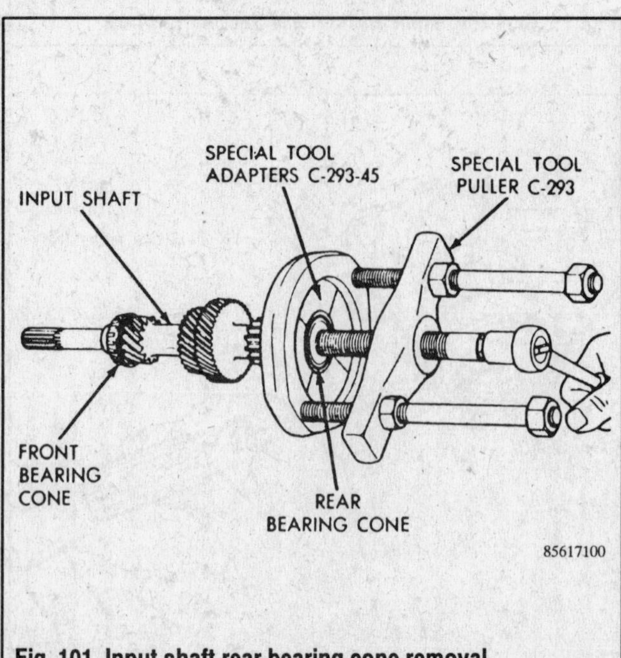

Fig. 101 Input shaft rear bearing cone removal

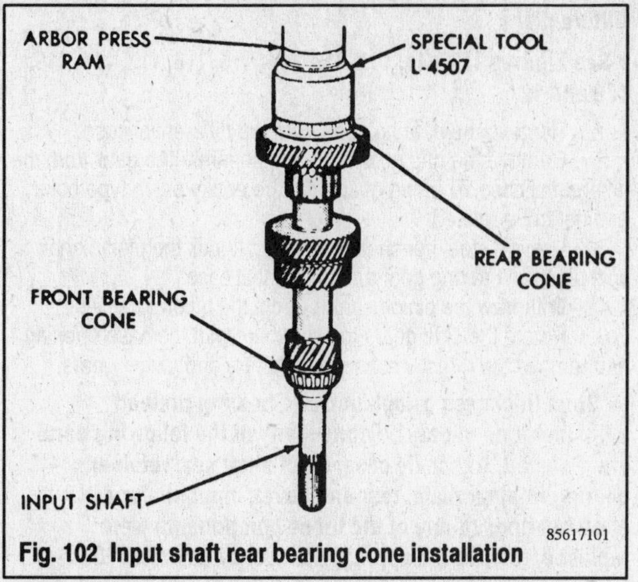

Fig. 102 Input shaft rear bearing cone installation

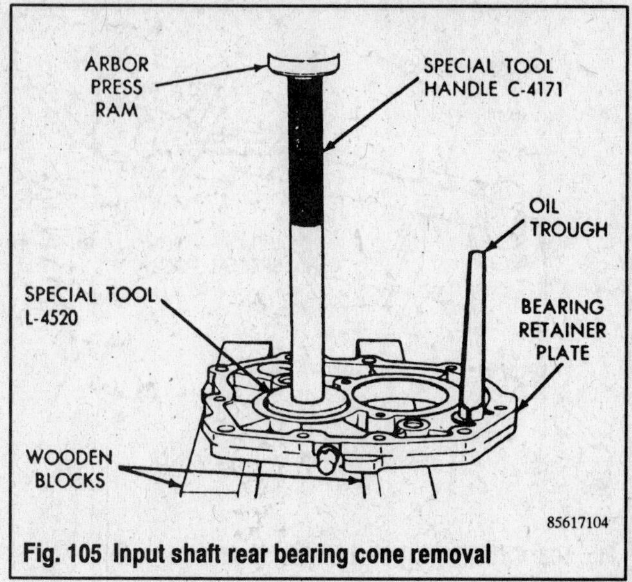

Fig. 105 Input shaft rear bearing cone removal

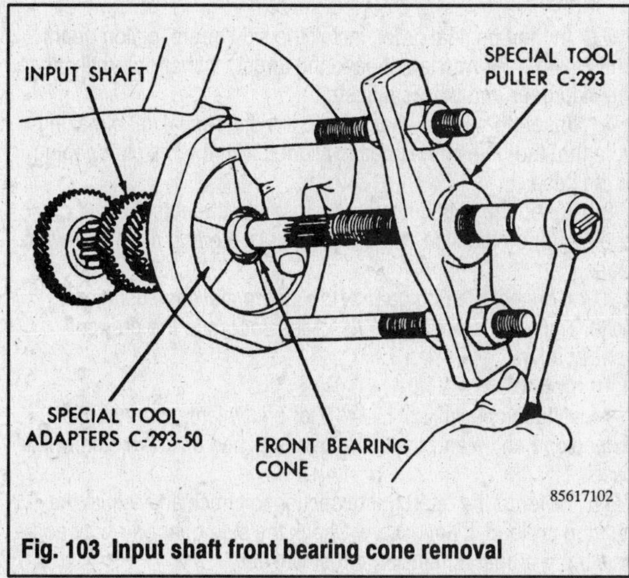

Fig. 103 Input shaft front bearing cone removal

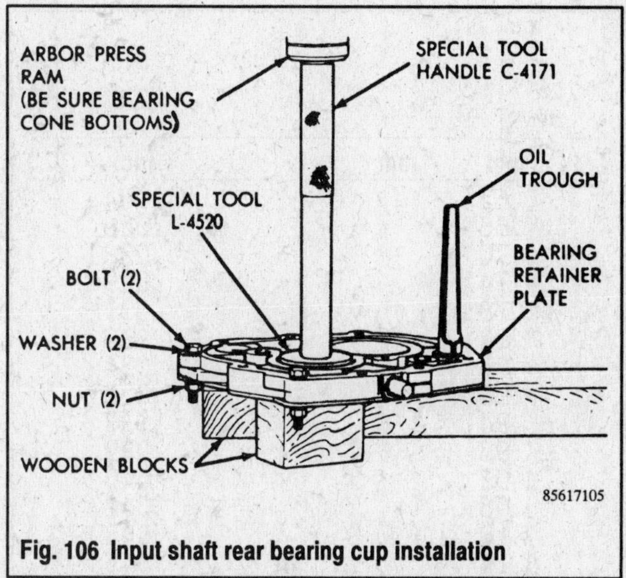

Fig. 106 Input shaft rear bearing cup installation

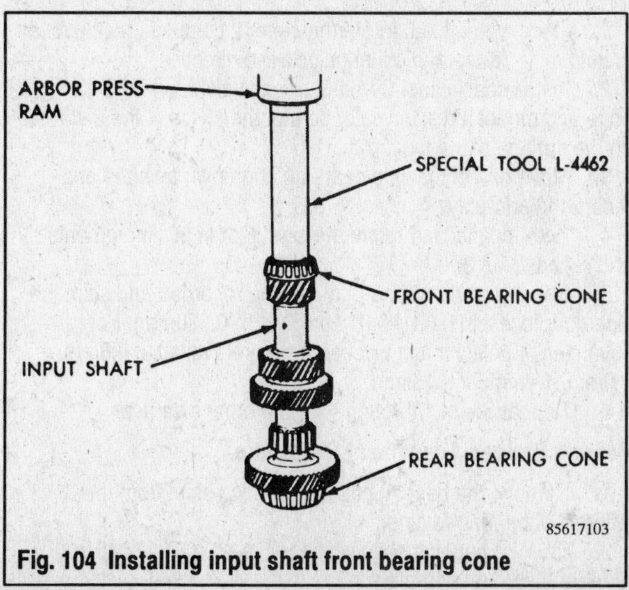

Fig. 104 Installing input shaft front bearing cone

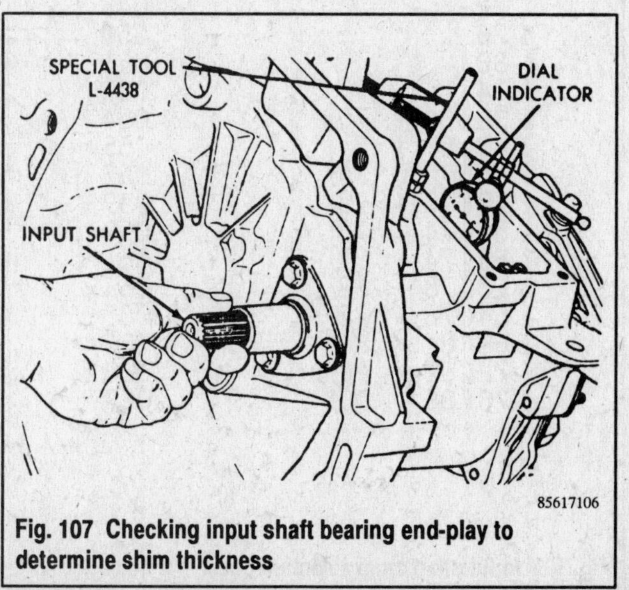

Fig. 107 Checking input shaft bearing end-play to determine shim thickness

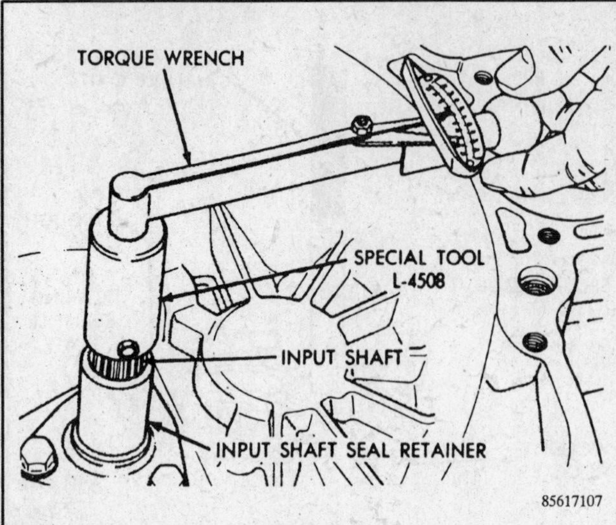

Fig. 108 Checking input shaft bearing turning torque

mm	mm	inch
.62		.024
.66		.026
.70		.028
.74		.029
.78		.031
.82		.032
.86		.034
.90		.035
.94		.037
.98		.039
1.02		.040
1.06		.042
1.10		.043
1.14		.045
1.18		.046
1.22		.048
1.26		.050
1.30		.051
1.34		.053
1.36	(.66 + .70)	.054
1.40	(.66 + .74)	.055
1.44	(.70 + .74)	.057
1.48	(.70 + .78)	.059
1.52	(.74 + .78)	.060
1.56	(.74 + .82)	.061
1.60	(.78 + .82)	.063
1.64	(.78 + .86)	.065
1.68	(.82 + .86)	.066
1.72	(.82 + .90)	.068
1.76	(.86 + .90)	.069

85617108

Fig. 109 Input shaft shim selection chart

Differential

See Figures 110, 111, 112, 113, 114, 115, 116, 117, 118, 119, 120 and 121

1. Remove the bearing cone from the differential case.
2. Remove the ring gear bolts and separate the gear from the differential case. The ring gear bolts are epoxy patch type bolts and not to be reused.
3. Using a steel punch and hammer, knock the pinion shaft split pin from the ring gear and differential case.
4. Withdraw the pinion shaft(s) from the differential case.
5. Rotate the side gears to align them with the case opening and remove the thrust washers, side gears and pinion gears.

Shim thickness calculation and bearing preload adjustment need only be done if any of the following parts are replaced: transaxle case, input shaft seal retainer, bearing retainer plate, rear end cover, input shaft or input shaft bearings. If any of the those components were replaced, refer to the appropriate section to adjust the bearing preload, proper bearing turning torque or side gear end-play.

6. In their original order, install the side gears, pinion gears and pinion gear washers. Leave the thrust washer out until after the side gear end-play is adjusted.
7. Insert the pinion shaft(s) into the differential case making sure that the hole in the shaft is aligned with the roll pin opening in the case.
8. Insert the pinion shaft roll pin(s) into the notched opening(s) on the side of the differential case and drive them into place.
9. Connect the ring gear to the differential case using new bolts. Tighten the bolts in a crisscross pattern to the proper specification.

To install:

10. Attach special tool L-4410, or equivalent, to a suitable extension handle and press the bearing cone onto the differential case.
11. Refer to the appropriate section to check and adjust the bearing preload, if necessary. Check the side gear end-play and select the proper dimension thrust washer.

Side Gear End-Play Adjustment

1. Once assembled, rotate the gears 2 complete revolutions in both a clockwise and counterclockwise direction.
2. Install special tool C-4996, or equivalent, on the bearing cone and mount a dial indicator so that the stylus of the dial rests on the surface of the tool.
3. Move one of the side gears up and down by hand and record the end-play.
4. Zero the dial and rotate the side gear in 90° increments and repeat Step 3.
5. Use the smallest end-play reading recorded and shim the side gear to within 0.001–0.013 in. (0.025–0.330mm). For shimming, 4 select thrust washer sizes are available: 0.8mm, 0.9mm, 1.0mm, and 1.2mm.
6. Repeat Steps 1 through 4 for the other side gear.

Bearing Preload Adjustment Procedure

1. Remove the bearing cup and existing shim from the differential bearing retainer.
2. Select a gauging shim which will give 0.001–0.010 in. (0.025–0.250mm) end-play.

➥ Measure the original shim from the differential bearing retainer and select a shim 0.015 in. (0.38mm) thinner than the original for the gauging shim.

3. Install the gauging shim in the differential bearing retainer and press in the bearing cup. Installation of the oil baffle is not necessary when checking differential assembly end-play.
4. Lubricate the differential bearings with A.T.F. (1984–87 models) or SAE 5W–30 engine oil (1988–91 models) and install the differential assembly in the transaxle case.
5. Inspect the extension housing for damage and replace it as necessary.
6. Position the transaxle with the bell housing facing down on the workbench and secure it with C-clamps. Position the dial indicator.
7. Apply a medium load to the ring gear, by hand, in the downward direction while rolling the differential assembly back and forth a number of times to settle the bearings. Zero the dial indicator. To obtain end-play readings, apply a medium load upward by hand while rolling the differential assembly back and forth a number of times to settle out the bearings. Record the end-play.
8. The shim required for proper bearing preload is the total of the gauging shim thickness, plus end-play, plus (constant) preload of 0.010 in. (0.25mm). Combine shims if necessary, to obtain a shim within 0.002 in. (0.05mm) of the shim(s).
9. Remove the differential bearing retainer.
10. Remove the bearing cup and gauging shim. Properly install the oil baffle making sure the oil baffle is not damaged. Install the shim(s) selected in Step 8 and press the bearing cup into the differential bearing retainer.
11. Using a 1/8 in. (3mm) bead of R.T.V. sealant for gaskets, install the differential bearing retainer and extension housing. Tighten the bolts to 21 ft. lbs. (28 Nm).
12. Using an appropriate tool and an inch lb. torque wrench, check the turning torque of the differential assembly. The turning torque should be 9–14 inch lbs. (1.0–1.6 Nm) for new bearings or a minimum of 6 inch lbs. (0.6 Nm) for used bearings. If the turning torque is too low, install a 0.002 in. (0.05mm) thicker shim.
13. Check the turning torque. Repeat Step 11 until the proper turning torque is obtained.

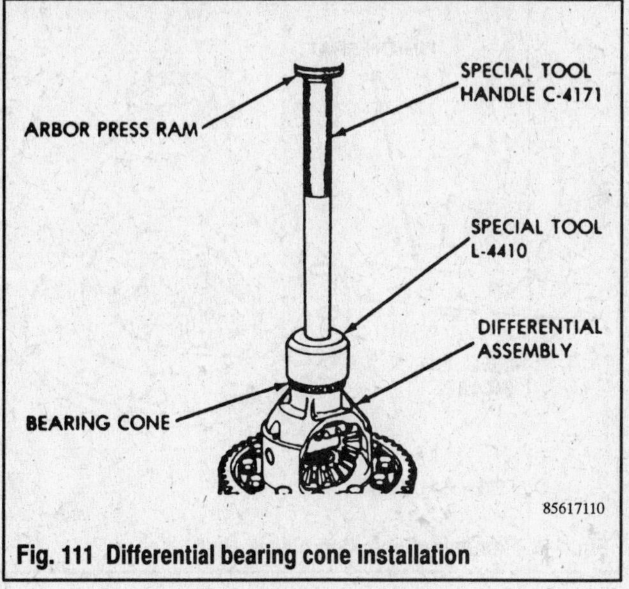

Fig. 111 Differential bearing cone installation

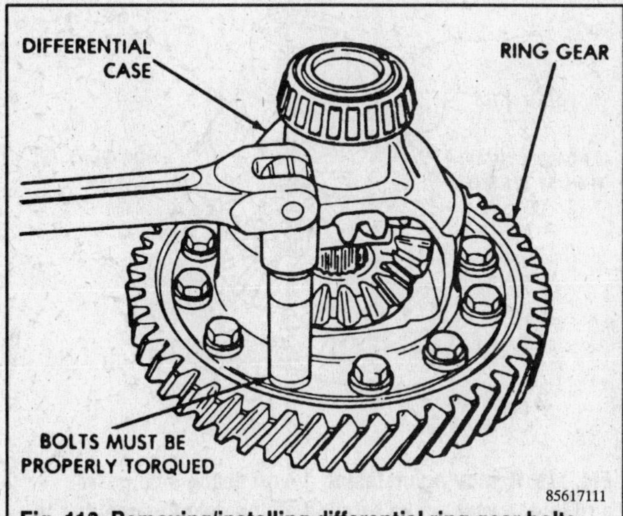

Fig. 112 Removing/installing differential ring gear bolts and ring gear

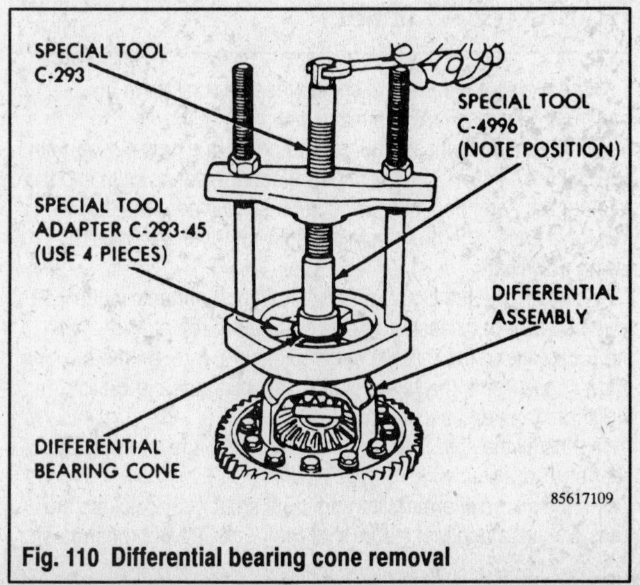

Fig. 110 Differential bearing cone removal

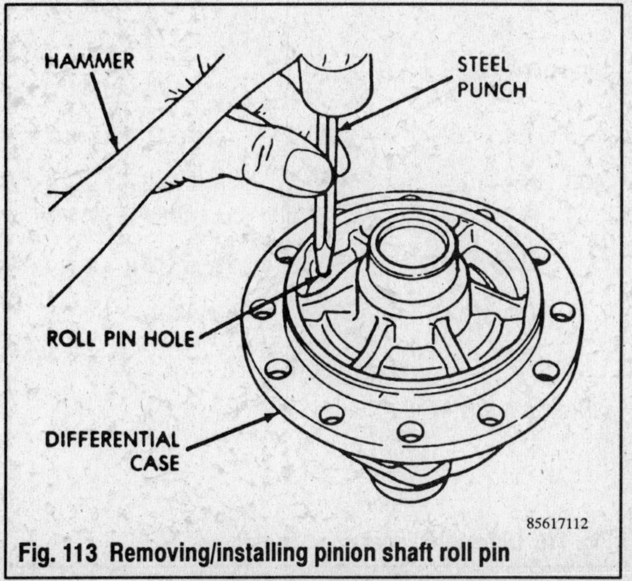

Fig. 113 Removing/installing pinion shaft roll pin

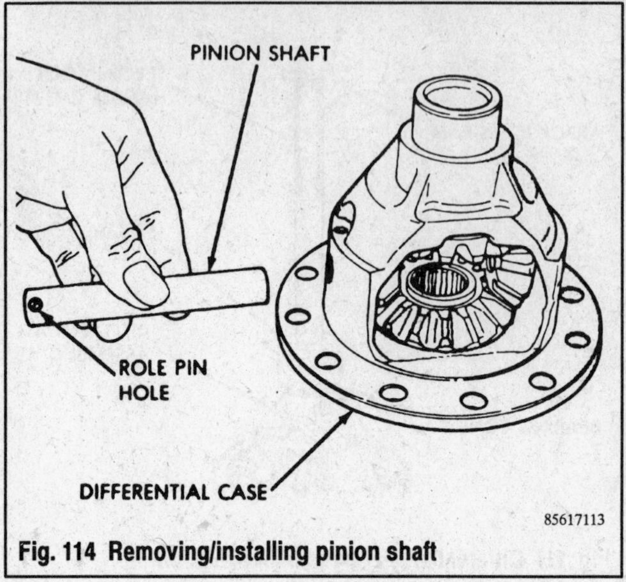

Fig. 114 Removing/installing pinion shaft

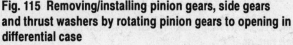

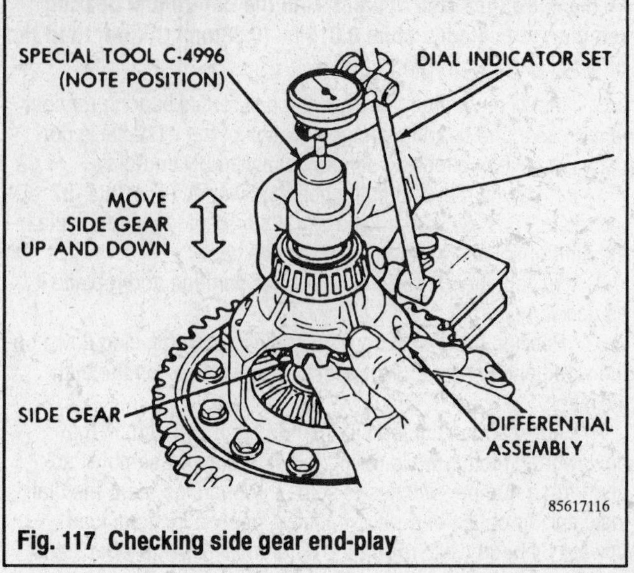

Fig. 117 Checking side gear end-play

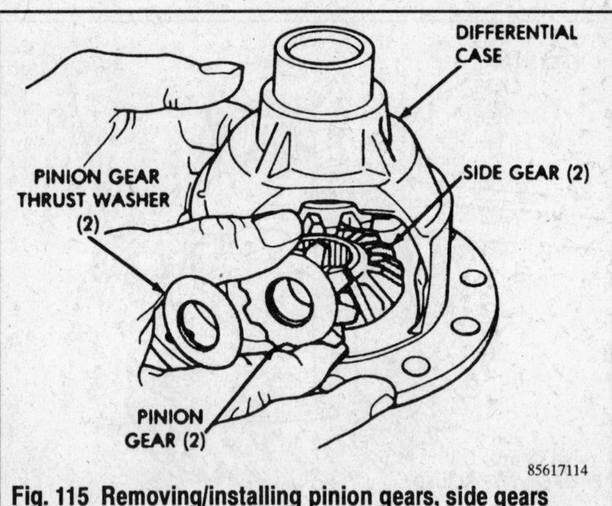

Fig. 115 Removing/installing pinion gears, side gears and thrust washers by rotating pinion gears to opening in differential case

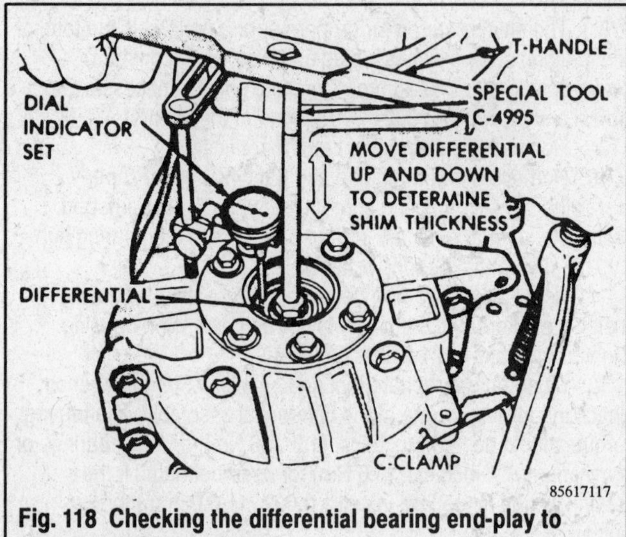

Fig. 118 Checking the differential bearing end-play to determine shim thickness

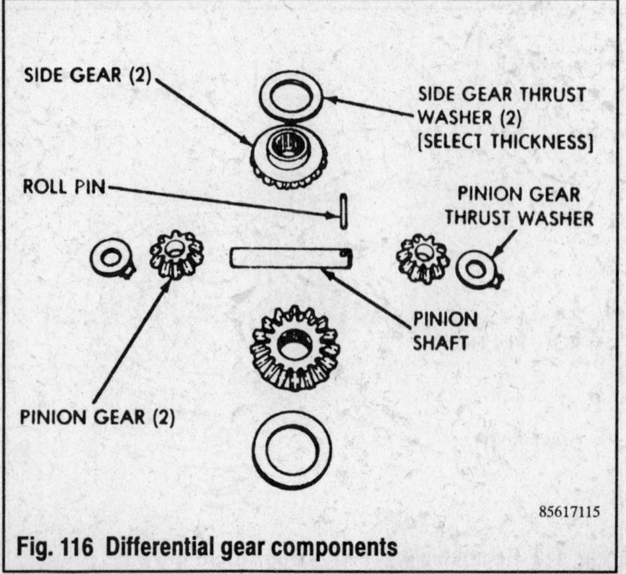

Fig. 116 Differential gear components

TRANSAXLE ASSEMBLY

1. Assemble the reverse shift lever components to the transaxle case and lock it in place with the E-clip.
2. Clean the input shaft bore and press in a new oil seal with special tool C-4674, or equivalent. Place the select shim into the retainer race and bolt the input shaft seal retainer onto the transaxle case. The drain hole on the retainer sleeve must be facing downward.
3. Assemble the clutch release shaft components in the reverse order of disassembly and secure the release lever with the E-clip. Insert the release shaft spline end through the bushing and engage it with the release shaft fork. Engage the E-clip on the shaft groove to secure the shaft.
4. Install the shift forks and shift rails onto the intermediate gear shaft assembly.
5. Install the intermediate and input shaft gear sets into the transaxle case and make sure that the gears are in proper mesh.

Once the gear sets are in place, rotate the 5th speed shifter to the right and the 1-2 and 3-4 shift forks to the left.

6. Install the reverse idler gear (with plastic stop) so that the roll pin on the end of the gear shaft aligns with the roll pin notch in the transaxle case. Lock the gear and engage the reverse shift lever. Make sure the plastic stop is firmly seated on the gear.

7. Install the 1-2, 3-4 and 5th speed shift fork rails into their respective locating holes.

8. Install and tighten the 1-2 shift fork set screw and 5th speed selector guide pin.

9. Remove all the excess sealant from the bearing retainer plate and run an 1/8 in. (3mm) bead of RTV around the plate's seating surface. Keep the RTV away from the bolt holes. Align the plate with the transaxle case and install it. The plate will align with the oil trough and the 5th speed shift rail. Install the intermediate shaft rear bearing snapring once the plate is in place and seated.

10. Install the bearing support plate with the retaining bolts. Tighten the bolts to specification.

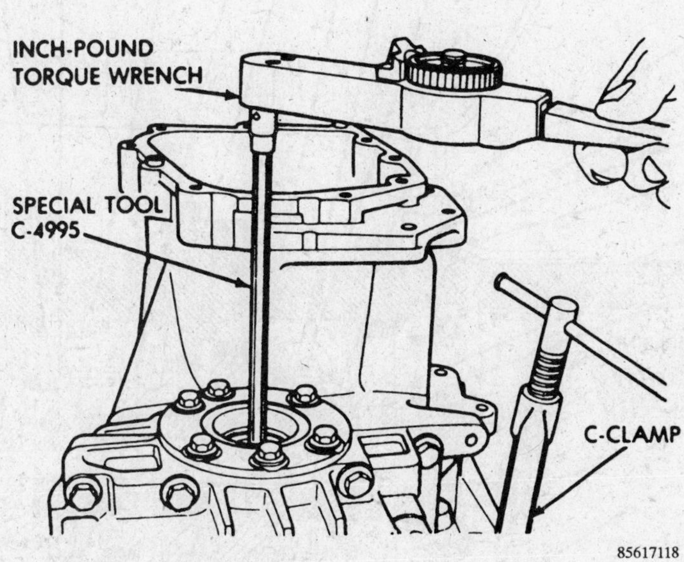

Fig. 119 Checking the differential bearing turning torque

Required Shim Combination	Total Thickness		Required Shim Combination	Total Thickness		Required Shim Combination	Total Thickness	
mm	mm	Inch	mm	mm	Inch	mm	mm	Inch
.50	.50	.020	.50 + .70	1.20	.047	1.00 + .70	1.70	.067
.75	.75	.030	.50 + .75	1.25	.049	1.00 + .75	1.75	.069
.80	.80	.032	.50 + .80	1.30	.051	1.00 + .80	1.80	.071
.85	.85	.034	.50 + .85	1.35	.053	1.00 + .85	1.85	.073
.90	.90	.035	.50 + .90	1.40	.055	1.00 + .90	1.90	.075
.95	.95	.037	.50 + .95	1.45	.057	1.00 + .95	1.95	.077
1.00	1.00	.039	.50 + 1.00	1.50	.059	1.00 + 1.00	2.00	.079
1.05	1.05	.041	.50 + 1.05	1.55	.061	1.00 + 1.05	2.05	.081
.50 + .60	1.10	.043	1.00 + .60	1.60	.063	1.05 + 1.05	2.10	.083
.50 + .65	1.15	.045	1.00 + .65	1.65	.065			

85617119

Fig. 120 Differential bearing shim selection chart

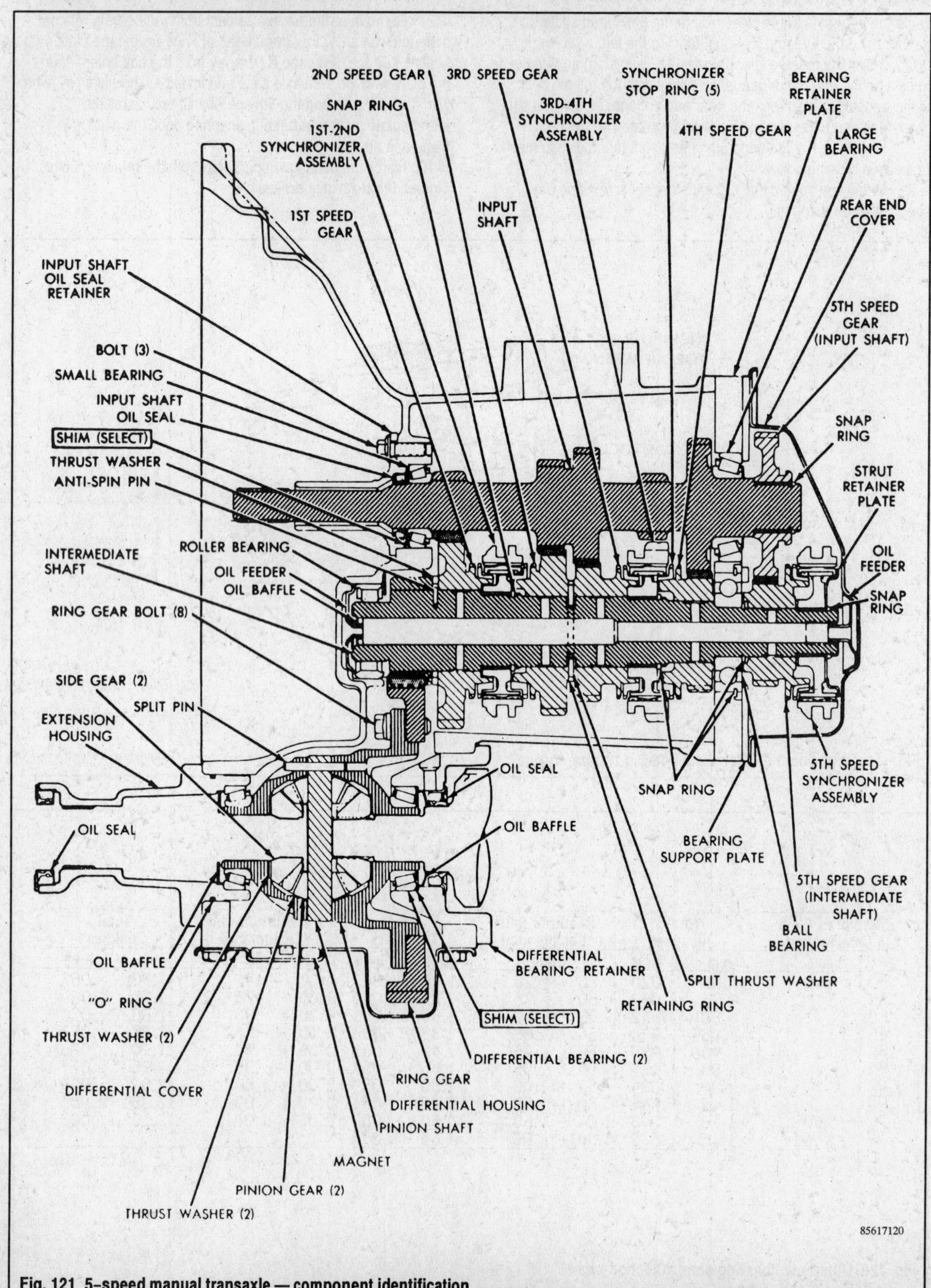

Fig. 121 5-speed manual transaxle — component identification

11. Install the 5th speed gear onto the input shaft. Install a new gear nut with special holding tool 6252, or equivalent. The holding tool must be used to install the gear nut and the old nut must not be reused. Tighten the nut to 190 ft. lbs. (258 Nm) and remove the holding tool.
12. Install the intermediate shaft 5th speed gear, synchronizer hub and struts using special tool C-4888, or an equivalent gear installer.
13. Position the 5th speed synchronizer sleeve and shift fork over the 5th speed shift rail and install it using the alignment marks for reference. Lock the fork to the rail with the set screw.
14. Install the 5th speed synchronizer strut retainer plate with the snapring.
15. Clean the excess sealant from the end cover and make sure the oil fill plug hole is clear. Run a bead of RTV around the cover's seating surface and place the cover on the bearing retainer plate. Install the end cover bolts and tighten to specification.
16. Clean the excess sealant from the selector shaft housing. If the back-up light switch was removed, install the switch with a new gasket. Run a $^1/_8$ in. (3mm) bead of RTV sealant around the cover's seating surface and install the housing with the housing bolts. Tighten the bolts to specification.
17. Apply RTV sealant to the portion of the differential bearing retainer that bolts to the ring gear to form a gasket.
18. Position the differential in the support saddles.
19. Connect the bearing retainer to the differential with the inner bolts and tighten the bolts to specification.
20. Remove the O-ring seal from the extension housing and replace it with a new one. Clean the old sealant from the base of the extension and run a bead of new sealant.
21. Connect the extension to the other side of the differential with the outer bolts. Tighten the bolts to specification.
22. Clean the excess sealant from the differential cover and run a $^1/_8$ in. (3mm) bead of RTV around the cover's seating surface. Install the differential cover with the cover bolts. Tighten the bolts to specification.
23. Install the remaining extension and differential bearing retainer (outer) bolts and tighten them to specification.
24. Remove the transaxle from the holding fixture and install it in the vehicle.

Halfshafts

The halfshafts used on your vehicle are of three piece construction and are unequal in length and material composition. A short solid interconnecting shaft is used on the left side and a longer tubular interconnecting shaft is installed on the right side.

The halfshaft assemblies are three piece units. Each shaft has a Tripod joint on the transaxle side, an interconnecting shaft and a Rzeppa joint on the wheel side. The Rzeppa joint mounts a splined stub shaft that connects with the wheel hub. The inner Tripod joint mounts a spring that maintains constant spline engagement with the transaxle. The design enables the halfshaft to be removed without dismantling the transaxle.

Models equipped with a turbo charged engine incorporate an equal length halfshaft system. This system includes an extra intermediate shaft installed on the right side. This helps to prevent torque steer induced by the power of the engine. The halfshaft removal procedure for all vehicles is the same.

REMOVAL & INSTALLATION

See Figures 122, 123, 124, 125, 126, 127, 128, 129, 130, 131, 132, 133, 134, 135, 136 and 137

1. Remove the cotter pin, lockwasher and spring washer from the front axle ends.
2. Have a helper apply the service brakes and loosen the front axle hub retaining nut.
3. Raise and support the front of the vehicle on jackstands.
4. Remove the hub nut, washer and wheel assembly. Drain transaxle fluid.

The speedometer drive pinion must be removed from the transaxle housing before the right side drive axle can be removed. Remove the retaining bolts and lift the pinion with cable connected from the housing.

5. Remove the clamp bolt that secures the ball joint stud with the steering knuckle.
6. Separate the ball joint from the knuckle by prying downward against the knuckle connecting point and the control arm. Take care not to damage the rubber boot.
7. Separate the outer CV-joint (Constant Velocity) splines from the steering knuckle hub by holding the CV housing and pushing the knuckle out and away. If resistance is encountered, use a brass drift and hammer to gently tap the outer hub end of the axle. Do not pry on the outer wear sleeve of the CV-joint.
8. After the outboard end of the drive axle has been removed from the steering knuckle, support the assembly and pull outward on the inner CV-joint housing to remove the assembly from the transaxle.

****WARNING**

Do not pull on the shaft or the assembly will disconnect. Pull only on the inner CV-joint housing.

9. Remove the halfshaft from under the vehicle and service as necessary.

To install:

10. When installing the halfshaft, hold the inner joint assembly by its housing, align and guide the shaft into the transaxle or intermediate shaft assembly.
11. Lubricate the outer wear sleeve and seal with multi-purpose grease. Push the steering knuckle outward and install the splined outer shaft into the drive hub.
12. Install the steering knuckle assembly. Tighten the ball joint clamp bolt to 70 ft. lbs. (95 Nm). Tighten the hub nut (splined shaft nut) to 180 ft. lbs. (250 Nm). Refill the transaxle with the proper lubrication fluid.

If after installing the axle assembly, the inboard boot appears collapsed, vent the boot by inserting a thin round rod between the boot and the shaft. Massage the boot until is expands. Install a new clamp to prevent dirt from entering the boot.

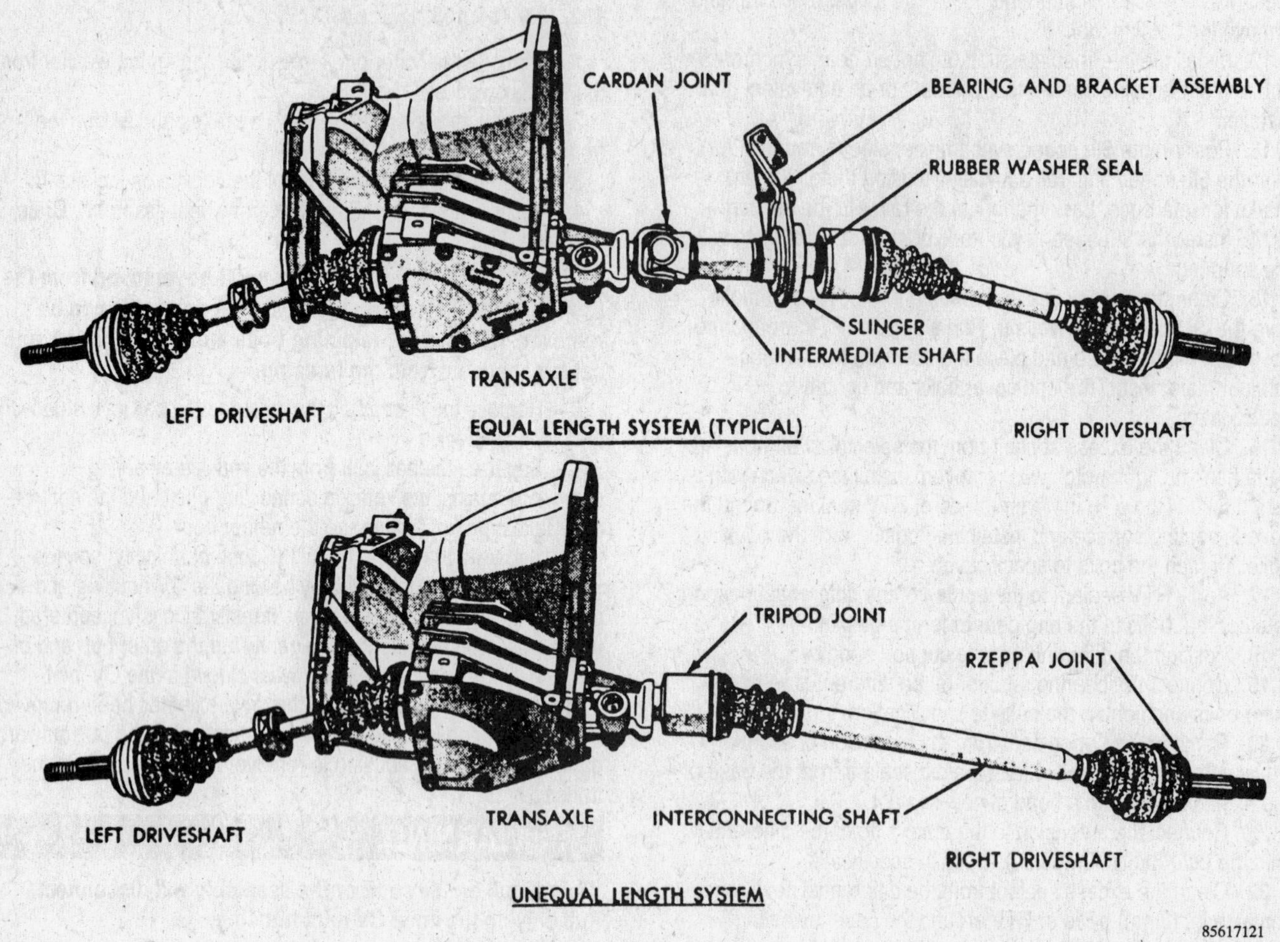

CARDAN JOINT
BEARING AND BRACKET ASSEMBLY
RUBBER WASHER SEAL
SLINGER
INTERMEDIATE SHAFT
TRANSAXLE
LEFT DRIVESHAFT
EQUAL LENGTH SYSTEM (TYPICAL)
RIGHT DRIVESHAFT
TRIPOD JOINT
RZEPPA JOINT
TRANSAXLE
INTERCONNECTING SHAFT
LEFT DRIVESHAFT
RIGHT DRIVESHAFT
UNEQUAL LENGTH SYSTEM
85617121

Fig. 122 Halfshaft type and identification

STEERING KNUCKLE
LOWER CONTROL ARM
PRY BAR
85617122

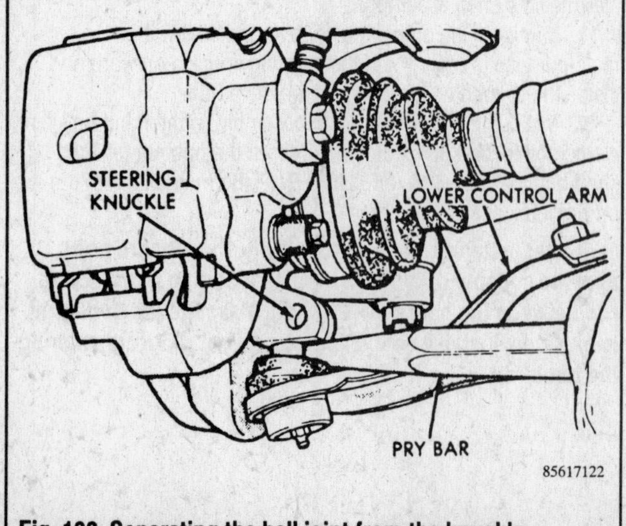

Fig. 123 Separating the ball joint from the knuckle

WEAR SLEEVE
TRANSAXLE EXTENSION
SUPPORT BOTH JOINTS AT HOUSING
85617123

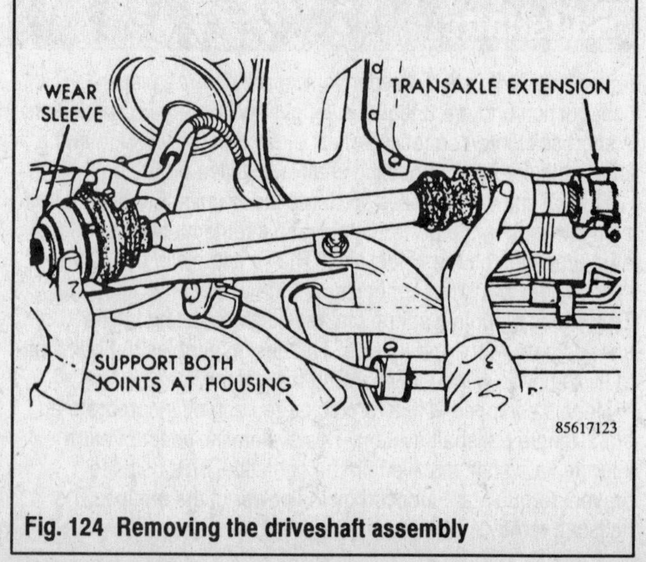

Fig. 124 Removing the driveshaft assembly

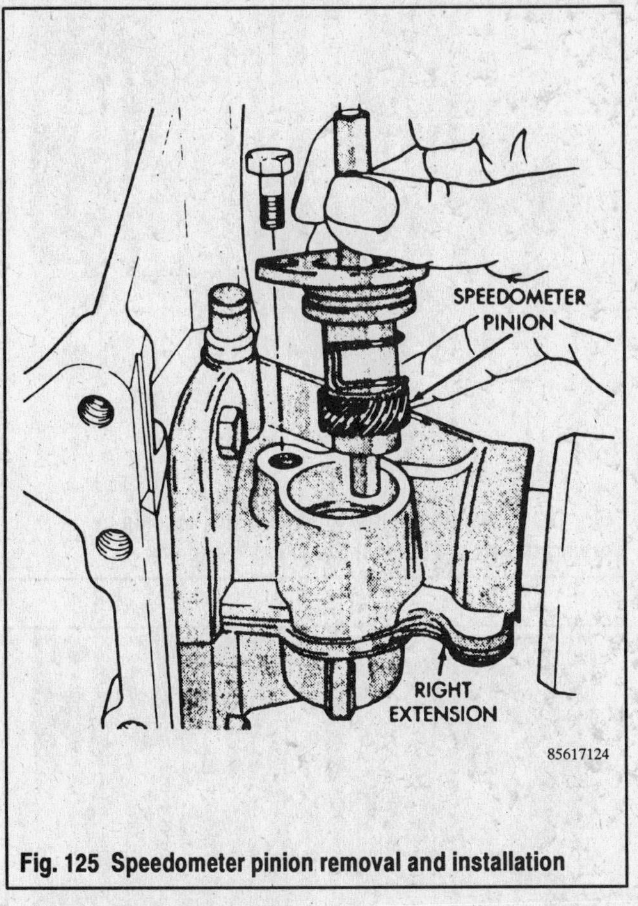

Fig. 125 Speedometer pinion removal and installation

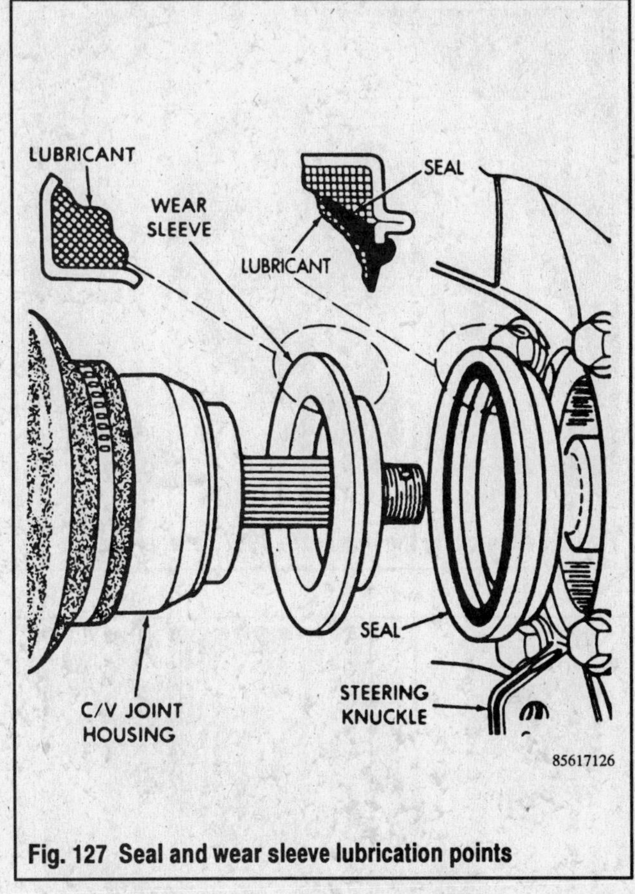

Fig. 127 Seal and wear sleeve lubrication points

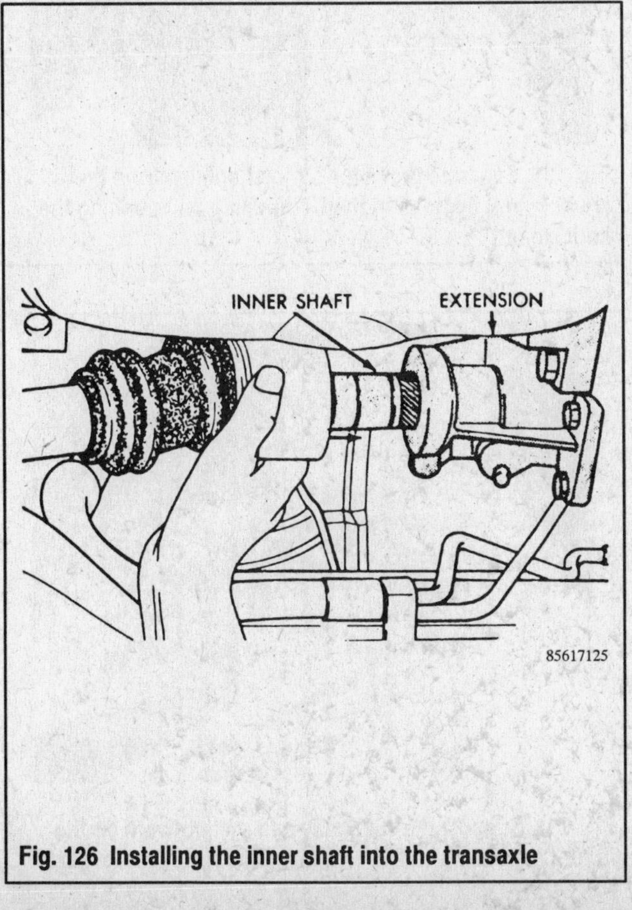

Fig. 126 Installing the inner shaft into the transaxle

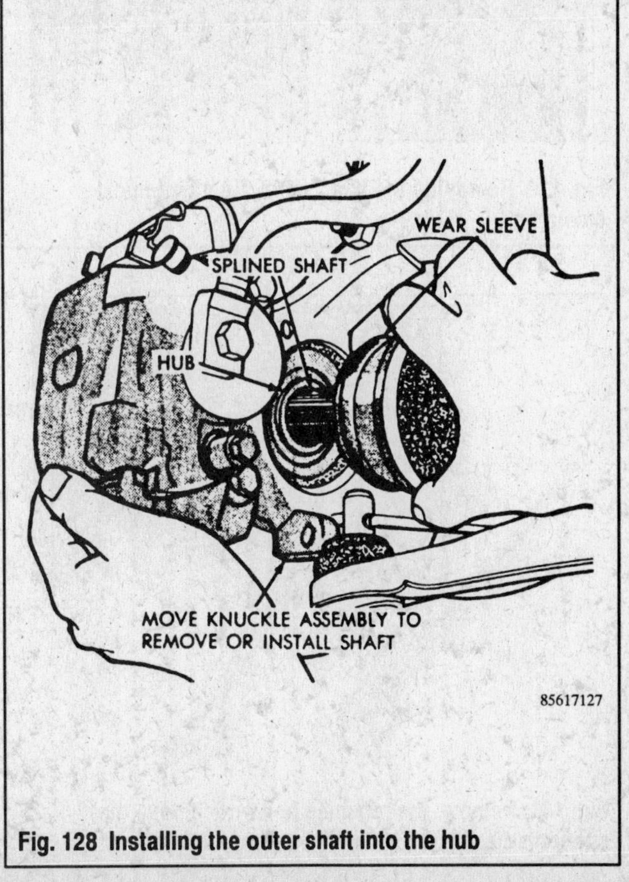

Fig. 128 Installing the outer shaft into the hub

85617128

Fig. 129 Removing the hub nut — 1987 Voyager shown

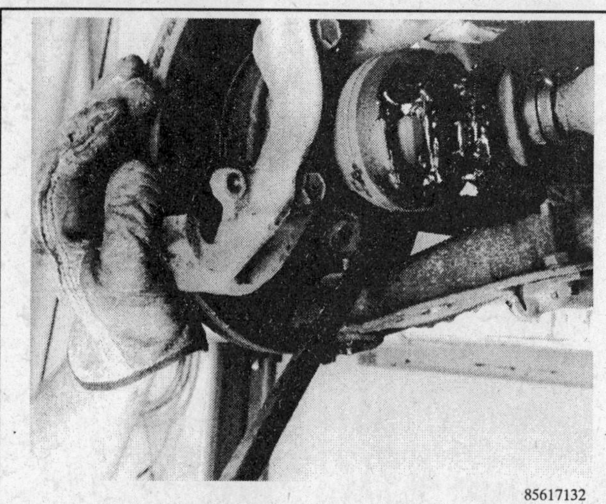

85617132

Fig. 132 Separate the ball joint from the knuckle by prying downward against the knuckle and arm

85617130

Fig. 130 Removing the ball joint to steering knuckle clamp bolt

85617133

Fig. 133 Separate the outer CV-joint splines from the knuckle hub by holding the CV-housing and pushing the knuckle out

85617131

Fig. 131 Remove the retaining bolt and remove the speedometer pinion from the transaxle assembly

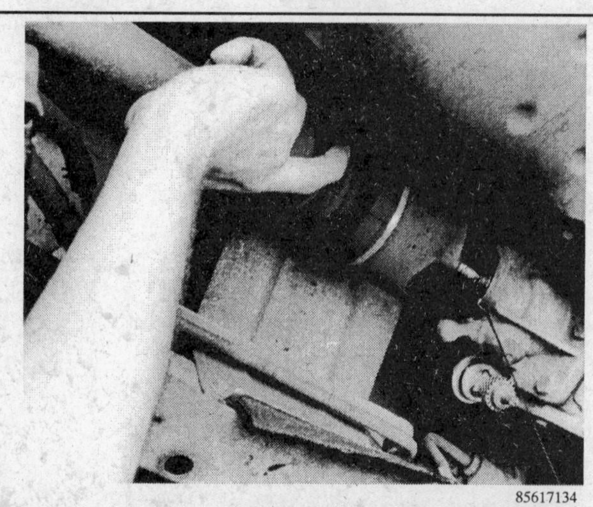

85617134

Fig. 134 Support the assembly and pull outward on the inner CV-housing to free the assembly from the transaxle

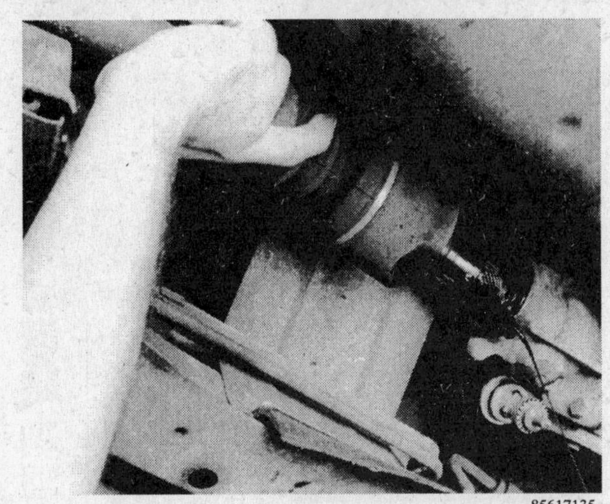
85617135

Fig. 135 Separating the assembly from the transaxle

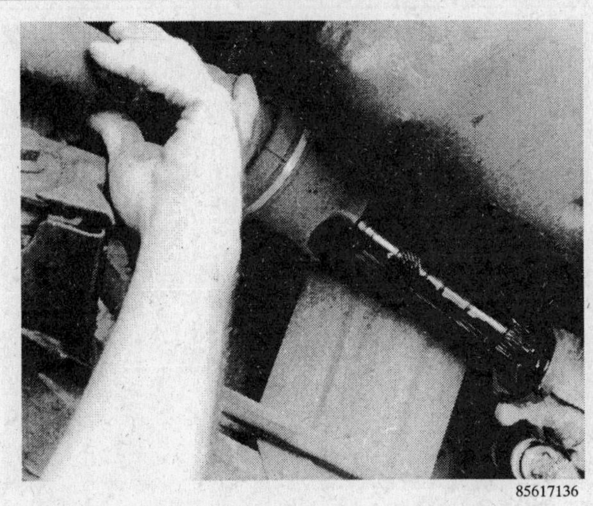
85617136

Fig. 136 Removing the assembly from the transaxle

85617137

Fig. 137 Removing the seal from the housing using a suitable prying tool

CV-JOINT OVERHAUL

Inner Joint

See Figures 138, 139, 140, 141, 142, 143, 144, 145, 146 and 147

1. With the halfshaft assembly removed from the vehicle, remove the clamps and boot.
2. Depending on the unit (GKN or Citroen) separate the tripod assembly from the housing as follows:

CITROEN TYPE

1. Since the trunion ball rollers are not retained on bearing studs, a retaining ring is used to prevent accidental tripod/housing separation, which would allow roller and needle bearings to fall away.In the case of the spring loaded inner CV-joints, if it weren't for the retaining ring, the spring would automatically force the tripod out of the housing whenever the shaft was not installed in the vehicle.
2. Separate the tripod from the housing by slightly deforming the retaining ring in 3 places, with a suitable tool.

****WARNING**

Secure the rollers to the studs during separation. With the tripod out of the housing secure the assembly with tape.

GKN TYPE

1. Spring loaded GKN inboard CV-joints have tabs on the can cover that prevent the spring from forcing the tripod out of the housing. These tabs must be bent back with a pair of pliers before the tripod can be removed. Under normal conditions it is not necessary to secure the GKN rollers to their studs during separation due to the presence of a retainer ring on the end of each stud. This retention force can easily be overcome if the rollers are pulled or impacted. It is also possible to pull the rollers off by removing or installing the tripod with the connecting shaft at too high an angle, relative to the housing.
2. Remove the snapring from the shaft end groove, then remove the tripod with a brass punch.

To install:

3. Remove as much grease as possible from the assembly. Look at the ball housing races, and the components for excessive wear.

DO NOT CLEAN THE INNER HOUSING WITH MINERAL SPIRITS OR SOLVENT. Solvents will destroy the rubber seals that are hidden in the housing and permit grease leakage. If wear is excessive, replace as necessary.

4. Fasten the new boot onto the interconnecting shaft. Install the tripod on the shaft as follows:
   a. GKN type: slide the tripod onto the shaft with the non-chamfered end facing the tripod retaining ring groove.
   b. Citroen type: slide the tripod onto the shaft (both sides are the same).
5. Install the retainer snapring into the groove on the interconnecting shaft locking the tripod in position.
6. On GKN type: put two of the three packets of grease into the boot and the remaining pack into the housing. On Citroen type: put two thirds of the packet of grease into the boot and the remaining grease into the housing.

7. Position the spring into the housing spring pocket with the cup attached to the exposed end of the spring. Place a small amount of grease in the spring cup.

8. On G.K.N type: slip the tripod into the housing and bend down the retaining tabs. Make sure the tabs are holding the housing firmly.

9. On Citroen type: remove the tape holding the rollers and needle bearings in place. Hold the rollers and needles in place and install the housing.

10. Install the retaining ring into the machined groove in the housing with a punch and plastic hammer. Hold the retaining collar in position with two C-clamps while engaging the retainer ring.

****WARNING**

When installing the tripod, the spring must be centered in the housing to insure proper positioning.

11. Position the boot over the retaining groove in the housing and clamp in position.

85617140

Fig. 140 Removing the spring and cup

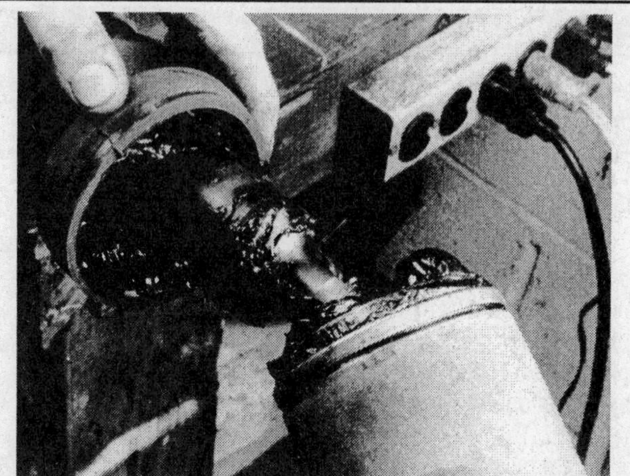

85617138

Fig. 138 After removing the clamps, pull the boot to expose the tripod retention system — 1987 Voyager with Citroen type CV-joint

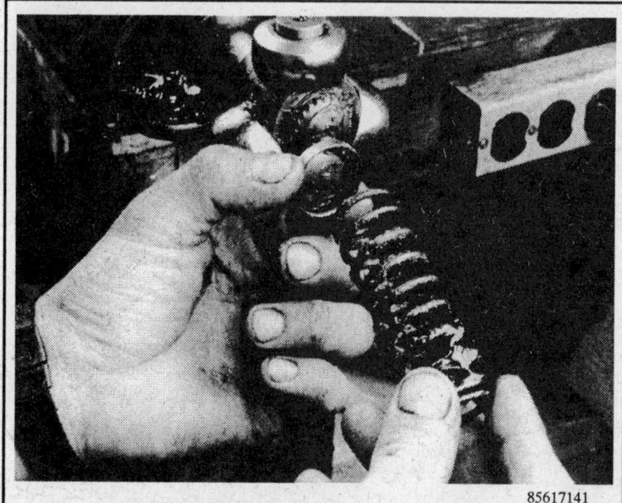

85617141

Fig. 141 Separating the cup from the spring

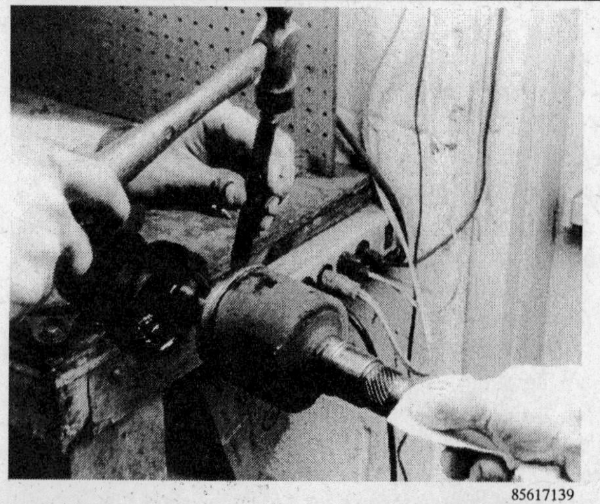

85617139

Fig. 139 Secure the rollers, then tap the retainer ring in 3 locations to separate the tripod from the housing

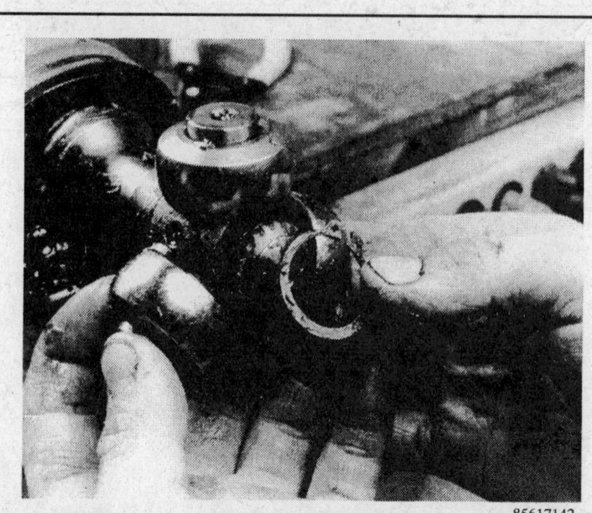

85617142

Fig. 142 Remove the snapring from the end of the shaft

85617143

Fig. 143 After removing the snapring from the end of the shaft remove the tripod

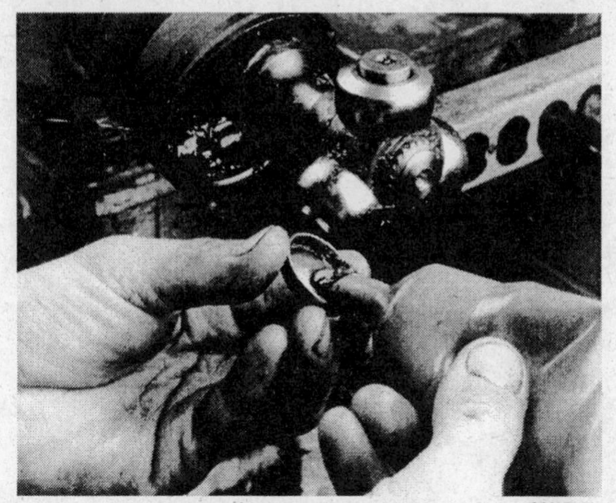

85617144

Fig. 144 Place a small amount of grease in the spring cup

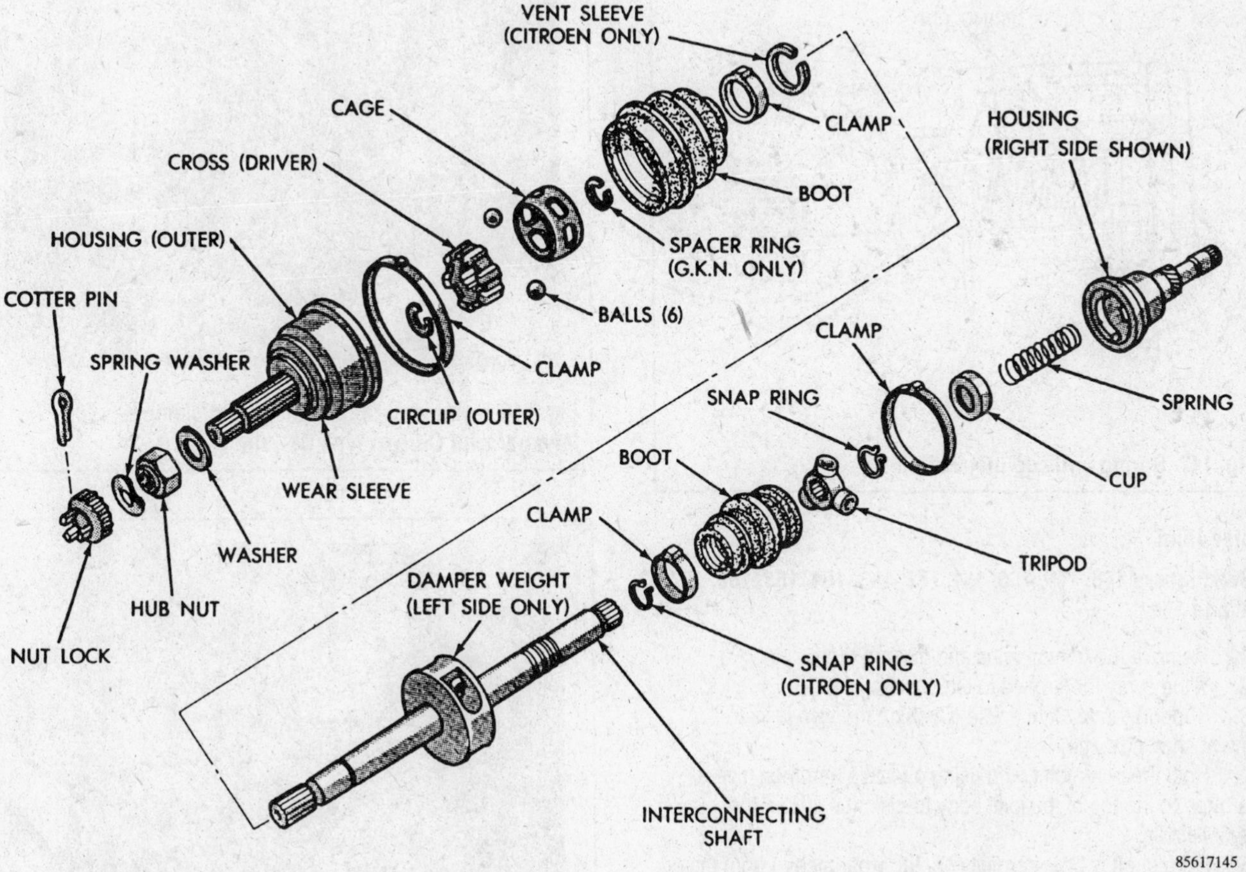

VENT SLEEVE (CITROEN ONLY)
CAGE
CLAMP
HOUSING (RIGHT SIDE SHOWN)
CROSS (DRIVER)
BOOT
HOUSING (OUTER)
SPACER RING (G.K.N. ONLY)
COTTER PIN
BALLS (6)
CLAMP
SPRING WASHER
CLAMP
SNAP RING
SPRING
CIRCLIP (OUTER)
BOOT
CUP
WEAR SLEEVE
CLAMP
TRIPOD
WASHER
DAMPER WEIGHT (LEFT SIDE ONLY)
HUB NUT
NUT LOCK
SNAP RING (CITROEN ONLY)
INTERCONNECTING SHAFT

85617145

Fig. 145 Exploded view of the halfshaft assembly

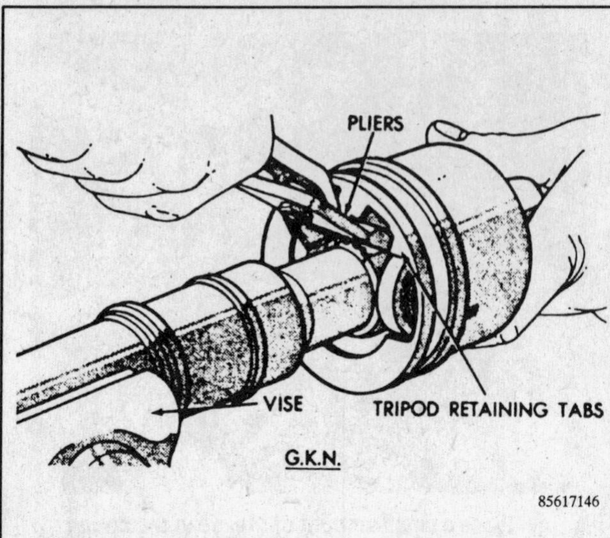

Fig. 146 Separating the tripod from the housing on a GKN type CV-joint

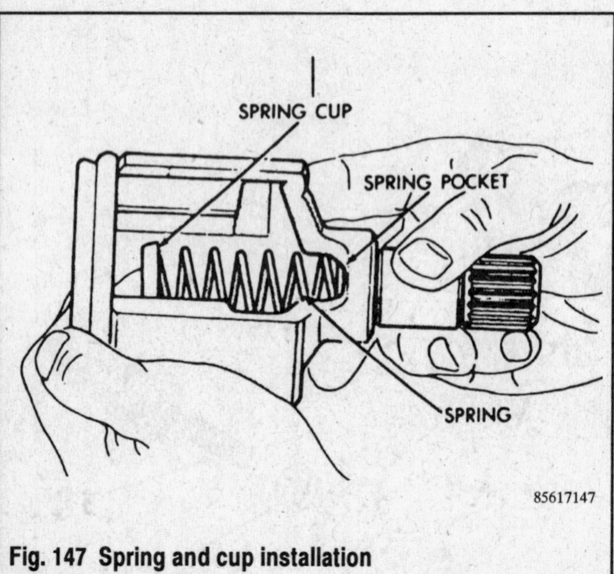

Fig. 147 Spring and cup installation

Outer Joint

➧ See Figures 148, 149, 150, 151, 152, 153, 154, 155, 156, 157, 158 and 159

1. Remove the boot clamps and discard them.
2. Wipe away the grease to expose the joint.
3. Support the shaft in a vise (Cushion the vise jaws to prevent shaft damage).
4. Hold the outer joint, and using a plastic hammer, give a sharp tap to the top of the joint body to dislodge it from the internal circlip.
5. If the shaft is bent carefully pry the wear sleeve from the CV-joint machined ledge.
6. Remove the circlip from the shaft and discard it.

➥ Replacement boot kits will contain this circlip.

7. Unless the shaft is damaged do not remove the heavy spacer ring from the shaft.

➥ If the shaft must be replaced, care must be taken that the new shaft is of the proper construction, depending on whether the inner joint is spring loaded or not. If the CV-joint was operating satisfactorily, and the grease down not appear contaminated, just replace the boot. If the outer joint is noisy or badly worn, replace the entire unit. The repair kit will include boot, clamps, retaining ring (circlip) and lubricant.

8. Wipe off the grease and mark the position of the inner cross, cage and housing with a dab of paint.
9. Hold the joint vertically in a vise. Do not crush the splines on the shaft.
10. Press down on one side of the inner race to tilt the cage and remove the balls from the opposite side.
11. If the joint is tight, use a hammer and brass drift pin to tap the inner race. Repeat this step until all balls have been removed. DO NOT hit the cage.
12. Tilt the cage and inner race assembly vertically and position the two opposing, elongated cage windows in the area between the ball grooves. Pull the cage out of the housing.
13. Turn the inner cross 90° and align the race lands with an elongated hole in the cage. Remove the inner race.

Fig. 148 Removing the housing boot clamp — 1987 Voyager with Citroen type CV-joint

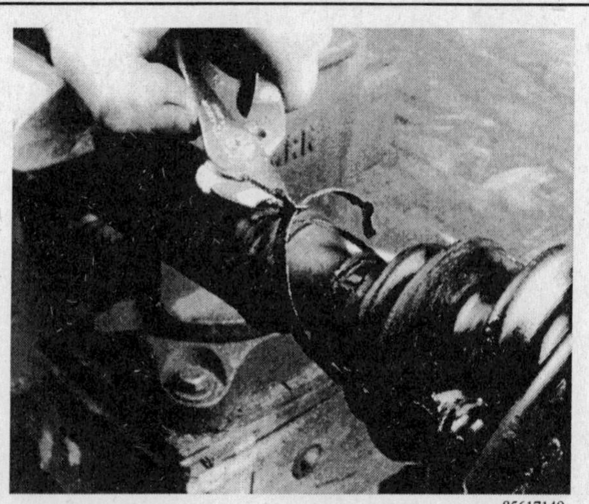

Fig. 149 Removing the shaft boot clamp

To install:

14. Position a new wear sleeve on the joint housing and install it using a suitable driver. Lubricate all of the components before assembly.
15. Align the parts according to paint markings.
16. Install one of the inner race lands into the cage window and feed the race into the cage.
17. Turn the cross 90° and align the opposing cage windows with the land, pivot another 90° and complete the land installation.
18. When properly installed, the cross counter bore should be facing outward from the joint on GKN type. The cross and cage chamfers will be facing out on Citroen type.
19. Apply the grease to the ball races. Install the balls into the raceway by tilting the cage and inner race assembly.
20. Fasten the boot to the shaft and install the new retainer circlip provided.
21. Position the outer joint on the splined end of the stub shaft and engage the splines and tap sharply to engage the circlip. Attempt to pull the shafts apart to see if the circlip is properly seated.
22. Position the large end of the boot and secure with a clamp and install the halfshaft.

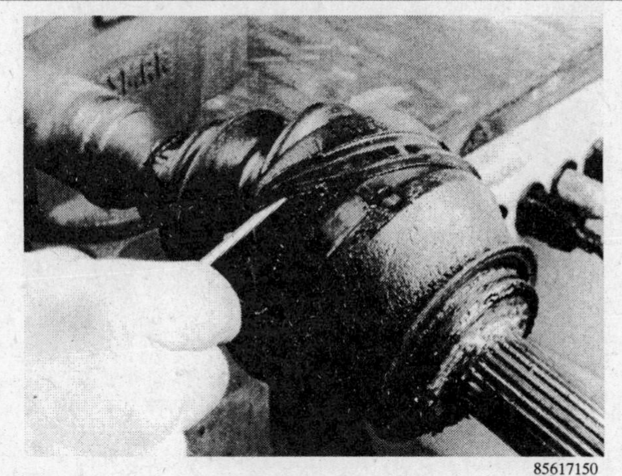

85617150

Fig. 150 After removing the clamps, pull the the boot back from the housing

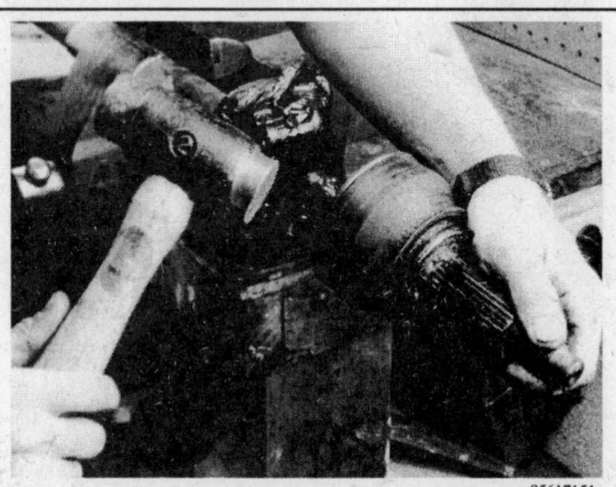

85617151

Fig. 151 Use a soft hammer and tap on the joint body to dislodge it from the internal circlip

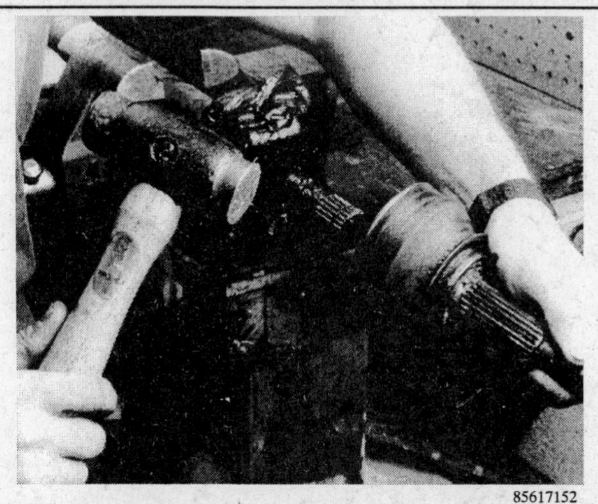

85617152

Fig. 152 Removing the inner housing and shaft from the interconnecting shaft

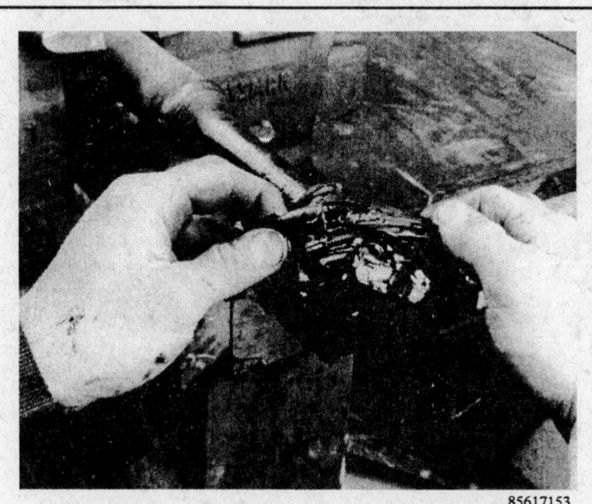

85617153

Fig. 153 Slide the boot and grease from the shaft

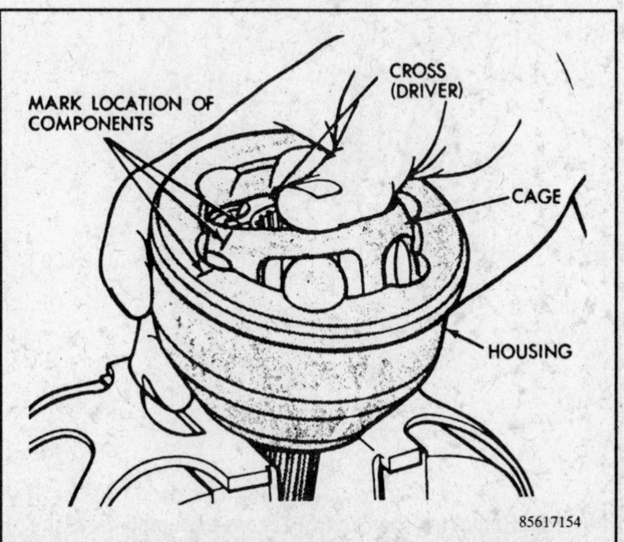

85617154

Fig. 154 Rotate the cage and cross to remove the balls

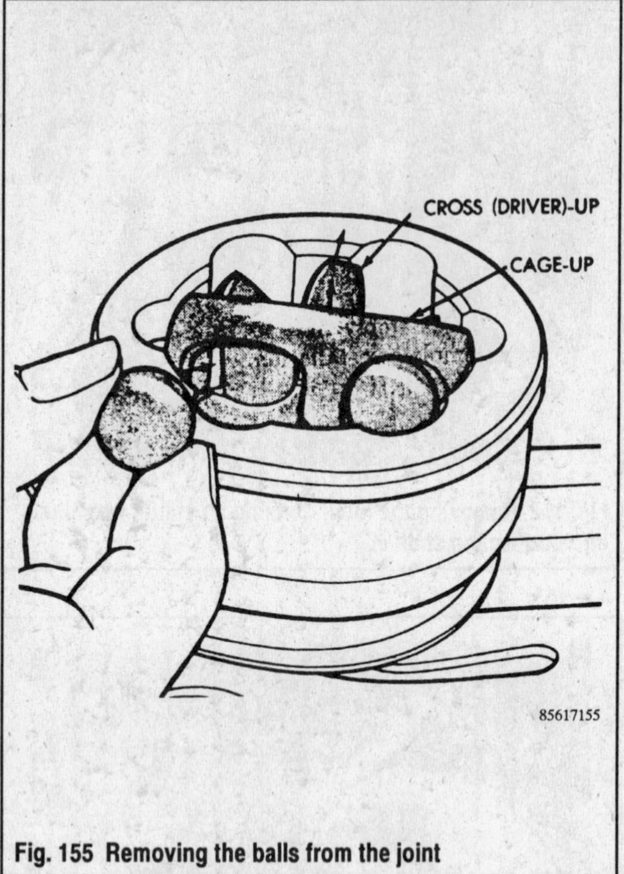

Fig. 155 Removing the balls from the joint

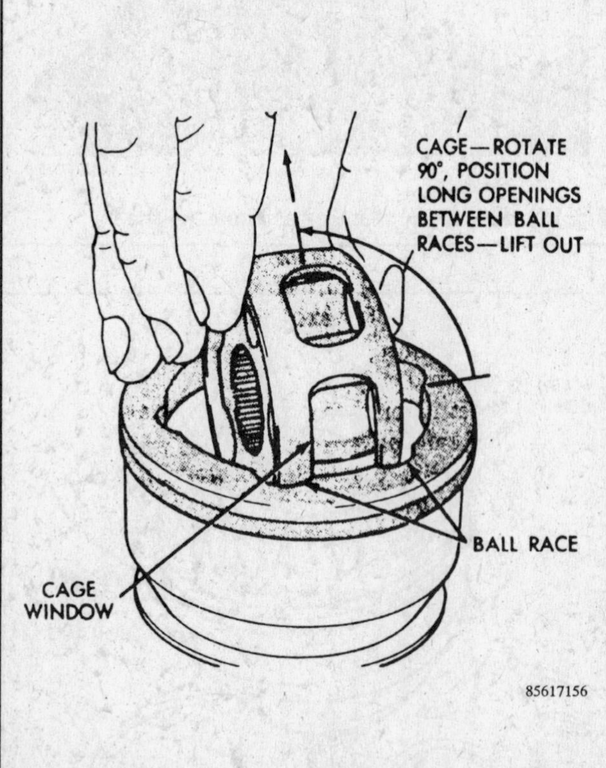

Fig. 156 Removing the case and cross assembly from the housing

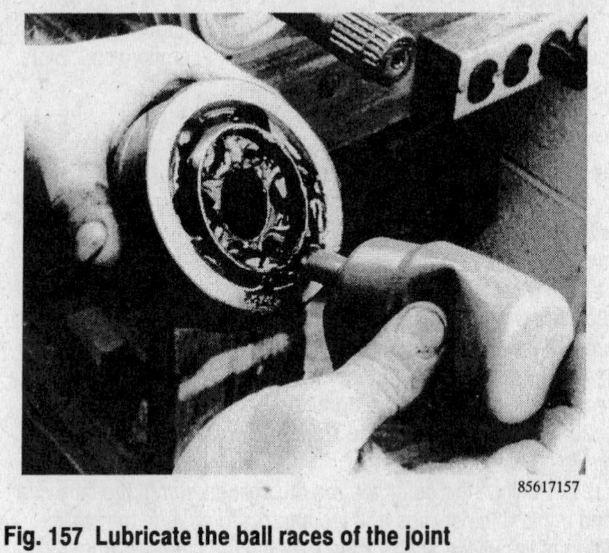

Fig. 157 Lubricate the ball races of the joint

Fig. 158 Gently tap the outer shaft and housing with a soft hammer onto the interconnecting shaft

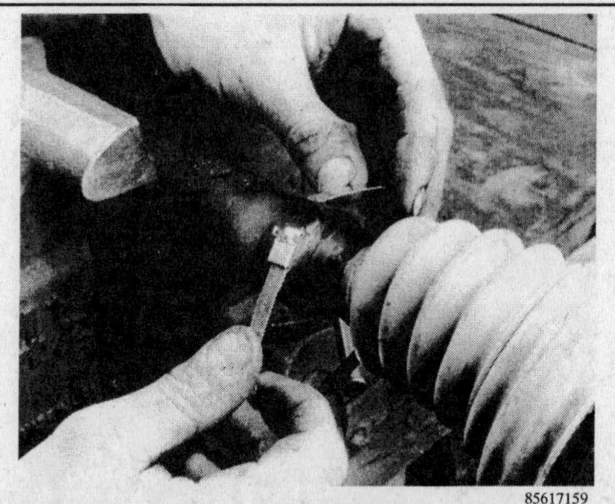

Fig. 159 After filling the new boot with the correct amount of grease install the boot retaining clamps

CLUTCH

Understanding the Clutch

All models are equipped with a self-adjusting clutch. No free-play adjustment is possible.

****CAUTION**

The clutch driven disc may contain asbestos, which has been determined to be a cancer causing agent. Never clean clutch surfaces with compressed air! Avoid inhaling any dust from any clutch surface! When cleaning clutch surfaces, use a commercially available brake cleaning fluid.

The purpose of the clutch is to disconnect and connect engine power at the transaxle. A vehicle at rest requires a lot of engine torque to get all that weight moving. An internal combustion engine does not develop a high starting torque (unlike steam engines) so it must be allowed to operate without any load until it builds up enough torque to move the vehicle. Torque increases with engine rpm. The clutch allows the engine to build up torque by physically disconnecting the engine from the transaxle, relieving the engine of any load or resistance.

The transfer of engine power to the transaxle (the load) must be smooth and gradual; if it weren't, drive line components would wear out or break quickly. This gradual power transfer is made possible by gradually releasing the clutch pedal. The clutch disc and pressure plate are the connecting link between the engine and transaxle. When the clutch pedal is released, the disc and plate contact each other (the clutch is engaged) physically joining the engine and transaxle. When the pedal is pushed inward, the disc and plate separate (the clutch is disengaged) disconnecting the engine from the transaxle.

Most clutches utilize a single plate, dry friction disc with a diaphragm-style spring pressure plate. The clutch disc has a splined hub which attaches the disc to the input shaft. The disc has friction material where it contacts the flywheel and pressure plate. Torsion springs on the disc help absorb engine torque pulses. The pressure plate applies pressure to the clutch disc, holding it tight against the surface of the flywheel. The clutch operating mechanism consists of a release bearing, fork and cylinder assembly.

The release fork and actuating linkage transfer pedal motion to the release bearing. In the engaged position (pedal released) the diaphragm spring holds the pressure plate against the clutch disc, so engine torque is transmitted to the input shaft. When the clutch pedal is depressed, the release bearing pushes the diaphragm spring center toward the flywheel. The diaphragm spring pivots the fulcrum, relieving the load on the pressure plate. Steel spring straps riveted to the clutch cover lift the pressure plate from the clutch disc, disengaging the engine drive from the transaxle and enabling the gears to be changed.

The clutch is operating properly if:

1. It will stall the engine when released with the vehicle held stationary.
2. The shift lever can be moved freely between 1st and reverse gears when the vehicle is stationary and the clutch disengaged.

Driven Disc and Pressure Plate

➥ Chrysler recommends the use of special tool C-4676 for disc alignment.

REMOVAL & INSTALLATION

➧ See Figure 160

1. Remove the transaxle.
2. Matchmark the clutch cover and flywheel for easy reinstallation.
3. Insert special tool C-4676, or its equivalent, to hold the clutch disc in place.
4. Loosen the cover attaching bolts. Do this procedure in a diagonal manner, a few turns at a time to prevent warping the cover.
5. Remove the cover assembly and disc from the flywheel.
6. Remove the clutch release shaft and slide the release bearing off the input shaft seal retainer.
7. Remove the fork from the release bearing thrust plate.
8. Inspect the components. Replace as necessary.

To install:

9. Install the throw out bearing, fork and component parts.
10. Mount the clutch assembly on the flywheel (Mate the matchmarks if old unit is used). Install the clutch disc alignment tool. Hold the alignment tool in position and loosely install the pressure plate retaining bolts.
11. Tighten the bolts a few turns at a time in rotation. Tighten to 21 ft. lbs. (28 Nm).

RELEASE CABLE ADJUSTMENT

The clutch release cable cannot be adjusted. When the cable is properly installed, a spring in the clutch pedal adjusts the cable to the proper position, regardless of clutch disc wear.

CLUTCH CABLE REPLACEMENT

➧ See Figures 161 and 162

1. Remove the clip from the cable mounting bracket on the shock tower.
2. Remove the retainer from the clutch release lever at the transaxle.
3. Pry the ball end of the cable from the positioner adjuster and remove the cable.
4. Installation is the reverse of removal.

Clutch Pedal

➧ See Figures 161 and 162

REMOVAL & INSTALLATION

1. Disconnect the negative battery cable.
2. Under the drivers side of the instrument panel, remove the clutch pedal return spring from the pedal and bracket.
3. Remove the retainer bolt from the clutch cable, at the top of the pedal arm. Release the cable from the pedal bracket.
4. Remove the lockring washers and bushing from the pedal pivot. Carefully slide the pedal assembly off of the pivot.

To install:

5. Install the pedal in position on the pivot and install the lockring. Reconnect the clutch release cable.
6. Check the operation of the pedal and make sure the clutch release is working.
7. Connect the negative battery cable.

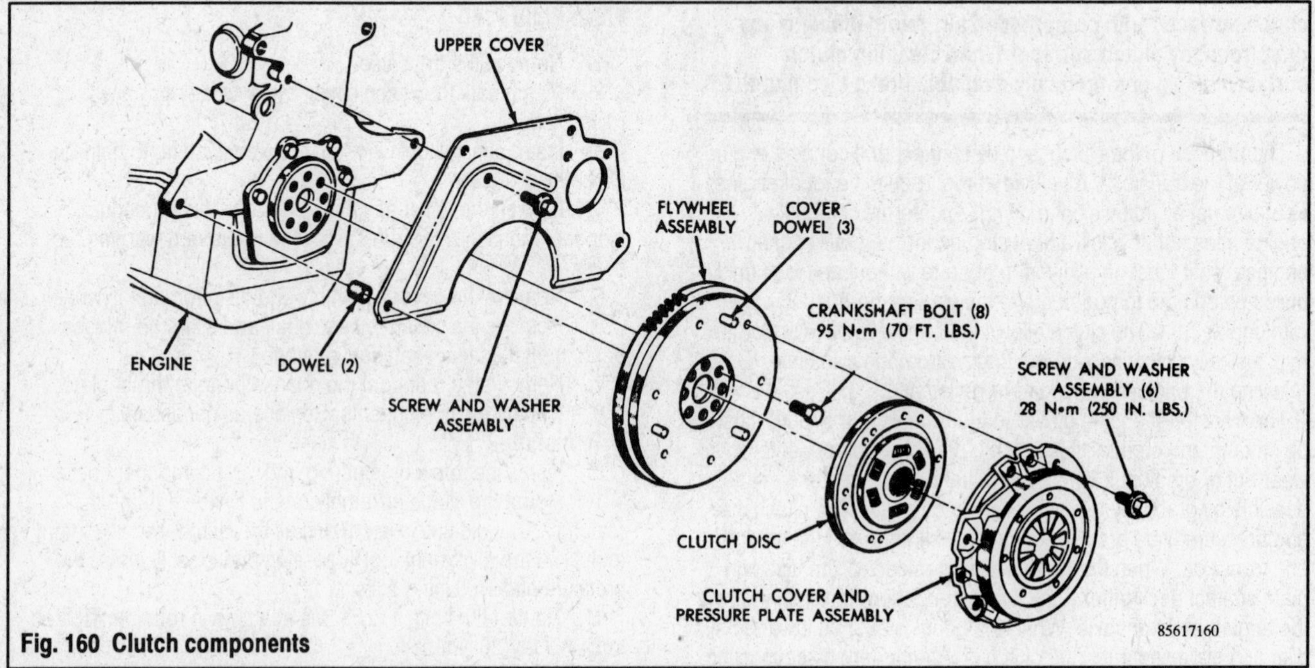

Fig. 160 Clutch components

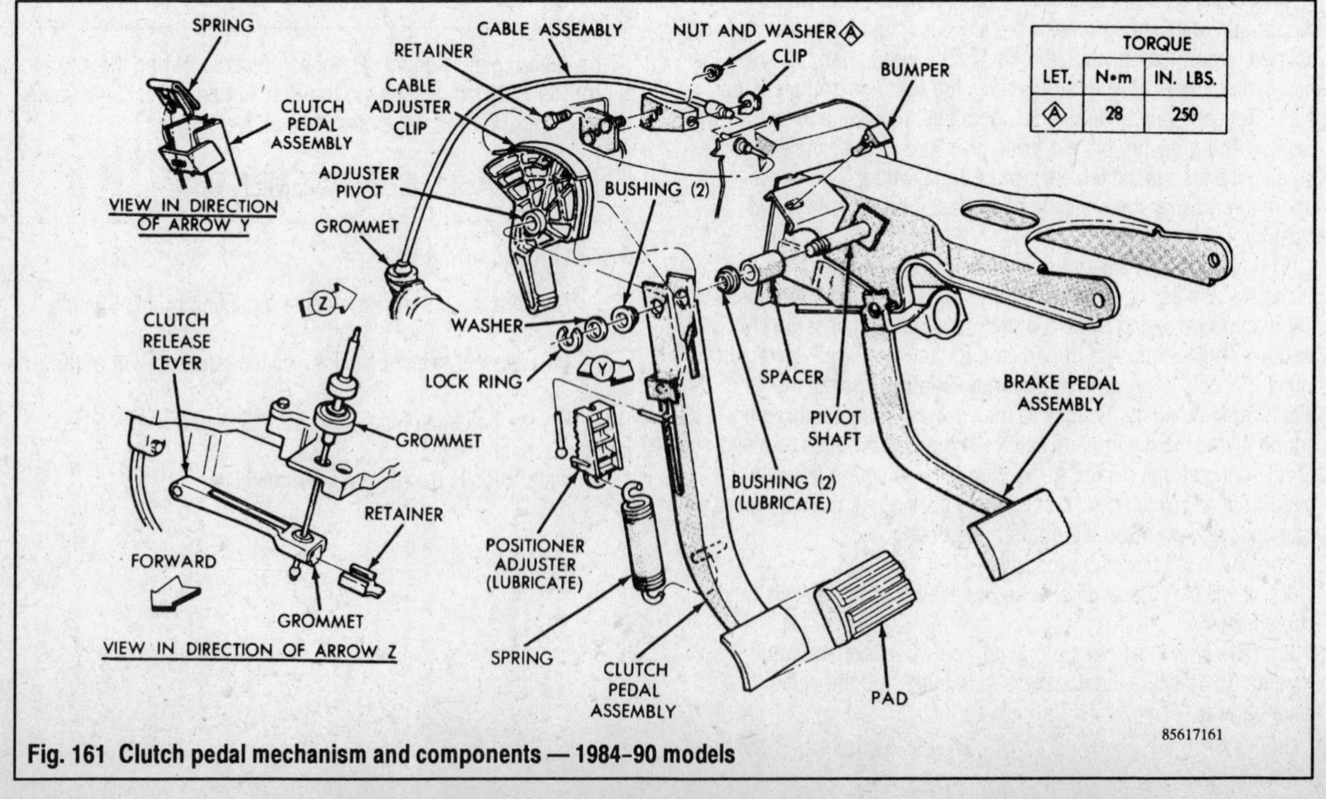

	TORQUE	
LET.	N•m	IN. LBS.
Ⓐ	28	250

Fig. 161 Clutch pedal mechanism and components — 1984-90 models

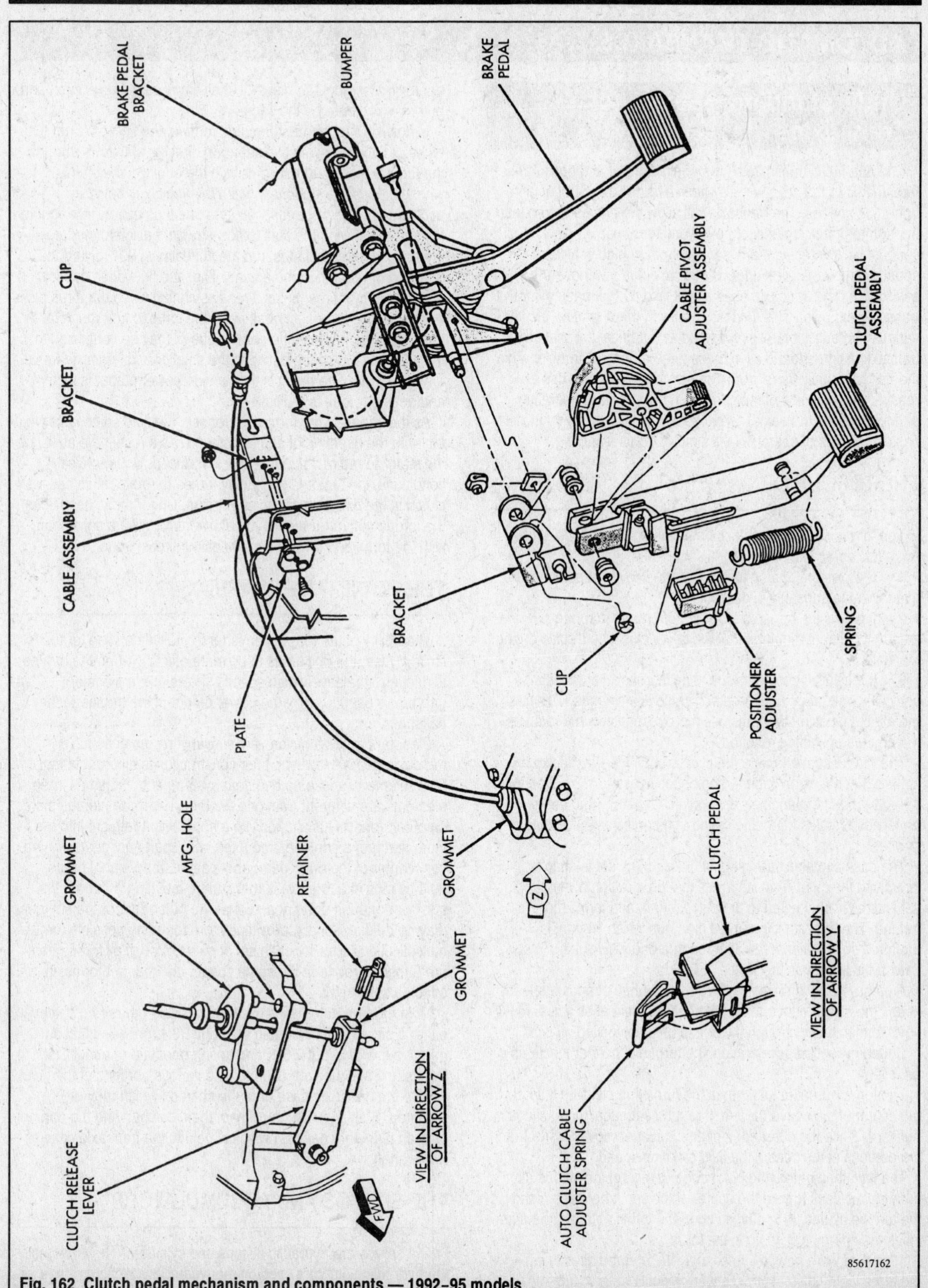

Fig. 162 Clutch pedal mechanism and components — 1992–95 models

AUTOMATIC TRANSAXLE

Understanding Automatic Transaxles

The automatic transaxle allows engine torque and power to be transmitted to the drive wheels within a narrow range of engine operating speeds. The transaxle will allow the engine to turn fast enough to produce plenty of power and torque at very low speeds, while keeping it at a sensible rpm at high vehicle speeds. The transaxle performs this job entirely without driver assistance. The transaxle uses a light fluid as the medium for the transaxle of power. This fluid also works in the operation of various hydraulic control circuits and as a lubricant. Because the transaxle fluid performs all of these three functions, trouble within the unit can easily travel from one part to another. For this reason, and because of the complexity and unusual operating principles of the transaxle, a very sound understanding of the basic principles of operation will simplify troubleshooting.

THE TORQUE CONVERTER

The torque converter replaces the conventional clutch. It has three functions:

1. It allows the engine to idle with the vehicle at a standstill, even with the transaxle in gear.
2. It allows the transaxle to shift from range to range smoothly, without requiring that the driver close the throttle during the shift.
3. It multiplies engine torque to an increasing extent as vehicle speed drops and throttle opening is increased. This has the effect of making the transaxle more responsive and reduces the amount of shifting required.

The torque converter is a metal case which is shaped like a sphere that has been flattened on opposite sides. It is bolted to the rear end of the engine's crankshaft. Generally, the entire metal case rotates at engine speed and serves as the engine's flywheel.

The case contains three sets of blades. One set is attached directly to the case. This set forms the torus or pump. Another set is directly connected to the output shaft, and forms the turbine. The third set is mounted on a hub which, in turn, is mounted on a stationary shaft through a one-way clutch. This third set is known as the stator.

A pump, which is driven by the converter hub at engine speed, keeps the torque converter full of transaxle fluid at all times. Fluid flows continuously through the unit to provide cooling.

Under low speed acceleration, the torque converter functions as follows:

The torus is turning faster than the turbine. It picks up fluid at the center of the converter and, through centrifugal force, slings it outward. Since the outer edge of the converter moves faster than the portions at the center, the fluid picks up speed.

The fluid then enters the outer edge of the turbine blades. It then travels back toward the center of the converter case along the turbine blades. In impinging upon the turbine blades, the fluid loses the energy picked up in the torus.

If the fluid were now to immediately be returned directly into the torus, both halves of the converter would have to turn at approximately the same speed at all times, and torque input and output would both be the same.

In flowing through the torus and turbine, the fluid picks up two types of flow, or flow in two separate directions. It flows through the turbine blades, and it spins with the engine. The stator, whose blades are stationary when the vehicle is being accelerated at low speeds, converts one type of flow into another. Instead of allowing the fluid to flow straight back into the torus, the stator's curved blades turn the fluid almost 90° toward the direction of rotation of the engine. Thus the fluid does not flow as fast toward the torus, but is already spinning when the torus picks it up. This has the effect of allowing the torus to turn much faster than the turbine. This difference in speed may be compared to the difference in speed between the smaller and larger gears in any gear train. The result is that engine power output is higher, and engine torque is multiplied.

As the speed of the turbine increases, the fluid spins faster and faster in the direction of engine rotation. As a result, the ability of the stator to redirect the fluid flow is reduced. Under cruising conditions, the stator is eventually forced to rotate on its one-way clutch in the direction of engine rotation. Under these conditions, the torque converter begins to behave almost like a solid shaft, with the torus and turbine speeds being almost equal.

THE PLANETARY GEARBOX

The ability of the torque converter to multiply engine torque is limited. Also, the unit tends to be more efficient when the turbine is rotating at relatively high speeds. Therefore, a planetary gearbox is used to carry the power output of the turbine to the halfshafts.

Planetary gears function very similarly to conventional transaxle gears. However, their construction is different in that three elements make up one gear system, and, in that all three elements are different from one another. The three elements are: an outer gear that is shaped like a hoop, with teeth cut into the inner surface; a sun gear, mounted on a shaft and located at the very center of the outer gear; and a set of three planet gears, held by pins in a ring-like planet carrier, meshing with both the sun gear and the outer gear. Either the outer gear or the sun gear may be held stationary, providing more than one possible torque multiplication factor for each set of gears. Also, if all three gears are forced to rotate at the same speed, the gear set forms, in effect, a solid shaft.

Most modern automatics use the planetary gears to provide either a single reduction ratio of about 1.8:1, or two reduction gears: a low of about 2.5:1, and an intermediate of about 1.5:1. Bands and clutches are used to hold various portions of the gear sets to the transaxle case or to the shaft on which they are mounted. Shifting is accomplished, then, by changing the portion of each planetary gear set which is held to the transaxle case or to the shaft.

THE SERVOS AND ACCUMULATORS

The servos are hydraulic pistons and cylinders. They resemble the hydraulic actuators used on many familiar machines, such as bulldozers. Hydraulic fluid enters the cylinder, under pressure, and forces the piston to move to engage the band or clutches.

The accumulators are used to cushion the engagement of the servos. The transaxle fluid must pass through the accumulator on the way to the servo. The accumulator housing contains a thin piston which is sprung away from the discharge passage of the accumulator. When fluid passes through the accumulator on the way to the servo, it must move the piston against spring pressure, and this action smooths out the action of the servo.

THE HYDRAULIC CONTROL SYSTEM

The hydraulic pressure used to operate the servos comes from the main transaxle oil pump. This fluid is channeled to the various servos through the shift valves. There is generally a manual shift valve which is operated by the transaxle selector lever and an automatic shift valve for each automatic upshift the transaxle provides: i.e., 2-speed automatics have a low/high shift valve, while 3-speeds have a 1-2 valve, and a 2-3 valve.

There are two pressures which effect the operation of these valves. One is the governor pressure which is affected by vehicle speed. The other is the modulator pressure which is affected by intake manifold vacuum or throttle position. Governor pressure rises with an increase in vehicle speed, and modulator pressure rises as the throttle is opened wider. By responding to these two pressures, the shift valves cause the upshift points to be delayed with increased throttle opening to make the best use of the engine's power output.

Most transaxles also make use of an auxiliary circuit for down shifting. This circuit may be actuated by the throttle linkage or the vacuum line which actuates the modulator, or by a cable or solenoid. It applies pressure to a special down shift surface on the shift valve or valves.

The transaxle modulator also governs the line pressure, used to actuate the servos. In this way, the clutches and bands will be actuated with a force matching the torque output of the engine.

The three speed automatic transaxle and differential are combined in a single housing and share the same Dexron®II type lubricant. Filter, fluid changes, and band adjustments are not require for average vehicle use. However, if the vehicle is used for constant heavy duty hauling, commercial use or more than 50% operation in heavy traffic, the fluid and filter should be changed every 15,000 miles.

Fluid Pan and Filter

REMOVAL & INSTALLATION

See Figures 163, 164, 165, 166, 167, 168 and 169

1. Raise and support the front of the vehicle on jackstands.
2. Remove the splash shield if it will interfere with the fluid pan removal.
3. Place a suitable container that will hold at least four quarts of fluid under the oil pan.
4. Loosen all of the pan bolts slightly until the fluid starts to drain and then unfasten the bolts around the point where the fluid is draining to increase the flow.
5. When the bulk of the fluid has drained, remove the oil pan. Clean the dirt from the pan and magnet.
6. Remove RTV sealant or gasket material from the pan and case mounting surfaces.
7. Remove the filter from the bottom of the valve body.

To install:

8. Install a new filter and gasket. Tighten the mounting screw to 40 inch lbs. (4 Nm).
9. Apply a unbroken bead of RTV sealant to the oil pan and install on case. Tighten the mounting bolts to 165 inch lbs. (18 Nm).
10. Remove the differential cover. Use a clean cloth and wipe the cover and magnet to remove dirt. Clean the mounting surfaces of the cover and case.
11. Apply an unbroken bead of RTV sealant to the differential cover and reinstall. Tighten the mounting bolts to 165 inch lbs. (18 Nm). Install the splash shield, etc. and lower the vehicle.
12. Pour four quarts of Dexron II type fluid through the dipstick fill tube. Start the engine, with the parking and service brakes applied, move the gear selector through the various positions ending up in Park.
13. Add sufficient fluid, if necessary, to bring the level to 1/8 in. (3mm) below the Add mark.
14. Check the fluid level after engine and transaxle have reached the normal operating temperature. The level should be within the Hot range on the dipstick.

Always make sure that the dipstick is fully seated in its tube to prevent dirt from entering the transaxle.

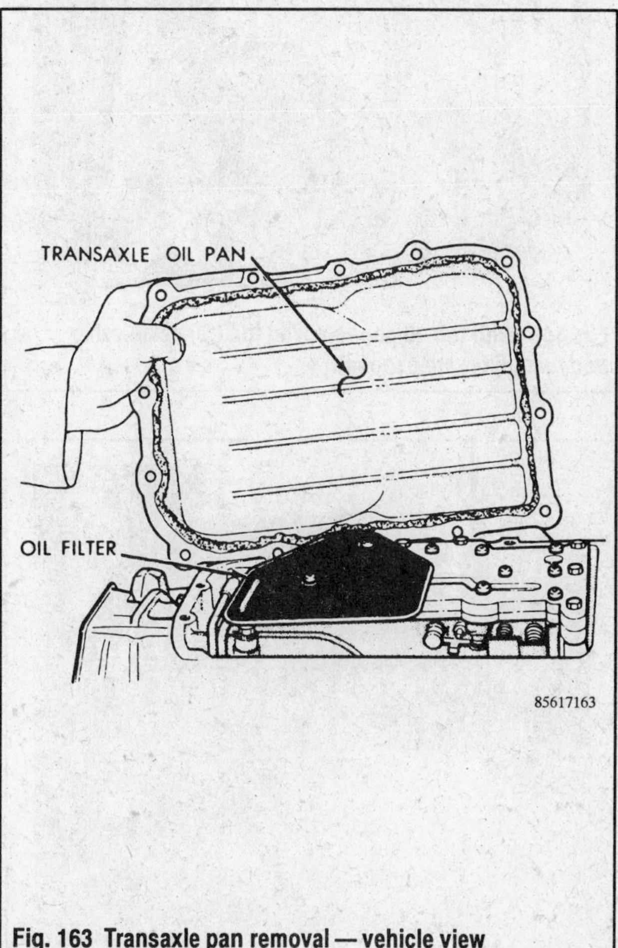

Fig. 163 Transaxle pan removal — vehicle view

85617165

Fig. 164 Removing the transaxle oil pan — 1987 Voyager shown

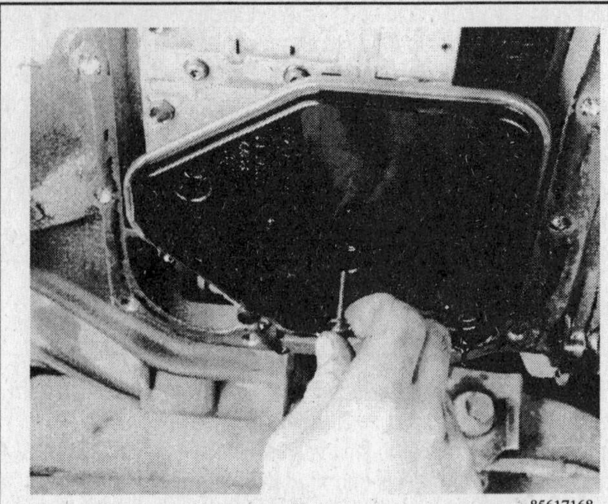
85617168

Fig. 167 Removing the transaxle oil filter retaining screws

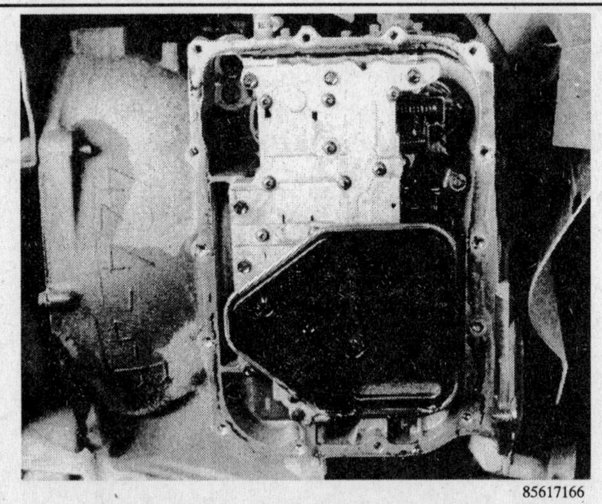
85617166

Fig. 165 With the oil pan removed the transaxle valve body and filter are exposed

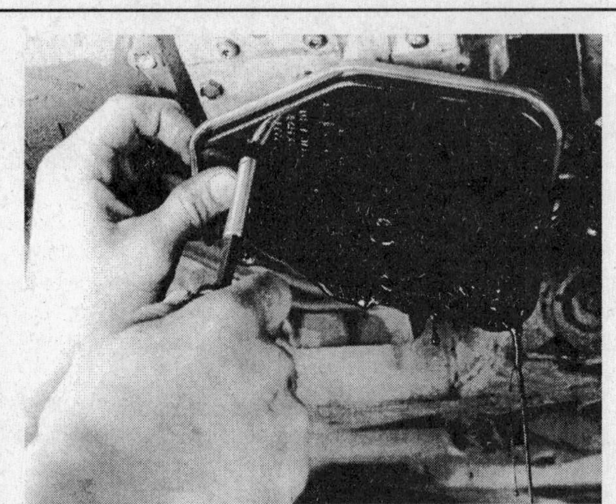
85617169

Fig. 168 Removing the transaxle oil filter retaining screws

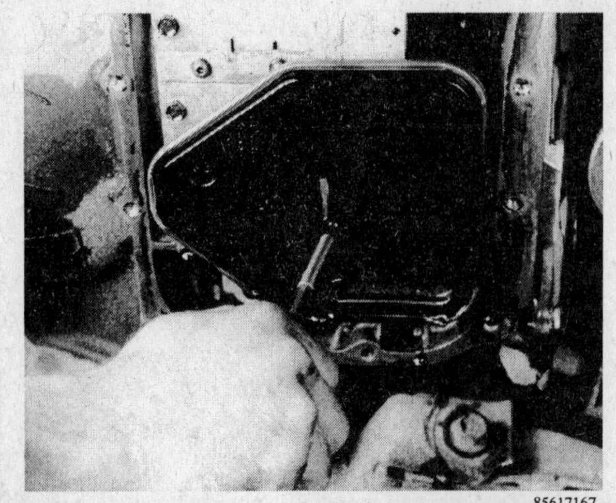
85617167

Fig. 166 Removing the transaxle oil filter retaining screws

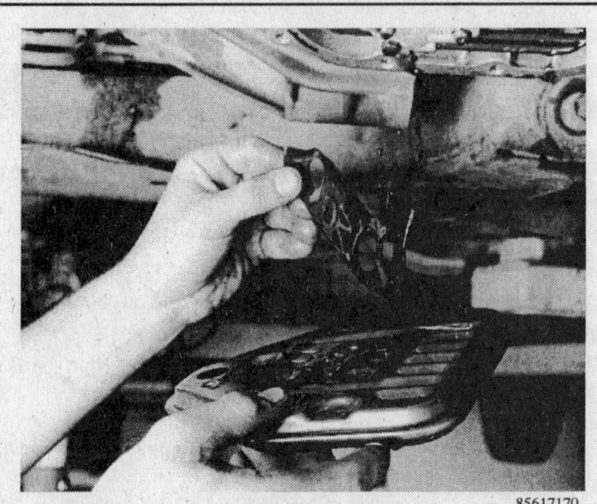
85617170

Fig. 169 Removing the transaxle oil filter and gasket

Adjustments

See Figure 170

KICKDOWN CABLE

1. Run the engine until the normal operating temperature is reached. Be sure the choke is fully opened.
2. Loosen the adjustment bracket lock bolt mounted on transaxle to engine flange.
3. Be sure that the adjustment bracket can slide freely. Clean as necessary.
4. Slide the bracket toward the engine as far as possible. Release the bracket and move the throttle lever to the right as far as it will go. tighten the adjustment lock bolt to 105 inch lbs. (12 Nm).

A-604 UPSHIFT & KICKDOWN LEARNING PROCEDURE

A-604 Ultradrive Transaxle

In 1989, the A-604 4 speed, electronic transaxle was introduced; it is the first to use fully adaptive controls. The controls perform their functions based on real time feedback sensor information. Although, the transaxle is conventional in design, its functions are controlled by the ECM.

Since the A-604 is equipped with a learning function, each time the battery cable is disconnected, the ECM memory is lost. In operation, the transaxle must be shifted many times for the learned memory to be reconstructed by the ECM; during this period, the vehicle will experience rough operation. The transaxle must be at normal operating temperature when learning occurs.

1. Maintain constant throttle opening during shifts. Do not move the accelerator pedal during upshifts.
2. Accelerate the vehicle with the throttle $^1/_8$–$^1/_2$ open.

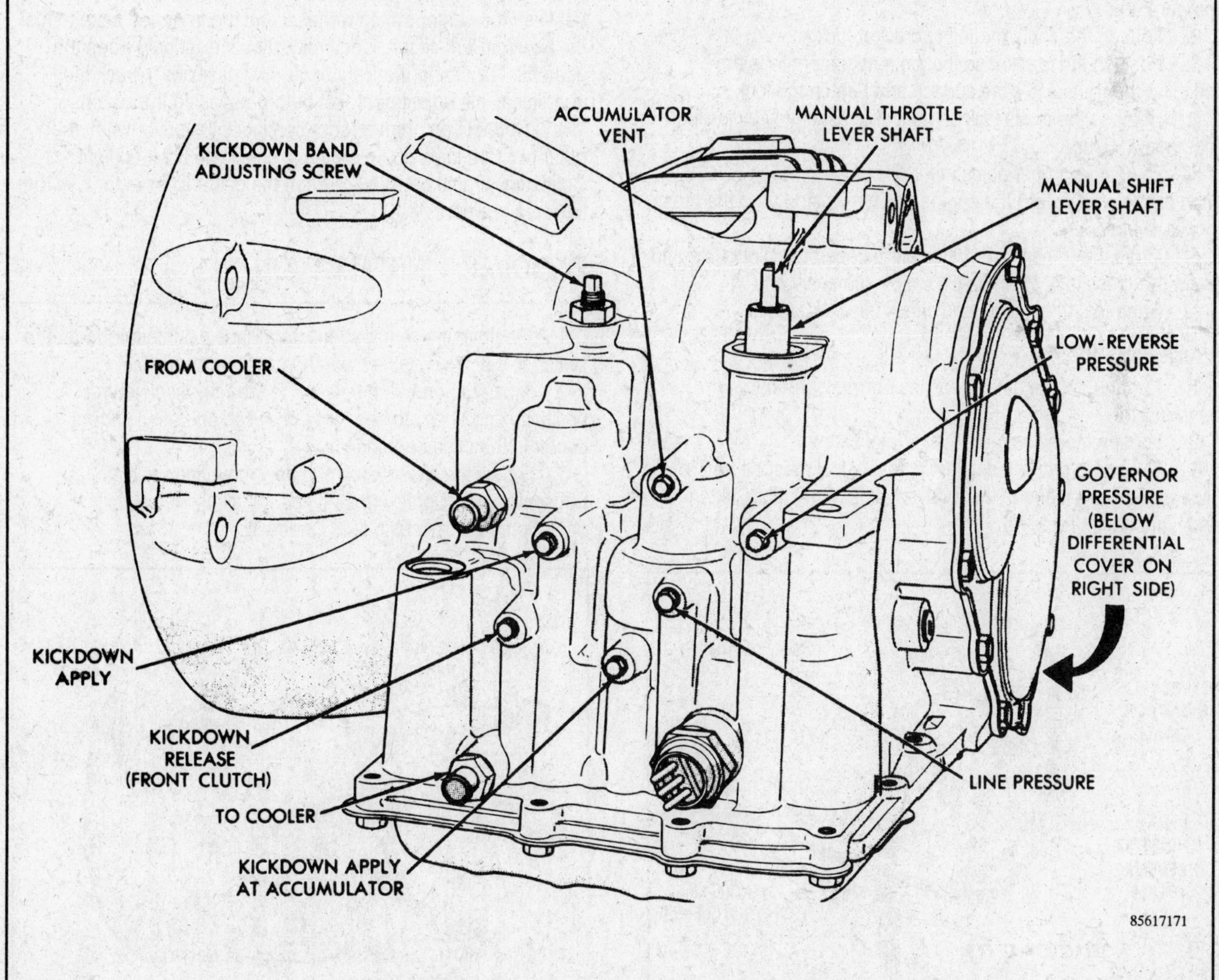

Fig. 170 Transaxle adjustment and maintenance points — 3-speed Torqueflite transaxle

3. Make 15 to 20 1st to 2nd, 2nd to 3rd and 3rd to 4th gear upshifts. Accelerating from a full stop to 50 mph each time at the aforementioned throttle opening.

4. With the vehicle speed below 25 mph (40 km/h), make 5 to 8 wide open throttle kick downs to 1st gear from either 2nd or 3rd gear. Allow at least 5 seconds of operation in 2nd or 3rd gear prior to each kickdown.

5. With the vehicle speed greater than 25 mph (40 km/h), make 5 to 8 part throttle to wide open throttle kick downs to either 3rd or 2nd gear from 4th gear. Allow at least 5 seconds of operation in 4th gear, preferably at road load throttle prior to performing the kickdown.

THROTTLE PRESSURE CABLE/ROD ADJUSTMENT

4-Cylinder Models

➧ See Figure 171

1. Run the engine until it reaches normal operating temperature.
2. Loosen the cable mounting bracket lock screw.
3. Position the bracket so that both alignment tabs are touching the transaxle case surface and tighten the lock screws.
4. Release the cross lock on the cable assembly by pulling the cross lock up.
5. To ensure proper adjustment, the cable must be free to slide all the way toward the engine against its stop after the cross lock is released.
6. Move the transaxle throttle control lever fully clockwise and press the cross lock down until it snaps into position.
7. Road test the vehicle and check the shift points.

6-Cylinder Models.

1. Run the engine until it reaches normal operating temperature.
2. Loosen the adjustment swivel lock screw.
3. To ensure proper adjustment, the swivel must be free to slide along the flat end of the throttle rod. Disassemble, clean and lubricate as required.
4. Hold the transaxle throttle control lever firmly toward the engine and tighten the swivel screw.
5. Road test the vehicle and check the shift points.

Neutral Starting/Back-up Light Switch

➧ See Figure 172

The neutral starting/back-up light switch is screwed into the side of the automatic transaxle. If the vehicle fails to start in either the Park or Neutral positions, or starts in any of the drive gears a problem with the switch is indicated.

TESTING

1. The Neutral/Park sensing part of the switch is the center terminal, while the back-up lights are controlled by the outer two terminals.
2. Disengage the wiring connector from the switch.
3. Using an ohmmeter or continuity tester, connect the leads between the center switch terminal and the transaxle case to test the Neutral/Park circuit. Continuity should exist only when the gearshift is either in the Park or Neutral positions. Check the gearshift cable adjustment first before replacing the switch.
4. Connect an ohmmeter or continuity tester, between the outer two terminals of the switch to check the back-up light. Continuity should be present when the gearshift selector is in the Reverse position.

REMOVAL & INSTALLATION

1. Remove the wiring connector. Place a container under the switch to catch transaxle fluid and unscrew the switch.
2. Move the gearshift selector to the Park and Neutral positions and check to see that the switch operating fingers center in the case opening.
3. Screw the new switch and new mounting seal into the transaxle case. Tighten to 24 ft. lbs. (33 Nm). Retest switch operation. Add transaxle fluid if needed.

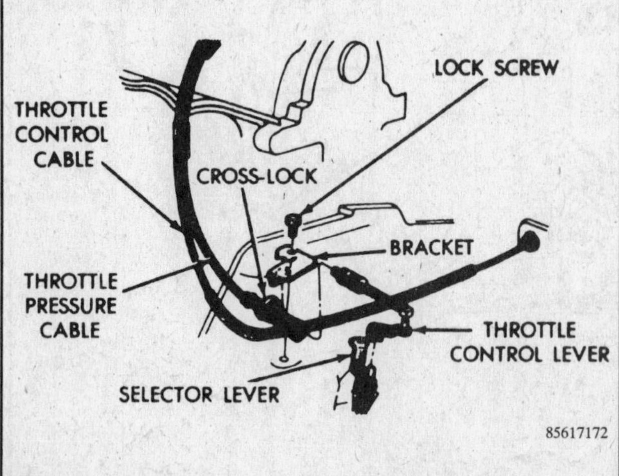

Fig. 171 Throttle pressure cable mounting — 3-speed transaxles

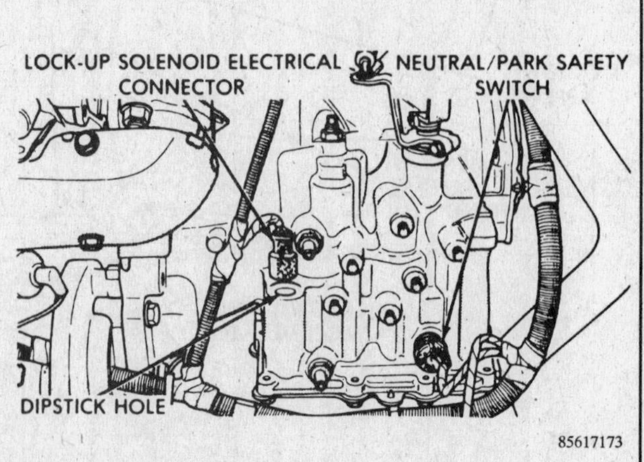

Fig. 172 Lock-up solenoid and neutral safety switch location, 3-speed transaxles

Transaxle Assembly

REMOVAL & INSTALLATION

➥ If the vehicle is going to be rolled while the transaxle is out of the vehicle, obtain 2 outer CV-joints to install to the hubs. If the vehicle is rolled without the proper torque applied to the front wheel bearings, the bearings will be destroyed.

1. Disconnect the negative battery cable. If equipped with a 3.0L, 3.3L or 3.8L engine, drain the coolant.
2. Remove the dipstick.
3. Install an engine support fixture.
4. Remove the air cleaner assembly if it is preventing access to the upper bell housing bolts.
5. Remove the upper bell housing bolts and water tube, where applicable. Disengage all electrical connectors from the transaxle.
6. If equipped with a 2.2L or 2.5L engine, remove the starter attaching nut and bolt at the top of the bell housing.
7. Raise the vehicle and support safely. Remove the tire and wheel assemblies.
8. Remove the axle end cotter pins, nut locks, spring washers and axle nuts.
9. Remove the ball joint retaining bolts and pry the control arm from the steering knuckle.
10. Position a drain pan under the transaxle where the axles enter the differential or extension housing.
11. Remove the axles from the transaxle or center bearing.
12. Unbolt the center bearing and remove the intermediate axle from the transaxle, if equipped.
13. Drain the transaxle. Disconnect and plug the fluid cooler hoses.
14. Disconnect the shifter and kickdown linkage from the transaxle, if equipped.
15. Unfasten the speedometer cable adaptor bolt and remove the adaptor from the transaxle.
16. Remove the starter.
17. Remove the torque converter inspection cover, matchmark the torque converter to the flexplate and remove the torque converter bolts.
18. Using the proper equipment, support the weight of the engine.
19. Remove the front motor mount and bracket.
20. On vehicles equipped with DIS ignition system, remove the crankshaft position sensor from the bell housing.
21. Position a suitable jack under the transaxle.
22. Remove the lower bell housing bolts.
23. Remove the left side splash shield.
24. Remove the transaxle mount bolts.
25. Carefully pry the engine from the transaxle.
26. Slide the transaxle rearward until the locating dowels disengage from the mating holes in the transaxle.

➥ Attach a small C-clamp to the edge of the bell housing. This will hold the torque converter in place during transaxle removal.

27. Pull the transaxle completely away from the engine and remove it from the vehicle.
28. To prepare the vehicle for rolling, support the engine with a suitable support or reinstall the front motor mount to the engine. Then reinstall the ball joints to the steering knuckle and install the retaining bolt. Install the obtained outer CV-joints to the hubs, install the washers and tighten the axle nuts to 180 ft. lbs. (244 Nm). The vehicle may now be safely rolled.

To install:

29. Install the transaxle securely on the jack. Rotate the converter so it will align with the positioning of the flexplate.

****WARNING**

If equipped with a 41TE Transaxle, and the torque converter has been replaced, a Torque Clutch Break-in Procedure must be performed. This procedure will reset the transaxle control module break-in status. Failure to perform this procedure may cause transaxle shutter. To properly do this a DRB scan tool is required to read or reset the break-in status.

30. Apply a coating of high temperature grease to the torque converter pilot hub.
31. Raise the transaxle into place and push it forward until the dowels engage and the bell housing is flush with the block.
32. Install the transaxle to bell housing bolts.
33. Raise the transaxle up (using the jack) and fasten the left side mount bolts. Install the torque converter bolts and tighten to 55 ft. lbs. (74 Nm).
34. Install the front motor mount and bracket. Remove the engine and transaxle support fixtures.
35. Install the starter to the transaxle. Fasten the bolt finger-tight if equipped with a 2.2L or 2.5L engine.
36. Install a new O-ring to the speedometer cable adaptor and engage it to the extension housing, make sure it snaps in place. Tighten the retaining bolt.
37. Connect the shifter and kickdown linkage to the transaxle, if equipped.
38. Install the axles and center bearing, if equipped.
39. Install the ball joints to the steering knuckles. Tighten the axle nuts to 180 ft. lbs. (244 Nm) and install new cotter pins.
40. Install the splash shield and the wheels.
41. Lower the vehicle and install the dipstick.
42. Install the upper bell housing bolts and water pipe, if removed.
43. If equipped with 2.2L or 2.5L engine, install the starter attaching nut and bolt at the top of the bell housing.
44. Raise the vehicle again and tighten the starter bolt from underneath the vehicle. Lower the vehicle.
45. Engage all electrical wiring disconnected from the transaxle.
46. Install the air cleaner assembly, if it was removed. Fill the transaxle with the proper amount of Dexron®II.
47. Connect the negative battery cable and check the transaxle for proper operation. On the A-604 transaxle perform the upshift and kickdown learn procedure found earlier in this section.

POWER TRANSFER UNIT

➧ See Figures 173 and 174

Identification

For 1991–95 models, Chrysler made available an All Wheel Drive (AWD) version of the Caravan/Voyager. The AWD equipped vehicles use the same basic drivetrain layout as the front wheel drive versions, with the exception of the rear driveline module. To transfer the power from the engine and transaxle, to the rear driveline module, these vehicles use an Power Transfer Unit (PTU). The PTU is connected to the transaxle where the right halfshaft extension housing would be.

The PTU is a separate unit from the transaxle. It uses a standard hypoid type ring and pinion. The PTU is sealed from the transaxle and has its own oil sump. The unit uses SAE 85W-90 gear lube and holds 1.22 qts.

The PTU is not a repairable unit and can only be replaced. If you suspect the PTU has failed, take the vehicle to an authorized service center.

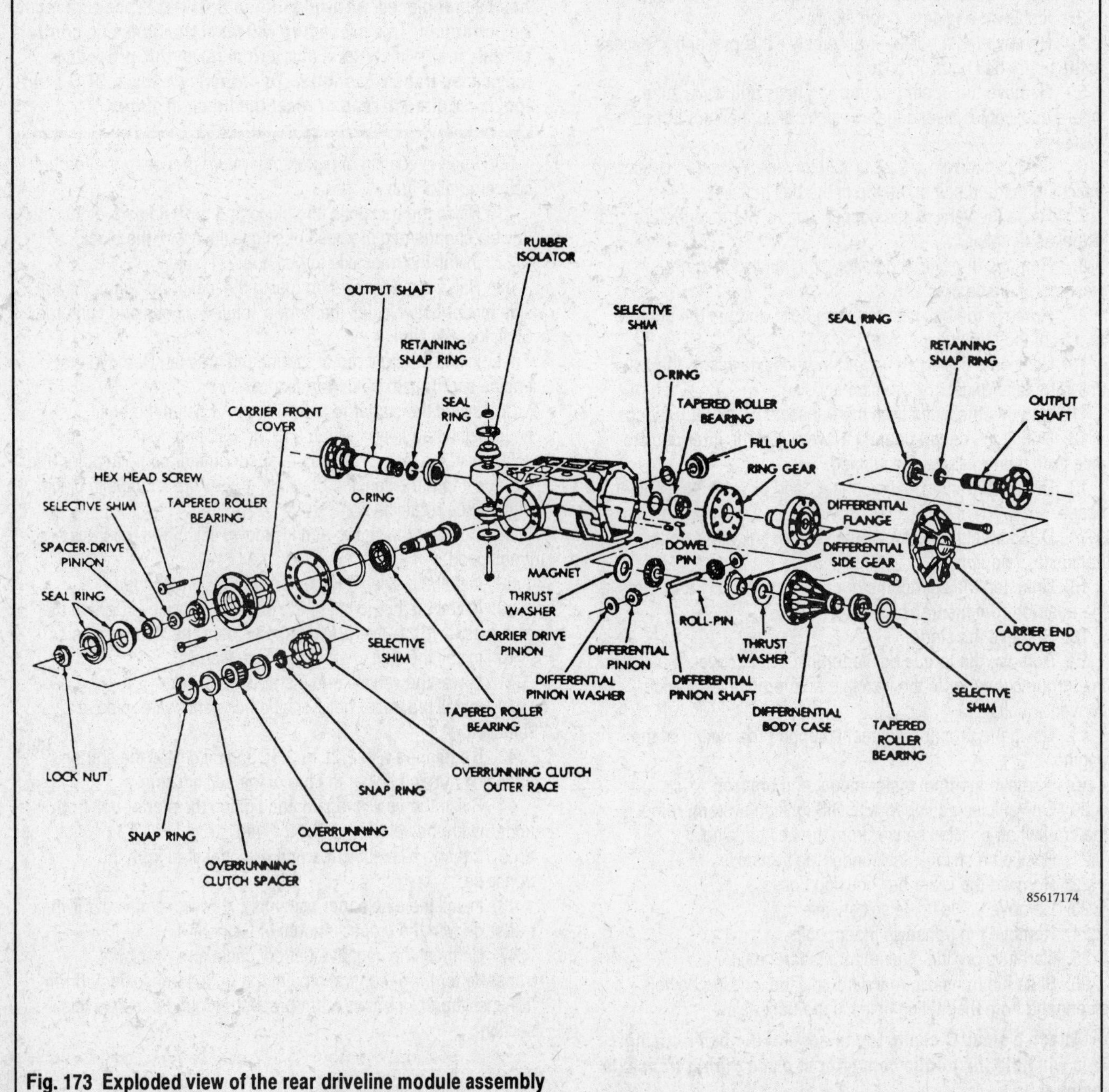

Fig. 173 Exploded view of the rear driveline module assembly

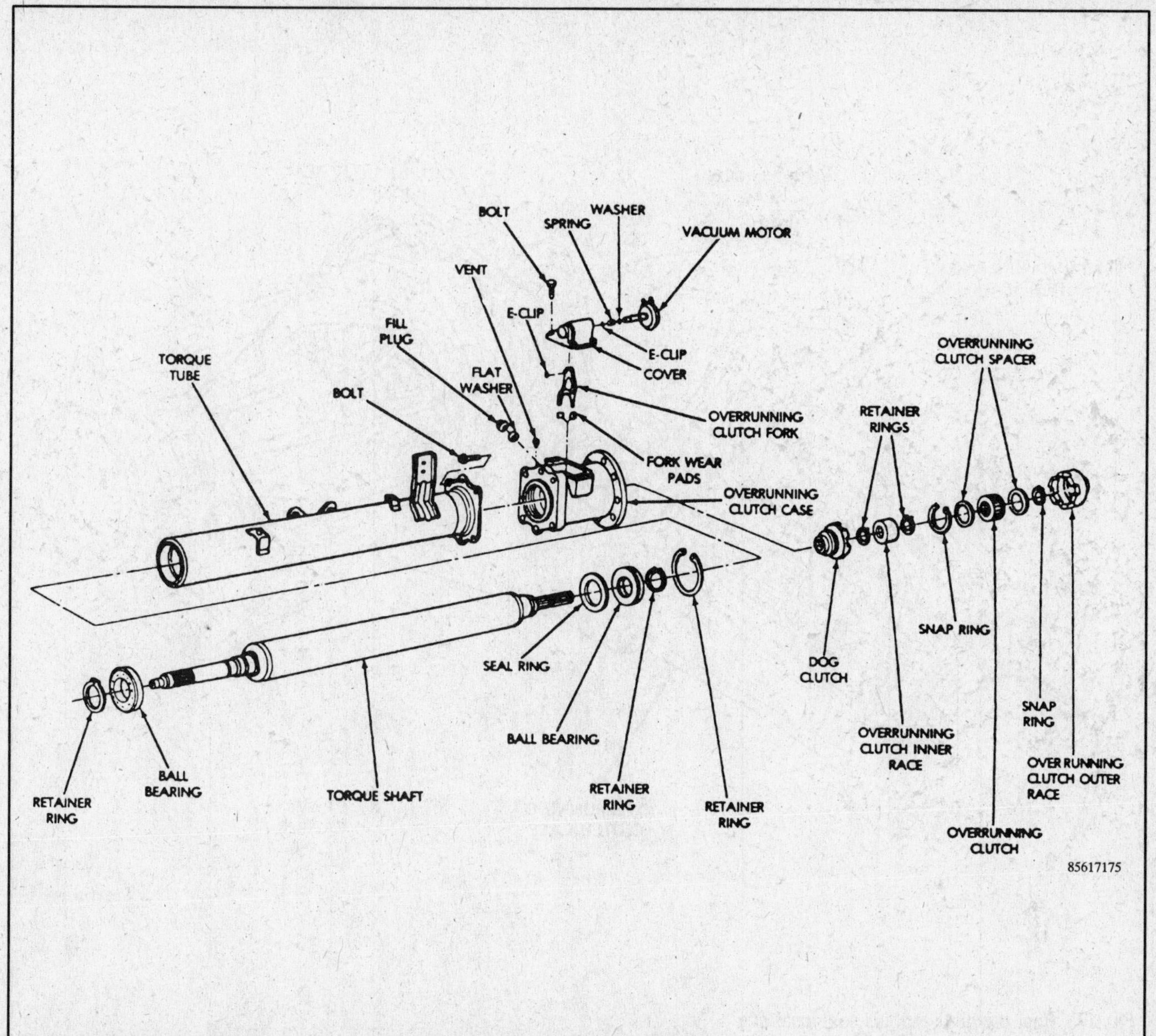

Fig. 174 Exploded view of the torque tube and overrunning clutch assemblies

REAR DRIVE LINE MODULE

Identification

As an option in 1991, Chrysler offered All Wheel Drive (AWD) on Caravan/Voyager models. These models are basically the same as the front wheel drive versions, with the exception of the components needed for driving the rear wheels as well.

The power is transferred to the rear wheels through the Power Transfer Unit (PTU) attached to the transaxle. The power travels through the PTU to a torque tube that contains the center driveshaft. The power then enters an overrunning clutch assembly, attached to the front of the rear differential carrier.

The overrunning clutch assembly is separate from the rear carrier. The overrunning clutch assembly has an vacuum operated dog clutch, it is lubricated with Mopar ATF type 7176. The rear carrier is lubricated with SAE 85W-90 gear lube.

Rear Drive Line Assembly Module

➧ See Figure 175

REMOVAL &INSTALLATION

1. Raise and safely support the rear of the vehicle.
2. Remove the right and left inner halfshaft joint mounting bolts.
3. Support the inner side of the halfshaft, by hanging it from the frame using a piece of wire. Do not allow the shafts to hang freely or the joints will be damaged.
4. Remove the mounting bolts from the rear side of the propeller shaft at, the rear carrier.

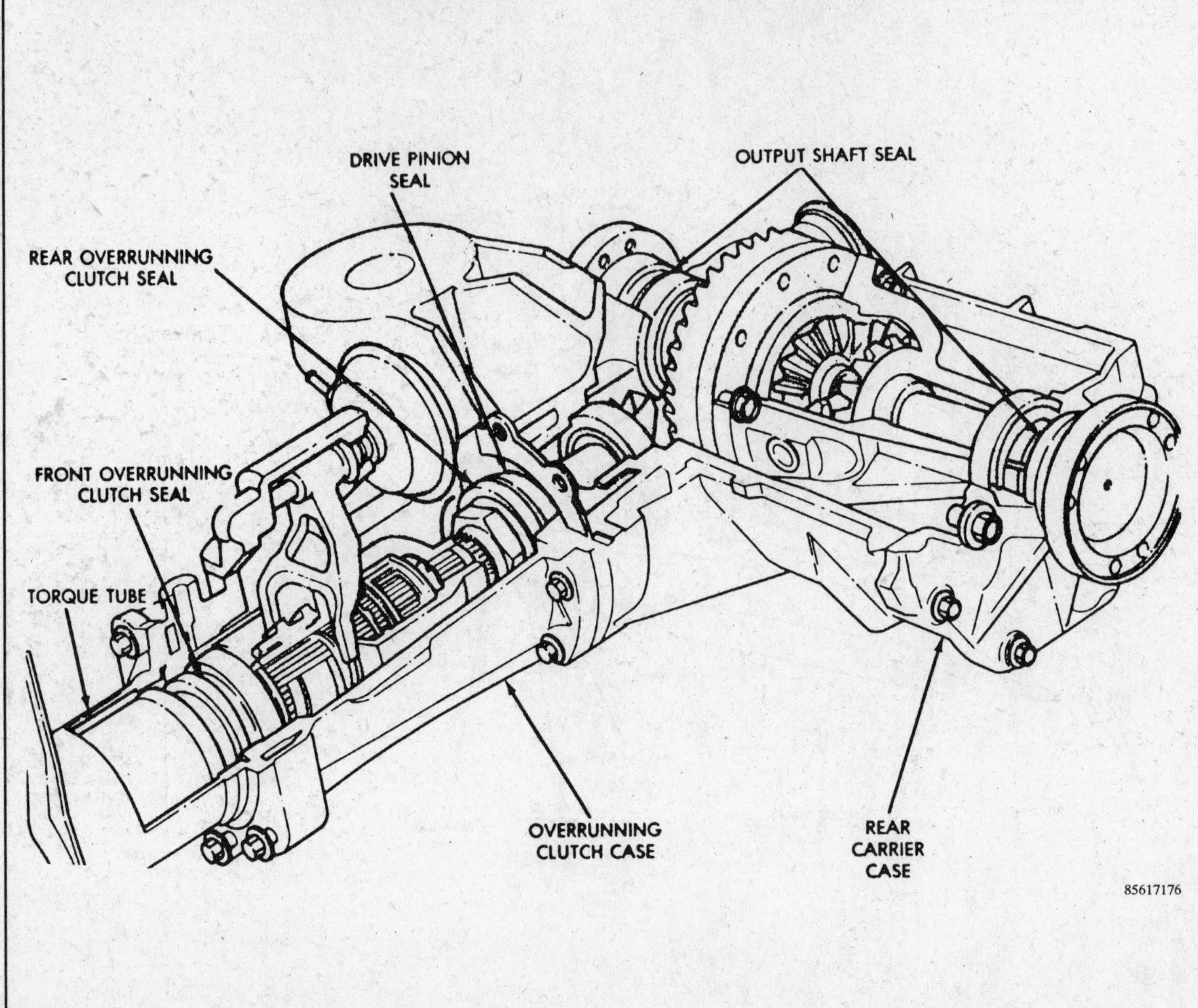

Fig. 175 Rear driveline module seal locations

5. Support the propeller shaft.
6. Remove the viscous coupling retaining nut and slide the viscous coupling off the rear driveline assembly.
7. Disengage the vacuum line at the driveline module.
8. Disengage the electrical lead from the assembly.
9. Support the rear of the driveline module with a jack.
10. Remove the rear driveline module front mounting bolts. Partially lower the unit from the vehicle.
11. Remove the rear driveline module from the vehicle.

To install:

12. Position the driveline module in the vehicle. Install the front mounting bolts and tighten to 40 ft. lbs. (54 Nm).
13. Reconnect the vacuum line and electrical lead. Install the viscous coupling and nut. Tighten the nut to 120 ft. lbs. (162 Nm).
14. Connect the propeller shaft to the driveline module, tighten to 21 ft. lbs. (28 Nm).
15. Connect the rear halfshafts to the rear driveline module. Tighten the bolt to 45 ft. lbs. (61 Nm).
16. Lower the vehicle. Check the operation of the drive train.

Rear Halfshaft

REMOVAL & INSTALLATION

1. Raise and safely support the rear of the vehicle.
2. Remove the rear wheel.
3. Remove the cotter pin, nut, lock and spring washer from the rear hub.
4. Remove the inner halfshaft retaining bolts.
5. The halfshaft is spring loaded, push it in slightly and then tilt it down to remove it. Pull it out from under the vehicle.

To install:

6. Insert the end of the halfshaft into the rear hub assembly.
7. Position it on the rear carrier unit and install the retaining bolts.
8. Tighten the retaining bolts to 45 ft. lbs. (61 Nm).
9. Install the hub nut, spring and lock washers, and cotter pin.
10. Install the wheel and tire assembly.

Drive Pinion

REMOVAL & INSTALLATION

➧ **See Figures 176, 177, 178, 179, 180, 181 and 182**

1. Raise and safely support the vehicle.
2. Remove the rear driveline module from the vehicle.
3. Remove the overrunning clutch case-to-rear carrier bolts. Separate the overrunning clutch case from the rear carrier.
4. Remove the overrunning clutch outer race snapring and slide the clutch race off of the shaft.
5. Using a spline socket and a wrench, remove the pinion nut.
6. Unfasten the front carrier cover retaining bolts and remove the carrier cover.
7. Place a block of wood under the end of the pinion shaft. Tap the end of the pinion against the wood to remove the spacer from the shaft.

To install:

8. Install the front carrier onto the case and tighten the retaining nuts to 105 inch lbs. (12 Nm).
9. Clean and inspect the seal area, apply a light coat of oil to the drive pinion seal.
10. Install the seal using a seal installer. The seal must be installed with the spring towards the rear of the case.
11. Apply a light coat of oil onto the drive pinion spacer and slide it onto the pinion shaft with the tapered side facing out.
12. Apply a light coat of oil to the overrunning clutch seal and install with a seal installer, the seal must be installed with the spring facing outward.
13. Install the pinion nut and tighten to 150 ft. lbs. (203 Nm).
14. Install the overrunning clutch outer race and snapring.
15. Apply Loctite® sealer to the overrunning clutch sealing surface and install the clutch case to the rear carrier. Tighten to 21 ft. lbs. (28 Nm).
16. Install the rear driveline module into the vehicle. Check and fill the fluid as required.

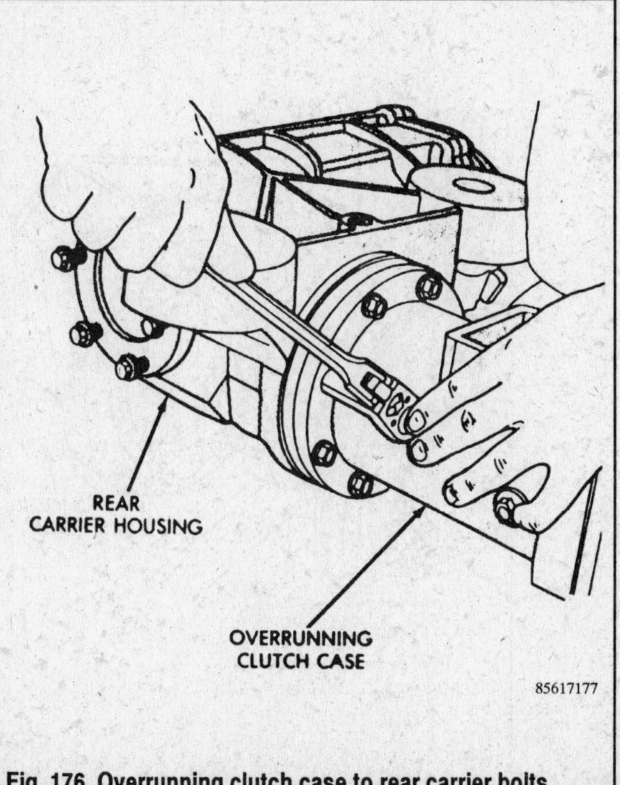

Fig. 176 Overrunning clutch case to rear carrier bolts

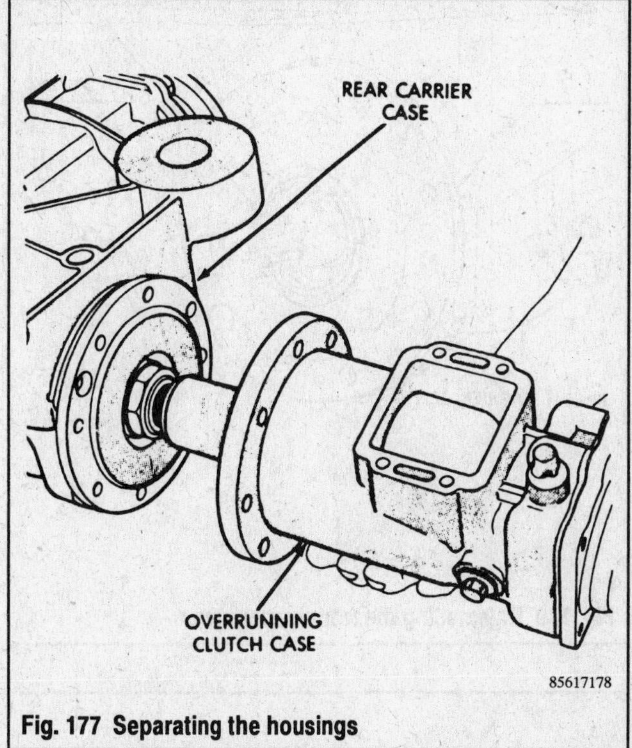

Fig. 177 Separating the housings

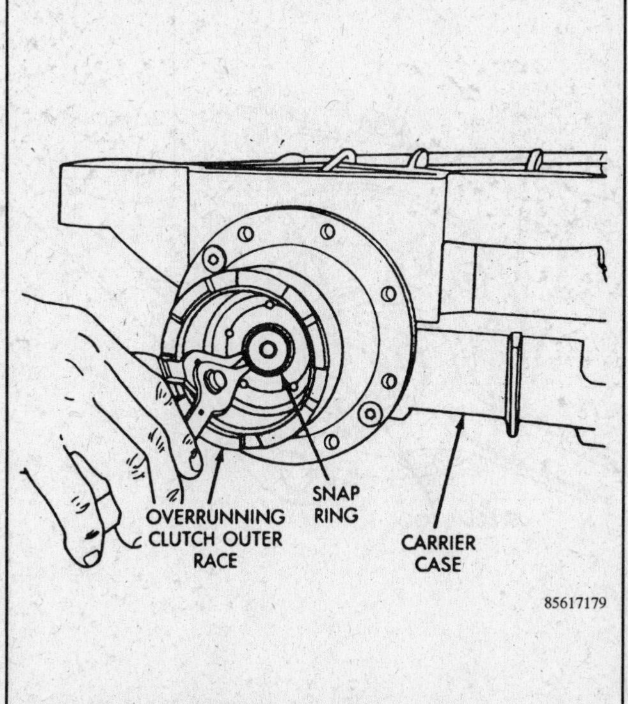

Fig. 178 Overruning clutch snapring removal

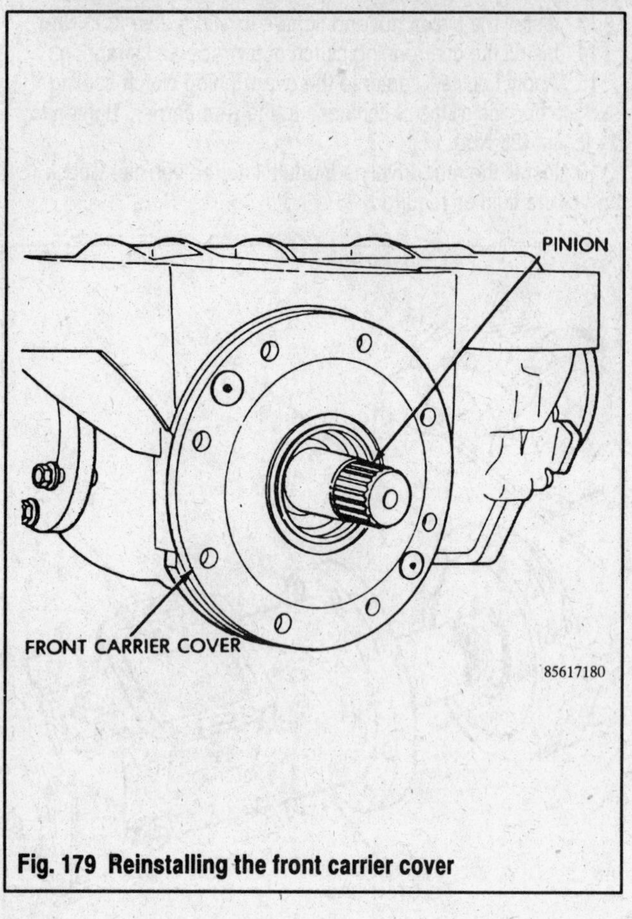

Fig. 179 Reinstalling the front carrier cover

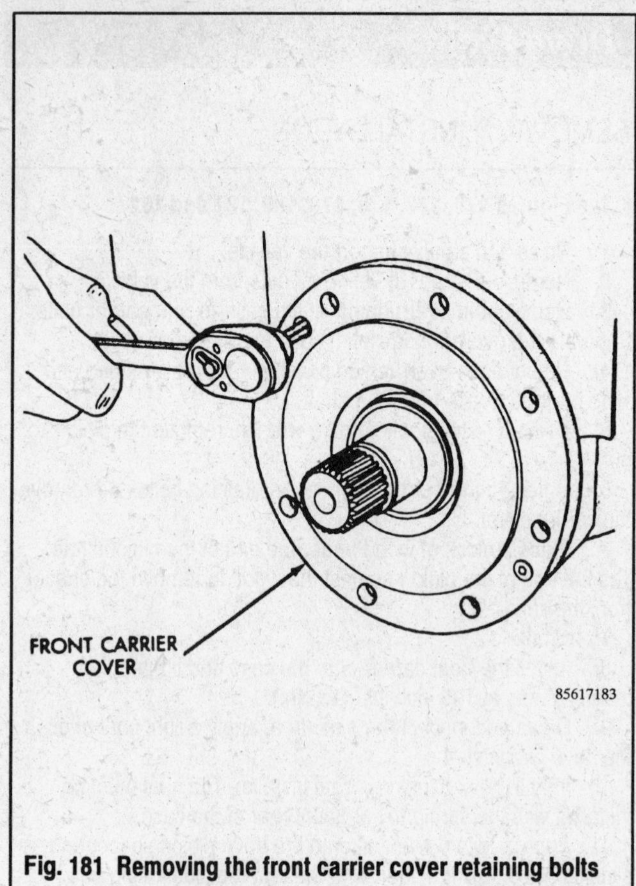

Fig. 181 Removing the front carrier cover retaining bolts

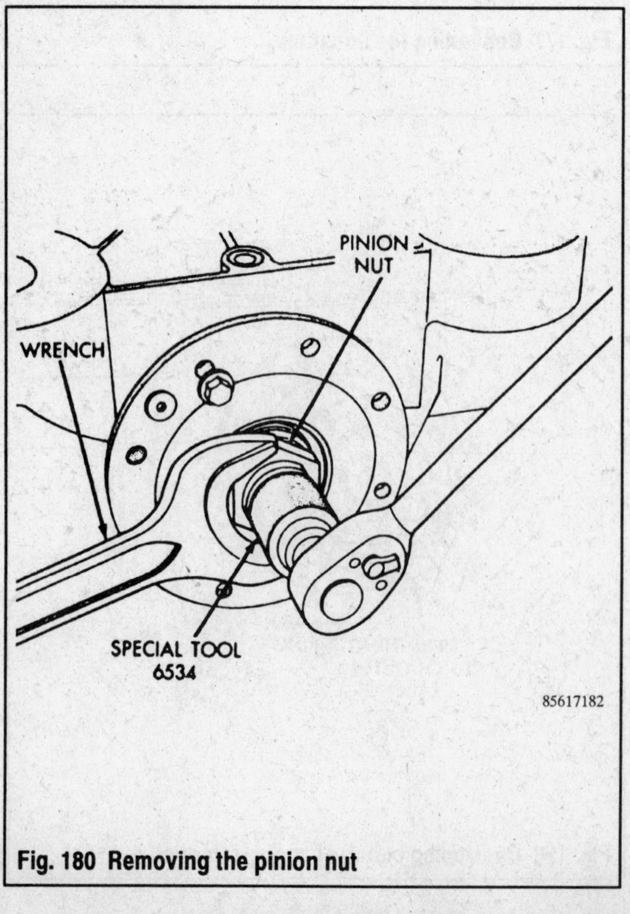

Fig. 180 Removing the pinion nut

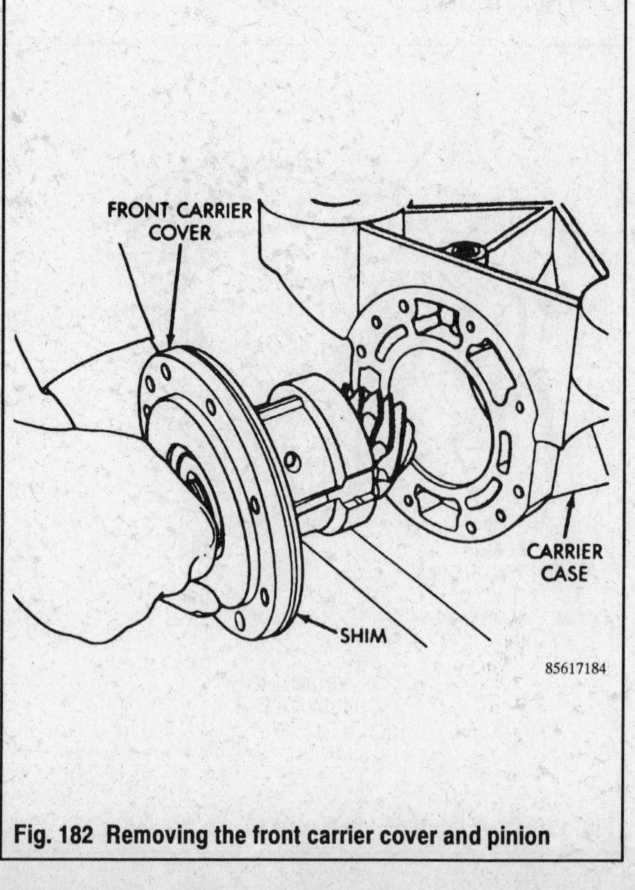

Fig. 182 Removing the front carrier cover and pinion

Differential Side Gears

➧ See Figures 183 and 184

REMOVAL & INSTALLATION

1. Raise and safely support the rear of the vehicle.
2. Disconnect both rear halfshafts from the axle carrier assembly.
3. Using 2 prybars, remove the output shaft.
4. Unfasten the end cover retaining bolts and remove the end cover.
5. Remove the differential assembly from the rear driveline case.
6. Remove the ring gear bolts and separate the differential case from the differential body.
7. Using a punch and hammer, remove the differential pinion shaft pin.
8. Slide the differential pinion shaft out of the differential case.

To install:

9. Replace the pinion gears, shaft or washers as required.
10. Reverse steps 8-5 to assemble the differential. Tighten the ring gear bolts to 70 ft. lbs. (95 Nm).
11. Install the differential into the module case. Clean and inspect sealer surfaces.
12. Apply Loctite® gasket eliminator or equivalent, and install the end cover. Tighten, in the sequence shown, to 21 ft. lbs. (28 Nm).
13. Install the rear halfshafts and lower the vehicle.

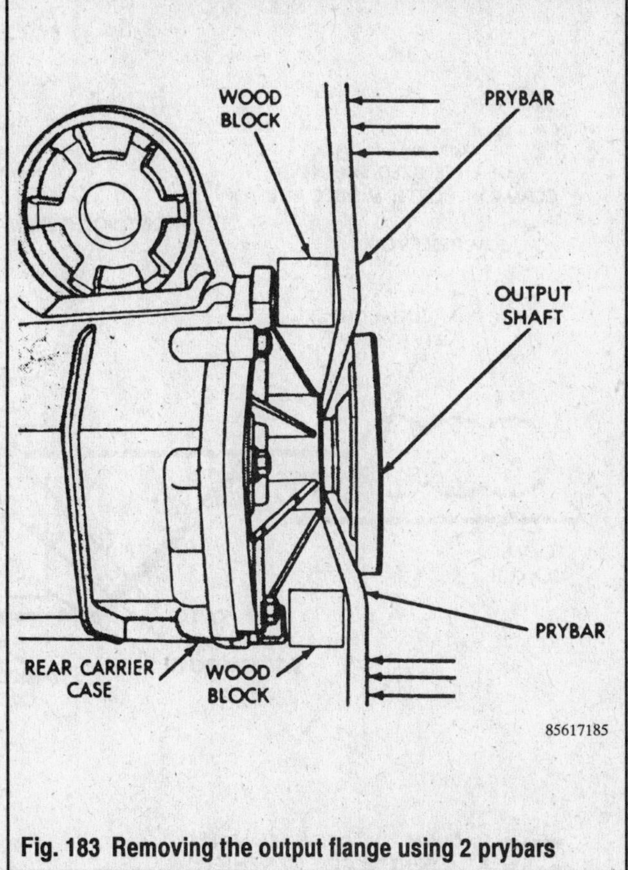

Fig. 183 Removing the output flange using 2 prybars

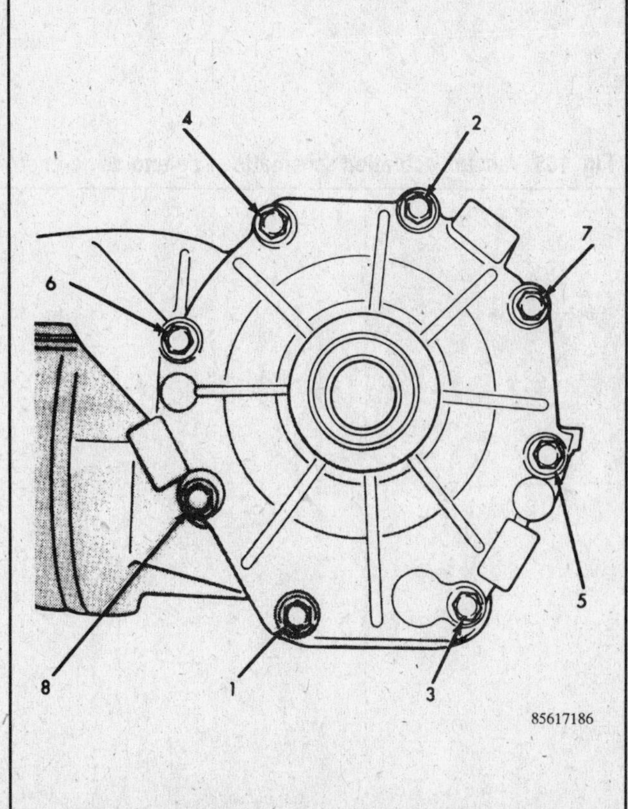

Fig. 184 Differential side gear bolt tightening sequence

Torque Tube

REMOVAL & INSTALLATION

1. Raise and safely support the vehicle.
2. Remove the rear driveline module assembly from the vehicle.
3. Remove the viscous coupling, snapring and torque tube bearing shield.
4. Remove torque tube to overrunning clutch case bolts.
5. Slide the torque tube off of the torque shaft.

To install:

6. Engage the torque tube onto the torque shaft. Install the torque tube to the overrunning clutch case bolts, tightening to 21 ft. lbs. (28 Nm).
7. Install the bearing shield and snapring.
8. Install the viscous coupling.
9. Install the driveline module into the vehicle. Lower The vehicle.

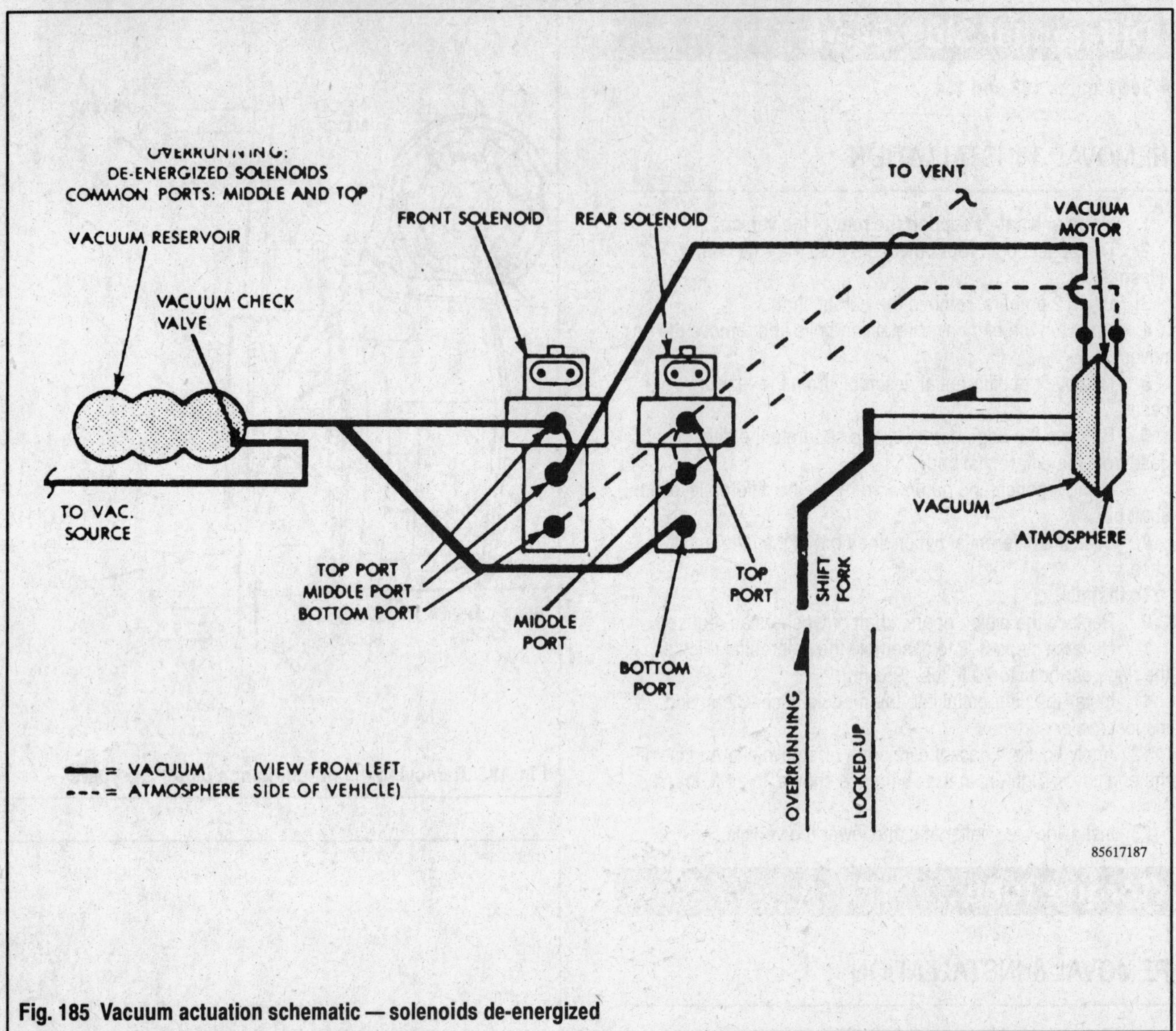

Fig. 185 Vacuum actuation schematic — solenoids de-energized

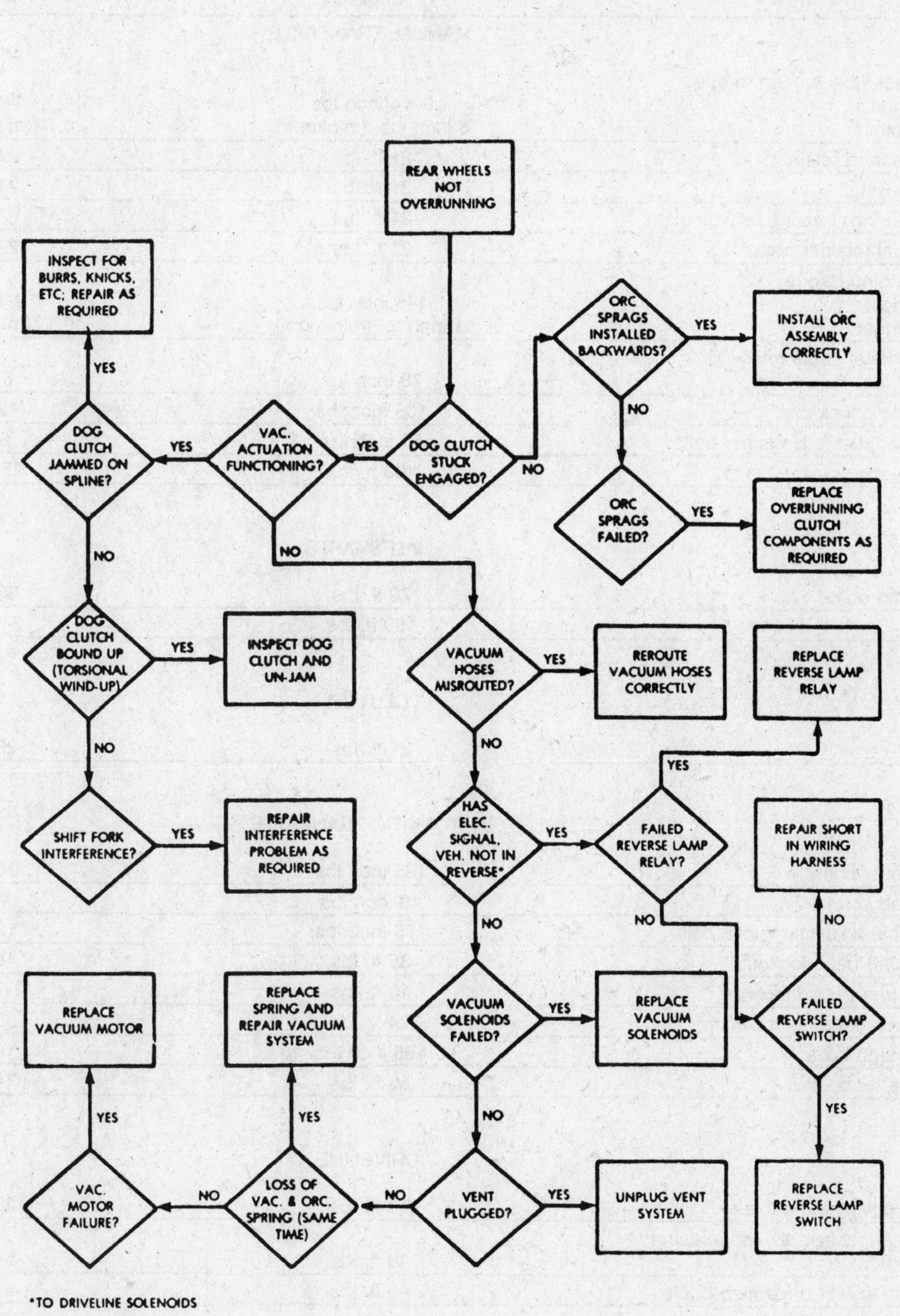

Fig. 186 Rear driveline vacuum shift motor diagnosis

TORQUE SPECIFICATIONS

Component	English	Metric
	MANUAL TRANSAXLE	
Differential assembly turning torque		
New bearings:	9–14 inch lbs.	1–2 Nm
Used bearings:	6 inch lbs. (minimum)	0.7 Nm (minimum)
Differential bearing retainer:	21 ft. lbs.	29 Nm
Extension housing:	21 ft. lbs.	29 Nm
Input shaft bearings bearing retainer plate:	21 ft. lbs.	29 Nm
Input shaft seal retainer bolts:	21 ft. lbs.	29 Nm
Input shaft turning torque		
New bearings:	1–5 inch lbs.	0.1–0.6 Nm
Used bearings:	1 inch lb. (minimum)	0.1 Nm (minimum)
Selector/crossover cable retaining screws:	70 inch lbs.	8 Nm
Selector housing lock pin:	105 inch lbs.	12 Nm
Shift linkage adjustment/retainer bolts:	55 inch lbs.	6Nm
5th speed gear nut:	190 ft. lbs.	258 Nm
	HALFSHAFTS	
Ball joint clamp bolt:	70 ft. lbs.	95 Nm
Hub nut:	180 ft. lbs.	245 Nm
	CLUTCH	
Pressure plate bolts:	21 ft. lbs.	29 Nm
	AUTOMATIC TRANSAXLE	
Differential cover bolts:	165 inch lbs.	18 Nm
Filter mounting screw:	40 inch lbs.	4 Nm
Kickdown cable adjustment lock bolt:	105 inch lbs.	12 Nm
Kickdown (front) band locknut:	35 ft. lbs.	48 Nm
Low/reverse (rear) band locknut:	10 ft. lbs.	(14 Nm
Neutral Start/Back-up Light Switch:	24 ft. lbs.	33 Nm
Oil pan mounting bolts:	165 inch lbs.	18 Nm
Torque converter bolts:	55 ft. lbs.	74 Nm
	DRIVELINE	
Driveshaft-to-driveline module:	21 ft. lbs.	28 Nm
Rear drive line assembly module front mounting bolts:	40 ft. lbs.	54 Nm
Rear halshafts-to-rear driveline module:	45 ft. lbs.	61 Nm
Viscous coupling nut:	120 ft. lbs.	162 Nm

85617C01

FRONT SUSPENSION
FRONT END ALIGNMENT 8-16
FRONT HUB AND BEARING 8-13
LOWER BALL JOINT 8-8
LOWER CONTROL ARM 8-9
MACPHERSON STRUTS 8-2
PIVOT BUSHING 8-10
STEERING KNUCKLE 8-12
STRUT SPRING 8-6
SWAY BAR 8-10
REAR SUSPENSION
GENERAL INFORMATION 8-17
REAR AXLE ALIGNMENT 8-23
REAR SPRINGS 8-18
REAR WHEEL BEARINGS 8-21
SHOCK ABSORBERS 8-20
SWAY BAR 8-20
SPECIFICATIONS CHARTS
TORQUE SPECIFICATIONS 8-45
WHEEL ALIGNMENT SPECIFICATIONS 8-16
STEERING
BOOT SEALS 8-44
IGNITION LOCK CYLINDER 8-27
IGNITION SWITCH 8-28
IGNITION SWITCH AND LOCK CYLINDER ASSEMBLY 8-28
MULTI-FUNCTION SWITCH 8-26
POWER STEERING PUMP 8-44
STEERING COLUMN 8-30
STEERING GEAR 8-41
STEERING LINKAGE 8-40
STEERING WHEEL 8-24
TURN SIGNAL SWITCH 8-25
WHEELS
WHEEL ASSEMBLIES 8-2

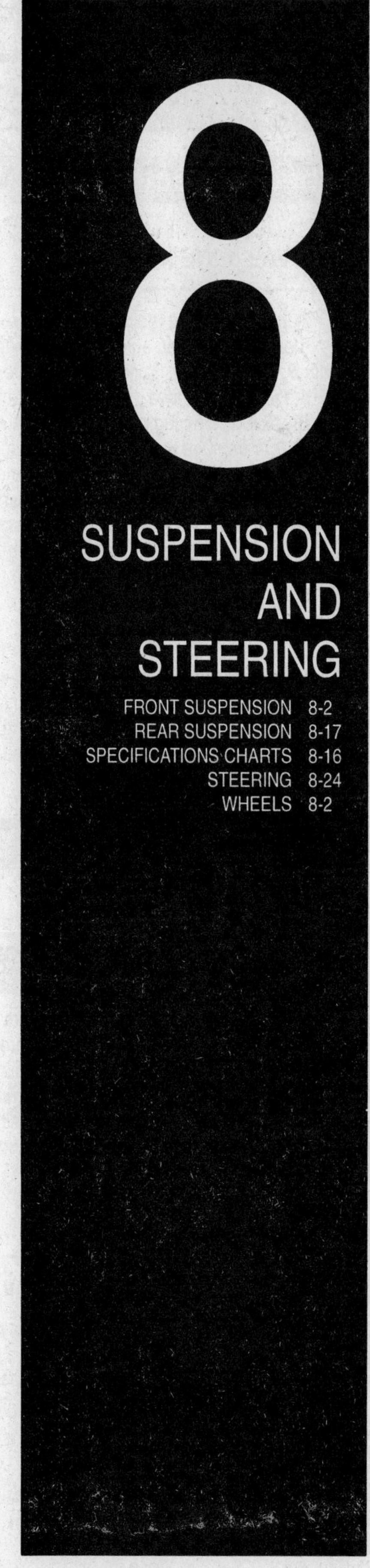

8 SUSPENSION AND STEERING

FRONT SUSPENSION 8-2
REAR SUSPENSION 8-17
SPECIFICATIONS CHARTS 8-16
STEERING 8-24
WHEELS 8-2

WHEELS

Wheel Assemblies

REMOVAL & INSTALLATION

1. Apply the parking brake and block the opposite wheel.
2. If equipped with an automatic transaxle, place the selector lever in **P**; with a manual transaxle, place the shifter in Reverse.
3. If equipped, remove the wheel cover or hub cap.
4. Break loose the lug nuts. If a nut is stuck, never use heat to loosen it or damage to the wheel and bearings may occur. If the nuts are seized, one or two heavy hammer blows directly on the end of the bolt head usually loosens the rust. Be careful as continued pounding will likely damage the brake drum or rotor.
5. Raise the vehicle until the tire is clear of the ground. Support the vehicle safely using jackstands.
6. Remove the lug nuts, then remove the tire and wheel assembly.

To install:

7. Make sure the wheel and hub mating surfaces as well as the wheel lug studs are clean and free of all foreign material. Always remove rust from the wheel mounting surfaces and the brake rotors/drums. Failure to do so may cause the lug nuts to loosen in service.
8. Position the wheel on the hub or drum and hand-tighten the lug nuts. Tighten all the lug nuts, in a crisscross pattern, until they are snug.
9. Remove the supports and lower the vehicle. Tighten the lug nuts, in a crisscross pattern to 95 ft. lbs. (130 Nm). Always use a torque wrench to achieve the proper lug nut torque and to prevent stretching the wheel studs.
10. Repeat the torque pattern to assure proper wheel tightening.
11. If equipped, install the hub cab or wheel cover.

INSPECTION

Check the wheels for any damage. They must be replaced if they are bent, dented, heavily rusted, have elongated bolt holes, or have excessive lateral or radial runout. Wheels with excessive runout may cause a high-speed vehicle vibration.

Replacement wheels must be of the same load capacity, diameter, width, offset and mounting configuration as the original wheels. Using the wrong wheels may affect wheel bearing life, ground and tire clearance, or speedometer and odometer calibrations.

FRONT SUSPENSION

See Figures 1, 2 and 3

MacPherson Struts

A MacPherson Type front suspension, with vertical shock absorbers attached to the upper fender reinforcement and the steering knuckle, is used. Lower control arms, attached inboard to a crossmember and outboard to the steering knuckle through a ball joint, provide lower steering knuckle position. During steering maneuvers, the upper strut and steering knuckle turn as an assembly.

REMOVAL & INSTALLATION

See Figures 4, 5, 6, 7, 8, 9, 10, 11, 12 and 13

1. Loosen the front wheel lug nuts slightly. Raise and support the front of the vehicle on jackstands.
2. Remove the wheel and tire assemblies.

If the original strut assemblies are to be installed, mark the camber eccentric bolt and strut for installment in same position.

3. Unfasten the lower camber bolt and nut (at the steering knuckle), along with the knuckle bolt and nut. Remove the brake hose-to-strut bracket mounting bolt.
4. Remove the upper mounting nuts and washers on the fender shield in the engine compartment. Remove the strut assembly from the vehicle.

To install:

5. Inspect the strut assembly for signs of leakage. A slight amount of seepage is normal, fluid streaking down the side of the strut is not. Replacer the strut if leakage is evident. Service the strut and spring assembly as required.
6. Position the strut assembly under the fender well and loosely install the upper washers and nuts. Position the lower mount over the steering knuckle, then loosely install the mounting and camber bolts and nuts. Attach the brake hose retaining bracket, then tighten the mounting bolt to 10 ft. lbs. (14 Nm).
7. Tighten the upper mount nuts to 20 ft. lbs. (27 Nm). Index the camber bolt to reference mark and snug the nut. Install the nut on the mounting bolt, then tighten slightly.
8. Mount a 4 in. (10cm) C-clamp over the inner edge of the strut and outer edge of the steering knuckle. Tighten the clamp just enough to eliminate any play between the knuckle and the strut. check the alignment of the camber bolt and strut reference marks. Tighten the mounting and camber nuts to 75 ft. lbs. (102 Nm) plus an additional $^1/_4$ turn more. Remove the C-clamp.
9. Install the wheel and tire assembly and lower the vehicle.

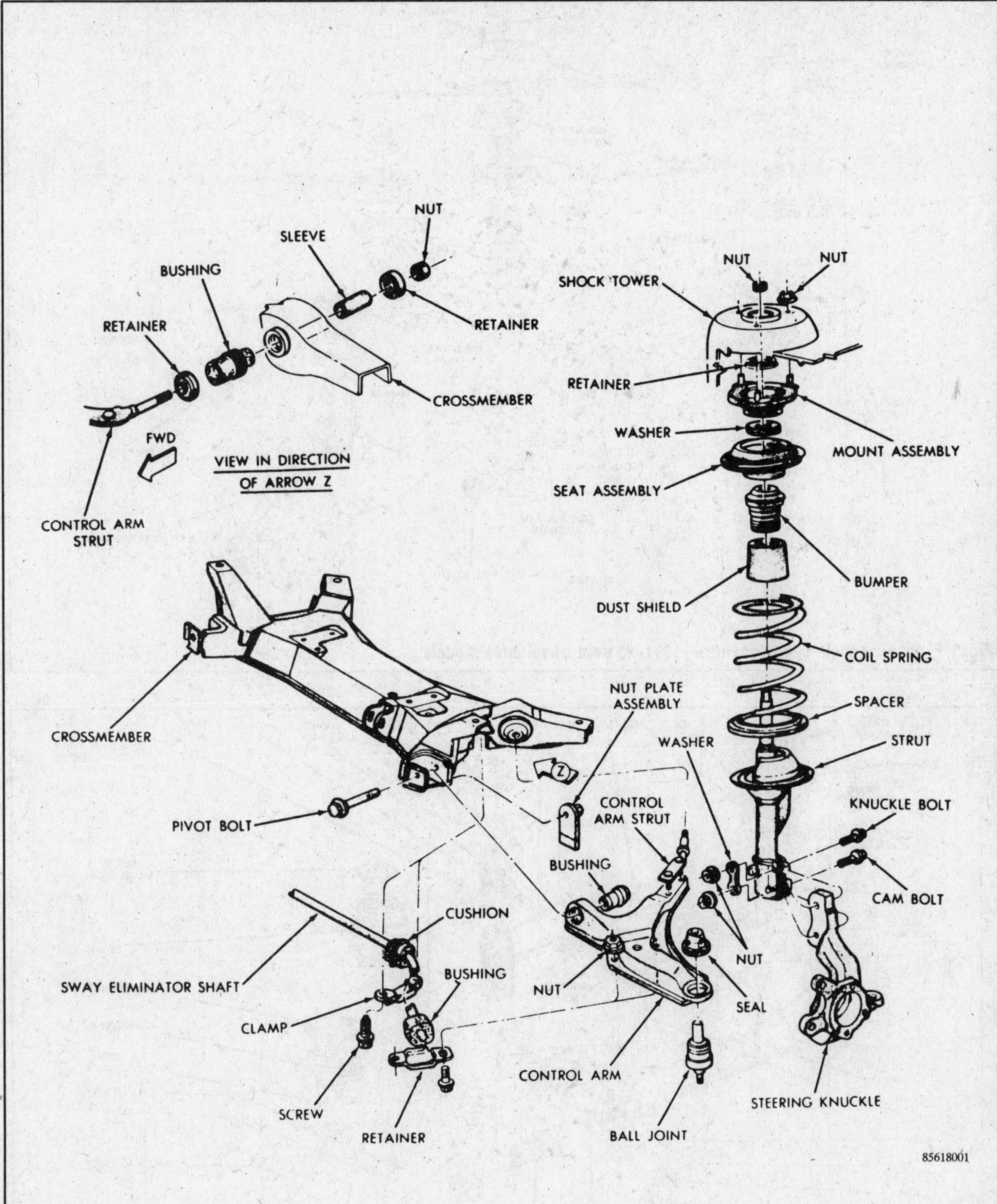

Fig. 1 Front suspension components — 1984–90 models

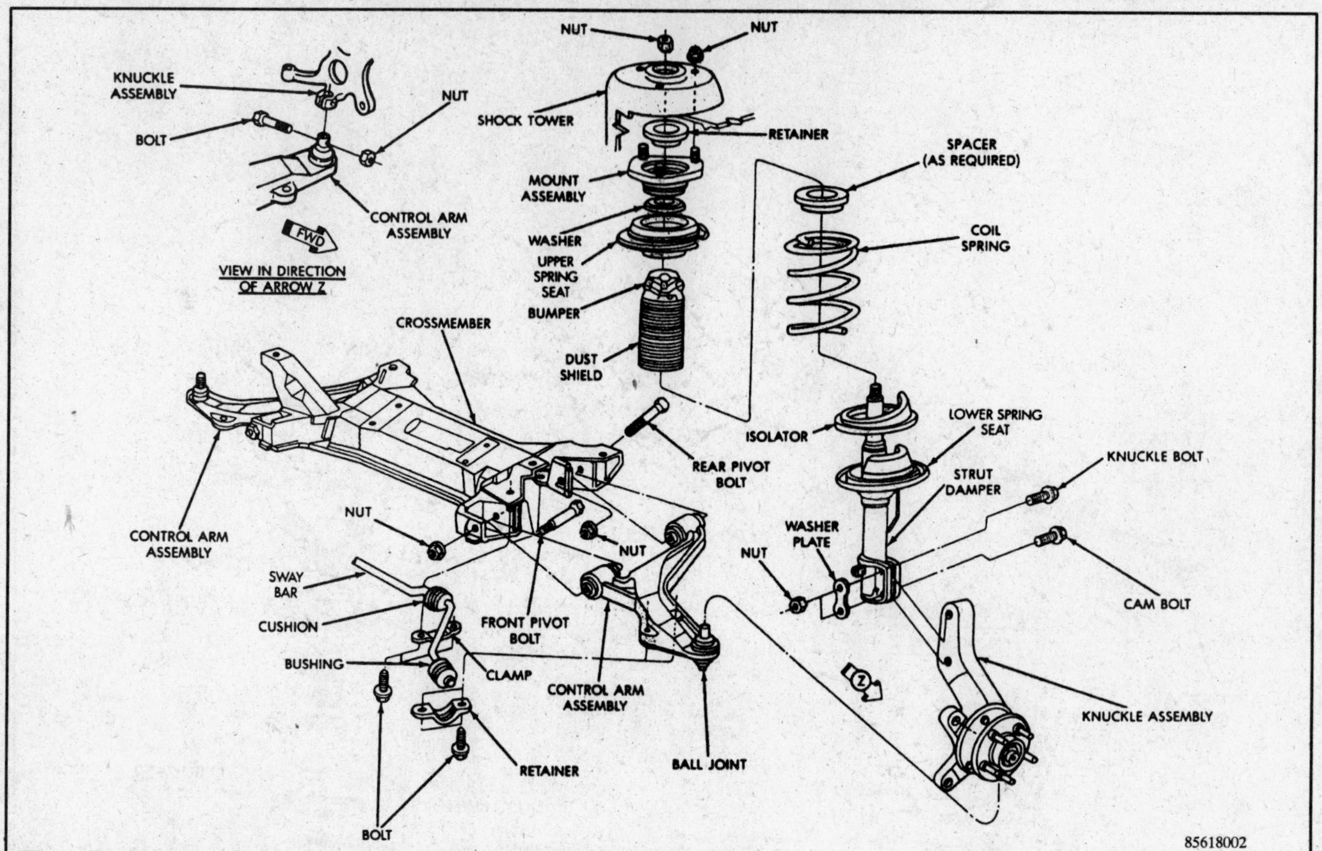

85618002

Fig. 2 Front suspension components — 1991–95 front wheel drive models

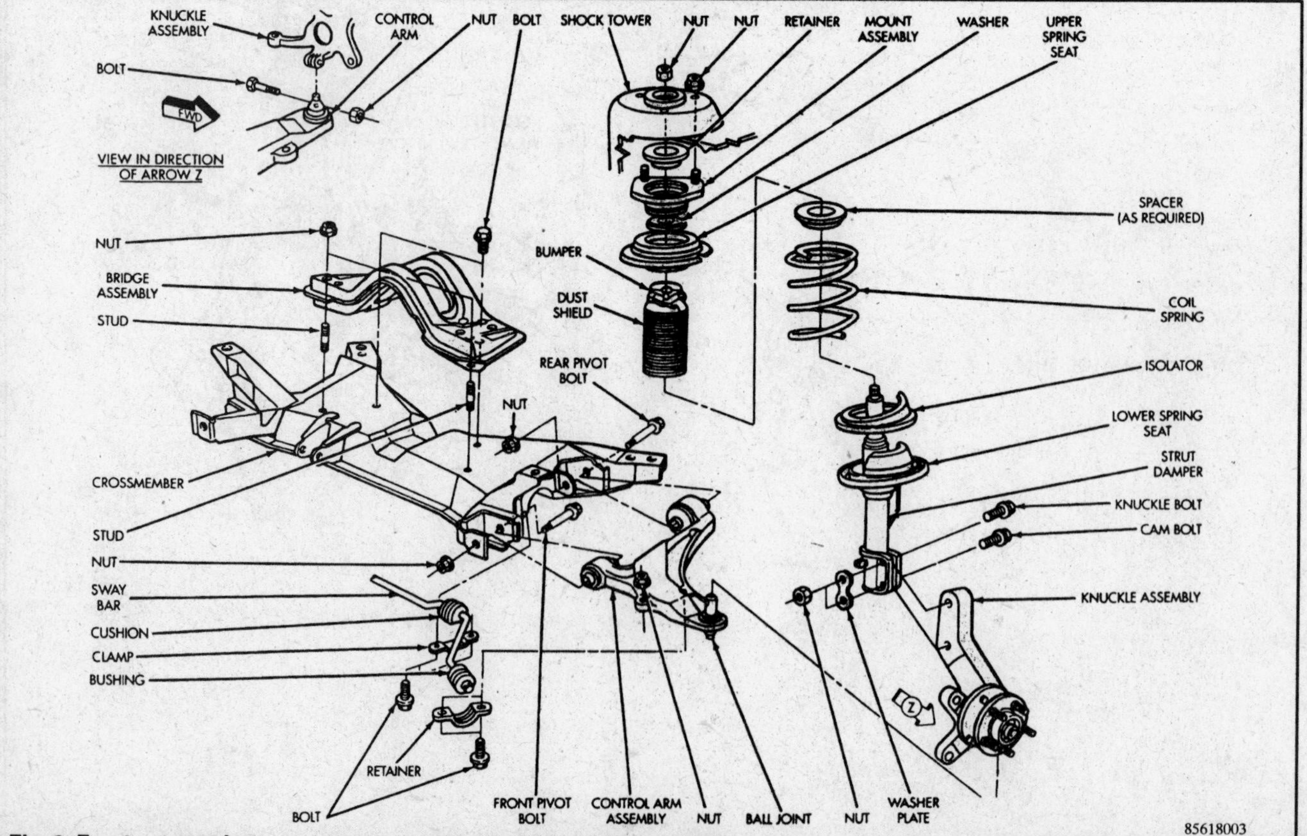

85618003

Fig. 3 Front suspension components — 1991–95 all wheel drive models

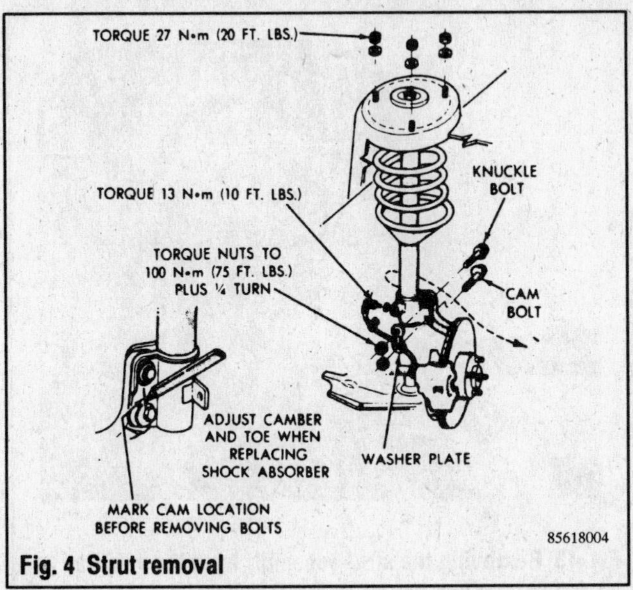

Fig. 4 Strut removal

Fig. 7 Mark the strut cam adjusting bolt for installation

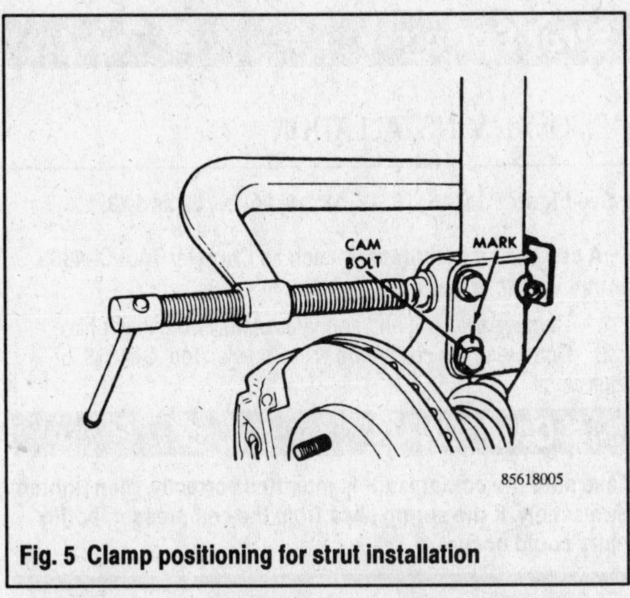

Fig. 5 Clamp positioning for strut installation

Fig. 8 Remove the brake hose to strut bracket mounting bolt

Fig. 6 Strut cam bolt location — 1987 Voyager shown

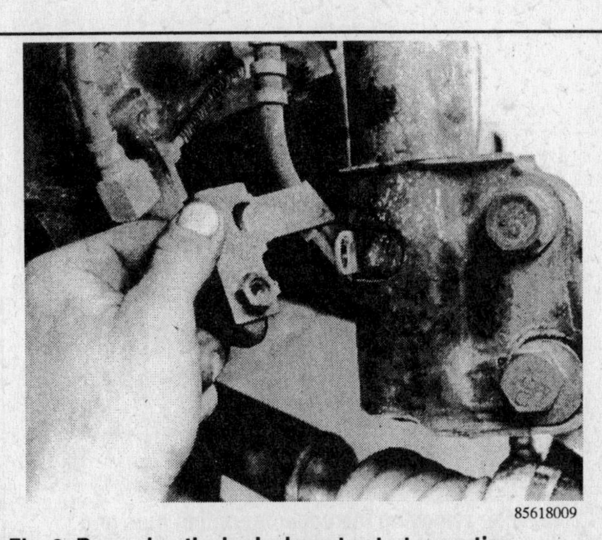

Fig. 9 Removing the brake hose to strut mounting bracket

85618010

Fig. 10 Remove the strut cam and knuckle lower retaining nuts and washer

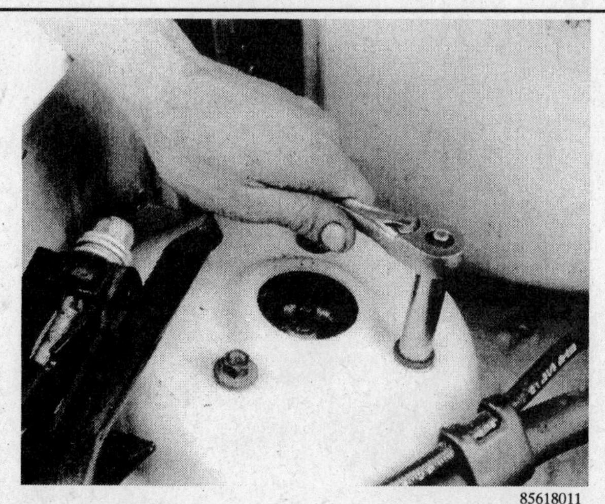
85618011

Fig. 11 Remove the upper mounting nuts and washers on the fender shield in the engine compartment

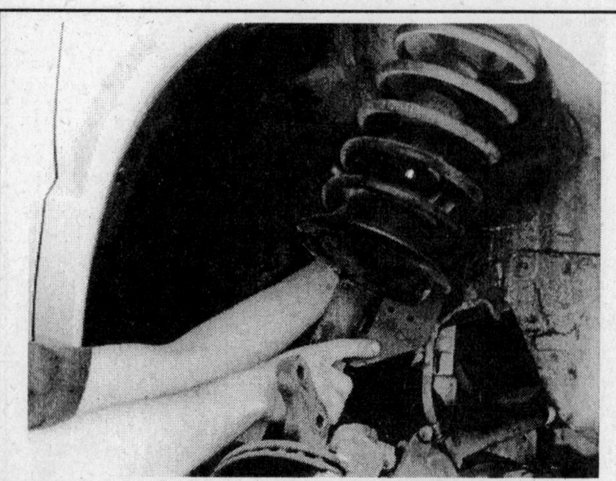
85618012

Fig. 12 After removing the upper mounting nuts and washers on the fender shield, lower the strut down and out

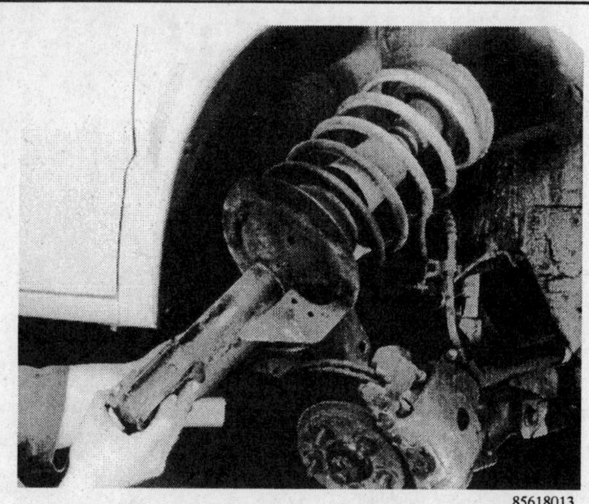
85618013

Fig. 13 Removing the strut assembly from the vehicle

Strut Spring

REMOVAL & INSTALLATION

See Figures 14, 15, 16, 17, 18, 19, 20, 21, 22 and 23

A coil spring compressor such as Chrysler Tool C-4838, or equivalent, is required.

1. Remove the strut and spring assembly from the vehicle.
2. Compress the coil spring with Chrysler Tool C-4838, or equivalent.

****CAUTION**

Make sure the compressor is mounted correctly, then tighten jaws evenly. If the spring slips from the compressor, bodily injury could occur.

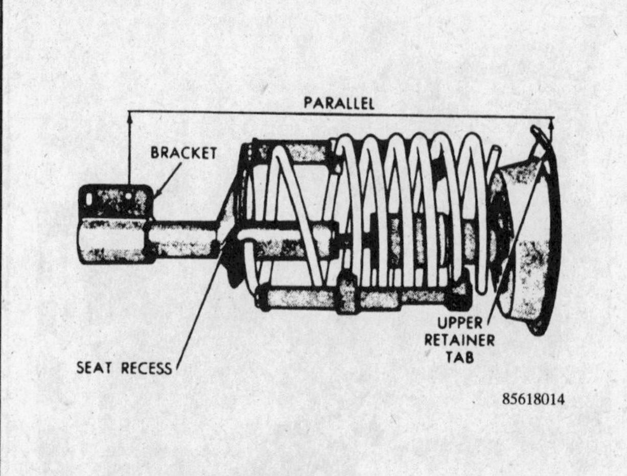

85618014

Fig. 14 A coil spring compressor Chrysler Tool C-4838 shown in the installed position

85618015

Fig. 15 An alternative coil spring compressor to the Chrysler Tool C-4838 is shown in the installed position

85618016

Fig. 16 With the the coil compressed, hold the center rod from turning and remove the assembly nut

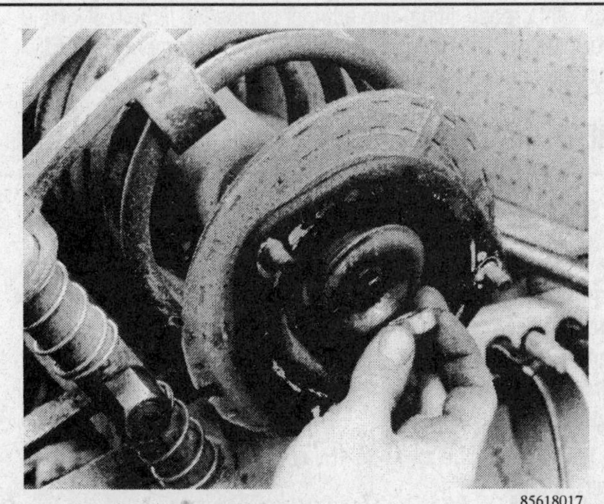
85618017

Fig. 17 Removing the nut from the shaft

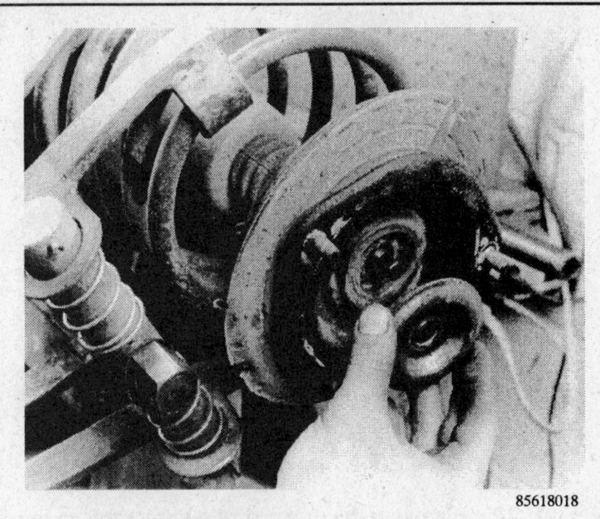
85618018

Fig. 18 Removing the washer from the shaft

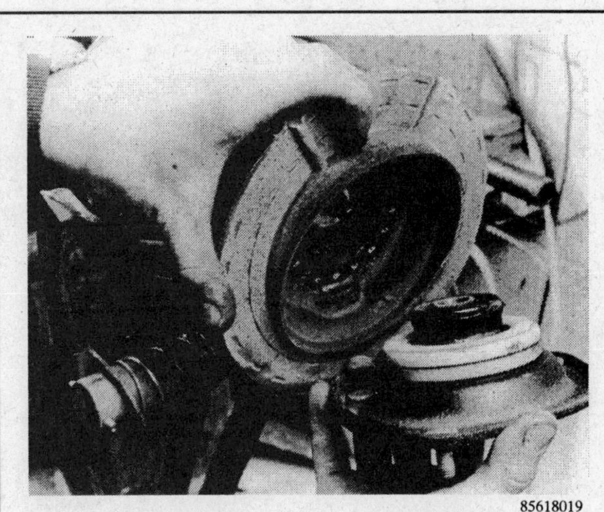
85618019

Fig. 19 Removing the upper strut mount from the shaft

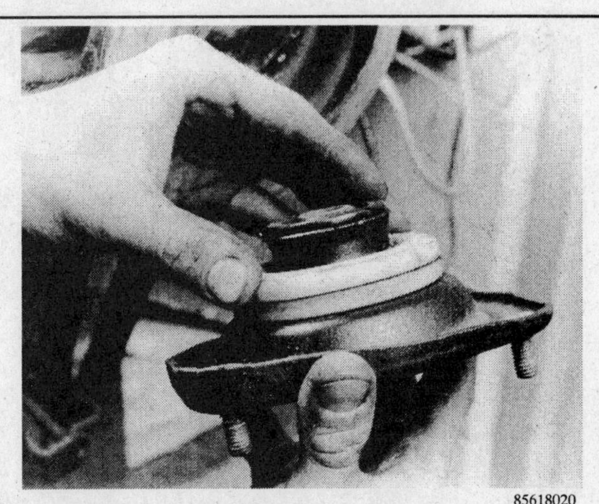
85618020

Fig. 20 The the upper strut mount shown removed from the shaft

Fig. 21 After removing the upper strut mount, remove the washer from the shaft

Fig. 22 Removing the rubber insulator

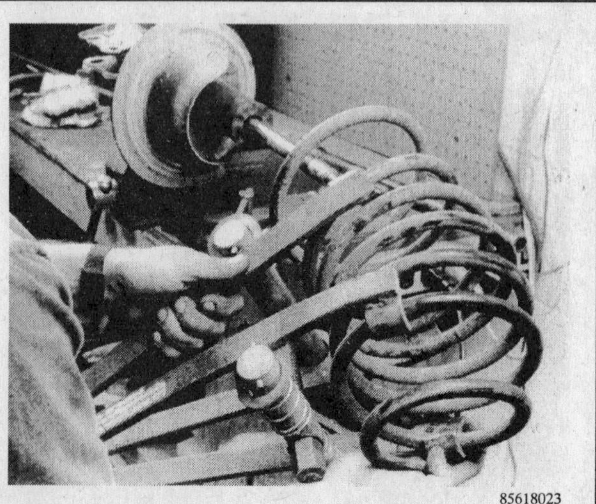

Fig. 23 Removing the coil spring from the strut

3. Hold the strut center rod from turning and remove the assembly nut.

➥ The coil springs on each are rated differently. Be sure to mark the spring for side identification.

4. Remove the mount assembly and the coil spring. Inspect the assembly for rubber isolator deterioration, distortion, cracks and bonding failure. Replace as necessary.
5. Check the mount bearings for binding and the retainers for bends and cracks. Replace as necessary.

To install:

6. Compress the spring and install it on the strut.
7. Install the upper mount assembly. The spring seat tab and the end of the coil spring must be aligned. Install assembly nut and tighten while holding the center strut rod in position. Tighten the nut to 60 ft. lbs. (82 Nm).
8. Release the coil spring compressor.
9. Install the strut assembly on the vehicle.
10. Lower the vehicle, remove the jackstands and test drive the vehicle.
11. Misalignment of the upper coil spring seat can cause interference between the coil spring and the inside of the mounting tower. A scraping noise on turns will be an indication if the problem. To correct:
    a. Raise and support the vehicle to take the weight off of the front wheels.
    b. Use two wrenches, one on the top of the center strut rod and one on the assembly nut. Turn both the strut rod and nut in the same direction. The spring will wind up and snap into position.
    c. Check the torque on the assembly nut — it should be 60 ft. lbs. (82 Nm).

Lower Ball Joint

The lower front suspension ball joints operate with no free-play. The ball joint housing is pressed into the lower control arm with the joint stud retained in the steering knuckle with a (clamp) bolt.

INSPECTION

With the weight of the vehicle resting on the ground, grasp the ball joint grease fitting, and attempt to move it. If the ball joint is worn the grease fitting will move easily. If movement is noted, replacement of the ball joint is recommended.

REMOVAL & INSTALLATION

➧ See Figure 24

➥ Special Chrysler Tools C-4699-1 and C-4699-2, or their equivalents, are required to remove and install the ball joint form the lower control arm. If the tools are not on hand, remove the control arm and have an automotive machine shop press the ball joint out and in. Refer to the Lower Control Arm Section.

1. Remove the lower control arm. Pry off the seal from the ball joint.
2. Position a receiving cup, special tool C-4699-2, or its equivalent, to support the lower control arm.

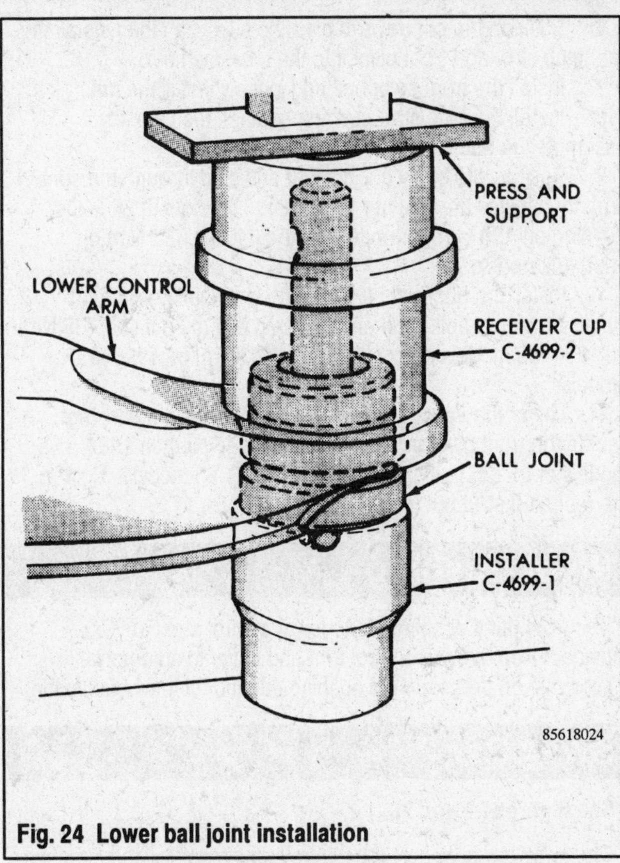

Fig. 24 Lower ball joint installation

3. Install a $1\frac{1}{8}$ in. deep socket over the stud and against the joint upper housing.
4. Press the joint assembly from the arm.

To install:

5. Position the ball joint housing into the control arm cavity.
6. Position the assembly in a press with special tool C-4699-1, or its equivalent, supporting the control arm.
7. Align the ball joint assembly, then press it until the housing ledge stops against the control arm cavity down flange.
8. To install a new seal, support the ball joint housing with tool C-4699-2 and place a new seal over the stud, against the housing.
9. With a $1\frac{1}{2}$ in. socket, press the seal onto the joint housing with the seat against the control arm. Install control arm.

Lower Control Arm

REMOVAL & INSTALLATION

➧ **See Figures 25 and 26**

1. Raise the vehicle and support it with jackstands.
2. Remove the front inner pivot through bolt, the rear stub strut nut, retainer and bushing, and the ball joint-to-steering knuckle clamp bolts.
3. Separate the ball joint stud from the steering knuckle by prying between the ball stud retainer on the knuckle and the lower control arm.

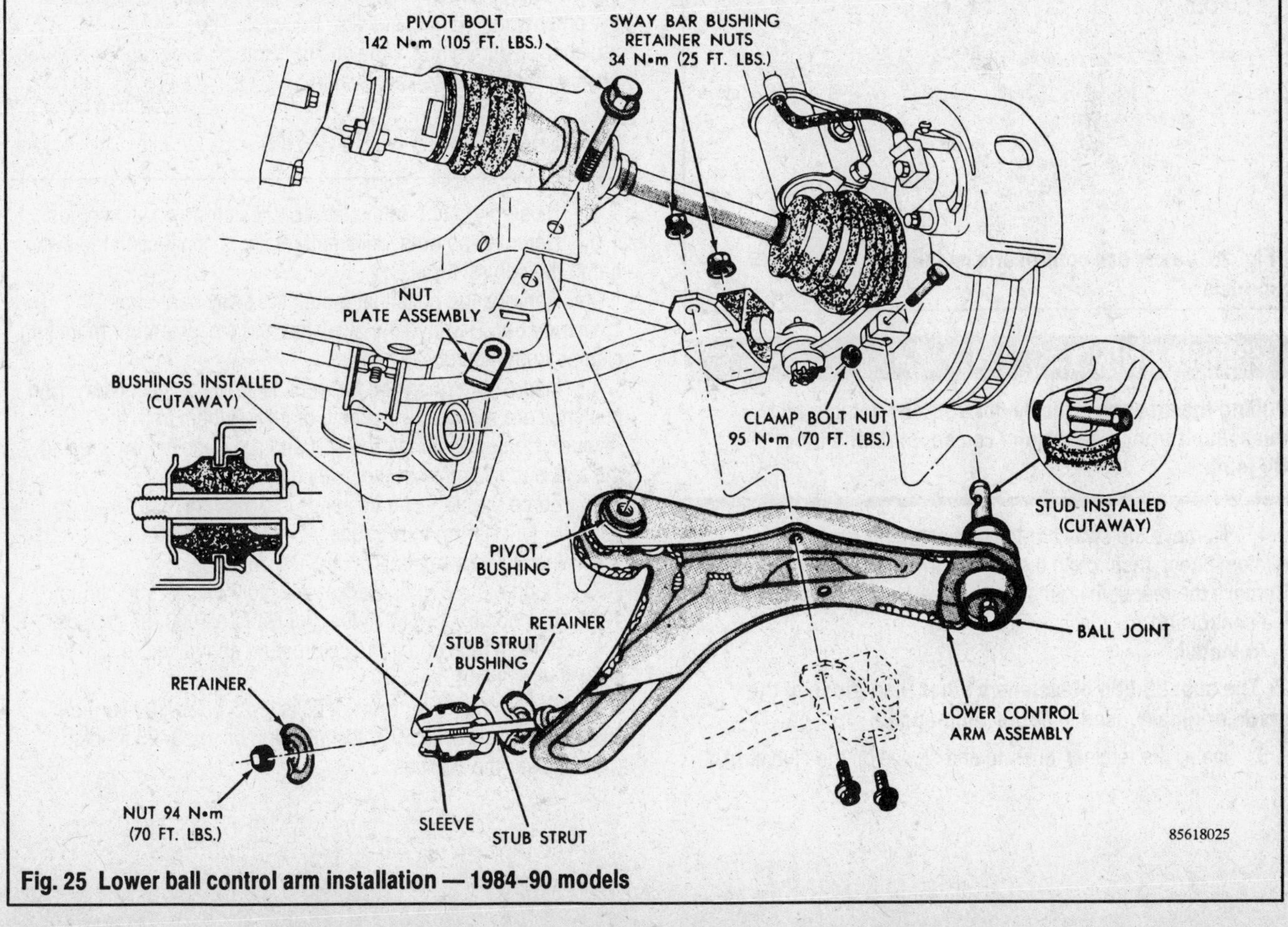

Fig. 25 Lower ball control arm installation — 1984–90 models

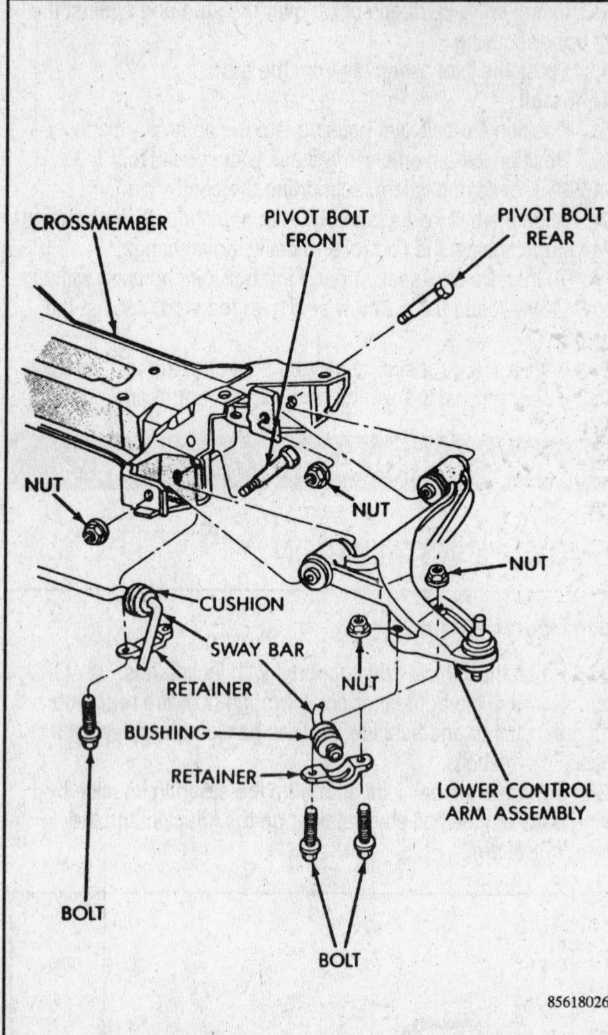

Fig. 26 Lower ball control arm installation — 1991-95 models

**WARNING

Pulling the steering knuckle out from the vehicle after releasing it from the ball joint can separate the inner CV-joint.

4. Remove the sway bar-to-control arm nut and reinforcement, then rotate the control arm over the sway bar. Remove the rear stub strut bushing, sleeve and retainer. Remove the control arm.

To install:

The substitution of fasteners other than those of the grade originally used is not recommended.

5. Install the retainer, bushing and sleeve on the stub strut.
6. Position the control arm over the sway bar, then install the rear stub strut and front pivot into the crossmember.
7. Install the front pivot bolt and loosely install the nut.
8. Install the stub strut bushing retainer, then loosely assemble the nut.
9. Position the sway bar bracket and stud through the control arm, then install the retainer nut. Tighten the nuts to 25 ft. lbs. (34 Nm) on 1984-1989 models, or to 50 ft. lbs. (68 Nm) on 1990-95 models.
10. Install the ball joint stud into the steering knuckle and install the clamp bolt. Tighten the clamp bolt to 70 ft. lbs. (95 Nm) on 1984-89 models or to 105 ft. lbs. (143 Nm) on 1990-95 models.
11. Lower the vehicle, so the weight is on the wheels, then tighten the front pivot bolt to 105 ft. lbs. (143 Nm) on 1984--89 models or to 125 ft. lbs. (170 Nm) on 1990-95 models. Tighten the rear stub strut nut to 70 ft. lbs. (95 Nm).

Pivot Bushing

The front pivot bushing of the lower control arm can be replaced. Remove the control arm and have an automotive machine shop press the old bushing out and the new bushing in.

Sway Bar

See Figures 27 and 28

The sway bar connects the control arms together and attaches to the front crossmember of the vehicle, in this way a bump, jounce or rebound affecting one wheel is partially transmitted to the other wheel to help stabilize body roll. The sway bar is attached to the control arms and crossmember by rubber-isolated bushings. All part are serviceable.

REMOVAL & INSTALLATION

1. Raise and support the front of the vehicle on jackstands.
2. Remove the nuts, bolts and retainers connecting the sway bar to the control arms.
3. Remove the bolts that mount the sway bar to the crossmember. Remove the sway bar and crossmember mounting clamps from the vehicle.
4. Inspect the bushings for wear. Replace as necessary. End bushings are replaced by cutting or driving them from the retainer. Center bushings are split and are removed by opening the split and sliding from the sway bar.
5. Force the new end bushings into the retainers, allowing about $^1/_2$ in. (13mm) to protrude.
6. Install the sway bar.
7. Tighten the center bracket bolts to 25 ft. lbs. (34 Nm) on 1984-89 models, or to 50 ft. lbs. (68 Nm) on 1990-95 models.
8. Place a jack under the control arm and raise the arm to normal ride height.
9. Tighten the outer bracket bolts to 25 ft. lbs. (34 Nm) on 1984-89 models or to 50 ft. lbs. (68 Nm) on 1990-95 models.
10. Lower the vehicle.

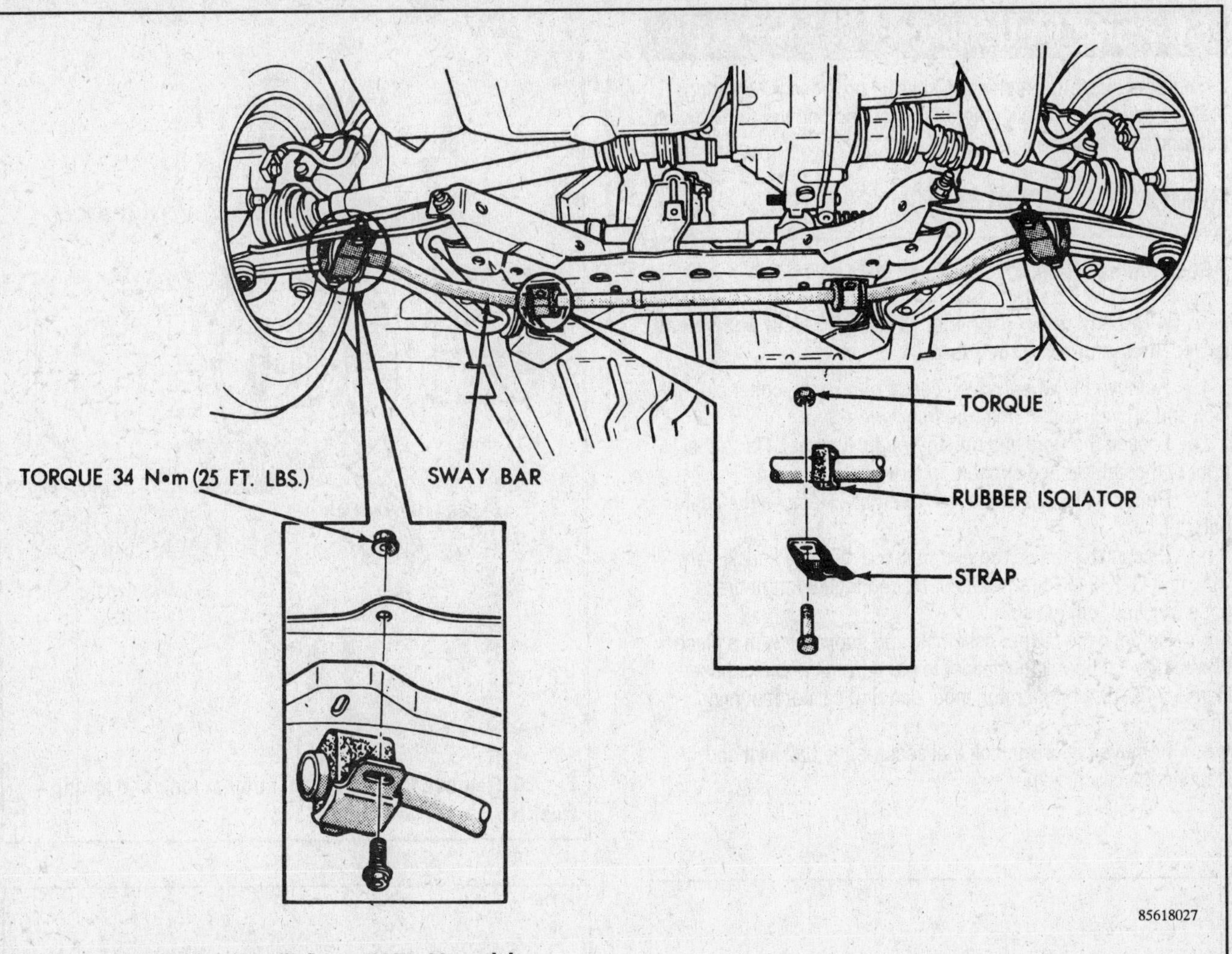

TORQUE 34 N•m (25 FT. LBS.)
SWAY BAR
TORQUE
RUBBER ISOLATOR
STRAP
85618027

Fig. 27 Front sway bar installation — 1984-90 models

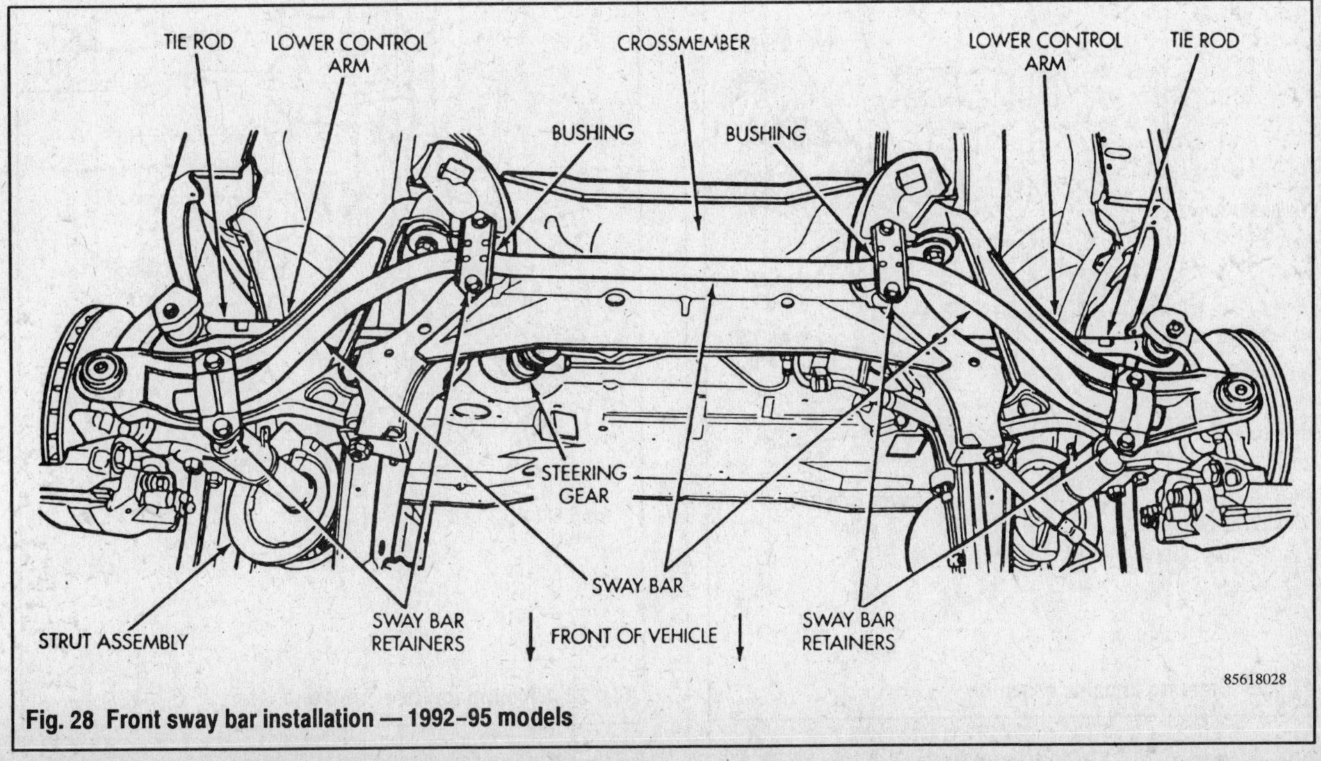

Fig. 28 Front sway bar installation — 1992-95 models

Steering Knuckle

The front suspension steering knuckle provides for steering, braking and front end alignment while supporting the front driving hub and axle assembly.

REMOVAL & INSTALLATION

See Figures 29, 30, 31, 32, 33 and 34

A tie rod end puller (Chrysler Tool C-3894A or equivalent) is necessary for this procedure.

1. Remove the wheel cover, center hub cover, cotter pin, nut lock and spring washer from the front wheel.
2. Loosen the front hub nut and wheel lug nuts. Raise the front of the vehicle and support on jackstands.
3. Remove the wheel and tire assembly. Remove the center hub nut.
4. Disconnect the tie rod end from the steering knuckle arm with Tool C-3894A, or equivalent. Disconnect the front brake hose bracket from the strut.
5. Remove the caliper assembly and support it with a piece of wire. Do not permit the caliper to hang from the brake hose. Remove the disc brake rotor, inner pad and caliper mounting adapter.
6. Remove the clamp bolt that secures the ball joint and steering knuckle together.

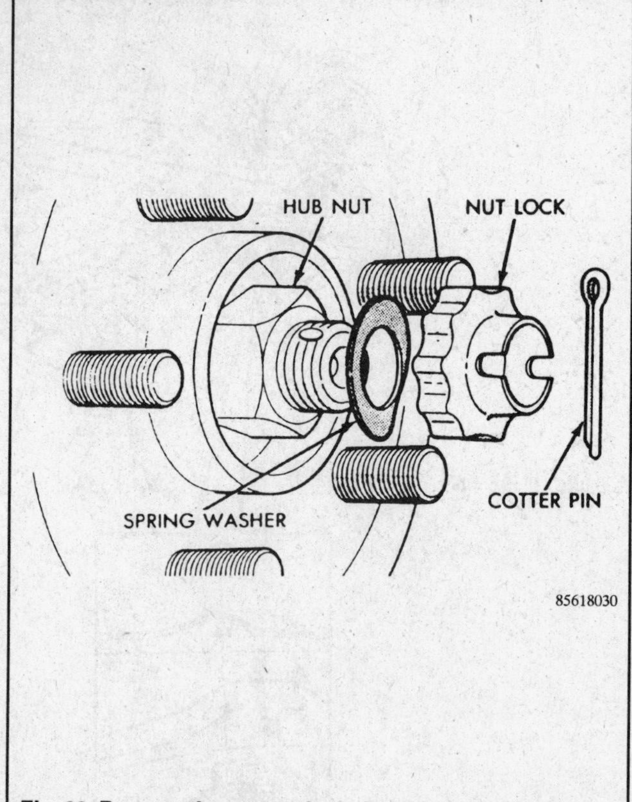

Fig. 30 Remove the cotter pin, hub nut lock and spring washer

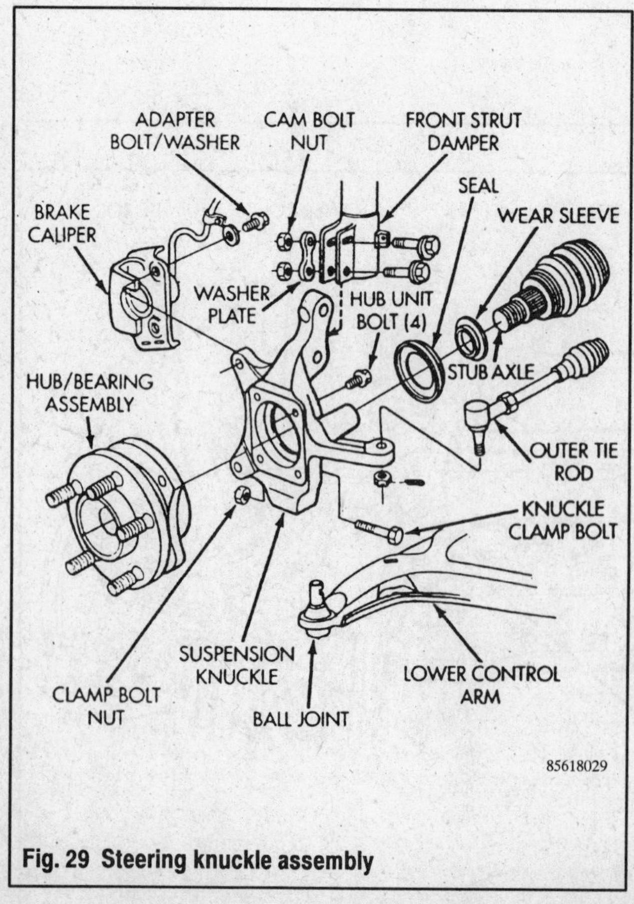

Fig. 29 Steering knuckle assembly

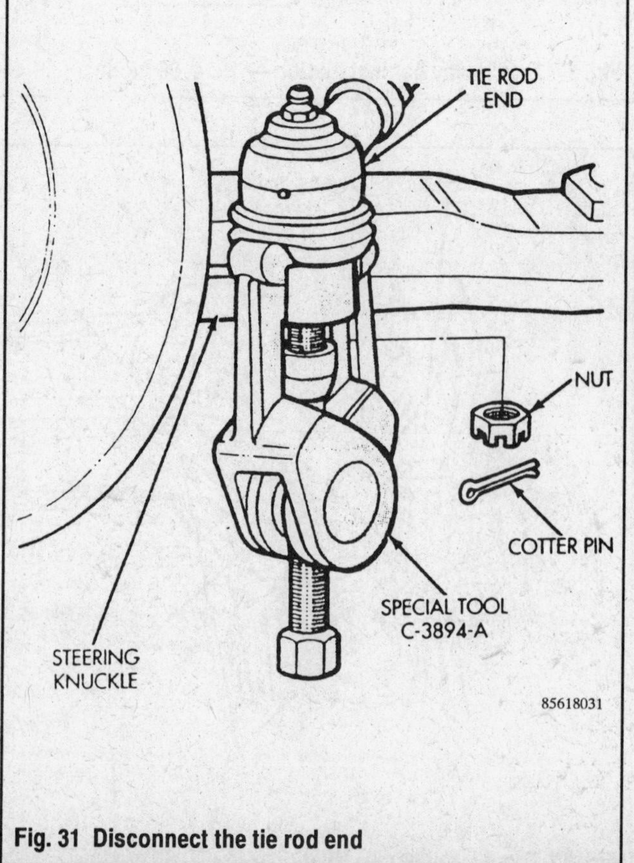

Fig. 31 Disconnect the tie rod end

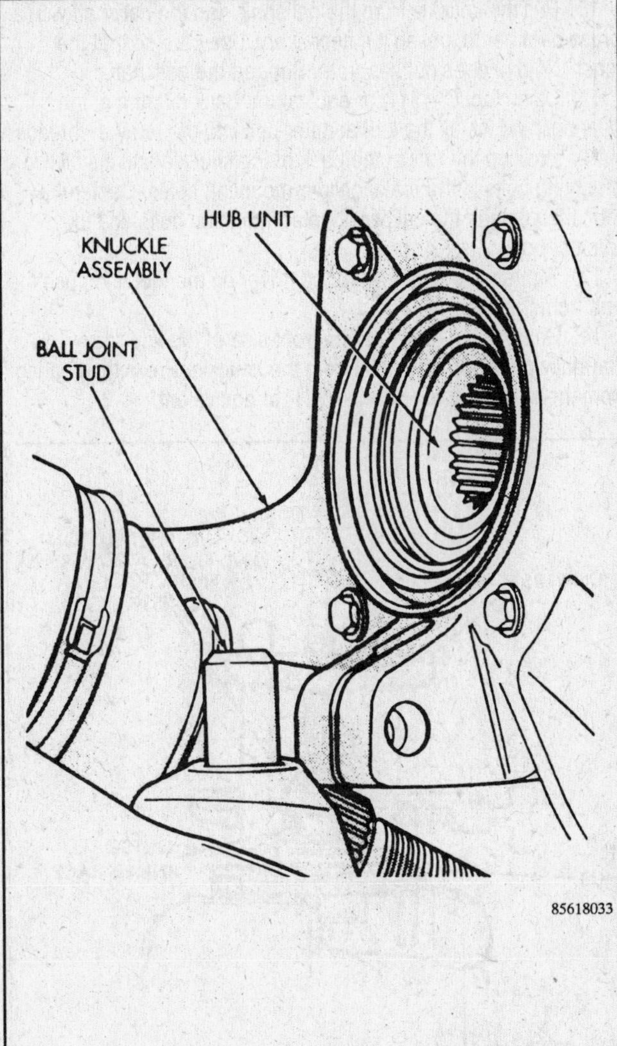

Fig. 32 Separate the ball ball joint stud from the knuckle assembly

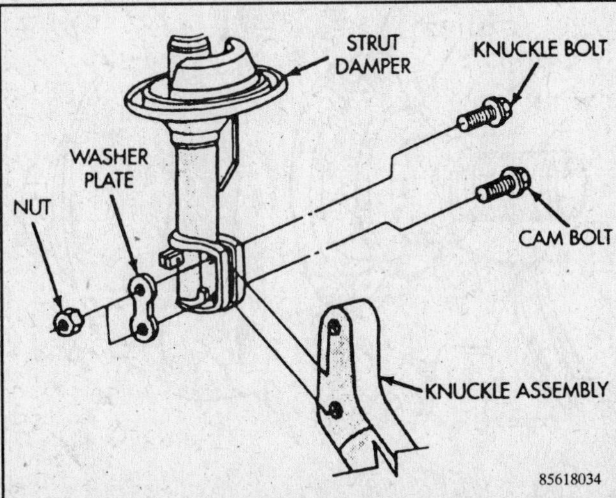

Fig. 33 Remove/install the steering knuckle from the strut assembly

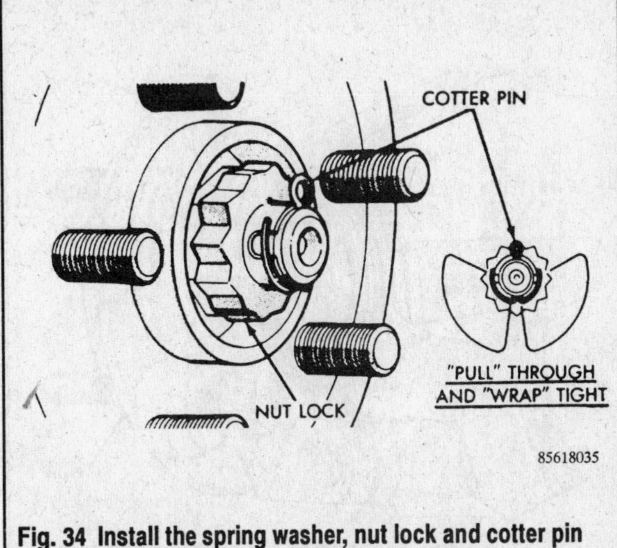

Fig. 34 Install the spring washer, nut lock and cotter pin

7. Insure that the splined halfshaft is loose in the hub by tapping lightly with a brass drift and hammer. Separate the ball joint and steering knuckle. Pull the knuckle assembly out and away from the halfshaft. Remove the steering knuckle from the strut assembly.

To install:

8. Service hub, bearing, seal and steering knuckle as necessary.
9. Install the steering knuckle to the strut assembly. Install the halfshaft through the hub and steering knuckle. Connect the ball joint to the knuckle, then tighten the clamp bolt to 70 ft. lbs. (95 Nm) on 1984–89 models or to 105 ft. lbs (143 Nm) on 1990–95 models.
10. Install the tie rod end, then tighten the retaining nut to 35 ft. lbs. (48 Nm). Install and bend the cotter pin.
11. Install the brake adapter, pads, rotor and caliper. Connect the brake hose bracket to the strut.
12. Install the center hub washer and retaining nut. Have an assistant apply the brakes while you tighten the nut to 180 ft. lbs. (245 Nm).
13. Install the spring washer, nut and new cotter pin.
14. Install the wheel and tire assembly.
15. Tighten the lug nuts to 95 ft. lbs. (130 Nm).
16. Lower the vehicle.

Front Hub and Bearing

REMOVAL & INSTALLATION

Press In Type

See Figures 35, 36, 37, 38, 39 and 40

All 1984–88 models and some 1989–90 eight passenger models use the press-in type front hub and bearing. A special set of tools, C-4811 or the equivalent, is required to remove and install the hub and bearing. If the special tool is not on hand, remove the steering knuckle and take it to an automotive machine shop for bearing replacement.

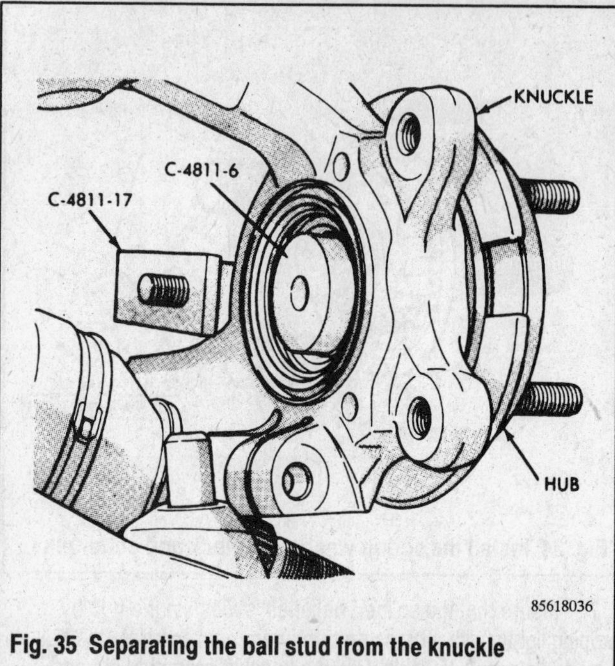

Fig. 35 Separating the ball stud from the knuckle

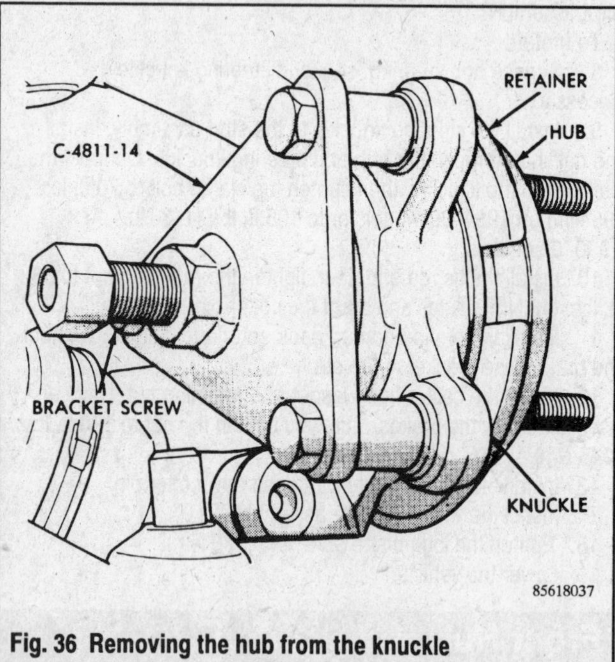

Fig. 36 Removing the hub from the knuckle

1. Remove the cotter pin, nut lock and spring from the front halfshaft hub nut. Loosen the hub nut. Loosen the wheel lug nuts slightly.
2. Raise and safely support the vehicle on jackstands.
3. Remove the wheel assembly.
4. Remove the center hub nut.
5. Disconnect the tie rod end from the steering arm.
6. Disconnect the brake hose from the strut retainer.
7. Remove the ball joint clamp nut.
8. Remove the brake caliper, suspend it with wire so that no strain is put on the brake hose. Remove the disc rotor.
9. Separate the knuckle from the control arm ball joint.
10. Pull the knuckle from the halfshaft. Tap the halfshaft with a brass hammer to loosen it if necessary. Use care so that the inner CV-joint does not separate. Support the halfshaft.
11. Using tool C-4811, or equivalent. Back out one of the bearings and install the tool adapter bolt into the retainer threads.
12. Position the tool at the back of the knuckle and install two mounting bolts in the brake caliper mounting holes. Center the tool, then tighten the caliper adapter mounting bolts and the retainer bolt.
13. Tighten the center threaded driver on the tool and push the hub from the knuckle.
14. Remove the tool from the front side of the knuckle. Carefully pry the grease seal from the knuckle. Press the bearing from the knuckle using tool C-4811, or equivalent.

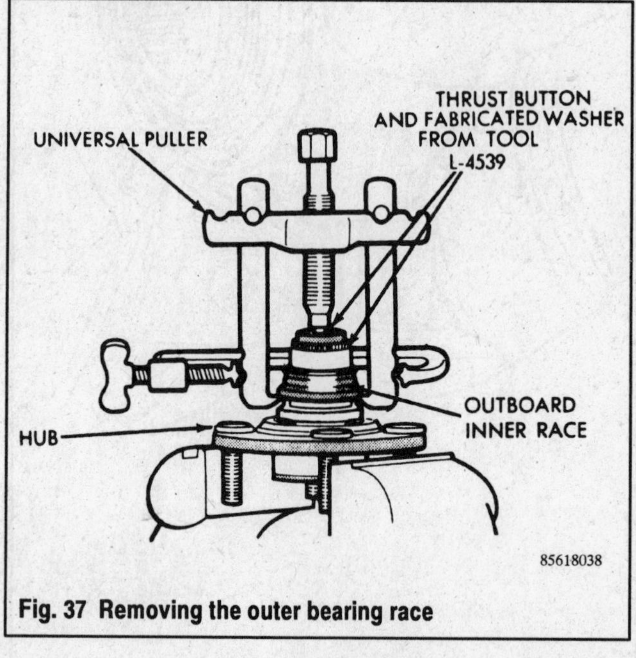

Fig. 37 Removing the outer bearing race

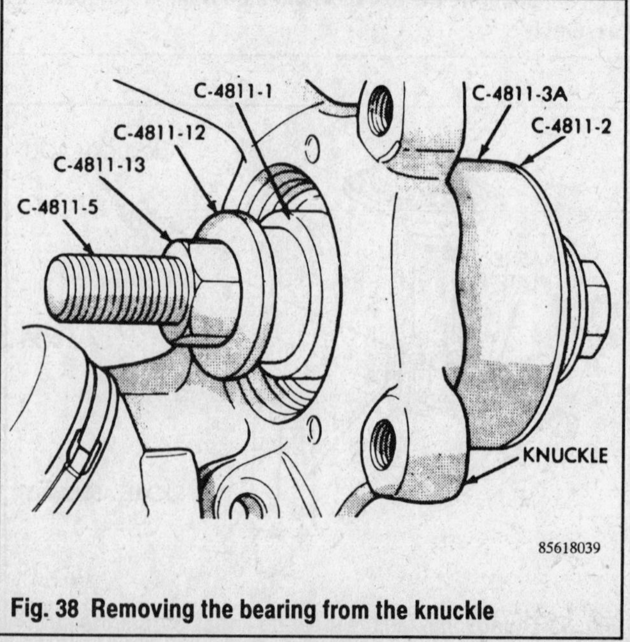

Fig. 38 Removing the bearing from the knuckle

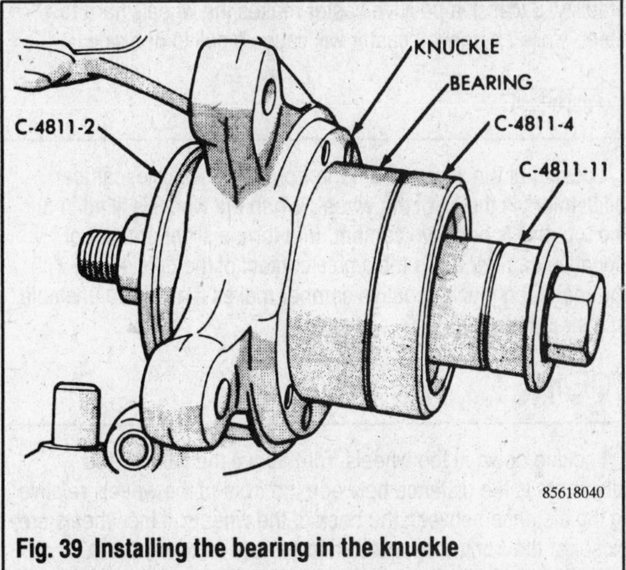

Fig. 39 Installing the bearing in the knuckle

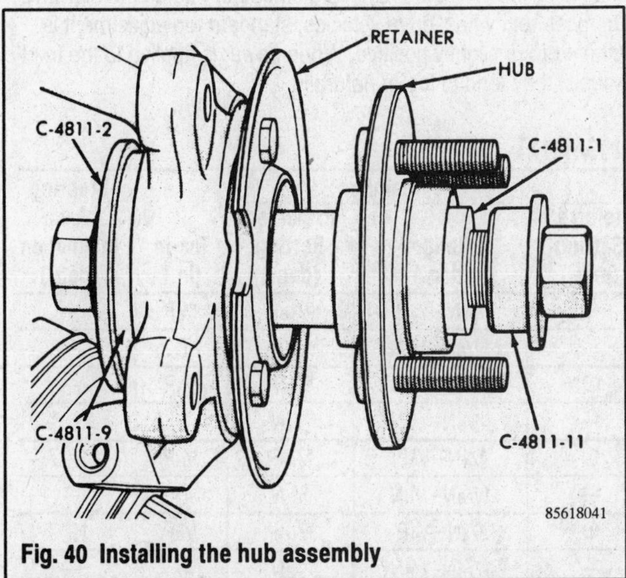

Fig. 40 Installing the hub assembly

To install:

15. Install a new bearing by using the puller adapter of tool C-4811. Install a new seal and lubricate. Install the bearing retainer and bolts, tighten the bolts to 20 ft. lbs. (27 Nm).

16. Press the hub into the bearing. Install a new wear/wipe seal. Install the halfshaft. Attach the ball joint and tie rod end. Install the brake rotor and caliper. Secure the brake hose. Tighten the clamp bolt to 70 ft. lbs. (95 Nm). Tighten the tie rod end nut to 35 ft. lbs. (48 Nm).

17. Install the washer and hub nut. Tighten the nut firmly. Install the wheel assemblies, then tighten the lug nuts firmly.

18. Lower the vehicle. Tighten the center hub nut to 180 ft. lbs. (245 Nm). Tighten the wheel lugs to 95 ft. lbs. (130 Nm).

Bolt-In Type

➧ **See Figure 41**

On some 1989–90 eight-passenger model vehicles and all 1991–95 models, a bolt in knuckle bearing is used. The bearing unit is serviced as a complete assembly. The unit is attached to the steering knuckle by four mounting bolts that are removed through a provided access hole in the hub flange.

1. Loosen the center splined retaining hub nut while the vehicle is on the ground. Loosen the wheel lug nuts slightly.
2. Raise and safely support the vehicle on jackstands.
3. Remove the wheel assembly. Remove the hub nut and washer.

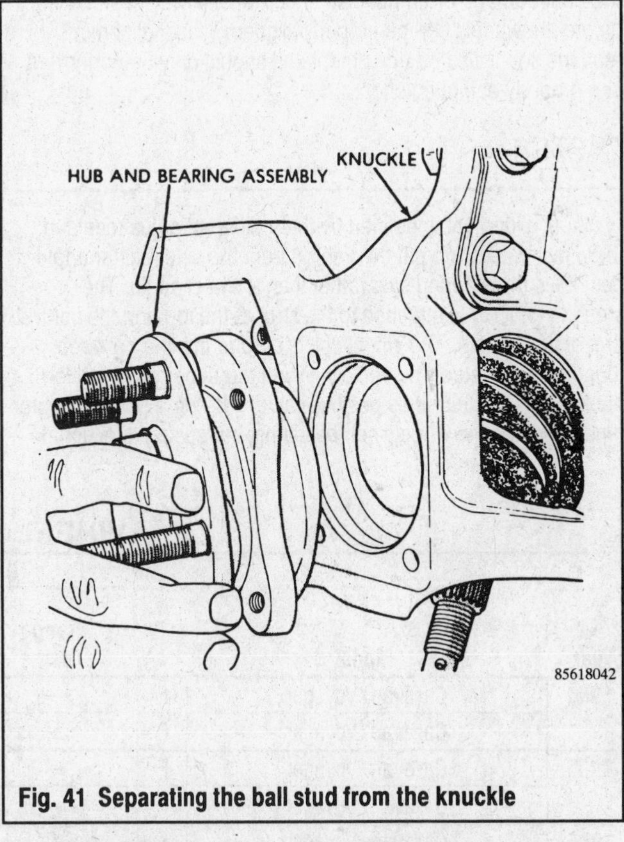

Fig. 41 Separating the ball stud from the knuckle

4. Disconnect the tie rod end from the steering arm and the clamp bolt that retains the ball joint to the knuckle.
5. Remove the disc brake caliper and suspend it with wire so that there is no strain on the brake hose. Remove the rotor.
6. Separate the knuckle from the ball joint. Pull the knuckle assembly away from the halfshaft. Take care not separate the halfshaft inner CV-joint. Support the halfshaft.
7. Remove the four hub and bearing retaining bolts. Remove the assembly.

To install:

8. Install the new bearing assembly, then tighten the mounting bolts in a crisscross manner to 45 ft. lbs. (61 Nm).
9. Install a new wear sleeve seal. Lubricate the sealing surfaces with multi-purpose grease. Install the halfshaft through the hub.
10. Install the steering knuckle onto the lower control arm. Tighten the clamp bolt to 70 ft. lbs. (95 Nm) on 1984–89 models or to 105 ft. lbs. (143 Nm) on 1990–91 models.
11. Install the tie rod end. Tighten the nut to 35 ft. lbs. (48 Nm). Install the brake disc rotor and caliper assembly.
12. Install and tighten the hub nut reasonably tight. Install the wheel assembly, tighten the lug nuts fairly tight.
13. Lower the vehicle, then tighten the hub nut to 180 ft. lbs. (245 Nm) and the wheel lugs to 95 ft. lbs. (130 Nm).

Front End Alignment

If the tires are worn unevenly, if the vehicle is not stable on the highway or if the handling seems uneven in spirited driving, wheel alignment should be checked. If an alignment problem is suspected, first check tire inflation and look for other possible causes such as worn suspension and steering components, accident damage or unmatched tires. Repairs may be necessary before the wheels can be properly aligned. Wheel alignment requires sophisticated equipment and should only be performed at a properly equipped shop.

CASTER

Wheel alignment is defined by three different adjustments in three planes. Looking at the vehicle from the side, caster angle describes the steering axis rather than a wheel angle. The steering knuckle is attached to the strut at the top and the control arm at the bottom. The wheel pivots around the line between these points to steer the vehicle. When the upper point is tilted back, this is described as positive caster. Having a positive caster tends to make the wheels self-centering, increasing directional stability. Excessive positive caster makes the wheels hard to steer, while an uneven caster will cause a pull to one side.

CAMBER

Looking at the wheels from the front of the vehicle, camber adjustment is the tilt of the wheel. When the wheel is tilted in at the top, this is negative camber. In a turn, a slight amount of negative camber helps maximize contact of the outside tire with the road. Too much negative camber makes the vehicle unstable in a straight line.

TOE-IN

Looking down at the wheels from above the vehicle, toe alignment is the distance between the front of the wheels relative to the distance between the back of the wheels. If the wheels are closer at the front, they are said to be toed-in or to have a negative toe. A small amount of negative toe enhances directional stability and provides a smoother ride on the highway. On most front wheel drive vehicles, standard toe adjustment is either zero or slightly positive. When power is applied to the front wheels, they tend to toe-in naturally.

WHEEL ALIGNMENT

Year	Model		Caster Range (deg.)	Caster Preferred Setting (deg.)	Camber Range (deg.)	Camber Preferred Setting (deg.)	Toe-in (in.)	Steering Axis Inclination (deg.)
1984	Caravan/Voyager	F	—	①	1/4N–3/4P	5/16P	1/8P	—
	Caravan/Voyager	R	—	—	1 1/8N–1/8N	1/2N	0	—
1985	Caravan/Voyager	F	—	①	1/4N–3/4P	5/16P	1/8P	—
	Caravan/Voyager	R	—	—	1 1/8N–1/8N	1/2N	0	—
1986	Caravan/Voyager	F	—	①	1/4N–3/4P	5/16P	1/8P	12.7
	Caravan/Voyager	R	—	—	1 1/8N–1/8N	1/2N	0	—
1987	Caravan/Voyager	F	—	①	1/4N–3/4P	5/16P	1/8P	12.7
	Caravan/Voyager	R	—	—	1 1/8N–1/8N	1/2N	0	—
1988	Caravan/Voyager	F	—	①	1/4N–3/4P	5/16P	1/8P	12.7
	Caravan/Voyager	R	—	—	1N–1/2P	0	0	—
1989	Caravan/Voyager	F	—	①	1/4N–3/4P	5/16P	1/8P	12.7
	Caravan/Voyager	R	—	—	1N–1/2P	0	0	—
1990	Caravan/Voyager	F	—	①	1/4N–3/4P	5/16P	1/8P	12.7
	Caravan/Voyager	R	—	—	1N–1/2P	0	0	—
1991	Caravan/Voyager/Town & Country	F	—	1 1/16P	1/4N–3/4P	5/16P	1/8P	12.2
	Caravan/Voyager/Town & Country	R	—	—	1N–1/2P	0	0	—
1992	Caravan/Voyager/Town & Country	F	—	1 5/16P	1/8N–3/4P	5/16P	1/16P	12.2
	Caravan/Voyager/Town & Country	R	—	—	13/16N–7/16P	1/4P	0	—
1993	Caravan/Voyager/Town & Country	F	—	1 5/16P	1/4N–1P	3/4P	1/16P	12.2
	Caravan/Voyager/Town & Country	R	—	—	13/16N–7/16P	1/4P	0	—
1994	Caravan/Voyager/Town & Country	F	—	1 5/16P	1/4N–3/4P	5/16P	1/16P	NA
	Caravan/Voyager/Town & Country	R	—	—	13/16N–7/16P	1/4P	0	NA
1995	Caravan/Voyager/Town & Country	F	—	1 5/16P	1/4N–3/4P	5/16P	1/16P	NA
	Caravan/Voyager/Town & Country	R	—	—	13/16N–7/16P	1/4P	0	NA

① Van: 7/16P; Wagon: 1 11/16P

85618C01

REAR SUSPENSION

General Information

➧ See Figures 42, 43 and 44

The rear suspension consists of a tube and casting axle, shock absorbers and leaf springs. Stub axles are mounted to the axle and spring by U-bolts. It is possible to align both the camber and toe of the rear wheels.

The rear leaf springs are mounted by shackles and a fixed end bushing. the shackle angles have been selected to provide increasing suspension rates as the vehicle is loaded. These angles provide a comfortable unloaded ride and ample suspension travel when the vehicle is loaded.

The rear shock absorbers are mounted at an angle, forward at the top and parallel to the springs. Greater stability and ride control are provided by this design.

****WARNING**

Do not install after market load leveling devices, air shocks or helper springs on your vehicle. These devices will cause the rear brake height sensing valve to adjust for a lighter load than is actually being carried.

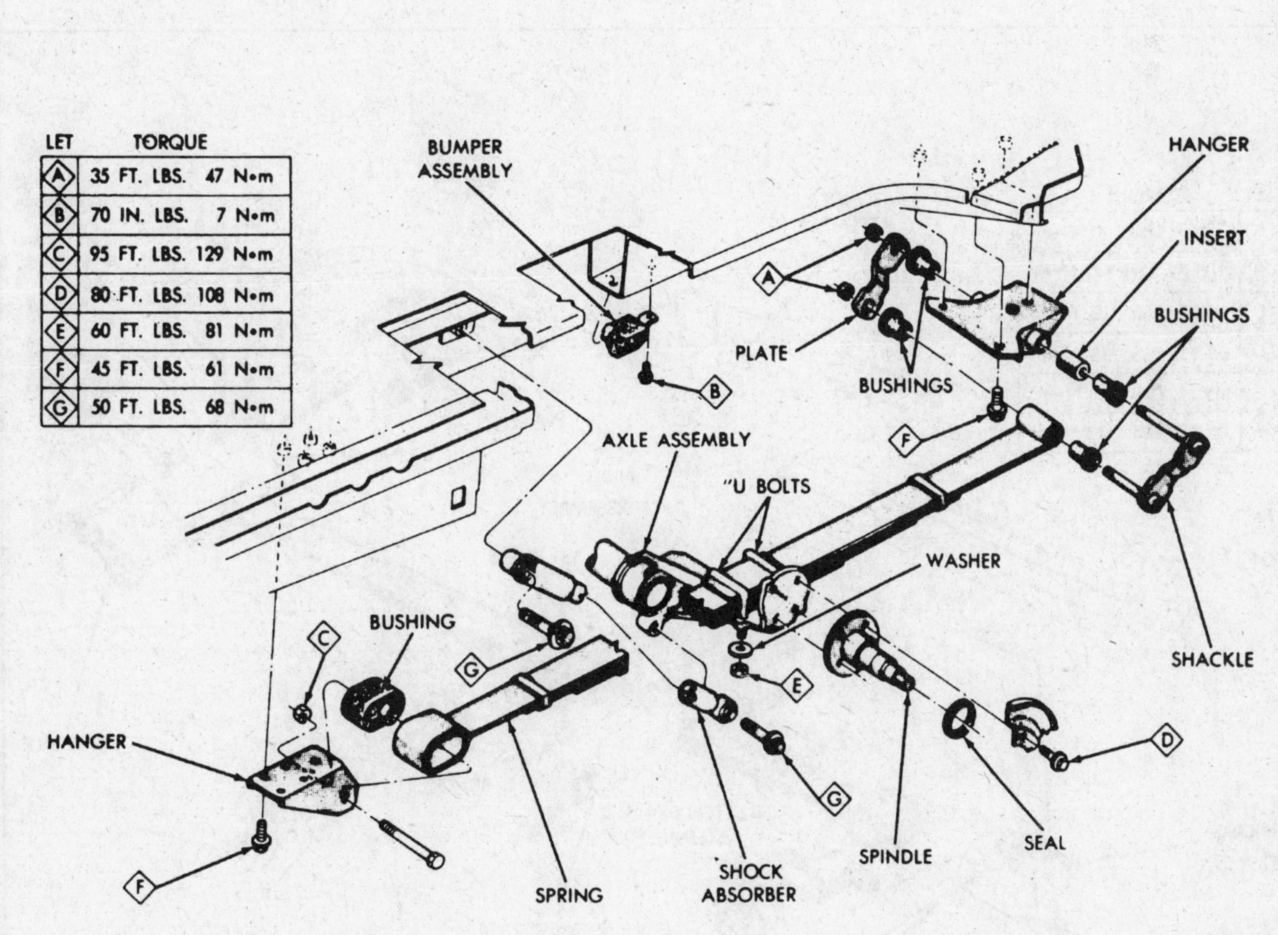

Fig. 42 Rear suspension components — 1984–88 models

Rear Springs

REMOVAL & INSTALLATION

Front Wheel Drive Models

➧ See Figures 42 and 43

1. Raise and support the rear of the vehicle on jackstands. Locate the jackstands under the frame contact points just ahead of the rear spring fixed ends.
2. Raise the rear axle just enough to relieve the weight on the springs and support on jackstands.
3. Disconnect the rear brake proportioning valve spring. Disconnect the lower ends of the shock absorbers at the rear axle bracket.
4. Loosen and remove the nuts from the U-bolts. Remove the washer and U-bolts.
5. Lower the rear axle assembly to permit the rear springs to hang free. Support the spring and remove the four bolts that mount the fixed end spring bracket. Remove the rear spring shackle nuts and plate. Remove the shackle from the spring.
6. Remove the spring. Remove the fixed end mounting bolts from the bracket and remove the bracket. Remove the front pivot bolt from the front spring hanger.

To install:

7. Install the spring on the rear shackle and hanger. Start the shackle nuts but do not completely tighten.
8. Assembly the front spring hanger on the spring. Raise the front of the spring and install the four mounting bolts. Tighten the mounting bolts to 45 ft. lbs. (61 Nm).
9. Raise the axle assembly and align the spring center bolts in correct position. Install the mounting U-bolts. Tighten the nuts to 60 ft. lbs. (82 Nm).
10. Install the rear shock absorber to the lower brackets.
11. Lower the vehicle to the ground so that the full weight is on the springs. Tighten the mounting components as follows: Front fixed end bolt, 95 ft. lbs. (130 Nm); Shackle nuts, 35 ft. lbs. (48 Nm); Shock absorber bolts, 50 ft. lbs. (68 Nm).
12. Raise and support the vehicle. Connect the brake valve spring and adjust the valve.

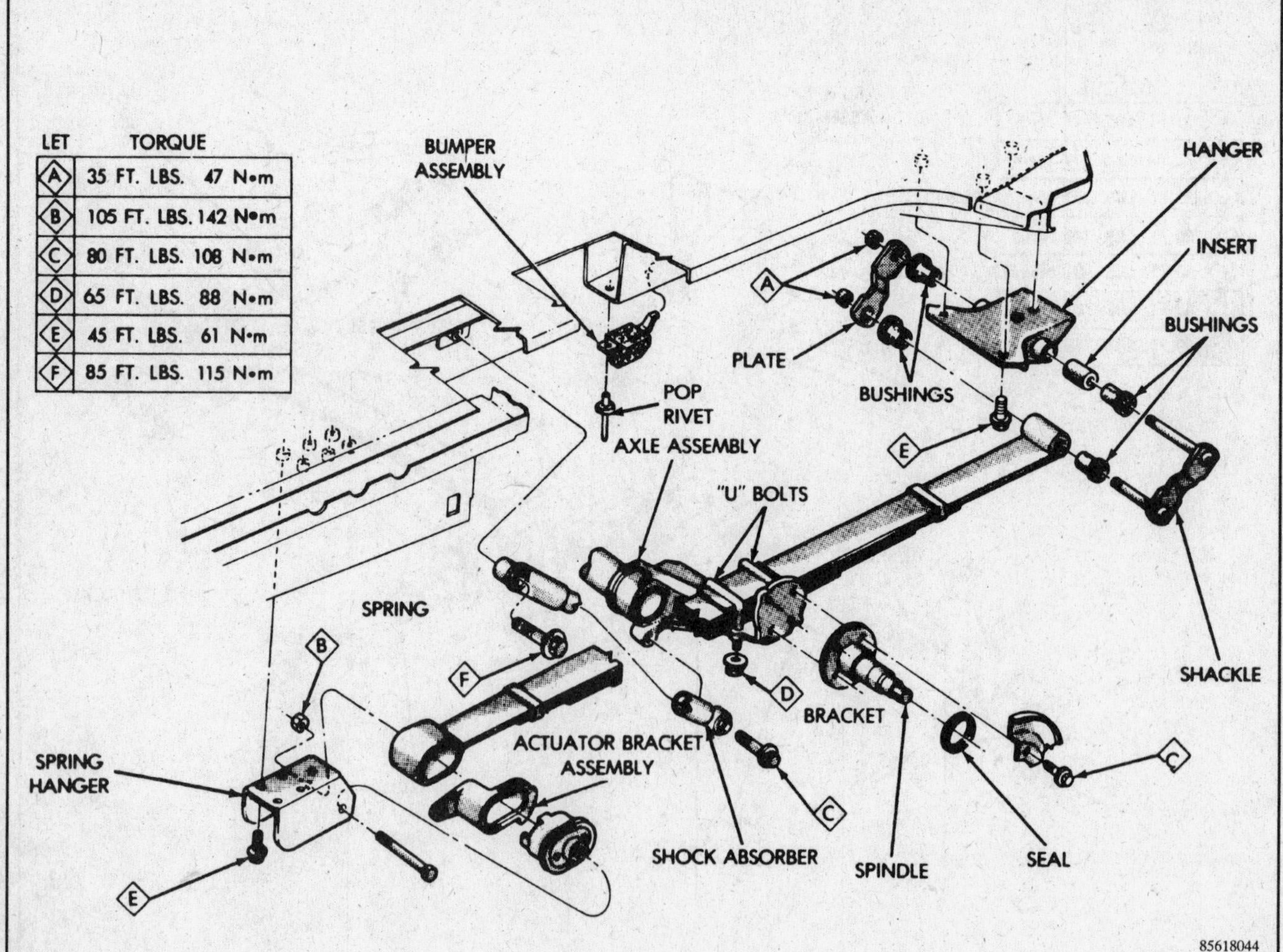

LET	TORQUE
A	35 FT. LBS. 47 N•m
B	105 FT. LBS. 142 N•m
C	80 FT. LBS. 108 N•m
D	65 FT. LBS. 88 N•m
E	45 FT. LBS. 61 N•m
F	85 FT. LBS. 115 N•m

Fig. 43 Rear suspension components — 1989–95 models (Except AWD models)

All Wheel Drive Models

➧ See Figure 44

1. Raise and support the rear of the vehicle on jackstands. Locate the jackstands under the chassis, ahead of the springs.
2. Raise the rear axle just enough to relieve the weight on the springs and support on jackstands.
3. Disconnect the rear brake proportioning valve spring. Disconnect the lower ends of the shock absorbers at the rear axle bracket.
4. Loosen and remove the nuts from the U-bolts. Remove the washer and U-bolts.
5. Lower the rear axle assembly to permit the rear springs to hang free. Support the spring and remove the four bolts that mount the fixed end spring bracket. Remove the rear spring shackle nuts and plate. Remove the shackle from the spring.
6. Remove the spring. Remove the fixed end mounting bolts from the bracket and remove the bracket. Remove the front pivot bolt from the front spring hanger.
7. Separate the rear shackle plate from the shackle and pin assembly. Remove the shackle and pin assembly from the spring.

To install:

8. Assemble the shackle and pin assembly, bushing and shackle plate on rear of spring and spring hanger. Start the shackle and pin assembly through bolts, do not tighten.
9. Assemble the front spring hanger to the front of the spring eye and install pivot bolt and nut. Do not tighten.

➥ Pivot bolt must installed inboard to prevent structural damage during spring installation.

10. Raise the front of the spring into position and install the 4 hanger bolts, tighten them to 45 ft. lbs. (61 Nm). Connect the actuator assembly for the proportioning valve.
11. Raise the axle assembly into position, centered under the spring center bolt.
12. Install the U-bolts, nuts and washers. Tighten the U-bolt nuts to 65 ft. lbs. (88 Nm).
13. Install the shock absorbers and start the bolts.

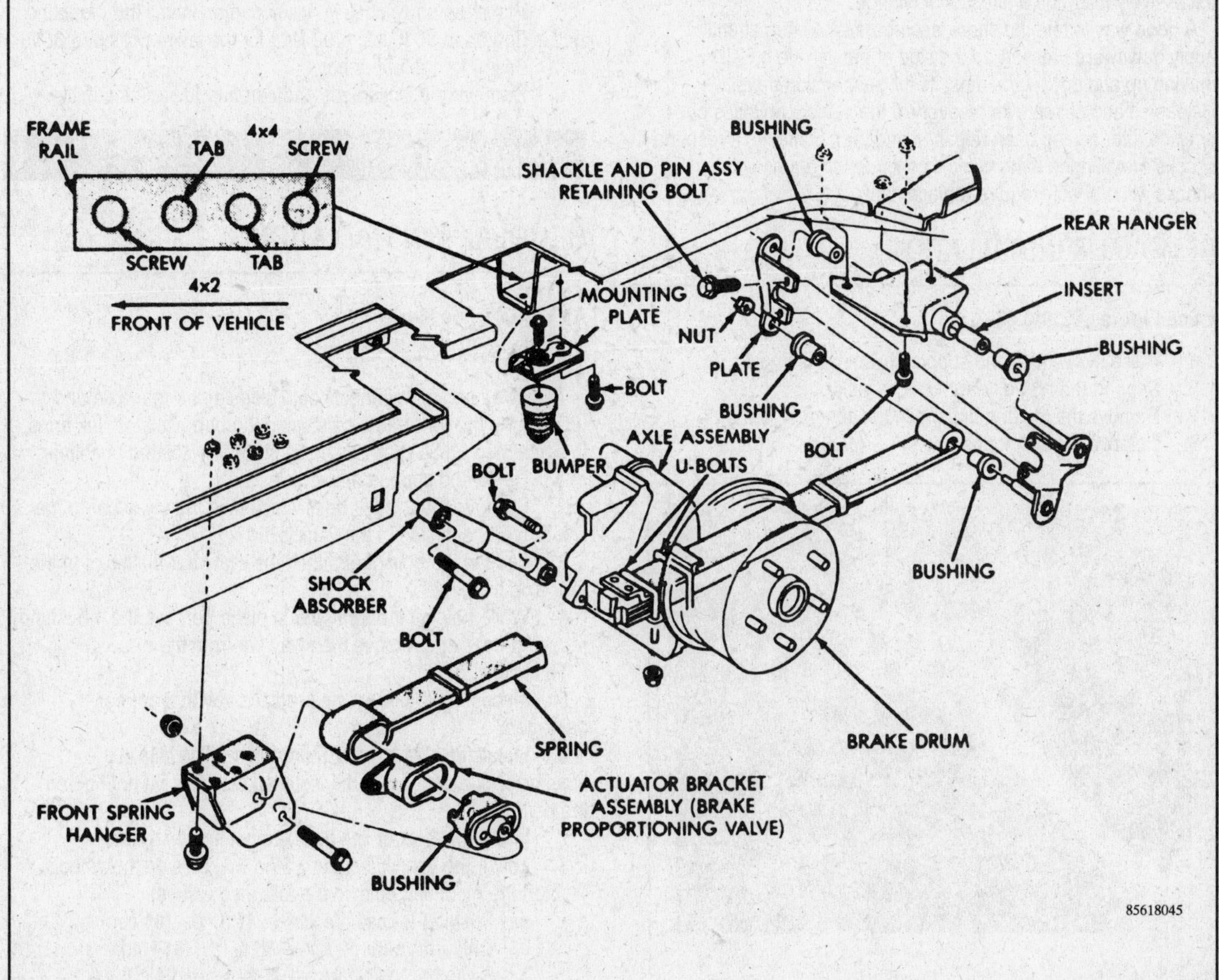

Fig. 44 Rear suspension components — 1991–95 (AWD models)

14. Lower the vehicle to the ground, with the full weight of the vehicle on the wheels. Tighten all of the fasteners in the following sequence and to the listed values:
   a. Front pivot bolts — 105 ft. lbs. (143 Nm)
   b. Shackle and pin assembly through-bolt nuts — 35 ft. lbs. (48 Nm)
   c. Shackle and pin assembly retaining bolts — 35 ft. lbs. (48 Nm)
   d. Shock absorber upper bolts — 85 ft. lbs. (116 Nm)
   e. Shock absorber lower bolts — 80 ft. lbs. (109 Nm)

15. Raise the vehicle and connect the rear brake proportioning valve spring.

Shock Absorbers

TESTING

Shock absorbers require replacement if the vehicle fails to recover quickly after hitting a large bump or if it sways excessively following a directional change.

A good way to test the shock absorbers is to intermittently apply downward pressure to the side of the vehicle until it is moving up and down for almost its full suspension travel. Release it and observe its recovery. If the vehicle bounces once or twice after having been released and then comes to a rest, the shocks are all right. If the vehicle continues to bounce, the shocks will probably require replacement.

REMOVAL & INSTALLATION

➧ See Figures 45 and 46

1. Raise the vehicle and support it with jackstands.
2. Support the rear axle with a floor jack.
3. Remove the top and bottom shock absorber bolts.
4. Remove the shock absorbers.

85618046

Fig. 45 Removing the top shock absorber retaining bolt

85618047

Fig. 46 Removing the bottom shock absorber retaining bolt

To install:

5. Place the new shock in position, then install the mounting bolts. Tighten to 80 ft. lbs. (109 Nm) for the lower bolts and 85 ft. lbs (116 Nm) for the upper bolts.
6. Remove the jackstands and carefully lower the vehicle.

Sway Bar

REMOVAL & INSTALLATION

All Wheel Drive Models

➧ See Figures 47 and 48

The sway bar interconnects both sides of the rear axle and attaches to the rear frame rails using 2 rubber isolated link arms. It is attached to the rear axle through rubber isolated bushings.

1. Raise and support the vehicle.
2. Remove the 2 lower bolts which hold the sway bar to the link arm on each side of the vehicle.
3. Loosen the bolts that attach the sway bar bushings to the rear axle housing.
4. While holding the sway bar in place, remove the 4 bushing retaining bolts and remove the sway bar from the axle.

To install:

5. Inspect the bushings and replace any that appear damaged.
6. Install the sway bar to the rear axle. The slits in the bushing should face up in the installed position. Do not tighten the bolts.
7. Install the 2 lower link bolts, do not tighten these.
8. Lower the vehicle so that all the weight is on the wheels. Tighten the mounting bolts to the following values:
   a. Bushing-to-axle bracket — 45 ft. lbs. (61 Nm)
   b. Link arm-to-frame rail — 45 ft. lbs. (61 Nm)
   c. Sway bar-to-link arm — 45 ft. lbs. (61 Nm)
   d. Link arm bracket-to-frame rail — 24 ft. lbs. (32 Nm)

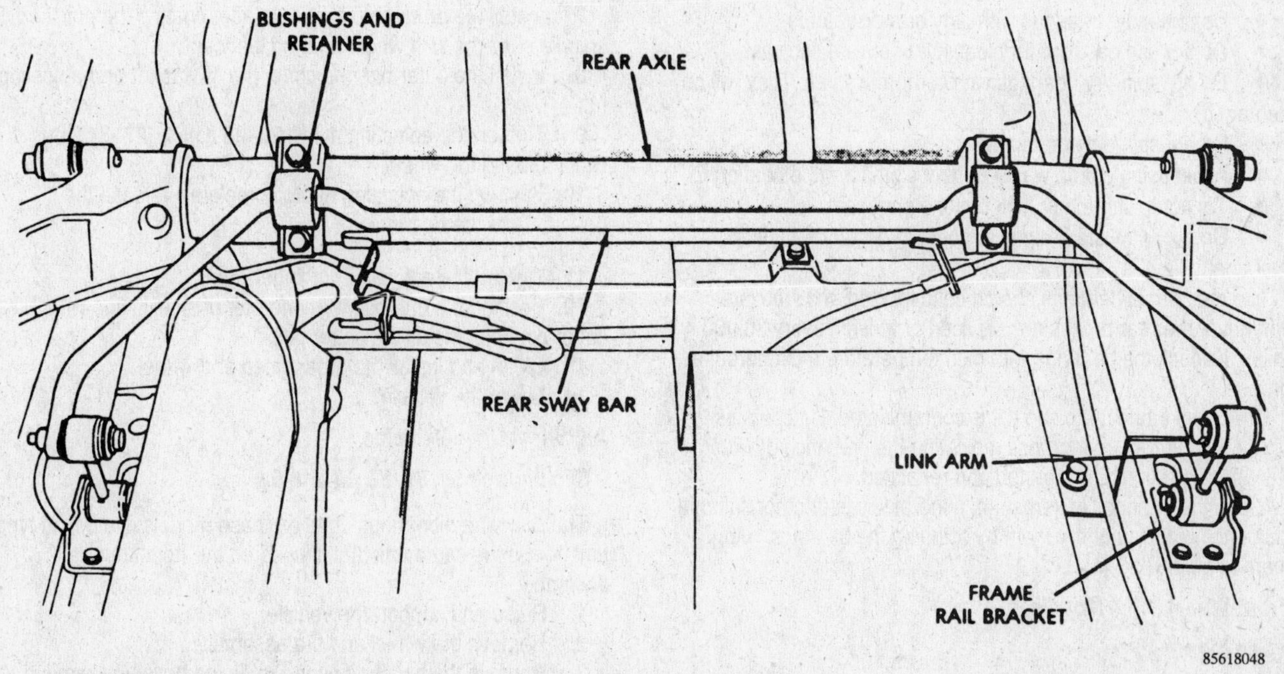

Fig. 47 Rear sway bar mounting — all wheel drive models

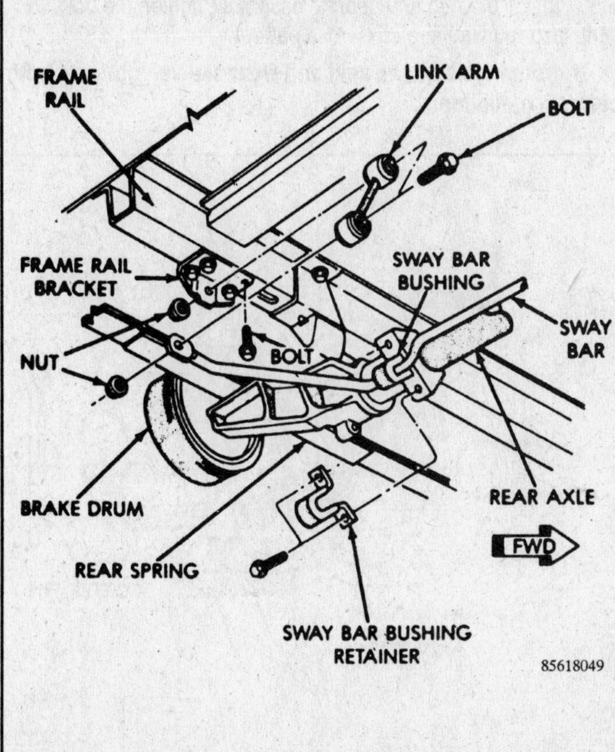

Fig. 48 Rear sway bar removal and installation — all wheel drive models

Rear Wheel Bearings

SERVICING

➔ Sodium-based grease is not compatible with lithium-based grease. Read the package labels and be careful not to mix the two types. If there is any doubt as to the type of grease used, completely clean the old grease from the bearing and hub before replacing.

Before handling the bearings, there are a few things that you should remember to do and not to do.

Remember to DO the following:

- Remove all outside dirt from the housing before exposing the bearing.
- Treat a used bearing as gently as you would a new one.
- Work with clean tools in clean surroundings.
- Use clean, dry canvas gloves, or at least clean, dry hands.
- Clean solvents and flushing fluids are a must.
- Use clean paper when laying out the bearings to dry.
- Protect disassembled bearings from rust and dirt. Cover them up.
- Use clean rags to wipe bearings.
- Keep the bearings in oil-proof paper when they are to be stored or are not in use.
- Clean the inside of the housing before replacing the bearing.

Do NOT do the following:

- Don't work in dirty surroundings.
- Don't use dirty, chipped or damaged tools.
- Try not to work on wooden work benches or use wooden mallets.
- Don't handle bearings with dirty or moist hands.
- Do not use gasoline for cleaning; use a safe solvent.
- Do not spin-dry bearings with compressed air. They will be damaged.
- Do not spin dirty bearings.
- Avoid using cotton waste or dirty cloths to wipe bearings.
- Try not to scratch or nick bearing surfaces.
- Do not allow the bearing to come in contact with dirt or rust at any time.

The rear wheel bearings should be inspected and lubricated whenever the rear brakes are serviced or at least every 30,000 miles. Repack the bearings with high temperature multi-purpose grease.

Check the lubricant to see if it is contaminated. If it contains dirt or has a milky appearance indicating the presence of water, the bearings should be cleaned and repacked.

Clean the bearings in kerosene, mineral spirits or other suitable cleaning fluid. Do not dry them by spinning the bearings. Allow them to air dry.

Front Wheel Drive Models

➧ See Figure 49

1. Raise and support the vehicle with the rear wheels off the floor.
2. Remove the wheel grease cap, cotter pin, nut-lock and bearing adjusting nut.
3. Remove the thrust washer and bearing.
4. Remove the drum from the spindle.
5. Thoroughly clean the old lubricant from the bearings and hub cavity. Inspect the bearing rollers for pitting or other signs of wear. Light discoloration is normal.

To install:

6. Repack the bearings with high temperature multi-purpose EP grease and add a small amount of new grease to the hub cavity. Be sure to force the lubricant between all rollers in the bearing.
7. Install the drum on the spindle after coating the polished spindle surfaces with wheel bearing lubricant.
8. Install the outer bearing cone, thrust washer and adjusting nut.
9. Tighten the adjusting nut to 20–25 ft. lbs. (27–34 Nm) while rotating the wheel.
10. Back off the adjusting nut to completely release the preload from the bearing.
11. Tighten the adjusting nut finger-tight.
12. Position the nut-lock with one pair of slots in line with the cotter pin hole. Install the cotter pin.
13. Clean and install the grease cap and wheel.
14. Lower the vehicle.

All Wheel Drive Vehicles

➧ See Figures 50, 51, 52, 53 and 54

The rear wheel bearings used on these models is a bolt in type unit, this is the same unit that is used on the front knuckle assembly.

1. Raise and support the vehicle.
2. Remove the wheel and tire assembly.
3. Remove the halfshaft flange retaining bolts and remove the halfshaft assembly.
4. Remove the wheel bearing mounting bolts and remove the wheel bearing and hub assembly.

To install:

5. Install the hub and bearing assembly, tighten the bolts to 96 ft. lbs (130 Nm) in a crisscross pattern.

➥ Thoroughly clean the seal and wear sleeve, lubricate both before installation.

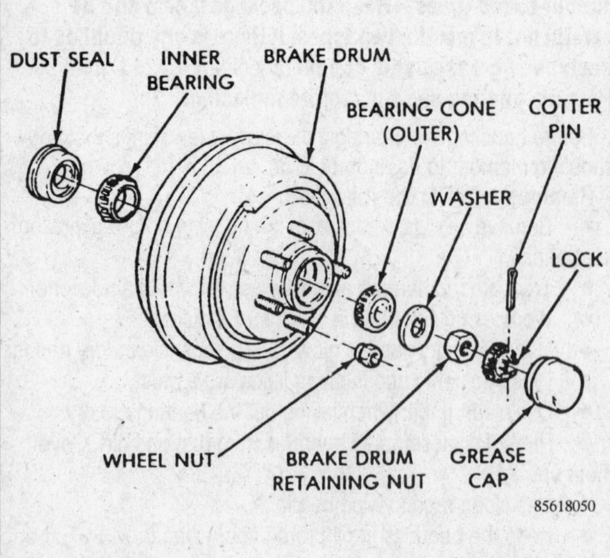

Fig. 49 Rear brake drum and bearings — front wheel drive models

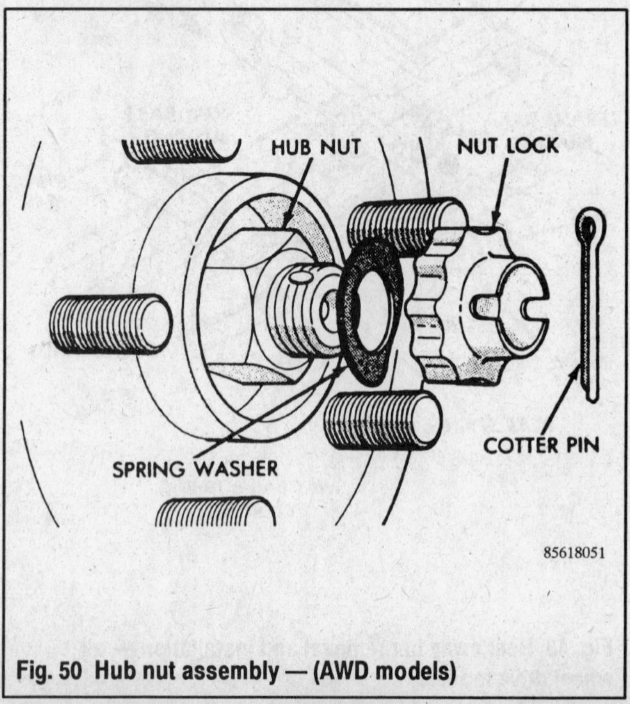

Fig. 50 Hub nut assembly — (AWD models)

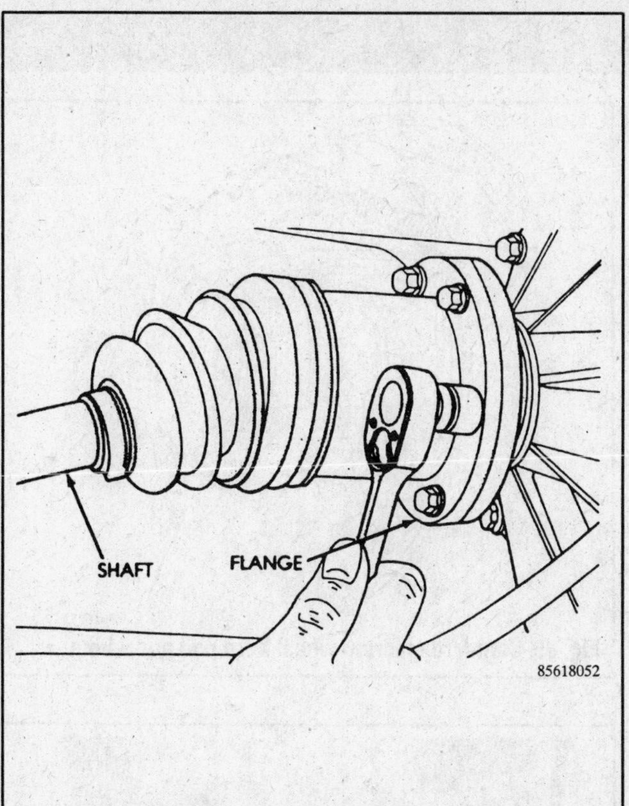

Fig. 51 Half shaft flange retaining bolts — (AWD models)

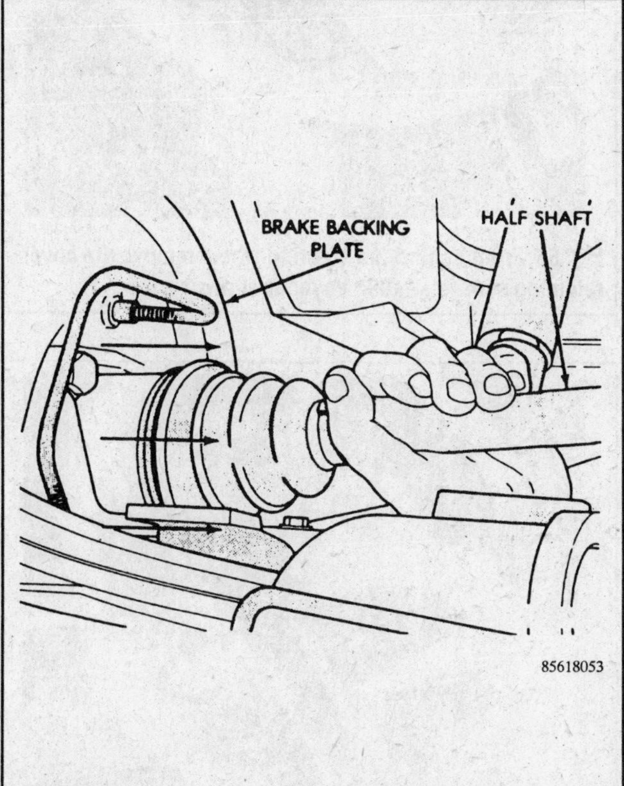

Fig. 52 Half shaft removal — (AWD models)

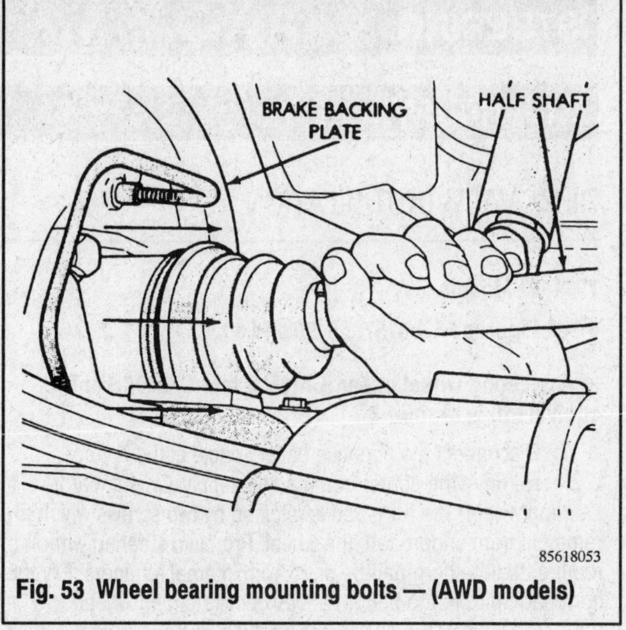

Fig. 53 Wheel bearing mounting bolts — (AWD models)

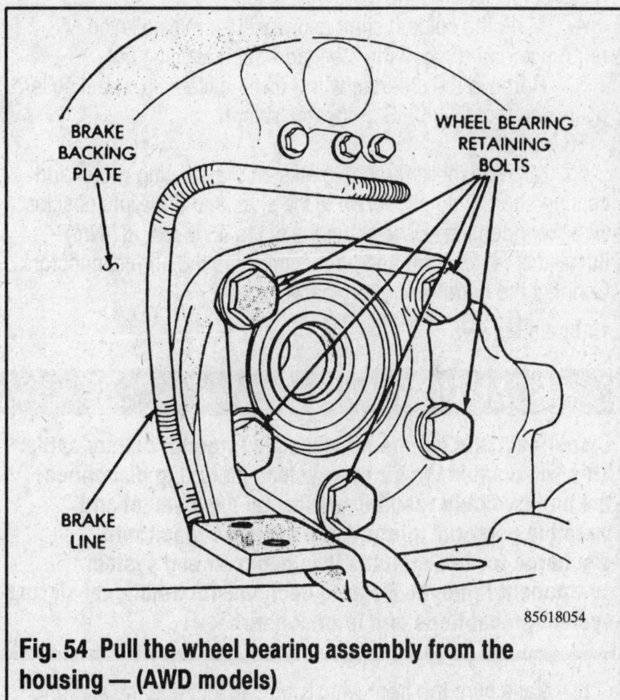

Fig. 54 Pull the wheel bearing assembly from the housing — (AWD models)

6. Install the halfshaft.
7. Install the washer and hub nut, with the brakes applied tighten the nut to 180 ft. lbs. (245 Nm).
8. Install the spring washer, nut lock and new cotter pin.
9. Install the wheel and tire assembly.

Rear Axle Alignment

Camber and Toe adjustment are possible through the use of shims. Shims are added or subtracted between the spindle mounting surface and the axle mounting plate. Each shim equals a wheel angle change of 0.3° (degree).

STEERING

Steering Wheel

REMOVAL & INSTALLATION

1984–91 Models

See Figures 55, 56, 57, 58, 59 and 60

A steering wheel puller (Chrysler tool C–3428B or the equivalent) is required.

1. Disconnect the negative battery cable at the battery.
2. Remove the center horn pad assembly. On standard steering wheels the horn pad is retained by two screws which are removed from underneath the wheel. Premium steering wheels require that the horn pad be pried from internal retainers. Pry the horn pad up from the bottom edges of the steering wheel.
3. Disconnect the horn wires from the center pad, if necessary. Remove the pad.
4. Mark the column shaft and wheel for reinstallation reference and remove the steering wheel retaining nut.
5. Remove the steering wheel using a steering wheel puller (Chrysler Tool C–3428B or the equivalent).

To install:

6. Align up the reference marks on the steering wheel and column shaft. Push wheel on to the shaft and draw into position with the mounting nut. Tighten the nut to 45 ft. lbs. (61 Nm). Install the center horn pad after connecting the horn connectors. Connect the negative battery cable.

1992–95 Models

****CAUTION**

Disconnect and isolate the negative (ground) battery cable. This will disable the air bag system. Failure to disconnect the battery could result in accidental deployment and possible personal injury. Allow system capacitor to discharge for two minutes then begin air bag system component removal. Refer to Section 6 for additional air bag system precautions and information.

1. Make sure the front wheels are straight and the steering column is locked in place.
2. Disconnect the negative battery cable at the battery and isolate.
3. Wait 2 minutes for the reserve capacitor to discharge before removing non deployed module.
4. Remove the 4 nuts attaching the air bag module from the back side of the steering wheel.
5. Lift the module and disengage the connector from the rear of the module.
6. Remove the vehicle speed control switch and connector, if so equipped or cover.
7. Mark the column shaft and wheel for reinstallation reference and remove the steering wheel retaining nut.
8. Remove the steering wheel using a steering wheel puller (Chrysler Tool C–3428B or the equivalent).

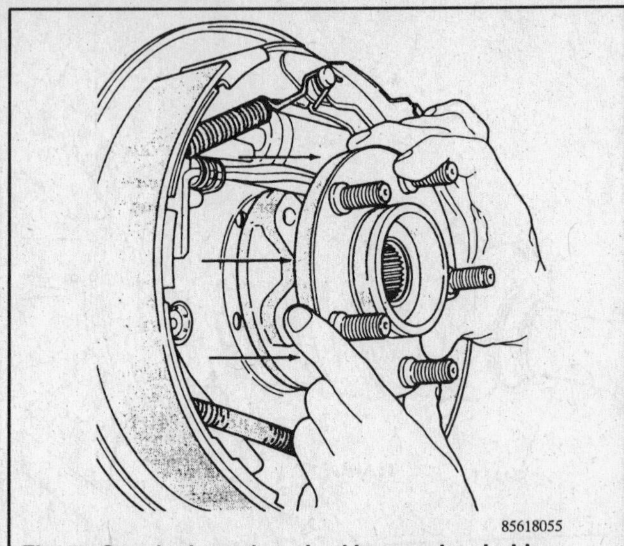

Fig. 55 Standard steering wheel horn pad and wiring

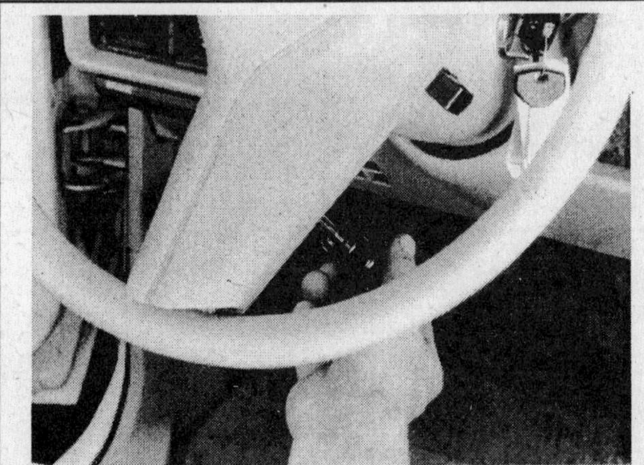

Fig. 56 From behind the steering wheel remove the cover retaining screws — 1987 Voyager shown

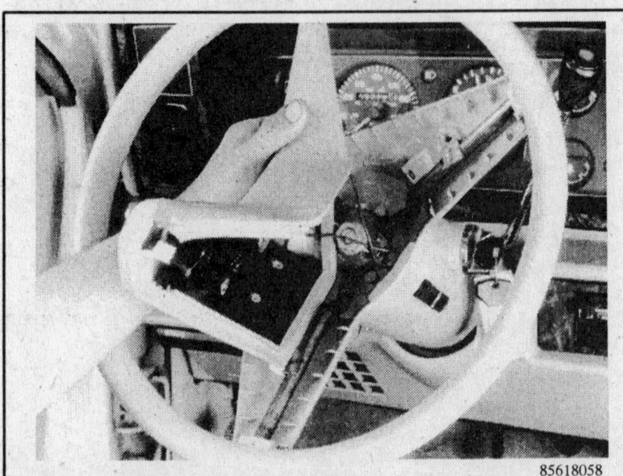

Fig. 57 Removing the horn pad from the steering wheel. The horn wires may be left connected, if desired

Fig. 58 Mark the shaft and wheel for reinstallation reference and remove the steering wheel retaining nut

Fig. 59 Remove the steering wheel using a steering wheel puller (Chrysler Tool C-3428B or the equivalent)

Fig. 60 The steering wheel shown removed with the horn pad attached

To install:

****CAUTION**

If the clockspring is not properly positioned or if the front wheel were moved, follow the clockspring centering procedure as outlined in Section 6 before installing the steering wheel.

9. With the front wheels in a straight ahead position, position the steering wheel on the steering column, making sure to fit the flats on the hub of the steering wheel with the formations on the inside of the clockspring.
10. Pull the air bag and speed control wires through the lower, larger hole in the steering wheel and horn wire through the smaller hole at the top. Be sure not to pinch the wires.
11. Install, then tighten the nut to 45 ft. lbs. (61 Nm).
12. Install the horn wire connector.
13. Connect the 4-way connector to the vehicle speed control switch and attach the switch to the steering wheel.
14. Connect the air bag lead wire to the air bag module and secure the module to the steering wheel. Tighten to 80-100 inch lbs. (9-11 Nm).
15. Do not connect the negative battery until you perform an Air Bag System check. Refer to Section 6 for additional air bag system precautions and information.

Turn Signal Switch

REMOVAL & INSTALLATION

1984-90 Models

See Figures 61, 62, 63 and 64

1. Disconnect the negative battery cable at the battery.
2. Remove the steering wheel. Remove the lower steering column cover, silencer panel and reinforcement.

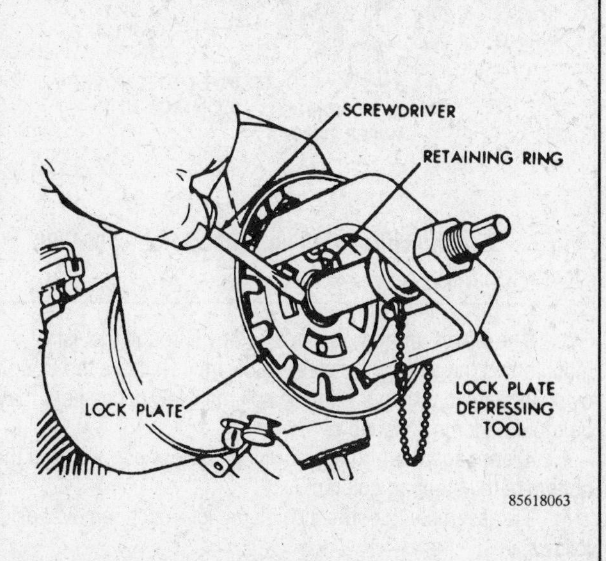

Fig. 61 Depressing the lock plate — 1984-90 models

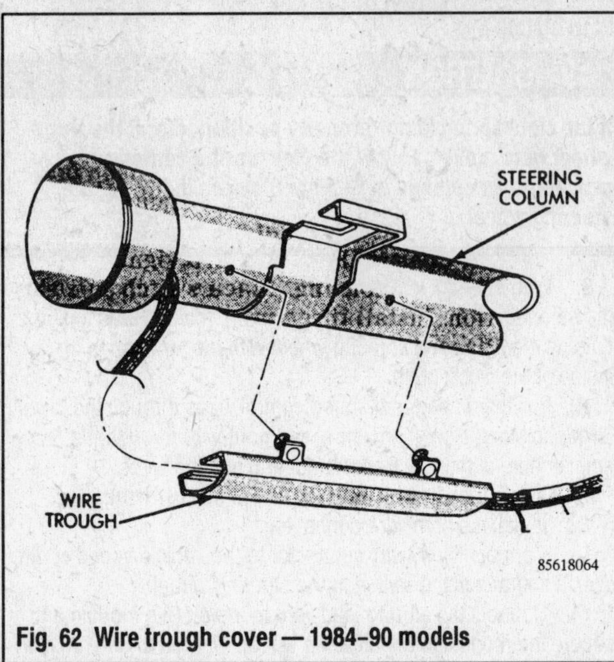

Fig. 62 Wire trough cover — 1984-90 models

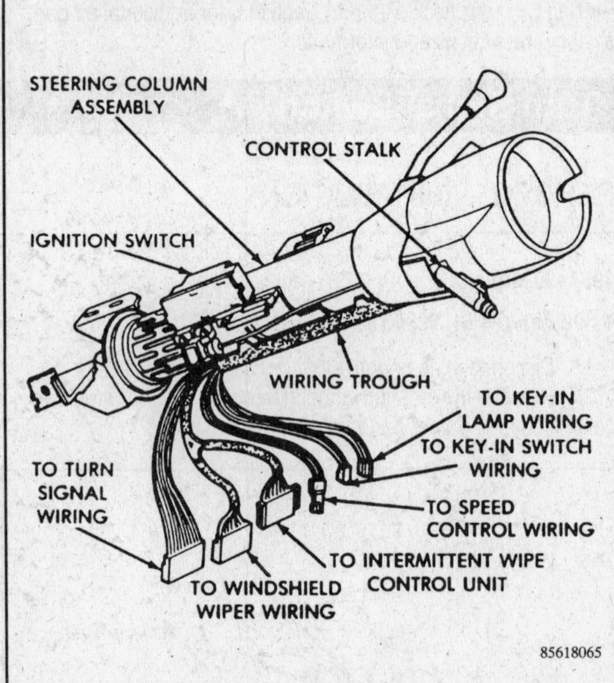

Fig. 63 Steering column wiring connectors — 1984-90 models

3. The wiring harness is contained by a trough that is mounted on the side of the steering column. Remove the trough by prying the connectors from the column. New connectors may be required for installation.

4. Disengage the turn signal wiring harness connector at the bottom of the steering column.

5. Disassemble the steering column for switch removal as follows:

6. On standard columns; remove the screw holding the wiper-washer switch to the turn signal switch. Allow the control stalk and switch to remain in position. Remove the three screws that attach the bearing retainer and turn signal switch to the upper bearing housing. Remove the turn signal and hazard warning switch assembly by gently pulling the switch up from the column while straightening the wires and guiding them up through the column opening. Be sure to disengage the ground connector.

7. On models with tilt wheel; remove the plastic cover (if equipped) from the lock plate. Depress the lock plate and pry the retaining ring form mounting groove. (Chrysler Tool C-4156 or equivalent is used to compress the lock plate). Remove the lock plate, canceling cam and upper bearing spring. Place the turn signal switch in right turn position. Remove the screw that attaches the link between the turn signal and wiper-washer switches. Remove the screw that attaches the hazard warning switch knob. Remove the three screws attaching the turn signal switch to the steering column. Remove the turn signal and hazard warning switch assembly by gently pulling the switch up from the column while straightening and guiding the wires up through the column opening.

To install:

8. On models with the standard column; lubricate the turn signal switch pivot hole with a white lube (such as Lubriplate). Thread the connector and wires through the column hole carefully. Position the turn signal switch and bearing retainer in place on the upper bearing housing and install the three mounting screws. Position the turn signal lever to turn signal pivot and secure with the mounting screws. Be sure the dimmer switch rod is in mounting pocket.

9. On models with tilt wheel; thread connector and wire harness through column hole. Position the turn signal switch in the upper column housing. Place the switch in the right turn position. Install the three mounting screws. Install the link between the turn signal switch and the wiper-washer switch pivot and secure mounting screw. Install the lock plate bearing spring, canceling cam and new retainer clip using Tool C-4156 or equivalent. Install the hazard warning knob, screw.

10. Connect the wiring harness plug. Install the cover through wiring cover to the steering column.

11. Install the steering wheel and retaining nut. Connect battery cable and test the switch for operation.

Multi-Function Switch

REMOVAL & INSTALLATION

1991-95 Models

➥ On these models the turn signal switch is part of the multi-function switch.

****CAUTION**

Disconnect and isolate the negative (ground) battery cable. This will disable the air bag system. Failure to disconnect the battery could result in accidental deployment and possible personal injury. Allow system capacitor to discharge for two minutes then begin air bag system component removal. Refer to Section 6 for additional air bag system precautions and information.

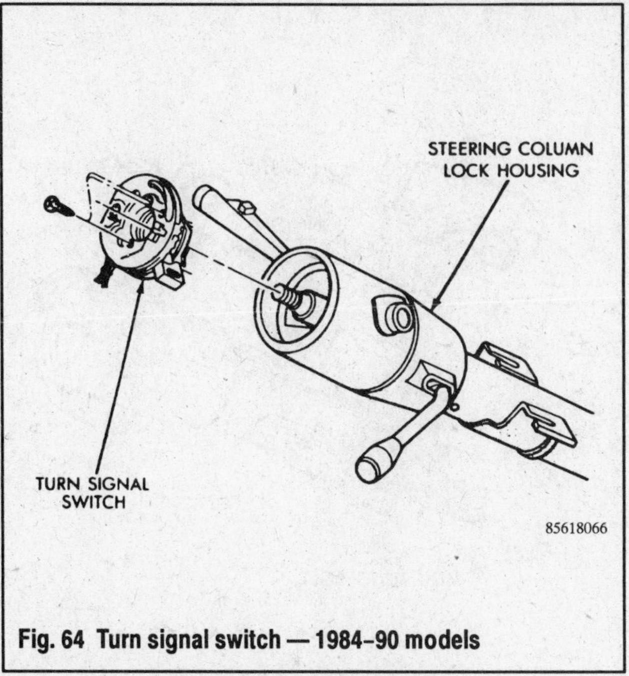

Fig. 64 Turn signal switch — 1984–90 models

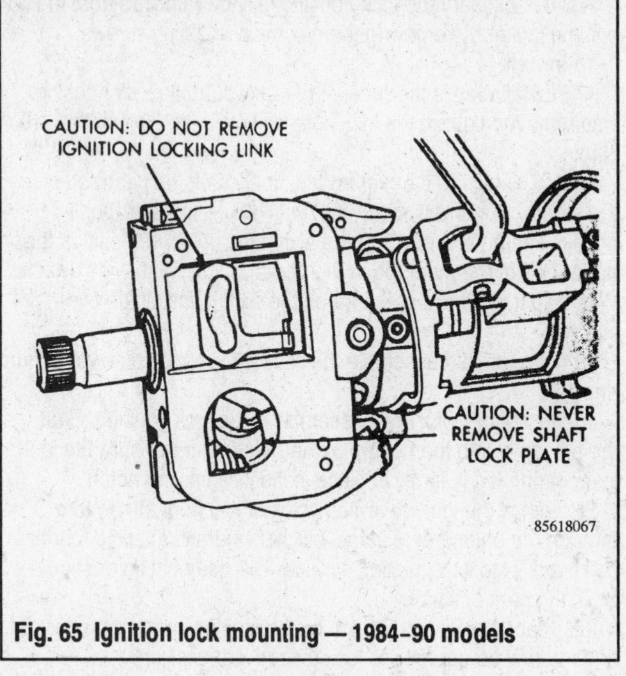

Fig. 65 Ignition lock mounting — 1984–90 models

1. Disconnect the negative battery cable.
2. With tilt column, remove the tilt lever.
3. Remove both upper and lower steering column covers.
4. Remove the multi-function switch tamper proof mounting screws.
5. Pull the switch away from the column and loosen the connector screw. The screw will remain in the connector.
6. Remove the wiring connector from the multi-function switch.

To install:

7. Install the wiring connector to the switch, then tighten the connector retaining screw to 17 inch lbs. (2 Nm).
8. Mount the multi-function switch to the column, then tighten the retaining screws to 17 inch lbs. (2 Nm).
9. With tilt column, install the tilt lever.
10. Connect the negative battery cable.

Ignition Lock Cylinder

REMOVAL & INSTALLATION

1984–90 Models

➧ **See Figures 65 and 66**

1. Disconnect the negative battery cable.
2. Follow the turn signal switch removal removal procedures.
3. Unclip the horn and key light ground wires.
4. Remove the four screws that hold the bearing housing to the lock housing.
5. Remove the snapring from the upper end of the steering shaft.
6. Remove the bearing housing from the shaft.
7. Remove the lock plate spring and lock plate from the steering shaft.
8. Remove the ignition key, then remove the screw and lift out the buzzer/chime switch.

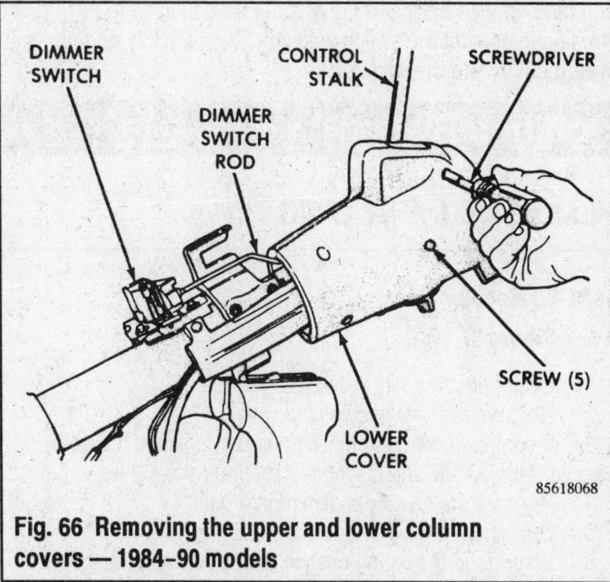

Fig. 66 Removing the upper and lower column covers — 1984–90 models

9. Remove the two screws attaching the ignition switch to the column jacket.
10. Remove the ignition switch by rotating the switch 90 degrees on the rod then sliding off the rod.
11. Remove the two mounting screws from the dimmer switch and disengage the switch from the actuator rod.
12. Remove the two screws that mount the bell crank and slide the bell crank up in the lock housing until it can be disconnect from the ignition switch actuator rod.
13. To remove the lock cylinder and lock levers place the cylinder in the lock position and remove the key.
14. Insert a small diameter screwdriver or similar tool into the lock cylinder release holes and push into the release spring loaded lock retainers. At the same time pull the lock cylinder out of the housing bore.
15. Grasp the lock lever and spring assembly and pull straight out of the housing.

16. If necessary the lock housing may be removed from the column jacket by removing the hex head retaining screws.

To install:

17. Installation is the reverse of removal. If the lock housing was removed tighten the lock housing screws to 90 inch lbs. (10 Nm).

18. To install the dimmer switch, firmly seat the push rod into the switch. Compress the switch until two $^{1}/_{8}$ in. (3mm) drill shanks can be inserted into the alignment holes. Reposition the upper end of the push rod in the pocket of the wash/wipe switch. With a light rearward pressure on the switch, install the two screws.

19. Grease and assemble the two lock levers, lock lever spring and pin.

20. Install the lock lever assembly in the lock housing. Seat the pin firmly into the bottom of the slots and make sure the lock lever spring leg is firmly in place in the lock casting notch.

21. Install the ignition switch actuator rod from the bottom through the oblong hole in the lock housing and attach it to the bell crank onto its mounting surface. The gearshift lever should be in the park position.

22. Place the ignition switch on the ignition switch actuator rod and rotate it 90 degrees to lock the rod into position.

23. To install the ignition lock, turn the key to the lock position and remove the key. Insert the cylinder far enough into the housing to contact the switch actuator. Insert the key and press inward and rotate the cylinder.

Ignition Switch

REMOVAL & INSTALLATION

1984-90 Models

➧ See Figure 67

1. Disconnect the negative battery cable.
2. Remove the steering column cover.
3. If equipped with automatic transaxle, position the gear selector into DRIVE and disconnect the indicator cable.
4. Remove the lower panel reinforcement.
5. Drop the steering column for switch replacement.
6. Disengage the wiring connector from the ignition switch.
7. Position the ignition lock cylinder into the LOCK position.
8. Tape the ignition switch rod to the steering column to prevent the rod from falling out of the lock cylinder assembly.
9. Remove the screws attaching the ignition switch to the column jacket.
10. Remove the ignition switch by rotating the switch 90 degrees and pulling up to disengage from the rod.

To install:

11. Rotate the switch 90° and push down to engage the rod.
12. Install the screws to the ignition switch mounting plate but do not tighten.
13. Remove the tape holding the rod to the column.
14. Adjust the switch by pushing up on the switch to take up rod system slack. This must be done with the key cylinder in the LOCK position and the key removed.
15. Tighten the screws attaching the switch to the column.
16. Connect the wiring connector to the ignition switch.
17. Install the steering column.

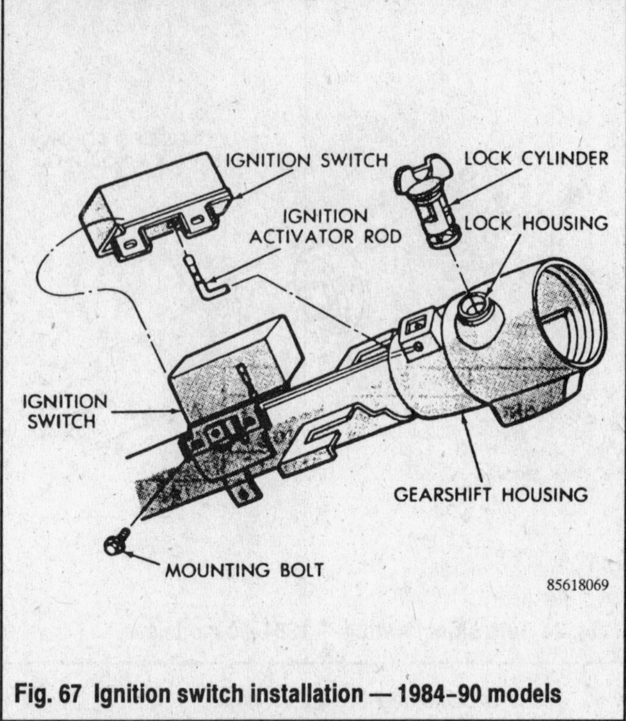

Fig. 67 Ignition switch installation — 1984-90 models

18. Install the steering column cover.
19. Connect the negative battery cable.

Ignition Switch and Lock Cylinder Assembly

REMOVAL & INSTALLATION

✻✻CAUTION

Disconnect and isolate the negative (ground) battery cable. This will disable the air bag system. Failure to disconnect the battery could result in accidental deployment and possible personal injury. Allow system capacitor to discharge for two minutes then begin air bag system component removal. Refer to Section 6 for additional air bag system precautions and information.

1991-95 Models

➧ See Figures 68, 69, 70, 71, 72 and 73

1. Disconnect the negative battery cable.
2. If equipped with a tilt column, remove the tilt lever by turning it counterclockwise.
3. Remove the upper and lower covers from the column.
4. Remove the ignition switch mounting screws. Use a tamper proof Torx® bit Snap-on TTXR15A2, TTXR20A2 or equivalent to remove the screws.
5. Pull the switch away from the column, release the connector locks on the 7 terminal wiring connector, then remove the connector from the ignition switch.
6. Release the connector lock on the 4-terminal wiring connector, then remove the connector from the ignition switch.

7. To remove the key cylinder from the ignition switch:

a. Turn the key to the **LOCK** position. Using a small screwdriver, depress the key cylinder retaining pin until it is flush with the key cylinder surface.

b. Rotate the key clockwise to the **OFF** position. The key cylinder will unseat from the ignition switch. When the key cylinder is unseated, it will be approximately $^1/_8$ in. (3mm) away from the ignition switch halo light ring. DO NOT attempt to remove the key cylinder at this time.

c. With the key cylinder in the unseated position, rotate the key counterclockwise to the **LOCK** position and remove the key.

d. Remove the key cylinder from the ignition switch.

To install:

8. Engage the electrical connectors to the ignition switch and make sure the switch locking tabs are fully seated.

9. Before attaching the ignition switch to a tilt steering column, the transmission shifter must be in the PARK position. Also the park lock dowel pin and the column lock flag must be properly indexed before installing the switch.

a. Place the transmission shifter in the **PARK** position

b. Place the ignition switch in the **LOCK** position. The switch is in the lock position when the column lock flag is parallel to the ignition switch terminals.

c. Position the ignition switch park lock dowel pin so it will engage the steering column park lock slider linkage.

d. Apply a light coating of grease to the column lock flag and the park lock dowel pin.

10. Place the ignition switch against the lock housing opening on the steering column. Ensure that the ignition switch park lock dowel pin enters the slot in the park lock slider linkage in the steering column.

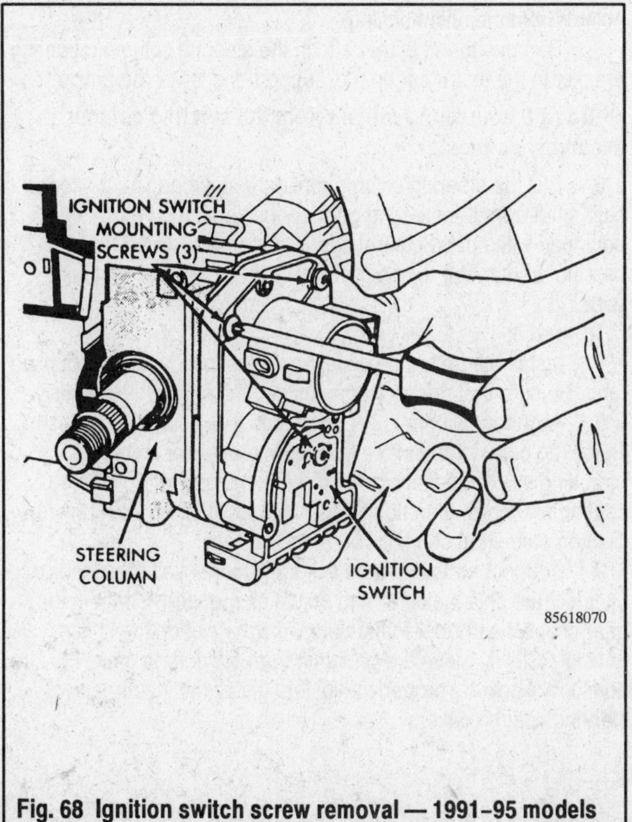

Fig. 68 Ignition switch screw removal — 1991-95 models

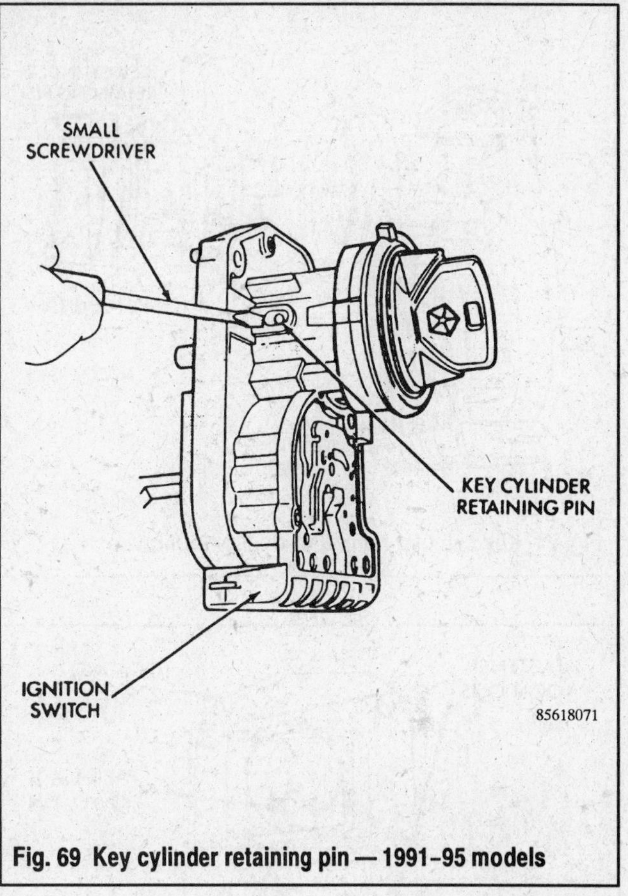

Fig. 69 Key cylinder retaining pin — 1991-95 models

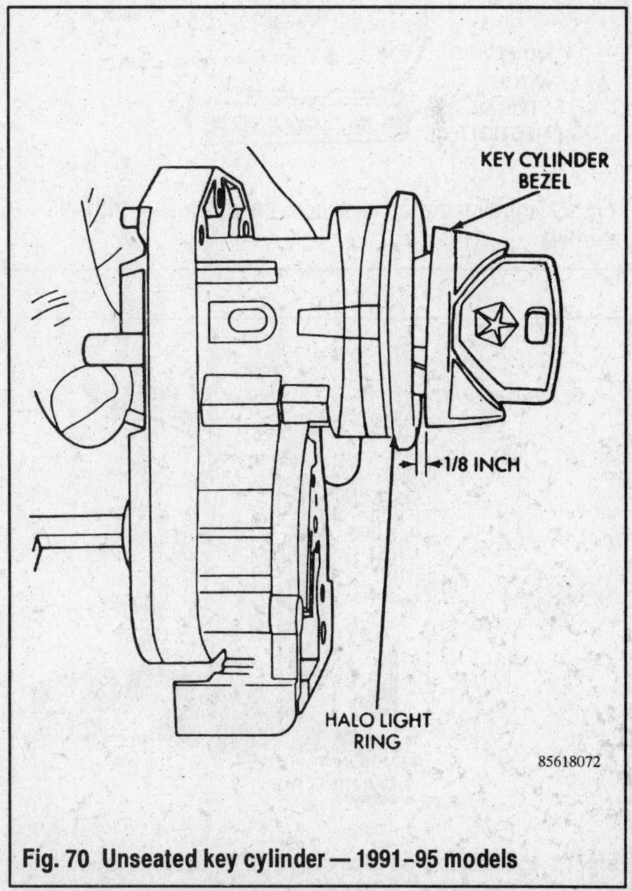

Fig. 70 Unseated key cylinder — 1991-95 models

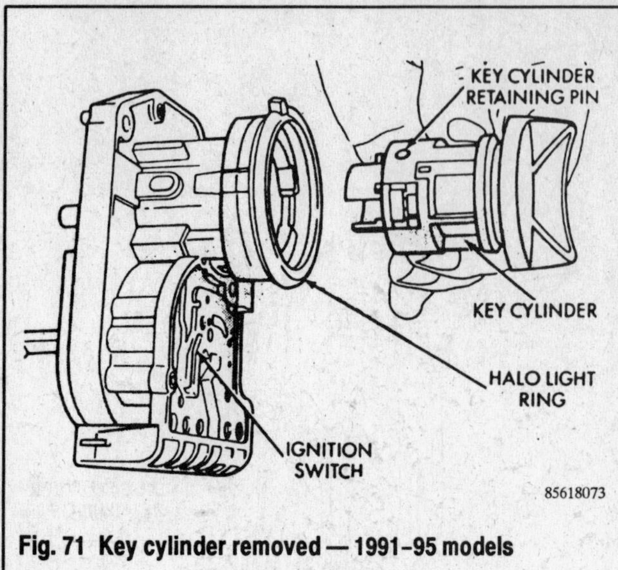

Fig. 71 Key cylinder removed — 1991-95 models

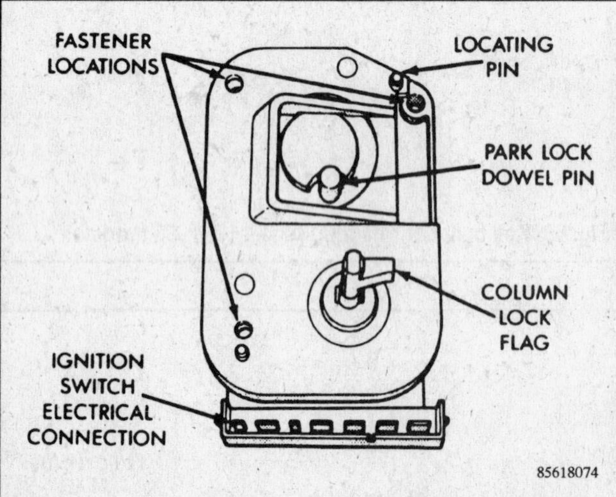

Fig. 72 Ignition switch view from the column — 1991-95 models

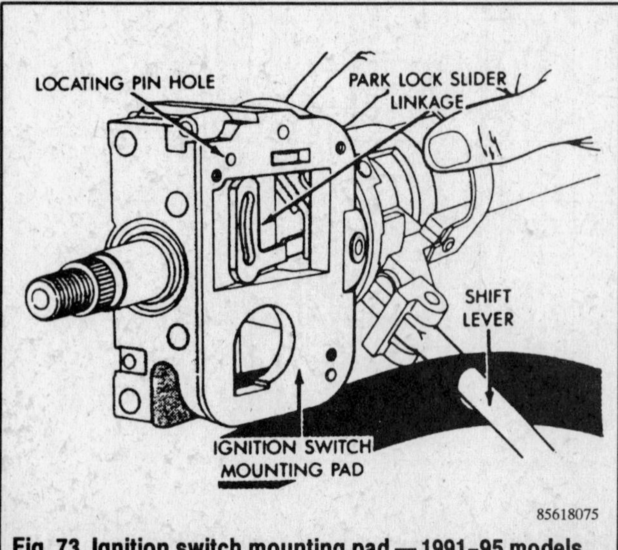

Fig. 73 Ignition switch mounting pad — 1991-95 models

11. Install the ignition switch mounting screws, then tighten the screws to 17 inch lbs. (2 Nm).
12. If the vehicle is equipped with a tilt steering column, install the tilt lever.
13. To install the ignition lock cylinder:
    a. With the key cylinder and the ignition switch in the **LOCK** position, insert the key cylinder into the ignition switch until it bottoms.
    b. Insert the ignition key into the lock cylinder. While pushing the key cylinder in toward the ignition switch, rotate the ignition key until the end of travel.
14. Connect the negative battery cable.
15. Check for proper operation.

Steering Column

REMOVAL & INSTALLATION

1984-90 Models

➧ See Figures 74 and 75

1. Disconnect the negative battery cable from the battery. If the vehicle is equipped with a column mounted shift, pry the shift cable rod from the lever grommet at the bottom of the steering column. Remove the cable clip and cable from lower bracket.
2. Disengage the wiring harness connector at the bottom of the steering column.
3. Remove the instrument panel lower steering column cover and disconnect the bezel. On models with floor shift, unsnap and remove shroud cover extensions.
4. If automatic, remove the selector indicator set screw and pointer from the shift housing.
5. Remove the nuts that attach the steering column mounting bracket to the instrument panel support and lower the bracket.

➝ Do not remove the roll pin from the steering column assembly connector.

6. Pull the steering column rearward, disengaging the lower stub shaft from the steering gear connector. If the vehicle is equipped with speed control and a manual transmission, take care not to damage the control switch mounted on the clutch pedal.

To install:

7. Install the anti-rattle coupling spring into the lower coupling tube. Be sure that the spring snaps into the slot in the coupling.
8. Align the column lower shaft stub with coupling and insert. Raise the column and place bracket into position on the mounting studs. Loosely install the mounting nuts. Pull the column rearward, then tighten the nuts to 105 inch lbs. (12 Nm). Tighten stub shaft connector.
9. Connect and adjust the linkage. Connect all harnesses. Connect the shift indicator and adjust as required. Connect the gear shift indicator operating cable into the slot on the shift housing. Slowly move the gearshift from 1st gear to park (P). The pointer will now be properly adjusted. Install the instrument steering column cover.

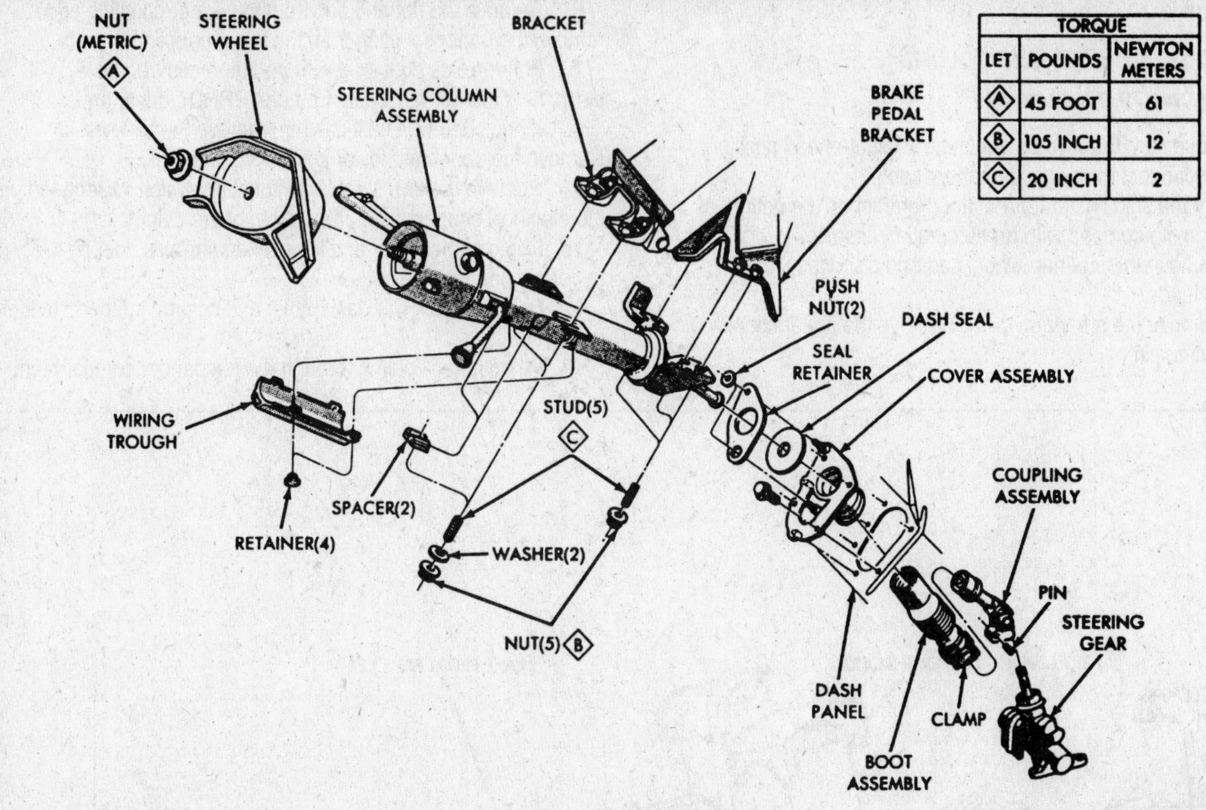

TORQUE		
LET	POUNDS	NEWTON METERS
A	45 FOOT	61
B	105 INCH	12
C	20 INCH	2

85618076

Fig. 74 Exploded view of the steering column assembly — 1984–90 models

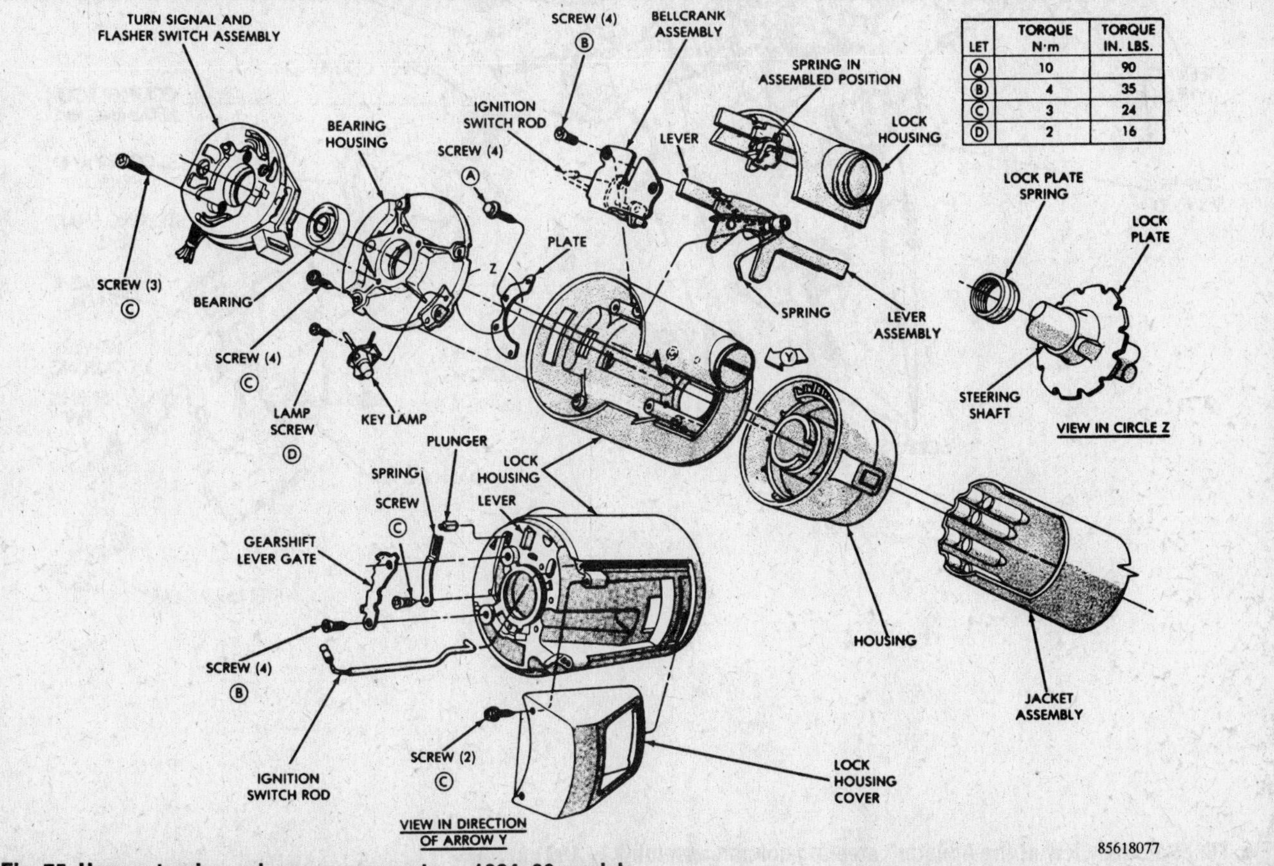

LET	TORQUE N·m	TORQUE IN. LBS.
A	10	90
B	4	35
C	3	24
D	2	16

85618077

Fig. 75 Upper steering column components — 1984–90 models

1991 Models

WITH ACUSTAR® STEERING COLUMN

See Figures 76, 77, 78 and 79

1. Make sure the wheels are in the straight-ahead position.
2. Disconnect the negative battery cable.
3. Pry the shift link rod out of the grommet on the bottom of the column, if equipped with an automatic transaxle.
4. Remove the steering wheel pad and disconnect the electrical leads.
5. Remove the steering wheel. Remove the upper coupling bolt retaining pin.
6. Remove the nut and bolt from the upper coupling and remove the upper coupling from the lower coupling.
7. For vehicles equipped with an automatic transaxle, disconnect the PRNDL cable from the PRNDL driver arm.
8. If equipped with a tilt column, remove the tilt lever. Remove the upper and lower ignition shroud trim.
9. Remove the turn signal/multifunction switch. Disengage the electrical connectors at the bottom of the column.
10. Remove the upper and lower fixed shrouds, loosen the upper support bracket bolts.
11. Remove the lower dash panel and column support standoff bracket bolts.
12. Remove the column through the passenger compartment.

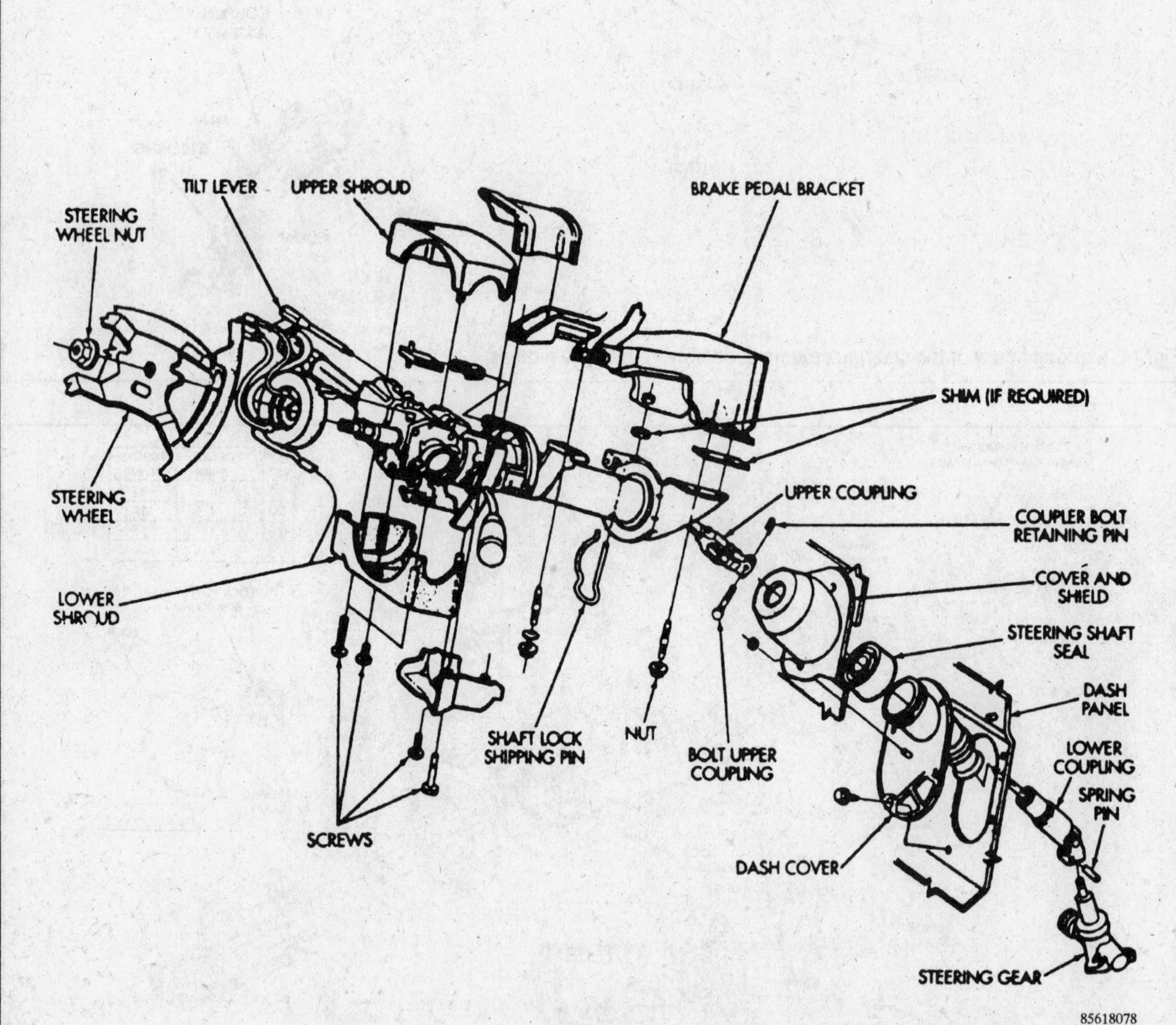

Fig. 76 Exploded view of the Acustar® steering column assembly — 1991 models

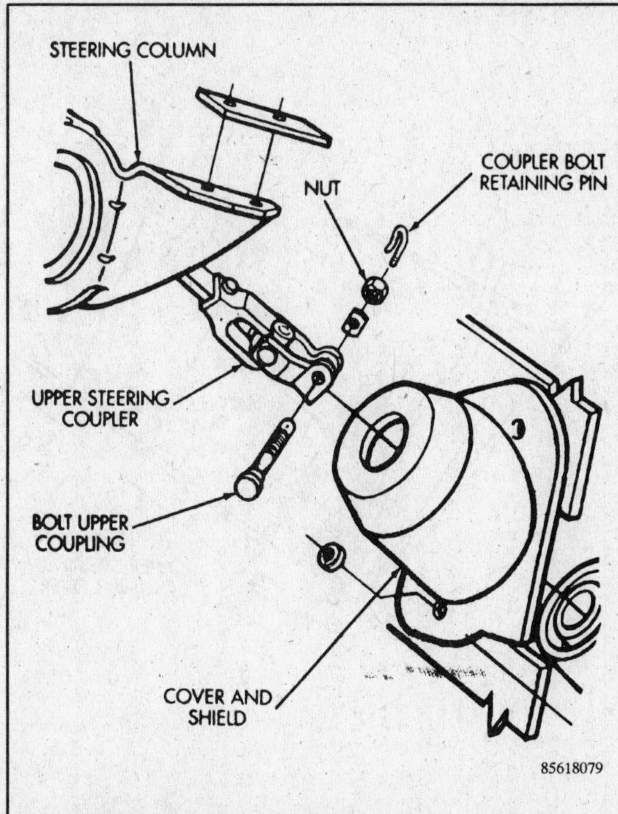

Fig. 77 Steering column coupler removal — 1991 with Acustar® steering column

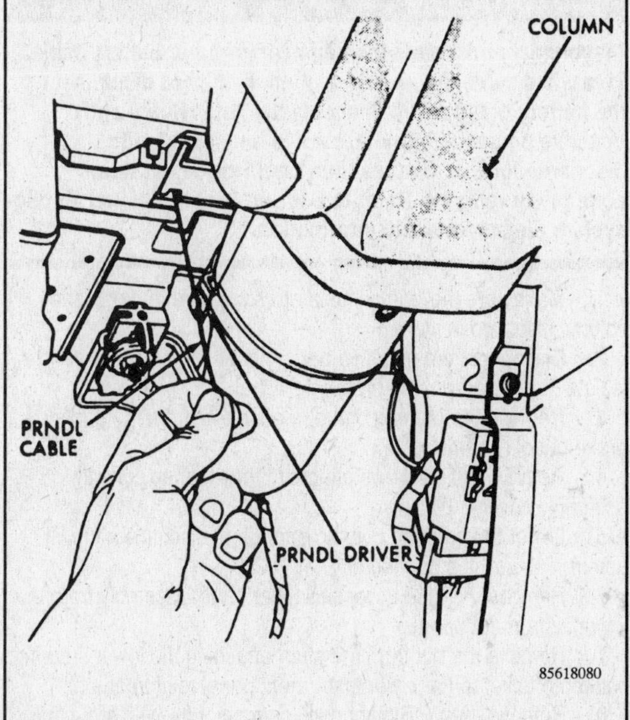

Fig. 78 PRNDL cable removal — 1991 with Acustar® steering column

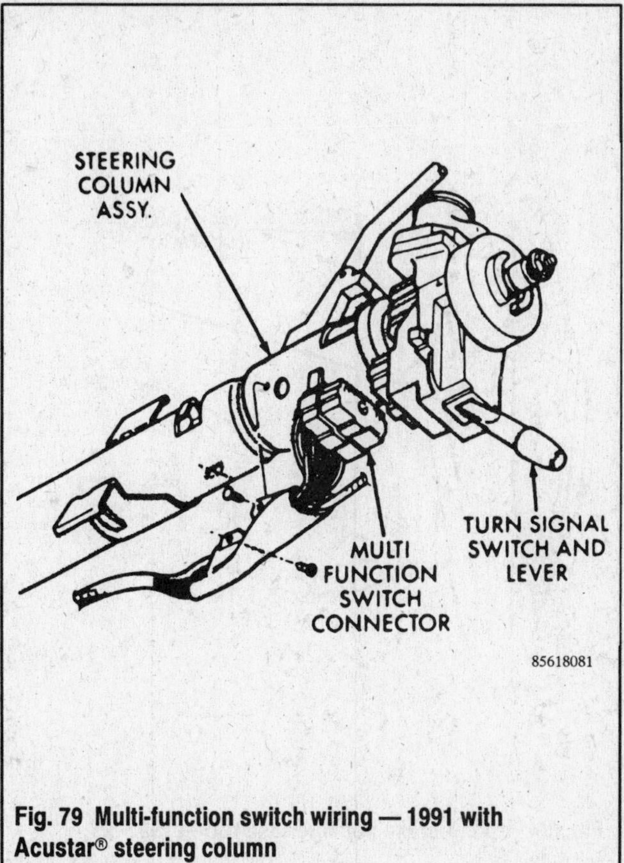

Fig. 79 Multi-function switch wiring — 1991 with Acustar® steering column

To install:

13. Install a replacement grommet on the shift rod arm and lubricate it.
14. Install the column in the vehicle, position it on the attaching studs and loosely assemble the upper bracket nuts.
15. Make sure the wheels are still in a straight-ahead position and align the upper and lower coupling. Install the coupling nut, then tighten to 21 ft. lbs. (28 Nm). Install the retaining pin.
16. Install the multifunction switch and connect the column wiring.
17. Install the upper fixed shroud.
18. Make sure the 2 plastic retainer are fully seated on the column bracket, then tighten the bracket bolts to 105 inch lbs. (12 Nm).
19. Install the lower shroud. Position the shift lever, if equipped with an automatic transaxle, in the farthest down position and install the PRNDL cable.
20. Install the tilt lever and the lower dash panel cover. Install the steering wheel. Connect the shift link rod.
21. Check the transaxle linkage adjustment through all of the gear positions.
22. Connect the negative battery cable.

1992-95 Models

See Figures 80, 81, 82, 83, 84, 85, 86, 87, 88, 89, 90, 91, 92, 93, 94, 95, 96, 97, 98, 99, 100 and 101

Before performing repair procedures that require the removal or disconnecting of any air bag system component, refer to the Air Bag Systems Check procedures outlined in Section 6

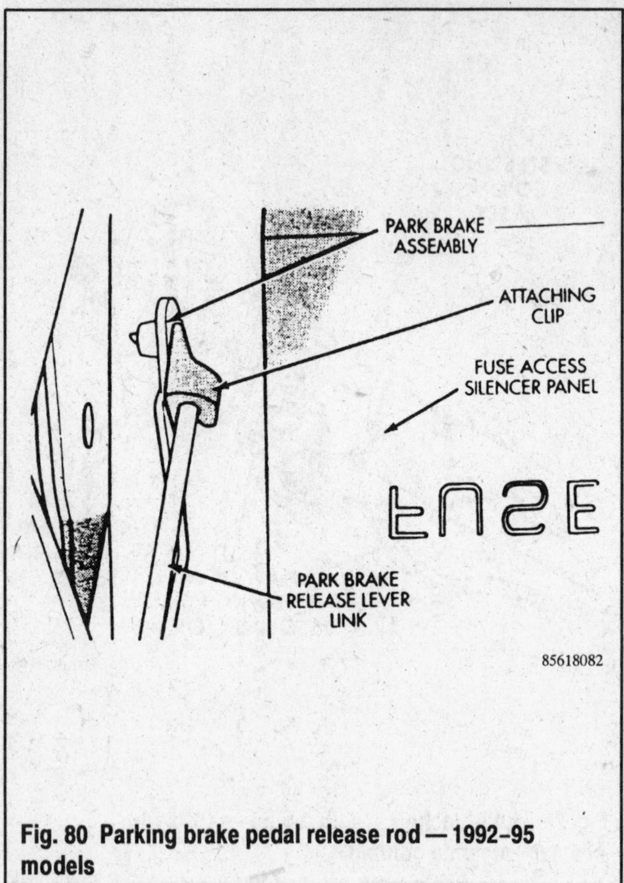

Fig. 80 Parking brake pedal release rod — 1992-95 models

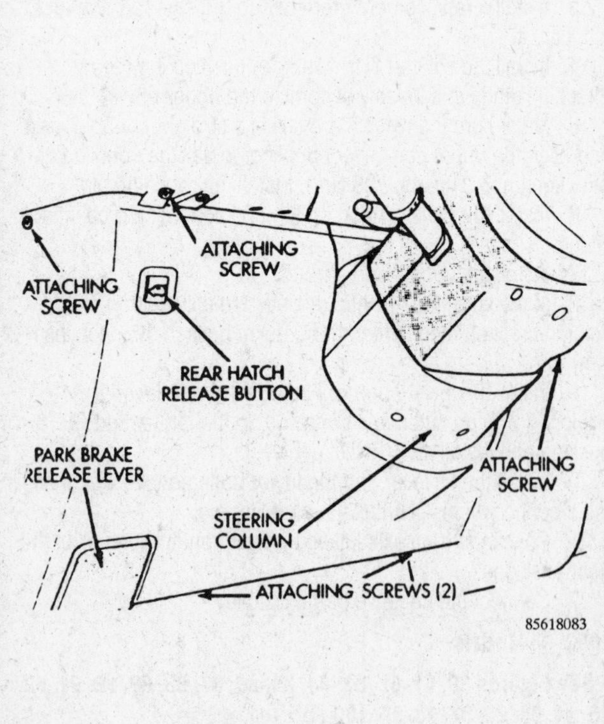

Fig. 81 Lower steering column cover removal — 1992-95 models

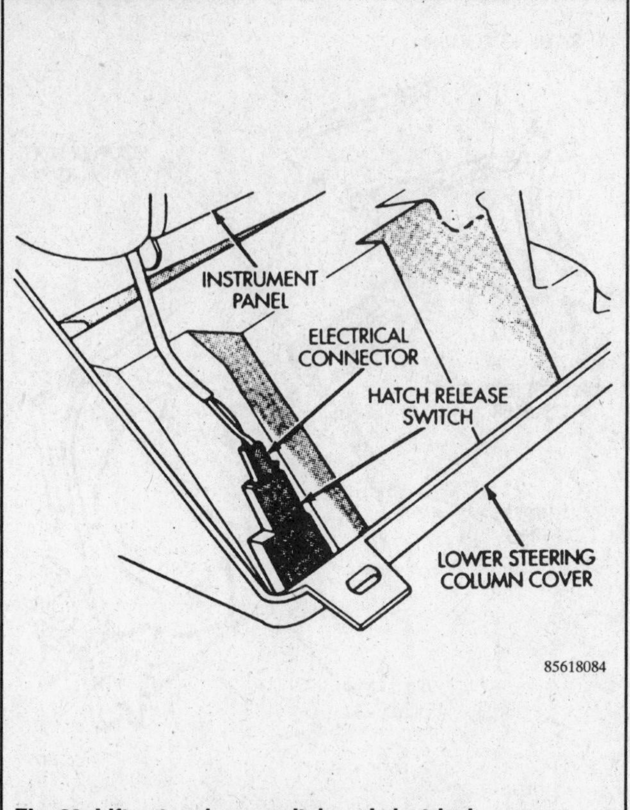

Fig. 82 Lift gate release switch and electrical connector — 1992-95 models

**CAUTION

Disconnect and isolate the negative (ground) battery cable. This will disable the air bag system. Failure to disconnect the battery could result in accidental deployment and possible personal injury. Allow system capacitor to discharge for two minutes then begin air bag system component removal. Refer to Section 6 for additional air bag system precautions and information.

1. Make sure the front wheels are straight and the steering column is locked in place.
2. Disconnect the negative battery cable at the battery and isolate the cable from the battery terminal.
3. Remove the parking brake release rod, from the parking brake pedal assembly.
4. Remove the 5 screws attaching the steering column assembly cover.
5. Lower the steering column enough to disconnect the lift gate release switch connector.
6. Remove the fuse access/silencer panel assembly from the lower instrument panel.
7. Remove the nut from the stud, attaching the lower steering column bracket to the lower instrument panel reinforcement.
8. Remove the DRB diagnostic connector from its mounting bracket, on the lower instrument panel reinforcement.
9. Remove the 4 attaching bolts and lower instrument panel reinforcement from the lower instrument panel.

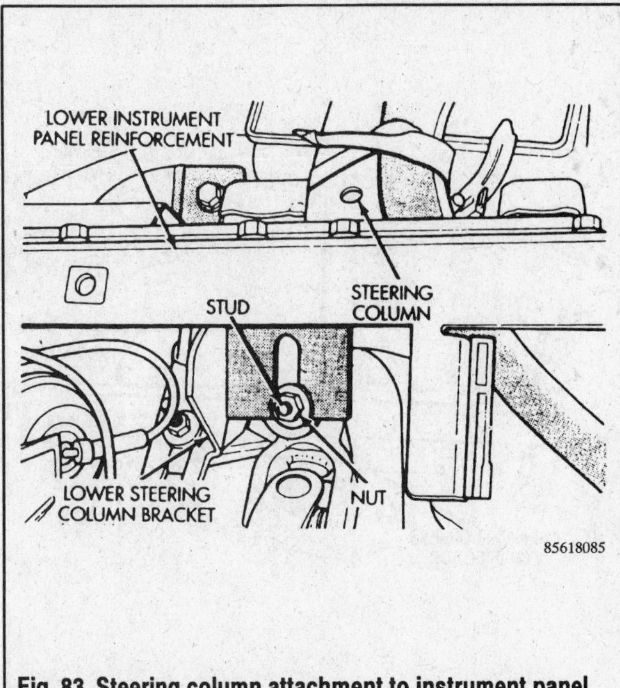

Fig. 83 Steering column attachment to instrument panel reinforcement — 1992-95 models

10. Position the steering wheel in the locked position and remove the key from the lock cylinder. Remove the 4 nuts attaching the air bag module from the steering wheel, then remove the air bag module from the steering wheel and disconnect the electrical lead at the air bag module.

11. Disengage the steering wheel horn switch wiring connector from the steering wheel wiring harness.

12. Remove the steering column wiring harness connector from the speed control switch assembly.

13. Remove the steering wheel retaining nut and remove the steering wheel using a puller as outlined earlier.

14. Remove the 3 screws attaching the upper steering column shrouds to the steering column, then remove the upper and lower halves of the upper steering column shroud, from the steering column.

15. Remove the 3 screws attaching the lower steering column shrouds to the steering column, then remove the upper and lower steering column shroud, from the steering column.

16. Remove the wiring harness connectors from the clock spring and ignition switch, then remove the halo light and key in buzzer wiring harness connector from the ignition switch assembly.

17. Remove the 0.27 in. (7 mm) hex head bolt from the rear of the multi-function switch connector.

18. Disengage the connector from the switch.

19. Remove the clock spring from the steering column assembly.

20. If the clock spring will not lift off the steering column do the following:.

a. Insert a screwdriver in the area of the clock spring's lower locking tab as shown.

b. Place the screwdriver against the locking tab of the clock spring assembly, then push the locking tab back and disengage the tab from the steering column.

c. Remove the clock spring from the column.

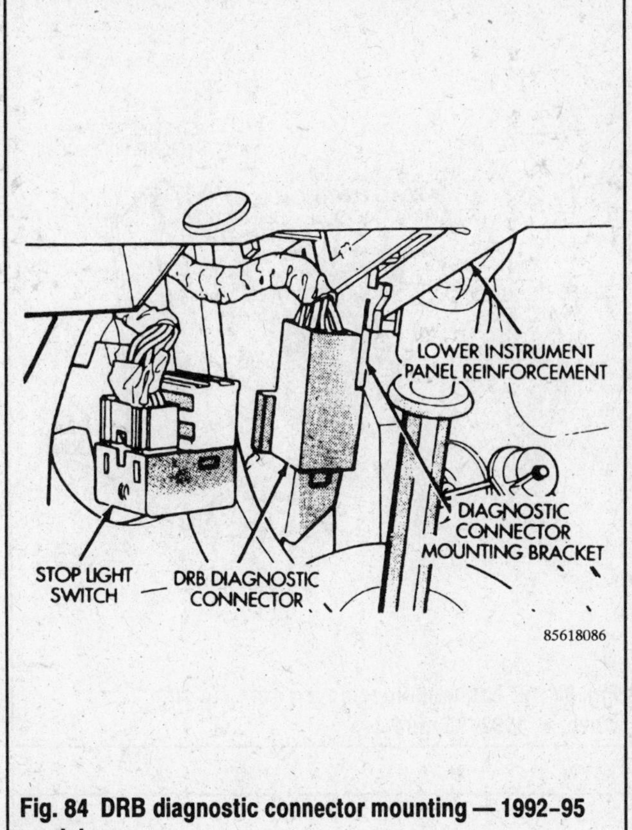

Fig. 84 DRB diagnostic connector mounting — 1992-95 models

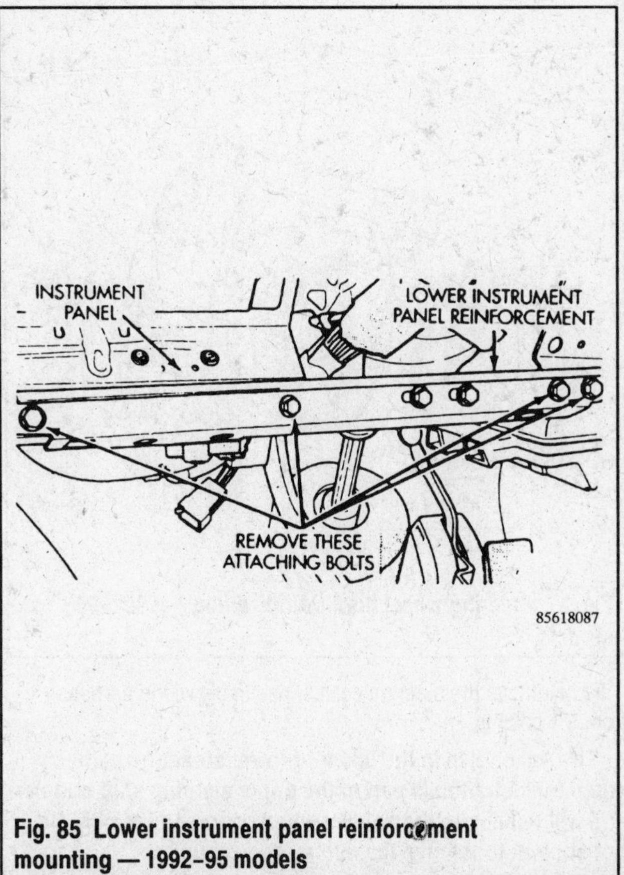

Fig. 85 Lower instrument panel reinforcement mounting — 1992-95 models

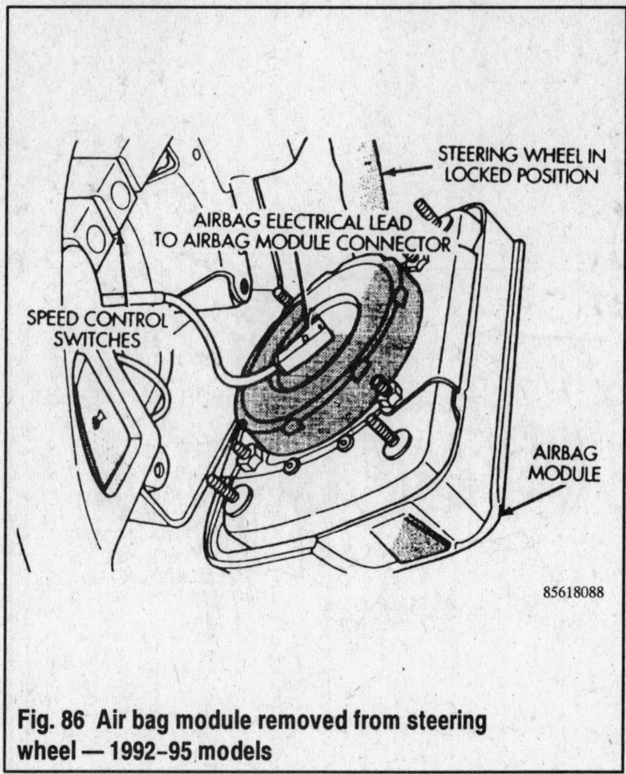

Fig. 86 Air bag module removed from steering wheel — 1992-95 models

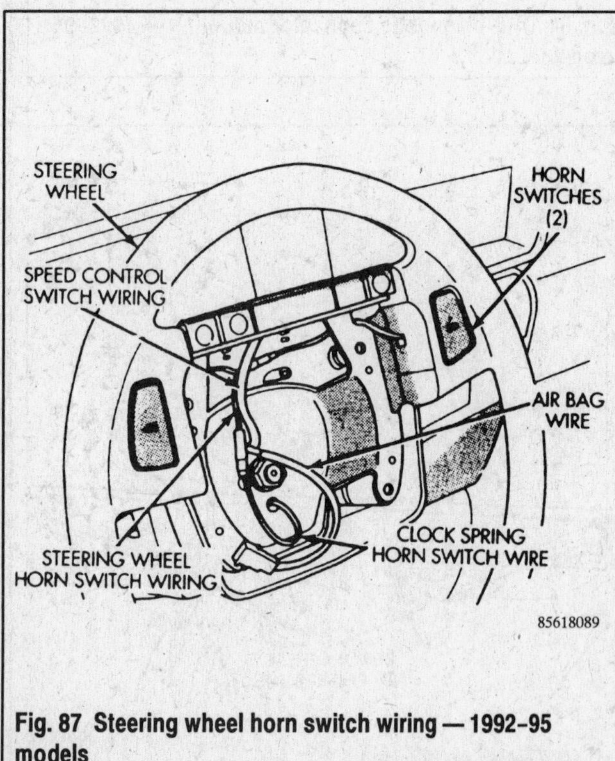

Fig. 87 Steering wheel horn switch wiring — 1992-95 models

21. Remove the steering column assembly wiring harness from the column.

➝ The nut shown in the upper-to-lower steering shaft coupler illustration is part of the upper steering shift coupler and will remain on the coupler when removing the bolt. Do not attempt to remove the nut from the coupler.

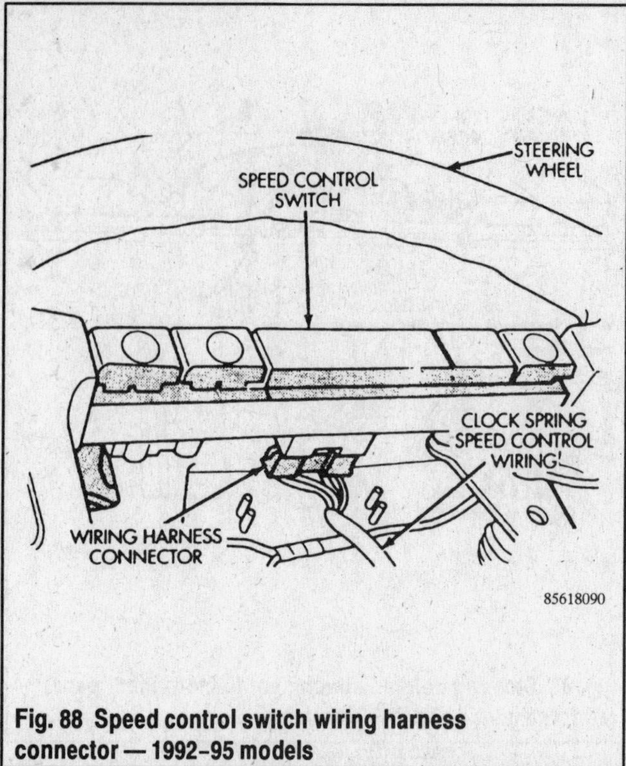

Fig. 88 Speed control switch wiring harness connector — 1992-95 models

22. Remove the 3 nuts, attaching the lower mounting bracket of the steering column assembly to the dash panel reinforcement/steering column lower mounting bracket, then remove the 2 nuts attaching the upper mounting bracket of the steering column assembly to the dash board liner.

****WARNING**

During the following Step, do not allow the weight of the steering column assembly to be supported by the gear shift indicator cable.

23. Lower the steering column assembly from the dash board of the vehicle enough to access the gear shift indicator cable assembly, on the jacket of the steering column.

24. Position the gear shift lever on the steering column in the park position and remove the gear shift indicator assembly from the steering column jacket. Remove the indicator assembly, by first releasing the lock bar on the column insert and squeezing the legs of the column insert together and then lift the assembly from the column.

25. Lower the steering column to the floor of the vehicle, then remove the clip attaching the gear shift cable to the lower bracket of the steering column assembly.

26. Remove the gear shift cable from the shift lever of the steering column

27. Carefully remove the steering column assembly from the vehicle.

To install:

28. Install a new gear shift cable attaching grommet into the steering column shift lever.

29. Prior to installing the steering column in the vehicle, install a ground clip on the left side capsule slot. The plastic capsules should be pre-assembled in the bracket slots. Remove the

shipping lock pin, located on the lower column jacket when installing a new jacket. Place the steering column on the floor of the vehicle.

30. Install the gear shift cable on the lower mounting bracket of the steering column assembly. Install the gear shift cable into the new grommet on the steering column gear shift lever, then install the clip, attaching the shift cable to the steering column bracket.

31. Route the gear shift indicator assembly and its cable under the left upper mounting bracket of the steering column. Hook the eye of the gear shift indicator cable onto the lever of the steering column gear shift tube. Insert the flange of the gear shift indicator assembly into the steering column jacket. Squeeze the legs of the steering column insert together and install the tabs under the steering column jacket. Engage the lock bar to secure the shift indicator assembly into the steering column jacket.

32. Install the lower mounting bracket of the steering column assembly on the studs of the dash panel/reinforcement steering column mounting bracket then loosely install the 3 mounting nuts. Lift the steering column aligning studs in the dash board liner with insert in the upper mounting bracket of the steering steering column and loosely install the 2 mounting nuts.

33. Slide the steering column down until the lower bracket of the steering column assembly is against the studs in the dash panel reinforcement/steering column bracket. Center the steering column assembly assembly in the dash panel opening, then tighten the mounting nuts at the upper bracket of the steering column assembly, then tighten all 5 steering column assembly mounting nuts to 105 inch lbs. (12 Nm).

34. Install the upper steering shaft coupler on the lower steering shaft coupler and install the upper coupler bolt. Tighten the nut on the upper steering coupler bolt to 21 ft. lbs. (28 Nm). Be sure to reinstall the retaining pin in the steering coupler retaining bolt.

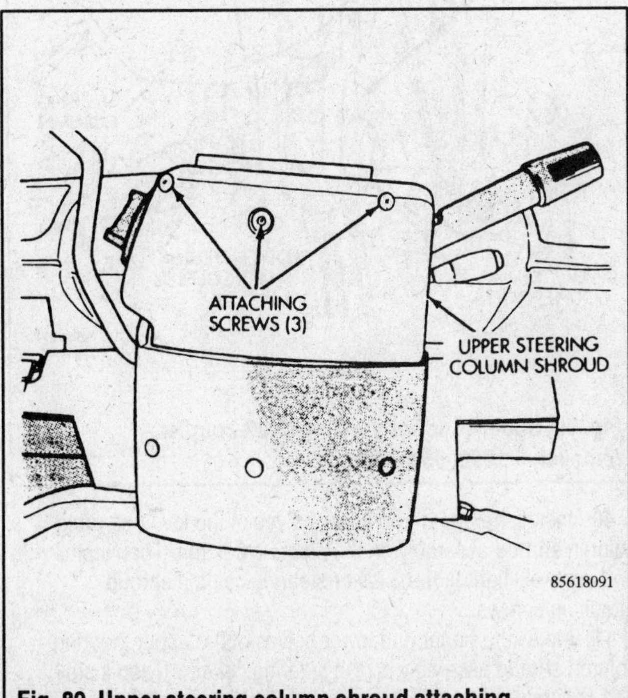

Fig. 89 Upper steering column shroud attaching screws — 1992-95 models

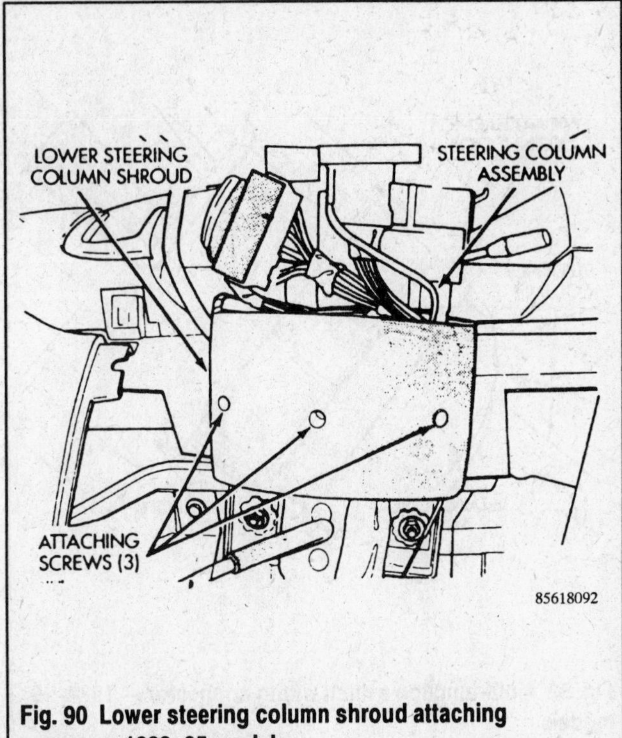

Fig. 90 Lower steering column shroud attaching screws — 1992-95 models

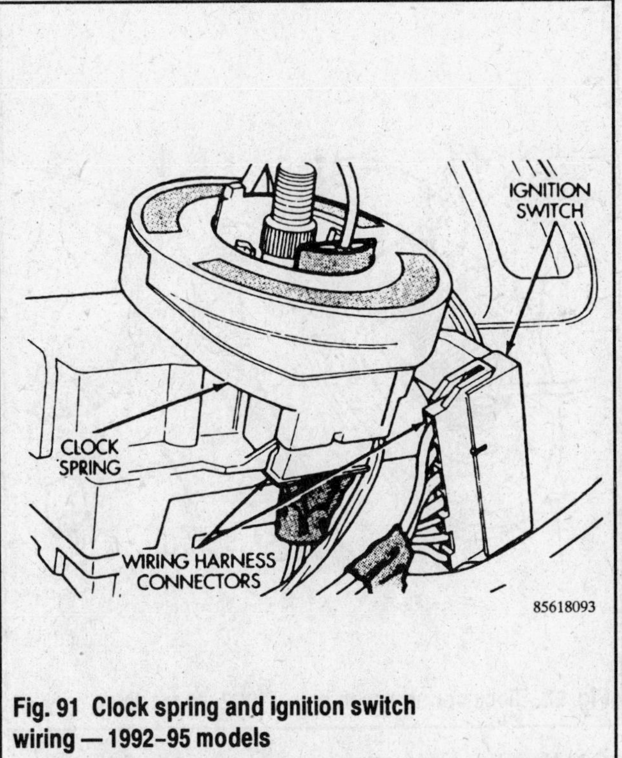

Fig. 91 Clock spring and ignition switch wiring — 1992-95 models

35. Install the clock spring on the steering column assembly, making sure the locking tabs on the clock spring are engaged with the steering column assembly.

36. Install the wiring harness connector onto the multi-function switch. Tighten the multi-function switch wiring harness connector retaining bolt to 17 inch lbs. (2 Nm).

37. Install the wiring harness connectors onto the clock spring and ignition switch assembly.

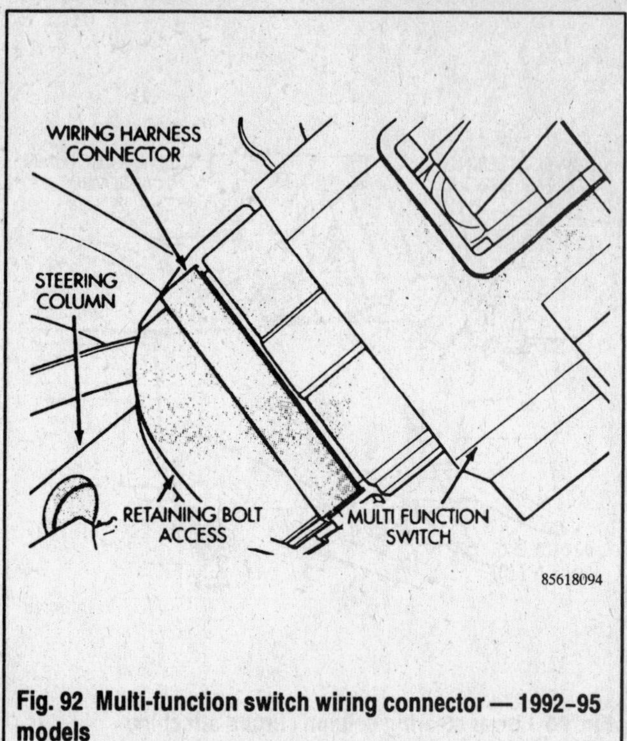

Fig. 92 Multi-function switch wiring connector — 1992–95 models

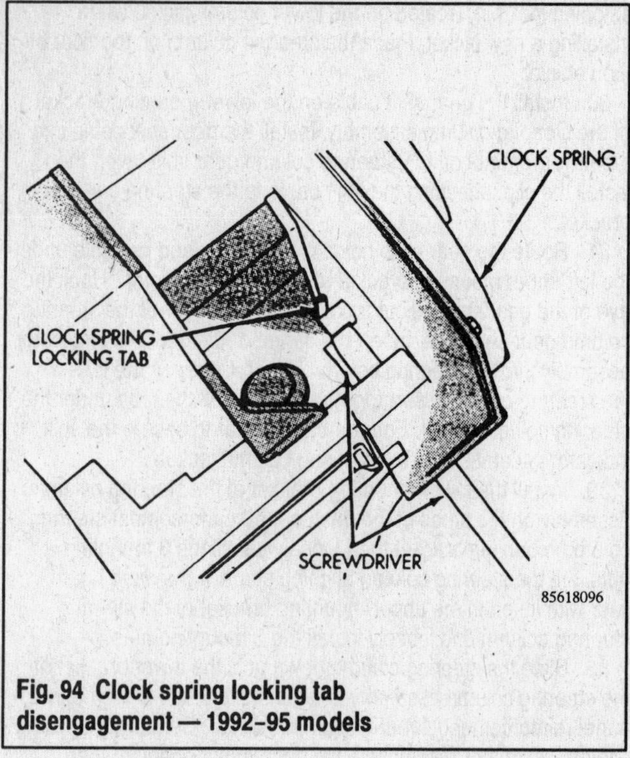

Fig. 94 Clock spring locking tab disengagement — 1992–95 models

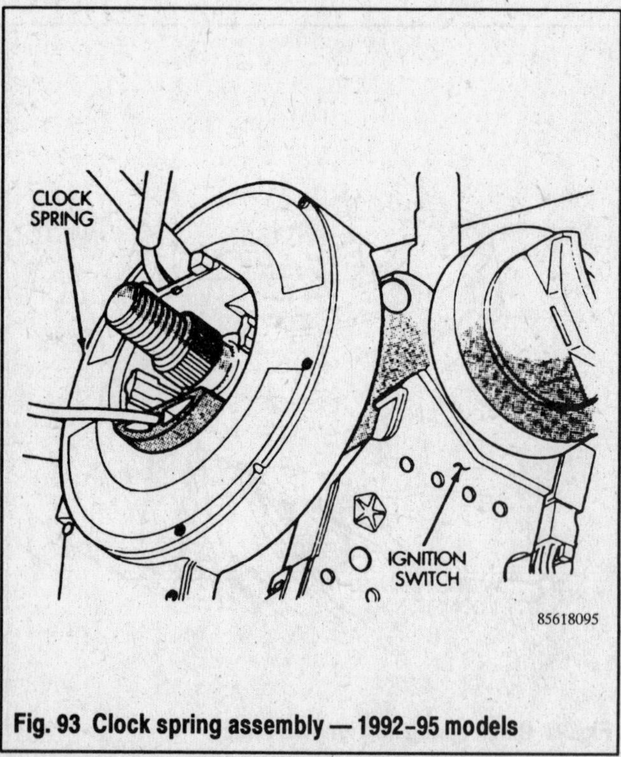

Fig. 93 Clock spring assembly — 1992–95 models

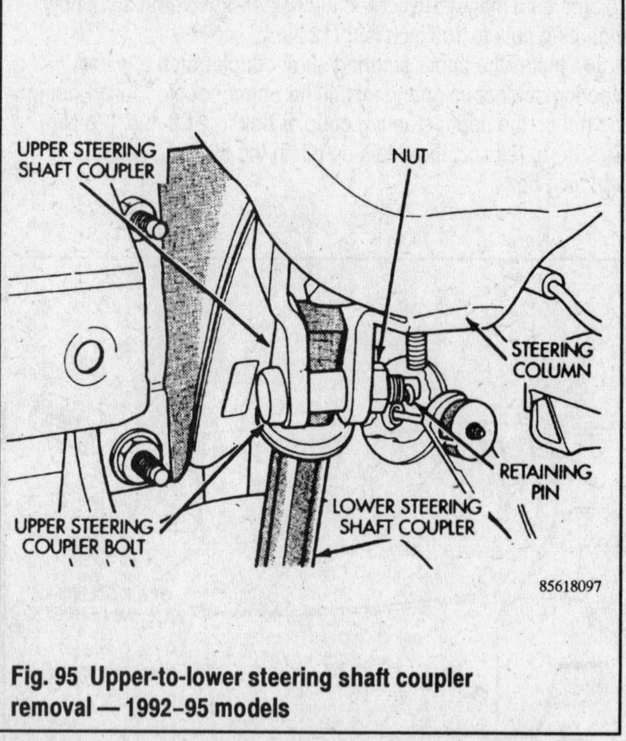

Fig. 95 Upper-to-lower steering shaft coupler removal — 1992–95 models

38. Move the shift lever to the neutral position and check the pointer location in the PRNDL window on the instrument cluster. If the pointer does not indicate neutral, adjust the actuator assembly to center the pointer on N (neutral), and then check the pointer in other gear positions.

39. Install the clips attaching the steering column assembly wiring harness to the steering column assembly.

40. Install the upper and lower halves of the lower steering column shroud assembly on the steering column. Then install and securely tighten the 3 lower steering column shroud attaching screws.

41. Install the upper and lower halves of the upper steering column shroud assembly on the steering column. Then install and securely tighten the 3 upper steering column shroud attaching screws.

42. Install the tilt lever on the column.

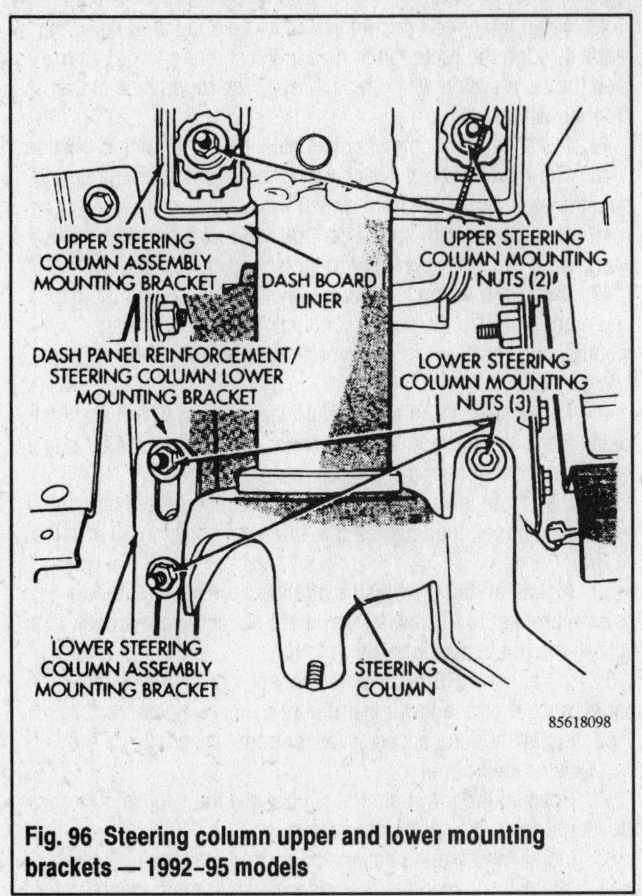

Fig. 96 Steering column upper and lower mounting brackets — 1992-95 models

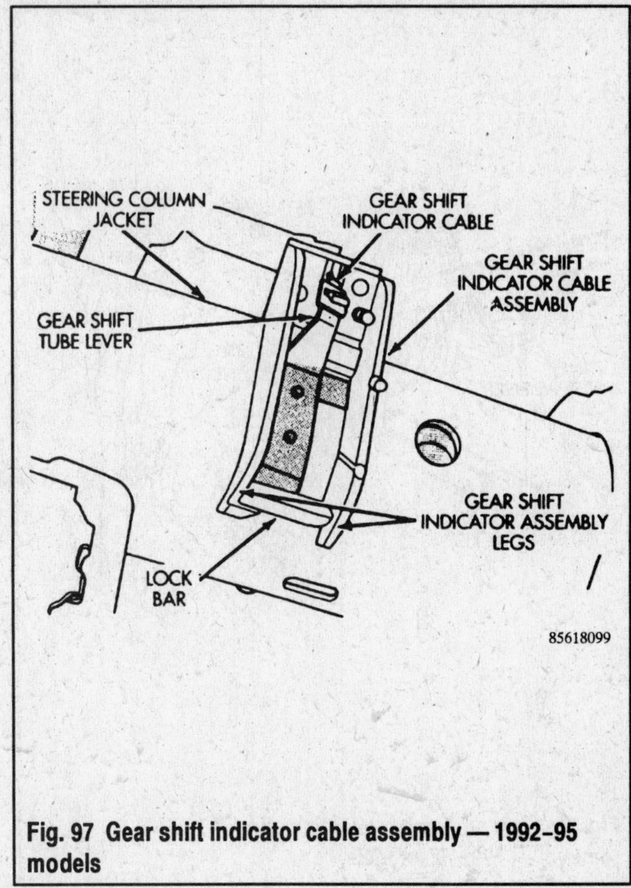

Fig. 97 Gear shift indicator cable assembly — 1992-95 models

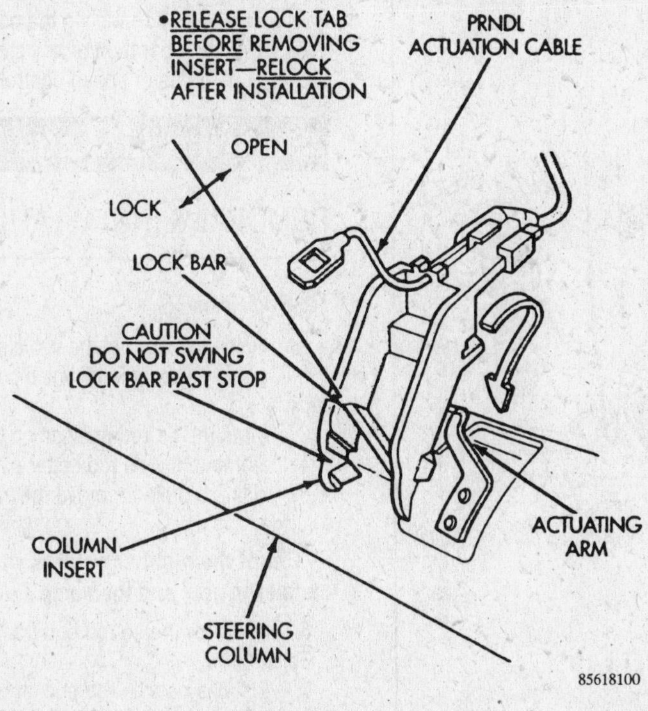

Fig. 98 Gear shift indicator cable removal from the steering column — 1992-95 models

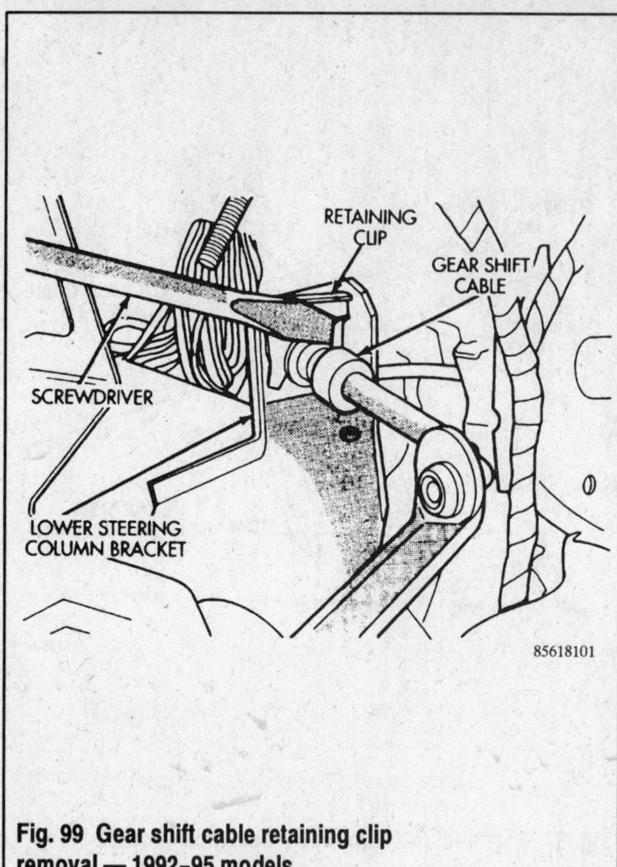

Fig. 99 Gear shift cable retaining clip removal — 1992-95 models

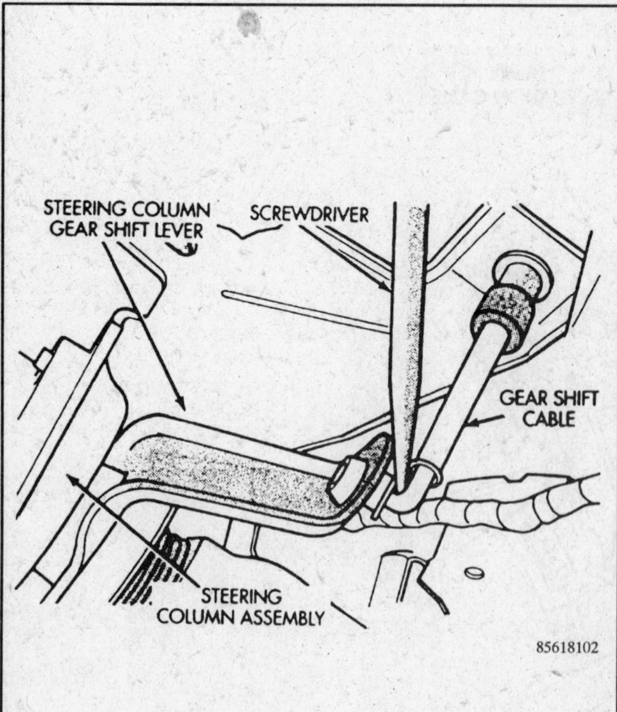

Fig. 100 Gear shift cable removal from steering column — 1992-95 models

43. Feed the speed control switch and air bag module wiring leads through the rectangular hole in the steering wheel, then feed the horn switch wiring lead through the round hole in the steering wheel.
44. Install the steering wheel as outlined earlier in this Section.
45. Connect the horn switch wiring lead from the clock spring, onto the steering wheel horn switch wiring.
46. If equipped with speed control, connect the speed control wiring from the clock spring onto the speed control switch.
47. Install the wiring lead from the clock spring onto the air bag module. Make the wiring connection onto the air bag module, by pressing straight in on the connector. Make sure it is fully seated.
48. Install the air bag module into the steering wheel and then install the 4 air bag module attaching nuts. Tighten all 4 air bag module attaching nuts to 100 inch lbs. (11 Nm).
49. Install the lower instrument panel reinforcement onto the instrument panel, then tighten the 4 retaining bolts to 50 inch lbs. (6 Nm).
50. Install the nut on the stud attaching the lower steering column bracket to the lower instrument panel reinforcement, then tighten the nut to 100 inch lbs. (11 Nm).
51. Install the DRB diagnostic connector onto the instrument panel bracket on the lower instrument panel reinforcement.
52. Install the fuse access/silencer panel assembly on the lower instrument panel.
53. Position the lower steering column in the vehicle. Connect the lift gate release switch connector.
54. Install the steering column cover and 5 attaching screws.
55. Install the parking brake release rod, to the parking brake pedal assembly and lock attaching clip.
56. Readjust then test the transmission shift linkage.
57. Perform the Air Bag System Check procedures outlined in Section 6 before connecting the negative battery cable.
58. Test the operation of any steering column functions such as the horn, lights or speed control system.

Steering Linkage

REMOVAL & INSTALLATION

Tie Rod Ends

1. Raise the front of the vehicle and support on jackstands.
2. Loosen the jam nut which connects the tie rod end to the rack.
3. Mark the tie rod position on the threads.
4. Remove the tie rod cotter pin and nut.
5. Using a puller, remove the tie rod from the steering knuckle.

➥ Count the number of turns when removing tie rod end. Install the new end the same amount of turns.

6. Unscrew the tie rod end from the rack.

To install:

7. Install a new tie rod end, screw in the same number of turns as when removed. Tighten the jam nut to 55 ft. lbs. (75 Nm).
8. Check the wheel alignment.

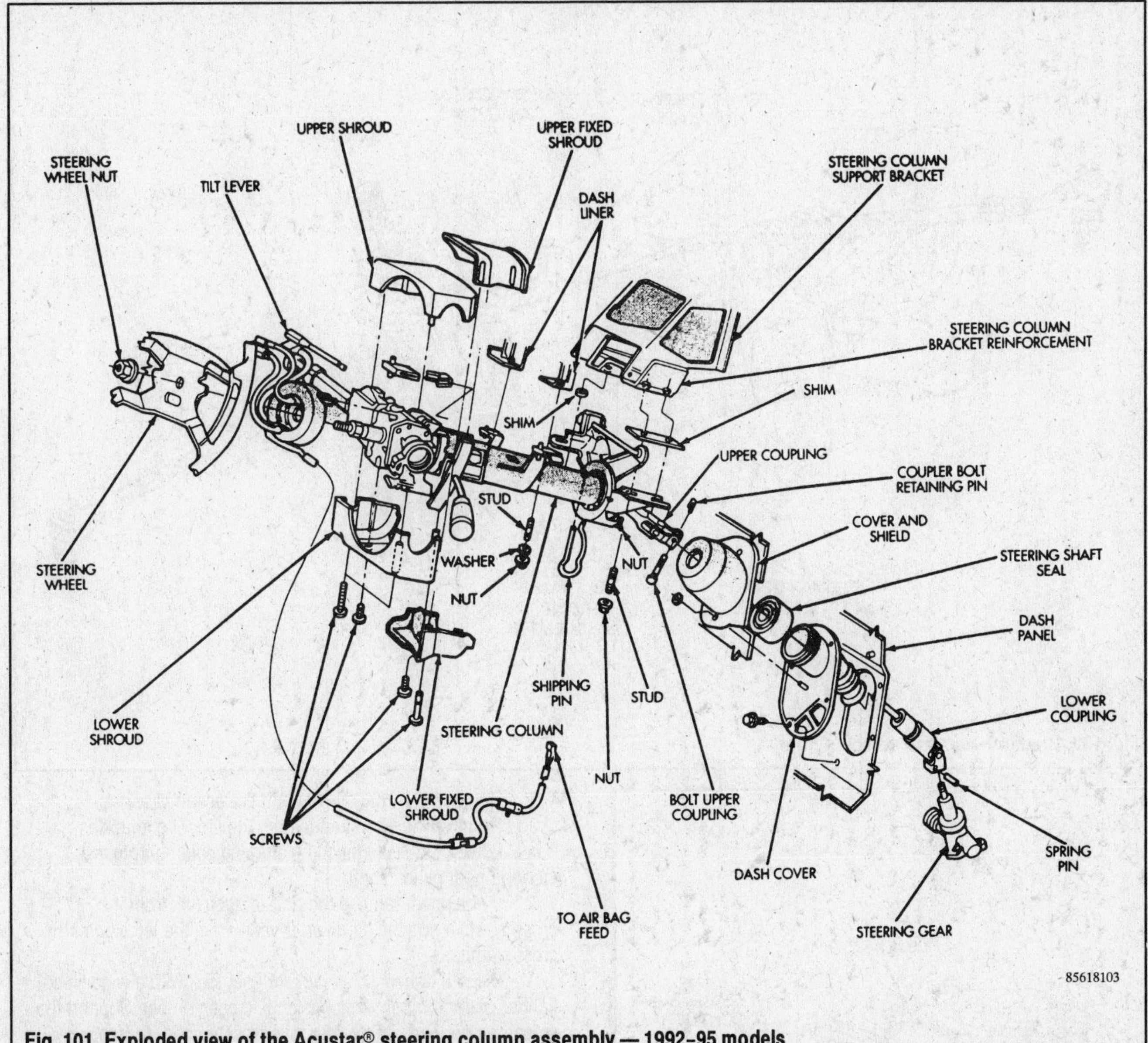

Fig. 101 Exploded view of the Acustar® steering column assembly — 1992-95 models

Steering Gear

The steering system (either manual or power) used on these vehicles is of the rack and pinion design.

The manual steering gear assembly consists of a tube which contains a toothed rack and a housing containing a straddle mounted, helical-cut pinion gear. Tie rods are connected to each end of the rack and an adjustable end (on each side) connects to the steering knuckles. A double universal joint attaches the pinion to the steering column shaft. Steering wheel movement is transmitted by the column shaft and the rack and pinion converts the rotational movement of the pinion to transverse movement of the rack. The manual steering gear is permanently lubricated at the factory and periodic lubrication is not necessary. The manual steering gear cannot be adjusted or serviced. If a malfunction occurs, the entire assembly must be replaced.

The power steering gear is similar to appearance, except for a rotary valve assembly and two fluid hose assemblies. The rotary valve assembly directs fluid from the power steering pump, through hoses, to either side of an internal rack piston. As steering wheel effort is applied, an internal torsion bar twists causing the rotary valve to direct the fluid behind an internal rack piston, which in turn builds up hydraulic pressure and assists in the turning effort.

Rubber boots seal the tie rods and rack assembly. Inspect the boots periodically for cuts, tears or leakage. Replace the boots as necessary.

REMOVAL & INSTALLATION

Front Wheel Drive Models

➧ See Figures 102 and 103

1. Loosen the wheel lugs slightly. Raise and support the front of the vehicle at the frame point below the front doors, not on the front crossmember. Use jackstands for supporting.

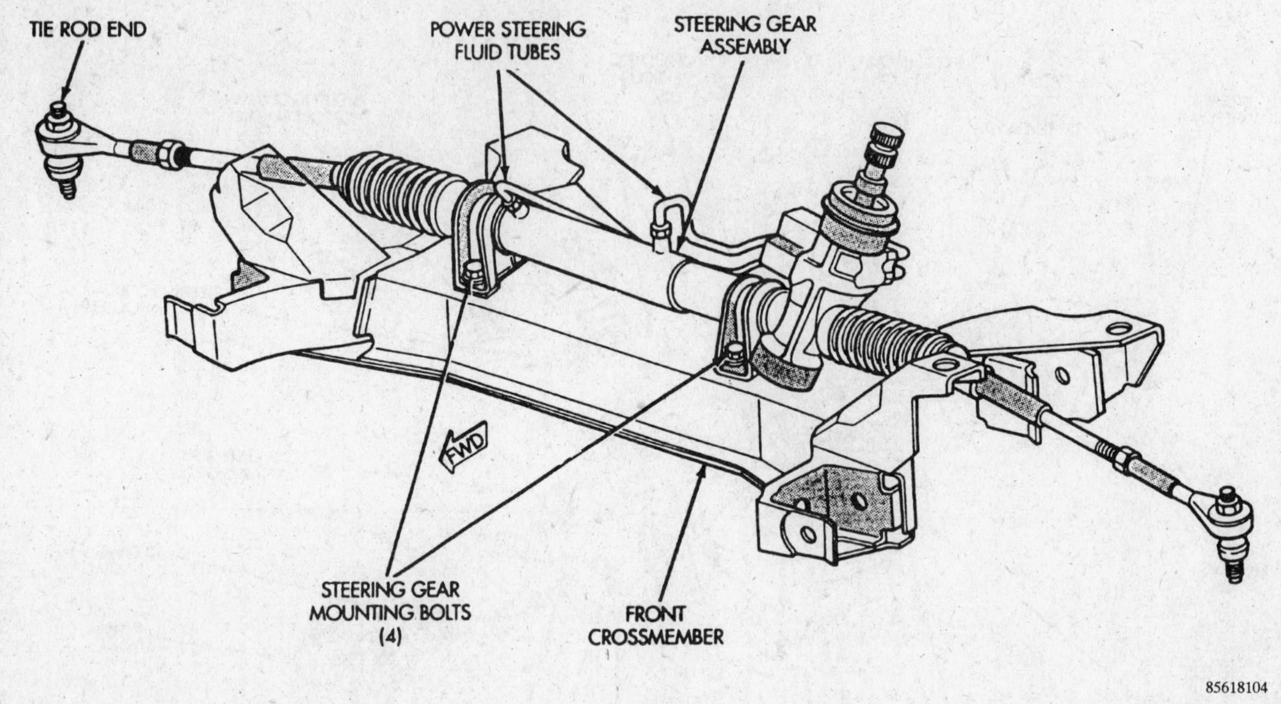

Fig. 102 Steering gear and crossmember

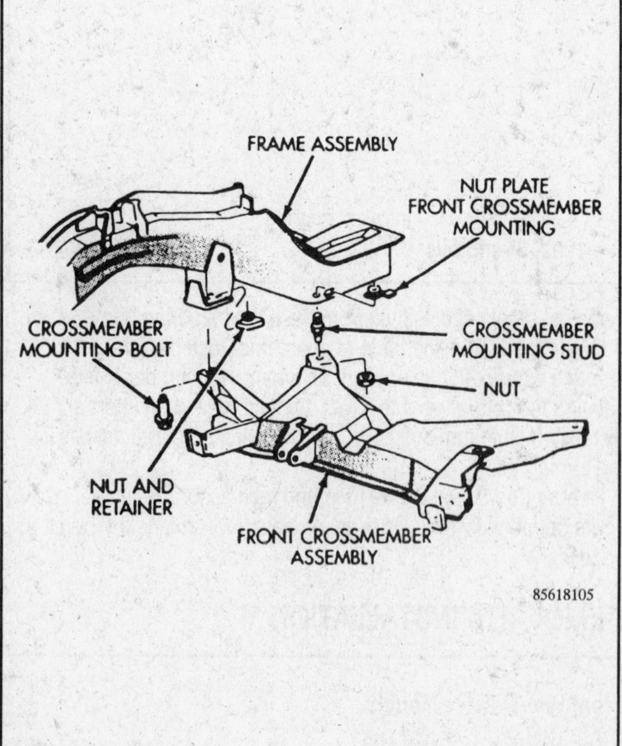

Fig. 103 Crossmember remove or replace

2. Remove the front wheels and tire assemblies.
3. Remove the tie rod ends from the steering knuckles.
4. Lower and disconnect the steering column from the steering gear pinion shaft.
5. If equipped, remove the anti-rotation link from the crossmember and the air diverter valve from the left side of the crossmember.
6. Place a transmission jack, or floor jack with a wide lifting flange, under the front suspension K-crossmember. Support the crossmember and remove the four crossmember to frame attaching bolts. Slowly lower the crossmember until enough room is gained to remove the steering gear assembly. Place stands under the crossmember, if available.
7. Remove the splash and boot shields. If equipped with power steering, disconnect the power steering hoses.
8. Remove the bolts that attach the steering gear assembly to the crossmember. Remove the assembly from the left side of the vehicle.

To install:

9. Align the gear pinion with the column. Installation is in the reverse order of removal. On models with manual steering, be sure the master serration of the steering gear aligns with the steering column connector. The right rear crossmember bolt is the alignment pilot for reinstallation. Install first, then tighten.
10. Attach the gear to the K-frame and secure the K-frame. Secure the anti-rotation link. Secure the K-frame. Tighten all crossmember attaching bolts to 90 ft. lbs. (122 Nm). Steering gear mounting bolts are tightened to 21 ft. lbs. (28 Nm).

11. Connect the tie rod ends. Fill power steering reservoir (if equipped), start engine, turn the steering wheel from lock-to-lock and check for fluid leaks.

12. Check toe adjustment.

All Wheel Drive (AWD) Models

➧ See Figure 104, 105, 106 and 107

Before removing the steering gear on AWD models, the steering column must be removed to provide clearance for steering rack removal.

1. Raise and support the vehicle. Remove the wheel and tire assemblies.
2. Remove the steering column assembly from the vehicle.
3. Remove the tie rod ends from the steering knuckle using a suitable puller.
4. Remove the 2 bolts and the 2 nuts that attach the bridge assembly to the crossmember. The bolts and nuts can be reached through the access holes in the top of the bridge assembly.
5. Remove the crossmember-to-frame rail attaching bolts. Use a jack to lower the crossmember so that it is suspended from the lower control arms. It is necessary to remove the crossmember completely from the vehicle.
6. Disconnect and plug the power steering lines from the steering gear. Remove the hose retaining bracket from the crossmember.
7. Remove the 4 bolts that retain the steering gear to the bridge assembly.

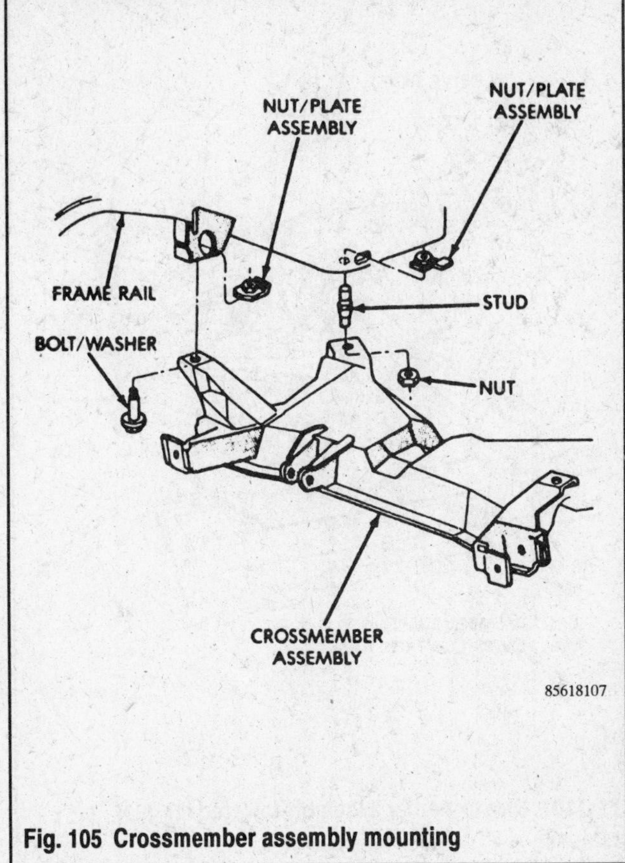

Fig. 105 Crossmember assembly mounting

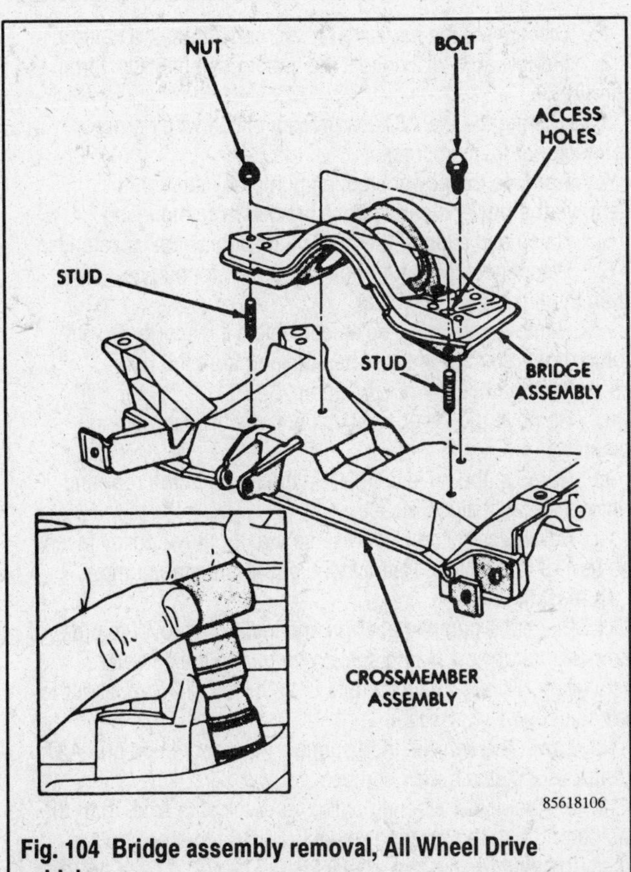

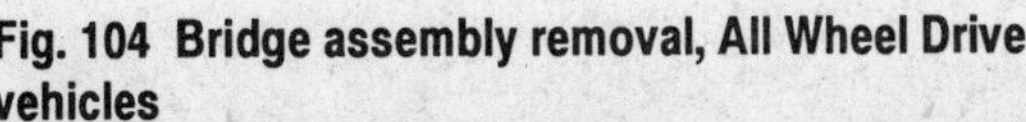

Fig. 104 Bridge assembly removal, All Wheel Drive vehicles

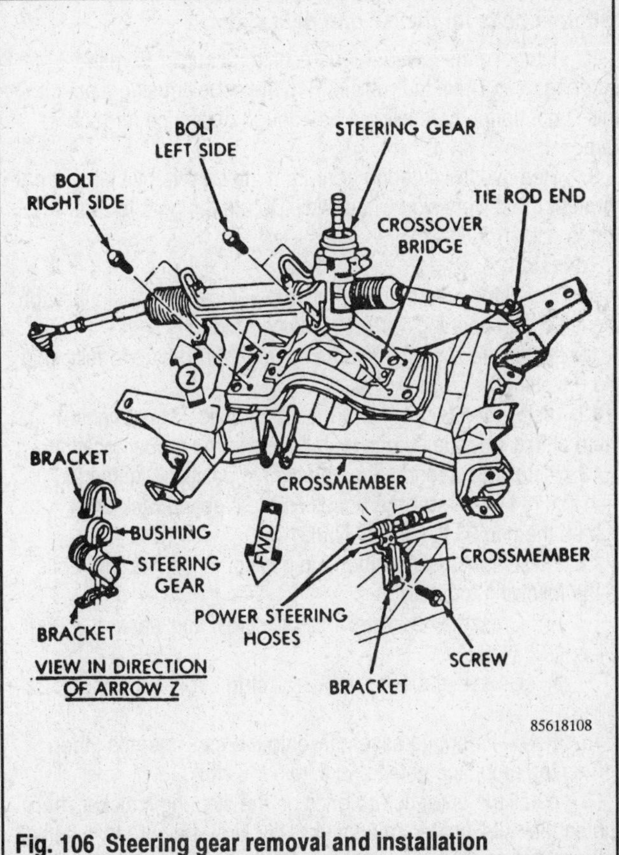

Fig. 106 Steering gear removal and installation

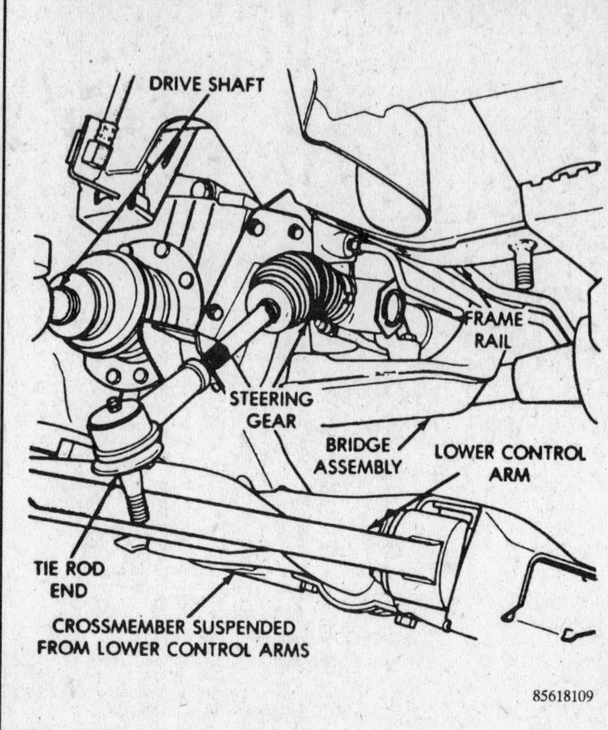

Fig. 107 Crossmember assembly lowered for gear removal

➜ Note the position of each bolt as it is removed, there are different bolts for the left and right sides.

8. Remove the lower steering column coupler from the steering gear. Drive the roll pin from the coupler using a punch. If this is not done, there will not be enough clearance for rack removal.
9. Remove the steering gear from the vehicle by pulling it out through the drivers side wheel well. Rotate the gear to clear the frame rail.

To install:

10. Install the steering gear into the vehicle. Work it in through the left wheel opening, rotating it as needed.
11. Install the steering column coupler, make sure to fully seat the roll pin.
12. Install the steering gear mounting bolts. Do not tighten them at this time, be sure to install them in the proper locations.
13. Install the steering hose bracket in position, tighten to 70 inch lbs. (8 Nm). Install the hoses on the steering rack, then tighten them to 23 ft. lbs. (31 Nm).
14. Raise the crossmember into position and install the bolts to the following torques:
    a. Crossmember-to-frame rail screw and washer — 90 ft. lbs. (122 Nm).
    b. Crossmember-to-frame rail stud nut — 90 ft. lbs. (122 Nm)
15. Install the bridge assembly onto the crossmember, then tighten the mounting nuts to 50 ft. lbs. (68 Nm).
16. Install the outer tie rod ends on the steering knuckle, then tighten the nuts, tighten to 38 ft. lbs. (52 Nm). Be sure to install a new cotter pin.
17. Install the wheel and tire assemblies. Lower the vehicle.
18. Install the steering wheel assembly.
19. Connect the negative battery cable. Start the vehicle and check the power steering lines for leaks. Check the fluid level.

Boot Seals

REMOVAL & INSTALLATION

1. Raise and support the front of the vehicle on jackstands.
2. Disconnect the tie rod end from the steering knuckle. Loosen the jam nut and unscrew the end. Count the number of turns required when removing the end.
3. Cut the inner boot clamp, use pliers to expand the outer clamp and remove.
4. Locate and mark for reinstallation, the location of the breather tube.
5. Use a small tool to lift the boot from inner mounting groove and slide boot from the shaft.
6. Install the new boot and clamps. Locate the breather tube to the reference mark. Lubricate the boot and the mounting groove with silicone type lubricant. Install the tie rod end the same number of turns as counted when removing.

Power Steering Pump

REMOVAL & INSTALLATION

1. Disconnect the negative battery cable from the battery.
2. If applicable, disconnect the vapor hose (canister) from the carburetor.
3. Disengage the A/C compressor clutch wire harness connector at the compressor.
4. Remove the power steering pump adjustment bolt. Remove the power steering hose bracket from mounting.
5. Raise and support the front of the vehicle on jackstands.
6. Disconnect the return hose from the steering gear and drain the fluid into a container.
7. Remove the right side splash shield if it interferes with pump removal. After the fluid has drained from the pump, disconnect the hoses from the pump.
8. Remove the lower pivot bolt and nut from the pump mounting.
9. Remove the drive belt. Move the pump to the rear and remove the adjusting bracket.
10. Rotate the pump clockwise so that the drive pulley faces the rear of the vehicle. Remove the power steering pump.

To install:

11. Place the pump in position and install it in reverse order of removal. Install new O-ring seal on the pump hoses before installation. Tighten the tube nuts to 25 ft. lbs. (34 Nm). Refer to belt adjustments in Section 1.
12. Lower the vehicle, then connect the vapor hose and A/C compressor clutch switch harness..
13. Fill the power steering pump reservoir with fluid. Start the engine and turn the steering wheel from stop-to-stop, several times, to bleed the system. check the fluid level.

TORQUE SPECIFICATIONS

Component	English	Metric
WHEELS		
Wheel lug nuts	95 ft. lbs.	129 Nm
FRONT SUSPENSION		
Ball joint-to-knuckle clamp bolt		
1984–89	70 ft. lbs.	95 Nm
1990–91	105 ft. lbs.	145 Nm
Ball joint stud-to-steering knuckle clamp bolt		
1984–89	70 ft. lbs.	95 Nm
1990–91	105 ft. lbs.	143 Nm
1992–95	100 ft. lbs.	136 Nm
Brake hose retaining bracket	10 ft. lbs.	14 Nm
Coil spring assembly nut	60 ft. lbs.	82 Nm
Front Hub and Bearing		
Press-in-type		
Bearing retainer bolts	20 ft. lbs.	27 Nm
Bolt-in type		
Bearing mounting bolts	45 ft. lbs.	61 Nm
Hub retaining nut	180 ft. lbs.	245 Nm
Lower control arm front pivot bolt		
1984–89	105 ft. lbs.	143 Nm
1990–91	125 ft. lbs.	170 Nm
1992–95	95 ft. lbs.	129 Nm
MacPherson strut		
Upper mount nuts	20 ft. lbs.	27 Nm
Lower mounting and camber nuts	75 ft. lbs. + 1/4 turn	102 Nm + 1/4 turn
Rear stub strut nut	70 ft. lbs.	95 Nm
Steering knuckle-to-lower control arm clamp bolt		
1984–89	70 ft. lbs.	95 Nm
1990–95	105 ft. lbs.	143 Nm
Sway bar bracket stud nuts		
1984–89	25 ft. lbs.	34 Nm
1990–95	50 ft. lbs.	68 Nm
Sway bar center bracket bolts		
1984–89	25 ft. lbs.	34 Nm
1990–95	50 ft. lbs.	68 Nm
Sway bar outer bracket bolts		
1984–89	25 ft. lbs.	34 Nm
1990–95	50 ft. lbs.	68 Nm
Tie rod end nut	35 ft. lbs.	48 Nm
REAR SUSPENSION		
Hub and bearing assembly bolts		
All wheel drive	96 ft. lbs.	130 Nm
Shock absorber bolts		
Front wheel drive	50 ft. lbs.	68 Nm
All wheel drive		
Upper bolts	85 ft. lbs.	115 Nm
Lower bolts	80 ft. lbs.	108 Nm

85618C02

TORQUE SPECIFICATIONS

Component	English	Metric
Spring		
Front wheel drive models		
Hanger bolts	45 ft. lbs.	61 Nm
U-bolt nuts	60 ft. lbs.	82 Nm
Front fixed end bolt	95 ft. lbs.	129 Nm
Shackle nuts	35 ft. lbs.	48 Nm
All wheel drive models		
Hanger bolts	45 ft. lbs.	61 Nm
U-bolt nuts	65 ft. lbs.	88 Nm
Front pivot bolts	105 ft. lbs.	142 Nm
Shackle and pin assembly through-bolt nuts	35 ft. lbs.	47 Nm
Shackle and pin assembly retaining bolts	35 ft. lbs.	47 Nm
Sway Bar		
All Wheel Drive Models		
Bushing-to-axle bracket	45 ft. lbs.	61 Nm
Link arm-to-frame rail	45 ft. lbs.	61 Nm
Sway bar-to-link arm	45 ft. lbs.	61 Nm
Link arm bracket-to-frame rail	24 ft. lbs.	33 Nm
STEERING		
Crossmember-to-frame rail screw	90 ft. lbs.	122 Nm
Crossmember-to-frame rail stud nut	90 ft. lbs.	122 Nm
K-frame-to-crossmember attaching bolts	90 ft. lbs.	122 Nm
Outer tie rod ends-to-steering knuckle nuts	38 ft. lbs.	52 Nm
Power steering bridge assembly-to-crossmember	50 ft. lbs.	68 Nm
Power steering hose bracket	70 inch lbs.	8 Nm
Power steering hoses-to-steering rack	23 ft. lbs.	31 Nm
Power steering pump tube nuts	25 ft. lbs.	34 Nm
Steering column bracket mounting stud nuts	105 inch lbs.	12 Nm
Steering gear mounting bolts		
1984–90	21 ft. lbs.	28 Nm
1991–95	50 ft. lbs.	68 Nm
Steering wheel nut	45 ft. lbs.	61 Nm
Tie rod end jam nut	55 ft. lbs.	75 Nm
Upper and lower steering shaft coupling nut	21 ft. lbs.	28 Nm

85618C03

BENDIX SYSTEM 10 ANTI-LOCK BRAKE SYSTEM
BLADDER ACCUMULATOR 9-48
COMPONENT REPLACEMENT 9-43
CONTROLLER ANTI-LOCK BRAKE (CAB) MODULE 9-48
DIAGNOSIS AND TESTING 9-37
HIGH PRESSURE AND RETURN HOSES 9-46
HYDRAULIC ASSEMBLY 9-47
HYDRAULIC RESERVOIR 9-48
PROPORTIONING VALVES 9-48
PUMP/MOTOR ASSEMBLY 9-46
SYSTEM DESCRIPTION 9-33
TONE RINGS 9-51
WHEEL SPEED SENSORS 9-49
BENDIX SYSTEM 4 ANTI-LOCK BRAKE SYSTEM
ANTI-LOCK BRAKE SYSTEM DEFINITIONS 9-54
ANTI-LOCK BRAKE SYSTEM OPERATION 9-54
BENDIX ANTI-LOCK 4 SYSTEM BLEEDING 9-62
CONTROLLER ANTI-LOCK BRAKE (CAB) MODULE 9-59
MAJOR COMPONENTS 9-54
MODULATOR ASSEMBLY 9-56
PROPORTIONING VALVE 9-59
SYSTEM DESCRIPTION 9-51
SYSTEM SELF-DIAGNOSTICS 9-51
WARNING SYSTEM OPERATIONS 9-54
WHEEL SPEED SENSORS 9-60
BRAKE SYSTEM
ADJUSTMENTS 9-3
BASIC OPERATING PRINCIPLES 9-2
BLEEDING THE BRAKE SYSTEM 9-11
BRAKE HOSES 9-9
BRAKE LIGHT SWITCH 9-4
FLUID RESERVOIR 9-5
HEIGHT SENSING FUEL PROPORTIONING VALVE 9-7
MASTER CYLINDER 9-4
POWER BOOSTERS 9-3
POWER BRAKE BOOSTER 9-6
PRESSURE DIFFERENTIAL SWITCH/WARNING LIGHT 9-7
FRONT DISC BRAKES
BRAKE DISC (ROTOR) 9-23
CALIPER 9-22
DISC BRAKE PADS 9-13
REAR DRUM BRAKES
BRAKE DRUMS 9-24
BRAKE SHOES 9-26
PARKING BRAKE 9-31
WHEEL CYLINDERS 9-30
SPECIFICATIONS CHARTS
BRAKE SPECIFICATIONS 9-66
TORQUE SPECIFICATIONS 9-66

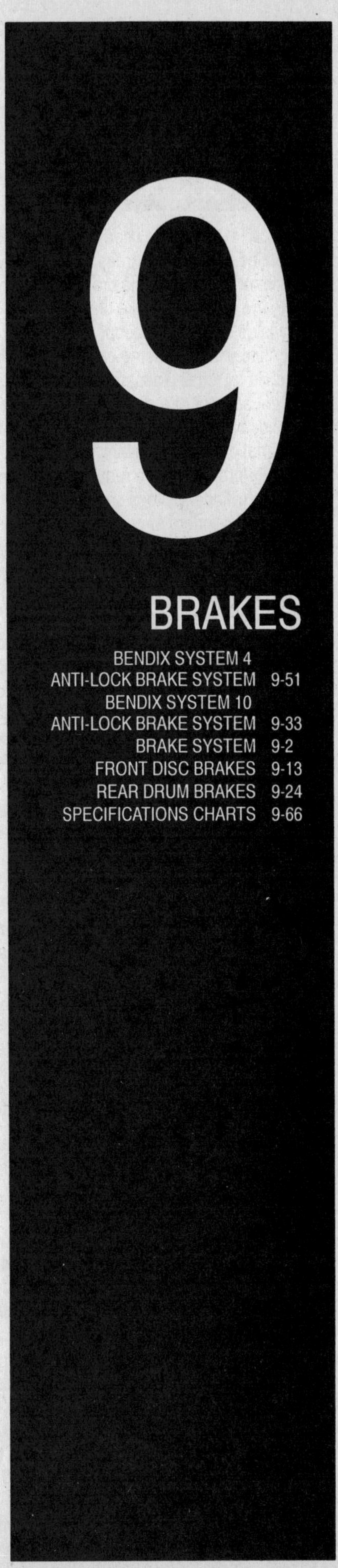

9

BRAKES

BENDIX SYSTEM 4 ANTI-LOCK BRAKE SYSTEM 9-51
BENDIX SYSTEM 10 ANTI-LOCK BRAKE SYSTEM 9-33
BRAKE SYSTEM 9-2
FRONT DISC BRAKES 9-13
REAR DRUM BRAKES 9-24
SPECIFICATIONS CHARTS 9-66

BRAKE SYSTEM

Basic Operating Principles

Hydraulic systems are used to actuate the brakes of all automobiles. The system transports the power required to force the frictional surfaces of the braking system together from the pedal to the individual brake units at each wheel. A hydraulic system is used for two reasons.

First, fluid under pressure can be carried to all parts of an automobile by small pipes and flexible hoses without taking up a significant amount of room or posing routing problems.

Second, a great mechanical advantage can be given to the brake pedal end of the system, and the foot pressure required to actuate the brakes can be reduced by making the surface area of the master cylinder pistons smaller than that of any of the pistons in the wheel cylinders or calipers.

The master cylinder consists of a fluid reservoir and a double cylinder and piston assembly. Double type master cylinders are designed to separate the front and rear braking systems hydraulically in case of a leak.

Steel lines carry the brake fluid to a point on the vehicles frame near each of the vehicles wheels. The fluid is then carried to the calipers and wheel cylinders by flexible tubes in order to allow for suspension and steering movements.

In drum brake systems, each wheel cylinder contains two pistons, one at either end, which push outward in opposite directions.

In disc brake systems, the cylinders are part of the calipers. One cylinder in each caliper is used to force the brake pads against the disc.

All pistons employ some type of seal, usually made of rubber, to minimize fluid leakage. A rubber dust boot seals the outer end of the cylinder against dust and dirt. The boot fits around the outer end of the piston on disc brake calipers, and around the brake actuating rod on wheel cylinders.

The hydraulic system operates as follows: When at rest, the entire system, from the piston(s) in the master cylinder to those in the wheel cylinders or calipers, is full of brake fluid. Upon application of the brake pedal, fluid trapped in front of the master cylinder piston(s) is forced through the lines to the wheel cylinders. Here, it forces the pistons outward, in the case of drum brakes, and inward toward the disc, in the case of disc brakes. The motion of the pistons is opposed by return springs mounted outside the cylinders in drum brakes, and by spring seals, in disc brakes.

Upon release of the brake pedal, a spring located inside the master cylinder immediately returns the master cylinder pistons to the normal position. The pistons contain check valves and the master cylinder has compensating ports drilled in it. These are uncovered as the pistons reach their normal position. The piston check valves allow fluid to flow toward the wheel cylinders or calipers as the pistons withdraw. Then, as the return springs force the brake pads or shoes into the released position, the excess fluid reservoir through the compensating ports. It is during the time the pedal is in the released position that any fluid that has leaked out of the system will be replaced through the compensating ports.

Dual circuit master cylinders employ two pistons, located one behind the other, in the same cylinder. The primary piston is actuated directly by mechanical linkage from the brake pedal through the power booster. The secondary piston is actuated by fluid trapped between the two pistons. If a leak develops in front of the secondary piston, it moves forward until it bottoms against the front of the master cylinder, and the fluid trapped between the pistons will operate the rear brakes. If the rear brakes develop a leak, the primary piston will move forward until direct contact with the secondary piston takes place, and it will force the secondary piston to actuate the front brakes. In either case, the brake pedal moves farther when the brakes are applied, and less braking power is available.

All dual circuit systems use a switch to warn the driver when only half of the brake system is operational. This switch is located in a valve body which is mounted on the firewall or the frame below the master cylinder. A hydraulic piston receives pressure from both circuits, each circuit's pressure being applied to one end of the piston. When the pressures are in balance, the piston remains stationary. When one circuit has a leak, however, the greater pressure in that circuit during application of the brakes will push the piston to one side, closing the switch and activating the brake warning light.

In disc brake systems, this valve body also contains a metering valve and, in some cases, a proportioning valve. The metering valve keeps pressure from traveling to the disc brakes on the front wheels until the brake shoes on the rear wheels have contacted the drums, ensuring that the front brakes will never be used alone. The proportioning valve controls the pressure to the rear brakes to lessen the chance of rear wheel lock-up during very hard braking.

Warning lights may be tested by depressing the brake pedal and holding it while opening one of the wheel cylinder bleeder screws. If this does not cause the light to go on, substitute a new lamp, make continuity checks, and, finally, replace the switch as necessary.

The hydraulic system may be checked for leaks by applying pressure to the pedal gradually and steadily. If the pedal sinks very slowly to the floor, the system has a leak. This is not to be confused with a springy or spongy feel due to the compression of air within the lines. If the system leaks, there will be a gradual change in the position of the pedal with a constant pressure.

Check for leaks along all lines and at wheel cylinders. If no external leaks are apparent, the problem is inside the master cylinder.

DISC BRAKES

Instead of the traditional expanding brakes that press outward against a circular drum, disc brake systems utilize a disc (rotor) with brake pads positioned on either side of it. Braking effect is achieved in a manner similar to the way you would squeeze a spinning phonograph record between your fingers. The disc (rotor) is a casting with cooling fins between the two braking surfaces. This enables air to circulate between the braking surfaces making them less sensitive to heat buildup and more resistant to fade. Dirt and water do not affect braking action since contaminants are thrown off by the centrifugal action of the rotor or scraped off the by the pads. Also, the equal clamping action of the two brake pads tends to ensure uniform, straight line stops.

Disc brakes are inherently self-adjusting. There are three general types of disc brake:

1. A fixed caliper.
2. A floating caliper.
3. A sliding caliper.

The fixed caliper design uses two pistons mounted on either side of the rotor (in each side of the caliper). The caliper is mounted rigidly and does not move.

The sliding and floating designs are quite similar. In fact, these two types are often lumped together. In both designs, the pad on the inside of the rotor is moved into contact with the rotor by hydraulic force. The caliper, which is not held in a fixed position, moves slightly, bringing the outside pad into contact with the rotor. There are various methods of attaching floating calipers. Some pivot at the bottom or top, and some slide on mounting bolts. In any event, the end result is the same.

All the vehicles covered in this book employ the sliding caliper design.

DRUM BRAKES

Drum brakes employ two brake shoes mounted on a stationary backing plate. These shoes are positioned inside a circular drum which rotates with the wheel assembly. The shoes are held in place by springs. This allows them to slide toward the drums (when they are applied) while keeping the linings and drums in alignment. The shoes are actuated by a wheel cylinder which is mounted at the top of the backing plate. When the brakes are applied, hydraulic pressure forces the wheel cylinder's actuating links outward. Since these links bear directly against the top of the brake shoes, the tops of the shoes are then forced against the inner side of the drum. This action forces the bottoms of the two shoes to contact the brake drum by rotating the entire assembly slightly (known as servo action). When pressure within the wheel cylinder is relaxed, return springs pull the shoes back away from the drum.

Most modern drum brakes are designed to self-adjust themselves during application when the vehicle is moving in reverse. This motion causes both shoes to rotate very slightly with the drum, rocking an adjusting lever, thereby causing rotation of the adjusting screw.

****WARNING**

Clean, high quality brake fluid is essential to the safe and proper operation of the brake system. You should always buy the highest quality brake fluid that is available. If the brake fluid becomes contaminated, drain and flush the system and fill the master cylinder with new fluid. Never reuse any brake fluid. Any brake fluid that is removed from the system should be discarded.

Power Boosters

Power brakes operate just as standard brake systems except in the actuation of the master cylinder pistons. A vacuum diaphragm is located on the front of the master cylinder and assists the driver in applying the brakes, reducing both the effort and travel he must put into moving the brake pedal.

The vacuum diaphragm housing is connected to the intake manifold by a vacuum hose. A check valve is placed at the point where the hose enters the diaphragm housing, so that during periods of low manifold vacuum brake assist vacuum will not be lost.

Depressing the brake pedal closes off the vacuum source and allows atmospheric pressure to enter on one side of the diaphragm. This causes the master cylinder pistons to move and apply the brakes. When the brake pedal is released, vacuum is applied to both sides of the diaphragm, and return springs return the diaphragm and master cylinder pistons to the released position. If the vacuum fails, the brake pedal rod will butt against the end of the master cylinder actuating rod, and direct mechanical application will occur as the pedal is depressed.

The hydraulic and mechanical problems that apply to conventional brake systems also apply to power brakes, and should be checked for if the tests below do not reveal the problem.

Test for a system vacuum leak as described below:

1. Operate the engine at idle without touching the brake pedal for at least one minute.
2. Turn **OFF** the engine, and wait one minute.
3. Test for the presence of assist vacuum by depressing the brake pedal and releasing it several times. Light application will produce less and less pedal travel, if vacuum was present. If there is no vacuum, air is leaking into the system somewhere.

Test for system operation as follows:

4. Pump the brake pedal (with engine **OFF**) until the supply vacuum is entirely gone.
5. Put a light, steady pressure on the pedal.
6. Start the engine, and operate it at idle. If the system is operating, the brake pedal should fall toward the floor if constant pressure is maintained on the pedal.

Power brake systems may be tested for hydraulic leaks just as ordinary systems are tested.

Your vehicle is equipped with pin slider type caliper front disc brakes and automatic adjuster equipped rear drum brakes. The brake system is diagonally split, with the left front and right rear brakes on one hydraulic system and the right front and left rear on the other. Should one side of the split system fail, the other should provide enough braking power to bring the vehicle to a stop. Other components included in the brake system are: A brake warning switch, master cylinder, a lead sensing dual proportioning valve, a brake booster and the necessary hoses and lines.

Adjustments

Periodic brake adjustment is not necessary as the front calipers are inherently self-adjusting, and the rear brakes are equipped with self-adjusters. In the event of a brake reline or component service requiring brake shoe removal, initial manual adjustment of the rear brake shoes will speed up servicing time. Front brake pads adjust themselves as the brake pedal is applied. After installing new front brake pads pump the brake pedal several times until a firm feeling is obtained. The pads will be incorrect adjustment.

DRUM BRAKES

1. To make an initial rear brake shoe adjustment, raise and support the rear of the vehicle on jackstands, so that both wheels are off the ground and can turn freely.
2. Remove the adjusting hole cover at the back of the brake mounting plates.
3. Be sure the parking brake is fully released and that there is slack in the brake cables.
4. Insert a brake adjusting tool through the hole in the backing plate until the adjuster star wheel is engaged. move the adjusting tool upward to turn the star wheel. Continue until a slight drag is felt when the wheel is rotated.
5. Insert a thin screwdriver or piece of stiff rod through the backing plate slot and push the adjuster lock tab away from the star wheel. Move the adjusting tool down while holding the locking tab out of the way. Back off the star wheel until the wheel turns freely without any brake drag. Install the adjusting slot cover.
6. Repeat the procedure for the other rear wheel. Adjust the parking brake after initial rear brake adjustment is finished. Check parking brake adjustment after applying several times, insure freedom from brake drag.

Brake Light Switch

The brake light switch is a self adjusting unit installed on the brake pedal shaft pivot pin.

REMOVAL & INSTALLATION

1. Remove the old switch from the retaining bracket.
2. Install the new brake light switch into the bracket and push the switch as far forward as it will go.
3. The brake pedal will move forward slightly when the switch is pushed forward.
4. Pull back on the brake pedal gently. As the brake pedal is pulled back, the switch striker will move toward the switch. When the brake pedal can not be pulled back any further, the switch will ratchet to the correct position. Very little movement is required, and no further adjustment is required.

Master Cylinder

The master cylinder is of tandem design, having an anodized aluminum body and a glass reinforced nylon reservoir. If the cylinder bore is pitted or scratched, the body must be replaced as honing will remove the anodized surface. The reservoir is indexed to prevent incorrect installation and the cap diaphragms are slotted to allow internal pressure to equalize. A secondary outlet tube leading from the master cylinder is connected to the differential valve mounted underneath the master cylinder. The front part of the valve supplied the right rear and left front brakes. The rear portion supplied the right rear and left front. The rear portion of the valve is connect to the primary outlet tube of the master cylinder.

REMOVAL & INSTALLATION

See Figures 1, 2, 3 and 4

1. Disconnect the primary and secondary brake lines at the master cylinder. Tape or plug the ends of the lines.
2. Remove the nuts attaching the master cylinder to the power brake booster.
3. Wrap a rag around the brake line fitting holes, slide the master straight away from the booster and remove from the vehicle. take care not to spill any brake fluid on the finish. Flush off with water if any fluid is spilled.

To install:

4. Bench bleed the master cylinder. For more details, refer to the bleeding procedure outlined in this section.
5. Install the master cylinder over the mounting studs.
6. After aligning the master cylinder pushrod and mounting studs, hold the cylinder in position and start the attaching nuts but do not tighten completely.
7. Install the brake lines but do not tighten completely.
8. After the brake lines are installed, tighten the cylinder mounting nuts fully and then the brake lines.
9. Finish bleeding the brake system.

85619001

Fig. 1 Disconnecting the brake lines at the master cylinder — 1987 Voyager shown

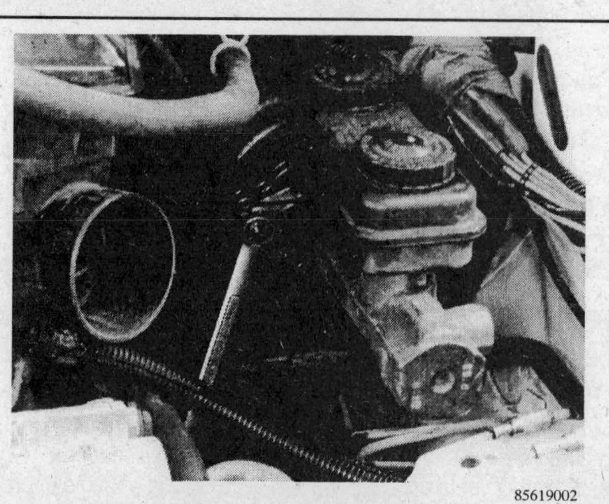

85619002

Fig. 2 Removing the master cylinder attaching nuts

85619003

Fig. 3 Removing the master cylinder away from the booster

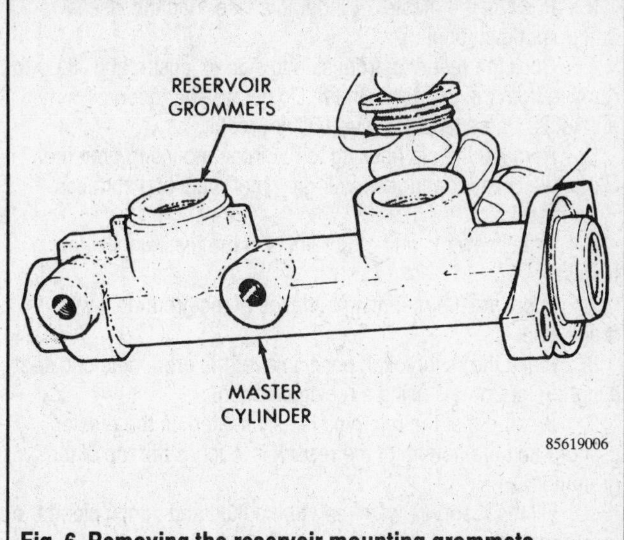

Fig. 6 Removing the reservoir mounting grommets

OVERHAUL

See Figures 4, 5, 6 and 7

The aluminum master cylinder cannot be rebuilt; service is limited to replacement.

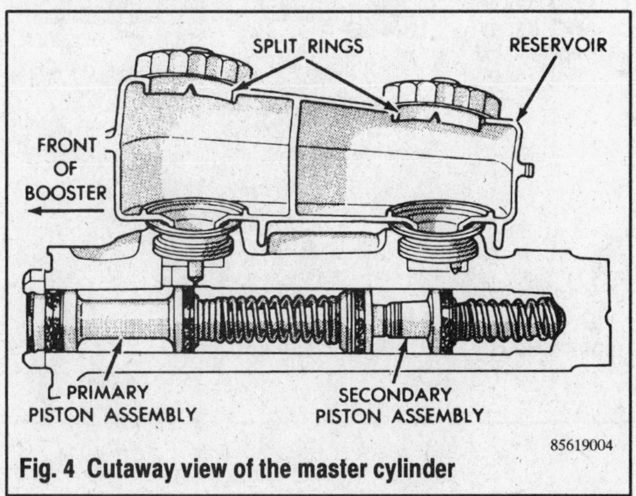

Fig. 4 Cutaway view of the master cylinder

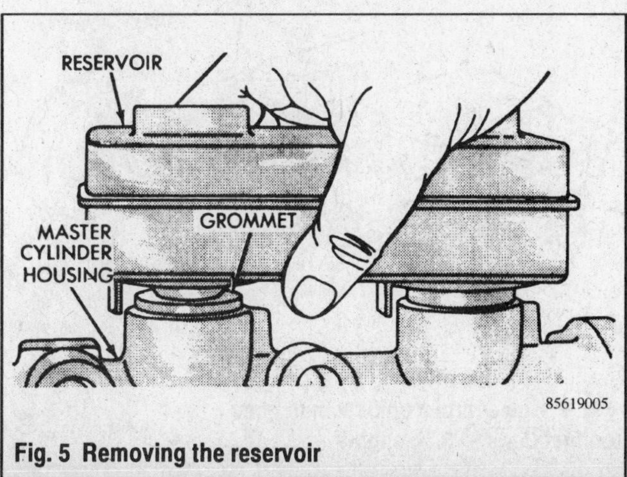

Fig. 5 Removing the reservoir

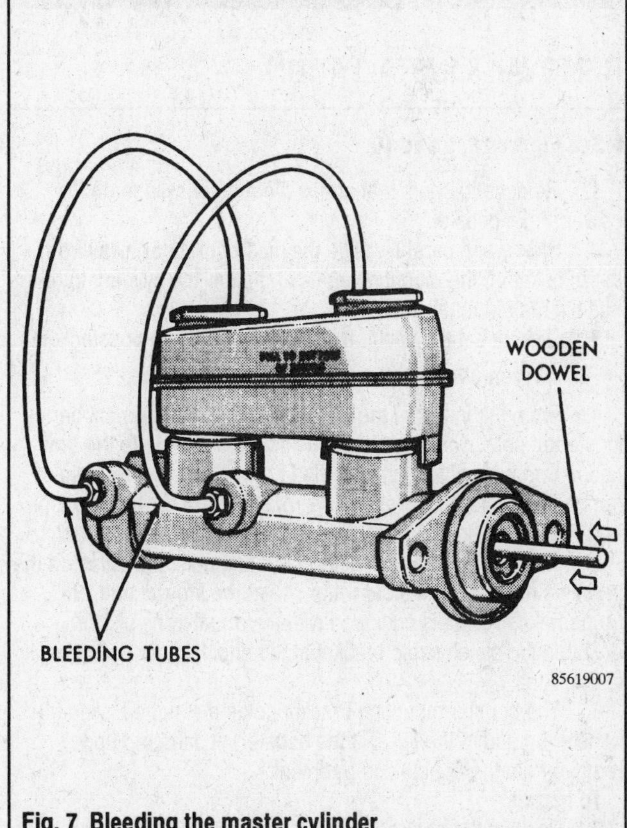

Fig. 7 Bleeding the master cylinder

Fluid Reservoir

REMOVAL & INSTALLATION

1. Remove the master cylinder from the vehicle. Clean the outside of the reservoir and cylinder.
2. Remove the reservoir caps and empty the brake fluid. Do not reuse the old fluid.

3. Position the master cylinder in a vise. Pad the vise jaws and do not over tighten.
4. Rock the reservoir from side to side to loosen and lift up to remove from the master cylinder. Do not pry the reservoir with any tools. Damage to the reservoir will result.
5. Remove the old housing to reservoir mounting grommets. Clean the cylinder and reservoir grommet mounting surfaces.

To install:

6. Install new mounting grommets in the master cylinder housing.
7. Lubricate the mounting surfaces of the grommets with brake fluid.
8. Place the reservoir in position over the grommets and seat it into the grommets using a rocking motion.
9. Be sure that the reservoir is fully seated on the master cylinder and the bottom of the reservoir touches the top of the grommets.
10. Fill the reservoir with fresh brake fluid and bench bleed the master cylinder.

Power Brake Booster

REMOVAL & INSTALLATION

➧ **See Figures 8, 9 and 10**

1. Remove the nuts that attach the master cylinder to the power brake booster.
2. Slowly and carefully slide the master cylinder away from the booster, off the mounting studs and allow the cylinder to rest against the fender shield.
3. Disconnect the vacuum hose from the brake booster.

➔ Do not remove the check valve.

4. From the inside of the vehicle under the instrument panel, locate the point where the booster linkage connects to the brake pedal. Use a small tool and position between the center tang of the booster linkage to brake pedal retaining clip. Rotate the tool and pull the retainer from the pin. disconnect the brake pedal.
5. Remove the brake booster mounting nuts and unfasten the brackets mounting the steel water line at the firewall and left frame rail. On models equipped with a manual transmission, unfasten the clutch cable bracket at the shock tower and move it to the side.
6. The booster mounting bracket holes are slotted, slide the booster up and to the left. Tilt the booster inboard and up to remove from the engine compartment.

To install:

7. Position the power booster over the firewall mounting studs. Install the mounting nuts, then tighten to 16–25 ft. lbs. (22–34 Nm).
8. install the steel heater line bracket and clutch cable bracket, if equipped.
9. Carefully install the master cylinder, then tighten the mounting bolts to 16–25 ft. lbs. (22–34 Nm).
10. Connect the vacuum line to the power brake booster.
11. Connect the pedal linkage to the booster push rod after lubricating the pivot point with white grease. Install a new retainer clip. Check the brake and stoplight operation.

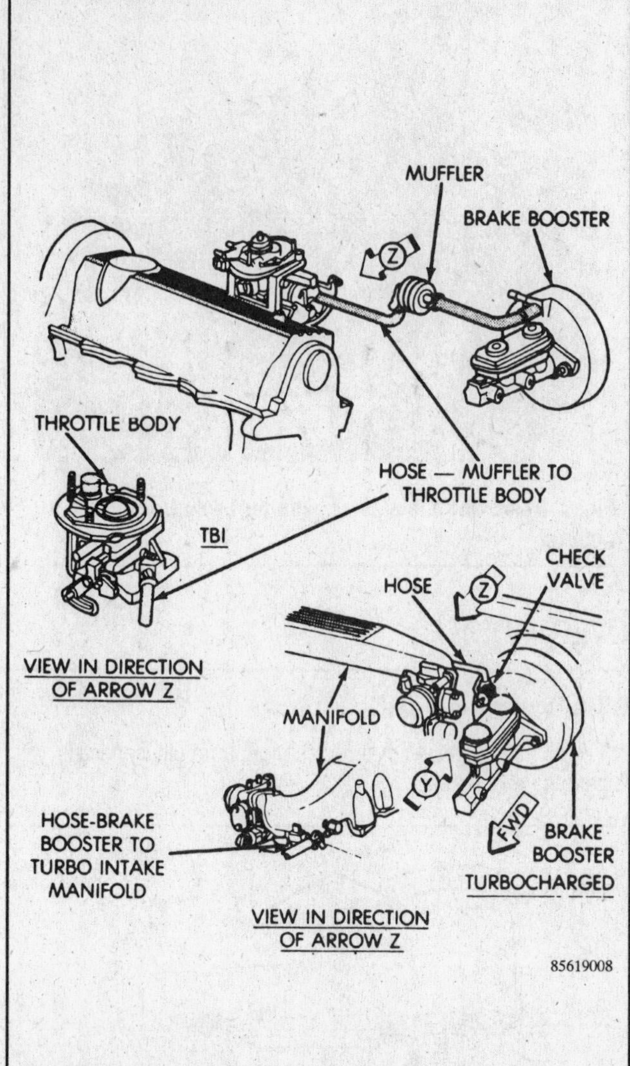

Fig. 8 Power brake unit/vacuum hose connections — 2.2L and 2.5L engines

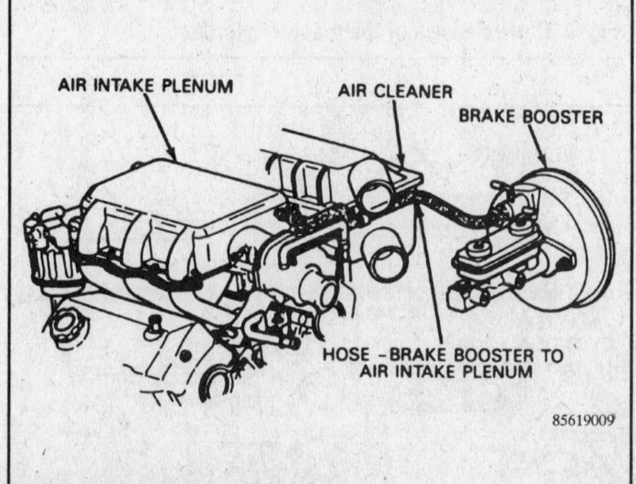

Fig. 9 Power brake unit/vacuum hose connections — 3.0L engine

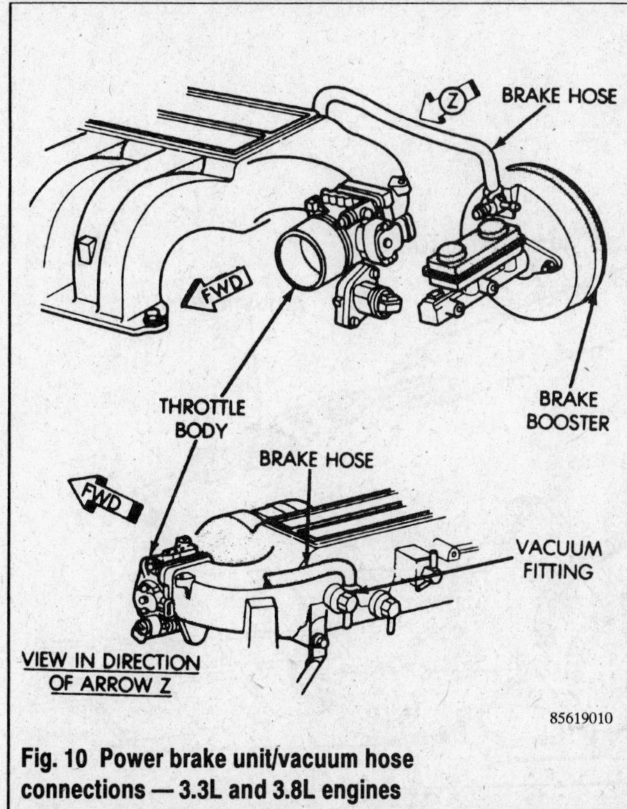

Fig. 10 Power brake unit/vacuum hose connections — 3.3L and 3.8L engines

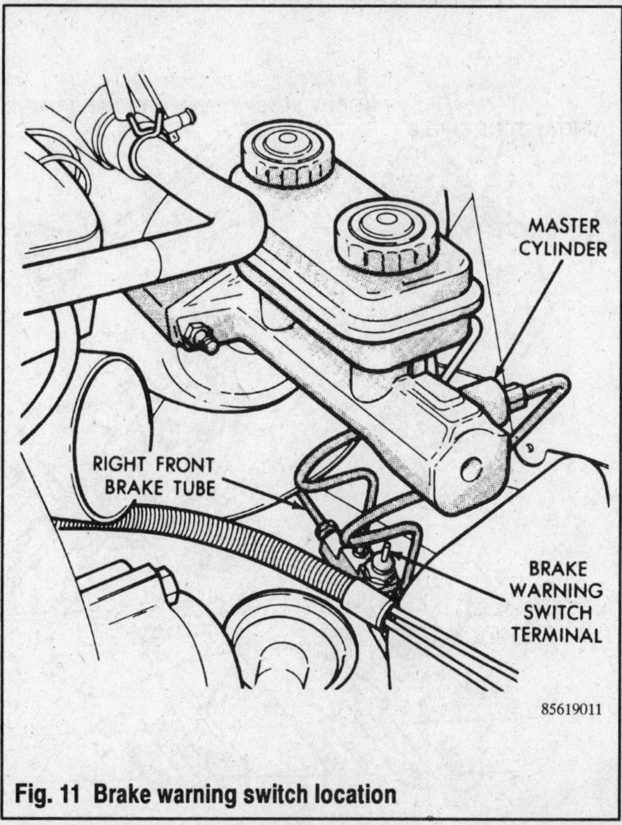

Fig. 11 Brake warning switch location

Pressure Differential Switch/Warning Light

See Figure 11

As mentioned before, the hydraulic brake system on your vehicle is diagonally split; the left front and right rear are part of one system and the right front and left rear part of the other. Both systems are routed through a pressure differential switch (located under the master cylinder) which is designed to warn the driver should a failure occur. If hydraulic pressure is lost in one side of the split system the switch will activate a warning light on the instrument panel, indicating that the brake system should be checked and repaired, if necessary. After repairs to the system have been made, the switch will automatically center itself and the light will go out.

TESTING

1. Raise the front or rear of the vehicle and safely support with jackstands.
2. Open a caliper or wheel cylinder bleeder valve while a helper holds pressure on the brake pedal.
3. As fluid is lost through the bleeder, the dash lamp should light.
4. If the lamp fails to light, check for a burned out bulb, disconnected socket, or a broken or disengaged wire at the switch.
5. Replace the warning switch if the rest of the circuit members check out.
6. Fill the master cylinder and bleed the brakes after repairs have been completed.

Height Sensing Fuel Proportioning Valve

See Figures 12 and 13

All vehicles are equipped with a height sensing dual proportioning valve. The valve is located under the rear floor pan just forward of the rear axle. The valve automatically provides the proper brake balance between the front and rear brakes regardless of the vehicle load condition. the valve modulates the rear brakes sensing the loading condition of the vehicle through relative height movement between the rear axle and load floor.

The valve is mounted on a crossmember and connected to an adjustable lever on the rear axle by a large spring. When the vehicle is unloaded or lightly loaded, the hydraulic line pressure is minimized. As the vehicle is more heavily loaded and the ride height lowers, the spring moves the valve control arm to allow higher rear brake pressure.

Because ride height determines rear brake pressure, the use of after market load leveling or capacity increasing devices should be avoided.

The proportioning section of the valve transmits full input pressure up to a certain point, called the split point. Beyond the split point the valve reduces the amount of pressure increase to the rear brakes according to a certain ratio. This means that on light brake pedal application equal pressure will be transmitted to the front and rear brakes. On harder pedal application, pressure transmitted to the rear brakes will be lower to prevent rear wheel lock-up and skid.

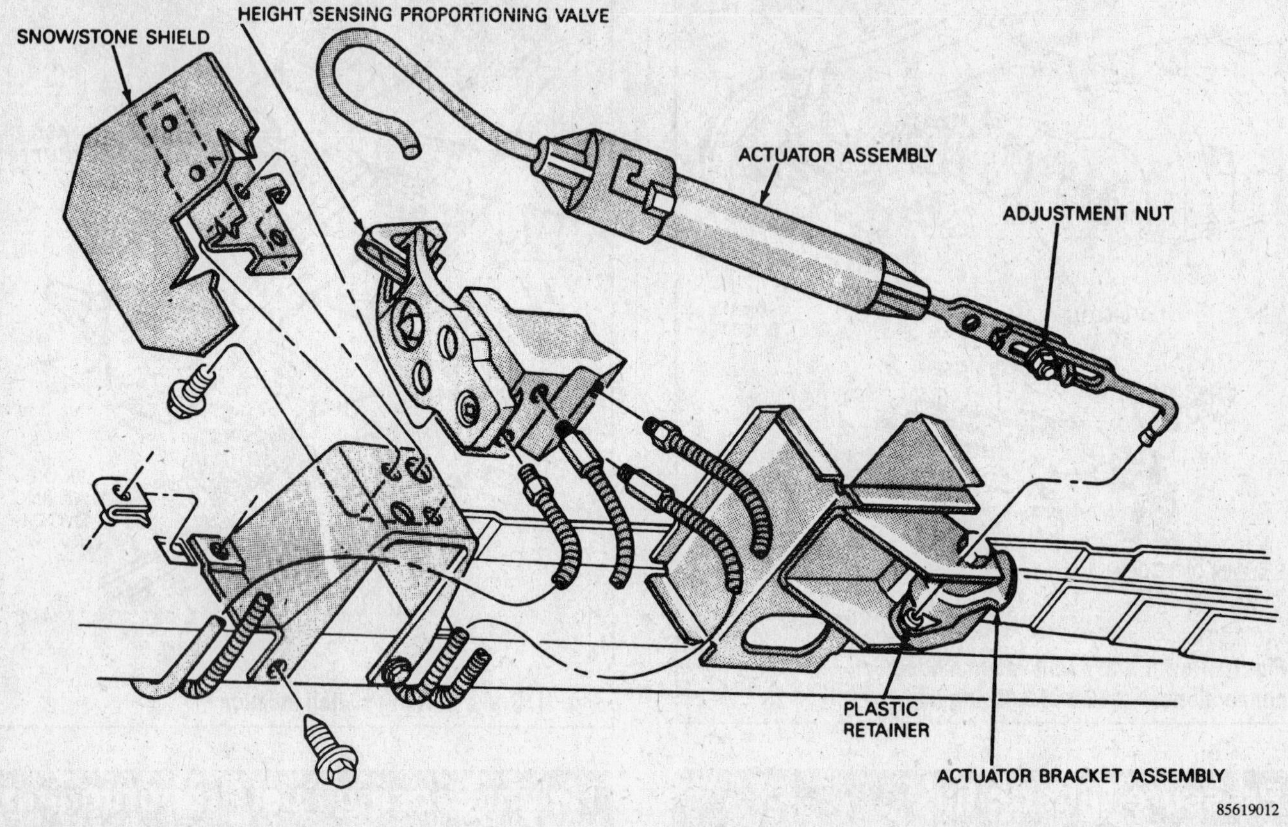

Fig. 12 Height sensing dual proportioning valve assembly — late model, non ABS equipped vehicles

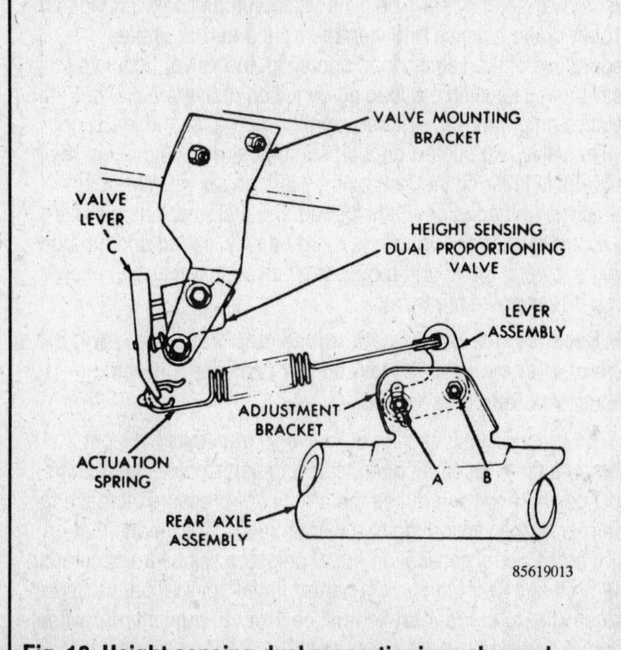

Fig. 13 Height sensing dual proportioning valve and adjustment points — early models

TESTING

➜ Two pressure gauges and adapter fittings (tool set C-4007A or equivalent) are required of the following test.

If premature rear wheel lock-up and skid is experienced frequently, it could be an indication that the fluid pressure to the rear brakes is excessive and that a malfunction has occurred in the proportioning valve or an adjustment is necessary.

1. If a pressure gauge and adapter fittings are on hand, proceed with the following test.
2. Disconnect the external spring at the valve lever.
3. Install one pressure gauge and T-fitting in line from either master cylinder port to the brake valve assembly.
4. Install the second gauge to either rear brake outlet port between the valve assembly and the rear brake line. Bleed the rear brakes.
5. Have a helper apply and hold pedal pressure to get a reading on the valve inlet gauge and outlet gauge. The inlet pressure should be 500 psi (3447 kPa) and the outlet pressure should be 100–200 psi. (690–1379 kPa).
6. If the required pressures are not present, replace the valve.
7. If the test pressures are all right, adjust the external spring and arm.

VALVE REMOVAL, INSTALLATION AND ADJUSTMENT

1. Raise and support the rear of the vehicle. Position jackstands at the rear contact pads so that the rear axle will hang free with the tires off the ground.
2. Loosen the rear axle mounted adjustable lever assembly and remove the actuating spring.
3. Unfasten the brake lines from the proportioning valve and remove the valve.

To install:

4. Install the brake lines loosely in the proportioning valve and mount the valve in position.
5. Tighten the brake lines, fill the master cylinder to the correct fluid level and bleed the brakes.
6. Confirm that the axle is hanging free and at full rebound position with the wheels and tires mounted.
7. Confirm that the actuating spring is connected between the proportioning valve and axle adjusting lever. The axle adjusting lever mounting bolts should be loose so that the bracket can be moved.
8. Push the control lever on the proportioning valve towards the valve until it is against the body and hold it in that position.
9. Move the axle lever up and away to apply tension to the spring.
10. When all free play is taken out of the spring, but the spring is not stretched, tighten the mounting bolt that goes through the slotted side of the adjustment bracket. Tighten the anchor bolt. Both mounting bolts should be tightened to 150 inch lbs. (17 Nm).

Brake Hoses

See Figures 14 and 15

REMOVAL & INSTALLATION

Right and left brake hoses are not interchangeable.

1. Remove the connector at the caliper.
2. Remove the mounting bracket from the strut support.
3. Remove the upper keyed end from the upper body mount and disconnect the hose from the steel line.
4. Always use a flare wrench to prevent rounding of the line fittings.

To install:

5. Install the new hose to the caliper first. Always use a new copper washer after making sure the mounting surfaces are clean. Tighten the caliper hose fitting.
6. Install the strut bracket, then attach the steel line fitting.
7. Position the upper keyed end of the hose to the body bracket and secure it.
8. Rear brake hoses should be attached first to the trailing arm bracket and the to the floor pan tubes.
9. Keep the hose as straight as possible, avoid twisting.
10. Bleed the brake system.

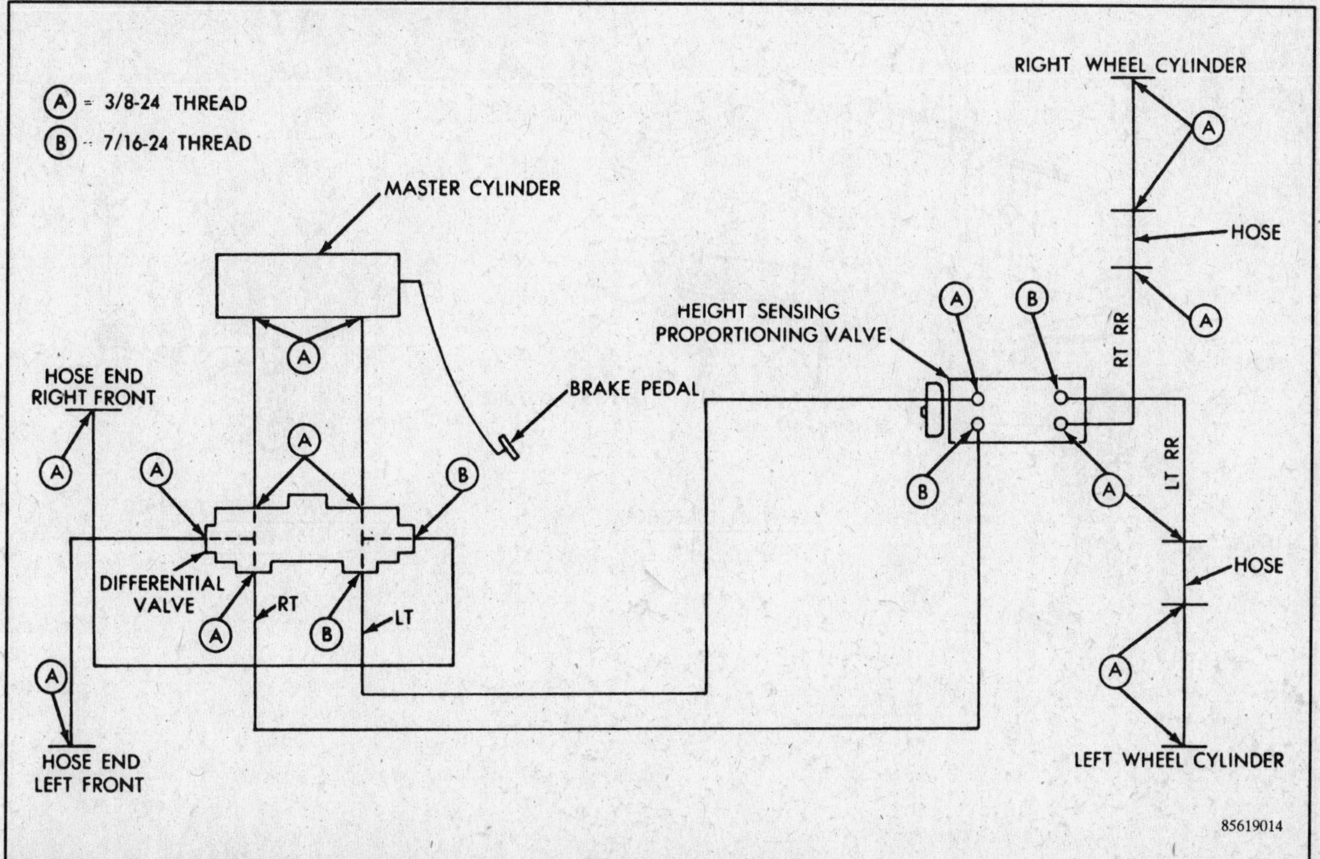

Fig. 14 Proper nut thread size and tube routing — non ABS equipped vehicles

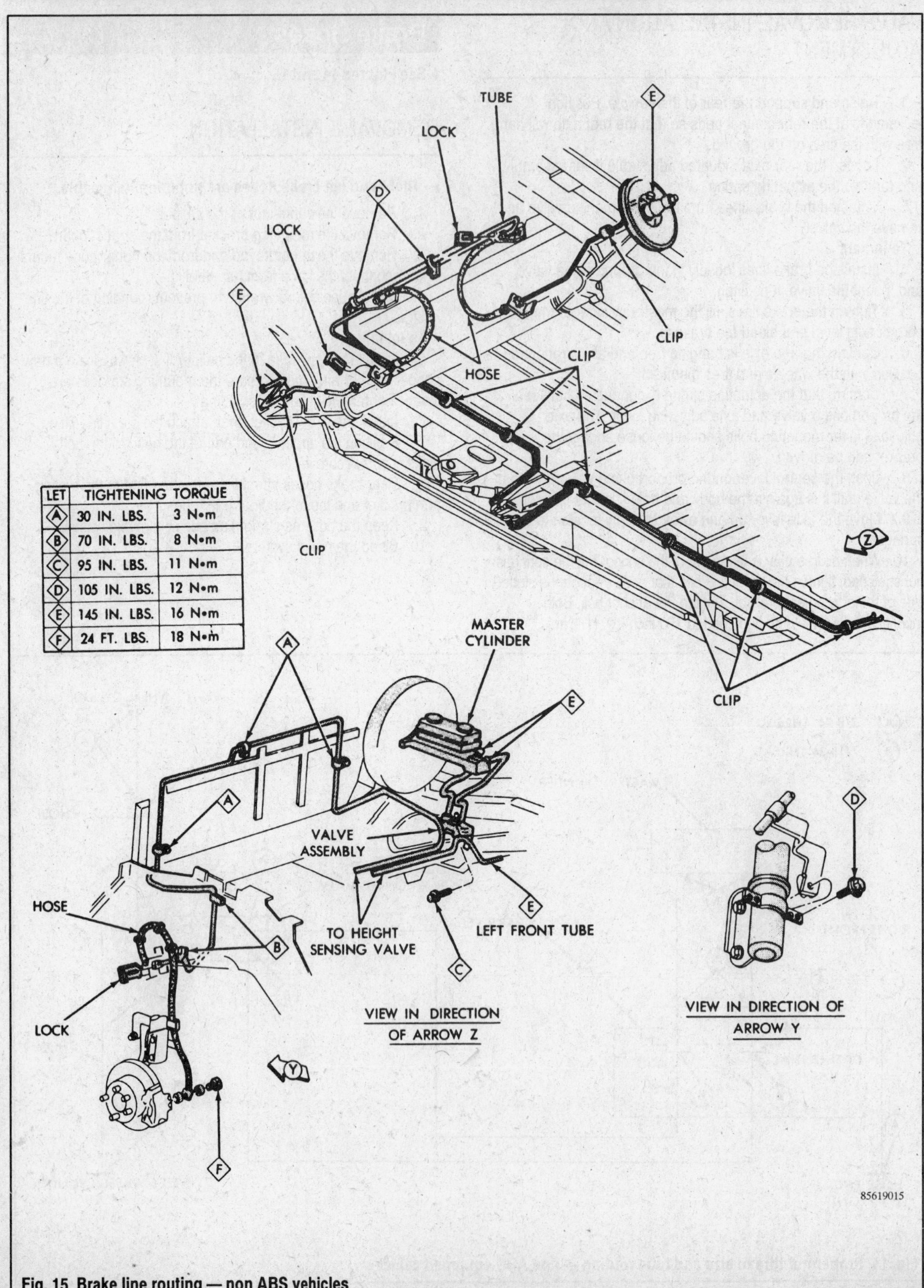

LET	TIGHTENING TORQUE	
A	30 IN. LBS.	3 N•m
B	70 IN. LBS.	8 N•m
C	95 IN. LBS.	11 N•m
D	105 IN. LBS.	12 N•m
E	145 IN. LBS.	16 N•m
F	24 FT. LBS.	18 N•m

Fig. 15 Brake line routing — non ABS vehicles

Bleeding the Brake System

The purpose of bleeding the brakes is to expel air trapped in the hydraulic system. The system must be bled whenever the pedal feels spongy, indicating that compressible air has entered the system. It must also be bled whenever the system has been opened or repaired. You will need a helper to help bleed the system. Always use fresh brake fluid.

BENCH BLEEDING

Always bench bleed the master cylinder before installing it on the vehicle.

1. Place the master cylinder in a vise.
2. Connect two lines to the fluid outlet orifices, then bend the lines upwards and insert the opened ends into the reservoir.
3. Fill the reservoir with brake fluid.
4. Using a wooden dowel, depress the pushrod slowly, allowing the pistons to return. Repeat this procedure several times until the air bubbles are all expelled.
5. Remove the bleeding tubes from the master cylinder, plug the outlets and install the caps.

➥ It is not necessary to bleed the entire system after replacing the master cylinder, provided that master cylinder has been bled and filled upon installation. However, if a soft pedal is experienced, bleed the entire system.

SYSTEM BLEEDING

➧ See Figures 16, 17, 18, 19, 20, 21 and 22

****CAUTION**

Do not allow brake fluid to spill on the vehicle's finish; it will remove the paint. In case of a spill, flush the area with water.

The sequence for bleeding is right rear, left front, left rear and right front.

1. If the vehicle is equipped with power brakes, remove the vacuum by applying the brakes several times. Do not run the engine while bleeding the brakes.
2. Clean all the bleeder screws. You may want to give each one a shot of penetrating solvent to help loosen the fitting. Seizure is a common problem with bleeder screws, which then break off, sometimes requiring replacement of the part to which they are attached.
3. Check the fluid level in the master cylinder and fill with DOT 3 brake fluid, if necessary.

➥ Brake fluid absorbs moisture from the air. Don't leave the master cylinder or the fluid container uncovered any longer than necessary. Be careful handling the brake fluid,it is a great paint remover. If any brake fluid spills on the vehicle's finish, flush off with water immediately. Check the level of the fluid often when bleeding, and refill the reservoirs as necessary. Don't let them run dry, or you will have to repeat the process.

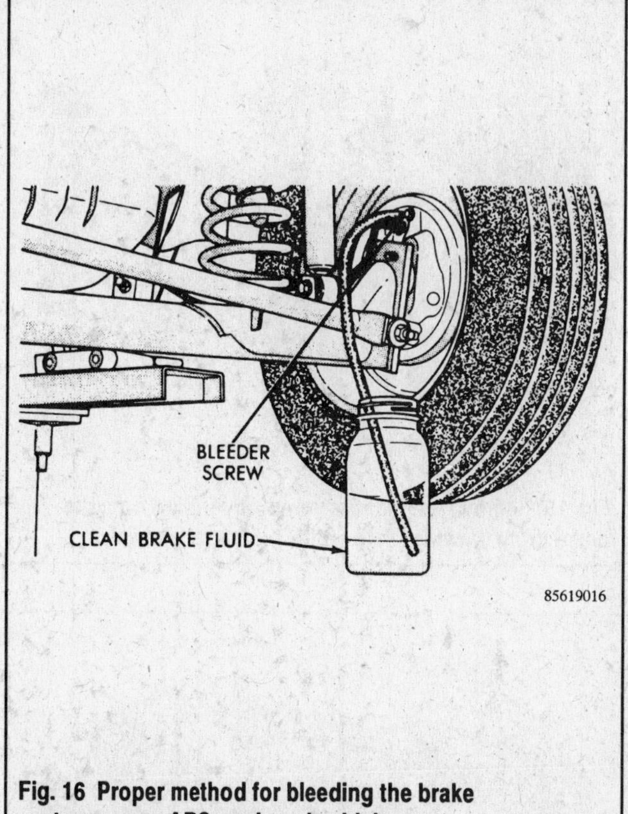

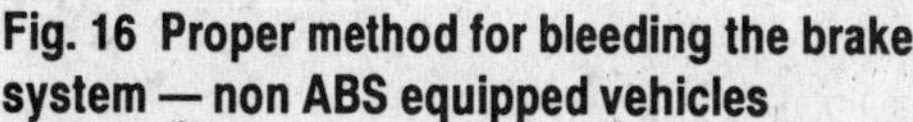

Fig. 16 Proper method for bleeding the brake system — non ABS equipped vehicles

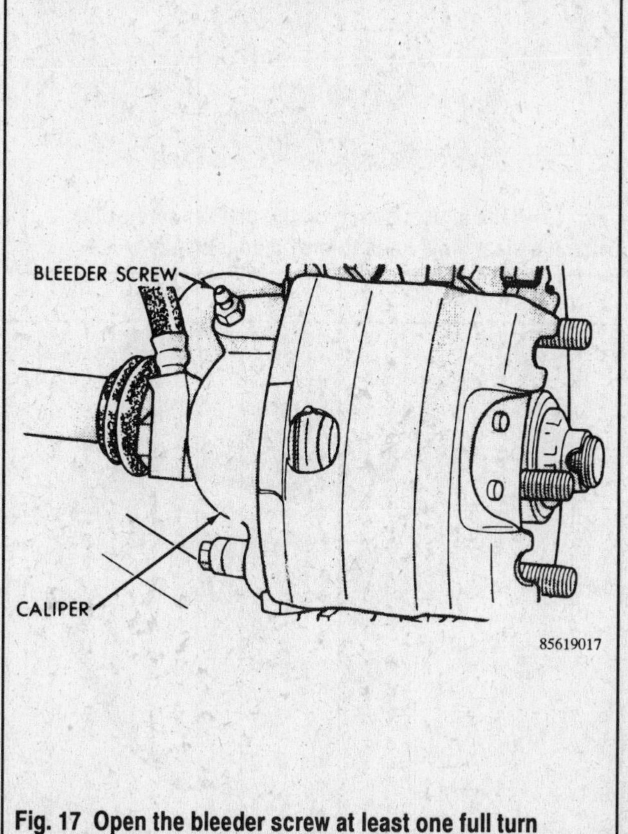

Fig. 17 Open the bleeder screw at least one full turn

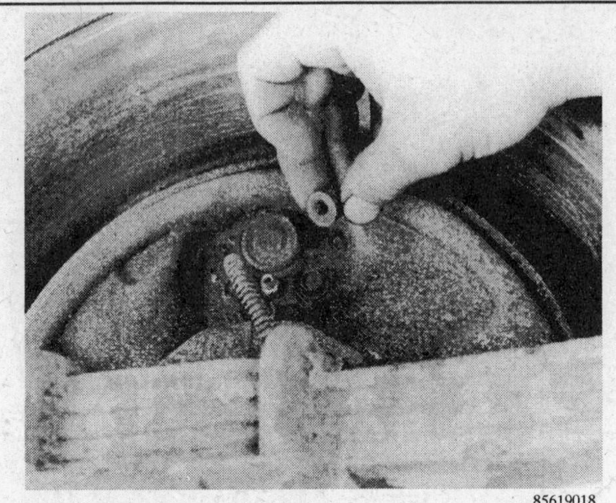

85619018

Fig. 18 Remove the bleeder screw cover plug from the brake drum backing plate — 1987 Voyager shown

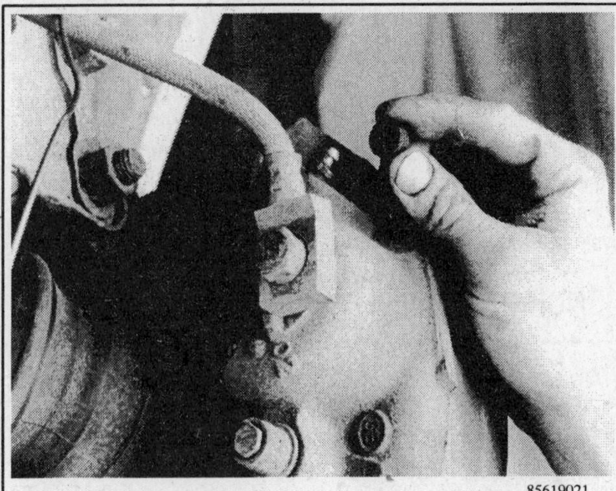

85619021

Fig. 21 Remove the bleeder screw cover plug from the brake caliper

85619019

Fig. 19 Place a box wrench on the bleeder screw then attach a clear vinyl hose to the bleeder nipple

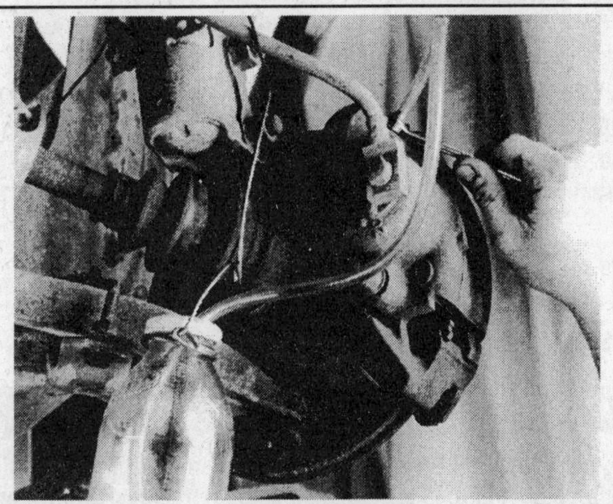

85619022

Fig. 22 Open the bleeder screw and bleed the fluid into a clean jar half filled with brake fluid

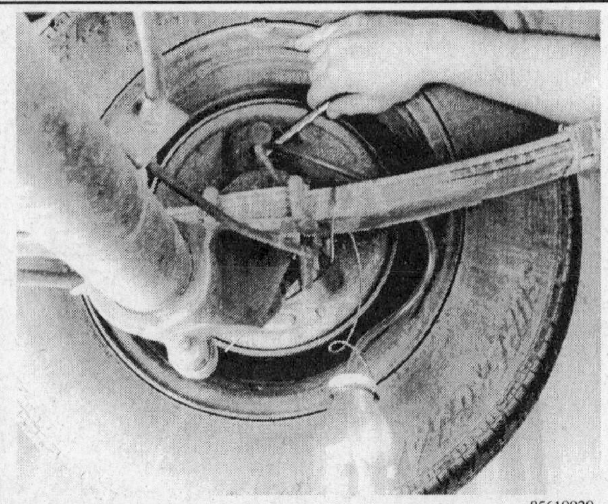

85619020

Fig. 20 Open the bleeder screw and bleed the fluid into a clean jar half filled with brake fluid

4. Attach a length of clear vinyl tubing to the bleeder screw at the wheel cylinder or caliper. Insert the other end of the tube into a clear, clean jar half filled with brake fluid. Start at a rear cylinder first, then bleed the opposite side front cylinder.

5. Have your assistant slowly depress the brake pedal. As this is done, open the bleeder screw $^1/_3$–$^1/_2$ of a turn on wheel cylinders and at least one turn on calipers, and allow the fluid to run through the tube. Then close the bleeder screw before the pedal reaches the end of its travel.

6. Have your assistant slowly release the pedal after the bleeder screw is closed. Repeat this process until no air bubbles appear in the expelled fluid.

7. Repeat the procedure on the other calipers and cylinders, checking the level of fluid in the master cylinder reservoir often.

8. After you're done, there should be no sponginess in the brake pedal feel. If there is, either there is still air in the line, in which case the process should be repeated, or there is a leak somewhere, which of course must be corrected before moving the vehicle.

FRONT DISC BRAKES

**CAUTION

Brake shoes contain asbestos, which has been determined to be a cancer causing agent. Never clean the brake surfaces with compressed air! Avoid inhaling any dust from any brake surface! When cleaning brake surfaces, use a commercially available brake cleaning fluid.

The Kelsey-Hayes single pin type caliper (1984–87 models) and the Kelsey-Hayes double pin type caliper (1987–95 models) front disc brakes are of the single position, floating caliper type. The caliper "floats" through a rubber bushing, inserted into the inboard portion of the caliper, via a guide pin that is threaded into the mounting adapter. The mounting adapter for the caliper is fitted with two machined abutments that position and align the caliper. The guide pin and bushing, on the Kelsey-Hayes single pin type caliper, control the movement of the caliper when the brakes are applied, providing a clamping force. The Kelsey-Hayes double pin type caliper, uses two steel guide pins and mounting bushings to control the movement of the caliper upon brake application.

Disc Brake Pads

INSPECTION

1. Loosen the front wheel lug nuts slightly. Raise and support the front of the vehicle safely on jackstands.
2. Remove the front wheels.
3. When the front wheels are removed, the cutout built into the caliper housing will be exposed. Look through the opening and check the lining thickness of the inner and outer pads.
4. If a visual inspection does not give a clear picture of lining wear, a physical check will be necessary.
5. Refer to the procedure covering pad removal and installation for instructions.

REMOVAL & INSTALLATION

Kelsey-Hayes Single Pin Type

See Figures 23, 24, 25, 26, 27, 28, 29 and 30

Three anti-rattle clips are provided on each brake caliper, take note of locations for installation purposes.

1. Loosen the wheel lug nuts slightly. Raise and safely support the front of the vehicle on jackstands.
2. Remove the front wheel and tire assemblies.
3. Siphon about one quarter of the brake fluid from the master cylinder and replace the cover caps.
4. Using the proper size socket wrench, remove the threaded caliper guide pin.
5. Insert a small prybar between the front edge of the caliper and the adapter rail. Apply steady upward pressure to loosen the adhesive seals.

Do not use a C-clamp to retract the plastic composition piston or damage to the piston could result.

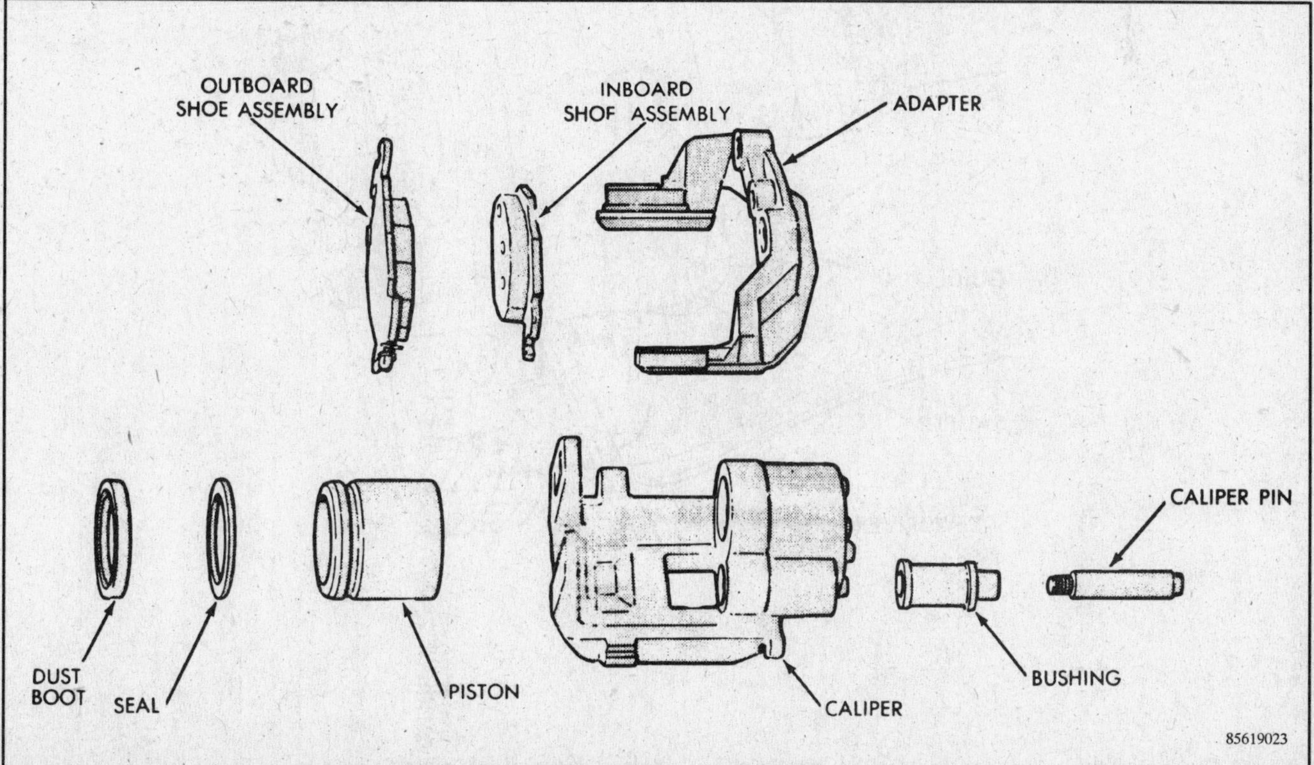

Fig. 23 Exploded view of the Kelsey Hayes single pin disc caliper

6. Remove the caliper by slowly sliding it up and off the adapter and disc rotor.

7. Support the caliper by hanging it out of the way on wire. Do not allow the caliper to be supported by the brake hose.

8. Observe the location of the anti-rattle clips. One clip is on the top of the inboard (closes to axle) brake pad. Another clip is on the bottom of the outboard brake pad, and the third is installed on the top finger of the caliper.

9. Slide the outboard brake pad from the adapter and remove the brake disc rotor if necessary.

10. Remove the inboard pad.

11. Measure the brake lining and pad thickness. If the combined thickness at the thinnest point of the is $^{1}/_{8}$ in. (3mm) or less replace both front wheel brake pad assemblies.

To install:

12. Check around the caliper piston and boot for signs of brake fluid leakage. Inspect the dust boot around the caliper piston for cuts and breaks. If the boot is damaged or fluid leakage is visible, the caliper should be serviced. Check the adapter and caliper mounting surfaces for rust and dirt, clean them with a wire brush.

13. Remove the protective paper from the gaskets mounted on the metal part of the brake pads.

14. Install the anti-rattle clips in position.

15. Install inner brake pad on the adapter.

16. Install the brake disc rotor and outer brake pad.

17. Press the caliper back into the caliper until it bottoms. If may be necessary to place a small piece of wood on the piston and use a C-clamp to retract the piston. If so, tighten the clamp with slow steady pressure. Stop when resistance is felt.

18. Lower the caliper over the brake pads and disc rotor.

19. Install the caliper guide pin, then tighten to 25–35 ft. lbs. (34–48 Nm). Take care not to cross thread the guide pin.

20. After both calipers have been installed, fill the master cylinder and bleed the brakes if the caliper were rebuilt. If the calipers were not serviced, pump the brakes until a firm brake pedal is obtained.

21. Install the front wheels and lower the vehicle.

22. After the vehicle is lowered, check the lug nut torque, then tighten to required specification to 95 ft. lbs. (130 Nm).

23. Road test the vehicle and make several firm but not hard stops to wear off any dirt from the pads or rotor.

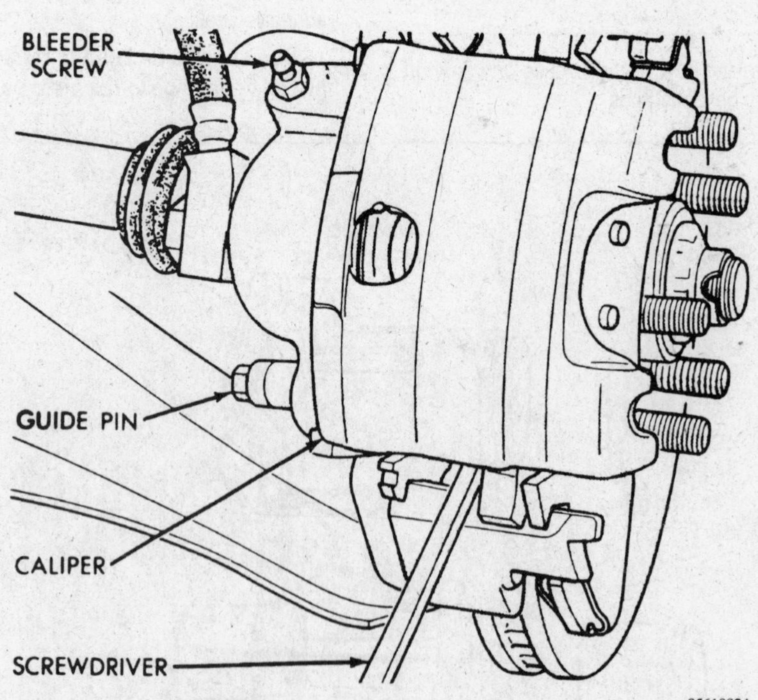

Fig. 24 Loosening the caliper assembly with a small prybar — Kelsey Hayes single pin disc caliper

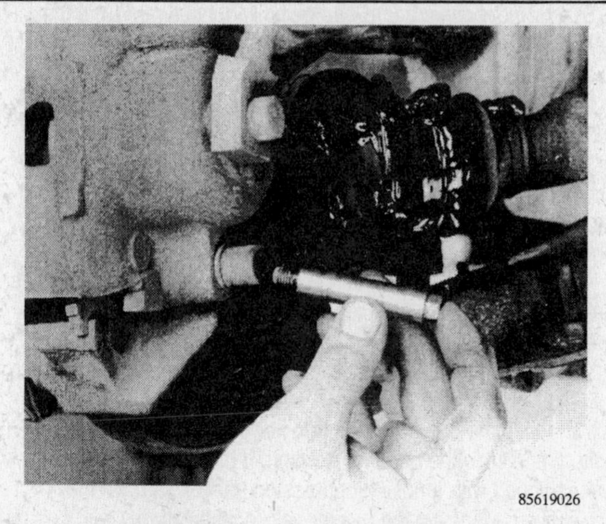

85619026

Fig. 25 Remove the single threaded caliper guide

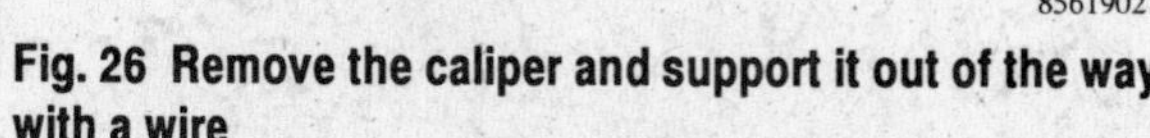

85619027

Fig. 26 Remove the caliper and support it out of the way with a wire

85619028

Fig. 27 Slide the outboard shoe from the caliper

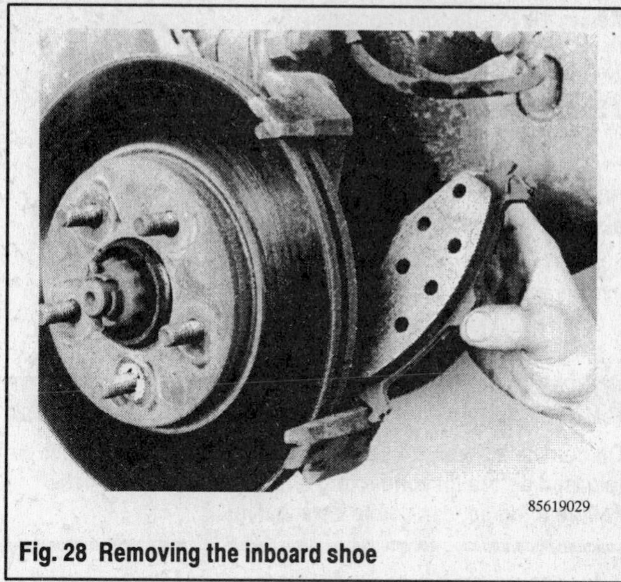

85619029

Fig. 28 Removing the inboard shoe

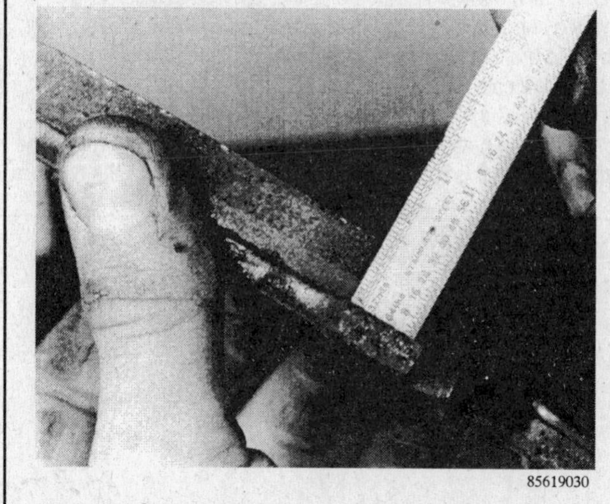

85619030

Fig. 29 Measure the brake lining and pad thickness

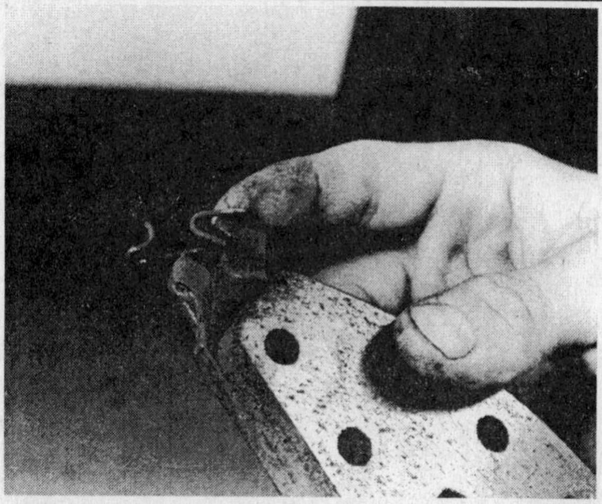

85619031

Fig. 30 Note one of the anti-rattle clips shown on the top of the inboard brake pad

Kelsey-Hayes Double Pin Type

1987–90 MODELS

➧ See Figures 31, 32, 33, 34, 35, 36 and 37

➥ The caliper is equipped with one hold-down spring running across the outboard fingers of the caliper, and is also equipped with an inner shoe to piston mounting clip.

1. The Kelsey-Hayes double pin type caliper uses two mounting pins. Loosen the wheel lugs slightly.
2. Raise and safely support the front of the vehicle.
3. Remove the wheel and tire assembly.

****CAUTION**

On models equipped with ABS, the system pressure must be released before disconnecting any of the hydraulic lines. Failure to do so, can cause personal injury.

4. Loosen, but do not remove the two steel caliper guide pins. Back the pins out until the caliper can be moved freely.
5. Pull the lower end of the caliper out from the steering knuckle support. Roll the caliper up and away from the disc rotor. The disc brake pads will remain located in their caliper positions.
6. Take care, while servicing the pads, that strain is not put on the brake hose.
7. Pry the outboard pad toward the bottom opened end of the caliper. The pad is retained by a captive clip. Remove the pad.
8. Remove the inboard pad by pulling it outward from the caliper piston. It is retained by a captive clip.

To install:

9. Inspect the caliper. Check for piston seal leaks and boot damage. Service the caliper as required.
10. Press the caliper piston slowly back into the caliper bore. Use a small block of wood and a C-clamp, if necessary. Tighten the clamp slowly, and make sure the piston is not cocked. Gently bottom the piston in the caliper.
11. The inboard pads are interchangeable, the outboard pads are marked with an **L** or **R** relating to the side of the vehicle they are to be used on.
12. Place the inboard pad clip into the caliper piston and push into position on the piston.
13. Place the outboard pad retainer clip over the ears of the caliper and slide the pad into position. If the replacement pads are equipped with a noise suppression gasket, remove the protective paper from the gasket before installation.
14. Lower the caliper over the disc rotor and align the hold-down spring under the machined surface of the steering knuckle. Install the caliper mounting pins, take care not to cross thread, then tighten the pins to 18–26 ft. lbs. (25–35 Nm). Pump the brake pedal several times to move the pads against the rotor. If the caliper has been rebuilt, or other system service completed, bleed the brake system.
15. Install the wheel and tire assembly. Lower the vehicle. Do not move the vehicle until a firm brake pedal is verified.

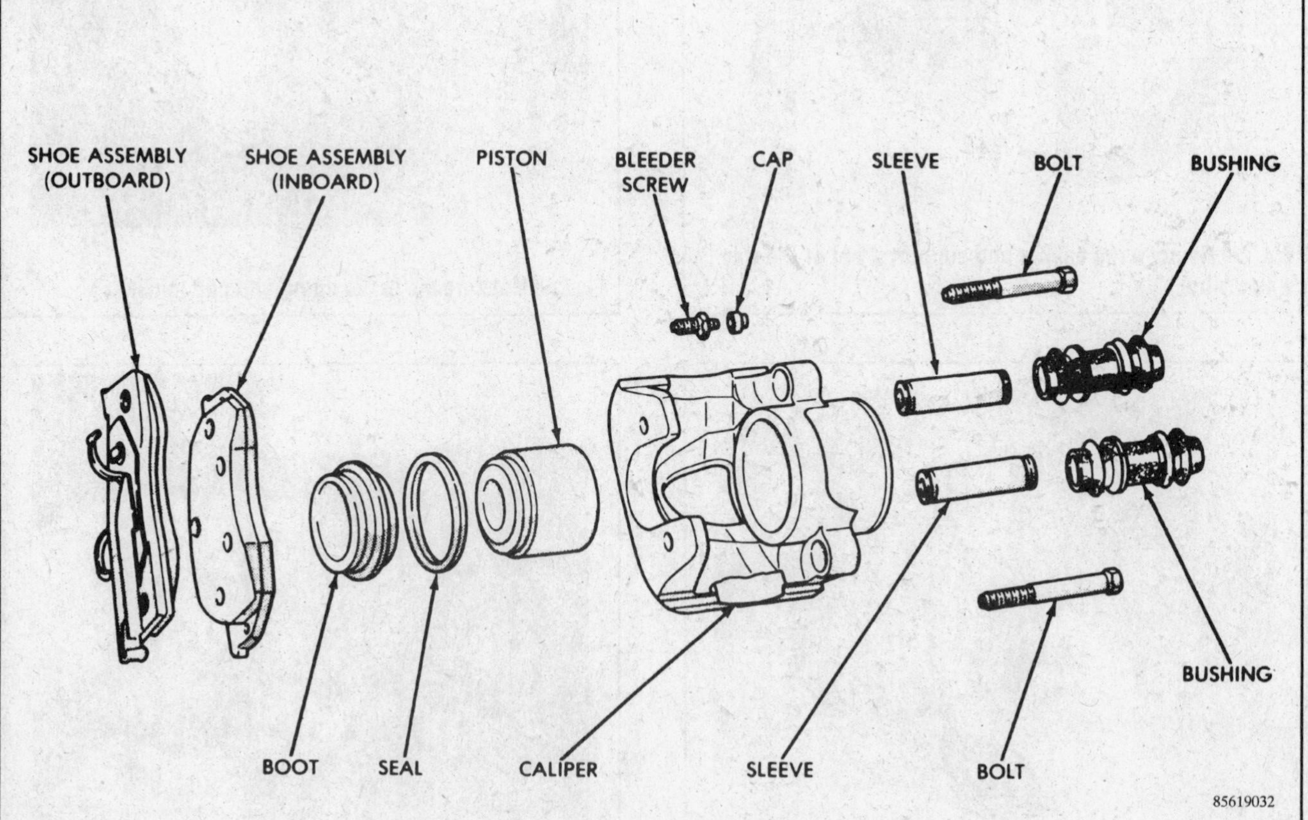

Fig. 31 Exploded view of the Kelsey Hayes double pin disc caliper — 1987–90 models

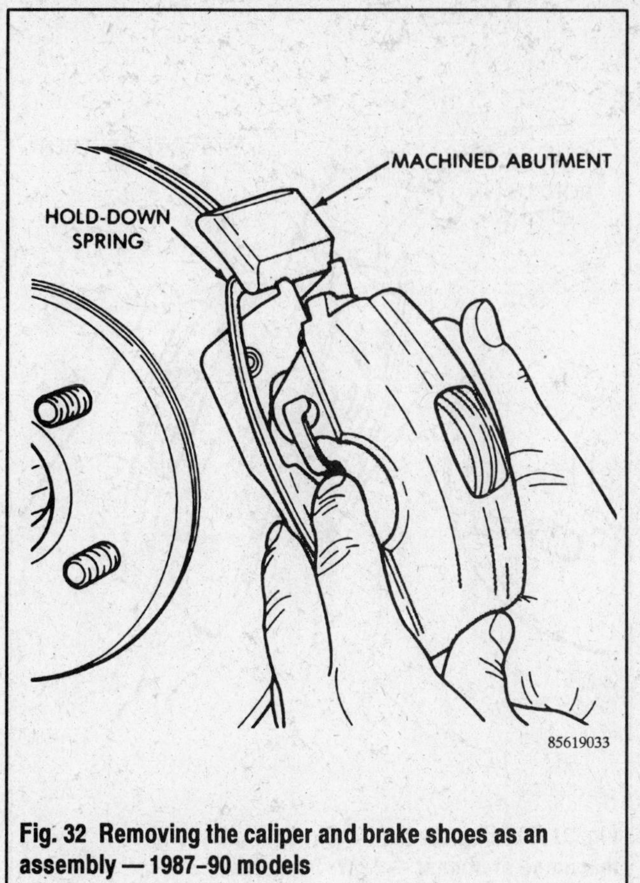

Fig. 32 Removing the caliper and brake shoes as an assembly — 1987-90 models

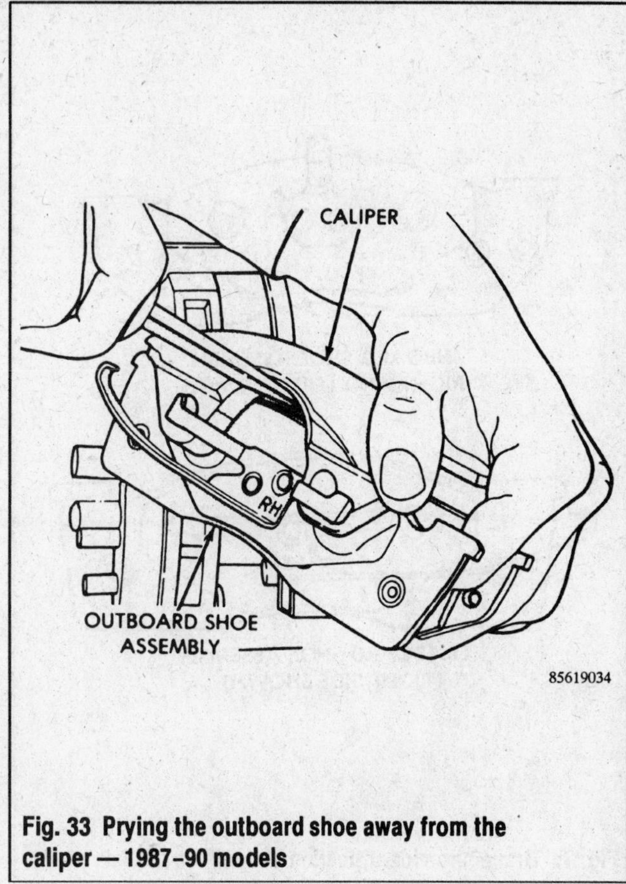

Fig. 33 Prying the outboard shoe away from the caliper — 1987-90 models

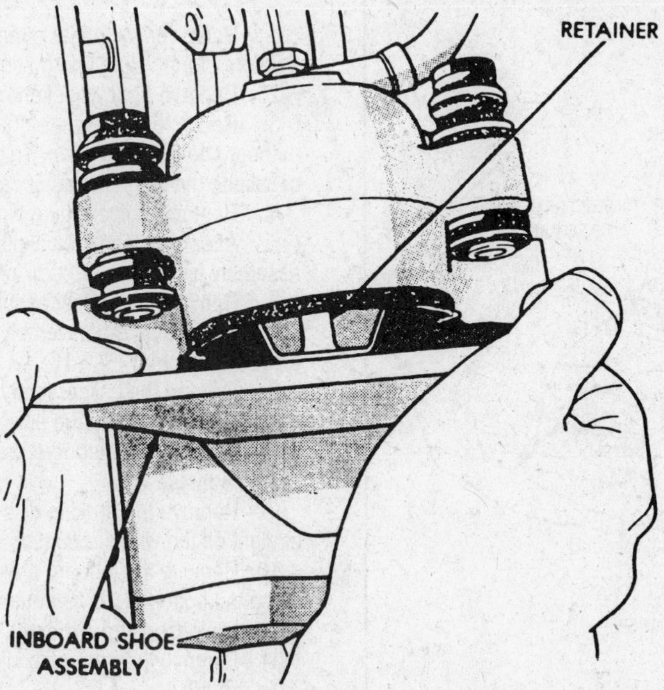

Fig. 34 Removing/installing the inboard shoe assembly — 1987-90 models

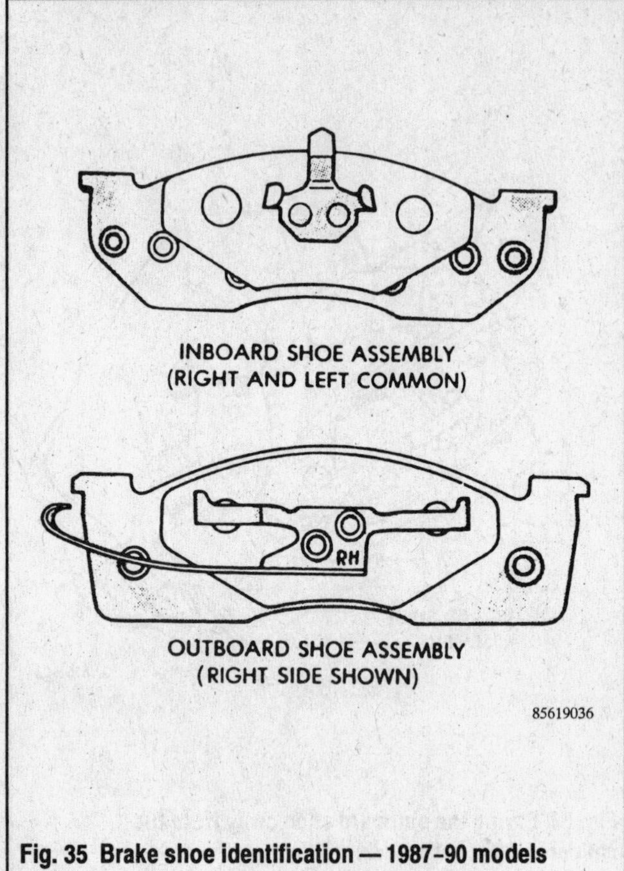

Fig. 35 Brake shoe identification — 1987-90 models

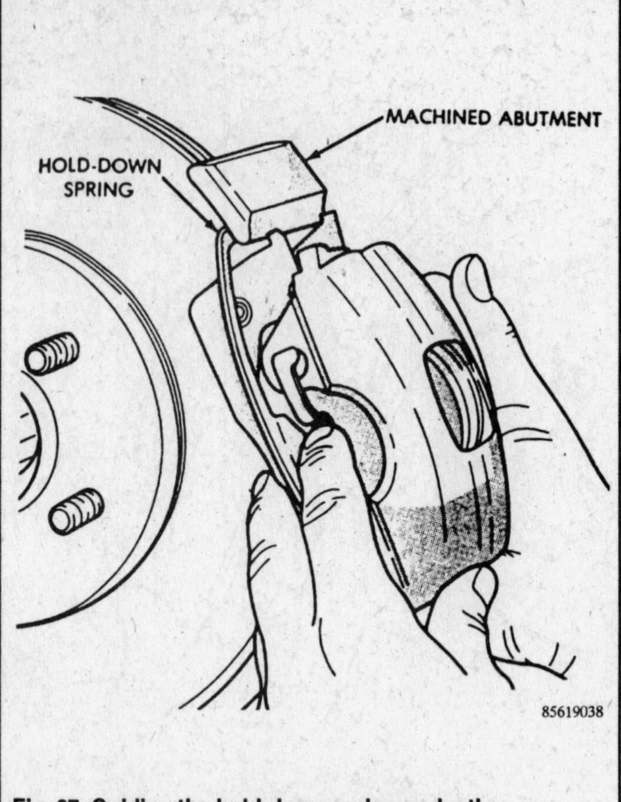

Fig. 37 Guiding the hold-down spring under the machined abutment — 1987-90 models

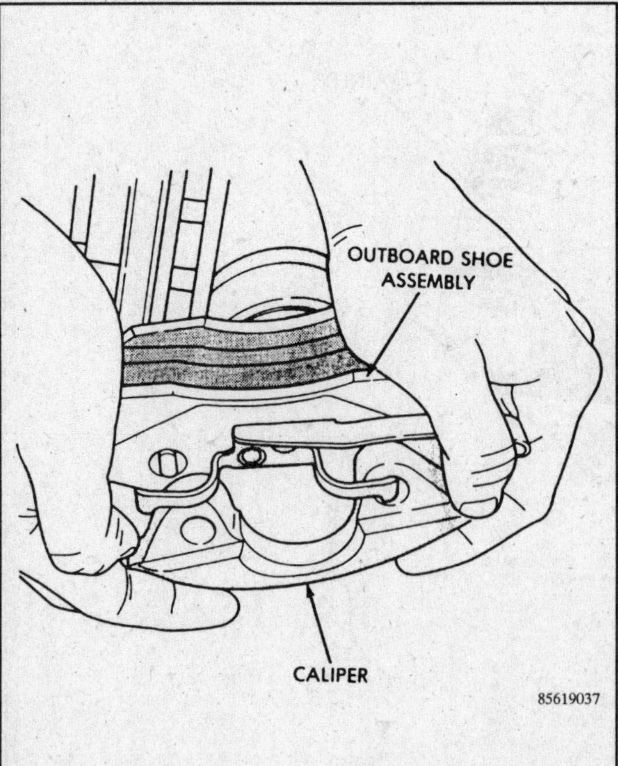

Fig. 36 Installing the outboard shoe onto the caliper — 1987-90 models

1991-95 MODELS

➧ See Figures 38, 39, 40, 41, 42, 43, 44 and 45

1. Raise vehicle on jackstands or centered on a hoist. See Section 1 for hoisting information.
2. Remove front wheel and tire assemblies.
3. Reach to the inside of the caliper assembly and pull it outboard as far as you can. This will push piston back into bore of caliper, making removal of caliper from adapter easier.
4. Remove caliper guide pin bolts.
5. After removing the caliper guide pin bolts lift the caliper assembly away from the braking disc with a pry bar.
6. Remove the caliper assembly from braking disc and adapter by sliding the assembly out and away from the braking disc and adapter.
7. Support the caliper firmly to prevent the weight of the caliper from damaging the flexible brake hose.
8. Remove the outboard brake shoe assembly from the caliper adapter.
9. Remove the braking disc (rotor) from the hub by pulling it straight off the wheel mounting studs.
10. Remove the inboard brake shoe assembly by sliding it out along the bottom adapter abutment until the brake shoe assembly loosens from the anti-rattle clip.
11. Remove the anti-rattle clip from the top adapter abutment.

To install:

12. Thoroughly clean both adapter abutment rails. If there is any build-up of rust on the adapter abutment rails, remove it using a wire brush do not sand rails.

13. Lubricate both adapter abutments with a liberal amount of Mopar Multipurpose Lubricant, or equivalent.

14. Install the anti-rattle clip on the upper abutment of the caliper mounting adapter.

15. Remove the protective paper from the noise suppression gasket on both the inner and outer brake shoe assemblies, if equipped.

16. Install the new inboard brake shoe assembly on the adapter by sliding it along the adapter abutments. Be careful not to get any grease from the adapter abutment on the surface of the brake lining material. Ensure the inboard brake shoe assembly is correctly positioned against anti-rattle clip.

17. Reinstall the braking disc on the hub, by installing it over the wheel studs until it is seated against the face of the hub.

18. Slide the new outboard brake shoe assembly on the adapter abutment.

19. Carefully lower the caliper over the braking disk and brake shoe assemblies. Make sure that the caliper guide pin bolt, bushings and sleeves are clear of the adapter.

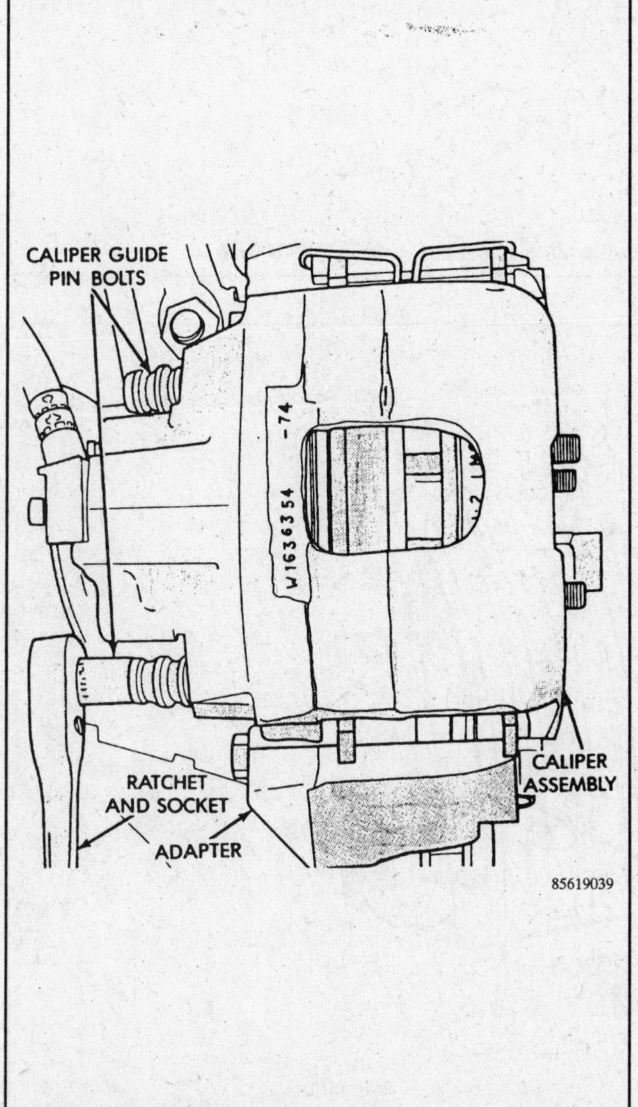

Fig. 38 Removing/installing the caliper guide pin bolts, Kelsey Hayes double pin disc caliper — 1991-95 models

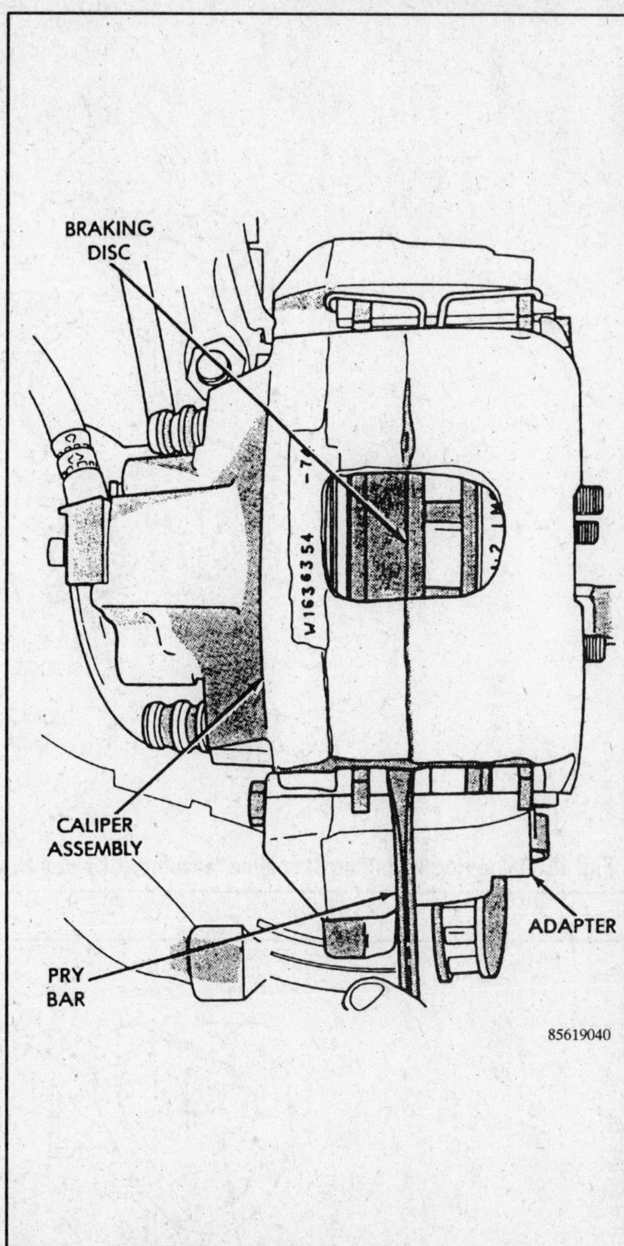

Fig. 39 Loosening the caliper assembly from the adapter and rotor, Kelsey Hayes double pin disc caliper — 1991-95 models

20. Install the caliper guide pin bolts, then tighten them to 25-35 ft. lbs. (34-48 Nm). Extreme caution should be taken not to cross the threads of the caliper guide pin bolts.

21. Install the wheel and tire assembly. Tighten the wheel mounting stud nuts in proper sequence until all nuts are tightened to half specification. This is important. Then repeat the tightening sequence to the full specified torque of 95 ft. lbs. (130 Nm).

22. Remove jackstands or lower the hoist.

23. Before moving vehicle, pump the brake pedal several times to insure the vehicle has a firm brake pedal to adequately stop vehicle.

24. Road test the vehicle and make several stops to wear off any foreign material on the brakes and to seat the brake shoe linings.

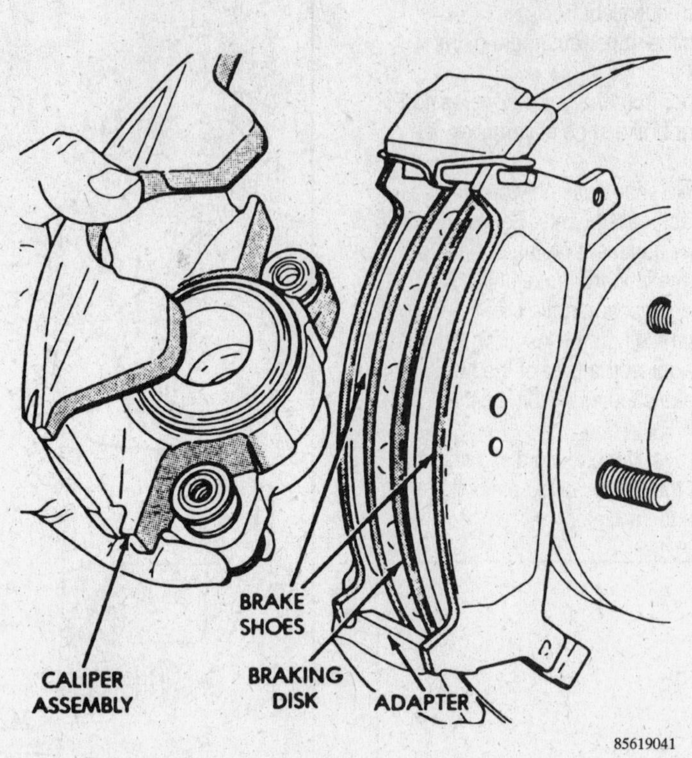

Fig. 40 Removing/installing the caliper assembly, Kelsey Hayes double pin disc caliper — 1991–95 models

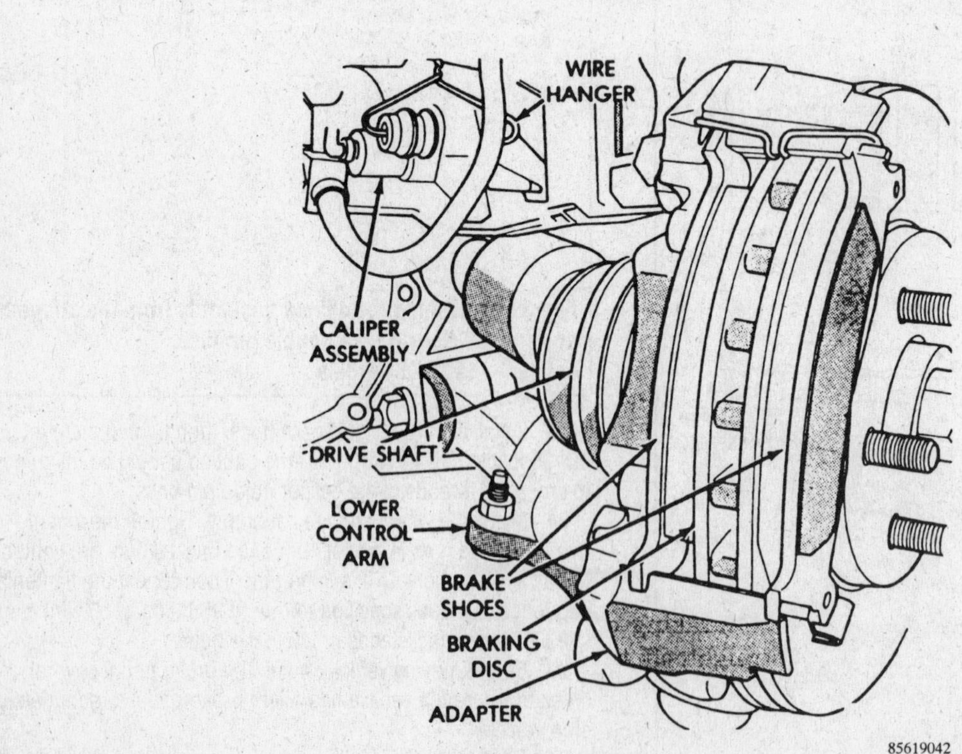

Fig. 41 Remove the tension from the brake hose by using a wire hanger to store the caliper out of the way, Kelsey Hayes double pin disc caliper — 1991–95 models

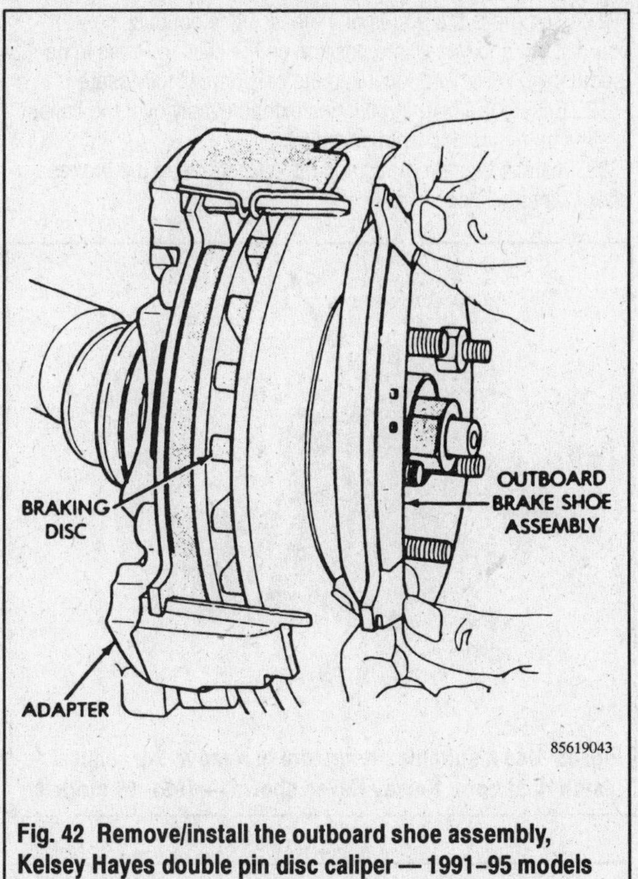

Fig. 42 Remove/install the outboard shoe assembly, Kelsey Hayes double pin disc caliper — 1991–95 models

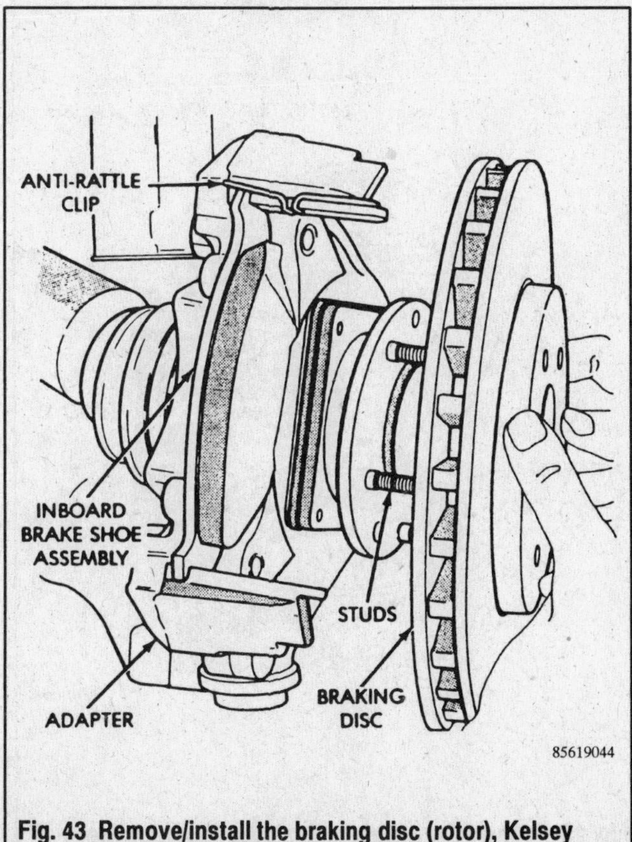

Fig. 43 Remove/install the braking disc (rotor), Kelsey Hayes double pin disc caliper — 1991–95 models

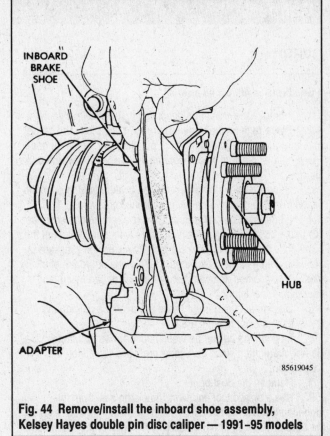

Fig. 44 Remove/install the inboard shoe assembly, Kelsey Hayes double pin disc caliper — 1991–95 models

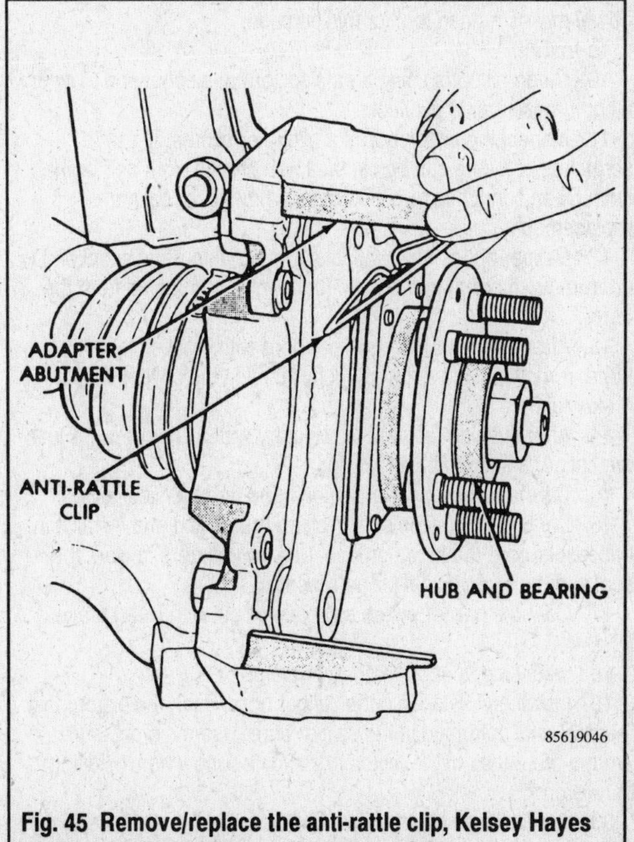

Fig. 45 Remove/replace the anti-rattle clip, Kelsey Hayes double pin disc caliper — 1991–95 models

Caliper

OVERHAUL

➧ **See Figures 46, 47, 48 and 49**

1. Remove the caliper as described in the previous section.
2. Place rags on the upper control arm and place the caliper on top of the rags. Take care not to put strain on the brake hose. Place a small block of wood between the caliper piston and outer fingers.
3. Have a helper slowly depress the brake pedal to push the piston from the caliper bore using hydraulic pressure.
4. If both front caliper pistons are to be removed, disconnect the brake hose, to the first caliper, at the frame bracket; plug the brake tube and repeat Steps 2 and 3. Never use air pressure to blow the pistons from their bores. The pistons are made of a plastic composition and can damage easily, or can fly out and cause personal injury.
5. Disconnect the flexible brake line from the caliper and remove the caliper to work area.
6. Position the caliper between padded jaws of a bench vise. Do not overtighten since excessive pressure can distort the caliper bore.
7. Remove the dust boot.
8. Use a plastic tool and work the piston seal from the mounting groove. Do not use a metal tool; damage can result to the bore or burrs can be created on the edges of the machined seal groove.
9. Remove the guide pin bushing from the caliper. A wooden dowel makes a good tool for this purpose.

To install:

10. Clean all parts using a safe solvent or alcohol and blow dry if compressed air is available.
11. Inspect the piston bore for pitting or scores. Light scratches or pitting can be cleaned with crocus cloth and brake fluid. Deep scratches or pitting require honing, or caliper replacement.
12. Caliper hones are available from an auto parts supplier. Do not remove more than 0.001 in. (0.025mm) of material from the bore.
13. After cleaning up the caliper bore with crocus cloth or hone, remove all the dirt and grit by flushing the caliper with brake fluid.
14. After flushing the caliper, wipe dry with a lintless rag. Flush the caliper a second time and dry.
15. Carefully reclamp the caliper in the padded vise jaws.
16. Dip the new piston seal in clean brake fluid and install it in the caliper bore mounting groove. Use your fingers to work the seal into the groove until properly seated.
17. Coat the caliper piston and piston boot with clean brake fluid.
18. Install the boot on the caliper piston.
19. Install the piston into the caliper bore. Push the piston past the seal until bottomed in the caliper bore. Use even pressure around the edges of the piston to avoid cocking when installing the piston.
20. Position the lip of the dust boot into the counter bore of the caliper. Use a seal driver or suitable tool to install the boot edge.
21. Compress the edges of the new guide pin bushing with your fingers and install into position on the caliper. Press in on the bushing while working it into the caliper until fully seated.
22. Ensure the bushing flanges extend evenly over the caliper casting on both sides when installed.
23. Install the brake pads and the caliper. Bleed the brakes after caliper service.

Fig. 46 Use a suitable prying tool to remove the caliper piston dust boot, Kelsey Hayes shown — 1991-95 models

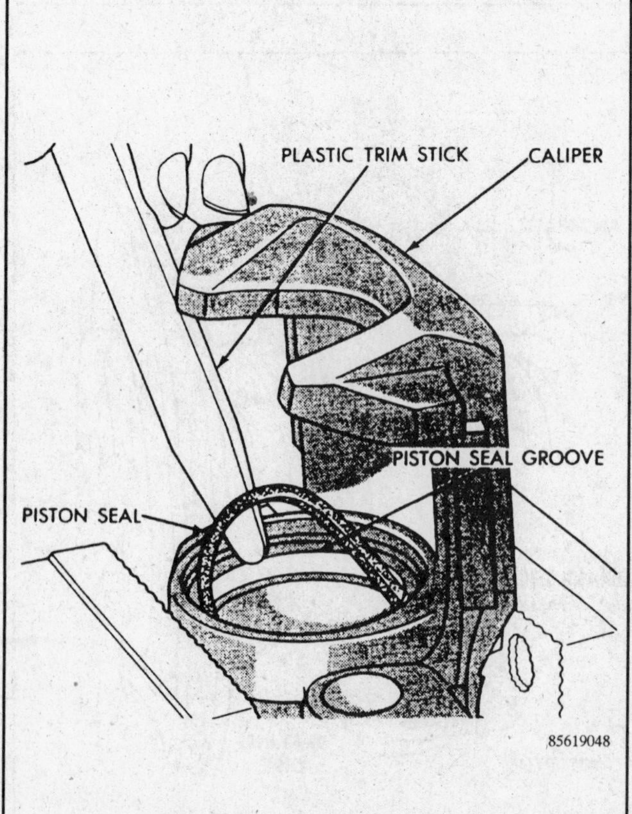

Fig. 47 Remove the caliper piston dust boot from the piston — 1991-95 Kelsey Hayes shown

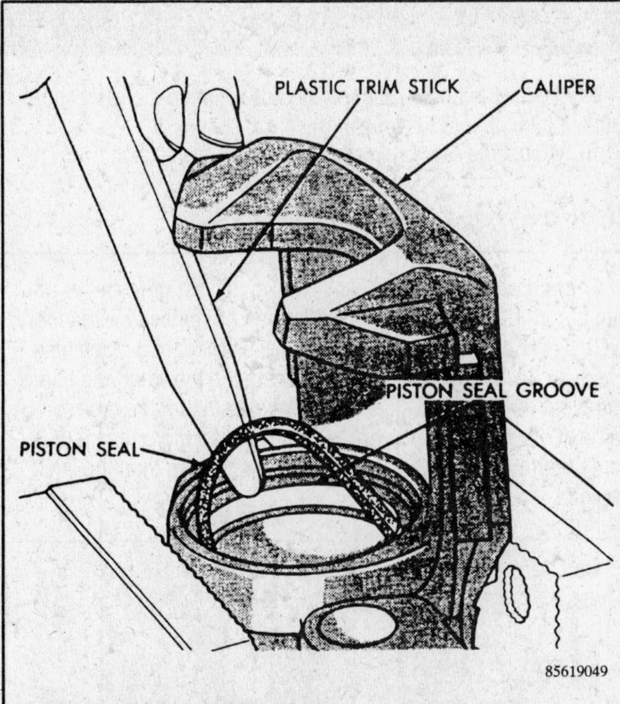

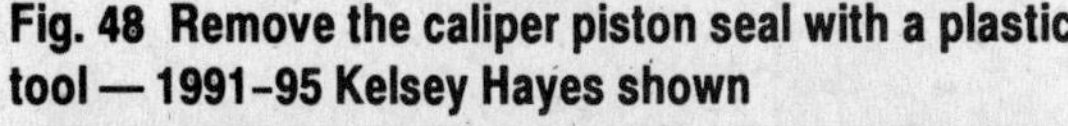
Fig. 48 Remove the caliper piston seal with a plastic tool — 1991-95 Kelsey Hayes shown

Fig. 49 Do not use a metal tool to remove the seal, even this tool could scratch the bore or burr the seal groove — 1991-95 Kelsey Hayes shown

Brake Disc (Rotor)

REMOVAL & INSTALLATION

➧ **See Figures 50 and 51**

1. Loosen the wheel lugs slightly.
2. Raise and support the front of the vehicle on jackstands.
3. Remove the front wheel and tire assembly.
4. Relieve the brake system pressure if equipped with ABS.
5. Remove the disc brake caliper and outer brake pad.
6. Remove the disc brake rotor.

To install:

7. Service as necessary.
8. Place the rotor in position and install the caliper assembly. Refer to the brake pad removal and installation procedures for detailed information, if necessary.

INSPECTION

If excessive run-out, wobble or thickness variation is present, feedback through the brake pedal will be felt when the brakes are applied. Pedal pulsation, chatter, surge and increased pedal travel can be caused when the disc rotor is worn unevenly or deeply scored. Remove the rotor and have an automotive machine shop measure the wear and check for run out. The machine shop can refinish the braking surfaces if replacement is not necessary.

Fig. 50 Removing the rotor retaining clip from the wheel stud

Fig. 51 Removing the rotor from the studs

REAR DRUM BRAKES

**CAUTION

Brake shoes contain asbestos, which has been determined to be a cancer causing agent. Never clean the brake surfaces with compressed air! Avoid inhaling any dust from any brake surface! When cleaning brake surfaces, use a commercially available brake cleaning fluid.

Brake Drums

REMOVAL & INSTALLATION

See Figures 52, 53, 54, 55, 56, 57, 58, 59, 60 and 61

Front Wheel Drive Vehicles

1. Raise and support the rear of the vehicle on jackstands.
2. Remove the wheels and tire assemblies.
3. Remove the brake shoe adjusting slot cover from the rear of backing plate.
4. Insert a thin tool through the adjusting slot and hold the adjusting lever away from the star wheel.
5. Insert an adjusting tool and back off the star wheel by prying downward with the tool.
6. Remove the center hub dust cover, nut, washer, brake drum, hub and wheel bearings.

To install:

7. Inspect the brake lining and drum for wear.
8. Inspect the wheel cylinder for leakage. Service as required.
9. Remove, clean, inspect and repack the wheel bearings.
10. Install the brake drum and tighten the hub nut to 20–25 ft. lbs. (27–34 Nm), then back off the nut until bearing pressure is released.
11. Retighten the nut finger tight, align the cotter pin hole and install the cotter pin.
12. Adjust the rear brakes as described in the beginning of this section.

All Wheel Drive Vehicles

1. Raise and support the rear of the vehicle on jackstands.
2. Remove the wheels and tire assemblies.
3. Remove the brake shoe adjusting slot cover from the front the of the brake drum.
4. Insert a thin tool through the adjusting slot and hold the adjusting lever away from the star wheel.
5. Insert an adjusting tool and back off the star wheel by prying downward with the tool.
6. Remove the brake drum from the hub assembly.

The rear hub and bearing does not come off with the brake drum on all wheel drive models

To install:

7. Inspect the brake lining and drum for wear.
8. Inspect the wheel cylinder for leakage. Service as required.
9. Install the brake drum on the hub. Tighten the wheel stud nuts to 95 ft. lbs. (130 Nm).
10. Adjust the rear brakes as outlined in this section.

INSPECTION

Check the brake drum for any cracks, scores, grooves, or an out-of-round condition. Slight scores can be removed with emory cloth, while extensive scoring or grooves will require machining. Have an automotive machine shop measure the wear and check the drum for run out. The shop will be able to turn the drum on a lathe, if necessary. Never have a drum turned more than 0.060 in. (1.5mm). If the drum is cracked, or worn more than the limit, replace.

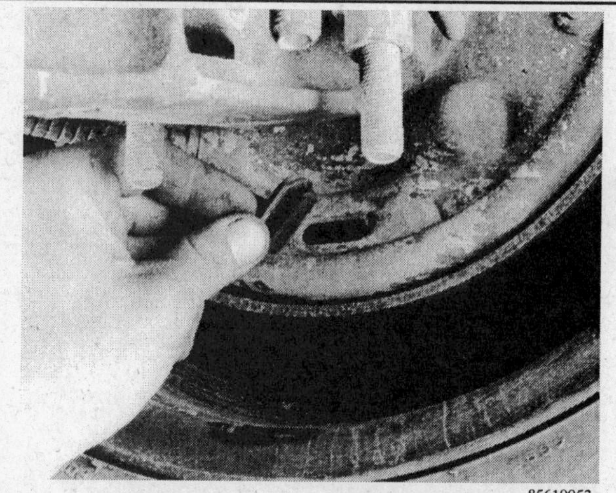

85619053

Fig. 52 Removing the rear drum adjusting hole cover plug

85619054

Fig. 53 Backing off the adjuster star wheel

8561955A

Fig. 54 Removing the dust cover from the axle stub

8561955B

Fig. 55 Removing the dust cover the washer from the axle stub

8561955C

Fig. 56 Removing the cotter pin from the axle stub nut

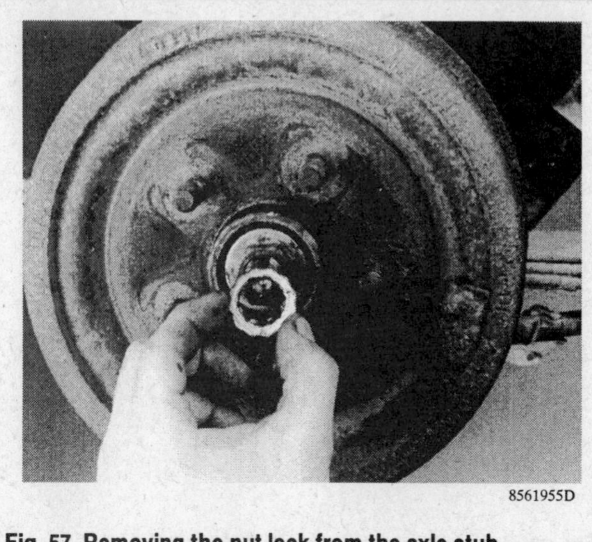

8561955D

Fig. 57 Removing the nut lock from the axle stub

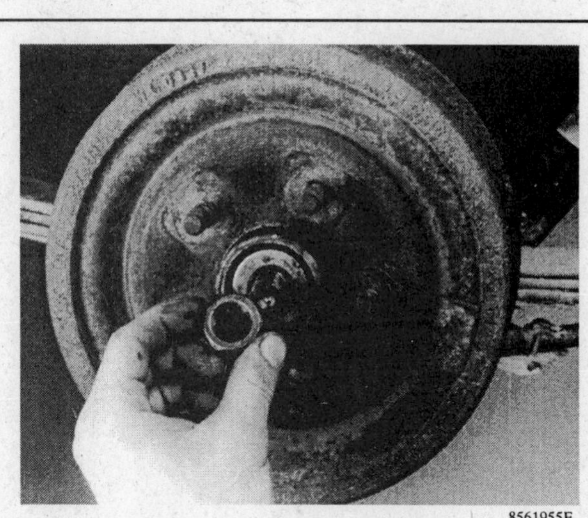

8561955E

Fig. 58 Removing the nut from the axle stub

85619055

Fig. 59 Removing the washer from the axle stub

Fig. 60 Removing the bearing from the axle stub

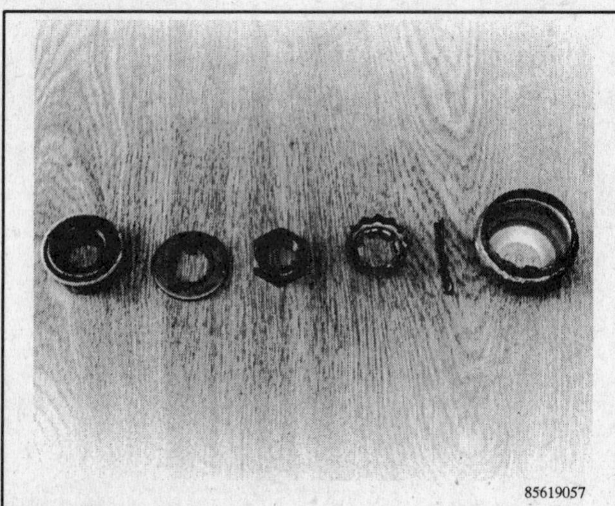

Fig. 61 All of these parts must be removed to remove the rear brake drum

Brake Shoes

REMOVAL & INSTALLATION

See Figures 62, 63, 64, 65, 66, 67, 68, 69, 70, 71, 72, 73, 74, 75, 76, 77, 78 and 79

A pair of brake springs pliers or spring removal/installation tool and a retainer cap spring tool are good tools to have on hand for this job.

1. Raise and support the rear of the vehicle on jackstands.
2. Remove the rear wheels and brake drums.

Remove and install the brake shoes on one side at a time. Use the assembled side for reference.

****CAUTION**

Brake shoes contain asbestos, which has been determined to be a cancer causing agent. Never clean the brake surfaces with compressed air! Avoid inhaling any dust from any brake surface! When cleaning brake surfaces, use a commercially available brake cleaning fluid.

3. Using a pair of brake spring pliers or an appropriate tool, remove the shoe return springs from the top anchor. Take note that the secondary shoe spring is on top of the primary shoe spring.
4. Slide the closed eye of the adjuster cable off of the anchor stud.
5. Unhook the spring end and remove the cable, overload spring, cable guide and anchor plate.
6. Remove the adjusting lever from the spring by sliding forward to clear the pivot. Work the lever out from under the spring.
7. Remove the spring from the pivot.
8. Unhook the bottom shoe-to-shoe spring from the secondary (back) shoe and disengage from the primary (front) shoe.
9. Spread the bottom of the brake shoes apart and remove the star wheel adjuster.
10. Remove the parking brake strut and spring assembly.

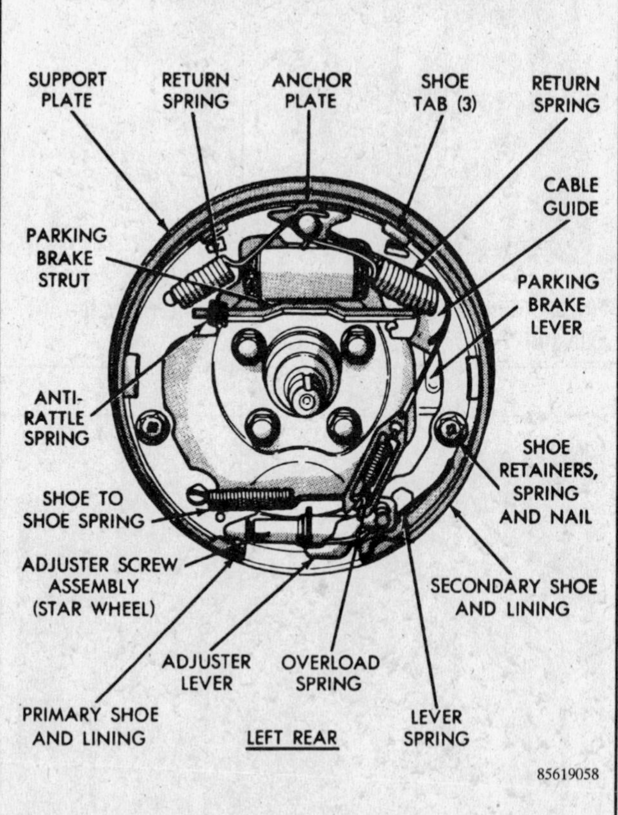

Fig. 62 Rear drum brake assembly components — front wheel drive models

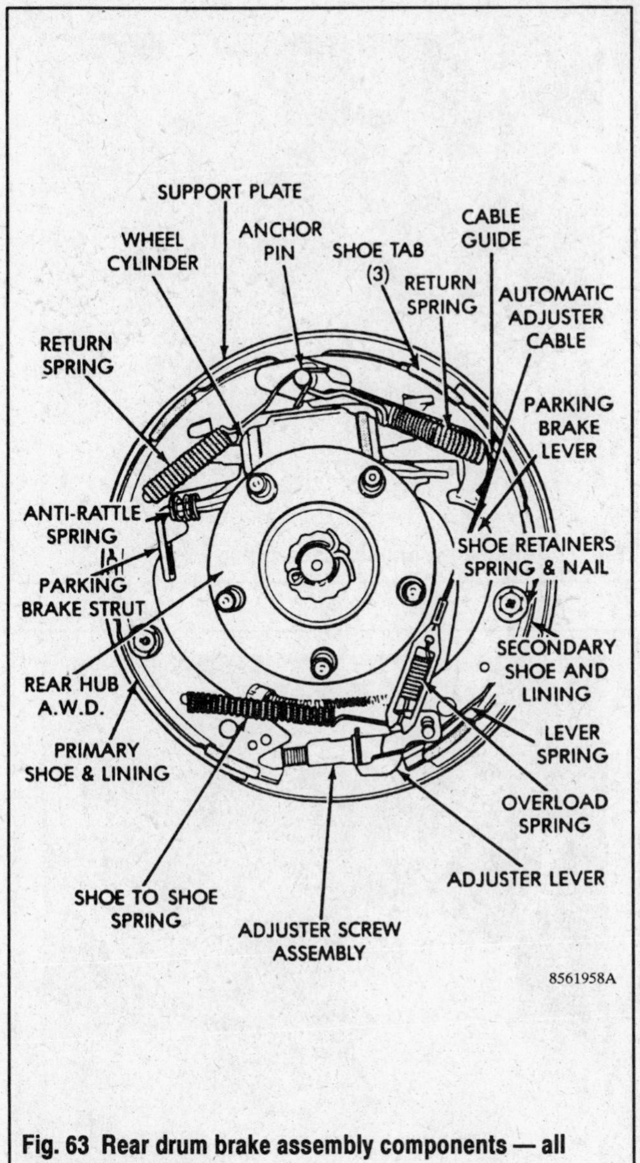

Fig. 63 Rear drum brake assembly components — all wheel drive models

Fig. 64 Rear drum brake assembly components

Fig. 65 Using a special brake tool to remove the return springs from the top anchor

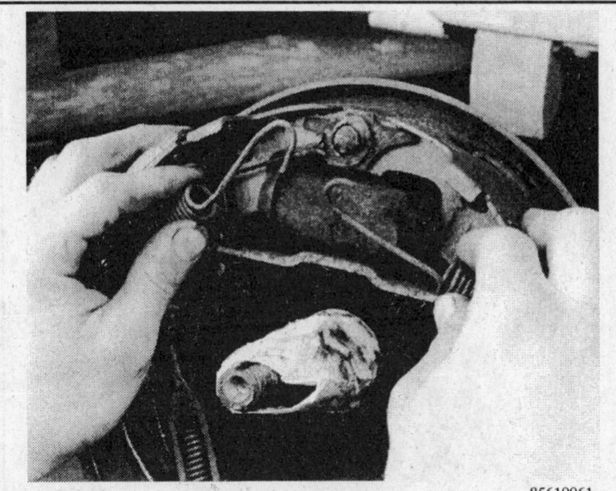

Fig. 66 The return springs shown removed from the top anchor

Fig. 67 Slide the closed eye of the adjuster cable from the top anchor

85619063

Fig. 68 Removing the anchor plate from the top anchor

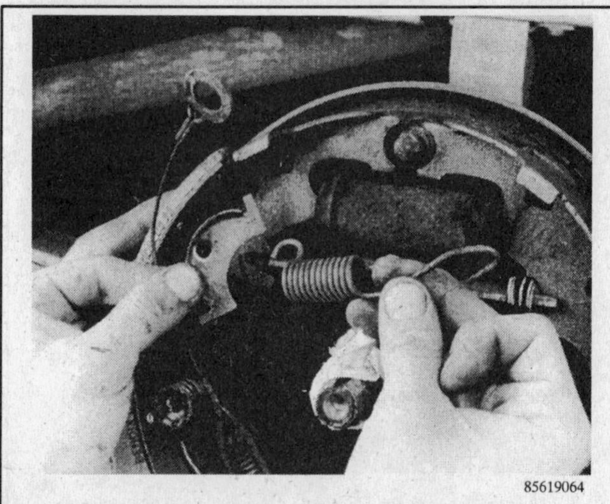

85619064

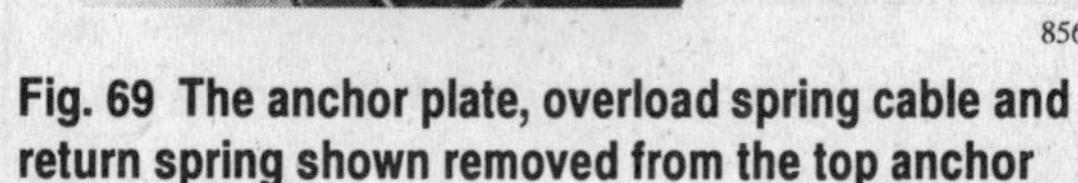

Fig. 69 The anchor plate, overload spring cable and return spring shown removed from the top anchor

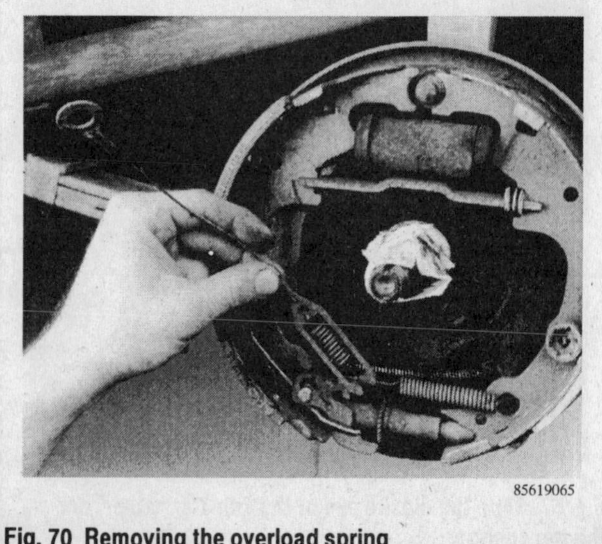

85619065

Fig. 70 Removing the overload spring

85619066

Fig. 71 Unhook the shoe to shoe spring

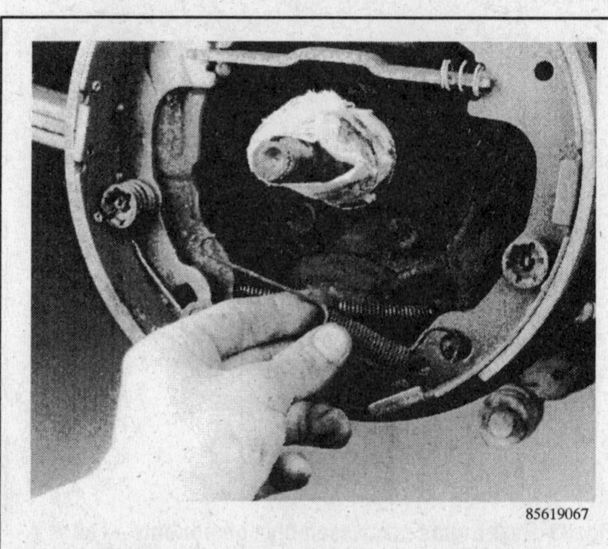

85619067

Fig. 72 The shoe to shoe spring shown removed

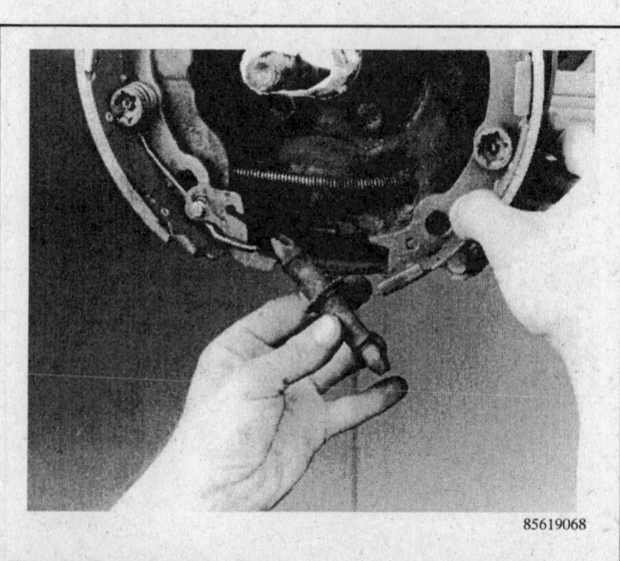

85619068

Fig. 73 Remove the adjuster assembly (star wheel)

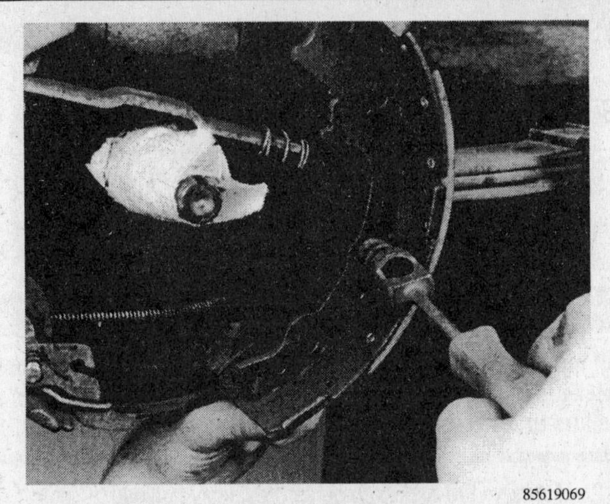
85619069

Fig. 74 Removing the shoe retainers, spring and nail

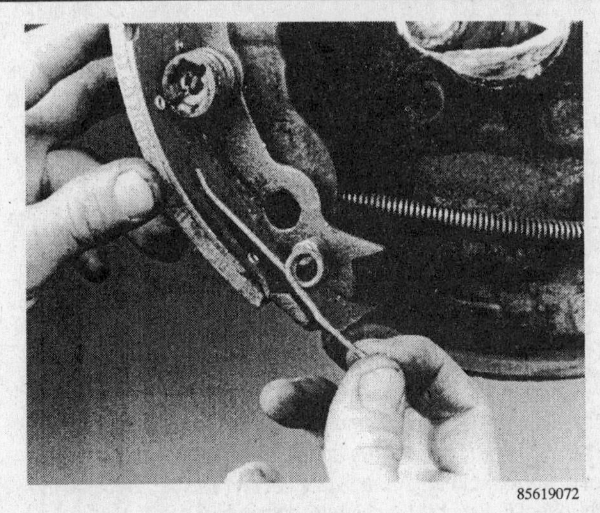
85619072

Fig. 77 Removing the lever spring

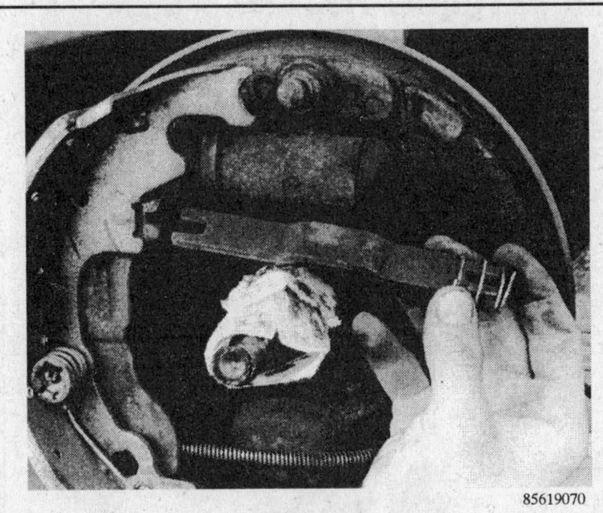
85619070

Fig. 75 Removing the parking brake strut

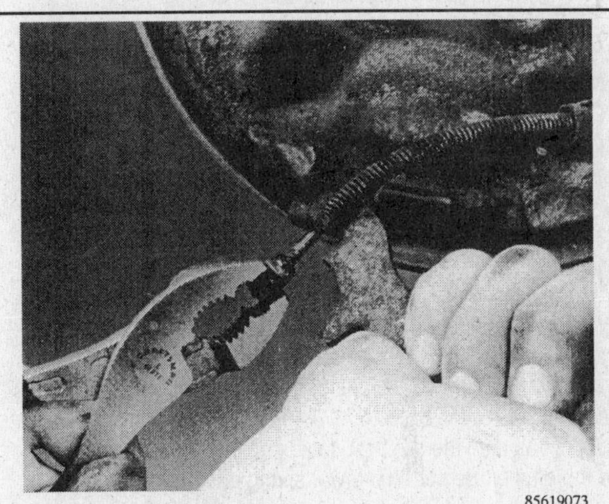
85619073

Fig. 78 Disengaging the parking brake cable from the parking brake lever

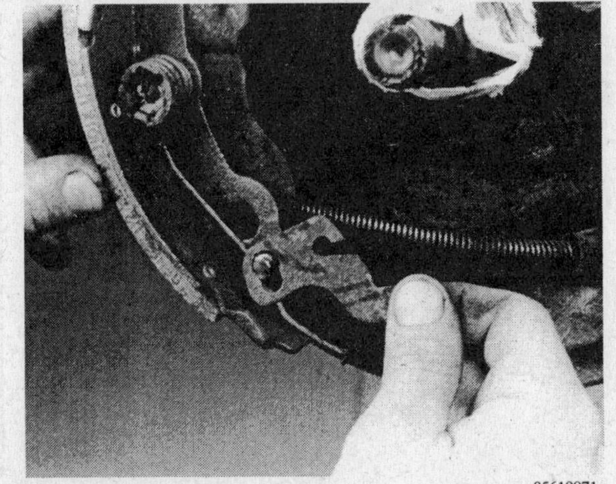
85619071

Fig. 76 Disengage the adjuster lever by sliding it forward to clear the pivot

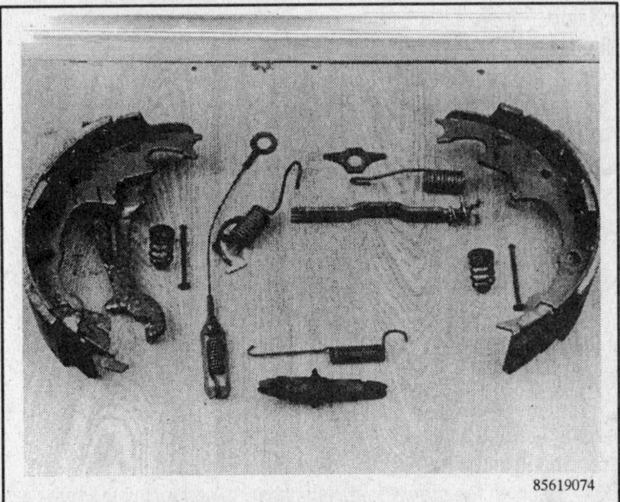
85619074

Fig. 79 Exploded view of the rear drum brakes — front wheel drive vehicle

11. Locate the shoe retainer nail head at the rear of the brake backing plate. Support the nail head with a finger, then press in and twist the spring retainer washer with the special retainer tool or a pair of pliers. If you are using pliers, take care not to slip and pinch your fingers.
12. Remove the retainer, spring, inner washer and nail from both shoes.
13. Remove the parking brake lever from the secondary brake shoe.
14. Remove the shoes from the backing plate and disconnect the parking brake lever from the brake cable.

To install:

15. Clean the backing plate with a safe solvent.
16. Inspect the raised show support pads for rough or rusted contact areas. Clean and smooth as necessary.
17. Clean and inspect the adjuster star wheels, apply a thin film of lubricant to the threads, socket and washer. Replace the star wheel if rust or threads show damage.
18. Inspect the hold-down springs, return springs and adjuster spring. If the springs have been subjected to overheating or if their strength is questionable, replace the spring.
19. Inspect the wheel cylinder. If signs of leakage are present (a small amount of fluid inside the end boot is normal) rebuild or replace the cylinder.
20. Lubricate the shoe contact area pads on the backing plate with high temperature resistant white lubrication.
21. Engage the parking brake lever with the cable and install the lever on the secondary brake shoe. Engage the end of the brake shoe with the wheel cylinder piston and the top anchor. Install the retainer nail, washer, spring and retainer.
22. Position the primary shoe in like manner and install hold-down pin assembly.
23. Install the top anchor plate.
24. Install the parking brake strut and spring in position, press the lower part of the brake.
25. Straighten the adjuster cable and install the eye end over the top anchor. Be sure the lower spring end hook is facing inward.
26. Install the primary (front) shoe return spring. Place the cable guide in position on the secondary (rear) shoe (keep cable out of the way) and engage the return spring.
27. Check the cable guide and ensure proper mounting position. Squeeze the anchor ends of the return springs with pliers until they are parallel.
28. Carefully install the star wheel between the brake shoes. The wheel end goes closest to the secondary (back) shoe.
29. Wind out the star wheel until snug contact between the brake shoes will hold it in position.
30. Install the adjusting lever spring over the pivot pin on the lower shoe web of the secondary shoe.
31. Install the adjuster lever under the spring and over the pivot pin. Slide the lever rearward until it locks in position.
32. Thread the adjuster cable over the guide and hook the end of the overload spring on the adjuster lever. Make sure the cable is float on the guide and the eye end is against the anchor.
33. Check the operation of the adjuster by pulling the cable rearward. The star wheel should rotate upward as the adjuster lever engages the teeth.
34. Back off the star wheel, if necessary, and install the hub and drum. Adjust the brakes as outlined in this section.
35. Repeat the procedures on the other rear wheel.

Wheel Cylinders

REMOVAL & INSTALLATION

➧ **See Figure 80**

1. Raise the rear of the vehicle and support it safely with jackstands.

****CAUTION**

On models equipped with ABS, the system pressure must be released before disconnecting any of the hydraulic lines. Failure to do so, can cause personal injury.

2. Remove the brake drums as previously outlined.
3. Visually inspect the wheel cylinder boots for signs of excessive leakage. Replace any boots that are torn or broken.

➥ **A slight amount of fluid on the boots may not be a leak but may be a preservative fluid used at the factory.**

4. If a leak has been discovered, remove the brake shoes and check for contamination. Replace the linings if they are soaked with grease or brake fluid.
5. Disconnect the brake line from the wheel cylinder.
6. Remove the wheel cylinder attaching bolts, then pull the wheel cylinder out of its support.

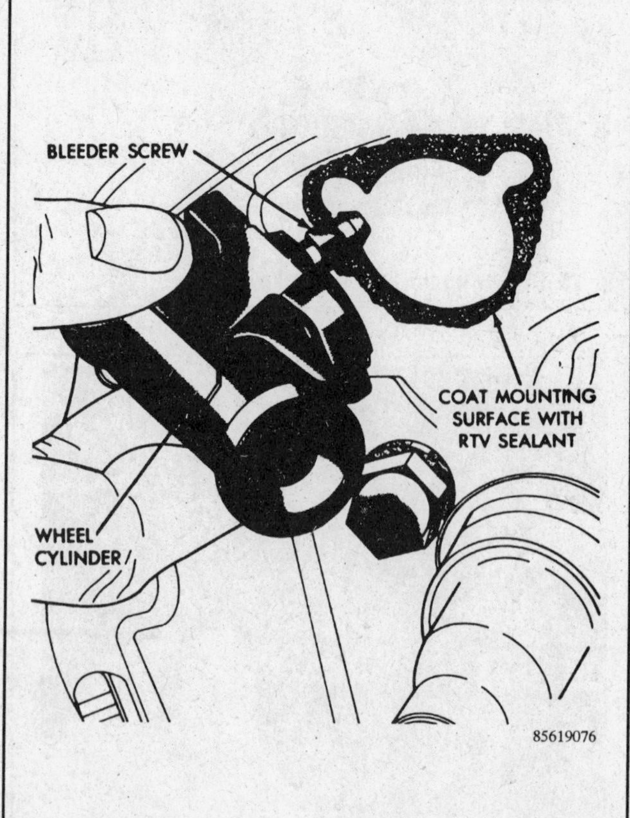

Fig. 80 Removing the wheel cylinder from the backing plate

To install:

7. Position the wheel cylinder onto the backing plate and loosely install the mounting bolts.
8. Start the brake line into the cylinder.
9. Tighten the mounting bolts and the brake line.
10. Install the brake shoes and brake drum.
11. Adjust the brake shoes.
12. Bleed the brake system.

OVERHAUL

➧ See Figure 81

1. Pry the boots away from the cylinder and remove the boots and pistons.
2. Disengage the boot from the piston.
3. Slide the piston into the cylinder bore and press inward to remove the other boot, piston and spring.
4. Wash all parts (except rubber parts) in clean brake fluid thoroughly. Do not use a rag; lint will adhere to the bore.
5. Inspect the cylinder bores. Light scoring can usually be cleaned up with crocus cloth. Heavier scores can be cleaned up with a cylinder hone. Black stains are caused by the piston cups and are no cause of concern. Bad scoring or pitting means that the wheel cylinder should be replaced.
6. Dip the pistons and new cups in clean brake fluid, or apply lubricant that is sometimes packaged in the rebuilding kit prior to assembly.

To install:

7. Coat the wheel cylinder bore with clean brake fluid.
8. Install the expansion spring with the cup expanders.
9. Install the cups in each end of the cylinder with the open ends facing each other.
10. Assemble new boots on the piston and slide them into the cylinder bore.
11. Press the boot over the wheel cylinder until seated.
12. Apply RTV on the mounting surface of the backing plate.
13. Install the wheel cylinder, and connect brake lines.
14. Install brake shoes, and drum.
15. Adjust and bleed brakes.

Parking Brake

ADJUSTMENT

1. Raise and support the rear of the vehicle on jackstands.
2. Apply and release the parking brake several times.
3. Clean the parking park adjustment bolts with a wire brush and lubricate the threads.
4. Back off the adjusting nut until there is slack in the cable.
5. Check the rear brake adjustment, adjust as necessary.
6. Tighten the parking brake cable adjuster until a slight drag is felt when turning the rear wheel.
7. Loosen the cable until no drag is felt on either rear wheel.
8. Back off adjusting nut two full turns more.
9. Apply and release the parking brake several times to ensure there is no rear wheel drag and lower the vehicle.

REMOVAL & INSTALLATION

➧ See Figure 82

Front Cable

1. Raise and support the front of the vehicle on jackstands.
2. Back off the adjuster nut until the cable can be released from the connectors.
3. Lift the floor mat for access to the floor pan. Force the seal surrounding the cable from the floor.
4. Pull the cable forward and disconnect from the lever clevis.
5. Remove the front cable from support bracket and vehicle.

To install:

6. Feed the new cable through the floor pan hole.
7. Attach the front end of the cable to the parking brake lever clevis and support.
8. Engage the intermediate cable, then adjust it as described earlier.

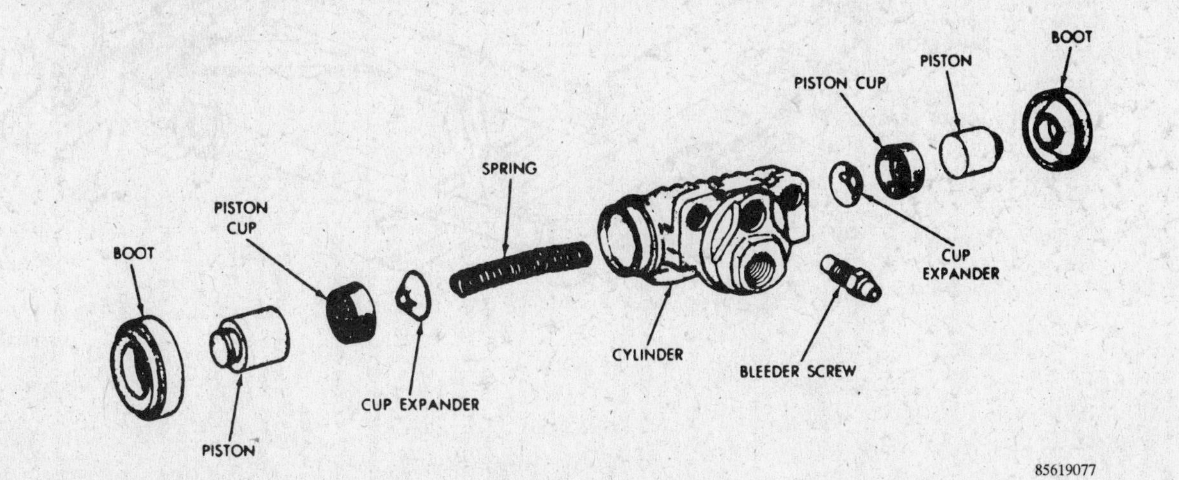

Fig. 81 Exploded view of the wheel cylinder assembly

Intermediate Cable

1. Back off the parking brake adjuster.
2. Disengage the front cable and rear cables from the intermediate cable connector.
3. Remove the intermediate cable.

To install:

4. Install the new cable, then adjust the cable as described above.

Rear Cables

1. Raise and support the rear of the vehicle on jackstands.
2. Back off the cable adjustment and disconnect the rear cable (that is to be replaced) from the intermediate cable.
3. Remove the rear cable from the mounting clips.
4. Remove the rear wheel and the brake shoes from the side requiring replacement.
5. Disconnect the cable from the rear brake apply lever. Compress the cable lock with a mini-hose clamp and pull the cable from the backing plate.

To install:

6. Install the new cable through the brake backing plate and engage the locks.
7. Attach the cable to the apply lever.
8. Install the brake shoes, drum and wheel assembly.
9. Adjust the service brakes and parking brake.

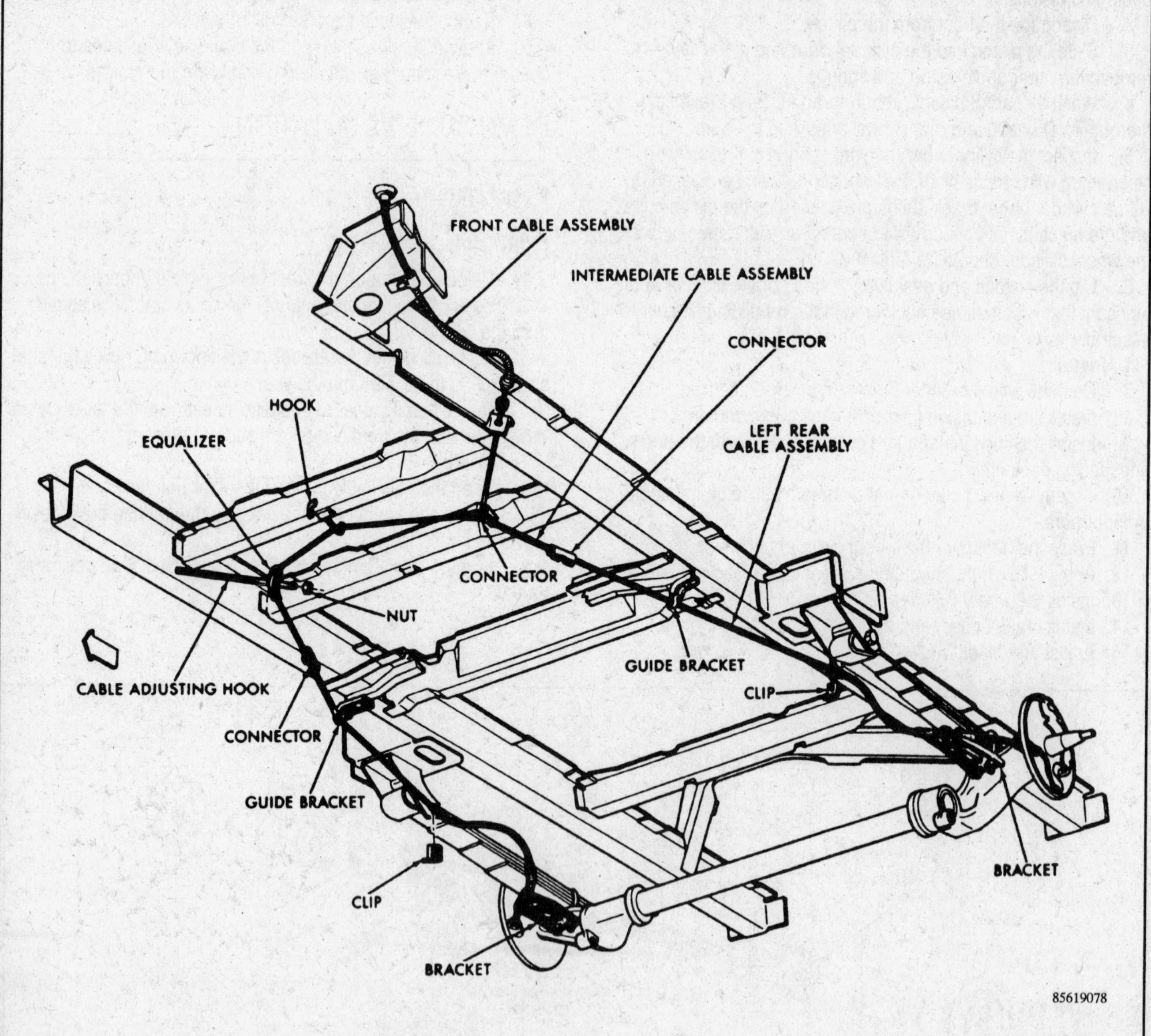

Fig. 82 Parking brake cable routing

BENDIX SYSTEM 10 ANTI-LOCK BRAKE SYSTEM

System Description

➧ See Figure 83

Found on 1991 Caravan/Voyager/Town and Country (AS body), the Bendix System 10 will prevent wheel locking under heavy braking. By preventing wheel lock-up, maximum braking effort is maintained while preventing loss of directional control. Additionally, some steering capability is maintained during the stop. The ABS system will operate regardless of road surface conditions.

There are conditions for which the ABS system provides no benefit. Hydroplaning is possible when the tires ride on a film of water, losing contact with the paved surface. This renders the vehicle totally uncontrollable until road contact is regained. Extreme steering maneuvers at high speed or cornering beyond the limits of tire adhesion can result in skidding which is independent of vehicle braking. For this reason, the system is named anti-lock rather than anti-skid.

Under normal braking conditions, the ABS system functions in the same manner as a standard brake system. The primary difference is that power assist is gained from hydraulic pressure rather than a conventional vacuum booster.

The system is a combination of electrical and hydraulic components, working together to control the flow of brake fluid to the wheels when necessary. The pump and motor assembly pressurizes brake fluid from the reservoir and stores it within an accumulator for use in both normal power-assisted and ABS braking. The Controller Anti-lock Brake (CAB) is the electronic brain of the system, receiving and interpreting speed signals from 4 sensors at the wheels. The CAB will enter anti-lock mode when it senses impending wheel lock at any wheel and immediately controls the line pressure(s) to the affected wheel(s). The hydraulic assembly serves as both an integral master cylinder and the hydraulic booster assembly for the brake system. It contains the wheel circuit valves used to control the brake fluid pressure to each wheel circuit.

During anti-lock braking, line pressures are controlled or modulated by the rapid cycling of electronic valves within the hydraulic assembly. These valves can allow pressures within the system to increase, remain constant or decrease depending on the needs of the moment as registered by the CAB. The front wheels are controlled individually while the rear wheels receive the same electrical signal, based on the wheel with the greatest locking tendency. Anti-lock function is available above 3–5 mph (4.5–8 km/h).

The operator may hear a popping or clicking sound as the pump and/or control valves cycle on and off during normal operation. The sounds are due to normal operation and are not indicative of a system problem; under most conditions, the sounds are only faintly audible. If ABS is engaged, the operator may notice some pulsation in the pedal. If additional force is applied to the pedal during an ABS-engaged stop, the operator will notice extremely hard pedal feel. This is due to isolation of the master cylinder during ABS operation. Some pulsing may also be felt in the body of the vehicle due to suspension movement as brake pressures apply and release at the individual wheels.

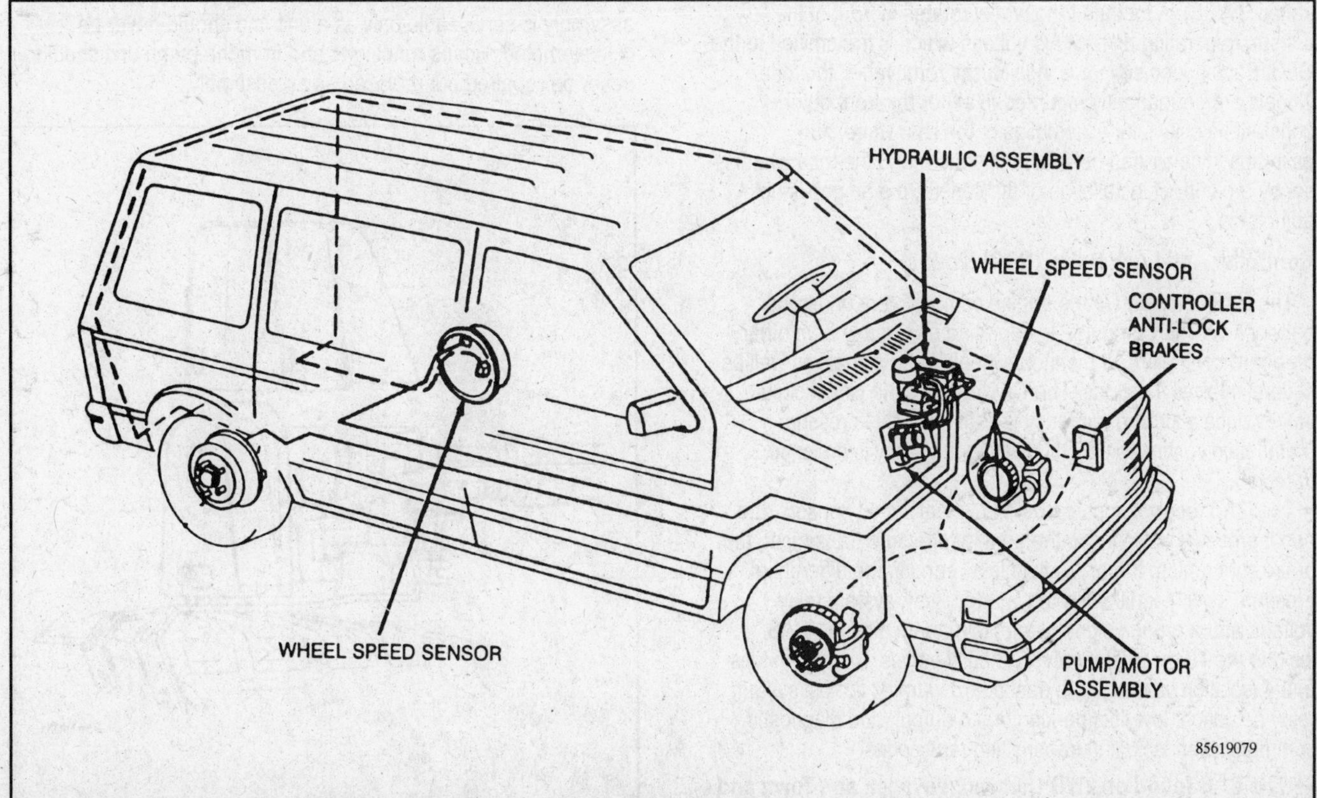

Fig. 83 Bendix system 10 anti-lock brake system — component layout

Although the ABS system prevents wheel lock-up under hard braking, as brake pressure increases, wheel slip is allowed to reach as high as 30%. This means that the rolling velocity of a given wheel is 30% less than that of a free-rolling wheel at a given speed. This slip will result in some tire chirp during ABS operation. The sound should not be interpreted as lock-up but rather as an indication of the system holding the wheel(s) just outside the point of lock-up. Additionally, since the ABS system turns off below 4 mph (7 km/h), the final few feet of an ABS-engaged stop may be completed with the wheels locked.

The Bendix system is equipped with built-in diagnostic capability. At every start-up, the CAB illuminates the dashboard warning lights and turns them off after checking the circuitry. When the vehicle reaches 3–5 mph (4.5–8 km/h), the CAB conducts a system check, briefly activating all the control valves to confirm their operation. This system check may be noticed by the operator as a series of rapid clicks during initial drive-off; the sound is normal and not indicative of a problem. Some fault conditions will cause the CAB to set and retain a trouble code which may be retrieved for diagnostic purposes. Stored fault codes will remain stored until cleared by the DRB II.

The CAB will illuminate the appropriate dashboard warning lamp according to the fault detected. It is possible to have a fault affecting only the ABS function; in this case, the ABS system will be disabled but the vehicle will retain normal braking capability.

SYSTEM COMPONENTS

Wheel Speed (WSS) Sensors

➧ See Figure 84

The speed of each wheel is monitored by a wheel speed sensor (WSS). A toothed tone wheel rotates in front of the sensor, generating a small AC voltage which is transmitted to the CAB. Each speed sensor is individually removable; the tone wheels are permanently mounted to either the front outer constant velocity joint assemblies or the rear wheel hub assembly. The air gap between the sensor and the tone wheel is set by the correct installation of the sensor; the air gap is not adjustable.

Controller Anti-Lock Brake (CAB) Module

The CAB is located in the engine compartment under the battery tray. This computer — operating separately from other on-board controllers — monitors wheel speed signals as well as several internal functions. The CAB controls the wheel circuit valves once a locking tendency is detected. This pressure modulation continues until the locking tendency is no longer detected.

The CAB receives inputs from the wheel speed sensors, the boost pressure transducer, the primary pressure transducer, the brake light switch, the brake fluid level sensor, the differential pressure switch, ignition switch, starter relay, system relay voltage and a ground signal. Outputs managed by the CAB include the 10 modulator valves (3 build valves, 3 decay valves and 4 isolation valves), both dashboard warning lamps, system relay actuation, low fluid/parking brake output, and diagnostic communication including transmitting fault codes.

➜ The CAB found on 2WD Caravan, Voyager, and Town and Country vehicles is different from that on the AWD versions. The controllers must not be interchanged.

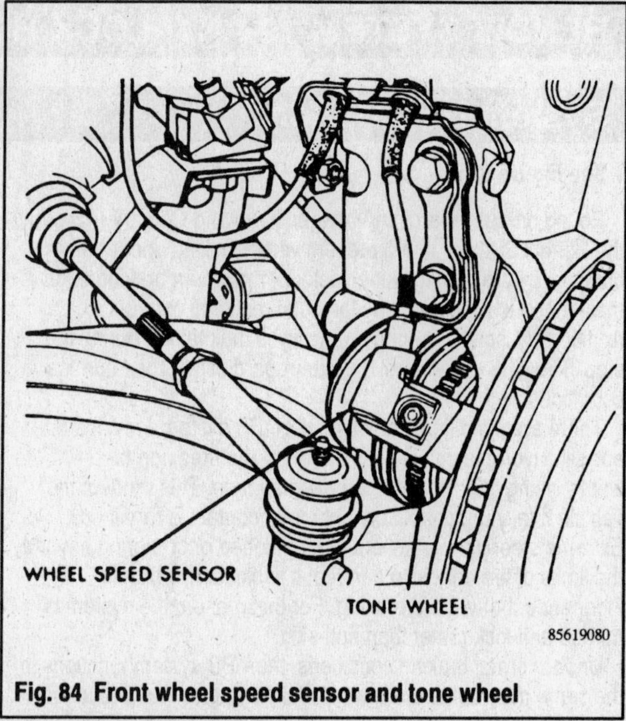

Fig. 84 Front wheel speed sensor and tone wheel

Pump and Motor Assembly

➧ See Figure 85

The integral motor and pump assembly is mounted on rubber isolators to a to a transaxle bracket below the hydraulic assembly. Fluid is taken from the master cylinder reservoir, pressurized and sent to storage in both the piston accumulator and the hydraulic bladder accumulator. The pump/motor assembly is serviceable only as a unit and should never be disassembled. Hoses running to and from the pump unit should never be repaired but replaced as an assembly.

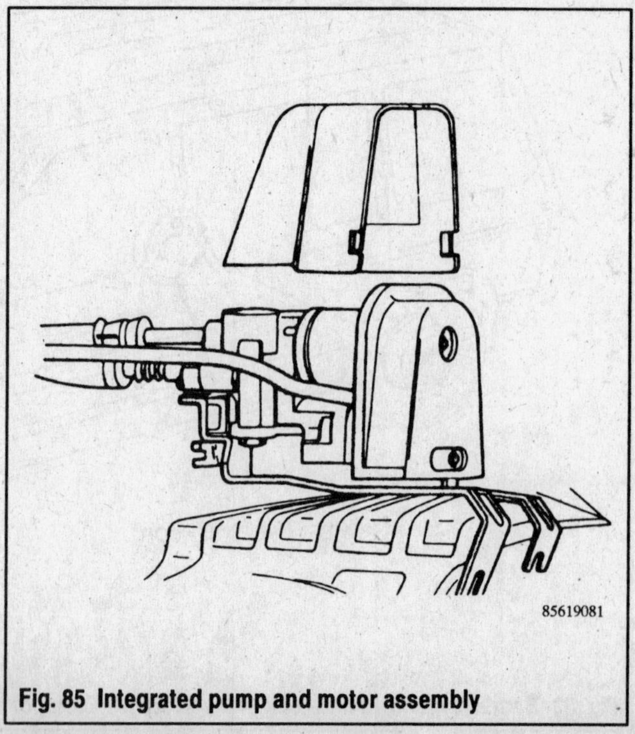

Fig. 85 Integrated pump and motor assembly

Hydraulic Assembly

➧ See Figure 86

The integral hydraulic assembly is located on the firewall and provides the function of the power booster and master cylinder. Other components provide the brake pressure modulation and system monitoring required by the ABS system. The hydraulic assembly consists of several components with individual function as outlined in this section. Note that although the components and their function may be discussed and tested separately, most components are not serviced individually.

BOOSTER/MASTER CYLINDER

The master cylinder uses a diagonally split configuration in normal braking. The 2 circuits are isolated so that a leak in one will not affect the other. During brake pedal application, the pushrod applies force to the boost control valve, allowing pressurized fluid from the accumulator to flow into the master cylinder chamber. This pressure within the booster servo applies pressure to the primary and secondary master cylinder pistons. The pressures generated by the primary and secondary pistons are used to apply the brakes during normal braking.

The pressure within the hydraulic booster is directly proportional to the pressure applied to the brake pedal. As with vacuum operated boosters, brake efficiency depends on road surface and the force applied to the pedal.

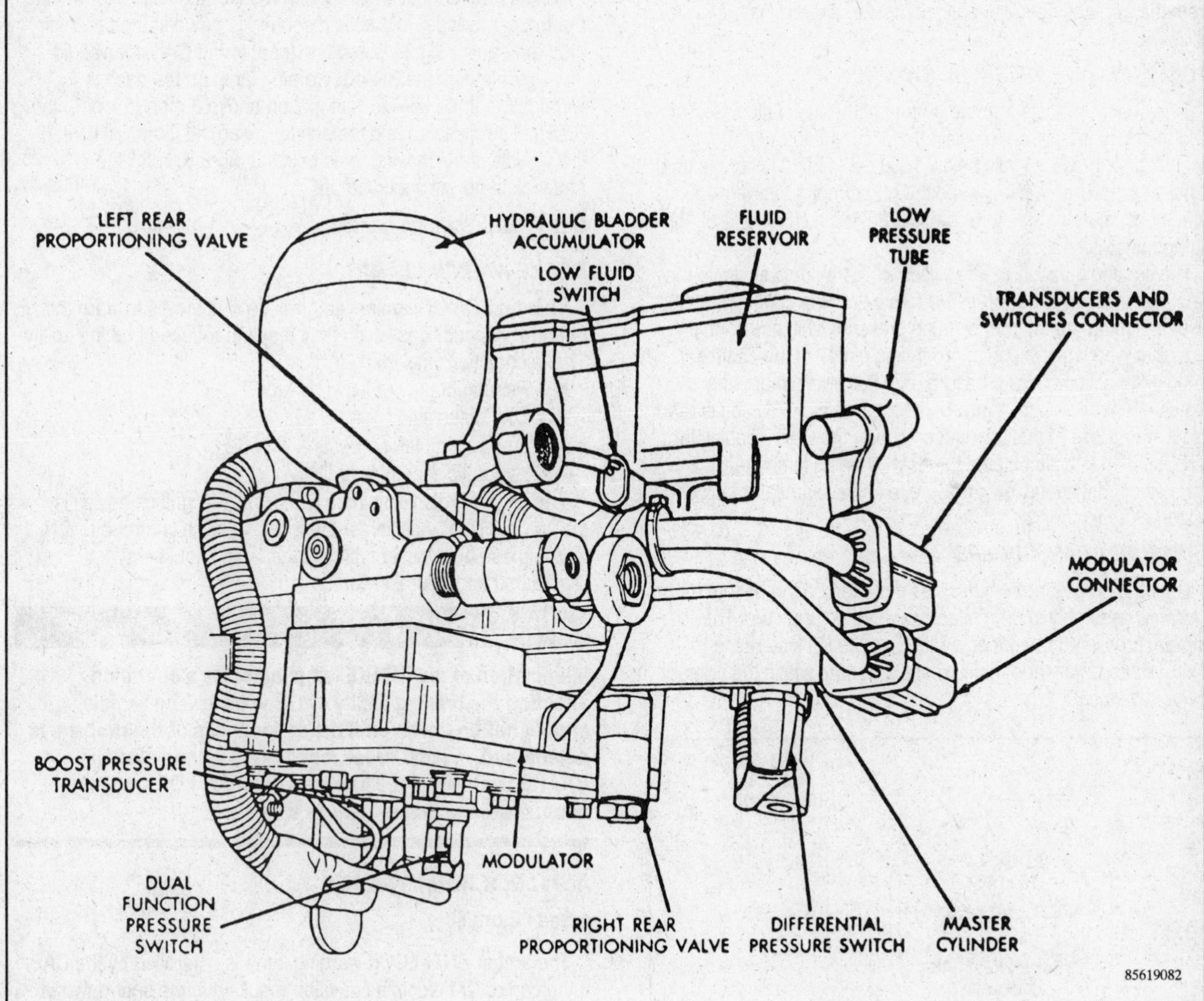

Fig. 86 Hydraulic assembly component location

HYDRAULIC ACCUMULATORS

➧ See Figure 87

The external or bladder accumulator stores brake fluid from the pump under very high pressure; the pressurized fluid is available for hydraulic assist (boost) and/or ABS braking. The accumulator uses a diaphragm and nitrogen pre-charge of about 1000 psi (6895 kPa). Normally, the pump will charge the accumulator to a working pressure of 1600–2000 psi (11,030–13,790 kPa). For this reason, all safety precautions must be observed before working on the hydraulic system. The pressures within the accumulator are sufficient to cause serious personal injury or damage to the vehicle.

The piston accumulator is an integral part of the pump/motor assembly. It contains a pre-charge of approximately 460 psi (3171 kPa) nitrogen gas. This accumulator cannot be removed from the pump/motor assembly; component service is not possible.

DUAL FUNCTION PRESSURE SWITCH

This switch is located on the bottom of the hydraulic assembly and monitors the pressure within the accumulator. When accumulator pressure falls below 1600 psi (11,030 kPa), the dual function pressure switch causes the pump/motor to energize. When accumulator pressure reaches 2000 psi (13,790 kPa), the pump/motor is shut off.

The second purpose of this switch is to provide a signal to the CAB when accumulator pressure falls below the 1000 psi (6895 kPa) minimum. An internal warning pressure switch is normally closed at working pressures, grounding pin 17 at the controller. Should the accumulator pressure drop below minimum, the switch opens, a voltage signal is detected at the CAB and is read as low pressure. At this warning pressure, the CAB disables the ABS function and illuminates the dash warning lamps. After 2 minutes of continuous low pressure, a low accumulator fault code is stored in memory.

PRESSURE TRANSDUCERS

The boost pressure transducer is mounted on the bottom of the hydraulic assembly and monitors boost servo pressure. The primary pressure transducer is found on the left side of the hydraulic assembly and monitors the pressure within the primary master cylinder.

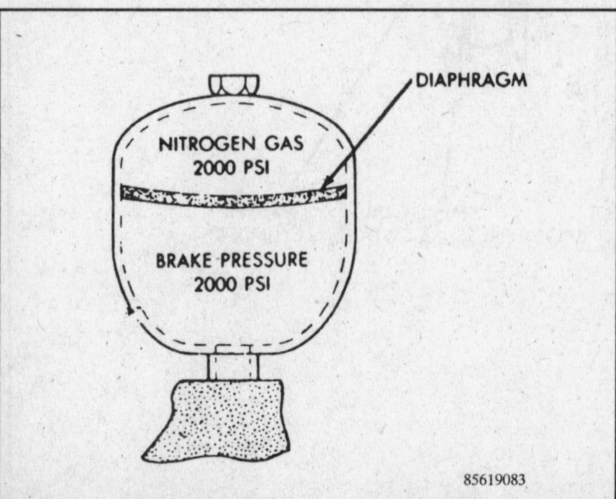

Fig. 87 Hydraulic bladder external accumulator

Both transducers generate a signal of 0.25–5.0 volts directly proportional to the fluid pressure. The CAB compares these signals and confirms proper operation. If either of the signals exceeds a pre-planned range, the CAB will disable the anti-lock system.

DIFFERENTIAL PRESSURE SWITCH

The differential pressure switch is used to detect a pressure differential between the primary and secondary master cylinder hydraulic circuits. When the pressure difference is 300 psi (2068 kPa) or more, this switch grounds the output of the primary pressure transducer. The CAB receives 0.0 volts from the transducer and reacts by shutting down the ABS function and illuminating the dash warning lights.

FLUID LEVEL SENSOR

A float and magnetic reed switch monitor the fluid level within the master cylinder hydraulic reservoir. Located in the reservoir cap, the sensor signal is used an input to the CAB. If low fluid level is detected, the BRAKE warning lamp on the dash is illuminated. If the vehicle is in motion above 3 mph (5 km/h), the ABS will be disabled and the anti-lock warning lamp will light. If the vehicle is not moving, or is below 3 mph (5 km/h) the anti-lock lamp will not come on.

Dashboard Warning Lamps

BRAKE WARNING LAMP

The red BRAKE warning lamp will be illuminated to warn the operator of conditions which may result in reduced braking ability. These conditions include:

- Parking brake not fully released.
- Low brake fluid.
- Low accumulator pressure.
- Hydraulic assembly or CAB

The lamp will also illuminate whenever the ignition switch is put in the **START** position or the ignition switch is turned to **ON**. Under these bulb test conditions, the lamp should stay illuminated for about 2 seconds.

****CAUTION**

Illumination of the BRAKE lamp indicates a condition affecting the braking ability of the vehicle. The vehicle should not be driven until the seriousness of the problem is determined. In most cases, conditions illuminating the BRAKE lamp will also illuminate the ANTI-LOCK warning lamp, disabling that system as well.

ANTI-LOCK WARNING LAMP

➧ See Figure 88

The amber ANTI-LOCK warning lamp is controlled by the CAB. If the controller detects a condition resulting in the shut-down of the ABS function, the ANTI-LOCK lamp will be lit. The ANTI-LOCK lamp is normally lit until the CAB completes its self-tests; if no faults are found, the lamp is turned off.

Display of the ANTI-LOCK warning lamp by itself indicates only that the ABS function has been disabled. Power-assisted normal braking is still available and the vehicle may be driven with reasonable care.

➥ When starting the vehicle, the ANTI-LOCK lamp may stay on 1-to-30 seconds depending on the residual press the left front headlight (AS body) The relay controls the operation of the pump/motor assembly and is energized by a signal from the dual function pressure switch. The relay may be serviced individually.

The system relay controls the modulator valves and the anti-lock warning lamp relay. The system relay, near the pump/motor relay, controls power to the CAB after the start-up cycle.

The anti-lock warning lamp relay controls the dashboard warning lamp. When the relay is energized by the CAB, the dash lamp is held **OFF**. Thus, the lamp will light when the CAB fails, is disconnected or causes the ABS function to be discontinued. The CAB has the capability to turn the light on by itself by providing a separate ground.

Proportioning Valves

In place of the usual differential pressure proportioning valve, this system incorporates individual valves in each rear brake line. Located in the brake outlet ports of the hydraulic assembly, these screw-in valves limit rear brake pressure after a certain pressure is reached. This improves front-to-rear brake balance during normal braking. Each proportioning valve may be serviced individually.

Diagnostic Connector

The ABS diagnostic connector is located on the left side of the steering column under the dash. The blue 6-pin connector is used for connecting diagnostic tools such as the DRB II.

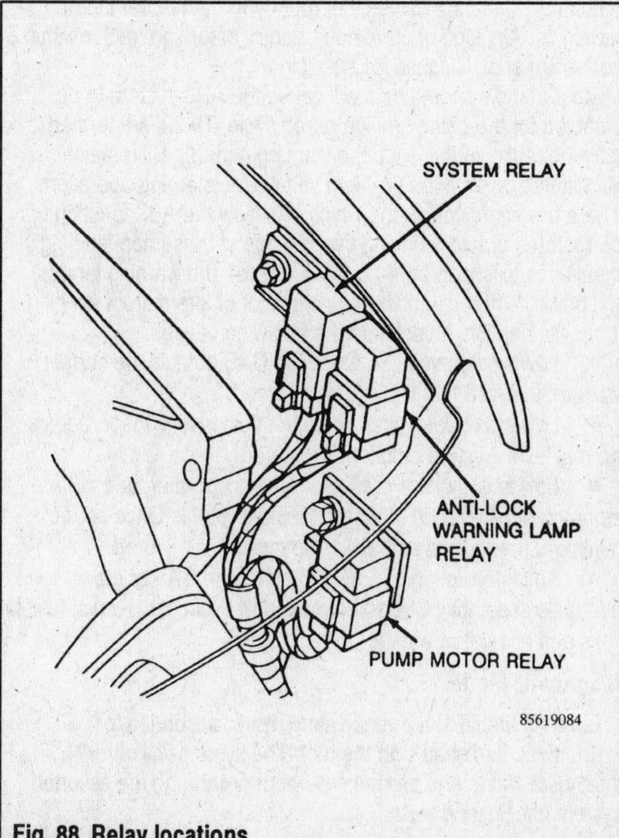

Fig. 88 Relay locations

Diagnosis and Testing

➧ See Figures 89, 90, 91, 92, 93, 94, 95 and 96

SERVICE PRECAUTIONS

****CAUTION**

This brake system uses hydraulic accumulators which, when fully charged, contain brake fluid at very high pressure. Before disconnecting any hydraulic lines, hoses or fittings be certain that the accumulator pressure is completely relieved. Failure to depressurize the accumulators may result in personal injury and/or vehicle damage.

- Certain components within the ABS system are not intended to be serviced or repaired individually. Only those components with removal and installation procedures should be serviced.
- The accumulator contains high pressure nitrogen gas to assist in pressurizing the system. The gas pressure is maintained even after fluid pressure in the system is reduced. Never puncture or attempt to disassemble this component.
- Do not use rubber hoses or other parts not specifically specified for the ABS system. When using repair kits, replace all parts included in the kit. Partial or incorrect repair may lead to functional problems and require the replacement of components.
- Lubricate rubber parts with clean, fresh brake fluid to ease assembly. Do not use lubricated shop air to clean parts; damage to rubber components may result.
- Use only DOT 3 brake fluid from an unopened container.
- If any hydraulic component or line is removed or replaced, it may be necessary to bleed the entire system.
- A clean repair area is essential. Always clean the reservoir and cap thoroughly before removing the cap. The slightest amount of dirt in the fluid may plug an orifice and impair the system function. Perform repairs after components have been thoroughly cleaned; use only denatured alcohol to clean components. Do not allow ABS components to come into contact with any substance containing mineral oil; this includes used shop rags.
- The Controller Anti-lock Brakes (CAB) is a microprocessor similar to other computer units in the vehicle. Ensure that the ignition switch is **OFF** before removing or installing controller harnesses. Avoid static electricity discharge at or near the controller.

1. Turn the ignition switch **OFF** and leave it **OFF** during repairs unless specifically directed otherwise. Alternately, the negative battery cable may be disconnected; it must remain disengaged throughout the repairs.
2. Firmly apply and release the brake pedal a minimum of 40 times, using at least 50 lbs. (222 N) of pedal force.
3. The pedal feel will become noticeably harder when the accumulator is completely discharged. Once this is felt, apply the brake pedal forcefully a few additional times. This will remove all hydraulic pressure from the system.

4. Do not turn the ignition switch **ON** or reconnect the battery cable after depressurizing the system unless service procedures specifically require it or all service operations have been performed.

➜ After the reserve pressure is depleted, the fluid level in the reservoir may rise above the MAX fill mark. This is normal; the reservoir will not overflow unless the system was overfilled to begin with.

5. Always wear safety goggles when disconnecting lines and fittings.

DIAGNOSTIC PROCEDURE

Diagnosis of the ABS system consists of 3 general steps, performed in order. The visual or preliminary inspection is always required before any other steps are taken. A functional test drive is performed to confirm the existence of a problem. The functional test will indicate the need for specific diagnostic tests to be performed.

Some diagnostic tests will require the ignition being left **ON** for a period of time. This could lead to lowered battery voltage and erroneous voltage readings within the system. Unless the battery is known to be in sound condition, connect a slow-charger to the battery when performing extended testing.

Visual Inspection

Before diagnosing an apparent ABS problem, make absolutely certain that the normal braking system is in correct working order. Many common brake problems (dragging lining, seepage, etc.) will affect the ABS system. A visual check of specific system components may reveal problems creating an apparent ABS malfunction. Performing this inspection may reveal a simple failure, thus eliminating extended diagnostic time.

1. Depressurize the system.
2. Inspect the brake fluid level in the reservoir.
3. Inspect brake lines, hoses, master cylinder assembly, brake calipers and cylinders for leakage.
4. Visually check brake lines and hoses for excessive wear, heat damage, punctures, contact with other parts, missing clips or holders, blockage or crimping.
5. Check the calipers and wheel cylinders for rust or corrosion. Check for proper sliding action if applicable.
6. Check the caliper and wheel cylinder pistons for freedom of motion during application and release.
7. Inspect the wheel speed sensors for proper mounting and connections.
8. Inspect the tone wheels for broken teeth or poor mounting.
9. Inspect the wheels and tires on the vehicle. They must be of the same size and type to generate accurate speed signals. Check also for approximately equal tire pressures.
10. Confirm the fault occurrence with the operator. Certain driver induced faults, such as not releasing the parking brake fully, will set a fault code and trigger the dash warning light(s). Excessive wheel spin on low-traction surfaces, high speed acceleration or riding the brake pedal may also set fault codes and trigger a warning lamp. These induced faults are not system failures but examples of vehicle performance outside the parameters of the CAB.
11. The most common cause of intermittent faults is not a failed sensor but a loose, corroded or dirty connector. Incorrect installation of the wheel speed sensor will cause a loss of wheel speed signal. Check harness and component connectors carefully.

Functional Check

If the visual inspections do not lead to resolution of the problem, the test drive, or functional check must be preformed. Keep in mind that the vehicle being driven, may have a problem affecting its braking ability; check the brakes at a very low speed in a safe location before beginning an extended drive. A recommended method of testing and test driving for an ABS fault is:

1. Turn the ignition **ON** without starting the engine. Wait until both the BRAKE and ANTI-LOCK warning lights turn off. This will allow the pump to charge the system; if either or both warning lamps do not go off, proceed to Step 3.
2. Turn the ignition switch **OFF** for 15 seconds.
3. Start the engine. Wait for displays to achieve normal operation.
4. Place the shift lever in **P**. Using a full pedal stroke, slowly depress the brake pedal and release it.
5. Drive the vehicle carefully for a short distance. Achieve a speed of at least 20 mph (32 km/h); bring the vehicle to a full stop then accelerate to at least 20 mph (32 km/h).
6. If either the BRAKE or ANTI-LOCK warning lamps comes on, a fault has been detected by the CAB and, in most cases, a fault code has been entered into the memory.

Intermittent Faults

Most intermittent faults are caused by loose or faulty connections or wiring. Always check suspect circuits for poor mating of connector halves, improperly formed or damaged terminals. Any sign of corrosion or entry of foreign matter within a connector shell is cause for suspicion.

Most of the system faults will cause the ABS system to be disabled for the entire ignition on-off cycle. These are termed latching faults; in this case the warning lamp(s) will remain illuminated, even if the problem self-corrects during operation. There are some conditions which will allow the ABS function to be restored during a driving cycle; if one of these non-latching conditions exists and then ceases to exist, the warning lamp(s) will go off. When diagnosing a complaint of intermittent warning lamp illumination, investigate the following causes:

- Low system voltage. Once the CAB detects the correct voltage, the ABS function will be restored.
- Low brake fluid level. Once the fluid level sensor reads a normal level, system function is restored.
- Low accumulator pressure. May occur after long or hard stopping or as a result of riding the brake pedal. Once correct minimum pressure is achieved, the system is restored.
- Any interruption of power to either the CAB or the hydraulic assembly. Check the main power circuits, relays, fusible links and all related wiring.

Diagnostic Mode

Connect the DRB II or equivalent tester, according to instructions furnished with the tool. The system will enter diagnostic mode and prompt the operator through the assorted system checks and tests.

DRB-II MESSAGE	WARNING LAMPS		POSSIBLE CAUSES	DETECTED	LATCHING
	BRAKE	ANTI-LOCK			
CAB FAULT	—	ON	—Internal CAB fault	Anytime key on	YES
MODULATOR FAULT	—	ON	—Shorted or open solenoid or solenoid driver —Loose connector pin —Internal CAB fault	After drive-off until next ignition reset	YES
RIGHT REAR / LEFT REAR / RIGHT FRONT / LEFT FRONT SENSOR	—	ON	—Missing sensor signal caused by defective wheel speed sensor —CAB fault	Vehicle speed above 15 mph	YES
RIGHT REAR / LEFT REAR / RIGHT FRONT / LEFT FRONT CONTINUITY	—	ON	—Open or short in sensor, wiring or CAB	After start-up check, vehicle not in motion	YES
SYSTEM RELAY FAULT	—	ON	—System relay stuck on	During start-up check	YES
SOLENOID UNDERVOLTAGE FAULT	—	ON	—Low battery, low vehicle voltage —Open circuit on system relay output —System relay malfunction	During drive-off check	NO
ANTILOCK LAMP RELAY	—	—	—Open or stuck relay —Open wiring	During start-up check	NO
ANTILOCK LAMP	*	—	—Failed bulb or open wiring *If this code is set and a 2nd fault is detected, the brake lamp will light	During start-up check	—
LOW FLUID/PARK BRAKE FAULT	ON	ON ABOVE 3 MPH	—Low brake fluid —Parking brake engaged —Short to ground on low fluid wire	Anytime key on	NO
PRIMARY PRESSURE/ DIFFERENTIAL PRESSURE FAULT	ON DURING BRAKING	ON DURING BRAKING	—Hydraulic leak —Air in circuits —Malfunctioning pressure transducers	Anytime with brakes applied	NO
BOOST PRESSURE FAULT	ON DURING BRAKING	ON DURING BRAKING	—Malfunction in hydraulic booster or pressure transducers	Anytime with brakes applied	NO
EXCESS DECAY FAULT	—	ON	—Modulator fault —Incorrect tone wheels —Sensor fault —Hydroplaning —Long stop on ice	During ABS operation, if any 2 decay valves operate for more than 2 seconds	NO
LOW ACCUMULATOR FAULT	ON	ON	Malfunction in pump/motor system: —Dual function pressure switch —Pump/motor relay —Pump/motor assembly —Wiring faults	Anytime. Warning lamps light immed. Fault code sets after 2 min. of continuous detection	NO
NO RESPONSE	—	—	—Open circuit in diagnostic or data wiring or loose connectors —Defective CAB —Ignition off	Not a fault code. DRB-II cannot communicate with CAB.	—

85619085

Fig. 89 DRB-II Fault Messages — Bendix ABS System 10

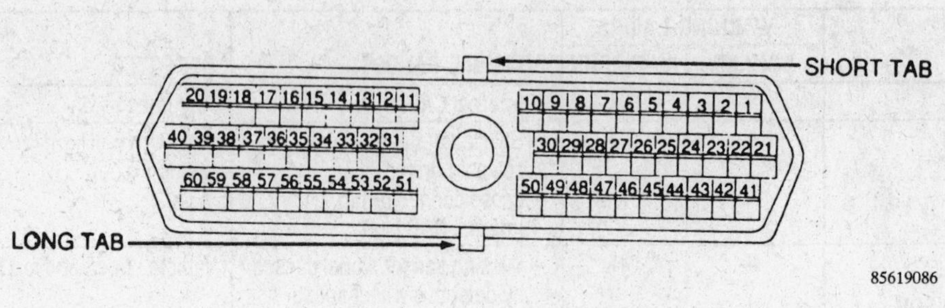

Fig. 90 ABS controller-60 pin connector — pin identification

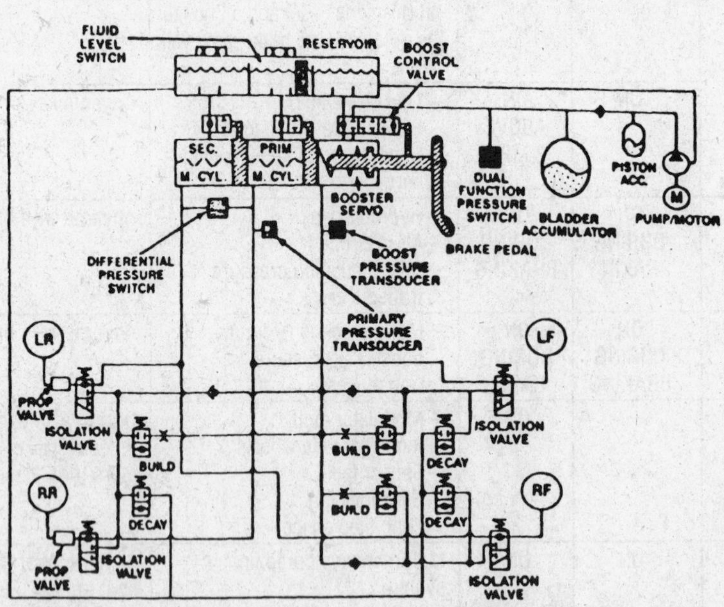

Isolation Valves—open, allowing fluid to flow from primary and secondary circuits to wheel brakes.

Decay and Build Valves—closed.

The brake pedal is in the released position, the booster servo circuit is closed to accumulator pressure. Booster servo circuit, primary and secondary circuits receive fluid from fluid reservoir. All brake circuits closed (check valves) to fluid from booster servo circuit.

85619087

Fig. 91 System schematic: Normal driving brakes off — Bendix ABS System 10

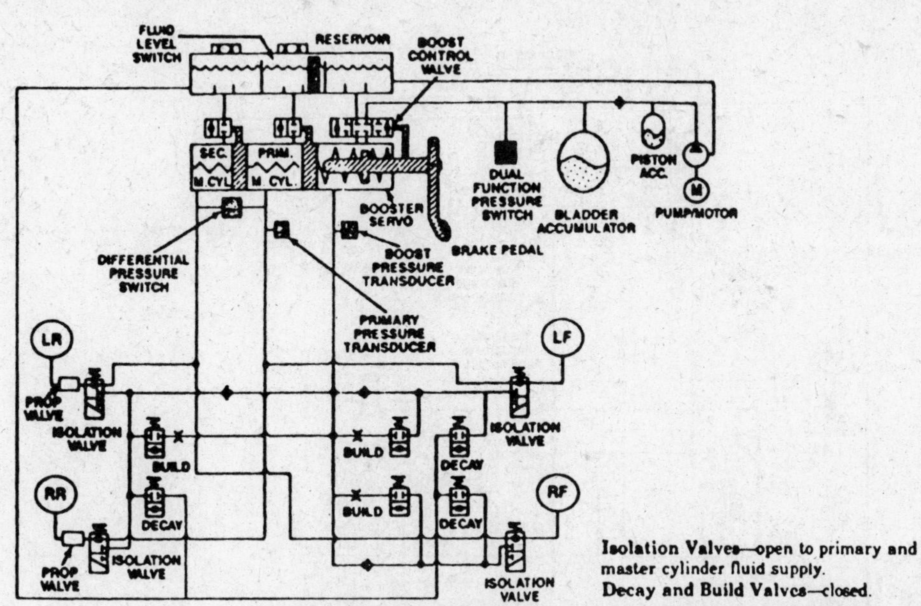

Isolation Valves—open to primary and secondary master cylinder fluid supply.
Decay and Build Valves—closed.

The brake pedal is applied. The travel of the brake pedal closes primary, secondary and booster servo circuits from fluid supply at the fluid reservoir. Brake fluid from the primary and secondary circuits flows through the open isolation valves and applies the wheel brakes. Fluid from the booster servo circuit does not flow to the wheel brakes. The fluid flow is blocked by the closed build valves and check valves.

Power Assist—The boost control valve shuttles between its three positions to provide power assisted braking

85619088

Fig. 92 System schematic: Normal driving brakes applied — Bendix ABS System 10

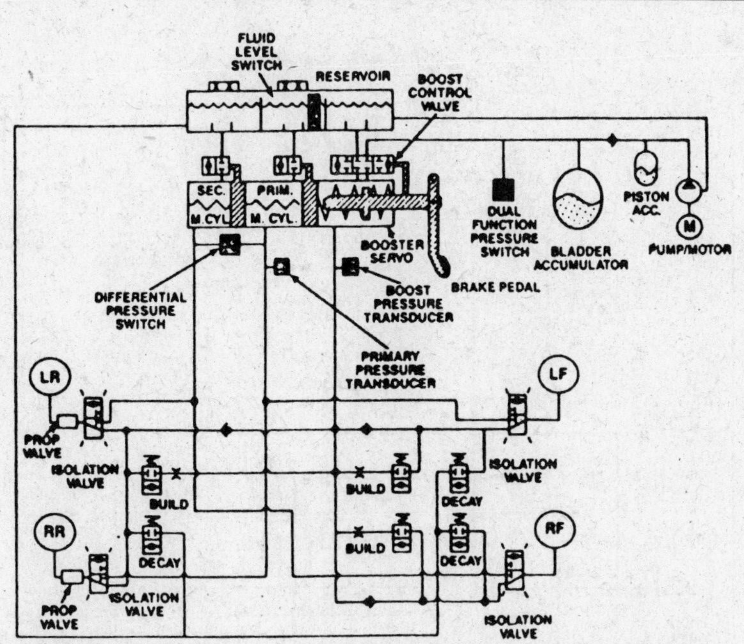

For explanation purposes, assume all speed sensors are sending the same wheel speed information, requiring the same modulation at the same rate.

Isolation Valves—closed, isolating the wheel brakes from master cylinder primary and secondary fluid supplies. Build and decay valves are closed preventing any fluid from reaching the open isolation valves.
Decay and Build Valves—closed.

85619089

Fig. 93 System schematic: ABS braking-hold pressure — Bendix ABS System 10

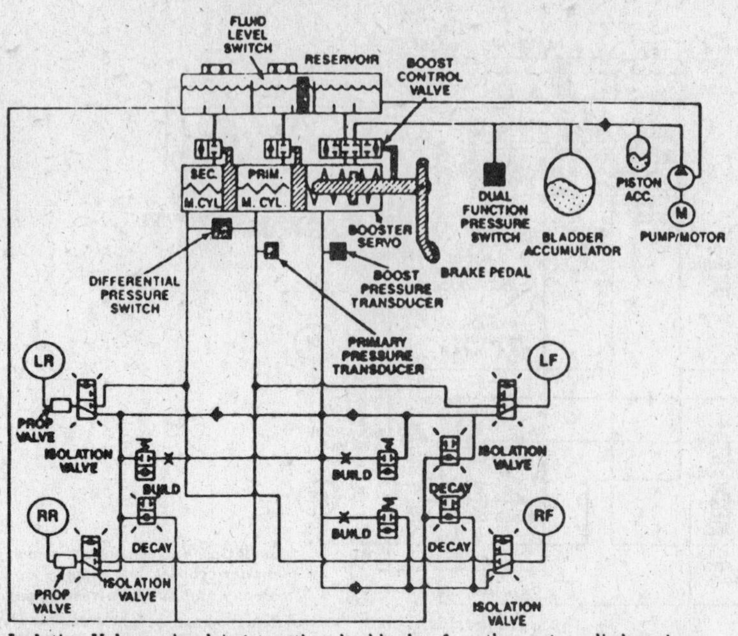

Isolation Valves—closed, isolating the wheel brakes from the master cylinder primary and secondary fluid supplies.

Decay Valves—open, allowing release of fluid through decay valve to the fluid reservoir.

Build Valves—closed, blocking booster servo circuit fluid to wheel brakes.

85619090

Fig. 94 System schematic: ABS braking-Decay pressure — Bendix ABS System 10

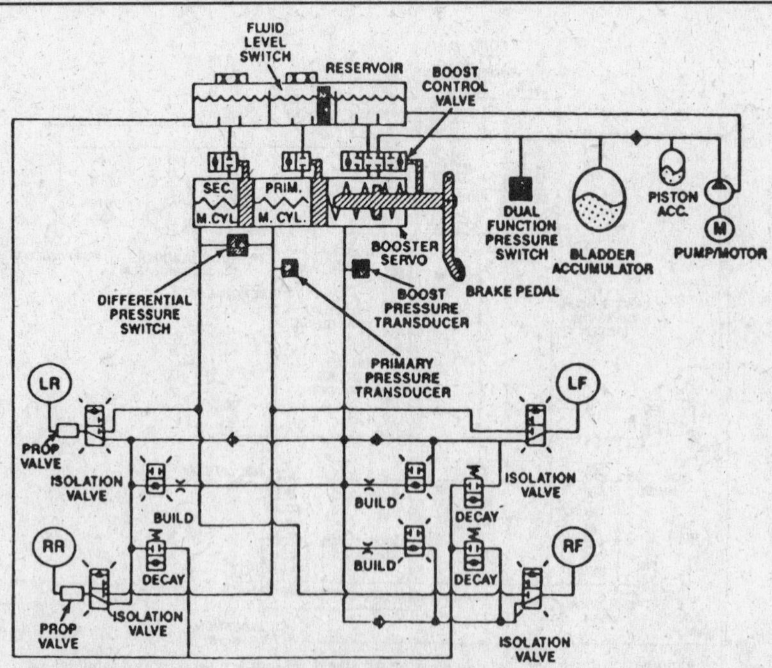

Isolation Valves—closed, isolating wheel brakes from master cylinder primary and secondary fluid supplies and open to booster servo circuit pressure through open build valves.

Decay Valves—closed.

Build Valves—open, allowing booster servo circuit pressure to flow to wheel brakes through the isolation valves.

Power Assist—The boost control valve shuttles between its three positions to provide power assisted braking.

85619091

Fig. 95 System schematic: ABS braking-Build pressure — Bendix ABS System 10

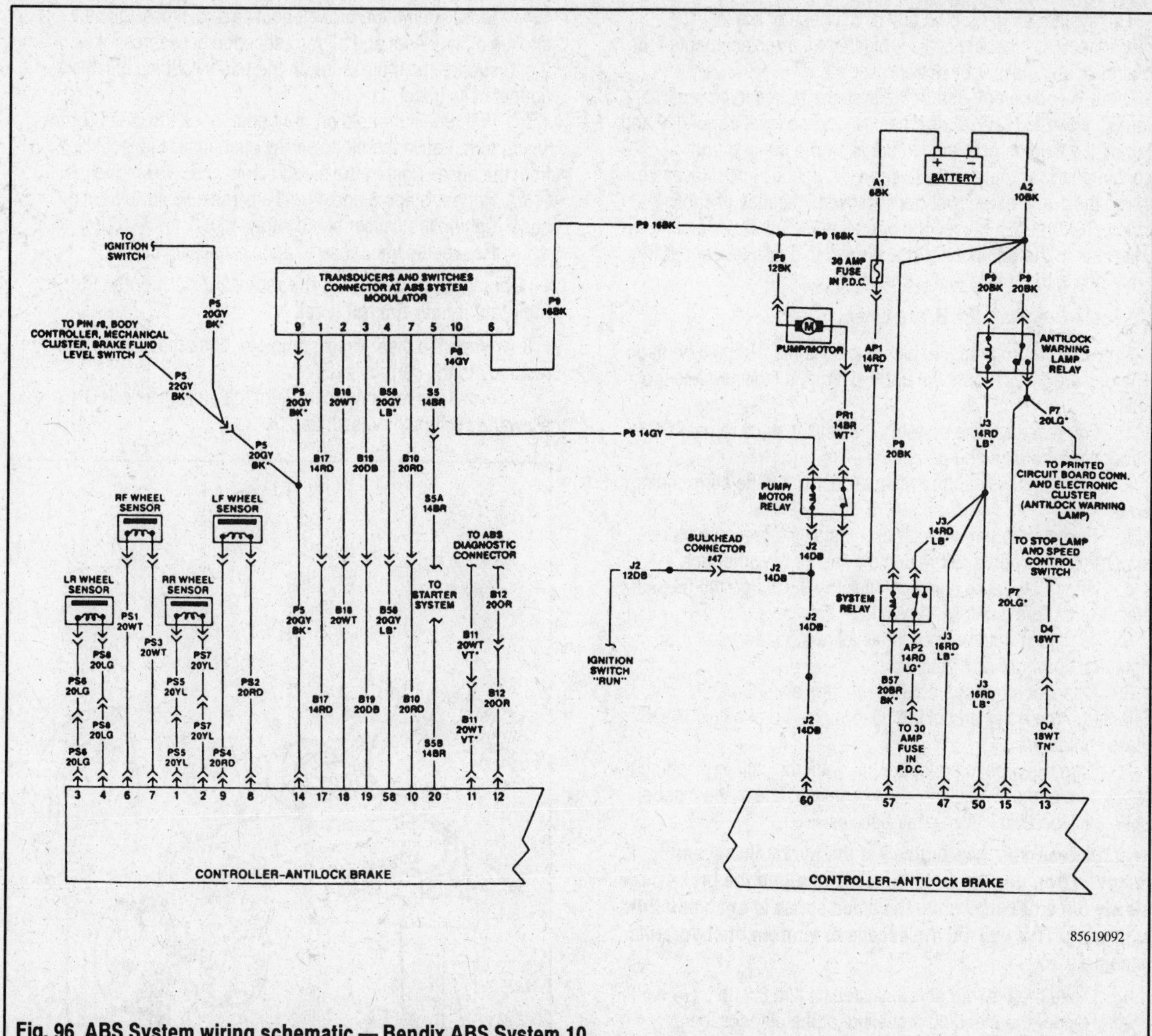

Fig. 96 ABS System wiring schematic — Bendix ABS System 10

Component Replacement

**CAUTION

This brake system uses a hydraulic accumulator which, when fully charged, contains brake fluid at very high pressure. Before disconnecting any hydraulic lines, hoses or fittings be certain that the accumulator pressure is completely relieved. Failure to depressurize the accumulator may result in personal injury and/or vehicle damage.

FILLING THE SYSTEM

1. Turn the ignition **OFF** and leave it **OFF** during inspection.
2. Depressurize the system.
3. Thoroughly clean the reservoir cap and the surrounding area.
4. Carefully remove the reservoir cap, keeping all dirt out of the reservoir.
5. Inspect the fluid level; fill to the top of the white screen in the front strainer if required. Do not overfill.

Use only fresh DOT 3 brake fluid from unopened containers. Do not use any fluid containing a petroleum base. Do not use any fluid which has been exposed to water or moisture. Failure to use the correct fluid will affect system function and component life.

6. Replace the reservoir cap.

BLEEDING THE SYSTEM

See Figures 97, 98 and 99

The brake system must be bled any time air is permitted to enter the system, through loosened or disconnected lines.It is important to realize that air in the system, will cause a primary pressure fault to be set in the controller.

The system must be bled any time a hose or line is disconnected. Bleeding is also required after replacement of the hydraulic unit, caliper or wheel cylinder.

When bleeding any part of the system, the reservoir must remain close to FULL at all times. Check the level frequently and top off the fluid as needed. Do not allow the pump to run continuously for more than 60 seconds. If it becomes necessary to run the pump extensively, allow several minutes of cooling time between each 60 second operation period. Severe damage will occur to the pump if it is not allowed to cool. Never operate the pump with no fluid in the system.

Pressure Bleeding the Brake Lines

Only diaphragm pressure bleeding equipment should be used. The diaphragm prevents the entry of dirt and moisture into the fluid.

1. Depressurize the system. The ignition must remain **OFF** throughout the bleeding procedure.
2. Thoroughly clean the reservoir caps and the surrounding area.
3. Remove both reservoir caps. Install the pressure bleeder adapter on one port and the dummy cap on the other port.
4. Attach pressure bleeding equipment. Charge the pressure bleeder to approximately 20 psi (137 kPa).
5. Brakes should be bled in the following order: Left rear, right rear, left front and right front.
6. Connect a transparent hose to the caliper bleed screw. Submerge the other end of the hose in clean brake fluid in a clear glass container.
7. Turn the pressure bleeder on; open the caliper bleed screw $^1/_2$–$^3/_4$ turn and allow fluid into the container. Leave the bleeder open until the fluid is free of air bubbles.

➥ If the reservoir was drained or the hydraulic assembly removed from the car before bleeding, pump the brake pedal slowly once or twice while the bleed screw is open and fluid is flowing. This will aid the escape of air from the hydraulic assembly.

8. Close the bleeder screw, tightening it to 8 ft. lbs. (10 Nm).
9. Repeat the bleeding procedure at the other calipers.
10. When bleeding is complete, close the pressure bleeder valve and slowly unscrew the adapter from the fluid reservoir. Failure to release reservoir pressure slowly will result in brake fluid spraying both the vehicle and those around it.
11. Use a clean syringe or similar device to remove the excess fluid from the reservoir. The system must not be left over filled.
12. Install the reservoir caps. Turn the ignition switch **ON**; the pump should charge the system, stopping after approximately 30 seconds or less.

Manual Bleeding of the Brake Lines

The individual lines may be bled manually at each wheel using the traditional 2 person method.

1. Depressurize the system. The ignition must remain **OFF** throughout the bleeding procedure.
2. Calipers should be bled in the following order: Left rear, right rear, left front and right front.
3. Connect a transparent hose to the caliper bleed screw. Submerge the other end of the hose in clean brake fluid in a clear glass container.
4. Slowly pump the brake pedal several times. Use full strokes of the pedal and allow 5 seconds between strokes. After 2 or 3 strokes, hold pressure on the pedal keeping it at the bottom of its travel.
5. With pressure held on the pedal, open the bleed screw $^1/_2$–$^3/_4$ turn. Leave the bleed screw open until fluid stops flowing from the hose. Tighten the bleed screw and release the pedal.
6. Repeat Steps 3 and 4 until air-free fluid flows from the hose. Tighten the caliper bleed screw to 8 ft. lbs. (10 Nm).
7. Repeat the sequence at each remaining caliper.

➥ Check the fluid level in the reservoir frequently and maintain it near the full level.

8. When the bleeding is complete, bring the fluid level in the reservoir to the correct level.
9. Install the reservoir cap. Turn the ignition switch **ON** and allow the system to pressurize.

Fig. 97 The dummy cap must be installed when using pressure bleeding equipment

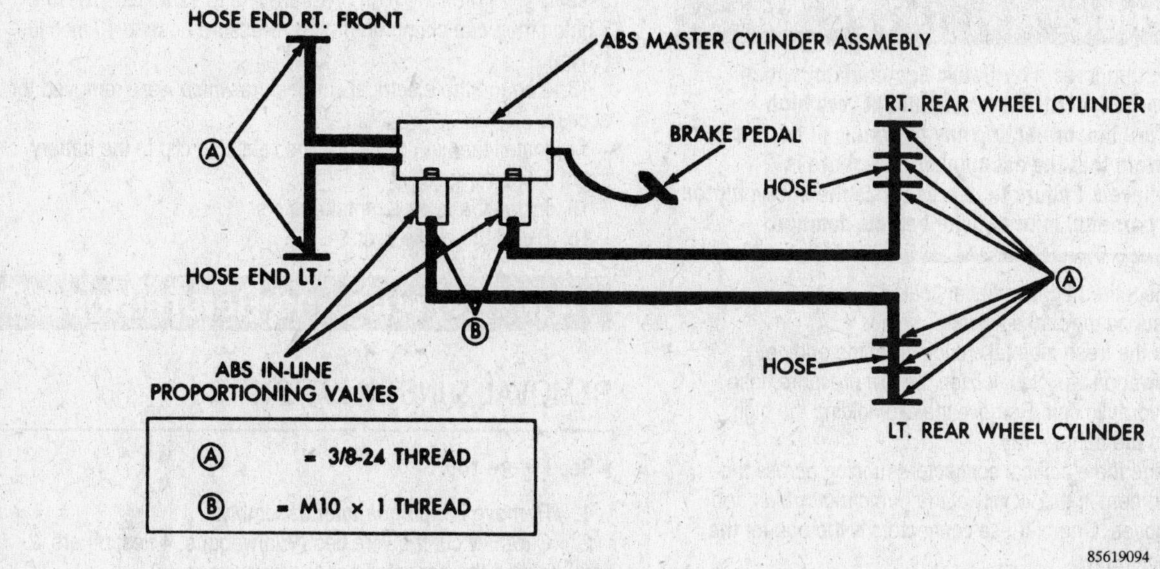

Fig. 98 Proper nut thread size and tube routing

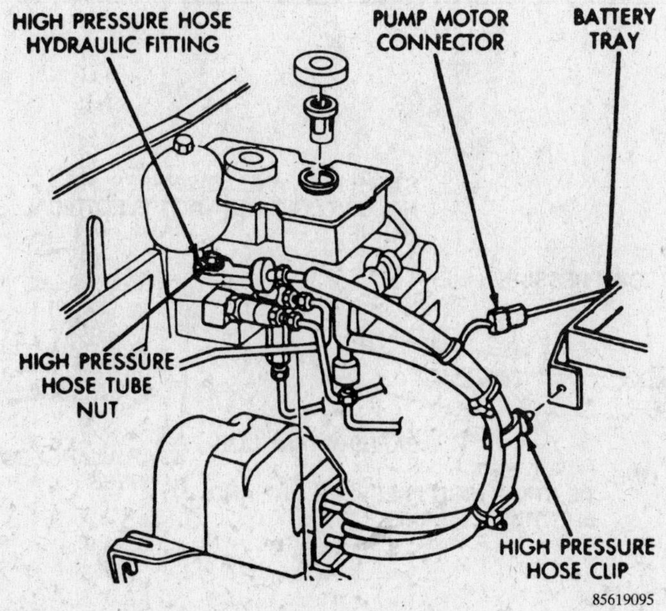

Fig. 99 Hose and line routing in the engine compartment

Pump/Motor Assembly

REMOVAL & INSTALLATION

****CAUTION**

This brake system uses a hydraulic accumulator which, when fully charged, contains brake fluid at very high pressure. Before disconnecting any hydraulic lines, hoses or fittings be certain that the accumulator pressure is completely relieved. Failure to depressurize the accumulator may result in personal injury and/or vehicle damage.

1. Disconnect the negative battery cable.
2. Depressurize the brake system.
3. Remove the fresh air intake ducts from the engine.
4. On Van/wagon vehicles, loosen the low pressure hose clamp at the hydraulic unit. Remove the clip holding the high pressure line to the battery tray.
5. Disengage the electrical connectors running across the engine compartment in the vicinity of the pump/motor high and low pressure hoses. One of these connectors is the one for the pump/motor assembly.
6. Disconnect the high and low pressure hoses from the hydraulic assembly. Cap or plug the reservoir fitting.
7. Disengage the pump/motor electrical connector from the engine mount.
8. Unfasten the heat shield bolt from the front of the pump bracket. Remove the heat shield.
9. Lift the pump/motor assembly from the bracket and out of the vehicle.

To install:

10. Fit the pump motor assembly onto the bracket; install the heat shield and its retaining bolt.
11. Install the pump/motor electrical connector to the engine mount.
12. Connect the high and low pressure hose to the hydraulic assembly. Tighten the high pressure line to 12 ft. lbs. (16 Nm). Tighten the hose clamp on the low pressure hose to 10 inch lbs. (1 Nm).
13. Engage the electrical connectors which were removed for access.
14. Install the high pressure line retaining clip to the battery tray if it was removed.
15. Install the fresh air intake ducts.
16. Bleed the brake system.

High Pressure and Return Hoses

REMOVAL & INSTALLATION

➧ See Figure 100

1. Remove the pump/motor assembly.
2. Carefully cut the wire ties (Van/wagons, 4 ties; others, 2 ties)) holding the hoses and wiring harnesses.
3. Unfasten the banjo bolt from the pump/motor assembly and remove the hoses.

To install:

4. Lubricate the rubber O-ring for the high and low pressure hoses with clean brake fluid before installation.
5. Place the hoses in position and install the banjo bolt.
6. Use care when routing the wiring along the hoses; install new wire ties in the proper locations. Noted that the wiring harness is not held within all the wire ties.
7. Install the pump/motor assembly.

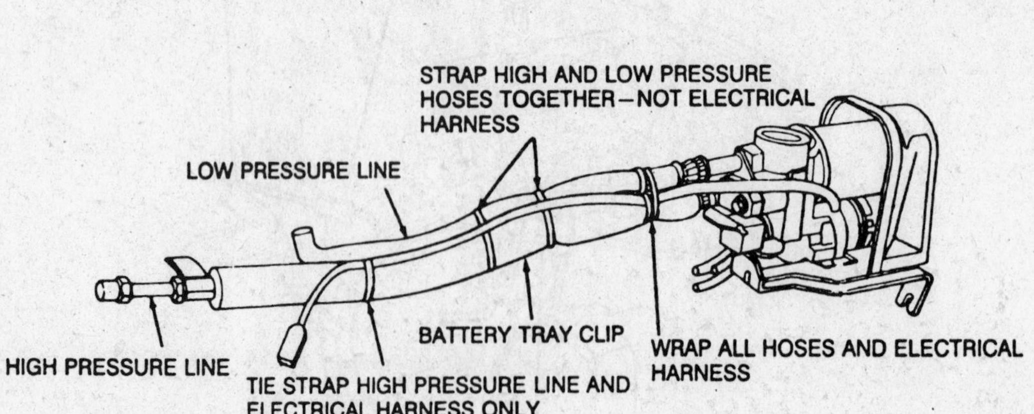

Fig. 100 Correct position of the tie straps

Hydraulic Assembly

REMOVAL & INSTALLATION

➧ See Figure 101

****CAUTION**

This brake system uses a hydraulic accumulator which, when fully charged, contains brake fluid at very high pressure. Before disconnecting any hydraulic lines, hoses or fittings be certain that the accumulator pressure is completely relieved. Failure to depressurize the accumulator may result in personal injury and/or vehicle damage.

1. Depressurize the brake system.
2. Remove the air cleaner assembly.
3. Remove the windshield washer fluid bottle.
4. Disengage all electrical connectors at the hydraulic assembly.
5. Use a syringe to remove as much fluid as possible from the reservoir.
6. Unfasten and remove the banjo bolt holding the high pressure hose to the hydraulic assembly.
7. Remove the hose from the steel tube and cap the tube.
8. Disconnect the brake lines from the hydraulic assembly.
9. Use a small flat tool to release the retainer clip on the brake pedal pin. The center tang on the clip must be moved back enough to allow the lock tab to clear the pin. Disconnect the pushrod from the pedal pin.
10. Under the dash at the firewall, remove the 4 bolts holding the hydraulic assembly.
11. Remove the hydraulic assembly from the engine compartment.

To install:

12. Position the hydraulic assembly and install the retaining nuts. Tighten the nuts to 21 ft. lbs. (28 Nm).
13. Coat the contact surface of the pedal pin with all-purpose grease. Connect the pushrod to the pedal pin and install a new retainer clip. Make certain the lock tab on the retainer is firmly engaged.

****WARNING**

The hydraulic assembly pushrod must be in the correct position before assembly.

14. Install the brake lines, then tighten them to 12 ft. lbs. (16 Nm).
15. If the proportioning valves were removed, reinstall, then tighten them to 30 ft. lbs. (40 Nm).

➥ **Be certain the brake tubes are connected to the proper location.**

16. Install the return hose to the reservoir or the steel tube.
17. Before connecting the pressure hose to the hydraulic assembly, make certain the washers are in their correct positions. Install the hose, then tighten the banjo bolt to 13. ft. lbs. (17 Nm).
18. Fill the reservoir to the top of the strainer screen.
19. Engage all the electrical connectors to the hydraulic assembly.
20. Bleed the entire brake system.
21. Install the air cleaner and washer bottle (Van/wagon) and the fresh air intake duct and clamps.

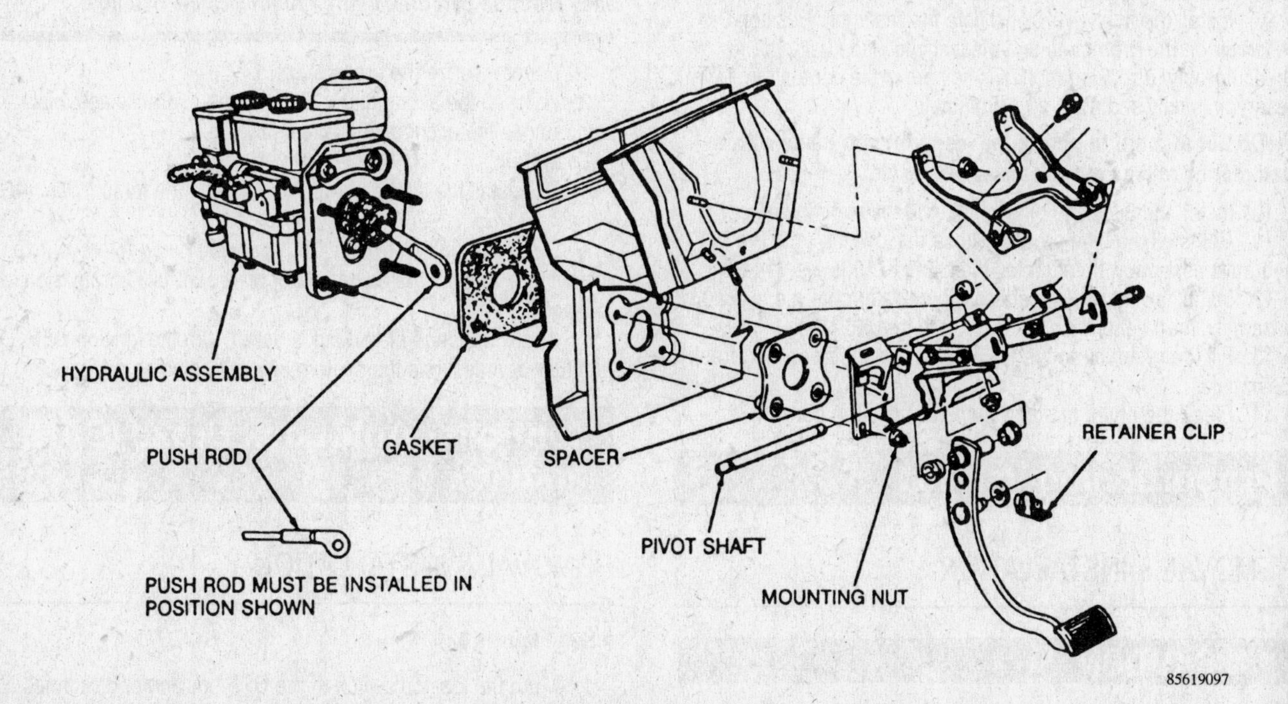

Fig. 101 Hydraulic assembly mounting and under dash connections

Hydraulic Reservoir

REMOVAL & INSTALLATION

✻✻CAUTION

This brake system uses a hydraulic accumulator which, when fully charged, contains brake fluid at very high pressure. Before disconnecting any hydraulic lines, hoses or fittings be certain that the accumulator pressure is completely relieved. Failure to depressurize the accumulator may result in personal injury and/or vehicle damage.

1. Depressurize the brake system.
2. Using a syringe or similar tool, remove as much brake fluid as possible from the reservoir.
3. Disconnect the high pressure hose banjo fitting and remove the hydraulic bladder accumulator from the hydraulic assembly.
4. Remove the 3 retaining pins holding the reservoir to the hydraulic assembly.
5. Use a blunt prying tool carefully installed between the reservoir and hydraulic assembly body to lift the reservoir. Use a rocking motion to gently lift the reservoir free of the grommets.

➥ Be extremely careful to avoid damaging or puncturing the reservoir.

6. Remove the fluid level sensor switch from the reservoir.
7. Use fingers only to remove the grommets from the hydraulic assembly. Discard the grommets.

To install:

8. Lubricate new grommets with clean brake fluid and install them onto the hydraulic assembly. Always use new grommets.
9. Install the fluid level switch into the reservoir. Position the reservoir on the grommets and press it into place using hand pressure only. A rocking motion is helpful; make certain the reservoir is fully seated in all 3 grommets.

➥ Do not attempt to pound the reservoir into place with a hammer or other tools. Damage will result.

10. Install the 3 locking pins to hold the reservoir in place.
11. Reinstall the high pressure hose banjo fitting onto the hydraulic assembly, then tighten the fitting to 10 ft. lbs. (14 Nm).
12. Install the hydraulic bladder accumulator onto the hydraulic assembly, then tighten the fitting to 30 ft. lbs. (40 Nm).
13. Fill the reservoir to the top of the strainer screen with fresh clean fluid.
14. Bleed the entire brake system including the booster.

Proportioning Valves

REMOVAL & INSTALLATION

✻✻CAUTION

This brake system uses a hydraulic accumulator which, when fully charged, contains brake fluid at very high pressure. Before disconnecting any hydraulic lines, hoses or fittings be certain that the accumulator pressure is completely relieved. Failure to depressurize the accumulator may result in personal injury and/or vehicle damage.

1. Depressurize the brake system.
2. Remove the air cleaner and intake duct.
3. Disconnect the high pressure and return hoses from the hydraulic unit.
4. Remove the brake tube and fitting from the proportioning valve.
5. Remove the proportioning valve from the hydraulic assembly.

To install:

6. Install the valve to the hydraulic assembly, then tighten it to 30 ft. lbs. (40 Nm).
7. Install the brake line, then tighten to 12 ft. lbs. (16 Nm).
8. Install the high pressure and return hoses. Tighten the high pressure hose fitting to 12 ft. lbs. (16 Nm.).
9. Install the air cleaner and the duct work.
10. Only the affected brake circuit needs bleeding.

Bladder Accumulator

REMOVAL & INSTALLATION

✻✻CAUTION

This brake system uses a hydraulic accumulator which, when fully charged, contains brake fluid at very high pressure. Before disconnecting any hydraulic lines, hoses or fittings be certain that the accumulator pressure is completely relieved. Failure to depressurize the accumulator may result in personal injury and/or vehicle damage.

1. Depressurize the brake system.
2. Loosen the accumulator fitting at the hydraulic assembly and remove the accumulator assembly.

To install:

3. Reinstall the accumulator, then tighten the to 30 ft. lbs. (40 Nm).
4. Turn the ignition switch **ON**. Allow the pump to pressurize the system. Inspect the accumulator area carefully for any sign of leakage.
5. If any seepage or leaking is noted, turn the ignition **OFF** and fully depressurize the system before beginning any repairs.

Controller Anti-Lock Brake (CAB) Module

REMOVAL & INSTALLATION

➧ See Figure 102

1. Turn the ignition switch to the **OFF** position or disconnect the negative battery cable.
2. Remove the speed control servo (cruise control).

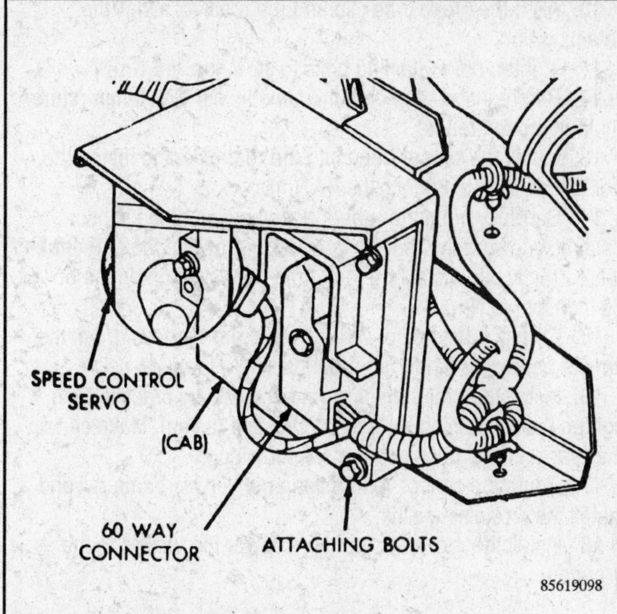

Fig. 102 Controller Anti-lock Brake (CAB) module mounting location

3. Double check that the ignition switch is **OFF** or that the battery cable is disconnected.
4. Disengage the 60-pin wiring connector at the CAB.
5. Unfasten the 3 CAB mounting bolts and remove the controller from the vehicle.

To install:

6. Install the CAB, then tighten the mounting bolts.
7. After checking that the ignition is **OFF** or the battery disengaged, connect the 60-pin harness to the controller. Make certain that the connector is properly seated and locked in place. Do not force the connector into place.
8. Reinstall the speed control servo.
9. If the vehicle is elevated, lower it to the ground. Connect the negative battery cable if it was removed.
10. Drive the vehicle following the test drive procedures listed under the diagnosis and testing portion of this section. If a warning lamp is on and/or a fault code set (not previously present), closely inspect the 60-pin connector at the CAB for looseness or improper mating.

Wheel Speed Sensors

REMOVAL & INSTALLATION

Front Wheel

See Figure 103

1. Elevate and safely support the vehicle.
2. Remove the wheel and tire.
3. Remove the screw from the sensor retaining clip.
4. Carefully remove the sensor wiring grommet from the fender shield.
5. Disconnect the sensor wiring from the ABS harness.
6. Remove the screws holding the sensor wiring tube to the fender well.
7. Remove the retainer grommets from the bracket on the strut.
8. Remove the fastener holding the sensor head.
9. Carefully remove the sensor head from the steering knuckle. Do not use pliers on the sensor head; if it is seized in place, use a hammer and small punch to tap the edge of the sensor ear. The tapping and side-to-side motion will free the unit.

To install:

10. Coat the sensor with high temperature multi-purpose grease.
11. Connect the speed sensor to the ABS harness.
12. Push the sensor assembly grommet into the hole in the fender shield. Install the retainer clip and screw.
13. Install the sensor grommets into the brackets on the fender shield and strut.
14. Install the retainer clip at the strut.
15. On Van/wagons, install the sensor wiring tube, then tighten the retaining bolts to 35 inch lbs. (4 Nm).
16. Install the sensor to the knuckle.
17. Install the retaining screw, then tighten it to 60 inch lbs. (7 Nm).

Proper installation of the sensor and its wiring is critical to system function. Make certain that wiring is installed in all retainers and clips. Wiring must be protected from moving parts and not be stretched during suspension movements.

18. Install the tire and wheel.
19. Lower the vehicle to the ground.

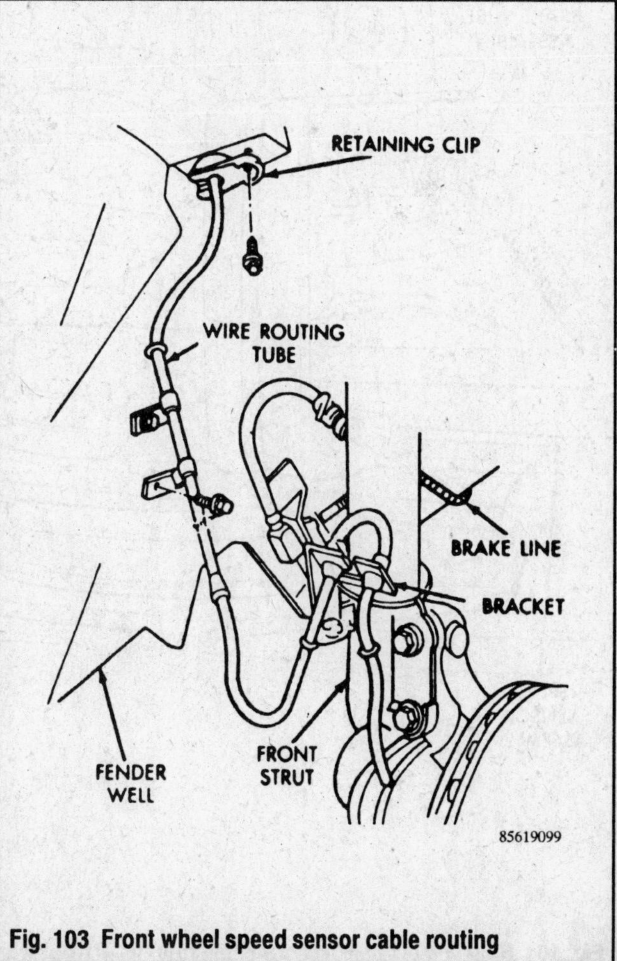

Fig. 103 Front wheel speed sensor cable routing

Rear Wheel

➧ See Figures 104 and 105

1. Elevate and safely support the vehicle. Remove the wheel and tire.
2. Remove the sensor assembly grommet from the underbody and pull the harness through the hole in the body.
3. Disconnect the sensor wiring from the ABS harness.
4. Remove the 4 clips holding the sensor wiring along the underside.
5. Remove the attaching bracket holding the wiring to the frame rail.
6. On FWD Van/wagons, unfasten the nuts from the rear axle U-bolts. Remove the sensor mounting bracket.
7. Remove the fastener holding the sensor head.
8. Carefully remove the sensor head from the adapter assembly. Do not use pliers on the sensor head; if it is seized in place, use a hammer and small punch to tap the edge of the sensor ear. The tapping and side-to-side motion will free the unit.

To install:

9. Position the sensor bracket under the brake tube and start the outer attaching bolt by hand.
10. Align the brake tube clip and the bracket; install the retaining bolt.
11. Tighten both retaining bolts to 12 ft. lbs. (16 Nm).
12. Before installation coat the sensor with high temperature, multi-purpose grease.
13. Install the sensor head into the rear axle and fasten the bolt and tighten to 60 inch lbs. (7 Nm).
14. Carefully bend the rubber hose section of the sensor assembly toward the rear of the vehicle. Position the anti-rotation tab correctly and install the frame rail bracket. Tighten the bolt to 50 inch lbs. (5 Nm).
15. Connect the sensor wiring to the rear harness. Push the sensor assembly wiring grommet back into the hole.
16. Install the rear sensor grommet retaining bracket, then tighten the 2 retaining bolts to 50 inch lbs. (5 Nm). Make certain the bracket does not pinch the sensor wiring.
17. Route the sensor wiring along the vehicle frame rail and install the 4 retaining clips.
18. install the rear wheel and tire; lower the vehicle to the ground.

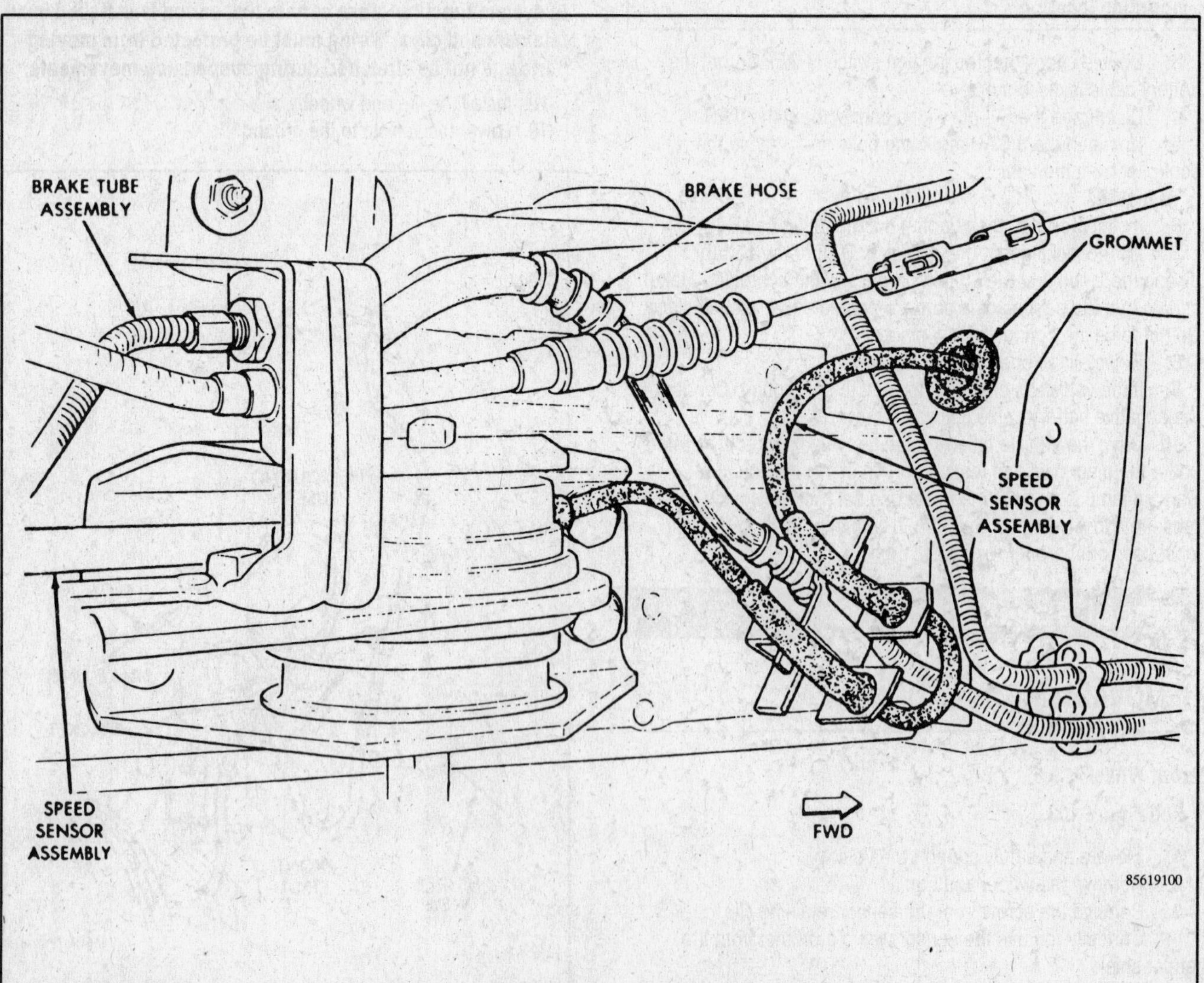

Fig. 104 Rear wheel speed sensor cable routing — front wheel drive equipped vehicles

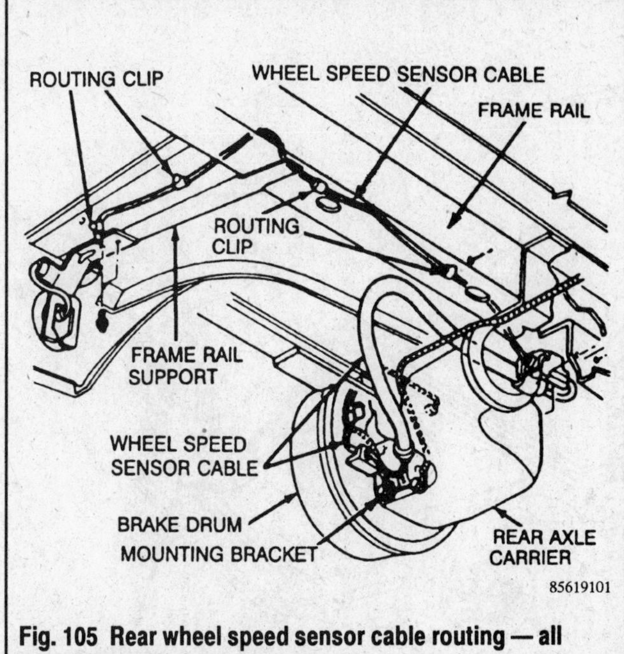

Fig. 105 Rear wheel speed sensor cable routing — all wheel drive equipped vehicles

Tone Rings

REMOVAL & INSTALLATION

The front toothed wheel or tone ring is an integral part of the outer Constant Velocity (CV) joint. Should the ring become unusable, the CV-joint must be replaced. Likewise, the rear tone ring is an integral part of the hub assembly and cannot be replaced individually.

The tone rings may be inspected in place on the vehicle. After gaining access, inspect for any evidence of contact between the speed sensor and the ring. If any contact occurred, the cause must be found and corrected before new parts are installed.

Teeth on the wheels should be unbroken and uncracked. The teeth and the valleys on the ring should be reasonably clean. Excessive run out of the tone ring can cause an erratic wheel speed signal. Replace the ring if run out exceeds 0.010 in. (0.25mm).

The air gap between the tone ring and the sensor is not adjustable. It is established by the correct installation of the wheel speed sensor.

BENDIX SYSTEM 4 ANTI-LOCK BRAKE SYSTEM

➧ **See Figures 106, 107, 108 and 109**

System Description

➥ **The Bendix System 4 Anti-lock Brake system was introduced on 1994–95 models.**

The purpose of the anti-lock brake system is to prevent wheel lock-up under heavy braking conditions on virtually any type of road surface. Anti-lock braking is desirable because a vehicle which is stopped without locking its wheels will retain directional stability and some steering capability. This allows a driver to retain greater control of the vehicle during heavy braking.

Under normal braking conditions, the Bendix Anti-lock 4 Brake System functions the same as a standard non-Anti-lock brake system.

When a wheel locking tendency is detected during a brake application, the vehicle brake system will enter the Anti-lock mode. During Anti-lock Braking, hydraulic pressure in the four wheel circuits is modulated to prevent wheels from locking. Each wheel circuit is designed with a set of electrical valves and hydraulic line to provide modulation, although for vehicle stability, both rear wheel valves receive the same electrical signal. The system can modulate pressure at each wheel, depending on signals generated by the wheel speed sensors (WSS) and received at the CAB.

The Bendix Anti-lock 4 Brake System, uses the following standard brake system components. Master cylinder, power booster, brake caliper assemblies, braking discs, pedal assembly, brake lines and hoses. The unique parts of the Bendix Anti-lock 4 Brake System consists of the following components, modulator assembly, unique proportioning valves, unique junction block, wheel speed sensors, tone wheels, and electronic control unit.

The hydraulic system, on the Bendix Anti-lock 4 brake system is diagonally split. Diagonally split hydraulic brake systems, have the left front and right rear brakes on one hydraulic system and the right front and left rear on the other. A diagonally split hydraulic brake system, will maintain half of the vehicles braking capability if there is a failure in either half of the hydraulic system.

The Bendix Anti-lock 4 Brake System uses two types of brake line fittings and tubing flares on the modulator assembly. The different types are the ISO style and double inverted style with their corresponding fittings at different joint locations. When servicing a vehicle equipped with Bendix Anti-lock 4 Brake System, be sure correct tube fitting and tube flare is always used in the correct location. Be sure that fittings and flares are never mismatched.

System Self-Diagnostics

The Bendix Anti-lock 4 Brake System has been designed with the following self diagnostic capabilities. The self diagnostic ABS start up cycle begins when the ignition switch is turned to the on position. At this time an electrical check is completed on the ABS components such as Wheel Speed Sensor Continuity and System and other Relay continuity. During this check the amber anti-lock light is on for approximately 1-to-2 seconds.

Further Anti-lock Brake System functional testing is accomplished once the vehicle is set in motion, knows as drive-off.

1. The solenoid valves and the pump/motor are activated briefly to verity function.
2. The voltage output from each of the wheel speed sensors is verified to be within the correct operating range. If a vehicle is not set in motion within 3 minutes from the time the ignition switch is turned to the on position. The solenoid valve test is bypassed but the pump/motor is activated briefly to verify that it is operating correctly.

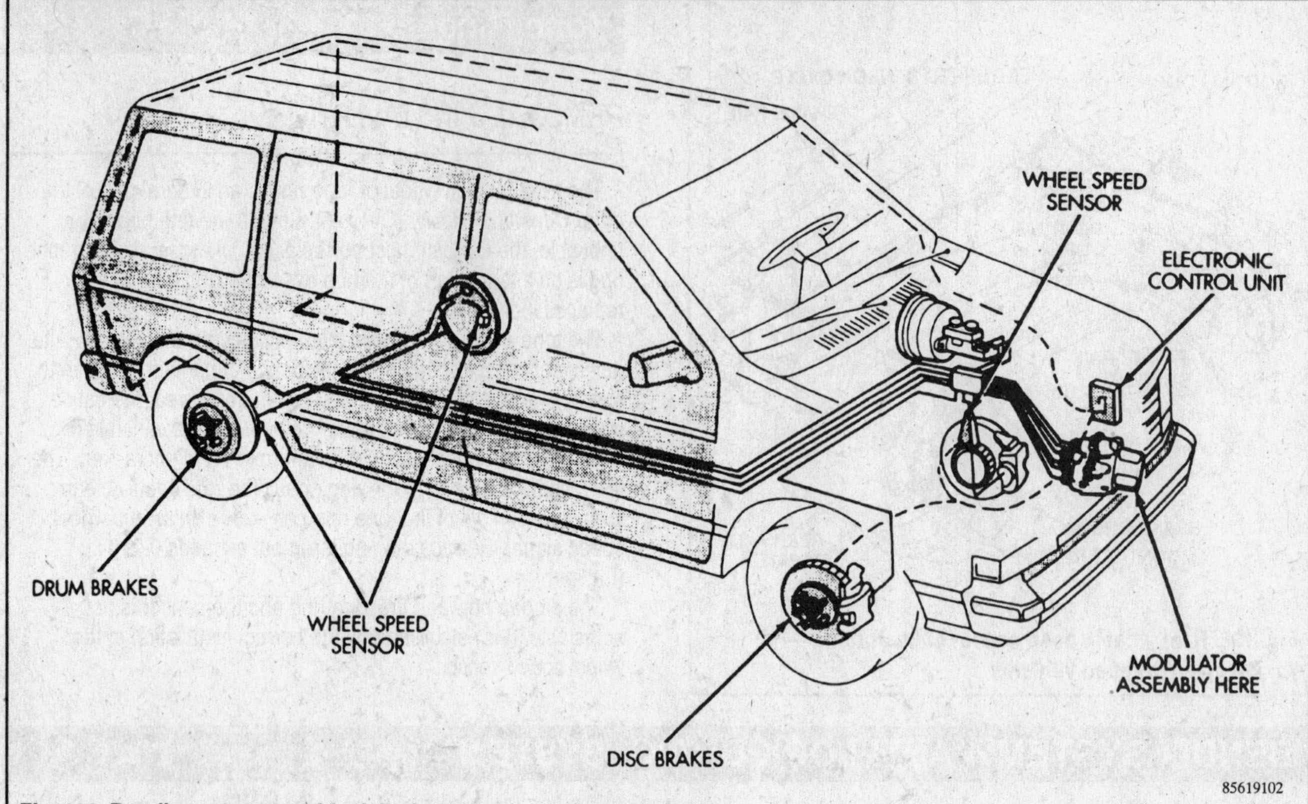

Fig. 106 Bendix system 4 anti-lock brake system — component layout

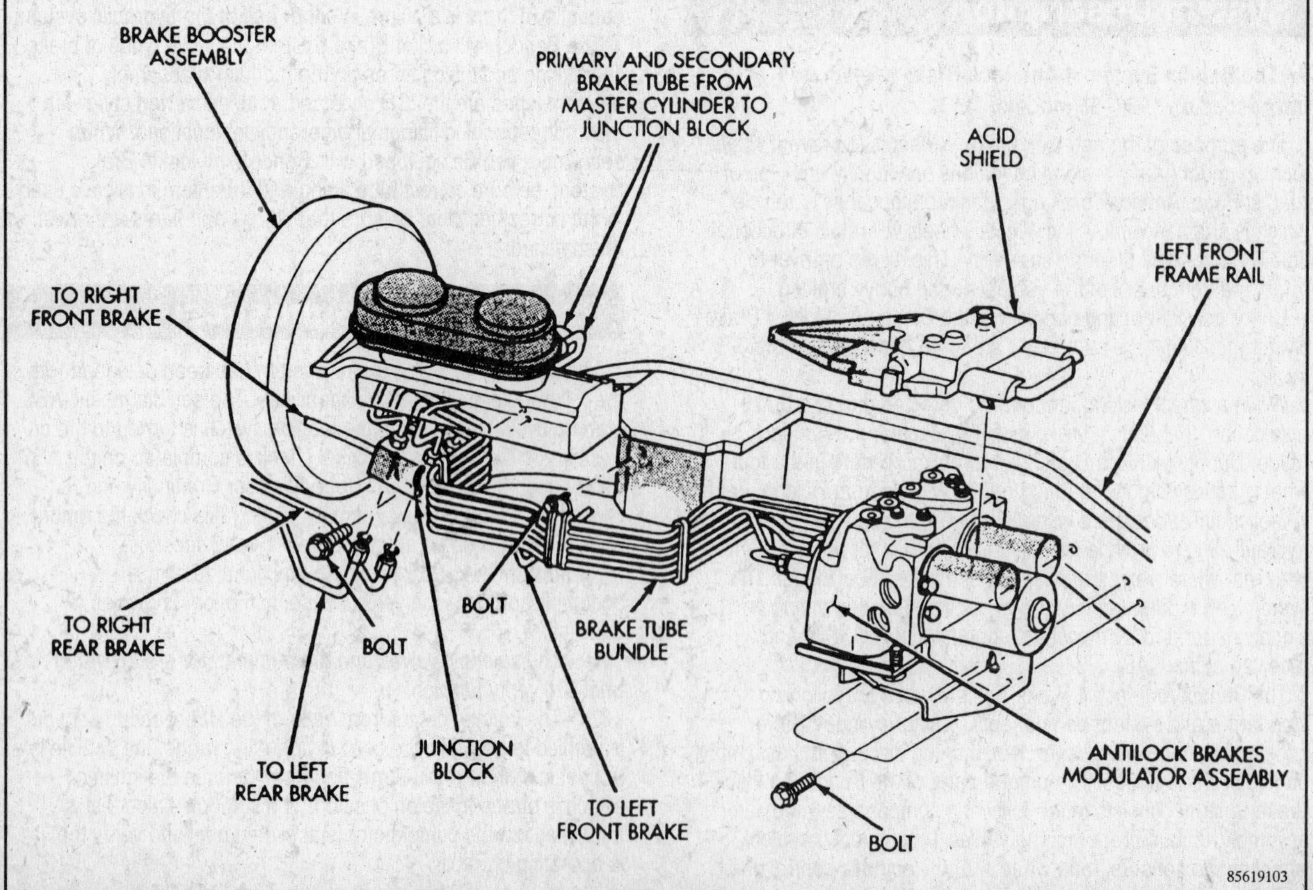

Fig. 107 Bendix system 4 anti-lock brake system — component layout

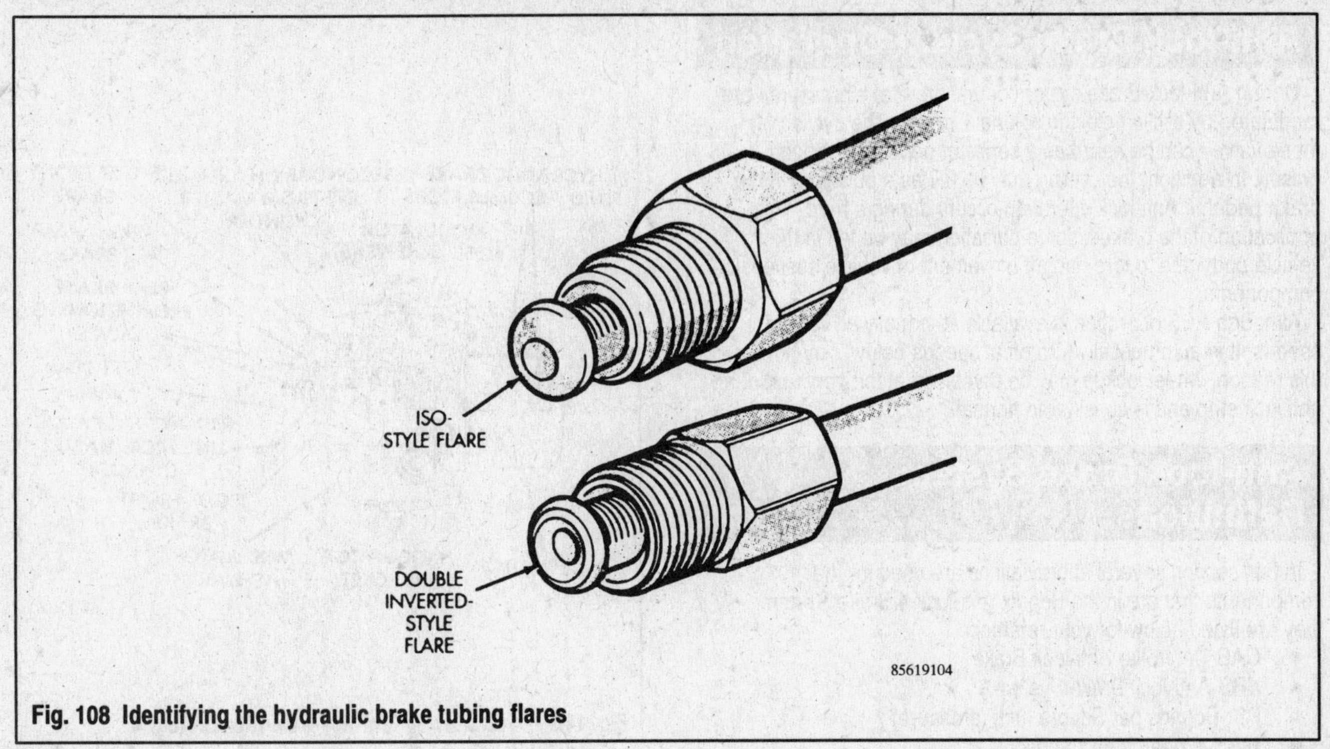

Fig. 108 Identifying the hydraulic brake tubing flares

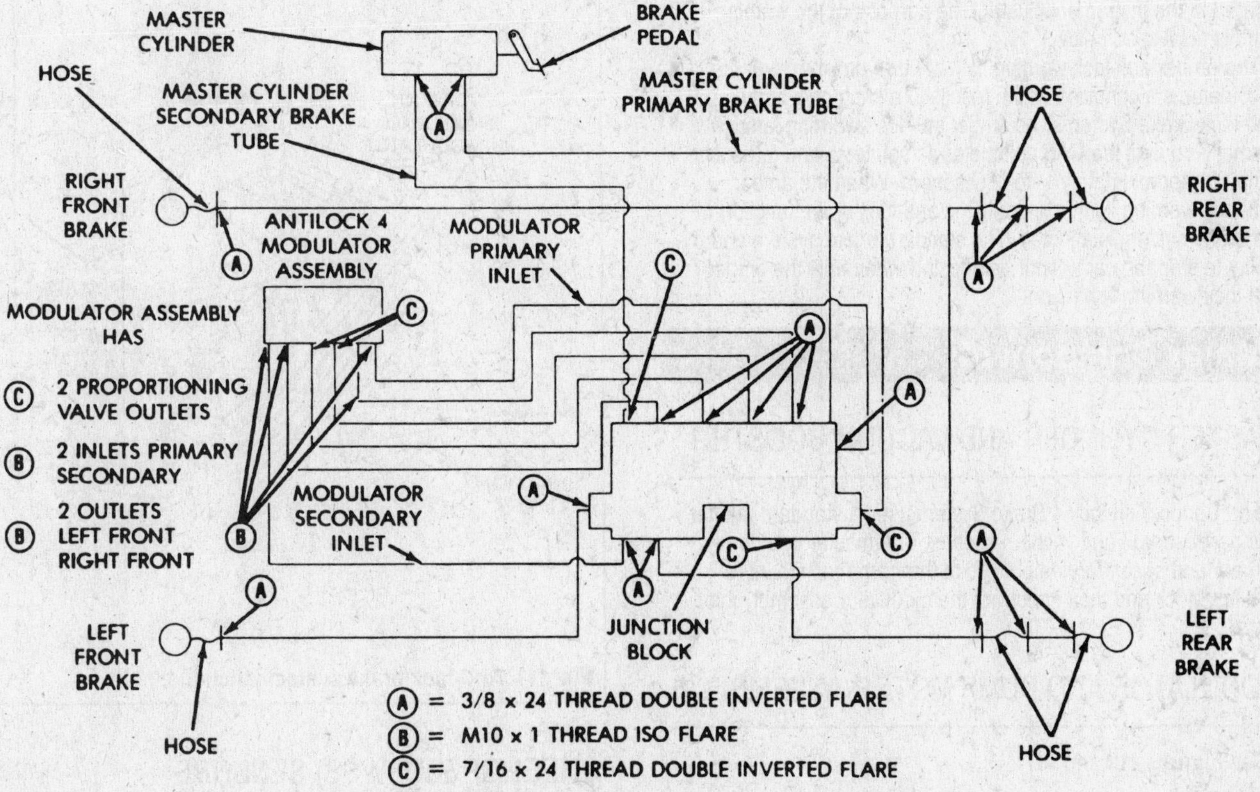

MASTER CYLINDER

BRAKE PEDAL

HOSE

MASTER CYLINDER SECONDARY BRAKE TUBE

MASTER CYLINDER PRIMARY BRAKE TUBE

HOSE

RIGHT FRONT BRAKE

ANTILOCK 4 MODULATOR ASSEMBLY

MODULATOR PRIMARY INLET

RIGHT REAR BRAKE

MODULATOR ASSEMBLY HAS

(C) 2 PROPORTIONING VALVE OUTLETS

(B) 2 INLETS PRIMARY SECONDARY

(B) 2 OUTLETS LEFT FRONT RIGHT FRONT

MODULATOR SECONDARY INLET

LEFT FRONT BRAKE

JUNCTION BLOCK

LEFT REAR BRAKE

HOSE

HOSE

(A) = 3/8 x 24 THREAD DOUBLE INVERTED FLARE

(B) = M10 x 1 THREAD ISO FLARE

(C) = 7/16 x 24 THREAD DOUBLE INVERTED FLARE

85619105

Fig. 109 Bendix system 4 anti-lock brake system tube routing and fitting locations

Anti-lock Brake System Operation

During Anti-lock Brake system operation, brake pressures are modulated by cycling electric solenoid valves. The cycling of these valves can be heard as a series of popping or ticking noises. In addition, the cycling may be felt as a pulsation in the brake pedal. If Anti-lock operation occurs during a hard application of the brakes, some pulsation may be felt in the vehicle body due to fore and aft movement of vehicle suspension components.

Although ABS operation is available at virtually all vehicle speeds, it is automatically turn off at speeds below 7 mph. For this reason, wheel lockup may be perceived at the very end of an anti lock stop and is considered normal.

Anti-lock Brake System Definitions

In this section several abbreviations are used for the components that are in the Bendix Anti-lock 4 Brake System, they are listed below for your reference.

- CAB-Controller Anti-lock Brake
- ABS-Anti-lock Brake System
- PSI-Pounds per Square Inch (pressure)
- WSS-Wheel Speed Sensor
- AC-Alternating Current

Warning System Operations

The ABS system uses an amber anti-lock warning lamp, located in the instrument cluster. The purpose of the warning lamp is discussed below.

The amber anti-lock warning light will turn on whenever the CAB detects a condition which results in a shutdown of the Anti-lock Brake System. The amber anti-lock warning lamp is normally on until the CAB completes its self tests and turns the lamp off (approximately 1-to-2 seconds). When the amber anti-lock warning light is on, only the anti-lock brake function of the brake system is affected. The standard brake system and the ability to stop the car will not be affected when only the amber anti-lock warning light is on.

Major Components

MASTER CYLINDER AND VACUUM BOOSTER

The Bendix Anti-lock 4 Brake System uses a standard master cylinder/reservoir and vacuum booster. The master cylinder primary and secondary outputs go to the frame rail mounted junction block and then directly to the modulator assembly inlet ports.

MODULATOR AND PUMP MOTOR/ASSEMBLY

➧ See Figures 110 and 111

The modulator assembly contains the electronic valves used for brake pressure modulation, and the pump/motor assembly.

The pump/motor function, as part of the modulator assembly, is to pump low pressure brake fluid from the modulator sump into the ABS accumulator, as required.

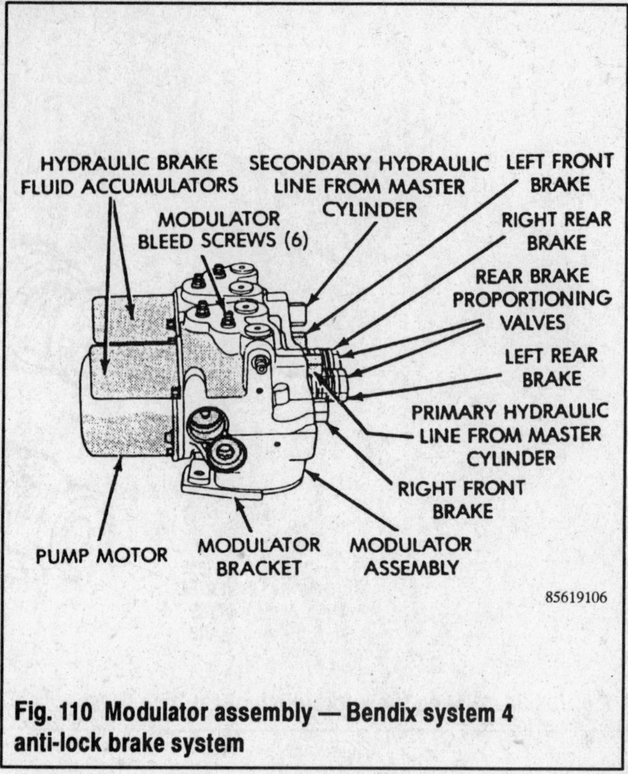

Fig. 110 Modulator assembly — Bendix system 4 anti-lock brake system

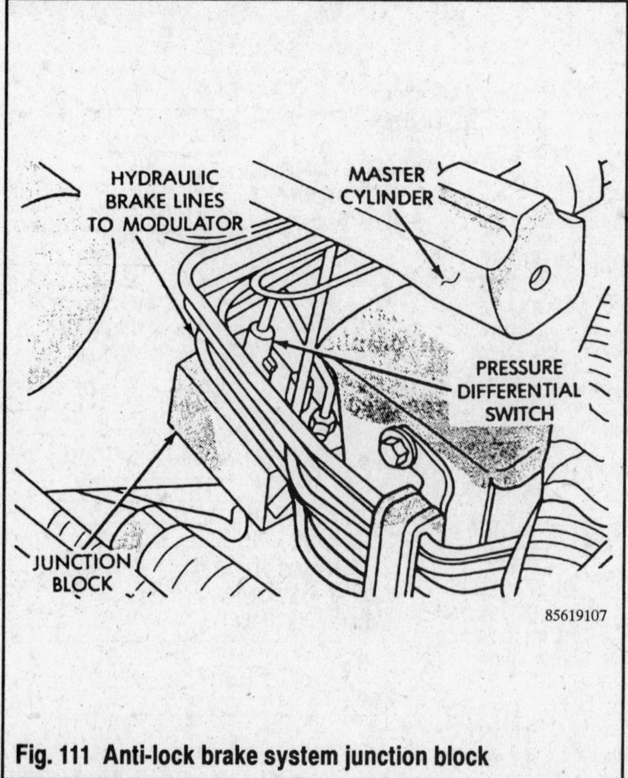

Fig. 111 Anti-lock brake system junction block

WHEEL SPEED (WSS) SENSORS

➧ See Figures 112, 113, 114 and 115

A Wheel Speed Sensor (WSS) is located at each wheel to transmit wheel speed information to the CAB.

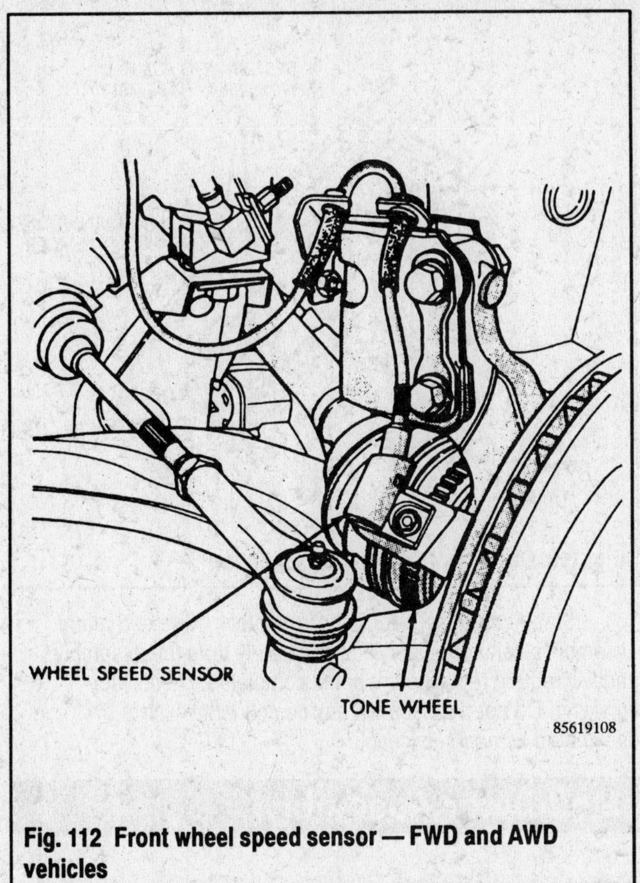

Fig. 112 Front wheel speed sensor — FWD and AWD vehicles

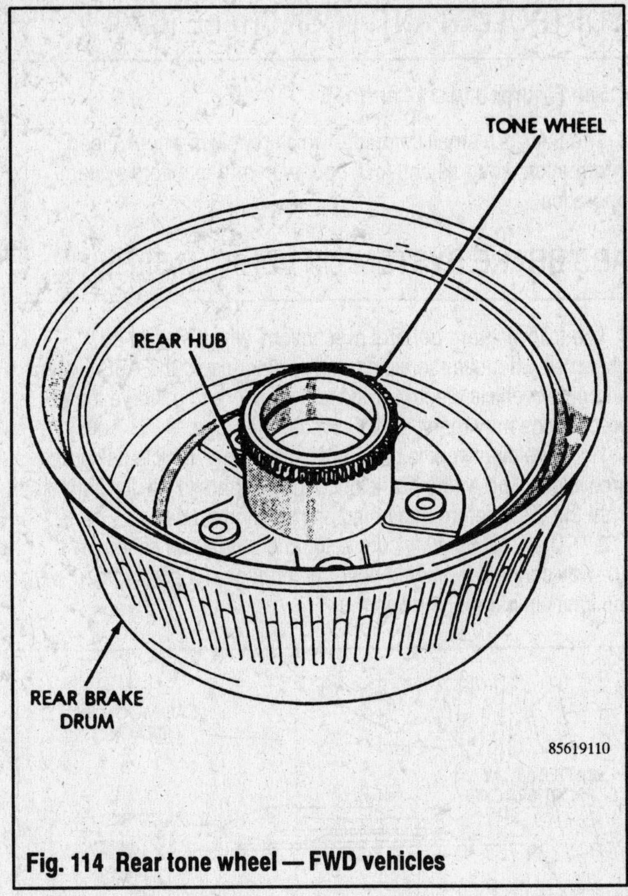

Fig. 114 Rear tone wheel — FWD vehicles

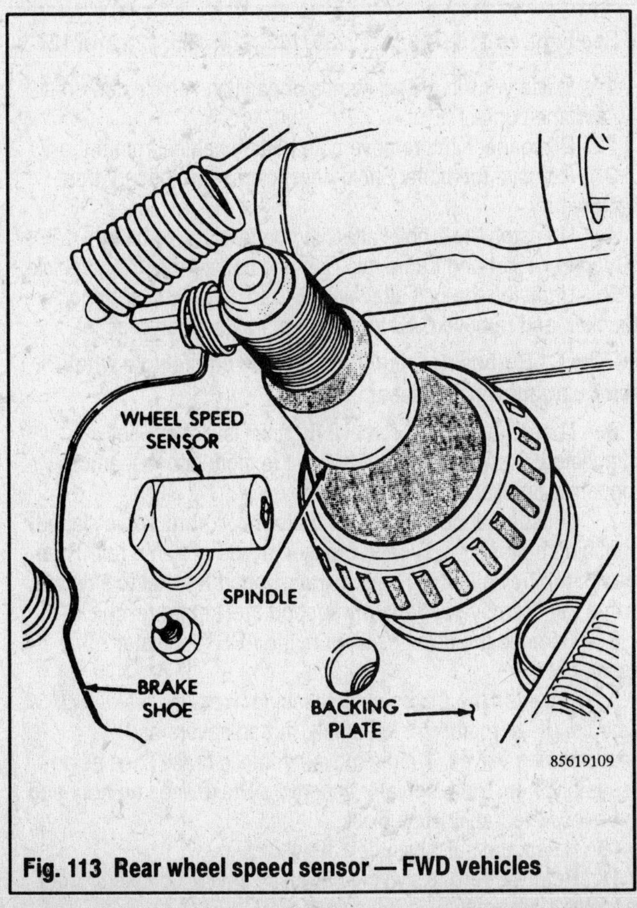

Fig. 113 Rear wheel speed sensor — FWD vehicles

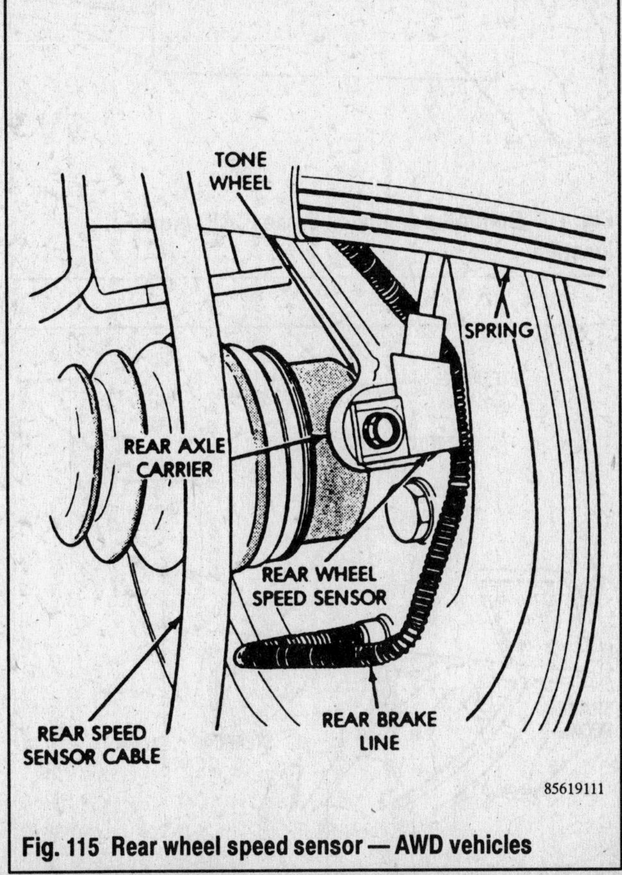

Fig. 115 Rear wheel speed sensor — AWD vehicles

CONTROLLER ANTI-LOCK BRAKE (CAB)

➧ **See Figures 116, 117 and 118**

The CAB is a small computer which receives wheel speed information, controls anti-lock operation and monitors system operation.

ABS BRAKE SYSTEM ON VEHICLE SERVICE

The following are general precautions which should be observed whenever servicing and or diagnosing the ABS system and other vehicle electronic systems. Failure to observe these precautions may result in ABS system damage.

1. If welding work is to be performed on a vehicle using an arc welder. The wiring harness connector should be disconnected from the CAB before beginning any welding operation.
2. The CAB 60–way connector and modulator assembly 10–way connector, should never be engaged or disengaged with the ignition in the on position.

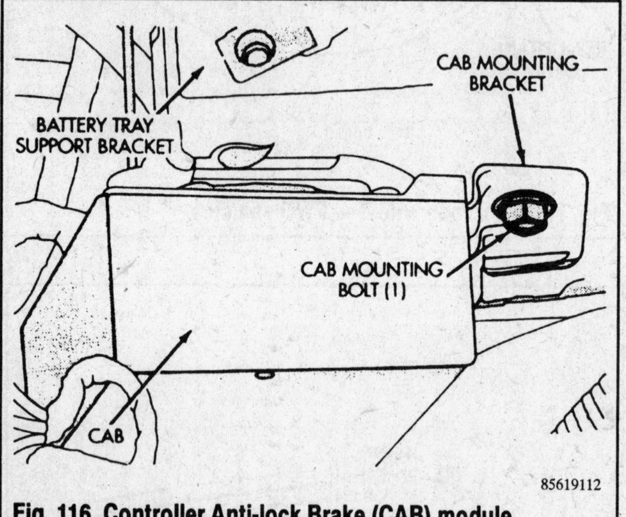

Fig. 116 Controller Anti-lock Brake (CAB) module location

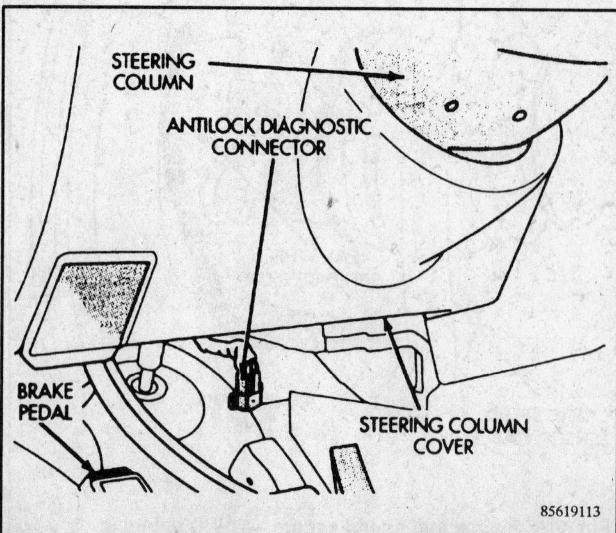

Fig. 117 Anti-lock brake diagnostic connector location

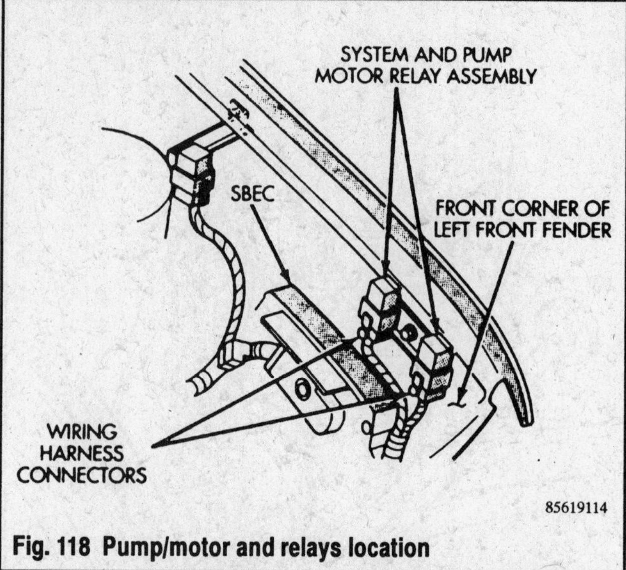

Fig. 118 Pump/motor and relays location

3. Some components of Bendix Anti-lock 4 Brake System assemblies can not be serviced separately from the assembly and will require replacement of the complete assembly for servicing. Do not disassemble any component which is designated as non-serviceable.

Modulator Assembly

REMOVAL & INSTALLATION

➧ **See Figures 119, 120, 121, 122, 123, 124, 125, 126 and 127**

1. Raise vehicle on jackstands or position vehicle centered on a frame contact hoist.
2. Disconnect and remove both battery cables from battery.
3. Remove the battery hold-down clamp and battery from battery tray.
4. Unfasten the 2 bolts attaching battery tray to battery tray support bracket and frame rail. Remove battery tray from vehicle.
5. Unfasten the bolt attaching CAB to battery tray support bracket, and remove CAB from battery tray support bracket.

➝ The CAB does not require removal from vehicle when removing modulator assembly.

6. Loosen but do not remove (bracket is slotted) bolt attaching battery tray support bracket to modulator assembly mounting bracket.
7. Loosen but do not remove bottom bolt, (bracket is slotted) attaching battery tray support bracket to side of frame rail. Then loosen top bolt attaching battery tray support bracket to side of frame rail. Remove battery tray support bracket from vehicle.
8. Remove the acid shield, from the ABS modulator assembly.
9. Unfasten the 6 tube nuts attaching hydraulic brake line tube bundle to modulator assembly, thread savers and proportioning valves. Then remove hydraulic brake lines as an assembly, from the modulator assembly. Brake lines do not need to be loosened at junction block.
10. Raise and safely support the vehicle.
11. Remove vehicle's wiring harness 10–way connector from modulator assembly.

12. If vehicle is equipped with speed control, remove bolt attaching speed control servo assembly to modulator assembly bracket.

13. The speed control servo does not need to be removed from vehicle, but should be moved out of the way.

14. Loosen but do not remove the 2 bolts at front of modulator assembly bracket, attaching it to frame rail.

15. Loosen, but do not remove bolt at rear of modulator bracket, attaching bracket to frame rail.

16. Lower the vehicle.

17. Remove the modulator assembly and the mounting bracket as an assembly from vehicle.

18. Remove the modulator assembly from the mounting bracket.

19. The mounting bracket will need to be transferred to replacement modulator assembly, if a new modulator is to be installed.

To install:

➔ Before installing modulator assembly back on mounting bracket, inspect the 3 modulator assembly to bracket isolators for any signs of deterioration or damage. Replace all 3 isolators if any show signs of damaged or deterioration, before mounting modulator assembly on bracket. Install the modulator assembly on mounting bracket.

**CAUTION

Be sure mounting isolators are correctly positioned on mounting bracket and modulator assembly, before installing and torquing modulator mounting bolts.Install the 3 bolts attaching anti-lock modulator assembly to mounting bracket. Then tighten the 3 modulator assembly to mounting bracket bolts to 21 ft. lbs. (28 Nm).

20. Mount the modulator and the mounting bracket assembly, on the 3 mounting bolts on the side of the frame rail.

21. Tighten rear bolt attaching modulator assembly mounting bracket to frame rail to 125 inch lbs. (14 Nm)

22. Raise and safely support the vehicle.

23. Tighten the 2 front modulator assembly to frame rail mounting bolts to 125 inch lbs. (14 Nm)

24. Mount the speed control servo and bracket, on the modulator assembly mounting bracket.

25. Install mounting bolt for speed control servo, then tighten to 21 ft. lbs. (28 Nm).

26. Install vehicle's wiring harness 10-way connector onto modulator assembly. Be sure lock on vehicle wiring harness connector is fully engaged with tab on modulator assembly electrical connector.

27. Lower the vehicle.

28. Align the 6 disconnected hydraulic brake lines with their appropriate fitting locations on modulator assembly. Then thread the 6 brake line tube nuts by hand into the proportioning valves and thread savers on modulator assembly.

29. Using a crow foot and torque wrench, tighten the 6 hydraulic brake line tube nuts to 13 ft. lbs. (18 Nm). When torquing the tube nuts, hold the thread savers and proportioning valves with an open end wrench to prevent them from turning.

30. Using approved battery jumper cables, attach battery, to the vehicles negative and positive battery cables.

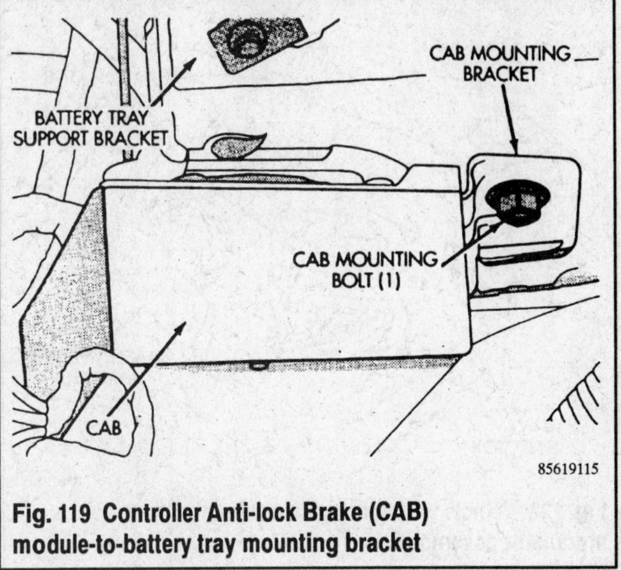

Fig. 119 Controller Anti-lock Brake (CAB) module-to-battery tray mounting bracket

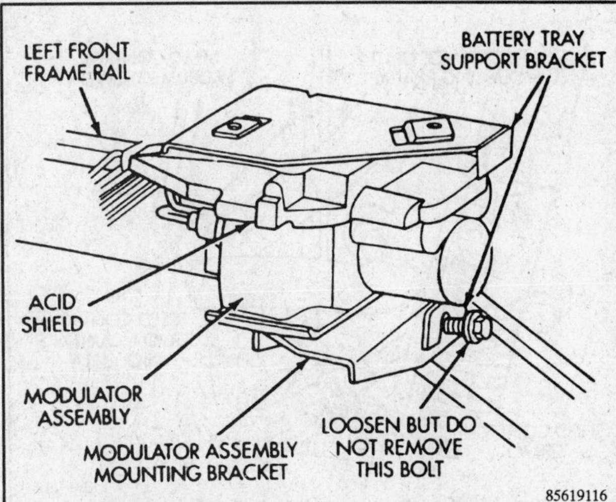

Fig. 120 Battery tray support bracket-to-modulator bracket attaching bolt

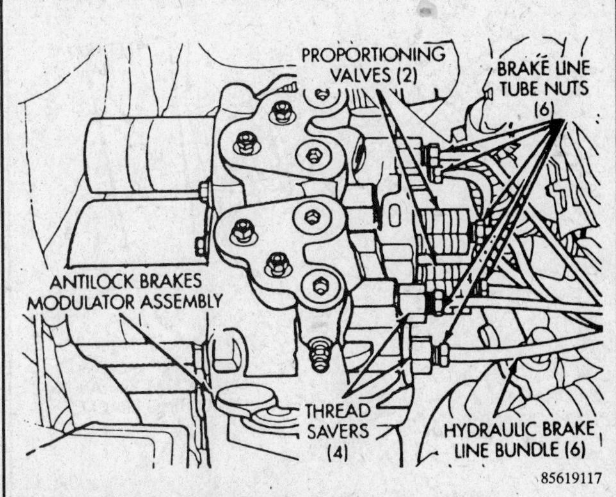

Fig. 121 Hydraulic brake line connections to the modulator assembly

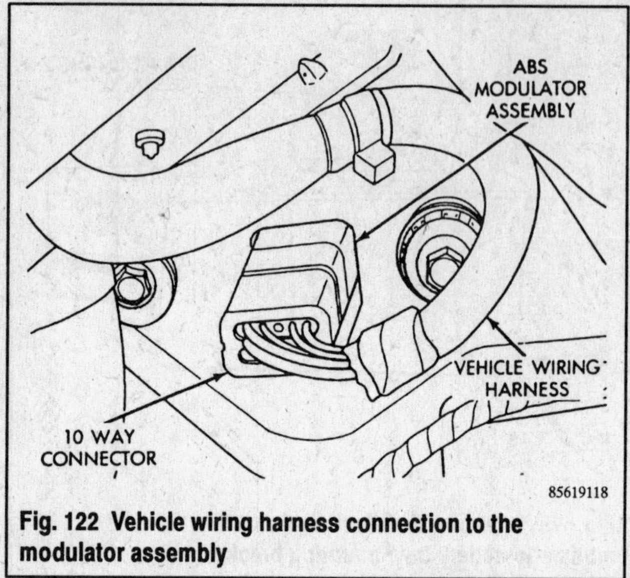

Fig. 122 Vehicle wiring harness connection to the modulator assembly

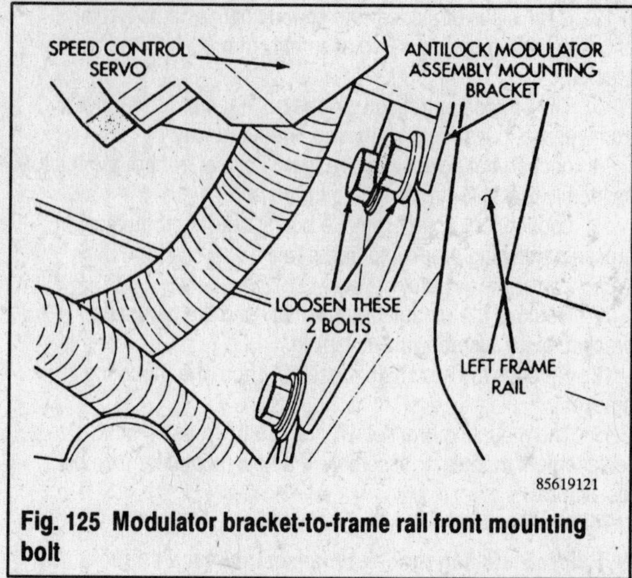

Fig. 125 Modulator bracket-to-frame rail front mounting bolt

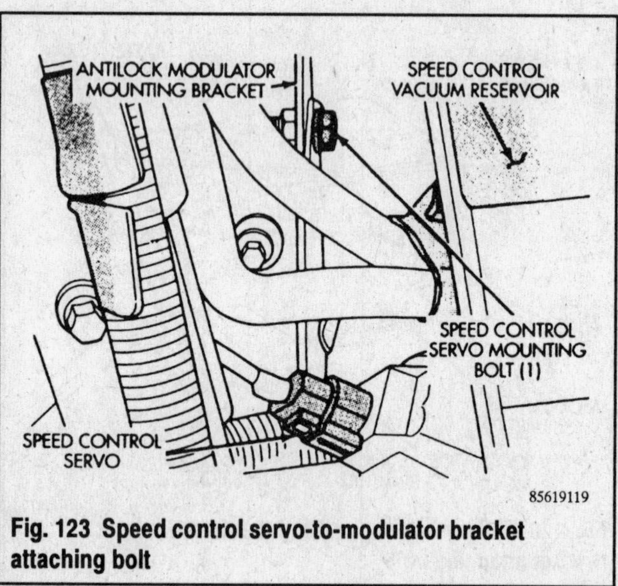

Fig. 123 Speed control servo-to-modulator bracket attaching bolt

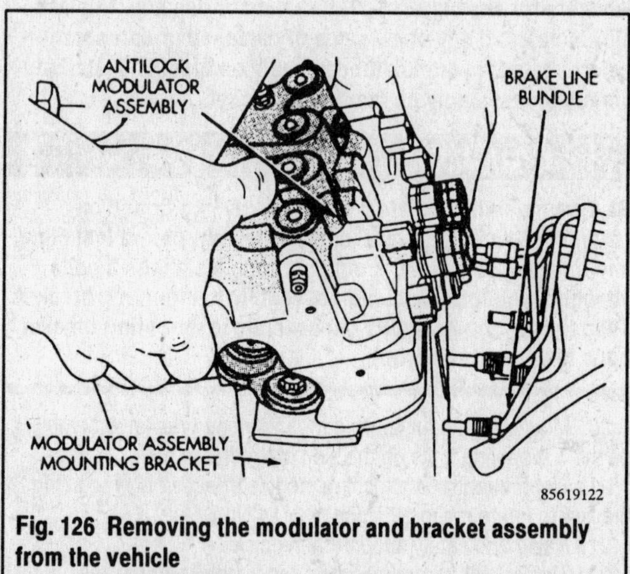

Fig. 126 Removing the modulator and bracket assembly from the vehicle

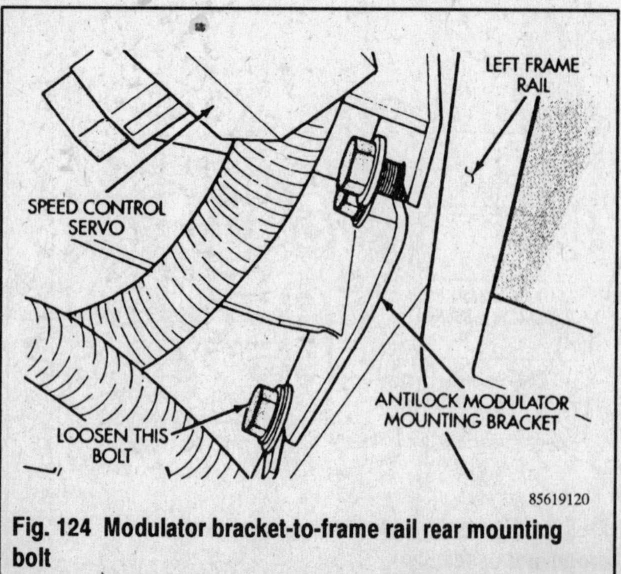

Fig. 124 Modulator bracket-to-frame rail rear mounting bolt

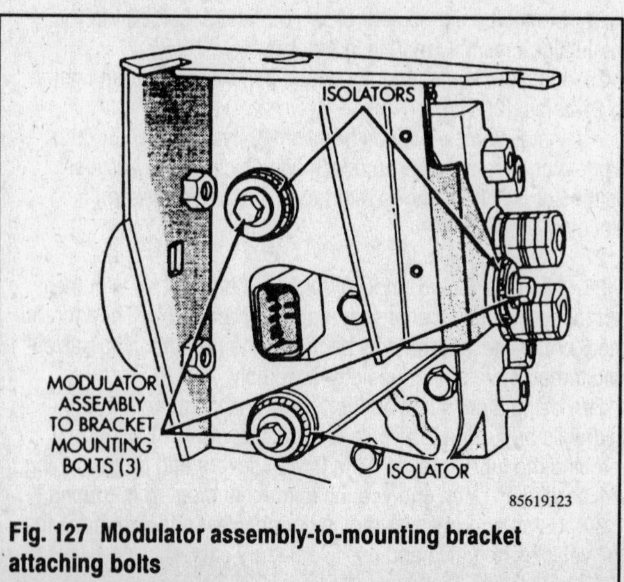

Fig. 127 Modulator assembly-to-mounting bracket attaching bolts

31. Bleed the vehicles base brake and anti-lock brake hydraulic systems. Refer to the Bendix Anti-lock 4 Brake bleeding procedure in this section for the required bleeding procedure.
32. Install the acid shield onto modulator assembly. Be sure the acid shield is securely attached to the modulator assembly before installing the battery tray support bracket.
33. Install the battery tray support bracket in the vehicle.
34. Install the 1 attaching bolt support bracket to the frame rail and tighten the 3 bolts attaching the battery tray support bracket to the frame rail and the modulator bracket to 125 inch lbs. (14 Nm).
35. Install the CAB module/mounting bracket assembly, on battery tray support bracket.
36. Install the CAB assembly mounting bolt, then tighten to 14 inch lbs. (6 Nm).
37. Install the battery tray. Fasten the 2 bolts mounting the battery tray to the battery tray support bracket and the fender shield.
38. Install the battery on battery tray. Fasten and securely tighten the battery hold down clamp.
39. Install the battery cables on the battery. Securely tighten the clamping bolts on the battery cable terminals.
40. Reset any electrical components of the vehicle which were affected by the removal of the battery.
41. Road test the vehicle to verify correct operation of the vehicles's base and anti-lock brake systems.

Proportioning Valve

REMOVAL & INSTALLATION

Screw-in proportioning valves can be identified by numbers stamped on the body of the valve. Be sure to replace with the correct numbered valve. Proportioning valves should never be disassembled.

1. Raise vehicle on jackstands or position vehicle centered on a frame contact hoist.
2. Disconnect and remove both battery cables from battery.
3. Remove the battery hold-down clamp and battery from battery tray.
4. Unfasten the 2 bolts attaching battery tray to battery tray support bracket and frame rail. Remove battery tray from vehicle.
5. Unfasten the bolt attaching CAB to battery tray support bracket, and remove CAB from battery tray support bracket.

The CAB does not require removal from vehicle when servicing the modulator assembly.

6. Loosen but do not remove (bracket is slotted) the bolt attaching the battery tray support bracket to the modulator assembly mounting bracket.
7. Loosen but do not remove the bottom bolt, (bracket is slotted) attaching the battery tray support bracket to the side of the frame rail.
8. Loosen the top bolt attaching the battery tray support bracket to the side of the frame rail. Remove the battery tray support bracket from the vehicle.
9. Remove the acid shield, from the ABS modulator assembly.
10. Remove the brake tube from the proportioning valve.
11. Remove the proportioning valve from the modulator.

To install:

12. Lightly coat the proportioning valve to modulator sealing ring with fresh clean brake fluid.
13. Install the proportioning valve into the modulator assembly by hand, until the O-ring seal is fully seated against the modulator assembly, then using a crow foot, tighten the proportioning valve to 26 ft. lbs. (35 Nm).
14. Install the hydraulic brake line on the proportioning valve and hand start the tube nut into the proportioning valve. Tighten the tube nut to 13 ft. lbs. (18 Nm).
15. Using approved jumper cables, attach the battery to the vehicles negative and positive battery cables.
16. Bleed the vehicles base brake and anti-lock brake hydraulic systems as outlined in this section.
17. Install the acid shield onto the modulator assembly. Be sure acid shield is securely attached to the modulator assembly before installing the battery tray support bracket.
18. Install the battery tray support bracket in the vehicle. Fasten the 1 bolt attaching support bracket to frame rail and tighten the 3 bolts attaching the battery tray support bracket to the frame rail and the modulator bracket to 125 inch lbs. (14 Nm).
19. Install the CAB module/mounting bracket assembly, on the battery tray support bracket. Fasten the CAB assembly mounting bolt and tighten to 14 inch lbs. (6 Nm).
20. Install battery tray. Then install the 2 bolts mounting battery tray to battery tray support bracket and fender shield.
21. Install battery on battery tray.
22. Install and securely tighten battery hold down clamp.
23. Install battery cables on battery. Securely tighten clamping bolts on battery cable terminals.
24. Reset any electrical components of the vehicle which were affected by the removal of the battery.
25. Road test vehicle to verify correct operation of the vehicles's base and Anti-lock brake systems.

Controller Anti-lock Brake (CAB) Module

REMOVAL & INSTALLATION

See Figures 128 and 129

1. Turn the ignition **OFF**.
2. Disconnect and remove both battery cables from battery.
3. Remove the battery hold-down clamp and the battery from battery tray.
4. Unfasten the 2 bolts attaching the battery tray to the battery tray support bracket and the frame rail. Remove battery tray from vehicle.
5. Unfasten the bolt attaching the CAB to the battery tray support bracket and remove the CAB from the battery tray support bracket.

****WARNING**

Before removing the 60-way connector from the CAB verify that the vehicle's ignition is in the OFF or LOCK position or damage to the controller could result.

6. Loosen the bolt retaining the wiring harness 60-way connector to the CAB, then disengage the 60-way connector from the CAB by pulling it straight out without twisting.
7. Remove the CAB and mounting bracket from the vehicle.

To install:

****WARNING**

Before installing the 60-way connector from the CAB verify that the vehicle's ignition is in the OFF or LOCK position or damage to the controller could result.

8. Install the the bolt retaining the wiring harness 60-way connector to the CAB and tighten to 38 inch lbs. (4 Nm).
9. Install the battery tray support bracket in the vehicle.
10. Fasten the 1 bolt attaching the support bracket to the frame rail and tighten the 3 bolts attaching the battery tray support bracket to frame rail and modulator bracket to 125 inch lbs. (14 Nm).

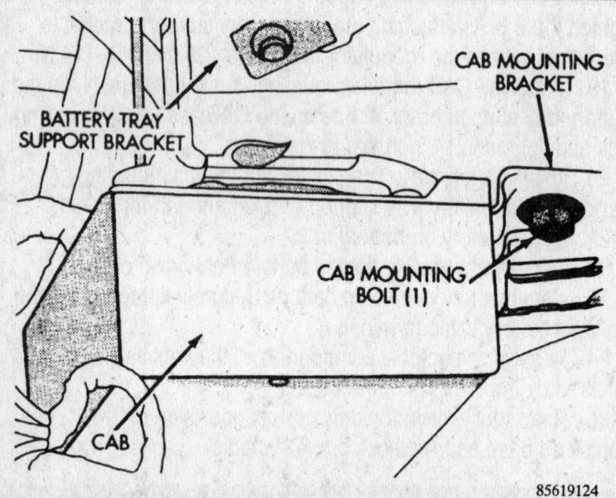

Fig. 128 Controller Anti-lock Brake (CAB) module mounting to battery tray support bracket

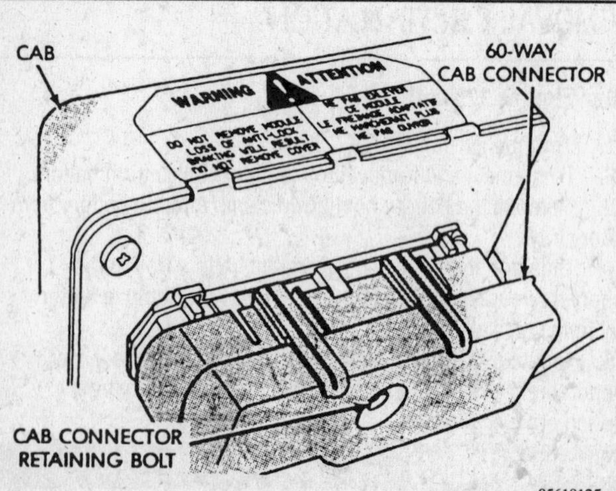

Fig. 129 Controller Anti-lock Brake (CAB) module 60-way connector and retaining bolt

11. Install the CAB module/mounting bracket assembly, on battery tray support bracket.
12. Fasten the CAB assembly mounting bolt, then tighten to 14 inch lbs. (6 Nm).
13. Install the battery tray. Fasten the 2 bolts mounting battery tray to battery tray support bracket and fender shield.
14. Install the battery on the battery tray.
15. Install and securely tighten the battery hold down clamp.
16. Install the battery cables on the battery. Securely tighten the clamping bolts on the battery cable terminals.
17. Reset any electrical components of the vehicle which were affected by the removal of the battery.
18. Road test vehicle to verify correct operation of the vehicles's base and Anti-lock brake systems.

Wheel Speed Sensors

REMOVAL & INSTALLATION

Front Wheel

➧ **See Figure 130**

1. Elevate and safely support the vehicle.
2. Remove the wheel and tire.
3. Remove the screw from the sensor retaining clip.
4. Carefully remove the sensor wiring grommet from the fender shield.
5. Disconnect the sensor wiring from the ABS harness.
6. Remove the screws holding the sensor wiring tube to the fender well.
7. Remove the retainer grommets from the bracket on the strut.
8. Remove the fastener holding the sensor head.
9. Carefully remove the sensor head from the steering knuckle. Do not use pliers on the sensor head; if it is seized in place, use a hammer and small punch to tap the edge of the sensor ear. The tapping and side-to-side motion will free the unit.

To install:

10. Before installation, coat the sensor with high temperature multi-purpose grease.
11. Connect the speed sensor to the ABS harness.
12. Push the sensor assembly grommet into the hole in the fender shield. Install the retainer clip and screw.
13. Install the sensor grommets into the brackets on the fender shield and strut.
14. Install the retainer clip at the strut.
15. On Van/wagons, install the sensor wiring tube, then tighten the retaining bolts to 35 inch lbs. (4 Nm).
16. Install the sensor to the knuckle.
17. Install the retaining screw, then tighten it to 60 inch lbs. (7 Nm).

➥ Proper installation of the sensor and its wiring is critical to system function. Make certain that wiring is installed in all retainers and clips. Wiring must be protected from moving parts and not be stretched during suspension movements.

18. Install the tire and wheel. Lower the vehicle to the ground.

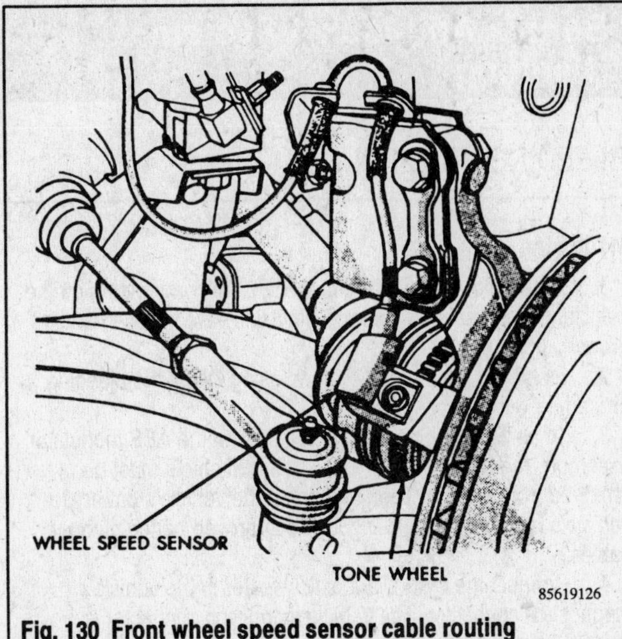

Fig. 130 Front wheel speed sensor cable routing

Rear Wheel

➧ See Figures 131, 132 and 133

1. Elevate and safely support the vehicle.
2. Remove the wheel and tire.
3. Remove the sensor assembly grommet from the underbody and pull the harness through the hole in the body.
4. Disconnect the sensor wiring from the ABS harness.
5. Remove the 4 clips holding the sensor wiring along the underside.
6. Remove the attaching bracket holding the wiring to the frame rail.
7. On FWD Van/wagons, unfasten the nuts from the rear axle U-bolts.
8. Remove the sensor mounting bracket.
9. Remove the fastener holding the sensor head.
10. Carefully remove the sensor head from the adapter assembly. Do not use pliers on the sensor head; if it is seized in place, use a hammer and small punch to tap the edge of the sensor ear. The tapping and side-to-side motion will free the unit.

To install:

11. Position the sensor bracket under the brake tube and start the outer attaching bolt by hand.
12. Align the brake tube clip and the bracket; install the retaining bolt.
13. Tighten both retaining bolts to 12 ft. lbs. (16 Nm).
14. Before installation coat the sensor with high temperature, multi-purpose grease.
15. Install the sensor head into the rear axle and fasten the bolt. Tighten the bolt to 60 inch lbs. (7 Nm).
16. Carefully bend the rubber hose section of the sensor assembly toward the rear of the vehicle. Position the anti-rotation tab correctly and install the frame rail bracket. Tighten the bolt to 50 inch lbs. (5 Nm).
17. Connect the sensor wiring to the rear harness. Push the sensor assembly wiring grommet back into the hole.
18. Install the rear sensor grommet retaining bracket, then tighten the 2 retaining bolts to 50 inch lbs. (5 Nm). Make certain the bracket does not pinch the sensor wiring.
19. Route the sensor wiring along the vehicle frame rail and install the 4 retaining clips.
20. install the rear wheel and tire; lower the vehicle to the ground.

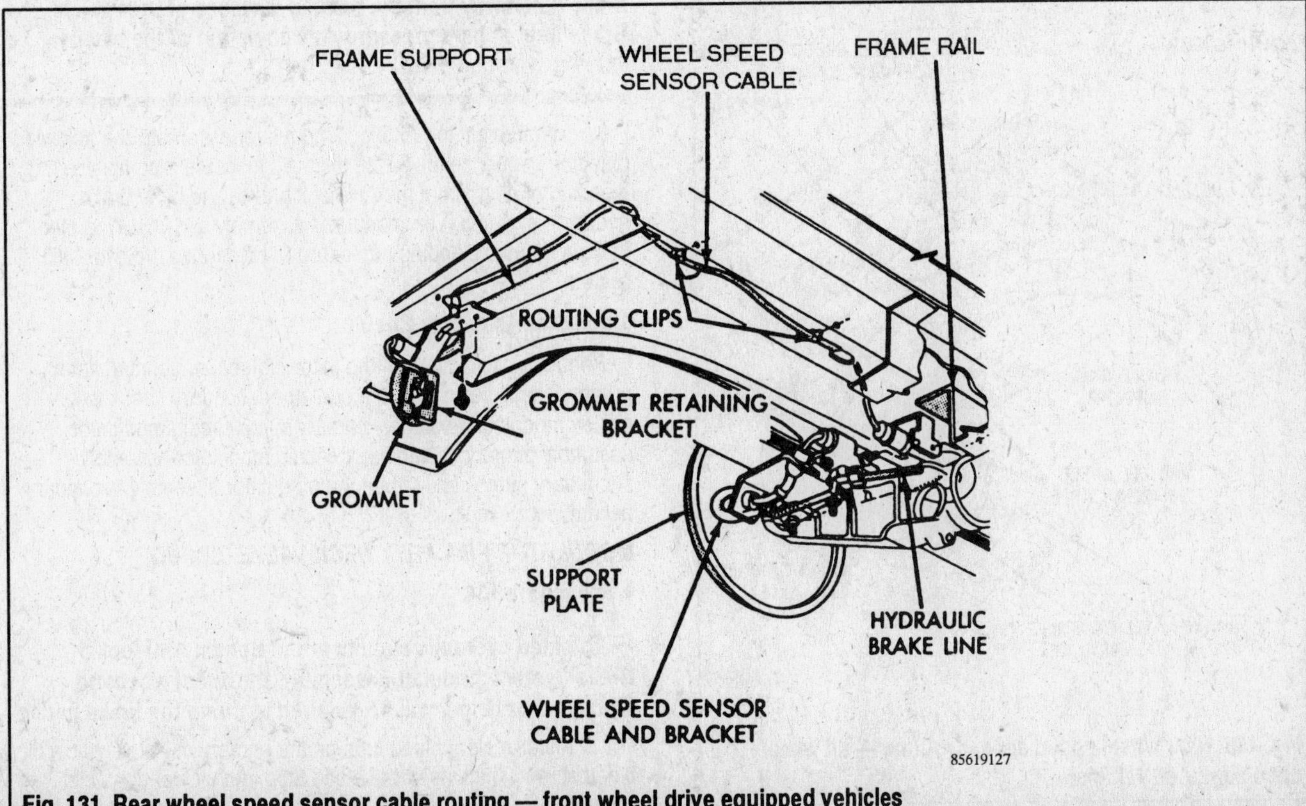

Fig. 131 Rear wheel speed sensor cable routing — front wheel drive equipped vehicles

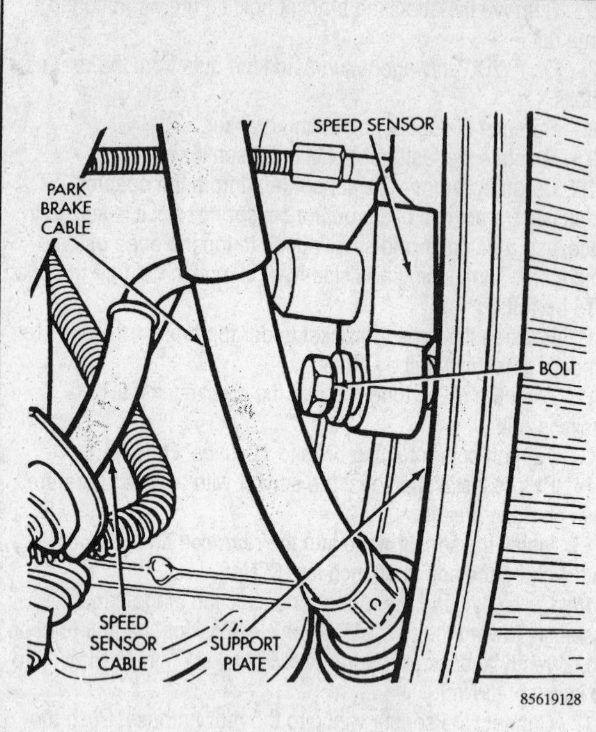

Fig. 132 Rear wheel speed sensor attaching bolt — front wheel drive equipped vehicles

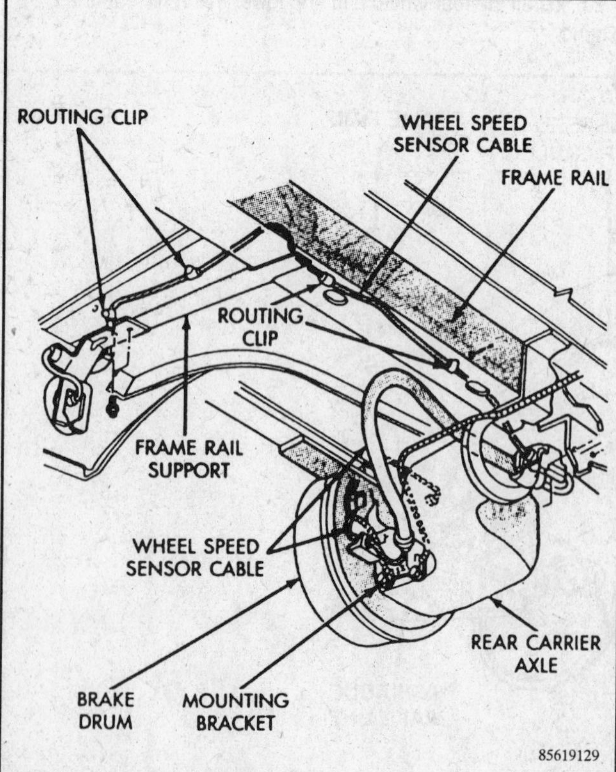

Fig. 133 Rear wheel speed sensor routing — all wheel drive equipped vehicles

Bendix Anti-lock 4 System Bleeding

BLEEDING PROCEDURE

Modulator

1. Assemble and install all brake system components on the vehicle, making sure all hydraulic fluid lines are installed and properly tightened.
2. Bleed the base brake system, using ONLY the bleeding procedure outlined in this section.
3. To perform the bleeding procedure on the ABS modulator assembly, the battery, battery tray and acid shield must be removed from vehicle. Then reconnect the vehicle's battery to vehicle's battery cables, using ONLY approved battery jumper cables.
4. Connect the DRB Diagnostics Tester to the vehicle's diagnostics connector. The vehicle diagnostic connector is located behind the fuse panel access cover on the lower section of the dash panel left of the steering column. The diagnostic connector is a blue 6 way connector.
5. Using the DRB check to make sure the CAB does not have any stored fault codes. If it does, remove them using the DRB..

****WARNING**

When bleeding the modulator assembly wear safety glasses. A clear bleed tube must be attached to the modulator bleed screws and submerged in a clear container filled part way with fresh clean brake fluid. Direct the flow of brake fluid away from the painted surfaces of the vehicle. Brake fluid at high pressure may come out of the bleeder screws, when opened.

6. When bleeding Anti-lock modulator assembly, the following bleeding sequence MUST be followed to insure a complete bleeding of all air from the Anti-lock brake, and base brake hydraulic systems. The modulator assembly can ONLY be bled using a manual bleeding procedure to pressurize the hydraulic system.

Modulator Assembly Circuit

Bleed the circuits only in the following sequence: modulator primary check valve circuit, modulator secondary check valve circuit, modulator assembly primary sump circuit, modulator assembly primary accumulator circuit, modulator assembly secondary sump circuit, then the modulator assembly secondary accumulator circuit.

MODULATOR PRIMARY CHECK VALVE CIRCUIT

➧ **See Figure 134**

➜ To bleed hydraulic circuits of the Bendix Anti-lock 4 Brake System modulator assembly, the aid of a second mechanic or helper will be required to pump the brake pedal.

1. Install a clear bleed tube on the primary check valve circuit bleed screw. Then insert the bleed tube into a clear container partially filled with fresh clean brake fluid.

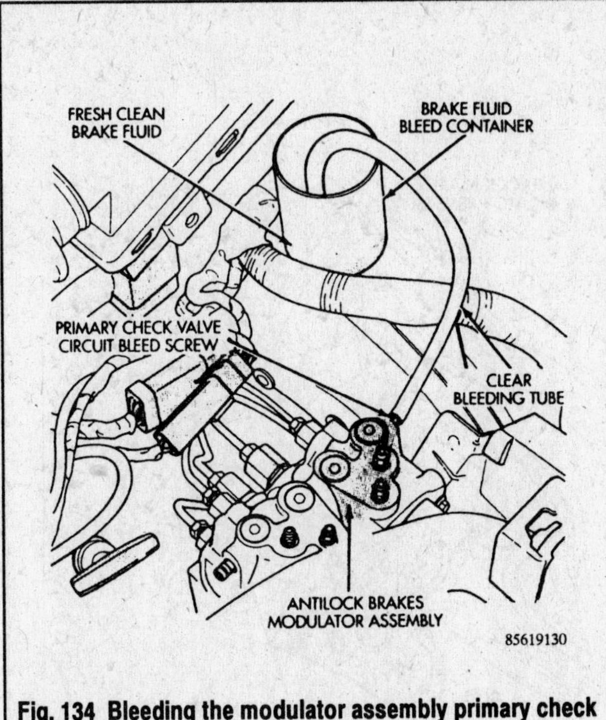

Fig. 134 Bleeding the modulator assembly primary check valve circuit

2. Pump brake pedal several times, then apply and hold a constant medium to heavy force on brake pedal.
3. Open primary check valve circuit bleed screw at least 1 full turn to ensure an adequate flow of brake fluid. Continue bleeding primary check valve circuit until brake pedal bottoms.
4. After brake pedal bottoms, close, then tighten bleed screw. Release the brake pedal. Do not release the brake pedal prior to closing, then tightening the bleed screw.
5. Continue bleeding the modulator assembly, repeating Steps 2 through 4 until a clear, bubble free flow of brake fluid is evident.
6. When all air is bled from primary check valve circuit, tighten bleed screw and remove bleed hose from bleed screw. Do not remove bleed hose before tightening bleed screw, air may re-enter modulator.
7. Tighten modulator assembly primary bleed screw to 80 inch lbs. (9 Nm).

MODULATOR SECONDARY CHECK VALVE CIRCUIT

➧ **See Figure 135**

1. Move the clear bleed tube to the secondary check valve circuit bleed screw. Then insert the bleed tube into a container partially filled with fresh clean brake fluid.
2. Pump brake pedal several times, then apply and hold a constant medium to heavy force on brake pedal.
3. Open secondary check valve circuit bleeder screw, at least 1 full turn to ensure an adequate flow of brake fluid. Continue to bleed secondary check valve circuit until the brake pedal bottoms.
4. After brake pedal bottoms, close, then tighten bleed screw and release brake pedal. Do not release brake pedal prior to closing and tightening bleed screw.
5. Continue bleeding secondary check valve circuit, repeating Steps 2 through 4, until a clear, bubble free flow of brake fluid is evident.

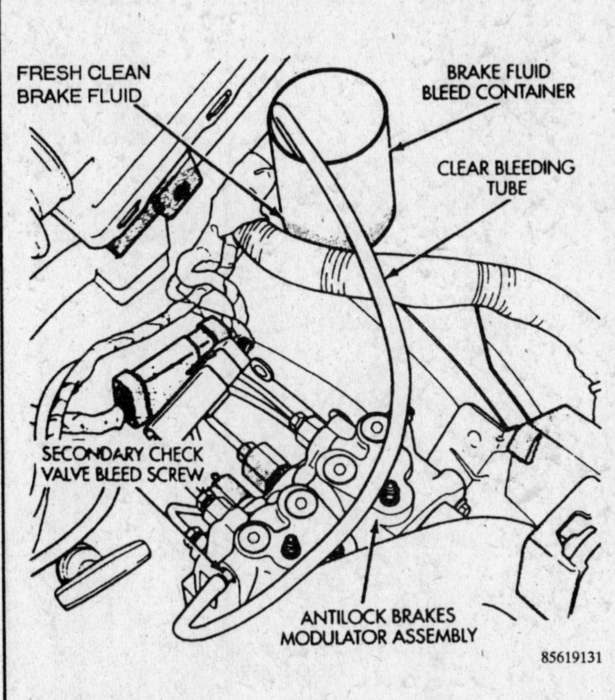

Fig. 135 Bleeding the modulator assembly secondary check valve circuit

6. When air is bled from primary check valve circuit, tighten bleed screw and remove bleed hose from bleed screw. Do not remove bleed hose before tightening bleed screw, air may re-enter modulator.
7. Tighten modulator assembly primary bleed screw to 80 inch lbs. (9 Nm).

MODULATOR ASSEMBLY PRIMARY SUMP CIRCUIT

➧ **See Figure 136**

1. Move clear bleed tube to primary sump bleed screw. Then install bleed tube into a container partially filled with fresh clean brake fluid.
2. Pump brake pedal several times, then apply and hold a constant medium to heavy force on brake pedal.
3. Open modulator assembly primary sump circuit bleed screw at least 1 full turn. This will ensure an adequate flow of brake fluid from the primary sump circuit.
4. Using the DRB, select the bleed ABS hydraulic unit mode. Then select the primary circuit. (The RF and LR solenoids will alternately fire for five seconds). Using the DRB, continue to select the primary circuit until an air-free flow of brake fluid from primary sump bleed screw is maintained or brake pedal bottoms. If an air-free flow is not maintained before brake pedal bottoms, close bleed screw and repeat Steps 2 to 4, until an air free flow is maintained.
5. After an air-free flow of brake fluid is maintained from primary sump bleed screw, close and lightly tighten bleeder screw. Then release brake pedal. Do not release brake pedal prior to closing and tightening bleeder screw.
6. After primary sump bleed screw is closed, remove bleed hose from primary sump bleed screw.
7. Tighten modulator assembly primary sump bleed screw to 80 inch lbs. (9 Nm).

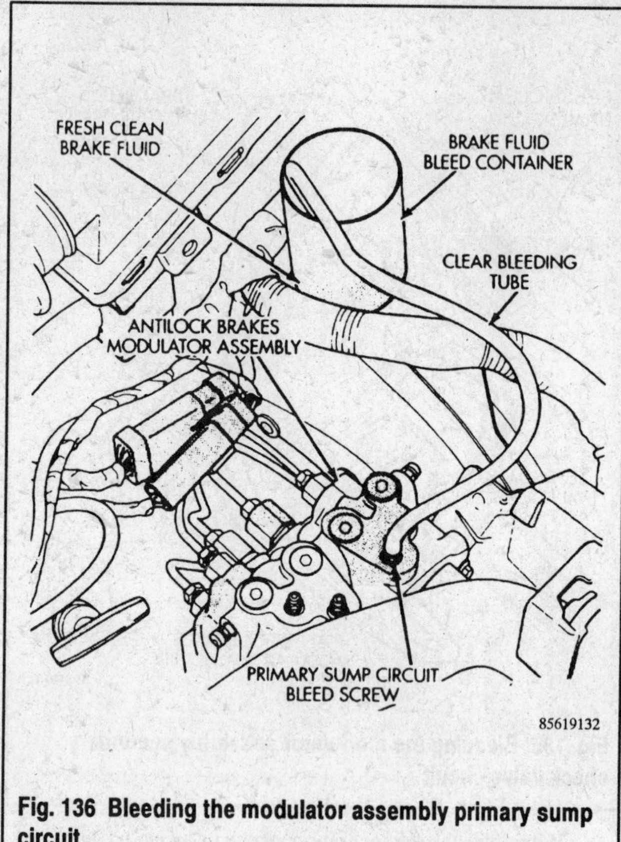

Fig. 136 Bleeding the modulator assembly primary sump circuit

MODULATOR ASSEMBLY PRIMARY ACCUMULATOR CIRCUIT

➧ **See Figure 137**

1. Transfer the clear bleed tube to the primary accumulator bleed screw. Then insert the bleed tube into a container partially filled with fresh clean brake fluid.
2. Pump brake pedal several times, then apply a constant medium to heavy force on the brake pedal. Using the DRB, select the bleed ABS hydraulic unit mode. Then select the primary circuit valves. (The RF and LR modulator assembly solenoids will fire for 5 seconds).
3. Open the modulator assembly primary accumulator circuit bleed screw at least one full turn. This will ensure an adequate flow of brake fluid from the primary accumulator circuit. Continue bleeding primary accumulator circuit until an air-free flow of brake fluid from bleed screw is maintained or the brake pedal bottoms. If an air-free flow of brake fluid is not maintained before brake pedal bottoms, close bleed screw and repeat Steps 1 and 2 until an air free flow is maintained.
4. After an air-free flow of brake fluid is maintained from the primary accumulator bleed screw, close and lightly tighten bleed screw. Then release pressure from brake pedal. Do not release force from brake pedal prior to closing and tightening bleed screw.

➛ **For the next modulator assembly bleeding procedure, use of the DRB is not required. This step of the bleed procedure does not require modulator solenoids to be operated for bleeding to be performed.**

5. Pump brake pedal several times, then apply and hold a constant medium to heavy force on the brake pedal.

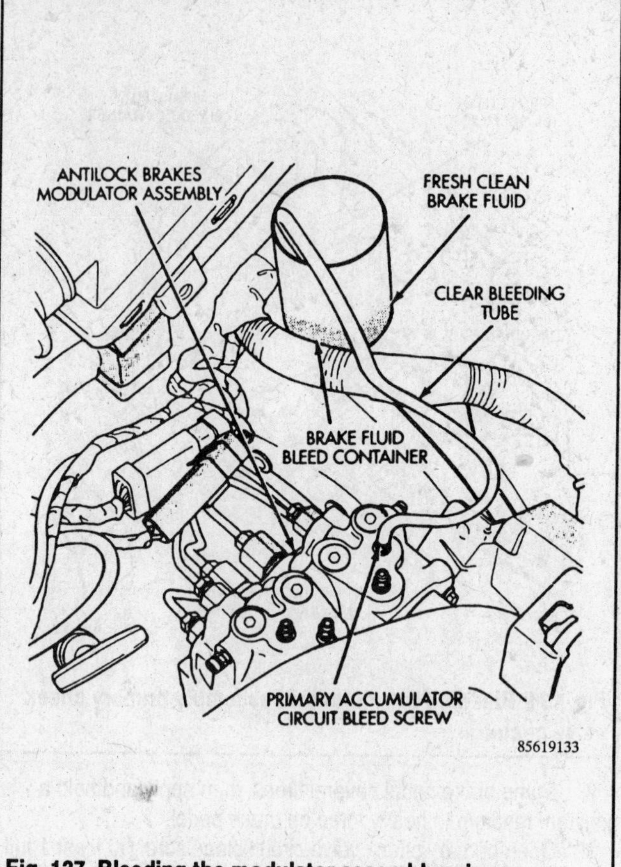

Fig. 137 Bleeding the modulator assembly primary accumulator circuit

6. Again without firing modulator solenoids, open primary accumulator circuit bleed screw 1 full turn. This will ensure an adequate flow of brake fluid from the primary accumulator circuit.
7. Bleed primary accumulator circuit until a clear, air-free flow of brake fluid is maintained from the accumulator bleed screw or the brake pedal bottoms. If an air-free flow of brake fluid is not maintained from the bleed screw before the brake pedal bottoms. First, close bleed screw and then repeat Steps 4 and 5 of this bleeding procedure until an air-free flow is maintained.
8. After an air-free flow of brake fluid is maintained from the primary accumulator circuit bleed screw, close and lightly tighten bleed screw. Then release force from brake pedal. Do not release force from brake pedal prior to closing and tightening bleeder screw.
9. After primary accumulator bleed screw is closed, remove bleed hose from bleed screw.
10. Tighten primary accumulator bleed screw to 80 inch lbs. (9 Nm).

MODULATOR ASSEMBLY SECONDARY SUMP CIRCUIT

➧ **See Figure 138**

1. Transfer the clear bleed tube to the secondary sump bleed screw on the modulator assembly. Then insert the bleed tube into a container partially filled with fresh clean brake fluid.
2. Pump brake pedal several times, then apply and hold a constant medium to heavy force on brake pedal.
3. Open the secondary sump circuit bleed screw at least 1 full turn. This will ensure an adequate flow of brake fluid is expelled from the secondary sump circuit.

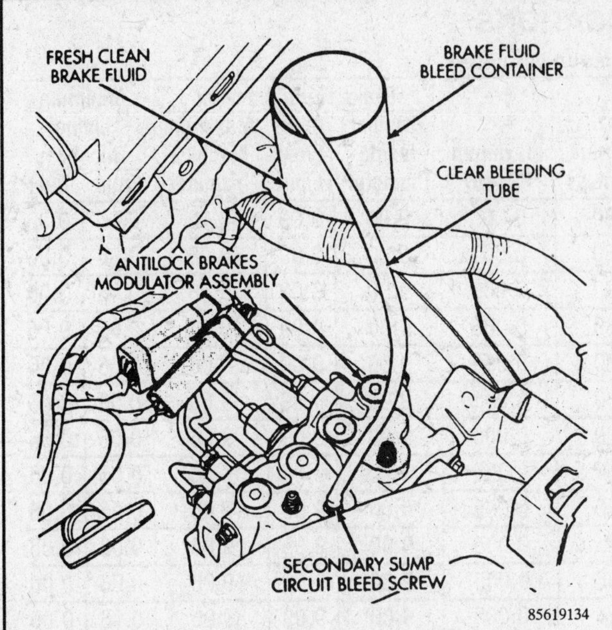

Fig. 138 Bleeding the modulator assembly secondary sump circuit

4. Using the DRB, select the bleed ABS hydraulic unit mode. Then select the secondary circuit valves. (The LF and RR solenoids will alternately fire for five seconds). Continue bleeding secondary sump circuit until an air-free flow of brake fluid from secondary sump bleed screw is maintained or brake pedal bottoms. If an air-free flow of brake fluid is not maintained before brake pedal bottoms, close bleed screw and repeat Steps 2 through 4 until an air-free flow is maintained.

5. After an air-free flow of brake fluid is maintained from secondary sump bleed screw, close and lightly tighten bleed screw. Then release force from brake pedal. Do not release brake pedal prior to closing and tightening bleeder screw.

6. After secondary sump bleed screw is closed, remove bleed hose from bleed screw.

7. Tighten secondary sump bleed screw to 80 inch lbs. (9 Nm).

MODULATOR ASSEMBLY SECONDARY ACCUMULATOR CIRCUIT

See Figure 139

1. Transfer the bleed tube to the secondary accumulator bleed screw. Then insert the bleed tube into a container partially filled with fresh clean brake fluid.

2. Apply constant, medium to heavy force on the brake pedal.

3. Using the DRB, select the bleed ABS hydraulic unit mode,and then select the secondary circuit valves. (The LF and RR modulator assembly solenoids will fire for 5 seconds).

4. Open the secondary accumulator circuit bleed screw at least one full turn. This will ensure an adequate flow of brake fluid is expelled from the secondary accumulator circuit. Continue to bleed primary accumulator circuit, until an air-free flow of brake fluid from the bleed screw is maintained or brake pedal bottoms. If an air-free flow of brake fluid is not maintained from bleed screw before brake pedal bottoms, close bleed screw and then repeat Steps 1 and 2 until an air free flow is maintained.

5. After an air-free flow of brake fluid is maintained from the bleed screw, close and lightly tighten the bleed screw. Then release force from the brake pedal.

6. Do not release the force from brake pedal prior to closing and tightening the bleeder screw.

For the next modulator assembly bleeding procedure, use of the DRB is not required. This step of the bleeding procedure does not require the modulator solenoids to be operated for bleeding to be performed.

7. Pump the brake pedal several times, then apply and hold a constant medium to heavy force on the brake pedal.

8. Again without firing modulator assembly solenoids, open secondary accumulator circuit bleed screw at least 1 full turn. This will ensure an adequate flow of brake fluid is expelled from the secondary accumulator circuit.

9. Bleed secondary accumulator circuit until a clear, air-free flow of brake fluid is maintained from the secondary accumulator bleed screw or the brake pedal bottoms. If an air-free flow of brake fluid is not maintained from secondary accumulator bleed screw before brake pedal bottoms. Repeat Steps 5 and 6 of this bleeding procedure until an air-free flow is maintained from the bleeder screw.

10. After an air free flow of brake fluid is maintained from secondary accumulator circuit bleed screw, close and lightly tighten bleed screw. Then release force from brake pedal. Do not release force from brake pedal prior to closing and tightening bleed screw.

11. After secondary accumulator bleed screw is closed, remove bleed hose from bleed screw.

12. Tighten secondary accumulator bleed screw to 80 inch lbs. (9 Nm).

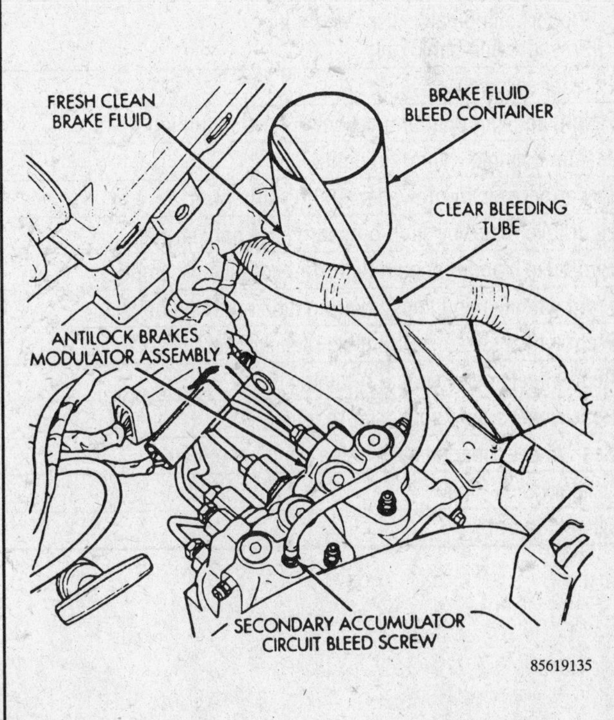

Fig. 139 Bleeding the modulator assembly secondary accumulator circuit

BRAKE SPECIFICATIONS

All measurements in inches unless noted.

Year	Model	Master Cylinder Bore	Brake Disc Original Thickness	Brake Disc Minimum Thickness	Brake Disc Maximum Runout	Brake Drum Diameter Original Inside Diameter	Brake Drum Diameter Max. Wear Limit	Brake Drum Diameter Maximum Machine Diameter	Minimum Lining Thickness Front	Minimum Lining Thickness Rear
1984	Caravan/Voyager	0.940	0.861	0.80	0.005	9.00	9.09	9.06	0.06	0.06
1985	Caravan/Voyager	0.940	0.861	0.80	0.005	9.00	9.09	9.06	0.06	0.06
1986	Caravan/Voyager	0.940	0.861	0.80	0.005	9.00	9.09	9.06	0.06	0.06
1987	Caravan/Voyager	0.940	0.861	0.80	0.005	9.00	9.09	9.06	0.06	0.06
1988	Caravan/Voyager	0.940	0.861	0.80	0.005	9.00	9.09	9.06	0.06	0.06
1989	Caravan/Voyager	0.940	0.861	0.80	0.005	9.00	9.09	9.06	0.06	0.06
1990	Caravan/Voyager	0.940	0.861	0.80	0.005	9.00	9.09	9.06	0.06	0.06
1991	Caravan/Voyager/Town & Country	0.940	0.861	0.80	0.005	9.00	9.09	9.06	0.06	0.06
1992	Caravan/Voyager/Town & Country	0.940	0.861	0.80	0.005	9.00	9.09	9.06	0.06	0.06
1993	Caravan/Voyager/Town & Country	0.940	0.940	0.88	0.005	9.00	9.09	9.06	0.06	0.06
1994	Caravan/Voyager/Town & Country	0.940	0.940	0.88	0.005	9.00	9.09	9.06	0.06	0.06
1995	Caravan/Voyager/Town & Country	0.940	0.940	0.88	0.005	9.00	9.09	9.06	0.06	0.06

85619C01

TORQUE SPECIFICATIONS

Component	English	Metric
Accumulator pump/motor assembly		
High pressure hose-to-hydraulic assembly	12 ft. lbs.	16 Nm
Low pressure hose-to-hydraulic assembly	10 inch lbs.	1 Nm
Hydraulic assembly attaching nuts	21 ft. lbs.	28 Nm
Brake line to hydraulic assembly	12 ft. lbs.	16 Nm
Proportioning valve attaching nuts	30 ft. lbs.	40 Nm
Pressure line banjo bolt	13 ft. lbs.	17 Nm
Bleeder screws	8 ft. lbs.	10 Nm
Height sensing dual proportioning valve mounting bolts	13 ft. lbs.	18 Nm
Master cylinder mounting bolts	17–25 ft. lbs.	23–34 Nm
Power booster-to-firewall mounting stud nuts	17–25 ft. lbs.	23–34 Nm
Hydraulic reservoir high pressure hose banjo fitting	10 ft. lbs.	13 Nm
Hydraulic bladder accumulator-to-hydraulic assembly	30 ft. lbs.	40 Nm
Front wheel speed sensor wiring tube retaining bolts	35 inch lbs.	4 Nm
Front wheel sensor-to-knuckle retaining screw	60 inch lbs.	7 Nm
Rear wheel speed sensor retaining bolts	60 inch lbs.	7 Nm
Rear wheel speed sensor-to-rear axle	60 inch lbs.	7 Nm
Rear wheel speed sensor frame rail bracket bolt	50 inch lbs.	5 Nm
Caliper guide pins	25–35 ft. lbs.	34–48 Nm
Wheel lug nuts	95 ft. lbs.	129 Nm

85619C02

EXTERIOR
ANTENNA 10-11
BUMPERS 10-8
EXTERIOR MOLDINGS AND BODY SIDE APPLIQUES 10-6
FENDERS AND SPLASH SHIELDS 10-11
FRONT DOOR HINGE 10-2
FRONT DOORS 10-2
GRILLE 10-10
HOOD 10-5
LIFTGATE 10-5
OUTSIDE MIRRORS 10-10
SLIDING DOOR 10-2

INTERIOR
DOOR GLASS REGULATOR 10-19
DOOR LOCKS AND LATCH 10-18
DOOR PANELS 10-13
ELECTRIC WINDOW MOTOR 10-19
FLOOR CARPETING AND SILENCERS 10-29
FRONT SEATS 10-22
HEADLINER 10-29
INSIDE REAR VIEW MIRROR 10-19
INTERIOR TRIM PANELS 10-14
REAR SEAT ASSEMBLY 10-24
ROOF TOP LUGGAGE RACK 10-30
SEAT BELT SYSTEMS 10-26
STATIONARY GLASS 10-21
WINDSHIELD GLASS 10-21

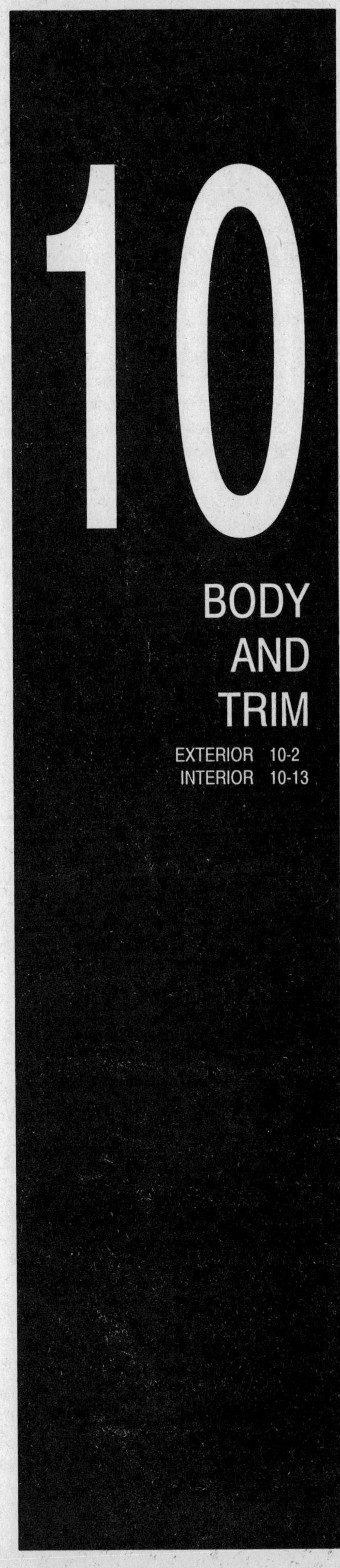

10 BODY AND TRIM

EXTERIOR 10-2
INTERIOR 10-13

EXTERIOR

Front Doors

REMOVAL & INSTALLATION

1984-90 Models

1. Open the front door and remove the inner door panel covering. Disconnect the interior light wiring harness and feed it through the access hole. Disconnect the door swing stop.
2. Open the door wide enough to gain access to the hinge bolts. Place a padded support under the door edge that will hold the door in a level position when the hinges been unbolted from the frame.
3. Scribe around the door hinge on the door frame. Remove the hinge mounting bolts, lower hinge first, then the upper, from the door frame.
4. Remove the door.

To install:

5. Place the door on the padded support and install the hinge mounting bolts until they are snug enough to support the door, but not tight enough to prevent door adjustment.
6. Adjust the door position until correctly aligned, then tighten the hinge bolts.
7. Adjust the striker as necessary.
8. Connect the door stop and interior light harness.
9. Install the inner trim panel.

1991-95 Models

1. Remove the door trim panel, silencer pad and water shield.
2. Disengage all wire connectors and wire harness hold-downs inside of the door, and push the harness through the access hole in the front of the door.
3. Open the door and support it with a jack, an assistant should also be used to hold the door.
4. Using a hammer and punch, drive the bottom hinge pin upward and remove the pin from the hinge.
5. Drive the upper hinge pin from the hinge and remove it. Separate the door from the vehicle.

To install:

6. Install the door assembly on the hinges.
7. Install the hinge pins, by tapping them into position.
8. The door should not require any re-alignment. Install the wiring harness into the door.
9. Install the trim panel.

ALIGNMENT

The front doors should be adjusted so that there is a $^1/_4$ in. (6mm) gap between the edge of the front fender and the edge of the door, and a $^1/_4$ in. (6mm) gap between the back edge of the door and the lock pillar. Adjust the door to position and raise or lower it so that the stamped edge line matches the body panel line. Secure the door in proper position after necessary adjustments.

Front Door Hinge

REMOVAL & INSTALLATION

1991-95 Models

1. Raise the front of the vehicle slightly.
2. Remove the wheel and tire assembly.
3. Remove the inner fender plastic splash shield retaining screws and remove the shield.
4. Support the door assembly. Remove the door retaining pin on the hinge to be replaced.
5. Remove the hinge plate retaining bolts from inside the fender well.
6. Remove the hinge assembly.

To install:

7. Install the hinge plate in position and install the retaining bolts. Do not tighten them completely.
8. Install the hinge pin and check the door alignment, there should be a $^1/_4$ in. (6mm) gap around the sides of the door.
9. Tighten the hinge mounting bolts.
10. Install the inner fender splash shield, then install the wheel.
11. Lower the vehicle.

Sliding Door

REMOVAL & INSTALLATION

See Figures 1, 2 and 4

When removing the sliding door as an assembly, it is not necessary to remove or loosen the bolts that would change the doors alignment.

1. Remove the sliding door upper track cover.
2. Remove the upper track over travel stop.
3. Remove the sill plate.
4. Remove the lower track over travel stop.
5. With the help of an assistant, roll the door back and out of tracks.

To install:

6. Position the door carefully on the tracks and roll it into position.
7. Install the track over travel stops.
8. Install the sill plate.
9. Install the upper track cover.

ALIGNMENT

See Figures 1, 2, 3 and 4

1. The gap between the back edge of the front door and the front edge of the sliding door should be $^5/_{16}$ in. (8mm). The gap between the sliding door edge and the quarter panel should be

1/4 in. (6mm). The stamped edge line of the front door the sliding door and the quarter panel should be in line.

2. Remove the hinge trim panels and adjust the sliding door in the direction(s) required. Refer to the illustration provided for adjustment direction.

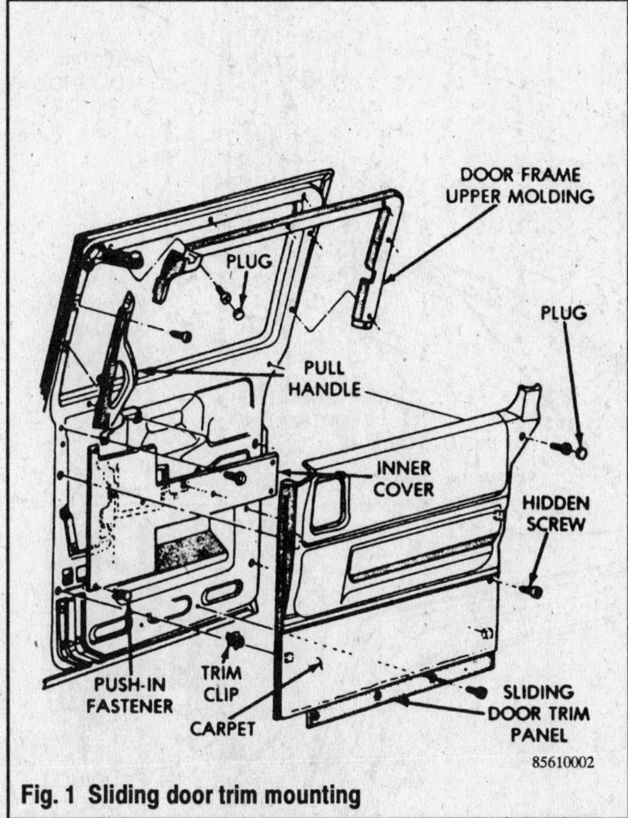

Fig. 1 Sliding door trim mounting

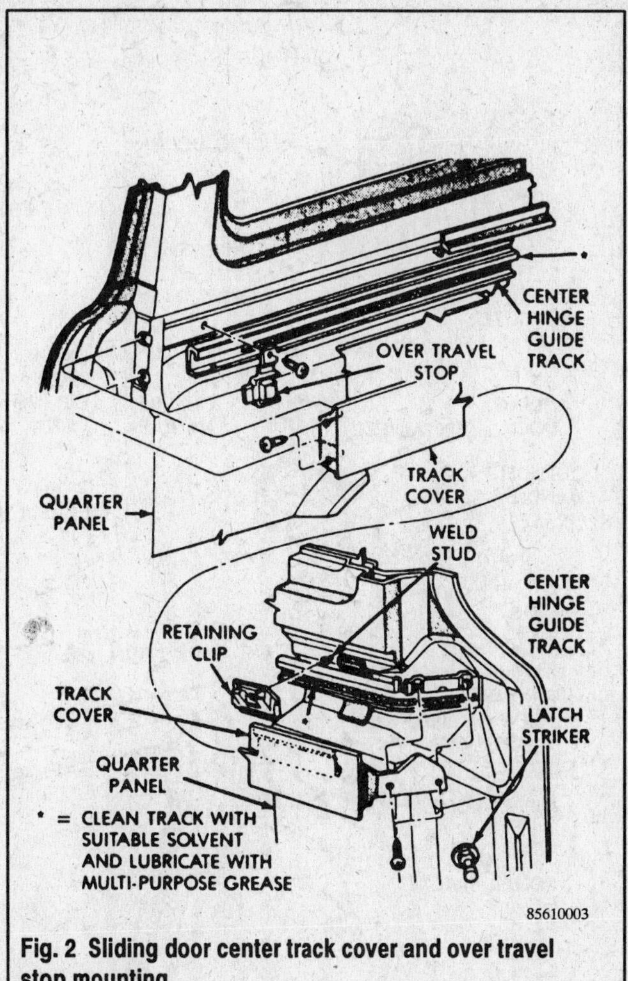

Fig. 2 Sliding door center track cover and over travel stop mounting

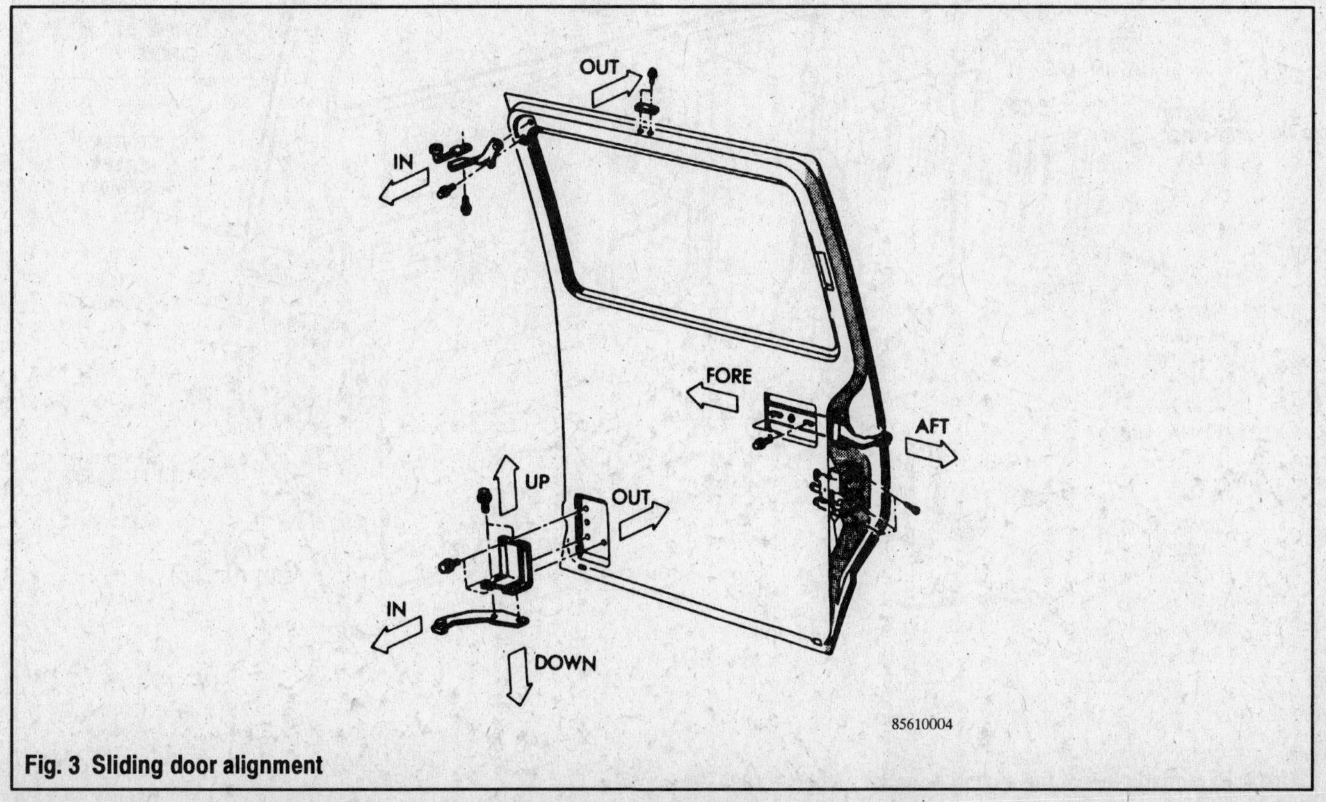

Fig. 3 Sliding door alignment

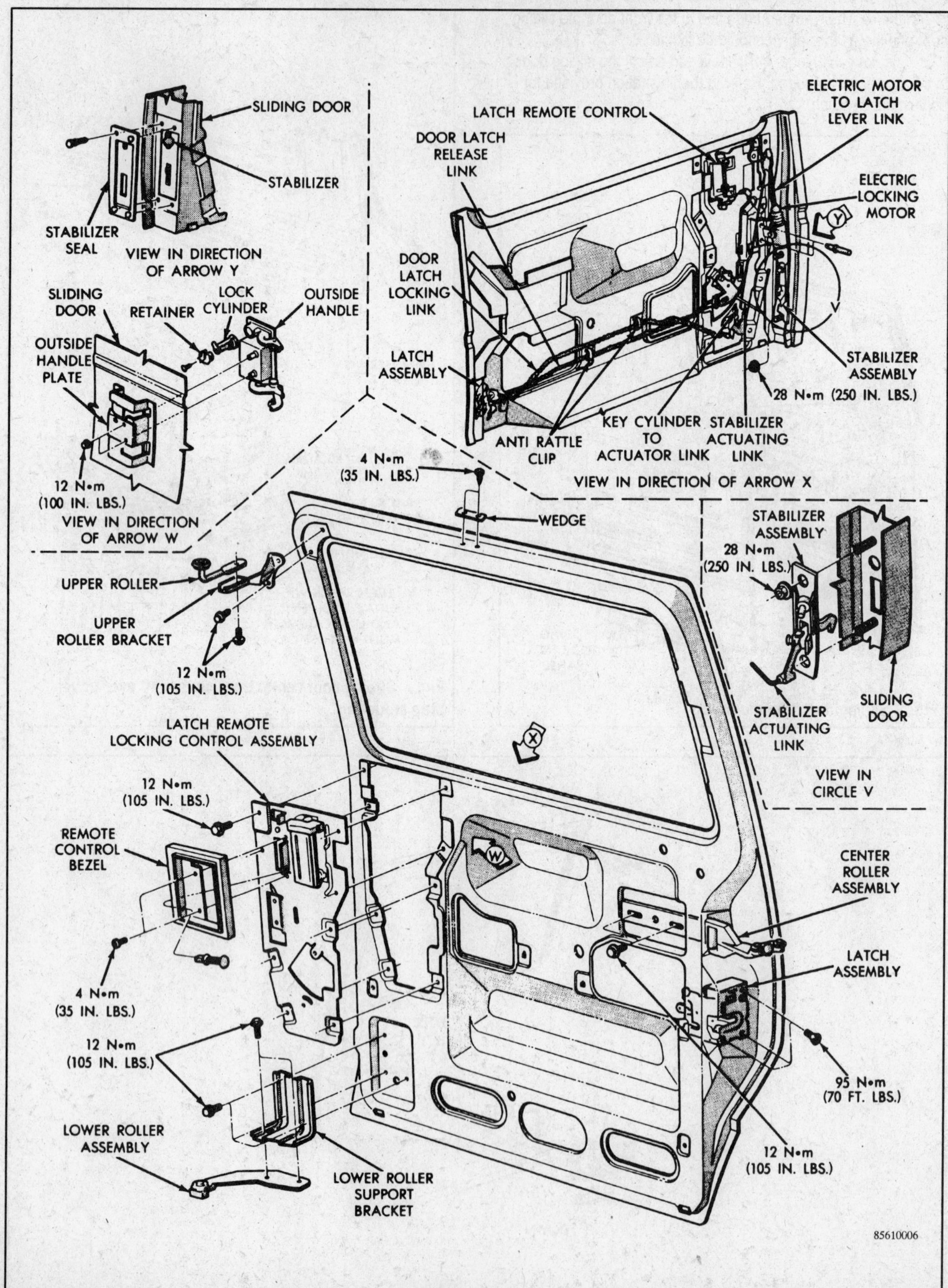

Fig. 4 Exploded view of the sliding door assembly — 1984–90 models

Liftgate

REMOVAL & INSTALLATION

➧ See Figure 5

1. Support the liftgate in the full opened position.
2. Scribe an alignment mark on the liftgate to mark the hinge positions.
3. Place masking tape on the roof edge and liftgate edge to protect the paint surfaces during removal and installation.
4. Remove the liftgate prop fasteners and remove the props.
5. Have a helper on hand to support the liftgate. Remove the hinge mounting bolts and remove the liftgate.

To install:

6. Raise the liftgate into position and install the hinge mounting bolts. Tighten the bolts until they are snug, but not tight enough to prevent liftgate adjustment.
7. Shift the liftgate until the hinge scribe marks are in position, then tighten the hinge mounting bolts.
8. Attach and secure the liftgate props.
9. Remove the top hood-to-hinge attaching bolts and loosen the bottom bolts until they can be removed by hand.
10. With the aid of a helper, support the hood and remove the hinge bolts.
11. Move the hood away from the vehicle and store it in a way to prevent it from being damaged.

To install:

12. With the aid of a helper, position the hood on the hinges and install the lower hinge bolt finger-tight.
13. Install the remaining hinge bolts and align the hinge marks. Tighten the bolts.

➥ When the hood is properly aligned there should be a 0.16 in. (4mm) clearance at the fenders, and the hood should be flush in height with the top of the fenders.

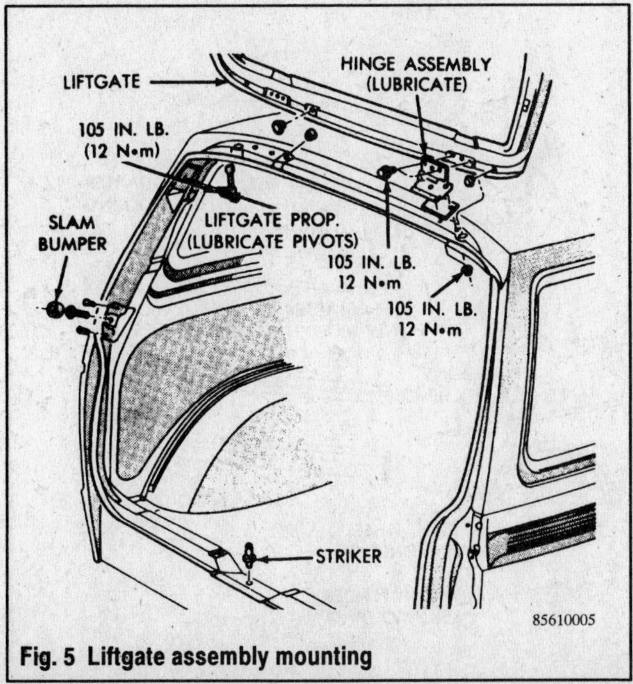

Fig. 5 Liftgate assembly mounting

14. Connect the under hood light and install the cowl cover. Install the wiper arms.
15. Check the hood latch operation.

Hood

REMOVAL & INSTALLATION

➧ See Figures 6, 7, 8 and 9

1. Raise the hood to its full open position.
2. Remove the cowl cover retaining screws.
3. Remove the wiper arms and the cowl cover.
4. Disengage the under hood light connector.
5. Mark all bolt and hinge attachment points with a grease pencil or equivalent, to provide reference marks for installation.

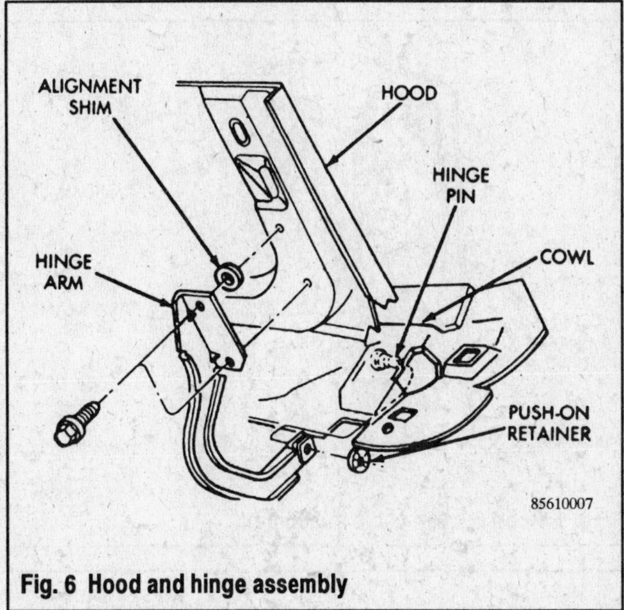

Fig. 6 Hood and hinge assembly

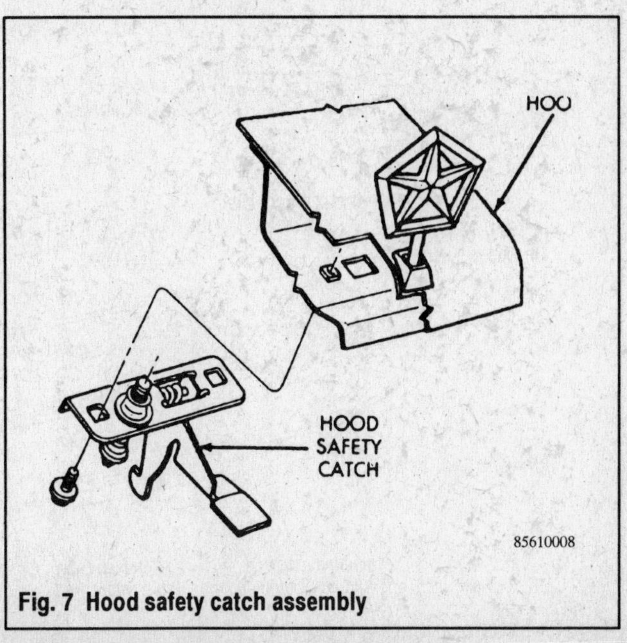

Fig. 7 Hood safety catch assembly

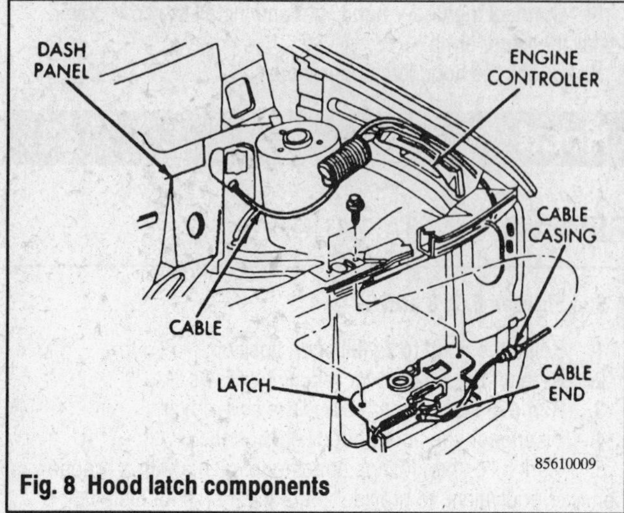

Fig. 8 Hood latch components

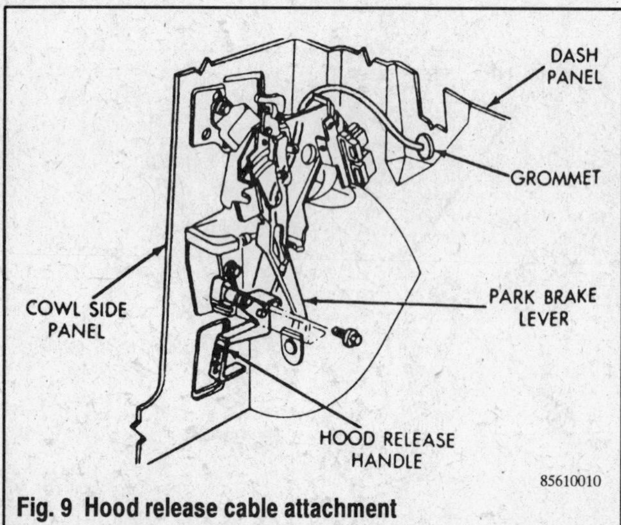

Fig. 9 Hood release cable attachment

Exterior Moldings and Body Side Appliques

REMOVAL & INSTALLATION

1991-95 Models

➧ See Figures 10 and 11

All of the 1991-95 models have various body moldings and applique panels, that are used to dress the appearance of the exterior of the vehicle. All of these trim pieces are either screwed or snapped in place.

1. Remove the screws that retain the trim piece being removed, these will be either under the edge of the trim or at the wheel openings. In some instances there will be clips holding the trim as well as screws. When removing front or rear bumper trim, be sure to remove all retaining bolts.
2. Once the screws are removed, lift the piece away from the vehicle, making sure no clips or screws are still in place.
3. When removing the side applique panels, they will need to be lifted slightly to release them from the tracks that retain them.

To install:

4. Install the replacement piece(s) in position and secure with screws or clips as needed. If replacing the trim piece, be sure to transfer any clips to the replacement.
5. Install all front or rear bumper retaining bolts.

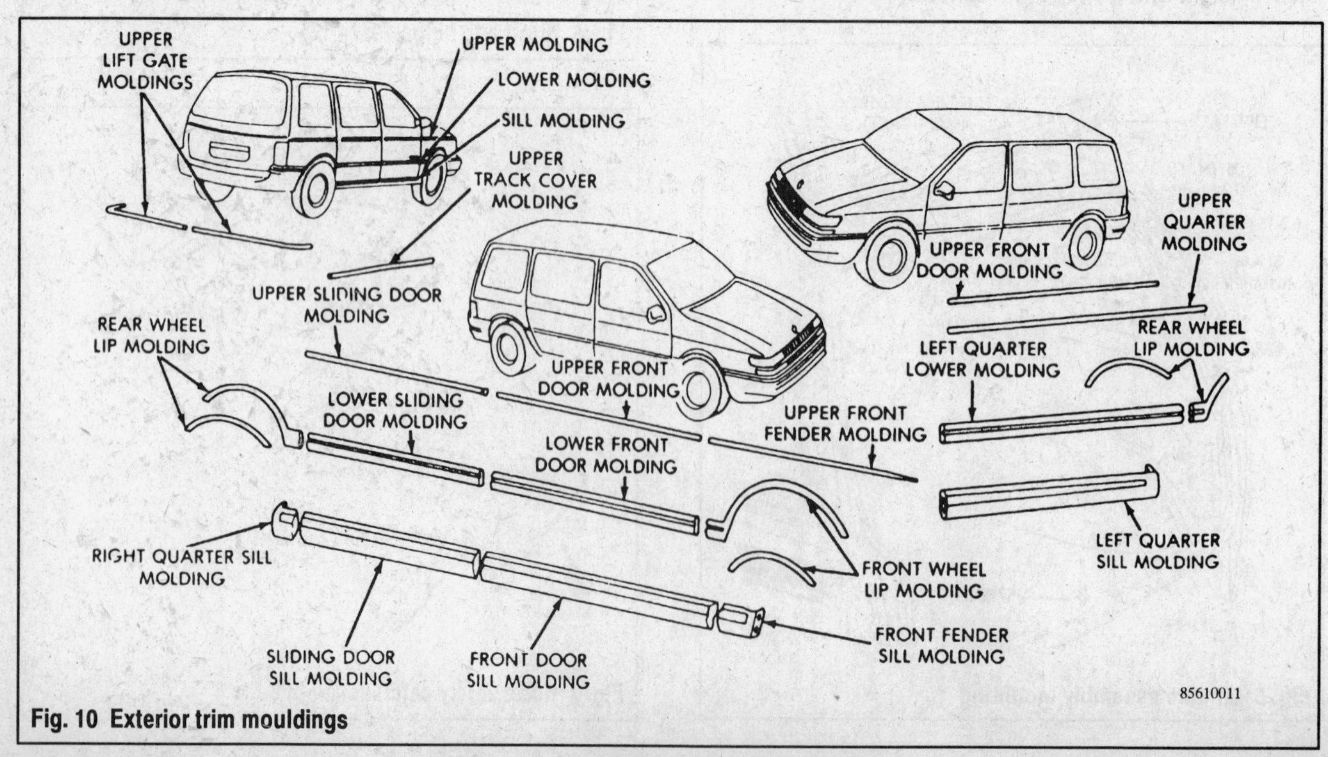

Fig. 10 Exterior trim mouldings

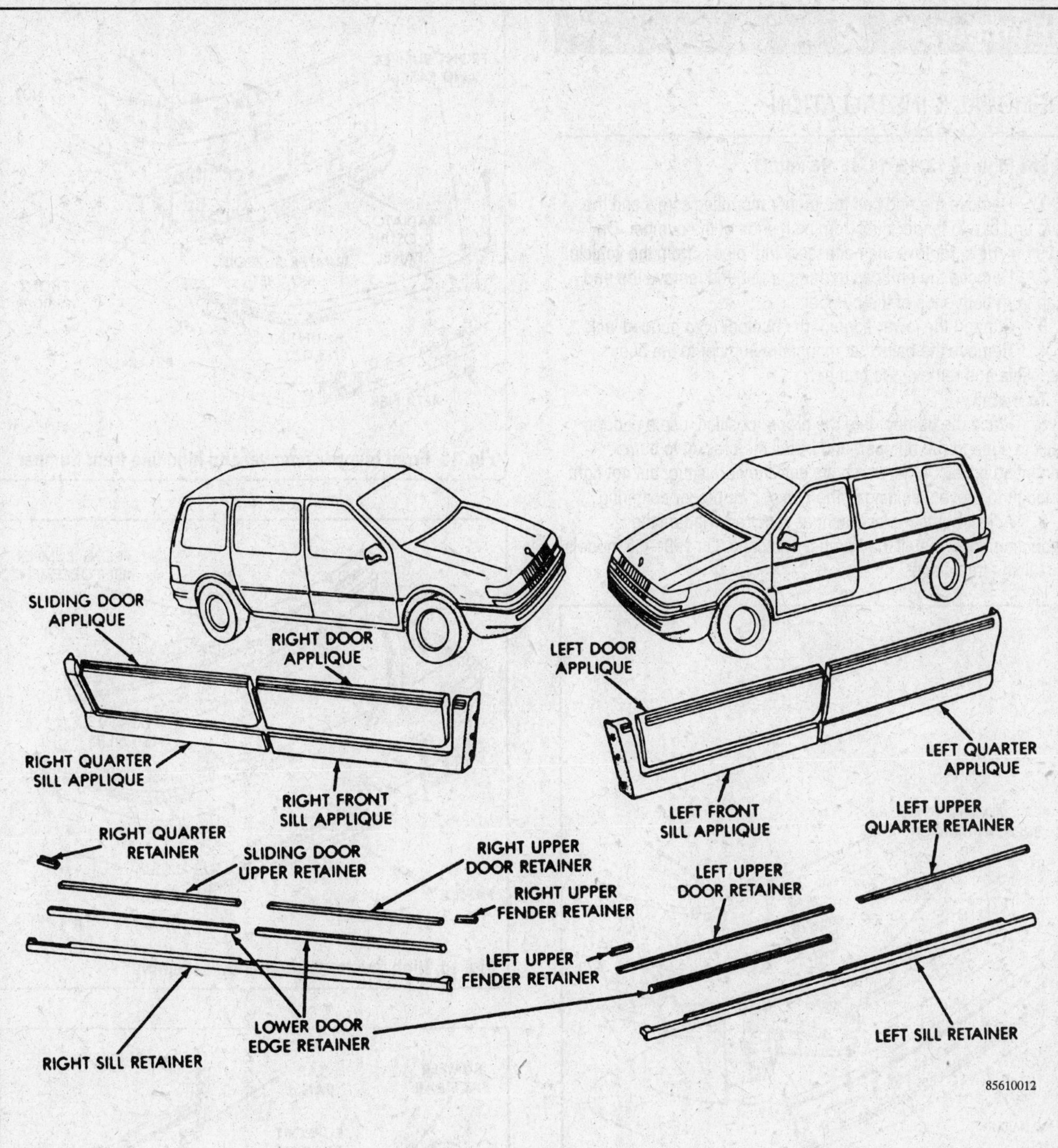

Fig. 11 Body side applique panels

Bumpers

REMOVAL & INSTALLATION

See Figures 12, 13, 14, 15, 16 and 17

1. Remove the end cap to bumper mounting screw and the two end cap to fender nuts from both ends of the bumper. On 1991 models, remove the necessary trim pieces from the vehicle.
2. Remove the end cap to bumper nut and remove the end cap from both ends of the bumper.
3. Support the lower edge of the bumper on a padded jack.
4. Remove the bolts that mount the bumper to the body brackets and remove the bumper.

To install:

5. Place the bumper into the proper position, use a padded jack to support the bumper, and install the bracket to bumper mounting bolts. Tighten the bolts until they are snug. but not tight enough to prevent shifting of the bumper for proper centering.
6. Adjust bumper placement as required. Tighten the mounting bolts. Install the bumper end caps. On 1991-95 models install the trim pieces.

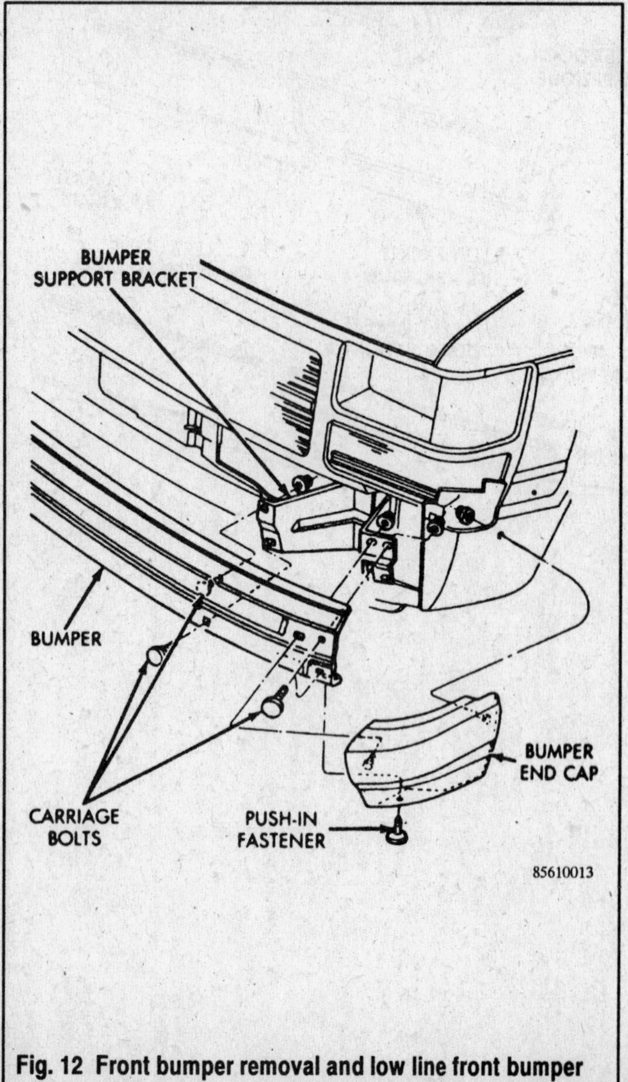

Fig. 12 Front bumper removal and low line front bumper

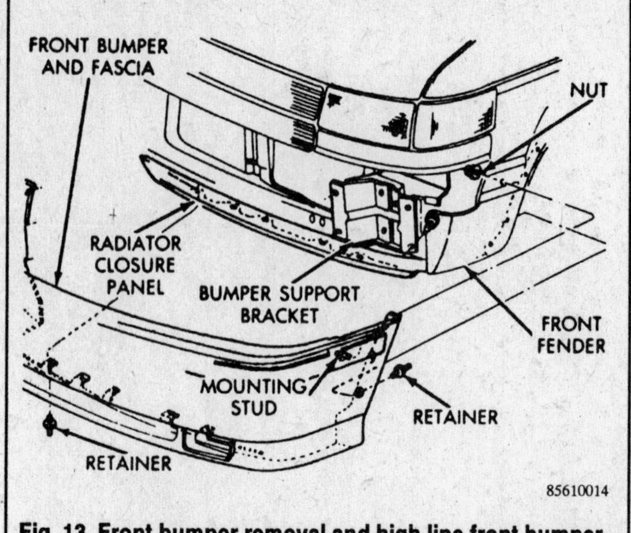

Fig. 13 Front bumper removal and high line front bumper

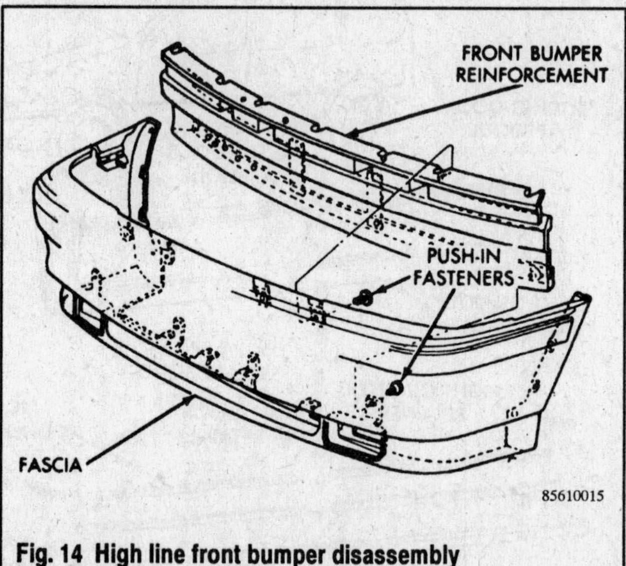

Fig. 14 High line front bumper disassembly

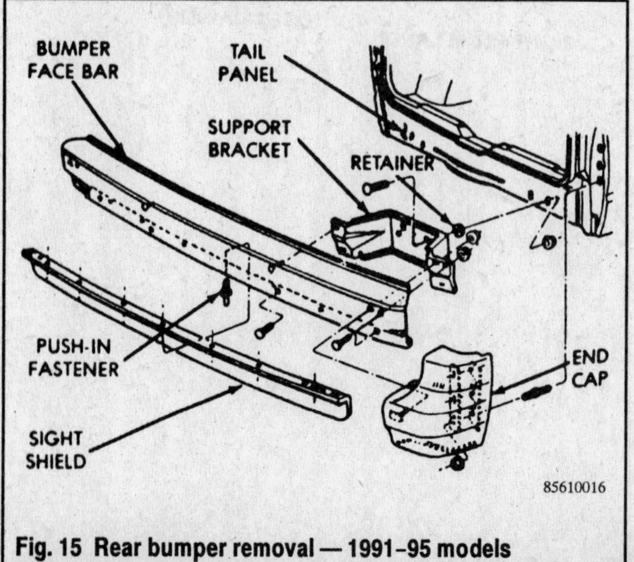

Fig. 15 Rear bumper removal — 1991-95 models

TAIL PANEL
RETAINER
RETAINER
BUMPER REINFORCEMENT
BUMPER SUPPORT
J-NUT
REAR BUMPER FASCIA
PUSH-IN FASTENER
85610017

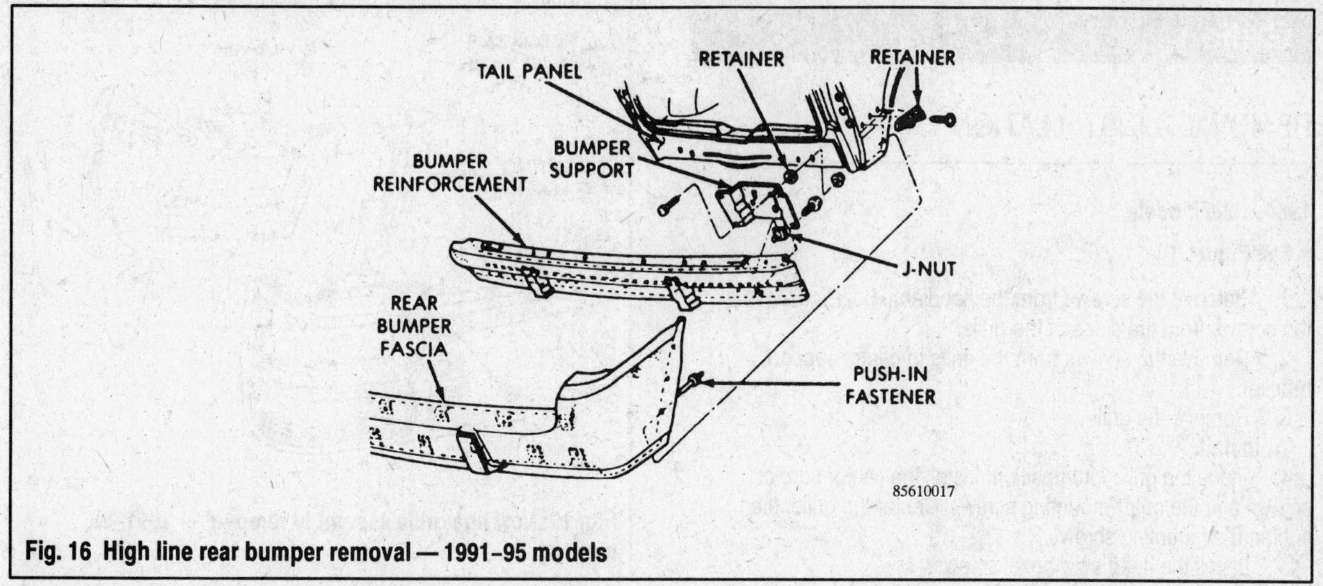

Fig. 16 High line rear bumper removal — 1991–95 models

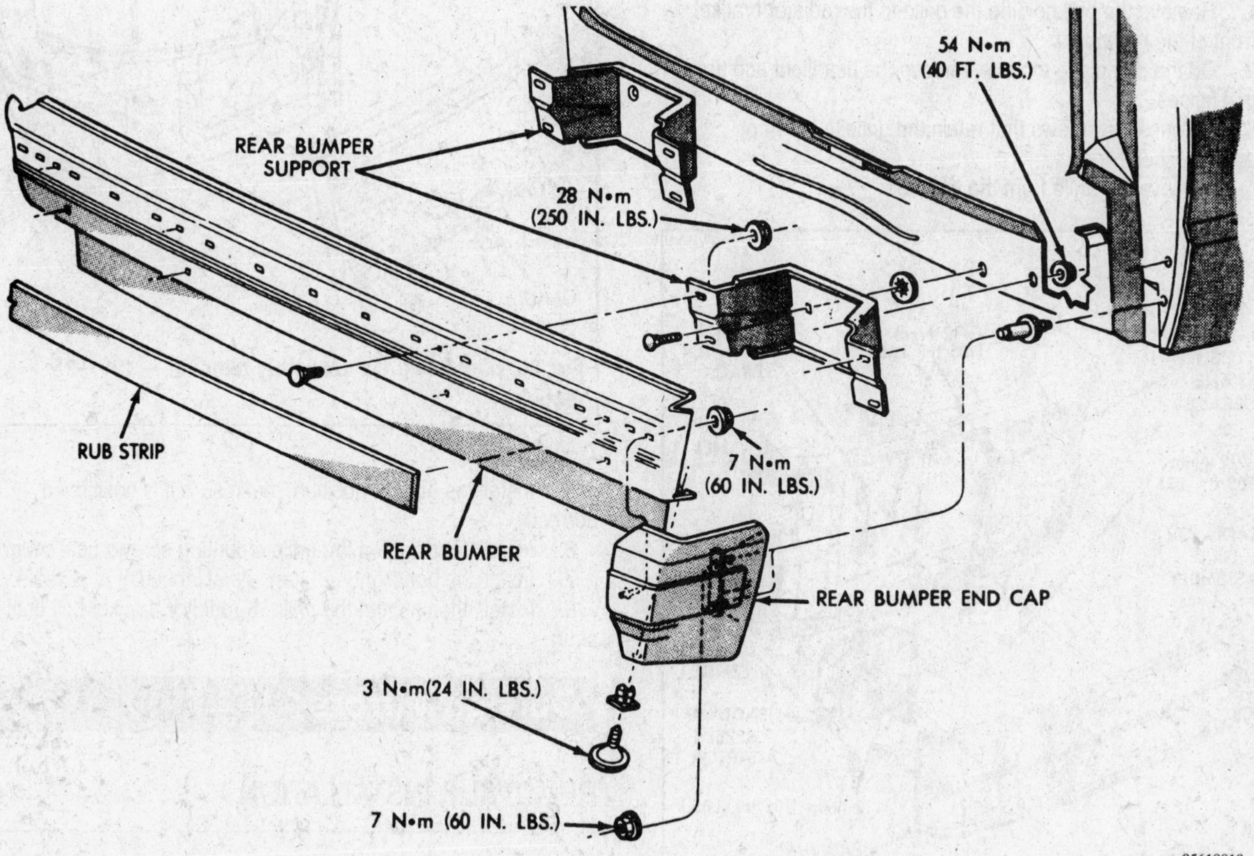

REAR BUMPER SUPPORT
54 N•m (40 FT. LBS.)
28 N•m (250 IN. LBS.)
RUB STRIP
7 N•m (60 IN. LBS.)
REAR BUMPER
REAR BUMPER END CAP
3 N•m(24 IN. LBS.)
7 N•m (60 IN. LBS.)
85610018

Fig. 17 Rear bumper removal — 1984–90 models

Grille

REMOVAL & INSTALLATION

1984–1990 Models

➧ See Figure 18

1. Remove the screws from the headlamp bezels. Remove the screws from the sides of the grille.
2. Remove the screws from the grille to center support bracket.
3. Remove the grille.

To install:

4. Place the grille into position. Install the center support screws and the outer mounting screws. Center the grille, then tighten the mounting screws.
5. Install the headlamp bezel screws.

1991–95 Models

➧ See Figures 19 and 20

There are 2 grille types used, one type incorporates the headlamp doors and the grille, the other is just the center grille assembly with separate headlamp doors.

1. Remove the bolt holding the grille to the radiator bracket, in front of the radiator.
2. On the one piece models, remove the headlight and turn signal lenses.
3. Remove the screws that retain the grille to the front headlight assemblies.
4. Remove the grille from the vehicle.

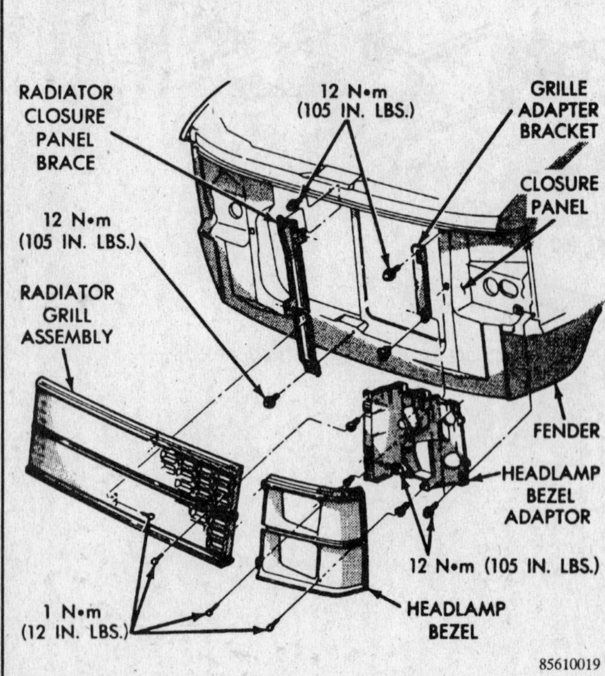

Fig. 18 Grille, headlamp bezel and adapter removal — 1984–1990 models

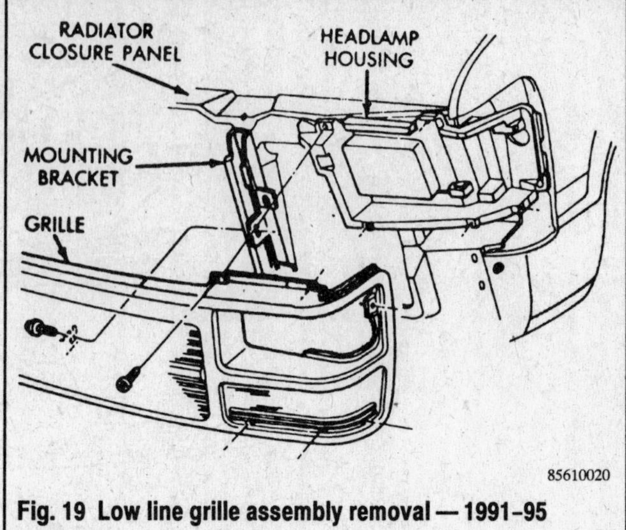

Fig. 19 Low line grille assembly removal — 1991–95 models

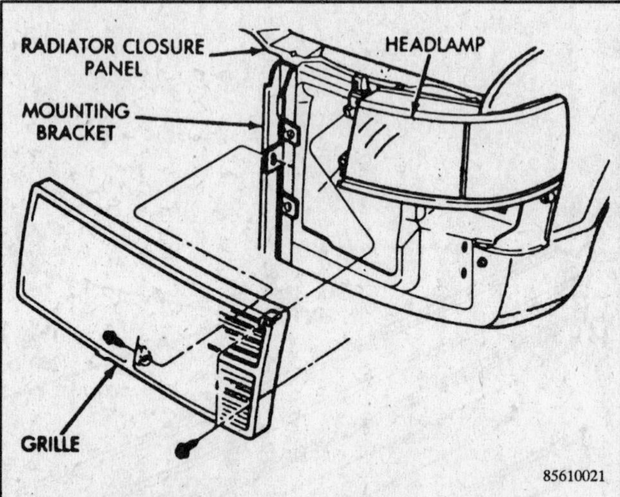

Fig. 20 High line grille assembly removal — 1991–95 models

To install:

5. Install the grille in position, make sure it is positioned correctly.
6. Install, then tighten the grille mounting screws until snug.
7. Install the headlight and turn signal lenses, if applicable.
8. Install, then tighten the grille-to-radiator bracket bolt until snug.

Outside Mirrors

REMOVAL & INSTALLATION

➧ See Figure 21

1. Remove the door trim panel.
2. Remove the adjustment knob with an Allen wrench. Remove the screw cover plug and the mirror inner bezel mounting screws. Remove the bezel.

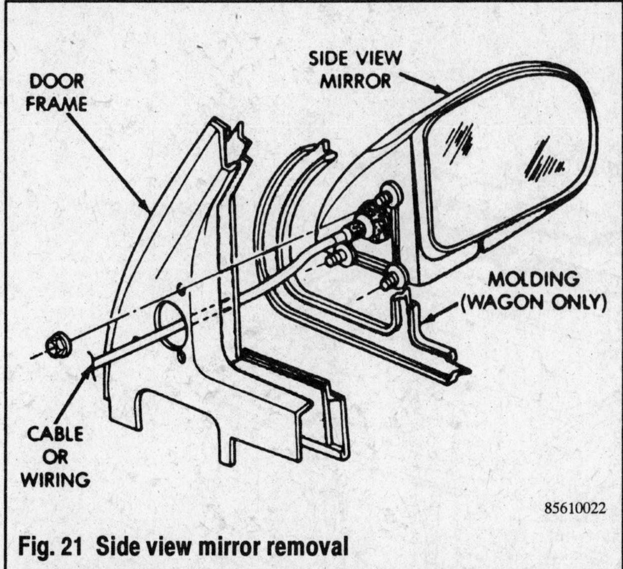

Fig. 21 Side view mirror removal

3. Remove the mirror mounting nuts and the mirror. If equipped with power mirrors, disconnect the electrical lead.

To install:

4. Place the mirror into position and install the mounting nuts. Connect the electrical lead, if equipped.
5. Place the bezel into position and install the mounting screws and cover plug.
6. Install the control knob and trim panel.

Antenna

Refer to the entertainment system portion of Section 6 for antenna servicing.

Fenders and Splash Shields

REMOVAL & INSTALLATION

➧ See Figures 22, 23, 24, 25, 26 and 27

1. Remove the splash shields from the inner fender wells.

➥ Raising the vehicle slightly and removing the wheel and tire, will make splash shield removal easier.

2. Remove the under vehicle splash shields where equipped, one will cover the transaxle and the other will cover the accessory drive belts.
3. Remove the grille and headlamp assemblies.
4. Remove the bolts holding the vehicle jacking pad under the vehicle and remove the pad.
5. Remove the bolts holding the fender to the hinge pillar from inside the wheel opening.
6. Remove the bolts holding the fender to the rocker panel.
7. Remove the bolts holding the fender to the lower radiator panel.

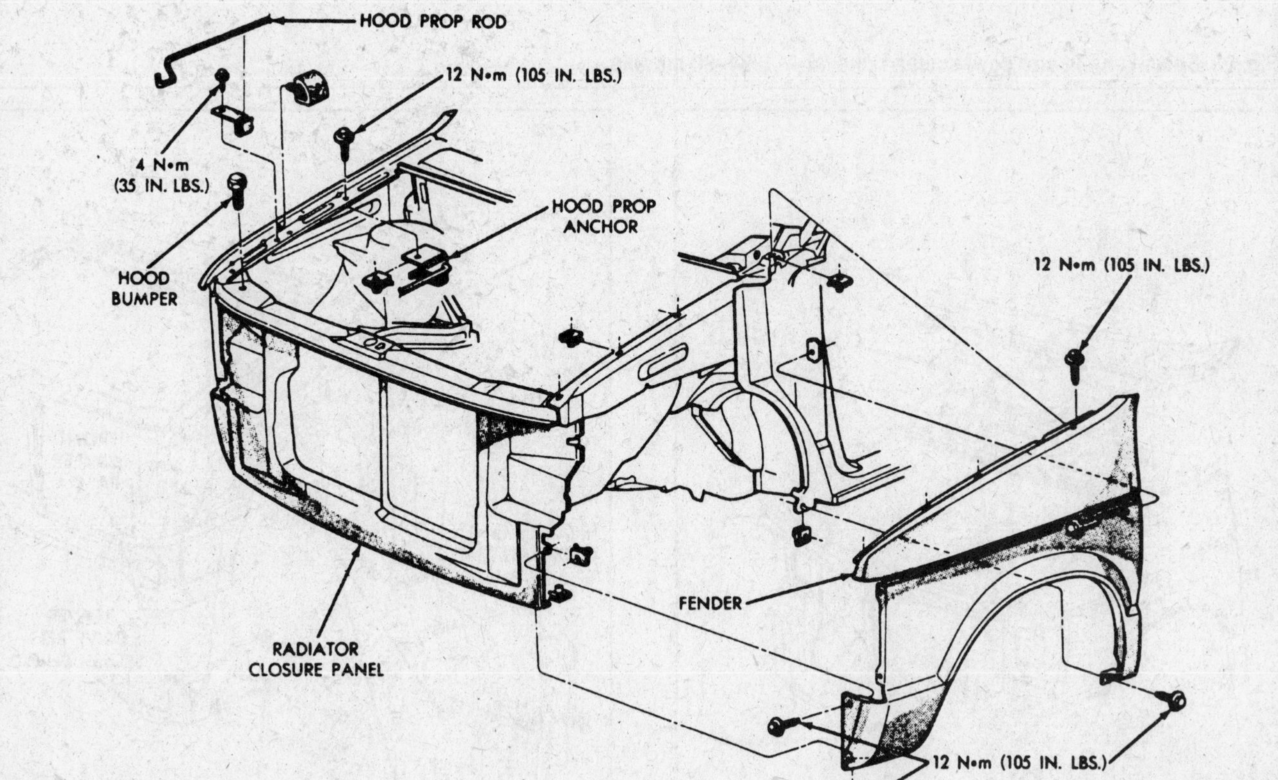

Fig. 22 Front fender removal and installation — 1984-90 models

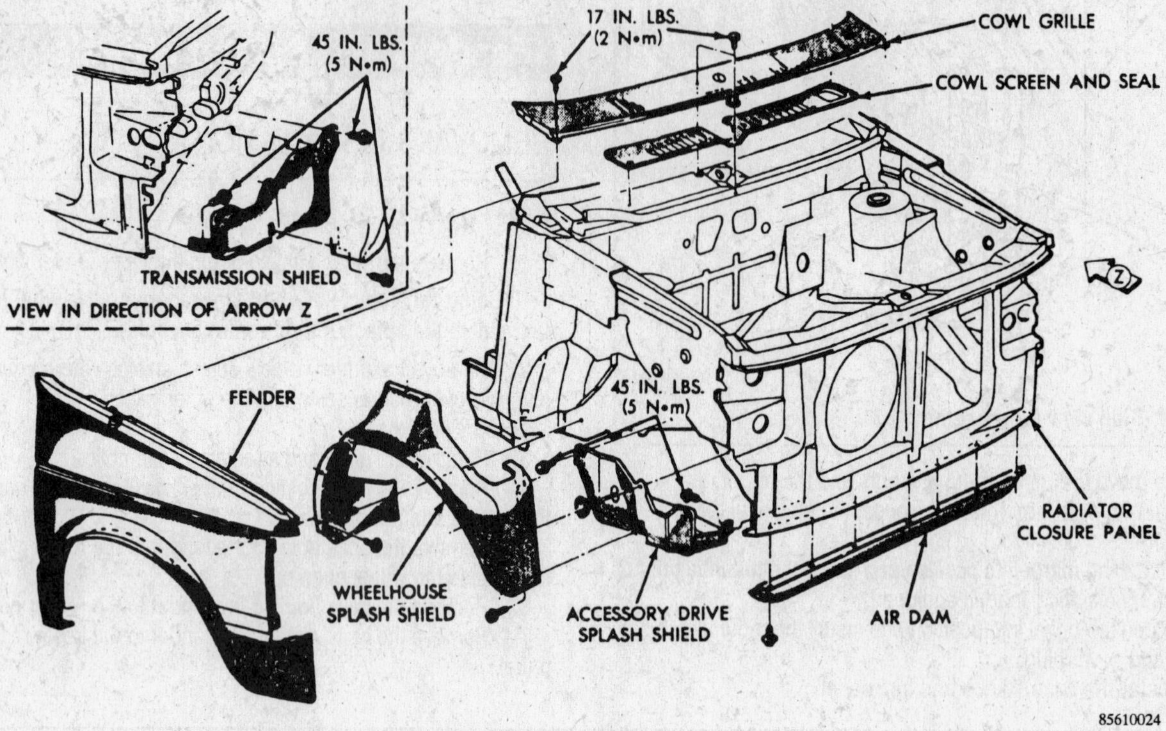

Fig. 23 Splash shield and cowl screen removal — 1984–90 models

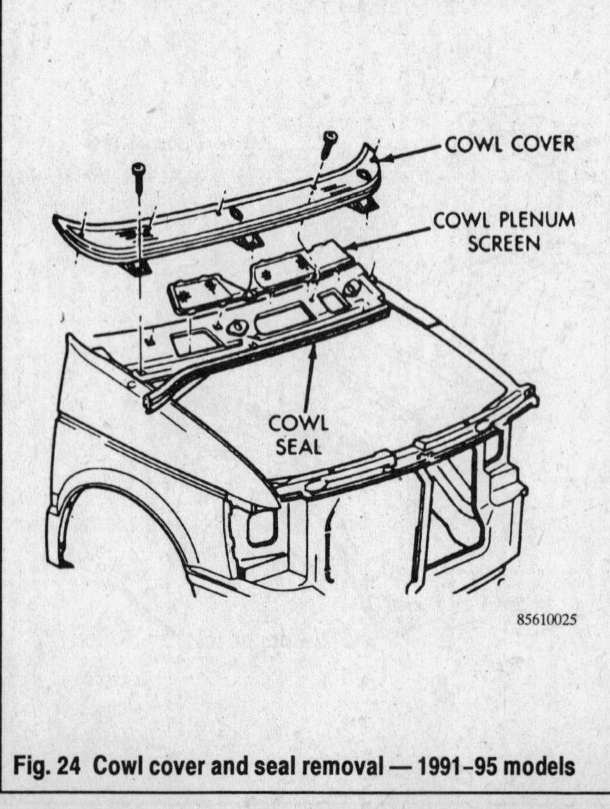

Fig. 24 Cowl cover and seal removal — 1991–95 models

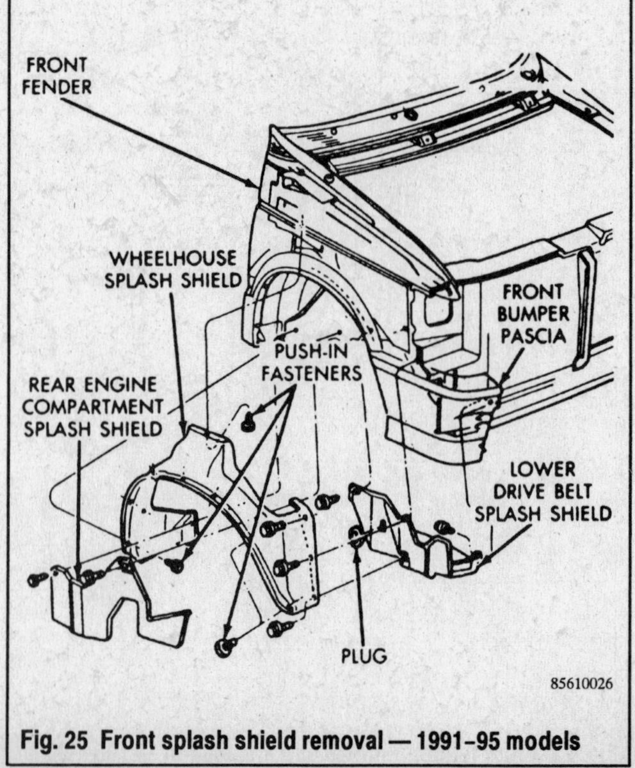

Fig. 25 Front splash shield removal — 1991–95 models

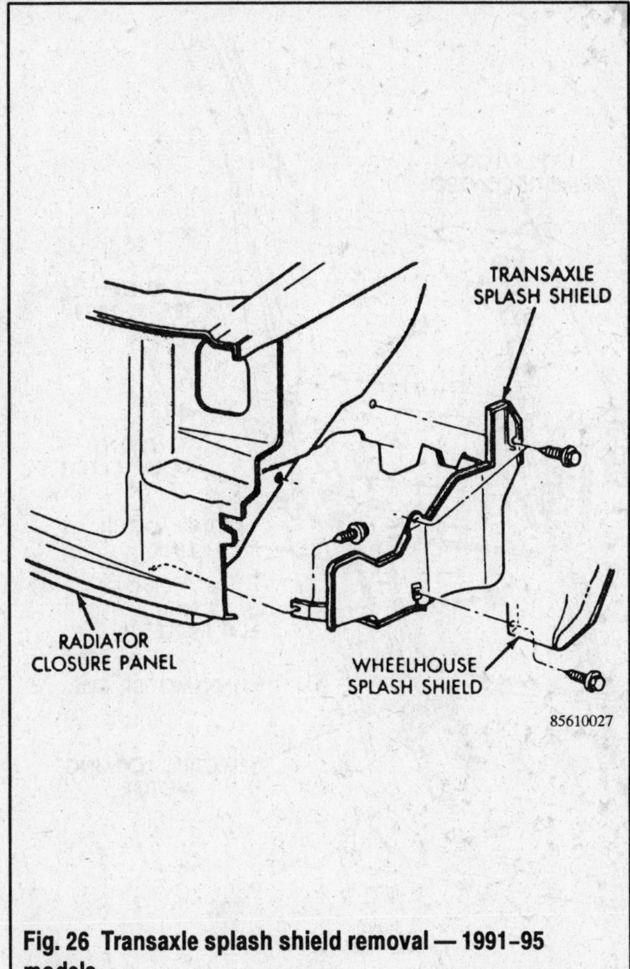

Fig. 26 Transaxle splash shield removal — 1991-95 models

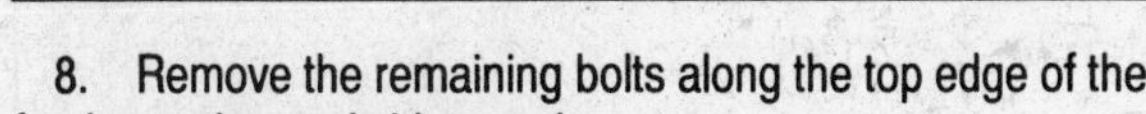

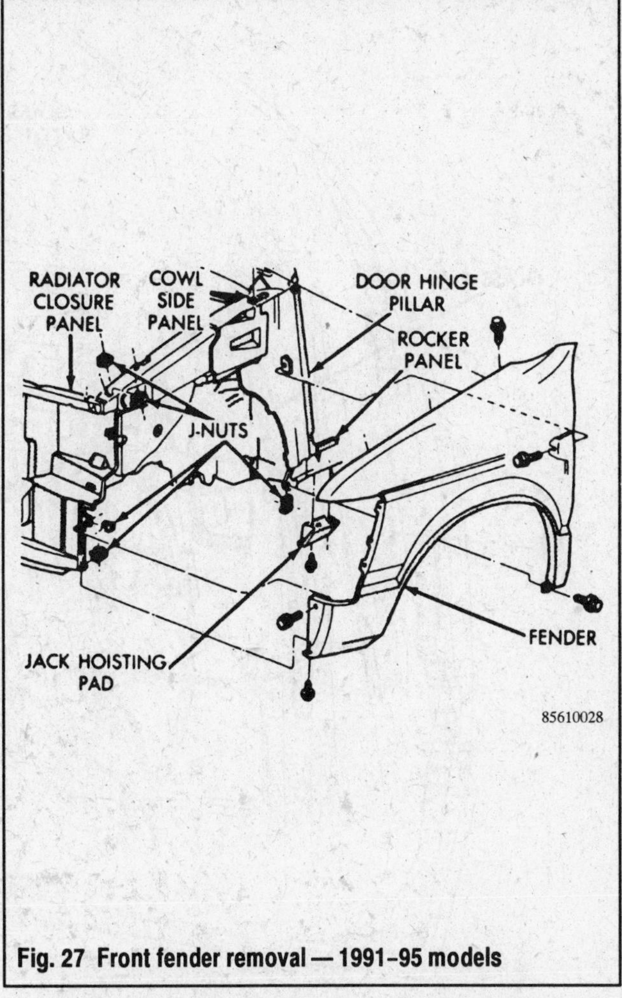

Fig. 27 Front fender removal — 1991-95 models

8. Remove the remaining bolts along the top edge of the fender on the cowl side panel.
9. Remove the fender from the vehicle.

To install:

10. Install the fender in position on the vehicle.
11. Install the fender retaining bolts, but do not tighten.
12. Align the fender to $^{1}/_{4}$ in. (6mm) gap at the door and $^{5}/_{16}$ in. (8mm) at the edge of the hood.
13. Tighten all of the fender mounting bolts.
14. Install the splash shields, using new retainers.

INTERIOR

Door Panels

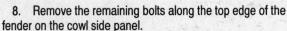

REMOVAL & INSTALLATION

➧ **See Figures 28 and 29**

1. Lower the door glass until it is 3 in. (76mm) from the full down position.
2. Unlock the door and remove the remote door latch control handle bezel by prying the front of the bezel out and rearward.
3. Remove the arm rest mounting screw, and on models with electric controls, pry out the power window switch bezel.
4. Remove the window crank handle on models with manual window regulators.
5. Remove the two edge inserts that cover the mounting screws for the door pull strap, and remove the mounting screws and strap.
6. Insert a wide flat tool between the panel and door frame and carefully twist the tool to release the retainer clips from the door.
7. If the vehicle is equipped with power locks, slide the switch bezel through the trim panel.
8. Disengage the courtesy lamp connector. Remove the door trim panel.
9. Remove the inner plastic cover and service the components as required.

To install:

10. Place sealer along the edges of the plastic liner and put the liner onto the door frame.
11. Position the trim panel, slide the power lock bezel through the panel, connect the courtesy lamp.
12. Position the panel clips over their mounting holes and push the panel against the door frame to lock the clips.
13. Install the pull strap, arm rest, widow handle/power switch, remote latch control/bezel.

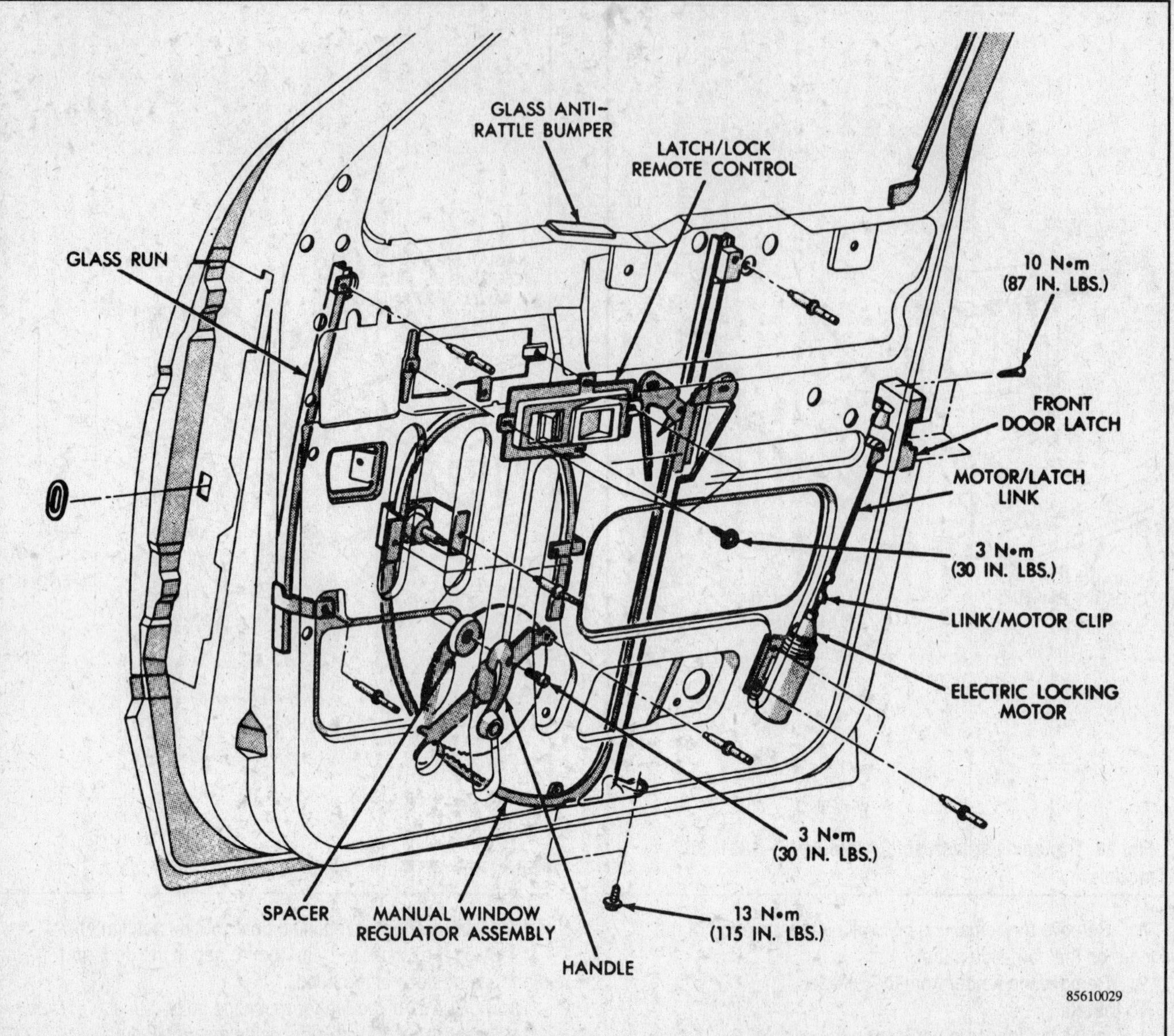

85610029

Fig. 28 Front door assembly component view — 1984-90 models

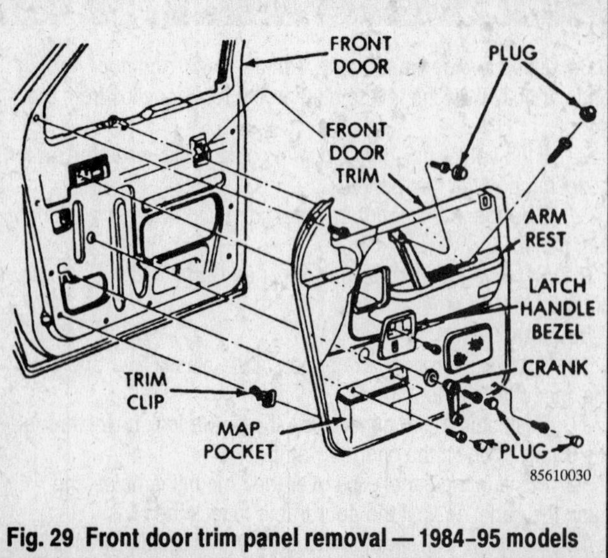

Fig. 29 Front door trim panel removal — 1984-95 models

Interior Trim Panels

REMOVAL & INSTALLATION

➧ See Figures 30, 31, 32, 33 and 34

All of the trim panels on the interior of the vehicle can be removed easily, by removing their retaining screws and separating them from each other. Almost all of the trim pieces are fastened with screws, most of the screws are visible, however a few have removable caps.

The interior trim panels can be removed without removing any of the interior components of the vehicle, such as seats, etc. Remove the panels carefully to avoid damaging them. In some cases, the trim may be attached with a hidden retaining clip. If the panel is fixed with a clip, remove it by gently prying it away from the clip.

The following is a recommended sequence for removing the trim pieces. Since the trim pieces overlap, this method of removal will avoid any damage.

1. Windshield surround trim and side garnish molding.
2. Front door scuff plate.
3. B-pillar trim, seat belt cover and seat belt assembly.
4. Sliding door upper track cover.
5. Sliding door scuff plate.
6. Liftgate scuff plate.
7. Quarter panel trim. On 1991 models, remove the upper quarter panel trim, then the lower. If equipped with rear air conditioning, remove the vents from the trim panels.

Install the trim panels by reversing the order in which they were removed. Be sure to position the panels correctly, this will help to avoid squeaks and possible warpage.

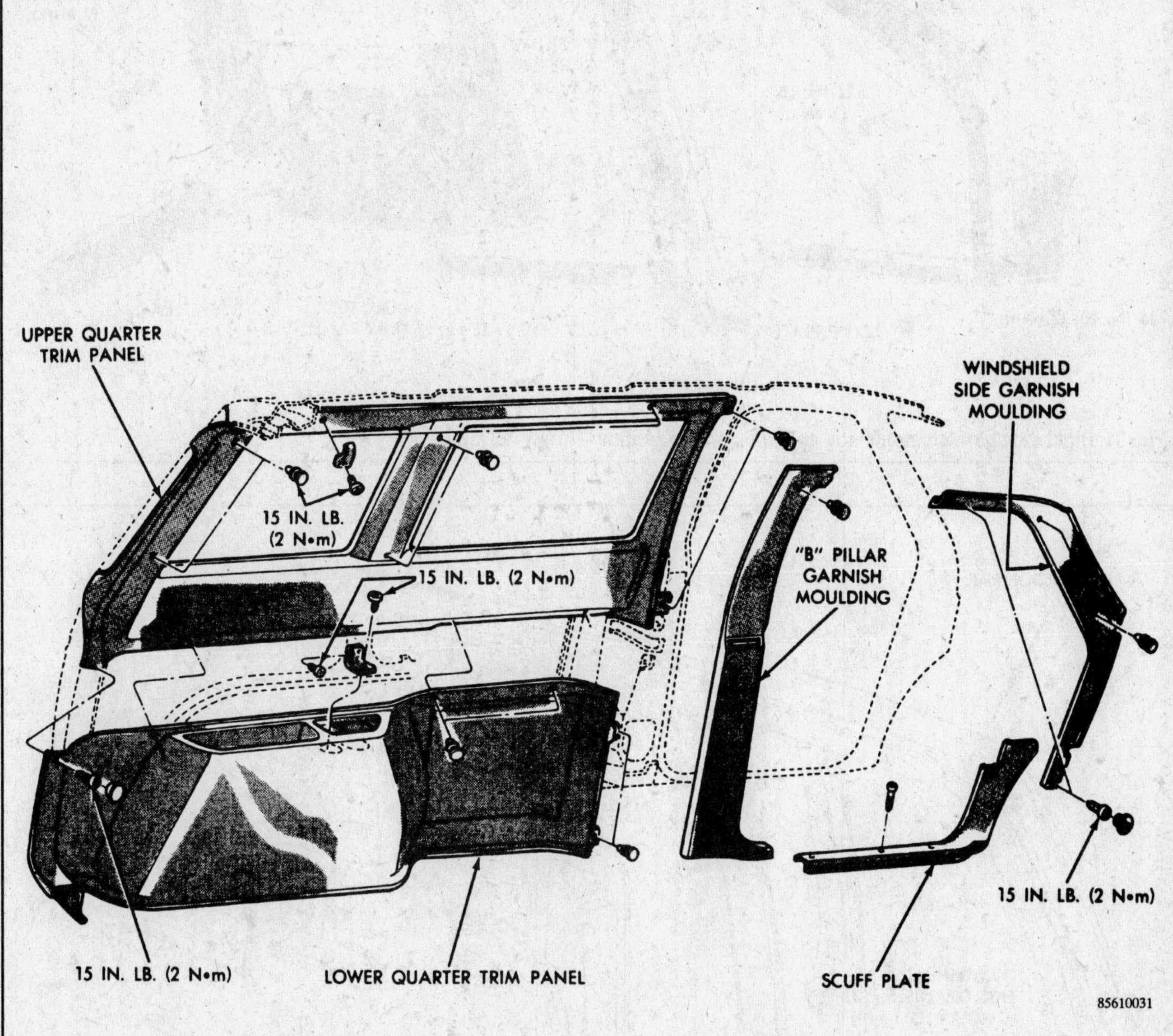

Fig. 30 Left side garnish mouldings and trim panel mounting — 1984-90 models

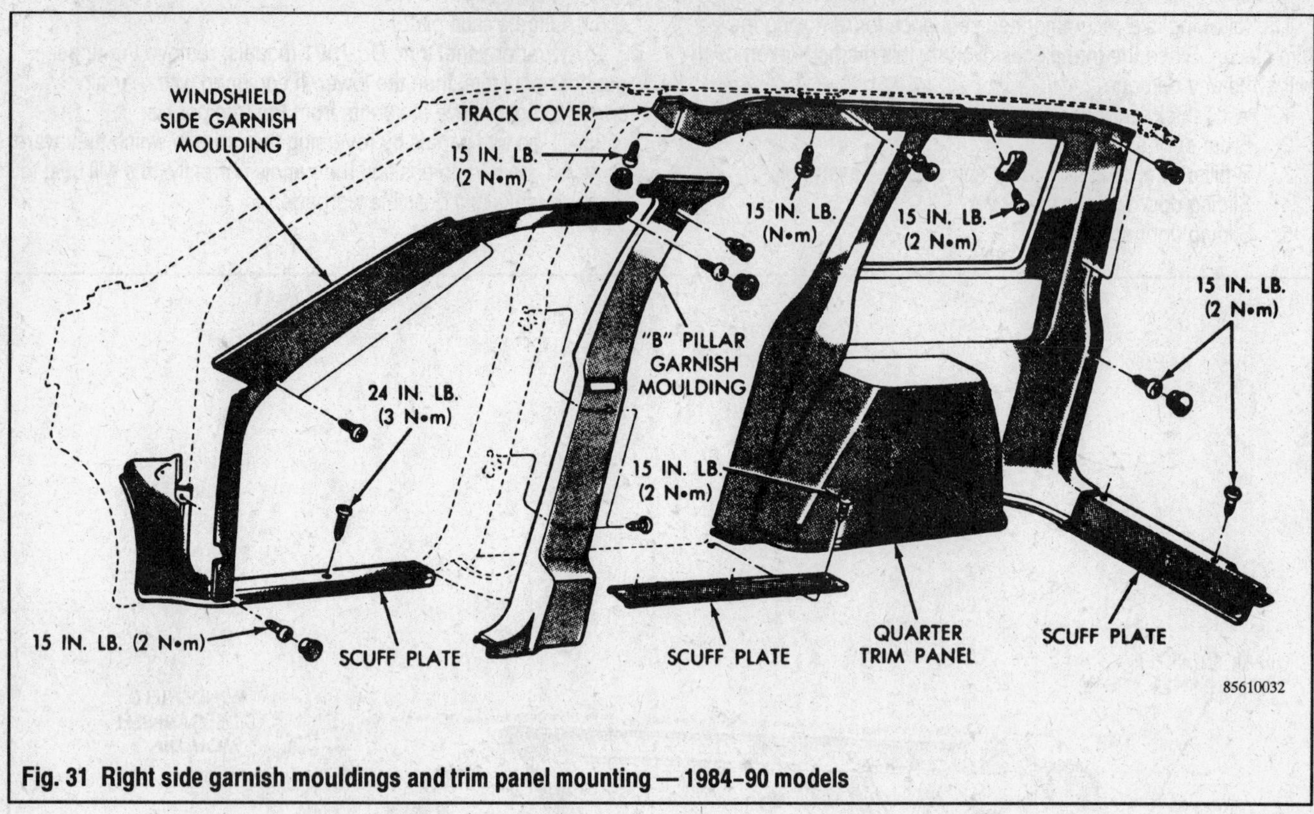

Fig. 31 Right side garnish mouldings and trim panel mounting — 1984–90 models

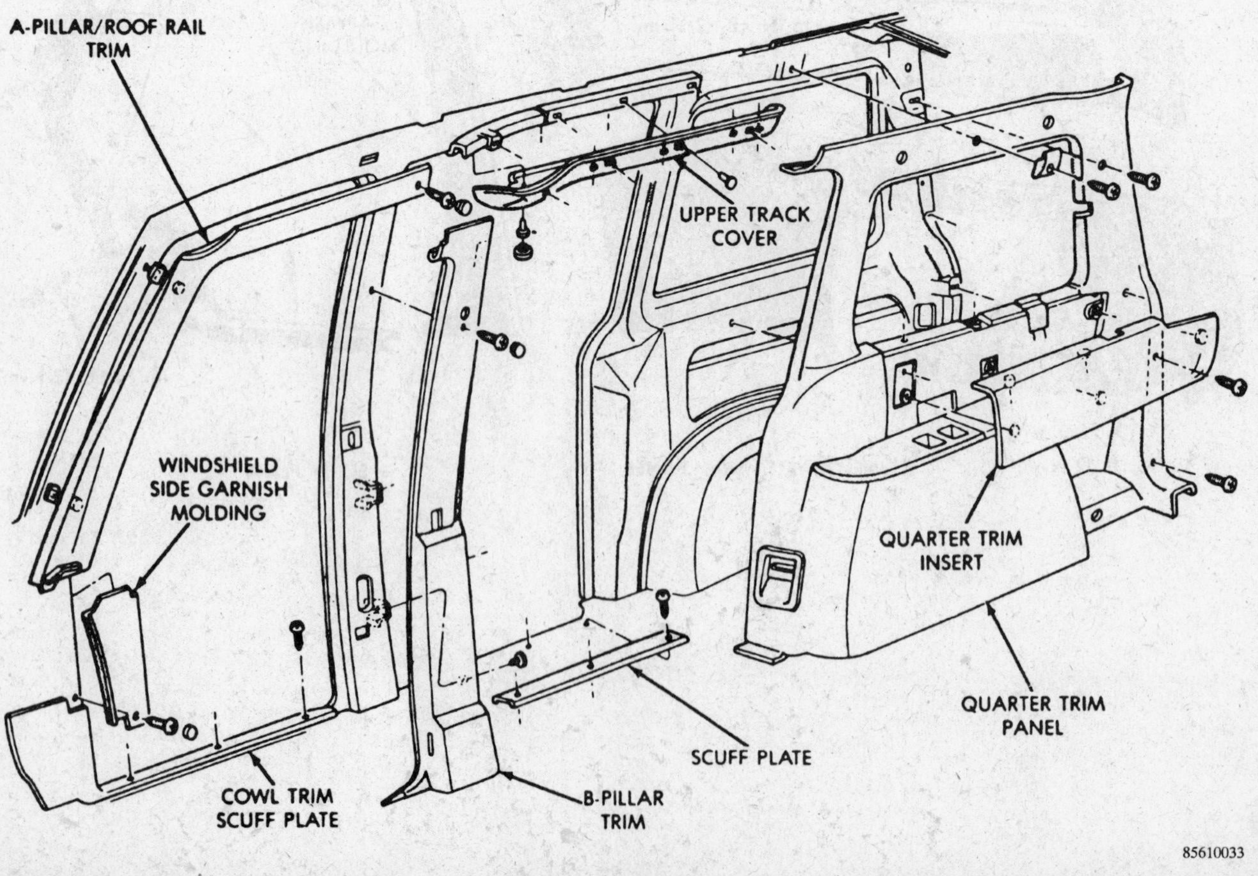

Fig. 32 Interior trim panel mounting — 1991–95 models

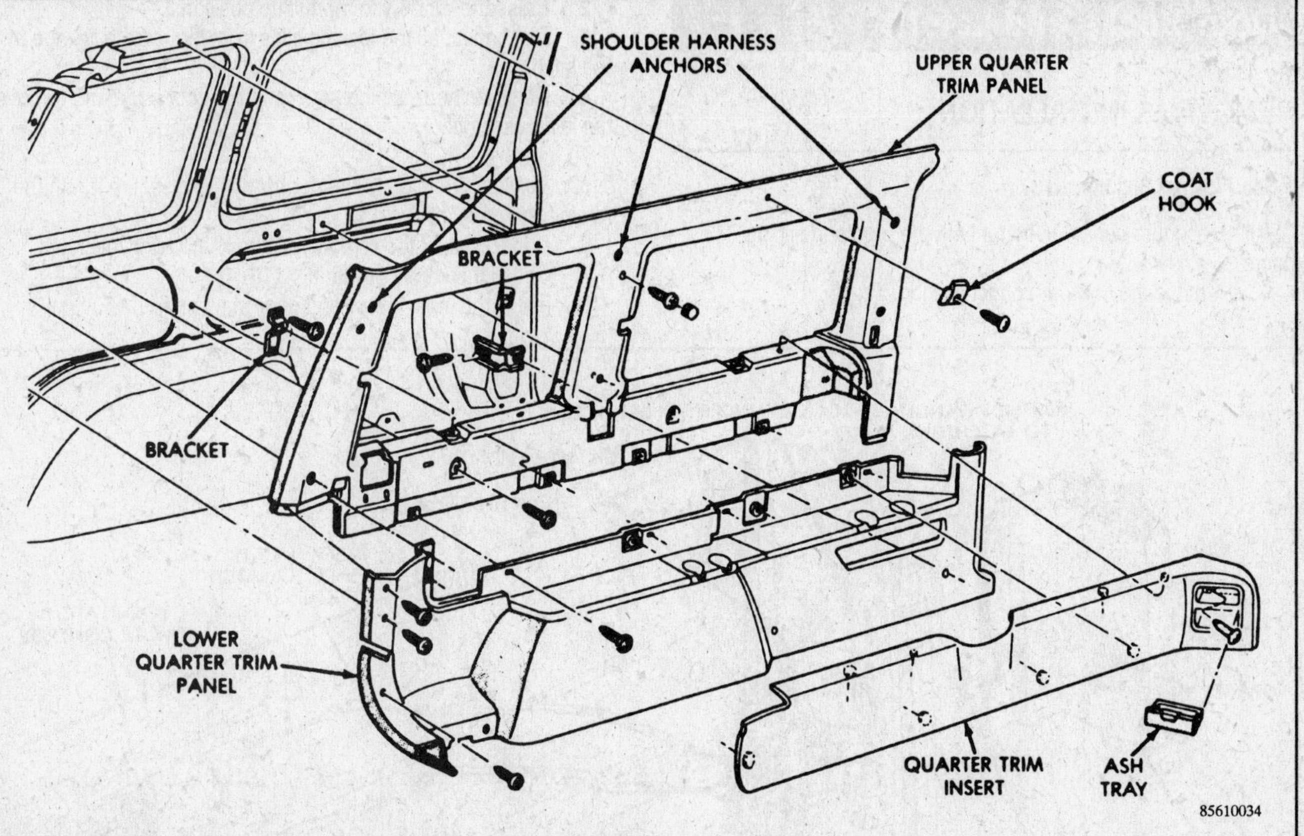

Fig. 33 Interior quarter trim panel mounting — 1991–95 models

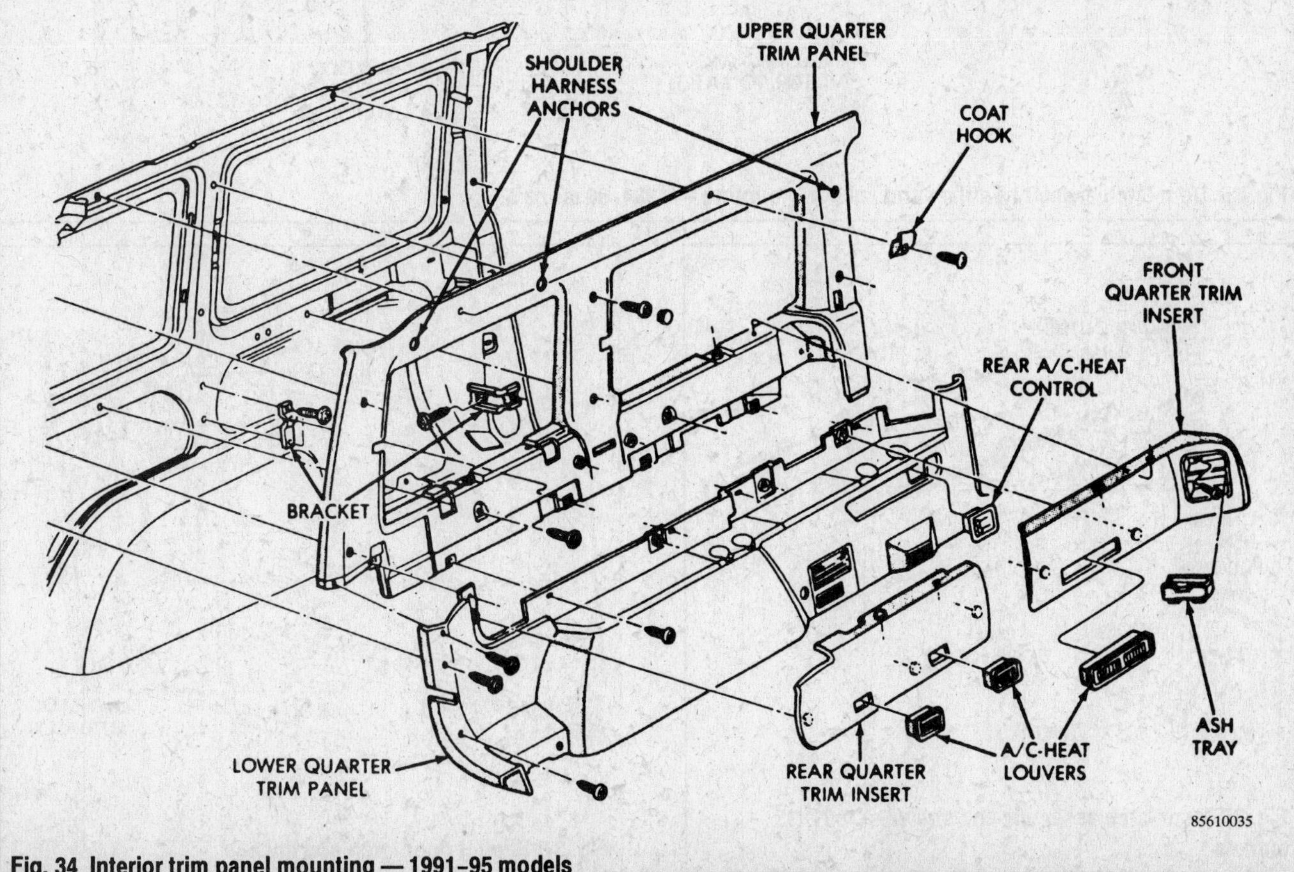

Fig. 34 Interior trim panel mounting — 1991–95 models

Door Locks and Latch

REMOVAL & INSTALLATION

➧ **See Figures 35, 36 and 37**

This procedure can be used for both the front and sliding doors.

1. Remove the door trim panel and inner cover.
2. Raise the window to the full up position.
3. Disconnect all the locking clips from the remote linkage at the latch.
4. Remove the retaining screws at the door edge and remove the latch assembly.

To install:

5. Position the latch to the door frame and secure it with the retaining screws.
6. Connect all of the remote linkage to the latch levers.
7. Check the latch operation.
8. Install the inner cover and door trim panel.

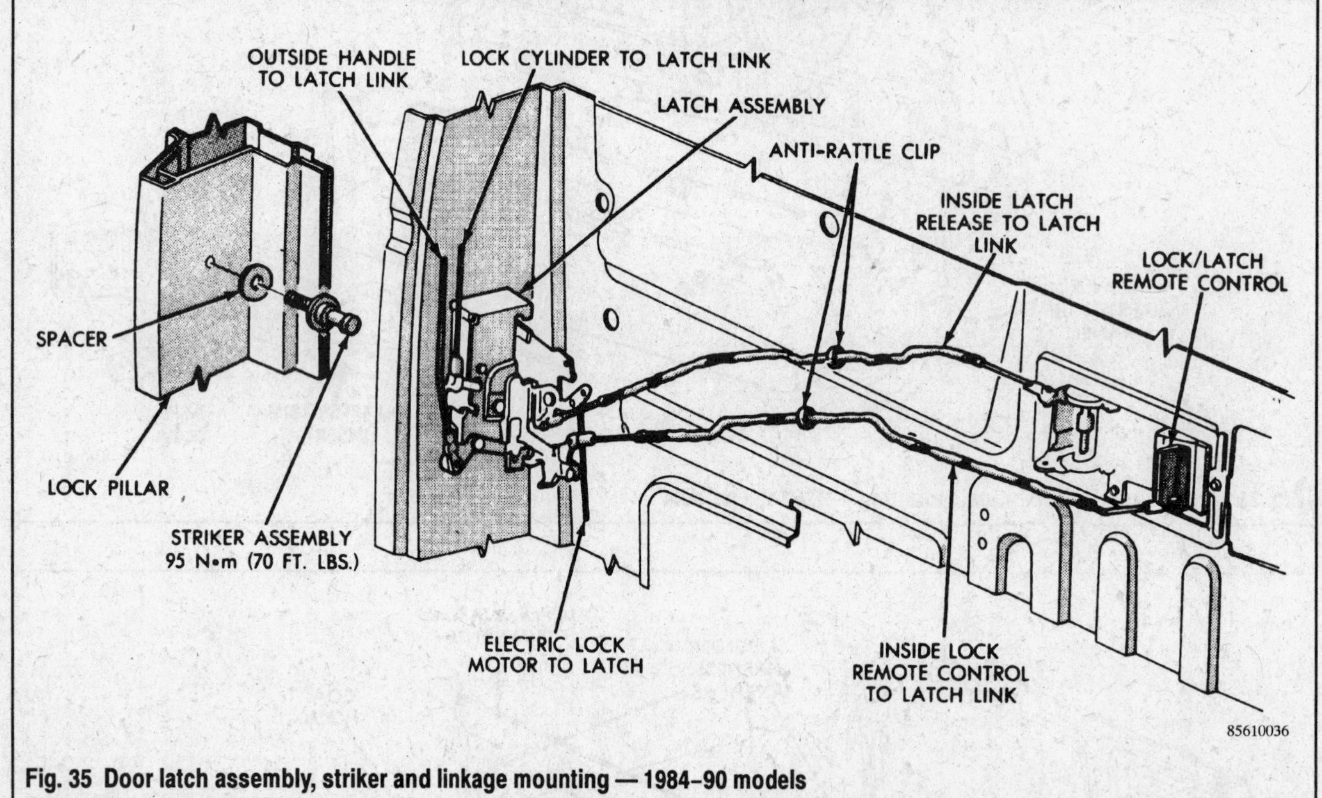

Fig. 35 Door latch assembly, striker and linkage mounting — 1984–90 models

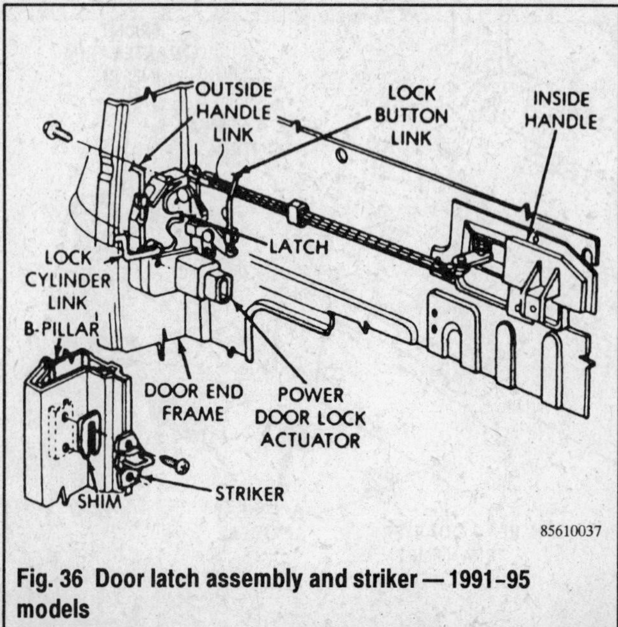

Fig. 36 Door latch assembly and striker — 1991–95 models

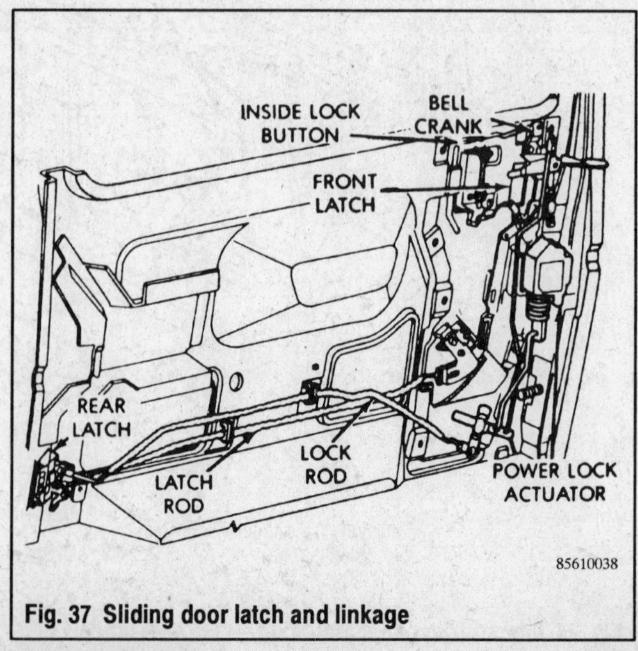

Fig. 37 Sliding door latch and linkage

Door Glass Regulator

REMOVAL & INSTALLATION

➧ **See Figures 38, 39, 40 and 41**

1. Remove the door trim panel and inner liner.
2. Remove the window glass from the regulator and the door.
3. If equipped with power windows, disconnect the wiring harness and remove the retainer clip.
4. Drill out the regulator mounting rivets. Their are five on vehicles equipped with electric windows, and six if equipped with manual windows.
5. Remove the regulator through the larger access hole. Rotate the regulator through the hole as required for removal.

To install:

6. Install the regulator to the mounting holes using $^{1}/_{4}$–20 X $^{1}/_{2}$ in. long screws and nuts. Tighten the screws to 90 inch lbs. (10 Nm).
7. Install the window glass, connect the motor wiring harness, and install the inner liner and door trim panel.

➝ The window glass is mounted to the regulator by two mounting studs and nuts. Raise the glass until the mounting nuts align with the large access hole. Remove the nuts. Raise the glass up through the door frame. Rotate the glass so that the mounting studs pass through the notch at the rear of the door and remove the glass from the door.

Electric Window Motor

REMOVAL & INSTALLATION

1. Remove the window regulator. For more details, refer to the window regulator procedure in this section.
2. Remove the electric motor mounting screws, then extract the motor from the door.

To install:

3. Position the window motor into the door, then secure it in place with the mounting screws.
4. Install the window regulator.

Inside Rear View Mirror

REPLACEMENT

The mirror is mechanically attached to the mirror button, and if it should become cracked or develop a mechanical problem which prevents easy adjustment, it can be replaced very simply by disconnecting it from the button. The button, in turn, serves to mount the mirror to the windshield. If it should be damaged or the adhesive bond should become partly broken, it can be removed and replaced after the mirror is detached. Note that removal of the button and/or remaining adhesive requires the use of a controllable electric heat gun. Also needed, if the button must be replaced, are a rag soaked in alcohol, ordinary kitchen cleanser, and fine-grit sandpaper. The new button is installed using a special adhesive kit 4054099 or an equivalent available in the aftermarket.

1. Loosen the setscrew with a standard screwdriver until all tension is removed. Slide the base of the mirror upward and off the mounting button.
2. If the mirror mounting button must be removed, first mark the location of the button on the outside of the windshield with a wax pencil. Then, apply low heat with the electric heat gun to soften the vinyl. When it is soft, peel the button off the glass.
3. Clean the surface of the windshield where the button was mounted with a rag soaked in alcohol and the cleanser. Then, wipe the surface with an alcohol soaked rag. Do not touch this area of the windshield glass!
4. Crush the vial in the plastic housing of the accelerator in the new button kit to saturate the applicator.
5. Remove the paper sleeve and then apply a generous amount of the accelerator to the onto the mounting surface of the mirror button.

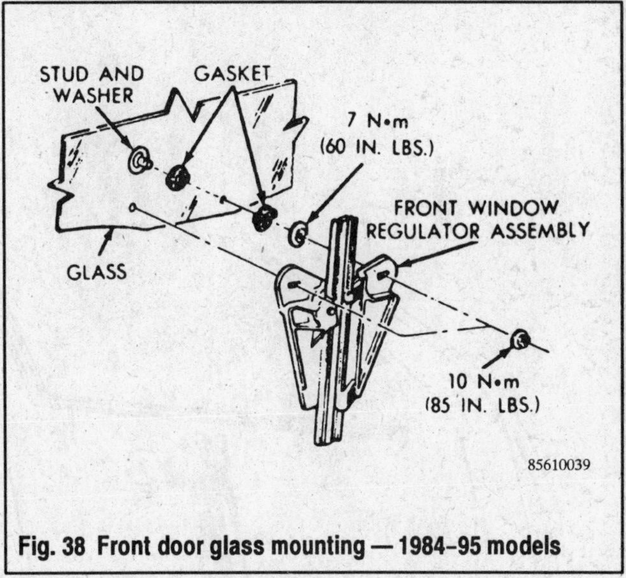

Fig. 38 Front door glass mounting — 1984–95 models

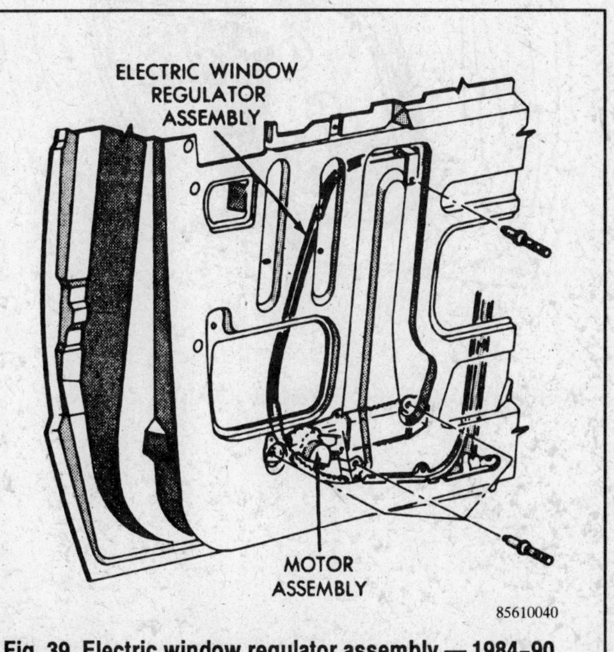

Fig. 39 Electric window regulator assembly — 1984–90 models

6. Allow the accelerator to dry for 5 minutes; during this time, be careful not to touch the mounting surface of the button.

7. Apply a thin film of the accelerator to the inner surface of the windshield where the button will be mounted. Allow this to dry for 1 minute.

8. Apply one drop of the adhesive to the center of the mounting surface of the button. Then, use the bottom of the adhesive tube, distribute the adhesive evenly over the entire button bonding surface.

➞ Precise alignment of the button is essential in the following step from the beginning, as the adhesive sets up very fast!

9. Position the bottom edge of the button against the lower edge of the mark made earlier with the button lined up side-to-side. Then, rock the button upward until it touches the windshield over its entire surface. Press it firmly to the glass and hold it there firmly for 1 full minute.

10. Remove the pressure, but allow 5 minutes more time for the button mounting adhesive to dry.

11. With an alcohol-dampened cloth, remove any adhesive which may have spread beyond the mounting surface of the button.

➞ Be careful not to over-tighten the mirror mounting screw in the following procedure, as the mirror mounting button could be distorted, destroying its bond with the windshield.

12. Slide the mirror downward and over the mount. Tighten the screw gently!

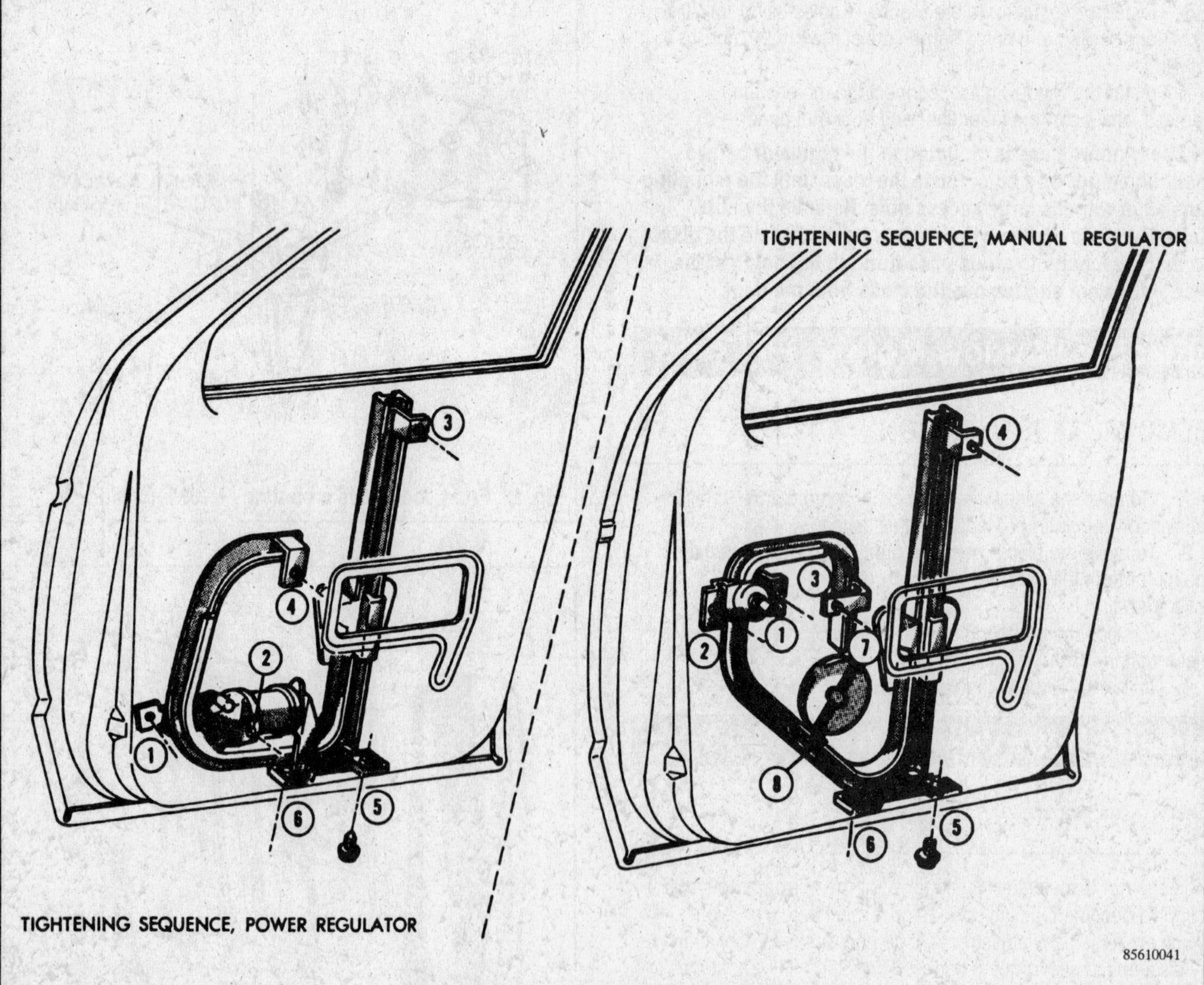

Fig. 40 Window regulator tightening sequence — 1984–90 models

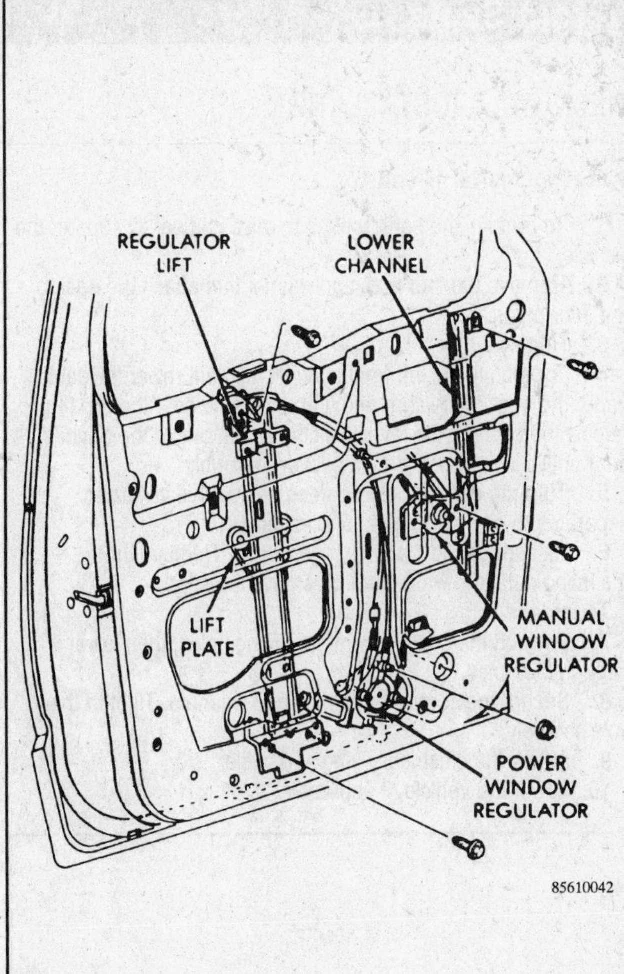

Fig. 41 Window regulator components — 1991-95 models

Windshield Glass

REMOVAL & INSTALLATION

➧ See Figures 42, 43 and 44

➥ The removal and installation of the windshield must be done carefully, improper installation can cause the windshield to crack or shatter. An assistant must be used to insure that the windshield is positioned properly in the opening.

1. Remove the inside rearview mirror.
2. Remove the cowl cover and the windshield moldings. The moldings can be removed by pulling upward.
3. Cut the urethane bonding from around the windshield using a sharp knife. Separate the windshield from the vehicle.

To install:

4. Clean the windshield area of old urethane bonding that may be loose. Clean the support spacers and reposition them on the studs.
5. With the aid of a helper, place the replacement windshield in the opening and position in the center of the opening. Mark the glass at the supports, once it is centered, using a grease pencil or masking tape. This will help position it properly.
6. Remove the windshield from the opening and place it on a suitable support, clean the inside of the glass. Apply clear glass primer in a 1 in. (25mm) path around the perimeter of the windshield and wipe with a clean cloth.
7. Apply a 0.6 in. (15mm) wide path of blackout primer around the top and sides of the windshield. Apply a 1 in. (25mm) path to the bottom of the windshield. Allow 3 minutes drying time.
8. Position the windshield bonding compression spacers around the opening for the windshield.
9. Apply a 10mm bead of urethane around the inside of the opening.
10. With the aid of a helper, install the windshield glass in position, aligning the reference marks made earlier. Push the windshield into position until it bottoms on the spacers and the top molding is flush with the roof line.
11. Clean any excess urethane from the glass using a suitable solvent. Install the moldings.
12. Use pieces of masking tape around the windshield to hold the moulding until the urethane cures.
13. Install the cowl cover and the inside mirror.
14. When the urethane cures, remove the tape and water test the windshield for leaks.

Stationary Glass

REMOVAL & INSTALLATION

All of the fixed glass in the vehicle is removed and installed in the same manner as the windshield glass.

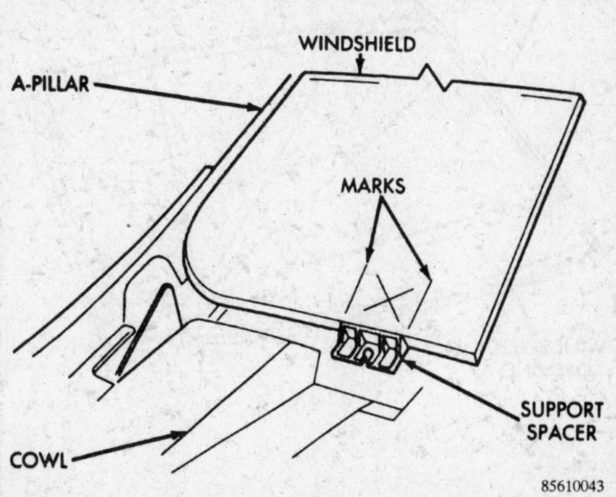

Fig. 42 Center the windshield and mark it at the support spacers

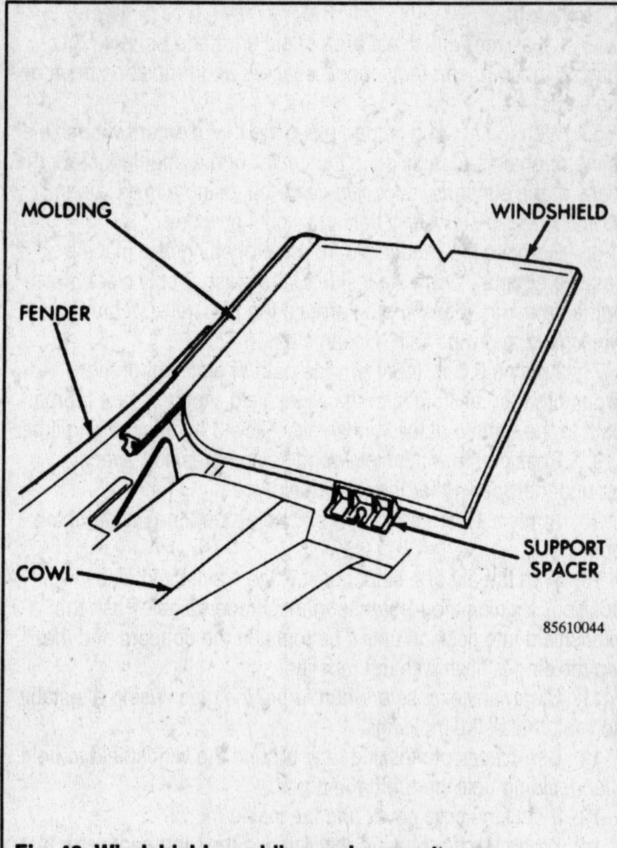

Fig. 43 Windshield moulding and support spacer

Fig. 44 Correct positioning of the urethane compression spacers

Front Seats

REMOVAL & INSTALLATION

➧ **See Figures 45, 46 and 47**

1. To remove the right front seat; raise and safely support the vehicle.
2. Remove the four nuts and washer that attach the seat to the floor pan.
3. Remove the seat.
4. To remove the left front seat: tilt the seat reward. Reach under the front of the seat and grab the cable near the clip that retains the cable to the lever. Pull the cable toward the driver's door until it is released from the lever assembly.
5. Turn the cable ninety degrees and push it inward to separate the cable from the lever assembly.
6. Disengage the electrical connectors. Remove the mounting nuts and washers and remove the seat.

To install:

7. Position the seat over the mounting holes, then lower it through the holes.
8. Secure the seat with the nuts and washers. Tighten the nuts securely.
9. Attach the electrical wiring and cable.
10. Lower the vehicle, if applicable.

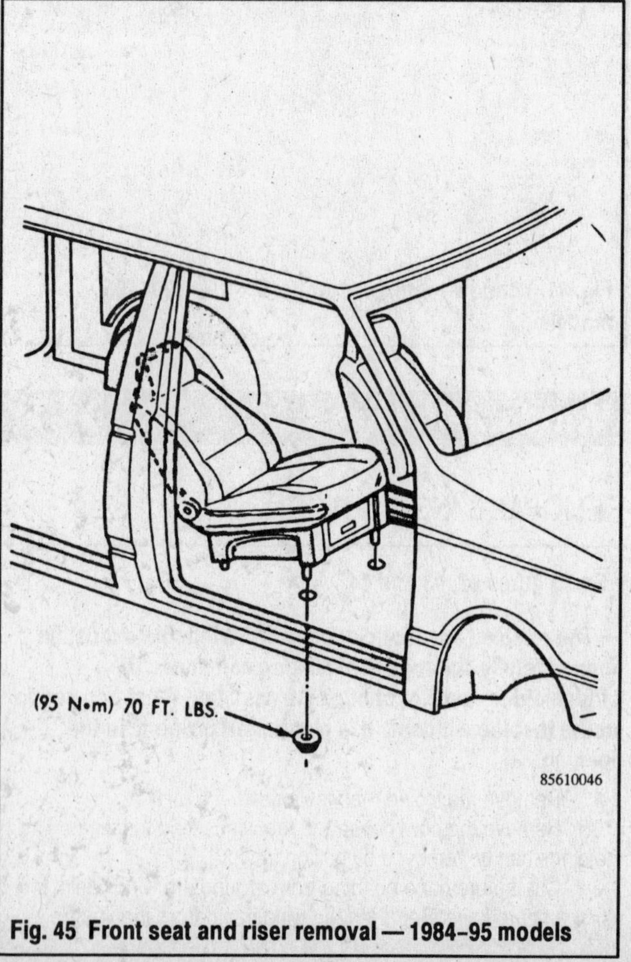

Fig. 45 Front seat and riser removal — 1984-95 models

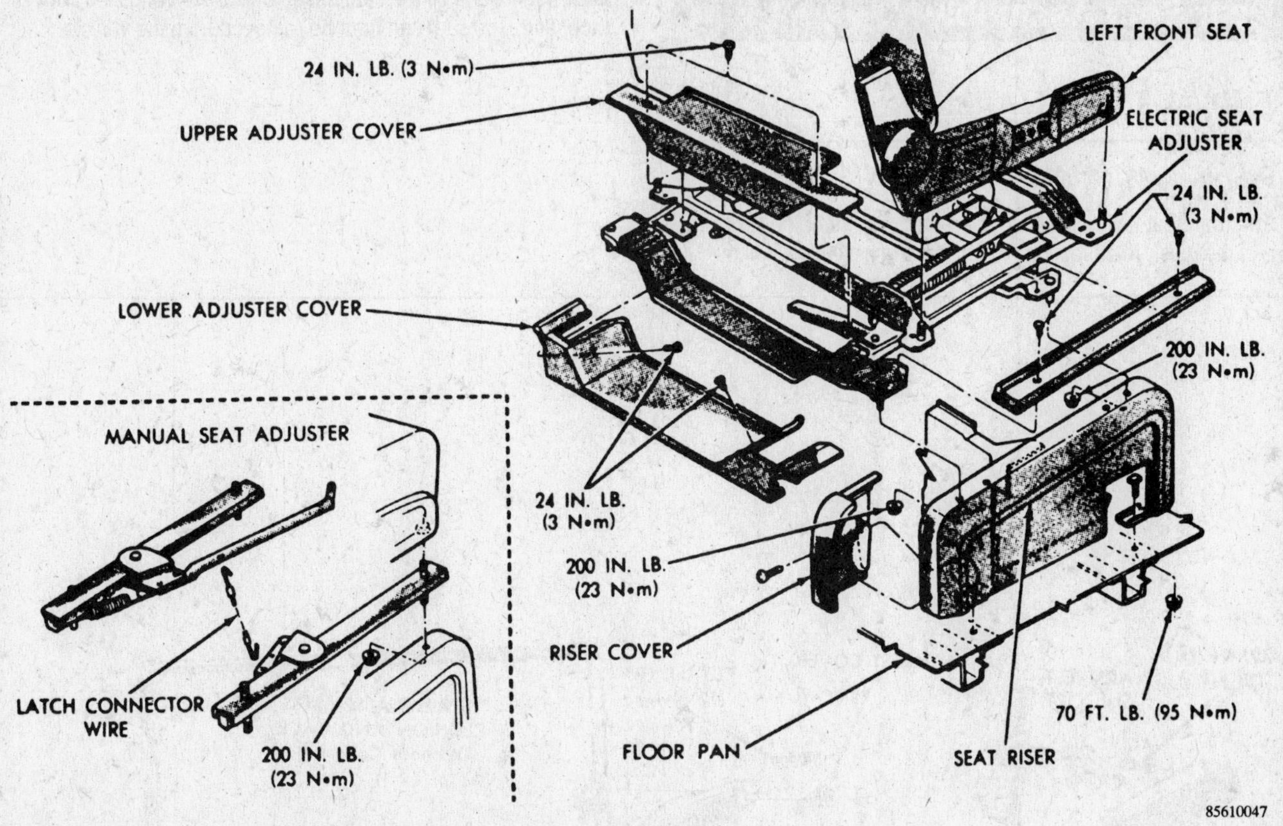

Fig. 46 Left front seat track and riser assembly — 1984–90 models shown

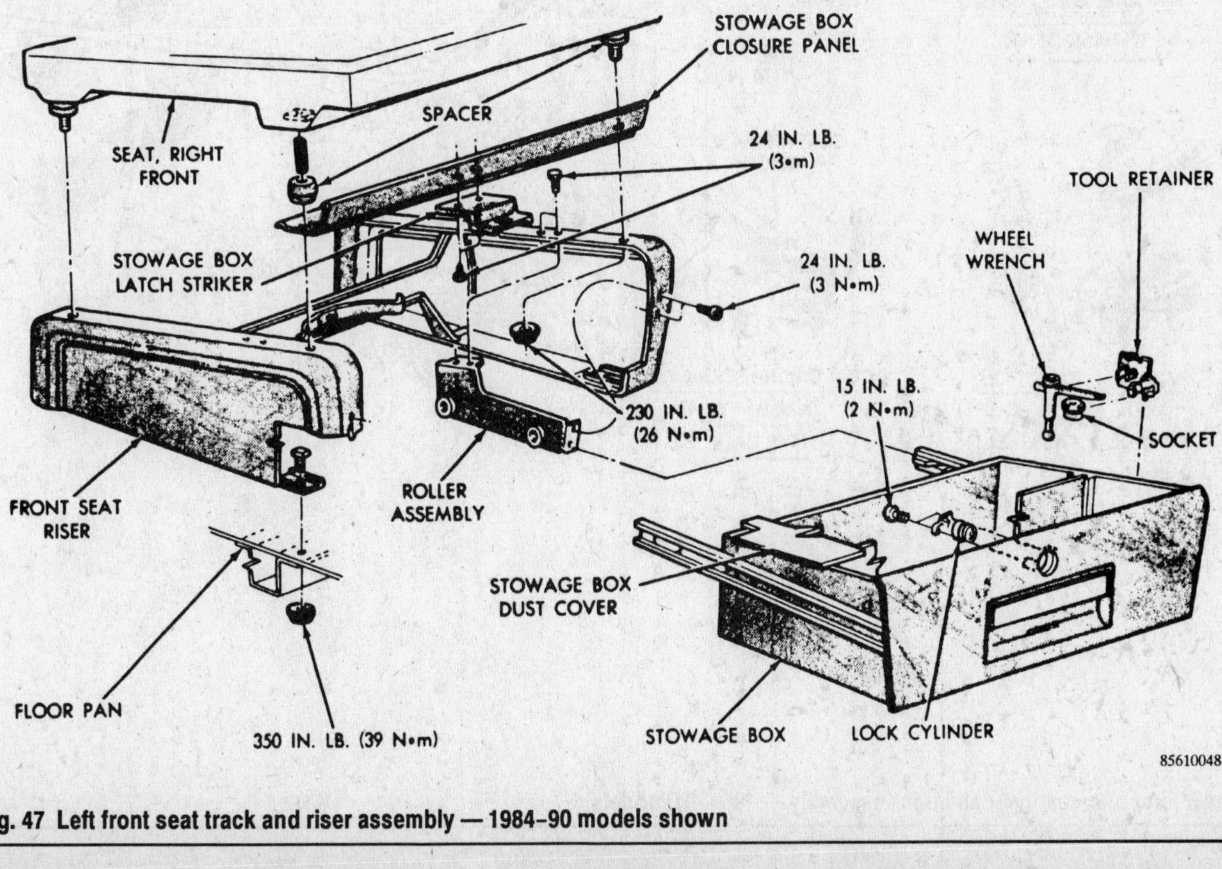

Fig. 47 Left front seat track and riser assembly — 1984–90 models shown

Rear Seat Assembly

REMOVAL & INSTALLATION

➧ See Figures 48, 49, 50, 51 and 52

The rear seat assemblies can be removed without tools. They are of the quick-release kind. To remove the assembly, pull the latch handle and tilt the seat assembly forward and lift it from its mounting. The seat can then be removed from the vehicle.

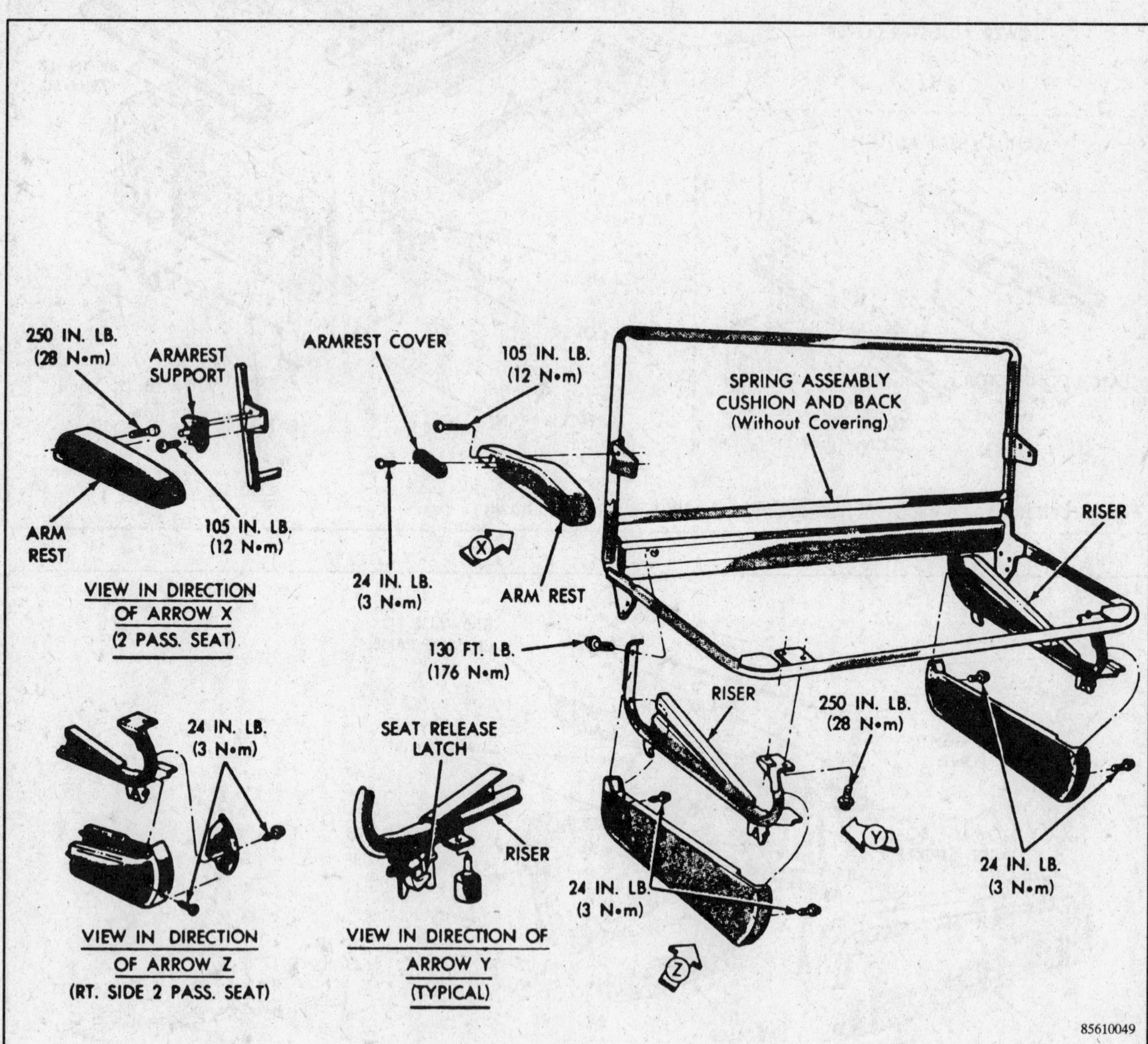

Fig. 48 First rear seat riser and track assembly — 1984–91 models

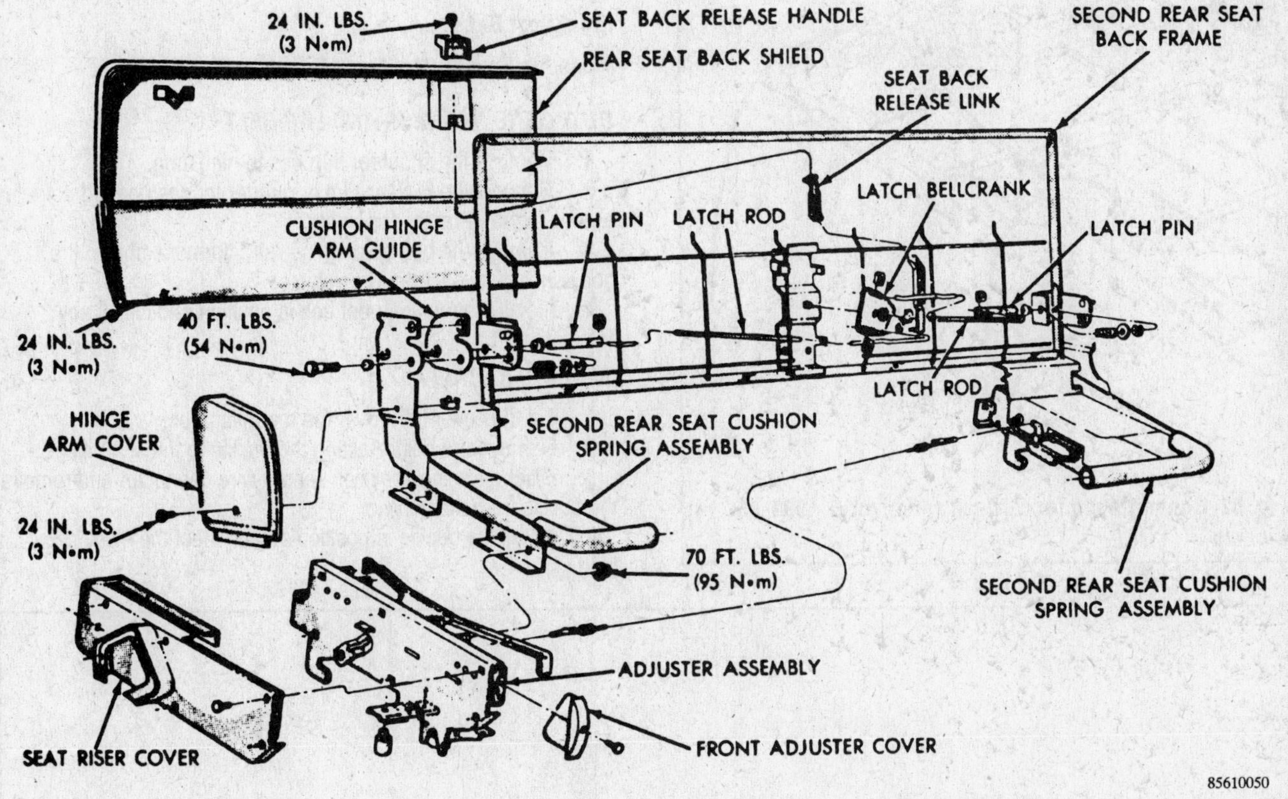

24 IN. LBS.
(3 N•m)
SEAT BACK RELEASE HANDLE
SECOND REAR SEAT
BACK FRAME
REAR SEAT BACK SHIELD
SEAT BACK
RELEASE LINK
LATCH BELLCRANK
CUSHION HINGE
ARM GUIDE
LATCH PIN
LATCH ROD
LATCH PIN
24 IN. LBS.
(3 N•m)
40 FT. LBS.
(54 N•m)
LATCH ROD
HINGE
ARM COVER
SECOND REAR SEAT CUSHION
SPRING ASSEMBLY
24 IN. LBS.
(3 N•m)
70 FT. LBS.
(95 N•m)
SECOND REAR SEAT CUSHION
SPRING ASSEMBLY
ADJUSTER ASSEMBLY
FRONT ADJUSTER COVER
SEAT RISER COVER
85610050

Fig. 49 Second rear seat riser and track assembly — 1984-91 models

TRACK
RISER
SEAT
FRAME
85610051

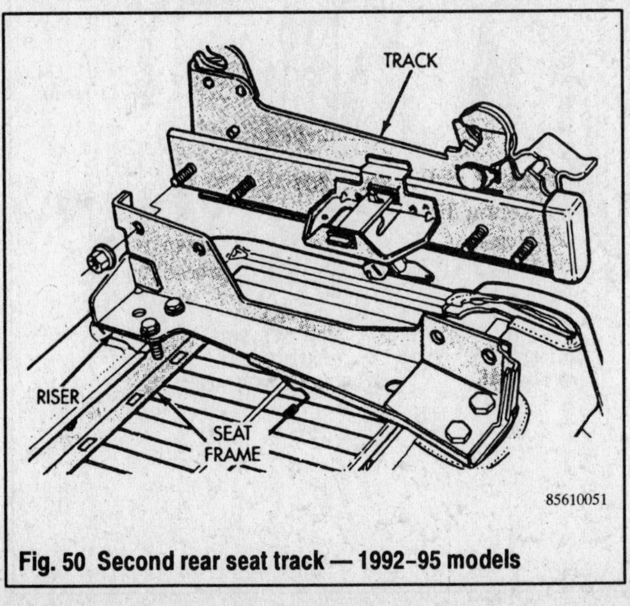

Fig. 50 Second rear seat track — 1992-95 models

RISER
FORWARD
RAIL
PIVOT
BRACKET
85610052

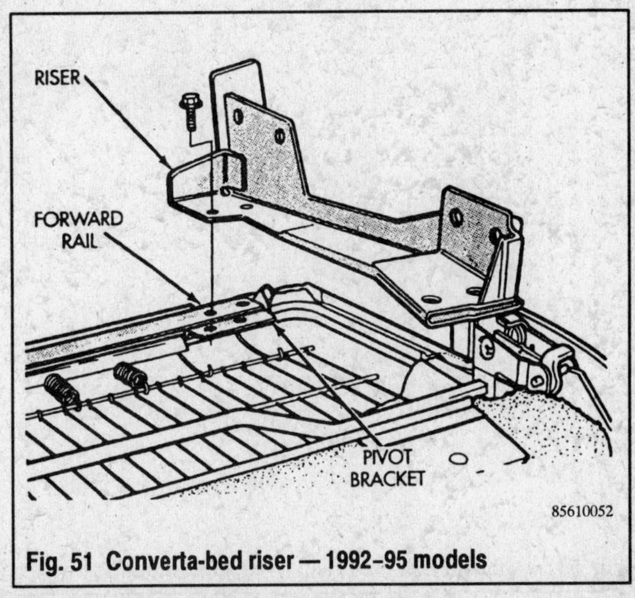

Fig. 51 Converta-bed riser — 1992-95 models

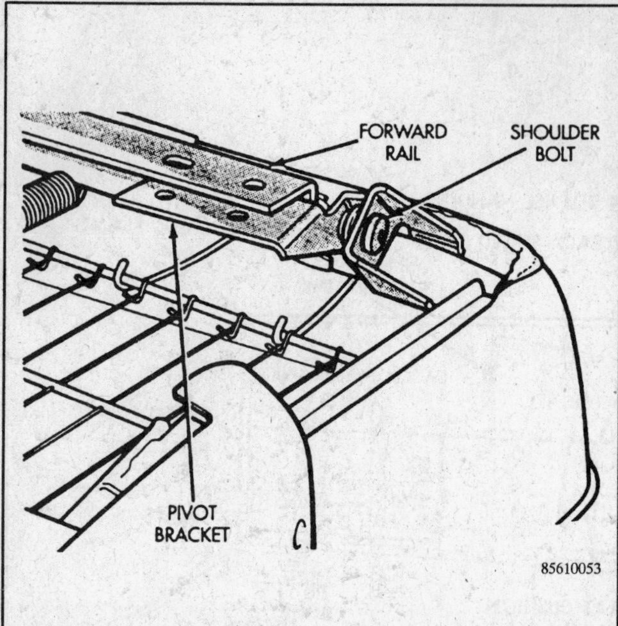

Fig. 52 Converta-bed forward rail and pivot — 1992–95 models

Seat Belt Systems

REMOVAL & INSTALLATION

Front Seat Belts

➧ **See Figures 53, 54, 55 and 56**

OUTBOARD HARNESS AND LAP BELT

1. Remove the shoulder harness turning loop.
2. Remove the B-pillar trim or quarter trim as needed, to gain access to the retractor assembly.
3. Remove the bolt holding the retractor assembly to the body and remove it from the vehicle.
4. Install the replacement belt in position and install any removed trim.

INBOARD BUCKLE

1. Lift the cover from over the mounting bolt.
2. Remove the bolt retaining the buckle to the seat riser.
3. Disengage the seat belt sensor wire connector and remove the buckle from the vehicle.
4. Install the buckle in position and connect the electrical lead.

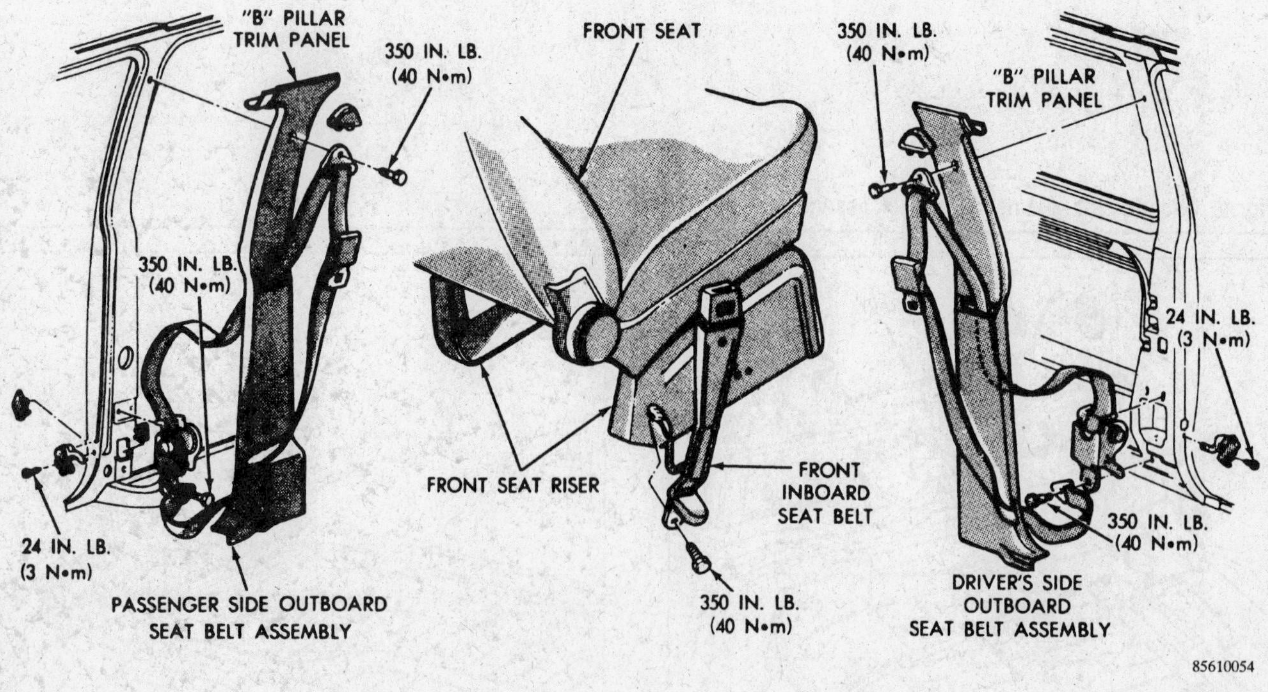

Fig. 53 Front seat belt mounting — 1984–90 models

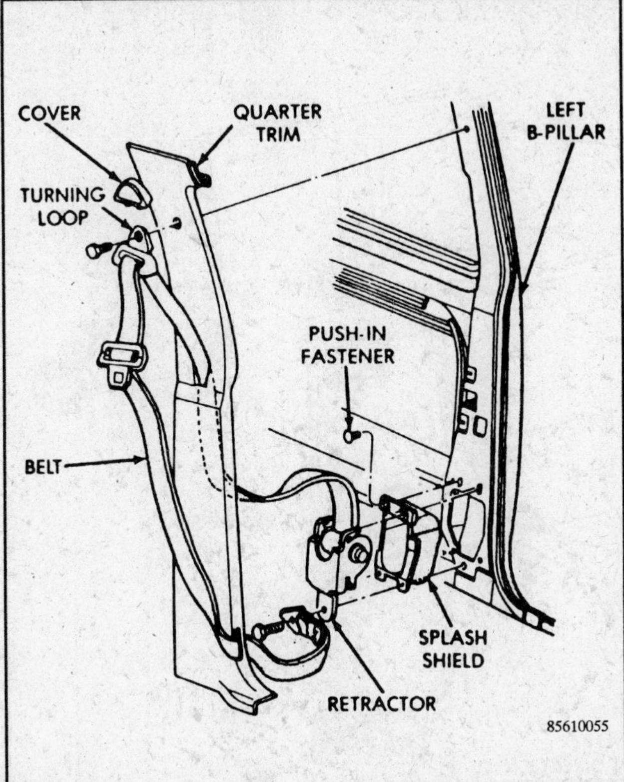

Fig. 54 Left front outboard seat belt mounting — 1991-95 models

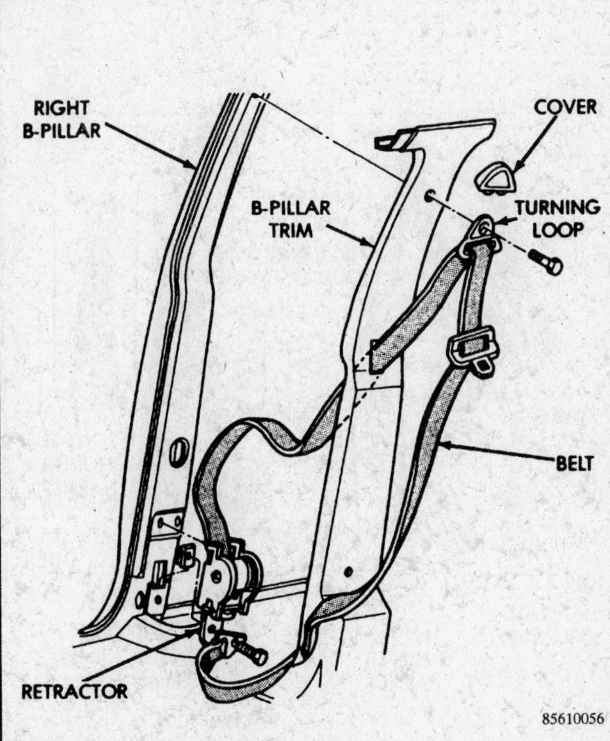

Fig. 55 Right front outboard seat belt mounting — 1991-95 models

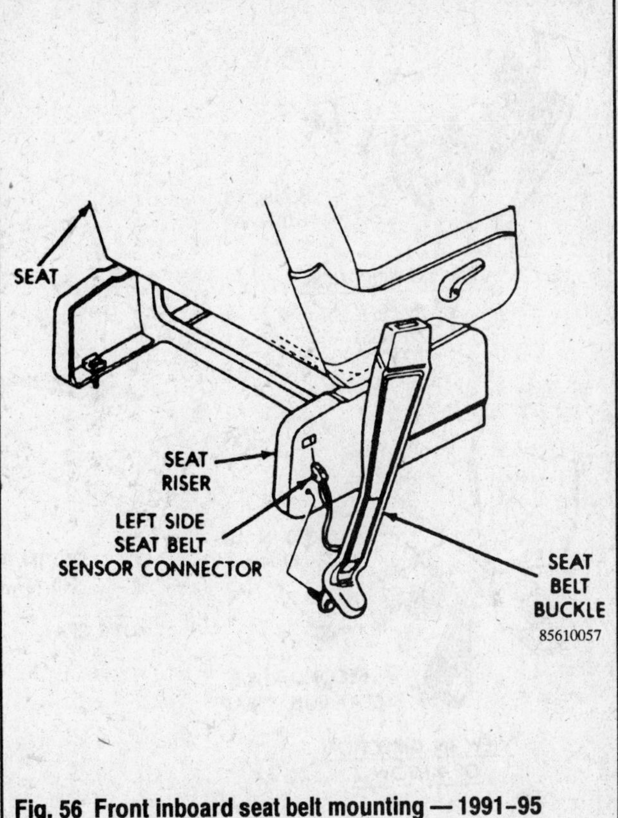

Fig. 56 Front inboard seat belt mounting — 1991-95 models

Rear Seat Belts

1984-90 MODELS

➧ See Figure 57

The rear seat belts in these vehicles are attached to the seat assembly mounting. The belt assemblies are retained by 1 bolt each. Remove the mounting bolt to remove the assembly. When installing replacement belts, tighten all mounting bolts to 30 ft. lbs. (40 Nm).

1991-95 MODELS

➧ See Figures 58 and 59

The seat belt assemblies in these vehicles are 3 point types mounted to the body in the same manner as the front belts.

1. Remove the interior trim as needed to gain access to the retractor assembly.
2. Remove the bolt holding the lower lap belt anchor to the floor bracket.
3. Remove the bolt retaining the retractor assembly to the inner quarter panel.
4. Remove the belt assembly from the vehicle.
5. Install the replacement belt in position and install any trim that was removed.

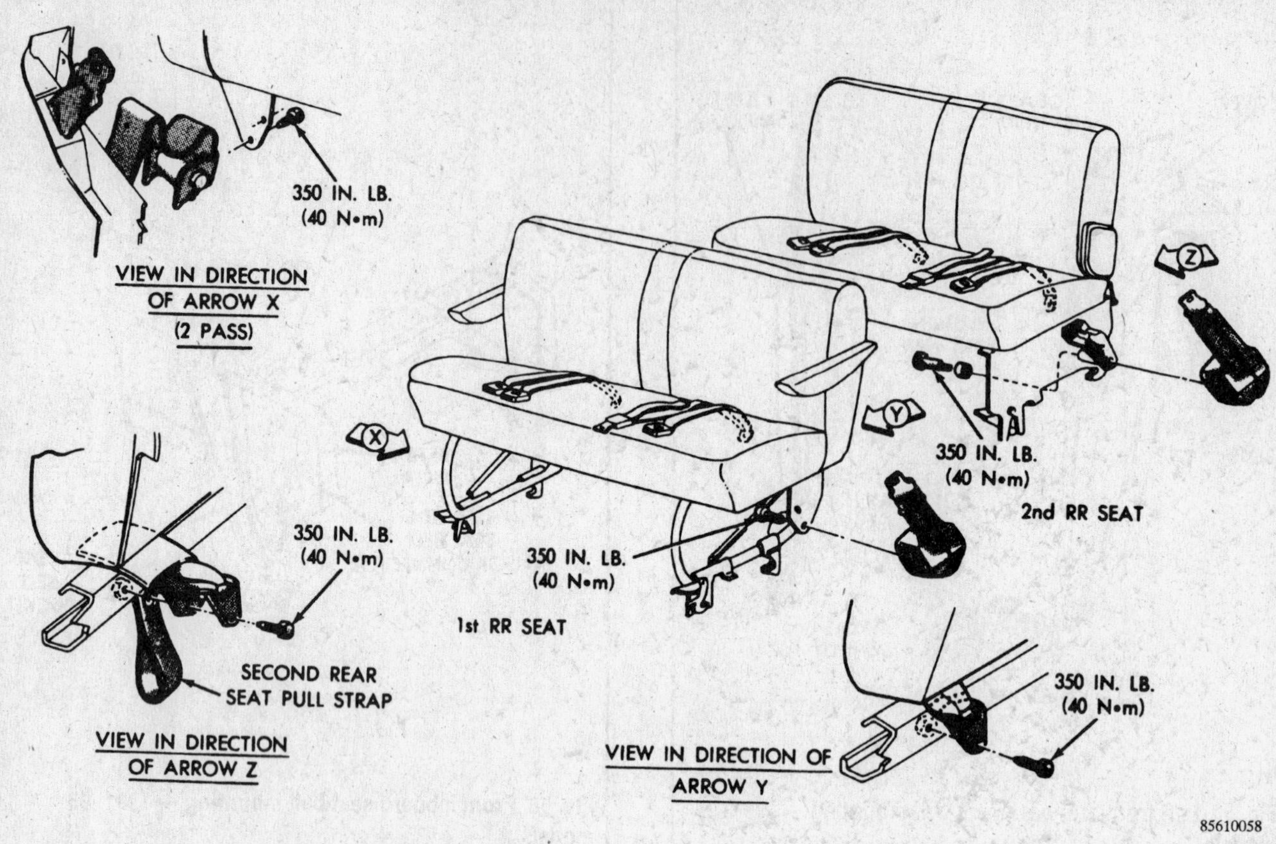

Fig. 57 Rear seat belt mounting — 1984–90 models

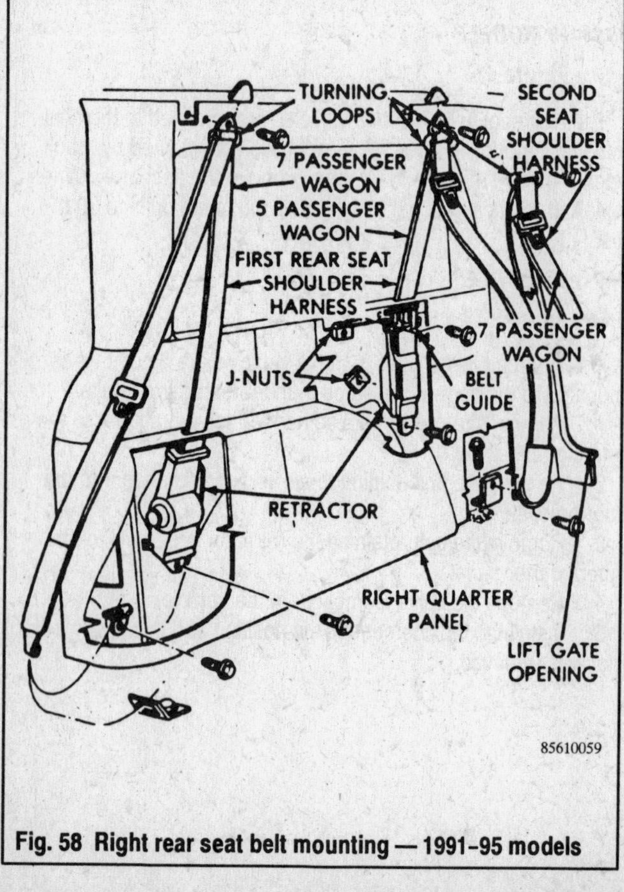

Fig. 58 Right rear seat belt mounting — 1991–95 models

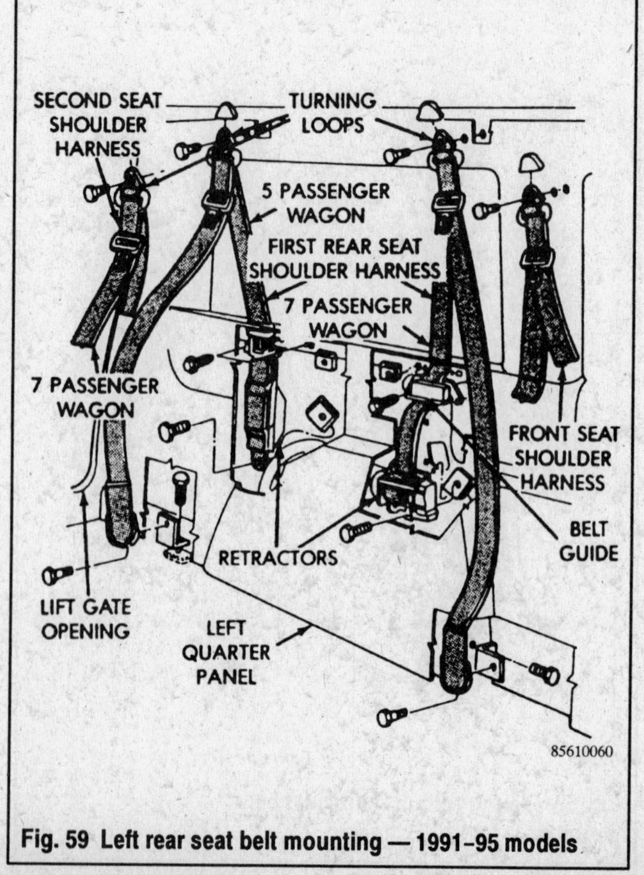

Fig. 59 Left rear seat belt mounting — 1991–95 models

Headliner

REMOVAL & INSTALLATION

➧ **See Figures 60 and 61**

1. If equipped with an overhead console, disengage the sun visors from the console. Remove the screws retaining the console to the roof, disconnect the wiring and remove the console.
2. Remove the inboard sun visor clips, if not equipped with an overhead console. Remove the sun visors.
3. Remove the upper moldings as needed, to gain access to the headliner.
4. Remove the sliding door upper track cover.
5. Remove the right quarter trim panel.
6. Remove the dome lamp, if equipped.
7. Separate the lining from the vehicle and remove it from the vehicle.

To install:

8. Install the headliner in the vehicle, make sure it is positioned properly.
9. Install the dome lamp and install the right quarter trim panel.
10. Install the sliding door upper track cover.
11. Install any trim moulding that was removed.
12. Install the sun visor clips and the overhead console. Install the sun visors.
13. Install the dome light, if equipped.

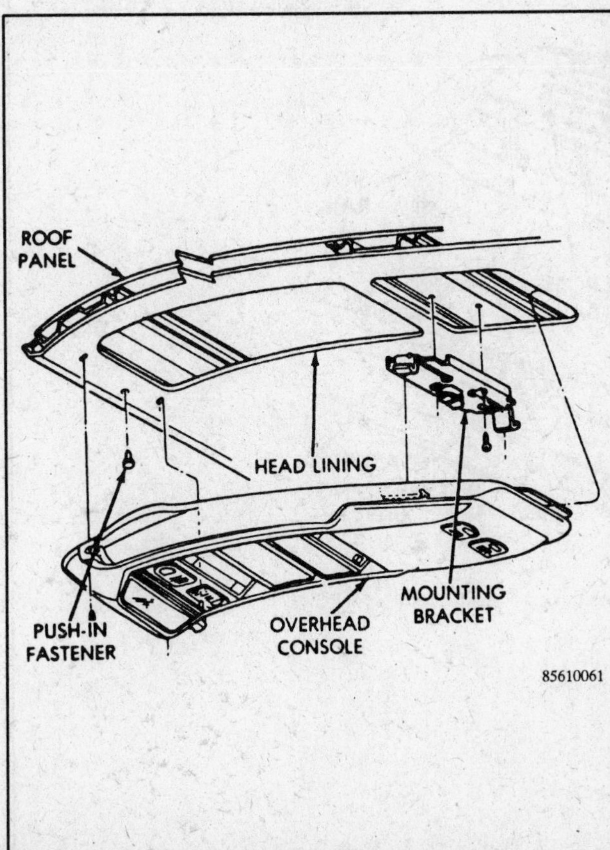

Fig. 60 Overhead console assembly mounting

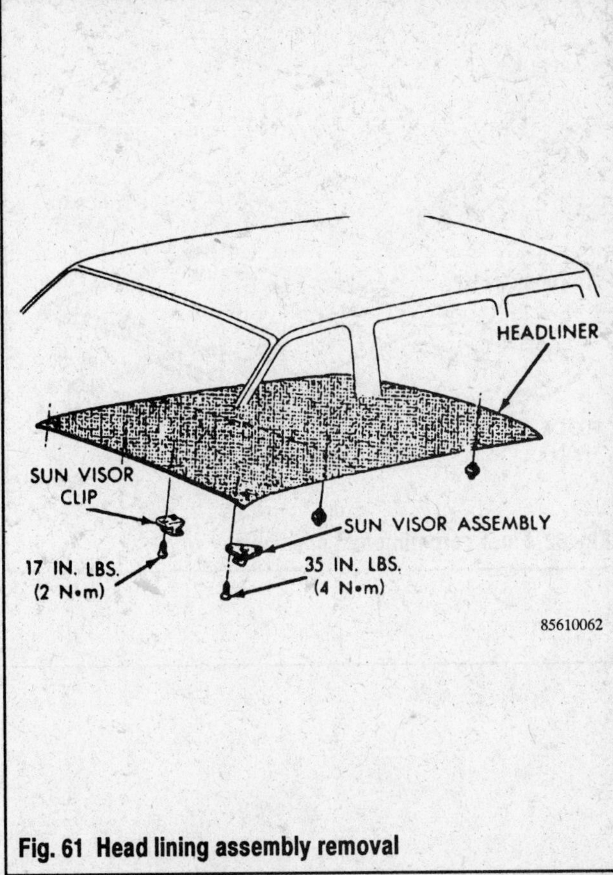

Fig. 61 Head lining assembly removal

Floor Carpeting and Silencers

REMOVAL & INSTALLATION

➧ **See Figure 62**

1. Remove the front console, if equipped.
2. Remove all of the seat assemblies from the vehicle.
3. Remove the inboard seat belt buckle assemblies. Remove the door sill scuff plates.
4. Remove the rear seat anchor bezels.
5. Lift the carpeting and fold it toward the center of the vehicle, remove it through the sliding door.
6. Lift the silencer pads from the floor and remove them from the vehicle.

To install:

7. Install the silencer pads in position first, make sure they are positioned correctly.
8. Place the carpeting in the vehicle through the sliding door. Unfold and position it.
9. Pull the carpet so that it is straight and even throughout the vehicle.
10. Install the rear seat anchor bezels. Install the rear seat assemblies.
11. Install the front seat assemblies. Install the inboard buckle assemblies.
12. Install the door sill scuff plates.
13. Install the center console assembly, if equipped.

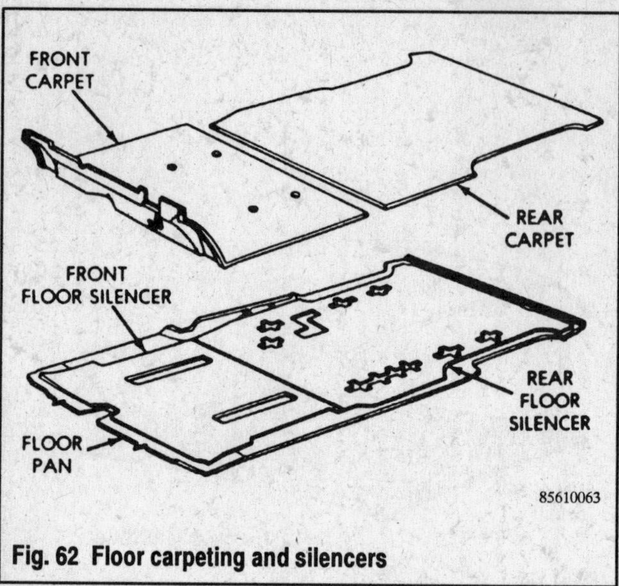

Fig. 62 Floor carpeting and silencers

Roof Top Luggage Rack

REMOVAL & INSTALLATION

See Figure 63

The center strips of the roof rack are stuck to the roof with an adhesive, they can be removed by heating them with a heat gun or lamp.

1. Slide the rail end covers from the side rails.
2. Remove the screws holding the rails to the roof.
3. Separate the luggage rack from the vehicle. Remove the center strips at this time, if they are to be removed.

To install:

4. Clean the area that the center strips mount to, if they were removed. All old adhesive must be removed.
5. Using new double sided trim tape, install the center strips.
6. Install the rack side rails to the roof. Make sure the gaskets are in position.
7. Install the rail end covers.

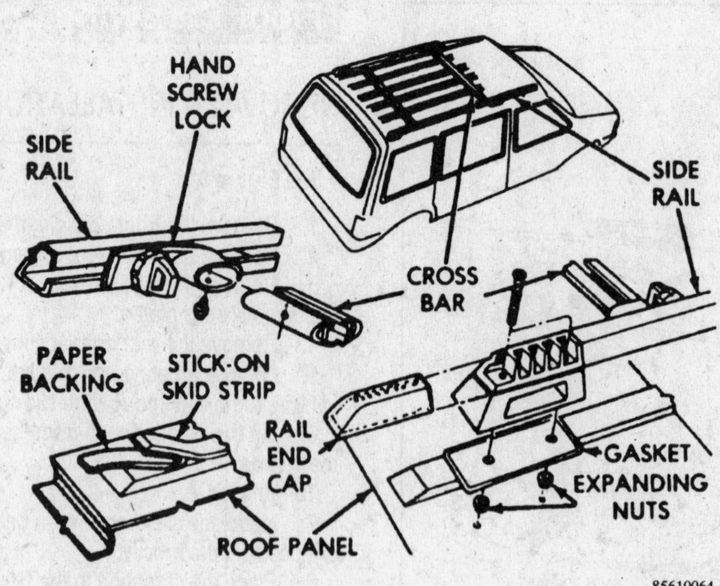

Fig. 63 Roof top luggage rack mounting

GLOSSARY

AIR/FUEL RATIO: The ratio of air-to-gasoline by weight in the fuel mixture drawn into the engine.

AIR INJECTION: One method of reducing harmful exhaust emissions by injecting air into each of the exhaust ports of an engine. The fresh air entering the hot exhaust manifold causes any remaining fuel to be burned before it can exit the tailpipe.

ALTERNATOR: A device used for converting mechanical energy into electrical energy.

AMMETER: An instrument, calibrated in amperes, used to measure the flow of an electrical current in a circuit. Ammeters are always connected in series with the circuit being tested.

AMPERE: The rate of flow of electrical current present when one volt of electrical pressure is applied against one ohm of electrical resistance.

ANALOG COMPUTER: Any microprocessor that uses similar (analogous) electrical signals to make its calculations.

ARMATURE: A laminated, soft iron core wrapped by a wire that converts electrical energy to mechanical energy as in a motor or relay. When rotated in a magnetic field, it changes mechanical energy into electrical energy as in a generator.

ATMOSPHERIC PRESSURE: The pressure on the Earth's surface caused by the weight of the air in the atmosphere. At sea level, this pressure is 14.7 psi at 32°F (101 kPa at 0°C).

ATOMIZATION: The breaking down of a liquid into a fine mist that can be suspended in air.

AXIAL PLAY: Movement parallel to a shaft or bearing bore.

BACKFIRE: The sudden combustion of gases in the intake or exhaust system that results in a loud explosion.

BACKLASH: The clearance or play between two parts, such as meshed gears.

BACKPRESSURE: Restrictions in the exhaust system that slow the exit of exhaust gases from the combustion chamber.

BAKELITE: A heat resistant, plastic insulator material commonly used in printed circuit boards and transistorized components.

BALL BEARING: A bearing made up of hardened inner and outer races between which hardened steel balls roll.

BALLAST RESISTOR: A resistor in the primary ignition circuit that lowers voltage after the engine is started to reduce wear on ignition components.

BEARING: A friction reducing, supportive device usually located between a stationary part and a moving part.

BIMETAL TEMPERATURE SENSOR: Any sensor or switch made of two dissimilar types of metal that bend when heated or cooled due to the different expansion rates of the alloys. These types of sensors usually function as an on/off switch.

BLOWBY: Combustion gases, composed of water vapor and unburned fuel, that leak past the piston rings into the crankcase during normal engine operation. These gases are removed by the PCV system to prevent the buildup of harmful acids in the crankcase.

BRAKE PAD: A brake shoe and lining assembly used with disc brakes.

BRAKE SHOE: The backing for the brake lining. The term is, however, usually applied to the assembly of the brake backing and lining.

BUSHING: A liner, usually removable, for a bearing; an anti-friction liner used in place of a bearing.

CALIPER: A hydraulically activated device in a disc brake system, which is mounted straddling the brake rotor (disc). The caliper contains at least one piston and two brake pads. Hydraulic pressure on the piston(s) forces the pads against the rotor.

CAMSHAFT: A shaft in the engine on which are the lobes (cams) which operate the valves. The camshaft is driven by the crankshaft, via a belt, chain or gears, at one half the crankshaft speed.

CAPACITOR: A device which stores an electrical charge.

CARBON MONOXIDE (CO): A colorless, odorless gas given off as a normal byproduct of combustion. It is poisonous and extremely dangerous in confined areas, building up slowly to toxic levels without warning if adequate ventilation is not available.

CARBURETOR: A device, usually mounted on the intake manifold of an engine, which mixes the air and fuel in the proper proportion to allow even combustion.

CATALYTIC CONVERTER: A device installed in the exhaust system, like a muffler, that converts harmful byproducts of combustion into carbon dioxide and water vapor by means of a heat-producing chemical reaction.

CENTRIFUGAL ADVANCE: A mechanical method of advancing the spark timing by using flyweights in the distributor that react to centrifugal force generated by the distributor shaft rotation.

CHECK VALVE: Any one-way valve installed to permit the flow of air, fuel or vacuum in one direction only.

CHOKE: A device, usually a moveable valve, placed in the intake path of a carburetor to restrict the flow of air.

CIRCUIT: Any unbroken path through which an electrical current can flow. Also used to describe fuel flow in some instances.

CIRCUIT BREAKER: A switch which protects an electrical circuit from overload by opening the circuit when the current flow exceeds a predetermined level. Some circuit breakers must be reset manually, while most reset automatically.

COIL (IGNITION): A transformer in the ignition circuit which steps up the voltage provided to the spark plugs.

COMBINATION MANIFOLD: An assembly which includes both the intake and exhaust manifolds in one casting.

COMBINATION VALVE: A device used in some fuel systems that routes fuel vapors to a charcoal storage canister instead of venting them into the atmosphere. The valve relieves fuel tank pressure and allows fresh air into the tank as the fuel level drops to prevent a vapor lock situation.

COMPRESSION RATIO: The comparison of the total volume of the cylinder and combustion chamber with the piston at BDC and the piston at TDC.

CONDENSER: 1. An electrical device which acts to store an electrical charge, preventing voltage surges. 2. A radiator-like device in the air conditioning system in which refrigerant gas condenses into a liquid, giving off heat.

CONDUCTOR: Any material through which an electrical current can be transmitted easily.

CONTINUITY: Continuous or complete circuit. Can be checked with an ohmmeter.

COUNTERSHAFT: An intermediate shaft which is rotated by a mainshaft and transmits, in turn, that rotation to a working part.

CRANKCASE: The lower part of an engine in which the crankshaft and related parts operate.

CRANKSHAFT: The main driving shaft of an engine which receives reciprocating motion from the pistons and converts it to rotary motion.

CYLINDER: In an engine, the round hole in the engine block in which the piston(s) ride.

CYLINDER BLOCK: The main structural member of an engine in which is found the cylinders, crankshaft and other principal parts.

CYLINDER HEAD: The detachable portion of the engine, usually fastened to the top of the cylinder block and containing all or most of the combustion chambers. On overhead valve engines, it contains the valves and their operating parts. On overhead cam engines, it contains the camshaft as well.

DEAD CENTER: The extreme top or bottom of the piston stroke.

DETONATION: An unwanted explosion of the air/fuel mixture in the combustion chamber caused by excess heat and compression, advanced timing, or an overly lean mixture. Also referred to as "ping".

DIAPHRAGM: A thin, flexible wall separating two cavities, such as in a vacuum advance unit.

DIESELING: A condition in which hot spots in the combustion chamber cause the engine to run on after the key is turned off.

DIFFERENTIAL: A geared assembly which allows the transmission of motion between drive axles, giving one axle the ability to turn faster than the other.

DIODE: An electrical device that will allow current to flow in one direction only.

DISC BRAKE: A hydraulic braking assembly consisting of a brake disc, or rotor, mounted on an axle, and a caliper assembly containing, usually two brake pads which are activated by hydraulic pressure. The pads are forced against the sides of the disc, creating friction which slows the vehicle.

DISTRIBUTOR: A mechanically driven device on an engine which is responsible for electrically firing the spark plug at a predetermined point of the piston stroke.

DOWEL PIN: A pin, inserted in mating holes in two different parts allowing those parts to maintain a fixed relationship.

DRUM BRAKE: A braking system which consists of two brake shoes and one or two wheel cylinders, mounted on a fixed backing plate, and a brake drum, mounted on an axle, which revolves around the assembly.

DWELL: The rate, measured in degrees of shaft rotation, at which an electrical circuit cycles on and off.

ELECTRONIC CONTROL UNIT (ECU): Ignition module, module, amplifier or igniter. See Module for definition.

ELECTRONIC IGNITION: A system in which the timing and firing of the spark plugs is controlled by an electronic control unit, usually called a module. These systems have no points or condenser.

END-PLAY: The measured amount of axial movement in a shaft.

ENGINE: A device that converts heat into mechanical energy.

EXHAUST MANIFOLD: A set of cast passages or pipes which conduct exhaust gases from the engine.

FEELER GAUGE: A blade, usually metal, of precisely predetermined thickness, used to measure the clearance between two parts.

FIRING ORDER: The order in which combustion occurs in the cylinders of an engine. Also the order in which spark is distributed to the plugs by the distributor.

FLOODING: The presence of too much fuel in the intake manifold and combustion chamber which prevents the air/fuel mixture from firing, thereby causing a no-start situation.

FLYWHEEL: A disc shaped part bolted to the rear end of the crankshaft. Around the outer perimeter is affixed the ring gear. The starter drive engages the ring gear, turning the flywheel, which rotates the crankshaft, imparting the initial starting motion to the engine.

FOOT POUND (ft. lbs. or sometimes, ft.lb.): The amount of energy or work needed to raise an item weighing one pound, a distance of one foot.

FUSE: A protective device in a circuit which prevents circuit overload by breaking the circuit when a specific amperage is present. The device is constructed around a strip or wire of a lower amperage rating than the circuit it is designed to protect. When an amperage higher than that stamped on the fuse is present in the circuit, the strip or wire melts, opening the circuit.

GEAR RATIO: The ratio between the number of teeth on meshing gears.

GENERATOR: A device which converts mechanical energy into electrical energy.

HEAT RANGE: The measure of a spark plug's ability to dissipate heat from its firing end. The higher the heat range, the hotter the plug fires.

HUB: The center part of a wheel or gear.

HYDROCARBON (HC): Any chemical compound made up of hydrogen and carbon. A major pollutant formed by the engine as a byproduct of combustion.

HYDROMETER: An instrument used to measure the specific gravity of a solution.

INCH POUND (inch lbs.; sometimes in.lb. or in. lbs.): One twelfth of a foot pound.

INDUCTION: A means of transferring electrical energy in the form of a magnetic field. Principle used in the ignition coil to increase voltage.

INJECTOR: A device which receives metered fuel under relatively low pressure and is activated to inject the fuel into the engine under relatively high pressure at a predetermined time.

INPUT SHAFT: The shaft to which torque is applied, usually carrying the driving gear or gears.

INTAKE MANIFOLD: A casting of passages or pipes used to conduct air or a fuel/air mixture to the cylinders.

JOURNAL: The bearing surface within which a shaft operates.

KEY: A small block usually fitted in a notch between a shaft and a hub to prevent slippage of the two parts.

MANIFOLD: A casting of passages or set of pipes which connect the cylinders to an inlet or outlet source.

MANIFOLD VACUUM: Low pressure in an engine intake manifold formed just below the throttle plates. Manifold vacuum is highest at idle and drops under acceleration.

MASTER CYLINDER: The primary fluid pressurizing device in a hydraulic system. In automotive use, it is found in brake and hydraulic clutch systems and is pedal activated, either directly or, in a power brake system, through the power booster.

MODULE: Electronic control unit, amplifier or igniter of solid state or integrated design which controls the current flow in the ignition primary circuit based on input from the pick-up coil. When the module opens the primary circuit, high secondary voltage is induced in the coil.

NEEDLE BEARING: A bearing which consists of a number (usually a large number) of long, thin rollers.

OHM:(Ω) The unit used to measure the resistance of conductor-to-electrical flow. One ohm is the amount of resistance that limits current flow to one ampere in a circuit with one volt of pressure.

OHMMETER: An instrument used for measuring the resistance, in ohms, in an electrical circuit.

OUTPUT SHAFT: The shaft which transmits torque from a device, such as a transmission.

OVERDRIVE: A gear assembly which produces more shaft revolutions than that transmitted to it.

OVERHEAD CAMSHAFT (OHC): An engine configuration in which the camshaft is mounted on top of the cylinder head and operates the valve either directly or by means of rocker arms.

OVERHEAD VALVE (OHV): An engine configuration in which all of the valves are located in the cylinder head and the camshaft is located in the cylinder block. The camshaft operates the valves via lifters and pushrods.

OXIDES OF NITROGEN (NOx): Chemical compounds of nitrogen produced as a byproduct of combustion. They combine with hydrocarbons to produce smog.

OXYGEN SENSOR: Used with the feedback system to sense the presence of oxygen in the exhaust gas and signal the computer which can reference the voltage signal to an air/fuel ratio.

PINION: The smaller of two meshing gears.

PISTON RING: An open-ended ring which fits into a groove on the outer diameter of the piston. Its chief function is to form a seal between the piston and cylinder wall. Most automotive pistons have three rings: two for compression sealing; one for oil sealing.

PRELOAD: A predetermined load placed on a bearing during assembly or by adjustment.

PRIMARY CIRCUIT: The low voltage side of the ignition system which consists of the ignition switch, ballast resistor or resistance wire, bypass, coil, electronic control unit and pick-up coil as well as the connecting wires and harnesses.

PRESS FIT: The mating of two parts under pressure, due to the inner diameter of one being smaller than the outer diameter of the other, or vice versa; an interference fit.

RACE: The surface on the inner or outer ring of a bearing on which the balls, needles or rollers move.

REGULATOR: A device which maintains the amperage and/or voltage levels of a circuit at predetermined values.

RELAY: A switch which automatically opens and/or closes a circuit.

RESISTANCE: The opposition to the flow of current through a circuit or electrical device, and is measured in ohms. Resistance is equal to the voltage divided by the amperage.

RESISTOR: A device, usually made of wire, which offers a preset amount of resistance in an electrical circuit.

RING GEAR: The name given to a ring-shaped gear attached to a differential case, or affixed to a flywheel or as part of a planetary gear set.

ROLLER BEARING: A bearing made up of hardened inner and outer races between which hardened steel rollers move.

ROTOR: 1. The disc-shaped part of a disc brake assembly, upon which the brake pads bear; also called, brake disc. 2. The device mounted atop the distributor shaft, which passes current to the distributor cap tower contacts.

SECONDARY CIRCUIT: The high voltage side of the ignition system, usually above 20,000 volts. The secondary includes the ignition coil, coil wire, distributor cap and rotor, spark plug wires and spark plugs.

SENDING UNIT: A mechanical, electrical, hydraulic or electromagnetic device which transmits information to a gauge.

SENSOR: Any device designed to measure engine operating conditions or ambient pressures and temperatures. Usually electronic in nature and designed to send a voltage signal to an on-board computer, some sensors may operate as a simple on/off switch or they may provide a variable voltage signal (like a potentiometer) as conditions or measured parameters change.

SHIM: Spacers of precise, predetermined thickness used between parts to establish a proper working relationship.

SLAVE CYLINDER: In automotive use, a device in the hydraulic clutch system which is activated by hydraulic force, disengaging the clutch.

SOLENOID: A coil used to produce a magnetic field, the effect of which is to produce work.

SPARK PLUG: A device screwed into the combustion chamber of a spark ignition engine. The basic construction is a conductive core inside of a ceramic insulator, mounted in an outer conductive base. An electrical charge from the spark plug wire travels along the conductive core and jumps a preset air gap to a grounding point or points at the end of the conductive base. The resultant spark ignites the fuel/air mixture in the combustion chamber.

SPLINES: Ridges machined or cast onto the outer diameter of a shaft or inner diameter of a bore to enable parts to mate without rotation.

TACHOMETER: A device used to measure the rotary speed of an engine, shaft, gear, etc., usually in rotations per minute.

THERMOSTAT: A valve, located in the cooling system of an engine, which is closed when cold and opens gradually in response to engine heating, controlling the temperature of the coolant and rate of coolant flow.

TOP DEAD CENTER (TDC): The point at which the piston reaches the top of its travel on the compression stroke.

TORQUE: The twisting force applied to an object.

TORQUE CONVERTER: A turbine used to transmit power from a driving member to a driven member via hydraulic action, providing changes in drive ratio and torque. In automotive use, it links the driveplate at the rear of the engine to the automatic transmission.

TRANSDUCER: A device used to change a force into an electrical signal.

TRANSISTOR: A semi-conductor component which can be actuated by a small voltage to perform an electrical switching function.

TUNE-UP: A regular maintenance function, usually associated with the replacement and adjustment of parts and components in the electrical and fuel systems of a vehicle for the purpose of attaining optimum performance.

TURBOCHARGER: An exhaust driven pump which compresses intake air and forces it into the combustion chambers at higher than atmospheric pressures. The increased air pressure allows more fuel to be burned and results in increased horsepower being produced.

VACUUM ADVANCE: A device which advances the ignition timing in response to increased engine vacuum.

VACUUM GAUGE: An instrument used to measure the presence of vacuum in a chamber.

VALVE: A device which control the pressure, direction of flow or rate of flow of a liquid or gas.

VALVE CLEARANCE: The measured gap between the end of the valve stem and the rocker arm, cam lobe or follower that activates the valve.

VISCOSITY: The rating of a liquid's internal resistance to flow.

VOLTMETER: An instrument used for measuring electrical force in units called volts. Voltmeters are always connected parallel with the circuit being tested.

WHEEL CYLINDER: Found in the automotive drum brake assembly, it is a device, actuated by hydraulic pressure, which, through internal pistons, pushes the brake shoes outward against the drums.

MASTER INDEX

AIR POLLUTION
- AUTOMOTIVE POLLUTANTS 4-2
  - HEAT TRANSFER 4-3
  - TEMPERATURE INVERSION 4-2
- INDUSTRIAL POLLUTANTS 4-2
- NATURAL POLLUTANTS 4-2

AUTOMOTIVE EMISSIONS
- CRANKCASE EMISSIONS 4-5
- EVAPORATIVE EMISSIONS 4-5
- EXHAUST GASES 4-3
  - CARBON MONOXIDE 4-4
  - HYDROCARBONS 4-3
  - NITROGEN 4-4
  - OXIDES OF SULFUR 4-4
  - PARTICULATE MATTER 4-4

AUTOMATIC TRANSAXLE
- ADJUSTMENTS 7-55
  - A–604 UPSHIFT & KICKDOWN LEARNING PROCEDURE 7-55
  - KICKDOWN CABLE 7-55
  - THROTTLE PRESSURE CABLE/ROD ADJUSTMENT 7-56
- FLUID PAN AND FILTER 7-53
  - REMOVAL & INSTALLATION 7-53
- NEUTRAL STARTING/BACK-UP LIGHT SWITCH 7-56
  - REMOVAL & INSTALLATION 7-56
  - TESTING 7-56
- TRANSAXLE ASSEMBLY 7-57
  - REMOVAL & INSTALLATION 7-57
- UNDERSTANDING AUTOMATIC TRANSAXLES 7-52
  - THE HYDRAULIC CONTROL SYSTEM 7-53
  - THE PLANETARY GEARBOX 7-52
  - THE SERVOS AND ACCUMULATORS 7-52
  - THE TORQUE CONVERTER 7-52

AUXILIARY HEATER/AIR CONDITIONER
- BLOWER MOTOR 6-31
  - REMOVAL & INSTALLATION 6-31
- BLOWER MOTOR RESISTOR 6-31
  - REMOVAL & INSTALLATION 6-31
- EVAPORATOR 6-31
  - REMOVAL & INSTALLATION 6-31
- EXPANSION VALVE 6-30
  - REMOVAL & INSTALLATION 6-30
- HEATER CORE 6-31
  - REMOVAL & INSTALLATION 6-31
- REFRIGERANT LINES 6-31
  - REMOVAL & INSTALLATION 6-31

BASIC ELECTRICAL THEORY
- BATTERY, STARTING AND CHARGING SYSTEMS 3-4
  - BASIC OPERATING PRINCIPLES 3-4
- UNDERSTANDING ELECTRICITY 3-2
  - BASIC CIRCUITS 3-2
  - TROUBLESHOOTING 3-3

BASIC FUEL SYSTEM DIAGNOSIS 5-2

BENDIX SYSTEM 10 ANTI-LOCK BRAKE SYSTEM
BLADDER ACCUMULATOR 9-48
REMOVAL & INSTALLATION 9-48
COMPONENT REPLACEMENT 9-43
BLEEDING THE SYSTEM 9-43
FILLING THE SYSTEM 9-43
CONTROLLER ANTI-LOCK BRAKE (CAB) MODULE 9-48
REMOVAL & INSTALLATION 9-48
DIAGNOSIS AND TESTING 9-37
DIAGNOSTIC PROCEDURE 9-38
SERVICE PRECAUTIONS 9-37
HIGH PRESSURE AND RETURN HOSES 9-46
REMOVAL & INSTALLATION 9-46
HYDRAULIC ASSEMBLY 9-47
REMOVAL & INSTALLATION 9-47
HYDRAULIC RESERVOIR 9-48
REMOVAL & INSTALLATION 9-48
PROPORTIONING VALVES 9-48
REMOVAL & INSTALLATION 9-48
PUMP/MOTOR ASSEMBLY 9-46
REMOVAL & INSTALLATION 9-46
SYSTEM DESCRIPTION 9-33
SYSTEM COMPONENTS 9-34
TONE RINGS 9-51
REMOVAL & INSTALLATION 9-51
WHEEL SPEED SENSORS 9-49
REMOVAL & INSTALLATION 9-49

BENDIX SYSTEM 4 ANTI-LOCK BRAKE SYSTEM
ANTI-LOCK BRAKE SYSTEM DEFINITIONS 9-54
ANTI-LOCK BRAKE SYSTEM OPERATION 9-54
BENDIX ANTI-LOCK 4 SYSTEM BLEEDING 9-62
BLEEDING PROCEDURE 9-62
CONTROLLER ANTI-LOCK BRAKE (CAB) MODULE 9-59
REMOVAL & INSTALLATION 9-59
MAJOR COMPONENTS 9-54
ABS BRAKE SYSTEM ON VEHICLE SERVICE 9-56
CONTROLLER ANTI-LOCK BRAKE (CAB) 9-56
MASTER CYLINDER AND VACUUM BOOSTER 9-54
MODULATOR AND PUMP MOTOR/ASSEMBLY 9-54
WHEEL SPEED (WSS) SENSORS 9-54
MODULATOR ASSEMBLY 9-56
REMOVAL & INSTALLATION 9-56
PROPORTIONING VALVE 9-59
REMOVAL & INSTALLATION 9-59
SYSTEM DESCRIPTION 9-51
SYSTEM SELF-DIAGNOSTICS 9-51
WARNING SYSTEM OPERATIONS 9-54
WHEEL SPEED SENSORS 9-60
REMOVAL & INSTALLATION 9-60

BRAKE SYSTEM
ADJUSTMENTS 9-3
DRUM BRAKES 9-4
BASIC OPERATING PRINCIPLES 9-2
DISC BRAKES 9-2
DRUM BRAKES 9-3
BLEEDING THE BRAKE SYSTEM 9-11
BENCH BLEEDING 9-11
SYSTEM BLEEDING 9-11
BRAKE HOSES 9-9
REMOVAL & INSTALLATION 9-9
BRAKE LIGHT SWITCH 9-4
REMOVAL & INSTALLATION 9-4
FLUID RESERVOIR 9-5
REMOVAL & INSTALLATION 9-5
HEIGHT SENSING FUEL PROPORTIONING VALVE 9-7
TESTING 9-8
VALVE REMOVAL, INSTALLATION AND ADJUSTMENT 9-9
MASTER CYLINDER 9-4
OVERHAUL 9-5
REMOVAL & INSTALLATION 9-4
POWER BOOSTERS 9-3
POWER BRAKE BOOSTER 9-6
REMOVAL & INSTALLATION 9-6
PRESSURE DIFFERENTIAL SWITCH/WARNING LIGHT 9-7
TESTING 9-7

CARBURETED FUEL SYSTEM 5-2
CARBURETOR 5-3
ADJUSTMENTS 5-3
ASSEMBLY 5-11
CLEANING AND INSPECTION 5-10
DISASSEMBLY 5-9
REMOVAL & INSTALLATION 5-7
MECHANICAL FUEL PUMP 5-2
REMOVAL & INSTALLATION 5-2
TESTING 5-2

CHRYSLER MULTI-POINT ELECTRONIC FUEL INJECTION
AUTOMATIC IDLE SPEED (AIS) MOTOR 5-15
REMOVAL & INSTALLATION 5-15
CHECK ENGINE LIGHT 5-12
DIAGNOSIS AND TESTING 5-13
FUEL INJECTOR RAIL ASSEMBLY 5-16
REMOVAL & INSTALLATION 5-16
FUEL INJECTORS 5-21
REMOVAL & INSTALLATION 5-21
FUEL PRESSURE DAMPENER 5-23
REMOVAL & INSTALLATION 5-23
FUEL PRESSURE REGULATOR 5-21
REMOVAL & INSTALLATION 5-21
FUEL PRESSURE TEST 5-13
2.5L TURBOCHARGED ENGINES 5-13
3.0L, 3.3L AND 3.8L ENGINES 5-14
FUEL SYSTEM PRESSURE RELEASE PROCEDURE 5-13
1987–92 MODELS 5-13
1993–95 MODELS 5-13
GENERAL INFORMATION 5-12
HEATED OXYGEN SENSOR 5-23
REMOVAL & INSTALLATION 5-23
POWERTRAIN CONTROL MODULE (PCM) 5-23
REMOVAL & INSTALLATION 5-23
THROTTLE BODY 5-14

REMOVAL & INSTALLATION 5-14
THROTTLE POSITION SENSOR (TPS) 5-15
REMOVAL & INSTALLATION 5-15
WASTEGATE CALIBRATION 5-14
INSPECTION 5-14

CHRYSLER HALL EFFECT ELECTRONIC IGNITION
SINGLE MODULE ENGINE CONTROLLER (SMEC) AND SINGLE BOARD ENGINE CONTROLLER (SBEC) SYSTEMS 2-29
1988–95 MODELS 2-29
SBEC, SBEC II AND PCM COMPONENT REMOVAL & INSTALLATION 2-34
SBEC, SBEC II AND PCM SYSTEMS DIAGNOSIS & TESTING 2-31
SMEC COMPONENT REMOVAL & INSTALLATION 2-33
SMEC SYSTEM DIAGNOSIS & TESTING 2-30
SYSTEM COMPONENTS 2-30
SYSTEM OPERATION 2-29
SPARK CONTROL COMPUTER (SCC) SYSTEM 2-18
SCC SYSTEM COMPONENTS 2-18
SYSTEM DIAGNOSIS & TESTING 2-20
TESTING FOR POOR ENGINE PERFORMANCE 2-22
SPARK CONTROL COMPUTER (SCC) SYSTEM — COMPONENT REPLACEMENT 2-24
REMOVAL & INSTALLATION 2-24

CHRYSLER OPTICAL DISTRIBUTOR SYSTEM
COMPONENT REPLACEMENT AND TESTING 2-37

CHRYSLER SELF-DIAGNOSTIC SYSTEM
GENERAL INFORMATION 4-17
ACTUATOR TEST MODE (ATM) CODES 4-18
CHECK ENGINE LIGHT 4-18
ENGINE RUNNING TEST CODES 4-18
ENTERING SELF-DIAGNOSTICS 4-18
EXITING THE DIAGNOSTIC TEST 4-19
FAULT CODES 4-18
INDICATOR CODES 4-18

CHRYSLER SINGLE POINT FUEL INJECTION SYSTEM
AUTOMATIC IDLE SPEED (AIS) MOTOR ASSEMBLY 5-29
REMOVAL & INSTALLATION 5-29
FUEL FITTINGS 5-26
REMOVAL & INSTALLATION 5-26
FUEL INJECTOR 5-27
REMOVAL & INSTALLATION 5-27
FUEL PRESSURE REGULATOR 5-26
REMOVAL & INSTALLATION 5-26
GENERAL INFORMATION 5-24
DIAGNOSIS & TESTING 5-24
FUEL SYSTEM PRESSURE RELEASE 5-25
FUEL SYSTEM PRESSURE TEST 5-24
SERVICE PRECAUTIONS 5-24
VISUAL INSPECTION 5-24
THROTTLE BODY 5-25
REMOVAL & INSTALLATION 5-25
THROTTLE BODY TEMPERATURE SENSOR 5-28
REMOVAL & INSTALLATION 5-28
THROTTLE POSITION SENSOR (TPS) 5-28
REMOVAL & INSTALLATION 5-28

CIRCUIT PROTECTION
FUSE BLOCK 6-57
FUSIBLE LINKS 6-57
REPLACEMENT 6-57

CLUTCH
CLUTCH PEDAL 7-50
REMOVAL & INSTALLATION 7-50
DRIVEN DISC AND PRESSURE PLATE 7-49
CLUTCH CABLE REPLACEMENT 7-49
RELEASE CABLE ADJUSTMENT 7-49
REMOVAL & INSTALLATION 7-49
UNDERSTANDING THE CLUTCH 7-49

DIRECT IGNITION SYSTEM (DIS)
DIS SYSTEM COMPONENT REPLACEMENT 2-39
REMOVAL & INSTALLATION 2-39
DIS SYSTEM DIAGNOSIS AND TESTING 2-38
FAILURE TO START TEST 2-38
SPARK AT COIL TEST 2-39
GENERAL INFORMATION 2-38

ENGINE ELECTRICAL
ALTERNATOR 3-9
ALTERNATOR PRECAUTIONS 3-9
CHARGING SYSTEM TROUBLESHOOTING 3-9
REMOVAL & INSTALLATION 3-10
DISTRIBUTOR 3-8
INSTALLATION 3-9
REMOVAL 3-8
DISTRIBUTOR CAP 3-8
REMOVAL & INSTALLATION 3-8
DISTRIBUTOR ROTOR 3-8
IGNITION COIL 3-7
REMOVAL & INSTALLATION 3-7
TESTING 3-7
REGULATOR 3-13
REMOVAL & INSTALLATION 3-13
STARTER 3-13
REMOVAL & INSTALLATION 3-14
SOLENOID REPLACEMENT 3-16
STARTER GEAR & CLUTCH REPLACEMENT 3-17
TEST PROCEDURES (ON VEHICLE) 3-13

ENGINE MECHANICAL 3-17
AIR CONDITIONING CONDENSER 3-54
REMOVAL & INSTALLATION 3-54
AUTOMATIC TRANSAXLE OIL COOLER 3-55
REMOVAL & INSTALLATION 3-55
BALANCE SHAFTS 3-93
REMOVAL & INSTALLATION 3-95
CAMSHAFT AND BEARINGS 3-89
INSPECTION 3-93
REMOVAL & INSTALLATION 3-89
CHECKING ENGINE COMPRESSION 3-19
COMBINATION MANIFOLD 3-49
REMOVAL & INSTALLATION 3-49
CRANKSHAFT AND MAIN BEARINGS 3-105
CLEANING & INSPECTION 3-107

REMOVAL & INSTALLATION 3-105
CYLINDER HEAD 3-58
CLEANING & INSPECTION 3-65
REMOVAL & INSTALLATION 3-58
RESURFACING 3-65
ELECTRIC COOLING FAN 3-54
REMOVAL & INSTALLATION 3-55
TESTING 3-54
ENGINE 3-28
ENGINE/TRANSAXLE POSITIONING 3-33
REMOVAL & INSTALLATION 3-28
ENGINE BLOCK HEATER 3-101
REMOVAL & INSTALLATION 3-101
ENGINE OVERHAUL TIPS 3-17
INSPECTION TECHNIQUES 3-18
OVERHAUL TIPS 3-18
REPAIRING DAMAGED THREADS 3-18
TOOLS 3-17
EXHAUST MANIFOLD 3-47
REMOVAL & INSTALLATION 3-47
FREEZE PLUGS 3-100
REMOVAL & INSTALLATION 3-100
FRONT CRANKSHAFT SEAL RETAINER 3-104
REMOVAL & INSTALLATION 3-104
FRONT TIMING COVER AND SEAL 3-75
REMOVAL & INSTALLATION 3-75
INTAKE MANIFOLD 3-44
REMOVAL & INSTALLATION 3-44
INTERMEDIATE SHAFT 3-93
REMOVAL & INSTALLATION 3-93
OIL PAN 3-67
REMOVAL & INSTALLATION 3-67
OIL PUMP 3-72
INSPECTION 3-74
REMOVAL & INSTALLATION 3-72
PISTONS AND CONNECTING RODS 3-96
CLEANING & INSPECTION 3-99
INSTALLATION 3-100
REMOVAL 3-96
RADIATOR 3-52
REMOVAL & INSTALLATION 3-52
REAR MAIN SEAL 3-102
REMOVAL & INSTALLATION 3-102
ROCKER (VALVE) COVER 3-35
REMOVAL & INSTALLATION 3-35
ROCKER ARMS AND SHAFTS 3-38
REMOVAL & INSTALLATION 3-38
SILENT SHAFTS 3-96
REMOVAL & INSTALLATION 3-96
SILENT SHAFT CLEARANCE 3-96
SOLID MOUNT COMPRESSOR BRACKET 3-34
REMOVAL & INSTALLATION 3-34
THERMOSTAT 3-41
REMOVAL & INSTALLATION 3-41
TIMING BELT/CHAIN 3-80
REMOVAL & INSTALLATION 3-80
TIMING SPROCKETS/GEARS 3-87
REMOVAL & INSTALLATION 3-87
TURBOCHARGER 3-52
REMOVAL & INSTALLATION 3-52
VALVES 3-65
CHECKING VALVE SPRINGS 3-66
INSPECTION 3-66
INSTALLATION 3-67
REMOVAL 3-65
WATER PUMP 3-55
OVERHAUL 3-57
REMOVAL & INSTALLATION 3-55
ENTERTAINMENT SYSTEM
ANTENNA 6-36
REMOVAL & INSTALLATION 6-36
RADIO 6-35
REMOVAL & INSTALLATION 6-35
EMISSION CONTROLS 4-5
AIR INJECTION SYSTEM 4-13
REMOVAL & INSTALLATION 4-13
CRANKCASE VENTILATION SYSTEM 4-6
DUAL AIR ASPIRATOR SYSTEM 4-16
REMOVAL & INSTALLATION 4-16
SYSTEM TEST 4-16
ELECTRIC CHOKE ASSEMBLY 4-17
TESTING 4-17
ELECTRONIC FEEDBACK CARBURETOR (EFC) SYSTEM 4-16
EMISSION MAINTENANCE LIGHT 4-17
EVAPORATIVE EMISSION CONTROLS 4-6
BOWL VENT VALVE 4-8
CANISTER PURGE SOLENOID 4-7
CHARCOAL CANISTER 4-6
DAMPING CANISTER 4-6
DUTY CYCLE CANISTER PURGE SOLENOID 4-7
GAS TANK FILLER CAP 4-8
ROLL OVER VALVE 4-7
EXHAUST EMISSION CONTROLS 4-8
HEATED INLET AIR SYSTEM 4-8
REMOVAL & INSTALLATION 4-10
SYSTEM INSPECTION 4-8
EXHAUST GAS RECIRCULATION (EGR) SYSTEM 4-10
SYSTEM INSPECTION 4-10
OXYGEN FEEDBACK SOLENOID 4-17
OXYGEN SENSOR 4-16
HEATED OXYGEN SENSOR 4-16
NON-HEATED OXYGEN SENSOR 4-16
PULSE AIR FEEDER SYSTEM 4-15
VEHICLE EMISSION CONTROL INFORMATION LABEL 4-5
EXHAUST SYSTEM 3-107
EXHAUST (CONVERTER/RESONATOR) PIPE 3-107
REMOVAL & INSTALLATION 3-107
MUFFLER 3-108
REMOVAL & INSTALLATION 3-108
SAFETY PRECAUTIONS 3-107
TAIL PIPE 3-108
REMOVAL & INSTALLATION 3-108
EXTERIOR
ANTENNA 10-11

BUMPERS 10-8
REMOVAL & INSTALLATION 10-8
EXTERIOR MOLDINGS AND BODY SIDE APPLIQUES 10-6
REMOVAL & INSTALLATION 10-6
FENDERS AND SPLASH SHIELDS 10-11
REMOVAL & INSTALLATION 10-11
FRONT DOOR HINGE 10-2
REMOVAL & INSTALLATION 10-2
FRONT DOORS 10-2
ALIGNMENT 10-2
REMOVAL & INSTALLATION 10-2
GRILLE 10-10
REMOVAL & INSTALLATION 10-10
HOOD 10-5
REMOVAL & INSTALLATION 10-5
LIFTGATE 10-5
REMOVAL & INSTALLATION 10-5
OUTSIDE MIRRORS 10-10
REMOVAL & INSTALLATION 10-10
SLIDING DOOR 10-2
ALIGNMENT 10-2
REMOVAL & INSTALLATION 10-2

FASTENERS, MEASUREMENTS AND CONVERSIONS
BOLTS, NUTS AND OTHER THREADED RETAINERS 1-8
STANDARD AND METRIC MEASUREMENTS 1-14
TORQUE 1-11
TORQUE ANGLE METERS 1-14
TORQUE WRENCHES 1-11

FIRING ORDERS 2-17

FLUIDS AND LUBRICANTS
BODY LUBRICATION 1-63
CHASSIS LUBRICATION 1-62
COOLING SYSTEM 1-58
CHECK THE RADIATOR CAP 1-60
CLEANING THE RADIATOR 1-60
DRAIN AND REFILL 1-59
FLUID RECOMMENDATION 1-58
LEVEL CHECK 1-59
DIFFERENTIAL 1-57
DRIVE LINE MODULE 1-58
FLUID RECOMMENDATION 1-58
ENGINE 1-52
OIL AND FILTER CHANGE 1-54
OIL LEVEL CHECK 1-52
OIL RECOMMENDATIONS 1-52
FLUID DISPOSAL 1-52
FUEL RECOMMENDATIONS 1-52
MASTER CYLINDER 1-60
FLUID RECOMMENDATION 1-60
LEVEL CHECK 1-61
POWER STEERING PUMP 1-61
FLUID RECOMMENDATIONS 1-61
LEVEL CHECK 1-61
POWER TRANSFER UNIT (PTU) 1-57
DRAIN AND REFILL 1-57
FLUID RECOMMENDATION 1-57
REAR WHEEL BEARINGS 1-63
SERVICING 1-63
STEERING GEAR 1-62
TRANSAXLE 1-55
DRAIN AND REFILL 1-57
FLUID LEVEL CHECK 1-55
FLUID RECOMMENDATION 1-55

FRONT DISC BRAKES
BRAKE DISC (ROTOR) 9-23
INSPECTION 9-23
REMOVAL & INSTALLATION 9-23
CALIPER 9-22
OVERHAUL 9-22
DISC BRAKE PADS 9-13
INSPECTION 9-13
REMOVAL & INSTALLATION 9-13

FRONT SUSPENSION
FRONT END ALIGNMENT 8-16
CAMBER 8-16
CASTER 8-16
TOE-IN 8-16
FRONT HUB AND BEARING 8-13
REMOVAL & INSTALLATION 8-13
LOWER BALL JOINT 8-8
INSPECTION 8-8
REMOVAL & INSTALLATION 8-8
LOWER CONTROL ARM 8-9
REMOVAL & INSTALLATION 8-9
MACPHERSON STRUTS 8-2
REMOVAL & INSTALLATION 8-2
PIVOT BUSHING 8-10
STEERING KNUCKLE 8-12
REMOVAL & INSTALLATION 8-12
STRUT SPRING 8-6
REMOVAL & INSTALLATION 8-6
SWAY BAR 8-10
REMOVAL & INSTALLATION 8-10

FUEL TANK 5-29

HEATING AND AIR CONDITIONING
AIR CONDITIONING COMPRESSOR 6-17
REMOVAL & INSTALLATION 6-17
BLOWER MOTOR 6-22
REMOVAL & INSTALLATION 6-22
BLOWER MOTOR RESISTOR 6-23
REMOVAL & INSTALLATION 6-23
CLIMATE CONTROL HEAD 6-27
REMOVAL & INSTALLATION 6-27
EXPANSION VALVE (H-VALVE) 6-29
REMOVAL & INSTALLATION 6-29
TESTING 6-29
FILTER/DRIER 6-28
REMOVAL & INSTALLATION 6-28
HEATER CORE AND EVAPORATOR 6-23
REMOVAL & INSTALLATION 6-23
HEATER/AIR CONDITIONING CONTROL CABLES 6-28
REMOVAL & INSTALLATION 6-28
HEATER/EVAPORATOR UNIT 6-20

REMOVAL & INSTALLATION 6-20

HOW TO BUY A USED VEHICLE
TIPS 1-69
ROAD TEST CHECKLIST 1-70
USED VEHICLE CHECKLIST 1-69

HOW TO USE THIS BOOK
AVOIDING THE MOST COMMON MISTAKES 1-2
AVOIDING TROUBLE 1-2
MAINTENANCE OR REPAIR? 1-2
WHERE TO BEGIN 1-2

INSTRUMENTS AND SWITCHES
CLUSTER LAMP BULBS 6-45
REMOVAL & INSTALLATION 6-45
CLUSTER LAMP SOCKETS 6-45
REMOVAL & INSTALLATION 6-45
FORWARD CONSOLE 6-49
REMOVAL & INSTALLATION 6-49
FUEL GAUGE 6-43
REMOVAL & INSTALLATION 6-43
HEADLAMP DIMMER SWITCH 6-52
ADJUSTMENT 6-52
REMOVAL & INSTALLATION 6-52
HEADLAMP SWITCH 6-52
REMOVAL & INSTALLATION 6-52
INSTRUMENT CLUSTER ASSEMBLY 6-41
REMOVAL & INSTALLATION 6-41
INSTRUMENT PANEL ASSEMBLY 6-47
REMOVAL & INSTALLATION 6-47
LOWER INSTRUMENT PANEL 6-45
REMOVAL & INSTALLATION 6-45
OIL PRESSURE GAUGE 6-44
REMOVAL & INSTALLATION 6-44
PRINTED CIRCUIT BOARD 6-44
REMOVAL & INSTALLATION 6-44
TEMPERATURE GAUGE 6-44
REMOVAL & INSTALLATION 6-44
UPPER INSTRUMENT PANEL 6-47
REMOVAL & INSTALLATION 6-47
VOLTMETER 6-43
REMOVAL & INSTALLATION 6-43
WINDSHIELD WIPER SWITCH 6-50
REMOVAL & INSTALLATION 6-50

INTERIOR
DOOR GLASS REGULATOR 10-19
REMOVAL & INSTALLATION 10-19
DOOR LOCKS AND LATCH 10-18
REMOVAL & INSTALLATION 10-18
DOOR PANELS 10-13
REMOVAL & INSTALLATION 10-13
ELECTRIC WINDOW MOTOR 10-19
REMOVAL & INSTALLATION 10-19
FLOOR CARPETING AND SILENCERS 10-29
REMOVAL & INSTALLATION 10-29
FRONT SEATS 10-22
REMOVAL & INSTALLATION 10-22
HEADLINER 10-29
REMOVAL & INSTALLATION 10-29
INSIDE REAR VIEW MIRROR 10-19
REPLACEMENT 10-19
INTERIOR TRIM PANELS 10-14
REMOVAL & INSTALLATION 10-14
REAR SEAT ASSEMBLY 10-24
REMOVAL & INSTALLATION 10-24
ROOF TOP LUGGAGE RACK 10-30
REMOVAL & INSTALLATION 10-30
SEAT BELT SYSTEMS 10-26
REMOVAL & INSTALLATION 10-26
STATIONARY GLASS 10-21
REMOVAL & INSTALLATION 10-21
WINDSHIELD GLASS 10-21
REMOVAL & INSTALLATION 10-21

JACKING
JACKING PRECAUTIONS 1-69

JUMP STARTING A DEAD BATTERY
JUMP STARTING PRECAUTIONS 1-67
JUMP STARTING PROCEDURE 1-67

LIGHTING
HEADLIGHTS 6-53
REMOVAL & INSTALLATION 6-53
SIGNAL AND MARKER LIGHTS 6-55
REMOVAL & INSTALLATION 6-55

MANUAL TRANSAXLE
4-SPEED TRANSAXLE OVERHAUL 7-8
DIFFERENTIAL 7-13
DIFFERENTIAL BEARING RETAINER 7-11
EXTENSION HOUSING 7-11, 7-31
INPUT SHAFT 7-11
INTERMEDIATE SHAFT 7-11
SELECTOR SHAFT HOUSING 7-11
TRANSAXLE CASE ASSEMBLY 7-14
TRANSAXLE CASE DISASSEMBLY 7-8
5-SPEED TRANSAXLE OVERHAUL 7-15
SUBASSEMBLY 7-22
TRANSAXLE ASSEMBLY 7-36
TRANSAXLE DISASSEMBLY 7-15
ADJUSTMENTS 7-2
BACK-UP LIGHT SWITCH 7-3
SHIFT LINKAGE 7-2
HALFSHAFTS 7-39
CV-JOINT OVERHAUL 7-43
REMOVAL & INSTALLATION 7-39
IDENTIFICATION 7-2
TRANSAXLE ASSEMBLY 7-6
REMOVAL & INSTALLATION 7-6
UNDERSTANDING THE MANUAL TRANSAXLE 7-2

MODEL IDENTIFICATION 1-16

POWER TRANSFER UNIT
IDENTIFICATION 7-58

REAR DRIVE LINE MODULE
DIFFERENTIAL SIDE GEARS 7-63
REMOVAL & INSTALLATION 7-63
DRIVE PINION 7-61

REMOVAL & INSTALLATION 7-61
IDENTIFICATION 7-59
REAR DRIVE LINE ASSEMBLY MODULE 7-59
REMOVAL &INSTALLATION 7-59
REAR HALFSHAFT 7-60
REMOVAL & INSTALLATION 7-60
TORQUE TUBE 7-63
REMOVAL & INSTALLATION 7-63

REAR DRUM BRAKES
BRAKE DRUMS 9-24
INSPECTION 9-24
REMOVAL & INSTALLATION 9-24
BRAKE SHOES 9-26
REMOVAL & INSTALLATION 9-26
PARKING BRAKE 9-31
ADJUSTMENT 9-31
REMOVAL & INSTALLATION 9-31
WHEEL CYLINDERS 9-30
OVERHAUL 9-31
REMOVAL & INSTALLATION 9-30

REAR SUSPENSION
GENERAL INFORMATION 8-17
REAR AXLE ALIGNMENT 8-23
REAR SPRINGS 8-18
REMOVAL & INSTALLATION 8-18
REAR WHEEL BEARINGS 8-21
SERVICING 8-21
SHOCK ABSORBERS 8-20
REMOVAL & INSTALLATION 8-20
TESTING 8-20
SWAY BAR 8-20
REMOVAL & INSTALLATION 8-20

ROUTINE MAINTENANCE AND TUNE-UP
AIR CLEANER 1-18
REMOVAL & INSTALLATION 1-18
AIR CONDITIONING 1-40
DISCHARGING, EVACUATING AND CHARGING 1-42
GENERAL SERVICING PROCEDURES 1-41
SAFETY PRECAUTIONS 1-40
SYSTEM INSPECTION 1-42
BATTERY 1-27
BATTERY FLUID 1-27
CABLES 1-29
CHARGING 1-30
GENERAL MAINTENANCE 1-27
REPLACEMENT 1-30
CRANKCASE VENT FILTER 1-26
VENT FILTER SERVICE 1-26
CV-BOOTS 1-40
INSPECTION 1-40
DRIVE BELTS 1-30
ADJUSTMENT 1-31
INSPECTION 1-30
REMOVAL & INSTALLATION 1-34
EVAPORATIVE CHARCOAL CANISTER 1-27
SERVICING 1-27
FUEL FILTER 1-20
REMOVAL & INSTALLATION 1-21
FUEL SYSTEM PRESSURE 1-24
RELEASE PROCEDURE 1-24
HOSES 1-38
INSPECTION 1-38
REMOVAL & INSTALLATION 1-39
PCV VALVE 1-25
OPERATION 1-25
REMOVAL & INSTALLATION 1-26
TESTING 1-26
TIRES AND WHEELS 1-47
CARE OF SPECIAL WHEELS 1-51
INSPECTION 1-49
TIRE DESIGN 1-48
TIRE INFLATION 1-47
TIRE ROTATION 1-47
TIRE STORAGE 1-49
TIRE USAGE 1-48
WINDSHIELD WIPERS 1-43
ELEMENT (REFILL) CARE AND REPLACEMENT 1-43

SERIAL NUMBER IDENTIFICATION
ENGINE IDENTIFICATION NUMBER (EIN) 1-16
ENGINE SERIAL NUMBER 1-18
TRANSAXLE 1-18
VEHICLE IDENTIFICATION NUMBER (VIN) 1-16

SERVICING YOUR VEHICLE SAFELY
DO'S 1-8
DON'TS 1-8

SPECIFICATIONS CHARTS
ADDITIONAL TORQUE SPECIFICATIONS 3-110
AUTOMATIC TRANSMISSION APPLICATIONS 1-72
BRAKE SPECIFICATIONS 9-66
CAPACITIES 1-74
CAMSHAFT SPECIFICATIONS 3-22
CRANKSHAFT AND CONNECTING ROD SPECIFICATIONS 3-23
ENGINE APPLICATIONS 1-71
GENERAL ENGINE SPECIFICATIONS 3-20
MANUAL TRANSMISSION APPLICATIONS 1-73
PISTON AND RING SPECIFICATIONS 3-24
STANDARD (ENGLISH) TO METRIC CONVERSION CHARTS 1-76
STANDARD AND METRIC CONVERSION FACTORS 1-15
TORQUE SPECIFICATIONS 1-75
TORQUE SPECIFICATIONS 3-26
TORQUE SPECIFICATIONS 5-30
TORQUE SPECIFICATIONS 7-66
TORQUE SPECIFICATIONS 9-66
TORQUE SPECIFICATIONS 8-45
TUNE UP SPECIFICATIONS 2-16
VALVE SPECIFICATIONS 3-21
WHEEL ALIGNMENT SPECIFICATIONS 8-16

STEERING

BOOT SEALS 8-44
REMOVAL & INSTALLATION 8-44
IGNITION LOCK CYLINDER 8-27
REMOVAL & INSTALLATION 8-27
IGNITION SWITCH 8-28
REMOVAL & INSTALLATION 8-28
IGNITION SWITCH AND LOCK CYLINDER ASSEMBLY 8-28
REMOVAL & INSTALLATION 8-28
MULTI-FUNCTION SWITCH 8-26
REMOVAL & INSTALLATION 8-26
POWER STEERING PUMP 8-44
REMOVAL & INSTALLATION 8-44
STEERING COLUMN 8-30
REMOVAL & INSTALLATION 8-30
STEERING GEAR 8-41
REMOVAL & INSTALLATION 8-41
STEERING LINKAGE 8-40
REMOVAL & INSTALLATION 8-40
STEERING WHEEL 8-24
REMOVAL & INSTALLATION 8-24
TURN SIGNAL SWITCH 8-25
REMOVAL & INSTALLATION 8-25

SUPPLEMENTAL RESTRAINT SYSTEM (AIR BAGS)
AIR BAG CONTROL MODULE (ACM) 6-15
REMOVAL & INSTALLATION 6-15
AIR BAG SYSTEM CHECK 6-14
WITH A SCAN TOOL 6-14
WITHOUT A SCAN TOOL 6-14
CLOCKSPRING 6-15
CLOCKSPRING CENTERING PROCEDURE 6-16
REMOVAL & INSTALLATION 6-16
DRIVER AIR BAG MODULE 6-14
REMOVAL & INSTALLATION 6-14
GENERAL INFORMATION 6-10
AIR BAG MODULE 6-10
CLOCKSPRING 6-12
DEPLOYED MODULE 6-12
DIAGNOSTIC MODULE 6-12
FRONT IMPACT SENSORS 6-11
HANDLING A LIVE MODULE 6-12
STORAGE 6-12
PASSENGER AIR BAG MODULE 6-14
REMOVAL & INSTALLATION 6-14
SERVICE PRECAUTIONS 6-13
STEERING COLUMN SWITCHES 6-16
REMOVAL & INSTALLATION 6-16

TOOLS AND EQUIPMENT
SPECIAL TOOLS 1-6

TOWING 1-66

TRAILER TOWING
COOLING 1-65
ENGINE 1-65
TRANSAXLE 1-65
GENERAL RECOMMENDATIONS 1-64
HANDLING A TRAILER 1-65
HITCH (TONGUE) WEIGHT 1-64
TRAILER WEIGHT 1-64
WIRING 1-65

TRAILER WIRING 6-56

TROUBLE CODES 4-20

TUNE-UP PROCEDURES
IDLE MIXTURE 2-14
ADJUSTMENT 2-14
IDLE SPEED 2-11
ADJUSTMENT 2-11
IGNITION TIMING 2-9
ADJUSTMENT 2-9
SPARK PLUG WIRES 2-9
SPARK PLUGS 2-2
INSPECTION & GAPPING 2-4
REMOVAL & INSTALLATION 2-2
SPARK PLUG HEAT RANGE 2-2
VALVE LASH 2-15
ADJUSTMENT 2-15

UNDERSTANDING AND TROUBLESHOOTING ELECTRICAL SYSTEMS
ADD-ON ELECTRICAL EQUIPMENT 6-10
SAFETY PRECAUTIONS 6-2
TROUBLESHOOTING 6-3
BASIC TROUBLESHOOTING THEORY 6-4
TEST EQUIPMENT 6-4
TESTING 6-6
UNDERSTANDING BASIC ELECTRICITY 6-2
AUTOMOTIVE CIRCUITS 6-3
CIRCUITS 6-2
SHORT CIRCUITS 6-3
THE WATER ANALOGY 6-2
WIRING HARNESSES 6-7
WIRING REPAIR 6-8

VACUUM DIAGRAMS 4-37

WHEELS
WHEEL ASSEMBLIES 8-2
INSPECTION 8-2
REMOVAL & INSTALLATION 8-2

WINDSHIELD WIPERS
LIFTGATE WIPER MOTOR 6-40
REMOVAL & INSTALLATION 6-40
WINDSHIELD WIPER LINKAGE 6-40
REMOVAL & INSTALLATION 6-40
WINDSHIELD WIPER MOTOR 6-39
REMOVAL & INSTALLATION 6-39
WIPER ARM (LIFTGATE) 6-39
REMOVAL & INSTALLATION 6-39
WIPER ARM (WINDSHIELD) 6-37
REMOVAL & INSTALLATION 6-37
WIPER BLADE 6-37

WIRING DIAGRAMS 6-58